Marcus Tullius Cicero, Albert Watson

Select Letters from Cicero

with english Introductions, Notes and Appendices

Marcus Tullius Cicero, Albert Watson

Select Letters from Cicero
with english Introductions, Notes and Appendices

ISBN/EAN: 9783742805539

Manufactured in Europe, USA, Canada, Australia, Japa

Cover: Foto ©ninafisch / pixelio.de

Manufactured and distributed by brebook publishing software
(www.brebook.com)

Marcus Tullius Cicero, Albert Watson

Select Letters from Cicero

CICERO

SELECT LETTERS

WITH

ENGLISH INTRODUCTIONS, NOTES, AND APPENDICES

BY

ALBERT WATSON, M.A.

FELLOW AND FORMERLY TUTOR OF BRASENOSE COLLEGE, OXFORD

Third Edition

PREFACE

TO THE FIRST EDITION.

I UNDERTOOK the preparation of an edition of Select Letters of Cicero for the Clarendon Press Series at the suggestion of the late Professor Conington, to whose advice and criticisms I was much indebted in the earlier part of my work.

The text which I have adopted is that of Baiter and Kayser's edition, Leipzig, 1860–69. In cases where I have departed from it, I have always referred to the departure in a note, and in the majority of them I have merely substituted the reading of the MS.[1] which Baiter recognizes as of sole or highest authority. I have not always adopted Baiter's punctuation, and have departed at times from his spelling, for the sake of clearness or of uniformity.

A list of the principal works which I have consulted in illustration of the letters will be found on p. xxii. foll.: and my obligations

[1] For the letters 'Ad Familiares' the Medicean MS. Plut. XLIX. No. IX is, according to Baiter, the sole authority, except one page of a Turin palimpsest. Hofmann, however, considers a Parisian MS., Notre Dame 178, to be of independent authority for the books which it contains—Ad Familiares 1. 1 to 8. 8, 6. The Medicean (M.) is of the eleventh century, and was discovered by Petrarch at Vercelli. A copy of it by his hand exists in the same collection as the original (Plut. XLIX, No. VII). For the letters 'Ad Quintum Fratrem' and 'Ad Atticum' another Medicean MS. (Plut. XLIX. No. XVIII), a copy of an original found by Petrarch at Verona in 1345 but since lost, seems to have the highest authority, but readings seem to have been preserved from another early MS. in the margin of Cratander's edition of 1528 (C.). Both the Medicean MSS. apparently contain suggestions from later hands. They are now kept in the Laurentian library at Florence. For the letters to Atticus a small portion of another MS. of the eleventh century, of which the greater part has been lost (W.), is also available. It exists in two portions, one at Munich, and one at Würzburg, and contains portions of books 11 and 12. Its text is reported to coincide to a great extent with C. Cp. Baiter's Prefaces to vols. IX and X of his edition; and Hofmann's Appendix, p. 219 of his edition of Select Letters of Cicero, Part I. See p. xxiii.

to many of them will also appear from my notes. This, however, is perhaps the proper place to acknowledge the great assistance which I have derived from Mommsen's history in preparing my introductions—especially on pp. 3, 4; 136–139; and to Brückner's Life of Cicero in Appendix V. I regret that Mr. J. R. King's notes[1] only refer to a small though very important part of Cicero's life.

Of works which may be less known to English students, I wish to mention the edition of all the letters in chronological order by Billerbeck; that of the letters to Atticus by Boot, with Latin notes; and those of select letters, with German notes, by Hofmann and Süpfle; also the works of A. W. Zumpt, Suringar, Drumann, Abeken, Rein, and the Onomasticon attached to Orelli's edition. The copious references given by Drumann and Suringar have been of great service. I have carefully verified almost all of them[2], and have given the source whence I have taken the very few that I have been unable to verify. The edition of select letters with Latin notes by Matthiae and Müller is, I believe, tolerably well known to English students. That with German notes by Frey has coincided with mine less than the other editions mentioned in the letters chosen, and I have therefore found it less useful than might otherwise have been the case. The first volume of the Corpus Inscriptionum Latinarum published under the superintendence of Theodor Mommsen (Berlin, 1863), will be found very useful in determining some questions of chronology; and M. Boissier's work, Cicéron et ses Amis (8vo. Paris, 1865), gives a very lively and interesting sketch of Cicero's public and private life.

In my selection of letters I have been principally guided by consideration of their historical importance or of their value as illustrating Cicero's character. Notwithstanding the absence of any letters of the important year 63 B.C., and their comparative paucity for the years 56–52 B.C., Cicero's correspondence furnishes, I think, the most detailed and trustworthy commentary on a very interesting period of Roman history, and the materials which it provides for an estimate of his own character are so

[1] The Philippic Orations of M. Tullius Cicero, with English notes, by the Rev. J. R. King (Clarendon Press Series), 8vo. Oxford, 1868; [Second Edition, 1878].

[2] i.e. of those used. Note to Second Edition.

abundant that their very abundance causes difficulty. His changing states of mind are so accurately reproduced in his letters that it is difficult to form a judgment with confidence as to the motives which had permanently most influence with him.

Among ancient works those which throw most light on the letters of Cicero are naturally his other works, especially his speeches. Though not so trustworthy as his letters with regard to matters of fact, they are still very valuable both as supplementing and as illustrating his correspondence.

Next in value to these I should place the writings of Caesar, and the epitomes of the lost books of Livy, so far as they illustrate the life of Cicero. The 'Catiline' of Sallust, though its historical character has been seriously questioned (cp. p. 10), may be added; and the second book of the history of M. Velleius Paterculus, though the latter seems to have been rather prejudiced.

Later writers, such as Appian, Dion Cassius, Plutarch, and Suetonius, are of course to be followed with caution except when they name their authorities. They had access, however, to independent contemporary, or nearly contemporary, sources of information; e.g. the public Acta; lost letters or speeches of Cicero, and of his correspondents; and the works of Libo[1], Livy, Oppius[2], Pollio[3], Tanusius Geminus[4], and others.

My introductions and notes will shew that I accept in the main Professor Mommsen's[5] view of the party struggles of Rome during the last century of the Commonwealth's existence. I do not, however, agree with all his judgments upon persons.

References to the contents of this book made in the notes are either to the pages or to the numbers of letters or of sections of Introductions and Appendices in this edition. But in notes to the Introductions and Appendices, where references are very

[1] App. Bell. Civ. 3. 77. [2] Plut. Caes. 17. [3] App. 2. 82; Plut. Caes. 46.
[4] Plut. Caes. 22.
[5] As far as the struggle between Caesar and Pompey is concerned, Dean Merivale and the majority of recent English writers on Roman history have anticipated or concurred with Mommsen in maintaining that Caesar's triumph was expedient. Friendly but candid biographical notices of some of Caesar's principal opponents will be found in Professor Goldwin Smith's article on 'The Last Republicans of Rome' in Macmillan's Magazine for April 1868.

numerous, I have, to avoid confusion, referred uniformly to the letters as arranged in the ordinary editions.

I wish now to acknowledge my obligations to the Delegates of the University Press for undertaking the publication of my book, and especially to the Dean of Christ Church, and to the late Canon Shirley, for suggestions on various points; and to the Rev. E. L. Hicks, Fellow and Tutor of Corpus Christi College, for his notes on the letters of the fourth period, and comments upon passages in the remainder of the work. I had hoped that Mr. Hicks would have been able to give me his valuable aid to a still greater extent, and regret very much that the state of his health, and his other engagements, have made it impossible for him to do so.

Brasenose College,
Oxford, 1870.

PREFACE

TO THE THIRD EDITION.

THE text of this edition does not differ from that of the second edition, except that some errors have been corrected. I have added, however, partly in the notes and partly in the list of additions and corrections, some various readings derived from sources mentioned below.

Since the publication of the second edition of this book our knowledge of three important MSS. has been much increased. 1. The Turonensis contains Ad Familiares 1. 1 to 7. 32, 1 'me conferri,' except the portion from 2. 16, 4 'hac orbis terrarum' to 4. 3, 4 'appareat cum me co'. It is kept in the library at Tours, and has been collated at Paris by or for M. Charles Thurot, who has published the collation with instructive comments. M. Thurot assigns the MS. to the latter part of the 12th century, but argues that it cannot have been derived from the Medicean (M). Both are derived, he thinks, from a common original. Readings from the Turonensis are quoted as from T. 2. Harleianus 2682 contains Ad Familiares 9–16, apparently only wanting the fragment 'Parmenses miserrimos' which Baiter calls 11. 13, b. F. Rühl (Rhein. Mus. xxx, 1875, pp. 26 and 135) assigns it to the 11th century. It is quoted as H. 3. Harleianus 2773 contains Ad Familiares 1. 1 to 8–9, 3 'puto etiam si ullam spem' except the portion between 1. 9, 20 after 'exarsi' and 2. 1, 2 'dignitate es consecutus.' This is quoted as B. F. Rühl assigns it to the 12th century, but it, as well as H, is stated in the British Museum Catalogue to belong to the 10th. I owe to the kindness of a friend a very careful report on the readings of both MSS. in a number of passages.

My knowledge of MS. readings is derived mainly, except where other sources are specified, from the Adnotatio critica of Baiter (1866–67) and from that of Orelli (1845).

I have also mentioned some suggestions of G. C. Cobet in Mnemosyne (8. 182–200, 1880), and of Professor Tyrrell.

My obligations to Professor Tyrrell, to Mr. G. E. Jeans, and to MM. Hofmann and Andresen will appear frequently in the notes, but I wish to acknowledge them here also.

I have read with great interest some notes by M. Cobet in Mnemosyne VII (1875) on Cicero's Philippics, the general drift of which is to shew that the friends of Antony were much more influential in the senate during the war of Mutina than would be gathered by a hasty reader of those orations. I do not find it needful to alter what I have said in the Introduction to Part V; but M. Cobet's remarks deserve to be carefully considered by students of the period there referred to.

A paper by L. Gurlitt discusses at some length the nature of the collection of letters 'Ad Familiares.' He believes that all the letters written by or to Cicero which we now possess, except those to Atticus, form part of one single collection made by Tiro, of which large portions have perished; that the seventy letters mentioned Ad Att. 16. 5, 5 were probably all contained in the thirteenth book 'Ad Familiares;' and that the collection was probably published after the final breach between Antony and Octavian, when attacks upon Antony would no longer give offence to the party dominant in Italy.

I need hardly refer to Mr. Froude's 'Caesar' and to Mr. Trollope's Life of Cicero. I am glad that writers of such established popularity should have employed themselves in making the great names of Roman history more familiar to English readers. These two books have furnished, wholly or partly, occasion for the appearance of articles in the Edinburgh Review for October, 1879, and in the Quarterly Review for October, 1879, and October, 1880, which I must regard as valuable contributions to Roman history without professing complete agreement with either of them.

I can hardly leave unnoticed the very able and unsparingly hostile criticism of Cicero's career and character prefixed by Mr. Pretor to his edition of the first book of the letters to Atticus. My introductions and occasional remarks will shew that I do not altogether agree with Mr. Pretor. As a more general comment I will here add that every candid reader must allow that Cicero was vain, excitable, egotistical, and often wanting in penetration and foresight as a statesman. But it should also,

I think, be remembered that his private life and his provincial administration were pure; that the state of public affairs threw extraordinary difficulties in the way of one who, while sincerely attached, as I believe Cicero to have been, to the old constitution of the Commonwealth, could not be blind to the selfishness and impracticability of most of its supporters; that if he was egotistical and exacting he was also ready to exert himself on behalf of others—on behalf, for instance, of members of the defeated party during the government of Caesar; and lastly that in more than one important political crisis he chose the more dangerous but honourable side when he might have secured safety and influence by submission.

In preparing either the second or the third edition I have been indebted in various ways to Professor Nettleship, to the Rev. M. Creighton of Merton College, to the Rev. C. W. Boase and to Mr. H. F. Pelham of Exeter College, to the Rev. J. R. King of Oriel College, to Mr. A. O. Prickard of New College, to the Rev. W. W. Merry and to Mr. W. W. Fowler of Lincoln College, to the Rev. W. Lock of Magdalen and Keble Colleges, and to the Rev. J. Wordsworth, Mr. C. B. Heberden, and Mr. F. Madan of Brasenose College.

I have read with pleasure a friendly but discriminating notice of the second edition of this work by Professor Iwan Müller in C. Bursian's Jahresbericht, 1874–5, p. 705.

The following are, I think, the most important alterations in the third edition as compared with the first: *repeated from the second*, those in the notes B, E, and F; in the notes on 'faenus,' p. 194, l. 3; 'Aristotelio more,' p. 214; 'lex curiata,' p. 217; 'Transpadani,' p. 222, l. 8; the intercalary month, p. 244, l. 9; the punishment of slaves, p. 476, l. 14, note; the mention of the 'lex Iulia municipalis,' p. 492; and the alterations in the twelfth Appendix: *appearing first in the third edition*, the fuller account of the Saturnalia on p. 483, and the increased number or length of the notes on Part V generally: especially on 'illis triumviris,' p. 556; on the dates of letters 139 and 140, see pp. 590 and 594; and on the position of Cularo, p. 593.

BRASENOSE COLLEGE,
Oxford, 1881.

CONTENTS.

	PAGE
Preface	v
Explanation of Signs and Abbreviations	xiv
Order of Letters in this selection	xvi
Names of correspondents	xx
List of books used	xxii
Chronological list of Cicero's writings	xxvii
Table of the principal events of Cicero's life	xxxii
Introduction to Part I.	1
Letters (1–19) and notes of Part I., 106–57 B.C.	25
Note A. Optimates	120
„ B. Provincia	120
„ C. Roman Letters and means of Correspondence	121
„ D. Origin of the collection of Cicero's Letters	121
„ E. On the meaning of the words 'Imperium' and 'Imperator'	122
Appendix I. State of the Roman Empire about the time of Cicero's entrance into public life	124
„ II. Campaigns of Pompey in the East	127
„ III. Life of Atticus	128
„ IV. On the Legality of the execution of Lentulus and his Accomplices	131
„ V. On Cicero's Estates and other Property	133
Introduction to Part II.	135
Letters (20–45) and notes of Part II., 57–49 B.C.	160
Note F. On the Commission granted to Pompey in September, 57 B.C.	286
Appendix VI. On the legal question at issue between Caesar and the Senate	287
„ VII. Distribution of the Roman forces at the beginning of the civil war between Caesar and Pompey	291

	PAGE
Introduction to Part III.	293
Letters (46–78) and notes of Part III., 49–48 B.C.	303
Introduction to Part IV.	393
Letters (79–104) and notes of Part IV., 48–45 B.C.	405
Appendix VIII. On the Calendar	487
„ IX. Caesar's laws, enacted from 49–44 B.C. ..	489
„ X. On the honours voted to Caesar	492
Introduction to Part V.	497
Letters (105–148) and notes of Part V., 44–43 B.C.	515
Appendix XI. State of the Roman provinces and armies from the death of Caesar to that of Cicero	611
„ XII. On the meaning of the words 'Colonia,' 'Municipium,' and 'Praefectura'	614
Index I. Of Greek words and phrases	621
„ II.[1] Of Latin words and phrases explained in the notes ..	624
„ III. Of proper names	648
Additions and Corrections	663

[1] [I have been rather doubtful at times whether to insert a word in II or III.]

EXPLANATION OF SIGNS AND ABBREVIATIONS.

* or . . in the text shews that words are wanting to complete the sense.

† shews that the words following it are corrupt.

[ ] shews that the words enclosed are considered by Baiter to be an interpolation.

Italics are used in the text where words or syllables have been added by Baiter.

I have referred to the Latin grammars of Madvig and Ramshorn, and occasionally to that of C. G. Zumpt, merely by the author's name.

a. d. = ante diem.
abl. or ablat. = ablative.
abs. or absol. = absolute.
acc. or accus. = accusative.
adj. = adjective.
Alt. Alter. = Alterthümer.
ap. = apud.
App. = Appendix.
App. = Appiani Alexandrini.
„ Bell. Civ. = De Bello Civili.
„ Mithr. = De Bello Mithridatico.
„ Parth. = De Rebus Parthicis. A spurious work, and apparently in great measure almost a literal transcript of some chapters of Plutarch's Life of Crassus. Cp. Long's note on Plut. Crass. 15.
„ Pun. = De Rebus Punicis.
„ Syr. = De Rebus Syriacis.
Ascon. = Q. Asconii Pediani Commentarius in Ciceronis Orationes, in Orelli's collection of Scholia to Cicero. Those portions of the Commentary which are not considered genuine I have quoted as Pseud. Ascon.
Att. = Atticus.
Bell. Afric. = Auctor de Bello Africano, a treatise usually published with Caesar's works.
Bell. Alex. = Auctor de Bello Alexandrino.
„ Hisp. = „ Hispano.
Billerb. = Billerbeck.
Caes. = C. Iulii Caesaris Commentarii.
„ Bell. Gall. = De Bello Gallico.
„ „ Civ. = „ Civili.
caus. = causae.
Cic. = M. Tullii Ciceronis.
„ Brut. = Brutus sive de Claris Oratoribus.
„ Div. in Caec. = Divinatio in Caecilium.
„ Divin. = de Divinatione.
„ In Clod. et. Cur. = Oratio in Clodium Curionem.
„ Pro Dom. or De Dom. = Oratio pro Domo Sua.
„ Fam. or Ad Fam. = Epistolae ad Familiares.
„ De Fin. or Fin. = De Finibus Bonorum et Malorum.
„ Orat. = Orator.
„ De Orat. = De Oratore.
„ Part. Orat. = Partitiones Oratoriae.
„ Prov. Cons. = De Provinciis Consularibus.
„ Ad Q. F. = Epistolae ad Quintum Fratrem.
„ Pro C. Rab. or Rab. = Pro C. Rabirio, perduellionis reo.
„ „ Rab. Post. = Pro C. Rabirio Postumo.
„ Rhet. ad Herenn. = Rhetoricorum ad Herennium.
„ Somn. Scip. = Somnium Scipionis, in De Rep. 6, 9.
„ In Vat. = Interrogatio in P. Vatinium testem[1].
Q. Cic. de Pet. Cons. = Q. Ciceronis de Petitione Consulatus liber.
conj. = conjunction, or conjunctive mood, according to the context.
constr. = construction.
Corn. Nep. = Cornelii Nepotis vitae excellentium Imperatorum.

[1] I have generally referred to Cicero's works without mentioning the author's name

cos. = consul.
cp. = compare.
d. at the beginning of letters = dicit; at the end, data or dabam.
def., defin. = definitivus.
Diog. Laert. = Diogenes Laertius de Vitis Philosophorum.
Dionys. = Dionysii Halicarnassensis Antiquitates Romanae.
e. q. v. = ego quidem, or quoque, valeo; e. v. = ego valeo.
Ep., Epp. = Epistle, Epistles.
Epit. = Epitome.
Fest. = Sex. Pompeius Festus de verborum significatione (ed. Müller, Lipsiae, 1839).
A. or Aul. Gell. = Auli Gellii.
" N. A. = Noctes Atticae.
gen. = genitive.
Hofm. = Hofmann.
ind., indic. = indicative mood.
inf., infin. = infinitive mood.
instr., instrum. = instrumenti.
Ioseph. = Flavii Iosephi.
" Antiq. = Antiquitates Iudaicae, Ἰουδαϊκὴ ἀρχαιολογία.
" Bell. Iud. = De Bello Iudaico, περὶ τοῦ Ἰουδαϊκοῦ πολέμου.
K., Kal. = Kalendae.
L. G. = Latin Grammar.
Lamprid. = Aelius Lampridius, among the Historiae Augustae Scriptores.
Macrob. = Aurelii Ambrosii Theodosii Macrobii.
" Sat. = Saturnalia.
metaph. = metaphorical.
mil. = militum.
obj. = objectivus.
obs., obss. = observation, observations.
Onom., Onomast. = Onomasticon.
Oros. = Orosii, Pauli, Historiarum adversus Paganos libri vii.
P. and B. = Messrs. Prichard and Bernard's edition.
pl. = plebis.
pl., plur. = plural; also plurimam (in addresses of letters).
Pliny = C. Plinii Secundi.
" H. N. = Historia Naturalis.
" Epp. = Epistolae.
Plut. = Plutarchus.
" De Defect. Orac. = De Defectu Oraculorum.
poss. possess. = possessive.
pr. = praetor: also pridie.
prep. = preposition.
procos. = proconsul.
propr. = propraetor.
q. = quod.
Quint. = M. Fabii Quintiliani.
" Inst. Orat. = Institutio Oratoria.
reff. = references.
s., sal. = salutem.
s. v. b. or b. e. = si vales bene or bene est.
Sall. = C. Sallustii Crispi.
" Cat. = De Catilinae Coniuratione.
" Iug. = De Bello Iugurthino.
sc., scil. = scilicet.
Schol. Bob. = Scholiasta Bobiensis in Ciceronem. In Orelli's Collection of Scholia.
sing. = singular.
Soph. = Sophocles.
Stob. = Ioannis Stobaei.
" Floril. = Florilegium (ἀνθολόγιον).
Strab. = Strabonis.
" Geogr. = Geographica.
Suet. = C. Suetonii Tranquilli.
" Claud. = Claudius.
" Iul. = Iulius.
" Oct. = Octavius.
" Tib. = Tiberius.
sup., supp. = supply.
sup., supr. = supra.
tr. = tribunus, tribuni.
Val. Max. M. (or P.) = Valerii Maximi Factorum et Dictorum Memorabilium libri ix.
v. = vide.
Varr. = M. Terentii Varronis.
" L. L. = De Lingua Latina.
" R. R. = De Re Rustica.
Vell. = M. Velleii Paterculi ex Historiae Romanae libris duobus quae supersunt.
voc., voce. = voce, vocibus.
Wiel. = Wieland and Gräter's translation.
Zumpt, A. W.
" C. E. = Commentationes Epigraphicae.
" S. R. = Studia Romana.

This list does not comprise all the abbreviations used, perhaps; but I hope that those which do not appear in it will be easily intelligible.

ORDER OF THE LETTERS IN THIS SELECTION COMPARED WITH THE ORDINARY ARRANGEMENT.

THIS SELECTION.			
1	Ad Att.	1.	1.
2	"	1.	2.
3	Ad Fam.	5.	7.
4	"	5.	1.
5	"	5.	2.
6	Ad Att.	1.	13.
7	"	1.	14.
8	"	1.	16.
9	"	2.	1.
10	"	2.	16.
11	"	2.	18.
12	"	2.	19.
13	"	2.	24.
14	"	2.	25.
15	Ad Q. F.	1.	2.
16	Ad Att.	3.	15.
17	Ad Fam.	14.	2.
18	"	14.	1.
19	Ad Att.	3.	23.
20	"	4.	1.
21	Ad Fam.	1.	1.
22	"	1.	2.
23	Ad Q. F.	2.	3.
24	"	2.	4.
25	Ad Att.	4.	5.
26	Ad Fam.	1.	7.
27	"	7.	5.
28	Ad Att.	4.	15.
29	Ad Fam.	1.	9.
30	"	2.	6.
31	Ad Att.	5.	11.
32	"	5.	16.
33	Ad Fam.	8.	4.
34	"	8.	8.
35	"	8.	6.
36	Ad Att.	5.	21.
37	Ad Fam.	2.	13.
38	Ad Att.	6.	2.
39	Ad Fam.	15.	5.
40	"	15.	6.
41	"	8.	14.
42	Ad Att.	6.	6.
43	Ad Fam.	14.	5.
44	Ad Att.	7.	7.
45	"	7.	9.
46	"	7.	10.
47	"	7.	11.
48	"	7.	13.
49	"	8.	11 A.
50	"	8.	11 B.
51	"	8.	12 D.
52	Ad Fam.	16.	12.
53	"	16.	15.
54	Ad Att.	8.	3.
55	"	8.	9.
56	"	8.	11.
57	"	8.	13.
58	"	8.	15 A.
59	"	8.	16.
60	"	9.	6 A.
61	"	9.	7.
62	"	9.	9.
63	"	9.	10.
64	"	9.	11 A.
65	"	9.	12.
66	"	9.	16.
67	"	9.	18.
68	"	10.	1.
69	Ad Fam.	8.	16.
70	"	2.	16.
71	Ad Att.	10.	8.
72	"	10.	8 A.
73	"	10.	8 B.
74	"	10.	16.
75	Ad Fam.	14.	7.
76	"	8.	17.

THIS SELECTION.			
77	Ad Fam.	9.	9.
78	Ad Att.	11.	4.
79	"	11.	5.
80	"	11.	6.
81	"	11.	9.
82	"	11.	12.
83	Ad Fam.	15.	15.
84	Ad Att.	12.	1.
85	"	12.	2.
86	Ad Fam.	9.	5.
87	"	9.	18.
88	"	7.	3.
89	"	9.	17.
90	"	4.	4.
91	"	6.	6.
92	"	6.	7.
93	"	13.	11.
94	"	4.	14.
95	"	4.	11.
96	Ad Att.	12.	21.
97	Ad Fam.	13.	16.
98	"	4.	5.
99	"	4.	6.
100	"	6.	2.
101	"	4.	12.
102	"	13.	4.
103	"	12.	18.
104	Ad Att.	13.	52.
105	"	14.	1.
106	"	14.	2.
107	Ad Fam.	11.	1.
108	Ad Att.	14.	12.
109	"	14.	13 A.
110	"	14.	13 B.
111	Ad Fam.	9.	14.
112	Ad Att.	14.	21.
113	Ad Fam.	11.	27.
114	"	11.	28.
115	"	12.	1.
116	"	11.	3.
117	Ad Att.	16.	7.
118	Ad Fam.	12.	2.
119	"	12.	23.
120	"	11.	4.
121	Ad Att.	16.	8.
122	"	16.	11.
123	Ad Fam.	11.	5.
124	"	12.	22.
125	"	11.	8.
126	"	12.	4.
127	"	10.	28.
128	"	12.	5.
129	"	10.	31.
130	"	10.	6.
131	"	10.	27.
132	"	10.	8.
133	"	10.	10.
134	"	12.	6.
135	"	10.	30.
136	"	11.	9.
137	"	11.	10.
138	"	12.	12.
139	"	10.	11.
140	"	10.	15.
141	"	10.	34.
142	"	10.	13.
143	"	11.	23.
144	"	10.	35.
145	"	11.	13 a.
146	"	10.	23.
147	"	12.	10.
148	"	10.	24.

ORDER OF THE LETTERS IN THE ORDINARY ARRANGEMENT COMPARED WITH THAT ADOPTED IN THIS SELECTION.

AD ATTICUM.		THIS SELECTION.	AD ATTICUM.		THIS SELECTION.
1. 1.	..	1	8. 15 A	..	58
1. 2.	..	2	8. 16.	..	59
1. 13.	..	6	9. 6 A.	..	60
1. 14.	..	7	9. 7.	..	61
1. 16.	..	8	9. 9.	..	62
2. 1.	..	9	9. 10.	..	63
2. 16.	..	10	9. 11 A.	..	64
2. 18.	..	11	9. 12.	..	65
2. 19.	..	12	9. 16.	..	66
2. 24.	..	13	9. 18.	..	67
2. 25.	..	14	10. 1.	..	68
3. 15.	..	16	10. 8.	..	71
3. 23.	..	19	10. 8 A.	..	72
4. 1.	..	20	10. 8 B.	..	73
4. 5.	..	25	10. 16.	...	74
4. 15.	..	28	11. 4.	..	78
5. 11.	..	31	11. 5.	..	79
5. 16.	..	32	11. 6.	..	80
5. 21.	..	36	11. 9.	..	81
6. 2.	..	38	11. 12.	..	82
6. 6.	..	42	12. 1.	..	84
7. 7.	..	44	12. 2.	..	85
7. 9.	..	45	12. 21.	..	96
7. 10.	..	46	13. 52.	..	104
7. 11.	..	47	14. 1.	..	105
7. 13.	..	48	14. 2.	..	106
8. 3.	..	54	14. 12.	..	108
8. 9.	..	55	14. 13 A.	..	109
8. 11.	..	56	14. 13 B.	..	110
8. 11 A.	..	49	14. 21.	..	112
8. 11 B.	..	50	16. 7.	..	117
8. 12 D.	..	51	16. 8.	..	121
8. 13.	..	57	16. 11.	..	122

AD FAMILIARES.		THIS SELECTION.
1. 1.	..	21
1. 2.	..	22
1. 7.	..	26
1. 9.	..	29
2. 6.	..	30
2. 13.	..	37
2. 16.	..	70
4. 4.	..	90
4. 5.	..	98
4. 6.	..	99
4. 11.	..	95
4. 12.	..	101
4. 14.	..	94
5. 1.	..	4
5. 2.	..	5
5. 7.	..	3
6. 2.	..	100
6. 6.	..	91
6. 7.	..	92
7. 3.	..	88
7. 5.	..	27
8. 4.	..	33
8. 6.	..	35
8. 8.	..	34
8. 14.	..	41
8. 16.	..	69
8. 17.	..	76
9. 5.	..	86
9. 9.	..	77
9. 14.	..	111
9. 17.	..	89
9. 18.	..	87
10. 6.	..	130
10. 8.	..	132
10. 10.	..	133
10. 11.	..	139
10. 13.	..	142
10. 15.	..	140
10. 23.	..	146
10. 24.	..	148
10. 27.	..	131
10. 28.	..	127

AD FAMILIARES.		THIS SELECTION.
10. 30.	..	135
10. 31.	..	129
10. 34.	..	141
10. 35.	..	144
11. 1.	..	107
11. 3.	..	116
11. 4.	..	120
11. 5.	..	123
11. 8.	..	125
11. 9.	..	136
11. 10.	..	137
11. 13 a.	..	145
11. 23.	..	143
11. 27.	..	113
11. 28.	..	114
12. 1.	..	115
12. 2.	..	118
12. 4.	..	126
12. 5.	..	128
12. 6.	..	134
12. 10.	..	147
12. 12.	..	138
12. 18.	..	103
12. 22.	..	124
12. 23.	..	119
13. 4.	..	102
13. 11.	..	93
13. 16.	..	97
14. 1.	..	18
14. 2.	..	17
14. 5.	..	43
14. 7.	..	75
15. 5.	..	39
15. 6.	..	40
15. 15.	..	83
16. 12.	..	52
16. 15.	..	53

AD QUINTUM FRATREM.

1. 2.	..	15
2. 3.	..	23
2. 4.	..	24

NAMES OF THE CORRESPONDENTS OF CICERO AND HIS FRIENDS (LETTERS FROM OR TO WHOM ARE INCLUDED IN THIS SELECTION), ARRANGED IN ALPHABETICAL ORDER.

Names.	*Letters addressed to.*	*Letters written by.*
M. Aemilius Lepidus	131.	141; 144.
M. Antonius	110; 116.	72; 109.
C. Asinius Pollio		129.
Q. Caecilius Metellus Celer	5.	4.
A. Caecina	91.	92.
M. Caelius Rufus	37; 70.	33; 34; 35; 41; 69; 76.
C. Cassius Longinus	83; 107; 115; 118; 126; 128; 134; 147.	116; 138.
M. Claudius Marcellus		95.
P. Cornelius Dolabella	111.	77.
P. Cornelius Lentulus Spinther	21; 22; 26; 29.	
L. Cornelius Balbus		58.
Q. Cornificius	103; 119; 124.	
C. Iulius Caesar	27; 64; 97.	60; 66; 73.
D. Iunius Brutus	123; 125.	107; 120; 136; 137; 143; 145.
M. Iunius Brutus	93; 107.	116.
A. Manlius Torquatus	100.	
M. Marius	88.	
C. Matius	113.	114.
L. Munatius Plancus	130; 133; 142.	132; 139; 140; 146; 148.
L. Papirius Paetus	87; 89.	
Cn. Plancius	94.	
Cn. Pompeius Magnus	3; 50.	49; 51.
M. Porcius Cato	40.	39.

Names.	*Letters addressed to.*	*Letters written by.*
C. Scribonius Curio	30.	
Ser. Sulpicius Galba		135.
Ser. Sulpicius Rufus	90; 99.	98; 101.
Terentia	17; 18; 43; 75.	
M. Terentius Varro	86.	
C. Trebonius	127.	
Q. Tullius Cicero	15; 23; 24.	
M. Tullius Tiro	52; 53.	
Q. Valerius Orca	102.	

The rest of the letters, including part of the 66th, are from Cicero to T. Pomponius Atticus.

EDITIONS OF CICERO'S EPISTLES,

AND OTHER BOOKS USED IN PREPARING THE PRESENT SELECTION.

TEXT.

Epistolae, recensuit J. G. Baiter. 2 vols. 8vo. Lipsiae. 1866–1867, being vols. IX, X of a complete edition of Cicero's works, by J. G. Baiter and C. L. Kayser, in 11 vols. Leipzig. 1860–1869.

Epistolae, recognovit A. S. Wesenberg, 2 vols. 12mo. Lipsiae. 1872–3.

Opera, volumen tertium epistolas continens, curaverunt I. C. Orellius et I. G. Baiterus, imp. 8vo. Turici. 1845.

Cobet, C. G., de locis quibusdam in Ciceronis epistolis. Mnemosyne, 8. 182–200. 1880.

Madvig, I. N. Adversaria Critica, vol. ii. 8vo. Hauniae. 1873.

Rühl, F. Rheinisches Museum, Ed. XXX. 1875, pp. 26 and 135.

" Wissenschaftliche Monatsblätter (Königsberg) 1878, pp. 25 and 85. On the Harleian MSS. 2682 and 2773.

Thurot, Charles. Ciceronis Epistolae ad Familiares, notice sur un manuscrit du XIIe siècle. Bibliothèque de l'école des hautes études. Dix-septième fascicule. Paris. 1874.

Emendationes alterae ad Ciceronis Epistolarum editionem, scripsit A. S. Wesenberg, 8vo. Lipsiae. 1873.

COMMENTARIES.

M. Tullii Ciceronis Scholiastae, ediderunt I. C. Orellius et I. G. Baiterus, imp. 8vo. Turici. 1833.

Billerbeck, Iulius, Epistolae temporis ordine dispositae, 4 vols. 8vo. Hannover. 1836.

Boot, I. G. Epistolarum ad Atticum libri XVI. Recensuit et adnotatione illustravit I. C. G. Boot, 2 vols. royal 8vo. Amstelod. 1865–1866.

Frey, Joseph. Ausgewählte Briefe Cicero's für den Schulgebrauch erklärt, 8vo. Leipzig. 1864.

Hofmann, Friedrich. Ausgewählte Briefe von M. Tullius Cicero, 1 Bändchen, 8vo. Berlin. 1860; 2 do., bearbeitet von Georg Andresen. Berlin. 1878.

Matthiae, Aug., and Müller, E. H. Epistolae selectae. Editio 4ta. 8vo. Lipsiae. 1849.

Parry, E. St. J., M.A. Ciceronis Epistolarum Delectus, 12mo. London. 1867.

Pretor, Alfred, M.A., Fellow of St. Catherine's College, Cambridge. The Letters of Cicero to Atticus, Book I, with notes, and an essay on the character of the Author, sm. 8vo. London and Cambridge. 1873.

[1] Prichard, Constantine E., the late, and Bernard, E. R., M.A. Selected Letters of Cicero, for the use of Schools (Clarendon Press Series), 12mo. Oxford. 1872.

Ross, Joannes, A. M. Epistolas ad Familiares edidit et commentario Anglico instruxit, 2 vols. 8vo. Cantab. 1749.

Süpfle, K. F. Epistolae selectae, 6te Auflage, 8vo. Karlsruhe, 1866.

Tyrrell, Robert Yelverton, M.A., Fellow of Trinity College and Professor of Latin in the University of Dublin. The Correspondence of Cicero, vol. I. Dublin and London. 1879.

Yonge, J. E., M.A. The Letters of Cicero, Part I, containing Books I, II, and III. New edition, sm. 8vo. London. 1872.

I have also occasionally referred to the notes of Manutius and to the edition of Schültz.

TRANSLATIONS.

Jeans, Rev. G. E., M.A. The Life and Letters of M. Tullius Cicero, being a new translation of the letters included in Mr. Watson's selection, with notes. London. 1880.

Metzger, K. L. F. M. Tullius Cicero's Sämmtliche Briefe übersetzt, Bändchen 1–5, 12mo. Stuttgart. 1859–1863.

Wieland, C. M. M. Tullius Cicero's Sämmtliche Briefe übersetzt und erläutert: vollendet von F. D. Gräter, 12 vols. 18mo. Leipzig. 1840–1841.

WORKS ILLUSTRATING THE LIFE OF CICERO.

Abeken. Life and Letters of Cicero translated by C. Merivale, 8vo. London. 1854.

[1] Referred to in the Notes as P. and B.

Boissier, Gaston. Cicéron et ses amis, 8vo. Paris. 1865.

Brückner, C. A. F. Leben des M. Tullius Cicero, 8vo. Göttingen. 1852.

Forsyth, W., Q.C. Life of Cicero, 2 vols. 8vo. London. 1864

Gurlitt, L. De M. Tullii Ciceronis epistulis earumque pristina collectione. Dissertatio inauguralis. Fribergae Sax. 1879.

Middleton, Conyers, D.D. Life of Cicero, 2 vols. 8vo. London. 1823.

Nake, Bruno. Der Briefwechsel zwischen Cicero und D. Brutus. In Jahrbücher für Classische Philologie. VIII. Supplement Bd. 1875–6, pp. 649–700.

„ De Planci et Ciceronis epistulis, in Jahresbericht über das Luisenstädtische Gymnasium in Berlin. Berlin. 1866.

Onomasticon Tullianum, curaverunt I. C. Orellius et I. G. Baiterus, 3 vols. royal 8vo. Turici. 1836–1838.

Quarterly Review, article on Cicero, October 1880.

Suringar, W. H. D. M. Tullii Ciceronis commentarii rerum suarum; accesserunt annales Ciceroniani, 8vo. Leidae. 1854.

„ M. Caelii Rufi et M. Tullii Ciceronis epistolae mutuae. Lugd. Bat. 1846.

Trollope, Antony. Life of Cicero, 2 vols. London. 1880.

WORKS ON THE GENERAL HISTORY OF THE TIME.

Arnold, Thomas, D.D. History of the later Roman Commonwealth, 2 vols. 8vo. London. 1845.

Champagny, Le Comte Franz de. Les Césars, 3ème édition, 3 tomes, 12mo. Paris. 1859.

Cobet, C. G. Annotationes ad Plutarchi vitam M. Bruti, Mnemosyne, VII, 1 and 225 (1879).

„ Ad Epistolas Ciceronis et Bruti, ib. 262.

„ Ad Ciceronis Philippicas, ib. 113.

Corpus Inscriptionum Latinarum, consilio et auctoritate academiae litterarum regiae Borussicae editum, vol. 1, folio. Berolini. MDCCCLXIII.

Drumann, W. Geschichte Roms. oder Pompeius, Caesar, Cicero und ihre Zeitgenossen, 6 vols. 8vo. Königsberg. 1834–1844.

Edinburgh Review. Article on Froude's Caesar, October 1879.

Fischer, E. W. Römische Zeittafeln, 4to. Altona. 1846.

Froude, J. A. Caesar. a sketch. London. 1879.

Guiraud, Paul. Le différend entre César et le sénat. Paris. 1878.

Liddell, Dean. History of Rome, 2 vols. 8vo. London. 1855.

Long, George, M.A. Civil Wars of Rome. Select Lives translated from Plutarch, with notes, 5 vols. in 2, 12mo. London. 1844–1848.
„ Decline of the Roman Republic, vols. 3–5, 8vo. London. 1869–1874.
Merivale, Rev. C., B.D. History of the Romans under the Empire, vols. 1–3, 8vo. London. 1850–1851.
Mommsen, Theodor. De Collegiis et Sodaliciis Romanorum, 8vo. Kiliae. 1843.
„ History of Rome, translated by Rev. W. P. Dickson, vol. 4, parts 1–2, 12mo. London. 1866.
„ Die Rechtsfrage zwischen Caesar und dem Senat, 4to. Breslau. 1857.
„ Römische Forschungen, vol. 1, 8vo. Berlin. 1864.
Napoléon III. Histoire de Jules César, tomes 1–2, imp. 8vo. Paris. 1865–1866.
Peter, Carl. Römische Geschichte, 2te Auflage, vol. 2, 8vo. Halle. 1866.
Quarterly Review, article on Caesar, October 1879.
Zumpt, A. W. Commentationes Epigraphicae, 2 vols. 4to. Berolini. 1850–1854.
„ Studia Romana, 8vo. Berolini. 1859.

GRAMMARS.

Madvig, I. N., translated by Woods, 4th edition, 8vo. Oxford and London, 1859.
Nägelsbach, C. F. Lateinische Stilistik für Deutsche, 4te Auflage, 8vo. Nürnberg. 1865.
Ramshorn, Ludwig. Lateinische Grammatik, 2te Ausgabe, 8vo. Leipzig. 1830.
Zumpt, C. G., translated by Schmitz, 6th edition, 8vo. London. 1861.

DICTIONARIES.

Forcellini et Facciolati totius Latinitatis Lexicon, 4 vols. in 2, 4to. Editio in Germania prima. Lipsiae. 1839.
Smith, Dr. William. Latin-English Dictionary, 8vo. London. 1855.
„ Dictionary of Greek and Roman Antiquities, 2nd edition, 8vo. London. 1856.
„ Dictionary of Biography and Mythology, 3 vols. 8vo. London. 1844–1849.
„ Dictionary of Geography, 2 vols. 8vo. London. 1856–1857.

LAW AND ANTIQUITIES, BESIDES THE ABOVE.

Becker, W. A., and Marquardt, J. Handbuch der Römischen Alterthümer, 3ter Theil, 8vo. Leipzig. 1851.

Lange, Ludwig. Römische Alterthümer, vol. 1, 2te Auflage, 8vo. Berlin. 1863; vol. 2. Berlin. 1862; vol. 3. Berlin. 1871.

Madvigii, I. N., Opuscula Academica, 8vo. Hauniae. 1834; vol. 2. ib. 1842.

[1] Marquardt, J. Römische Staatsverwaltung, vols 1–3. Leipzig. 1873–1878.

[1] Mommsen, Theodor. Römisches Staatsrecht, vols. 1, 2, 8vo. Leipzig. 1871–1875.

Rein, W. Criminalrecht der Römer, 8vo. Leipzig. 1844.

" Privatrecht der Römer, 8vo. Leipzig. 1858.

[1] These two works *form* part of a new edition of Becker and Marquardt's Handbook of Roman Antiquities.

CHRONOLOGICAL LIST OF CICERO'S WRITINGS.

* Defective. ** Very fragmentary. † Lost.

B.C. about

86 De Inventione Rhetorica libri ii. (cp. De Orat. 1. 2, 5; Quintil. Inst. Orat. 3. 6, 58).

** Translations of Aratus' Phaenomena, and of other poems of Aratus (cp. De Deor. Nat. 2. 41, 104).

** Translations from Homer (De Fin. 5. 18, 49).

* Translation of the Oeconomics of Xenophon (De Off. 2. 24, 87), and of † various Dialogues of Plato.

81 [1]* Oratio pro P. Quinctio (cp. A. Gell. N. A. 15. 28, 3).

80 " " Sex. Roscio Amerino (A. Gell. l. c.; Quintil. Inst. Orat. 12. 6, 4).

** " " L. Vareno.

79 † " " Muliere Arretina (Pro Caec. 33, 97).

† " " Titinia (Brut. 60, 217).

75 † " " Patriciis Adulescentibus apud Sex. Peducaeum (Plut. Cic. 6).

74 ** " Quaestoris decedentis, habita Lilybaei (Pseud. Ascon. Argum. in Divin. in Caec.).

71 " pro M. Tullio.

? † " " C. Mustio (In Verr. 2 Act. 1. 53, 139).

70 Divinatio in Caecilium; and In Verrem, Actio 1; Actio 2. 1–5.

69 * Oratio pro M. Fonteio.

" " A. Caecina.

68 First Letter to Atticus (Ad Att. 1. 5).

[1] Mr. Trollope (Cicero 1. 90 foll.) has given some reasons for placing the speech Pro P. Quinctio after that Pro Sex. Roscio Amerino.

B.C. about

* Oratio pro Q. Roscio Comoedo.

67 ** Oratio pro P. Oppio.

66 „ de Imperio Cn. Pompeii, seu pro Lege Manilia (Ib. 1; 24, 69).

„ pro A. Cluentio (cp. Ib. 53, 147).

** „ „ M. Fundanio et † C. Orchivio (cp. Q. Cic. de Pet. Cons. 5. 19).

** „ „ C. Manilio (cp. Plut. Cic. 9).

† „ „ Q. Mucio (cp. Orat. in Tog. Cand. 6).

65 ** Orationes Duae pro C. Cornelio (Ascon. in Cornel. 93, 94).

64 ** Oratio in Toga Candida (Ascon. Argum. pp. 109; 110).

** „ pro Q. Gallio (Ascon. ad Orat. in Tog. Cand. p. 113; Q. Cic. de Pet. Cons. 5, 19).

63 Orationes Consulares (cp. Ad Att. 2. 1. 3).

Oratio in Senatu, Kal. Ian., de Lege Agraria.

„ ad Quirites contra P. Rullum.

** „ de Othone.

* „ pro C. Rabirio.

** „ de Proscriptorum Filiis.

† „ cum Provinciam in Contione deponeret.

„ in Catilinam Orationes Quatuor.

Orationes duae, breves, de Lege Agraria (one no longer extant).

Oratio pro L. Murena (not mentioned Ad Att. l. c.)

† „ C. Pisone (Pro Flacco 39, 98).

62 † „ contra Contionem Q. Metelli (cp. Ad Fam. 5. 2, 8).

„ pro P. Sulla.

„ „ Archia Poeta (Schol. Bob. on 2, 3, of that speech).

† Letter to Pompey on his consulship (Pro Planc. 34, 85, and Schol. Bob. thereon).

First Letter 'Ad Familiares' (5. 7).

61 ** Oratio in Clodium et Curionem (Schol. Bob. Argum.: cp. Ad Att. 1. 16, 1).

60 † Commentarius consulatus sui, Graece scriptus (Ad Att. 1. 19, 10).

** Poem on his consulship (Ad Att. 2. 3, 3).

Translation of Aratus' Prognostica (Ad Att. 2. 1, 11).

† Oratio pro P. Scipione Nasica (Ad Att. 2. 1, 9).

59 † „ „ C. Antonio (De Domo 16, 41; Dion Cassius 38. 10).

B.C. about

† Oratio pro A. Thermo (Pro Flacco 39, 98).
* „ „ L. Flacco (Ad Att. 2. 25, 1).
59 ? ** Chorographia, a geographical work (cp. Ad Att. 2. 6, 1; Priscian. 6, 83, ap. Baiter. xi. 76).
57 ? Oratio Post Reditum in Senatu (Ad Att. 4. 1, 5).
? „ „ „ ad Quirites (Ad Att. 4. 1, 6).
? „ de Domo Sua (Ib. 4. 2, 2).
56 ** „ „ Rege Alexandrino (Ad Q. F. 2. 2. 3).
„ pro P. Sestio (Ib. 2. 4, 1).
„ in P. Vatinium (Ad Q. F. 2. 4, 1; Ad Fam. 1. 9, 7).
† „ pro L. Calpurnio Bestia (Ad Q. F. 2. 3, 6).
? „ de Haruspicum Responsis.
„ „ Provinciis Consularibus (Pro Balbo 27, 61; Ascon. Argument. in Pisonian.; cp. Ad Fam. 1. 7, 10).
? „ pro P. Asicio (Pro Cael. 10. 23, 24).
„ „ M. Caelio (Ad Q. F. 2, 13 [11 Bait.], 2; Pro Cael. 13, 32).
„ „ L. Cornelio Balbo.
† „ „ M. Cispio (Pro Planc. 31, 75).
55 „ in L. Pisonem (Ascon. in Pisonian. Intr.).
† „ pro L. Caninio Gallo (Ad Fam. 7. 1, 4).
De Oratore, libri iii. (Ad Fam. 1. 9, 23).
? ** De Temporibus Suis libri iii. versibus scripti (Ad Fam. 1. 9, 23).
54 † Oratio pro M. Crasso (Ad Fam. 1. 9, 20).
† „ de Reatinorum Causa (Ad Att. 4. 15, 5).
† „ pro C. Messio (Ad Att. 4. 15, 9).
† „ „ Druso (Ad Att. l. c.; Ad Q. F. 2. 16, 3).
** „ „ Vatinio (Ascon. in Scaurian. p. 131; Ad Q. F. 2. 16, 3).
* „ „ Scauro (Ascon. l. c.; Ad Q. F. 3. 1, 11).
„ „ Cn. Plancio (Ad Q. F. l. c.; Schol. Bob. ad Plancian. sub init.).
† „ „ A Gabinio (Pro. Rab. Post. 12, 32; Dion Cassius 39. 55).
„ „ C. Rabirio Postumo.
† „ „ Tenediorum Libertate (Ad Q. F. 2. 11, 2).
* De Re publica libri vi. (cp. Ad Att. 4. 16, 2).
53 ? Oratio de Aere Alieno Milonis (Schol. Bob. Argum).

B.C. about

52 Oratio pro T. Annio Milone (Ascon. in Milonian. p. 140).

† „ „ M. Saufeio (Ascon. l. c. 159).

† „ in T. Munatium Plancum Bursam (Dion Cassius 40, 55: cp. Ad Fam. 7. 2, 2).

? De Optimo Genere Oratorum, as a preface to a translation of Aesch. in Ctesiph. and Demosth. de Cor. (cap. 4, 10).

* De legibus libri iii. (Suringar, p. 721).

? Orationes duae pro P. Dolabella (Ad Fam. 3. 10, 5).

46 Oratio pro M. Marcello (Ad Fam. 4. 4, 4).

Paradoxa.

Brutus, sive De Claris Oratoribus.

Laus Catonis (Ad Att. 12. 4, 2; 12. 5, 2).

Orator (cp. 10, 35; Ad Att. 12. 6, 3).

? Partitiones Oratoriae.

Oratio pro Q. Ligario (Ad Fam. 6. 14, 2; Ad Att. 13. 12, 2).

45 ** Consolatio, sive De Luctu Minuendo (De Divin. 2. 1, 3; Pliny, Hist. Nat. Praef. § 22).

** Hortensius (Tusc. Disp. 3. 3, 6; 2. 2, 4).

* Academicorum libri iv. (Ad Att. 13. 12, 3; Tusc. Disp. 2. 2, 4).

De Finibus Bonorum et Malorum libri v. (Ad Att. 13. 12, 3; 13. 21, 4).

† Laudatio Porciae (Ad Att. 13. 37, 3).

Oratio pro Rege Deiotaro (Ad Fam. 9. 12, 2).

† Epistola ad Caesarem de Ordinanda Re publica (συμβουλευτικόν: cp. Ad Att. 12. 40, 2).

44 ? * Timaeus, sive de Universo.

Tusculanae Disputationes V. (Ad Att. 15. 4, 3).

De Deorum Natura libri iii. (De Divin. 1. 5, 8; 2. 1, 3).

De Divinatione libri ii.

De Fato (1. 1 and 2: cp. Ad Att. 15. 1, 3).

** De Gloria libri ii. (Ad Att. 16. 11, 1; 16. 6, 4).

Cato Maior, sive De Senectute (Ad Att. 14. 21, 3; 16. 11, 3; Divin. 2. 1, 3).

Laelius, sive De Amicitia.

De Officiis libri iii. (Ad Att. 16. 11, 4; 15. 13, 6).

Topica (Ad Fam. 7. 19).

Oratio de Pace (Philipp. 1. 1, 1).

Orationes Philippicae I–IV.

Ad Atticum 16. 15[1]. Dec.

[1] The last letter written to Atticus that has been preserved.

B.C. about	
43	Orationes Philippicae V–XIV.
	Ad Familiares 12. 10[1]. Quintil. Ineunte.
	„ „ 10. 24[2]. V. Kal. Sext.
Incerto anno	Oratio pro Popilio Laenate (Val. Max. 5. 3. 4).
	Translation from the Protagoras of Plato.
„	Marius, a poem (De Leg. 1. 1; De Divin. 1. 47, 106).

The above list has been compiled from notices of Cicero's life in Orelli's Onomasticon, in Baiter's Leipzig edition of Cicero, and in Suringar's Annales Ciceroniani.

[1] The last letter written by Cicero that has been preserved.
[2] „ „ „ to Cicero „ „

PRINCIPAL EVENTS IN THE LIFE OF CICERO[1].

Age of Cicero.		Date B.C.
	Birth of Cicero, Jan. 3	106
17	He serves under Cn. Pompeius Strabo in the Marsic war	89
18	Murder of P. Sulpicius. Flight of C. Marius .	88
19	Sulla goes to the East. Civil war. Return of Marius	87
20	Cicero writes the treatise 'De Inventione.' Death of C. Marius	86
23	Return of Sulla. Civil war renewed	83
25	Speech 'Pro Quinctio.' Legislation of Sulla .	81
26	Speech 'Pro Sex. Roscio Amerino'	80
27–28	Cicero travels in Greece and Asia	79–78
	Death of Sulla	78
29	Cicero returns to Rome and marries Terentia (?).	77
31–32	Serves as quaestor for a year for Lilybaeum .	75–74
36	Accuses Verres. First consulship of Pompey and Crassus	70
37	Curule aedileship	69
40	Praetorship. Speech 'Pro Lege Manilia' . .	66
41	Birth of his son Marcus	65
42	Election as consul	64
43	Consulship. Speeches against Catiline . .	63
45	Quarrel with Clodius	61
47	First consulship of Caesar. (First triumvirate) .	59
48–49	Exile of Cicero. He returns to Italy Aug. 5, 57 .	58–57
50	Reconciliation with Pompey and Caesar . .	56
53	Defeat and Death of Crassus	53
54	Murder of Clodius. Third and sole consulship of Pompey	52

[1] I have not thought it necessary to give the authorities for these dates. Those relating to Cicero's personal history will be found either on pp. xxvii–xxxi, or in the Introductions to the various Parts.

Age of Cicero.		Date B.C.
55-56	Government of Cilicia. Cicero returns to Italy Nov. 24, 50 B.C.	51-50
57-58	Civil war. Cicero joins Pompey in Greece, but returns to Italy after the battle of Pharsalus. Death of Pompey	49-48
59	Cicero is restored to Caesar's favour . . .	47
60	War in Africa. Death of Cato. Cicero divorces Terentia and marries Publilia . . .	46
61	Death of Tullia. War in Spain. Battle of Munda	45
62	Murder of Caesar. Cicero sets out for Greece, but returns. Delivers the first four Philippics .	44
63	Cicero delivers the last ten Philippics. War of Mutina. Death of Cicero, Dec. 7 . .	43

ADDITIONS AND CORRECTIONS.

Page 40, l. 10, *for* 'solam' *read* 'solum.'

p. 43, note on l. 10. From Plut. Cic. 19-20, compared with in Cat. 3, 2 6; 4. 5, 10; ad Att. 10. 1, 1, it appears that the sacrifice in the year of Cicero's consulship was offered on December 3 or 4.—I owe this reference to an article in the Quarterly Review, October 1880, on Cicero.

p. 58, l. 13, *om.* 'que' *after* 'rogatus.'

p. 62, l. 10, note on 'fabam mimum.' Professor E. Böckel in the altered and improved [8th] edition of Süpfle's selection brought out by him (Karlsruhe, 1880) quotes apparently with approval a note of Bücheler suggesting that the reference is to a mime or farce called Faba which had become proverbial for something insignificant.—I admire but cannot adopt Prof. Tyrrell's ingenious suggestion 'fabae midam:'—*see* Hermathena 7. 13 (1881).

p. 94, l. 15, note on 'nobiliorem' foll. Professor Tyrrell (Hermathena 7. 13-14, 1881) would read 'molliorem.' He thinks that the town referred to under the MS. reading Blainde or Blaknde in § 4 was not Blaudus but Blaundus, another town in Phrygia and that 'Blaundus' and 'blandus' being pronounced alike, 'molliorem' = 'blandiorem.'

p. 129, § 3, cp p 420, l. 5, note. Perhaps the evidence hardly enables us to fix the date of Attica's birth. Cicero, it is true, writing in 51 B.C., says of her 'quam numquam vidi' (cp. ad Att. 5. 19, 2), but Middleton, quoted by Tunstall (Observations on the Epistles between Cicero and Marcus Brutus, London, 1744, pp. 165, 166), suggests that the first years of her life may have been spent away from Rome. Boot thinks that she was born about 55 or 54 B.C. See his note on ad Att 5. 19, 2.

p. 165, note on l. 12, Marcellinum. *Read* 'who commanded at Aesernia.'

p. 203, l. 21, 'sicut et meis temporibus.' T. has 'sicut et cumeis temporibus;' B. 'sicut et cinneis temporibus.' F. Rühl, Monatsblätter, p. 26, suggests 'Cinnae or 'Cinnanis temporibus.'

p. 224, note on p. 223, l. 10. I cannot find evidence that L. Tullius was Cicero's cousin.

p. 257, l. 16, 'attigissem rem militaremque conlocassem.' T. has 'attigissem militem que collocassem;' B. 'atigissem militemque collocatem.'

p. 271, at top, *for* 'VIII. 7' *read* 'VIII. 14.'

p. 437, l. 3, 'postquam armis disceptari.' B. has 'postquam armis civilibus disceptari;' T. 'p. a. c. dicepiari.'

p. 471, l. 13, 'quem e re publica.' T. has 'quem de re publica;' B 'quam de re publica.'

„ note on l 16. The reading of T. seems to be 'maius mihi solatium afferre;' B. agrees with this except in reading 'solacium.'

p. 476, note on l. 7. B. agrees with T.

p. 583, l. 6. H. has 'passus D.'

p. 586, l. 11, 'hominibus inicial vacuitas.' H. has 'hominibus in itiata civitas.' F. Rühl, Rhein. Mus. xxx. p. 28, quotes Madvig as suggesting 'inicial vacua civitas.'

p. 604, l. 8. H. inserts 'numeroque hostium habueram' after 'ceperam.'

[illegible]

SELECT LETTERS

OF

M. TULLIUS CICERO.

PART I.

FROM CICERO'S BIRTH TO HIS RETURN TO ROME FROM EXILE, 57 B.C.

INTRODUCTION.

§ 1. M. TULLIUS CICERO was born at Arpinum Jan. 3, 106 B.C.[1] His father bore the same name, and was a Roman knight of considerable landed property; his mother, Helvia, is said[2] to have belonged to a good family. Cicero calls the poet Archias, who went to Rome in 102[3], one of his earliest teachers[4]; and hence it is probable that the family removed to Rome about that time.

Both the greatest orators of the time—L. Crassus and M. Antonius—took an interest in Cicero's education[5]; and his uncle Lucius accompanied Antonius, who received about this time a commission to suppress piracy, to the East[6].

After completing his earlier studies[7] Cicero began to attend the lessons of a Latin rhetorician, L. Plotius, for which, however, he afterwards substituted those of Greek teachers[8]. At the age of seventeen he often listened to the answers given on points of law by Q. Mucius Scaevola, the augur[9]; but his legal education was interrupted by the Social War, in which he[10] served under the consul Cn. Pompeius Strabo, and Scaevola died about this time. Cicero, however, resumed his studies under another Scaevola, cousin of his late teacher, and pontifex maximus. Among his teachers in philosophy were the Academic Philo and the Stoic Diodotus; in rhetoric, Apollonius, surnamed Molon, of Rhodes, who was then at Rome, and whose precepts were illustrated by the speeches of the eloquent tribune P. Sulpicius[11].

[1] Aul. Gell. N. A. 15. 28, 3; Plut. Cic. 2. [2] Plut. Cic. 1. [3] Pro Arch. 3, 5. [4] Ib. 1. [5] De Orat. 2. 1, 2. [6] Ib. [7] Suringar p. 533. [8] Fragm. 112 ap. Nobbe. [9] Brut. 89, 306. [10] Philipp. 12, 11, 27. [11] Brut. 89, 90.

§ 2. Cicero mentions, as early works of his, a translation[1] of the Economics of Xenophon, and a treatise on rhetoric; but whether the latter was any of the works now extant under his name, is doubtful[2].

He seems to have remained neutral during the civil wars of Marius and Sulla and their partisans or successors. After the final triumph of Sulla, he delivered the first of his speeches which has come down to us, that on behalf of P. Quinctius[3], and resumed, apparently[4], his attendance upon Molon's teaching.

At the age of 26, in 80 B.C., he boldly undertook the defence of Sex. Roscius, of Ameria, whom some of Sulla's creatures had conspired to accuse of parricide[5]; and, shortly afterwards, pleaded on behalf of a woman of Arretium, in a case involving the validity of Sulla's harsh measures with respect to that place[6].

Partly, perhaps, to avoid the hostility aroused by these acts, partly to rest from exertions which he was told were injuring his health, Cicero left Rome in 79 B.C. After spending six months at Athens, where he studied under Antiochus, a philosopher of the old Academy, he travelled in Asia, and found an opportunity of again receiving instruction from Molon, who had returned to Rhodes[7]. Cicero was absent from Rome about two years in all; and returned much stronger in health and taught how to husband his powers in speaking. He was now 29 years old: his first marriage[8] must have taken place in this year at latest. His wife, Terentia, was apparently a woman of good family, and certainly possessed a respectable landed property[9].

Q. Hortensius Hortalus and C. Aurelius Cotta enjoyed the highest reputation as orators at this time[10].

§ 3. In the year 76 B.C., Cicero was elected one of the quaestors by a large majority[11], and was assigned to the department of Lilybaeum[12], Sex. Peducaeus being propraetor of Sicily. During his residence in the island, Cicero discovered the tomb of Archimedes[13], and before returning to Rome delivered a speech to the Sicilians at Lilybaeum[14].

He seems to have discharged the duties of his office with zeal and honesty, and to have won the regard both of the Sicilians and of his own countrymen, to whom his diligence in supplying the capital with corn at a time of scarcity was most welcome[15].

From 73 to 71 B.C., Sicily was oppressed by C. Verres, while public

[1] De Off. 2. 24. 87. [2] De Orat. 1. 2, 5. [3] Pro Quinct. 24. 76. [4] Or began it: cp. Brut. 90, 312, with Ellendt p. 363. [5] Aul. Gell. N. A. 15. 28. [6] Pro Caec. 33. 97. [7] Brut. 91, 316. [8] Baiter and Orelli, Chronology of Cicero's life. [9] Ad Fam. 14. 1, 5; Plut. Cic. 8. [10] Brut. 92, 317. [11] In Pis. 1, 2; Brut. 92, 318. [12] Div. in Caec. 1, 2, Ascon. Comment.: cp. Pro Planc. 27, 65. [13] Tusc. Disp. 5. 23, 64. [14] Ascon. Comment. ad Div. in Caec. 1. [15] Pro Planc. 26, 64; Plut. Cic. 6.

attention was engrossed at Rome by the wars with Sertorius, Spartacus, and Mithridates. The war with Sertorius was brought to an end in 72, that with Spartacus in 71; but these triumphs of the Roman government were followed by dissensions among its supporters.

The only speech delivered by Cicero between the years 75 and 71 B.C. which has been preserved to us, is that on behalf of M. Tullius, spoken apparently in 71[1]; but the next year witnessed the memorable prosecution of Verres, with which Cicero's political career may be said to have begun. He was elected curule aedile during the proceedings[2].

§ 4. Eight years had elapsed since the death of Sulla, and no alterations of importance had been made in his institutions: the tribunes of the people were still deprived of their old power of initiating legislation; the courts of criminal justice were still exclusively composed of senators; and the appointment of censors had been discontinued for several years. Moreover, many important cities in Italy were still occupied by his military colonists; and their old inhabitants, with many others, were suffering from the effects of his proscriptions and confiscations. Nor had the efforts of the popular party to effect a counter revolution by arms been successful. Yet the aspect of affairs can have given little satisfaction to the more far-sighted members of the victorious party. Sulla had attempted to establish the supremacy of the senate both over the people and over all public officers; and his constitution required, for its successful working, wisdom and firmness on the part of the governing body, and obedience and self-sacrifice on the part of the highest civil and military officers. Now, there seem to have been few men in the senate of real foresight, even as to the interests of their own order; the majority were selfish, and, if not themselves criminal, inclined to look with indulgence on crimes committed by members of their own body[3]. And high officers were little inclined to respect either the letter or the spirit of the constitution. Usage required that a provincial governor should be, or should have been, consul or praetor; but Pompey, without having held either office, advanced a claim successfully for the government of one of the Spanish provinces.

Further, a minority in the senate had never approved the violent measures of Sulla. The equites were, probably, exasperated by the loss of their control of the courts of criminal justice. The exclusiveness of the government drove men like Cicero into the ranks of the opposition. Many Italian communities, especially in Etruria, had suffered loss of lands, or of local franchises, at the hands of Sulla, and the

[1] Suringar, Annal. Cic. sub ann. [2] In Verr. Act. 1. 9, 25; 13, 37. [3] Even Verres hoped for an acquittal by the aid of his influential connections: v. infra, § 6.

inhabitants of such places must either have gone to Rome to swell the turbulent and needy population of the capital, or have formed a dangerous element in the country districts, where their ranks were soon reinforced by numbers of bankrupt military colonists. Lastly, the metropolitan populace, composed in great measure of foreigners and freedmen, and the numerous slaves in Italy, many of them trained as gladiators, required the control of a far more effective police than the government had at its disposal.

§ 5. Pompey returned from Spain in 71 B.C., and seems to have put himself in communication with Crassus, with the more moderate party in the senate, and with the leaders of the democrats. He was anxious to obtain the distinctions of a triumph and consulship, and could not legally enjoy either[1]. The motives of Crassus in supporting him are not very clear; but to the democrats the aid of the greatest general of the time was invaluable.

The results of this powerful combination, which seems to have been effected in the summer of 71 B.C., speedily appeared. Pompey and Crassus were elected consuls for 70 B.C. Pompey obtained the triumph he desired, and, with his colleague, proposed or supported the measures desired by the democrats, namely,—

1. The abolition of the restrictions imposed by Sulla on the power of the tribunes, which were now removed by a Lex Pompeia tribunicia[2].

2. A remodelling of the courts of criminal justice. They were henceforth to be composed of senators, equites, and tribuni aerarii. This change was effected by a Lex Aurelia, proposed by L. Cotta, brother of the consul in 75 B.C., and bears the marks of compromise[3].

3. A re-establishment of the censorship[4].

These measures reversed all the more important political changes of Sulla. But they did little for the direct mitigation of the social and economical evils from which Rome and Italy were suffering.

§ 6. The prosecution of Verres took place during the summer of 70 B.C. The friends of the accused were anxious, first, to deprive Cicero of the conduct of the prosecution; secondly, to delay the trial till the next year, when Verres' advocate Hortensius would be consul, and the composition of the court might be more favourable. But Cicero's vigilance baffled them. He made only a short speech in opening the case, and then summoned the witnesses, whose disclosures were so

[1] Not the triumph, for he had held no magistracy: not the consulship, for he was too young, and had not been praetor or aedile. Cp. Cic. Philipp. 5. 17, 48: App. Bell. Civ. 1. 100. [2] App. Bell. Civ. 1. 121; Cic. De Legg. 3. 9, 22: 3. 11, 26. [3] Ascon. in Pison. p. 129, § 94; Ad Att. 1. 16, 3. [4] Div. in Caec. 3, 8; Schol. Gronov. ad loc. Fasti Consulares for 70 B.C.

overwhelming that Hortensius gave up the defence, and Verres went into exile. The affair may have contributed to the enactment of the Lex Aurelia mentioned above; and, to deepen the impression which it made, Cicero published five speeches which he might have delivered had the case gone on, and in which he summed up the evidence at great length [1].

During the three following years, 69–67 B.C., Cicero seems to have taken little part in politics. In his aedileship he received presents from the Sicilians, and applied them to the public service; an opportunity of winning popular favour which was the more welcome, as the moderate extent of his own fortune prevented his offering the usual entertainments to the people on a splendid scale [2]. In 69 he defended M. Fonteius on a charge of misgovernment in Gaul; and parts of his speech [3] diminish our respect for the spirit he shewed in accusing Verres. The speech on behalf of A. Caecina very likely belongs to the same year. In the next, 68, Cicero lost his father, and his first cousin Lucius [4]. His brother Quintus married Pomponia, sister of Atticus, about the same time. The earliest of Cicero's letters which have been preserved date from the same year, but contain little of general interest [5]. The speech Pro Q. Roscio Comoedo was probably delivered in 68 or 67 B.C. Roscius had previously given Cicero lessons in elocution [6].

§ 7. In the year 67 B.C., having reached the age required by law of candidates for the praetorship, Cicero sued for that office; and such was his popularity, that though the comitia were twice adjourned, he was at the head of the poll on all three occasions [7].

Various measures of more or less importance were carried during this year. C. Cornelius, one of the tribunes, proposed and carried laws restricting the powers of the senate to grant exemptions from the operation of particular laws, and binding the praetors to publish their edicts at once on coming into office, and to adhere to them [8]. His supporters behaved with great turbulence. L. Roscius Otho, another tribune, carried a law assigning to the equites special places in the theatre. Cicero was of an equestrian family, and, both on personal and public grounds, he approved this measure [9], as calculated to draw the equites nearer to the senate. He also approved of a far more important law of the same date [10], that of A. Gabinius commissioning Pompey to act against the pirates of Cilicia with very extensive powers.

The foreign history of Rome had been very chequered during the few

[1] The five books of the second Actio in Verrem. [2] Pro Muren. 19. 40; De Off. 2. 17. 59. [3] Cp. Pro Font. 3; 10; 14. [4] Ad Att. 1. 5. 1; 1. 6. 2. [5] Ib. 1. 5–7. [6] Drumann. 5. 346; Plut. Cic. 5. [7] Ad Att. 1. 11. 2; Pro Leg. Man. 1. 2. [8] Dion Cassius 36. 22; 23. [9] Pro Muren. 19. 40; Ad Att. 2. 1. 3. [10] Pro Leg. Man. 17. 52.

past years. In October 69 B.C., L. Lucullus had gained a splendid victory over Tigranes of Armenia, and had taken Tigranocerta; but he was unpopular with his army, and ill-supported by the home government. His lieutenants, also, in Armenia and Pontus, were defeated by Mithridates, and he was successively deprived of the government of Asia and Cilicia, and of the conduct of the war. The officer named to succeed him in the last duty, M'. Acilius Glabrio, declined, however, to act; but Lucullus could only stand on the defensive near the Upper Halys[1].

Pompey, on the other hand, executed his commission to suppress piracy with brilliant success, and passed the winter of 67–66 B.C. in Cilicia, preparing, apparently, to act against Q. Metellus in Crete[2], who declined to recognise the supremacy granted to Pompey, by the law of Gabinius, over all provincial governors.

§ 8. Such was the position of affairs when Cicero entered on his praetorship in the beginning of 66 B.C. He presided in the court which tried cases of extortion (quaestio repetundarum), and appears to have acted with integrity[3], especially on the trial of the wealthy C. Licinius Macer[4]. He delivered various speeches before other tribunals; among others, that on behalf of A. Cluentius Habitus.

The most important event of the year 66 B.C., both for Rome and for Cicero, was the enactment of the Lex Manilia, transferring to Pompey the command against Mithridates, with the government of Pontus, Bithynia, and Cilicia, while he was to retain the commission he held to act against the pirates. Cicero earnestly supported this measure, in a speech still extant[5], and his attachment to the great general had so important an influence on his subsequent career, that we may pause to consider briefly its nature and grounds.

Pompey had done more than any contemporary to reverse the measures of Sulla. Though not, like Cicero, a 'novus homo,' he was by no means of high nobility; and his supporters were mainly to be found among the equites, the middle classes in the country districts, and at times among the populace of the capital, as was the case, to a great extent, with Cicero himself. Both in Spain and in Asia Pompey had displayed courage and judgment; and he was a good husband and father. Thus, as a successful general, a moderate politician, and a Roman of old-fashioned morality, Pompey acquired an ascendancy over Cicero, which the errors and inconsistencies of his later conduct never entirely destroyed.

[1] Dion Cassius 35; Vell. 2. 33; App. Mithr. 90; 91; Plut. Lucull. 35. [2] He was cousin of Q. Metellus Pius, and had gained victories in Crete in 68–67. Dion Cassius 36. 1; 2; 28; Vell. 2. 34; Plut. Pomp. 29. [3] Plut. Cic. 9. [4] Ad Att. 1. 4. 2. [5] Pro Lege Manilia, or De Imperio Cn. Pompeii.

Tullia was betrothed in 66 B.C. to C. Calpurnius Piso, but apparently not married for some years[1].

It appears that Cicero's brother, Quintus, was elected curule aedile for 65 B.C.[2] P. Sulla and P. Autronius were elected consuls for the same year, but were convicted of bribery, which annulled their election. They then combined with Cn. Piso and L. Sergius Catilina to murder L. Cotta and L. Torquatus, who had been elected to fill their places. The plot was to be carried out on Dec. 31[3], but failed, owing to some misunderstanding. Catiline had just returned from governing Africa as propraetor, and probably feared a prosecution, envoys from the province having arrived at Rome to complain of his conduct.

In the year 65 B.C., Cicero defended C. Cornelius, the tribune of 67[4]; and perhaps delivered the speech 'de rege Alexandrino' of which some fragments have been preserved[5]. Having declined the administration of a province as propraetor[6], he began to prosecute his canvass for the consulship, which, however, he could not legally hold till 63[7]. The election for 64 resulted in favour of L. Iulius Caesar, maternal uncle of M. Antonius, the triumvir, and of C. Marcius Figulus[8]. Cicero mentions among his own antagonists, Catiline, C. Antonius, and two more respectable men, P. Galba and Q. Cornificius. He begged Atticus, who was then at Athens, to come to Rome to help him in his canvass, and to do all he could for him with the friends of Pompey[9]. Nor did he shrink from more questionable electioneering manoeuvres. For he thought of defending Catiline, of whose guilt he had no doubt, on a charge of extortion; hoping that, if acquitted, he would coalesce with his advocate[10]. Opinions differed, even among writers living within a century of Cicero's death, whether he actually defended Catiline or not[11]. Moreover, he declined to support Caecilius, uncle of Atticus, in a just suit against one Caninius Satyrus, out of regard both for Caninius himself, and for his powerful friend L. Domitius[12]. Catiline was acquitted, owing to the corruption of the judges and the treachery of his accuser, P. Clodius[13].

Cicero's son Marcus was born on the day of election of consuls for 64 B.C.[14] Atticus, in compliance with Cicero's request, returned to Rome from Athens, where he had lived 22 years[15].

In the next year, 64 B.C., Cicero's attention must have been mainly occupied by his canvass for the consulship. We have no letters of this date, nor does he seem to have made any remarkable speeches, with the

[1] Ad Att. 1. 3. 3. For an account of Piso, cp. infra, § 22. [2] Ad Att. 1. 4. 1. [3] In Cat. 1. 6. 15; Sall. Cat. 18. [4] Ascon. in Cornelian. 93. [5] Cp. Mommsen 4. 1. 166, note. [6] Pro Muren. 20, 42. [7] De Off. 2. 17, 59. [8] Ad Att. 1. 2, 1. [9] Ib. 1. 1, 2. [10] Ib. 1. 2, 1. [11] Ib. 1. 2, 2, note. [12] Ib. 1. 1, 3. [13] Ib. 1. 2, 1; Q. Cic. De Pet. Cons. 3, 10; In Pison. 10, 23. [14] Ad Att. 1. 2, 1. [15] Appendix 3, § 1.

exception of that 'in toga candida,' which we possess in fragments. It contained a violent attack on Catiline. Atticus seems to have been at Rome throughout the year.

It must have been about this time that Cicero received from his brother Quintus the letter 'de Petitione Consulatus.' He was elected consul by a large majority, in spite of the support which both Caesar and Crassus are said to have given to Catiline and C. Antonius. Antonius was elected by a small majority over Catiline[1].

63 B.C.

§ 9. Cicero had now attained the summit of his desires: he entered on his consulship Jan. 1, 63 B.C. On that day he addressed the senate against an agrarian law proposed by P. Rullus, and followed up this speech by one addressed to the people on the same subject; in which, however, he did not venture to attack the principle of an agrarian law, and spoke with respect of the Gracchi[2].

It has been already remarked, that little had been done to remedy the social distress and disorder which had resulted from Sulla's legislation. But the restoration of the old powers of the tribunate had made an opening for attempts to relieve it; and P. Servilius Rullus, one of the tribunes for 64–63 B.C.[3], made a proposal for the division of the state lands in Campania among the people, and for the purchase of other lands for a similar purpose[4]. This proposal respected private property, and might have created a valuable class of proprietors, while relieving the capital of its superfluous population[5]. But Rullus proposed to entrust the carrying out of the law to a commission armed with very extensive powers, of which Pompey should not be a member, and which should be appointed by a novel mode of election. All these provisions might give offence; and Cicero's declamations against the formidable powers to be given to the commission, and his appeals to popular jealousy of Capua, were sufficient to defeat the measure. It is possible that Rullus may have acted in concert with Caesar and others, and that the commission may have been intended to form a counterpoise to the power of Pompey. But such a supposition seems needless to

[1] Ascon. ad Orat. in Tog. Cand. 118. [2] De Leg. Agrar. 2. 5, 10. [3] I have occasionally described the tribunes' year of office thus, for the sake of clearness, as they entered on their functions in December and so held office during parts of two years. Where only one year is mentioned, that in which they passed the greater part of their term is referred to. [4] De Leg. Agrar. 2. 28, 76; 24–27. [5] The objects of an agrarian law cannot be better described than in Cicero's own words on another occasion: 'et sentinam urbis exhauriri et solitudinem Italiae frequentari posse arbitrabar.' Ad Att. 1. 19. 4. He protests, however, against the propriety of similar language when used by Rullus. Cp. de Leg. Agr. 2. 26, 70.

account for the introduction of a measure thoroughly in accordance with the policy of the popular party[1].

Cicero also opposed a measure for removing the political disabilities which Sulla had imposed on the children of proscribed persons[2]. He may have justified his opposition by the danger to be feared from the removal; but it can hardly be doubted that the failure of these two proposals turned the thoughts of many towards revolution.

The popular leaders succeeded, however, in reversing one of Sulla's reactionary enactments; for the tribune T. Labienus carried a law restoring the mode of appointing augurs, which Sulla had abolished, and by which candidates for admission into the college were nominated by two members of it, elected by 17 tribes chosen by lot out of the 35, and, finally, admitted by the college itself. It appears that this law also restored the election of the pontifex maximus to the people[3].

Cicero advocated in the senate a grant of unusual honours to Pompey. A 'supplicatio' of twelve days was voted in honour of his eastern victories[4].

Of the other speeches delivered by Cicero in this year, before his attention was engrossed by Catiline's conspiracy, the two most important were, one spoken to reconcile the people to the precedence enjoyed by the equites in the theatre under the law of L. Roscius Otho[5], and one in defence of C. Rabirius[6]. This man had taken an active part in suppressing the insurrection of Saturninus in the year 100 B.C., and was prosecuted for murder, or 'perduellio,' by Labienus. This trial involved the question whether the senate could invest the consuls with absolute powers of life and death; and Rabirius would probably have been condemned, if means had not been found to evade a decision[7] when the case came on appeal before the comitia centuriata.

Cicero introduced a measure relieving the provinces of a considerable burden, by limiting the duration of 'legationes liberae' to one year[8].

§ 10. It does not appear how soon Cicero became aware of the resumption of the treasonable designs of Catiline. He lost no time, however, in securing his colleague Antonius to the cause of order. Macedonia and Cisalpine Gaul had been assigned as the provinces to be governed by the consuls for 63 B.C., on the expiration of their year of office. Cicero allowed his colleague to obtain Macedonia[9], which he desired, and, renouncing his own claim to govern a province at all,

[1] Cp. A. W. Zumpt, Comment. Epigraph. 1. 271, 273, with Mommsen 4. 1, 170-177, and both with the second Oration De Leg. Agrar., passim. [2] Ad Att. 2. 1, 3. [3] Dion Cassius 37. 37; Cic. De Leg. Agrar. 2. 7. [4] De Prov. Cons. 11, 27; Ad Fam. 1. 9, 11. [5] Ad Att. 2. 1, 3. [6] Ib. [7] Dion Cassius 37. 27 and 28; Merivale 1. 124-127; Mommsen 4. 1, 159. [8] Cic. De Legg. 3. 8, 18. [9] Ad Att. 2. 1, 3, note; Ad Fam. 5. 5; Dion Cassius 37. 33.

contrived that Cisalpine Gaul should be secured to Q. Metellus Celer, one of the praetors for 63. Cicero addressed the people on the subject [1].

It is uncertain how far the conspirators were supported by men of high position discontented with the government. Both Caesar and Crassus were seriously suspected; but, if the latter was really privy to the plot, the anarchical designs of Catiline must have been represented by Cicero with much exaggeration, which is in any case probable [2].

Cicero was well informed by a spy among the conspirators, Q. Curius, of their proceedings [3]; and invited Catiline in the senate to clear himself. Catiline replied in language of obscure menace [4], but Cicero complained that the senate did not pass decrees sufficiently strong to meet the danger and left him to provide for his own safety at the consular comitia, which appear to have been held a few days afterwards, and at which D. Iunius Silanus and L. Licinius Murena were elected consuls for 62 B.C. Metellus Celer went to raise forces in Picenum and Gaul for the government, while Catiline, to avoid suspicion, offered himself for free custody in the house of some eminent senator. On October 21 the senate by a decree commissioned the consuls to provide for the safety of the state; and a plot of Catiline to murder Cicero and other eminent men on October 28 failed. He was not, however, discouraged; and at a meeting at the house of M. Porcius Laeca, on the night of Nov. 6–7, a fresh plot was formed to murder Cicero, but failed through timely information being conveyed to the intended victim. On the 8th Cicero denounced the conspirators before the senate [5], and Catiline left Rome that night. Next day Cicero addressed the people in terms of mingled exultation and warning [6].

§ 11. The next decisive step followed the disclosure of intrigues

[1] Ad Att. l. c.; Ad Fam. 5. 2, 3: cp. De Leg. Agrar. 1. 8, 26. [2] I am aware that high authorities speak more decidedly on this question. Lord Macaulay (Miscellaneous Works, 1. 157; Essay on History), Mr. De Quincey (Cicero, vol. vi. of Collected Works, pp. 231–233, and The Caesars, vol. ix. of Collected Works, p. 43), and Professor Beesly (Fortnightly Review, for May 30, 1865), all consider that the plot was a genuine popular movement, and state or imply a belief that Caesar supported it. Mommsen accepts in the main the ordinary view of the conspiracy, but thinks that the popular party, in its abasement and fear of Pompey, was willing to co-operate with the conspirators. Some of the evidence he produces is very striking (cp. vol. iv. 1, 181–183), but hardly, perhaps, conclusive. The nature of the conspiracy has been probably somewhat misrepresented, and the character of the conspirators blackened, by Cicero; but, in my judgment, the safest course is, with Merivale (1. 86), to call the reader's attention to the suspicious nature of the evidence, as derived mainly from Cicero, and to leave him to form his own conclusions. Sallust, indeed, supports Cicero in the main; but considerable doubt has been thrown upon the historical character of his work by Mommsen (4. 1, 184), Merivale (History 1. 87; 2. 88), and by a reviewer of Dean Merivale's work in the Edinburgh Review for July 1850. [3] Sall. Cat. 26. [4] Cic. Pro Muren. 25, 51. Lange, 3. 241, has made it probable that the scene here referred to took place some days earlier than I stated previously; perhaps on Sept. 22. Cp. Suet. Octav. 5; 94. [5] In Cat. 1. [6] Ib. 2. The principal authorities for the preceding paragraph are Cic. In Cat. 1. 3-5; pro Muren. 25; pro Sulla 18; Sall. Cat. 26–32.

between the conspirators and some envoys of the Allobroges then at Rome. The envoys disclosed the offers made to them, and were arrested on the night of Dec. 3–4. Documents were found upon them compromising Lentulus, Cethegus, and others, whereon the latter were also arrested. The senate, on Dec. 4, voted that they should be committed to custody, and that Cicero should be honoured by a 'supplicatio.' He addressed[1] the people on the same day, congratulating them on the virtual suppression of the plot. Next day, Dec. 5, the punishment of the conspirators was discussed in the senate, and, in spite of the efforts of C. Caesar, a majority voted for their execution. Cicero supported this course, though not very decidedly, in his fourth speech against Catiline. The execution took place that evening: Lentulus, Cethegus, and three others, were strangled in a dungeon near the Capitol[2].

At an earlier period of the year, Cicero had proposed and carried a law[3] increasing the penalties for bribery and other illegal practices at elections. Ser. Sulpicius, M. Cato, and others, prosecuted L. Murena, one of the consuls elect, under this law; but Cicero defended him, and he was acquitted. The speech is strangely omitted in a list given by Cicero of those of his consulate[4]. It was delivered after Catiline's flight from Rome[5].

On Dec. 31, one of the new tribunes, Q. Metellus Nepos, prevented Cicero from addressing the people on going out of office, saying that he had put Roman citizens to death without trial. Cicero declared, amid the applause of the people, that he had saved his country[6]. The incident was significant, for Metellus was a decided adherent of Pompey.

It is evident that, before the close of his consulship, Cicero had definitely quitted the popular party; even during his year of office a change of tone may be noticed[7]. Various causes may have contributed to produce this result; satisfied ambition and the flatteries of the leading nobles; the estrangement of the popular party from Pompey; and the suspicions under which its leaders lay of complicity with Catiline. The same causes naturally tended to strengthen the dominant party in the senate generally.

But Cicero saw that the senate could only maintain its position by keeping up a good understanding with the equites and with Pompey; and he worked hard to maintain such an understanding. His letters show how his exertions were baffled by the selfishness and personal jealousy of some senators, and by the ill-timed rigour of Cato[8].

[1] In Cat. 3. [2] Ib. 4; Sall. Cat. 55; Ad Att. 2. 1, 3; 12. 21, 1. [3] Pro Muren. 23; 32, 68. [4] Ad Att. 2. 1, 3, where that Pro C. Pisone is also omitted. [5] Pro Muren. 37. [6] Ad Fam. 5. 2, 7. [7] Compare his language about the Gracchi in January and November; De Leg. Agrar. 2. 5, 10; In Cat. 1. 1, 3 and 1. 2, 4. [8] Ad Att. 1. 17; 1. 18; 2. 1.

C. Octavius, afterwards emperor, was born on Sept. 23 in this year[1], and C. Caesar was elected one of the praetors for 62 B.C. He was also elected pontifex maximus, though Q. Catulus was brought forward against him[2].

62 B.C.

§ 12. Catiline, on hearing of the execution of his accomplices, had attempted to make his way into Cisalpine Gaul, with the forces which his partisan Manlius had collected at Faesulae. But Metellus Celer was prepared to meet him, and he accordingly turned upon the consul C. Antonius. A desperate battle followed, in which the loyal forces under M. Petreius, legate of Antonius, destroyed the rebels. Catiline himself fell[3]. Many men were brought to trial at Rome as his accomplices, and Cicero defended one of them, P. Sulla. He also spoke in the senate in defence of his late colleague, C. Antonius; and, in a court presided over by his brother Quintus, defended the claim of the poet Archias to Roman citizenship, which had been questioned[4].

Q. Cicero and C. Caesar were among the praetors. By the advice, probably, of the latter, the popular party seems to have sought a reconciliation with Pompey. Caesar proposed to transfer to him from Q. Catulus the dedication of the temple of Jupiter Capitolinus[5], but without success; and attempts made by Caesar, and by the tribune Metellus Nepos, to procure a popular vote entrusting Pompey with the command against Catiline, failed also, principally owing to the energetic resistance of Cato. Much rioting, however, followed; and both Metellus and Caesar were suspended from their functions by the senate. Nepos fled to the camp of Pompey; but Caesar, by a judicious mixture of deference and firmness, induced the senate to re-instate him in his office. He was soon afterwards denounced by L. Vettius and Q. Curius as an accomplice of Catiline; but Cicero declared the charge to be groundless, and its authors were disgraced or punished[6].

Cicero bought a large house on the Palatine from M. Crassus, for which he paid about £30,000 (XXXV.HS.) He had to borrow large sums of money from P. Sulla and from 'Teucris[7],' and, in a letter[8] to P. Sestius, said that he would rather join in a conspiracy than suppress one, as he owed so much money.

§ 13. The series of his letters begins anew, after a considerable interval,

[1] Suet. Octav. 5; Vell. 2. 36. [2] Vell. 2. 43; Dion Cassius 37. 37; Ovid. Fast. 3. 415. [3] Sall. Cat. 60. [4] Schol. Bob. in Orat. Pro Archia 2. 3. [5] It had been burned in 83 B.C.; cp. Tac. Hist. 3. 72. [6] Plut. Cic. 23; Cat. Min. 26–29; Suet. Iul. 15–17; Dion Cassius 37. 43 and 44; Abeken 54–61; Merivale 1. 147–149; 155–159; Mommsen 4. 1, 191 and 192. [7] Aul. Gell. N. A. 12, 12, 2; Ad Att. 1. 13, 6, note; Ad Fam. 5. 6, 2. [8] Ad Fam. l. c.

with one written to Pompey early in this year. Cicero had already sent him a detailed account of his consulship, and was vexed at receiving in reply what he thought an insufficient acknowledgment of his public services. This vexation is expressed frankly enough in a second letter[1]; the first and longer one has been lost. About the same time Cicero received an unreasonable letter[2] from Q. Metellus Celer, governor of Cisalpine Gaul, complaining of his behaviour to Metellus Nepos. Cicero's reply[3] was a temperate and dignified expostulation, shewing that he had not been the aggressor.

The two Metelli were probably brothers[4]. Q. Metellus Celer, praetor in 63 B.C., and afterwards governor of Cisalpine Gaul, had contributed, as has been said[5], to the suppression of Catiline's rebellion. He was generally on good terms with Cicero, but was a more uncompromising politician, being a determined member of the party of the optimates, and not inclined to make concessions either to the equites or to Pompey. He married a sister of P. Clodius, nicknamed Quadrantaria; was consul in 60 B.C., and died next year, as some believed, poisoned by his wife[6].

Q. Metellus Nepos, tribune in 63–62 B.C., has been already mentioned[7]. He subsequently gave up his quarrel with Cicero, and promoted, as consul, his restoration from exile in 57[8].

Towards the close[9] of the year, it was generally believed that P. Clodius had been detected in the house of C. Caesar while the yearly sacrifice to the Bona Dea was going on, prompted, it was supposed, by a passion for Caesar's wife Pompeia. Caesar refused to take any steps against Clodius, but divorced Pompeia, saying his wife must be 'above suspicion[10].'

A law proposed by the consuls (Lex Iunia Licinia) provided for proper publicity in the registration of laws—'ne leges clam in aerarium inferri liceret[11].'

61 B.C.

§ 14. The new consuls were M. Pupius Piso and M. Valerius Messalla. Cicero was satisfied with Messalla, but not with his colleague, who slighted him in the senate, and opposed a motion for enquiry into the scandalous affair of Clodius[12]. Cicero seems to have been rather despondent as to the issue of that transaction, and relaxed his own exertions[13].

[1] Ad Fam. 5. 7. 3. [2] Ib. 5. 1. [3] Ib. 5. 2. [4] Ib. 5. 1, note. [5] supra, § 12. [6] Pro Cael. 24. 59; Schol. Bob. in Sest. 62. [7] supra, §§ 11; 12. [8] infra, §§ 21; 23; cp. Orat. Post Red. in Sen. 10. 25; Post Red. Ad Quir. 6. 15; De Prov. Cons. 9. 22. [9] See, however, Ad Att. 1. 13. 3, note. [10] Ad Att. 1. 13. 3: cp. Suet. Iul. 74. [11] Schol. Bob. ad Cic. Pro Sest. 64, note 6; Cic. Philipp. 5. 3. 8. [12] Ad Att. 1. 13. 3. [13] Ib.

He also suspected Pompey of jealousy and insincerity[1]. It was from the camp of that general that Metellus Nepos had come to Rome to sue for the tribuneship; and, as has been mentioned[2], Metellus took refuge with Pompey when suspended by the senate. Pompey lingered needlessly in Asia, and when he landed in Italy (Jan., 61 B.C.) order had been restored there. He disbanded his forces accordingly, and returned to Rome with few attendants[3].

His first address to the people satisfied no party[4], and, subsequently[5], he would not commit himself to a definite approval either of the prosecution of Clodius, or of the proceedings of Cicero's consulship. He offended Metellus Celer by divorcing his wife, Mucia, half-sister of Metellus, on suspicion of an intrigue with Caesar; and Metellus joined many other senators in opposing the confirmation of Pompey's 'acts' in Asia. The increasing isolation of Pompey led him to court Cicero[6].

Meanwhile the trial of Clodius had taken place. It had been proposed that the judges who were to try him should be named by the praetor; but a tribune threatened opposition[7], and Hortensius advised the senate to give way, and allow the judges to be chosen by lot, as was usual, saying that no court could acquit where the case was so clear. The senate complied, and the result was that, owing to the grossest bribery, Clodius was acquitted by 31 votes to 26[8]. Cicero had given evidence[9] which contradicted a plea of alibi put forward by Clodius, and the latter determined to have revenge. He was of high patrician nobility, brother of Ap. Claudius Pulcher, and his three sisters were married to L. Lucullus, Q. Metellus Celer, and Q. Marcius Rex[10].

Towards the close of September, Pompey celebrated his triumph over Mithridates for two days[11]. He secured the election of one of his adherents, L. Afranius, as one of the consuls for 60 B.C.; but from the other, Q. Metellus Celer, he had only hostility to expect.

Somewhat later, the equites applied to the senate for an alteration of the hard terms on which they had farmed the revenues of Asia. Cicero supported their request from considerations of policy; but it was opposed by Cato and Metellus Celer, and, though the senate seemed disposed for concession, no decision seems to have been arrived at, and an unfriendly feeling between the senate and the equites remained[12].

Among the propraetors for this year were Q. Cicero in Asia[13],

[1] Ad Att. 1. 13, 4. [2] supra, § 12. [3] Plut. Pomp. 43. [4] Ad Att. 1. 14, 1. [5] Ib. 1. 14, 2. [6] Ib. 1. 16, 11; Dion Cassius 37. 49. [7] Ad Att. 1. 16, 2. [8] Ib. 5. [9] Ib. 2. 1, 5, note; Plut. Cic. 29. [10] Ad Att. 2. 1, 5; Ad Fam. 1. 9. 15, notes. [11] Plut. Pomp. 45; Vell. 2. 40, 3. [12] Ad Att. 1. 17; 18; 2. 1, 7 and 8. [13] Ad Q. F. 1. 1.

C. Pomptinus[1] in Transalpine Gaul, and C. Caesar in Farther Spain. Pomptinus had to repress a revolt of the Allobroges, who had already risen against C. Piso in 66 B.C.[2] Caesar was very successful, not only in reducing hostile tribes to submission, but in his financial measures for mitigating the distress of the provincials[3].

60 B.C.

§ 15. Pompey renewed his efforts to escape from his unsatisfactory position, and, in particular, to obtain grants of land for his soldiers, which he had promised them. With this object L. Flavius, one of the tribunes, brought in an agrarian law, which Cicero revised and supported, but without success[4]. Meanwhile the discussion in the senate about the petition of the equites continued, and Cato, much to Cicero's vexation, not only opposed it, but proposed measures of increased severity against judicial corruption, a proposal naturally unpleasant to the equites, from whom one-third of the judges were taken. In both cases the senate followed Cato's advice, and the equites, in consequence, regarded the behaviour of L. Flavius with indifference, even when he ordered the consul Metellus to be imprisoned for opposing his agrarian law[5].

Cicero, disgusted by the frivolity[6] of some of the nobles, and the perversity of others, and much courted by Pompey, inclined to the latter. Atticus seems to have criticised his conduct[7].

About this time Caesar returned from Spain, and began at once to sue for the consulship, without risking his chance of success by waiting outside the walls to claim a triumph. Cicero speaks of his popularity[8]. He had not yet reached the age required by law for the consulship, but this seems not to have been urged against him[9]; the law had been already broken in Pompey's case.

P. Clodius seems to have wished already to become a plebeian, as a qualification for holding the office of tribune; he had secured the services of one of the tribunes of this year, C. Herennius, but others frequently interposed[10].

The optimates[11] lost one of their wisest leaders in the spring, by the death of Q. Catulus. Cicero deeply lamented him[12].

Rumours had reached Rome early in the year, of movements in Gaul

[1] Dion Cassius 37. 47; 48. [2] Ad Att. 1. 13, 2. [3] Dion Cassius 37. 52; 53: Plut. Caes. 11; 12; Merivale 1. 173-176. [4] Dion Cassius 37. 49; Ad Att. 1. 19, 4. [5] Dion Cassius 37. 50; Ad Att. 1. 18, 3; 2. 1, 8. [6] Ib. 2. 1, 7 and 8. [7] Ib. 6. [8] Ib.: cp. App. Bell. Civ. 2. 8. [9] That age was 43 (cp. § 8); and Caesar was born in 100 B.C. Suet. Iul. 88. Pompey was 35 when first elected consul. [10] Ad Att. 1. 18, 4; 1. 19, 5; 2. 1, 4-5, notes. [11] See note A. [12] Ad Att. 1. 20, 3.

which might make an intervention necessary. The Aedui and Sequani were at war; the Helvetii were meditating a migration westwards, and the senate decreed that the two consuls, after their year of office had expired, should govern the two Gaulish provinces. Meanwhile envoys were sent to enquire into the state of affairs, and hinder other states of Gaul from joining the Helvetii. The senate complimented both Cicero and Pompey, by regarding their presence as indispensable at Rome, and did not allow them to serve as envoys[1]. The war rumours seem subsequently to have died away, to the satisfaction of every one except the consul Metellus, who had wished to earn a triumph in Gaul[2].

§ 16. About the summer, the celebrated combination of Caesar, Pompey, and Crassus, usually known as the first triumvirate, was effected. Cicero seems at first to have thought that he might exercise great influence over Pompey, and even over Caesar[3], and he was evidently flattered by some tempting offers which Balbus made him in Caesar's name[4]; but he feared the reproach of inconsistency. The triumvirs succeeded in securing the election of Caesar as one consul for 59 B.C.; but the optimates, by a prodigal expenditure of money, procured the election of M. Calpurnius Bibulus, a decided member of their party, as his colleague, instead of L. Lucceius, whom the triumvirs had supported[5].

Cicero seems to have occupied the early months of 60 B.C. in writing a Greek history of his consulship, which excited the envy of Posidonius, he says, by the correctness of its style[6]. He also revised a translation of parts of Aratus, which he had written[7] in early youth, and wrote a long letter to his brother Quintus, who was still governor of Asia. It might be called an Essay on the Duties of Provincial Governors[8].

59 B.C.

§ 17. Caesar lost no time in fulfilling what was probably his portion of the compact between the triumvirs. He proposed an agrarian law, with the object of providing both for Pompey's veterans and for needy citizens. The state lands in Campania seem to have been exempted[9] from the operation of the law in its original form, and the land required was probably to be provided by purchase. The proposal, however, met with violent opposition in the senate, before which Caesar laid it in the first instance; and he seems to have been provoked into bringing it

[1] Ad Att. 1. 19, 2–3. Caes. Bell. Gall 1. 2. [2] Ad Att. 1. 20, 5. [3] Ib. 2. 1, 6. [4] Ib. 2. 3, 3. [5] App. Bell. Civ. 2, 9; Suet. Iul. 19. [6] Ad Att. 2. 1, 2. [7] Ib. 2. 1, 11: De Nat. Deor. 2. 41, 104. [8] Ad Q. F. 1. 1. [9] Ad Att. 2. 16, 2; Dion Cassius 38. 1; A. W. Zumpt, Comment. Epigr. 2. 288.

forward again in a more sweeping form, the exemption of Campania being removed. A clause[1] was also appended, binding all senators and all candidates for any magistracy to take an oath publicly that they would respect its provisions. The law was to be executed by a commission of twenty, of which both Pompey and Crassus were to be members. Cicero scornfully remarks, that P. Clodius was not thought worthy of a place in so numerous a body[2].

The optimates naturally disapproved of this law, and the senate was still under their control. But, in spite of the vehement opposition of the consul Bibulus and of some of the tribunes, the law was sanctioned by the people, and was followed by another ratifying the acts of Pompey in Asia[3].

Other laws of the same date were:—

One making concessions to the equites with regard to provincial taxation[4].

One stating the liability to prosecution for extortion (repetundae) of all who should in any way share the spoils of a guilty provincial governor. This was the 'Lex Iulia de repetundis;' but Cicero says that it introduced no novelty[5].

One recognising the title of Ptolemy Auletes to the throne of Egypt. He was not of legitimate descent, and is said to have bought his recognition from the triumvirs for 6000 talents[6]. His brother, who ruled in Cyprus, was less fortunate[7].

Caesar also provided that the senate's proceedings and other news should be published in the 'acta,' or gazette[8].

But by far the most important event of this year was the enactment of the Lex Vatinia, assigning to Caesar the government of Cisalpine Gaul with Illyricum, and the command of three legions, for five years. P. Vatinius, one of the tribunes, brought this measure before the people[9].

The senate had attempted to prevent Caesar's obtaining such a position, by assigning to the two consuls for 59 B.C. the duty of repairing roads in Italy on the expiration of their year of office. But the manœuvre had failed; and now, to avoid affording another triumph to the popular party, the senate itself added to Caesar's province Transalpine Gaul, with a fourth legion[10].

§ 18. Caesar, about this time, gave his daughter Julia in marriage to Pompey, and himself married Calpurnia, daughter of L. Piso, one

[1] Ad Att. 2. 18, 2. [2] Ib. 2. 7, 3; Dion Cassius 38. 1. [3] App. Bell. Civ. 2. 10-12; Vell. 2. 44; Dion Cassius 38. 4-7. [4] Ad Att. 2. 16, 2; Pro Planc. 14, 35. [5] Pro Sest. 64, 135; Pro Rab. Post. 4. [6] Ad Att. 2. 16, 2; Mommsen 4. 1, 153; cp. 207. [7] v. infra, § 20. [8] Suet. Iul. 20. [9] See Appendix 6, § 1. [10] Suet. Iul. 22; Dion Cassius 38. 8.

of the consuls elect. The other was A. Gabinius, a dependent of Pompey[1].

P. Clodius, having been adopted into a plebeian family with questionable legality[2], was elected tribune for 58 B.C. He seems to have imposed on Cicero with regard to his intentions[3].

Notwithstanding the strength of their combination, and the promised support of the consuls elect, the triumvirs were afraid of serious opposition, and anxious to remove some of the more eminent optimates from Rome. A mysterious plot, disclosed in one of Cicero's letters, was supposed to have been formed with this object[4]. L. Vettius, a man whom Cicero had employed as an informer[5], told the younger Curio that he had determined to kill Pompey, and was arrested on Curio's denunciation. He then charged several of the leading nobles with complicity, but he contradicted himself so much that he was not believed, and was committed to prison, where he was shortly afterwards found dead. He was probably murdered by the contrivers of the plot. Cicero charges[6] Vatinius both with suborning and with murdering Vettius; and both Mommsen[7] and Abeken[8] regard the whole affair as an intrigue prompted by the triumvirs. Merivale[9], however, urges that if such had been the case, Vettius would hardly have named M. Brutus, whose mother, Servilia, was a favourite of Caesar. He therefore suspects that some of the more violent optimates were the true authors of the affair.

Cicero was much vexed by the behaviour of Pompey[10] at times. Of M. Bibulus he speaks with respect, not unmixed, however, with irony[11]. Before the close of the year he seems to have become thoroughly aware of the designs of Clodius[12], but to have been encouraged partly by the assurances of Pompey[13], partly by the evident unpopularity of the triumvirs[14]. He declined, therefore, an offer of Caesar to take him to Gaul as his legate, and also one of the 'legatio libera,' though the former tempted him considerably[15].

His principal speeches were,—one for his old colleague, C. Antonius, accused of misgovernment in Macedonia, who, however, was condemned[16]; two for A. Thermus, who was acquitted[17]; and one, still extant, for L. Valerius Flaccus, accused of misgovernment in Asia, but acquitted.

[1] App. Bell. Civ. 2. 14; Dion Cassius 38. 9; supra, § 7. [2] Cic. pro Dom. 13. [3] Ad Att. 2. 12, 2. [4] Ib. 2. 24. [5] Ib. sect. 2; cp. supra, § 12. [6] In Vat. 10; 11. [7] 4. 1, 206. [8] p. 111. [9] 2. 196. For the view of the emperor Napoleon III. cp. Ad Att. 2. 24, 2, note. [10] Ad Att. 2. 16, 2. [11] Ib. 2. 19, 2. [12] Ib. 2. 21, 6. [13] Ib. 2. 24, 5. [14] Ib. 2. 19, 4. [15] Ib. 2. 18, 3; 2. 19, 5. [16] Pro Dom. 16, 41; Pro Cael. 31, 74. [17] Pro Flacco 39, 98.

58 B.C.

§ 19. The new consuls, as has been said[1], were connected with the party of the triumvirs; and Clodius, now tribune, relying on their aid, prepared for his attack on Cicero. He previously, however, carried a number of measures intended to win the favour of various classes of citizens. He proposed:—

1. To abolish the small payment hitherto made by recipients of the public dole of corn[2].

2. To repeal the Lex Aelia Fufia, which secured that the auspices should be respected at the time of holding the comitia[3].

3. To repeal a decree of the senate against the formation of collegia—clubs, or guilds[4].

4. To curtail the powers of the censors[5].

These proposals would, taken together, find some support from almost all classes; for the powers of the censors were regarded with dislike by many of the nobles, and after Sulla's legislation the appointment of such officers had been discontinued for several years[6]. Having thus secured his position, Clodius proposed two more laws:—

5. Assigning Syria to Gabinius, and Macedonia, apparently with Achaia, to Piso, on the expiration of their consulship[7].

6. Enacting, 'That any one who had put Roman citizens to death without trial, should be forbidden fire and water[8].'

§ 20. The last measure was evidently directed against Cicero, and caused great consternation. The senators, the equites, and many thousand citizens, put on mourning, which the senators, however, were obliged to lay aside. L. Ninnius, a tribune, and L. Lamia, one of the equites, were active in support of Cicero. Opinions differed as to what he ought to do. He was not named in the law, and some advised him to stay till a more direct attack was made upon him. L. Lucullus, in particular, was eager to resort to force in his defence. To have done so would perhaps have been in the end the best policy for the optimates; in no other cause could they have won so much support from the mass of moderate and peaceable citizens; the country towns especially were devoted to Cicero[9]. But Pompey, to whom earnest appeals were made

[1] supra, § 18. [2] Dion Cassius 38. 13; Ascon. in Pisonian. 4. 9. [3] In Pis. 4. 9; 5. 10; In Vat. 2, 5; 7, 18. According to some, the Lex Aelia and Lex Fufia were different laws. [4] In Pis. 4. 9. On the nature of such 'collegia' cp. Ad Att. 3. 15. 4. note; Merivale, History 1. 202; Mommsen 4. 2, 296. [5] In Pis. 4, 9. [6] Div. in Caec. 3. 8 and Schol. Gronov. ad loc. [7] Pro Dom. 23, 60; In Pis. 16. [8] Vell. 2. 45. [9] Ad Att. 3. 15, 7; Plut. Cic. 31.

on his behalf, declined to interfere, except at the request of the consuls[1]; and the counsels of Cato and Hortensius, which Cicero's own family supported, prevailed. He left Rome, accordingly, towards the end of March[2]. On the very day of his departure, Clodius carried a law[3] banishing Cicero by name; but Cicero's friends got a clause inserted, allowing him to live anywhere beyond the limit of 400 miles from Rome[4]. After his departure, his house on the Palatine, and his villas at Formiae and Tusculum, were pillaged and destroyed; the consuls appropriated a good deal of the spoil, and Clodius dedicated the site of the house on the Palatine to Liberty[5].

Clodius then carried another law, giving Cato a commission to manage the annexation of Cyprus, which Cato accepted, though unwillingly[6].

Caesar, who had lingered near Rome, now hastened across the Alps to meet the Helvetii, whom he completely defeated[7] near Bibracte. He afterwards also defeated Ariovistus[8].

The legality of the execution of Lentulus, Cethegus, and their associates, depends on the extent of the powers conferred by the senate's vote commissioning the consuls to provide for the safety of the state. Cicero maintained[9] that he might have ordered Catiline's execution by virtue of that decree; but the prosecution of Rabirius had shewn that some of the popular leaders thought differently, and Cicero himself, by consulting[10] the senate as to the punishment to be inflicted on Lentulus and his accomplices, had seemed to doubt the extent of his own powers as consul. Cp. Appendix IV.

§ 21. After leaving Rome, Cicero repaired at first to the neighbourhood of Vibo, in Bruttium, where he had a friend named Sicca; and there he heard of the enactment forbidding him to live within 400 miles of Rome[11]. He was refused an asylum in Sicily by its propraetor, C. Vergilius[12], who, though a friend of Cicero, was afraid of offending the dominant party at Rome. Cicero decided, therefore, on going to Macedonia[13], declining an invitation[14] to the estate of Atticus in Epirus, and avoiding Greece for fear of meeting some of the accomplices[15] of Catiline who lived there. He went, accordingly, to Thessalonica[16], where, under the protection of the propraetor L. Appuleius—which appears, however, not to have been very heartily given[17]—and in the house of his own

[1] In Pis. 31, 77; Ad Att. 10. 4. 3. [2] Ad Att. 3. 1; 2. [3] In the comitia tributa: cp. Pro Sest. 30, 65. [4] Ad Att. 3. 4. 500 from Italy, according to Plutarch, Cic. 32; 3750 stadia from Rome, Dion Cassius 38, 17. See too Mr. Tyrrell's notes on Ad Att. 3. 2 and 4. [5] On the facts mentioned above, cp. Ad Fam. 14. 2. 3; Ad Att. 4. 1. 7, note; App. Bell. Civ. 2. 15; Dion Cassius 38. 14–17; Plut. Cic. 30–33. [6] Pro Sest. 28. [7] Caes. Bell. Gall. 1. 25; 26. [8] Ib. 51–53. [9] In Cat. 1. 2. 4. [10] supra, § 11. [11] Ad Att. 3. 4. [12] Pro Planc. 40, 96. [13] Ib. 41. [14] Ad Att. 3. 7. 1. [15] Ib. [16] Ib. 3. 8. 1; Pro Planc. 11, 28. [17] Ib. 41, 98.

devoted friend the quaestor, Cn. Plancius, he lived in security, though in deep dejection. He apprehended that his brother Quintus, then returning from his administration of Asia, might be persecuted for his sake[1]; suspected false dealing on the part of Hortensius and others[2]; and was tormented by fears for his wife and children. He earnestly dissuaded Terentia from selling part of her property to aid him in his exile[3].

Towards the close of the year his prospects brightened. On Caesar's departure from Rome, Pompey shewed himself unable to keep Clodius in order; and the ill-feeling between the two was increased by the escape of Tigranes[4]—an Armenian prince whom Pompey had brought to Rome as a hostage, but whom Clodius helped to escape—and by an alleged attempt of Clodius to procure the assassination of Pompey[5]. Moreover, eight[6] at least of the new tribunes were friendly to Cicero; and of the consuls elect, one[7], P. Lentulus Spinther, was a warm friend, the other, Q. Metellus Nepos, was much under the influence of Pompey, and proved a placable enemy[8].

Various attempts were made, even before the close of 58 B.C., to repeal the act banishing Cicero. Atticus, and his friend, Q. Terentius Culleo, one of the tribunes, thought of attacking it as a 'privilegium,' or law enacted against an individual, such laws being prohibited by the Twelve Tables. This course, however, did not seem advisable to Cicero[9].

L. Ninnius Quadratus, one of the tribunes for 59–58 B.C., had brought in a bill for his direct recall on June 1; but, though it met with the unanimous approval of the senate, one of the tribunes, P. (?) Aelius Ligus, interposed his veto[10].

On October 29, eight of the tribunes brought in a bill for Cicero's restoration, on which Atticus asked his opinion. It was not favourable; some of its clauses seemed to shew either negligence or treachery in its framers[11]. Cicero wrote from Dyrrhachium, whither he had gone, both to avoid meeting L. Piso's soldiers and to be nearer to Italy[12].

The new tribunes came into office on Dec. 10, after the consuls had already departed for their provinces[13]. T. Annius Milo, T. Fadius, and P. Sestius, were prominent among the tribunes[14], and the whole college promised to support Cicero. Two, however, Sex. Atilius Serranus and Q. Numerius Rufus[15], subsequently went over to his enemies.

In this year M. Scaurus, son of the celebrated princeps senatus, was

[1] Ad Att. 3. 9. 1; Ad Q. F. 1. 3. 4. [2] Ad Att. 3. 9. 2. [3] Ad Fam. 14. 1, 5. [4] Ad Att. 3. 8, 3; Dion Cassius 38. 30. [5] Pro Sest. 32, 69. [6] Ad Fam. 14. 1, 2; cp. Ad Att. 4. 1, 6; Pro Sest. 33. 72. [7] Ad Fam. 1. 1-9, passim. [8] Pro Sest. 33. 72; 62, 130. [9] Ad Att. 3. 15. 5. [10] Pro Sest. 31, 68. [11] Ad Att. 3. 23. 2. [12] Ib. 3. 22, 1 and 4. [13] Pro Sest. 33. 71. [14] Ad Att. 3. 23. 4; Post Red. in Sen. 8. [15] Pro Sest. 33. 72; 43. 94.

curule aedile, and distinguished himself by the splendour of his shows[1], which exhausted his fortune[2].

§ 22. Cicero's letters during this year do not shew him in a favourable light. We find him indulging in unmanly lamentations[3]; suspecting his best friends of lukewarmness or treachery without adequate grounds[4]; regretting the course he had been persuaded to take when it was too late to alter it[5]; and stooping to unworthy artifices in order to regain the favour of men whom he had offended[6]. It must be remembered, however, that he had been wounded in two most tender points,—his affection for his family and his love of fame. The patriotism which had nerved him for the really magnanimous resolution to leave Rome, rather than expose it to the chances of a civil conflict, did not support him under the daily weariness and annoyances of a life in exile. Moreover, the prospect of return was uncertain, and his life was insecure, except when he was under the direct protection of some official. In spite of the favourable signs already[7] mentioned, he was very despondent at the close of the year, especially on account of the departure of Atticus from Rome[8].

Of the men referred to in his letters of this date, the most important, besides those already mentioned, were M. Terentius Varro and Cicero's son-in-law, C. Piso.

The former, an eminent antiquary, will be often mentioned. He had been on good terms with Cicero[9], who looked for his support against Clodius, but afterwards suspected him of duplicity[10], and only partially regained confidence in him[11].

C. Calpurnius Piso, a connection of Cicero's enemy, the consul L. Piso, shewed the greatest devotion to his father-in-law, both by trying to conciliate the consul, his kinsman[12], and by declining to go into a province as quaestor, in order that he might watch over Cicero's interests at Rome[13]. He seems to have died soon after Cicero's return from exile[14]. Cicero always speaks of him in the highest terms[15].

57 B.C.

§ 23. The consul Lentulus proposed Cicero's recall on the 1st of January. He was supported by Pompey and by L. Cotta, and a decree would have passed on that very day, but that Sex. Atilius Serranus, one

[1] Pro Sest. 47, 101; 54. 116: De Off. 2. 16, 57: Pliny, H. N. 36, 15. [2] Ascon. ad Orat. pro Scaur. 131. [3] Ad Fam. 14. 1 and 2. [4] Ad Att. 3. 9, 2. [5] Ib. 3. 15. 4. [6] Ib. 3. 12, 2. [7] supra, § 21. [8] Ad Att. 3 25. [9] Ib. 2. 20. 1. [10] Ib. 2. 25. 1. [11] Ib. 3. 15, 3. [12] Pro Sest. 24. 54. [13] Post Red. in Sen. 15, 38. [14] Pro Sest. 31, 68. [15] Brut. 78, 272, alib.

of the tribunes, demanded a night for consideration[1]. The decree seems afterwards to have been regarded as legally passed[2]. Various difficulties prevented a renewal of the discussion till Jan. 23, when Cicero's friends brought a bill for his recall before the popular assembly. Clodius, however, interfered with his armed rabble, and Q. Cicero was grievously hurt[3]. No further steps seem to have been taken in Cicero's behalf for some months; in July, Clodius appears still to have been master of the streets of Rome[4].

The senate subsequently passed a series of decrees in favour of Cicero, but their precise number and dates are not easy to determine. Perhaps three may be distinguished.

1. Summoning the Italians to Rome for Cicero's protection; thanking the allies for attentions shewn him, and recommending his safety to officials in the provinces and to foreign princes[5]. This was passed, apparently, in the 'monument of Marius[6],' and was followed by a great demonstration at the theatre in honour of Cicero[7].

2. Declaring that Cicero's counsels had saved the state, and, perhaps, directing the consuls to propose a law for his recall[8]. This decree was passed apparently in the temple of Jupiter Capitolinus.

3. One passed on the day following, which contained expressions of gratitude to all who had come to Rome for the sake of supporting Cicero's recall; threats against any who should hinder the passing of a law in his favour[9]; and an invitation to himself to return if such a law did not pass within five days[10]. On this occasion the consul Metellus Nepos declared himself reconciled to Cicero[11].

This decree perhaps passed[12] on August 4, on which day a law for Cicero's recall was sanctioned by the comitia centuriata[13]. Milo, who had already indicted Clodius for riot, brought armed men into the Forum to protect the voters from disturbance[14].

§ 24. Cicero left Dyrrhachium, where he had been since the end of November, 58 B.C., on the very day on which the law passed. He landed next day at Brundisium, where he found Tullia awaiting his arrival; and, on the 8th, heard from his brother Quintus that the law for his restoration had passed. He then travelled to Rome, receiving everywhere a warm greeting, and reached the capital on Sept. 4. He was

[1] Pro Sest. 34. 74. [2] Ad Att. 3. 26. [3] Pro Sest. 35. [4] Pro Milon. 14. 38 and Ascon. thereon. [5] Pro Sest. 60, 128. [6] Ib. 54, 116. It was the temple of Honos and Virtus. Lange, 3. 305, places this in June. [7] Ib. 54–58. [8] Ib. 61. Lange, 3. 306, places this in July. [9] Ib.; Post. Red in Sen. 11, 27. [10] Pro Sest. 61. [11] Ib. 62, 130. [12] Ib. 61, 129; Post Red. in Sen. 11. 27; Ad Att. 4. 1. 4. [13] Ad Att. 4. 1, 4. [14] Post Red. in Sen. 8, 19; Dion Cassius 39. 8.

enthusiastically welcomed, and next day addressed the senate, thanking them for his recall, possibly in the speech which we now possess[1].

Only three of his letters belong to the first eight months of 57 B.C.; two to Atticus, one[2] apparently written about the middle of January, saying that he would return on the strength of the senate's expression of opinion, even if anything prevented the passing of a law; the other[3], an outburst of utter despair after the events of Jan. 23 were known to him. The third[4] was to the consul Metellus, appealing to him to forget his private grudges, and promising gratitude.

§ 25. The foreign affairs of this year were important. A. Gabinius, pro-consul of Syria, had to make war on the Jews, who had revolted against the government of Hyrcanus, which the Romans had set up. He governed ably, but was covetous and unscrupulous, and, if Cicero is to be believed, met with some serious reverses[5]. His late colleague, Piso, governed Macedonia rapaciously and disastrously[6].

Meanwhile Caesar was prosecuting his conquests in Gaul. He reduced most of the Belgian tribes to submission, defeating the Nervii in a great battle. He then sent P. Crassus against some of the north-western tribes[7].

Ptolemy Auletes had been driven from Egypt by his subjects in 58 B.C., and went to Rome to intrigue for his restoration. His subjects, on their part, sent envoys to protest against it; but Ptolemy had some of them murdered on their journey, and employed his money to prevent the survivors getting an audience before the senate. In 57 a decree of the senate directed that the next governor of Cilicia (the actual consul, P. Lentulus) should restore Ptolemy[8].

[1] The Orat. Post Red. in Sen.: cp. Ad Att. 4. 1, 5. [2] Ad Att. 3. 26. [3] Ib. 3. 27. [4] Ad Fam. 5. 4. [5] De Prov. Cons. 1–7; In Pis. 21: cp. Mommsen 4. 1, 153 and 154; 4. 2, 329; Joseph. Antiq. 14. 6. [6] De Prov. Cons. l. c.; In Pis. 17 foll. [7] Caes. Bell. Gall. 2. [8] Dion Cassius 39. 12 and 13; Plut. Cat. Min. 35. Cicero's biography is resumed in the Introduction to the Second Part.

SELECT LETTERS

OF

M. TULLIUS CICERO.

PART I.

I. To ATTICUS (AD ATT. I. 1).

ROME, JULY, 65 B.C. (689 A.U.C.)

1. With regard to my canvass for the consulship, I am resolved not to injure my prospects by putting myself forward too soon, but to wait for the 17th. Galba, Antonius, and Catiline will be among my competitors, if the last named escape the conviction which is his due. 2. Of the candidates for *next* year, Caesar is thought safe; I hope Thermus may be his colleague, as I should then be relieved of a formidable rival. I shall exert myself to the utmost here, and shall perhaps employ my first leisure in visiting Cisalpine Gaul, to conciliate its inhabitants. Do you urge Pompey's friends to attend at the election. 3. I have to ask your forgiveness for denying your uncle Caecilius a request, viz. that I would support his claims upon my friend A. Caninius. 4. I in vain represented to your uncle that he would be supported efficiently by men who had similar claims to his own upon Caninius; he still seemed somewhat offended, but you will find a sufficient excuse for my conduct in my present position. 5. I am glad you are so much pleased with your 'Hermathena.'

CICERO ATTICO SAL.

1 PETITIONIS nostrae, quam tibi summae curae esse scio, huius modi ratio est, quod adhuc coniectura provideri possit. Prensat unus P. Galba; sine fuco ac fallaciis, more maiorum,

For an account of Atticus, see Appendix 3.

1. Petitionis nostrae . . . ratio est, 'matters stand thus with regard to my canvass for the consulship.' Cp. 'rationem temperationem' Pro Muren. 2, 4.

2. Quod adhuc . . . possit, 'so far as we can look forward by conjecture at present.' On the mood of 'possit' after a relative limiting the verb, cp. Madv. 364, Obs. 2.

3. Prensat unus P. Galba, 'Galba alone is canvassing personally.' According to Manutius the term 'prensare' applied to a preliminary testing of public feeling, be-

negatur. Ut opinio est hominum, non aliena rationi nostrae fuit illius haec praepropera prensatio; nam illi ita negant volgo, ut mihi se debere dicant. Ita quiddam spero nobis profici, cum hoc percrebrescit, plurimos nostros amicos inveniri. Nos autem initium prensandi facere cogitaramus eo ipso tempore, quo tuum puerum cum his litteris proficisci Cincius dicebat, in campo, comitiis tribuniciis, a. d. XVI. Kalend. Sextiles. Competitores, qui certi esse videantur, Galba et Antonius et Q. Cornificius: puto te in hoc aut risisse aut ingemuisse. Ut frontem ferias, sunt qui etiam Caesonium putent. Aquilium non arbitramur,

fore the formal 'petitio' began. The translations of Wieland and Metzger both give 'more' its usual sense here; but some have thought that such a meaning is inconsistent with the mention of more competitors a few lines below, and either suppose that a new letter begins with 'competitores qui certi' foll., or translate 'more' by 'especially.' May not the meaning be that Galba alone was actively canvassing, though others allowed their names to be mentioned? For the word 'premare,' cp. Livy 1. 47 'circumire et prensare patres.'

P. Sulpicius Galba is well spoken of by Cicero, cp. In Verr. Act. 1. 10, 30; Pro Muren. 8, 17; De Harusp. Resp. 6, 12.

Sine fuco ac fallaciis, 'without any deceitful fine words.' Cp. 'fucosi suffragatores' Q. Cic. de Pet. Com. 9. 35.

More maiorum negatur, 'men say no with old-fashioned frankness.' Prof. Nettleship has pointed out to me a parallel passage in Plautus; cp. Truc. Prol. 6—

'En mehercle in vobis resident mores pristini
Ad denegandum ut celeri lingua utamini.'

1. Rationi, 'interest.' Cp. 'si rationes meas saluti vestrae anteposuissem' Post Red. ad Quir. 1, 1.

2. Ita negant . . . ut . . . dicant, 'in refusing him their support profess themselves under obligations to me.' On the constr. cp. Zumpt. L. G. 726.

3. Quiddam spero nobis profici . . . . inveniri, 'I hope it is proving of some use to me, that my friends are being found numerous.' For the pres. infin. with 'spero,' cp. Madv. 395, Obs. 3 ad fin. And for this sense of 'proficere,' cp. 'ad summam profectum aliquid puto,' Ep. 48, 1.

Cum . . . percrebrescit = 'percrebrescere.' Cp. Ep. 111, 3, note, and Madv. 358, Obs. 2.

5. Cogitaramus . . . dicebat = 'cogitavimus . . dicit.' The past tenses are used because they would be true of the time when the letter would reach its destination. Atticus would say, 'when Cicero wrote this, Cincius was saying.' Cp. Madv. 345.

6. Puerum, sc. 'tabellarium.'

Proficisci, for 'profecturum esse.' Cp. 'quando te proficisci istinc putes fac ut sciam' Ad Att. 2. 6, 2; Ter. Phorm. 3. 2, 47; Ep. 36, 11 'negavi me audire.'

Cincius. (L.) Agent, apparently, of Atticus, and often mentioned in Cicero's letters to him: e.g. 1, 7; 6. 2, 1.

In campo, sc. Martio.

7. a. d. xvi. Kal Sext. This would be about a year before the day of election. The formal 'professio' of the candidates generally took place a 'trinundinum,' or 17 days before the election: cp. Ep. 52, 3; Livy 3. 35; but the canvass, as we see from this passage, might begin much sooner.

8. Qui certi . . . . videantur. For the mood, see on this sect. 'quod . . possit,' line 2. 'Certi' appears to mean 'certain to stand.'

Antonius. (C.) Cicero's colleague in his consulship. He afterwards governed Macedonia, and on his return to Rome was condemned for misgovernment. Cp. Intr. to Part I, § 18.

Q. Cornificius. Spoken of with great respect by Cicero: cp. In Verr. Act. 1. 10, 30. His son was appointed to govern Africa by Caesar. Cp. Epp. 119; 124.

9. In hoc, sc. 'Cornificio,' 'at the last name.'

Risisse. At the pretensions of a 'new man' with no great personal qualifications; ingemuisse, at the impending defeat of a man of good character.

Ut frontem ferias; 'prae admiratione et dolore' Schütz. Cp. 'frons non percussa' Brut. 80, 278.

10. Caesonium. M. Caesonius was colleague of Cicero as curule aedile, and one of the judges on the trial of Verres. Cp. In Verr. Act. 1. 10, 29.

qui denegavit et iuravit morbum et illud suum regnum iudiciale opposuit. Catilina, si iudicatum erit meridie non lucere, certus erit competitor. De Auli filio et de Palicano non puto
2 te exspectare dum scribam. De iis, qui nunc petunt, Caesar certus putatur. Thermus cum Silano contendere existimatur, qui sic inopes et ab amicis et *ab* existimatione sunt, ut mihi videatur non esse ἀδύνατον Curium obducere. Sed hoc praeter me nemini videtur. Nostris rationibus maxime conducere vide-

Aquilium. C. Aquilius Gallus was a celebrated jurisconsult, author of the formula 'de dolo malo,' and teacher of the celebrated Servius Sulpicius. As the latter was Cicero's contemporary, Aquilius was probably somewhat older than Cicero, though praetor in the same year with him. Cp. Brut. 42, 153 and 154.

Non arbitramur, sc. 'competitorem fore.'

1. **Iuravit morbum,** 'protested that his health would not allow him to be a candidate.' Cp. 'perpetuum morbum iurabo' Ad Att. 12. 13. 1.

Regnum iudiciale opposuit, 'pleaded his sovereignty in the law courts,' i.e. his great business. Cp. 'omnis dominatio regnumque iudiciorum,' said of Hortensius, In Verr. Act. 1. 12, 35.

2. **Catilina:** cp. Intr. to Part I, § 8.

Si iudicatum erit meridie non lucere. I cannot find that this expression is elsewhere used. Apparently it means, 'if the judges decide that black is white.'

3. **De Auli filio.** L. Afranius, consul in 60 B.C., is said to have been called 'Auli filius' on account of his own insignificance; 'quasi terrae filius,' says Drumann (1. 35), but it seems a strange expression. Mr. Tyrrell retains the MS. reading 'Aufidio,' and refers to T. Aufidius once praetor in Asia: cp. pro Flacco 19. 45. Mr. Tyrrell remarks that Cicero does not call Afranius A. filius before 61 B.C. Afranius was a devoted adherent of Pompey; commanded his forces in Spain, with M. Petreius, in 49 B.C., and perished in the African campaign three years later. Cp. Intr. to Parts III, § 8; IV, § 10.

Palicano. M. Lollius Palicanus, tribune for 72-71 B.C., is mentioned In Verr. Act. 2. 2. 41, 100. He seems to have been held in great contempt, and it is said that the consul Piso declared in 67 B.C. that he would not announce Palicanus as elected even if he obtained a majority of the votes. Cp. Val. Max. 3. 8, 3.

4. **Nunc,** 'for this year's election,' i.e. to hold office in 64 B.C.

L. Iulius Caesar, consul 64 B.C. His sister Julia married (1) M. Antonius Creticus, to whom she bore the celebrated triumvir, (2) P. Lentulus, the associate of Catiline. Notwithstanding this near connection, Caesar voted, in December, 63 B.C., for the execution of Lentulus. See Ep 96, 1. After the murder of the dictator Caesar, Lucius tried to mediate between the senate and Antony: was proscribed by the triumvirs, and narrowly escaped death. Cp. Philipp. 8. 1. 1; 12. 7. 18; App. Bell. Civ. 4. 12; 4. 37. **Certus,** 'certain of success.'

5. **Q. Minucius Thermus.** Said to have become C. Marcius Figulus, by adoption, and so to have been consul in 64 B.C. But I cannot find any evidence for this, beyond the probability arising from a comparison of this passage with Ep. 2. 1, Drumann (5. 405) is satisfied with the probability.

Silano. D. Iunius Silanus, consul for 62 B.C. When consul elect, he proposed in the senate that Lentulus and his accomplices should be punished with death (cp. In Cat. 4. 4. 7), but afterwards supported a motion for delay.

Thermus cum Silano, foll., 'the struggle is thought to lie between Thermus and Silanus.'

6. **Ab amicis,** 'in respect of friends.' See Madv. 253, Observations, for the ablat.

7. **Curium obducere,** 'to bring forward Curius against them.' Boot says this is the only passage in Cicero where the word occurs in this sense. Manutius says 'contra illos in Campum Martium ducere.' Asconius (ad Orat. in tog. cand. 118) quotes from C. Licinius Calvus the words 'et talis Curius pereruditus' in illustration of Curius' love of gambling. The Curius referred to may have been the Q. Curius who betrayed to Cicero the secrets of Catiline and his associates. The context shows that he was a man of little consequence. Cicero's slighting mention of Thermus seems inconsistent with his wish not to have him for a competitor.

8. **Rationibus:** see note on sect. 1, p. 26.

tur Thermum fieri cum Caesare; nemo est enim ex iis, qui nunc petunt, qui, si in nostrum annum reciderit, firmior candidatus fore videatur, propterea quod curator est viae Flaminiae, †quae cum erit absoluta sane facile eum libenter nunc ceteri consuli acciderim. Petitorum haec est adhuc informata cogitatio. Nos in omni munere candidatorio fungendo summam adhibebimus diligentiam et fortasse, quoniam videtur in suffragiis multum posse Gallia, cum Romae a iudiciis forum refrixerit, excurremus mense Septembri legati ad Pisonem, ut Ianuario revertamur: cum perspexero voluntates nobilium, scribam ad te. Cetera spero prolixa esse, his dumtaxat urbanis competitoribus. Illam manum tu mihi cura ut praestes, quoniam propius abes,

2. **Si . . . reciderit**, 'if he shall be left over for my year.'

Firmior, 'more likely to succeed.'

3. **Curator . . viae Flaminiae**, 'commissioner for repairing the Flaminian road.' The Flaminian was the great north road, leading to the Adriatic by Ocriculum and Narnia; and the office of Thermus would give him opportunities of gaining influence with the population of the districts through which the road ran.

4. **Quae cum erit . . . . acciderim.** I have given the reading of the best MS. but it is not intelligible. Of conjectures, that of Manutius, 'quae tum erit absoluta, sane facile. Eum libenter nunc Caesari consulem addiderim,' keeps nearest to the MS.; that of Kayser, 'quae tum erit absoluta sane facile. Eum libenter municipia consulem accipient,' perhaps suits the context best. Mr. Tyrrell gives 'sane facile: eo libenter Thermum Caesari consulem accuderim' as an improvement on that of Manutius, and suggests himself 'eo libenter Thermum Ciceri (a lupine to a vetch) consulem accuderim.'

5. **Petitorum . . . . cogitatio**, 'this is the general impression which I have formed about the candidates up to the present time.' **Informo** = *ὑποτυπόω*. Forcell.

8. **Gallia Cispadana**: for the franchise of the Transpadane Gauls was not thoroughly recognized till after Caesar's victory over Pompey. Cp. Ep. 31, 2, note. On the importance of the support of the Gallic district to candidates, cp. 'municipia coloniasque Galliae a qua nos tum . . . petere consulatum solebamus' Philipp. 2. 30, 76.

Cum . . . refrixerit, 'when the heat of business shall have grown less intense in the courts at Rome.' In the autumn many days were taken up with the celebration of different public games, and were therefore unavailable for judicial business. Cp. In Verr. Act. 1. 10, 31. 'Refrigere' is opposed to 'calere.' Cp. Ep. 9. 6.

9. **Ad Pisonem.** C. Calpurnius Piso was consul in 67 B.C., and afterwards governor of Gallia Narbonensis. He proposed a law against bribery in his consulship, and it was carried. On his return from his province, he was accused of maladministration by C. Caesar; defended by Cicero, and acquitted, in 63 B.C. If he did not combine the government of Cisalpine with that of Narbonensian Gaul, Cicero may have visited the farther province as an excuse for canvassing the Cispadane Gauls on his way. **Legati.** Cicero would probably apply for the 'legatio libera,' a titular office which would enable him to visit the province with more dignity. Cp. Ep. 11, 3; Philipp. 1. 2, 6.

11. **Prolixa**, 'clear,' from the sense of flowing or streaming freely; hence 'favourable.' Forcell. Cp. 'rebus secundis atque prolixis' Cat. ap. Aul. Gell. 7 (or 6). 3.

Urbanis, either 'who are now at Rome' (Casaub. ap. Billerb.), or 'whose claims rest on civil services' (Boot, following Gronovius). Either version may, perhaps, be justified by the expression 'urbana militia' Pro Muren. 9. 19. The whole passage means, 'if I have only to deal with these competitors.' On the abl. abs. 'his,' see Madv. 277.

12. **Manum.** The friends and dependents of Pompey, who was now in Asia. Atticus, who was now at Athens, might have more opportunities for intercourse with the East, than Cicero in Italy. Boot, however, explains 'manus' as meaning 'opera, auxilium.'

Pompeii, nostri amici: nega me ei iratum fore, si ad mea comitia non venerit. Atque haec huius modi sunt. Sed est quod abs te mihi ignosci pervelim: Caecilius, avunculus tuus, a P. Vario cum magna pecunia fraudaretur, agere coepit cum eius fratre A. Caninio Satyro de iis rebus, quas cum dolo malo mancipio accepisse de Vario diceret; una agebant ceteri creditores, in quibus erat *L.* Lucullus et P. Scipio et is, quem putabant magistrum fore, si bona venirent, L. Pontius. Verum hoc ridiculum est de magistro. Nunc cognosce rem. Rogavit me Caecilius, ut adessem contra Satyrum: dies fere nullus est quin hic Satyrus domum meam ventitet; observat L. Domitium

1. **Ei, Pompeio.** Boot.

3. **Quod . . . pervelim,** 'for which I should be very glad of your forgiveness.' 'Pervelim' recurs Ad. Att. 11. 14. 3. For the mood, see Madv. 350 b, Obs. 1.

Caecilius. (Q.) Uncle of Atticus, and, like him, a great money-lender. He adopted Atticus by his will. Cp. Ad Att. 1. 12, 1; 2. 19, 5; 3. 20, 1.

4. **P. Vario.** Varius is not apparently mentioned elsewhere.

Agere coepit cum eius fratre, 'began legal proceedings against the brother of Varius.' If '*fratre*' has its usual meaning, one of the two brothers must have changed his name by adoption, or they may have been brothers on the mother's side.

5. **Dolo malo mancipio accepisse,** 'to have fraudulently purchased,' i.e. so as to defraud the creditors, by giving less than the real value. There was a legal action for 'dolus malus' (cp. § 1, note), which is defined (Digest 4. tit. 3, § 1) 'omnis calliditas, fallacia, machinatio ad circumveniendum, fallendum, decipiendum alterum adhibita.' The action seems to have been provided for cases of fraud which could not be brought under any more specific head. Cp. De Offic. 3. 14, 60.

6. **Diceret** = 'ut dicebat' with 'accepisset,' or 'accepisset' might stand alone. See Madv. 357 a, Obs. 2, and examples.

Una agebant, 'are acting in concert with Caecilius.'

7. **L. Lucullus.** So Baiter, but without giving any reason for his insertion of L. Boot follows Manutius in believing *Marcus* Lucullus to be referred to, but on the erroneous supposition that Lucius was at this time engaged in the Mithridatic War, whereas he left Asia in 66 B.C., and seems to have waited 'ad urbem,' three years for his triumph. Cp. Acad. Pr. 2. 1, 3; Drumann 4. 161. For an account of L. Lucullus, see Intr. to Part I, § 7; Appendix 1, § 1; and of Marcus, Ep. 21, § 3.

P. Scipio. Nasica, probably, adopted by Q. Metellus Pius subsequently. His daughter, Cornelia, was Pompey's third wife. He commanded a considerable force for Pompey in the campaign of 48 B.C., and was afterwards general of the army of the optimates in Africa. Some days after the battle of Thapsus, in 46 B.C., he killed himself, being hotly pursued by Caesar's partisans. See Intr. to Part IV, §§ 4; 10; Caes. Bell. Civ. 3. 37, alib.; Bell. Afric. 96; App. Bell. Civ. 2. 100; Livy, Epit. 114.

8. **Magistrum,** sc. 'auctionis.' If a debtor's property had to be sold, the 'magister' presided at the sale in the interest of the creditors. Cp. Pro Quinct. 15, 50; Ad Att. 6. 1, 15; 9. 11, 4: also Rein, Privatrecht, 944.

L. Pontius Aquila. A friend of Cicero. As tribune of the people, in 44–45 B.C., he offended Caesar by his independence. Cp. Ep. 112, 3, note. He was one of the conspirators against Caesar; after whose death he did good service to the senate in the war of Mutina, and was killed in one of the battles which obliged Antony to raise the siege of that place. See Philipp. 13. 13, 27; Ad Fam. 10. 33, 4.

Verum hoc . . . . magistro, 'it is ridiculous to dwell on the appointment of a "magister."'

9. **Rem,** 'the affair for which I wish you to forgive me.'

11. **Observat,** 'courts.' Cp. Ad Fam. 6. 10, 2, alib.

L. Domitium Ahenobarbum. This nobleman is mentioned as a witness against Verres. In Verr. Act. 2. 1. 53, 139. He was consul 54 B.C., and afterwards named as Caesar's successor in Transalpine Gaul by the senate. He supported the cause of the

maxime, me habet proximum; fuit et mihi et Q. fratri magno
usui in nostris petitionibus. Sane sum perturbatus cum ipsius 4
Satyri familiaritate, tum Domitii, in quo uno maxime ambitio
nostra nititur. Demonstravi haec Caecilio; simul et illud
ostendi, si ipse unus cum illo uno contenderet, me ei satis
facturum fuisse; nunc in causa universorum creditorum, hominum praesertim amplissimorum, qui sine eo, quem Caecilius
suo nomine perhiberet, facile causam communem sustinerent,
aequum esse cum et officio meo consulere et tempori. Durius
accipere hoc mihi visus est quam vellem et quam homines belli
solent, et postea prorsus ab instituta nostra paucorum dierum
consuetudine longe refugit: abs te peto, ut mihi hoc ignoscas
et me existimes humanitate esse prohibitum, *ne contra* amici
summam existimationem miserrimo eius tempore venirem, cum
is omnia sua studia et officia in me contulisset. Quod si voles
in me esse durior, ambitionem putabis mihi obstitisse; ego
autem arbitror, etiam si id sit, mihi ignoscendum esse: *ἐπεὶ οὐχ
ἱερήϊον οὐδὲ βοείην*. Vides enim, in quo cursu simus et quam
omnes gratias non modo retinendas, verum etiam acquirendas
putemus. Spero tibi me causam probasse, cupio quidem certe.
Hermathena tua valde me delectat et posita ita belle est, ut 5

optimates in the civil war with zeal, but without much skill or success, and was killed after Pharsalus, Cicero says by Antony. See Intr. to Part III, § 11.

1. **Me habet proximum**, 'gives me the next place in his regard.'

2. **Petitionibus.** M. Cicero had been quaestor, aedile, and praetor. His brother Quintus had been aedile, and in all probability quaestor.

3. **Ambitio nostra nititur**, 'my canvass rests its hopes of success.'

5. **Illo**, sc. 'Satyro.'

6. **Nunc in causa . . . . et tempori**, 'but under existing circumstances, seeing that all the creditors were interested, and they, too, men of distinction, able to take care of themselves, even without the aid of any advocate produced by Caecilius individually, it was fair that Caecilius should consider my obligations and my position,' i. e. not insist on my accusing a friend and an influential supporter. 'Adhibere' is more common than 'perhibere,' in the sense of 'to produce in one's support.'

10. **Belli** = 'humani.' Forcell. 'of good breeding.' Rare in Cicero, but occurs in Ep. 75. 3: De Fin. 2. 31, 102.

11. **Ab instituta . . . consuetudine**, 'from our intimacy which had begun a few days before.'

13. **Ne contra . . . venirem**, 'from appearing against a friend in his time of greatest need, and when his whole reputation was at stake.' For a conviction for 'dolus malus' seems to have implied 'infamia.' Rein, Criminalrecht, 916.

17. *ἐπεὶ οὐχ ἱερήϊον οὐδὲ βοείην
ἀρνύσθην, ἅ τε ποσσὶν ἀέθλια γίγνεται
ἀνδρῶν,
ἀλλὰ περὶ ψυχῆς θέον Ἕκτορος ἱπποδάμοιο.*—Il. 22, 159.

i.e. 'no small interests are at stake.'

18. **In quo cursu simus**, 'in what a career I am embarked.' Perhaps with an allusion to the passage from the Iliad quoted above, about the 'running' of Hector. On the conjunctive in dependent questions, see Madv. 356.

19. **Omnes gratias.** With this use of the plural, cp. 'multas bonas gratias' Pro Muren. 20. 42.

20. **Me causam probasse**, 'that I have made good my plea,' 'shewn sufficient grounds for my conduct.'

21. **Hermathena.** A statue with two

totum gymnasium eius ἀνάθημα esse videatur. Multum te amamus.

2. To ATTICUS (AD ATT. I. 2).

Rome, July or August, 65 B.C. (689 A.U.C.)

1. You will be pleased to hear that Terentia bore me a son on the day that Caesar and Figulus were elected consuls, and that she is doing well. I am anxious to hear from you. I think of pleading for Catiline on his trial, and, if I succeed, shall hope for his support at the election. 2. Please take care to be at Rome in January; I shall need your influence with certain nobles, who are supposed not to look with favour on my claims.

CICERO ATTICO SAL.

1 L. Iulio Caesare C. Marcio Figulo consulibus filiolo me auctum scito salva Terentia. Abs te tam diu nihil litterarum? ego de meis ad te rationibus scripsi antea diligenter. Hoc tempore Catilinam, competitorem nostrum, defendere cogitamus; iudices habemus, quos voluimus, summa accusatoris voluntate.

faces, one of Hermes, one of Athene; so we hear of a 'Hermeracles,' Ad Att. 1. 10, 3.

1. Gymnasium. Used of a place dedicated to literary and philosophical discussions, from the older philosophers having used the Greek gymnasia for such purposes. Forcell.

Eius ἀνάθημα, 'an offering to it,' 'dedicated to it.'

3. L. Iulio Caesare C. Marcio Figulo consulibus. Cicero amuses himself by expressing in one sentence the result of the consular comitia for 64 B.C., and the birth of his child. He must refer to the day of election, not to that of the new consuls coming into office, for he speaks of the trial of Catiline as not yet concluded, and it took place in 65 B.C. Cp. Fragm. Orat. in Tog. Cand. 'In iudiciis quanta vis esset didicit cum est absolutus, si aut illud iudicium aut illa absolutio nominanda est,' with Asconius' Comment. 111. See, too, Suringar, Annales, 601.

Filiolo. Cicero's namesake Marcus. He accompanied his father to Cilicia, and studied there, together with his cousin Quintus, but seems to have been slow in learning. He commanded a body of cavalry under Pompey in the civil war, cp. De Off. 2. 13, 45, and his father sent him, in 45 B.C., to study at Athens. Cp. Ad Att. 12. 32, 2; De Off. 1. 1, 1. When M. Brutus appeared in Greece, after Caesar's murder, the young Cicero did him good service against Dolabella and C. Antonius. Cp. Philipp. 10. 6, 13; Plut. Brut. 26, 3. After the battle of Philippi, he escaped to Sex. Pompeius, in Sicily, and perhaps returned to Italy by virtue of the amnesty which was one of the conditions of the peace of Misenum. Cp. App. Bell. Civ. 5. 72. He was consul 30 B.C., when the senate ordered the destruction of Antony's images. Dion Cassius 51. 19; Plut. Cic. 49. He was famous for his violent temper, and love of the pleasures of the table (cp. M. Seneca Suasor. 7; Pliny H. N. 14. 22, 28), and died, apparently, without male issue.

4. Auctum, 'enriched,' 'blessed.'

Salva Terentia, 'and that Terentia is doing well.'

Nihil litterarum, sc. 'accepero.'

6. Catilinam . . . cogitamus. It is doubtful if Cicero carried out this intention. Perhaps, if he had done so, he would hardly have spoken with such contempt of a court which had decided in his favour, as is shewn in the passage quoted above from the 'Oratio in Toga Candida.' But Asconius' argument, that if he had pleaded for Catiline, he would afterwards have charged the latter with ingratitude, is not convincing. Catiline was apparently brought to trial in this year on a charge of misgovernment arising out of his administration of Africa as propraetor. Cp. Ascon. ad Orat. in Tog. Cand. 111.

7. Quos voluimus, 'such as I wanted.'

Summa accusatoris voluntate, 'with the greatest good will on the part of the

Spero, si absolutus erit, coniunctiorem illum nobis fore in ratione petitionis; sin aliter acciderit, humaniter feremus. Tuo adventu nobis opus est maturo; nam prorsus summa hominum est opinio tuos familiares, nobiles homines, adversarios honori nostro fore: ad eorum voluntatem mihi conciliandam maximo te mihi usui fore video. Qua re Ianuario mense, ut constituisti, cura ut Romae sis.

3. To POMPEY (AD FAM. V. 7).

ROME, 62 B.C. (692 A.U.C.)

1. I rejoice over the contents of your despatches, which seem to hold out a good prospect of peace. Your new friends, so long your enemies, are confounded by the news. 2. I am not much annoyed by the tone of your private letter to me, 3. though I think you might have added your testimony to that of others, as to the value of my services. I allow you are greater than Africanus; do not place me much below Laelius.

M. TULLIUS M. F. CICERO S. D. CN. POMPEIO CN. F. MAGNO IMPERATORI.

S. T. E. Q. V. B. E. Ex litteris tuis, quas publice misisti, 1
cepi una cum omnibus incredibilem voluptatem; tantam enim spem otii ostendisti, quantam ego semper omnibus te uno fretus pollicebar; sed hoc scito, tuos veteres hostes, novos amicos, vehementer litteris perculsos atque ex magna spe deturbatos

accuser.' On the abl. (abs.), see Madv. 277. The accuser was P. Clodius, and he seems to have left several judges unchallenged, who were likely to favour the accused. See Rein, Criminalrecht, 658, 659. In Pison. 10, 23.

1. In ratione, 'in the matter of.' Cp. De Prov. Cons. 14. 35.

2. Humaniter, 'with equanimity.' Forcell.

Tuo adventu .... maturo, 'my interests require your speedy return.' For the abl., see Madv. 266, Obs.; and for the adject., used as an adverb. Ib. 300 b.

4. Tuos familiares. Probably Hortensius was one of them (cp. Ep. 14. 1), and perhaps L. Lucullus and M. Crassus were others. Cicero had offended many of the nobles, by arguing for the grant of excessive powers to Pompey. Cp. Intr. to Part I. § 8.

Honori, 'my election to the consulship.'

6. Ianuario . . . sis. Atticus seems to have complied with this request, and to have remained three years at Rome. Cicero's next letter to him is dated 61 B.C.

M.F., CN.F. = 'Marci filius, Cnaei filio.'

Magno. Pompey is said to have been greeted by Sulla with the title Magnus on his victorious return from Africa in B.C. 81. See Plut. Pomp. 13; Drumann 4. 335.

8. S. T. E. Q. V. B. E. = 'si tu exercitusque valetis bene est.' Cicero does not use this greeting often when he writes confidentially. Cp. note C on Part I.

Litteris tuis . . . misisti. The official despatches of Pompey, announcing his successes over Mithridates. On which, and on Pompey's proceedings in the East in general, see Intr. to Part I. § 7; Appendix 2.

10. Spem otii, 'hope of peace,' in the East, or perhaps 'of tranquillity at Rome.' Pompey's despatch may have announced an intention of supporting the senate. See Süpfle's notes on this letter.

11. Pollicebar. Especially in the Oration de Imperio Cn. Pompeii, or Pro Leg. Man.

Veteres hostes, novos amicos. These words probably refer to the Roman democrats, though Manutius thinks that M. Crassus

iacere. Ad me autem litteras, quas misisti, quamquam exiguam significationem tuae erga me voluntatis habebant, tamen mihi scito iucundas fuisse; nulla enim re tam laetari soleo quam meorum officiorum conscientia, quibus si quando non mutue respondetur, apud me plus officii residere facillime patior: illud non dubito, quin, si te mea summa erga te studia parum mihi adiunxerint, res publica nos inter nos conciliatura coniunctumque sit.

3 Ac ne ignores, quid ego in tuis litteris desiderarim, scribam aperte, sicut et mea natura et nostra amicitia postulat: res eas gessi, quarum aliquam in tuis litteris et nostrae necessitudinis et rei publicae causa gratulationem exspectavi; quam ego abs te praetermissam esse arbitror, quod vererere ne cuius animum offenderes. Sed scito ea, quae nos pro salute patriae gessimus, orbis terrae iudicio ac testimonio comprobari; quae, cum veneris, tanto consilio tantaque animi magnitudine a me gesta esse cognosces, ut tibi multo maiori, quam Africanus fuit, me non multo minorem quam Laelium facile et in re publica et in amicitia adiunctum esse patiare.

and L. Lucullus are meant. Pompey had served the optimates effectively in Italy, Africa, and Spain, but had afterwards combined with the democratic leaders, and with Crassus to reverse some of Sulla's most important measures. Intr. to Part I, § 5. The democrats had been alarmed, apparently, afterwards by the prospect of Pompey's victorious return from the East. Mr. H. F. Pelham thinks that the words 'veteres hostes' apply to Crassus and Caesar in regard to their supposed intrigues against Pompey in 65-63 B.C., and their possible complicity with Rullus and with Catiline: and that the words 'novos amicos' refer to the steps taken by Caesar and Q. Metellus Nepos in favour of Pompey. Cp. Intr. to Part I, p. 12.

1. Iacere, 'are prostrate.'

Litteras, quas misisti. Cicero appears to have written to congratulate Pompey on his successes, and to have added an account of his own consulship. Pompey's reply seems to have been rather cold, and any uncertainty as to his feelings would be very alarming to Cicero. Cp. Pro Sulla 24, 67; Pro Planc. 34, 85. On the acc. 'litteras,' attracted to 'quas,' see Madv. 319.

2. Significationem, 'expression.' Cp. Pro Sest. 49, 105.

4. Si . . . non mutue respondetur, 'if no fair return is made.' 'Mutuo' is the more common form. 'Mutue respondere' = 'par pari referre.' Forcell.

5. Apud me . . facillime patior, 'I am well content that the balance of services done should be on my side.' With this use of 'facile patior,' cp. below, § 3, and Ep. 29, 21.

6. Mea summa erga te studia. Cicero had supported, as praetor, the proposal of Manilius (cp § 1), and had proposed, as consul, a thanksgiving of twelve days in honour of Pompey's victories. Cp. Intr. to Part I, § 8: also De Prov. Cons. 11. 27; Ep. 29, 11.

10 Res eas gessi . . . . expectavi, 'I have performed achievements of which I expected some acknowledgment.' On the ind., see Madv. 362 a, and 366.

12. Quod vererere. The conjunctive is used to express the thoughts of Pompey. See Madv. 369.

Cuius. Q. Metellus Nepos, one of Pompey's most active associates, was on bad terms with Cicero; but it is needless to suppose a reference to any particular person.

Ne . . animum offenderes, 'lest you should give offence to.' Cp. 'ne Divitiaci animum offenderet' Caes. de Bell. Gall. 1. 19.

13. Ea quae nos . . gessimus. Cicero refers especially to the detection and suppression of Catiline's conspiracy.

16. Africanus. Probably the younger, who took Carthage. Billerb.

17. Quam Laelium. Accusative at-

4. Q. METELLUS CELER TO CICERO (AD FAM. V. 1).

CISALPINE GAUL, EARLY IN 62 B.C. (692 A.U.C.)

1. I regret both your unexpected insult to myself, and your attack on my unhappy brother. I am surprised that you shewed so little consideration for the dignity of my family, and for the claims of our former friendship. 2. One who, like me, is at the head of a province and an army, ought to have been spared this humiliation. You must not be surprised if you have to repent such a departure from old usage. However, no insult shall prevent me from discharging my duty to the State.

Q. METELLUS Q. F. CELER PROCOS. S. D. M. TULLIO CICERONI.

Si vales, bene est. Existimaram pro mutuo inter nos animo 1 et pro reconciliata gratia nec absentem *me* ludibrio laesum iri nec Metellum fratrem ob dictum capite ac fortunis per te oppugnatum iri; quem si parum pudor ipsius defendebat, debebat vel familiae nostrae dignitas vel meum studium erga vos remque publicam satis sublevare. Nunc video illum circumventum, me desertum, a quibus minime conveniebat. Itaque in luctu et 2

tracted to 'me.' It might be 'quam Laelius fuit.' See Madv. 402 b; and cp. Ep. 64, 2. The friendship between Scipio and Laelius was, like that of Pompey and Cicero, one between a general and a statesman and man of letters.

4. Q. METELLUS. For an account of Q. Metellus Celer, see Intr. to Part I, § 13.

PROCOS. Q. Metellus Celer had not been consul, but seems to have been called pro-consul as governing a consular province. Cp. § 2 of this letter, note.

1. Bene est. On the adverb as a predicate, cp. Madv. 209 b, Obs. 2.

Mutuo inter nos animo, 'our mutual regard' = 'voluntate.' Forcell.

2. Reconciliata gratia. In the following letter Cicero does not allow that there had been a quarrel.

Ludibrio. Apparently Metellus had received an exaggerated account of the amusement caused in the senate by Cicero's complaints of his silence. Cp. Ep. 5, 2.

3. Fratrem. The two Metelli, Celer and Nepos, notwithstanding the identity of praenomen, were probably brothers. Drumann (2. 25) gives from Manutius the following conjecture: that they were both sons of Q. Metellus Nepos, consul in 98 B.C.; that his eldest son and namesake died after his second son, the writer of this letter, had been adopted by Q. Metellus Celer, consul in 90 B.C.; and that he had then a third son, who bore both his praenomen and cognomen.

Ob dictum. See § 8 of the next letter.

Capite ac fortunis. On the ablat., see Madv. 253. 'In his personal rights and property.' 'Poenae capitales' included in the largest sense, all penalties affecting a man's life, liberty, citizenship, or reputation. But this use of the term was rather popular than legal. Strictly speaking, under the republic, the term 'poena capitalis' could only be applied to penalties involving loss of life, freedom, or citizenship; and, under the empire, it was usually restricted to capital punishments in our sense. See Rein, Criminalrecht, 286.

4. Si parum pudor ipsius defendebat, 'if he did not find a sufficient protection in the respect due to him.' Billerb. But Metzger translates, 'if his own attitude was deficient in modesty.' The last rendering suits the words best, I think; the first the context.

Debebat, sc. 'defendere.' On the indic., see Madv. 348 c.

5. Vos. Either 'the senate,' or 'Cicero's own party.'

6. Sublevare = 'iuvare.' Forcell.

Circumventum, 'oppressed,' 'endangered.'

7. Conveniebat, sc. 'me deseri.'

In luctu et squalore sum. 'Squalore'

squalore sum, qui provinciae, qui exercitui praesum, qui bellum gero: quae quoniam nec ratione nec maiorum nostrorum clementia administrastis, non erit mirandum, si vos paenitebit. Te tam mobili in me meosque esse animo non sperabam: me interea nec domesticus dolor nec cuiusquam iniuria ab re publica abducet.

5. TO METELLUS CELER (AD FAM. V. 2).

ROME, EARLY IN 62 B.C. (692 A.U.C.)

1. I am not quite clear to what you refer as an insult. It is true that I remarked with regret in the senate, that you had allowed your relations to estrange you from me; 2. but the amusement which followed was principally caused by my disappointment. 3, 4. As for our 'mutual regard,' ask yourself if your behaviour on your last visit to Rome was a fitting return for my constant anxiety to promote your honour. I resigned my claim to a province, no doubt, in the State's interest; but it was from regard to you that I contrived you should have one. 5. I do not allow that there has been any quarrel between us. 6. I admire your affection for your brother, but you should not be offended by my opposition to him on public grounds, nor by my resistance to his attacks on myself. 7. He did me great wrong on December 31; yet 8. I was still anxious for a reconciliation, but your brother replied by a censure of my best services as consul, and by further insults a few days afterwards, to which I could not help replying. 9. After all the provocations I had received, however, I took no active part in the proceedings against your brother; on the contrary, I supported the mildest proposals made. 10. I repeat, that I not only make allowance for your indignation, but admire it: I only ask you to consider my position impartially, as I have always thought of you as of a friend.

M. TULLIUS M. F. CICERO Q. METELLO Q. F. CELERI PROCOS. S. D.

1 Si tu exercitusque valetis, bene est. Scribis ad me te existimasse pro mutuo inter nos animo et pro reconciliata gratia

is not, perhaps, to be taken literally. The writer's brother was threatened with deprivation by the senate, and Metellus Celer says that such a demonstration put him in mourning, as for a relative against whom a criminal charge had been brought.

1. Provinciae. That of Cisalpine Gaul, which he owed to Cicero's renunciation of a province. See the next letter, § 3. Metellus had commanded a force in Umbria and Picenum during the year 63 B.C., and seems to have entered on his provincial government, with the command of a force of three legions, at the beginning of 62 B.C. Cp. In Cat. 2. 3. 5; Merivale 1. 143; A. W. Zumpt, Studia Romana 57-60.

Bellum gero. Either against the Salassi and other barbarians (Süpfle, Matth.), or against the relics of Catiline's forces. Metellus had been commissioned to prevent them from penetrating northwards. Sall. Cat. 57.

2. Quae refers to 'circumventum' and 'desertum.' For the use of pronouns referring to the contents of a sentence, cp. Madv. 312 b, and 315 b; and for the relative, instead of the demonstrative with a particle of transition, ib. 448. The sentence quae . . . administrastis, may be rendered, 'since your management of these affairs has been neither reasonable nor in accordance with our ancestors' lenity.'

5. Domesticus dolor, 'indignation for the slight to my family.'

Cuiusquam iniuria, 'any one's wrong doing.' Gen. poss., Madv. 280 and 283, Obs. 1.

numquam te a me ludibrio laesum iri. Quod cuius modi sit, satis intellegere non possum, sed tamen suspicor ad te esse adlatum, me, in senatu cum disputarem permultos esse qui rem publicam a me conservatam dolerent, dixisse a te propinquos tuos, quibus negare non potuisses, impetrasse ut ea quae statuisses tibi in senatu de mea laude esse dicenda reticeres. Quod cum dicerem, illud adiunxi, mihi tecum ita dispertitum officium fuisse in rei publicae salute retinenda, ut ego urbem a domesticis insidiis et ab intestino scelere, tu Italiam et ab armatis hostibus et ab occulta coniuratione defenderes, atque hanc nostram tanti et tam praeclari muneris societatem a tuis propinquis labefactatam, qui, cum tu a me rebus amplissimis atque honorificentissimis ornatus esses, timuissent ne quae mihi pars abs te voluntatis mutuae tribueretur. Hoc in sermone cum 2
a me exponeretur, quae mea exspectatio fuisset orationis tuae quantoque in errore versatus essem, visa est oratio non iniucunda, et mediocris quidam est risus consecutus, non in te, sed magis in errorem meum et quod me abs te cupisse laudari aperte atque ingenue confitebar. Iam hoc non potest in te non honorifice esse dictum, me in clarissimis meis atque amplissimis rebus tamen aliquod testimonium tuae vocis habere voluisse. Quod autem ita scribis, 'pro mutuo inter nos animo,' 3
quid tu existimes esse in amicitia mutuum, nescio; equidem hoc arbitror, cum par voluntas accipitur et redditur. Ego si hoc dicam, me tua causa praetermisisse provinciam, tibi ipse levior videar esse; meae enim rationes ita tulerunt atque eius

1. **Quod cuius modi sit**, 'what you mean thereby.' Billerb.

4. **Propinquos tuos.** Cicero probably means Metellus Nepos, and perhaps also P. Clodius, whose sister Claudia was wife of Metellus Celer.

7. **Quod cum dicerem**, 'In saying this, however.' See Madv. 358 for the mood.

12. **Rebus amplissimis.** These words refer, probably, to the important commissions which Cicero had procured for Metellus Celer.

13. **Ne quae mihi . . . tribueretur**, 'lest you should show me some good will in return.'

15. **Orationis tuae**, 'of a speech from you,' 'of some declaration on your part.' On this use of the possessive pronoun, see Madv. 297 a.

17. **Mediocris . . risus.** This Metellus seems to have considered an insult to himself. Cp. § 1 of the preceding letter.

23. **Mutuum**, 'reciprocity.'

24. **Ego si hoc dicam.** On the insertion of the personal pronoun, see Madv. 482.

25. **Praetermisisse provinciam.** In a speech delivered, apparently, late in the summer, or early in the autumn of 63 B.C. Cicero had renounced his claim to govern a province after the expiration of his year of office at Rome (cp. Ep. 9. 3), and thus Metellus, one of the praetors for 63 B.C., obtained the government of Gallia Cisalpina. See Intr. to Part I, § 10.

26. **Levior videar esse**, 'should seem to make foolish pretensions.' 'Levis' = 'vaniloquus.' Forcell. On the tense of 'dicam, videar,' see Madv. 347 b.

mei consilii maiorem in dies singulos fructum voluptatemque
capio: illud dico, me, ut primum in contione provinciam deposuerim, statim, quem ad modum eam tibi traderem, cogitare
coepisse. Nihil dico de sortitione vestra: tantum te suspicari
volo, nihil in ea re per collegam meum me inscienle esse
factum. Recordare cetera; quam cito senatum illo die facta
sortitione coëgerim, quam multa de te verba fecerim, cum tu
ipse mihi dixisti orationem meam non solum in te honorificam,
4 sed etiam in collegas tuos contumeliosam fuisse. Iam illud
senatus consultum, quod eo die factum est, ea perscriptione
est, ut, dum id exstabit, officium meum in te obscurum esse
non possit. Postea vero quam profectus es, velim recordere,
quae ego de te in senatu egerim, quae in contionibus dixerim,
quas ad te litteras miserim: quae cum omnia collegeris, tum
ipse velim iudices, satisne videatur his omnibus rebus tuus ad-
5 ventus, cum proxime Romam venisti, mutue respondisse. Quod
scribis de reconciliata *gratia* nostra, non intellego, cur recon-
6 ciliatam esse dicas, quae numquam imminuta est. Quod scribis
non oportuisse Metellum fratrem tuum ob dictum a me oppug-
nari, primum hoc velim existimes, animum mihi istum tuum

Meae rationes, 'my interests.' See Ep. 1, 1, note, p. 26.

2. Illud dico, 'this I do say,' referring to what follows. Madv. 485 b.

Deposuerim. 'Deponere' seems to have been a technical word for waiving a claim to the government of a province. Forcell. Cp Ep. 9, 5.

4. De sortitione vestra. The praetors for 63 B.C. had to cast lots, apparently, for the government of Cisalpine Gaul, which had become vacant by Cicero's renunciation; and C. Antonius, who presided at the allotment, probably contrived at Cicero's suggestion that it should result in favour of Metellus.

9. Contumeliosam. As exalting Metellus at the expense of his colleagues.

Iam illud. 'Iam transitionibus inservit'—'praeterea.' Forcell. Cp. 'iam hoc non potest' in § 2.

10. Perscriptione, 'form.' Cp. Nägelsb. Stilistik, § 9, p. 38.

12. Postea vero quam profectus es . . egerim. 'I should like you to remember how I pleaded your cause in the senate after your departure' for Picenum to act against Catiline.

14. Collegeris, 'have put together,' taken into account.'

15. Adventus. Probably Metellus drew near to Rome in the winter of 63–62 B.C., as a demonstration in support of his brother. He could not have entered the city without forfeiting his imperium; and perhaps this consideration suggested Süpfle's rendering of proxime Romam, 'to the immediate neighbourhood of Rome.' On the acc., see Madv. 172, Obs. 4. But more probably 'proxime' means 'just lately.' 'Romam venire' and 'Romae esse' could be said of an officer visiting or remaining in the immediate neighbourhood of Rome. Cp. Ep. 46, note; In Verr. Act. 2, 2, 6, 17; 'Romae et ad urbem;' and Mr. Long's note on Act. 1, 15, 45. 'Roma' included the suburbs without, as well as the 'urbs' within the 'pomoerium.' Cp. Paulus, Digest 50, 16, 2: ap. Long. The visit of Metellus is not elsewhere mentioned, apparently.

16. Mutue respondisse, 'to have shewn a similar spirit in return.'

17. De reconciliata gratia. Cicero will not allow that there had been a quarrel. The misunderstanding must, apparently, have arisen before the struggle between Cicero and Catiline had definitely begun, for Cicero and Metellus seem to have co-operated cordially against the conspirators.

vehementer probari et fraternam plenam humanitatis ac pietatis voluntatem; deinde, si qua ego in re fratri tuo rei publicae causa restiterim, ut mihi ignoscas; tam enim sum amicus rei publicae, quam qui maxime; si vero meam salutem contra illius impetum in me crudelissimum defenderim, satis habeas nihil me etiam tecum de tui fratris iniuria conqueri: quem ego cum comperissem omnem sui tribunatus conatum in meam perniciem parare atque meditari, egi cum Claudia, uxore tua, et cum vestra sorore Mucia, cuius erga me studium pro Cn. Pompeii necessitudine multis in rebus perspexeram, ut eum ab
illa iniuria deterrerent. Atqui ille, quod te audisse certo *scio*, 7
pr. Kal. Ianuarias, qua iniuria nemo umquam in minimo magistratu improbissimus civis adfectus est, ea me consulem adfecit, cum rem publicam conservassem, atque abeuntem magistratu contionis habendae potestate privavit; cuius iniuria mihi tamen honori summo fuit: nam, cum ille mihi nihil nisi ut iurarem permitteret, magna voce iuravi verissimum pulcherrimumque ius iurandum, quod populus item magna voce me vere iurasse iuravit. Hac accepta tam insigni iniuria, tamen illo ipso die misi 8
ad Metellum communes amicos, qui agerent cum eo, ut de illa mente desisteret; quibus ille respondit sibi non esse integrum: etenim paulo ante in contione dixerat ei, qui in alios animum advertisset indicta causa, dicendi ipsi potestatem fieri non oportere. Hominem gravem et civem egregium! qui, qua poena senatus consensu bonorum omnium eos adfecerat, qui urbem

3. **Ut mihi ignoscas.** After 'velim.' 'Ut' would more usually be omitted. See Madv. 372 b, Obs. 2.

4. **Quam qui maxime,** sc. 'est.' Madv. 310, Obs. 4.

Si . . . defenderim, 'supposing that I defended.' 'Si' = 'etiamsi.' Cp. Forcell. On 'defenderim,' see Zumpt, L. G. 524 and note. It is nearly = 'defendi.'

5. **Satis habeas,** 'be content.' Conj. for Imperat. Madv. 385, Obs.

6. **Nihil . . . conqueri,** 'that I abstain from making a complaint to you, as well as to the senate.'

7. **Omnem . . . conatum . . . meditari,** 'that he was laying his plans, and preparing the whole resources of his office, for my destruction.'

8. **Claudia.** Eldest sister of P. Clodius, and wife of Cicero's correspondent; a woman of bad reputation. Cp. Ep. 9. 5.

9. **Mucia.** Half-sister of the two Metelli, and wife of Pompey.

Pro . . . necessitudine, 'in consideration of my intimacy with Pompey.'

15. **Contionis habendae,** 'of addressing the people on the events of the year,' as was usual with magistrates retiring from office. Hofm.

17. **Ius iurandum.** Cicero swore 'rem publicam atque hanc urbem mea unius opera esse salvam.' Cp. In Pis. 3, 6.

20. **Qui agerent cum eo,** 'to entreat him,' a favourite use of the expression, see above, l. 8.

21. **Sibi non esse integrum,** 'that he had no choice,' 'that he was committed;' a common expression. Cp. Pro Muren. 4, 8.

22. **Qui in alios . . causa.** Referring to Cicero's treatment of Lentulus and his associates. See Intr. to Part I, § 11; also Appendix 4.

incendere et magistratus ac senatum trucidare, bellum maximum conflare voluissent, eadem dignum iudicaret eum, qui curiam caede, urbem incendiis, Italiam bello liberasset. Itaque ego Metello, fratri tuo, praesenti restiti: nam in senatu Kal. Ianuariis sic cum eo de re publica disputavi, ut sentiret sibi cum viro forti et constanti esse pugnandum. A. d. III. Non. Ianuar. cum agere coepisset, tertio quoque verbo orationis suae me appellabat, mihi minabatur; neque illi quicquam deliberatius fuit quam me, quacumque ratione posset, non iudicio neque disceptatione, sed vi atque impressione evertere. Huius ego temeritati si virtute atque animo non restitissem, quis esset qui me in consulatu non casu potius existimaret quam consilio fortem fuisse?

2 Haec si tu Metellum cogitare de me nescisti, debes existimare te maximis de rebus a fratre esse celatum; sin autem aliquid impertivit tibi sui consilii, lenis a te et facilis existimari debeo, qui nihil tecum de his ipsis rebus expostulem. Et, si intellegis non me dicto Metelli, ut scribis, sed consilio eius animoque in me inimicissimo esse commotum, cognosce nunc humanitatem meam, si humanitas appellanda est in acerbissima iniuria remissio animi ac dissolutio: nulla est a me umquam sententia dicta in fratrem tuum; quotienscumque aliquid est actum,

2. **Voluissent . . . . liberasset.** In 'voluissent' the conj. expresses the grounds of another's (Cicero's) conduct; in 'liberasset,' expresses the character suggested in 'eum.' See Madv. 369 and 364, Obs. 1. Cicero almost quotes the very words of a decree of the senate in his honour. Cp. In Cat. 3. 6. 15.

4. **Restiti.** Probably in the Oratio Metellina referred to Ep. 6, 5.

7. **Agere,** 'to argue for his proposal,' which was that Pompey should be recalled from the East, to restore order in Italy. Cp. Plut. Cato Min. 26. It does not appear whether this speech of Metellus was delivered in the senate or in the assembly.

8. **Neque illi quicquam . . . . fuit,** 'and he had not resolved more definitely on anything.' Nägelsb. Stilistik 72, 191. See, too, Ad Att. 15. 5. 3.

9. **Non iudicio neque disceptatione,** 'by no trial in a court of law.'

10. **Impressione,** 'by an attack.' Forcell. Tyrrell renders 'vi atque impressione,' 'violent browbeating.'

12. **Casu.** Cicero protests elsewhere against his successes being attributed to chance. Cp. Ad Att. 1. 20. 3; In Cat. 3. 12, 29; and, on the meaning of 'casus,' Ep. 101. 1, note.

14. **Celatum,** 'kept in the dark.' Cp. Philipp. 2. 13. 32; Madv. 228 a.

17. **Non me dicto.** On the position of the negative, see below, 'non ego oppugnavi fratrem tuum' § 10.

19. **Remissio animi ac dissolutio,** 'carelessness and indifference.' With this meaning of 'dissolutio' cp. De Off. 1. 28, 99. 'neglegere quid de se quisque sentiat non solum arrogantis est sed etiam omnino dissoluti.'

20. **Nulla est . . . sententia dicta.** Cicero, as a consular, would be asked his opinion individually by the presiding officer in the senate's debates. This would give him an opportunity either of arguing at length in favour of some proposal already before the senate, or of originating one of his own; but, in the case of Metellus, he does not seem to have taken advantage of either privilege.

21. **Quotienscumque aliquid est actum,** 'whenever his behaviour was dis-

sedens iis adsensi, qui mihi lenissime sentire visi sunt. Addam illud etiam, quod iam ego curare non debui, sed tamen fieri non moleste tuli atque etiam, ut ita fieret, pro mea parte adiuvi, ut senati consulto meus inimicus, quia tuus frater erat, sublevaretur. Qua re non ego oppugnavi fratrem tuum, sed fratri tuo repugnavi, nec in te, ut scribis, animo fui mobili, sed ita stabili, ut in mea erga te voluntate etiam desertus ab officiis tuis permanerem. Atque hoc ipso tempore tibi paene minitanti nobis per litteras hoc rescribo atque respondeo: ego dolori tuo non solam ignosco, sed summam etiam laudem tribuo; meus enim me sensus, quanta vis fraterni sit amoris, admonet. A te peto ut tu quoque aequum te iudicem dolori meo praebeas; si acerbe, si crudeliter, si sine causa sum a tuis oppugnatus, ut statuas mihi non modo non cedendum, sed etiam tuo atque exercitus tui auxilio in eius modi causa utendum fuisse. Ego te mihi semper amicum esse volui; me ut tibi amicissimum esse intellegeres, laboravi. Maneo in voluntate et, quoad voles tu, permanebo citiusque amore tui fratrem tuum odisse desinam quam illius odio quicquam de nostra benevolentia detraham.

covered in the senate.' For the measures taken against Metellus Nepos, see Intr. to Part I, § 12; Suet. Iul. 16.

1. Sedens. A senator seems only to have risen if he wished to speak at length, or to bring a new motion forward.

Addam illud etiam, 'I will add this, too, that I regarded with favour, and even supported, a decree of the senate relieving your brother from some of the penalties he had incurred; though, after what had passed (iam), I had no reason to trouble myself about it.' On 'illud' see above, § 3, note.

4. Ut senati consulto . . sublevaretur. The construction seems irregular here, though Süpfle says that these words depend upon 'fieri non moleste tuli.' The sentence seems to be resumed in a new form after the parenthetic clause 'non . . . debui,' and then a fresh subordinate clause, 'atque . . . adiuvi,' is introduced. Prof Tyrrell makes the final sentence depend on 'curare.' One would expect to find (1) 'me tulisse' and 'me adiuvisse,' or (2) 'meum inimicum sublevatum esse,' or (3) 'quod meus inimicus sublevatus est.' The form 'senati' is archaic. See Madv. 46, Obs. 2, and cp. Ad Fam. 2. 7. 4.

5. Sublevaretur, 'be relieved,' 'released from his perilous position.'

Non . . . oppugnavi . . . repugnavi, 'I did not attack your brother, but resisted his attacks.'

7. Etiam desertus ab officiis tuis, 'though you have ceased to pay me any attentions.' Cp. 'a ceteris oblectationibus deseror' Ad Att. 4. 10, 1. 'Ab' may either mean 'in respect of,' cp. Ep. 1. 2, note; or it may personify the 'officia,' cp. Zumpt, L. G. 451.

8. Paene minitanti: see the close of the preceding letter.

15. Exercitus tui auxilio. An ironical answer to Metellus' boast of his commanding position. See § 2 of the preceding letter. The riots which took place at Rome early in 62 B.C., hardly required an army of three legions to repress them. Cp. Intr. to Part I, § 12. Cicero has adopted many expressions from Metellus' letter ('dicto Metelli,' 'sublevaretur,' 'oppugnavi,' 'desertus,' 'animo mobili'), and retorts Metellus' reference to his army.

19. Detraham. Fut. indic. On the constr., cp. Pro Ligario 5. 16 'suam citius abiciet humanitatem quam extorquebit tuam.'

6. TO ATTICUS (AD ATT. I. 13).
ROME, JAN. 25, 61 B.C. (693 A.U.C.)

1. I have received three letters from you, but uncertainty as to your movements, and the want of a faithful messenger, have interfered with my promptitude in replying, 2. though interesting events have happened since our parting. The consul Piso has rather slighted me, but I am not sorry to be relieved from the need of shewing him any respect; his colleague honours me, and is devoted to the good cause. 3. The disagreement of the consuls is unfortunate, and I fear its effects may be aggravated by an affair of which you have probably heard, viz. that P. Clodius has been detected in the house of C. Caesar when the rites of the Bona Dea were being celebrated, and that Caesar has divorced his wife in consequence. Proceedings against Clodius are in progress, but are not pressed with the energy one could wish. 4. I cannot say that a certain friend of yours is behaving honestly or straightforwardly just now. 5. The praetors' provinces have not yet been allotted. I am obliged to you for your remarks and criticisms on various works which I have sent you. 6. A purchase lately made by the consul Messalla, shows that I have not made a bad one in my house. Teucris still keeps me waiting. I hope soon to write with more freedom.

CICERO ATTICO SAL.

1 Accepi tuas tres iam epistolas: unam a M. Cornelio, quam Tribus Tabernis, ut opinor, ei dedisti, alteram, quam mihi Canusinus tuus hospes reddidit, tertiam, quam, ut scribis, ancora soluta de phaselo dedisti; quae fuerunt omnes, *ut* rhetorum pueri loquuntur, cum humanitatis sparsae sale, tum insignes amoris notis: quibus epistolis sum equidem abs te lacessitus ad rescribendum, sed idcirco sum tardior, quod non invenio fidelem tabellarium; quotus enim quisque est, qui epistolam paulo graviorem ferre possit, nisi eam pellectione relevarit? accedit eo, quod mihi non*, ut quisque in Epirum proficiscitur: ego enim

1. A M. Cornelio. This man seems not to be mentioned elsewhere by Cicero.

2. Ut opinor. Atticus had not dated his letter, so Cicero had to guess whence it was written, and thought of one of the stages near to Rome on the Appian Way. Tres Tabernae was about 35 miles from Rome. For another explanation of 'ut opinor,' cp. Ep. 40, 1, note.

3. Canusinus tuus hospes, 'the friend with whom you lodged at Canusium,' on your way to Greece.

Ut scribis. These words call attention to the unusual phrase 'ancora soluta.' 'Ancoram tollere' is the usual phrase for weighing anchor. Perhaps there was a confusion with 'navem solvere.' Cp. Hor. Carm. 3. 2, 29. Prof. Tyrrell has 'ora soluta.'

4. De phaselo: cp. Ad Att. 14. 16, 1, 'phaselum epicopum.'

Rhetorum pueri = *ῥητόρων παῖδες*, 'pupils of rhetoricians.' Prof. Tyrrell thinks that the word describes 'the class or profession.'

8. Tabellarium, cp. Ep. 18, 6, note.

Paulo graviorem, 'conveying news of more than ordinary weight.' I owe this translation of 'paulo graviorem' to a notice of my book by Mr. J. R. King in the *Academy* for Feb. 15, 1871.

9. Pellectione, 'by reading it through.' *ἅπαξ λεγόμενον* apparently.

Relevarit, 'have lightened it,' as if by taking out some money which weighted it. An allusion to 'paulo graviorem' above.

10. Non *, ut. Various suggestions

te arbitror caesis apud Amaltheam tuam victimis statim esse ad
Sicyonem oppugnandum profectum; neque tamen id ipsum certum
habeo, quando ad Antonium proficiscare aut quid in Epiro temporis ponas: ita neque Achaicis hominibus neque Epiroticis paulo
liberiores litteras committere audeo. Sunt autem post discessum 2
a me tuum res dignae litteris nostris, sed non committendae eius
modi periculi, ut aut interire aut aperiri aut intercipi possint.
Primum igitur scito primum me non esse rogatum sententiam
praepositumque esse nobis pacificatorem Allobrogum, idque admurmurante senatu neque me invito esse factum; sum enim et ab
observando homine perverso liber, et ad dignitatem in re publica
retinendam contra illius voluntatem solutus, et ille secundus in
dicendo locus habet auctoritatem paene principis et voluntatem

have been made for amending this passage. Orelli's 'non perinde est,' 'it is not indifferent to me,' seems tautologous. Others are 'non notum est,' 'I am not aware of;' 'non prodest,' 'I derive no benefit from,' the various departures for Epirus.

1. **Amalthea**, or **Amaltheum**. A villa in Epirus belonging to Atticus, so called, apparently, from containing a room decorated with pictures from the story of Amalthea. Cp. Epp. 8, 18; 9. 10. Cicero says, in sport, that Atticus only went there to sacrifice before his campaign against the Sicyonians, i.e. before pressing on them his demands for repayment of debts they owed him.

3. **Antonium**. C. Antonius was now governor of Macedonia. Cicero had quarrelled with him, but had subsequently written to ask him to aid Atticus in recovering the money owing to him in that province. Cp. Ad Fam. 5, 5.

4. **Ponas**. 'Ponere' is properly used of money, 'to lay out,' 'invest;' hence of time, 'to spend.' On the tense of 'ponas' and 'proficiscare,' with a future signification, see Madv. 378 a, Obs. 3; and for the mood, Ib. 356.

Ita, 'on account of my uncertainty where you are.'

Neque Achaicis . . neque Epiroticis, 'neither to residents in Achaia nor to residents in Epirus,' who would be the most obvious letter carriers to those countries.

5. **Sunt autem . . . nostris**, 'affairs have, however, happened since your departure from me, important enough to form the subject of one of my letters to you.'

7. **Interire**, 'be lost or destroyed.'

Possint. The subject of this is in construction the 'res,' but in reality the 'litterae.'

8. **Primum . . . rogatum**. Cicero had probably been used to be asked his opinion first in the senate during the consulship of Silanus and Murena, 62 B.C., and was now vexed because the consul Piso gave precedence to a relative, C. Calpurnius Piso. The latter had been consul in 67 B.C., and had afterwards governed Gallia Narbonensis (cp. Ep. 1, 2, note), still barely pacified after a revolt of the Allobroges. 'Civitas male pacata,' are words Cicero uses of the district. In Cat. 3 9. 22. If Piso's colleague Messalla was present as is probable (see the end of this section) Piso probably presided as having been returned first at the election. This case would then shew that a plebeian consul might preside even if his colleague were a patrician. Cp. Manut. ad loc.

9. **Pacificatorem**, a rare word, apparently.

Admurmurante senatu, 'amidst hostile murmurs from the senate.' Forcell. says of the verb 'admurmuro,' 'in utramque partem accipitur.' Cp. in Pis. 14. 31.

10. **Neque me invito**, 'yet without reluctance on my part.' On the omission of an adversative conjunction, see Zumpt, L. G. 781.

Ab observando . . . perverso, 'from paying attention to a perverse man,' i.e. the consul Piso.

11. **Ad dignitatem . . . solutus**, 'at liberty to maintain a dignified political position, even if he (Piso) does not wish it.'

13 **Principis**, sc. 'loci,' 'of the first place.'

Et . . . devinctam, foll., 'while it leaves one's feelings free from any excessive sense of obligation.'

non nimis devinctam beneficio consulis. Tertius est Catulus, quartus, si etiam hoc quaeris, Hortensius. Consul autem ipse parvo animo et pravo, tantum cavillator genere illo moroso, quod etiam sine dicacitate ridetur, facie magis quam facetiis ridiculus, nihil agens cum re publica, seiunctus ab optimatibus, a quo nihil speres boni rei publicae, quia non volt, nihil [speres] mali, quia non audet. Eius autem collega et in me perhonorificus et partium studiosus ac defensor bonarum. Qui nunc leviter inter se dissident; sed vereor ne hoc, quod infectum est, serpat longius: credo enim te audisse, cum apud Caesarem pro populo fieret venisse eo

1. **Beneficio consulis**, 'arising from a compliment paid by the consul.'

Q. Lutatius Catulus was perhaps the most upright and consistent member of the Roman aristocracy. He had taken an active part in resisting the seditious movement of Lepidus in 78 B.C., and afterwards opposed the proposals made by A. Gabinius and C. Manilius, for investing Pompey with extraordinary powers in the East. He voted for the execution of Lentulus and his associates, in the debate of Dec. 5, 63 B.C. See, for notices of him, Pro Leg. Man. 20 and 21; Epp. 13, 4; 96, 1. He seems to have died 60 B.C.

1. Q. **Hortensius**, consul 69 B.C., was the leading orator at Rome before Cicero attained that position. He was a decided supporter of the optimates, and defended Verres. He incurred Cicero's suspicions afterwards, about the time of the latter's exile; but the two orators were presently reconciled, and lived on good terms till Hortensius' death in 50 B.C. See the Orations against Verres, passim; Epp. 7, 5; 8, 2-4; 14, 1; 21, 3; 41, 2. It was usual for the magistrate who presided in the senate, to ask the opinions (1) of the consuls elect (this would only apply to the later months of the year), (2) of the princeps senatus, (3) of any other consular whom he might choose. The order adopted at the beginning of the year was generally preserved throughout it. Cp. Ep. 96, 1, note; Philipp. 5. 13. 55; Smith's Dictionary of Antiquities, 1020.

3. **Cavillator** = σκώπτης, 'a scoffer:' apparently here only in Cicero.

Genere illo moroso, 'of the (well-known) perverse kind.' On the ablative ('qualitatis'), see Madv. 272. Cicero expresses a different opinion about Piso elsewhere. Cp. Pro Plancio 5, 12.

4. **Dicacitate**, 'wit.' 'Dicta' seem to have been distinguished from 'facetiae;' in the former the point lay in the expression, in the latter in the substance. Cp. Cic. de Orat. 2. 60, 243, and 2. 66, 264.

Facie, 'by his grimaces.'

5. **Nihil agens cum re publica**, 'not busying himself about the State's interest,' 'not taking any part in politics.' It is an unusual expression, but may be explained by supposing the 'res publica' to be personified. Boot.

7. **Collega**. M. Valerius Messalla Niger. See the next letter, § 6.

Partium . . bonarum. For the order of words, see Madv. 466; 467: and for the difference of 'et' and 'ac,' ibid. 433. **Studiosus** seems to be used as a substantive, 'a partisan.' Cp. Ep. 8, 8.

9. **Sed**, 'but,' i.e. in spite of Messalla's energy.

Hoc quod infectum est, 'this disorder,' or 'contagion.' Manh. supposes Cicero to fear lest Messalla should be corrupted by his colleague. Or is he afraid lest the dispute of the consuls should be aggravated by difference of opinion as to the affair of Clodius? This would explain 'enim' below. Prof. Tyrrell explains 'sed' '(to this I am indifferent) but I am afraid the contagion of these bad feelings towards each other will spread;' Mr. Pretor, 'in spite of my satisfaction at their rupture.'

10. **Cum . . . fieret**, 'when sacrifice was being offered' to the Bona Dea. The house of one of the consuls or praetors was chosen for the performance of this rite, and only women could lawfully be present. Caesar was now one of the praetors, and pontifex maximus. The time of the sacrifice is doubtful. According to Ovid (Fasti 5. 148), it took place in the spring; but Asconius (in Milonian. 138) speaks of Clodius as 'quaestor designatus' at the time, which would fix the date in one of the later months of the year, elections generally taking place in summer. Cicero's letters are hardly to

muliebri vestitu virum, idque sacrificium cum virgines instaurassent, mentionem a Q. Cornificio in senatu ſactam—is ſuit princeps, ne tu ſorte aliquem nostrum putes—; postea rem ex senatus consulto [ad virgines atque] ad pontifices relatam idque ab iis neſas esse decretum; deinde ex senatus consulto consules rogationem promulgasse; uxori Caesarem nuntium remisisse. In hac causa Piso amicitia P. Clodii ductus operam dat ut ea rogatio, quam ipse ſert et ſert ex senatus consulto et de religione, antiquetur: Messalla vehementer adhuc agit severe. Boni viri precibus Clodii removentur a causa; operae comparantur; nosmet ipsi, qui Lycurgei a principio ſuissemus, quotidie demitigamur; instat et urget Cato. Quid multa? vereor ne haec, neglecta a bonis, deſensa ab improbis, magnorum rei publicae malorum causa sit. Tuus autem ille amicus—scin quem dicam?— 4

be quoted for either view, as he supposes Atticus to have heard of the affair already.

1. Instaurassent, 'had resumed' on another day.

2. A Q. Cornificio: cp. Ep. 1, 1, note. He was probably of praetorian rank; Tyrrell, Pretor.

3. Princeps, 'the first to take notice of the affair.' A reproach against the more eminent senators, especially against the consulars, 'nostrum.'

Ne tu . . . putes. An ellipse for 'hoc dico ne.'

4. Idque . . decretum, 'they decreed that the occurrence was an offence against religion.' For the gender of 'id,' referring to a sentence, see Madv. 312 b, 315 b.

6. Rogationem. This proposal probably was that an enquiry should be made about the transaction. Corradus ap. Boot. A special law was needed for the trial of Clodius because apparently no statute provided a penalty for the offence of which he had been guilty. Cp. Ferrat. Ep. 2, 9, 106; ap. Drumann 2, 207.

Uxori. To Pompeia, daughter of Q. Pompeius Rufus. Her mother was a daughter of Sulla; her paternal grandfather had been Sulla's colleague in his first consulship, 88 B.C.

Nuntium remisisse, 'has sent notice of divorce.' For the phrase, cp. De Orat. 1. 40, 183; Topica, 4. An equivalent expression seems to have been 'repudium renuntiare,' cp. Ter. Phorm. Act. 4. Sc. 3. 72. On the force of re- in 'remittere' cp. Epp. 92. 1; 98. 1, notes. It appears that at Rome in Cicero's time either husband or wife could ordinarily procure a dissolution of marriage by simply giving or sending such a notice as that mentioned in the text. Cp. Ad Fam. 8. 7, 2. A common form seems to have been 'tuas res tibi habeto,' cp. Cic. Philipp. 2. 28, 69: and on the whole subject, Smith's Dict. of Antiq. art. 'Divortium,' 418; Rein, Privatrecht, 445-457.

7. P. Clodii. For an account of this demagogue, see Intr. to Part I, §§ 13; 14; 19-23.

8. Quam ipse fert. Id est cuius lator futurus est nam rogationi ferendae nondum dies venerat. Manut.

9. Adhuc. This word, perhaps, conveys a suspicion as to Messalla's firmness.

10. Removentur a causa, 'are being induced to take no part in the matter.' Boni viri, according to Boot, is here = optimates.

Operae, 'bands of men hired to shout and riot.' Cp. Philipp. 1. 9, 22.

11. Nosmet . . . fuissemus, 'I myself, though I had been rigorous enough at first.' For the conj. 'fuissemus,' expressing an opposition to the leading proposition, see Madv. 366, Obs. 3.

Lycurgei. A reference, either to the Spartan lawgiver, or, as Billerb. thinks, to an Athenian statesman, contemporary with Demosthenes. Cp. Brut. 34. 130.

Demitigamur, 'feel my anger diminishing.' The word seems only to occur here.

12. Cato, M. Porcius, tribune for 63-62 B.C. For notices of him, see Intr. to Parts I, §§ 11; 15; II, § 8; III, § 10; IV, § 10.

Haec, 'this outrage.' On the sing. sit cp. Madv. 216.

14. Amicus, Pompey. With the account here given of him, cp. 'solet aliud sentire et

de quo tu ad me scripsisti, postea quam non auderet reprehendere laudare coepisse, nos, ut ostendit, admodum diligit, amplectitur, amat, aperte laudat; occulte, sed ita, ut perspicuum sit, invidet. Nihil come, nihil simplex, nihil ἐν τοῖς πολιτικοῖς honestum, nihil illustre, nihil forte, nihil liberum. Sed haec ad te scribam alias subtilius; nam neque adhuc mihi satis nota sunt et huic terrae filio nescio cui committere epistolam tantis de rebus non audeo.

5 Provincias praetores nondum sortiti sunt: res eodem est loci, quo reliquisti. τοποθεσίαν, quam postulas, Miseni et Puteolorum, includam orationi meae. A. d. III. Non. Decembr. mendose fuisse animadverteram. Quae laudas ex orationibus, mihi crede, valde mihi placebant, sed non audebam antea dicere; nunc vero, quod a te probata sunt, multo mihi ἀττικώτερα videntur. In illam orationem Metellinam addidi quaedam: liber tibi mittetur,

6 quoniam te amor nostri philorhetora reddidit. Novi tibi quidnam scribam? quid? etiam. Messalla consul Autronianam

loqui, neque tantum valere ingenio ut non appareat quid cupiat' Ad Fam. 8. 1, 3; also Ad Att. 4. 9. 1.

1. **De quo . . . scripsisti.** 'Quem scripsisti' would be a more common construction, but cp. Madv. 395. Obs. 7; also Ad Fam. 10. 20, 1 'de te fama constans nec decipi posse nec vinci;' also Tusc. Disp. 5. 20, 57, and Kuhner's note.

Reprehendere. sc. 'me.' Cp. Ep. 7, 3.

4. **Nihil come . . . liberum,** 'no courtesy, frankness, political honour, elevation (illustre), energy, generosity.'

6. **Subtilius.** 'with more precision.'

Nam neque . . . et. For the combination of negative and affirmative particles, see Madv. 458 c.

Terrae filio, 'the mean and unknown fellow,' who bears this letter. Cp. 'tuus familiaris summo genere natus (iron.) terrae filius' Ad Fam. 7. 9, 3.

8. **Provincias . . . sortiti sunt.** I cannot find any explanation of the delay in the allotment of the praetorian provinces. Cicero was interested in the matter, because his brother Quintus was one of the praetors for 62 B.C. Cp. 'Asiam Quinto suavissimo fratri obtigisse audisti' Ad Att. 1. 15, 1.

Res eodem . . . reliquisti, 'the matter remains as you left it.' 'Eodem loci pro ibidem positum.' Forcell. Cp. 'eodem loci potentiam et concordiam esse' Tac. Ann. 4. 4.

9. **τοποθεσίαν,** 'topographical description.' Liddell and Scott.

Puteolorum. Drumann, 6, 393, infers from this passage that Cicero already possessed a villa at Puteoli, cp. Appendix, v. 7.

10. **Orationi meae.** What speech this was does not appear. Süpfle. Prof. Tyrrell can find no example of 'includere' with the dative, meaning 'to insert in,' or, as Mr. Pretor says, 'to enclose in.' Prof. Tyrrell suggests 'iecudam.'

A. d. III. Non . . . animadverteram, 'I had noticed, before you told me, that the date, Dec. 3, was wrong.' I cannot find as to what work Cicero makes this confession.

13. **ἀττικώτερα.** Apparently = 'more classical,' 'more correct,' with an allusion, perhaps, to Atticus' name. I cannot find that the word is used quite in this sense in classical Greek.

14. **Metellinam.** Against Metellus Nepos. Cp. Epp. 4; 5, 2.

15. **Philorhetora,** 'a lover of oratory.' The word seems only to be found here.

Novi tibi . . . etiam, 'shall I write you any more news? any? Yes.' Cp. 'aliud quid? etiam, quando te proficisci istinc putes, fac ut sciam' Ad Att. 2. 6, 2.

16. **Autronianam,** 'of P. Autronius Paetus.' This man had been elected consul for 65 B.C., but a conviction for bribery had prevented him from holding office, and he subsequently joined Catiline's conspiracy; was tried and condemned 'de vi,' and went into exile in 62 B.C.

domum emit HS. CXXXIIII. 'Quid id ad me?' inquies. Tantum, quod ea emptione et nos bene emisse iudicati sumus et homines intellegere coeperunt, licere amicorum facultatibus in emendo ad dignitatem aliquam pervenire. Teucris illa lentum negotium est, sed tamen est in spe. Tu ista confice. A nobis liberiorem epistolam exspecta. VI. Kal. Febr. M. Messalla M. Pisone coss.

7. To ATTICUS (AD ATT. I. 14).

ROME, FEB. 13, 61 B.C. (693 A.U.C.)

1. I have already told you how Pompey's first speech after his return satisfied nobody. He was afterwards asked in public what he thought of the senate's provision for the trial of Clodius, 2. and answered by dwelling at some length upon his respect for the senate. He renewed his declaration a few days later in that body, and 3. was followed by Crassus, who spoke in the highest terms of my services; rather, I thought, to Pompey's annoyance. 4. I then rose, and enlarged on the satisfactory position of affairs brought about by the union of parties. 5. The senate's energy and firmness have been admirable. When some young nobles and their dependents had riotously interrupted the proceedings against Clodius in the assembly, the senate, by an overwhelming majority, instructed the consuls to urge upon the people the acceptance of the bill providing for his trial. 6. All the magistrates, except the consul Piso and the tribune Fufius, are behaving very well; and Piso's sloth makes him the less dangerous. 7. Teucris has fulfilled her promise. My brother Quintus is anxious to buy a new house. I should be glad to see you reconciled to Lucceius. Let me hear what you are doing, and how affairs stand in Epirus.

CICERO ATTICO SAL.

Vereor ne putidum sit scribere ad te, quam sim occupatus, 1

1. HS. CXXXIIII = 'centies tricies quadringentis,' or 13,400,000 sesterces, between £110,000 and £120,000 according to various estimates. The sum seems enormous, as compared with 3,500,000 sesterces which Cicero had paid for his house. Cp. Ad Fam. 5. 6, 2.

2. Bene, 'cheaply.'

Homines intellegere . . pervenire. These words probably mean, 'men begin to see that there is no discredit in borrowing from one's friend to buy a house suited to one's aspirations.' It is implied that Messalla's house was bought in part with borrowed money.

4. Teucris. Many suppose C. Antonius, Cicero's colleague, to be meant. But another suggestion is, that Cicero refers to a rich woman from whom he had borrowed money. Mr. Pretor's note on Ad Att. 1. 12, induces me to look with more favour than I did previously on the identification of 'Teucris' with C. Antonius. A passage in Persius (1. 4.) may be quoted in illustration of the use of such a term for an effeminate Roman.

Negotium, 'creature.' Cp. 'varium et mutabile semper Femina' Virg. Aen. 4. 569, and the Greek χρῆμα.

5. Est in spe, 'there is hope that she will fulfil her promise.' The sentence is elliptical. For the phrase 'in spe esse,' cp. Ep. 19, 4: Ad Att. 8. 11 D, 8.

Tu ista confice: cp. 'tu mandata effice quae recepisti,' § 7 of the next letter. I cannot explain the allusion in either letter, but, from the context in both passages, it seems likely that Cicero is referring to his transactions with Teucris. Manutius, however, believes that in this passage Cicero is urging Atticus to get in the money owing him as soon as possible, that he may return to Rome the sooner.

7. Putidum, 'formal,' hence 'in bad taste.' Cp. 'nolo exprimi litteras putidius nolo obscurari neglegentius' De Orat. 3. 11. 41.

sed tamen distinebar, ut huic vix tantulae epistolae tempus
habuerim atque id ereptum e summis occupationibus. Prima
contio Pompeii qualis fuisset, scripsi ad te antea: non iucunda
miseris, inanis improbis, beatis non grata, bonis non gravis;
itaque frigebat. Tum Pisonis consulis impulsu levissimus tribunus pl. Fufius in contionem producit Pompeium—res agebatur
in circo Flaminio et erat in eo ipso loco illo die nundinarum
πανήγυρις—; quaesivit ex eo, placeretne ei iudices a praetore legi,
quo consilio idem praetor uteretur: id autem erat de Clodiana
2 religione ab senatu constitutum. Tum Pompeius μάλ' ἀριστοκρατικῶς locutus est senatusque auctoritatem sibi omnibus in rebus
maximi videri semperque visam esse respondit et id multis
verbis. Postea Messalla consul in senatu de Pompeio quaesivit,
quid de religione et de promulgata rogatione sentiret: locutus

1. Distinebar, 'I am so busy.' Cp. Ep. 1, 1, p. 26, note, for the tense, and 'quanta occupatione distinear' Ad Att. 2. 23. 1, for the meaning. 'Ita' before 'distinebar' would bring the passage more into accordance with usage.

2. Prima contio Pompeii. Pompey's first speech after his return from Asia.

3. Scripsi. In a letter now lost; perhaps the 'liberior epistola' promised at the close of the last.

4. Miseris, 'to the poor;' improbis, 'to the democrats;' beatis, 'to the wealthy;' bonis, 'to the well disposed or optimates.' See Mommsen, E. T. 4. 1, 194.

5. Frigebat, 'was coldly received.' The word is used of a flute-player, Brut. 50, 187; and see Nägelsb. 134. 388.

Tum, 'subsequently.'

6. Fufius. Q. Calenus. See Ep. 11, 1, note.

In contionem producit Pompeium, 'brings Pompey forward to address the people,' or perhaps 'causes Pompey to mount the rostra.' A Roman could only address a meeting of the people with the leave of a magistrate who had the power of convening it. 'Contio' was an assembly of the people for discussion, not for voting, and apparently, could be convened anywhere in or near Rome. See Smith, Dict. of Antiq. 348.

7. In circo Flaminio. This was in the Campus Martius, and so Pompey did not lose his imperium and his claim to a triumph by attending the meeting, as he would have done by entering the city. See Ep. 5, 4, note, and note E.

Nundinarum πανήγυρις, 'a solemn assembly—on market-day.' There is some irony in applying the term πανήγυρις to a concourse on such an ordinary occasion. The 'nundinae' were always 'dies fasti' for plebeians, and, after some time, became so for patricians also. Cp. Smith's Dictionary of Antiquities, sub voc., pp. 815, 816. Iulius Caesar (ap. Macrob. Sat. 1. 16, 29) 'negat nundinis contionem advocari posse;' but this passage seems to contradict his statement. Cp. Lange, Röm. Alt. 2. 100.

8. Ex eo, sc. 'Pompeio.'

Iudices . . . legi. Usually the judges were chosen by lot, for a particular trial, from the whole list, or 'album iudicum;' but, if corruption was to be apprehended, it was sometimes desired that they should be specially appointed by a consul or praetor. Cp. Pro Muren. 23, 47; Pro Milone 8, 21.

9. Quo consilio . . uteretur, 'whom the said praetor should employ at his council.' On the meaning of 'consilium,' see on § 5 of the next letter.

Id autem erat . . constitutum, 'that, you must know, was the proposal of the senate as to the sacrilege of Clodius.' 'Autem' simply continues the narrative. See Madv. 437 b. For this sense of 'religio,' cp. Philipp. 1. 6, 13.

10. μάλ' ἀριστοκρατικῶς locutus est, 'held the language of a thorough aristocrat.'

13. De Pompeio, 'of Pompey.'

14. De promulgata rogatione, 'about the proposal which had been made for the trial of Clodius.' See the last words of the previous section.

Locutus ita est . . ut, foll. A pleonasm. Cp. Madv. 481 b.

ita est in senatu, ut omnia illius ordinis consulta γενικῶς laudaret, mihique, ut adsedit, dixit se putare satis ab se etiam de istis rebus esse responsum. Crassus postea quam vidit illum 2
excepisse laudem ex eo, quod suspicarentur homines ei consulatum meum placere, surrexit ornatissimeque de meo consulatu locutus est, ut ita diceret, se, quod esset senator, quod civis, quod liber, quod viveret, mihi acceptum referre; quotiens coniugem, quotiens domum, quotiens patriam videret, totiens se beneficium meum videre. Quid multa? totum hunc locum, quem ego varie meis orationibus, quarum tu Aristarchus es, soleo pingere, de flamma, de ferro—nosti illas ληκύθους—, valde graviter pertexuit. Proximus Pompeio sedebam: intellexi hominem moveri, utrum Crassum inire eam gratiam, quam ipse praetermisisset, an esse tantas res nostras, quae tam libenti senatu laudarentur, ab eo praesertim, qui mihi laudem illam eo minus deberet, quod meis omnibus litteris in Pompeiana laude per-

1. γενικῶς, 'in general terms.' Schütz, Billerb., Matth. But Orell. and Metzger render 'without exception.' The first meaning seems most probable, for Pompey wished not to break with any party, which he would have done by unreserved approval of the senate's measures.

3. De istis rebus. Boot thinks the actual words of Pompey are quoted, who might say, on resuming his seat, 'satis a me de istis rebus responsum puto.' If the words are Cicero's, they may mean either 'on the two points upon which Messalla questioned him,' or 'on the affairs you (Atticus) know about,' i.e. my proceedings as consul.

Crassus. M. Licinius, afterwards triumvir. For notices of him, see Introd. to Part I, §§ 5: 16

Illum excepisse . . placere, 'that Pompey had won praise, because men *fancied* he approved of my consular measures.' Boot remarks on 'excipere,' that it is said, 'de rebus quae forte offeruntur. Minus aliquanto est quam accipere.'

6. Ut . . . diceret = 'saying,' explains 'ornatissime.' 'Ita' is used pleonastically and refers to what follows. Cp. Ep. 100, 7; Zumpt, L. G. 748.

8. Patriam, 'his own city.' Cp. Ep. 47, 1, note.

9. Quid multa? sc. 'dicam,' 'enough.' See Madv. 479 d, Obs. 1.

10. Aristarchus. A critic of proverbial severity. Cp. Hor. Ars Poet. 450; Cic. in Pis. 30, 73. He lived at Alexandria, about the middle of the second century before Christ.

11. Pingere, 'to embellish.' Translate est ornare. Forcell. Cp. Ep. 15. 3.

ληκύθους. Literally, 'oil flasks.' Forcell, Liddell and Scott, Matth., and Boot, think it has the same meaning as 'ampullae' in Hor. A. P. 97, 'swelling phrases.' Manutius thinks it means 'paint pots' = 'familiar rhetorical passages.' Cp. 'pingere' above, and 'pigmenta' Ep. 9. 1, note. For examples of such passages, cp. In Cat. passim; Pro Muren. 39, 85. Mr. Jeans renders 'paillettes' = 'spangles;' both he and Professor Tyrrell deny that the word is here equivalent to 'ampullae.' Prof. Tyrrell thinks that it means 'flasks for holding pigments.'

Valde graviter pertexuit, 'narrated with much dignity.' Cp. Lucret. 6. 42, 'inceptum pergam pertexere dictis.'

13. Moveri = 'moleste ferre.' On the infin. after such verbs, see Madv. 397.

Utrum . . praetermisisset, an, 'possibly at Crassus' establishing a claim for gratitude which he had failed to secure; possibly—'

16. Meis omnibus litteris, 'in all my literary efforts.' Cp. 'te neque illos (versus) neque ullas omnino litteras nosse' Philipp. 2. 8, 20; and for the abl., Madv. 253. Prof. Tyrrell denies the sense which I have given to 'litteris,' and reads 'meis orationibus, omnibus litteris,' taking the last two words to mean 'in every letter of the words I spoke.' On the plural sense of 'litterae,' cp. Ep. 79, 3.

In Pompeiana . . esset, 'had had his praises curtailed,' 'had been censured, that

4 strictus esset. Hic dies me valde Crasso adiunxit, et tamen ab illo aperte tecte quicquid est datum libenter accepi. Ego autem ipse, di boni! quo modo ἐνεπερπερευσάμην novo auditori Pompeio! si umquam mihi περίοδοι, si καρποί, si ἐνθυμήματα, si κατασκευαὶ suppeditaverunt, illo tempore. Quid multa? clamores. Etenim haec erat ὑπόθεσις: de gravitate ordinis, de equestri concordia, de consensione Italiae, de intermortuis reliquiis coniurationis, de vilitate, de otio. Nosti iam in hac materia sonitus nostros: tanti fuerunt, ut ego eo brevior sim, quod eos
5 usque istinc exauditos putem. Romanae autem se res sic habent: senatus Ἄρειος πάγος. Nihil constantius, nihil severius, nihil fortius: nam cum dies venisset rogationi ex senatus consulto ferendae, concursabant barbatuli iuvenes, totus ille grex Catilinae, duce filiola Curionis, et populum, ut antiquaret, roga-

Pompey might be praised.' e.g. Cicero had praised Pompey as the conqueror of Spartacus, whose insurrection had been suppressed almost entirely by Crassus. Cp. Pro Leg. Man. 11, 30.

2. Ab illo. Pompeio.

Aperte tecte, 'whether directly or indirectly.' Boot. Matth.

3. ἐνεπερπερευσάμην, 'sounded my own praises.' Epictetus uses the verb, but it is not found in classical Greek.

Novo auditori. Pompey had only recently returned from Asia. See above § 1, note, and Manut.

4. περίοδοι, 'well-turned periods.' Cp. Arist. Rhet. 3. 9; Cic. Orat. 61, 204.

καρποί. I cannot explain this word in such a connection, but it is apparently the reading of the best MS. καμπαί, which has been suggested, might mean 'transitions,' and occurs in Demet. Phal. ap. L. and S.

ἐνθυμήματα, 'conclusions from contraries,' 'antitheses.' Cp. Cic. Top. 13. 55, and for illustration, Pro Milon. 29. 79, quoted by Quintilian, Inst. Or. 5. 14. 2.

5. κατασκευαί, 'figures.' Mr. Pretor quotes Gronovius for the sense 'figurae elocutionis' and Ernesti for the sense 'constructive arguments,' confirmationes. See also Liddell and Scott, sub voc. Especially confirmation of what has gone before. Cp. Quintil. Inst. Or. 2. 4. Boot, quoting from J. C. T. Ernesti, says that the two first words refer to style, the two last to modes of proof.

Illo tempore, sc. 'suppeditarunt.'

Clamores, sc. 'secuti sunt,' 'cheers followed.'

6. ὑπόθεσις, 'my subject,' = 'argumentum.' Cic. Top. 21, 79.

De gravitate ordinis, 'about the dignified conduct of our [the senatorian] order,' which it had pursued in punishing Catiline's accomplices.

7. Intermortuis reliquiis. These words seem to refer to the surviving accomplices of Catiline, who were for the present harmless. 'Intermortuus' is a term used in cases of suspended animation or activity. Cp. Pro Muren. 7, 16.

8. Vilitate, 'the cheapness of provisions,' supposed to have resulted from Pompey's appointment as praefectus annonae, which had been made at Cicero's suggestion, in 63 B.C.

In hac materia, 'on this topic.'

9. Sonitus nostros, 'my thunders.'

10. Usque istinc, 'even from Epirus, where you are.'

11. Ἄρειος πάγος, 'a true Areopagus.' Cp. ἀρειοπαγίτας, used ironically in § 5 of the next letter, and Ep. 28, 4. The high character of the Areopagus at Athens was proverbial, and is much dwelt upon in the Eumenides of Aeschylus.

13. Barbatuli, 'with small, delicate beards.' Cp. 'bene barbatos' In Cat. 2. 10, 22. To wear such a beard after coming of age was a mark of foppishness. Cp. Smith's Dict. of Antiq., sub voc. Barba, 197.

14. Filiola Curionis. The younger Curio, notorious for his debauchery. Cp. Ep. 11, 1; Philipp. 2. 18, 44. For an account of his subsequent career, see note on Ep. 30, and Intr. to Part II, § 26, and to Part III, § 9.

bant; Piso autem consul, lator rogationis, idem erat dissuasor. Operae Clodianae pontes occuparant; tabellae ministrabantur ita, ut nulla daretur VTI ROGAS. Hic tibi rostra Cato advolat, convitium Pisoni consuli mirificum facit, si id est convitium, vox plena gravitatis, plena auctoritatis, plena denique salutis; accedit eodem etiam noster Hortensius, multi praeterea boni; insignis vero opera Favonii fuit. Hoc concursu optimatium comitia dimittuntur; senatus vocatur. Cum decerneretur frequenti senatu, contra pugnante Pisone, ad pedes omnium singillatim accidente Clodio, ut consules populum cohortarentur ad rogationem accipiendam, homines ad quindecim Curioni nullum senatus consultum facienti adsenserunt; ex altera parte facile CCCC. fuerunt. Acta res est. Fufius tribunus tum concessit. Clodius contiones miseras habebat, in quibus Lucullum, Hortensium, C. Pisonem, Messallam consulem contumeliose laedebat; me tantum 'comperisse omnia' criminabatur. Senatus et de

2. **Operae Clodianae**: see § 3 of the preceding letter, and note thereon.

Pontes. Narrow passages leading to and from the enclosures ('saepta') in the Campus Martius, where the tribes or centuries assembled separately before giving their votes. If the comitia were convoked for legislation, each voter ought to be furnished with two voting tablets (**tabellae**), one marked V.R. ('uti rogas'), affirmative, the other A. 'antiquo'), negative; and he would give his vote by throwing one of these into a basket ('cista') as he passed out of his 'saeptum.' But on the present occasion, owing to intimidation apparently, no tablets marked V.R. were supplied. See, on the mode of voting, Cic. de Leg. 3. 17. 38; Festus, sub voc. Sexagenarii, (334, Müller): Smith's Dict. of Antiq., sub vocc. Comitia 336; Tabella 1090.

3. **Tibi.** Dativus ethicus. See Madv. 248.

4. **Convitium . . facit**: cp. Ep. 121, 2.

5. **Salutis**, 'of beneficial advice,' 'patriotism.'

7. **Favonii.** M. Favonius was a determined aristocrat, jealous of Pompey, and a great admirer of Cato. He opposed the triumvirs in 59 B.C.; was aedile in 53 B.C., and probably praetor in 49 B.C.; served under Pompey in the civil war, and was pardoned by Caesar after the battle of Pharsalus. He did not conspire with Brutus and Cassius against Caesar, but joined them in the war which ensued, and was put to death after the battle of Philippi. He is frequently mentioned in Cicero's letters. See, too, Suet. Oct. 13.

11. **Curioni.** C. Scribonius Curio, father of the young man mentioned above, is probably here referred to, for his son can hardly have been of senatorial age. The father was consul in 76 B.C.; he afterwards governed Macedonia, and won victories over the Dardani. He generally supported the optimates, and his defence of Clodius on this occasion may have been dictated by hostility to Caesar, who had received a grievous wrong from Clodius. Cicero delivered a speech about this time, 'In Clodium et Curionem,' of which portions are extant. Curio died in 53 B.C.

Nullum senatus consultum facienti, 'who suggested that no decree of the senate should be made.'

13. **Acta res est**, 'the affair was settled.'

Concessit, 'yielded,' did not press his opposition.'

14. **Lucullum.** L. Lucullus, the famous general, is probably meant: on whom cp. Ep. 1, 3, note, and Pro Milon. 27, 73.

15. **Pisonem**: see the preceding letter, § 2, and note.

16. **Comperisse omnia.** Cicero seems often to have used this expression about the information he had procured as to Catiline's conspiracy, instead of publishing his proofs, and to have given offence thereby. Cp. Ad Fam. 5. 5. 2.

De provinciis praetorum: cp. § 5 of the preceding letter, and note.

provinciis praetorum et de legationibus et de ceteris rebus decer-
nebat, ut ante, quam rogatio lata esset, ne quid ageretur. Habes
6 res Romanas. Sed tamen etiam illud, quod non speraram, audi:
Messalla consul est egregius, fortis, constans, diligens, nostri
laudator, amator, imitator; ille alter uno vitio minus vitiosus,
quod iners, quod somni plenus, quod imperitus, quod ἀπρακτότατος, sed voluntate ita καχέκτης, ut Pompeium post illam contionem, in qua ab eo senatus laudatus est, odisse coeperit;
itaque mirum in modum omnes a se bonos alienavit, neque id
magis amicitia Clodii adductus fecit quam studio perditarum
rerum atque partium. Sed habet sui similem in magistratibus
praeter Fufium neminem. Bonis utimur tribunis pl., Cornuto
7 vero Pseudocatone. Quid quaeris? Nunc ut ad privata redeam,
Τεῦκρις promissa patravit. Tu mandata effice, quae recepisti.
Q. frater, qui Argiletani aedificii reliquum dodrantem emit
HS. DCCXXV., Tusculanum venditat, ut, si possit, emat, Pacilianam domum. Cum Lucceio in gratiam redi: video hominem valde

1. **Legationibus.** In this passage, embassies to and from foreign states are probably referred to; they were usually received and appointed in February. Cp. Ad Att. 1. 18, 7; Ad Fam. 1. 4, 1.

2. **Ut . . ne:** see Madv. 456, for this combination.

Habes res Romanas, 'there is an account of Roman affairs for you.' See note on § 6 of the next letter.

3. **Illud,** 'this,' referring to what follows. See Ep. 5, 9, note.

5. **Uno . . vitiosus,** 'has one fault which cancels some of the rest; he is lazy.'

6. **ἀπρακτότατος,** 'most indolent.'

7. **καχέκτης,** 'ill-affected.' Originally a medical term. Cp. Polyb. 1. 68.

Contionem: see the second section of this letter.

12. **Cornuto.** C. Cornutus was praetor in 57 B.C. Cp. Post Red. in Sen. 9, 23.

13. **Pseudocatone.** Does this word mean 'a second Cato,' or 'a sham Cato?' Perhaps the second version is nearest to Cicero's meaning.

Quid quaeris? 'enough.' The expression seems to be borrowed from conversation, and to be suggested by surprise exhibited on the face of the person with whom one is talking. Cp. also Ep. 8, 4, note.

14. **Τεῦκρις . . recepisti:** see on § 6 of the preceding letter.

15. **Argiletani.** The Argiletum seems to have been near the Forum Iulium, north of the Forum Romanum. See Smith's Dict. of Geogr. 2. 798, and cp. Virg. Aen. 8. 345.

Reliquum dodrantem. Q. Cicero was previously owner of one quarter of the house, and seems to have bought up the shares of the other joint owners. See, for the use of 'dodrans' and similar words, Madv. Suppl. II, B. 2.

16. **Venditat,** '*offers for sale.*' Forcell., and cp. Pliny Ep. 1. 24.

Pacilianam domum. I can find no explanation of this allusion.

17. **Lucceio.** L. Lucceius was a man of eminent literary attainments and great wealth. He coalesced with Caesar at the election of consuls for 59 B.C., but failed to secure his own election. He then seems to have devoted himself to literature, and Cicero wrote him a remarkable letter, asking for a flattering description of his own services. Cp. Ad Fam. 5. 12. The quarrel between Atticus and Lucceius seems to have been partly caused by Lucceius, as arbitrator, giving his decision against Atticus in some affair. Cp. Ad Att. 1. 11, 1. That letter, however, was written six years previously, and Wesenb. agrees with Madv. (Adv. Crit. 2. 234) in proposing to substitute 'redit' for 'redi,' arguing that Cicero is more likely to inform Atticus of a reconciliation between

petiturire. Navabo operam. Tu, quid agas, ubi sis, cuius modi istae res sint, fac me quam diligentissime certiorem. Idibus Febr.

8. TO ATTICUS (AD ATT. I. 16).

ROME, JUNE OR JULY, (?) 61 B.C. (693 A.U.C.)

1. I will explain to you my comparative inactivity of late, and the result of Clodius' trial. As long as there was any hope of success, I exerted myself to the uttermost; 2. but when Hortensius had made his fatal concession as to the appointment of the judges, I withdrew, not sharing his confidence as to the result. 3. Yet, even after the challenge of the judges, which went very much in favour of the accused, 4. in all the earlier stages of the trial everything looked promising for the prosecution; and, when I appeared to give evidence, I had a most flattering reception from the judges. 5. However, bribery and corruption of the most atrocious kind secured a slight majority for an acquittal. 6. This has been a heavy blow to the commonwealth, 7. but I am glad to say that bad citizens do not exult so much in their victory as one might have expected. 8. I have exerted myself to reassure the senate and all well-disposed citizens, and have attacked the corrupt judges, the consul Piso, and Clodius. 9. I said, on May 15, that the acquittal of Clodius only reserved him for heavier punishment, and (10.) completely silenced him in a lively altercation which followed my speech. 11. On the whole, I think my position is as good as ever in the regard of the well disposed, while my unpopularity with the populace has diminished, and I evidently enjoy Pompey's esteem in a high degree. 12. We look forward with much interest to the consular comitia. Pompey is actively supporting Afranius, and systematic corruption is feared. Special measures are being taken against it. 13. The election of Afranius would throw discredit on the consulship. 14. I regret that you will not attend Quintus in Asia, 15. am content with the inscriptions in your Amaltheum, 16. and have written to thank C. Antonius for his services to you. 17. I will attend to the affairs of Cincius. 18. Let me know all about your Amaltheum.

CICERO ATTICO SAL.

Quaeris ex me, quid acciderit de iudicio, quod tam praeter 1
opinionem omnium factum sit, et simul vis scire, quo modo ego minus, quam soleam, proeliatus sim: respondebo tibi *ὕστερον*

himself and Lucceius, both being at Rome, than to exhort Atticus, who was absent, to be reconciled to Lucceius. I hardly think we are sufficiently acquainted with the circumstances to justify adoption of the suggestion.

Hominem. Instead of a pronoun. It expresses no contempt, and is used of Pompey in the third section of this letter.

1. Petiturire, 'is very anxious to be a candidate' for the consulship, probably. Cp. Ad Att. 1. 17. 11; Ad Fam. 5. 12–15, for notices of L. Lucceius.

2. Istae res, 'the affairs you are engaged in.' Cp. Ep. 6, 1, notes, for an account of them.

4. De iudicio, 'in the matter of Clodius' trial.'

Quod . . factum sit, 'that it has ended in a way so contrary to general expectation.' The conjunctive is used because the sentence is a question quoted from Atticus. See Ep. 6, 1, note.

6. Minus . . proeliatus sim, 'took less part in the struggle than usual.' Apparently the word is only here used metaphorically, and Boot thinks it is adopted from Atticus' own letter.

ὕστερον πρότερον = 'ordine praepostero,' 'I will answer your last question first.'

πρότερον, Ὁμηρικῶς. Ego enim, quam diu senatus auctoritas mihi defendenda fuit, sic acriter et vehementer proeliatus sum, ut clamor concursusque maxima cum mea laude fierent: quod si tibi umquam sum visus in re publica fortis, certe me in illa causa admiratus esses; cum enim ille ad contiones confugisset in iisque meo nomine ad invidiam uteretur, di immortales! quas ego pugnas et quantas strages edidi! quos impetus in Pisonem, in Curionem, in totam illam manum feci! quo modo sum insectatus levitatem senum, libidinem iuventutis! saepe, ita me di iuvent! te non solum auctorem consiliorum meorum, verum etiam spectatorem pugnarum mirificarum desideravi.

2 Postea vero quam Hortensius excogitavit, ut legem de religione Fufius tribunus pl. ferret, in qua nihil aliud a consulari rogatione differebat nisi iudicum genus—in eo autem erant omnia—, pugnavitque ut ita fieret, quod et sibi et aliis persuaserat nullis illum iudicibus effugere posse, contraxi vela perspiciens inopiam iudicum, neque dixi quicquam pro testimonio, nisi quod erat ita notum atque testatum, ut non possem prae-

1. Ὁμηρικῶς, 'after the manner of Homer,' who 'in medias res Non secus ac notas auditorem rapit.' Hor. Ars. Poet. 148, 149.

Auctoritas. Perhaps the resolution mentioned in the fifth section of the preceding letter.

5. Ille: Clodius.

Contiones, 'addresses to the populace.'

6. Meo nomine . . uteretur, 'used my name to exasperate the people against me.' See § 5 of the preceding letter.

7. Quas ego . . edidi! 'in what battles I engaged, and how I overthrew my foes.' He keeps up the metaphor of 'proeliatus sum,' and is probably alluding to debates in the senate.

Pisonem. The consul of this year.

8. Manum, 'crew.'

9. Levitatem, 'want of principle, worthlessness.' Cp. Philipp. 2. 31, 77; A. Gell. N. A. 6 (7), 11 quoted by Mr. Mayor in his note on the passage in the Philippics. In later Latin it meant 'inconstancy.' Prof. Tyrrell remarks that 'senum' refers especially to Piso and Curio the elder; 'iuvenum' especially to Curio the younger. Cp. Ep. 7, 5–6.

10. Auctorem, 'as an adviser,' 'suggester.'

13. A consulari rogatione: see § 5 of the preceding letter.

14. Genus, 'mode of appointment.' The consuls had suggested that the praetor who presided at the trial should name the judges (cp. Ep. 7, 1), while the tribune Fufius Calenus proposed that the usual practice should be followed. The motives of Hortensius in supporting the latter proposal are explained presently. Professor Beesly (Fortnightly Review, June 1, 1866) believes that the real question in dispute between Fufius and the senate was, whether the court should be established by a vote of the centuries or of the tribes, and thus, indirectly, whether it should have power to pronounce sentence of death. Cp. Maine, Ancient Law, p. 388. But this conjecture seems needless to me. We learn from the oration Pro Murena 23, 47, that the selection of judges by a magistrate was thought more likely to lead to convictions than their appointment by lot, and this would account for the enemies of Clodius preferring the first way of appointment.

In eo . . erant omnia, 'on that everything depended.'

15. Ut ita fieret, 'that such a measure should be passed.'

16. Nullis illum . . posse, 'that Clodius could not escape, whoever the judges might be.' On the abl., see Ep. 1, 2, note.

Contraxi vela, 'I reefed my sails,' 'checked myself.' Cicero is fond of nautical metaphors.

17. Inopiam, 'the neediness:' common in this sense in Cicero.

18. Ita notum atque testatum, 'so well

terire. Itaque, si causam quaeris absolutionis, ut iam πρὸς τὸ
πρότερον revertar, egestas iudicum fuit et turpitudo; id autem
ut accideret, commissum est Hortensii consilio, qui, dum veritus
est ne Fufius ei legi intercederet, quae ex senatus consulto
ferebatur, non vidit illud, satius esse illum in infamia relinqui
ac sordibus quam infirmo iudicio committi; sed ductus odio pro-
peravit rem deducere in iudicium, cum illum plumbeo gladio
iugulatum iri tamen diceret. Sed iudicium si quaeris quale 5
fuerit, incredibili exitu, sic, uti nunc ex eventu ab aliis, a me
iam ex ipso initio consilium Hortensii reprehendatur. Nam
ut reiectio facta est clamoribus maximis, cum accusator tamquam censor bonus homines nequissumos reiiceret, reus tamquam
clemens lanista frugalissumum quemque secerneret, ut primum
iudices consederunt, valde diffidere boni coeperunt; non enim
umquam turpior in ludo talario consessus fuit: maculosi sena-
tores, nudi equites, tribuni non tam aerati quam, ut appellantur,
aerarii; pauci tamen boni inerant, quos reiectione fugare ille

known and attested.' Cp. 'testatam rem abiiciunt,' according to one reading in Pro Muren. 21, 45, and 'ut quasi testata esset nostra gratia,' Ep. 29, 10. On Cicero's evidence cp. Introduction to Part I, p. 14 and references.

1. πρὸς τὸ πρότερον, 'to your first question.' Cp. ὕστερον πρότερον p. 52, l. 6; 53, l. 1.

2. Id autem .. consilio, 'the mistake which made the choice of such judges possible, was owing to the advice of Hortensius.'

5. Satius esse . . sordibus, 'that it was better that Clodius should be left in disgrace and danger' of a trial. 'Sordes' means the mourning worn by persons accused.

7. Plumbeo .. tamen, 'that a leaden sword would be sharp enough to stab him.' For this use of 'tamen' with the corresponding particle suppressed cp. 'Cethegus qui paulo ante aliquid tamen responderat' In Cat. 3. 5. 10.

8. Iudicium, 'the trial.'

9. Incredibili, 'extraordinary,' because the judges shewed such a rigorous disposition at first. For the omission of 'fuit' after 'exitu,' see Madv. 478, 2.

Sic, uti nunc . . . reprehendatur. We might express this, 'so much so, that all disapprove the advice of Hortensius after the event, as I did before it.' 'Sic' = 'tale,' cp. Pro Rosc. Amer. 30. 84.

11. Reiectio, 'challenge.' A larger number of judges than was actually required for the trial was chosen by lot from the whole register or 'album iudicum,' and then reduced by names being struck off by the prosecutor and defendant. Cp. below in this section: also cp. In Verr. Act. 1. 6, 16; 10, 30.

Facta est. On the tense, see Madv. 338 b.

Clamoribus maximis, 'amid the loudest outcries.' Perhaps from the friends of both parties. Though Clodius was a favourite with the populace, his anxiety to get rid of upright judges may have disgusted many. On the abl., see Ep. 1, 2, note.

Accusator. L. Lentulus Crus, consul in 49 B.C. He was supported by two other Lentuli. Cp. Schol. Bob. ad Orat. in Clodium et Curionem 5. 3.

13. Clemens lanista. A trainer of gladiators, when asked to furnish combatants for a public show, would be glad to reserve his best men for future service, if possible. Prof. Tyrrell thinks that these words refer to the behaviour of a 'lanista' when buying slaves for service as gladiators, who might show his kindness by passing over the more respectable.

15. In ludo talario, 'in a gambling house.'

Consessus, 'company.'

Maculosi, 'under a stigma.' Cp. Tac. Hist. 1, 7, 'Capitonem ut avaritia et libidine foedum et maculosum.' It need not refer to the 'nota censoria.'

16. Nudi, 'needy,' 'beggared.' Tyrr.

Aerati, 'men of property.'

17. Aerarii. This word is here used with

non potuerat, qui maesti inter sui dissimiles et maerentes sede-
4 bant et contagione turpitudinis vehementer permovebantur. Hic, ut quaeque res ad consilium primis postulationibus referebatur, incredibilis erat severitas, nulla varietate sententiarum; nihil impetrabat reus; plus accusatori dabatur, quam postulabat; triumphabat—quid quaeris?— Hortensius se vidisse tantum; nemo erat qui illum reum ac non miliens condemnatum arbitraretur. Me vero teste producto credo te ex acclamatione Clodii advocatorum audisse quae consurrectio iudicum facta sit, ut me circumsteterint, ut aperte iugula sua pro meo capite P. Clodio ostentarint: quae mihi res multo honorificentior visa est quam aut illa, cum iurare tui cives Xenocratem testimonium dicentem prohibuerunt, aut cum tabulas Metelli Numidici, cum eae, ut mos est, circumferrentur, nostri iudices aspicere nolue-

a double meaning: its proper one is 'paymasters' when used with 'tribunal,' to describe one of the three orders of judges; but there seems to be in this case an allusion to the corruption of the court which tried Clodius. Cp. 'nummariis' in § 8. Prof. Tyrrell suggests 'non tam aerarii ut appellantur quam aerati' (bribed).

2. Contagione turpitudinis, 'their contact with corruption.'

3. Ad consilium. See next page.

Primis postulationibus, 'in the first requests' made by the two parties to the judges, e.g. to have witnesses compelled to attend.

6. Triumphabat: metaph. Cp. Ad Fam. 2. 12, 3, and Ep. 66, 2.

Quid quaeris? 'enough.' '"Noli quaerere" et "quid quaeris" sunt formulae quibus utimur cum rem ejusmodi dicturi sumus quae exspectatione major sit, quasi dicamus "ne plura quaeras" "sit hoc satis quod iam dicam."' Forcell. Cp. p. 51, note on l. 13.

. Se vidisse tantum, 'that he had shewn such penetration.'

7. Reum, 'a man accused' *only*.

Ac non, 'and not much rather.' See Madv. 438 a, Obs. 1.

8. Credo te . . facta sit, 'I think you must have heard how the judges rose after the outcries made by the partisans of Clodius.' The natural order of the words would be, 'quae consurrectio iudicum facta sit ex acclamatione.' Mr. Pretor and Mr. Jeans both understand the passage as meaning 'the outcries of the partisans of Clodius must have told you,' and refer in illustration of the hyperbole to Ad Att. 2. 14. 4, ad fin.

9. Advocatorum: cp. Ep. 12, 3; Philipp. 1. 7. 16.

10. Ut me circumsteterint. On the mood, see Madv. 356.

12. Iurare, 'to take an oath' when giving his testimony.

Tui cives. The Athenians, who had offered Atticus the rights of citizenship amongst them. See Appendix 3, § 1.

Xenocratem. Xenocrates was a fellow-student of Aristotle. Cp. Diog. Laert. 4. 2–4. Cicero (De Off. 1. 30) calls him 'philosophorum severissimum,' and often mentions him in his philosophical works. The incident here referred to is mentioned again by Cicero (Pro Balbo 5, 12).

13. Tabulas, 'his accounts,' which, on a charge of extortion or peculation, would be important documents.

Metelli Numidici. Q. Metellus Numidicus is more than once mentioned by Cicero, as an example of firmness and high principle. He commanded in the war against Jugurtha, 109–108 B.C., and did good service, but incurred the hostility of C. Marius, one of his principal officers, and was obliged, during the sixth consulship of Marius, to go into exile, for refusing to take an oath imposed by the consul on the senate. See Ep. 29, 16. It is doubtful when the occurrence to which Cicero here refers took place. Rein (Criminalrecht 649) says that Metellus was accused by a C. Curio after either his praetorship, 112 B.C., or his consulship, 109 B.C.

14. Circumferrentur, 'were handed round among the judges for inspection.'

runt; multo haec, inquam, nostra res maior. Itaque iudicum 8 vocibus, cum ego sic ab iis, ut salus patriae, defenderer, fractus reus et una patroni omnes conciderunt; ad me autem eadem frequentia postridie convenit, quacum abiens consulatu sum domum reductus. Clamare praeclari Ariopagitae se non esse venturos nisi praesidio constituto. Refertur ad consilium: una sola sententia praesidium non desideravit. Defertur res ad senatum: gravissime ornatissimeque decernitur; laudantur iudices; datur negotium magistratibus; responsurum hominem nemo arbitrabatur. *ἔσπετε νῦν μοι, Μοῦσαι, ὅππως δὴ πρῶτον πῦρ ἔμπεσε.* Nosti Calvum, ex Nannelanis illum, illum laudatorem meum, de cuius oratione erga me honorifica ad te scripseram: biduo per unum servum, et eum ex gladiatorio ludo, confecit totum negotium; arcessivit ad se, promisit, intercessit, dedit. Iam vero—o di boni rem perditam!—etiam noctes certarum mulierum atque adulescentulorum nobilium introductiones non nullis iudicibus pro mercedis cumulo fuerunt. Ita summo discessu bonorum, pleno foro servorum, XXV. iudices ita fortes tamen fuerunt, ut summo proposito periculo vel perire malu-

1. **Haec . . nostra res,** 'this reception of mine,' 'this incident in my life.'

Iudicum vocibus, 'owing to the expressions of the judges:' abl. caus., see Madv. 255.

3. **Conciderunt,** 'lost all confidence.' Cp. §§ 9, 10, notes; and Livy 28. 26, omnis ferocia concidit.

4. **Frequentia,** 'crowd.'

Abiens consulatu, 'at the expiration of my consulate.' See Intr. to Part I, § 11.

5. **Ariopagitae,** ironical. Cp. *τριακονταφυγόντας* Ep. 28, 4.

6. **Refertur ad consilium,** 'the votes of the court are taken.' 'Consilium,' 'generally, in passages relating to the administration of justice, means the body of judges acting under a praetor in any case. And perhaps that may be its meaning here; the judges, having previously signified their wishes by acclamation, may have declared them by a formal vote. Boot, however, considers the 'consilium' to have consisted of the praetor's legal advisers, not of the 'iudices.' Mr. Tyrrell agrees with Boot.

7. **Sententia,** 'vote.'

9. **Datur negotium magistratibus,** 'the protection of the court is entrusted to the magistrates.'

Responsurum hominem, 'that Clodius would make any defence.'

10. *ἔσπετε νῦν μοι, κ.τ.λ.*: cp. Hom. Il. 16. 112, 113.

11. **Calvum.** M. Crassus is probably meant. A Nannelus, or Nannius, was among the victims of Sulla's proscription, and Crassus seems to have bought some of his property under the name of Calvus. So Manutius. Cp. Plut. Crass. 2 and 6, with Q. Cicero De Pet. Cons. 2, 9. Mr. Tyrrell points out how much conjecture there is in this, and suggests that a Greek word gave rise to 'ex Nannelanis.' He adds 'possibly "callidum illum, illum laudatorem meum" is what he (Cicero) wrote.'

Laudatorem meum: see § 3 of the preceding letter.

13. **Ex gladiatorio ludo,** i.e. 'not one of the more educated of his class.'

14. **Arcessivit ad se,** sc. 'iudices.'

Intercessit, 'gave security.' Cp. Philipp. 2. 18, 45.

17. **Cumulo,** 'addition.'

Summo discessu bonorum, 'when the well-disposed spectators had altogether retired.' For this use of the adj., see Nägelsbach 78 a, 4, p. 213. On the abl., see Ep. 1, 2, note on p. 28.

19. **Periculo.** From the disorderly supporters of Clodius.

erint quam perdere omnia: XXXI. fuerunt, quos ſames magis quam ſama commoverit; quorum Catulus cum vidisset quendam, 'quid vos' inquit 'praesidium a nobis postulabatis? an ne nummi
6 vobis eriperentur [timebatis]?' Habes, ut brevissime potui, genus iudicii et causam absolutionis. Quaeris deinceps, qui nunc sit status rerum et qui meus: rei publicae statum illum, quem tu meo consilio, ego divino confirmatum putabam, qui bonorum omnium coniunctione et auctoritate consulatus mei fixus et ſundatus videbatur, nisi quis nos deus respexerit, elapsum scito esse de manibus uno hoc iudicio, si iudicium est, triginta homines populi Romani levissimos ac nequissimos nummulis acceptis ius ac ſas omne delere et, quod omnes non modo homines, verum etiam pecudes ſactum esse sciant, id Thalnam et Plautum et Spongiam et ceteras huius modi quisquilias statuere numquam
7 esse ſactum. Sed tamen, ut te de re publica consoler, non ita, ut sperarunt mali, tanto imposito rei publicae volnere alacris exsultat improbitas in victoria; nam plane ita putaverunt, cum religio, cum pudicitia, cum iudiciorum fides, cum senatus auctoritas concidisset, ſore ut aperte victrix nequitia ac libido poenas ab optimo quoque peteret sui doloris, quem improbis-
8 simo cuique inusserat severitas consulatus mei. Idem ego ille —non enim mihi videor insolenter gloriari, cum de me apud

1. Quos ſames . . commoverit, 'who feared famine more than infamy.'

4. Habes, sc. 'expositum.' 'Habere dicitur qui quippiam audiit intellexitque.' Forcell. Cp. Epp. 7, 8; 16, 10; 29, 20.

Ut brevissime potui, sc. 'exponere.' On the ellipse, see Madv. 479 d.

9. Nisi quis nos deus respexerit: cp. 'nisi idem deus . . respexerit rem publicam' Ad Att. 7. 1, 2.

Elapsum . . de manibus: cp. Pro Mur. 39, 85.

10. Uno hoc iudicio. For the abl., see on § 5.

Si iudicium est . . delere, 'If the overthrow of all law and justice, by thirty worthless men for wretched pelf, deserve the name of a trial.' The words populi Romani are governed by the following superlatives. See Madv. 284. 'The most worthless men in the whole Roman people.' Boot.

13. Sciant. For the mood, cp. Ep. 5, 8, and note (p. 39)

Thalnam et Plautum et Spongiam. These seem to be names given in derision to the judges. Orell. Onom.

14 Quisquilias, 'refuse.' Cp. Pro Sest. 43. 94.

15. Non ita . . in victoria. 'the unscrupulous are not so active and exulting in their triumph as the badly affected had hoped.'

16. Tanto imposito . . . volnere: cp. 'volneribus quae sunt imposita provinciae' Ad Att. 5. 17, 6. Improbitas and mali seem to be different designations of the same people = 'the disaffected and disorderly.'

18. Fides, 'integrity.'

19. Nequitia ac libido, 'criminal passion.'

20. Poenas . . . doloris. Cp. Ep. 108, 1, for the expression in a slightly different sense; also Pro Milone, 13. 35, punitor doloris sui.

21. Inusserat: cp. 'cur hunc dolorem cineri eius atque ossibus inussisti' In Verr. Act. 2. 1. 44. 113.

Idem ego ille, 'I also.' See Madv. 488.

te loquor, in ea praesertim epistola, quam nolo aliis legi—idem, inquam, ego recreavi adflictos animos bonorum, unum quemque confirmans, excitans; insectandis vero exagitandisque nummariis iudicibus omnem omnibus studiosis ac fautoribus illius victoriae παρρησίαν eripui, Pisonem consulem nulla in re consistere umquam sum passus, desponsam homini iam Syriam ademi, senatum ad pristinam suam severitatem revocavi atque abiectum excitavi, Clodium praesentem fregi in senatu cum oratione perpetua, plenissima gravitatis, tum altercatione huius modi; ex qua licet pauca degustes—nam cetera non possunt habere neque vim neque venustatem remoto illo studio contentionis, quem ἀγῶνα vos appellatis—: nam, ut Idibus Maiis in 9
senatum convenimus rogatusque ego sententiam multa dixi de summa re publica, atque ille locus inductus a me est divinitus, ne una plaga accepta patres conscripti conciderent, ne defice-

1. **Aliis legi**, 'to be read to others.' Boot. Madvig, on Cic. de Fin. 1. 4. 11, says that the words must mean this, and that the insertion of 'ab' would be required if they were to mean 'read by others.'

3. **Confirmans, excitans**, 'encouraging and arousing.'

4. **Nummariis**, 'corrupt.' Cp. In Verr. Act. 2. 3. 57. 131.

Studiosis ac fautoribus: see Ep. 6. 2, note.

5. **παρρησίαν eripui**, 'I deprived of all freedom of speech.'

Nulla in re . . sum passus, 'I gave no rest to him in anything,' 'deprived him of his self-command.' Cp. Ep. 23. 2.

6. **Desponsam**, 'promised,' but probably informally, not decreed. Cp. De Prov. Cons. 15. 37, where the irregular 'desponsio' is contrasted with the formal 'decretum.' Syria only became a province after the successes of Pompey in the East. See Appendices 1, § 1 and 2. Now to avoid favouritism it was usual to assign provinces to the consuls of each year before their election took place; hence the provinces for the consuls of 61 B.C. would be fixed in the first half of 62 B.C. Syria appears not to have been one of them, but *Piso* may have hoped, by his personal influence, to procure a change of the arrangements. See, on the general question of the allotment of the provinces, Appendix 6, § 4; Ep. 26. 10.

8. **Abiectum**, 'in its humiliation.'

Fregi = 'domui' (Forcell.), 'overpowered.'

9. **Perpetua**, 'set,' 'continuous.'

Altercatione, 'a dispute' carried on in short alternate speeches.

10. **Degustes**, 'have a taste of.' Cp. 'et tu Galba quandoque degustabis imperium' Tac. Ann. 6. 20.

Nam cetera . . venustatem, a few passages only, '*for* the rest would have no interest.'

Non . . neque. The general negative is not cancelled by the two which follow, but is applied to two distinct ideas. See Madv. 460, Obs. 2.

11. **Studio contentionis**, 'the heat of dispute.'

12. **ἀγῶνα**. Not quite classical in this sense, for it seems to be given as an equivalent for 'studium contentionis.' Quern. For its gender, see Madv. 316.

Vos, 'you Athenians.' See note on § 4. p. 55.

Nam, 'namely,' 'then.' Cp. 'enim,' in § 1, and Madv. 435. Obs. 4.

14. **Ille locus**, 'the following topic.' Cp. Ep. 5. 3, p. 37, note, for this sense of 'ille.'

Divinitus, 'with marvellous appropriateness.' Mr. Pretor, following Casaubon, renders 'by inspiration;' Prof. Tyrrell, 'by a happy inspiration,' or 'with wonderful effect.'

15. **Conciderent**: cp. 'concidit,' § 10. 'Concidere' = 'ruere, perire, deficere.' Forcell., who gives several examples from Cicero.

rent; volnus esse eius modi, quod mihi nec dissimulandum nec pertimescendum videretur; ne aut ignorando stultissimi *aut metuendo ignavissimi* iudicaremur; bis absolutum esse Lentulum, bis Catilinam; hunc tertium iam esse a iudicibus in rem publicam immissum. 'Erras, Clodi; non te iudices urbi, sed carceri reservarunt, neque te retinere in civitate, sed exsilio privare voluerunt. Quam ob rem, patres conscripti, erigite animos, retinete vestram dignitatem. Manet illa in re publica bonorum consensio; dolor accessit bonis viris, virtus non est imminuta; nihil est damni factum novi, sed, quod erat, inventum est: in
10 unius hominis perditi iudicio plures similes reperti sunt.' Sed quid ago? Paene orationem in epistolam inclusi. Redeo ad altercationem: surgit pulchellus puer, obiicit mihi, me ad Baias fuisse. Falsum, sed tamen quid huic? 'Simile est' inquam, 'quasi dicas in operto fuisse.' 'Quid' inquit 'homini Arpinati cum aquis calidis?' 'Narra' inquam 'patrono tuo, qui Arpinatis

2. Ignorando, 'by affecting ignorance.' Cp. 'ignoro causam, detestor exitum' Philipp. 8. 2, 7.

3. Lentulum. P. Cornelius Lentulus Sura, the accomplice of Catiline. Cp. Plut. Cic. 17. Lentulus had been charged with peculation in 81 or 80 B.C., and again in some later year; he seems on both occasions to have been acquitted, but the censors, L. Gellius and Cn. Lentulus Clodianus, expelled him from the senate in 69 B.C. See Rein, Criminalrecht 689.

4. Catilinam. In 65 B.C. for 'repetundae' (see Ep. 2. 1, note), and in 64 B.C. for the murder of M. Marius Gratidianus (Ascon. in Orat. in Tog. Cand. p. 116); perhaps also for incest with a Vestal (cp. Oros. 6, 3) in 73 B.C. Cp. Long, Decl. of Rom. Rep. 3. 326, 337.

5. Immissum, 'let loose upon,' like a wild beast.

Carceri. The Roman prison at this time was more a place of execution than of penal detention, though occasionally used for the custody of prisoners before trial.

6. Exsilio privare, 'to deprive you of the power of going into exile,' which appears from this passage to have been the penalty Clodius would have suffered for sacrilege. Cicero implies that, if he went on as he had begun, he would incur the last penalty of the law, and not be allowed to evade it by going into voluntary exile. For instances of such evasion, cp. Livy 3. 13; 26, 3.

8. Illa, 'the former:' that which had prevailed in his own consulship.

9. Dolor accessit bonis viris, 'the well-disposed have been made indignant.' Boot; 'have now the added stimulus of indignation' Tyrrell.

10. Nihil est damni factum novi, 'no new mischief has befallen us, but that which already existed has been brought to light.'

13. Pulchellus: cp. Ep. 11, 3. An allusion, perhaps, to the Claudii Pulchri, to whose family Clodius belonged, with an ironical notice of his personal appearance. Cp. 'postquam speculum tibi allatum est, longe te a pulchris abesse sensisti' Orat. in Clod. et Cur. 5. 4.

Me ad Baias fuisse. The luxury and dissipation of Baiae were notorious, and Clodius said a rustic from Arpinum ought not to have gone there. See note on l. 15 below.

14. Falsum, a remark to Atticus.

Simile est .. in operto fuisse, 'this is as serious a charge (iron.) as if you had said I had been in hiding like yourself.' Boot. 'In operto' = 'in adyto Bonae Deae.'

15. Quid . . . homini Arpinati . . . calidis? cp. 'quid homini Arpinati cum Baiis, agresti ac rustico' Orat. in Clod. et Cur. 4.

16 Patrono. The elder Curio. See note on § 5 of the preceding letter. Curio is said to have bought an estate once belong-

aquas concupivit; nosti enim marinas.' 'Quousque' inquit 'hunc regem feremus?' 'Regem appellas,' inquam 'cum Rex tui mentionem nullam fecerit?'—Ille autem Regis hereditatem spe devorarat.—'Domum' inquit 'emisti.' 'Putes' inquam 'dicere, iudices emisti.' 'Iuranti' inquit 'tibi non crediderunt.' 'Mihi vero' inquam 'XXV. iudices crediderunt, XXXI., quoniam nummos ante acceperunt, tibi nihil crediderunt.' Magnis clamoribus adflictus conticuit et concidit. Noster autem status est 11
hic: apud bonos iidem sumus, quos reliquisti, apud sordem urbis et faecem multo melius nunc, quam *cum* reliquisti: nam et illud nobis non obest, videri nostrum testimonium non valuisse: missus est sanguis invidiae sine dolore; atque etiam hoc magis, quod omnes illi fautores illius flagitii rem manifestam illam redemptam esse a iudicibus confitentur; accedit illud, quod illa contionalis hirudo aerarii, misera ac ieiuna plebecula, me ab hoc Magno unice diligi putat, et hercule multa et iucunda consuetudine coniuncti inter nos sumus, usque eo, ut nostri isti

ing to C. Marius at Baiae, which might be called 'aquae marinae.'

2. Rex. Q. Marcius Rex was brother-in-law of Clodius, who had expected a legacy from him apparently.

4. Spe devorarat, 'had already swallowed in his hopes.' Cp. Pro Domo 23. 60.

Domum .. emisti, 'you have bought a palace,' a censure on Cicero's extravagance, as unbecoming in a 'new man.' Cp. Epp. 6, 6; 25, 2.

Putes .. dicere, 'suppose you say.' 'Idem valet atque illud simile est quasi dicas.' Boot. 'Putes' seems to have the force of a potential. 'One would suppose.' Tyrrell.

5. Iuranti .. non crediderunt, 'the judges did not believe you on your oath.' Cicero gave evidence to disprove Clodius' plea of alibi, and, as the judges acquitted the defendant, it is argued that they did not believe Cicero. See Intr. to Part I. § 14.

7. Nihil crediderunt, 'gave you no credit.' A play on 'crediderunt.'

8. Concidit, 'lost heart.' Cp. § 5 of this letter, note; Philipp. 3. 9. 24 'paene concidit.'

9. Iidem sumus, quos reliquisti, 'I have as much influence as when you left me.'

10. Nam et illud .. confitentur. The construction of this passage is rather confused; perhaps the following version will give its general force. 'I do not suffer from the *ineffectiveness* of my testimony, and profit more (etiam hoc magis, sc. 'non obest') by the general confession that the court was bribed.' Or 'hoc' may be the abl., and then the meaning will be 'all the more as.' In the latter case, accedit illud may be substituted for the more natural 'et illud nobis prodest,' because of the long passage intervening between 'non obest' and 'accedit.' So Boot.

11. Nostrum testimonium, 'my evidence against Clodius.'

12. Missus est sanguis invidiae, 'my swelling unpopularity has been reduced by bleeding.' 'Materia subtracta est invidiae nostrae.' Forcell. Cp. 'Appius cum *ei* *depauperavit* provinciam curant sanguinem miserit' Ad Att. 6. 1. 2.

13. Rem manifestam .. a iudicibus, 'that the case was clear, and that the judges were bought off.'

15. Contionalis hirudo aerarii, 'the mob who drain the treasury' by demands for corn, &c.; 'the hundred headed leech,' Prof. Nettleship; 'that bloodsucker of the treasury the wretched starveling mob.' Tyrrell.

Plebecula, 'rabble,' apparently only occurs here in Cicero.

16. Magno. Pompey, then, must have been popular at this time.

comissatores coniurationis, barbatuli iuvenes, illum in sermonibus Cn. Ciceronem appellent; itaque et ludis et gladiatoribus mirandas ἐπισημασίας sine ulla pastoricia fistula auferebamus. Nunc est exspectatio comitiorum, in quae omnibus invitis trudit noster Magnus Auli filium, atque in eo neque auctoritate neque gratia pugnat, sed quibus Philippus omnia castella expugnari posse dicebat [in quae modo asellus onustus auro posset ascendere]; consul autem ille deterioris histrionis similis suscepisse negotium dicitur et domi divisores habere; quod ego non credo. Sed senatus consulta duo iam facta sunt odiosa, quod in consulem facta putantur, Catone et Domitio postulante, unum, ut apud magistratus inquiri liceret, alterum, cuius domi divisores habitarent, adversus rem publicam. Lurco autem tribunus pl.,

1. **Comissatores coniurationis**, 'the boon companions of the conspiracy,' who joined it merely to gratify their taste for sensual pleasures. 'Qui inter vinum de coniuratione egerunt.' Gronov. 'Consortes coniurationis Catilinariae quae per comissationes inita erat.' Forcell.

Barbatuli: see on § 5 of the preceding letter.

2. **Ludis et gladiatoribus**, 'at the games and gladiatorial shows.' Abl. of the date, see Madv. 276 Obs. 2.

3. **ἐπισημασίας**, 'demonstrations of opinion,' here 'applause.' Cp. Polyb. 6, 6.

Sine ulla .. fistula, 'without any sound of the shepherd's pipe,' i. e. hissing.

Pastoricius is found Pro Cael. 11, 26, and Varro, R. R. 2. 1, 1; but 'pastoralis' is more common.

4. **In quae .. trudit .. Auli filium**, 'into which contest Pompey is pushing Afranius, against everybody's wishes.' Forcell. does not give another instance of the use of 'trudere' in quite this sense. Prof. Nettleship suggests that Afranius may be compared to the ass alluded to in the saying quoted below from Philip. Cp. Hor. Epp. 1. 20, 15 for such a use of 'trudere.'

5. **A. filium**: cp. Ep. 1, 1, note.

In eo, 'in his cause.'

6. **Quibus**, sc. 'subsidiis.' For Philip's saying, cp. Plut. Apophthegm. Regum. (Philipp. 14)

8. **Ille**. Piso.

Deterioris histrionis, either 'playing a subordinate part to Pompey,' or 'inferior.' After what Cicero has said in Ep. 6, 2, he may now compare Piso to a bad actor in a farce. Another reading is 'Doterionis,' which may mean 'an actor charged to distribute presents in a play;' or as Mr. Jeans thinks there may be an allusion to Aristodemus and Neoptolemus, two actors mentioned by Demosthenes (de. fals. leg. pp. 344, 419, 441) as agents of Philip.

9. **Negotium**, sc. 'suffragiorum emendorum.' Matth.

Divisores, 'bribery agents.' Cp. Pro Muren. 26, 54.

10. **Odiosa**. To Pompey and his friends, or perhaps to the public.

11. **Domitio**: see Ep. 1, 3, note.

Postulante. On this use of the sing., see Madv. 213 a, and Obs.

Ut apud magistratus .. liceret, 'that there should be power to search in the houses of magistrates,' for money supposed to be deposited there, or for corrupt agents. I presume that, without such a decree, the magistrates' houses would be exempt from search.

12. **Cuius domi .. rem publicam**, sc. 'facere,' 'any magistrate at whose house corrupt agents should be detected, should be held guilty of an offence against the State.'

13. **Lurco**. M. Aufidius Lurco was lame, and Cicero remarks ironically, that his proposal might have been thought inauspicious, but for the suspension of the Aelian and Fufian laws. These laws were carried about 154 B.C. (Lange, Röm. Alt. 1, 295; 2. 477), and gave to the tribunes and to all magistrates, as against others of no higher rank than their own, the right of 'spectio' and 'obnuntiatio.' They also forbade the proposal of laws on the days appointed for elective meetings of the comitia. As the object of these laws, probably, was to limit the legislative activity of the tribunes, the postponement of the comitia on this occa-

qui magistratum simul cum lege Aelia iniit, solutus est et Aelia et Fufia, ut legem de ambitu ferret, quam ille bono auspicio claudus homo promulgavit: ita comitia in a. d. VI. Kal. Sext. dilata sunt. Novi est in lege hoc, ut qui nummos in tribus pronuntiarit, si non dederit, impune sit; sin dederit, ut quoad vivat singulis tribubus HS. CIↃ CIↃ CIↃ debeat. Dixi hanc legem P. Clodium iam ante servasse; pronuntiare enim solitum esse et non dare. Sed heus tu! videsne consulatum illum nostrum, quem Curio antea ἀποθέωσιν vocabat, si hic factus erit, fabam mimum futurum? qua re, ut opinor, φιλοσοφητέον, id quod tu facis, et istos consulatus non flocci facteon.
Quod ad me scribis, te in Asiam statuisse non ire, equidem 14
mallem ut ires, ac vereor ne quid in ista re minus commode
fiat; sed tamen non possum reprehendere consilium tuum, praesertim cum egomet in provinciam non sim profectus. Epigram- 15
matis tuis, quae in Amaltheo posuisti, contenti erimus, praesertim

sion, to enable Lurco to bring forward his proposal, was an evasion of their spirit.
Claudus. Apprehensions of disaster were felt at Sparta in connection with the succession of Agesilaus, who was lame. Cp. Plut. Ages. 3.

1. Simul cum lege Aelia, 'under the obligations of the Aelian law.' Hofm. suggests 'insimulatus lege alia;' Boot suggests 'qui magistratus simul cum lege Aelia coniit;' Mr. Munro, whom Prof. Tyrrell follows, 'insimulatum lege Aelia.' Matth. omits 'cum lege Aelia;' Wesenb. suggests 'cum iis,' i.e. Catone et Domitio.

3. a. d. VI Kal. Sext., July 27th.

4. Novi est in lege hoc, 'the law contains the following novelty.' It was not carried. Cp. 'facto senatus consulto de ambitu . . . nulla lex perlata' Ad Att. 1. 18, 3.

5. Pronuntiarit, 'promised.' Cp. 'pecuniam quam pro reo pronuntiasset' Pro Cluentio 29, 78, and Pro Plancio 18, 45.

6. HS. CIↃ CIↃ CIↃ = 3000 sesterces, or nearly £25 for each tribe. The whole sum to be paid (in each year apparently, quoad vivat) would be about £875.

9. ἀποθέωσιν. Frequent in Cicero, and used by Strabo.

Hic. Afranius.

10. Fabam mimum. Billerbeck explains as meaning 'a joke,' like the election of a king at the Saturnalia, when boys elected a king, using beans to vote with. 'A Twelfth Night Royalty.' Cp. 'pueri ludentes, Rex eris aiunt' Hor. Ep. 1. 1, 59; Tac. Annal. 13, 15. Hofm. suggests 'fabae hilum;' Orell. 'Famam mimum, a mimo aliquo Fama inscripto;' Schütz 'fabulam mimum;' Wesenb. 'fabulam ac mimum,' but thinks that 'fabulam' may be a gloss.

φιλοσοφητέον, 'one must turn philosopher:' quite classical.

11. Istos consulatus, 'those consulships which some prize so highly.'

Facteon. A Greek form for 'faciendum,' suggested by φιλοσοφητέον.

12. Quod . . scribis, 'as to the fact that you write,' 'as to your writing.' See Madv. 398 b, Obs. 2.

Te . . non ire, 'that you have decided not to go to Asia' as legate to Quintus. See Appendix 3, § 2.

13. Mallem ut ires, 'I should have preferred your going.' 'Ut' is more usually omitted in such cases. See Madv. 372 b, Obs. 2. On the tense of 'mallem,' ib. 350 b, Obs. 1.

In ista re, 'in the administration of Quintus. He was hasty, and inclined to harshness. Cp. Ep. 15, 6.

15. Epigrammatis, 'inscriptions.' Under the statues of eminent Romans in his Amaltheum in Epirus (cp. Corn. Nep. Att. 18), Atticus had verses inscribed, giving a short account of their exploits.

16. Posuisti, 'have placed under my statue.'

cum et Thyillus nos reliquerit et Archias nihil de me scripserit,
ac vereor ne, Lucullis quoniam Graecum poëma condidit, nunc
16 ad Caecilianam fabulam spectet. Antonio tuo nomine gratias
egi eamque epistolam Mallio dedi; ad te ideo antea rarius
scripsi, quod non habebam idoneum, cui darem, nec satis scie-
17 bam, quo darem. Valde te venditavi. Cincius si quid ad me
tui negotii detulerit, suscipiam; sed nunc magis in suo est
occupatus, in quo ego ei non desum. Tu, si uno in loco es
futurus, crebras a nobis litteras exspecta; ast plures etiam ipse
18 mittito. Velim ad me scribas, cuius modi sit Ἀμαλθεῖον tuum,
quo ornatu, qua τοποθεσίᾳ, et quae poëmata quasque historias
de Ἀμαλθείᾳ habes ad me mittas: lubet mihi facere in Arpinati.
Ego tibi aliquid de meis scriptis mittam: nihil erat absoluti.

9. To ATTICUS (AD ATT. II. 1).

ROME, JUNE, 60 B.C. (694 A.U.C.)

1. I am glad that I had sent you my account of my consulship in Greek before receiving yours; I thus escape the suspicion of plagiarism, though perhaps difference of style would in any case have prevented its arising. 2. My book has won the applause of Posidonius and others: if you like it, try to promote its circulation in Greece. 3. You shall have the speeches you ask for, and others also; I am forming a collection of my speeches as consul, which I will send you. 4. I do not want to hurry your return, though I wish you had arranged your movements differently: if Clodius becomes more

1. Thyillus. Apparently a Greek poet. Cp. Ad Att. 1. 9, 2; 1. 12, 2.

Nos reliquerit, 'has deserted us,' 'not finished his promised inscriptions.' Matth.

Archias. A. Licinius Archias, a poet of Greek extraction, for whose claims to the Roman franchise Cicero pleaded afterwards. See Intr. to Part I, § 12. Archias wrote a heroic poem in praise of the Luculli (cp. Pro Arch. 9, 21), and another in praise of Cicero. Atticus seems to have asked for anything Thyillus or Archias might have written about Cicero.

3. Caecilianam fabulam, 'a poem on the Metelli' probably. Archias was intimate both with Q. Metellus Numidicus and with his son Pius. Cp. Pro Arch. 3. Others think there is a reference to Statius Caecilius, a freedman of the Metelli, and an early Latin poet, whose language is criticised by Cicero, Brut. 74, 258.

Antonio. C. Antonius seems to have complied with a request of Cicero that he would interest himself in the affairs of Atticus in Macedonia: for an account of which request cp. Ad Fam. 5. 5.

4. Mallio. Of this Mallius little seems to be known. L. Manlius of Neapolis is mentioned (Ad Fam. 13. 30, 1), and T. Manlius, a 'negotiator' at Thespiae (Ad Fam. 13. 22, 1).

6. Quo, 'with what address.'

Venditavi, 'praised you.' Boot thinks the name of the person to whom Cicero recommended Atticus has been lost. Cicero may mean, 'to Antonius,' as Matth. thinks, though the long passage intervening since the mention of his name is rather against this.

Cincius: see Ep. 1, 1, note on p. 26.

11. τοποθεσίᾳ: cp. Ep. 6, 5, note, p. 45.

12. Ἀμαλθείᾳ, the Amalthea of mythology.

Facere, sc. 'simile quid,' Billerb., 'a similar apartment to your Amaltheum.'

In Arpinati, 'on my estate at Arpinum.' Cp. Ep. 10, 4.

13. Nihil erat absoluti, 'I have nothing finished.' For the tense, see Ep. 1, 1, note, p. 26.

violent, I shall summon you at once. Metellus is an excellent consul. 5. Clodius is eager to become tribune of the people; I attacked him lately in the senate, but we are on fair terms with each other, notwithstanding my jokes about him. 6. You complain of my intimacy with Pompey, but I hope to influence both him and Caesar for the public good. 7. In any case I should be disposed for conciliation; but now that some of our nobles think only of indulging frivolous tastes, while 8. others by ill-timed obstinacy have estranged the senate and the equites from each other, and so increased the power of the populace—such a policy as mine is all the more necessary. 9. Favonius has failed to secure his election, and did not make a very good impression as accuser of Scipio Nasica. 10. Cato's ill-timed rigour is the cause of your difficulties at Sicyon. 11. I take much pleasure in my different country estates, though their purchase has rather embarrassed me. We hope that Gaul is tranquil. When may we expect you at Rome? 12. Please take care of Paetus' legacy of books, and see that I get them safe. I wrote to Octavius on your behalf.

CICERO ATTICO SAL.

Kal. Iuniis eunti mihi Antium et gladiatores M. Metelli cupide 1
relinquenti venit obviam tuus puer: is mihi litteras abs te et commentarium consulatus mei Graece scriptum reddidit; in quo laetatus sum *me* aliquanto ante de isdem rebus Graece item scriptum librum L. Cossinio ad te perferundum dedisse: nam, si ego tuum ante legissem, furatum me abs te esse diceres. Quamquam tua illa—legi enim libenter—horridula mihi atque incompta visa sunt, sed tamen erant ornata hoc ipso, quod ornamenta neglexerant, et, ut mulieres, ideo bene olere, quia nihil olebant, videbantur. Meus autem liber totum Isocrati myrothecium atque omnes eius discipulorum arculas ac non nihil etiam Aristotelia pigmenta consumpsit; quem tu Corcyrae, ut mihi aliis litteris

1. Gladiatores M. Metelli, 'the gladiatorial show which M. Metellus was about to provide.' Cicero had no taste for such amusements. Cp. Ad Fam. 7. 1, 2 and 3. The Metellus here mentioned was brother of Q. Metellus Creticus, and one of the praetors in 69 B.C. Cicero mentions him as a friend of Verres. In Verr. Act. 1. 9, 26. It does not appear with what object he was now going to exhibit gladiators.

Cupide relinquenti. Prof. Tyrrell has 'cupido relinquendi.' He also remarks, 'we may gather from Ad Att. 4. 4 b, 2 that it was a practice with wealthy Romans to buy gladiators as a speculation, and to give a show as a specimen of their powers.'

3. Commentarium consulatus mei, 'a memoir of my consulship written in Greek' by Atticus. Cp. 'tuum' a few lines below, and Corn. Nep. Atticus 18.

5. L. Cossinio. This Cossinius was a friend of Cicero and Varro. He belonged to the same tribe (Lemonia) with Ser. Sulpicius, to whom Cicero recommends him in Ad Fam. 13. 23.

6. Quamquam, 'and yet,' correcting the previous remark. See Madv. 443. The roughness of Atticus' style would prevent Cicero's being suspected of plagiarism.

9. Ideo . . olebant: cp. 'mulier recte olet ubi nihil olet.' Plaut. Mostell. 1. 3. 116.

10. Isocrati. A common form for the genitive. See Madv. 42. 2.

Myrothecium. Apparently the word only occurs here. It seems to mean much the same as 'arcula.'

11. Arculas, 'jewel-, or scent-boxes.'

Aristotelia pigmenta, 'colours,' ornaments, such as Aristotle recommends in his Rhetoric.

significas, strictim attigisti, post autem, ut arbitror, a Cossinio accepisti; quem tibi ego non essem ausus mittere, nisi eum lente
2 ac fastidiose probavissem. Quamquam ad me scripsit iam Rhodo Posidonius se, nostrum illud *ὑπόμνημα cum* legeret, quod ego ad eum, ut ornatius de isdem rebus scriberet, miseram, non modo non excitatum esse ad scribendum, sed etiam plane perterritum. Quid quaeris? conturbavi Graecam nationem: ita, volgo qui instabant ut darem sibi quod ornarent, iam exhibere mihi molestiam destiterunt. Tu, si tibi placuerit liber, curabis ut et Athenis sit et in ceteris oppidis Graeciae; videtur enim posse aliquid
3 nostris rebus lucis adferre. Oratiunculas autem et quas postulas et plures etiam mittam. quoniam quidem ea, quae nos scribimus adulescentulorum studiis excitati, te etiam delectant. Fuit enim mihi commodum, quod in eis orationibus, quae Philippicae nominantur, enituerat civis ille tuus [Demosthenes], et quod se ab hoc refractariolo iudiciali dicendi genere abiunxerat, ut *σεμνότερόν*

1. Strictim, 'hastily,' = 'obiter.' Schütz. The book seems to have been published before Atticus received a special revised copy.

2. Lente ac fastidiose, 'deliberately and with pedantic rigour.'

3. Probavissem, 'had tested,' 'revised.' Cp. 'villam publicam probare,' said of the censors. Or perhaps 'approved after revision.'

4. Posidonius. A pupil of Panaetius, born at Apamea in Syria about 135 B.C. After spending some time at Athens and Rhodes, he removed to Rome, 51 B.C., and died there shortly afterwards. In mental philosophy he is said to have been eclectic, with a leaning towards the Stoics; in physics he rather followed Aristotle.

ὑπόμνημα, 'a memoir,' = 'commentarius.' The word is used in this sense by Polyb. 1, 1, 6. None of the memoirs referred to has been preserved.

7. Qui instabant. Some Greek contemporaries of Cicero probably.

8. Exhibere = 'facessere,' 'create.' Forcell. Cp. de Nat. Deor. 1. 17, 45.

9. Ut . . sit, 'that it be in circulation.'

10. Aliquid . . lucis adferre, 'to give some distinction to.' Billerb.

11. Oratiunculas, 'my little speeches.' Billerb. supposes Cicero to refer to short declamations, written for young students to practise oratory with: but is not he speaking of his political orations with affected modesty? Cp. '*fuit enim* mihi commodum' etc. below.

12. Quae . . scribimus, 'which I commit to writing, urged by the eagerness of young men to have them.' Cicero affects to suppose that only the young would care to have copies of his speeches. Cp. 'oratio iuventuti nostrae deberi non potest' Ad Att. 4. 2, 2.

13. Fuit enim . . nominarentur. The substance of this passage may be thus stated: 'I will comply with your request, for I have found it suit my purpose to combine the orations of my consulship in one collection, just as Demosthenes did his Philippics.' Enim, I think, explains 'plures.' Atticus had apparently only asked for some of the consular speeches; Cicero promises all. Prof. Tyrrell follows Orelli in suspecting the passage from 'Fuit enim,' l. 13, to 'offerebam' on the next page to be spurious. Orelli, indeed, suspects the preceding passage beginning with 'Oratiunculas.'

14. Quod . . enituerat. The indicative is used as giving a real reason. See Madv. 357. The eminence of Demosthenes dated from his exchange of the position of a legal advocate for that of a political leader; Cicero hopes that his consulship will form a similar epoch in his own career.

16. Refractariolo, 'quarrelsome.' Forcell. The word is only found here apparently.

Ut σεμνότερός . . videretur, 'that he might assume a more dignified and statesmanlike position.' πολιτικώτερος is often used in this sense by Cicero, as by the Greeks.

τιν et πολιτικώτερος videretur, curare ut meae quoque essent orationes, quae consulares nominarentur; quarum una est in senatu Kal. Ianuariis, altera ad populum de lege agraria, tertia de Othone, quarta pro Rabirio, quinta de proscriptorum filiis, sexta, cum provinciam in contione deposui, septima, qua Catilinam emisi, octava, quam habui ad populum postridie quam Catilina profugit, nona in contione, quo die Allobroges † invocarunt, decima in senatu, Nonis Decembribus. Sunt praeterea duae breves, quasi ἀποσπασμάτια legis agrariae. Hoc totum σῶμα curabo ut habeas; et quoniam te cum scripta, tum res meae delectant, isdem ex libris perspicies et quae gesserim et quae dixerim: aut ne poposcisses; ego enim tibi me non offerebam. Quod quaeris, quid 4
sit quod te arcessam, ac simul impeditum te negotiis esse significas, neque recusas quin, non modo si opus sit, sed etiam si velim,

1. **Ut meae quoque . . nominarentur**, 'that there should be a collection of my speeches also, under the title "consulares."'

2. **Una est.** This was on the agrarian law of Rullus apparently. Only the beginning has been preserved.

3. **Altera**, the second against Rullus.

De Othone. Spoken to reconcile the mass of the citizens to the precedence which the law of L. Roscius Otho granted to the equites in the theatre. The people raised an outcry against Otho when he appeared in the theatre, but Cicero invited them to attend him to the temple of Bellona, and there appeased them. The law of Otho had been carried in 67 B.C. Pliny (H. N. 7. 30) refers to this speech of Cicero, which has been lost, as have the fifth and sixth here mentioned, with one of the two short ones on the agrarian law.

4. **Pro Rabirio**: cp. Intr. to Part I, § 9; also Merivale 1. 124; Mommsen 4. 1, 159 (E. T.).

De proscriptorum filiis. Sulla's laws had excluded the sons of proscribed citizens from high office, and the repeal of this provision was discussed in Cicero's consulship. Cicero persuaded the people, apparently, that the repeal would do more harm than good. Cp. In Pis. 2, 4; and a fragment of the speech itself, quoted by Quintil. Inst. Orat. 11. 1, 85.

5. **Cum provinciam . . deposui**, 'when I publicly renounced my claim to govern a province.' The two provinces to be administered by the consuls for 63 B.C., after their year of office had expired were apparently Macedonia and Gallia Cisalpina. Cicero seems first to have allowed his colleague Antonius to choose Macedonia, and then to have waived his own claim to Gallia Cisalpina, which was allotted to Q. Metellus Celer. Cp. Ep. 5, 3 and 4.

Septima. This and the three following are the four orations against Catiline which we now possess.

6. **Emisi**: cp. In Cat. 2. 1, 1; Pro Sull. 5.

7. **Invocarunt.** Manutius suggests 'indicarunt,' 'made their disclosures.' Cp. In Cat. 3. 3-5 for the facts.

8. **Duae breves.** One of these is extant as the third against Rullus.

9. **ἀποσπασμάτια**, 'fragments.' The word occurs here only apparently.

σῶμα, 'collection.' Not, apparently, classical quite in this sense.

11. **Aut ne poposcisses**, 'or you should not have asked for them.' Cp. 'fortasse non nemo vir fortis . . . dixerit restitissem' Pro Sestio 20, 45; also Zumpt L. G. § 529, note; Nägelsbach 98, a 2, 267.

12. **Ego enim . . offerebam**, 'for I did not want to force myself upon you.' Cp. Pro Rosc. Am. 38, 112.

Quod quaeris . . significas, 'as for your enquiry about the reason for my asking you to come, which you couple with a reference to your business engagements.'

13. **Quod te arcessam**, an indirect question. See Ep. 6, 1, note, on p. 42. Prof. Tyrrell follows the Medicean MS. and Klotz in reading 'quo' = 'in quam rem' for 'quod.'

14. **Neque recusas**, 'and yet do not refuse.' We might expect 'tamen' to follow 'neque.'

accurras, nihil sane est necesse; verum tamen videbare mihi tempora peregrinationis commodius posse discribere: nimis abes diu, praesertim cum sis in propinquis locis, neque nos te fruimur et tu nobis cares. Ac nunc quidem otium est, sed, si paulo plus furor Pulchelli progredi posset, valde ego te istim excitarem. Verum praeclare Metellus impedit et impediet. Quid quaeris? est consul φιλόπατρις et, ut semper iudicavi, natura bonus. Ille autem non simulat, sed plane tribunus pl. fieri cupit; qua *de* re cum in senatu ageretur, fregi hominem et inconstantiam eius reprehendi, qui Romae tribunatum pl. peteret, cum in Sicilia aedilitatem se petere dictitasset, neque magno opere dixi esse nobis laborandum, quod nihilo magis ei liciturum esset plebeio rem publicam perdere, quam similibus eius me consule patriciis esset licitum. Iam, cum se ille septimo die venisse a freto neque sibi obviam quemquam prodire potuisse et noctu se introisse dixisset in eoque se in contione iactasset, nihil ei novi dixi accidisse, ex Sicilia septimo die Romam: tribus horis Roma Interamnam; noctu introisse: item

1. **Nihil . . est necesse,** sc. 'te accurrere.' For the use of 'nihil' for 'non' see Madv. 455. Obs. 4.

Videbare . . discribere, 'I thought you might have arranged the times of your residence abroad more conveniently than you proposed to do.'

3. **In propinquis locis.** Atticus was in Epirus probably.

4. **Cares,** 'feel the want of me,' 'have to do without me.'

5. **Pulchelli:** see Ep. 8, 10, note on p. 59.

Posset. 'Non poterat impediente Metello.' Boot.

Valde . . excitarem, 'I should press you earnestly to come hither from where you are.'

6. **Metellus.** The consul Q. Metellus Celer. Cp. Ep. 4. 1, note.

7. **φιλόπατρις,** 'patriotic.' Polyb. 1. 14.

Natura bonus, 'naturally well disposed,' though set against me formerly by his brother. Cp. Epp. 4 and 5. Cicero's satisfaction with the conduct of Metellus probably arose from the latter's resistance to a proposal of C. Herennius for transferring Clodius to the plebs. Cp. Ad Att. 1. 18, 4; Pro Cael. 24. 60; Dion Cass. 37. 51.

Ille, P. Clodius.

Non simulat, 'does not merely pretend to desire the office:' supp. 'cupere.' 'It is not a mere pretence to frighten me.' Prof. Tyrrell. Manutius thinks that the words mean 'makes no false pretences as to his reason for wishing to become a plebeian.'

9. **Fregi,** 'humbled.'

Qui Romae . . dictitasset. Clodius had been quaestor, and in Sicily had said, apparently, that the next office for which he should stand would be the aedileship. But on his return to Rome he changed his mind and expressed anxiety to be tribune. As a patrician he could only become tribune by renouncing his order and going over to the plebs.

11. **Neque:** see note on § 4.

Magno opere . . laborandum, 'that we should have any serious cause for anxiety.'

13. **Similibus eius . . patriciis.** Catiline, Lentulus, and Cethegus were patricians.

Cum se ille . . iactasset. Clodius took credit for activity shewn in his travelling rapidly from the straits to Rome, and for his modesty in avoiding a public reception.

14. **A freto,** 'from the straits' of Messina.

15. **In eo,** 'on that account,' 'in' = 'ob, propter.' Forcell.

17. **Tribus horis Roma Interamnam,** sc. 'isse.' Clodius affirmed that he was at Interamna on the night when the outrage at the rites of the Bona Dea occurred at Rome, but Cicero swore that he had seen him at Rome three hours before that event happened. Interamna on the Nar was more than sixty miles from Rome; Interamna on the Liris was still more distant.

ante; non esse itum obviam: ne tum quidem, cum iri maxime debuerit. Quid quaeris? hominem petulantem modestum reddo non solum perpetua gravitate orationis, sed etiam hoc genere dictorum; itaque iam familiariter cum ipso cavillor ac iocor; quin etiam, cum candidatum deduceremus, quaerit ex me, num consuessem Siculis locum gladiatoribus dare? Negavi. 'At ego' inquit 'novus patronus instituam; sed soror, quae tantum habet consularis loci, unum mihi solum pedem dat.' 'Noli' inquam 'de uno pede sororis queri; licet etiam alterum tollas.' 'Non consulare' inquies 'dictum:' fateor; sed ego illam odi male consularem: [ea] est enim seditiosa, [ea] cum viro bellum gerit, neque solum cum Metello, sed etiam cum Fabio, quod eos † in hoc esse moleste fert. Quod de agraria lege quaeris, sane iam videtur refrixisse. Quod me quodam modo molli brachio de Pompeii familiaritate obiurgas, nolim ita existimes, me mei praesidii causa cum illo coniunctum esse, sed ita res erat instituta, ut, si inter nos esset aliqua forte dissensio, maximas in re publica discordias versari esset necesse: quod a me ita praecautum atque ita pro-

1. **Non esse itum obviam**, 'he did not have a public reception.'

Ne tum quidem, 'no, not on his entry into Caesar's house.'

Cum iri . . debuerit. Prof. Tyrrell remarks that there is a play on two senses of 'obviam ire,' 'to go to meet,' and 'to check.'

3. **Perpetua gravitate orationis** = 'perpetuae orationis,' 'with a serious set speech.'

4. **Dictorum**, 'repartees.' Cp. Ep. 6, 2, note.

Cavillor, 'saepe sumitur pro "iocari," "dicteria dicere."' Forcell.

5. **Deduceremus**, 'were attending to or from his home;' an honour paid to candidates by their friends. Cp. Q. Cic. de Pet. Cons. 9, 36; Cic. pro Muren. 34, 70.

6. **Siculis**, 'my Sicilian clients.' Cicero and Clodius had both been quaestors in Sicily, and both apparently were regarded as patrons by the natives of that province. Cp. Div. in Caec. 1, 2. On the relation in general cp. Cic. de Off. 1. 11. 35.

Gladiatoribus, 'at the gladiatorial games.' See on the abl. Ep. 8, 11, note, on p. 61.

7. **Tantum . . loci**, 'so much of her husband's space,' 'so much room at her disposal as a consul's wife.' A sister of P. Clodius had married Q. Metellus Celer, but seems to have been notoriously unfaithful to him. Cicero says of Clodius 'qui non pluris fecerat Bonam Deam quam tres sorores' Ep. 29, 15. See, too, Ep. 5, 6, note.

10. **Male consularem**, 'so unworthy to be the wife of a consul.' Boot. Or perhaps 'so little of a consul's wife.'

12. **Fabio.** This Fabius is said to have been a previous lover of Claudia.

In hoc esse = 'hoc agere; operam dare ne P. Clodius tribunus fiat.' Boot.

13. **De agraria lege.** L. Flavius, tribune for 61-60, proposed an agrarian law which Pompey supported, as one of its objects was to provide lands for his veterans. See Intr. to Part I, § 15; Dion Cass. 37. 50: Ad Att. 1. 18, 6; Mommsen 4. 1. 195; Merivale 1. 181.

14. **Refrixisse**, 'to have lost interest.' Cp. Ad Fam. 15. 17, 2.

Molli brachio, 'with a gentle touch, or hand.' Cp. 'levi brachio' Ad Att. 4. 16, 6.

15. **Mei praesidii causa**, 'for the sake of my own safety.' Compare with Cicero's profession here the following passage, 'consultor quaedam nobis ad retinendas opes nostras tuta ut spero via . . utor Pompeio familiarissime' Ad Att. 1. 17. 10.

16. **Ita res erat instituta**, 'matters had taken such a shape.' Billerb. Cp. 'rem aliter institutam offendimus' Ad Fam. 5. 17, 2.

18. **Ita praecautum . . deponeret.**

visum est, non ut ego de optima illa mea ratione decederem, sed
ut ille esset melior et aliquid de populari levitate deponeret;
quem de meis rebus, in quas cum multi incitarant, multo scito
gloriosius quam de suis praedicare; sibi enim bene gestae, mihi
conservatae rei publicae dat testimonium. Hoc facere illum mihi
quam prosit nescio; rei publicae certe prodest. Quid, si etiam
Caesarem, cuius nunc venti valde sunt secundi, reddo meliorem,
7 num tantum obsum rei publicae? Quin etiam, si mihi nemo
invideret, si omnes, ut erat aequum, faverent, tamen non minus
esset probanda medicina, quae sanaret vitiosas partes rei publicae,
quam quae exsecaret. Nunc vero, cum equitatus ille, quem ego
in clivo Capitolino te signifero ac principe collocaram, senatum
deseruerit, nostri autem principes digito se caelum putent attingere, si mulli barbati in piscinis sint, qui ad manum accedant,

'my precautions and forethought do not imply my abandoning my principles, but have his improvement in view.' For this use of ita .. ut, see Zumpt L. G. 726, and Ep. 30, 1, note.

1. De optima illa .. ratione, 'from my former constitutional policy.'

2. Ille, Pompeius.

De populari levitate, 'of his weak subserviency to the populace.' Cp. Philipp. 5. 18, 49. Pompey had perhaps suggested the seditious proceedings of Metellus Nepos; had not held consistent language about the suppression of Catiline's conspiracy; and was now intriguing with Caesar and Crassus. See Intr. to Part I, § 16.

3. In quas, 'to attack which.'

Multo . . . gloriosius, 'in far more flattering terms.' Cp. 'iudicia gloriosa' Ep. 28, 9.

5. Hoc . . mihi quam prosit. The prominence given to Cicero might bring him into trouble, though the appearance of a good understanding between him and Pompey was beneficial to the state.

7. Caesarem. This is the first passage in Cicero's letters in which the future dictator is mentioned as a prominent politician.

Cuius . . . venti . . . sunt secundi, 'who has the wind in his sails now;' 'whose prospects are very good.' Cp. Ep. 30, 4, note.

8. Tantum, 'so much as you hint by your remonstrances.' Manut.

Quin etiam .. medicina, 'even if my position were more secure than it is, my present policy would be the best.' Cp. Ep. 29, 11.

9. Ut erat aequum, 'as they ought.' For the indic. see Madv. 348 a.

10. Medicina, 'a treatment.'

11. Equitatus is substituted for the more common 'equester ordo.'

12. In clivo, on the sloping road from the forum to the Capitol. The equites assembled there in large numbers to protect the senate when it sat in the temple of Concord to deliberate on the fate of Lentulus and his accomplices.

Te signifero ac principe. Atticus was one of the equites. The metaphors in this passage are throughout military. Cp. 'cum princeps, cum signifer esset iuventutis' pro Sull. 12, 34; 'belli princeps,' Philipp. 2. 29, 71. I owe these references to Prof. Nettleship.

13. Deseruerit. For the causes of this breach between the two orders, see Intr. to Part I, §§ 14, 15.

Principes. Especially Lucullus and Hortensius. The frivolity of the nobles is described in similar terms, Ad Att. 2. 18, 6.

Digito .. caelum .. attingere. Apparently this phrase is not found elsewhere. Forcell. explains it 'summe beatum et velut diis proximum se putare.'

14. Mulli barbati, 'mullets,' barba gemina insignuntur inferiori labro' Pliny, H. N. 9. 17, 30. Mr. Jeans remarks that 'the mullus barbatus of naturalists is the plain red mullet, distinguished from our common or striped red mullet (mullus surmuletus). All kinds of mullet have two long barbules on the under jaw.'

Qui ad manum accedant, 'tame enough to come when called.'

alia autem neglegant, nonne tibi satis prodesse videor, si perficio ut nolint obesse qui possunt? Nam Catonem nostrum non tu amas 8
plus quam ego; sed tamen ille optimo animo utens et summa fide nocet interdum rei publicae: dicit enim tamquam in Platonis πολιτείᾳ, non tamquam in Romuli faece, sententiam. Quid verius quam in iudicium venire qui ob rem iudicandam pecuniam acceperit? censuit hoc Cato, adsensit senatus: equites curiae bellum, non mihi; nam ego dissensi. Quid impudentius publicanis renuntiantibus? fuit tamen retinendi ordinis causa faciunda iactura: restitit et pervicit Cato; itaque nunc, consule in carcere incluso, saepe item seditione commota, aspiravit nemo eorum, quorum ego concursu itemque ii consules, qui post me fuerunt, rem publicam defendere solebant. Quid ergo? istos, inquies, mercede conductos habebimus? Quid faciemus, si aliter non possumus? an libertinis atque etiam servis serviamus? Sed, ut tu ais, ἅλις σπουδῆς. Favo- 9
nius meam tribum tulit honestius quam suam, Lucceii perdidit.

2. Obesse (rei publicae) qui possunt (obesse). Cicero refers especially to Caesar and Pompey.

Nam introduces and answers an objection. Cp. Philipp. 11. 8, 18.

5. πολιτείᾳ, 'the ideal commonwealth' of Plato.

Faece, 'rabble.' Cp. Ep. 8, 11. apud sordem urbis et faecem. Prof. Tyrrell thinks that it is a strange expression, and suggests 'Romulea faece,' or 'Romulae' of our degenerate Rome.

Verius, = 'aequius.' Forcell.

6. In iudicium venire, 'should be brought to trial.' I do not know what cases of corruption are here referred to; probably some among the equites acting as judges. Cp. Ad Att. 1. 17, 8 '[equites] graviter tulerunt, promulgatum ex senatus consulto fuisse, ut de eis, qui ob iudicandum *pecuniam* accepissent, quaereretur.' Boot thinks that the decree referred to the court which tried Clodius. So, too, Long, Decl. of Rom. Rep. 3. 388.

7. Bellum, sc. 'indixerunt.' On the ellipse, see Madv. 479 d.

8. Renuntiantibus, 'giving up their contract. For the fact, cp. note on § 7, and Ad Att. 1. 17. 9.

9. Fuit tamen .. iactura, 'it would have been wise to submit to the public loss,' which would result from modifying the terms of the contract, for they had been very favourable to the state.

10. In carcere incluso. The tribune Flavius ordered Metellus Celer to be arrested for his opposition to the agrarian law. But the interposition of the other tribunes and of Pompey procured his release, after a detention of a few hours. See Merivale 1. 183.

11. Aspiravit, 'shewed himself even in the distance.' Nägelsb. 152, 382. 'Shewed any inclination to support Metellus.' 'Aspirare,' according to Forcell., is a weaker word than 'accedere.'

Eorum, 'of the equites.'

13. Istos .. habebimus, 'shall we buy the support of the equites?'

14. Quid faciemus .. possumus, 'what shall we do if we cannot get their support in any other way?' Cicero answers.

An libertinis .. serviamus? 'shall we be dependent on freedmen and even on slaves?' of whom the popular assemblies in great measure consisted. A. W. Zumpt, Comment. Epigraph. 1. 276, note 2, thinks that the reference is to the dependents of the nobles. Cp. 'pedisequorum nostrorum' Ep. 10, 1, note.

15. ἅλις σπουδῆς, 'enough of serious topics.'

Favonius: see Ep. 7. 5, note.

16. Meam tribum. Cicero, as an Arpinate, voted in the Cornelian tribe. Cp. Livy 38, 36.

Tulit honestius, 'carried by a larger majority.'

Lucceii. What tribe this was does not appear. On Lucceius, see Ep. 7. 7, note.

Accusavit Nasicam honeste, ac moleste tamen dixit, ita ut Rhodi videretur molis potius quam Moloni operam dedisse; mihi, quod defendissem, leviter succensuit. Nunc tamen petit iterum rei publicae causa. Lucceius quid agat, scribam ad te, cum Caesarem videro, qui aderit biduo. Quod Sicyonii te laedunt, Catoni et eius aemulatori attribues Servilio. Quid? ea plaga nonne ad multos bonos viros pertinet? sed, si ita placuit, laudemus; deinde in discessionibus soli relinquamur! Amalthea mea te exspectat et [illegible]iget tui. Tusculanum et Pompeianum valde me delectant, nisi

[illegible] Nasicam. For an account of P. [illegible] Nasica, see on Ep. 1, 3. The present [illegible]ention may have been for bribery prac[illegible]ed against Favonius.

Honeste, 'from honourable motives.'

Moleste. Does this word mean 'spitefully,' or 'to the annoyance of his hearers?' As it seems to be used to discredit Favonius' training, I should prefer the second version. Prof. Nettleship suggests 'laboured,' 'strained,' as versions of 'molestus,' remarking that it means 'affected' in Catull. 42, 8; Ovid Art. Amat. 1. 6. Prof. Tyrrell retains the MS. 'inhoneste,' 'shabbily,' and 'modeste.'

Ita ut .. molis .. operam dedisse, 'so that it seemed he must have worked in a mill at Rhodes, and not studied under Molon.' There is a play on the words 'moleste,' 'molis,' 'Moloni.' Apollonius, surnamed Molon, a native of Alabanda, was a rhetorician of considerable reputation at Rhodes. See Intr. to Part I, §§ 1, 2; also Brut. 90, 312; Schol Bob. in Orat. Pro Planc. 34, 3. Mr. Long, however, in a note on Plut. Caes. 3, expresses a doubt of the identity of Molon and Apollonius. Civil Wars of Rome, vol. iii. p. 223.

3. Petit iterum, 'he is again a candidate.' Boot conjectures that after having failed in a contest for the praetorship he stood for the tribuneship.

Rei publicae causa, 'solely for the public good.' Slightly ironical.

5. Aderit biduo. Caesar was on his return from Lusitania, where he had been propraetor.

Laedunt, sc. 'by not paying their debts.' Cp. Ad Att. 1. 19, 9. A decree seems to have been passed, on the motion of Servilius, for checking the employment of violence in the exaction of debts alleged to be owing to Roman citizens from provincials and citizens of allied states. Sicyon was, apparently, an 'urbs libera.' Prof. Tyrrell on Ad Att. 1. 19, 9 thinks that the decree perhaps provided that debts incurred by *populi liberi* were not cognizable in Roman courts of law. The Servilius here mentioned is P. Servilius Vatia Isauricus, son of the first who bore the name Isauricus. He was praetor 54 B.C., and then apparently an opponent of the triumvirs, but sided with Caesar in the civil war, and was his colleague as consul in 48 B.C. After Caesar's death he acted generally with Cicero, and with the consuls Hirtius and Pansa; but afterwards was reconciled to Antony and Octavian. Cp. Ad Fam. 10. 12, 2–4; 13. 2, 1; Philipp. 11. 8, 19; 11, 10, 25.

6. Ea plaga nonne .. pertinet? 'does not that blow "affect the interests of" many good citizens?' Cicero refers to the decree of the senate mentioned above, which would be unwelcome to the moneyed class at Rome; or perhaps to the general estrangement of the equites from the senate. Prof. Nettleship remarks that 'pertinere ad' means 'to reach to.' Cp. Pro Rosc. Amer. 33, 94 ne ad plures oratio mea pertinere videatur.

7. Si ita placuit, 'if such was the senate's pleasure.'

Laudemus, 'let us approve what has been done.'

Deinde .. relinquamur, 'and then be left alone'—i.e. unsupported by the equites—'in all future discussions.' 'Discessiones' is not apparently used here in the technical sense, of divisions in the senate. Billerb. Wesenb. and Prof. Tyrrell retain the MS. 'dissensionibus' in their texts, but Prof. Tyrrell thinks 'discessionibus' a good conjecture.

8. Amalthea mea. Apparently a gymnasium attached to Cicero's villa at Arpinum, which he had named after that of Atticus in Epirus. Cp. Ep. 6, 1; 8, 15.

9. Indiget tui, 'wants you to set it in order.'

Tusculanum et Pompeianum. Cicero's villas near Tusculum and Pompeii, which are often referred to in his letters. Cp. Appendix 5, 1.

quod me, illum ipsum vindicem aeris alieni, aere non Corinthio, sed hoc circumforaneo obruerunt. In Gallia speramus esse otium. Prognostica mea cum oratiunculis propediem exspecta; et tamen, quid cogites de adventu tuo, scribe ad nos: nam mihi Pomponia nuntiari iussit, te mense Quintili Romae fore; id a tuis litteris, quas ad me de censu tuo miseras, discrepabat. Pactus, ut antea 12
ad te scripsi, omnes libros, quos frater suus reliquisset, mihi donavit. Hoc illius munus in tua diligentia positum est: si me amas, cura ut conserventur et ad me perferantur; hoc mihi nihil potest esse gratius, et cum Graecos, tum vero diligenter Latinos ut conserves velim. Tuum esse hoc munusculum putabo. Ad Octavium dedi litteras; cum ipso nihil eram locutus: neque enim ista tua negotia provincialia esse putabam, neque te in tocullionibus habebam; sed scripsi, ut debui, diligenter.

1. **Vindicem aeris alieni**, 'maintainer of credit,' 'protector of creditors.' Smith: Forcell. Cicero might claim this title on the ground both (1) of his opposition to the anarchical plots of Catiline, and (2) of a measure for an equitable settlement of debts, which seems to have been introduced during his consulship. Cp. Ad Fam. 5. 6, 2; In Cat. 2. 8, 18; Sall. Cat. 21.

Aere, used in a double sense. On the bronze of Corinth, cp. Smith's Dict. of Antiq. sub voc. Aes, p. 25. Cicero's buildings had burdened him with debts to the money-lenders who lived near the forum: 'aere circumforaneo.'

2. **In Gallia . . otium**, 'we hope that tranquillity prevails in Gaul.' Cp. 'spero enim . . et confido te iam ut volumus valere' Ad Att. 6. 9, 1; and see Ep. 1, 1, note, on p. 26. Prof. Tyrrell thinks that 'esse' may stand for 'futurum esse,' and may be one of Cicero's Plautinisms. The peace of Gaul was endangered or disturbed by the intention of the Helvetii to emigrate, and by quarrels between the Aedui and Ariovistus. Cp. Caes. de Bell. Gall. 1; and Mommsen 4. 1, 235–237.

3. **Prognostica mea**, 'my translation of the Prognostica of Aratus.' Passages from this work are quoted or referred to, Ad Att. 15. 16 b; and De Divin. 1. 7, 13.

Et tamen, 'and yet,' without waiting for their arrival.

4. **Pomponia**, sister of Atticus, and wife of Q. Cicero. The marriage was not very happy; cp. Ad Att. 5. 1; 6. 2, 1 and 2.

6. **De censu tuo.** Hoot compares 'ne abacus censeare curabo . . sub lustrum autem censeri germani negotiatoris est' Ad Att. 1. 18, 8.

Paetus. For an account of L. Papirius Paetus, see Ep. 87, note. His kinsman Ser. Claudius, had died, leaving a handsome library, apparently in Epirus.

Ut antea . . scripsi: cp. Ad Att. 1. 20, 7.

7. **Quos . . reliquisset**, 'which his brother, as he (Paetus) believed, had left;' or 'which his brother might have left.' See Madv. 368.

Frater, 'half-brother,' 'cousin,' or perhaps a brother who had passed by adoption into the Claudian family.

8. **Hoc illius . . positum est**, 'it depends on your care whether I ever profit by his gift.' Cp. Ad Att. 1. 20, 7 for Cicero's anxiety that Atticus should serve him in this matter.

10. **Cum Graecos, tum vero . . Latinos**, 'both the Greek books, and more especially the Latin;' 'cum . . tum' brings the second member of the comparison more prominently forward than 'tum . . tum.' See Zumpt L. G. 723.

11. **Tuum esse . . putabo**, 'I shall consider myself indebted to you for the books.'

Ad Octavium . . putabam, 'I have written to recommend you to Octavius: I did not speak to him on the subject, for before he left Rome I did not know that your business had to do with his province.'

13. **Provincialia** means apparently 'in the province of Octavius,' 'in Macedonia.' Wiel. Metzg. C. Octavius, father of the emperor Augustus succeeded C. Antonius as governor of Macedonia. He had been praetor,

10. TO ATTICUS (AD ATT. II. 16).

FORMIAE, EARLY IN MAY, 59 B.C. (695 A.U.C.)

1. I was at first much disturbed by your news about the Campanian domains, but regained my composure on considering that the proposed measure will not satisfy the populace, and will arouse the indignation of good citizens as threatening ruin to our finances. 2. I do not understand Pompey's language. Hitherto he has avoided committing himself to all Caesar's measures, but now seems inclined to throw off the mask. 3. I do not wish to take any part in politics at present, and think of devoting myself to literature. 4. My letter from Quintus shewed as much inconsistency as yours. He does not seem to have received one from me, as to the exaction of certain duties in his province. If I have to express an opinion on the subject here, I must declare against the publicani, but I had rather be silent. I hope that the quaestors will pay Quintus in our currency. Come to me at Arpinum.

CICERO ATTICO SAL.

1 Cenato mihi et iam dormitanti pridie K. Maias epistola est illa reddita, in qua de agro Campano scribis. Quid quaeris? primo ita me pupugit, ut somnum mihi ademerit, sed id cogitatione magis quam molestia; cogitanti autem haec fere succurrebant: primum ex eo, quod superioribus litteris scripseras, ex familiari te illius audisse prolatum iri aliquid, quod nemo improbaret, maius aliquid timueram; hoc mihi eius modi non videbatur. Deinde, ut me egomet consoler, omnis exspectatio largitionis agrariae in agrum Campanum videtur esse derivata, qui ager, ut dena iugera

but was never consul. Cicero expresses a very high opinion of him (Ep. 15, 7), and says that he would have been consul but for his premature death, Philipp. 5. 6, 15.

Neque . . habebam, 'nor did I class you among petty usurers.'

Toculliónibus. This word may be a diminutive from τόκος, but seems not to occur elsewhere. Prof. Tyrrell suggests 'a bit of an usurer' thinking that the diminutive has a softening force.

2. **De agro Campano.** One of Caesar's agrarian laws proposed the assignation of this district to the people. See Intr. to Part I, § 17.

Quid quaeris: see Ep. 7, 6, note, on p. 51.

3. **Pupugit,** 'excited.' The verb is often used metaphorically by Cicero.

Cogitatione . . molestia, 'more from the thoughts it suggested than from vexation.'

5. **Primum . . scripseras,** 'first from a statement in your last letter.'

Ex familiari . . illius, 'from some intimate friend of Caesar.'

6. **Prolatum . . improbaret,** 'that some proposal would be made which would satisfy everybody:' i.e. probably, from the context, every partisan of an agrarian law.

Maius aliquid, 'some more sweeping measure.'

7. **Hoc mihi . . videbatur,** 'this does not (see Ep. 1, 1, note) seem to answer to your description.' It would satisfy too few, Cicero means.

Eius modi refers either to 'maius aliquid' or to 'quod nemo improbaret.'

8. **Largitionis agrariae,** 'of gratuitous assignation of land.'

9. **Derivata,** 'diverted, or directed, to;' 'concentrated on' Tyrrell.

Ut dena iugera sint, 'supposing each settler to get ten jugera' only. It would not be a large allowance. For 'ut' =

sint, non amplius hominum quinque milia potest sustinere: reliqua omnis multitudo ab illis abalienetur necesse est. Praeterea, si ulla res est, quae bonorum animos, quos iam video esse commotos, vehementius possit incendere, haec certe est, et eo magis, quod portoriis Italiae sublatis, agro Campano diviso, quod vectigal superest domesticum praeter vicensimam? quae mihi videtur una contiuncula clamore pedisequorum nostrorum esse peritura. 8

Gnaeus quidem noster iam plane quid cogitet nescio:

> φυσᾷ γὰρ οὐ σμικροῖσιν αὐλίσκοις ἔτι,
> ἀλλ' ἀγρίαις φύσαισι, φορβειᾶς ἄτερ·

qui quidem etiam istuc adduci potuerit. Nam adhuc haec ἐσοφίζετο, se leges Caesaris probare, actiones ipsum praestare debere; agrariam legem sibi placuisse, potuerit intercedi necne, nihil ad se pertinere; de rege Alexandrino placuisse sibi aliquando confici;

'supposing that,' see Madv. 440 a. Obs. 4.

1. **Reliqua . . multitudo**, 'the rest of the numerous expectants.' Caesar did provide for 20,000 settlers, by dividing both the ager Stellatis and the ager Campanus among them. See above; also Velleius 2. 44; Suet. Iul. 20.

3. **Bonorum**, 'of the friends of the constitution.'

4. **Vehementius**, 'more violently, or seriously, than another.'

5. **Portoriis**. Customs-duties had been abolished in the Italian ports in 60 B.C. Cp. Dion Cass. 37, 51. But, according to Suet. Iul. 43, Caesar reimposed them on foreign goods: after he acquired supreme power, probably.

6. **Domesticum**, 'levied in Italy.'

Vicensimam manumissorum. A tax of five per cent. on the value of slaves emancipated. It was first imposed by a Lex Manlia, passed 357 B.C. Cp. Livy 7. 16 for the details.

Una contiuncula . . . nostrorum, 'will be abolished by the outcries of the rabble after one popular harangue.' 'Contiuncula' seems not to be found elsewhere. The ablative here expresses the more remote cause, clamore, the instrument, of what Cicero feared. See Madv. 255 and 254.

7. **Pedisequorum**, 'lackeys,' as the populace was so largely composed of freedmen. Cp. Ep. 9, 8, and note.

9. **φυσᾷ γὰρ κ.τ.λ.** Soph. Fragm. 723 ap. Dind.

αὐλίσκοις, 'pipes.'

10. **φύσαισι**, 'blasts,' lit. 'bellows.' It was usual for pipers to wear a mouth-band for compressing their cheeks while playing, called φορβεία or 'capistrum.' Cp. Smith, Dict. of Antiq. p. 238.

φορβειᾶς ἄτερ, 'wildly.'

11. **Qui quidem . . potuerit**, 'seeing that it was found possible to bring him even to the position you describe,' of advocating the agrarian law in its original shape. For the position of 'quidem' in such passages, see Madv. 471; and for an account of Caesar's legislation in this year, Intr. to Part I, § 17.

Adhuc, opposed to nunc vero below.

Haec ἐσοφίζετο, 'he resorted to the following evasions.'

12. **Actiones . . debere**, 'that Caesar must himself be responsible for the means he took to carry them.'

13. **Agrariam legem**: see Intr. as above.

Potuerit intercedi necne, 'whether a veto was possible or not.' Three tribunes did interpose. See Mommsen 4. 1, 202, E. T.

14. **De rege Alexandrino**. The recognition of the title of Ptolemy XII Auletes to the throne of Egypt had been brought about by the influence of the triumvirs: see Mommsen 4. 1, 152, 153; Merivale 1. 371, 376, 397. Cicero seems to have been offered an embassy to this prince. See Ad Att. 2. 5, 1.

Placuisse sibi . . confici, 'that he had approved of a settlement being made at length.'

Bibulus de caelo tum servasset necne, sibi quaerendum non fuisse;
de publicanis, voluisse *se* illi ordini commodare; quid futurum
fuerit, si Bibulus tum in forum descendisset, se divinare non
potuisse. Nunc vero, Sampsicerame, quid dices? vectigal te nobis
in monte Antilibano constituisse, agri Campani abstulisse? quid,
hoc quem ad modum obtinebis? 'Oppressos vos' inquit 'tenebo
exercitu Caesaris.' Non mehercule me tu quidem tam isto exercitu quam ingratis animis eorum hominum, qui appellantur boni,
qui mihi non modo praemiorum sed ne sermonum quidem umquam
8 fructum ullum aut gratiam rettulerunt. Quod si in eam me partem
incitarem, profecto iam aliquam reperirem resistendi viam: nunc
prorsus hoc statui, ut, quoniam tanta controversia est Dicaearcho,
familiari tuo, cum Theophrasto, amico meo, ut ille tuus τὸν

1. **Bibulus de caelo . . . servasset necne**, 'whether Bibulus had watched for omens in the sky or not.' A magistrate could suspend public business at Rome by declaring 'se servasse'—or 'servaturum'—'de caelo.' Cp. Philipp. 2. 32 and 33. **Tum**, 'when the agrarian law was being discussed.' See below. M. Calpurnius Bibulus, one of the consuls for this year, was one of the most obstinate of the optimates. For notices of his conduct as consul, see Intr. to Part I, §§ 17, 18, and reff. He governed Syria at the same time that Cicero was governing Cilicia, and excited Cicero's jealousy on various grounds. Cp. Ad Att. 6. 8, 5; 7. 2, 6. In the civil war between Caesar and Pompey, Bibulus commanded a fleet for the latter in the Adriatic, and died in consequence of his great exertions. Cp. Caes. Bell. Civ. 3. 18.

2. **De publicanis . . . commodare**, 'as for the publicani, he had been willing to do that order a service.' See Intr. as above; also Ad Att. 1. 17, 9; Pro Plancio 14. 35.

3. **Fuerit.** For the tense, see Madv. 383.

Tum = 'on the day when the agrarian law was brought forward.' Bibulus was then driven by violence from the forum. Cp. Dion Cass. 38. 6.

4. **Nunc vero . . abstulisse?** 'but now,' after the sacrifice of the Campanian domains, 'what will you say? that you have increased our resources in the East, while diminishing them in Italy?' If Pompey did say this he used a good argument; the improvement of the Roman revenues by conquests in the East rendered the produce of the Campanian domains less indispensable to the treasury.

Sampsiceramus, a prince of Emesa. Here a nickname for Pompey.

Vectigal . . in . . Antilibano constituisse, 'that you have established a source of revenue for us on Antilibanus,' by making Judaea and Syria tributary. Antilibanus was a mountain range running to the east of Coele Syria.

5. **Quid . . obtinebis**, 'how will you defend, or make good, this?' 'Quid' seems pleonastic. See Zumpt 769, and cp. Madv. 449, and 395. Obs. 7.

7. **Exercitu Caesaris.** Caesar's army would threaten the capital from Cisalpine Gaul, and recruits or soldiers on leave of absence might mingle with the populace at Rome.

Quidem: see note on p. 74, l. 11.

9. **Qui mihi . . rettulerunt**, 'who, far from showing their gratitude by material rewards, have not even thanked me in words.'

Praemiorum . . sermonum are instances of the genitivus definitivus. See Madv. 286, Obs. 2. Cicero's meaning seems to be that he should not fear Caesar's army if he were sure of the support of the nobles. Or perhaps that he did not care to exert himself for so ungrateful a faction.

10. **Si in eam . . incitarem**, 'if I aroused myself to oppose that party,' i.e. the party of the triumvirs. On this use of 'in,' see Ep. 9, 6, note on p. 69.

12. **Dicaearcho.** Dicaearchus of Messana was a philosopher of the Peripatetic school, and is often mentioned by Cicero. He was one of Aristotle's younger pupils, and lived about 350–285 B.C.

13. **Theophrasto.** Theophrastus of

πρακτικὸν βίον longe omnibus anteponat, hic autem *τὸν θεωρητικόν*, utrique a me mos gestus esse videatur; puto enim me Dicaearcho adfatim satis fecisse, respicio nunc ad hanc familiam, quae mihi non modo, ut requiescam, permittit, sed reprehendit, quia non semper quierim. Qua re incumbamus, o noster Tite, ad illa praeclara studia et eo, unde discedere non oportuit, aliquando revertamur. Quod de Quinti fratris epistola scribis, ad me quoque 4
fuit *πρόσθε λέων, ὄπιθεν δὲ* —. Quid dicam nescio: nam ita deplorat primis versibus mansionem suam, ut quemvis movere possit; ita rursus remittit, ut me roget, ut annales suos emendem et edam. Illud tamen, quod scribit, animadvertas velim, de portorio circumvectionis; ait se de consilii sententia rem ad senatum reiecisse: nondum videlicet meas litteras legerat, quibus ad eum re consulta et explorata rescripseram non deberi. Velim, si qui Graeci iam Romam ex Asia de ea causa venerunt, videas et, si tibi videbitur, iis demonstres, quid ego de ea re sentiam. Si possum discedere, ne causa optima in senatu pereat, ego satis

Eresus, succeeded Aristotle as the head of the Peripatetic school. Cicero derives the terms *πρακτικὸς* and *θεωρητικὸς βίος* from Aristotle. Cp. Arist. Eth. 1. 5; 10. 7: Polit. 7. 2.

3. **Familiam**, 'school of philosophy.' Forcell.

5. **Illa praeclara studia**, 'our old and noble pursuits.' The study of philosophy is referred to.

6. **Eo**, 'to a life of study and retirement.'

Oportuit. On the mood, see Ep. 9, 7, note.

8. *πρόσθε λέων ὄπιθεν δὲ δράκων μέσση δὲ χίμαιρα*. Il. 6. 181. Cicero complains of the inconsistency of his brother's letter, and Atticus seems to have received one, to which he made the same objection: hence quoque, 'as to you.'

9. **Mansionem.** His prolonged residence in Asia as governor.

10. **Remittit**, 'grows less earnest;' 'tones down.' Prof. Tyrrell.

Annales. Perhaps Quintus was referring to his official journals; perhaps to some historical work.

11. **De portorio circumvectionis.** These words are variously explained. Billerb. supposes them to mean a tax on goods conveyed from one town of the province to another: Boot that the portorium was a duty levied on goods re-exported in default of a purchaser.

12. **De consilii sententia**, 'with the approval of his legal advisers.' See Ep. 8, 5, note, and Smith's Dict. of Antiq. sub voc. 'conventus.'

14. **Re consulta**, 'having considered the matter.' Forcell. Cp. Livy 2. 28.

Non deberi, 'that there is no obligation to pay.'

Si qui . . venerunt, 'I beg you to see such Greeks as have already come.' Cicero often uses 'videre' in this sense in his letters.

17. **Discedere**, sc. 'de sententia' 'renounce my opinion on the case.' Schütz. If this be the meaning of 'discedere,' 'si possum' must mean 'if I can consistently with my duty,' cp. supr. § 2, 'potuerit intercedi necne.' But perhaps 'discedere' has the same sense as in Ep. 13, 16, and the general sense may be 'if I can get out of the affair on any terms which will save the best of causes from ruin.' Prof. Nettleship suggests that 'de re' may have dropped out after 'discedere,' if I can get out of the matter.'

Causa optima. The cause of the constitution, which depended on a good understanding being maintained between the senate and the equites. The denial of the obligation of the provincials to pay the tax referred to would annoy the equites, for their gains as farmers of the revenue would depend in part on its payment.

Pereat, 'should be lost.'

faciam publicanis, εἰ δὲ μή,—vere tecum loquar—in hac re malo universae Asiae et negotiatoribus; nam eorum quoque vehementer interest. Hoc ego sentio valde nobis opus esse. Sed tu id videbis. Quaestores autem, quaeso, num etiam de cistophoro dubitant? nam si aliud nihil erit, cum erimus omnia experti, ego ne illud quidem contemnam, quod extremum est. Te in Arpinati videbimus et hospitio agresti accipiemus, quoniam maritumum hoc contempsisti.

11. To ATTICUS (AD ATT. II. 18).

ROME, MAY OR JUNE, 59 B.C. (695 A.U.C.)

1. Your letters show great anxiety to hear the news. I can only say that we live under great restraint. Curio's opposition to our masters is very popular, and their tool, Fufius, is insulted wherever he appears. 2. Tyranny cannot put down all expression of opinion, which, indeed is rather freer than it was just lately. The law about the Campanian domains, prescribes an oath to be taken by all candidates for office: Laterensis has won great credit by refusing to take it. 3. I reproach myself with want of independence, yet cannot prevail upon myself to accept Caesar's offers of protection. 4. Various circumstances trouble me; come at once if I send for you.

CICERO ATTICO SAL.

1 Accepi aliquot epistolas tuas, ex quibus intellexi, quam suspenso animo et sollicito scire averes, quid esset novi: tenemur

1. Malo, sc. 'satisfacere.' On the ellipse, see Madv. 478, Obs. 3.

2. Asiae. The province of Asia, which comprehended the districts on the coast of the Aegean, with part of Phrygia. Cp. Smith, Dict. of Geogr. 1. 238, 239.

Negotiatoribus. This word generally means bankers, or money-lenders; but it is difficult to see how they should have a different interest from the equites, unless the exaction of the 'portorium' was likely to make their provincial debtors insolvent. See Smith, Dict. of Antiq. 794.

3. Hoc ego .. opus esse .. videbis, 'I see that this is a matter of great importance to us, but I leave it to your judgment.'

Nobis, either 'to my brother and me,' or 'to our party.' Boot suggests 'bonis,' which would give the same sense as the last version. 'Opus esse' is less strong than 'necesse esse.' It means only 'very desirable,' not 'indispensable.' Cp. Ep. 29, 25.

4. Etiam .. dubitant? 'are they still hesitating?' as to the mode of payment.

Cistophoro. The cistophorus was a Greek coin, stamped with the cista, serpents, and other emblems. According to Hultsch, Metrologie, 270 (Berlin 1862), the cistophorus was worth three denarii. Q. Cicero wished to have his official stipend in denarii, but the quaestors preferred to give him orders on Asiatic money-changers for cistophori, of which Pompey had a great many struck before leaving Asia. Cp. Ad Att. 2. 6, 2.

5. Nam si .. extremum est, 'If we can get nothing better, I shall not complain of the last resource,' i.e. payment in the cistophorus. Quintus apparently would lose on the exchange into Roman currency, the nominal value of the cistophorus being higher than the real.

7. Hospitio agresti, 'entertainment in a country house.'

Maritumum. Cicero was now at his villa near Formiae.

10. Scire averes. Atticus was probably in Epirus.

Tenemur undique, 'we are hemmed in on all sides.' See Mommsen 4. 1, 205.

undique, neque iam quo minus serviamus recusamus, sed mortem et eiectionem quasi maiora timemus, quae multo sunt minora; atque hic *est* status, qui una voce omnium gemitur neque verbo cuiusquam sublevatur: σκοπὸς est, ut suspicor, illis, qui tenent, nullam cuiquam largitionem relinquere. Unus loquitur et palam adversatur adulescens Curio: huic plausus maximi, consalutatio forensis perhonorifica, signa praeterea benevolentiae permulta a bonis impertiuntur; Fufium clamoribus et convitiis et sibilis consectantur. His ex rebus non spes, sed dolor est maior, cum videas civitatis voluntatem solutam, virtutem alligatam. Ac ne 2 forte quaeras κατὰ λεπτὸν de singulis rebus, universa res eo est deducta, spes ut nulla sit aliquando non modo privatos, verum etiam magistratus liberos fore. Hac tamen in oppressione sermo in circulis dumtaxat et in conviviis est liberior, quam fuit; vincere incipit timorem dolor, sed ita, ut omnia sint plenissima desperationis. Habet etiam Campana lex exsecrationem

1. **Neque . . recusamus . . minora,** 'we no longer object to be slaves, and fear death and exile as greater evils than slavery, whereas they are really not nearly so great.'

2. **Eiectio** seems not to be used elsewhere as simply equivalent to banishment.

3. **Hic est status . . sublevatur,** 'our position is one which all only lament, and no one says a word to relieve.' A word meaning 'only' is often omitted in such passages. See Nägelsb. 84, 231.

4. σκοπὸς, 'the aim.'

Qui tenent, sc. 'rem publicam;' or perhaps 'now,' 'our masters.' Cp. 'tenemus,' above. For the more absolute use, cp. 'in me dum qui tenent' Ad Att. 7. 12, 3.

5. **Nullam . . relinquere,** 'to leave no one else any opportunity of giving.' Cp. Suet. Iul. 20, quoted by Prof. Tyrrell. Florus 3. 17, where M. Livius Drusus says, 'nihil se ad largitionem ulli reliquisse nisi si quis aut caenum dividere vellet aut caelum.'

6. **Adulescens Curio:** cp. Ep. 7, 5, note.

Consalutatio, 'multorum salutatio.' Forcell. A rare word apparently.

7. **Forensis,** 'when he appears in the forum.' Forcell.

8. **Fufium.** Q. Fufius Calenus was tribune 62–61 B.C., and employed his influence on behalf of Clodius. He seems to have been praetor in this year (59 B.C.), and served under Caesar in the Gaulish and civil wars. During the war of Mutina, Antony's wife and children found a refuge in his house, and he often pleaded for conciliation in the senate, to Cicero's annoyance. See Intr. to Part V, § 13; Philipp. 12, 1, 3, alib.

10. **Voluntatem . . alligatam,** 'that the people's wishes are free, but their power for action is under restraint.'

Ac ne . . quaeras, supp. 'I will tell you.' Cp. 'ut ne quid praetermittam, Camonius ad me litteras misit' Ad Att. 12, 11.

11. **κατὰ λεπτὸν,** 'bit by bit.' The expression does not seem to be used by classical Greek authors.

Universa . . deducta, 'in general things have come to this.'

14. **Circulis,** 'clubs,' 'coteries.'

Dumtaxat qualifies the previous statement: 'speech is freer in social gatherings at least.'

15. **Ita, ut . . desperationis,** 'without preventing a general despondency' from prevailing. For this use of 'ita, ut,' see Ep. 1, 1, note.

16. **Habet . . Iuliis.** 'The law about the Campanian domains, prescribes an oath to be taken publicly by all candidates for any magistracy, "that they will not suggest any other mode of occupation than that which the Julian laws direct."' Billerb. On the Julian laws see Intr. to Part I, § 17.

Etiam, = 'moreover.'

Exsecrationem. An oath, in which the juror imprecates curses on himself if he breaks it. Forcell. Boot thinks the words 'in contione' suspicious. See upon them, A. W. Zumpt, Comment. Epigraph. 1. 284, foll. and Intr. as above. I have translated

in contione candidatorum, si mentionem fecerint, qua aliter ager possideatur atque ut ex legibus Iuliis: non dubitant iurare ceteri; Laterensis existimatur laute fecisse, quod tribunatum pl. petere destitit, ne iuraret. Sed de re publica non libet plura scribere: displiceo mihi nec sine summo scribo dolore. Me 3
tueor, ut oppressis omnibus, non demisse, ut tantis rebus gestis, parum fortiter. A Caesare valde liberaliter invitor [in legationem illam], sibi ut sim legatus, atque etiam libera legatio voti causa datur. Sed haec et praesidii apud pudorem Pulchelli non habet satis et a fratris adventu me ablegat; illa et munitior est et non impedit quo minus adsim, cum velim: hanc ego teneo, sed usurum me non puto; neque tamen scit quisquam.

them 'publicly.' Prof. Tyrrell thinks they refer to the orations 'in toga candida' made by the candidates.

3. Laterensis. M. Iuventius. He accused Cn. Plancius in 54 B.C., and was praetor next year. In 44-43 B.C. he was legate to M. Lepidus in Gallia Narbonensis, and served the Commonwealth faithfully in that capacity till, in despair at the dissimulation and treason of his general, he slew himself. See Ep. 146. 4.

Laute, apparently 'admirably,' a rare meaning of the word. Prof. Nettleship suggests 'to have kept his hands clean.' He remarks that 'lautus' is contrasted with 'sordes,' Philipp. 1. 8. 20. But I think that the contrast in that passage is hardly direct enough, and doubt if it was thought of by Cicero.

5. Displiceo . . dolore. According to some, a quotation from Lucilius. Boot thinks the verse escaped Cicero by accident. 'Displiceo mihi,' 'I am out of humour.' Cp. Philipp. 1. 5. 12.

Me tueor, 'I maintain my position,' 'behave myself.'

6. Ut oppressis omnibus, 'considering the general oppression.'

Non demisse, 'without humiliation.'

8. Sibi ut sim legatus. Cp. Ad Fam. 14. 3. 1. Caesar was annoyed by Cicero's refusal of his offer. Cp. Ad Att. 9. 2 a, 1.

Libera . . datur, 'a titular legation, for the sake of discharging a vow, is offered me.' 'Libera' means 'free from the usual limitation to a particular province.' This privilege was granted either to enable a Roman who had business in the provinces to travel with more cheapness and comfort, or, as here, to afford an honourable retirement from public life. Cp. Ad Att. 15. 11. 4. The burden of providing for such legati was severely felt by the provinces, and Cicero, in his consulship, limited the duration of the privilege to one year (cp. De Legg. 3. 8. 18), a limitation afterwards sanctioned by Caesar apparently (cp. Ad Att. 15. l. c.).

9. Haec, 'the legatio libera.'

Apud pudorem Pulchelli, 'in presence of, or against, the moderation (ironical) of Clodius.' Cicero would still be legally a private person if he accepted this office, and so liable to prosecution. Prof. Tyrrell renders 'resting as it does on the honour of Clodius.' Professor Nettleship suggests that 'pudorem' may be corrupted from 'furorem' which, as Baiter remarks, 'alii' read: but Boot thinks that if Cicero had written 'furorem' he would have written 'adversus,' or 'contra' 'furorem.'

10. A fratris . . ablegat, 'removes me from Rome just about the time of my brother's return.' Q. Cicero left Asia in 58 B.C. Cp. Ad Q. F. 1. 3. 4.

Munitior, 'safer,' for it would secure him Caesar's protection.

11. Non impedit . . cum velim. Cicero might spend a short time in Gaul as Caesar's legate, and then return to Rome. Math.

Hanc . . teneo, 'I cling to this post,' of legate to Caesar. Cicero after all refused it. He seems to have wavered much as to his conduct at this crisis. Prof. Tyrrell renders 'I have already got the legatio libera (hanc).'

12. Scit quisquam. If these words are genuine, 'quid facturus sim,' or words to that effect, must be supplied. Orell. suggests 'scio quid sequar.'

Non lubet fugere, aveo pugnare. Magna sunt hominum studia. Sed nihil adfirmo, tu hoc silebis. De Statio manu misso et non 4
nullis aliis rebus angor equidem, sed iam prorsus occallui. Tu vellem ego vel cuperem adesses: nec mihi consilium nec consolatio deesset. Sed ita te para, ut, si inclamaro, advoles.

12. TO ATTICUS (AD ATT. II. 19).

ROME, JULY, 59 B.C. (695 A.U.C.)

1. Nothing, even in these troubled times, disquiets me more than the manumission of Statius. I care less for the threats of Clodius, but should be glad of your presence and advice. 2. The present state of things is generally odious; no one can be more unpopular than the so-called popular leaders. Bibulus is the idol of the populace; Pompey has lost all hold on its affections. I try to avoid offending our rulers, without discrediting my previous life. 3. At all public entertainments people shew their feelings; this was the case especially when the actor Diphilus attacked Pompey at the games of Apollo. The younger Curio had an enthusiastic reception on the same occasion, and it is said that our masters meditate measures of retaliation, both against the equites and against the populace. 4. Clodius threatens me, but Pompey promises his protection. I am not inclined, however, to accept a place on the Commission of Twenty, 5. nor even the post of legate to Caesar. I prefer to meet force by force, but have not made my final decision. In future I shall only write distinctly if I can quite depend on my messenger; otherwise I shall substitute other names for yours and mine. I shew proper attention to your uncle.

CICERO ATTICO SAL.

Multa me sollicitant et ex rei publicae tanto motu et ex iis 1
periculis, quae mihi ipsi intenduntur, et sescenta sunt; sed mihi nihil est molestius quam Statium manu missum:

1. **Aveo pugnare**, i.e. 'to resist the attack which Clodius threatened, instead of evading it.'

Magna . . studia, 'people are zealous in my cause.' Boot, who quotes Ad Att. 2. 22, 3 'renovatur memoria consulatus, studia significantur.'

2. **Nihil adfirmo**, 'I say nothing for certain.'

Silebis = 'sile.' See Madv. 384, Obs.

Statio. Statius was a slave, for whom Q. Cicero was thought to have too much regard, and whose manumission caused unfriendly remarks. Cp. Epp. 12, 1; 15, 1.

3. **Occallui**, 'have grown thick-skinned.' Apparently this is the only passage in which the word is used by an author of the best period metaphorically; but Forcell. quotes passages from Pliny the younger and Columella, where it has a similar meaning.

4. **Vellem ego vel cuperem**, 'I should wish, or rather earnestly desire.' Orell. suggests 'vellem ego accurreres.' The MS. has 'vellem ego ve cuperem.' On 'vellem,' and on the conj. mood after it, see Ep. 8, 14, note, on p. 62.

7. **Intenduntur**, 'are threatened.'

Sescenta, 'very numerous.'

8. **Quam Statium manu missum**, sc. 'esse,' 'than the manumission of Statius.' For more about him, cp. Ep. 15, 1.

Nec meum imperium : ac mitto imperium : non simultatem meam
Revereri saltem !

Nec quid faciam scio, neque tantum est in re, quantus est
sermo. Ego autem ne irasci possum quidem iis quos valde
amo : tantum doleo, ac mirifice quidem. † Cetera in magnis rebus ; minae Clodii contentionesque, *quae* mihi proponuntur,
modice me tangunt : etenim vel subire eas videor mihi summa
cum dignitate vel declinare nulla cum molestia posse. Dices
fortasse : 'dignitatis ἅλις, tamquam δρυός : saluti, si me amas,
consule.' Me miserum ! cur non ades ? nihil profecto te praeteriret ; ego fortasse τυφλώττω et nimium τῷ καλῷ προσπέπονθα.
Scito nihil umquam fuisse tam infame, tam turpe, tam perae- 2
que omnibus generibus, ordinibus, aetatibus offensum, quam
hunc statum, qui nunc est, magis mehercule, quam vellem, non
modo quam putaram. Populares isti iam etiam modestos homines
sibilare docuerunt. Bibulus in caelo est, nec qua re scio, sed ita
laudatur, quasi

Unus homo nobis cunctando restituit rem.

1. Nec meum imperium . . saltem, 'does he not regard my orders? or at least fear a quarrel with me?' a quotation from Terence, Phorm. II. 1, 2.

Mitto, 'I say nothing of.' On the infin. revereri, expressing surprise, see Madv. 399.

3. Neque . . sermo, 'however, there is not as much in the affair as people say.'

5. Cetera in magnis rebus, 'my other causes of annoyance have to do with important matters.' In appos. with minae. Kayser suggests 'ceterum in magnis rebus minae.'

6. Quae mihi proponuntur, 'with which I am threatened.'

8. Declinare, 'to avoid.' Cp. Ad Att. 8. 11 D, 7.

9. δρυός. Quoted, apparently, from a proverb about men leaving off acorns when they could get corn. 'You have had enough of dignity, think of safety.' Cp. Orell. Onomast. sub voc. Mr. Jeans renders by a French proverb 'le siècle du gland est passé,' which he quotes from Voltaire. See a letter of Voltaire to M. de la Chalotais written on November 3, 1762, in the 'Correspondance générale de Voltaire.' "Le siècle du gland est passé, vous donnerez du pain aux hommes." '

11. τυφλώττω, 'I am blind,' i.e. to my true interest. Cp. Polyb. 2. 61.

Nimium . . προσπέπονθα, 'am too passionately devoted to.' Cp. Plut. Sert. 26.

12. Peraeque, 'quite equally.' Cp. In Verr. Act. 2. 3. 52, 121.

13. Generibus, perhaps 'parties,' cp. Pro Sest. 45. 96 ; perhaps 'professions,' cp. A. W. Zumpt's Excursus on the Lex Curiata de Imperio, in his edition of Cicero's orations on the agrarian law of Rullus, p. 170.

Offensum, 'odious,' 'offensive.' Prof. Tyrrell suggests 'distasteful.'

14. Quam vellem, 'than I should wish.' Cp. Ep. 8. 10, note.

15. Putaram, i.e. before his return to Rome. Not, I think, the epistolary tense.

Populares, 'the chiefs of the popular party, the triumvirs.'

16. In caelo est, 'is exalted to the skies.' Cicero seems to have appreciated properly the foolish obstinacy of Bibulus, who only opposed a passive resistance to the triumvirs. Cp. Intr. to Part I, § 18. But he afterwards called him 'praestantissimum civem' Philipp. 2. 10, 23.

18. Unus homo . . rem. A quotation from Ennius, on Q. Fabius Cunctator ; hence the indicative 'restituit' is retained.

Pompeius, nostri amores, quod mihi summo dolori est, ipse se
adflixit: neminem tenet voluntate; ne metu necesse sit iis
uti, vereor. Ego autem neque pugno cum illa causa propter
illam amicitiam, neque approbo, ne omnia improbem, quae
antea gessi: utor via. Populi sensus maxime theatro et spec- 2
taculis perspectus est: nam gladiatoribus qua dominus qua
advocati sibilis conscissi; ludis Apollinaribus Diphilus tragoedus
in nostrum Pompeium petulanter invectus est:

Nostra miseria tu es magnus—

millies coactus est dicere;

Eandem virtutem istam veniet tempus cum graviter gemes

totius theatri clamore dixit itemque cetera. Nam eius modi sunt ii versus, uti in tempus ab inimico Pompeii scripti esse videantur.

1. **Nostri amores**, 'my favourite:' common enough in Cicero in this sense.

Se adflixit, 'has ruined himself.'

2. **Neminem tenet voluntate**, 'he can reckon on no one's voluntary support,' lit. 'controls none by their own choice.' 'holds no one by any bonds of good will.' Tyrrell. 'Voluntate' = 'voluntarie.' Forcell. Cp. 'sentiant se nullius partis voluntatem tenere,' Ad Att. 2. 21, 5.

Iis, 'for the populares.'

3. **Cum illa causa**, 'with the cause referred to,' that of the men in power.

4. **Illam amicitiam**, 'my friendship for Pompey.' Cp. 'nostri amores' above.

5. **Utor via**, 'I go straight on' (Matth.), i.e. I presume, without turning to support either side.

Theatro et spectaculis, 'at the theatre and at public shows.' The conjunction seems rather harsh, for 'theatro,' if it stood by itself, would rather be explained as the local ablative. On the ablatives 'spectaculis, gladiatoribus,' see Ep. 8, 11, note. The gladiatorial show referred to was perhaps that exhibited by A. Gabinius. Cp. Ep. 13, 3.

6. **Qua . . qua**, 'both . . and.' Cp. Ep. 65, 1, and Forcell, who gives 'cum . . tum' as equivalents.

Dominus, 'the man who gave the entertainment.' Cp. 'dominus epuli' in Vat. 13, 31. Or perhaps more probably 'our master' Caesar. Prof. Tyrrell thinks that Pompey is meant.

7. **Advocati**, 'partisans.' See Ep. 8, 4.

Conscissi, 'hissed,' lit. 'torn,' 'pelted.' Cp 'conscindi' Ep. 59, 1.

Ludis Apollinaribus. These games dated from 212 B.C., and were celebrated on July 5 by the praetor urbanus. Cp. Livy 25. 12; 27. 23.

Diphilus seems not to be elsewhere mentioned. According to Valerius Maximus (6. 2, 9), he pointed to Pompey when delivering these passages. Valerius Maximus quotes the passage 'Miseria nostra magnus es,' which Prof. Tyrrell says is more rhythmical, and suggests as an alternative 'nostra miseria tu magnus es.' He would also omit 'neque' before 'leges' in another quotation below, supposing both passages to form part of trochaic tetrameters.

9. **Nostra miseria**, 'at the cost of our misery.' On the ablative, cp. Madv. 258.

11. **Virtutem istam**, 'that valour (Caesar's) which you praise.' Boot. Manutius says 'virtutem.' Opes, facultates, vires in civitate. Prof. Tyrrell says 'the spectator would refer "virtutem" to the victories of Pompeius, and "gemes" to himself.'

12. **Itemque cetera**, 'and the rest of the passage likewise.' The lines here quoted are placed by Ribbeck among the fragments 'ex incertis incertorum fabulis.'

Nam eius modi . . videantur, 'are such as to seem written to suit the present time by some enemy of Pompey.' The expression is elliptical. 'This was not strange, for' cp. Madv. ad Cic. de Fin. Excursus, p. 791, who, however, thinks that '*et* eius modi' would be more in accordance with Cicero's usage; in which case I presume that there should be only a comma after 'videantur.' Prof. Tyrrell has a colon.

Si neque leges neque mores cogunt—

Et cetera magno cum fremitu et clamore sunt dicta. Caesar cum venisset mortuo plausu, Curio filius est insecutus: huic ita plausum est, ut salva re publica Pompeio plaudi solebat. Tulit Caesar graviter: litterae Capuam ad Pompeium volare dicebantur. Inimici erant equitibus, qui Curioni stantes plauserant, hostes omnibus; Rosciae legi, etiam frumentariae, minitabantur: sane res erat perturbata. Equidem malueram, quod erat susceptum ab illis, silentio transiri, sed vereor ne non liceat: non ferunt homines, quod videtur esse tamen ferendum. Sed est iam una vox omnium, magis odio firmata quam prae-
4 sidio. Noster autem Publius mihi minitatur, inimicus est; impendet negotium, ad quod tu scilicet advolabis. Videor mihi nostrum illum consularem exercitum bonorum omnium, etiam satis bonorum, habere firmissimum. Pompeius significat studium erga me non mediocre; idem adfirmat verbum de me illum non esse facturum; in quo non me ille fallit, sed ipse

1. Cogunt, 'have any constraining force,' i. e. over tyrants.

2. Caesar . . plausu, 'Caesar having arrived when the applause (called forth by the passage given above) had ceased.' It is implied that no applause greeted him.

3. Curio: see on § 1 of the preceding letter.

5. Capuam. Pompey was probably at Capua, employed as one of the commission of twenty charged with the execution of Caesar's agrarian laws.

6. Dicebantur is not, probably, the epistolary imperfect. Prof. Tyrrell takes a different view, however.

Erant, sc. 'populares isti.' Cp. § 2. The demeanour of the equites seems curious, considering what the triumvirs did to conciliate them. Cp Ep. 10, 2, note; Intr. to Part I, § 17. Mr. Long (Decl. of Rom. Rep. 3. 429. 430) thinks that Caesar's law for releasing the 'publicani' from their bargain had not yet been introduced; but this seems hardly probable. May not the equites present in the theatre have been carried away by a momentary impulse? Mr. H. F. Pelham suggests that the 'equites' here referred to may be the 'equitum centuriae,' mainly consisting of young patricians.

7. Hostes omnibus, 'open enemies to all their countrymen.'

Rosciae . . minitabantur, 'they were threatening to abrogate the Roscian law, and even that providing corn for the people.' On the Roscian law, see Ep. 9, 3, note. Its repeal would of course offend the equites, as that of the other law would offend the populace. The Lex Frumentaria here referred to was probably the Lex Cassia Terentia, enacted 73 B.C. (cp. Orell. Onomast.), which provided for the sale of corn at low fixed rates.

8. Malueram. On the indic., see Madv. 348 c.

9. Ab illis, 'by Pompey and Caesar.'

11. Magis . . praesidio, 'emboldened by hatred rather than by the possession of any real force.'

12. Noster . . Publius, 'our friend Publius,' i.e. Clodius, who is often spoken of simply by his praenomen.

13. Impendet, 'threatens us.' The threat would be fulfilled when Clodius should be tribune.

Scilicet, 'of course.' Forcell. gives 'nimirum' as one of the equivalents for 'scilicet,' and says 'habet vim affirmandi.'

14. Nostrum illum . . firmissimum, 'to be able to place full reliance in that force of well-disposed, or even fairly well-disposed, citizens which my consulate embodied.'

17. Illum, 'Clodium.'

Non me ille . . fallitur. Cicero thought that Pompey was kept in the dark as to the attack planned against himself by Clodius. Cp. Ad Att. 2. 21, 6.

fallitur. Cosconio mortuo sum in eius locum invitatus: id
erat vocari in locum mortui; nihil me turpius apud homines
fuisset, neque vero ad istam ipsam ἀσφάλειαν quicquam alienius;
sunt enim illi apud bonos invidiosi, ego apud improbos meam
retinuissem invidiam, alienam adsumpsissem. Caesar me sibi 8
volt esse legatum. Honestior declinatio haec periculi; sed
ego hoc non repudio. Quid ergo est? Pugnare malo. Nihil
tamen certi. Iterum dico, utinam adesses! sed tamen, si erit
necesse, arcessemus. Quid aliud? quid? Hoc opinor: certi sumus
perisse omnia; quid enim ἀκκιζόμεθα tam diu? sed haec scripsi
properans et mehercule timide. Posthac ad te aut, si perfidelem
habebo, cui dem, scribam plane omnia, aut, si obscure scribam,
tu tamen intelleges. In iis epistolis me Laelium, te Furium
faciam; cetera erunt ἐν αἰνιγμοῖς. Hic Caecilium colimus et
observamus diligenter. Edicta Bibuli audio ad te missa: iis
ardet dolore et ira noster Pompeius.

1. Cosconio. We may perhaps infer from this passage compared with Ad Att. 9. 2 a, 1, and Vell. 2, 45, that Cicero was invited to succeed Cosconius as a member of the Commission of Twenty appointed to divide the public lands in Campania. C. Cosconius was praetor in 63 B.C., and afterwards governor of Farther Spain. Cp. Pro Sulla, 14, 42; In Vat. 5, 12.

Id erat . . mortui, 'that was an invitation to take a dead man's place,' 'to pass from political existence.' A play on the words 'in locum mortui,' which might merely mean 'to succeed a dead man.'

2. Apud homines. So Boot and Orell. Baiter has 'apud hominem,' which, I presume, must mean 'in the eyes of Pompey.'

3. Ad istam ipsam ἀσφάλειαν, 'with a view to that very security you advise me to think of.' For this sense of 'iste,' cp. Ep. 7, 2, note.

4. Illi, 'the commissioners' probably.

6. Honestior . . periculi, 'this is a more honourable way of avoiding the danger' than the acceptance of a place among the XX viri would be. For Caesar's offer, cp. § 3 of the previous letter.

7. Hoc non repudio, 'I do not shrink from danger.' Boot. Wesenb. denies that 'repudio' can have this meaning, and suggests 'refugio.'

Quid ergo est? 'what then do I mean.'

9. Quid aliud . . omnia, 'what more have I to say? This, I think; that we are sure that all is lost.' Cicero's agitation shews itself in the abruptness of the style. Billerb.

10. ἀκκιζόμεθα, 'dissemble.' See Plat. Gorg. 497 A.

11. Perfidelem. This word seems not to occur elsewhere.

12. Obscure, 'under a disguise.' Cp. ἐν αἰνιγμοῖς a few lines below. It is opposed to 'plane.'

13. Me Laelium . . faciam, 'I shall call myself Laelius, and you Furius.' 'Facio' is often used by Cicero in this sense. The name Furius was perhaps suggested by the younger Laelius having had a friend of that name, L. Furius Philus, who was consul 136 B.C. Cicero has compared himself to Laelius once before; see Ep. 3, 3.

14. αἰνιγμοῖς. αἴνιγμα is the more common form, but αἰνιγμός is found, Eur. Rhes. 754; Aristoph. Ranae 61.

Caecilium. Atticus had an uncle named Q. Caecilius, who afterwards adopted him. Cp. Ep. 1, 3, note.

15. Edicta, 'proclamations.' Bibulus, during the last six months of his consulship, shut himself up in his house, and merely issued proclamations declaring Caesar's acts void. Cp. App. Bell. Civ. 2. 12; Dion Cassius 38, 6.

Iis, 'at,' or 'about them.' On the abl., see Madv. 255.

16. Pompeius. There is more about the behaviour of Pompey at this time, in Ad Att. 2, 21, 3.

18. To ATTICUS (AD ATT. II. 24).

Rome, August, 59 B.C. (695 A.U.C.) [Baiter].

1. I sent you a most pressing summons by Numestius, but do not be anxious; the affair for which I wanted you will not, I hope, turn out so ill as I feared. 2. Vettius, my old agent, has contrived a plot for the ruin of the younger Curio and others. He charged Curio with conspiring for the murder of Pompey, but had in reality suggested that crime to Curio, who warned Pompey through his own father. 3. Vettius was guilty of many contradictions, and was imprisoned, but afterwards brought before the people by Caesar. He made several changes in the list of alleged conspirators, and hinted that I was one of them, without naming me. 4. He now awaits his trial for 'vis,' and, if convicted, will probably ask to be allowed to inform against others. In that case there must be more trials, but I do not fear their result. I receive many promises of support, but am sick of life, so wretched are the times. The bold language of Considius has dispelled our fears of a massacre, but I have still reason enough to envy Catulus. I show no weakness, however. 5. Pompey bids me not to fear Clodius, and is generally most friendly in his language. I am most anxious for your advice and sympathy.

CICERO ATTICO SAL.

1 Quas Numestio litteras dedi, sic te iis evocabam, ut nihil
acrius neque incitatius fieri posset: ad illam celeritatem adde
etiam, si quid potes. Ac ne sis perturbatus; novi enim te et
non ignoro, quam sit amor omnis sollicitus atque anxius, sed
2 res est, ut spero, non tam exitu molesta quam auditu. Vettius
ille, ille noster index, Caesari, ut perspicimus, pollicitus est
sese curaturum, ut in aliquam suspitionem facinoris Curio filius
adduceretur; itaque insinuatus in familiaritatem adulescentis

1. Numestio. Numerius Numestius is mentioned Ad Att. 2. 20, 1; 2. 22, 7. Cicero received him as a friend on the recommendation of Atticus.

Litteras perhaps refers to Ad Att. 2. 23. On quas . . litteras, see Ep. 3, 2, note, on p. 33.

2. Acrius . . incitatius, 'more earnest and pressing.' Forcell.

Ad illam celeritatem, 'to the speed I then requested.' See Madv. 483.

3. Ac ne sis perturbatus, 'but do not be alarmed at my vehemence.'

Enim, supp. 'as you will naturally be, if I do not reassure you.'

5. Res, 'the affair in which I want your aid.'

Exitu, 'in its actual result.'

Vettius. One L. Vettius had been employed by Cicero as an informer during his consulship (cp. Dion Cassius 37. 41), and had tried to establish the complicity of Caesar in Catiline's plot (Suet. Iul. 17; Abeken, p. 61). The plot described in this letter is also mentioned at less length in the orations Pro Sest. 63, 132, and In Vatin. 10. Mommsen (4. 1. 206) accepts Cicero's account of this affair; the Emperor Napoleon III (César 1. 399 foll.) suggests, not improbably, that the plot was devised by some adherents of the triumvirs, without the knowledge of their chiefs; Merivale (1. 196) thinks that there was a real plot among some of the violent young nobles against the triumvirs.

6. Ille noster index. Atticus had been in Rome during Cicero's consulship, and his familiarity with the events of that year would make any further description of Vettius needless.

8. Insinuatus. The verb is both act. and neut. Cp. Forcell.

et cum eo, ut res indicat, saepe congressus rem in eum locum deduxit, ut diceret sibi certum esse cum suis servis in Pompeium impetum facere eumque occidere. Hoc Curio ad patrem detulit, ille ad Pompeium; res delata ad senatum est. Introductus Vettius primo negabat se umquam cum Curione constitisse; neque id sane diu: nam statim fidem publicam postulavit; reclamatum est. Tum exposuit manum fuisse iuventutis duce Curione, in qua Paulus initio fuisset et Q. Caepio hic Brutus et Lentulus, flaminis filius, conscio patre; postea C. Septimium, scribam Bibuli, pugionem sibi a Bibulo attulisse: quod totum irrisum est, Vettio pugionem defuisse, nisi ei consul dedisset, eoque magis id eiectum est, quod a. d. III. Idus Mai. Bibulus Pompeium fecerat certiorem, ut caveret insidias; in quo ei Pompeius gratias egerat. Introductus Curio filius dixit ad ea, quae Vettius dixerat, 5 maximeque in eo tum quidem Vettius est reprehensus, quod dixerat adulescentium consilium, ut in foro [cum] gladiatoribus

1. **Rem in eum locum deduxit**, 'went so far as to say.' Bout. Cp. 'quem in locum res deducta sit, vides' Ad Fam. 4. 2, 3.

2. **Sibi certum esse**, 'that he was resolved.'

5. **Negabat.** By appearing to fear a disclosure of what had passed between him and Curio, Vettius hoped to bring suspicion upon Curio. Manut.

Cum Curione constitisse, 'that he had had interviews with Curio.' Cp. In Verr. Act. 1. 7, 19.

6. **Fidem publicam**, 'indemnity for his disclosures.' Cp. In Cat. 3. 4, 8.

Reclamatum est, 'there were outcries against it.' Cp. Ep. 22, 2. We must suppose that Vettius persevered in his statement, though conscious that he did so at his own peril.

8. **Paulus.** L. Aemilius Paulus was son of M. Lepidus, consul in 78 B.C. Paulus was quaestor in Macedonia in 59 B.C., praetor in 53 B.C., consul in 50 B.C. He at first was one of the optimates, and is often praised by Cicero; but Caesar bought his services in the year 50 B.C. for a sum of 1500 talents (Plut. Caes. 29). Though brother of the triumvir Lepidus, he was among the proscribed in 43 B.C., but escaped to the camp of M. Brutus, and was afterwards pardoned. His basilica was celebrated among the great public buildings of the time.

Fuisset, orat. obl.: see Ep. 3, 3, note.

Q. Caepio . . Brutus. More commonly known as M. Brutus, Caesar's murderer. He had been adopted by his maternal uncle, Q. Servilius Caepio. For more notices of him, cp. Ep. 36, 10, and Intr. to Part IV, § 13; to Part V, §§ 2; 4; 7; 11; 13. The words 'hic Brutus' are probably inserted to distinguish him from other men named Q. Caepio. Manut.

Lentulus. L. Lentulus Niger is mentioned (Philipp. 3. 10, 25) as a friend of Antony, who disapproved of his policy. He survived the battle of Actium. His father, who bore the same name, was flamen of Mars; accused Clodius 61 B.C.; stood for the consulship against Piso and Gabinius in 59 B.C.; and was one of the court before which Cicero pleaded 'De Domo Sua.' He died 56 B.C.

12. **Id eiectum est.** A theatrical expression = 'explosum,' 'discredited.'

13. **In quo**, 'in which matter.' Forcell. explains 'in' in this sense as equivalent to 'quod attinet ad.' Cp. Ep. 9, 5, note, on p. 67.

14. **Ad ea . . dixerat**, 'in answer to the charges of Vettius.'

15. **In eo . . quod**, 'because.'

Tum quidem, 'on that occasion.' Vettius may have been guilty of other misstatements equally serious at other times.

16. **Consilium**, supp. 'fuisse' from the next clause. Cp. Madv. 478. On 'ut' with the conj. after 'consilium fuisse,' cp. ib. 372 a.

Gladiatoribus: see Ep. 12, 3. Billerb. retains 'cum,' but explains it as meaning 'at the time of.'

Gabinii Pompeium adorirentur, in eo principem Paulum fuisse, quem constabat eo tempore in Macedonia fuisse. Fit senatus consultum, ut Vettius, quod confessus esset se cum telo fuisse in vincula coniiceretur; qui eum emisisset, eum contra rem publicam esse facturum. Res erat in ea opinione, ut putarent id esse actum, ut Vettius in foro cum pugione et item servi eius comprehenderentur cum telis, deinde ille se diceret indicaturum, idque ita factum esset, nisi Curiones rem ante ad Pompeium detulissent. Tum senatus consultum in contione recitatum est. Postero autem die Caesar, is, qui olim, praetor cum esset, Q. Catulum ex inferiore loco iusserat dicere, Vettium in rostra produxit eumque in eo loco constituit, quo Bibulo consuli aspirare non liceret. Hic ille omnia, quae voluit, de re publica dixit, ut qui illuc factus institutusque venisset. Primum Caepionem de oratione sua sustulit, quem in senatu acerrime nominarat, ut appareret noctem et nocturnam deprecationem intercessisse; deinde, quos in senatu ne tenuissima quidem suspitione attigerat, eos nominavit: Lucullum, a quo solitum esse ad se mitti C. Fannium, illum, qui in P. Clodium subscripserat, L.

1. Gabinii. A. Gabinius was consul 58 B.C., and may have exhibited gladiatorial shows the year before, in order to win favour with the populace. For further notices of him, cp. Intr. to Part I, §§ 7; 18; 19: to Part II, §§ 6; 7; 10; to Part IV, § 4.

3. Cum telo. It was illegal, apparently, to bear arms in Rome. Cp. In Cat. 1. 6, 15; Ascon. in Milonian. p. 145.

4. Emisisset, sc. 'e vinculis,' 'should have procured his release.' This decree was passed to prevent, if possible, an appeal to the tribunes on behalf of Vettius. Cp. Caesar's proposal, quoted In Cat. 4. 4. 8, and 4. 5. 10.

5. Res erat . . putarent, 'the general impression about the occurrence was that people thought.' On the pleonasm, cp. Madv. 481 b; Zumpt 750.

6. Id esse actum, that it had been intended, or arranged.

Item: cp. Ep. 12, 3, note.

10. Olim. Caesar was praetor in 62 B.C., when Catulus came forward to speak about the rebuilding of the Capitol. Cp. Intr. to Part I, § 12; Suet. Iul. 15.

11. Ex inferiore loco, opposed to 'e rostris.'

12. Produxit. But this was actually done by Vatinius. On the practice, cp. Ep. 7. 1, note, and Livy 6. 33.

13. Aspirare, 'to approach.' Cp. Ep. 9. 8, note.

Voluit. 'Non Vettius, sed Caesar.' Manut. Orell. ap. Billerb., and Boot propose 'hic omnia, ille quae voluit.' Prof. Tyrrell approves, but takes 'hic' as an adverb = 'in the rostra.'

14. Factus, 'schooled,' 'prepared.' Cp. De Orat. 3. 48, 184; Hor. Sat. 1. 10, 58.

Caepionem . . sustulit, 'removed the name of Caepio from his statement.'

15. Acerrime, 'with the greatest earnestness, or decision.'

Nominarat. Perhaps 'nominare' was a technical term for a denunciation or information. Cp. Suet. Iul. 17; Livy 39. 17 'qui nominatos profugissent.'

16. Deprecationem. Intercession from Brutus' mother, Servilia, reported to be on intimate terms with Caesar.

18. Lucullum. Probably L. Lucullus is meant.

Solitum esse, supp. 'dixit' from 'nominavit.' See Madv. 401 a; 403 a.

19. C. Fannium. Either a tribune of the year 59 B.C. (cp. Pro Sest. 53. 113), who was afterwards killed about the time of the battle of Pharsalus, fighting on the side of Pompey (cp. Ep. 80. 6), or, if his not being called tribune here makes a difficulty, perhaps a C. Fannius who went as envoy

Domitium, cuius domum constitutam fuisse, unde eruptio fieret; me non nominavit, sed dixit consularem disertum, vicinum consulis, sibi dixisse Ahalam Servilium aliquem aut Brutum opus esse reperiri; addidit ad extremum, cum iam dimissa contione revocatus a Vatinio fuisset, se audisse a Curione his de rebus conscium esse Pisonem, generum meum, et M. Laterensem.
Nunc reus erat apud Crassum Divitem Vettius de vi et, cum 4
esset damnatus, erat indicium postulaturus; quod si impetrasset iudicia fore videbantur: ea nos, utpote qui nihil contemnere soleamus, *non contemnebamus, sed* non pertimescebamus. Hominum quidem summa erga nos studia significabantur, sed prorsus vitae taedet: ita sunt omnia omnium miseriarum plenissima. Modo caedem timueramus, quam oratio fortissimi senis, Q. Con-

from Lepidus to Sextus Pompeius in 43 B.C. (cp. Philipp. 13. 6, 13); afterwards joined Sextus, but finally deserted him.

Subscripserat. Indic. as a remark of Cicero's own. 'Subscribere in' means to act as subordinate accuser, 'junior counsel for the prosecution.' Mr. Tyrrell thinks that the word is used of the chief accuser as well, but I think it is more commonly used as above.

L. Domitium. For an account of him, see Ep. 1, 3, note.

1. Eruptio, 'the attack on Pompey.'

2. Vicinum. Cicero's house stood on the Palatine (see Intr. to Part I, § 12), and so would be near the official residence of Caesar, who, as pontifex maximus, lived in the Via Sacra. Cp. Suet. Iul. 46.

3. Ahalam Servilium . . Brutum, 'some one like Servilius Ahala or Brutus.' C. Servilius Ahala, as master of the horse to L. Quinctius Cincinnatus, killed Sp. Maelius. Cp. Livy 4. 14. The Brutus referred to is of course the L. Brutus who expelled the second Tarquin.

4. Opus esse reperiri, 'it was desirable should be discovered.' On the constr., see Madv. 366, and Obs. For the meaning of 'opus esse,' cp. Ep. 10, 4, note; Ep. 29, 15, note.

5. Revocatus, 'recalled for further examination.' Cp. In Vat. 11, 26.

Vatinio. For an account of P. Vatinius, see Intr. to Parts I, §§ 17; 18; II, §§ 2; 8; 10; IV, § 4.

6. Pisonem. C. Calpurnius Piso Frugi married Cicero's daughter Tullia in 64 B.C., after a betrothal of four years: see the close of Ad Att. 1. 3, 3. He is often mentioned in connection with Cicero's banishment. Cp. Intr. p. 32; Epp. 17, 2; 18, 4. He was quaestor in 58 B.C., and apparently died next year, before Cicero's return from exile.

M. Laterensem: see Ep. 11, 2, note.

7. Reus erat. Here 'erat' is the epistolary tense, and the following tenses must be altered accordingly in translation.

Apud Crassum Divitem. This man seems to have been one of the praetors for 59 B.C. But according to Mommsen Staatsrecht 2. 1, 548, the 'quaestio de vi' was not presided over by a praetor but by a quaesitor taken from among the judges who might be changed often in the year. Matth. says the praenomen of this Crassus was Publius. Little seems to be known of him, except that some suppose him to have been a Crassus reduced from great wealth to poverty. See Val. Max. 6. 9, 12.

De vi. Carrying weapons in a public place seems to have been a violation of the statutes 'de vi.' See Smith, Dict. of Antiq. p. 1209; Rein, Criminalrecht 734.

Cum esset damnatus, 'after condemnation.' 'Cum' seems here to have nearly the force of 'si.'

8. Indicium, 'leave to act as informer.' Forcell.

9. Iudicia, 'a number of prosecutions.'

10. Soleamus. In the present, as a general remark. 'Pertimescebamus' imperf., as referring to the time of writing. See Madv. 345. The MS. has 'soleremus,' but Orell. and Baiter both substitute the conj., which is more in accordance with usage after utpote qui. Prof. Tyrrell reads 'soleremus.'

11. Quidem. On the position of this word, see Madv. 471.

13. Modo, 'lately.'

sidii, discusserat; ea, quam quotidie timere potueramus, subito exorta est. Quid quaeris? nihil me *infortunatius, nihil* fortunatius est Catulo, cum splendore vitae, † tum hoc tempore. Nos tamen in his miseriis erecto animo et minime perturbato sumus, honestissimeque dignitatem nostram et magna cura tuemur. Pompeius de Clodio iubet nos esse sine cura et summam in nos benevolentiam omni oratione significat. Te habere consiliorum auctorem, sollicitudinum socium, omni in cogitatione coniunctum cupio; qua re, ut Numestio mandavi tecum ut ageret, item atque eo si potest acrius te rogo, ut plane ad nos advoles: respiraro, si te videro.

14. To ATTICUS (AD ATT. II. 25).

ROME, AUGUST, (?) 59 B.C. (695 A.U.C.)

1. I shall be obliged if, in future, when I praise any of your friends in a letter to you, you will let him know what I have said. In particular, I should like you to tell Varro that I am satisfied with him, though I can hardly say so truly: you know his disposition. Hortensius, on the contrary, was most eloquent in praise of me when he spoke of the praetorship of Flaccus. Please let him know what I think of his speech. 2. I expect you soon, and am anxious for your support. My personal prospects are pretty good: the commonwealth is in a desperate position, and those who have ruined it are thoroughly detested.

CICERO ATTICO SAL.

1 Cum aliquem apud te laudaro tuorum familiarium, volam illum scire ex te me id fecisse, ut nuper me scis scripsisse ad te de Varronis erga me officio, te ad me rescripsisse eam rem

Caedem, 'a massacre,' like those of Marius and Sulla. To explain ea, some word suggested by 'caedes' must be supplied. The context seems to require 'danger.' Such a case of zeugma is not unnatural in a letter.

Q. Considii. Q. Considius Gallus reproached Caesar in the senate with his violent proceedings, and Caesar apparently behaved with more moderation afterwards. Cp. Plut. Caes. 14. Verres rejected Considius as a judge. In Verr. Act. 2. 1. 7. 18.

1. Discusserat, 'dispelled our fears of,' 'got rid of.' Forcell.

The best MS. has apparently 'ea inquam.' Wesenb. suspects that the in- of inquam conceals a substantive, which may refer to a plot for assassination, contrasted with the 'massacre' caedes, before referred to as possible.

3. Catulo. Catulus died 60 B.C. Cp. Ad Att. 1. 20. 3.

Tum hoc tempore, sc. 'mortis,' 'in having died when he did.' Orell. suggests 'tum quod tempore,' sc. 'opportuno mortem obiit,' Boot, after Lambinus, 'mortis tempore.' Cp. De Orat. 3. 3. 12.

9. Tecum ut ageret: cp. Ep. 5. 8, note, on p. 38.

Item, 'again,' 'in like manner.'

10. Eo . . acrius, 'with more vehemence still, if possible,'

13. Me . . scripsisse: cp. 'Varro mihi satis facit' Ad Att. 2. 21, 6.

14. Varronis. M. Terentius Varro, the

summae tibi voluptati esse; sed ego mallem ad illum scripsisses mihi illum satis facere, non quo faceret, sed ut faceret. Mirabiliter enim moratus est, sicut nosti, *ἑλικτὰ καὶ οὐδέν*—. Sed nos tenemus praeceptum illud, *τὰς τῶν κρατούντων*. At hercule alter tuus familiaris, Hortalus, quam plena manu, quam ingenue, quam ornate nostras laudes in astra sustulit, cum de Flacci praetura et de illo tempore Allobrogum diceret! sic habeto, nec amantius nec honorificentius nec copiosius potuisse dici: ei te
2 hoc scribere a me tibi esse missum sane volo. Sed quid tu scribas? quem iam ego venire atque adesse arbitror; ita enim egi tecum superioribus litteris. Valde te exspecto, valde desidero, neque ego magis, quam ipsa res et tempus poscit. His de negotiis quid scribam ad te, nisi idem, quod saepe? re publica nihil desperatius, iis, quorum opera, nihil maiore odio: nos, ut opinio et spes et coniectura nostra fert, firmissima benevolentia hominum muniti sumus. Qua re advola: aut expedies nos omni molestia aut eris particeps. Ideo sum brevior, quod, ut spero,

celebrated antiquary, author, amongst other works, of the treatises 'De Re Rustica,' and 'De Lingua Latina.' For other notices of him, see Intr. to Part III, § 8, and Ad Fam. 9. 1–8.

2. Non quo . . faceret, 'not that he really did so, but that he might.' 'Quo' = 'quia.' On its force with the conj., see Madv. 357 b, Obs. It introduces a reason not the real one.

3. Moratus est. Either from 'moror,' 'he has interposed strange delays,' or from 'mos,' 'he is strangely constituted.' Cp. De Part. Orat. 23, 82. The passage which follows means, 'whose thoughts are all crooked, and not honest or straightforward.' It is from Euripides, who (Androm. 448–449) says of the Spartans,

ἑλικτὰ κοὐδὲν ὑγιὲς ἀλλὰ πᾶν πέριξ φρονοῦντες.

4. Nos tenemus, 'I remember.' Forcell. *τὰς τῶν κρατούντων ἀμαθίας φέρειν χρεών.* Eur. Phoen. 393. The connection of this passage with what goes before, may be that Cicero was unwilling to offend Varro as a friend of Pompey. The 'masters' are no doubt Pompey and Caesar.

5. Hortalus Q. Hortensius: see Ep. 6, 2, note.

Quam plena manu, 'how liberally' = 'copiose,' 'large.' Forcell.

6. Cum . . diceret, 'in speaking about.' See Madv. 358, Obs. 4.

Flacci. L. Valerius Flaccus was praetor in 63 B.C., and afterwards governed Asia. On his return to Rome he was accused of extortion by D. Laelius, and defended by Cicero and Hortensius, in 59 B.C. Much of Cicero's speech is extant. The praises for which Cicero is so grateful to Hortensius very likely formed part of the latter's speech on the trial of Flaccus. On the services of Flaccus, as praetor, against Catiline's accomplices, and on the intrigues of the latter with envoys of the Allobroges, cp. In Cat. 3. 2, 3; Sall. Cat. 45. On the Allobroges, cp. Ep. 139, note.

7. Sic habeto, 'be assured of this:' a not uncommon use of the words in Cicero. Cp. De Rep. 6. 24, 26. The following clause supplies the place of an accusative.

8. Ei te hoc . . volo, 'I much wish that you should let him know that I have sent you this message.'

9. Missum = 'nuntiatum.' Cp. 'ad me mittunt' Ad Att. 2. 2, 3.

10. Quem . . arbitror, 'who, I suppose, are already on your way, and at hand.'

12. Ipsa res et tempus, 'the state of affairs in itself at the present crisis.'

His de negotiis, 'about the state of things here,' at Rome.

14. Iis. Probably Caesar and Pompey are meant.

Quorum opera, sc. 'factum est ut nihil esset desperatius.'

coram brevi tempore conferre quae volumus [1] licebit. Cura ut valeas.

15. TO HIS BROTHER QUINTUS (AD Q. F. I. 2).

ROME, ABOUT NOV., 59 B.C. (695 A.U.C.) (?)

I. 1. I was at once pleased and annoyed by the arrival of Statius; you will miss him, but gossip about your intimacy with him will have ceased here before your own return. 2. I never suspected him myself, and only wrote you word what others were saying, that you might avoid suspicion. Statius could remark for himself what people said, and how his name especially occurred in their complaints of you. 3. People's requests to be recommended to him, and his own unguarded expressions, shewed me how matters stood; but I do not think anything would have been said about him, had not the rigour of your administration given offence. II. 4. I will now answer your letters. You complain that I recommended Zeuxis of Blaudus to you. This is part of a more general question. I have been anxious to conciliate the Greeks, whose complaints of you were producing considerable effect, and in many cases I have succeeded. 5. As for Zeuxis himself, I received him kindly to silence his complaints of you, and I do not think you should have shewn such eagerness to punish him. 6. Nor is it only your Greek enemies that I try to pacify; I have appeased L. Caecilius, and in fact everybody except Tuscenius. I do not complain of your severity to the father of T. Catienus; but why need you write in such threatening language to the son, who is now at Rome? or to C. Fabius about the two Licinii? 7. I have never complained of anything in you, except violence of language and occasional carelessness in your letters. Do you suppose I am not sorry when I hear of the popularity of Vergilius and Octavius, who are more conciliatory than you, though inferior in literary cultivation? III. 8. I hope you will be as careful as possible in your correspondence, and suppress, if you can, all letters likely to injure you. 9. You know I have often warned you on this point; do what you can during the remainder of your term of office. 10. L. Flavius has just complained of your arbitrary interference with L. Naso's property, which I cannot approve of. 11. I do not want to serve Flavius at the expense of your character: but see if you cannot do something for a man in whom Pompey and Caesar are interested. IV. 12. I am sorry I wrote to you hastily about Hermia, and hope you will excuse me. I am glad you are on good terms with Censorinus and others. 13. You have taken my warnings rather too seriously. If we had not so many enemies, I should not have thought of censuring you in anything. 14. Please to consult the wishes of Attalus of Hypaepi, and try to procure for our friend Aesopus the restoration of his runaway slave Licinius, who is said to be detained at Ephesus. V. 15. The position of affairs here is desperate; C. Cato's life has been seriously endangered by a riot, owing to his having called Pompey a 'private dictator.' 16. My own prospects, however, are fair; all good citizens are enthusiastic in my support, and Pompey and Caesar promise all that I can wish. I do not trust them too much, however. The consuls, tribunes, and praetors elected for next year seem, on the whole, very well disposed to me; so do not despond.

1. Conferre quae volumus, 'to discuss together what we choose.' Forcell.

MARCUS QUINTO FRATRI.

Statius ad me venit a.d. VIII. K. Novembr. Eius adventus, quod 1
ita scripsisti, direptum iri te a tuis, dum is abesset, molestus mihi
fuit; quod autem exspectationem sui concursumque eum, qui erat
futurus, si una tecum decederet neque antea visus esset, sustulit,
id mihi non incommode visum est accidisse: exhaustus est enim
sermo hominum et multae emissae iam eius modi voces, ἀλλ' αἰεί
τινα φῶτα μέγαν· quae te absente confecta esse laetor. Quod 2
autem idcirco a te missus est, mihi ut se purgaret, id necesse
minime fuit: primum enim numquam ille mihi fuit suspectus,
neque ego, quae ad te de illo scripsi, scripsi meo iudicio, sed cum
ratio salusque omnium nostrum, qui ad rem publicam accedimus,
non veritate solum, sed etiam fama niteretur, sermones ad te
aliorum semper, non mea iudicia perscripsi; qui quidem quam
frequentes essent et quam graves, adventu suo Statius ipse cognovit: etenim intervenit non nullorum querelis, quae apud me
de illo ipso habebantur, et sentire potuit sermones iniquorum in
suum potissimum nomen erumpere. Quod autem me maxime 3
movere solebat, cum audiebam illum plus apud te posse, quam
gravitas istius aetatis, imperii prudentia postularet—quam multos
enim mecum egisse putas, ut se Statio commendarem? quam
multa autem ipsum ἀσφαλῶς mecum in sermone ita protulisse

1. Statius: see Ep. 12, 1, note.

2. Direptum iri, 'would be plundered,' by the wastefulness and peculation of his other attendants.

3. Exspectationem sui, 'the expectation of his return,' which was cut short by his sudden appearance. The MS. has 'tui,' which might mean 'the expectation of seeing you enter Rome with him.'

Erat futurus. For this use of the imperf. ind., see Madv. 348 a.

4. Decederet, 'left the province.' Cp. Pro Muren. 18. 37.

5. Exhaustus .. sermo, 'people's gossip is used up on the subject.'

6. ἀλλ' αἰεί τινα φῶτα μέγαν καὶ καλὸν ἐδέγμην. Hom. Od. 9. 513. The words are used by Polyphemus of the appearance of Ulysses. Here they refer to the insignificant aspect of Quintus' favourite

7. Quae te absente confecta .. laetor, 'and I am glad this talk has been brought to an end before your return.' 'Confectus'='finitus.' Forcell.

Quod autem .. fuit: see Ep. 10, 14, note.

11. Ratio salusque, 'the interest and safety.' For this sense of 'ratio,' see Ep. 1, 1, note, on p. 26.

12. Niteretur, 'depends upon.' It follows the tense of 'perscripsi.' See Madv. 383, Obs. 1.

15. Intervenit .. querelis, 'he was himself witness of the complaints of some people.' Forcell. gives 'adesse,' 'interesse' as equivalents of the verb.

Querelis, dat. See Madv. 245 a.

17. Quod autem: an anacoluthon. 'Id' would be more natural. Billerb. The break in the construction begins after 'postularet.' For a somewhat similar anacoluthon, cp. In Cat. 2. 6, 12. Wesenb. thinks that an apodosis is implied in 'materiam .. dedisse,' as though Cicero had intended to write 'quod autem .. id fuit quod materiam Statius dedit.'

21. ἀσφαλῶς. Perhaps 'unsuspectingly.'

Ita protulisse. Baiter's suggestion;

'id mihi non placuit; monui, suasi, deterrui?' quibus in rebus etiamsi fidelitas summa est, quod prorsus credo, quoniam tu ita iudicas, tamen species ipsa tam gratiosi liberti aut servi dignitatem habere nullam potest. Atque hoc sic habeto—nihil enim nec temere dicere nec astute reticere debeo—, materiam omnem sermonum eorum, qui de te detrahere vellent, Statium dedisse; antea tantum intellegi potuisse, iratos tuae severitati esse non nullos, hoc manumisso iratis quod loquerentur non defuisse.

4 II. Nunc respondebo ad eas epistolas, quas mihi reddidit L. Caesius, cui, quoniam ita te velle intellego, nullo loco deero; quarum altera est de Blaudeno Zeuxide, quem scribis certissimum matricidam tibi a me intime commendari. Qua de re et de hoc genere toto, ne forte me in Graecos tam ambitiosum factum esse mirere, pauca cognosce. Ego cum Graecorum querelas nimium valere sentirem propter hominum ingenia ad fallendum parata, quoscumque de te queri audivi quacumque potui ratione placavi. Primum Dionysopolitas qui erant inimicissimi lenivi, quorum principem Hermippum non solum sermone meo, sed etiam familiaritate devinxi; ego Apamensem Hephaestum, ego levissimum hominem, Megaristum Antandrium, ego Niciam Smyrnaeum, ego

'to have used expressions like these.' The MS. has 'potuisse,' sc. 'dicere.'

1. Id mihi . . deterrui. Expressions of Statius quoted.

Quibus in rebus, 'in which behaviour' or 'expressions even if used with the utmost fidelity.'

2. Etiamsi is followed by the indic., if the condition be not expressly negatived, see Madv. 361, Obs. 2.

Quoniam tu ita iudicas. Quintus refers to the fidelity of Statius Ad Fam. 16. 16, 2.

3. Dignitatem . . potest, 'is inconsistent with proper self-respect on your part,' 'puts you in quite an undignified light' Tyr. On 'nullam' = 'non,' see Madv. 455, Obs. 5.

4. Nihil . . nec: cp. p. 58, note on l. 10.

5. Astute: cp. Ep. 70, 6, note.

Materiam . . dedisse, 'has furnished all the materials for the remarks of those who wish to censure you.' On the mood of 'vellent' see Ep. 5, 8, note.

8. Hoc manumisso: see Ep. 12, 1, note.

9. L. Caesius, agent of Q. Cicero, and mentioned Ad Q. F. 1. 1, 14.

10. Nullo loco, 'on no occasion.' It seems a rare use of the word.

11. Blaudeno. Probably 'of Blandus,' a town near Ancyra, in Phrygia. Of this Zeuxis nothing more seems to be known. The termination '-enus' recurs often in adjectives formed from the names of towns to the east of the Aegean. Cp. Abydenus, Lampsacenus, Hypaepenus.

12. Intime, 'cordially,' 'earnestly,'—a rare meaning of the word.

De hoc genere toto, 'on this whole subject' of my relations with the Greeks. 'Genus' = 'res.' Forcell.

13. Ambitiosum, 'anxious for the good opinion of.' Forcell., Metzg.

14. Nimium valere, 'have too much weight at Rome.'

17. Dionysopolitas. Dionysopolis was a town of Phrygia in the conventus of Apamea; for a notice of the latter place, see Ep. 32, 2, note. The Greeks whose names are found in this passage, are not, apparently, mentioned elsewhere.

18. Familiaritate, 'by admitting him to intimacy.'

19. Devinxi, 'placed under an obligation.'

20. Antandrium. Antandros was a coast town of Asia Minor, opposite Lesbos.

nugas maximas omni mea comitate complexus sum, Nymphontem
etiam Colophonium: quae feci omnia, non quo me aut hi homines
aut tota natio delectaret—pertaesum est levitatis, adsentationis,
animorum non officiis, sed temporibus servientium—, sed, ut ad 5
Zeuxim revertar, cum is de M. Cascellii sermone secum habito,
quae tu scribis, ea ipsa loqueretur, obstiti eius sermoni et hominem in familiaritatem recepi. Tua autem quae fuerit cupiditas
tanta, nescio, quod scribis cupisse te, quoniam Smyrnae duos
Mysos insuisses in culeum, simile in superiore parte provinciae
edere exemplum severitatis tuae et idcirco Zeuxim elicere omni
ratione voluisse, quem adductum in iudicium fortasse dimitti non
oportuerat, conquiri vero et elici blanditiis, ut tu scribis, ad
iudicium necesse non fuit, cum praesertim hominem, quem ego
et ex suis civibus et ex multis aliis quotidie magis cognosco
nobiliorem esse prope quam civitatem suam. 'At enim Graecis 6
solis indulgeo.' Quid? L. Caecilium nonne omni ratione placavi?
quem hominem! qua ira! quo spiritu! quem denique praeter
Tuscenium, cuius causa sanari non potest, non mitigavi? Ecce
supra caput homo levis ac sordidus, sed tamen equestri censu,

1. Nugas maximas, 'the most worthless creatures.' Cp. 'amicos habet meras nugas' Ad Att. 6. 3. 5. See too Nägelsb. 15. 48.

Omni comitate complexus sum, 'treated with the utmost courtesy.' This use of the verb seems common.

2. Non quo . . delectaret: cp. p. 90, note on l. 2. There are no corresponding words here to 'non quo.'

3. Levitatis. Cp. Ep. 8. 1, note.

4. Non officiis . . servientium, 'who regard in their attentions people's circumstances, rather than the claims of good services' done by them.

Sed, resumptive: cp. Ep. 13. 2.

5. M. Cascellius seems to have been a merchant of Asia. The conversation reported by Zeuxis had probably been unfavourable to Q. Cicero, and Marcus thought it advisable to check the talkativeness ('sermoni') of Zeuxis by admitting him among his friends.

6. Quae tu scribis . . loqueretur, 'began to talk at Rome just as one might expect from your letter.' Reported the very threat mentioned in your letter to me. In substance, Tyrr.

7. Quae fuerit cupiditas . . nescio, 'I know not how to account for such passion as is shewn in your writing.'

9. Insuisses in culeum. Referring to the well-known punishment of parricides. Cp. Pro Rosc. Am. 25, 26; Iuv. 8, 214.

Superiore parte, 'in the upper, or inland, part of your province.'

10. Elicere, 'to inveigle,' from a place where he was in safety.

11. Quem adductum . . oportuerat, 'who, if brought to trial, ought not perhaps to have been discharged.' On the indic. 'oportuerat,' see Ep. 4. 1, note.

15. Nobiliorem quam civitatem suam, 'more famous than his native town,' perhaps ironical. Prof. Tyrrell suggests 'mobiliorem.'

At enim, 'but you will say.' This phrase, introducing an objection, is frequent in orations.

16. L. Caecilium. P. Sulla had a half-brother named L. Caecilius Rufus; but the man here mentioned was more probably a Roman trader, of whom nothing else is known.

17. Praeter Tuscenium. Tuscenius had apparently been already punished in some way by Q. Cicero. Cp. Ad Q. F. 1. 2. 19.

18. Cuius causa sanari non potest, 'whose case is past remedy.'

19. Supra caput, 'troubles, or threatens, us:' lit. 'hangs over our heads.' Cp. Sall.

Catienus: etiam is lenietur; cuius tu in patrem quod fuisti asperior, non reprehendo; certo enim scio te fecisse cum causa; sed quid opus fuit eius modi litteris, quas ad ipsum misisti? 'Illum crucem sibi ipsum constituere, ex qua tu eum ante detraxisses; te curaturum, fumo ut combureretur, plaudente tota provincia.' Quid vero ad C. Fabium nescio quem?—nam eam quoque epistolam T. Catienus circumgestat—'renuntiari tibi Licinium plagiarium cum suo pullo miluino tributa exigere.' Deinde rogas Fabium, ut et patrem et filium vivos comburat, si possit; si minus, ad te mittat, uti iudicio comburantur. Eae litterae abs te per iocum missae ad C. Fabium, si modo sunt tuae, cum
7 leguntur, invidiosam atrocitatem verborum habent; ac, si omnium mearum praecepta litterarum repetes, intelleges esse nihil a me nisi orationis acerbitatem et iracundiam et, si forte, raro litterarum missarum indiligentiam reprehensam; quibus quidem in rebus si apud te plus auctoritas mea quam tua sive natura paulo acrior sive quaedam dulcedo iracundiae sive dicendi sal facetiaeque valuissent, nihil sane esset, quod nos poeniteret. Et mediocri me dolore putas adfici, cum audiam, qua sit existi-

Cat. 52 'dux hostium cum exercitu supra caput est.' Prof. Tyrrell remarks that the phrase is used by Livy and Sallust, but not elsewhere by Cicero.

1. Catienus seems only to be mentioned in this letter.

3. Ad ipsum. To the *younger* Catienus probably.

4. Ex qua . . detraxisses. Perhaps Q. Cicero had passed over some offence of the younger Catienus, and described his service in these exaggerated terms. The son of a man of equestrian *fortune* can hardly have really been in danger of crucifixion, except from a governor like Verres.

5. Fumo ut combureretur, 'should be stifled with smoke.' Cp. Lamprid. in Alex. Sev. 36 for a description of the punishment; but Wesenb. quotes Plaut. Curc. 1. 1. 54. '*fumo comburi nihil potest*,' and suggests 'in furno,' quoting Ursinus for 'furno.'

6. Quid vero. Sc. 'opus fuit scribere,' or 'quod scripsisti,' 'what need was there for you to write?' or 'what do you say about having written?' Wesenb. places the ? after 'vero' and would supply 'scribis,' 'say further, you write.'

Ad C. Fabium. This man seems not to be mentioned elsewhere.

7. Licinium plagiarium. This man's name seems to be only mentioned here. 'Plagiarius' means a kidnapper, and is used by the writers on law, though apparently not by Cicero, except in this passage.

8. Cum suo pullo miluino, 'with his little kite,' i.e. his son apparently, or, as Manutius thinks, a slave.

Tributa exigere. These words probably mean, 'is collecting taxes,' i.e. 'levying contributions,' without any official authority.

10. Iudicio, 'after a legal trial,' 'according to law.' On the abl., see Ep. 4. 8, note.

11. Invidiosam atrocitatem verborum, 'an odious harshness, or *ferocity*, of expression.'

14. Si forte, raro . . indiligentiam, 'and, it may be, occasionally hastiness in your correspondence.' Prof. Tyrrell renders 'carelessness shewn in neglecting to write often enough.' 'Indiligentia' seems not to occur elsewhere in Cicero. Forcell.

17. Sal facetiaeque. From Cic. Orat. 26 it appears that 'sal' was the more general term, and comprehended both '*facetiae*,' elegant and amusing stories, and 'dicta,' bon mots. Cp. p. 43, note on l. 4.

19. Cum audiam, 'on hearing.' Cp. 'quis non cum haec videat irriserit?' De

matione Vergilius, qua tuus vicinus C. Octavius? nam si te interioribus vicinis tuis, Ciliciensi et Syriaco, anteponis, valde magnum facis! atque is dolor est, quod cum ii, quos nominavi, te innocentia non vincant, vincunt tamen artificio benevolentiae colligendae, qui neque Cyrum Xenophontis neque Agesilaum noverint; quorum regum summo imperio nemo umquam verbum ullum asperius audivit.

III. Sed haec a principio tibi praecipiens quantum profecerim, 2
non ignoro: nunc tamen decedens, id quod mihi iam facere videris, relinque quaeso quam iucundissimam memoriam tui. Successorem habes perblandum; cetera valde illius adventu tua requirentur. In litteris mittendis, *ut* saepe ad te scripsi, nimium te exorabilem praebuisti: tolle omnes, si potes, iniquas, tolle inusitatas, tolle contrarias. Statius mihi narravit scriptas ad te solere adferri, ab

Legg. 2. 1. 2. If it meant 'whenever I hear,' the indic. would probably be used. See Madv. 359.

1. Vergilius. C. Vergilius was propraetor of Sicily in 59–58 B.C. He was a friend of Cicero, but dared not offer an asylum to him as an exile (see Pro Planc. 40). Vergilius served afterwards against Caesar in Africa (Bell. Afric. 28).

C. Octavius: see Ep. 9. 12, note.

2. Interioribus, 'farther up the country, farther East.' The governor of Syria at this time was either L. Marcius Philippus or Cn. Lentulus Marcellinus. Cp. App. Syr. 51. The governor of Cilicia was perhaps T. Ampius Balbus (cp. Ad Fam. 1. 3. 2), perhaps M. Pupius Piso, consul for 61 B.C. Cp. A. W. Zumpt, Studia Romana 63.

Valde magnum facis! 'that is a great deal to boast of!' ironical.

3. Is dolor . . vincunt, 'I am indignant at their surpassing you.' Cp. Madv. for the difference of 'quod' with the indic. from the accus. and inf. 398 a. b.

4. Artificio . . colligendae, 'skill in winning good-will.' 'Colligere' = 'comparare.' Forcell.

5. Qui, 'though they.' See Ep. 6, 3, note. Quintus, it is implied, was familiar with the works of Xenophon.

6. Quorum . . imperio, 'from whom, though both kings with absolute power.' On the abl. see Ep. 6, 2, note, on p. 43. The reference is to the works of Xenophon bearing the titles Cyropaedia and Agesilaus.

8. Quantum, perhaps 'how little!' Cp. 'in scobe quantus Consistit sumtus' Hor. Sat. 2. 4. 81, and, as some maintain,

'quanti sua funera vendant
Quid refert.'—Iuv. Sat. 8. 192, 3.

Cp. also Mr. King's note on the use of 'quantumcumque,' Philipp. 7. 3. 8. But Prof. Tyrrell thinks that Cicero here refers to the real merits of his brother's administration and understands 'quantum' in the usual sense.

10. Successorem. It is not known who succeeded Q. Cicero in his province.

11. Perblandum. A rare word. See Livy 23. 10.

Cetera . . requirentur, 'your other qualities will be much missed on his arrival.' On the abl. 'adventu,' see Ep. 8, 11, note.

12. In litteris . . praebuisti, 'in issuing rescripts,' or perhaps, as Prof. Tyrrell says, 'requisitionary letters' of which that to the agents of L. Flavius mentioned below § 10, may be a sample, 'you have shown yourself too accessible to entreaties.'

13. Tolle, 'destroy,' or perhaps 'rescind.'

Iniquas . . contrarias, 'illegal, unusual in form, or contrary to other letters.'

14. Scriptas . . solerent, 'that your rescripts are brought to you ready written and read by him, after which he tells you if they contain anything illegal [or 'unfair;' Tyrr.], but that before he joined you there was no sifting of them; that this carelessness had given birth to the collections of select correspondence which were so much criticised.' 'Scriptas,' 'ab iis qui eas a Quinto petivissent,' 'by the petitioners themselves.' Manut. I presume that those who were aggrieved by Q. Cicero's conduct collected and circu-

se legi, et, si iniquae sint, fieri te certiorem; antequam vero ipse
ad te venisset, nullum delectum litterarum fuisse; ex eo esse
9 volumina selectarum epistolarum, quae reprehendi solerent. Hoc
de genere nihil te nunc quidem moneo; sero est enim, ac scire
potes multa me varie diligenterque monuisse: illud tamen, quod
Theopompo mandavi, cum essem admonitus ab ipso, vide per
homines amantes tui, quod est facile, ut haec genera tollantur
epistolarum, primum iniquarum, deinde contrariarum, tum absurde
et inusitate scriptarum, postremo in aliquem contumeliosarum.
Atque ego haec tam esse, quam audio, non puto, et, si sunt occupationibus tuis minus animadversa, nunc perspice et purga. Legi
epistolam, quam ipse scripsisse Sulla nomenclator dictus est, non
10 probandam; legi non nullas iracundas. Sed tempore ipso de
epistolis: nam cum hanc paginam tenerem, L. Flavius, praetor
designatus, ad me venit, homo mihi valde familiaris. Is mihi, te
ad procuratores suos litteras misisse, quae mihi visae sunt iniquis-
simae, ne quid de bonis, quae L. Octavii Nasonis fuissent, cui

lated such of his rescripts as were most likely to make him unpopular.

1. **Sint.** Wesenb. suggests 'essent' as required by the following tenses.

3. **Hoc de genere:** see note on § 4 of this letter.

5. **Varie** = 'multis de rebus.' Manut.

Illud tamen refers to what follows. See Ep. 5, 9, note.

6. **Theopompus** seems to have been one of the retinue of Q. Cicero.

Vide per homines . . ut tollantur, 'take care that any friends of yours, who may meet with such letters, destroy them,' 'that any men, on whose friendship you can count, destroy them.' Manutius thinks that 'tollantur' means 'be discontinued.'

8. **Absurde**, prob. 'in bad taste.'

10. **Haec tam esse quam audio**, 'that there are so many faults of this kind as I hear.' Prof. Tyrrell has 'that these faults exist to such a degree.' Orell. does not think the insertion of any word necessary.

Occupationibus tuis, 'by reason of your occupations.' We might expect the insertion of 'prae,' but cp. 'Gallicanis legionibus' in Cat. 2, 3, 5, according to some editions. See also Madv. 255.

11. **Perspice et purga**, 'look through and sift.'

12. **Ipse**, supp. 'without your reading it,' or, perhaps, as Schütz suggests, 'without your dictating it.' Quintus must have sealed the letter as it was brought to him.

Sulla. Not mentioned elsewhere. Perhaps a freedman of the Sulla family, though it was not usual for freedmen to assume the cognomen of their patrons.

Nomenclator. An attendant, whose business it was to tell his master the names of men who were approaching, as they walked in the streets together. The services of such an attendant were especially useful to candidates for public offices on their canvass. Cp. Pro Muren. 36, 77.

13. **Tempore ipso de epistolis**, 'I was writing about your letters at a very opportune time.' On the ellipse, see Ep. 9, 8, note on p. 70.

14. **Cum . . tenerem**, 'while I held this very page,' 'was writing these very lines.'

L. Flavius. Perhaps the tribune for 61-60 B.C., who brought forward an agrarian law in Pompey's interest, and had the consul Metellus Celer arrested for opposing him. Cp. Ep. 9, 6 and 8, notes. He fought on Caesar's side in the civil war. Cp. Ep. 68, 2.

16. **Procuratores**, 'agents.'

17. **L. Octavius Naso** is not mentioned elsewhere. He seems to have died in Asia, leaving Flavius his heir; who would naturally wish to convert the inheritance into

L. Flavius heres est, deminuerent ante, quam C. Fundanio pecuniam solvissent; itemque misisse ad Apollonidenses, ne de bonis, quae Octavii fuissent, deminui paterentur prius, quam Fundanio debitum solutum esset. Haec mihi veri similia non videntur; sunt enim a prudentia tua remotissima. 'Ne deminuat heres?' Quid si infitiatur? quid si omnino non debet? quid? praetor solet iudicare deberi? Quid? ego Fundanio non cupio? non amicus sum? non misericordia moveor? Nemo magis; sed vis iuris eius modi est quibusdam in rebus, ut nihil sit loci gratiae. Atque ita mihi dicebat Flavius scriptum in ea epistola, quam tuam esse dicebat, te aut quasi amicis tuis gratias acturum aut quasi inimicis incommoda *ad*laturum. Quid multa? Ferebat graviter, et 11
vehementer mecum querebatur orabatque, ut ad te quam diligentissime scriberem: quod facio et te prorsus vehementer etiam atque etiam rogo, ut et procuratoribus Flavii remittas de deminuendo et Apollonidensibus ne quid perscribas, quod contra Flavium sit, amplius. Et Flavii causa et scilicet Pompeii facies omnia. Nolo medius fidius ex tua iniuria in illum tibi liberalem

money as soon as possible, through his agents.

1. Deminuerent. 'Deminuere' = 'alienare.' Forcell. Cp. Pro Balb. 1, 2.

C. Fundanius may perhaps be identified with a Roman knight who deserted to Caesar in the second Spanish war. Cp. Bell. Hisp. 11. He seems to have had claims against the estate of Octavius, and to have prevailed on Q. Cicero to interfere with the ordinary course of law on his behalf.

2. Apollonidenses. Apollonis was a town of Mysia, about 40 miles from Pergamum, and as far from Sardis. Cp. Pro Flacc. 29. 71.

6. Quid si infitiatur, 'what if Flavius denies the debt.'

Praetor. More correctly 'propraetor.' But Verres is called 'praetor' In Verr. Act. 2. 1. 12, 34, and 2. 12, 31; cp. also Ep. 36. 11. The proper course was for the magistrate or governor (praetor or propraetor) to lay down the law, and to name a judge or judges to try the question of fact; not for the magistrate ('iudicare') to try the question of fact as Q. Cicero had done. See the second passage quoted above.

7. Ego . . non cupio, 'do I not wish Fundanius well?' See Madv. 344 a.

8. Vis. The best MS. has 'via,' which might mean 'course,' 'method.' Cp. 'non tam iustitiae quam litigandi tradunt vias' De Legg. 1. 6, 18.

9. Ita . . scriptum, sc. 'esse.'

11. Te aut . . aut foll., 'that according to their [the procuratores'] behaviour in this matter you would treat them as friends or enemies.'

12. Ferebat graviter, 'he took it ill.' 'Ferre graviter' is more commonly followed by an accusative, or by a sentence, but the ellipse is not unnatural in a letter.

13. Diligentissime, 'as earnestly as possible.' Forcell.

15. Remittas, 'make a concession to,' 'withdraw your prohibition.' The verb is used in a similar sense with 'aliquid,' Philipp. 1. 5, 12. Cp. Tac. Ann. 1, 8 'Remisit Caesar adroganti moderatione.'

16. Perscribas. The MS. M. has 'prescribas' for 'praescribas,' 'dictate,' which Prof. Tyrrell reads.

17. Scilicet, 'assuredly.' Cp. Ep. 12. 4.

Facies omnia, 'make all these concessions.' For this use of the fut. ind., cp. Ep. 11. 5, note. Flavius was a political friend of Pompey. See below; also Ad Att. 1. 18. 6; 1. 19. 4; Intr. to Part I, § 15.

18. Nolo . . me videri, 'I by no means wish you should think I am doing a favour (to Pompey and Flavius) at the expense of a wrong done by you to Fundanius.'

me videri, sed te oro, ut tu ipse auctoritatem et monumentum aliquod decreti aut litterarum tuarum relinquas, quod sit ad Flavii rem et ad causam accommodatum: fert enim graviter homo et mei observantissimus et sui iuris dignitatisque retinens se apud te neque amicitia nec iure valuisse; et, ut opinor, Flavii aliquando rem et Pompeius et Caesar tibi commendarunt, et ipse ad te scripserat Flavius et ego certe. Qua re si ulla res est, quam tibi me petente faciendam putes, haec ea sit. Si me amas, cura, elabora, perfice, ut Flavius et tibi et mihi quam maximas gratias agat: hoc te ita rogo, ut maiore studio rogare non possim.

12 IV. Quod ad me de Hermia scribis, mihi mehercule valde molestum fuit. Litteras ad te parum fraterne scripseram; quas oratione Diodoti, Luculli liberti, commotus, de pactione statim quod audieram, iracundius scripseram et revocare cupiebam: huic
13 tu epistolae non fraterne scriptae fraterne debes ignoscere. De Censorino, Antonio, Cassiis Scaevola, te ab iis diligi, ut scribis, vehementer gaudeo. Cetera fuerunt in eadem epistola graviora, quam vellem: *ὀρθὰν τὰν ναῦν* et *ἅπαξ θανεῖν*. Maiora ista erunt:

Medius fidius, = 'ita me deus fidius adiuvet.' The words 'deus fidius' are variously explained as equivalent to (Ζεὺς πίστιος) the god of good faith; 'dius filius,' Hercules or Sancus (see Zumpt, L. G. 361, note); and 'per divi fidem.' Paul. Diac. ap. Festum, p. 147, Müller. On the acc. and infin. after 'volo,' 'cupio,' etc., see Madv. 389, Obs. 4.

1. Auctoritatem, 'an official declaration.' Cp. In Verr. Act. 2, 3. 62, 146.

Monumentum, 'record.' On the gen. 'decreti,' see Ep. 10, 2, note, on p. 78.

2. Relinquas. Tempus enim discessionis appropinquabat. Manut.

Quod sit . . accommodatum, 'framed to promote the cause and interest of Flavius.' On the conj. 'sit,' see Ep. 5, 8, note.

4. Retinens, 'tenacious of.' Nägelsb. 72, 196. On the gen., see Madv. 289 a, and cp. 'avitae nobilitatis inter angustias fortunae retinens' Tac. Ann. 2. 38.

Se . . valuisse, 'that neither regard for friendship nor regard for justice prevailed with you on his behalf.'

5. Iure. 'Cum iudicare praetor non debueris' Manut.

8. Elabora. With 'perfice' this word may mean, 'bring it to pass by your exertions.'

11. Hermia; apparently a slave of M. Cicero. Cp. Ep. 83, 1.

13. Diodoti. Diodotus seems not to be mentioned elsewhere.

Pactione. What Cicero here refers to is not known. Manut. says 'inter Graecos et publicanos facta,' and cites Ad Q. F. 1. 1, 12.

Statim quod, 'immediately after.' Cp. 'inde quod' Ter. Heaut. 1. 1, 2; and 'tertius dies est quod' Plin. Epp. 4. 27.

15. De Censorino. The man here mentioned may have been L. Marcius Censorinus, praetor 43 B.C., and an adherent of M. Antonius. He is often noticed in the Philippics. Cp. Philipp. 11. 5, 11; 13. 14, 36; 12. 8, 20. It is uncertain who were the Cassii and Antonius here mentioned.

16. Scaevola. Q. Mucius Q. F. Q. N. Scaevola, tribune in 55-54 B.C., opposed the claim of C. Pomptinus to a triumph (cp. Ad Att. 4. 16, 12). He was legate to Appius Claudius in Cilicia (cp. Ad Fam. 3. 5. 5), and Caesar seems to have counted on his support (Ep. 62, 3) in the senate in 49 B.C.

17. Graviora, 'more serious.' Prof. Tyrrell says 'more strongly expressed than I could have wished.'

18. *ὀρθὰν τὰν ναῦν*. In Stobaeus, *ὅτι δεῖ γενναίως φέρειν τὰ προσπίπτοντα*, p. 108 (106) 83 ad fin. we find, *καλῶς τὸ τοῦ κυβερνήτου ἐκεῖνο 'Ἀλλ' οὖν γε ὦ Πόσειδον, ὀρθήν*, translated by Seneca, Epp. Mor. 85

meae obiurgationes fuerunt amoris plenissimae; quae sunt non nulla, sed tamen mediocria et parva potius. Ego te numquam ulla in re dignum minima reprehensione putassem, cum te sanctissime gereres, nisi inimicos multos haberemus. Quae ad te aliqua *cum* monitione aut obiurgatione scripsi, scripsi propter diligentiam cautionis meae, in qua et maneo et manebo et, idem ut facias, non desistam rogare. Attalus Hypaepenus mecum egit, ut se ne 14
impedires, quo minus, quod ad Q. Publicii statuam decretum est, erogaretur: quod ego te et rogo et admoneo, ne talis viri tamque nostri necessarii honorem minui per te aut impediri velis. Praeterea Aesopi [tragoedi], nostri familiaris, Licinius servus, tibi notus, aufugit: is Athenis apud Patronem Epicureum pro libero fuit; inde in Asiam venit. Postea Plato quidam Sardianus, Epicureus, qui Athenis solet esse multum et qui tum Athenis fuerat, cum Licinius eo venisset, cum eum fugitivum esse postea ex Aesopi litteris cognosset, hominem comprehendit et in custodiam Ephesi tradidit, sed in publicam an in pistrinum non satis ex

(12. 3. 33) 'Neptune numquam hanc navem nisi rectam.' It means here, 'be assured that I will govern my province rightly.' I owe this correction of my former note to Prof. Tyrrell.

ἅπαξ θανεῖν. From Aesch. Prom. Vinct. 769 (Paley), where Io says

κρεῖσσον γὰρ εἰσάπαξ θανεῖν
ἢ τὰς ἁπάσας ἡμέρας πάσχειν κακῶς.

Quintus means that he had rather die than be constantly abused.

Maiora ista erunt, 'such expressions will do for greater troubles,' Orell. ap. Billerb. 'You speak in too tragic tones.' Wesenb. proposes to omit 'erunt' as repeated from the following 'fuerunt,' and to read 'quaestus sum' for 'quae sunt.'

1. Quae sunt non nulla . . potius. If these words are genuine, they may perhaps be translated, 'which have some severity (deserve the name obiurgationes to some extent), but only a moderate or rather a small amount of it.' On the gender of 'nonnulla,' cp. Madv. 211 b, Obs. 1. Prof. Tyrrell reads 'quaerunt' = 'requirunt,' 'my reproaches require some changes in your conduct.'

3. Cum . . gereres, 'considering that you behave very well.' On the tense, cp. note on § 2 of this letter.

5. Cum monitione. As 'monitio' is said to occur in only one other passage of Cicero's writings (Lael. 24. 89), Wesenb. suggests 'cum admonitione.'

Diligentiam cautionis meae, 'my careful foresight.' See on the gen., Ep. 10, 2, note.

7. Attalus is only mentioned here.

Hypaepenus. Hypaepi was a city of Lydia, on the southern slope of Mount Tmolus, and about 42 miles from Ephesus.

8. Q. Publicii. Baiter adopts this from Schütz for the MS. reading 'Publiceni.' Publicius was praetor in 65 B.C. (cp. Pro Cluent. 45, 126), and may have afterwards governed Asia.

9. Erogaretur, 'should be paid from the provincial treasury.' Attalus was not improbably the contractor for this statue.

Quod ego te et rogo, 'as to which I both entreat you.' Cp. De Nat. Deor. 1. 9. 24.

11. Aesopi: cp. 'gravis Aesopus' Hor. Epp. 2. 1, 82. He was an eminent tragic actor, on friendly terms with Cicero, who commends his political principles as well as his professional talent. Cp. Pro Sest. 56, 120; also Rhet. ad Herenn. 3. 21.

Licinius. Evidently distinct from the man mentioned before in this letter. Neither his name nor that of Plato of Sardis seems to be found elsewhere in Cicero's writings.

12. Patron, who succeeded Phaedrus as an Epicurean teacher at Athens, seems to have been intimate with Cicero. Cp. Ep. 31, 6: Ad Fam. 13. 1.

17. In publicam, sc. 'custodiam,' 'to

litteris eius intellegere potuimus: tu, quoquo modo est, quoniam Ephesi est, hominem investiges velim summaque diligentia vel tecum deducas. Noli spectare, quanti homo sit; parvi enim pretii est, qui iam nihili est; sed tanto dolore Aesopus est adfectus propter servi scelus et audaciam, ut nihil ei gratius facere possis, quam si illum per te recuperarit.

V. Nunc ea cognosce, quae maxime exoptas: rem publicam funditus amisimus, adeo ut Cato, adulescens nullius consilii, sed tamen civis Romanus et Cato, vix vivus effugeret, quod, cum Gabinium de ambitu vellet postulare, neque praetores diebus aliquot adiri possent vel potestatem sui facerent, in contionem escendit et Pompeium privatum dictatorem appellavit; propius nihil est factum, quam ut occideretur. Ex hoc, qui sit status totius rei publicae, videre potes. Nostrae tamen causae non videntur homines defuturi: mirandum in modum profitentur, offerunt se, pollicentur. Equidem cum spe sum maxima, tum maiore etiam animo, spe, superiores fore nos, animo, ut in hac re

the public prison,' distinguished from pistrinum, a private place of punishment for slaves.' 'a mill' where they had to grind; frequently referred to in the Roman comedians.

1. Est. Prof. Tyrrell reads 'potest.'

2. Vel tecum, 'even in your own company,' i.e. 'on your return to Rome.' Quintus had not much longer to stay in his province. Wesenb. suggests that 'vel Romam mittas,' or other words to that effect, should be inserted after 'diligentia.'

4. Nihili. So Baiter. The MS. has 'nihil,' which Forcell. explains as = 'nullius pretii.'

8. Adeo ut . . effugeret. On the mood, see Madv. 355, and for the tense, ib. 382.

Cato. C. Porcius Cato is probably meant, a man of shifting principles and strong prejudices. He had a quarrel with Ptolemy, also with P. Lentulus Spinther, Pompey, Milo, and Cicero; but was reconciled to the three last. Cp. Ep. 23, 3 and 4. He was tribune 57-6 B.C.; was accused of illegal conduct two years afterwards, but acquitted. Cp. Ad Att. 4. 15. 4; 4. 16. 5; 4. 17. 2.

Nullius consilii, gen. qualitatis. See Madv. 287.

9. Et Cato, 'and a Cato.'

10. Gabinium. Aulus Gabinius was now consul elect. For more particulars about him, see Ep. 13, 3, and references there.

Postulare, 'to demand leave to accuse,' the first step in a prosecution.

Diebus aliquot, ablat. of a space of time. See Madv. 276.

11. Adiri . . facerent, 'allowed no access to, or communication with, them.' Forcell.

In contionem, 'to the rostra,' where, as a private citizen, he had no right to appear, except at the bidding of a magistrate. See Ep. 7, 1, note.

12. Privatum dictatorem, 'a dictator in a private station,' 'an unrecognised dictator.'

Propius . . occideretur. On the general form of this sentence, see Madv. 373.

Propius factum, 'nearer happening.' Cp. 'propius fidem' Liv. 4. 17; 'propius virtutem' Sall. Cat. 11.

14. Nostrae . . causae. Cicero was threatened with an attack by Clodius.

15. Profitentur, 'declare themselves for me.'

16. Pollicentur, 'make promises.' Forcell. It has an accusative a few lines below.

17. Spe, superiores . . animo. The MS. has 'sperent superiores fore nos, confident animo ut.' The reading in the text is that of Madvig and Baiter.

Animo . . ut . . pertimescam, for the conj., explaining 'animo,' cp. Ep. 13, 3, note.

publica ne casum quidem ullum pertimescam. Sed tamen se res sic habet: si diem nobis dixerit, tota Italia concurret, ut multiplicata gloria discedamus; sin autem vi agere conabitur, spero fore studiis non solum amicorum, sed etiam alienorum, ut vi resistamus. Omnes et se et suos amicos, clientes, libertos, servos, pecunias denique suas pollicentur; nostra antiqua manus bonorum ardet studio nostri atque amore; si qui antea aut alieniores fuerant aut languidiores, nunc horum regum odio se cum bonis coniungunt. Pompeius omnia pollicetur et Caesar, quibus ego ita credo, ut nihil de mea comparatione deminuam. Tribuni pl. designati sunt nobis amici; consules se optime ostendunt; praetores habemus amicissimos et acerrimos cives, Domitium, Nigidium, Memmium, Lentulum; bonos etiam alios, *hos* singulares:

In hac re publica. 'Quicunque nunc est et quocunque eventurus rei publicae status' Orell. ap. Billerb.

1. Sed tamen, resumptive; 'however, as I was going to say.' See Madv. 480.

Se res sic habet, 'the case stands as follows.' Forcell.

2. Si diem .. dixerit, sc. Clodius, 'if he indicts me,' 'proceeds legally.'

Ut .. discedamus, 'that we shall get out of the affair,' or 'ex iudicio,' as Manut. followed by Tyrrell. 'Discedere dicitur qui re confecta quidpiam aut obtinuit aut perdidit' Forcell. On the mood, see § 15 above; and on the tense, Ep. 6, 1, note on p. 42.

3. Spero fore .. ut vi resistamus. On the first abl., see Ep. 18, 3, note; on the second, Ep. 4, 2, note. 'I hope the zeal of my friends will enable me to resist force with force.' On the position of 'ut,' see Madv. 465 b.

6. Nostra antiqua manus, 'my old supporters.' Cp. 'consularis exercitus' Ep. 12, 4.

8. Horum regum, i.e. the triumvirs.

9. Quibus ego ita credo .. ut deminuam, 'but I do not allow my confidence in them to suspend my own preparations.' On 'ita .. ut,' see Ep. 9, 6, note. 'Comparatio' seems not to be common in this sense without an objective genitive following.

10. Tribuni plebis designati. Among them were L. Ninnius Quadratus, P. (?) Aelius Ligus, perhaps Q. Terentius Culleo, P. Clodius. Cicero can hardly have meant to include the last among his friends, and P. Aelius also proved hostile. Cp. Pro Sestio, 31, 68. The complete list given in previous editions was taken from Billerbeck's note, but I have not been able to find authority for most of the names.

11. Consules, sc. 'designati.' L. Piso and A. Gabinius. Cicero's hopes were not well founded.

Se optime ostendunt, 'shew themselves very well disposed.' Cp. the use of the adverb in such expressions 'ut dicta impune erant' Tac. Ann. 1. 72, and Ep. 4, 1, note. Wesenb., however, suggests 'optimos.'

Praetores, sc. 'designatos,' Manut. 'among the praetors,' elect, 'for praetors.' See Madv. 227 a.

12. Domitium. L. Ahenobarbum. See Ep. 1, 3, note.

Nigidium. P. Nigidius Figulus was a senator of philosophical tastes. Cp. Ad Fam. 4. 13, 3. He was one of the senators chosen to report on the informations laid against Lentulus and others in 63 B.C. Cp. Pro Sulla 14, 42. He was subsequently banished by Caesar, and seems to have died in exile.

13. Memmium. C. Memmius Gemellus was a man of talent, but of bad character. He was quaestor to Pompey in Spain (cp. Pro Balbo 2, 5), and afterwards curule aedile in 60 B.C. (cp. Ad Att. 1. 18, 3), when he summoned Vatinius before him for trial (cp. In Vat. 14). Memmius attacked Caesar, was reconciled to him for a short time, and quarrelled with him again (cp. Ad Att. 4. 15, 7; 4. 16, 6), was accused of bribery, and banished in 54 or 53 B.C. Cp. Ad Q. F. 3. 2, 3; Ad Att. 6. 1, 23; Ad Fam. 13. 1. Lucretius dedicated to him his poem 'de rerum natura.' Cp. Lucr. de Rer. Nat. 1. 17. 43.

Lentulum. L. Lentulus Crus interceded for Cicero with the consul Piso in 58 B.C.

qua re magnum fac animum habeas et spem bonam. De singulis tamen rebus, quae quotidie gerantur, faciam te crebro certiorem.

16. TO ATTICUS (AD ATT. III. 15).

THESSALONICA, AUGUST 17, 58 B.C. (696 A.U.C.)

1. I have received four letters from you, which I will answer in order. 2. In the first, you exhort me to be firm; I am really ashamed of my own composure, considering what I have lost and what I suffer. I willingly accept your defence of Cato and others. 3. I do not think the freedman of Crassus, whom you mention in your second, was honest in what he said. The proceedings in the senate, of which you speak in your third, were satisfactory—but other accounts differ from yours. Varro's language, quoted in your fourth, gives hopes of Caesar. 4. If you will serve me now, I will make amends for past neglect. Had you been thoroughly devoted to my cause, you would have advised me to resist Clodius; I allow, however, that I did not shew more penetration or resolution than yourself. 5. What occurred to you and Culleo is worth consideration, but I think a repeal of the act of banishment would be preferable to a mere declaration of its illegality, and not subject to more difficulties. The first law of Clodius would have done no harm, if I had been wise. 6. I fear you are concealing some facts from me. How do my friends propose to evade the provisions made by Clodius against the repeal of his law? I shall wait at Thessalonica for the gazette of Aug. 1. 7. I again appeal to you, either to do me real and effective service, or to let me know the worst. I only charge you with want of zeal, not with perfidy. 8. Let me then have accurate news, and write in my name to those who you think wish to hear about me.

CICERO ATTICO SAL.

1 Accepi Idibus Sextilibus quattuor epistolas a te missas: unam, qua me obiurgas, ut sim firmior; alteram, qua Crassi libertum ais tibi de mea sollicitudine macieque narrasse; tertiam, qua demonstras acta in senatu; quartam de eo, quod a Varrone scribis
2 tibi esse confirmatum de voluntate Pompeii. Ad primam tibi hoc

(In Pis. 31), and afterwards supported his claim to a triumph (Ad Fam. 16. 11, 3). He was consul in 49 B.C., and fought on the side of Pompey in the civil war. Cp. Epp. 80, 6; 87, 2. He fled to Egypt after the battle of Pharsalus, and was put to death by order of Ptolemy XIII, Dionysius, or of his advisers. Cp. Caes. Bell. Civ. 3. 104.

Alios, 'others among the number.' The four other praetors were L. Flavius, T. Ampius Balbus, M. Terentius Varro, M. Nonius Sufenas. The election of praetors had thus resulted, on the whole, unfavourably for the triumvirs; it is not probable that any of their decided adherents were among the number of successful candidates, except perhaps Flavius and Nonius.

1. Fac .. habeas: see Madv. 372 b, Obs. 4.

2. Gerantur. On the mood, see Ep. 5, 8, note; Madv. 369.

4. Obiurgas ut sim firmior. Condensed for 'obiurgas et rogas ut' Boot.

scribo, me ita dolere, ut non modo a mente non deserar, sed id ipsum doleam, me tam firma mente ubi utar et quibuscum non habere. Nam si tu me uno non sine maerore cares, quid me censes, qui et te et omnibus? et, si tu incolumis me requiris, quo modo a me ipsam incolumitatem desiderari putas? nolo commemorare, quibus rebus sim spoliatus, non solum quia non ignoras, sed etiam ne rescindam ipse dolorem meum: hoc confirmo, neque tantis bonis esse privatum quemquam neque in tantas miserias incidisse. Dies autem non modo non levat luctum hunc, sed etiam auget; nam ceteri dolores mitigantur vetustate, hic non potest non et sensu praesentis miseriae et recordatione praeteritae vitae quotidie augeri: desidero enim non mea solum neque meos, sed me ipsum. Quid enim sum? Sed non faciam ut aut tuum animum angam querelis aut meis volneribus saepius manus adferam. Nam quod purgas eos, quos ego mihi scripsi invidisse, et in eis Catonem, ego vero tantum illum puto ab isto scelere afuisse, ut maxime doleam plus apud me simulationem aliorum quam istius fidem valuisse. Ceteros quod purgas, debent mihi purgati esse, tibi si sunt. Sed haec sero agimus. Crassi libertum 8
nihil puto sincere locutum. In senatu rem probe scribis actam.

1. **Ita dolere, ut . . non deserar**: see Ep. 9, 6, note. And on 'ut non' as distinguished from 'ne,' see Madv. 456.

2. **Ubi utar et quibuscum**, 'a sphere and society in which to show my firmness.'

3. **Quid me censes**, sc. '*facere*.' See Ep. 8, 6, note.

4. **Omnibus**, sc. 'carere.' For the omission, see Madv. 478 and Obs. 3.

Incolumis, 'whose position is unimpaired;' used in a political sense often by Cicero, as is 'calamitas.'

7. **Rescindam**, 'tear open, as if a half-healed wound. Cp. Ovid. Trist. 3. 11, 63, 64

> 'Ergo quicumque es rescindere crimina noli
> De quo gravi duras vulnere tolle manus.'

9. **Dies**, 'lapse of time.' Cp. 'ipsa die quae debilitat cogitationem.' Ad Fam. 1. 6, 1.

13. **Sed me ipsum.** Cp. for the thought 'non enim vidisses fratrem tuum, non eum quem reliqueras' Ad Q. F. 1. 3, 1, and Fam. 14. 1, 3.

Non faciam ut, pleonastic. See Madv. 481 b.

14. **Manus adferam**, 'feel,' 'handle.' Cp. the quotation from Ovid on l. 7, above.

15. **Quod purgas**: see Ep. 8, 14, note.

Quos ego mihi scripsi invidisse. He refers especially to Hortensius. Cp. Ad Att. 3. 9, 2, where he says of Hortensius 'nondum perspicis . . quorum scelere perierimus?' also Ad Q. F. 1. 3, 8.

16. **Ego vero**, 'I certainly.' See Madv. 454, and cp. 'ego vero libenter desino' Pro Muren. 4, 9.

Tantum . . afuisse, 'so far do I think he was from sharing that crime.'

17. **Simulationem aliorum**, 'the pretended friendship of others.' Perhaps of the consuls and of Pompey. Cp. Epp. 12, 4; 15, 16.

18. **Debent mihi . . si sunt**, 'I ought to acquit their conduct of blame if you do.' Prof. Tyrrell finds a difficulty here. Do not the words simply illustrate Cicero's confidence in his friend's judgment?

19. **Crassi . . locutum**, 'I do not think the freedman of Crassus spoke honestly.' Cicero comments in order on the four letters he had received from Atticus. Cp. § 1. The allusion to the freedman of Crassus is obscure.

20. **Rem . . actam.** These words refer

Sed quid Curio? an illam orationem non legit? quae unde sit prolata nescio. Sed Axius, eiusdem diei scribens ad me acta, non ita laudat Curionem. At potest ille aliquid praetermittere; tu, nisi quod erat profecto non scripsisti. Varronis sermo facit exspectationem Caesaris, atque utinam ipse Varro incumbat in causam! quod profecto cum sua sponte, tum te instante faciet. 4 Ego, si me aliquando vestri et patriae compotem fortuna fecerit, certe efficiam ut maxime laetere unus ex omnibus amicis, meaque officia et studia, quae parum antea luxerunt—fatendum est enim—, sic exsequar, ut me aeque tibi ac fratri et liberis nostris restitutum putes. Si quid in te peccavi, ac potius quoniam peccavi, ignosce; in me enim ipsum peccavi vehementius. Neque haec eo scribo, quo te non meo casu maximo dolore esse adfectum sciam, sed profecto, si, quantum me amas et amasti, tantum amare deberes ac debuisses, numquam esses passus me, quo tu abundabas, egere consilio, nec esses passus mihi persuaderi utile nobis esse legem de collegiis perferri. Sed tu tantum lacrimas

to a debate in the senate on June 1, when P. (?) Aelius Ligus interposed to prevent a decree being passed in Cicero's favour.

Probe = 'bene,' (Forcell.), 'satisfactorily.'

1. Curio. The elder, probably. The younger is generally distinguished by the epithet 'meus,' 'adulescens,' or 'filius.'

An illam .. non legit? Cicero composed a speech against Curio, which got published by some mistake (cp. Ad Att. 3. 12, 2), and so Cicero was surprised to hear that Curio had spoken in his behalf. The speech to which Cicero refers was perhaps a revised edition of that 'In Clodium et Curionem' of which considerable fragments are extant.

2. Axius: see Ep. 18, 5, note.

Acta, 'the occurrences.'

Non ita, 'not so very much.' See Madv. 462 a. Prof. Tyrrell suggests 'does not quote Curio to that effect.'

3. Ille, sc. Axius.

4. Nisi quod erat, 'except what really happened.'

Varronis sermo .. Caesaris, 'what Varro told you gives me hopes of Caesar.' 'Caesaris:' gen. obj. See Madv. 283.

5. Incumbat in causam, 'exert himself in support of my cause.' Cp. Ep. 19, 5, note.

9. Parum .. luxerunt, 'were not so remarkable as they should have been.'

10. Exsequar, 'will discharge or fulfil.'

11. Ac potius, 'or rather.'

12. In me enim .. vehementius, 'I was guilty of a worse offence against myself,' in not trying by all means to attach you. Cicero means that the friendship of Atticus was more valuable to him than his to Atticus.

Neque haec .. quo te non .. sciam, 'my reason for writing is not that I am not aware of your grief.' On 'quo non' with the conjunct., see Ep. 14, 1, note.

14. Si, quantum .. debuisses. If the text is genuine the meaning must be, 'if your affection for me had rested on an obligation to me.' So in substance Hofm., Tyrrell, Jeans. Boot accepts the reading of Pius given as that of 'prisci codices,' 'si tantum amorem re exhibuisses.'

15. Quo tu .. consilio, 'to lack the advice you were so abundantly qualified to give.'

17. De collegiis, 'about the clubs.' Probably the 'collegia compitalicia,' clubs for celebrating the 'ludi compitalicii,' are especially referred to. Such bodies might easily be employed for political purposes, and many of them had been abolished by a law, or by a decree of the senate, passed apparently in 64 B.C. Clodius, however, had restored these clubs, and had founded others consisting, according to Cicero, of the lowest of the people. The organization of the populace was improved, and the

praebuisti dolori meo. quod erat amoris, tamquam ipse ego; quod meritis meis perfectum oportuit, ut dies et noctes, quid mihi faciendum esset, cogitares, id abs te meo, non tuo scelere praetermissum est. Quod si non modo tu, sed quisquam fuisset, qui me Pompeii minus liberali responso perterritum a turpissimo consilio revocaret, quod unus tu facere maxime potuisti, aut occubuissem honeste aut victores hodie viveremus. Hic mihi ignosces: me enim ipsum multo magis accuso, deinde te quasi me alterum; et simul meae culpae socium quaero, ac si restituor, etiam minus videbimur deliquisse, abs teque certe, quoniam nullo nostro, tuo ipsius beneficio diligemur. Quod te cum Culleone scribis de pri- 5

popularity of Clodius increased by this measure. Cp. In Pis. 4, and Asconius' comment; Pro Sest. 25, 55; Mommsen 4. 2, 296 (cp. 303), and De Collegiis, etc., pp. 73-78; Long, Decl. of Rom. Rep. 3. 214; 215.

Tantum lacrimas, 'only tears and not advice,' but you did as much for me as I did for myself.

1. Tamquam ipse ego, sc. 'praebui.'

Quod .. perfectum oportuit, 'what I ought to have earned by a proper display of affection to you.' See a few lines above, 'si .. deberes.' On the mood of 'oportuit,' see Ep. 4. 1, note. On the omission of 'esse' after 'perfectum,' see Madv. 407, Obs. 1.

3. Scelere, 'neglect' (Tyrr.).

4. Quod si .. fuisset, 'but if there had been found—I do not say you, but any one.'

5. Pompeii .. perterritum. Cicero in one place represents Pompey as replying to representations made to him on behalf of Cicero, 'that he could not oppose a tribune without the authority of the consuls and of the senate' (In Pis. 31, 77); in another place, 'that he could do nothing displeasing to Caesar' (Ad Att. 10. 4. 3). The last reply probably expressed the real state of the case.

Turpissimo consilio, i.e. 'that of retiring from Rome to avoid a conflict.'

7. Hic, = 'in hac re' (Forcell.), 'for my remonstrances on this subject.'

Ignosces: see Ep. 11. 3, note.

8. Te quasi me alterum: cp. Ep. 20, 7.

9. Etiam minus .. deliquisse, 'shall seem to have deserved even less than the moderate amount of blame with which I have visited our joint offence.' Cicero only charged himself with want of penetration, and Atticus with that and want of zeal. Compare with this passage § 7 of this letter. If Cicero were restored, their shortcomings would be thought less serious than if he remained in exile.

10. Quoniam nullo nostro .. diligemur, 'shall be dear to you for services done, if not received, by you.' On the abl. 'beneficio,' cp. Madv. 255. With the sentiment, cp. Thucyd. 2. 40; Arist. Eth. Nic. 4. 3. (7.) 25. 'Nullo,' = 'non.' See Ep. 15. 3. note.

11. Quod te .. locutum, 'your conversation with Culleo as to the law against me being a "privilegium" may do some good.' 'Your or his suggestion may be of some value.' Prof. Tyrrell suggests 'tecum Culleonem,' remarking that there could be no reason for the mention of Culleo if the suggestion did not originate with him. On 'quod .. scribis,' see Ep. 8, 14, note.

Cum Culleone. Q. Terentius Culleo was one of the tribunes for 59-58 B.C., and also one of the pontifices minores. Cp. De Harusp. Resp. 6. 12. After the battle of Mutina he left Antony and joined Lepidus, but probably acted as a go-between. Cp. Ep. 141, notes.

De privilegio. The laws of the Twelve Tables forbade all legislation against individuals, and all capital trials except before the people assembled in the comitia centuriata. Cp. Cic. de Legg. 3. 19. 44. Now Cicero had been banished by a law, naming him individually, and passed in the comitia tributa; thus doubly illegal. Atticus, or Culleo, seems to have argued that it might be declared void by a simple decree of the senate; but Cicero remarks that such a decree would be as open as a law to the veto of a tribune (sin erit .. intercedet). According to the oration De Domo, 18, the law for Cicero's banishment ran 'velitis

vilegio locutum, est aliquid, sed multo est melius abrogari: si enim nemo impediet, quid est firmius? sin erit, qui ferri non sinat, idem senatus consulto intercedet. Nec quicquam aliud opus est abrogari: nam prior lex nos nihil laedebat; quam si, ut est promulgata, laudare voluissemus aut, ut erat neglegenda, neglegere, nocere omnino nobis non potuisset. Hic mihi primum meum consilium defuit, sed etiam obfuit. Caeci, caeci, inquam, fuimus in vestitu mutando, in populo rogando, quod, nisi nominatim mecum agi coeptum esset, fieri perniciosum fuit. Sed pergo praeterita; verum tamen ob hanc causam, ut, si quid agetur,
6 legem illam, in qua popularia multa sunt, ne tangatis. Verum est stultum me praecipere, quid agatis aut quo modo: utinam modo agatur aliquid! Multa occultant tuae litterae, credo, ne vehementius desperatione perturber. Quid enim vides agi posse aut quo modo? Per senatumne? ast tute scripsisti ad me, quoddam caput legis Clodium in curiae poste fixisse, NE REFERRI NEVE DICI LICERET. Quo modo igitur Domitius se dixit relaturum? quo

iubeatis ut M. Tullio aqua et igni interdictum sit.'

1. **Sed multo . . melius abrogari**, 'but a regular repeal is much more desirable.'

2. **Qui ferri non sinat**, 'if there be any tribune disposed to prevent the enactment of a law' recalling Cicero.

3. **Nec quicquam . . abrogari**, 'nor does anything else require repeal,' except the special law for my banishment.

4. **Prior lex**: see Intr. to Part I, § 19. It is the sixth law there mentioned.

5. **Laudare**. Cicero might have praised a law drawn up in such general terms, especially as he held that Lentulus and his accomplices had been, not citizens, but public enemies. Cp. in Cat. 4. 5, 10; Intr. to Part I, § 20; Appendix 4.

7. **Defuit, sed etiam obfuit**. Orell. would insert 'non solum' before 'defuit;' Baiter thinks that after 'defuit' 'nec solum defuit' may have dropped out.' Boot, however, argues from the omission of 'non solum' by the MSS. in similar passages, that 'sed etiam' may be equivalent to 'quinetiam,' cp. especially Ad Q. F. 1. 1. 15, 44. Forcell. agrees with Boot.

8. **In vestitu . . rogando**, 'in putting on mourning and supplicating the people.' The senate did so too. Cp. Pro Sest. 11, 26.

Quod nisi . . fuit, 'which was a mischievous step, unless (as was not the case) proceedings had been begun against me by name.' On the indic. 'fuit,' see Madv. 348 b. On **mecum agi**, see Ep. 1, 3, note.

9. **Pergo praeterita**, sc. 'commemorare.' 'I continue to harp on the past.' See Ep. 8, 6, note, and cp. 'pergo reliqua' Ad Att. 4. 11, 1.

10. **Ob hanc causam . . ne tangatis**, 'I do so to prevent your meddling with the law mentioned above, which contains many popular provisions.' The 'prior lex' asserted sound constitutional doctrine.

Ut . . ne: see Ep. 7, 5, note.

Si quid agetur, 'if any steps are taken on my behalf.'

15. **Quoddam caput legis**, 'a certain section of his law' for my banishment.

16. **Ne referri . . liceret**, 'that no motion should be brought forward, and no speech made.' Cp. in Cat. 4. 4, 8 for a similar proviso. A speech might be made in the senate upon a point not directly comprised in the motion under discussion. To make such a speech was called 'egredi relationem.' Cp. Tac. Ann. 2. 38. For instances of the practice, see Philipp. 3. 5, 13; 7. 1, 1.

17. **Domitius**: see Ep. 15, 16, note.

Se relaturum. Domitius could hardly do this in the presence and in spite of the opposition of the consuls. He may have

modo autem iis, quos tu scribis, et de re dicentibus et, ut referretur, postulantibus Clodius tacuit? Ac, si per populum, poteritne nisi de omnium tribunorum pl. sententia? Quid de bonis? quid de domo? poteritne restitui? aut, si non poterit, egomet quo modo potero? Haec nisi vides expediri, quam in spem me vocas? sin autem spei nihil est, quae est mihi vita? Itaque exspecto Thessalonicae acta Kal. Sext., ex quibus statuam in tuosne agros confugiam, ut neque videam homines, quos nolim, et te, ut scribis, videam et propius sim, si quid agatur—idque intellexi cum tibi, tum Q. fratri placere —, an abeam Cyzicum. Nunc, Pomponi, 7
quoniam nihil impertisti tuae prudentiae ad salutem meam, quod aut in me ipso satis esse consilii decreras aut te nihil plus mihi debere quam ut praesto esses, quoniamque ego proditus, inductus, coniectus in fraudem, omnia mea praesidia neglexi, totam Italiam [in me] erectam ad me defendendum destitui et reliqui, me meosque meis tradidi inimicis inspectante et tacente te, qui, si non plus ingenio valebas quam ego, certe timebas minus: si potes, erige adflictos et in eo nos iuva; sin omnia sunt obstructa, id ipsum fac ut sciamus et nos aliquando aut obiurgare aut comiter consolari desine. Ego si tuam fidem accusarem, non me potissimum tuis tectis crederem: meam amentiam accuso, quod a te tantum *me* amari, quantum ego vellem, putavi; quod si fuisset, fidem eandem, curam maiorem adhibuisses, me certe ad exitium praecipitantem retinuisses, istos labores, quos nunc in naufragiis

reckoned on their being absent, or departing for their province before the end of the year.

1. Iis. Among these L. Ninnius was prominent. Cp. Post Red. in Sen. 2, 3.

2. Per populum, sc. 'agetur,' 'if the matter shall be brought forward in the assembly of the people.'

Poteritne, sc. 'agi.'

4. Restitui, 'be rebuilt.' Cp. Intr. to Part I, § 20; to Part II, § 1.

5. Potero, sc. 'restitui,' 'be restored to my old position.' Cp. Ep. 17. 3.

Haec . . expediri, 'unless you see that these points are in the way of being settled.' Cp. Ep. 16. 10 'adsequi.'

7. Thessalonicae. For Cicero's movements, see Intr. to Part I. § 21.

Acta Kal. Sext., 'the gazette of the first of August.' The publication of the proceedings of the senate and of other news dated from Caesar's first consulship, 59 B.C. See Intr. to Part I, § 17.

Tuos . . agros. Cicero refers to the property of Atticus in Epirus, which is often mentioned in his letters.

13. Ut praesto esses, 'to be at hand,' ready to give advice if asked.

Inductus, 'cajoled,' 'deceived.'

14. In fraudem, 'into a snare.'

17. Timebas minus, 'were less alarmed,' and so ought to have given better and cooler advice.

18. Erige adflictos, 'raise me up in my deep fall.' Metag.

In eo, 'in this matter.' See note on 'in quo' Ep. 13. 2, p. 86.

Sin . . obstructa, 'but if all paths to safety are closed.'

20. Non me . . crederem, 'I should not choose your roof in preference to all others as a refuge.'

22. Me amari. Perhaps the insertion of 'me' is needless. See Madv. 401.

24. Praecipitantem. The verb is not uncommonly used intransitively. Cp. de Rep. 6, 19 sec. to our reading; Forcell.

8 nostris suscipis, non subisses. Qua re fac ut omnia ad me perspecta et explorata perscribas, meque, ut facis, velis esse aliquem, quoniam, qui fui et qui esse potui, iam esse non possum, et ut his litteris non te, sed me ipsum a me esse accusatum putes. Si qui erunt, quibus putes opus esse meo nomine litteras dari, velim conscribas curesque dandas. Data XIIII. Kal. Sept.

17. To his Wife and Children (Ad Fam. XIV. 2).

Thessalonica, Oct. 5, 58 B.C. (696 A.U.C.)

1. I do not write longer letters to any one than to you, unless it is absolutely necessary. 2. Piso deserves my warmest thanks, and I have written to him. The support of the new tribunes will be effectual if we can count on Pompey; but I am afraid of Crassus. Your embarrassments distress me very much, and I wish you would allow me to rely on the aid of others, instead of impoverishing yourself. 3. The restoration of the site of our house will be most important if we can obtain it. I beg you will be careful of your health. 4. I will not go to a more distant asylum, as you wish me to stay here. I hope you will write frequently.

TULLIUS S. D. TERENTIAE ET TULLIOLAE ET CICERONI SUIS.

1 Noli putare me ad quemquam longiores epistolas scribere, nisi si quis ad me plura scripsit, cui puto rescribi oportere; nec enim habeo quod scribam, nec hoc tempore quicquam difficilius facio. Ad te vero et ad nostram Tulliolam non queo sine plurimis

In naufragiis nostris, 'in the wreck of my fortunes.' An instance of the metaphorical use of the word is found also 2 Philipp. 36, 92.

1. Non subisses, 'would not have subjected yourself to.' For if Cicero had not been banished, Atticus would not have had so much trouble in trying to procure his restoration.

2. Explorata, = 'certa.' Cicero suspected that Atticus coloured his prospects too brightly, and requests accordingly that only trustworthy news may be sent him.

Esse aliquem, 'to be of some consequence;' 'somebody.' Cp. Iuv. 1. 74 'Si vis esse aliquis.'

3. Potui. On the indic. see note on § 5 'fuit.'

Ut .. putes. These words depend on 'fac:' the expression is pleonastic. See note on § 2.

4. Si qui erunt .. dari .. dandas, 'if there be any men to whom you think letters ought to be written in my name.' The practice of employing secretaries would prevent the handwriting exciting suspicion, and perhaps Cicero had left his seal with Terentia. See Ep. 81, 2. Forcell. however explains meo nomine as = 'on my account.'

For an account of Terentia and Tullia, see Intr. to Parts I, §§ 2; 24; II, § 26; IV, §§ 1; 7.

7. Nisi si, almost = 'nisi,' but is used when the exception is a conditional clause. Forcell. See also Madv. 442 c. Mr. King in his note on Philipp. 2. 28, 70 remarks that 'nisi si' is most commonly thus used with indefinite pronouns and adverbs.

8. Nec .. habeo quod scribam. 'Non habeo quod scribam' = 'nihil habeo,' or 'mihi deest quod scribam;' 'non habeo quid scribam' = 'nescio quid scribam,' implying a dependent question. See Madv. 363, and Obs 2; Zumpt 562.

9. Difficilius, owing to his dejection. Manut.

lacrimis scribere; vos enim video esse miserrimas, quas ego
beatissimas semper esse volui idque praestare debui, et, nisi tam
timidi fuissemus, praestitissem. Pisonem nostrum merito eius 2
amo plurimum: eum, ut potui, per litteras cohortatus sum gratiasque egi, ut debui. In novis tribunis pl. intellego spem te
habere: id erit firmum, si Pompeii voluntas erit, sed Crassum
tamen metuo. A te quidem omnia fieri fortissime et amantissime video, nec miror, sed maereo casum eius modi, ut tantis
tuis miseriis meae miseriae subleventur: nam ad me P. Valerius,
homo officiosus, scripsit, id quod ego maximo cum fletu legi,
quem ad modum a Vestae ad tabulam Valeriam ducta esses.
Hem, mea lux, meum desiderium, unde omnes opem petere
solebant! te nunc, mea Terentia, sic vexari, sic iacere in lacrimis et sordibus! idque fieri mea culpa, qui ceteros servavi, ut
nos periremus! Quod de domo scribis, hoc est de area, ego vero 3

2. Praestare, 'guarantee.'

Tam timidi. Cicero still dwells on his supposed error in avoiding a struggle with Clodius. The change from the plural 'fuissemus' to 'praestitissem' may be made to avoid monotony.

3. Pisonem: see Ep. 13, 3, note.

Merito eius: see Madv. 255, and cp. 'merito tuo feci' Ep. 31, 6.

5. Novis tribunis plebis. Cicero refers to those elected for 58-57 B.C., of whom Milo was one of the most active. See Intr. to Part I, § 21.

6. Si . . voluntas erit, sc. 'firma' (Hofm., Billerb.), 'if the friendly disposition of Pompey shall continue.'

Crassum: cp. Ad Att. 2, 22, 5, and Ad Q. F. 1. 3, 7, from which it would seem that Cicero had been disappointed in Crassus, but did not despair of his aid.

8. Casum eius modi, ut, 'a misfortune which causes.' See Madv. 364, and Obs. 1. A similar construction is found Ep. 13, 3 'adulescentium consilium . . ut.'

Tantis tuis miseriis. Explained by what immediately follows.

9. P. Valerius seems to have been a friend of Cicero to whom Atticus had lent money. Cp. Ep. 36, 14; 117, 1.

11. A Vestae. On the gen., see Madv. 280, Obs. 3. Cicero's house stood near the temple of Vesta, and Terentia, who had a half-sister, Fabia, among the Vestals (cp. Ascon. ad Orat. in Tog. Cand. p. 93), may have taken refuge in the temple when her husband's house was demolished at the bidding of Clodius.

Ad tabulam . . ducta esses. Hofm. and Süpfle think that 'tabula' means a bank where Terentia had to borrow money. Prof. Tyrrell thinks that Terentia had to make some declaration at the bank about her husband's property—probably that no effects had been made away with. Others think that it means a court where she had to give securities for payment, perhaps that of the tribunes. Cp. In Vat. 9, 21 'cum . . ab tabula Valeria collegae tui mitti laberent.' 'Ducta esses,' 'had been obliged to repair,' at the bidding of her creditors, or perhaps of a magistrate. 'Tabula Sestia' is mentioned Pro Quinct. 6, 25. Cp. Manut.

12. Lux: cp. Ep. 43, 1.

Desiderium, 'an object of desire, or regret.' Cp. Hor. Carm. 1. 14, 18, 'nunc desiderium.'

Opem petere: i.e. 'to ask her to use her influence with her husband on their behalf.'

13. Te . . sic vexari. The infin. expresses indignation. See Ep. 12, 1, note.

14. Qui . . servavi . . ut . . periremus, 'who preserved all my countrymen for my own and my family's ruin.' The 'ut' expresses result, or, as Süpfle says, purpose in a large sense. See Madv. 355, and cp. a quotation from Pacuvius applied to Caesar: 'men' servasse ut essent qui me perderent?' Suet. Iul. 84. Cicero owed his banishment to his having complied with the senate's recommendation to have Lentulus and his accomplices executed.

15. Hoc est de area. Cicero corrects himself thus because his house had been destroyed. Cp. De Dom. 24, 62.

tum denique mihi videbor restitutus, si illa nobis erit restituta; verum haec non sunt in nostra manu: illud doleo, quae impensa facienda est, in eius partem *te* miseram et despoliatam venire. Quod si conficitur negotium, omnia consequemur; sin eadem nos fortuna premet, etiamne reliquias tuas misera proiicies? Obsecro te, mea vita, quod ad sumptum attinet, sine alios, qui possunt, si modo volunt, sustinere, et valetudinem istam infirmam, si me amas, noli vexare: nam mihi ante oculos dies noctesque versaris; omnes labores te excipere video; timeo, ut sustineas. Sed video in te esse omnia: qua re, ut id, quod
4 speras et quod agis, consequamur, servi valetudini. Ego, ad quos scribam, nescio, nisi ad eos, qui ad me scribunt, aut ad eos, de quibus ad me vos aliquid scribitis. Longius, quoniam ita vobis placet, non discedam, sed velim quam saepissime litteras mittatis, praesertim, si quid est firmius, quod speremus. Valete, mea desideria, valete. D. a. d. III. Non. Oct. Thessalonica.

18. TO HIS WIFE AND CHILDREN (AD FAM. XIV. 1).

BEGUN AT THESSALONICA; FINISHED AT DYRRHACHIUM, NOV. 25, 58 B.C. (696 A.U.C.)

1. Everybody bears witness to your zeal and energy in my cause. I am deeply grieved for the calamity which has befallen you and our children, especially as it is owing to my folly. 2. If I had followed my own judgment, we should now be in an

2. Quae impensa . . venire, 'that you should have to share the necessary expenditure.' On the attraction of 'impensa' to 'quae,' and on the position of the two words, cp. Ep. 13, 1. Money was probably wanted, as Süpfle suggests, to buy votes and hire bands of gladiators (cp. Ep. 18, 5, and Intr. to Part I, § 23); also for Cicero's support in exile.

4. Si conficitur negotium, 'if my restoration is effected.' With this combination of the pres. 'conficitur' and the fut. consequemur, cp. 'qui si condemnatus desierunt homines dicere' in Verr. Act. 2. 1. 7, 6.

7. Sustinere, 'to contribute for my support.'

Valetudinem . . infirmam. Yet Terentia is said to have lived to be 103 years old. Cp. Pliny, H. N. 7. 48; Val. Max. 8. 13, 6.

9. Timeo ut sustineas, sc. 'labores,' 'I fear you may not be able to bear them.' See Madv. 376.

10. In te esse omnia, 'that all our hopes depend on you.' Cp. Ep. 8, 2, note, on p. 53.

11. Agis, 'you are attempting.'

Ad quos scribam nescio. Terentia may have suggested that her husband might write to more people and exert himself more than he did, and these words may be his justification.

15. Si quid est . . speremus, 'if there are any surer grounds for hope.'

16. D. = data.

Thessalonica. Acc. to Hofm. (on Ad Att. 3. 8; Ad Fam. 4. 14), the place where a letter is written is more often given in the ablative than in the genitive. Cp. Epp. 32 extr., 129 extr., alib.

excellent position. To regain what is lost will be difficult; but, with the support you mention as probably to be relied on, not impossible. 3. I will act as our friends suggest about my slaves. This place is now healthy, and Plancius urges me to remain here, though I should prefer a more retired residence, and one less exposed to treacherous attacks. 4. Piso is most devoted to us all. I do not complain of your behaviour to Quintus, but I wished you to keep up as good an understanding as possible. 5. Do not think of selling any of your property to provide for my wants; consider our son's prospects. 6. Take care of your health, and send me messengers that I may hear how you are going on.

P.S. 7. I have come to Dyrrhachium, a free city devoted to me, and near to Italy.

TULLIUS TERENTIAE SUAE, TULLIOLAE SUAE, CICERONI SUO SALUTEM DICIT.

Et litteris multorum et sermone omnium perfertur ad me, 1
incredibilem tuam virtutem et fortitudinem esse teque nec
animi neque corporis laboribus defatigari. Me miserum! te
ista virtute, fide, probitate, humanitate in tantas aerumnas
propter me incidisse! Tulliolamque nostram, ex quo patre
tantas voluptates capiebat, ex eo tantos percipere luctus! Nam
quid ego de Cicerone dicam? qui cum primum sapere coepit,
acerbissimos dolores miseriasque percepit. Quae si, tu ut scribis,
fato facta putarem, ferrem paulo facilius, sed omnia sunt mea
culpa commissa, qui ab iis me amari putabam, qui invidebant,
eos non sequebar, qui petebant. Quod si nostris consiliis usi 2
essemus neque apud nos tantum valuisset sermo aut stultorum
amicorum aut improborum, beatissimi viveremus: nunc, quoniam sperare nos amici iubent, dabo operam, ne mea valetudo
tuo labori desit. Res quanta sit, intellego, quantoque fuerit

1. Perfertur, 'news is brought,' 'I learn.'

3. Me miserum! cp. Madv. 236.

Te . . incidisse: cp. Ep. 12, 1, note.

4. Ista virtute: cp. Ep. 6, 2, note.

5. Ex quo patre. On the order of the words, cp. Ep. 13, 1, and Madv. 319.

7. De Cicerone. His son Marcus was born 65 B.C. Cp. Ep. 2, 1.

Qui cum primum . . percepit, 'who since he began to notice anything, has experienced nothing but the most bitter sufferings.'

9. Fato, 'in the natural course of things' as often.

10. Ab iis, 'by his rivals among the optimates.' Manutius thinks that Hortensius, Arrius, and Pompey are referred to. Cp. as to Hortensius Ad Att. 3. 9, 2. Cicero suspected Cato at one time; cp. Ep. 16, 8.

11. Qui petebant, 'who sought my friendship;' i.e. Caesar, who had offered him a post as his legate. Cp. Ep. 11, 3.

12. Aut stultorum . . aut improborum, 'of friends who were either foolish, "like Atticus and perhaps Cato" (Tyrr.) or treacherous "like Arrius and Hortensius"' (Tyrr.).

13. Beatissimi. On the adject. as adverb, see Ep. 1, 2, note on p.

14. Ne mea . . desit, 'to prevent the state of my health making your exertions fruitless.' That the state of my health may not 'fail to second your exertions.' Tyrr. 'Ut valeam, ne tu pro mea salute frustra laborem suscipias.' Manut.

Valetudo is a neutral word, meaning either good or ill-health. Forcell.

ſacilius manere domi quam redire; sed tamen, si omnes tribunos
pl. habemus, si Lentulum tam studiosum, quam videtur, si vero
3 etiam Pompeium et Caesarem, non est desperandum. De ſamilia,
quo modo placuisse scribis amicis, ſaciemus; de loco, nunc quidem iam abiit pestilentia, sed quam diu ſuit, me non attigit.
Plancius, homo officiosissimus, me cupit esse secum et adhuc
retinet. Ego volebam loco magis deserto esse in Epiro, quo
neque Hispo veniret nec milites, sed adhuc Plancius me retinet;
sperat posse fieri, ut mecum in Italiam decedat: quem ego diem
si videro et si in vestrum complexum venero ac si et vos et
me ipsum recuperaro, satis magnum mihi ſructum videbor per-
4 cepisse et vestrae pietatis et meae. Pisonis humanitas, virtus,
amor in omnes nos tantus est, ut nihil supra possit: utinam
ea res ei voluptati sit! gloriae quidem video ſore. De Q. ſratre
nihil ego te accusavi, sed vos, cum praesertim tam pauci sitis,
5 volui esse quam coniunctissimos. Quibus me voluisti agere
gratias, egi et me a te certiorem ſactum esse scripsi. Quod

1. **Si omnes tribunos**: cp. § 2 of the previous letter.

2. **Lentulum.** P. Lentulus Spinther had been elected consul for 57 B.C. For more particulars about him, see Epp. 21; 22; 26; 29. and Intr. to Part II, § 2.

Si vero, 'if moreover,' 'certainly if.' See Madv. 437 d.

3. **De familia**, 'about our slaves.' Apparently Cicero had been advised to emancipate them, and Terentia was anxious as to the bearing this step might have on her interests. Cp. Ad Fam. 14. 4. 4.

4. **De loco**, 'as to the state of this place,' Thessalonica.

5. **Attigit**, 'attacked.'

6. **Cn. Plancius** was now quaestor to L. Appuleius in Macedonia, and rendered Cicero great services, giving him an asylum in his official residence. Cp. Pro Planc. 41, 42. He was tribune in 57–56 B.C., and next year was elected curule aedile, but accused of bribery by M. Iuventius Laterensis. Cicero defended him successfully in a speech still extant. He is mentioned as living in exile during the civil war. Cp. Ad Fam. 4. 14; 15; and Pro Planc. passim.

Me cupit esse: see Ep. 15. 11, note.

8. **Hispo.** Supposed by Orelli, (Onomast. s. v.) to have been an officer sent by the consuls to watch Cicero in exile. Wesenb. suggests 'Piso,' i.e. the consul of 58 B.C., who went to Macedonia as proconsul.

Veniret, 'might come.' See Ep. 5. 8, note on 'liberamur.'

11. **Me ipsum**, 'my former self,' 'my old position.' Cp. 'mihi restitutus' in § 3 of the preceding letter, and 'desidero.. me ipsum' Ep. 16. 2.

12. **Vestrae pietatis et meae**, 'of your devotion to me, and of mine to my country.'

13. **Ut nihil supra possit**, sc. 'esse.' See Madv. 478, Obs. 3.

14. **Voluptati.** Referring to the pleasure Piso would derive from Cicero's return. Manut.

15. **Nihil .. accusavi**, 'I made no complaint of your conduct.' Apparently there had been a misunderstanding between Q. Cicero and Terentia, and Cicero had written to his wife urging her to a reconciliation, in terms which she thought implied a censure upon her.

16. **Quibus .. gratias.** Terentia had probably mentioned the names of some men who had been active in trying to secure Cicero's recall.

17. **Me a te certiorem factum**, 'that I had been informed by you of their services.' Cicero was very anxious to gain credit for his own courtesy in such cases. Cp. Ep. 14, 1.

Quod .. scribis. On the constr., see Ep. 8, 14, note.

ad me, mea Terentia, scribis te vicum vendituram, quid, obsecro
te,—me miserum!—quid futurum est? et, si nos premet eadem
fortuna, quid puero misero fiet? Non queo reliqua scribere—
tanta vis lacrimarum est—, neque te in eundem fletum addu-
cam. Tantum scribo: si erunt in officio amici, pecunia non
deerit; si non erunt, tu efficere tua pecunia non poteris. Per
fortunas miseras nostras, vide, ne puerum perditum perdamus.
Cui si aliquid erit, ne egeat, mediocri virtute opus est et
mediocri fortuna, ut cetera consequatur. Fac valeas et ad me 6
tabellarios mittas, ut sciam, quid agatur et vos quid agatis.
Mihi omnino iam brevis exspectatio est. Tulliolae et Ciceroni
salutem dic. Valete. D. a. d. VI. K. Decemb. Dyrrhachii.

Dyrrhachium veni, quod et libera civitas est et in me officiosa 7
et proxima Italiae; sed si offendet me loci celebritas, alio me
conferam, ad te scribam.

19. TO ATTICUS (AD ATT. III. 23).

DYRRHACHIUM NOV. 29, 58 B.C. (696 A.U.C.)

1. I have received your three letters. In the first you encourage me to await the new year with fortitude, and state the grounds of your hope; in the next you mention the bill promulgated by eight tribunes. I will notice some points that have occurred to me on this subject. 2. The bill of the present tribunes had three heads: one as to my

1. Vicum. Probably a village (or country seat, Tyrr.) forming part of Terentia's portion.

3. Quid puero . . . fiet? 'what will become of our boy?' See Madv. 167.

5. Erunt in officio, 'do their duty.' Forcell.

6. Efficere, 'bring about my restoration.' Or perhaps, as Manutius thinks, 'ut ego in hac misera fortuna ne egeam.'

7. Perditum perdamus, 'ruin utterly.' Manutius says 'perditum, calamitate nostra; perdamus, vico vendito.'

8. Cui si aliquid . . consequatur. 'for whom, if he has enough to save him from positive need, even moderate merit and good fortune will do the rest.'

10. Tabellarios, 'letter carriers,' freq.

Quid agatur, 'what is going on in general,' 'the news.'

Vos quid agatis, 'what you are doing,' 'how you are getting on.'

11. Iam brevis exspectatio est, 'my suspense must soon end,' as I expect soon to hear from you. Manut.

13. Dyrrhachium. A postscript begins here. Dyrrhachium, on the coast of Epirus, was previously called Epidamnus, and is now called Durazzo. On its importance in the civil war between Caesar and Pompey, cp. Intr. to Part III, §§ 10; 11. It was much attached to Cicero. Cp. Pro Planc. 41. 97 'Dyrrhachium quod erat in fide mea.'

Libera civitas. The free towns enjoyed certain municipal privileges, which will be found enumerated by Marquardt Staatsverwaltung 1. 351, 352; see also Smith's Dict. of Antiq. sub voc. 'Provincia.' esp. p. 966. Among them was that of settling disputes by their own laws and before their own magistrates. Cp. A. W. Zumpt, Comment. Epigr. 1. 156; Ep. 38, 4, note. Prof. Tyrrell remarks that a Roman exile would there be more 'sui iuris.'

14. Celebritas, 'the busy, crowded nature of the place.'

15. Ad te scribam. Wesenb. thinks that something has fallen out, and suggests the insertion of 'quod cum faciam' after 'conferam.'

restoration, which was not sufficiently comprehensive; another, the usual provision for indemnity: a third, and very mischievous one, 3. declaring that the bill should be invalid so far as it was inconsistent with previous legislation. 4. There was no necessity for such a provision, and Clodius seems to have appreciated its value to him. I should be glad if you could discover how my friends failed to see its import. I hope the new tribunes will be more careful. 5. In your third letter you point out the causes which delay my restoration. If there is any hope, try to effect our object at one blow; if none, as I rather believe, support my family to the best of your ability. I shall go to Epirus as soon as I hear of the first measures taken; let me know how the new tribunes begin.

CICERO ATTICO SAL.

1 A. d. v. Kal. Decembr. tres epistolas a te accepi: unam datam a. d. VIII. Kal. Novembres, in qua me hortaris, ut forti animo mensem Ianuarium exspectem, eaque, quae ad spem putas pertinere, de Lentuli studio, de Metelli voluntate, de tota Pompeii ratione, perscribis. In altera epistola praeter consuetudinem tuam diem non adscribis, sed satis significas tempus; lege enim ab octo tribunis pl. promulgata scribis te eas litteras eo ipso die dedisse, id est a. d. IIII. Kal. Novembres, et, quid putes utilitatis eam promulgationem attulisse, scribis: in quo si iam haec nostra salus cum hac lege desperata erit, velim pro tuo in me amore hanc inanem meam diligentiam miserabilem potius quam ineptam putes, sin est aliquid spei, des operam ut maiore

3. **Ad spem pertinere**, sc. 'faciendam,' 'to be hopeful signs.' Boot. Cp. 'si ista . . . . quicquam ad spem explorati haberent' Ad Att. II. 20, 1.

4. **Lentuli**: see on § 2 of the preceding letter.

Metelli, 'of Q. Metellus Nepos,' consul elect for 57 B.C. He had been on bad terms with Cicero (see Epp. 4; 5, notes), who wrote to deprecate his hostility (cp. Ad Fam. 5. 4).

Voluntate, 'good will.'

5. **Ratione**, 'attitude,' 'policy.' See Ep. 9, 6, note.

Perscribis, 'write carefully.' Forcell.

Praeter, 'contrary to.'

6. **Sed . . tempus**, 'but indicate the date clearly enough.'

Lege . . promulgata. A proposal for the recall of Cicero, which seems to have been brought forward by eight of the tribunes for 59-58 B.C., but not to have passed. The two dissentient tribunes were probably P. Clodius and P. (?) Aelius Ligus. Cp Ep. 16, 6.

7. **Promulgata**. The notice which ought to be given by the proposer of a law, at least seventeen days, or three nundinae, before it first came on for discussion, was called 'promulgatio.' Cp. 'ubi promulgatio trinum nundinum' Philipp. 5. 3. 8.

8. a. d. IIII. Kal. Nov. = Oct. 29.

9. **Utilitatis**. Manutius suggests that this step of the eight tribunes might have some influence on their successors, and that it shewed a change of feeling in their body, as earlier in the year none of them had ventured to veto the proposals of Clodius.

Attulisse = 'contulisse,' 'has contributed.'

In quo . . desperata erit, 'in which matter, if my prospects and the enactment of the law (which seeks to secure them) are already hopeless when this reaches you.' On **in quo**, cp. Ep. 13, 2, note on p. 85.

11. **Hanc . . diligentiam . . putes**, 'that you will think the useless trouble I am about to expend in examining the law deserving of pity rather than of ridicule.'

12. **Maiore diligentia**, 'with more consideration.'

diligentia posthac a nostris magistratibus defendamur. Nam 2
ea veterum tribunorum pl. rogatio tria capita habuit, unum de
reditu meo, scriptum incaute; nihil enim restituitur praeter
civitatem et ordinem, quod mihi pro meo casu satis est, sed,
quae cavenda fuerint et quo modo, te non fugit. Alterum
caput est tralaticium de impunitate, SI QVID CONTRA ALIAS
LEGES EIVS LEGIS ERGO FACTVM SIT. Tertium caput, mi Pomponi, quo consilio et a quo sit inculcatum, vide: scis enim Clodium sanxisse, ut vix aut omnino non posset nec per senatum nec per populum infirmari sua lex. Sed vides numquam esse observatas sanctiones earum legum, quae abrogarentur: nam, si id esset, nulla fere abrogari posset; neque enim ulla est, quae non ipsa se saepiat difficultate abrogationis. Sed, cum lex abrogatur, illud
ipsum abrogatur, quo modo eam abrogari oporteat. Hoc, quod 3
re vera ita est, cum semper ita habitum observatumque sit, octo
nostri tribuni pl. caput posuerunt hoc: SI QVID IN HAC ROGA-

1. **Nostris**, 'inclined to support me:' cp. l. 16, below. Prof. Tyrrell approves the conjecture of Manutius, 'novis.'

2. **Veterum tribunorum.** The tribunes for 59-58 B.C.: Clodius' colleagues.

4. **Ordinem**, 'my rank as a senator.'

Pro meo casu, 'considering my misfortune.'

5. **Quae cavenda fuerint**, 'what should have been provided for.' Cicero refers especially to the restoration of the site of his house, and to indemnity for his losses.

6. **Tralaticium**, 'ordinary,' 'universally adopted.' Forcell.

De impunitate, 'indemnifying the proposers.' It is explained just below.

SI QVID .. FACTVM SIT, 'in case the carrying out of this law involves the breach of any others.' ERGO = 'causa.' Forcell. On the tense of 'factum sit,' see Madv. 379. The apodosis of the sentence is omitted; it would run 'id ei qui fecerit ne fraudi esto.' Boot.

8. **A quo sit inculcatum**, 'by whom its insertion was procured.' Cicero suspected that Clodius got the obnoxious clause inserted, apparently.

9. **Sanxisse .. sua lex**, 'added a sanction, with a view to [or 'such as to,' (Tyrr.)] prevent, or render very difficult, the repeal of his law.' For a similar sense of 'sancire,' cp. 'sancit in posterum,' etc. In Cat. 4. 5. 10. The words from ut vix to sua lex express the object rather than the precise form of the clause in question.

Vix aut omnino non = 'vix aut ne vix quidem.' On the repeated negatives, non .. nec .. nec, see Ep. 8, 8, note.

12. **Quae non ipsa .. abrogationis**, 'which does not try to guard itself by interposing difficulties in the way of its repeal.' On the mood of 'abrogarentur' and 'saepiat,' see Madv. 364, and Obs. 1.

13. **Illud ipsum**, 'that very provision against repeal.'

14. **Quo modo .. oporteat**, 'in the way in which the law itself must be repealed.' Prof. Tyrrell says that this would need 'oportet,' and suggests 'quo minus'—'the sanction forbidding its abrogation.' Cicero means that it would be as easy to repeal the protecting clauses as the law which it protected. Wesenb. reads 'quo non .. oporteat,' words which must be taken as explanatory of 'illud ipsum,' and as equivalent to those suggested by Prof. Tyrrell.

Hoc, quod re vera .. observatumque sit, 'though this is really the practice, and has been always maintained and observed,' i.e. 'though men proposing to repeal a law are never deterred from doing so by a clause intended to prevent its repeal.'

15. **Habitum** = 'actum,' 'practised.' Forcell.

16. **Nostri**: cp. l. 1, above.

TIONE SCRIPTVM EST, QVOD PER LEGES PLEBISVE SCITA, hoc est quod per legem Clodiam, PROMVLGARE, ABROGARE, DEROGARE, OBROGARE SINE FRAVDE SVA NON LICEAT, NON LICVERIT, QVODVE EI QVI PROMVLGAVIT, DEROGAVIT, OB EAM REM POENAE
4 MVLTAEVE SIT, E. H. L. N. R. Atque hoc in illis tribunis pl. non laedebat; lege enim collegii sui non tenebantur; quo maior est suspitio malitiae alicuius, cum id, quod ad ipsos nihil pertinebat, erat autem contra me, scripserunt, ut novi tribuni pl., si essent timidiores, multo magis sibi eo capite utendum putarent. Neque id a Clodio praetermissum est; dixit enim in contione a. d. III. Nonas Novembres hoc capite designatis tribunis pl. praescriptum esse, quid liceret; tamen in lege nulla esse eius modi caput te non fallit, quo, si opus esset, omnes

1. Hoc est quod per legem Clodiam. Cicero's remark, to shew how the proposal of the eight tribunes had been marred by carelessness or treachery. For of course its object was to repeal the law of Clodius, and any clause saving the provisions of that law would make the new one nugatory. It is possible that the tribunes did not consider the 'privilegium' against Cicero as a law.

2. ABROGARE, 'to repeal altogether.'

DEROGARE, 'to repeal in part.' Cp. De Inv. Rhet. 2. 45, 134; Rhet. ad Herenn. 2. 10, 15.

3. OBROGARE, 'to pass a new law in opposition to an old one;' 'legis prioris infirmandae causa,' cp. Paulum Diaconum, excerpt. in lib. Pomp. Fest. lib. xiii, p. 187, Muller.

SINE FRAVDE SVA, 'without incurring a penalty.'

NON LICEAT, NON LICVERIT, 'is (at the time of voting on the law), or was (at the time of its promulgation), illegal.' Hofm.

4. POENAE MULTAEVE SIT, 'may involve punishment or fine.' The more general term is put first.

5. E. H. L. N. R. 'Eius hac lege nihil rogatur' (Boot), 'this law is so far void.'

Hoc in illis . . non laedebat, 'the violation of the law of Clodius could do no harm as far as those tribunes (of 59–58 B.C.) were concerned.' On the imperf. 'laedebat,' see Madv. 337, Obs. 1. 'Hoc' refers to 'si quid' of the passage quoted at the end of the previous section.

6. Lege enim . . non tenebantur, 'for they were not bound by a law sanctioned by their body,' 'there was no law sanctioned by their body to bind them,' i.e. Clodius' law had not been sanctioned by the majority of their body, and could not be treated as their act, or bind them as such. Boot, Wiel. Corradus (ap. ed. Graev. 1684) whom Wesenb. follows, approves of the substitution of 'collegae' for 'collegii,' thinking that the meaning is that an enactment originating with Clodius could not bind his own colleagues: cp. 'soluti cum essent' below. Perhaps 'collegii,' may mean 'originating with one of their own body.' Prof. Tyrrell, 'emanating from their own college.' Hofmann thinks that Clodius only provided against the repeal of his law by tribunes who should hold office in *subsequent years*, because he relied on his right of 'intercessio' to frustrate any attempt of his colleagues to repeal it.

7. Malitiae, 'trickery,' 'foul play.'

Cum id . . scripserunt, 'in their having added a clause needless for their own safety and injurious to me.' See, on the constr., Ep. 1, 1, note.

8. Ut novi . . putarent, 'so that the new tribunes would think it far more needful for *them* to insert that clause.' With this use of 'ut,' expressing result, cp. Ep. 15. 13, note, and 'ut odia . . erumperent' Pro Muren. 23. 47.

10. Neque id a Clodio praetermissum est, 'nor did Clodius fail to see the significance of their action.' Tyrr.

11. Hoc capite . . quid liceret, 'that the limits of the powers of the tribunes elect were defined by this clause.'

13. Quo si . . uterentur. The MS. has 'quod,' which might be rendered, 'yet if that clause were necessary.' [In the reading

in abrogando *uterentur*. Ut Ninnium aut ceteros fugerit investiges velim et quis attulerit et qua re octo tribuni pl. ad senatum de me referre non dubitarint—scilicet quod observandum illud caput non putabant—, iidem in abrogando tam cauti fuerint, ut id metuerent, soluti cum essent, quod ne iis quidem, qui lege tenentur, est curandum. Id caput sane nolim novos tribunos pl. ferre, sed perferant modo quidlubet: uno capite, quo revocabor, modo res conficiatur, ero contentus. Iam dudum pudet tam multa scribere; vereor enim ne re iam desperata legas, ut haec mea diligentia miserabilis tibi, aliis irridenda videatur. Sed si est aliquid in spe, vide legem, quam T. Fadio scripsit Visellius: ea mihi perplacet; nam Sestii nostri, quam tu tibi probari scribis, mihi non placet. Tertia est epistola 8
pridie Idus Novembr. data, in qua exponis prudenter et diligenter, quae sint quae rem distinere videantur, de Crasso, de Pompeio, de ceteris: qua re oro te ut, si qua spes erit, posse studiis bonorum, auctoritate, multitudine comparata, rem confici,

adopted in the text, 'eo,' must be supplied with opus esset; in the MS. reading, with 'uterentur.'] Prof. Tyrrell retains 'quod.' For the two constructions of opus est, see Madv. 266.

1. In abrogando, 'in proposing the repeal of other laws.' If the clause were needful, Cicero says it would be always used in proposals similar to that of the eight tribunes, whereas it had not been found in any.

Ut, 'how.' On the mood of 'fugerit,' see Ep. 6, 1, note.

Ninnium. L. Ninnius Quadratus, tribune for 59–58 B.C., was active in promoting Cicero's recall. He is mentioned Ep. 74, 4; Pro Sest. 31, 68; De Domo 48, 125.

Ceteros, 'his seven colleagues.' See on § 1.

2. Quis attulerit, 'to whom we owe it,' 'who it was who added the saving clause.' Tyrr.

3. Scilicet, 'no doubt.'

Illud caput. The clause by which Clodius had tried to prevent the repeal of his law. Cp. § 1, and Ep. 16, 6.

4. Iidem . . fuerint, 'and yet have been so cautious in proposing a repeal.' For this use of 'idem,' see Madv. 488.

5. Soluti: cp. the first words of this section, and note there.

Qui lege tenentur. 'Aliorum collegiorum tribunos plebis intelligit.' Manut.

9. Ne . . legas, 'that you may read this letter after my prospects are already ruined.'

11. Si est aliquid in spe: see Ep. 6, 6, note on p. 46.

Quam . . Visellius, 'which Visellius has drawn up for T. Fadius,' i.e. for Fadius to propose as tribune. T. Fadius Gallus was quaestor 63 B.C., and tribune in 58–57 B.C. Cp. Post Red. in Sen. 8. He must have been elected before this letter was written, and Visellius seems to have advised him as to the best form in which to draw up a proposal for Cicero's recall. In 52 B.C., probably, Cicero wrote to console Fadius in exile. Cp. Ad Fam. 5. 18. C. Visellius Varro was son of a sister of Cicero's mother; his father's name was C. Visellius Aculeo. He was a friend of Caesar (cp. De Prov. Cons. 17, 40), and is mentioned as a learned jurisconsult (Brut. 76, 264).

12. Perplacet seems only to be found here in Cicero's writings.

Sestii. P. Sestius, quaestor in 63 B.C., supported Cicero zealously against Catiline and his associates. He was one of the tribunes for 58–57 B.C., and took an active part in promoting Cicero's restoration. See the oration Pro Sestio, passim. He appears to have been with Pompey at the beginning of the civil war, but to have been received into favour by Caesar. Cp. Ad Att. 7. 17, 2, with Ad Att. 11. 7, 1, and Bell. Alex. 34.

15. Rem distinere, 'to delay a measure for my recall.' Cp. Philipp. 12. 12, 28.

17. Auctoritate. I am not sure whether this word has here the technical meaning

des operam ut uno impetu perfringatur, in eam rem incumbas ceterosque excites; sin, ut ego perspicio cum tua coniectura, tum etiam mea, spei nihil est, oro obtestorque te, ut Q. fratrem ames, quem ego miserum misere perdidi, neve quid eum patiare gravius consulere de se, quam expediat sororis tuae filio, meum Ciceronem, cui nihil misello relinquo praeter invidiam et ignominiam nominis mei, tueare, quoad poteris, Terentiam, unam omnium aerumnosissimam, sustentes tuis officiis. Ego in Epirum proficiscar, cum primorum dierum nuntios excepero: tu ad me velim proximis litteris, ut se initia dederint, perscribas. Data pridie Kal. Decembr.

of 'a resolution of the senate,' or if it means 'by the influence of leading men.' Prof. Tyrrell takes the latter view. Cp. Philipp. 13. 13, 28, where Cicero says, that if some of his eminent contemporaries had been alive, Antony would have been less aggressive. 'Auctoritati cessisset audacia.'

Multitudine comparata. Either 'by the help of a large number of voters from the country districts,' where Cicero was very popular (see Intr. to Part I. §§ 20; 24); or, 'by a force of gladiators and others,' hired to oppose Clodius in street fighting. Such a body, under Milo's direction, contributed effectively to secure Cicero's recall (Intr. ubi supra).

1. Ut .. perfringatur, 'that we may break through all obstacles,' 'carry the matter through' at once.

In eam rem incumbas, 'exert yourself to that end.'

4. Miserum misere perdidi. Cicero had borrowed considerable sums from his brother, and had drawn part of his official income from the treasury. Quintus seems to have been much embarrassed in consequence (cp. Ad Q. F. 1. 3. 7), and his brother was alarmed lest he should take some hasty resolution.

5. Filio. The younger Q. Cicero. His mother was Pomponia, sister of Atticus.

6. Misello: rare. Forcell.

7. Unam omnium. These words strengthen the following superlative. Cp. Madv. 310, Obs. 1.

9. Primorum dierum, the first days after the new tribunes came into office, which they would do on Dec. 10. Cp. 'spes reliqua est in novis tribunis plebis, et in primis quidem diebus' Ad Fam. 14. 3. 3.

10. Ut se initia dederint, 'how the new tribunate begins.' Cp. 'prout tempus ac res se daret' Livy 18. 5. 9, according to some editors. On the conj., see Ep. 8, 4, note.

NOTE A. *Optimates.*

At the risk of seeming pedantic, I have often used this word to describe one of the parties of the later Roman Commonwealth; that for which Sulla had conquered, which opposed the concession of extraordinary powers to Pompey, supported Cicero in his consulship, struggled in vain against the first triumvirate, and finally coalesced with Pompey against Caesar. It cannot properly be called conservative, for some of its members were reactionary; nor aristocratic, for many of the noblest families in Rome were well represented among its adversaries; nor republican, for many of Caesar's supporters were probably long ignorant of the scope of his plans, and not less devoted than their opponents to a republican form of government. The most prominent optimates between 63 and 49 B.C. were Q. Catulus, L. Lucullus, Q. Hortensius, Q. Metellus Celer, M. Bibulus, L. Domitius Ahenobarbus, M. Cato, and M. Marcellus. The senate seems to have been under the control of the leaders of the optimates till about 57 on the whole, though Pompey had many personal adherents among its members. Hence, in notes to the letters of the first period, the senate is often spoken of as identical with that party; but such identification would be a mistake for the years following Cicero's return from exile. See Intr. to Part II, § 3, foll.

NOTE B. *Provincia.*

This word, of which the derivation is uncertain, seems originally to have meant 'a department of the public service;' or, as Mommsen (Rechtsfrage 4, cp. Staatsrecht, 1, 81) and Marquardt (Staatsverwaltung, 1, 339) maintain, a special department allotted for the exercise of the 'imperium.' Thus the conduct of the war against a particular enemy might be called 'provincia.' Cp. Livy 2. 40 ad fin.; 31. 6. After the institution of the praetorship, 'iuris dictio' would probably be called the praetor's 'provincia;' and when a second praetor was added to administer justice between citizens and foreigners, his duties would form a second 'provincia.' Now, when at the close of the First Punic War the Romans acquired considerable territory in Sicily, the government of such territory was entrusted to a new praetor, and called his 'provincia;' and so the word was applied in general to any administrative district of the Roman empire, (1) having definite boundaries, (2) subject to direct taxation, and (3) ruled by a Roman governor. (Marquardt, 1, 340.) The old meaning was, however, retained side by side with the new. Cp. Ad Q. F. 1. 1, 43: Pro Muren. 20, 41. The provinces, in the later sense, were probably from the first distinguished from Italy, and after the Roman franchise had been granted to most of the inhabitants of Italy south of the Po—as it had been before Cicero entered upon public life (cp. Smith, Dict. of Geogr. 1, 945, sub voc. Gallia Cis.)—the distinction must have become more marked. Land was generally held on different terms in Italy and in the provinces, except in specially privileged districts of the latter, and the inhabitants of the provinces were subject, generally speaking, to personal taxes and to arbitrary punishments from which Italians were exempt. Cp. In Verr. 2 Act. 2–5 passim; esp. 5. 66. 169. The Roman or Latin franchise might however be conferred either on individuals or on communities in the provinces (cp. Ep. 108, 1; Dion Cassius 41, 24) but neither appears to have necessarily implied the exemption of those who enjoyed it from the usual provincial burdens (Marquardt 1, 360, notes). Nor am I aware of any grant of the Roman or Latin franchise on a great scale before the time of the dictator Caesar, except in the case of genuine Roman or Italian colonies. The case of the Transpadani (cp. Appendix 1, § 2; Ep. 31, 2, notes) hardly forms an exception, as the province of Cisalpine Gaul held a peculiar position. Other towns in the provinces differed considerably in their privileges; probably according to their services to Rome, and the circumstances under which they had submitted to her supremacy. Cp. Epp. 18, 7; 38, 4, notes.

Cisalpine Gaul, in the year 43 B.C., was a province, but most of its inhabitants were Roman citizens. Cp. A. W. Zumpt, Studia Romana, 30–37. Perhaps the term 'provincia' was applied to it in a sense intermediate between the older political or military and the later local meaning, as seems to have been the case with Cilicia before 64 B.C. The general authorities for this note, besides the passages already quoted, have been, Mommsen, Die Rechtsfrage zwischen Caesar und dem Senat, pp. 1–11; Römisches Staatsrecht, 1, 70–88. Smith's Dictionary of Antiquities, sub vocc., 'colonia,' 'provincia,' 'Latinitas;' Marquardt, Römische Staatsverwaltung, 1. 338–365; Corpus Inscr. Lat. 1. 78; 96 foll.

NOTE C. *Roman Letters and means of Correspondence.*

The letter was written either (cp. Ad Att. 12. 1, 1) with a stylus on 'tabulae,' thin slips of wood or ivory covered with wax and folded together with the writing inwards, which was protected from defacement by the tablets having projecting rims—or (cp. Q. F. 2. 15 b, 1) with a reed pen and ink on papyrus or parchment. In either case it was secured by a thread passing round it and sealed. As letters were usually dictated to a secretary, the seal was often the only guarantee for genuineness, and was preserved unbroken; the receiver cut the thread when he opened the letter.

The outside address of the letter was very simple (cp. Ad Att. 8. 5, 2). The letter began with a friendly wish from the writer to the receiver, 'salutem dicit,' or 'salutem plurimam dicit;' sometimes simply 'salutem.' These words were generally expressed by their initial letters. The use or omission of the full names and titles of the writer and receiver depended naturally on the degree of formality which the writer wished to observe.

The greeting was often followed by the words 'si vales bene est,' but Cicero rarely uses these words in confidential letters, except to Terentia. Letters often ended with the word 'vale,' but this was frequently dispensed with.

There was no regular post at Rome; officials might employ attendants named 'statores' to carry their letters (cp. Ad Fam. 2. 17, 1; 2. 19, 2), but Cicero speaks in another passage of employing the messengers of the publicani or tax-gatherers, who would naturally keep up a constant communication between the capital and the provinces (cp. Ad Att. 5. 16, 1). Private people had to trust to their own or their friends' slaves or freedmen; letter-carriers were called 'tabellarii.' Cicero often expresses apprehensions that his letters may be tampered with—(e.g. Ad Att. 1. 13, 1; 4. 15, 7), and occasionally disguises his meaning,—writing in Greek or substituting fictitious for real names (Ad Att. 2. 19, 5; cp. 1. 13, 4; 6. 4 and 5). Cp. Süpfle, Einl. 36–38; Smith's Dictionary of Antiquities, sub vocc. 'atramentum,' 'calamus,' 'liber,' 'stilus,' 'tabellarius,' 'tabulae.'

NOTE D. *Origin of the collection of Cicero's Letters.*

Cicero, writing to Atticus in 44 B.C., says that there was no regular collection of his letters, but that Tiro had collected about seventy, and that he himself meant to add to and publish them. Ad Att. 16. 5, 5. Perhaps the letters Ad Familiares and Ad Quintum Fratrem were published by Tiro, having been procured in part from copies existing in Cicero's house, in part from those who had received them. The title Ad Familiares is modern, or at least post-classical; in ancient times each book was distinguished by the name of the person to whom the first letter in it was addressed, e.g. book I. was called Ad P. Lentulum.

The letters to Atticus were probably published either by Atticus himself or after his death by his orders. Cornelius Nepos, writing shortly before the death of Atticus, mentions 11—or according to a suggestion, 16—books of them; Vit. Att. 16.

Letters of Cicero are quoted or referred to by Seneca, Epp. 97. 4; 118, 1; Quintil. Inst. Orat. 6. 3. 109; 8. 3. 35; Suet. Iul. 9; Octav. 3; Tib. 7. Cp. Hofmann, 10–13; Süpfle 39. 40; Boissier, Recherches sur la manière dont furent recueillies et publiées les lettres de Cicéron 8–35.

NOTE E. *On the meaning of the words 'Imperium' and 'Imperator.'*

'Imperium' differed from 'potestas' both in the powers which it comprised, and in the fact that it could only be regularly granted by a distinct vote of the people (cp. Paul. Diac. Excerpt. p. 50), the 'lex curiata de imperio'—which, however, does not seem in Cicero's time to have been universally regarded as necessary: cp. Ep. 29, 25, note. In the time of the kings, 'Imperium' seems to have comprised military, judicial, and administrative prerogatives, and to have passed into the hands of the first consuls, subject only to two limitations; that it was made annual, and divided between two persons. According to Mommsen (Staatsrecht 1. 48–50), 'potestas' when the word is not used pleonastically (as by Cicero In Verr. Act. 1. 13. 37), nor as including 'imperium,' expresses merely a negative notion, that of official power without 'imperium.' 'Imperium' he explains as describing the power of those magistrates on whom the supreme authority formerly possessed by the kings had devolved. The view of Lange (Röm. Alt. 1. 232–241; 264–269)—that 'potestas,' described the patriarchal powers of the king or magistrate, considered as a 'paterfamilias,' on a great scale, while 'imperium' described the powers conveyed to him by the voluntary act of a body of independent 'patres familias'—is ingenious and plausible, but hardly demonstrable.

The constitutional history of Rome is, to a great extent, a history of the further limitation of the 'Imperium' by subdivision, by direct legislation, and by the increasing strictness of the senate's control over public officers. The institution of the praetorship in 366 B.C. was an important step in this direction. 'Iuris dictio' was apparently regarded as an exercise of the 'imperium' (see p. 120) and was then transferred from the consuls to the praetor.

Before considering the meanings which the word 'Imperium' bore in Cicero's time, it will be convenient to point out an important change which had taken place in the system of Roman administration.

For many years the foreign provinces of Rome were governed by praetors during their year of office, unless a formidable war happened to be going on in or near to any of them, in which case the conduct of the war was often entrusted to a consul. But a change was made during the later years of the commonwealth's existence, owing to the gradual increase in the number of the provinces, and to the greater demand for the services of the praetors at Rome. These two causes made it necessary to entrust the government of provinces often to proconsuls or propraetors; and, after Sulla had organized six permanent criminal courts, these, together with the two civil courts, required the superintendence of all the praetors, though their number was at that time increased to eight. Cp. Smith, Dict. of Antiq. sub vocc. 'iudex,' 'praetor.'

They might, however, be employed on military service in case of extreme need; and Q. Metellus Celer was so employed in 63 B.C. Cp. Ep. 4, notes and references.

At some time during Cicero's life it became usual for the consuls also to remain in Italy during their year of office. Mommsen thinks that this change dated from the legislation of Sulla, but allows that there were many exceptions during the following twenty years. Rom.

Hist. 3. 367; Rechtsfrage 9-11; 29-34. Others have fixed on the year 74 B.C. as that with which the new system began; A. W. Zumpt thinks that it dated from 59 B.C. Cp. Studia Romana, pp. 72. 73.

In the time then of Cicero's political activity we can recognise two kinds of 'Imperium,' (1) that held by consuls or praetors[1] during their year of office at Rome (cp. In Verr. 2 Act. 13. 37; In Pis. 13. 29; Messalla ap. A. Gell. 13. 15): (2) that held by provincial governors, or by commissioners specially invested with it: in Mommsen's words the 'imperium domi' and 'imperium militiae:' terms which do not so much perhaps define the quality of the 'imperium' as the sphere of its exercise. Cp. Mommsen, Staatsrecht, pp. 95; 100.

The military 'Imperium'[2] was not ordinarily exercised by the consuls in Italy after the change above referred to had taken place, nor indeed, was there ordinarily occasion for its exercise. Sallust (Cat. 29) seems to have thought that a special vote of the senate was needed to invest a consul with it. As the more important judicial functions had been long since transferred to the praetors and permanent courts, the ordinary 'Imperium' of the consuls must have consisted, apparently, in practice of little more than the right of convoking the 'comitia centuriata' for elections and for legislation; a right which probably rested upon the 'Imperium.' Cp. A. Gell. 13. 15; 15. 27; Varro L. L. 6. 88-93.

The 'Imperium' of provincial governors comprised, like that of the old Roman kings, military, administrative, and judicial powers; and was probably only limited locally while the governor's term of office lasted. After that term had expired, he might of course be prosecuted for misgovernment. He seems to have entered on the exercise of his 'Imperium' in a certain sense when he left Rome with proper ceremony ('paludatus'); but not to have held it in its entirety till he reached his province. Cp. Mommsen Rechtsfrage 34; 35. He lost it altogether, except for the day of a triumph, when he recrossed the pomoerium, or ancient sacred limit of the city of Rome. Cp. Ep. 29. 25; Philipp. 3. 11, 27 and Mr. King's note; Ulpian, Digest. 1. 16. 16. It could be granted to private persons by the people—as more than once to Pompey (cp. Intr. to Part I, §§ 4; 7; 8);—and was apparently conferred by the senate, though with some irregularity, on various persons in 49 B.C. (cp. Caes. Bell. Civ. 1. 6) and on Octavian in 43 B.C. (cp. Philipp. 5. 16. 45).

The unconstitutional combination of powers in the hands of Pompey during his third consulship was altogether exceptional. Cp. Intr. to Part II, §§ 14; 15; Mommsen 4. 1, 324. 325.

The title 'Imperator' seems during the republican period to have been of a purely military character. Perhaps it could legally be assumed by any officer who had been invested with the military 'Imperium.' Cp. Dion Cassius 43. 44; A.W. Zumpt, S.R. 212. 233. In practice, however, I think that it seems only to have been borne by officers possessed of 'imperium' who had obtained successes in war, and had consequently been greeted as 'Imperatores' by their soldiers. Cp. Ad Att. 5. 20. 3; Tac. Ann. 3. 74; Mommsen, Röm. Staatsrecht, 105. It was often confirmed by a vote of the senate. Cp. Philipp. 14. 4; 5; In Pis. 19. 44.

For an account of the title 'Imperator' prefixed to the names of the emperors, cp. Dion Cassius (53. 17), who considers it equivalent to that of king or dictator; also Mommsen 4. 1. 470; 471; A. W. Zumpt, S. R. 232; 233.

---

[1] It is doubtful if the possession of 'imperium' was necessary for the praetors who presided in the criminal courts, or 'quaestiones perpetuae.' Cp. Mommsen, Rechtsfrage, p. 10, note.

[2] I use this term as the nearest equivalent for 'Imperium militiae' in Mommsen's work, though admitting that it is not quite accurate.

APPENDIX I.

State of the Roman Empire about the time of Cicero's entrance into public life.

§ 1. In the East, Nicomedes III. of Bithynia had died in 74 B.C., and had bequeathed his kingdom to the Romans. In the same year, however, Mithridates renewed hostilities, and at first obtained considerable successes, till the arrival of L. Lucullus in Asia changed the aspect of affairs. Mithridates was defeated, and driven to seek a refuge with his son-in-law, Tigranes of Armenia. The Roman frontier, however, was still fluctuating; on the whole, it may have nearly coincided with the course of the Halys. The Romans had three provinces in the East; Asia, comprising Mysia, Lydia, most of Caria and part of Phrygia (cp. Cic. pro Flacco 27, 65); Bithynia, bounded on the north-west by the Propontis and the Thracian Bosphorus and ending at the mouth of the Sangarius, while its eastern frontier was advanced during the Mithridatic war from the Sangarius to the Halys or even somewhat further; and Cilicia, which, however, can have comprised little or none of Cilicia proper as a permanent possession before the suppression of piracy by Pompey (cp. Intr. to Part I, § 7; Appendix 2). Lycia had received its freedom from Sulla as a reward for its attachment to Rome.

In the district between the Adriatic and the Euxine, the Romans had exerted themselves to secure their frontier, and to conquer or bridle the robber-tribes of Dalmatia and Thrace, and great, though not complete, success had attended their efforts. This they owed in great measure to the ability of M. Lucullus, governor of Macedonia in 73–71 B.C. Macedonia, to which Illyricum was probably long annexed, was the only Roman province in this region; Thrace was still governed nominally by its own princes, and Dalmatia was only watched by the governors of Cisalpine Gaul, to which Illyricum was subsequently attached.

§ 2. Farther west were the two Gaulish provinces. The Cisalpine, though treated as a part of Italy for some time after its conquest by the Romans, and though its southern districts were inhabited by Roman citizens, seems to have been organized as a province at some time before 63 B.C.[1] (cp. pp. 9; 10; 35; 36); it extended from the Alps

[1] Cp however, A. W. Zumpt, Studia Romana, pp. 45-71, who places its organization as a province in 59 B.C.

to the Rubicon and the Macra. Many of the towns in the northern, or Transpadane, district had received the Latin franchise in 89 B.C., and were eager to exchange it for the Roman. They thus naturally became allies of the democratic party at Rome, which, they hoped, would gratify their wishes.

The Transalpine province, or Narbonensis, consisted of a broad strip of land stretching from the Alps to the Pyrenees, and encircling the nominally independent territory of Massilia. Its outposts seem to have been—on the west, Lugdunum Convenarum (St. Bertrand) and Tolosa (Toulouse); on the north and north-east, Vienna (Vienne) and Genava (Geneva). An unruly spirit prevailed in considerable districts of this territory, especially among the Allobroges.

The two provinces into which the Roman conquests in Spain were divided had just been reorganized by Pompey, after the death of Sertorius and the dispersion of his followers. The influence of Pompey was predominant, at least in the Hither province, for many years.

§ 3. In Africa the Roman frontier might be occasionally, but not seriously, threatened by the tribes of the interior. The province called Africa consisted mainly of the territory which Carthage had retained just before the third Punic war, which had perhaps been increased after the war with Jugurtha by the addition of the Tripolis (Leptis, Aea, and Sabrada), and was very important from its fertility, which enabled it to supply Rome with much corn. The neighbouring kings of Numidia could hardly be formidable, unless aided by dissensions or corruption among the Romans.

Cyrene, with the four neighbouring towns of Apollonia or Sozusa, Teucheira or Arsinoe, Euesperides or Berenice, and Barca or Ptolemais, had been bequeathed to the Romans by Apion, an Egyptian prince, in 95 B.C., and reduced to a province, probably in 75 or 74 B.C. Cp. A. W. Zumpt, S. R. 48, who refers to a fragment of Sallust, 2. 47, ap. Kritz.

The three great islands of the western Mediterranean had long been subject directly to Rome. Sicily had been seriously impoverished by three years of misgovernment under C. Verres, and its important supplies of corn must have been much diminished.

Sardinia, with which Corsica was combined as one province, also produced much corn. These islands had principally to fear insurrections of slaves and depredations of pirates.

Greece was probably subject to the governors of Macedonia; the organization of a distinct province of Achaia belonging to a later period. Cp. Epp. 34, 8; 90, 2, notes.

Crete was conquered in 67 B.C. by Q. Metellus, and was annexed, according to some, to Cyrene, according to others, to Macedonia. A. W. Zumpt holds the latter view (C. E. 2. 187–189, and 240). Cp. Ad Fam. 8. 8, 8, note.

§ 4. Thus it will be noticed, that while the extent of the Roman dominions was imposing, the frontier was almost everywhere ill-defined, and the communications insecure. Transalpine Gaul was exposed to great danger from armed migrations, such as those of the Cimbri and Teutones in 106 B.C., of Ariovistus and the Suevi in 71, and of the Helvetii somewhat later. In Spain, the most prosperous theatre of Roman colonization, the work of conquest was by no means completed. The frontier of Macedonia was threatened by northern tribes, who afterwards combined into the formidable and well-organized kingdom of Dacia. In the East, Mithridates was not yet subdued; and even the subsequent defeat of his son-in-law Tigranes only made the Parthian monarchy of the Arsacidae the more formidable.

But these dangers were infinitely aggravated by three evils, for which the Roman government was directly or indirectly responsible; the misgovernment of the provinces; the excessive development of slave cultivation in Italy; and the spread of piracy in the Mediterranean. Mithridates, Sertorius, and afterwards Catiline, relied in no small degree on the discontent of the provincials; Spartacus, with an army of slaves and gladiators, ravaged Italy for nearly three years (73–71 B.C.), and the pirates, in spite of partial reverses, were long masters of the Mediterranean, and even threatened the coasts of central Italy.

Seldom had the Roman empire been in greater danger than when these corsairs kept up a communication between the Spanish insurgents and Mithridates, and encouraged the revolted slaves in Italy. It was a most fortunate circumstance for Rome that, when the insurrection of Spartacus began, the war with Sertorius had passed its most critical moment.

The ancient authorities consulted for the facts mentioned in this Appendix are: Livy, Epitt. 70 and 91–97; Plutarch's Lives of Lucullus, Pompey, Crassus, Sertorius; Velleius 2. 29–31; Appian, Bell. Civ. 1. 107–121; Mithridatica 61; 67–96; Dion Cassius 35; 36. 1–6. The modern: Merivale 1, 21–66; Mommsen 4, chaps. 1 and 2; Zumpt, Comment. Epigr. 2. 157–241; Studia Romana, pp. 1–57; Mr. King's notes on the Tenth Philippic; the articles on the various provinces in Smith's Dictionary of Geography; Fischer's Römische Zeittafeln; and Marquardt, Römische Staatsverwaltung, 1. 90–337.

APPENDIX II.

Campaigns of Pompey in the East.

After executing, with complete success, his commission to suppress piracy (cp. Intr. to Part I, § 7), Pompey had passed the winter of 67–66 B.C. in Cilicia, where he received the news of the extended powers conferred upon him by the law of Manilius (supra, § 8). He levied a considerable force, and with it met Lucullus at Danala[1], in Galatia, where, after a warm discussion, he amalgamated that general's forces with his own. Before the close of the year he had completely defeated Mithridates at Nicopolis, and driven him across the Phasis, while Tigranes sued for peace, and obtained it on paying a large sum of money, and surrendering all his possessions except Armenia Proper. The close of 66, and nearly the whole of 65, were occupied with successful campaigns against the Albanians and Iberians; the close of 65, and the beginning of 64, with the suppression of the last efforts at resistance in Pontus.

Pompey then marched southwards, to complete the conquest of Syria which some of his officers had begun. By the end of 63 B.C. the Roman sovereignty was completely established there, and Pompey then began to organize his conquests. Two new provinces, Syria and Crete[2], were formed; three older ones, Asia, Bithynia, and Cilicia, were reconstituted. Bithynia received part of Pontus; the new province of Cilicia comprised, besides Cilicia proper, which had been won by Pompey, Pamphylia, Pisidia, Isauria, Lycaonia, and part of Phrygia. Pompey founded many towns in Cilicia, Cappadocia, and elsewhere, and gave a corporate existence to others. Many of the captive pirates were settled in these towns.

He had also in 63 B.C. defeated the Jews under Aristobulus, and taken Jerusalem, but he did not reduce Judaea to the condition of a Roman province, preferring to leave its government to Hyrcanus, a rival of Aristobulus.

Meanwhile, Mithridates tried to organize means of resistance in the Tauric Chersonese, but his suspicious cruelty caused a revolt, headed by his son Pharnaces, and he died by his own hand in 63 B.C.

Thus, towards the end of 63 B.C., Pompey had completed his task. The Parthians were probably indignant at the advance of the Roman power, but showed no disposition to begin hostilities. Cp. Vell. 2. 33;

[1] Cp. Strab. 12. 5, 2. [2] Cp. Appendix 1, § 3.

37–40; Appian, Mithridatica 97–115; Syriaca 50–51; Plut. Pomp. 30–42; Dion Cassius 36. 28–37; 37. 1–20; Mommsen. 4. 1, chap. 4; Drumann, 4. 429–475; Fischer, Römische Zeittafeln, pp. 213–226; Smith's Dictionary of Geography; Marquardt, 1. 179; 191–193; 236–239.

APPENDIX III.

Life of Atticus.

§ 1. T. Pomponius Atticus was born apparently about 109 B.C., and consequently was about three years older than Cicero. He studied with Cicero, C. Marius the younger, and L. Torquatus, the consul of 65. He lent money to C. Marius and others, to help them in escaping from Italy. About 86 or 85 apparently he left Rome, and stayed twenty-two years at Athens, where his liberality made him generally popular, and the rights of citizenship were offered him by the Athenians. Atticus declined the offer, though Cicero speaks of the Athenians as his fellow citizens[1].

When Sulla visited Athens in 84 B.C. he was much pleased with Atticus, who declined, however, to follow him to Italy.

In 79 B.C. Cicero went to Athens, and the two friends listened in company to Antiochus, Phaedrus, and Zeno[2].

The length of time which Atticus spent at Athens may account for his cognomen. He returned to Rome in 65 B.C. at Cicero's request, to support him in his canvass for the consulship. No letters addressed to him during the years 64–62 have been preserved, but it does not follow that he was at Rome all that time. In December, 63, he induced the equites to make a demonstration in support of Cicero[3]—a service for which his position as a member of an old equestrian family gave him great advantages. At the end of 62 or beginning of 61 he embarked at Brundisium for Epirus[4].

§ 2. He declined to attend Quintus Cicero to Asia as his legate, and was not on very good terms with him, thinking that Quintus did not treat his sister well (v. Infr. § 7). Private affairs mainly occupied his thoughts, but he seems to have warned Cicero against forming too close an union with Pompey[5]. He returned to Rome for a few months at the end of 60 B.C.[6], but went back to Epirus in May, 59[7]. Cicero frequently begged him to return. But Atticus stayed in Epirus till November, and when he returned to Rome, Cicero thought that he did not shew sufficient zeal in

[1] Ad Att. 1. 16, 4; but cp. 6. 6, 2. [2] Intr. to Part I, § 2. [3] Add Att. 2. 1, 7. [4] Ib. 1, 13. 1. [5] Ib. 2. 1, 6. [6] Ib. 2. 2. [7] Ib. 2. 18, 1 and 4; 2. 20, 2.

his service[1]. Atticus was liberal, however, both to Cicero and to his family during the time of his exile, and tried to console him by holding out hopes of a speedy return, which Cicero hardly shared[2]. Atticus was adopted by the will of his uncle about this time, and inherited ten million sesterces from him[3]. He left Rome about the end of 58, and presently met Cicero at Dyrrhachium[4].

§ 3. After Cicero's restoration from exile, Atticus seems for some time to have taken little part in politics. He returned to Rome early in 56 B.C., and married Pilia[5], with whom he seems to have lived very happily. Atticus again left Rome about May 10, 54[6], and after a short stay in Epirus went to Asia, and wrote to Cicero from Ephesus[7]. He returned to Italy in the winter, apparently, and remained there about three years[8]. He had a daughter born to him in 51[9].

Cicero, during his proconsulate, requested the aid of Atticus in various matters—especially to prevent his being detained in Cilicia[10]. He was also anxious to defend his own behaviour to Brutus[11]. Atticus returned to Rome suffering from a fever, September 19, 50 B.C.[12]

§ 4. During the civil war, which began in the next year, Atticus seems not to have given Cicero any very distinct advice, and was probably guided by what seemed his friend's inclinations[13]. He was liberal to Cicero, and to his family[14], but remained neutral in the struggle—an attitude which satisfied Caesar more than Pompey. After Cicero's return to Brundisium, Atticus was his confidant in the trouble caused by the unnatural conduct of his brother and nephew[15], and by the alleged selfishness of Terentia[16].

About this time, probably, Atticus interceded for Buthrotum, which had incurred Caesar's displeasure, and saved its lands from confiscation by giving security for the payment of a considerable sum of money[17].

§ 5. During the year 45 B.C. Atticus and Cicero generally lived apart, but kept up a constant correspondence[18]. After Caesar's death Atticus took no decided part in politics, but lent large sums to Brutus privately. He was again anxious about Buthrotum, and entreated Cicero to intercede with various people on behalf of its inhabitants[19].

Atticus seems to have approved of Caesar's murder, and of the

[1] Ad Att. 3. 15. 4 and 7. [2] Ib. 3. 9. 2; 3. 23. 5. [3] Ib. 3. 20. 1. [4] Ib. 3. 25 and 27. [5] Ad. Q. F. 2. 3. 7. [6] Ad Att. 4. 14. 1. [7] Ib. 4. 15. 2; 4. 17. 3. [8] Ib. 5. 21, 1. [9] infra, § 7; Ad Att. 5. 19. 2. [10] Ad Att. 5. 15. 1; 5. 21. 3. [11] Ib. 5. 21, 10–13. [12] Ib. 6. 9, 1. [13] Ib. 9. 10, 4–10. [14] Ib. 11. 2, 4; 11. 3. 1. [15] Ib. 11. 15. 2. [16] Ib. 11. 24. 3. [17] Ib. 12. 6 4; 16. 16 A. 4 and 5. [18] Ib. 12. 12 to 13. 52. [19] Ib. 15. 14, 1; 16. 16, with the letters appended.

vigorous acts of Dolabella[1]—and to have been adroit, as before[2], in anticipating what advice Cicero wished him to give. When, however, the war of Mutina had gone decidedly against Antony, Atticus assisted his wife Fulvia—a service in return for which Antony exempted not only Atticus himself, but two of his friends, from proscription.

After the battle of Philippi, Atticus kept up a friendly correspondence both with Antony and with Octavian; the latter often consulted him on poetical and antiquarian questions. Atticus' health had generally been very good, but when about 77 years old he was visited by a painful disorder, aggravated perhaps in the first instance by maltreatment. He abstained from food, thinking the case desperate, and died March 31, 32 B.C.

§ 6. He was extremely wealthy; besides his uncle's legacy, he had inherited two million sesterces from his father. About the year 69 B.C. he had bought a considerable estate near Buthrotum in Epirus, and he had perhaps properties at Sybota and in Corcyra[3], and large sums at interest in Sicyon, Macedonia, and Delos[4]. He seems to have been moderate in his demands of interest, but prompt in exacting repayment.

His expenditure, both on his houses and on his table, was moderate—at least compared with that of other wealthy Romans; he had a fine house with gardens on the Quirinal, a villa close to Rome, and estates at Ardea, at Nomentum, and near Lucretilis. On his estate at Buthrotum stood the Amaltheum—an apartment or shrine containing groups of mythological personages, and busts of eminent Romans, with a few lines of poetry under each, of his own composition. Cicero's was among them. Cicero asked Atticus to collect works of art for him in Greece[5].

The slaves of Atticus were valuable as copyists or readers; some of them seem to have been trained as gladiators[6].

His knowledge of and fondness for literature were remarkable; he wrote a Greek account of Cicero's consulship, a compendium of Roman history, and various genealogical works. He spoke and wrote both Greek and Latin with great elegance and propriety. His knowledge of dates and of antiquities generally was remarkable, and his power of rapid calculation still more so[7]. In philosophy he seems to have inclined to Epicureanism[8].

[1] Ad Att. 14. 14, 2; 14. 16, 2; Ad Fam. 9. 14. [2] Ad Att. 16. 7. 3–5. Cp. supra § 4.
[3] Ad Att. 1. 5. 7; 4. 8 a, 1; 5. 9, 1. [4] Ib. 1. 13. 1; 9. 9. 4; Ad Fam. 5. 5.
[5] Ad Att. 1. 6–9. [6] Ib. 4. 4 b. 2; 4. 8 a, 2. [7] Ib. 5. 21, 13.
[8] Ib. 14. 20, 5, alib.

§ 7. He was placable and affectionate as a son, husband, and father, and an honest, if not very energetic, friend. He was on intimate terms with many of his eminent contemporaries; traces may be found of an intimacy between him and the Claudii[1]; and among his acquaintance were Pompey[2], Q. Hortensius, M. Varro, Q. Gellius Canus, A. Torquatus, Q. Metellus Celer. Caesar was pleased by his not leaving Italy during the first civil war[3].

His sister Pomponia married Q. Cicero, but the marriage was not happy, and seems to have been terminated by a divorce about 45 or 44 B.C.[4]

Atticus had a daughter—Pomponia or Caecilia Attica—born 51 B.C.[5] She married M. Agrippa, at Antony's suggestion, about 36; their daughter Vipsania Agrippa was betrothed when hardly a year old to Tiberius Nero, afterwards emperor, whom she subsequently married, and lived happily with him till Augustus required him to separate from her[6].

The authorities for the above biography, besides the passages quoted in the notes, have been the life of Atticus by Cornelius Nepos, and that by Drumann in the fourth volume of his Roman history.

APPENDIX IV.

ON THE LEGALITY OF THE EXECUTION OF LENTULUS AND HIS ACCOMPLICES.

The Lex Porcia, enacted, probably, in the year 197 B.C., provided that no Roman citizen should be scourged or put to death by the sentence of a magistrate. Cp. Livy 10. 9; Sall. Cat. 51; Cic. pro Rab. 4, 12. Subsequently, a Lex Sempronia (C. Gracchi) provided that no commissions should be appointed, without the consent of the people, for trying cases in which the 'caput' of a Roman citizen was endangered. Cp. Pro Rab. l. c., and the quotation from Ahrens in Orelli's Index Legum, Onomast. vol. 3.

Neither of these laws, of course, would interfere with the old capital prosecutions for 'perduellio,' before the people assembled in the comitia centuriata; but such prosecutions were very rare in the later years of the Commonwealth.

[1] Ad Att. 2. 9; 2. 15, 2; 2. 22, 4; 10. 8, 3. [2] Ib. 3. 13, 1. [3] supra, § 4.
[4] Ad Att. 1. 17, 1–4; 5. 1, 3; 6. 2, 1–2; 14. 13, 5; 14. 17, 3. [5] supra, § 3.
[6] Suet. Tib. 7; Tac. Ann. 1. 12; 2. 43.

It is clear that the execution of Lentulus and his accomplices was in direct violation of the Porcian law, and of others probably, unless the decree by which the senate invested the consuls with extraordinary powers (viderent consules ne quid detrimenti res publica caperet) deprived those who should subsequently be guilty of seditious practices of their rights as citizens. Cicero argues that such was the legal effect of that decree, and that Lentulus and his associates were outlaws. Cp. In Cat. 1. 11, 28; 4. 5, 10; Pro Rab. 7–11. And Sallust (Cat. 29) says of the effect of that decree, 'ea potestas per senatum more Romano magistratibus maxima permittitur . . . coercere *omnibus modis* socios atque cives.' These words, however, do not assert the strict legality of punishments inflicted by virtue of the decree, and Sallust makes Caesar (cap. 51) plead energetically that Lentulus could not be put to death by the senate's order. The senate does not seem to have had the power of disfranchising Roman citizens (cp. In Verr. 2 Act. 1, 5, 13); according to the author of the speech 'De Domo' (29, 30), no one could be deprived of citizenship, even by a vote of the people, without his own consent.

Still less had the senate the power of sentencing citizens to death. The question is, whether it could invest the consuls with such power.

In practice, its right to do so had not passed unquestioned. L. Opimius had been accused before the people for his severities in putting down the insurrection of C. Gracchus; he was, however, acquitted (cp. Livy Epit. 61); and C. Rabirius had been prosecuted, in the very year of Cicero's consulship, for having killed a man when co-operating in the suppression of the revolt of Saturninus (cp. Intr. to Part I, § 9). The truth seems to be, that the senate had usurped illegal powers; that its usurpation had been largely, though not universally, approved, and that therefore it is an exaggeration to speak, as Mommsen does, of the execution of Lentulus as a 'judicial murder' (4. 1, 179 and 181); and that opinions seem to have been much divided at Rome, as among modern scholars, on the question. In addition to Mommsen, Rein, Criminalrecht, p. 562; Lange, Röm. Alt. 1. 615 and 616; Arnold, Later Roman Commonwealth, 1. 331; Drumann 5. 553; all maintain the illegality of the act, and Dean Liddell (2. 398) implies the same view. Niebuhr (Lectures, 2. 25), decidedly, and the authors of the articles 'consul' and 'dictator' in Smith's Dictionary of Antiquities, doubtfully, take the other side; Merivale (1. 84) is doubtful.

APPENDIX V.

ON CICERO'S ESTATES, AND OTHER PROPERTY.

§ 1. 1. At Arpinum. This was inherited by Cicero from his father[1]; it was retired, and Cicero stayed there, seems to have found it an agreeable residence in spring or summer[2]. He had there an Amaltheum[3]. His brother Quintus had two estates near it, called Arcanum and Laterium[4].

2. At Tusculum. This had formerly been the property of Sulla, then of Q. Catulus[5]. The villa was richly adorned with statues and pictures, and had a gymnasium attached to it[6]. Cicero offered this property for sale[7] in 57 B.C., but afterwards changed his mind, for we find him in possession of it[8] at a later period.

3. At Antium. This was an agreeable and retired spot[9]. Cicero seems to have sold it before 45 B.C. to M. Lepidus[10].

4. At Formiae. This was one of his oldest possessions. He spent some money upon it, but found the situation bustling[11].

5. At Pompeii. He spent much on the decoration of his villa there, and seems to have kept possession of it till his death[12].

6. At Cumae. A delightful spot, but in too crowded a neighbourhood[13]. It is first mentioned after his return from exile[14]. The treatise 'De Republica' was partly written there[15].

7. At Puteoli. Only mentioned in his later letters[16]. Cicero composed the 'Academica' there, and was perhaps visited there by Caesar[17] towards the end of 45 B.C.

8. At Astura. This is not mentioned before 45 B.C., and perhaps was purchased in that year[18].

Cicero had also several houses at which he could lodge for a night, in travelling from one estate to another ('deversoria'), e.g. at Tarracina[19] perhaps, Sinuessa[20], Cales[21], Anagnia[22].

§ 2. He parted with his father's house at Rome to his brother[23], and

[1] De Leg. Agrar. 3. 2, 8.
[2] Ad Att. 9. 6, 1: cp. Ad Fam. 14. 7, 3.
[3] Ad Att. 1. 16, 18; 2. 1, 11.
[4] Ib. 5. 1, 3; 10. 1, 1; Ad Q. F. 2. 7.
[5] Pliny H. N. 22. 6; Ad Att. 4. 5, 2.
[6] Ib. 1. 1, 5, note; 1. 3–11.
[7] Ib. 4. 2, 7.
[8] Ib. 12. 41, 3.
[9] Ib. 2. 6.
[10] Ib. 13. 47 b, 1.
[11] Ib. 2. 14, 2; 4. 2, 7.
[12] Ib. 2. 1, 11; 14. 16, 1.
[13] Ib. 5. 2, 2; 14. 16, 1.
[14] Ib. 4. 9, 1.
[15] Ad Q. F. 3. 5, 1.
[16] Ad Att. 14. 7, 1; but cp. Ib. 4. 10, 1, and 1. 13, 5. Perhaps, as Mr. Jeans thinks, (intr. to Ep. 109) it was a bequest from M. Cluvius,—see next page and Ad Att. 14. 7, 1; 14. 9, 1.
[17] Ad Att. 13. 52; Pliny H. N. 31. 2, 3.
[18] Ad Att. 12. 19, 1.
[19] Ad Fam. 7. 23, 3.
[20] Ib. 12. 20.
[21] Ad Att. 8. 3, 3.
[22] Ib. 12. 1, 1.
[23] Ad Q. F. 2. 3, 7; Plut. Cic. 8.

bought, for three millions and a half of sesterces, a magnificent one on the Palatine, which had belonged to M. Livius Drusus, and afterwards to M. Crassus[1]. It was destroyed by Clodius in 58 B.C., and the money granted by the consuls for its restoration in 57 was insufficient, especially as the rebuilding went on slowly, and was hindered by violence[2].

§ 3. The dowry which Cicero received with Terentia, amounted to 400,000 sesterces, and a legacy bequeathed to him tolerably early in life, amounted to 360,000[3]. In 68 B.C. he already owned the estates at Formiae and Tusculum, and paid 20,400 sesterces for statues[4].

The Stoic Diodotus, who had lived some time in his house, left him ten million of sesterces in 59 B.C.[5] But his exile caused him great embarrassments, from which he seems never altogether to have extricated himself[6], and he subsequently borrowed money from Milo, Vestorius, and Caesar[7].

He suspected Philotimus, a freedman of Terentia, of culpable mismanagement or peculation[8].

Cicero received a legacy during his absence in Cilicia, which he calls 'Preciana'[9].

He made 2,200,000 sesterces by his government of Cilicia, but Pompey took this money[10], and the war gave rise to other embarrassments[11], owing partly to the depreciation of landed property, partly to the extravagance of Dolabella; partly, perhaps, to the mismanagement of Terentia[12].

He received, however, various legacies: one from Galeo[13], one from Fufidius[14], and one from M. Cluvius[15] which produced at first 80,000, and afterwards 100,000 sesterces a year. This was in the summer of 45 B.C.

His divorce from Terentia in 46 B.C., and the expense of his son's education, led to fresh, but not very serious, embarrassments[16]. His property seems still to have been substantially unimpaired in the summer of 44[17]. He needed Atticus' help at times, owing to his difficulty in getting in money owed him, e.g. from Faberius[18].

This Appendix gives the substance of the 40th section of Brückner's Life of Cicero.

[1] Ad Fam. 5. 6, 2; Vell. 2. 14; Intr. to Part I, § 12. [2] Ad Att. 4. 5. 3; 4. 7. 3; Ad Q. F. 2. 3. 7. [3] Plut. Cic. 8. [4] Ad Att. 1. 4. 3; 1. 5, 7; 1. 7. [5] Ib. 2. 20, 6. [6] Ad Fam. 14. 1, 5; 14. 4, 4. [7] Ad Att. 5. 10, 4; 4. 6, 4. [8] Ib. 6. 4. 3. [9] Ib. 6. 9. 2. [10] Ib. 11. 1, 2; Ad Fam. 5. 20, 9. [11] Ad Att. 11. 2, 2 and 3; 11. 4, 1. [12] Ad Fam. 9. 18, 4; Ad Att. 11. 25, 3; 11. 24, 3. [13] Ib. 11. 12, 4. [14] Ib. 11. 14, 3. [15] Ib. 13. 46, 3; 14. 9. 1; 14. 10, 3. [16] Intr. to Part IV, § 7; Ad Att. 16. 1, 5. [17] Ib. 16. 6, 2. [18] Ib. 12. 21, 2.

PART II.

From Cicero's return from exile, Sept. 4, 57 B.C., to the outbreak of hostilities between Caesar and Pompey, early in January, 49 B.C.

INTRODUCTION.

§ 1. Cicero returned from exile Sept. 4, and returned thanks next day to the senate and people for his restoration. The enthusiasm of his reception, probably, did much to encourage the optimates.

On Sept. 7, wishing, Plutarch[1] says, to promote a better understanding between Pompey and the leaders of the optimates, he proposed that a commission should be given to the former for supplying Rome with corn. Pompey's term of office was to be five years, and he was to have power to name fifteen legates. C. Messius[2] proposed to invest him with far more extensive powers, but it does not appear that his proposal was adopted.

On Sept. 29 Cicero pleaded before the pontifices—perhaps in the speech 'De Domo Sua,' which we still possess—against the legality of the consecration of the site of his house by Clodius. The court decided in his favour[3]; and the senate, on the two following days, passed votes empowering the consuls to reimburse him for the destruction both of his house and of his villas. The work of rebuilding was speedily begun; and though interrupted by Clodius, was protected by Milo.

About the same time Cicero removed from the Capitol the tablets recording the acts of Clodius' tribunate. This displeased Cato, who had received an honourable commission from Clodius[4].

[1] Cp. Plut. Pomp. 49. [2] Ad Att. 4. 1, 7. [3] Ib. 4. 2, 2. [4] Plut. Cic. 34. Dion Cassius (39. 21) speaks of 'the pillars that were set up about Cicero's exile.'

Caesar, during this summer, subdued the Belgae, of whom the Nervii were the most famous[1] tribe, and received the submission of several tribes on the north-west coast. Towards the close of the year his legate, Ser. Galba, was employed in reducing the Veragri, Nantuates, and Seduni, near the lake of Geneva[2], to submission. In honour of these victories, Cicero supported a vote of fifteen days thanksgivings—an unprecedented distinction[3].

Thus far Cicero, since his return to Rome, had done nothing to displease, and a great deal to gratify, the triumvirs. The next few months witnessed a change of his political attitude.

We have seen that Pompey had quarrelled with Clodius. Cicero's restoration could only increase the latter's animosity, and he affected to support Crassus, who had always been jealous of Pompey, and was perhaps anxious to be sent on a public commission to Alexandria[4].

The curious result followed, that a temporary good understanding was effected between the leaders of the optimates[5] and Clodius. This was promoted by the interest which Cato had in maintaining the legality of the acts of Clodius[6]. But it must have tended to bring Milo and Pompey into a closer union.

56 B.C.

§ 2. Our knowledge of the events of the early months of this year is derived mainly from letters to P[7]. Lentulus Spinther, now governor of Cilicia, and to Q. Cicero[8], now in Sardinia, and acting as legate to Pompey. Clodius had been elected curule aedile[9], and so escaped for a year any danger of prosecution, from which magistrates were exempt during their year of office[10].

In January, Cicero argued in the senate, that P. Lentulus Spinther should be allowed to restore Ptolemy XII. at[11] Alexandria. But opinions in the senate were much divided; a passage from the Sibylline books, forbidding the employment of an army in the transaction, was circulated not without effect; Cicero himself was probably somewhat distracted by the rival claims of Pompey and Lentulus, and the affair was adjourned indefinitely[12].

Next month Clodius accused Milo of riotous proceedings ('vis'[13]).

[1] Caes. Bell. Gall. 2. [2] Ib. 3. 1-3. [3] Ib. 2. 35; Cic. De Prov. Cons. 11, 27. [4] Ad Q. F. 2. 3. 2; cp. Plut. Pomp. 48. [5] Ad Fam. 1. 9. 19. [6] supra, pp. 20; 135. [7] Ad Fam. 1. 1-6. [8] Ad Q. F. 2. 2-4. [9] Pro Sest. 44. 95. [10] Cp., however, Varro ap. A. Gell. 13. 13. [11] Ad Fam. 1. 1 and 2. [12] Ad Q. F. 2. 2. 3. [13] Ib. 2. 3. 1; Pro Sest. l. c. The accusation seems to have been preferred before the 'comitia tributa.' Cp. Ep. 23. 2. note. Peter, 2. 237.

We have no account of the issue of the trial, but it seems unlikely that a conviction should have passed unnoticed.

On Feb. 3, Cicero defended L. Bestia on a charge of bribery before the praetor Domitius; the trial gave him an opportunity of sounding public feeling by political[1] allusions. Still more was this the case on the trial of P. Sestius for riot, in March. He had been active the year before in promoting Cicero's restoration, and the charge was no doubt based in part upon his conduct at that time. Other experienced advocates spoke for the defence; Cicero last, as usual. His speech was a political manifesto. He still treated Pompey and Caesar with courtesy on the whole[2]; but professed unlimited respect for the senate[3], and during the course of the proceedings found an opportunity of inveighing bitterly against Vatinius, one of the witnesses for the prosecution, especially on account of his behaviour in 59 B.C.[4] This cannot have been agreeable to Caesar, though Cicero affected[5] not to consider him responsible for the measures of Vatinius.

Sestius was unanimously acquitted[6]; and this may have encouraged Cicero to shew greater independence for a time.

He soon came again into collision with Clodius. Various prodigies were reported, and the opinion of haruspices was taken as to what they portended, and what was the cause of the divine displeasure intimated by them. The haruspices reported, among other causes, that the gods were displeased because sacred rites were treated as profane; and Clodius instantly, in a speech to the people, applied this to the rebuilding of Cicero's house. Cicero thought it necessary to argue in the senate against this interpretation. His speech 'De Haruspicum Responsis,' is mainly an attack upon Clodius, and he hints[7] that the optimates should not be deluded by his flatteries.

The answer of the haruspices seems, however, to have been procured in the interest of the optimates, and not of Clodius only. It contained a warning against dissensions among the nobles which might lead to the concentration of all powers in the hands of one man[8], with reference perhaps to the proposal of C. Messius. The confused state of parties was shewn by the acquittal of Sex. Clodius, prosecuted by Milo at the instance of Pompey; for he owed his acquittal to the votes of the senatorial[9] portion of his judges.

§ 3. A political crisis had been for some time approaching. Various

[1] Ad Q. F. 2. 3, 6. [2] There is an exception: 33, 71. [3] Especially 65, foll. [4] Intr. to Part I, § 18. [5] In Vat. 9, 22. [6] Ad Q. F. 2. 4, 1. [7] De Har. Resp. 23, 48. [8] Ib. 19, 40: cp. supra, § 1. [9] Ad Q. F. 2. 6, 6.

circumstances had raised the spirits of the optimates, as we have seen; the enthusiasm with which the Italians had greeted Cicero's return; the election of consuls favourable, or not adverse, to the old constitution; the acquittal of Sestius, indicating the temper of the tribunals; the quarrels among the triumvirs and their instruments. Even Cicero was inspired with unwonted confidence and decision, and became for a moment the spokesman of the optimates[1].

The revenue was in an unsatisfactory state, and ill able to meet the heavy demands made upon it for the supply of corn to the capital, and for the pay of Caesar's army. Now a considerable income had been sacrificed by the allotment of the Campanian domain under the agrarian laws[2] of 59 B.C., and Cicero, on April 5, proposed that the senate should, on May 15, discuss the legality of such allotment. No doubt the object of this motion was the repeal of the laws of 59, and it was thus a direct challenge to Caesar. It is probable that Cicero hoped too much from a suspected estrangement of Pompey from Caesar. The conduct of the former, with respect both to the proposal of Messius[3], and to the restoration of Ptolemy[4], betrayed eagerness to obtain an important military command; and he was probably jealous of Caesar. Thus Cicero seems not to have been surprised when, at an interview shortly after his own proposal had been made in the senate, Pompey shewed[5] no sign of displeasure. But he failed to consider that the agrarian laws of 59 had been as much Pompey's work as Caesar's; that the friendship of those two leaders was secured by a marriage connection; and that several of the optimates (especially Favonius, M. Bibulus, and Curio) disliked Pompey, and would not abstain from their offensive patronage of Clodius.

Caesar, probably warned of the state of affairs at Rome, had left his Transalpine province and was now at Ravenna, where Crassus[6], among others, waited on him. The result of their representations seems to have been that Caesar was much incensed against Cicero, and probably somewhat disturbed by the doubtful behaviour of Pompey. The latter, however, would not submit to so decided an attack on his past policy as that made by Cicero's motion. He left Rome for a visit to Sardinia and Africa, and, on his way to one of the northern ports of Italy, had a conference with Caesar at Luca. Many senators and men holding high office were drawn to the place by this important meeting.

§ 4. Both Pompey and Caesar had reason to wish for a re-establish-

[1] Ad Fam. 1. 9, 8. [2] Intr. to Part I, § 17. [3] Ad Att. 4. 1, 7.
[4] Ad Fam. 1. 1, 3; 1. 2, 3. [5] Ib. 1. 9, 9. [6] Ib. 1. 9, 9.

ment of friendly relations. Pompey, unable to conduct affairs at Rome by himself, had to choose between a reconstruction of the triumvirate and a surrender to the optimates, who had shewn little consideration for him. As for Caesar, his provincial government would expire in March, 54 B.C.; he would then have either to resign it or to declare war on the government. The conquest of Gaul was not completed, and it was probably doubtful if, without Pompey's aid, he could get his government prolonged. An understanding between the two leaders was soon arrived at, and its objects seem to have been two; to check the rising spirit of independence in the capital and in Italy, and to secure the position of Pompey and Caesar. The support of Crassus had perhaps been already promised at Ravenna.[1]

Pompey and Crassus were to sue for the consulship for 55 B.C., and so to prevent the election of L. Domitius Ahenobarbus, who might have proved a formidable enemy. Caesar's government of Gaul was to be prolonged for five years, and Pompey and Crassus were to have other governments for a like period. The position of Crassus had always been a subordinate one, but his wealth and connections made him a valuable ally, and, as he could never aspire to the first place, he might be of much use as a mediator between his more eminent colleagues.

The measures necessary to carry out these stipulations were only proposed in the next year, but it is reasonable to suppose that they were settled now.

The first intimation which Cicero received of the new compact, seems to have been from Quintus, with whom Pompey remonstrated in Sardinia on his brother's[1] conduct. This placed Cicero in a position of great difficulty; he had to choose between submission to the triumvirs, and an opposition in which most of his allies would be factious, selfish, and impracticable, which would probably be fruitless, and might dismiss him to a second and more hopeless exile.

He chose submission; withdrew, apparently, his motion on the Campanian domains[2], and made some apology to Caesar for his recent[3] opposition.

§ 5. No part of Cicero's career seems to have caused him more regret and vexation; he attempted to justify it by elaborate[4] excuses and petulant recrimination[5]. Personal fear and jealousy no doubt influenced him to a considerable extent, but other considerations should not be lost sight of. He had never professed an absolute devotion to the optimates; he had more than once argued in favour of investing Pompey with

[1] Ad Fam. 1. 9, 9. [2] Ad Q. F. 2. 8, 1. [3] Ad Att. 4. 5, 1. [4] Ad Fam. 1. 9, 9 to 18. [5] Ad Att. 4. 5.

extraordinary powers; and the main object of his political life had been to maintain a good understanding between him, the optimate leaders, and the equites. Now this seemed impracticable; and, if the events of 59–58 B.C. might detach Cicero from Pompey, what had happened since his return to Rome was hardly likely to put him on good terms with the optimates. Even his exile seems to have inspired him with almost as much resentment towards his irresolute supporters as towards his more open enemies[1]. After all, however, he can hardly be acquitted of rashness in his defiance, and of weakness in his recantation; and the next few years form, perhaps, the part of his career which his biographer will regard with least pleasure.

It was, however, a time of great activity for Cicero as an orator, especially in the law courts; and the speeches which have been preserved, numerous as they are, give no adequate notion of his exertions.

The speech in defence of M. Caelius Rufus, accused of sedition and of attempted poisoning, seems to belong to this spring or summer, but it is not easy to fix its precise date. It was successful, and seems to have led to a lasting friendship between Cicero and his client. Intimacy with Catiline had been made a charge against Caelius, and, in replying to it, Cicero introduced a portrait of Catiline more favourable than those with which we are most familiar[2].

§ 6. About this time Cicero argued[3] in the senate in favour of a grant of money for the pay of Caesar's troops, and of his being allowed to name ten legates. Shortly afterwards he had to attest his recantation by a still more decided step.

A discussion took place in the senate about the assignation of provinces to the consuls of 55 B.C., provision for which was generally made beforehand. Some proposed that either Cisalpine or Transalpine Gaul should be one, which of course would imply the withdrawal of one province from Caesar. Cicero, however, notwithstanding the remonstrances of some of[4] the optimates, and of the consul[5] Philippus, opposed the suggestion successfully, saying that it was essential that Piso and Gabinius[6] should be recalled as soon as possible, and that difficulties would arise if one of Caesar's provinces were assigned to one of the consuls[7] for 55. He also extolled the successes of Caesar[8], and attacked the inconsistency of those optimates who questioned the validity of the Julian laws while defending that of the Clodian[9]. In a letter[10] written to

[1] Ad Att. 3. 9. 2; Ad Fam. 1. 9. 13. [2] Pro Caelio 5 and 6. [3] De Prov. Cons. 11, 28. [4] Ib. 8, 18, foll. [5] Ib. 9. 21. [6] Infra, §§ 8; 9. [7] De Prov. Cons. 7, 17. [8] Ib. 13; 14; cp. Intr. to Part I, § 25. [9] De Prov. Cons. 19. [10] Ad Fam. 1. 7, 10.

P. Lentulus Spinther about this time, Cicero describes the debate as though he had taken no prominent part in it himself.

Either in the summer or autumn he pleaded for the rights of citizenship of L. Cornelius Balbus, which had been conferred by Pompey in Spain. The validity of the act depended on strictly legal points, but the trial enabled Cicero to shew his devotion to Pompey by panegyric [1].

The confidence which Pompey derived from the renewal of his alliance with Caesar seems to have removed his anxiety to be employed in Egypt; and he authorized Cicero to write to Lentulus, in terms [2] which must be considered as a cautious encouragement to intervention.

During the last few months of the year, little of importance happened at Rome. Cicero suffered a severe loss in the death [3] of L. Lentulus Niger, flamen of Mars, for whom he had felt much esteem. He was also much annoyed by the humiliating position to which he had been reduced, and seems to have avoided the capital as much as possible. In a curious letter [4] to L. Lucceius, Cicero entreated him to write an eulogistic account of his services and sufferings, and not to confine himself strictly to the truth.

Tullia was betrothed [5] in the spring to Furius Crassipes, but a marriage does not seem to have ensued. Atticus married Pilia on Feb 12 [6], and Cicero often notices her in his later letters.

§ 7. In Gaul, Caesar reduced the Veneti, and afterwards the Morini and Menapii. P. Crassus, one of his officers, conquered the Aquitani, and another, Sabinus, the Unelli [7].

In Syria, Gabinius seems to have gained successes over Aristobulus, who had escaped from Italy [8]. He thought himself entitled to a 'supplicatio,' but the senate, greatly to Cicero's satisfaction, refused it on May [9] 15. Cicero accuses [10] him of corruption and extortion, very possibly with good grounds; but the unpopularity of Gabinius with the 'publicani' may have arisen from his consulting the interests of the provincials—the Jews and Syrians, of whom Cicero speaks as 'born for slavery.'

Piso had been as unscrupulous, and less successful, in Macedonia. He had oppressed and despoiled the subjects of Rome, and Cicero says [11] that his army melted away without meeting an enemy. Perhaps this was the reason why he was recalled sooner than Gabinius. The senate resolved that Piso should be succeeded, at the beginning of 55 B.C., by

[1] Pro Balbo 1. [2] Ad Fam. 1. 7. 4–6. [3] Ad Att. 4. 6, 1. [4] Ad Fam. 5. 12. [5] Ad Q. F. 2. 4. 2; Ad Fam. 1. 7, 11. [6] Ad Q. F. 2. 3, 7. [7] Caes. Bell. Gall. 3. 7, foll. [8] Joseph. Antiq. 14. 6; Wars 1. 8. [9] Ad Q. F. 2. 8, 1. [10] De Prov. Cons. 4 and 5. [11] Ib. 3.

Q. Ancharius Priscus, apparently[1] one of the praetors for 56; while Gabinius was to be succeeded by (the consul) M. Crassus at the beginning of 54.

It appears that C. Cato, one of the tribunes, interfered with the election of consuls for 55 B.C.; hence an interregnum[2] intervened, followed by a very turbulent election, at which Pompey and Crassus were chosen. Their most formidable opponent was L. Domitius Ahenobarbus.

55 B.C.

§ 8. The new consuls applied themselves at once to securing their position. The election of praetors took place without delay, and, owing to gross bribery, Vatinius was elected and Cato defeated[3]. A law was proposed by C. Trebonius, assigning to the consuls the government of Spain and Syria for five years. Pompey obtained Spain, and Crassus Syria. Another law[4] prolonged Caesar's government of Gaul for five years. It was perhaps proposed by the consuls[5]. Cicero declares[6] that he earnestly dissuaded Pompey from sanctioning this enactment.

About the same time Crassus, with the approval of his colleague, carried a law against illegal political combinations—'sodalicia.' These clubs were now probably strongholds of the optimates, and seem to have been skilfully managed, as the election for curule officers for 57 and 56 B.C. had been, on the whole, adverse to the triumvirs. The judges in trials under the new law were to be taken from three tribes, the accuser naming four, of which the accused might reject one[7].

L. Piso, after his return from Macedonia, had inveighed bitterly against Cicero, who replied by the speech 'In Pisonem,' still extant. It consists principally of mere abuse; but in chap. 21 we find the important fact recorded, that Gabinius had already occupied Alexandria and restored Ptolemy.

Shortly afterwards Pompey opened his new theatre, with shows of extraordinary splendour. Cicero expressed[8] great disgust for the more cruel parts of the entertainment, and the sensibility of the spectators generally was aroused by the slaughter of eighteen elephants.

[1] In Pis. 36, 89; Pro Sest. 53, 113. [2] Ad Att. 4. 15. 4. [3] Plut. Cat. Min. 42; Dion Cassius 39. 32; Livy, Epit. 105. [4] Cp. Appendix 6, § 1. Dion Cassius (39. 33) represents that Caesar's friends threatened opposition if this were not done; but it seems more likely that the whole of this legislation was carried on in concert. [5] Appendix 6, § 1, notes. [6] Philipp. 2. 10. 24. [7] Schol. Bob. ad orat. Pro Planc. c. 15; Dion Cassius 39. 37. [8] Ad Fam. 7. 1, 3; cp. Ad Att. 2. 1, 1.

Cicero, about the same time, was prevailed [1] upon to defend L. Caninius Gallus, the turbulent tribune of 57–56 B.C., a task for which he seems to have felt great repugnance [2].

In November, apparently, Crassus set out to assume the government of his province [3]. Cicero had been at variance with him earlier in the year; they were now, however, reconciled by the intervention of Caesar and Pompey, and Crassus accepted Cicero's hospitality just before his departure [4].

Cicero refers [5] to this time as one of great literary activity on his part. Its most important results seem to have been the three books [6] 'De Oratore.'

A 'Lex Pompeia' of this year seems to have fixed a higher pecuniary [7] qualification for the office of judge than had previously existed, and perhaps [8] refused exemptions to those who desired them.

At the election of praetors for 54 B.C., M. Cato [9] was one of the successful candidates. The election of aediles was disturbed by riot and bloodshed; Pompey's toga was stained with blood, and the sight of [10] it gave his wife, Julia, a shock from which she never altogether recovered. She died next year.

§ 9. The events of the war in Gaul were important. The campaign opened with the destruction of the Usipetes and Tencteri, who had crossed the Rhine, and were attacked rather [11] treacherously by Caesar. He was anxious to deepen the impression thus made, threw a bridge over the Rhine, and spent some days on its right bank with the intention of striking terror into the population. Afterwards he received the submission of the Morini, and made his first expedition [12] into Britain, which, however, produced no decisive results [13].

In Syria, Gabinius, after restoring Ptolemy XII. at Alexandria, had returned to his province, and was preparing for war with Parthia. A family quarrel in the Arsacid dynasty gave him a pretext for interference. Phraates, king of Parthia, had been murdered by his sons Mithridates and Orodes; and, when the latter seemed likely to secure the throne, Mithridates fled to [14] Gabinius, who, however, could not assist him at once, as his intention was diverted by the affairs [15] of Egypt.

[1] By Pompey, probably. [2] Ad Fam. 7. 1. 4. [3] Ad Att. 4. 13. 2. [4] Ad Fam. 1. 9, 20. [5] Ib. 1. 8. 3. [6] Ad Att. 4. 13. 2; Ad Fam. 1. 9. 23. [7] Philipp. 1. 8. 20; Ascon. in Pisonian. 39. 94. p. 129. [8] In Pison. 39. 94; Mommsen 4. 2, 317, foll. [9] Plut. Cat. Min. 44. [10] Id. Pomp. 53. [11] Caes. Bell. Gall. 4. 4; 13 and 14. [12] Ib. 20–37. [13] Ad Q. F. 3. 1. 9 and 10. [14] Dion Cassius 39. 56. [15] Cp. preceding page.

54 B.C.

§ 10. The consuls for this year were L. Domitius Ahenobarbus and Appius Claudius Pulcher. The former was one of the most obstinate and determined of the optimates; the latter an incapable and covetous man of no definite political convictions. The extraordinary commands, however, now held by the triumvirs, made it the less important who held the ordinary political offices.

Cicero seems still to have acquiesced completely in the government of the triumvirs. Among his forensic speeches, of which he delivered an unusual number in this year, we read of one[1] in July on behalf of C. Messius, now a legate of Caesar; of one[2], delivered somewhat later, for Vatinius, whom Cicero had denounced so bitterly at the time of Sestius' trial; and even of one[3] delivered in the autumn for Gabinius, whom he had considered his worst enemy.

Gabinius had been accused somewhat earlier by a Lentulus, and acquitted by a bare majority, to the great disgust of Cicero, who bore testimony[4] against him. Gabinius had attacked Cicero[5] violently in the senate, but on his trial expressed a wish for reconciliation. The speech 'Pro Rabirio Postumo,' now extant, was delivered on a trial which grew out of that of Gabinius, whose unjust gains Rabirius was accused of sharing.

Of Cicero's other speeches of this date, that[6] delivered in the senate on behalf of M. Crassus must have possessed much political interest. The consuls and other eminent senators attacked Crassus, probably for his measures[7] against the Parthians. The speech still extant on behalf of Cn. Plancius, Cicero's old friend and protector in exile, supplies good illustrations of the proceedings at a Roman election. Plancius had been accused of bribery by another friend of Cicero, M. Iuventius Laterensis. A third, in which Cicero pleaded for the people of Reate against the people of Interamna, in a case relating to the management of the course of the Velinus, shews that a friendly connection was still[8] maintained between Cicero and the people of Reate.

§ 11. The letters belonging to this year are—several in the Fourth Book to Atticus, and in the end of the Second and beginning of the Third Book to his brother Quintus, with various others, of which the most interesting are—a laboured[9] defence of his recent political conduct, and a recommendation[10] of a friend to Caesar.

[1] Ad Att. 4. 15, 9. [2] Ad Q. F. 2. 16, 3. [3] Pro Rab. Post. 12, 32. [4] Ad Q. F. 3. 4, 1. [5] Ib. 3. 2, 2. [6] Ad Fam. 5. 8, 1. [7] Dion Cassius 40, 12; Plut. Crassus 16. [8] In Cat. 3. 2, 5; cp. Ad Att. 4. 15, 5. [9] Ad Fam. 1. 9. [10] Ib. 7. 5.

Quintus Cicero seems, at the beginning of this year, to have transferred his services from Pompey to Caesar [1], apparently without opposition from Pompey. He became one of Caesar's most efficient officers, and his presence was a security for his brother's good behaviour. The general tone of the letters of Marcus to Quintus at this time is one of great political despondency, and he repeatedly warns his brother to be cautious in writing [2]. He feared the possible results of an interregnum, followed by a dictatorship; expressed interest in Messalla, as a candidate for the consulship for 53 B.C., and in Milo for 52 [3], though regretting the latter's extravagance and estrangement from Pompey. He received a letter of Caesar's [4] from Britain, and expressed generally great regard for him, and admiration for the firmness with which he bore his daughter's [5] loss.

Cicero's leisure was occupied to a great extent in the composition of the six books on the [6] Commonwealth, which we possess in a fragmentary state. A poem, in [7] three books, on his exile and return, may also belong to this year, and he addressed another [8] to Caesar on his victories in Gaul.

The political corruption now prevailing at Rome was illustrated by the proceedings of the candidates for the consulship in this year, two of whom made a scandalous bargain with the actual consuls, which was presently disclosed in the [9] senate. No election took place till the seventh month of 53 B.C., according to Dion Cassius [10].

In the summer of this year, as has been mentioned by anticipation [11], Pompey's wife, Julia, died, and received a splendid funeral. Her death was a great blow to Caesar, both as a father and as a politician.

§ 12. In the East, Crassus replaced Gabinius as proconsul of Syria, and prepared for war with the Parthians. Mithridates [12] had been defeated and killed during the absence of Gabinius in Egypt, but there was still much dissension in Parthia. Crassus, however, employed his first summer in levying heavy contributions on the provincials, and in plundering the temples of Syria and Palestine. His only military measure was a march into Mesopotamia, in which he met with few enemies, and secured some positions of importance for the next year's campaign [13].

Caesar, meanwhile, after visiting Illyricum, made a second expedition

[1] Ad Att. 4. 17, 3. [2] Ad Q. F. 3. 8, 2; 3. 9, 3. [3] Ib. 3. 8, 6; 3. 9, 2. [4] Ib. 3. 1, 28. [5] Ib. 3. 1, 10; 3. 8 and 6, 4; 3. 8, 1 and 3. [6] Ib. 2. 14, 1; 3. 5, 1; Ad Att. 4. 14, 1; De Legg. 3. 2, 4. [7] Ad Fam. 1. 9, 23: where, however, Baiter (xi. 130 foll.) supposes that Cicero refers to the poem on his consulship. [8] Ad Q. F. 3. 8, 3; 3. 9, 6. [9] Ad Att. 4. 18, 7, note. [10] 40. 17. [11] supra, § 8. [12] supra, § 9. [13] Dion Cassius 40. 13; Plut. Crass. 17.

to[1] Britain. It was on a much larger scale than the first, but seems only to have secured a nominal recognition of Roman supremacy from the British prince Cassivellaunus, who consented to pay tribute and to give hostages. Towards the end of the year a formidable[2] insurrection broke out in Gaul, one of its principal leaders being Ambiorix, king of the Eburones, who lived between the Rhine and the Meuse. The scattered Roman legions were exposed to great peril.

53 B.C.

§ 13. This year, as a previous statement implies, opened with a series of interregna[3]. Pompey at length[4] employed his influence to bring about an election of consuls, and Cn. Domitius Calvinus and M. Valerius Messalla were chosen, both of whom afterwards supported Caesar. Much confusion prevailed before the election, some urging that military tribunes should be appointed, others that Pompey should be dictator.

By far the most important event of the year was the defeat of Crassus, followed, on June 9[5], by his murder. This was a terrible blow to Caesar, for it deprived him, at a very critical moment, of a counterpoise to Pompey's ascendancy. Caesar was engaged during the greater part of the year in a desperate struggle with the Belgae, who destroyed two legions, and reduced a third, commanded by Q. Cicero, to great extremities[6]. At the end of the year he had, however, restored the supremacy of the Roman arms, and was able to return, as usual, to North Italy for the winter[7], in order to watch the course of political events. Pompey was still on good terms with him, and allowed him to form a legion out of men of Cisalpine Gaul who had taken the military oath of obedience to Pompey himself[8].

Cicero was probably little affected by the death of Crassus[9], whom he seems never to have regarded with cordial affection. Crassus' son Publius, who perished a day or two before his father, had, however, always shewn great respect for Cicero[10], who was chosen to fill the place in the college of augurs which had become vacant by Publius' death[11].

Cicero was much interested in Milo's prospects as a consular candi-

[1] Caes. Bell. Gall. 5. 8–23. [2] Ib. 5. 25, foll. [3] supra, § 11: cp. Ad Fam. 7. 11, 1. [4] Plut. Pomp. 54; Dion Cassius 40. 45. [5] Ov. Fast. 6. 465; Mommsen 4. 1. pp. 336. 337. [6] Caes. Bell. Gall. 5. 25 to 6. 44. [7] Ib. 6. 44. [8] Ib. 6. 1; 8. 54; Ad Fam. 8. 4. 4. [9] De Divin. 1. 9. 22. [10] Ad Fam. 5. 8, 4. [11] Ib. 3. 10, 9; Philipp. 2. 2, 4; Plut. Cic. 36.

date, and recommended him to Curio[1]. But this year, like its predecessor, closed without any election of consuls having been made, and was followed by an interregnum.

Atticus seems to have spent the year at Rome, otherwise we should hardly be without some letters to him. Cicero's main correspondents at this time were the younger Curio[2], now quaestor in Asia, and C. Trebatius Testa[3], a lawyer who had gone, with Cicero's recommendation, to push his fortunes in Caesar's camp.

52 B.C.

§ 14. Great turbulence and corruption prevailed during this winter; the partisans[4] of the consular candidates, P. Plautius Hypsaeus, T. Annius Milo, and Q. Metellus Scipio, were all active. P. Clodius was a candidate for the praetorship, but was killed by Milo's retinue in an affray near Bovillae[5] on Jan. 17 or 18. Much rioting followed, and the senate-house was burnt at Clodius' funeral. Milo did not renounce his hopes of the consulship: but to stop the violence which still prevailed, the senate, at the suggestion of M. Bibulus, proposed that Pompey should be appointed sole consul. This election took place on the 24th of an intercalary month, inserted between February and March. Pompey was created consul 'absens et solus quod nulli alii umquam contigit[6],' and became virtually dictator. Nor was he required to lay down his government of Spain, which was administered by his legates. He could not wish for a more exalted position, and a growing estrangement may now be traced between him and Caesar, whose alliance he no longer thought necessary. Pompey refused Caesar's proposal of a new marriage connection, and married Cornelia[7], the daughter of Q. Metellus Scipio. Her father became his colleague for the last five months of his consulship.

Pompey now proposed and carried a series of important measures.

1. Laws against riot ('vis') and corruption ('ambitus'), which prescribed a briefer and stricter process and heavier penalties. Perhaps[8] that on 'vis' declared it illegal to keep arms in Rome.

2. A law 'de iure magistratuum[9],' providing that candidates must attend to canvass in person, and that five years[10] should elapse between holding office at Rome and the government of a province[11]. Pompey

[1] Ad Fam. 2. 6. [2] Ib. 2. 1–6. The elder Curio seems to have died about this time. [3] Ib. 7. 10–18. [4] Livy, Epit. 107. Argum. ad orat. De Aere Alieno Milonis. [5] Ascon. Argum. in Milonianam. [6] Livy, Epit. 107. [7] Plut. Pomp. 55; Mommsen 4. 2, 341, 347. 348. [8] Pliny H. N. 34. 39. Cp. Merivale 2. 51. [9] A. W. Zumpt, Comm. Epigr. 2. 204, 205. [10] Suet. Iul. 28; Dion Cassius 40. 56. [11] Perhaps these provisions were embodied in two distinct laws. Cp. App. VI. § 3. notes.

violated this law, however, in his own case, by procuring an enactment which

3. Secured him the [1] government of Spain for five years more.

The general effect of these measures was— 1. To limit [2] the freedom of forensic oratory. 2. To check the activity of political clubs by the greater probability of the punishment of illegal practices. 3. To place the provincial governments [3] more directly under the control of the senate. 4. To embarrass Caesar, by requiring him to sue for the consulship in person, as he would thus abandon the protection of his army, and would be exposed to great danger. For 5. the operation of the laws against riot and corruption was extended retrospectively to the year 70 B.C. [4]; and thus the proceedings of Caesar in 60–59 B.C. might be called in question under it.

Pompey had, however, approved of a law brought in by the ten tribunes, among whom M. Caelius was prominent, dispensing in Caesar's favour with the necessity of a personal canvass for the consulship; and when it was pointed out to him that the law 'de iure magistratuum' withdrew this concession, Pompey granted it again by an appended clause [5] of questionable validity. Cicero attached great importance [6] to this concession, but is inconsistent in the account [7] he gives of his own behaviour in the matter.

§ 15. Milo was accused of riotous proceedings ('vis') early in April by Ap. Claudius Pulcher (major), P. Valerius Nepos, and M. Antonius. Cicero spoke in Milo's defence on April 8th, but without his usual ability and success. The court was beset by a turbulent rabble, and guarded by soldiers; and the unusual sight seems to have terrified Cicero. Milo was condemned by 38 to 13 [8] votes. He went into exile at Massilia, and Cicero sent him there a copy of the speech we now possess. Milo acknowledged it by an ironical compliment [9].

Cicero succeeded better in two speeches delivered on behalf of M. Saufeius, who had been at the head of Milo's followers in the affray [10] at Bovillae, and was brought to trial on two charges in consequence. M. Caelius Rufus joined Cicero in his defence; having already interested himself in [11] that of Milo. Cicero was also much gratified by the con-

[1] This period would probably date from some day in 51 B.C., and thus Pompey would have in reality about three additional years. For the Lex Trebonia already gave him the government of Spain from 55–50 B.C.: cp. supra, § 8. [2] Brut. 94. 324; De Fin. 4. 1, 1; Tac. Dial. de Orat. 38. [3] Appendix 6, § 3. [4] App. Bell. Civ. 2. 23; Mommsen 4. 2, 341, 342: cp., however, Merivale 2. 50. But I cannot discover Dean Merivale's authority for limiting the retrospective operation of the law to 55 B.C. [5] Suet. Iul. 28; Caes. Bell. Civ. 1. 32; Dion Cassius 40. 56; Mommsen 4. 2, 349. [6] Philipp. 2. 10, 24. [7] Ad Att. 7. 1, 4; Philipp. l. c. [8] Ascon. in Milonian. p. 158. [9] Dion Cassius 40. 54. [10] Ascon. in Milonian. 159. [11] Pro Milone 33. 91.

demnation of T. Munatius Plancus Bursa[1], one of the violent supporters of Clodius. Pompey tried in vain to protect Bursa, whose trial took place in December, after his year of office as tribune had expired.

Cicero seems to have had much occupation in the courts of law[2], but probably found leisure to begin his work 'De Legibus[3],' and possibly to compose a short treatise 'De Optimo Genere Oratorum[4],' as a preface to a translation of Demosthenes' and Aeschines' speeches 'De Corona.' The fourth book, 'De Finibus[5],' professes to have been written now, but really belongs to a later time. Few of the letters of this date have been preserved, and these have little political interest.

At some time early in the year, before Pompey was named sole consul, the senate declared the country in danger, and empowered the interrex, the tribunes, and Pompey, to provide for its safety[6]; authorizing Pompey to bind the military population of Italy by an oath of obedience to himself. He had already a considerable force at his disposal, consisting of men levied nominally for service in Spain[7]. He seems to have retained his proconsular imperium since 55 B.C., but to have been authorized to enter the city without forfeiting his proconsular 'imperium[8].'

Tacitus[9] says that Pompey was in this year 'auctor idem et subversor' of his own laws; referring probably to his getting his government of Spain prolonged; to the exemption in Caesar's favour above[10] referred to; to his having sent into court an eulogy of Plancus[11]; and to his interposing[12] to prevent the conviction of his father-in-law Scipio for bribery. In the two last cases he violated the rules prescribed by his own laws against riot and corruption.

§ 16. In Gaul, Caesar was occupied in dealing with a most formidable insurrection, at the head of which stood Vercingetorix, king of the Arverni. It began with a massacre of the Romans settled at Genabum (Orleans), and was marked by the capture of Avaricum by the Romans, and by a repulse of Caesar before Gergovia, followed by a revolt of the Aedui, old friends of the Romans. Finally, however, Vercingetorix was obliged to shut himself up in Alesia, where Caesar blockaded him. A vast force of Gauls marched to the relief of the place, but failed to force the Roman lines, and Vercingetorix was compelled to surrender. Caesar spent the rest of the year at Bibracte[13] (Autun).

[1] Ad Fam. 7. 2, 2; Philipp. 6. 4, 10 alib.; Ascon. in Milonian. Argum. 145 foll.
[2] Ad Fam. 7. 2, 4. [3] Baringer 721. [4] De Opt. Gen. Orat. 10.
[5] De Fin. 4. 1, 1; Ad Att. 13. 12, 3; 13. 21. 5. [6] Ascon. in Milonian. § 67, p. 157; Mommsen 4. 2. 325. [7] Caes. Bell. Gall. 6. 1; Mommsen 4. 2. 311 and 325.
[8] Ascon. in Milonianam, p. 138; Dion Cassius 40. 53; App. Bell. Civ. 2. 23. [9] Ann. 3. 28. [10] above, § 14. [11] above, l. 2; Dion Cassius 40. 55.
[12] Mommsen 4. 2. 326; Plut. Pomp. 55. [13] Caes. Bell. Gall. 7.

His successes were rewarded by the senate with a thanksgiving of twenty days[1].

In the East, little of importance had happened. The Romans had lost their hold on Mesopotamia and Armenia, but the Parthians made no serious attack upon the Roman provinces; thus C. Cassius, who had been quaestor in Crassus' army, and now commanded in Syria, was able to reorganize the remains of the Roman army, and, with the help of Herod Antipater, to subdue a rising of the Jews, who were enraged by Crassus' plunder of their temple[2].

51 B.C.

§ 17. The consuls for this year were M. Claudius Marcellus, a leader of the optimates and a man of high personal character, and Servius Sulpicius Rufus, an eminent and upright jurist, but no politician. At some time early in the summer, Marcellus ordered a citizen of Novum Comum to be scourged[3], wishing to shew his contempt for Caesar, by whom that town had been reconstituted. Sulpicius, on the other hand, pleaded for moderation[4], and pointed out the calamities which must attend civil war.

It has been mentioned that Pompey's law 'de iure magistratuum' provided that provinces should be governed by ex-magistrates, not immediately after their year of office at Rome, but after an interval of five years[5]. This law does not seem to have been retrospective; but the senate, acting in its spirit, decreed that all men qualified by office, who had not yet governed provinces, should assume such governments, apparently according to seniority[6]. Cicero accordingly had to cast lots for a consular province, and obtained Cilicia, while Bibulus subsequently obtained Syria.

Cicero's province comprised[7], besides Cilicia proper, Pisidia, Pamphylia, Cyprus, Isauria, Lycaonia, and three other districts north of Taurus, of which the capitals appear to have been Cibyra, Synnada and Apamea[8]. The senate recommended Ariobarzanes[9] of Cappadocia to his protection.

He succeeded Appius Claudius Pulcher, brother of P. Clodius, and had to complain of much discourtesy, especially of the unwillingness[10] of Appius to grant him a meeting. Cicero had little taste for his new functions, especially as the forces allotted for the defence of his province seemed inadequate[11], and a Parthian invasion was not improbable. He

[1] Caes. Bell. Gall. 7. 90. [2] Dion Cassius 40. 28: Mommsen 4. 2, 339. [3] Ep. 31, 2, note; A. W. Zumpt, Comment. Epigraph. 1. 308 foll. [4] Ad Fam. 4. 3. 1 and 2. [5] above, § 14: cp. Dion Cassius 40. 56. [6] Cp. Ad Fam. 3. 2, 2 and 8. 8, 8. [7] Ep. 36, 6 and 9. [8] Ep. 36, 9. [9] Ad Fam. 2. 17, 7; cp. 15. 5, 1. [10] Ib. 3. 6, 3; Ad Att. 5. 16, 4. [11] Ib. 5. 15, 1.

had, however, able officers among his legates; his brother Quintus, C. Pomptinus, M. Anneius, and L. Tullius[1] are mentioned. As quaestor he had L. Mescinius Rufus[2], afterwards succeeded by C. Caelius Caldus[3]. Cicero's son and nephew also accompanied him with their tutor Dionysius[4].

§ 18. He started from a villa near Pompeii on May 10, and passing through Beneventum and Venusia spent three days at Tarentum, where he had a conversation with Pompey[5]. He then went to Brundisium, where he met some officers of Appius[6]. He was very anxious that the force in Cilicia should not be diminished by disbandment, and wrote to Appius on the subject. After a detention of some days at Brundisium, owing to ill health and the non-arrival of his legate Pomptinus[7], he reached Actium June 14, and Athens June 24, where he spent ten days[8]. Thence he sailed by Gyarus, Scyrus, and Delos to Ephesus[9], where he arrived July 22. During the earlier part of the voyage he had suffered considerably from stormy weather, for which the light Rhodian vessel on which he sailed was ill suited. He had been able when at Athens to do a service[10] to the heads of the Epicurean school there by writing to C. Memmius, then an exile at Mytilene.

About the same time an affair connected with Milo's exile gave Cicero much annoyance. Milo's property had been sold for the benefit of his creditors, and Philotimus, a freedman of Terentia, was one of the purchasers. Cicero heard that Milo was offended at this; but represented that he had acted on good advice for the benefit of Milo, and would gladly get out of the business[11].

§ 19. After a stay of three days at Ephesus, Cicero reached Tralles July 27, and there received a despatch from his predecessor[12]. He then entered his province, and arrived at Laodicea on[13] July 31. He found the country in a deplorable state, owing to the exactions of Appius[14], and at once applied himself to redress some of its more serious grievances[15]. The change made a great impression on the provincials, but Appius was offended[16], and thought that Cicero might have some sinister motive for his reforms. Cicero was especially vigilant in repressing all exactions by[17] his retinue, but was perhaps less[18] successful than he supposed.

[1] Ad Att. 5. 4. 2; 5. 20. 5; 5. 21, 9; Ad Fam. 13. 55. 1. [2] Ib. 5. 20; 13. 26: Ad Att. 6. 3. 1. [3] Ib. 6. 2, 10; 6. 6, 3: Ad Fam. 2. 15. 4. [4] Ad Att. 6. 1, 12. [5] Ib. 5. 2, 1; 5. 6, 1; 5. 7. [6] Ad Fam. 3. 3. 1; 3. 4. 1. [7] Ad Att. 5. 8, 1. [8] Ib. 5. 11, 4. [9] 5. 13. 1. [10] Ib. 5. 11, 6; Ad Fam. 13. 1. [11] Ad Att. 5. 8. [12] Ad Fam. 3. 5. 1. [13] Ad Att. 5. 15. 1. [14] Ib. 5. 16, 2. [15] Ib. 5. 16. 3; 5. 20, 1. [16] Ad Fam. 3. 7. 3; 3. 8. 5; Ad Att. 6. 1, 2. [17] Ib. 5. 16. 3; 5. 20, 6; 5. 21, 5. [18] Ib. 7. 1, 5.

He had directed M. Anneius, one of his legates, to assemble his forces at Iconium[1]. He himself appeared in the camp on Aug. 24. His administration had conciliated[2] the subjects and allies of Rome, and he raised a large force of retired soldiers—'evocati.' He thus felt tolerably secure when on Sept. 1 news arrived[3] that a large Parthian army had crossed the Euphrates. He decided to leave Cilicia to its natural defences, and to take up a position at Cybistra on the borders of Cappadocia, whence he might watch the wavering princes of the neighbourhood[4]. He there received an offer from Deiotarus, king of Galatia, under whose protection[5] the young Ciceros were staying, to support him with all his forces. This offer Cicero gladly accepted; but having heard first that the Parthians were threatening Cilicia, and afterwards that they had retired from Antioch, he sent to Deiotarus to say that he need not come.

§ 20. The protection of Cicero's army had emboldened some of the accomplices in a plot against Ariobarzanes of Cappadocia to make disclosures[6] which led to its frustration. Cicero now marched southwards, and entered Cilicia proper, arriving at Tarsus on[7] Oct. 5. Shortly afterwards he attacked with success the mountaineers of the Amanus between Cilicia and Commagene, and was saluted Imperator. The year's operations ended with the capture of the strong town of Pindenissus, which surrendered Dec. 17, after a siege of 57 days[8]. Cicero allowed his soldiers to retain all the plunder except the horses, and sold his prisoners for the benefit of the treasury, apparently[9]. Then, leaving his brother in command for the winter, he went to Laodicea. He rejected all[10] offers of statues and temples to be raised in his honour.

The dreaded Parthian invasion had taken place, but with little result. Surenas, the victor of Charrae, had incurred the suspicion of King Orodes, who ordered his execution; and Pacorus, son of Orodes, advised by a chief named Osaces, now commanded. The Parthians were repulsed near Antioch by Cassius, and Osaces was mortally wounded[11]. But Cicero did not think much of the success, and Bibulus, who presently arrived in Syria, suffered some losses. He was successful, however, in fomenting discord in the Parthian royal family[12].

Cicero was kept well informed about the course of events at Rome by his correspondents there, especially by M. Caelius, who was elected

[1] Ad Fam. 15. 4. 2 and 3. [2] Ad Att. 5. 18, 2. [3] Ib. 5. 18, 1; Ad Fam. 15. 4. 3. [4] Ib. 15. 4. 4. [5] Ib. 15. 4. 7. [6] Ib. 15. 2, 6-8. [7] Ad Att. 5. 20, 3. [8] Ad Fam. 15. 4. 10. [9] Ad Att. 5. 20, 5. [10] Ad Att. 5. 21, 7. [11] Ib. 5. 20, 3; Ad Fam. 2. 10, 2; Mommsen 4. 2, 339. Merivale (1. 510) thinks that Surenas 'was a title, not an appellative': Mommsen (4. 2, 329–337) speaks simply of 'the vizier.' [12] Ad Fam. 8. 6, 4; Ad Att. 5. 20, 4; Dion Cassius 40. 30.

curule aedile[1] for 50 B.C. Cicero complained[2], however, that Caelius did not write enough on serious subjects. He was very anxious that the confusion caused by the debates on the consular provinces should not lead to a prolongation of his own government; and the letters of Caelius[3] and Atticus did not remove this apprehension. He wrote to congratulate[4] L. Paulus and C. Marcellus on their election as consuls—though his real opinion[5] of Paulus was not favourable—and C. Curio[6] on his election as tribune.

§ 21. On Sept. 29 an important discussion took place in the senate as to the recall of Caesar from his provinces; but the interposition of two tribunes, C. Caelius and C. Vibius Pansa, prevented the adoption of any decisive resolution. The question was to be resumed in 50 B.C., after March 1[7]. The estrangement of Pompey from Caesar was no secret, and was attested by various remarks[8] of the former. Curio had announced his intention of attacking Caesar, but the first days of his tribunate were not marked by any active steps[9]. M. Caelius complained[10] that both consuls shewed little energy, and that Paulus was anxious for a provincial government. Cicero urged all his correspondents to do their best to prevent his being detained in Cilicia. He was importuned by Caelius to send[11] him panthers for his shows as aedile, but did not like to impose on the provincials the burden of providing them[12].

His long correspondence[13] with Appius Claudius, already alluded to, must have been annoying. Appius had shewn little consideration for him[14], in avoiding an interview which Cicero desired, and in detaining some of his forces. Yet he afterwards spoke like an injured man[15].

P. Lentulus Spinther triumphed this year for successes in Cilicia[16].

§ 22. Caesar had to subdue many desultory risings in Gaul. He brought the Carnutes and Bituriges to submission with little difficulty, but had to wage a more obstinate struggle with the tribes of the north-east. There the Atrebates under Commius, and the Bellovaci under Correus, took up arms and were aided by Ambiorix with the remnant of the Eburones. Correus, however, fell, and the Bellovaci submitted; whereon Caesar, sending Labienus against the Treviri, himself marched to the West, where the Carnutes and others were again in arms. They soon, however, submitted; and the last resistance in the West was

[1] Ad Fam. 2. 9. 1. [2] Ib. 2. 8, 1. [3] Ib. 8. 5, 2; Ad Att. 5. 21, 3. [4] Ad Fam. 15. 7; 15. 12. [5] Ad Att. 6. 1, 7. [6] Ad Fam. 2. 7. [7] Ib. 8. 8, 5: cp. A. W. Zumpt, Comment. Epigr. 2. 208-211. [8] Ad Fam. 8. 4, 4; 8. 8, 9. [9] Ib. 8. 4, 2; 8. 6, 5; 8. 8, 10; 8. 10, 3. [10] Ib. 8. 10, 3. [11] Ib. 8. 4, 5; 8. 6, 5, alib. [12] Ad Att. 6. 1, 21. [13] Ad Fam. 3. 1-8, esp. 6 and 8. [14] above, § 17; Ad Fam. 3. 6, 4. [15] above, § 19; Ad Fam. 3. 8, 4. [16] Ad Att. 5. 21, 4.

offered by a mixed crowd collected at Uxellodunum, probably on the Oltis (Lot), under Drappes and Lucterius. Caesar, however, forced the place to surrender, and treated his prisoners with great severity. Meanwhile Labienus had subdued the Treviri, and Caesar wintered at Nemetocenna (Arras) in the country of the Atrebates. There he received promises of submission from Commius, against whom he had sent M. Antonius[1].

In the summer Caesar had sent back one legion to North Italy, perhaps to shew that he did not want all his men north of the Alps[2].

50 B.C.

§ 23. The consuls for this year were C. Marcellus, cousin of the consul of the preceding year, and L. Aemilius Paulus. Both were reputed stanch optimates.

Cicero left Tarsus on Jan. 5[3] for his northern districts, where his arrival was eagerly looked for. A frequent mode of extortion practised by previous governors had been to require money for exempting cities from the burden of receiving soldiers during winter; this practice was discontinued by Cicero. He continued to provide for the interests of the Roman publicani, and, by expostulation with the magistrates of various towns, enabled those communities to make good some arrears of taxes which had been left unpaid, owing to gross peculation[4].

He occupied the greater part of the spring[5] in administering justice at Laodicea to his northern and western districts, and declares that he shewed patience, lenity, and affability, both on the bench and in his own house.

His temperate representations to the corn dealers caused them to bring out their hoards, and so to relieve the distress which a failure of the harvest had brought about[6]; and he shewed such respect for the laws of the different communities that they thought, he says, that they had regained their independence[7].

Various circumstances, however, disquieted him. He was uneasy about the provision made for a successor in his province, especially as one of his best officers, Pomptinus, left him[8] about this time. M. Caelius was still teasing him to send panthers to Rome; and he was compelled by his sense of justice to refuse M. Brutus[9] a favour. To a modern reader Cicero will seem rather to have erred on the side of indulgence in

[1] Caes. Bell. Gall. 8. 1-48; Mommsen 4. 1, 282. [2] Caes. Bell. Gall. 8. 24. [3] Ad Att. 5. 21, 7. [4] Ib. 6. 2, 5. [5] Feb. 13 to May 1. Ad Att. 5. 21, 9; 6. 2, 4 and 5. [6] Ib. 5. 21, 8. [7] Ib. 6. 2, 4. [8] Ib. 5. 21, 9. [9] Ib. 5. 21, 10-13; 6. 2, 7-9.

the last-mentioned affair; but perhaps few of his contemporaries would have shewn so much firmness as he did. He was again alarmed by the prospect of a Parthian invasion, and had little confidence in his neighbour Bibulus, but seems to have had some hope[1] that Pompey might take the command in the East. The rumour of invasion, however, died away; and he was thus relieved of some of his difficulty in selecting a temporary successor. He chose his quaestor[2], C. Caelius Caldus, though with some hesitation on account of his youth and want of firmness.

§ 24. On May 7, Cicero set out for Cilicia proper, and seems to have spent the month of June there, arriving at Tarsus on the 5th[3]. He found brigandage prevalent in the province, but there was nothing to hinder his return to Rome, and he made up two copies of his accounts to be deposited at Apamea and Laodicea, as he was required by the Julian law[4] to deposit them at two towns in his province. He seems to have amassed a considerable sum of money during his proconsulship, but his officers were offended by his paying into the treasury the surplus of his year's allowance for expenses[5].

He was still at Tarsus on July 17[6], and seems to have embarked at Sida[7] in Pamphylia on Aug. 3. Thence he sailed to Rhodes[8], to enable his son and nephew to see the island, and was much distressed there by hearing of the death of Q. Hortensius. From Rhodes he sailed to Ephesus, where, on Sept. 29[9], he received very alarming political reports from Rome, and embarked next day. He landed at the Piraeus on Oct. 14[10].

From Athens, where he made no long stay, he wrote to Terentia, begging her to come as far as she could without injury to her health to meet him[11]. He then went to Patrae, where he arrived early in November, and left Tiro, his favourite freedman[12], there. After visiting Alyzia[13], near Leucas, he reached Actium in Corcyra[14] Nov. 7, and Corcyra two days later. He spent about a week there, and after being much detained by storms, landed at Brundisium on Nov. 24. Terentia arrived there by land the same day[15]. He was very anxious about Tiro's health[16], also about political prospects[17] at Rome; and was eager to urge his claim to a triumph[18].

§ 25. At Brundisium he learned[19] that Atticus was convalescent from

[1] Ad Att. 6. 1, 14. [2] Ib. 6. 6, 3. [3] Ib. 6. 4, 1. [4] Ad Fam. 5. 20, 2. [5] Ad Att. 7. 1, 6; 11. 1, 2; Ad Fam. 5. 20, 9. [6] Ib. 2. 17, 1. [7] Ib. 3. 12, 4. [8] Ib. 2. 17, 1; Ad Att. 6. 7, 2; Brut. 1, 1. [9] Ad Att. 6. 8, 1. [10] Ib. 6. 9, 1. [11] Ad Fam. 14. 5, 1. [12] Ib. 16. 6, 2; 16. 9, 1. [13] Ib. 16. 2. [14] Ib. 16. 6, 2; 16. 9, 1.—This was, I now think, the well-known Actium in Acarnania, not the 'Actium Corcyrae' mentioned ad Att. 7. 2. 3. [15] Ad Att. 7. 2, 2. [16] Ad Fam. 16. 1–15. [17] Ad Att. 7. 1. [18] Ib. 7. 1, 5; Ad Fam. 16. 1, 1. [19] Ad Att. 7. 2, 2.

a serious illness. Political news became more and more alarming[1]; and Cicero seems to have wished for vigorous war with Parthia, to divert men's minds from domestic troubles. From Brundisium he went to Aeculanum[2] in Samnium on Dec. 6; and thence to an estate[3] of L. Pontius in northern Campania, where, probably, he had a conversation[4] on political affairs with Pompey, who spoke of civil war as inevitable. They met again near Formiae, when Pompey again expressed his apprehensions, and spoke of a violent attack made upon himself on Dec. 21 by M. Antonius, one of the new tribunes[5].

Cicero asked Atticus his[6] opinion on the crisis; denounced[7] the short-sightedness which had allowed Caesar to grow so powerful; expressed his longing for peace; but said[8] that if war began he should probably side with Pompey, rather against his reasonable convictions. He was anxious[9] therefore to pay his debts to Caesar before taking up arms against him. At the conclusion of the year he was probably at Tarracina[10].

§ 26. The affairs at Rome in which Cicero had taken most interest during this year were:—

(1.) The marriage of his daughter. He thought of Tiberius Claudius[11] Nero for her, but heard that she and Terentia both preferred P. Cornelius Dolabella—a dissipated man who had just divorced his own wife, but of good family and agreeable manners[12]. This match was rather embarrassing to Cicero; for he had recently been reconciled to Appius Claudius, and was now doing his best to serve him; whereas Dolabella accused[13] Appius of treasonable conduct.

Dolabella had been elected[14] one of the 'quindecimviri sacris faciundis,' defeating L. Lentulus Crus, contrary to general expectation.

(2.) The discussion on the honours due to his successes in Cilicia. The senate voted him 'supplicationes' early in this year[15]; both the consuls[16], with M. Caelius and Curio, supported the grant, but Cato[17] opposed it; and his artful defence of his conduct naturally excited Cicero's indignation, when he learned that Cato had supported the claims of Bibulus to a like honour. Caesar[18] seems to have been pleased at the estrangement of Cicero and Cato.

Cicero seems to have hoped that the vote would be followed by an

[1] Ad Att. 7. 2, 8. [2] Ib. 7. 5. 1. [3] Ib. 7. 5. 12. [4] Ib. 7. 4. 2; cp. 7. 5. 12. [5] Ib. 7. 8, 4 and 5. [6] Ib. 7. 9. [7] Ib. 7. 1, 3-4; 7. 7. 6. [8] Ib. 7. 3. 4-5; 7. 6. 2; 7. 7, 7. [9] Ib. 7. 8, 5. [10] Ib. 7. 5. 3. [11] Ib. 6. 6. 1. [12] Ad Att. 6. 6. 1; Ad Fam. 8. 6, 1 and 2. [13] cp. Ad Att. and Ad Fam. ll. cc., with Ad Fam. 3. 11, 2 and 3; 3. 12, 1. [14] Ib. 8. 4. 1; it was in 51 B.C. [15] Perhaps not before May or June. Cicero knew of the vote before he left his province at the end of July or beginning of August; cp. Ad Att. 6. 7, 2; Ad Fam. 3. 12, 4. [16] Ad Fam. 2. 15, 1; 15. 11, 1; 8. 11. 1. [17] Ib. 15. 5; Ad Att. 7. 2, 7. [18] Ib. l. c.

acknowledgment of his claims to a triumph. His exploits may hardly seem to have justified such a hope, but very likely they were as great as those of Lentulus Spinther, who triumphed[1] in 51 B.C. Cicero was especially anxious for a triumph, as a means of restoring him to the dignity he enjoyed before his exile[2].

§ 27. (3.) The progress of the discussion in the senate about the measures to be taken against Caesar.

At the beginning of the year both consuls and the tribune Curio passed for decided enemies[3] of Caesar; but he managed to secure at least the neutrality of the consul Paulus by a bribe of 1500 talents, and the active support of Curio by a still larger one. Hence, when it was proposed in the senate[4] that Caesar should be required to lay down his command, Curio praised the proposal, but suggested, amid great applause, that a similar demand should be addressed to Pompey[5]. The discussion began, apparently, on or soon after March 1[6], but, owing to the interposition of Curio, the senate came to no decision[7]. Nor were the optimates more successful when the measures to be adopted against Curio were discussed soon afterwards[8]. Towards the close of the year, shortly before the tribunes went out of office, the senate adopted, by an immense majority, Curio's proposal that both Pompey and Caesar should be required to lay down their commands; but the consul Marcellus angrily declared the sitting at an end—apparently before a formal decree had been passed[9]. Presently afterwards a rumour reached Rome[10] that a large part of Caesar's army had crossed the Alps. Such a movement might have been lawfully carried out by Caesar as proconsul; but without even waiting to ascertain the truth, the consul Marcellus hastened[11] out of the city with Lentulus, consul elect, to Pompey, who was in the suburbs; placed a sword in his hand, and bid him levy troops for the defence of the constitution.

Under the pretext that men were wanted for the Parthian war, the senate required Caesar and Pompey to furnish one legion each for that service. Pompey required the 15th, which he had lent to Caesar. Thus Caesar was rather unfairly deprived of two legions. He obeyed, however, the senate's orders. The two legions were stationed at Capua, but were not well satisfied with the transfer[12]. Pompey now left Rome for a tour in central and southern Italy; during which, as before mentioned[13], he met Cicero.

[1] Ad Att. 5. 21, 4. [2] Ib. 6. 6, 4. [3] App. Bell. Civ. 2. 26; Ad Fam. 8. 6, 5; 8. 11, 1. [4] App. Bell. Civ. 2. 27. [5] Ib. [6] Ad Fam. 8. 8, 5. [7] App. Bell. Civ. 2. 29. [8] Ad Fam. 8. 13, 2. [9] App. Bell. Civ. 2. 30. [10] Ib. 2. 31; Ad Att. 6. 9, 5. [11] App. Bell Civ. 2. 31; Plut. Pomp. 58, 59. [12] App. Bell. Civ. 2. 29; Caes. Bell. Gall. 8. 54, 55; Ad Att. 7. 13, 2. [13] above, § 25.

Curio, after the close of his tribunate, hastened to Caesar at Ravenna, to lay before him an account of the state of affairs, and returned to Rome, bearing Caesar's final proposals, on Jan. 1[1], 49 B.C. Among the new tribunes, Q. Cassius Longinus and M. Antonius were devoted to Caesar; Antonius had been chosen augur in the room of Q. Hortensius in 50[2].

§ 28. (4.) The trials of Appius Claudius Pulcher, Cicero's predecessor in Cilicia. Appius was acquitted both of treason[3] and of corruption[4], and presently afterwards was elected censor. He exercised his functions with great vigour[5], expelling the historian Sallust, among others, from the senate.

Caesar was able to devote much time this year to the work of pacifying Transalpine Gaul, which he effected in great measure by indulgence[6]. He visited Cisalpine Gaul, however, to recommend M. Antonius to the inhabitants as a candidate for the augurship, and himself for the consulship[7] in 48 B.C. His progress through the different towns was triumphant. He then returned to Nemetocenna, and concentrated ten legions[8] on the frontiers of the Treviri. The 15th he had left south of the Alps, and when Pompey required it, Caesar replaced it by the 13th[9]. Of the rest of his army, four legions under C. Fabius wintered among the Aedui, and four under C. Trebonius among the Belgae. Caesar himself went to Ravenna[10] for the winter. Labienus had been in charge of Cisalpine Gaul, and Caesar would not[11] listen to rumours of his intended desertion.

The result of the election of consuls for 49 B.C. had disappointed Caesar. He had hoped that Ser. Sulpicius Galba[12], one of his officers, would be chosen; but the two successful candidates were L. Lentulus Crus and C. Claudius Marcellus, both decidedly hostile to Caesar. Marcellus was cousin of his namesake, the consul of the previous year, and brother of M. Marcellus, the consul of 51[13].

[1] App. Bell. Civ. 2. 31 and 32. [2] Ad Fam. 8. 13, 1; Caes. Bell. Gall. 8. 50; Cic. Philipp. 2. 2, 4. [3] Ad Fam. 3. 11, 2. [4] Ib. 3. 12, 1. [5] Ib. 8. 14, 4; Dion Cassius 40. 63: cp. Hor. Sat. 1. 6, 20 'censorque moveret Appius.' [6] Caes. Bell. Gall. 8. 49. [7] Ib. 8. 50. [8] He had all his army except one legion, which was south of the Alps. Now he subsequently furnished two legions to Pompey, and had still nine in all. 9 + 2 = 11 − 1 = 10: cp. Caes. Bell. Gall. 8. 52 and 54. [9] Ib. 8. 54. [10] Caes. Bell. Civ. 1. 5. [11] Caes. Bell. Gall. 8. 52. [12] Ib. 8. 50. [13] Mommsen 4. 2. p. 358; Fasti Consulares sub ann.; Drumann 2. 398.

SELECT LETTERS

OF

M. TULLIUS CICERO.

PART II.

20. To ATTICUS (AD ATT. IV. 1).

ROME, SEPTEMBER, 57 B.C. (697 A.U.C.)

1. I write immediately after my return, to say that, while I think I had previously some reason to complain, your late services have made me ample amends; 2. and I wish you were here to share my satisfaction. In future I will make up for past neglect. 3. I have regained my old position to a greater extent than I could have hoped, but my property has been seriously impaired. 4. I left Dyrrhachium on August 4, and arrived next day at Brundisium, where Tullia met me, and I presently learned that the law for my recall had been carried. Both at Brundisium and along the road to Rome I received the warmest congratulations from every one, 5. and on my arrival literally every one of the slightest importance came to meet me, while the parts of the city through which I passed to the Capitol were thronged by a vast multitude. Next day, Sept. 5, I returned thanks to the senate. 6. Two days afterwards there were disorders, caused by the dearness of corn. I suggested, in accordance with Pompey's known wishes, that he should be entrusted with a commission to supply it; and the senate passed a decree to that effect. I then addressed the people. 7. Next day, in a full senate, a bill was drawn up giving Pompey the management of the supply of corn for five years, with power to name fifteen legates, of whom he named me first. Messius proposed that he should have still more ample powers. The way in which I shall receive compensation for my house will depend on the judgment of the pontifices. 8. You see my position. I am in difficulties, as you know, about my property, and have some family troubles which I do not mention. My brother is most devoted to me. Pray come speedily; some of those who lately served me are already beginning to fall away.

CICERO ATTICO SAL.

CUM primum Romam veni, fuitque cui recte ad te litteras 1
darem, nihil prius faciendum mihi putavi, quam ut tibi absenti de reditu nostro gratularer; cognoram enim—ut vere scribam—te in consiliis mihi dandis nec fortiorem nec prudentiorem quam me ipsum, me etiam propter meam in te observantiam nimium in custodia salutis meae diligentem, eundemque te, qui primis temporibus erroris nostri aut potius furoris particeps et falsi timoris socius fuisses, acerbissime discidium nostrum tulisse plurimumque operae, studii, diligentiae, laboris ad conficiendum reditum meum contulisse: itaque hoc tibi vere adfirmo, in 2
maxima laetitia et exoptatissima gratulatione unum ad cumulandum gaudium conspectum aut potius complexum mihi tuum defuisse; quem semel nactus si umquam dimisero, ac nisi etiam praetermissos fructus tuae suavitatis praeteriti temporis omnes exegero, profecto hac restitutione fortunae me ipse non satis dignum iudicabo. Nos adhuc in nostro statu, quod difficillime 3
recuperari posse arbitrati sumus, splendorem nostrum illum forensem et in senatu auctoritatem et apud viros bonos gratiam magis, quam optaramus, consecuti sumus; in re autem familiari, quae

1. Recte, 'with prudence.' See Ep. 6, 1, note.

3. Cognoram, 'I had known' before my exile.

5. Me etiam. Most MSS. have apparently 'nec etiam,' which Wesenb. retains.

Propter meam in te observantiam, 'on account of my regard for your advice.' Cicero had complied with Atticus' advice not to risk a struggle with Clodius in 58 B.C., and thought afterwards that his compliance shewed timidity.

6. Eundemque te, 'but that you notwithstanding.' See Madv. 488.

7. Erroris nostri, 'my mistake' in retiring from Rome. See Intr. to Part I, §§ 20; 22. The whole passage is a delicate reproof of Atticus for the want of penetration and zeal which he had shewn, in Cicero's opinion, early in 58 B.C. A similar mixture of praise and blame may be found, Ep. 16, 7.

13. Quem = 'te,' implied in 'tuum.' See Madv. 317 a.

Si umquam. This is a conjecture adopted by Baiter. 'Numquam' seems to have some MS. authority.

Nisi . . exegero, 'unless I shall reclaim and enjoy even those delights from your friendliness, which I failed to grasp in past time.'

14. Praetermissos suggests a fault on Cicero's part, and is not therefore superfluous. On the double genitive, 'suavitatis, temporis,' see Madv. 288, and cp. Ad Fam. 9. 8, 2 'superiorum temporum fortuna reipublicae.' 'Exigere' is a word used for the exaction of arrears of taxes, frequent in the writings of Cicero and Caesar.

16. In nostro statu, 'with regard to my political position.' Billerb.

Quod . . sumus. There seems to be a confusion between 'quod difficillimum arbitrati eramus,' and 'quae difficillime recuperari arbitrati sumus.'

17. Forensem. In foro partam, multorum causis defendendis. Manut.

19. In re . . familiari, 'with regard to my property.' It had suffered mainly from the demolition of his house at Rome, and the plunder of his villas. His losses must have amounted to at least £20,000. 'Viciens DCCL millia H.S.' Ad Att. 4. 2, 5.

quem ad modum ſracta, dissipata, direpta sit, non ignoras, valde laboramus tuarumque non tam ſacultatum, quas ego nostras esse iudico, quam consiliorum ad colligendas et constituendas reli-
4 quias nostras indigemus. Nunc, etsi omnia aut scripta esse a tuis arbitror aut etiam nuntiis ac rumore perlata, tamen ea scribam brevi, quae te puto potissimum ex meis litteris velle cognoscere. Pr. Nonas Sextiles Dyrrhachio sum proſectus, ipso illo die, quo lex est lata de nobis; Brundisium veni Nonis Sextilibus: ibi mihi Tulliola mea ſuit praesto natali suo ipso die, qui casu idem natalis erat et Brundisinae coloniae et tuae vicinae Salutis; quae res animadversa *a* multitudine summa Brundisinorum gratulatione celebrata est. Ante diem VI. Idus Sextiles cognovi, [cum Brundisii essem,] litteris Quinti, mirifico studio omnium aetatum atque ordinum, incredibili concursu Italiae legem comitiis centuriatis esse perlatam: inde a Brundisinis honestissimis ornatus iter ita ſeci, ut undique ad me
5 cum gratulatione legati convenerint. Ad urbem ita veni, ut nemo ullius ordinis homo nomenclatori notus ſuerit, qui mihi obviam non venerit, praeter eos inimicos, quibus id ipsum [se inimicos esse] non liceret aut dissimulare aut negare. Cum venissem ad portam Capenam, gradus templorum ab infima plebe completi erant, a qua plausu maximo cum esset mihi gratulatio significata, similis et ſrequentia et plausus me usque ad Capitolium celebravit, in ſoroque et in ipso Capitolio miranda multitudo ſuit. Postridie in senatu, qui ſuit dies

3. Constituendas, 'setting in order.'
4. Omnia, 'all Roman news.'
8. Lex, the law for his recall. See Intr. to Part I. § 23.
10. Natalis. The colony of Brundisium was founded 244 B.C. Boot, however, referring to A. W. Zumpt (Comment. Epigraph. 1. 239), thinks that the date of its reconstitution by Drusus, the rival of C. Gracchus, in 122 B.C., is referred to.
11. Salutis. The temple of Salus, on the Quirinal, and near the house of Atticus, was vowed by C. Iunius, consul, in 311, built 307, and dedicated 303 B.C. See Livy 10. 1.
13. Cum Brundisii essem. If these words are genuine I think, with Mr. Jeans, that they mean 'being,' or, 'as I was,' 'still at Brundisium,' and so did not miss the letter.
16. Ornatus. Orell. proposes to add 'decretis.' But may not the words mean, 'having received attentions from the most respectable men of Brundisium?' Cp. Pro Reg. Deiot. 1, 2 'regem quem ornare antea cuncto cum senatu solebam.'
17. Legati, 'deputies from the various towns.'
Ita . . ut, 'in such style that.'
18. Nomenclatori: see Ep. 15. 9, note.
19. Id ipsum, 'that very fact' of their hostility. Hofm., Billerb.
21. Templorum. Among the temples near that gate were two, or one with two 'cellae' of Honos and Virtus. The celebrated M. Claudius Marcellus ordered the building in 208 B.C.; having originally vowed one temple in the Gallic wars, 222 B.C. Cp. Livy 27. 25; Smith's Dict. of Geogr. 2. 819.
Ab infima plebe, on the force of the preposition cp. Ep. 104. 1, note.
24. Celebravit, 'attended.' Metzg.

Nonarum Septembr., senatui gratias egimus. Eo biduo cum 6
esset annonae summa caritas et homines ad theatrum primo, deinde ad senatum concurrissent, impulsu Clodii mea opera frumenti inopiam esse clamarent, cum per eos dies senatus de annona haberetur et ad eius procurationem sermone non solum plebis, verum etiam bonorum Pompeius vocaretur idque ipse cuperet, multitudoque a me nominatim, ut id decernerem, postularet, feci et accurate sententiam dixi. Cum abessent consulares, quod tuto se negarent posse sententiam dicere, praeter Mesallam et Afranium, factum est senatus consultum in meam sententiam, ut cum Pompeio ageretur ut eam rem susciperet lexque ferretur; quo senatus consulto recitato continuo cum more hoc insulso et novo plausum meo nomine recitando dedissent, habui contionem; omnes magistratus praesentes praeter unum praetorem et duos tribunos pl. dederunt. Postridie 7

1. **Gratias egimus**: see Intr. to Part II, § 1. On the plural 'egimus' after 'venissem,' cp. Ep. 17, 1, note.

Eo biduo, 'two days afterwards.' Cp. Caes. Bell. Civ. 1, 41 'eo biduo Caesar cum equitibus in castra pervenit.'

2. **Ad theatrum.** The Ludi Magni were celebrated Sept. 4–10. Süpfle.

3. **Ad senatum**, 'before the senate house.'

Concurrissent . . clamarent. For the omission of a conjunction, cp. Ep. 54, 7 'etsi Scipionem cum cohortibus duabus praemiserat, legionem a Fausto conscriptam in Siciliam sibi placere a consule duci scripserat.' More curious is the want of a conjunction between **cum esset** and **cum . . haberetur**, with which, cp. Philipp. 2. 43, 110, 'supplicationes . . . contaminari passus es, pulvinaria noluisti?'

Mea opera, 'by my fault.' Perhaps Clodius meant, 'owing to the crowds that had come to greet Cicero.' Boot.

7. **Ut id decernerem**, 'that I should vote for that measure.' Cp. In Cat. 4. 5, 10.

8. **Feci**, 'I complied.'

Accurate, 'elaborately.'

9. **Quod . . negarent . . dicere**, 'because, as they said, they could not express their opinions in safety.' See Madv. 357 a, and Obs. 2. On **Afranius**, see Ep. 1, 1, note; on **Messalla**, Ep. 6, 2, note.

11. **Ut . . ageretur . . ferretur**, 'that Pompey should be entreated to undertake the business, and that a law should be proposed.' See Madv. 372 a.

12. **Recitato**, 'having been read to the assembly.' The names of the senators who suggested or approved the course adopted would be read (to the assembly) probably.

13. **Meo nomine recitando**, 'while my name was being read.' The gerundive in passages like this seems to supply the place of a present passive participle. Hofm. Baiter inserts 'in' before 'meo,' but perhaps unnecessarily. Cp. 'partis honoribus eosdem in fori gesti labores quos petendis' Philipp. 6. 6, 17; also Ep. 33, 1; Madv. 416, Obs. 1; Nägelsb. 96, 260.

14. **Dedissent**, sc. 'qui aderant.' The MSS. have 'dedisset,' and Süpfle suggests 'cum contio' for 'contionem.' Wesenb. suggests the insertion of 'quam' before 'omnes.'

Contionem. Perhaps the Oratio Post Red. ad Quirites.

Omnes magistratus . . dederunt, sc. 'contionem,' 'all the magistrates were present, and agreed in inviting me to speak, with the exception of one praetor and two tribunes of the plebs.' 'Contionem dare,' = 'in contionem producere,' on which phrase cp. p. 47, note on l. 6. The praetor referred to is supposed to have been Ap. Claudius Pulcher, the tribunes Q. Numerius Rufus and Sex. Atilius Serranus. Cp. Ad Att. 4. 2, 4; Pro Sestio 33, 72; 34, 74; In Pison. 15, 35; Ascon. in Pisonian., p. 126. Livy (2. 56) makes Appius Claudius refuse to the tribunes of the commons the title of 'magistratus populi;' cp. Mommsen, Staatsrecht, 1. 46–48 and notes. But the present passage agrees with one in De Orat. 1. 7, 25; and the distinction between 'populus' and 'plebs' had lost much of its importance in Cicero's time. See the notes of Manutius

senatus frequens; et omnes consulares nihil Pompeio postulanti negarunt; ille legatos quindecim cum postularet, me principem nominavit et *ad* omnia me alterum se fore dixit. Legem consules conscripserunt, qua Pompeio per quinquennium omnis potestas rei frumentariae toto orbe terrarum daretur; alteram Messius, qui omnis pecuniae dat potestatem et adiungit classem et exercitum et maius imperium in provinciis, quam sit eorum, qui eas obtineant: illa nostra lex consularis nunc modesta videtur, haec Messii non ferenda. Pompeius illam velle se dicit, familiares hanc. Consulares duce Favonio fremunt; nos tacemus, et eo magis, quod de domo nostra nihil adhuc pontifices responderunt: qui si sustulerint religionem, aream praeclaram habebimus; superficiem consules ex senatus consulto aestimabunt: sin aliter, demolientur, suo nomine locabunt, rem totam aestimabunt. Ita sunt res nostrae, ut in secundis, fluxae, ut in adversis, bonae. In re familiari valde sumus, ut scis, perturbati. Praeterea sunt quaedam domestica, quae litteris non

and of Mr. J. E. Yonge on Ad Fam. 1. 7, 2; and my own on Ep. 34. 5.

1. Senatus frequens, sc. 'fuit,' 'there was a full meeting of the senate.' On the ellipse, see Madv. 479 a. Wesenb. suggests the insertion of 'fuit.'

2. Me principem . . . dixit, 'named me first, and said I should be a second self to him in everything.'

5. Toto orbe terrarum, 'throughout the world.' See Madv. 275 c.

6. C. Messius was now tribune. For another notice of him, cp Epp. 28, 9. His proposal would have given Pompey enormous power, and would have placed Caesar under his command.

8. Nostra . . . consularis, 'that law proposed by the consuls, and based on my suggestion.' Boot.

10. Hanc, sc. 'eam velle.'

Duce Favonio. Favonius, for an account of whom see notes on Ep. 7. 5, had only been quaestor, but his energy probably induced men of higher position to accept his guidance.

Fremunt, 'raise an outcry.' Cp. Ad Att. 2. 7, 3 'Arrius consulatum sibi ereptum fremit.'

11. Pontifices. Cicero pleaded before them on Sept. 29 (cp. Ad Att. 4. 2, 2), and on the two following days the senate passed decrees for the restitution of his property. His uncertainty as to the decision of the pontifices made him unwilling to offend any powerful party that might be represented in their body.

12. Sustulerint religionem, 'declare against the religious character of the place,' declare the consecration by Clodius null.'

13. Superficiem, 'the building which had stood there.' The consuls would make an estimate how much Cicero ought to have for rebuilding what had been destroyed. Cp. Ad Att. 4. 2, 5 'nobis superficiem aedium consules de consilii sententia aestimarunt H. S. vicies.'

14. Sin aliter . . aestimabunt, 'but if they decide otherwise, the consuls will demolish Clodius' buildings, contract for a new temple in their own names, and fix the amount of my whole losses.' i.e. provide me with a site, as well as with compensation for the buildings. Hofm. This proceeding would inflict a slight on Clodius; for, while recognizing the validity of his dedication of the site, the consuls would pull down his temple of Liberty.

15. Ita sunt . . bonae, 'such is my position; shaken, for a prosperous man; good, for one who has suffered reverses.'

16. In re . . perturbati, 'my property, as you know, is in great disorder.'

17. Quaedam domestica. These words refer, perhaps, to disputes with Terentia. In another letter he mentions the affection of his brother and daughter, but says nothing of his wife. Cp. Ad Att. 4. 2, 7.

committo. Q. fratrem insigni pietate, virtute, fide praeditum sic amo, ut debeo. Te exspecto et oro ut matures venire eoque animo venias, ut me tuo consilio egere non sinas. Alterius vitae quoddam initium ordimur. Iam quidam, qui nos absentes defenderunt, incipiunt praesentibus occulte irasci, aperte invidere: vehementer te requirimus.

21. To P. LENTULUS SPINTHER (AD FAM. I. 1).

ROME, JAN. 13, 56 B.C. (698 A.U.C.)

1. I wish I could serve you as effectively as you served me; but the money of the king's envoys, the hypocritical plea of a religious difficulty, and the eagerness of the king's friends to serve Pompey are obstacles in my way. 2. I am always warning Pompey to have regard to his own honour, but indeed he hardly seems to need any warnings, and serves you zealously. Marcellinus, you know, has a quarrel with you; but, except on this question, promises you his support. 3. On Jan. 13 the subject was discussed in the senate. Hortensius, Lucullus, and I, advised that you should be empowered to restore the king, but not by force of arms. Crassus and others proposed in substance that Pompey should restore him; Bibulus desires to exclude Pompey from the commission; Servilius thinks there ought to be no restoration at all. There is a general impression that Pompey would like to be employed. 4. My opinion carries the less weight with the public, because of my obligations to you, which are thought to prejudice me in your favour.

M. CICERO S. D. P. LENTULO PROCOS.

Ego omni officio ac potius pietate erga te ceteris satis facio 1
omnibus, mihi ipse numquam satis facio; tanta enim magnitudo est tuorum erga me meritorum, ut, quia tu nisi perfecta re de me non conquiesti, ego, quia non idem in tua causa efficio, vitam mihi esse acerbam putem. In causa haec sunt: Hammonius,

3. Eoque animo . . . sinas. Perhaps a fresh allusion to Atticus' alleged indifference just before Cicero's exile. Cp. § 1.

Alterius vitae . . ordimur, 'I am now beginning, in a certain sense, a second life,' 'a new career.' Cicero means, either (1) that he has to build up his fortunes again (cp. Ep. 42, 4, where he speaks of his παλιγγενεσία), or (2) that he intends to act in concert with Pompey and Caesar, or (3) that he will henceforth renounce politics. Cp. Ad Att. 4. 6. 2. Boot prefers the first of these three explanations, I think with reason, for Cicero does not seem to have given up an independent political career yet. Cp. Epp. 25; 29, 5-20.

4. Quidam probably refers to some of the leaders of the optimates, who might regard Cicero's approaches to Pompey with suspicion.

7. Omni . . pietate, 'in the satisfaction of every claim of duty—I might say of affection.'

9. Meritorum, i.e. in promoting Cicero's restoration from exile. Cp. Intr. to Part I, §§ 21-23: Pro Sest. 33, 72.

Nisi perfecta re, 'till my restoration had been effected.'

10. In tua causa, in tuo negotio, in reductione regis. Manut.

11. In causa haec sunt, 'the causes of my ill-success are as follows.'

Hammonius seems not to be elsewhere mentioned.

regis legatus, aperte pecunia nos oppugnat; res agitur per eosdem creditores, per quos, cum tu aderas, agebatur. Regis causa si qui sunt qui velint, qui pauci sunt, omnes rem ad Pompeium deferri volunt; senatus religionis calumniam non religione, sed male-
2 volentia et illius regiae largitionis invidia comprobat. Pompeium et hortari et orare, etiam liberius accusare et monere, ut magnam infamiam fugiat, non desistimus; sed plane nec precibus nostris nec admonitionibus relinquit locum: nam cum in sermone quotidiano, tum in senatu palam sic egit causam tuam, ut neque eloquentia maiore quisquam nec gravitate nec studio nec contentione agere potuerit, cum summa testificatione tuorum in se officiorum et amoris erga te sui. Marcellinum tibi esse iratum scis: is hac regia causa excepta ceteris in rebus se acerrimum tui defensorem fore ostendit. Quod dat, accipimus: quod instituit referre de religione et saepe iam retulit, ab eo deduci
3 non potest. Res ante Idus acta sic est;—nam haec Idibus mane scripsi;—Hortensii et mea et Luculli sententia cedit religioni de exercitu—teneri enim res aliter non potest—, sed ex illo senatus

1. Regis. Ptolemy XII. Auletes is the king referred to. Cp. Intr. to Part II, § 2.

2. Creditores: men who perhaps were hostile to Lentulus, and furnished Hammonius with the money which he employed in bribing senators. Cicero makes a similar statement, Ad Q. F. 2. 2, 3. His client, C. Rabirius Postumus (cp. sup. p. 144), seems to have been one of the 'creditores.' Cp. Pro Rab. Post. 2; 3.

Regis causa .. velint, 'those who may be interested in the king's cause.' Cp. Ad Fam. 7. 17, 2 'si me aut sapere aliquid aut velle tua causa putas.'

4. Calumniam, 'the plea maliciously set up.' Cp. Ad Fam. 1. 4. 2 'nomen inductum fictae religionis,' Ad Q. F. 2. 2, 3 'calumnia extracta res est.'

Non religione .. invidia, 'not from religious feeling, but from ill-will to the king, and under the influence of the odium which his largesses have aroused.'

7. Infamiam. Pompey would be charged both with ingratitude and ambition if he opposed the claims of Lentulus. Cp. 'tuorum in se officiorum' a few lines below.

11. Officiorum. Cp. Epp. 20, 7; 26, 3, note.

Marcellinum. Cn. Cornelius Lentulus Marcellinus is thought to have been the son of a P. Lentulus who had passed by adoption from the family of the Marcelli into that of the Lentuli. The paternal grandfather of the Marcellinus here mentioned seems to have been M. Marcellus Æserninus (cp. Cic. Brut. 36, 136), who commanded at Aesernia in the Marsic war, and was forced to surrender that place to the revolted allies. Cp. Livy, Epit. 73; Drumann 2, 404; 405. The grandson had supported, as patron of Sicily, the prosecution of Verres (Div. in Caec. 4. 13). He was consul in 56 B.C. with L. Marcius Philippus, and showed a decided hostility to Clodius.

14. Quod instituit .. non potest, 'he cannot be diverted from his intention of bringing the religious question before the senate.' On this use of the pronouns, see Madv. 398 b.

17. Hortensii .. exercitu, 'Hortensius, Lucullus, and I are for respecting people's scruples as to the employment of an army, otherwise our end [the restoration of Ptolemy by you] cannot be obtained at all.' For this sense of 'teneri' see Forcell. The Lucullus here referred to was M. Lucullus, adopted by M. Terentius Varro. He was consul 73 B.C.; did good service as governor of Macedonia, and supported Cicero's measures in 63 B.C. In Pis. 19, 44; Philipp. 2. 5, 12. His more celebrated brother Lucius seems to have died in 57 or 56 B.C.

18. Ex illo senatus consulto. Appa-

consulto, quod te referente factum est, tibi decernit, ut regem reducas, quod commodo rei publicae facere possis; ut exercitum religio tollat, te auctorem senatus retineat. Crassus tres legatos decernit, nec excludit Pompeium; censet enim etiam ex iis, qui cum imperio sint; Bibulus tres legatos, ex iis, qui privati sunt. Huic adsentiuntur reliqui consulares praeter Servilium, qui omnino reduci negat oportere, et Volcatium, qui, Lupo referente, Pompeio decernit, et Afranium, qui adsentitur Volcatio. Quae res auget suspitionem Pompeii voluntatis, animadvertebatur Pompeii familiares adsentiri Volcatio. Laboratur vehementer; inclinata res est: Libonis et Hypsaci non obscura concursatio et contentio

rently a decree providing that the proconsul of Cilicia should restore Ptolemy.

2. Quod . . . possis, 'so far as you can do it without injury to the state.' On the mood, cp. Madv. 364, Obs. 2, and for the abl. commodo, Ad Fam. 4. 2, 4 'quod tuo commodo fiat.'

Ut exercitum . . retineat, 'so that while we do without an army, in obedience to religious scruples, the senate should retain you as manager of the business.' For the omission of an adversative conjunction before 'retineat,' see Madv. 437 d, Obs.

3. Legatos, 'commissioners,' for the restoration of Ptolemy.

4. Ex iis qui . . sint . . sunt. The change of mood is curious. In the first clause Cicero probably intends to describe a class, in the second to state a fact. 'From such as may be invested with "imperium" . . from men in a private station.' Wesenb. reads 'sint' in both clauses. Mr. J. E. Yonge follows Kleyn in preferring 'sunt' in both. Pompey was now chief commissioner for supplying the capital with corn. Cp. Ep. 20, 7, and Mommsen 4. 2, pp. 303, 304.

6. Servilium. P. Servilius Vatia Isauricus supported the government against the insurrection of Saturninus in the year 100 B.C.; was consul in 79 B.C., and served with distinction against the pirates. He generally acted with the optimates, but voted for the Manilian law. He reconciled Q. Metellus Nepos to Cicero in 57 B.C., and is often mentioned in Cicero's letters. Cp. Pro Rab. 7. 21; Pro Leg. Man. 23. 68; Post Red. in Sen. 10. 25.

7. Volcatium. L. Volcatius Tullus, consul in 66 B.C., is said to have intended to refuse any votes which should be offered for Catiline as candidate for the consulship. He remained neutral in the civil war between Caesar and Pompey. Cp. Fragm. Orat. in Tog. Cand. 11; Ad Att. 7. 3, 3; 9. 10, 7; 9. 19, 2.

Lupo. P. Rutilius Lupus, one of the tribunes for this year, is mentioned Ad Q. F. 2. 1, 1. He was praetor in 49 B.C., and at first supported Pompey, but afterwards went over to Caesar. Cp. Ad Att. 9. 1, 2.

Referente. It seems doubtful if a tribune could force a question to a division in the senate in spite of the opposition of the consuls or other presiding magistrates. From § 2 of the following letter, from Ad Fam. 10. 16, 1; and from Pro Sest. 11, 26; 31, 68; 32, 70, we might infer the affirmative—but the statement in Caes. Bell. Civ. 1. 1 seems inconsistent with such a supposition. The last passage refers, however, to a session in which great irregularities were certainly tolerated, and, on the whole, the affirmative appears most probable. For the date of the motion of Lupus, cp. §§ 1, 2 of the following letter.

8. Quae res, periphrastic for 'quod.' On the relative referring to the contents of a sentence, see Madv. 318 b, Zumpt L. G. 678. With the account here given of Pompey's behaviour, cp. Cicero's remarks in Ep. 20, 7. He seems to have expected people to divine his thoughts when not expressed, and to have been disappointed when they took his words literally. See below.

10. Laboratur . . res est. I am now, having regard to the word 'laboraremus' at the end of the letter, inclined to agree with Manutius, who says of 'laboratur,' 'difficultas negotii non sine quadam animi sollicitudine ostenditur,' and of 'inclinata res est' that the expression is used when things 'aliter se habent ac volumus.' Prof. Nettleship treats both words as military expressions, and would I think nearly agree with Manutius.

11. Libonis. L. Scribonius Libo, now tribune, and consul in 34 B.C., was intimate

omniumque Pompeii familiarium studium in eam opinionem rem adduxerunt, ut Pompeius cupere videatur; cui qui nolunt, idem
4 tibi, quod eum ornasti, non sunt amici. Nos in causa auctoritatem eo minorem habemus, quod tibi debemus; gratiam autem nostram exstinguit hominum suspitio, quod Pompeio se gratificari putant. Ut in rebus multo ante, quam profectus es, ab ipso rege et ab intimis ac domesticis Pompeii clam exulceratis, deinde palam a consularibus exagitatis et in summam invidiam adductis, ita versamur. Nostram fidem omnes, amorem tui absentis praesentes tui cognoscent. Si esset in iis fides, in quibus summa esse debebat, non laboraremus.

22. To P. LENTULUS SPINTHER (AD FAM. I. 2).
ROME, JAN. 15, 56 B.C. (698 A.U.C.)

1. A dispute between Marcellinus and Caninius prevented the senate from coming to any decision on the 13th, but a speech of mine made a great impression in your favour. Next day part of the proposal of Bibulus was approved; 2. that of Hortensius

with Cicero, M. Varro, and M. Brutus, but Cicero does not seem to have thought well of him. His daughter married Sextus Pompeius, and he commanded a fleet in the Adriatic against Caesar in the civil war. He is afterwards mentioned as corresponding with his son-in-law Sextus Pompeius. Cp. Acad. Post 1. 1, 3; Ad Att. 8. 11 B, 2; 9. 11, 4; 16. 4, 2; Caes. Bell. Civ. 3. 16; 3. 24.

Hypsaei. P. Plautius Hypsaeus, quaestor to Pompey in the Mithridatic war, had promoted Cicero's restoration from exile. Cp. Pro Flacco 9; Ad Att. 3. 8, 3. He was subsequently a candidate for the consulship in 52 B.C.; but was convicted of bribery and exiled: cp. sup. p. 147; App. Bell. Civ. 2. 24.

Concursatio. Forcell gives as an equivalent for this word 'discursio petendi causa,' 'canvassing.'

2. Cui qui nolunt, 'and those who do not wish him well,' that is, Bibulus and his friends. Cp. above, § 3. Forcell. explains 'nolunt' by 'non favent:' cp. p. 98, l. 7, note.

3. Ornasti, 'honoured.' Cp. Ep. 20, 4, note. Lentulus had proposed that Pompey should be at the head of a commission for supplying corn. Cp. Ep. 20, 6 and 7.

4. Debemus, absol. 'are indebted to.' Cp. Pro Planc. 28, 68.

5. Suspitio, 'people's suspicion that Pompey wants to undertake the business himself.' Cicero's influence would be principally with men who would be unwilling to offend Pompey.

Quod . . . putant. I had thought that these words mean, 'do Pompey a favour by declining to support me.' But Metzger and Mr. J. E. Yonge understand the whole passage as referring to the unpopularity of Pompey. 'People suspect that Pompey would be pleased if they supported my proposal on your behalf, and therefore decline to support it.' Mr. Jeans seems to take the same view.

6. Ut in rebus . . ita versamur, 'we have to deal with a case embittered long before your departure by the king himself, and by the intimate associates of Pompey, and afterwards thrown into confusion ("openly opposed," J. E. Y.) and put in an odious light by men of consular rank.' Wiel. explains 'exagitatis' by 'pushed on,' 'bitzig betrieben;' Forcell. by 'tractatis.' With the general structure of the sentence Nägelsbach, 156, 440, compares ὡς οὖν τοιούτου τοῦ πράγματος ὄντος οἵου—οὕτω δὴ ἐγὼ κ.τ.λ. Cicero gives a slightly different account of his conduct in this matter to his brother Quintus. Cp. Ad Q. F. 2. 2, 3 'nos et officio erga Lentulum mirifice et voluntati Pompeii praeclare satis fecimus.'

10. In iis. In some of Pompey's friends? or in Bibulus and his associates? Manutius says 'videtur consulares indicare.' On the indic. 'debebat,' cp. Ep. 4. 1, note.

never went to a division, owing to the difficulties interposed by Lupus. 3. I spent the evening with Pompey; nothing could sound fairer than his own language: but when I hear what his friends say, I suspect some underhand dealing. 4. I write on January 15; the senate meets to-day, and I hope we shall be able to maintain a good position there, and also to prevent any resolution unfavourable to you being legally taken by the people. I will write you word how things go on, and will do my best to secure that they shall go on well.

M. CICERO S. D. P. LENTULO PROCOS.

Idibus Ianuariis in senatu nihil est confectum, propterea quod 1
dies magna ex parte consumptus est altercatione Lentuli consulis et Caninii tribuni pl. Eo die nos quoque multa verba fecimus maximeque visi sumus senatum commemoratione tuae voluntatis erga illum ordinem permovere. Itaque postridie placuit, ut breviter sententias diceremus; videbatur enim reconciliata nobis voluntas esse senatus, quod cum dicendo, tum singulis appellandis rogandisque perspexeram. Itaque cum sententia prima Bibuli pronuntiata esset, ut tres legati regem reducerent, secunda Hortensii, ut tu sine exercitu reduceres, tertia Volcatii, ut Pompeius reduceret, postulatum est, ut Bibuli sententia divideretur. Quatenus de religione dicebat, cui quidem rei iam obsisti non poterat, Bibulo adsensum est; de tribus legatis frequentes ierunt in alia

1. Confectum, 'settled.' Cp. Ad Att. 12. 19, 1 'tu .. confice de columnis.'

3. Caninii. L. Caninius Gallus was one of the tribunes for this year. He was a friend of M. Varro and of M. Marius. Cicero pleaded for him in 55 B.C., but does not seem to have approved his conduct as tribune. He was praetor in 53 B.C., governed Achaia, perhaps combined with Macedonia, next year, and died in 44 B.C. Cp. Ad Fam. 9. 2, 1; 7. 1, 4; Ad Q. F. 2. 2, 3; Ad Att. 16. 14. 4. A. W. Zumpt, C. E. 2. 201–202.

Nos quoque. Cicero here means himself alone, but 'diceremus' in the next clause seems to refer to the senate at large.

5. Itaque .. diceremus, 'and so next day it was resolved that our opinions should be expressed briefly.' This would be in favour of Lentulus, whose friends desired a speedy decision. It does not appear whether a formal vote is implied in placuit.

6. Nobis, 'to you and me.'

7. Dicendo, 'during my speech.' Cp. Ep. 20, 6, note. But Madvig (Advers. Crit. II. 233) thinks that the sense here requires that 'in' should be prefixed to 'dicendo.'

Singulis appellandis rogandisque, 'in addressing and making requests to individuals.' Cp. Forcell. sub voce.

8. Prima; used adverbially. Cp. Madv. 300 b.

9. Pronuntiata esset, 'had been read out for discussion.' Cp. Forcell.

11. Divideretur, 'should be submitted in separate votes.' In this case the questions would be? (1) Are religious scruples to prevent the employment of an armed force? and, (2) Are three commissioners chosen from men not invested with 'imperium,' to restore Ptolemy? Cp. Pro Milon. 6. 14, and Asconius' note.

13. Frequentes ierunt in alia omnia, 'rejected the motion in a full house,' or perhaps, 'by a large majority.' The presiding officer in submitting a motion to the senate, used, according to Pliny (Ep. 8. 14. 19), the following words, 'qui haec sentitis in hanc partem; qui alia omnia, in illam partem ite, qua sentitis.' Those who were in favour of the motion went to the side of the mover; those who were against it, to the other side: thus 'in alia omnia ire' became a technical expression for voting against a motion. Cp. Forcell. sub voc. 'eo' and Festus, 261, Müller.

2 omnia. Proxima erat Hortensii sententia, cum Lupus, tribunus pl., quod ipse de Pompeio retulisset, intendere coepit, ante se oportere discessionem facere quam consules. Eius orationi vehementer ab omnibus reclamatum est; erat enim et iniqua et nova. Consules neque concedebant neque valde repugnabant, diem consumi volebant; id quod est factum: perspiciebant enim in Hortensii sententiam multis partibus plures ituros, quamquam aperte Volcatio adsentirentur. Multi rogabantur, atque id ipsum consulibus invitis; nam ii Bibuli sententiam valere cupierunt.

3 Hac controversia usque ad noctem ducta senatus dimissus est. Ego eo die casu apud Pompeium cenavi nactusque tempus hoc magis idoneum quam umquam antea, quod post tuum discessum is dies honestissimus nobis fuerat in senatu, ita sum cum illo locutus, ut mihi viderer animum hominis ab omni alia cogitatione ad tuam dignitatem tuendam traducere: quem ego ipsum cum audio, prorsus eum libero omni suspitione cupiditatis; cum autem eius familiares omnium ordinum video, perspicio, id quod iam omnibus est apertum, totam rem istam iam pridem a certis homi-

1. **Proxima erat**, 'stood next for discussion.' For its substance, see § 3 of the preceding letter.

2. **Quod ipse . . . retulisset**, 'because he had himself opened a debate on the question whether Pompey should go.' Perhaps Lupus had taken this step towards the close of 57 B.C., after the consuls for that year had departed for their provinces, when we know that he was active in the senate. He might on this ground claim priority for the motion of Volcatius, as having been first brought before the senate. Cp. § 3 of the preceding letter; Ad Q. F. 2. 1, 1. Ross in his note on the present passage says, 'Lupus claimed the privilege of dividing the house upon his question, because he was a magistrate, before the consuls divided it upon that of Hortensius, who was a private senator.'

Intendere coepit, 'began to maintain strongly,' = 'contendere.' Forcell.

3. **Discessionem facere**, 'to divide the house,' said of the presiding officer. Cp. Philipp. 14. 7. 21.

4. **Nova**, 'unprecedented.'

5. **Diem consumi volebant.** On the constr., cp. Madv. 389, Obs. 4. The consuls wished the day to be spent in a debate, not concluded by a fresh division.

6. **Enim** refers to 'volebant.'

8. **Adsentirentur.** The conjunctive is used because the words express the view of the consuls. Cp. Madv. 369.

Rogabantur, 'were asked their opinion.'

Id ipsum introduces an addition to the previous proposition, 'and that too.' Cp. Madv. 484 c; Zumpt L.G. 698–9. Wesenb. inserts 'non' before 'invitis,' supposing, I presume, that the consuls were glad of the delay caused by the debate on Lupus' motion.

9. **Valere cupierunt**, 'were eager for the success of.' As part of the motion of Bibulus had been rejected (sup. § 1, note), Madvig (Advers. Crit. II. 233) thinks that the sense here requires 'cupierant.' So, too, Wesenb. The powers of the consuls and tribunes in controlling the debates of the senate do not seem to have been accurately defined. See a previous note on this section, and one on § 3 of the preceding letter.

11. **Hoc magis**: 'hoc' is here the ablative, 'so much the more.' It corresponds to quod . . fuerat a few lines below.

12. **Umquam**, = 'ullum.'

Discessum, 'your departure for your province,' which seems to have taken place towards the close of 57 B.C., for Cicero, writing to his brother in the December of that year, mentions a meeting of the senate, in terms implying that no consuls were present at it. Ad Q. F. 2. 1, 1.

16. **Cupiditatis**, 'of selfish ambition.'

18. **Totam rem . . corruptam**, 'that the whole affair has been ruined by certain people.' Cp. Sall. Iugurth. 64 'res familiares

nibus, non invito rege ipso consiliariisque eius, esse corruptam. Haec scripsi a. d. XVI. Kal. Februarias ante lucem; eo die senatus 4 erat futurus. Nos in senatu, quem ad modum spero, dignitatem nostram, ut potest in tanta hominum perfidia et iniquitate, retinebimus; quod ad popularem rationem attinet, hoc videmur esse consecuti, ut ne quid agi cum populo aut salvis auspiciis aut salvis legibus aut denique sine vi posset. De his rebus pridie, quam haec scripsi, senatus auctoritas gravissima intercessit; cui cum Cato et Caninius intercessissent, tamen est perscripta: eam ad te missam esse arbitror. De ceteris rebus, quicquid erit actum, scribam ad te, et, ut quam rectissime agatur, omni mea cura, opera, diligentia, gratia providebo.

23. TO HIS BROTHER QUINTUS (AD Q. F. II. 3).
ROME, FEB. 15, 56 B.C. (698 A.U.C.)

1. The audiences to foreign envoys have been postponed, and C. Cato has proposed to put an end to the government of Lentulus. 2. Milo appeared on the 2nd, and again on the 7th; Pompey wished to speak in his defence, but the uproar raised by Clodius' partisans drowned his voice, and a scene of riot and confusion followed. 3. On the 9th the senate passed a resolution censuring some of these proceedings. C. Cato praised me, while inveighing against Pompey; and the latter, in replying to him, attacked Crassus and said he would take care of his own life. 4. I understand from Pompey that Crassus and others are supporting Clodius and C. Cato against him. He is preparing for defence, and many people will come from the country, both to support him and to oppose C. Cato's attacks upon Lentulus and Milo. 5. I have promised my support to Sestius, who has been indicted both for bribery and riot. The senate is

corruperit.' 76 'praeda corrupta.' Cicero insinuates that Pompey was playing an underhand game by means of his friends. Cp. § 3 of the previous letter.

1. Consiliariis. Cp. Ep. 19, 2.

3. Erat, epistolary tense, = 'est.'

4. Ut potest, sc. 'fieri,' 'as far as is possible.' Forcell.

Perfidia et iniquitate. Is the doubtful policy of Pompey's friends referred to? Cp. § 4 of the preceding letter, and note.

5. Popularem rationem, 'the plan of bringing the question before the people,' entertained probably by Pompey's adherents. Caninius, one of the tribunes, was hostile to Lentulus (cp. infr. § 4: Ep. 26, 3, note), and C. Cato proposed to deprive Lentulus of his 'imperium.' Ep. 23, 1, note. The latter, however, does not seem to have been a friend of Pompey.

Hoc videmur .. posset, 'I think we secured that no measure should be brought before the people without violation of the laws or disregard of the auspices, nor even without a breach of the peace.' Cicero means that he and his friends had secured tribunes to veto any such measure, and other magistrates to declare 'se servaturos de caelo'—on which power cp. Ep. 10, 2, note. The tribunes on whom he most relied were, apparently, L. Racilius, Cn. Plancius, and Antistius Vetus. Cp. Ad Q. F. 2. 1, 3. On the pleonastic use of ut ne, cp. Madv. 372 b: see also p. 51, 2. note.

7. De his rebus, 'on these points,' i.e. possible irregular proceedings in the assembly.

8. Auctoritas, 'a resolution of the senate.' The term was used when a tribune's veto had prevented a regular decree, 'consultum,' from being passed. Cp. Ep. 26, 4.

Intercessit, merely 'was passed.' Cp. Ep. 29, 21.

9. Cato, C. Porcius Cato. Cp. p. 101, l. 8, note.

Est perscripta, 'was regularly drawn up.'

trying to check popular corruption. 6. On Feb. 11, I defended Bestia, and took the opportunity of saying something in praise of Sestius. 7. Thus far I wrote on Feb. 12. My position is influential, and I owe it in great measure to your devotion. I have hired you a house, but hope your own will be ready in a few months. Good tenants have taken that in the Carinae. I have not had a letter since that you wrote from Olbia. Be careful of your health, and remember that you are in Sardinia.

MARCUS QUINTO FRATRI SALUTEM.

1 Scripsi ad te antea superiora; nunc cognosce, postea quae sint
acta: a Kal. Febr. legationes in Idus Febr. reiiciebantur; eo die
res confecta non est. A. d. IIII. Non. Febr. Milo adfuit; ei Pompeius advocatus venit; dixit Marcellus, a me rogatus; honeste
discessimus. Prodicta dies est in VII. Idus Febr. Interim reiectis
legationibus in Idus referebatur de provinciis quaestorum et de
ornandis praetoribus; sed res multis querelis de re publica interponendis nulla transacta est. C. Cato legem promulgavit de
2 imperio Lentuli abrogando: vestitum filius mutavit. A. d. VII.

1. **Superiora**, the events of Dec., 57 B.C. and Jan., 56 B.C. Cp. Ad Q. F. 2. 1; 2. 2, and Intr. to Part II, §§ 1; 2.

2. **Legationes**, 'the audiences given to foreign envoys, and discussion of their requests.'

Reiiciebantur = 'differebantur' (Forcell.), 'were put off.' The imperfect is used to describe what was actually passing on that day. Cp. Madv. 337.

Eo die, 'on the first of February.'

3. **Res**, 'the question who should restore Ptolemy.' Cp. Epp. 21; 22.

Adfuit, = 'comparuit in iudicio' (Forcell.), 'appeared to stand his trial.' Cp. sup. p. 136; and for other notices of Milo, see Intr. to Part I, § 23; to Part II, §§ 14; 15; and to Part III, § 12.

4. **Advocatus**, 'as a supporter,' one who aided by his presence or by his counsel on points of law, differing from the 'patronus' who pleaded. Cp. Forcell. and Pseudo Ascon. ad Div. in Caec. sect. 11.

Dixit, 'spoke in his defence.' It does not appear to which of the Marcelli Cicero refers.

Honeste discessimus, 'we got honourably out of the affair.' Manutius thinks the words mean 'left the place of trial without suffering insult:' whereas on the next day of the court's sitting there was much disorder. Cp. Ad Att. 2. 21, 6; Ad Q. F. 2. 4, 1. As proceedings in a criminal trial, and not in the senate, are referred to, the technical meaning of 'discedere' seems out of place here.

5. **Prodicta dies est**, 'the trial was adjourned.' Cp. the expression 'diem dicere,' which is frequent in Livy, for giving notice of a trial.

6. **De provinciis quaestorum**, 'to which provinces the quaestors should be assigned.' We read elsewhere of an *allotment* of provinces among the quaestors, but perhaps the arrangement depended very much upon the senate. Cp. In Verr. 2 Act. 1. 13, 34; Pro Muren. 8, 18; Philipp. 2. 20, 50. According to Mommsen and Marquardt it is not strictly accurate to speak of the 'provinces' of the quaestors as they had no 'imperium.' Cp. note B. p. 120.

De ornandis praetoribus. 'Provinciam ornare' is a more common expression, meaning, to supply with the proper officers and forces. The meaning appears to be the same as if Cicero had written 'de provinciis praetorum ornandis.' Cp. Ad Att. 3. 24, 1 'de consulibus ornandis.' The praetors seem to have had their provinces allotted early in the year. Cp. Ep. 6, 5; Ad Att. 1. 15, 1.

7. **Multis querelis .. interponendis**, 'as many complaints on the position of affairs intervened;' abl. caus.

8. **Legem promulgavit .. abrogando**, 'gave notice of a proposal to put an end to the command of Lentulus.' This proposal is called 'nefaria Catonis promulgatio' Ad Fam. 1. 5 a, 2. The consul Marcellinus interposed to prevent its being carried out.

9. **Lentuli**. So the MS. Baiter substitutes Lentulo. The dative of the person is certainly more common after 'abrogare,' but cp. Livy 22. 25.

Filius. His namesake, P. Lentulus

Id. Febr. Milo adfuit; dixit Pompeius, sive voluit: nam, ut surrexit, operae Clodianae clamorem sustulerunt, idque ei perpetua oratione contigit, non modo ut adclamatione, sed ut convitio et maledictis impediretur. Qui ut peroravit—nam in eo sane fortis fuit, non est deterritus, dixit omnia atque interdum etiam silentio, cum auctoritate † peregerat—, sed ut peroravit, surrexit Clodius: ei tantus clamor a nostris—placuerat enim referre gratiam—, ut neque mente nec lingua neque ore consisteret. Ea res acta est, cum hora sexta vix Pompeius perorasset, usque ad horam VIII., cum omnia maledicta, versus denique obscenissimi in Clodium et Clodiam dicerentur. Ille furens et exsanguis interrogabat suos in clamore ipso, quis esset, qui plebem fame necaret. Respondebant operae: 'Pompeius.' Quis Alexandriam ire cuperet. Respondebant: 'Pompeius.' Quem ire vellent. Respondebant: 'Crassum.' Is aderat tum, Miloni animo non amico. Hora fere nona quasi signo dato Clodiani nostros consputare coeperunt: exarsit dolor. Urgere illi, ut loco nos moverent; factus est a nostris impetus; fuga operarum; eiectus de rostris Clodius; ac nos quoque tum

Spinther, who was augur in 57 B.C., and after Caesar's murder supported the party of Brutus and Cassius. Cp. Pro Sest. 69, 144; Ad Fam. 12. 14; 12. 15. He is said by Dion Cassius (39, 17) to have been adopted by a Torquatus. Manut.

Mutavit: i.e. as a sign of mourning. Manut.

1. Sive voluit, 'or rather, wished to speak.' On the ellipse, cp. Madv. 478, Obs. 3.

2. Operae Clodianae, 'the hired partisans of Clodius.' See Ep. 6. 3, note.

Perpetua oratione, 'during his whole speech.' Cp. Madv. 276, Obs. 2.

3. Non modo ut. On the position of 'ut,' cp. Madv. 465 b, Obs.

Adclamatione, 'outcry.' Cp. Ad Q. F. 2. 1, 3, where the words 'maxima adclamatione senatus' are used of the reception given to an unpopular motion.

4. Peroravit, 'concluded his speech.' Forcell.

5. Dixit . . peregerat, either 'dixit' or 'peregerat' seems superfluous. Lambinus would insert 'semper' before 'peregerat,' which does not mend the construction, but makes the sense plainer.

Silentio, 'without interruption.'

6. Sed ut, resumptive, 'when, I say.'

7. A nostris, 'by our partisans.'

Referre gratiam, iron. 'to return his favours,' 'to pay him out.' Cp. De Amic. 15. 53.

Ut neque . . consisteret, 'that he was master neither of his senses, his voice, nor his countenance.'

8. Ea res acta est, 'that scene lasted.'

9. Ad horam VIII, 'till nearly two o'clock.' See Ep. 101, 2, note.

10. Cum omnia . . dicerentur. On the mood, cp. Madv. 358, Obs. 3.

11. Clodiam: cp. Epp. 5, 6, note; 9, 5; 29, 15.

Exsanguis, 'pale.'

In clamore ipso, 'in the midst of the outcries against him.'

12. Fame necaret, i.e. by keeping back supplies of corn, or by neglecting his duties as commissioner for supplying it. Cp. Ep. 20, 6-7, note 5.

16. Consputare. This word seems only to be found here.

18. Fuga operarum, sc. 'facta est.' Cp. Madv. 479 d.

De rostris. It would seem then that the forum had been the scene of the previous occurrences. Cp. infr. § 6; sup. p. 136; and Lange, Röm. Alt. 2. 503, who thinks that Clodius, as aedile, prosecuted Milo before the comitia tributa.

fugimus, ne quid in turba. Senatus vocatus in curiam; Pompeius domum: neque ego tamen in senatum, ne aut de tantis rebus tacerem aut in Pompeio defendendo—nam is carpebatur a Bibulo, Curione, Favonio, Servilio filio—animos bonorum virorum offenderem. Res in posterum dilata est; Clodius in Quirinalia pro-
2 dixit diem. A. d. VI. Id. Febr. senatus ad Apollinis fuit, ut Pompeius adesset. Acta res est graviter a Pompeio. Eo die nihil perfectum est. A. d. V. Id. Febr. ad Apollinis senatus consultum factum est, ea, quae facta essent a. d. VI. Id. Febr., contra rem publicam esse facta. Eo die Cato vehementer est in Pompeium invectus et cum oratione perpetua tamquam reum accusavit; de me multa me invito cum mea summa laude dixit: cum illius in me perfidiam increparet, auditus est magno silentio malevolorum. Respondit ei vehementer Pompeius Crassumque descripsit, dixitque aperte se munitiorem ad custodiendam vitam

1. Ne quid in turba, sc. 'pateremur.'

Pompeius domum, sc. 'ivit.' Cp. Madv. 479 d.

3. Carpebatur, 'was attacked,' probably for his inconsistency in having formerly patronized Clodius, and for his ambition and dissimulation. Cp. Ep. 22, 3, note.

4. Bonorum virorum, 'of the optimates.' Cp. Ep. 6, 3.

5. Res, 'the discussion of these outrages in the senate.'

Quirinalia, a festival in honour of the deified Romulus, celebrated on Feb. 17.

Prodixit diem: see note on § 1.

6. Ad Apollinis. This temple of Apollo was built in 430 B.C., and stood near the Circus Flaminius and Forum Olitorium (cp. Livy, 4. 29; Smith, Dict. of Geogr. 2. 833), and may have been near Pompey's house also. As it was outside the walls, Pompey could attend a meeting there without laying down his military 'imperium;' but he had entered the city to speak on behalf of Milo in the forum (sup. § 2), and did so afterwards to bear testimony on behalf of Sestius (cp. Ep. 29, 7); it seems probable therefore that the senate was now convoked outside the walls because Pompey was anxious that the senate should meet near a house which he had lately built for himself in the Campus Martius, and was reluctant to enter the 'urbs' on account of the prevailing disorder. Cp. Manutius ad loc; on the general constitutional question involved, Notes, E. p. 123; and F.; Epp. 5. 4, note; 35. 1, note; 44. 4, note; and as to Pompey's house, Plut. Pomp. 40, and Long's note; Smith Dict. of Geogr. 2. 834, Roma; Becker and Marquardt, 1. 616, note 1302. Manutius thinks that Pompey was 'legibus solutus' released from ordinary restrictions. See his note on Ad Fam. 8. 4. 4.

7. Acta res .. a Pompeio, 'Pompey spoke with weight.'

9. Ea, quae facta essent: cp. § 2 of this letter. But we should expect 'vii. Id.' here, having no notice of any disturbances as having taken place on 'vi. Id.'

Contra rem publicam facta esse. The usual form adopted by the senate in censuring any proceedings as seditious or treasonable.

10. Cato. Apparently C. Cato, now tribune. Cp. Drumann 5. 204.

13. Cum .. increparet: cp. § 2, note.

Illius, 'of Pompey,' who had betrayed Cicero to Clodius in 58 B.C.

Magno silentio malevolorum, 'amid deep silence on the part of my ill-wishers.' Cp. on the ablat., Madv. 257. Those who wished to estrange Pompey from Cicero would naturally abstain from interrupting a speech which seemed likely to serve their ends.

15. Descripsit, 'gave a description of without naming,' 'alluded to.' Nagelsbach 237, 397.

Munitiorem, 'better secured,' or 'provided.' Forcell. gives 'firmatus,' 'armatus,' among synonymes. On the addition of fuisset to mark difference of time, cp. Madv. 303 b, Obs. 2.

suam fore, quam Africanus fuisset, quem C. Carbo interemisset.
Itaque magnae mihi res iam moveri videbantur: nam Pompeius 4
haec intellegit nobiscumque communicat, insidias vitae suae fieri,
C. Catonem a Crasso sustentari, Clodio pecuniam suppeditari,
utrumque et ab eo et a Curione, Bibulo ceterisque suis obtrectatoribus confirmari, vehementer esse providendum ne opprimatur
contionario illo populo a se prope alienato, nobilitate inimica,
non aequo senatu, iuventute improba. Itaque se comparat, homines ex agris arcessit; operas autem suas Clodius confirmat:
manus ad Quirinalia paratur; in eo multo sumus superiores ipsius
copiis; et magna manus ex Piceno et Gallia exspectatur, ut
etiam Catonis rogationibus de Milone et Lentulo resistamus.
A. d. IIII. Idus Febr. Sestius ab indice Cn. Nerio Pupinia ambitus 5
est postulatus et eodem die a quodam M. Tullio de vi. Is erat
aeger: domum, ut debuimus, ad eum statim venimus eique nos
totos tradidimus, idque fecimus praeter hominum opinionem, qui

1. Africanus, the younger. Cp. Ep. 3. 3, note. He was son of L. Aemilius Paulus, the conqueror of Pydna, and was adopted by a son of the elder Africanus. For an account of his death, cp. Mommsen 3. pp. 104, 105.

C. Papirius Carbo was tribune in 131 B.C., and succeeded Ti. Gracchus as one of the leaders of the popular party. He is often mentioned by Cicero.

Interemisset, orat. obl. Cp. Madv. 369.

2. Videbantur is, I think, the epistolary imperfect.

3. Haec: pleonastic, referring to what follows. Cp. Madv. 485 b, Zumpt L. G. 744.

5. Ab eo, sc. Crasso.

A Curione, by the elder Curio, whom Cicero had denounced in 61 B.C. for supporting Clodius. Cp. Ep. 7, 5, note.

6. Confirmari, 'are being encouraged.' Forcell.

Ne opprimatur, sc. Pompeius.

7. Contionario, 'frequenting the assemblies.' The word seems not to occur elsewhere, but cp. Ep. 8, 11, 'contionalis hirudo aerarii.'

8. Iuventute improba, 'while the young are so reckless.' See Merivale 1. pp. 97, 98, and the references there given.

Se comparat: a rare expression, without mention of the object for which preparations are made. 'Copias comparare' is more common.

9. Ex agris. Especially from Picenum, which was devoted to Pompey. See below.

Confirmat, 'is increasing.'

10. In eo, 'as regards that affair,' the trial of Milo.

Ipsius, sc. Clodii. Cicero seems to mean that he and Pompey could oppose Clodius successfully, without any unusual exertions, but that to oppose C. Cato it was desirable to summon some of the country people to Rome.

11. Et. Wesenb. has 'sed,' which is also the reading of the best MS.

Gallia, Cispadana probably. Cp. Ep. 1, 4, note. Cicero perhaps means to include in it the 'ager Gallicus' between Ancona and the Rubicon, which is often mentioned in connection with Picenum. Cp. In Cat. 2. 3. 5; De Senect. 4, 11; Livy 23. 14; Polyb. 2. 21.

12. Rogationibus. That about Milo seems to be only mentioned here; that about Lentulus has been mentioned in § 1 of this letter.

13. Sestius. P. Sestius, tribune for 58–57 B.C., had been most active in promoting Cicero's restoration from exile, and Cicero afterwards defended him. Cp. § 1 of the following letter, and Intr. to Part II, § 2.

Indice, 'the informer.' Cp. Ep. 15. 4, note.

Pupinia, 'of the Pupinian tribe.' It was one of the 16 or 17 original 'tribus rusticae.' On the ablat., cp. Madv. 275, Obs. 3.

14. Postulatus. Cp. Ep. 35, 1, note.

M. Tullio Albinovano. Cp. In Vat. 1, 3.

Is, Sestius.

15. Ei . . nos totos tradidimus, 'placed my services altogether at his disposal.'

nos ei iure succensere putabant, ut humanissimi gratissimique et ipsi et omnibus videremur, itaque faciemus. Sed idem Nerius index edidit ad adligatos Cn. Lentulum Vatiam et C. Cornelium: † ista ei. Eodem die senatus consultum factum est, ut sodalitates decuriatique discederent, lexque de iis ferretur, ut, qui non discessissent, ea poena, quae est de vi, tenerentur.

6 A. d. III. Idus Febr. dixi pro Bestia de ambitu apud praetorem Cn. Domitium in foro medio, maximo conventu, incidique in eum locum in dicendo, cum Sestius multis in templo Castoris volneribus acceptis subsidio Bestiae servatus esset. Hic προοικονομησάμην quiddam εὐκαίρως de iis, quae in Sestium adparabantur crimina, et eum ornavi veris laudibus, magno adsensu omnium. Res homini fuit vehementer grata: quae tibi eo scribo, quod me de retinenda Sestii gratia litteris saepe monuisti.

7 Pridie Idus Febr. haec scripsi ante lucem; eo die apud Pom-

1. Iure succensere. Perhaps Sestius had shown some of his ill-temper (see § 1 of the following letter) in his behaviour to Cicero. Or perhaps Cicero thought that he, like the consuls for 57 B.C., had been lukewarm (cp. sup. p. 134) in securing him reimbursement for his losses.

Ut .. videremur. The conjunctive here expresses consequence rather than design, and depends on 'facimus praeter opinionem.' Cp. Madv. 358.

2. Itaque faciemus, 'and so will I behave myself.' 'I will do as I said' (Manut.). For 'itaque,' meaning not 'therefore,' but 'and so,' cp. Pro Cluent. 19, 51; Pro Reg. Deiot. 7, 19.

3. Ad adligatos, 'in addition to the other accused.' Metzg. 'Ad' seems rarely to have quite this sense in Cicero's writings: cp. however, in Vat. 8, 20; also Livy 24. 45. For this sense of 'adligati,' cp. Pro Cluentio 13, 39, and Prof. Ramsay's note. If 'adlegatos' be read, it may mean 'to the deputies appointed to receive informations.' Forcell. Wesenb. suggests 'edidit alligatos,' 'reported as implicated.'

Cn. Lentulus Vatia seems not to be mentioned elsewhere.

C. Cornelius was tribune in 68–67 B.C. He brought in bills for removing abuses in the procedure of the senate and of the praetors' courts, which were carried, and others which were not. Thus he incurred the enmity of the optimates, was accused in 65 B.C., and defended by Cicero. Cp. Ascon. in Cornel. 93.

4. Ista ei. Orell. suggests 'itaque rei facti sunt.'

5. Sodalitates, clubs formed for influencing elections, probably. Cp. Q. Cic. de Pet. Cons. 5. 19; Pro Plancio 18; 19; De Senect. 13. 45; Mommsen 4. 1. 317. They were originally religious or social clubs. Cp. p. 105, note on l. 17, on collegia.

Decuriati. Men organised—perhaps in companies of ten—for corruption and intimidation. Cp. Pro Sest. 15. 34; Pro Plancio 18.

Discederent, sc. 'de campo.' Billerb.

6. Tenerentur, = 'obnoxii essent,' 'should be liable to the penalties of.' Forcell.

7. Bestia. L. Calpurnius Bestia is mentioned, Philipp. 11. 5. 11.

8. Cn. Domitium. Cn. Domitius Calvinus was consul 53 B.C. He commanded one wing of Caesar's army at Pharsalus, and was afterwards, at the head of a rather miscellaneous army, defeated by Pharnaces. Cp. Intr. to Parts III, § 11; IV, § 3, and Caes. Bell. Civ. 3. 89.

Maximo conventu, 'amid a great concourse.' On the abl., cp. § 3 of this letter, and note.

Incidique in eum .. cum, 'I came in my speech to the topic of Sestius' escape.' 'Cum' = 'quod.' Cp. De Fin. 3. 1. 9. The affair to which Cicero refers took place on Jan. 23, 57 B.C. See Intr. to Part I, § 23.

10. προοικονομησάμην, not a classical word. The sense seems to require 'dealt with beforehand;' or as Manutius says, 'tanquam bonus causae Sestianae gubernator praemunivi quiddam opportune.'

15. Haec, 'thus far.' The postscript appears to begin with 'cetera sunt.' But Wesenb. thinks that all the passage from

ponium in eius nuptiis eram cenaturus. Cetera sunt in rebus nostris huius modi, *ut* tu mihi fere diffidenti praedicabas, plena dignitatis et gratiae; quae quidem tua, mi frater, patientia, virtute, pietate, suavitate etiam, tibi mihique sunt restituta. Domus tibi ad lucum Pisonis Luciniana conducta est; sed, ut spero, paucis mensibus post K. Quintiles in tuam commigrabis. Tuam in Carinis mundi habitatores Lamiae conduxerunt. A te post illam Olbiensem epistolam nullas litteras accepi. Quid agas et ut te oblectes, scire cupio maximeque te ipsum videre quam primum. Cura, mi frater, ut valeas et, quamquam est hiems, tamen Sardiniam istam esse cogites. XV. K. Martias.

24. TO HIS BROTHER QUINTUS (AD Q. F. II. 4).
ROME, MARCH, 56 B.C. (698 A.U.C.)

1. Sestius has been unanimously acquitted, and during the trial I inveighed bitterly against his enemy Vatinius, amid general applause. I think Sestius must be quite satisfied with me. 2. Your son Quintus is pursuing his studies, as well as I could wish, under Tyrannio. I hope I have formed a satisfactory engagement for Tullia with Crassipes. The 'feriae Latinae' are at an end, but to-day and to-morrow are still considered holidays.

'Pridie' to 'cogites' was written on the 13th, and that Cicero did not find a messenger till the 14th.

Pomponium. Atticus should properly have been called Caecilius now. Cp. Ad Att. 3. 20. He married Pilia, who is not unfrequently referred to in Cicero's later letters.

1. Cetera sunt . . praedicabas, 'my position in all particulars not here referred to is one of the same dignity and influence (huiusmodi) as you often told me it would be when I was inclined to distrust your statements.' Cp. Zumpt, 831, L. G., note. 'Huiusmodi' refers to the account given of his position earlier in the letter. Cp. Madv. 485.

4. Suavitate etiam. 'Etiam' expresses surprise; Quintus was naturally harsh and passionate. The good qualities here praised were probably shown in negotiations with various political leaders for his brother's recall from exile.

Domus . . conducta est. The house of Q. Cicero on the Palatine was now being rebuilt. Cp. Ad Q. F. 2. 2, 2; 2. 4, 2.

5. Ad lucum Pisonis, 'near the pleasure grounds (?) of Piso.' It does not appear who the Piso was who gave his name to the spot, nor can I discover the meaning of Luciniana, for which Lucceiana and Liciniana have been suggested as emendations.

6. Paucis mensibus. It does not appear whether these months were calculated from the date of the letter, or from July 1, which seems to have been an usual term for house-letting. Cp. Suet. Tib. 35. Perhaps Baiter's punctuation is in favour of the latter date, and so are the words 'ante hiemem' in § 2 of the next letter.

In tuam, 'to your own on the Palatine,' cp. ep. 24, 2.

7. In Carinis. The Carinae was one of the finest situations in Rome, on the slope of the Esquiline.

Mundi habitatores Lamiae, 'respectable tenants of the family of the Lamiae.'

8. Olbiensem, 'from Olbia' in Sardinia. This place was situated on the east coast of the island, not far from its north-east corner, and had a good harbour. It is now called Terranova.

10. Quamquam . . cogites, 'though it is winter, and therefore the least dangerous season, remember that your (istam) residence is in Sardinia,' a notoriously unhealthy island.

MARCUS QUINTO FRATRI SALUTEM.

1 Sestius noster absolutus est a. d. V. Idus Martias, et, quod vehementer interfuit rei publicae, nullam videri in eius modi causa dissensionem esse, omnibus sententiis absolutus est. Illud, quod tibi curae saepe esse intellexeram, ne cui iniquo relinqueremus vituperandi locum, qui nos ingratos esse diceret, nisi illius perversitatem quibusdam in rebus quam humanissime ferremus, scito hoc nos in eo iudicio consecutos esse, ut omnium gratissimi iudicaremur; nam defendendo moroso homini cumulatissime satis fecimus, et, id quod ille maxime cupiebat, Vatinium, a quo palam oppugnabatur, arbitratu nostro concidimus dis hominibusque plaudentibus. Quin etiam Paulus noster cum testis productus esset in Sestium, confirmavit se nomen Vatinii delaturum, si Macer Licinius cunctaretur, et Macer ab Sestii subselliis surrexit ac se illi non defuturum adfirmavit. Quid quaeris? homo petulans et audax [Vatinius] valde perturbatus
2 debilitatusque discessit. Quintus tuus, puer optimus, eruditur egregie: hoc nunc magis animum adverto, quod Tyrannio docet

1. **Quod** refers to the following sentence. **nullam . . esse.** Cp. Madv. 449, last example.

3. **Dissensionem,** 'difference of opinion among the judges.'

Illud refers to the sentence **ne cui . . locum.**

4. **Ne cui . . ferremus,** 'lest I should leave ill-natured people an opportunity of blaming me as ungrateful, unless in some things I put up with Sestius' perversity as good humouredly as possible.'

8. **Defendendo,** 'in my defence of him.' Cp. Ep. 10, 6, note.

Moroso: 'morosus' = δύσκολος (Forcell.), 'peevish,' 'cross-grained.'

Cumulatissime, 'most abundantly.' The word recurs in the same sense, Ad Fam. 10. 29.

9. **Ille,** Sestius.

Vatinium. P. Vatinius appeared as a witness against Sestius, and Cicero took advantage of his appearance to attack him in an invective, which takes its place among Cicero's speeches as the 'Interrogatio in P. Vatinium testem.' Cp. Intr. to Part II, § 2.

10. **Arbitratu nostro,** 'as one could wish.'

Concidimus. Forcell. explains 'concidere' as = 'evertere.'

11. **Paulus.** L. Aemilius, consul 50 B.C.

13. **Licinius Macer** seems to be only mentioned here.

Ab Sestii subselliis, 'from the benches where the friends of Sestius were seated.' Billerb. Cp. Ep. 34, 1, note; Pro Cluent. 19. 54; 24. 65.

14. **Illi non defuturum,** 'would satisfy the wishes of Paulus.'

16. **Discessit,** 'left the court,' or 'got out of the affair.' Cp. § 1 of the preceding letter.

Quintus tuus. The younger Q. Cicero, a youth of good abilities, but passionate and changeable. Cp. Ad Att. 6. 2, 2; 10. 4, 5 and 6.

17. **Tyrannio.** Usually identified with a teacher of Amisus named Theophrastus, and surnamed Tyrannio for his overbearing demeanour to his fellow pupils: cp. Suidas (Gaisford, 3639); Smith, Dict. of Biogr. 3. 1196; Strab. 12. 3. 17; 13. 1. 54. He was brought prisoner to Rome by L. Lucullus, where he taught in noble families, and became rich. He is often mentioned in Cicero's letters to Atticus. According to Suidas, as corrected by Kuster, he died in 58 B.C., but Clinton, Fasti Hell. III on 71 B.C., p. 165, and on 58 B.C., p. 185 has pointed out that the one here mentioned probably lived till 46 B.C.

apud me. Domus utriusque nostrum aedificatur strenue. Redemptori tuo dimidium pecuniae curavi. Spero nos ante hiemem contubernales fore. De nostra Tullia, tui mehercule amantissima, spero cum Crassipede nos confecisse. Dies erant duo, qui post Latinas habentur religiosi; ceterum confectum Latiar erat.

25. TO ATTICUS (AD ATT. IV. 5).

NEAR ANTIUM, APRIL (?), 56 B.C. (698 A.U.C.)

1. Do not suppose I value any one's criticism more than yours. If you must know why I did not send you my recantation, I was rather ashamed of it, but the perfidy of my political associates left me no choice. 2. You advised me to take my present course, and I wish by this open avowal to pledge myself for the future. The jealousy of the leaders of the optimates, and their evident exultation over any misunderstanding between Pompey and me, really absolves me from any further obligation to them. I will choose more powerful protectors in future. 3. You will say, 'I wish you had done so long ago.' I acknowledge my folly. Tullia's dowry exhausts money I might have spent on travelling. I hope to visit you soon. Your slaves have made themselves useful in my library.

CICERO ATTICO SAL.

Ain tu? an me existimas ab ullo malle mea legi probarique 1
quam a te? Cur igitur cuiquam misi prius? Urgebar ab eo, ad

1. **Domus.** The houses of both brothers were, apparently, contiguous on the Palatine, and were now being rebuilt; hence Cicero's hope that he and his brother would soon be 'contubernales' under one roof.

Redemptori tuo, 'your contractor for the building.'

2. **Dimidium pecuniae**, 'half the sum agreed on.' On the neut. adj. 'dimidium' with 'pecuniae,' cp. Madv. 284. Obs. 5.

Curavi, sc. 'solvendum.' Cp. Forcell.

Spero . . confecisse, 'I hope we have settled her betrothal with Furius Crassipes.' It seems doubtful if a marriage ever took place. Cp. Ascon. In Pisonian. p. 122; Plut. Cic. 41. Cicero, however, calls Furius 'gener.' Ep. 29, 30. On the betrothal, cp. Ep. 25, 3, note. Crassipes was an adherent of Caesar.

4. **Dies erant . . Latiar erat**, 'to-day and to-morrow are still considered holidays, but the Latin festival ended' yesterday. The pres. **habentur** is used because the time of composing the letter is not specially referred to in that word. Cp. Madv. 345.

5. **Latiar**, sc. 'solenne.' The festival originally consisted only of one day, but three others were added after the expulsion of the kings, the first secession of the plebs, and the Licinian legislation respectively. The Latinae were 'conceptivae,' fixed by the consuls every year (cp. Smith's Dict. of Antiq. sub voc. 'Feriae,' p. 529), and were probably held early, as the consuls could not leave Rome till after they had been celebrated (cp. Livy 21. 63; 22. 1; 25. 12). In this year the festival was celebrated twice. Cp. Ad Q. F. 2. 6, 4. The letter ends abruptly; but I have not thought it necessary to follow Baiter in adding a portion of Ad Q. F. 2. 6 to complete it. The MS. has 'cetero confectum erat Latiar erat exiturum,' which is hardly explicable. Wesenb. doubts the use of 'Latiar' as an adjective and thinks that 'confectum erat' refers to the betrothal.

6. **Ain tu?** 'do you speak in earnest?' referring, apparently, to a letter in which Atticus had complained of Cicero's not sending him a copy of the παλινῳδία afterwards mentioned. Wesenb. and Boot omit 'an.'

7. **Cur igitur . . prius?** Atticus' question is anticipated.

quem misi, et non habebam exemplar. Quid? etiam—dudum enim circumrodo, quod devorandum est—subturpicula mihi videbatur esse παλινῳδία. Sed valeant recta, vera, honesta consilia: non est credibile, quae sit perfidia in istis principibus, ut volunt esse et ut essent, si quicquam haberent fidei. Senseram, noram inductus, relictus, proiectus ab iis; tamen hoc eram animo, ut cum iis in re publica consentirem: iidem erant, qui fuerant.
2 Vix aliquando te auctore resipui. Dices ea tenus te suasisse, qua facerem, non etiam ut scriberem. Ego mehercule mihi necessitatem volui imponere huius novae coniunctionis, ne qua mihi liceret labi ad illos, qui etiam tum, cum misereri mei debent, non desinunt invidere. Sed tamen modici fuimus ὑποθέσει, ut scripsi: erimus uberiores, si et ille libenter accipiet et ii subringentur, qui villam me moleste ferunt habere, quae Catuli fuerat, a Vettio me emisse non cogitant; qui domum

Ab eo. Billerb. thinks 'by Pompey,' who was to transmit the document, whatever its nature, to Caesar.

1. **Exemplar**, 'a copy.'

Quid? etiam (cp. Ep. 6. 6, note), 'Is there anything more to say? Yes.'

2. **Circumrodo quod devorandum est**, 'I am gnawing round the morsel I shall have to swallow.'

Subturpicula, 'rather shameful.' This word seems not to occur elsewhere.

3. **παλινῳδία**. Cicero has been supposed by various scholars to apply this term to (1) an address to Caesar expressing regret for the past, and wishes for a better understanding in future; (2) a poem in three books, 'De Temporibus Suis' (cp. Ep. 29. 21, note); (3) the oration 'De Provinciis Consularibus;' (4) the oration 'Pro Balbo.'

Valeant . . consilia, 'I bid good-bye to straightforward, true, and honourable principles.'

4. **Principibus**, 'chief men in the state.' Cicero probably refers to the leaders of the optimates, mentioned as 'quidam' in Ep. 20, 8. L. Domitius Ahenobarbus, M. Bibulus, and M. Cato, were prominent among them.

5. **Senseram . . inductus . . ab iis.** I had thought that the nominative might be used as in Virg. Aen. 2. 377, 'sensit medios delapsus in hostes,' but Mr. Jeans has pointed out that there seems to be no instance in prose of this usage (cp. Madv. 401, Obs. 3) and I now agree with Boot in thinking that the sentence is elliptical. 'I knew what their honour was worth, for I had been cajoled by them.' For this sense of 'inductus,' cp. Ep. 16. 7; Philipp. 2. 32. 79.

7. **Iidem erant**, i.e. 'in their jealousy and impracticability.' Cp. § 2.

8. **Resipui**, 'returned to my senses.'

Dices . . ut scriberem, 'you will say that your advice only suggested the course of conduct I should *pursue*, not that I should make a formal profession of it in writing.'

10. **Necessitatem . . coniunctionis**, 'a necessity of adhering to this new connection' with Caesar.

11. **Illos**: the '*principes*' mentioned above.

12. **ὑποθέσει**, 'in my treatment of the subject,' i.e. in my praise of Caesar and Pompey. Isocrates and Xenophon seem to use the word in this sense. Cp. Liddell and Scott's Lexicon, sub voc.

13. **Scripsi** probably refers to a lost letter.

Erimus uberiores, 'I shall treat it more fully.'

Ille, Caesar.

14. **Subringentur**, 'shall be annoyed.' The word seems to occur here only.

15. **A Vettio.** Perhaps this man is not elsewhere mentioned.

Domum . . oportuisse, 'who says I ought not to have rebuilt my house, but rather to have sold the site,' i.e. on his return from exile, to relieve himself from his money difficulties. On the jealousy excited by Cicero's fine house at Rome, cp. Ep. 8, 10, note.

negant oportuisse me aedificare, vendere aiunt oportuisse. Sed
quid ad hoc, si, quibus sententiis dixi quod et ipsi probarent,
laetati sunt tamen me contra Pompeii voluntatem dixisse? Finis.
Sed quoniam, qui nihil possunt, ii me nolunt amare, demus
operam ut ab iis, qui possunt, diligamur. Dices 'vellem iam 2
pridem.' Scio te voluisse et me asinum germanum fuisse. Sed
iam tempus est me ipsum a me amari, quando ab illis nullo
modo possum. Domum meam quod crebro invisis, est mihi
valde gratum. Viaticum Crassipes praeripit. Tu de via recta
in hortos. Videtur commodius ad te: postridie scilicet; quid
enim tua? sed viderimus. Bibliothecam mihi tui pinxerunt
constrictione et sittybis: eos velim laudes.

1. Sed quid ad hoc, 'what do you say to this?'

2. Si, quibus . . dixisse, 'if, as is true, they are pleased that those very votes of mine which they approved gave offence to Pompey?' 'Si'='si quidem.' Billerb. For the facts, cp. Ep. 29. 10.

3. Finis, 'no more of them,' i.e. such perversity does not deserve another thought. Baiter reads 'finis sit: quoniam.' But perhaps a verb is needless after 'finis,' considering the excitement under which the letter was evidently written.

4. Qui nihil possunt, i.e. the leaders of the optimates.

5. Qui possunt, i.e. Caesar and Pompey.
Iam pridem, sc. 'operam dedissem.'

6. Germanum, 'real,' 'genuine:' often used in Cicero's philosophical works in this sense. Cp. De Off. 3. 17, 69, alib.

8. Invisis, 'visit to look after it.' Cicero wrote from the neighbourhood of Antium to Atticus at Rome.

9. Viaticum Crassipes praeripit, 'the expenses of Tullia's betrothal to Furius Crassipes will require all the money I might spend on travelling.' Cicero had thought of travelling under the pretext of a 'votiva legatio.' Cp. Ad Att. 4. 2, 6. On Tullia's betrothal, cp. § 2 of the preceding letter.

De via recta in hortos. Boot thinks the words are a quotation from a letter of Atticus to Cicero, asking him on his arrival at Rome ('de via') to come at once ('recta') to the gardens, which would be in the suburbs. Cicero preferred to spend the first night at Atticus' house in Rome (videtur commodius ad te, sc. 'me ire'), and to visit the gardens next day ('postridie'). For the expression 'recta,' cp. De Off. 3. 20, 80 'Marius a subselliis in rostra recta.'

10. Quid enim tua? sc. 'refert.'

11. Tui, 'your slaves' or freedmen. Dionysius and Menophilus are mentioned as engaged in such work. Ad Att. 4. 8 a, 2—a reference which I owe to Manutius.

Pinxerunt, 'have ornamented,' Forcell.

12. Constrictione, 'constrictio'='actus constringendi.' Forcell. Perhaps this means 'by fastening my books in cases.'

Sittybis, 'cases' of parchment, for keeping rolls of papyrus or parchment clean. Cp. Smith's Dict. of Antiq., sub voc. 'liber,' p. 704. Boot reads 'sillybis,' 'with titles' printed on slips of parchment. Cp. Ad Att. 4. 4 b, 1. This perhaps makes better sense. The best MS. has 'sit tybis.'

26. To P. LENTULUS SPINTHER (AD FAM. I. 7).
ROME, MAY OR JUNE (?), 56 B.C. (698 A.U.C.)

1. I am glad you are satisfied with my conduct towards you, and pleased with my letters. 2. It is difficult to describe how individuals behave towards you; but you have many jealous rivals, as I had. Hortensius, Lucullus, and L. Racilius are among your warmest friends. 3. Pompey was not in the senate when your affairs were under consideration; your recent letter to him has done much to promote a good understanding between you, and 4. you may consider what I write to have his sanction.[1] We suggest, then, that you should go to Alexandria with a proper force, and secure and pacify Egypt; the king could then return, and a breach of the senate's decrees would be avoided. 5. We think, however, that you should not attempt this without a sure prospect of success; and you can judge better than we can of the probabilities of the case. 6. If you think this plan dangerous, there may be another way; but you will be best able to judge. 7. I thank you for your congratulations on my present position, to my attainment of which you have so largely contributed; but you must know that the perversity of certain nobles has compelled me to change my policy. 8. They treat you no better; and this shews me that it has not been simply as an upstart that I have met with so much envy. 9. I entreat you to devote yourself to that pursuit of glory which you have so long followed; great things are expected of you, and I hope that in your provincial administration you will have regard to your future position at Rome. 10. In politics, a violent, but unequal, struggle is going on; the mistakes of the optimates have made the side which has might seem to have right also. The senate has granted Caesar all his requests. I do not dwell on this unpleasant topic, but mention it, that you may combine caution with independence. 11. I thank you for your congratulations on my daughter's engagement. Your son is everything you can wish, and I hope you will train him to resemble his father.

M. CICERO S. D. P. LENTULO PROCOS.

1 Legi tuas litteras, quibus ad me scribis gratum tibi esse, quod crebro certior per me fias de omnibus rebus et meam erga te benevolentiam facile perspicias: quorum alterum mihi, ut te plurimum diligam, facere necesse est, si volo is esse, quem tu me esse voluisti; alterum facio libenter, ut, quoniam intervallo locorum et temporum diiuncti sumus, per litteras tecum

MAY. From § 11 we learn that Cicero had already received Lentulus' congratulations, sent from Cilicia on his daughter's betrothal to Crassipes, which took place on April 4th. Cp. Ad Q. F. 2. 5. 1, and see Guiraud, César et le sénat, p. 83.

3. **Alterum .. facere** refers rather irregularly to the action suggested by **benevolentiam**; and to make the sense clearer **ut te plurimum diligam** is added in explanation: **alterum facio** refers in like manner to the action on Cicero's part implied in **certior .. fias**, and the following words are again added in explanation. Perhaps the sense of the whole passage **quorum .. colloquar** may be given as follows: 'but I must needs love you if I am not to be ungrateful, and it is a pleasure to converse with you by letter. On neither ground can I claim gratitude from you.'

4. **Is esse .. voluisti**, 'to be worthy of the position which I owe to your aid.' Manut.

5. **Quem tu me esse voluisti**, 'such as you wished I should be' when you promoted my recall from exile.

quam saepissime colloquar. Quod si rarius fiet quam tu exspectabis, id erit causae, quod non eius generis meae litterae sunt, ut eas audeam temere committere: quotiens mihi certorum hominum potestas erit, quibus recte dem, non praetermittam. Quod scire vis, qua quisque in te fide sit et voluntate, difficile 2
dictu est de singulis: unum illud audeo, quod antea tibi saepe significavi, nunc quoque re perspecta et cognita scribere, vehementer quosdam homines et eos maxime, qui te et maxime debuerunt et plurimum iuvare potuerunt, invidisse dignitati tuae, simillimamque in re dissimili tui temporis nunc et nostri quondam fuisse rationem, ut, quos tu rei publicae causa laeseras, palam te oppugnarent, quorum auctoritatem, dignitatem voluntatemque defenderas, non tam memores essent virtutis tuae quam laudis inimici. Quo quidem tempore, ut perscripsi ad te antea, cognovi Hortensium percupidum tui, studiosum Lucullum, ex magistratibus autem L. Racilium et fide et animo singulari. Nam nostra propugnatio ac defensio dignitatis tuae propter magnitudinem beneficii tui fortasse plerisque officii maiorem auctoritatem habere videatur quam sententiae. Praeterea quidem de 3
consularibus nemini possum aut studii erga te aut officii aut amici animi esse testis: etenim Pompeium, qui mecum saepissime non solum *a* me provocatus, sed etiam sua sponte de te communicare

1. Quod = 'et hoc.' Cp. Madv. 448.

2. Id . . causae = 'ea causa.' Cp. Madv. 285 b.

3. Temere = 'cuivis,' 'to any one who offers.' Cp. pp. 41, 45 for Cicero's caution in this matter.

Certorum, 'trustworthy.' Forcell.

4. Potestas erit, 'I shall have at my command.' Cp. Ad Att. 16. 16 E, 1 'potestas eius rei;' also the expression 'potestatem sui facere,' of magistrates granting access to themselves, p. 101, note on l. 11.

Recte. Cp. Ep. 20, 1, note.

Praetermittam, sc. 'dare' or 'scribere.'

5. Quod scire vis, 'as to your wish to know.' Cp. Madv. 398 b, Obs. 2.

7. Significavi, 'pointed out to you.'

8. Quosdam, 'consulares, videtur significare.' Manut. I should hardly have thought the reference so general.

Et maxime debuerunt, sc. 'iuvare.' On the order of the words, cp. Madv. 473 a, b.

10. In re dissimili. Cp. § 8, 'gaudeo tuam dissimilem fuisse fortunam.'

Tui temporis, 'your time of need.' Cp. Pro Planc. 31, 79.

Nunc, sc. 'esse.'

12. Quorum auctoritatem, 'while those whose influence.' For the omission of a conjunction, cp. Madv. 437, d, Obs.

15. Percupidum. This word seems not to occur elsewhere.

16. Magistratibus. On the application of this term to the tribunes of the commons, cp. Ep. 20, 6, note.

L. Racilium. One of the tribunes for this year. Cp. Ep. 21, 4, note.

17. Nam introduces and answers an objection: 'I say nothing of myself, for—.' Cp. p. 70, l. 2, note.

18. Fortasse . . . sententiae, 'may seem to have more importance as a discharge of duty, than as an impartial expression of opinion.' Hofm.

19. Praeterea, 'with these exceptions.'

22. Provocatus, 'invited,' 'drawn out.'

Communicare. More usually active than neuter.

solet, scis temporibus illis non saepe in senatu fuisse; cui quidem litterae tuae, quas proxime miseras, quod facile intellexerim, periucundae fuerunt. Mihi quidem humanitas tua vel summa potius sapientia non iucunda solum, sed etiam admirabilis visa est: virum enim excellentem et tibi tua praestanti in eum liberalitate devinctum, non nihil suspicantem propter aliquorum opinionem suae cupiditatis te ab se abalienatum, illa epistola retinuisti; qui mihi cum semper tuae laudi favere visus est, etiam ipso suspitiosissimo tempore Caniniano, tum vero lectis tuis litteris perspectus est a me toto animo de te ac de

4 tuis ornamentis et commodis cogitare. Qua re ea, quae scribam, sic habeto, me cum illo re saepe communicata de illius ad te sententia atque auctoritate scribere: quoniam senatus consultum nullum exstat, quo reductio regis [Alexandrini] tibi adempta sit, eaque, quae de ea scripta est, auctoritas, cui scis intercessum esse, ut ne quis omnino regem reduceret, tantam vim habet, ut magis iratorum hominum studium quam constantis senatus con-

1. **Temporibus illis**: cp. Ep. 23, 2. Pompey retired to his house for some time to avoid the violence of the followers of Clodius, and had also to attend to the supply of corn.

2. **Quod facile intellexerim**, 'as I can easily understand,' a modest expression. Cp. Madv. 350 b. Or perhaps, 'as I could easily perceive.' Metzg. Pompey's real feelings were not always easy to interpret; cp. Ep. 28, 7, note.

3. **Humanitas**, 'courtesy,' 'tact,' J.E.Y.

6. **Liberalitate.** Lentulus had proposed that Pompey should be commissioned to supply Rome with corn. Cp. Ep. 20, 7.

Non nihil . . abalienatum, 'entertaining a certain suspicion that you had been estranged from him because some people thought him grasping.' Pompey might fancy that Lentulus had heard reports of his eagerness to be employed in restoring Ptolemy.

8. **Retinuisti.** The word is rarely used in this way without some words to explain it. Cp. § 7 'in communi causa retinere.'

Cum semper . . tum vero, 'both always . . and especially.' Cp. Madv. 435 a, Obs. 3, and 437 d.

9. **Tempore Caniniano**, 'the time when Caninius was so active.' Cp. Ep. 22, 1 and 4. We learn from Plutarch (Pomp. 49) that Caninius proposed that Pompey should restore Ptolemy, but without an army.

10. **Perspectus est.** The impersonal construction would be more common. Cp. Madv. 400 c.

11. **Ea, quae scribam**, i.e. the whole passage from 'Quoniam senatus' to 'placere dixerunt.'

12. **Sic habeto**, 'be assured.' Cp. Ep. 30, 5; also Ad Fam. 2. 10. 1, and 16. 4. 4 'sic habeto neminem esse qui me amet quin idem te amet.' For the order of the words from **de illius** to **scribere**, cp. Madv. 467 a, and 469, Obs. 2. The indicatives **exstat . . habet** are curious, taken in connection with 'te perspicere posse.' Perhaps Cicero begins by using the actual words which Pompey would have used in a direct address, and then passes into the oratio obliqua, writing 'te perspicere posse' instead of 'tu perspicere potes.'

15. **Auctoritas**: cp. Ep. 22, 4, note. The proposal of Bibulus, mentioned above on pp. 166, 168, is perhaps referred to; but in neither passage is there mention of its having been vetoed by a tribune, **intercessum esse**.

16. **Ut ne quis . . reduceret.** These words depend upon 'auctoritas scripta est.'

Tantam, 'only so much,' 'so little.' Cp. Ep. 15, 7, note.

Ut magis . . videatur, 'as to seem to express the party feelings of angry men rather than the fixed purpose of a consistent senate.'

silium esse videatur, te perspicere posse, qui Ciliciam Cyprumque teneas, quid efficere et quid consequi possis, et, si res facultatem habitura videatur, ut Alexandriam atque Aegyptum tenere possis, esse et tuae et nostri imperii dignitatis, Ptolemaide aut aliquo propinquo loco rege conlocato te cum classe atque exercitu proficisci Alexandriam, ut, eam cum pace praesidiisque firmaris, Ptolemaeus redeat in regnum; ita fore, ut et per te restituatur, quem ad modum senatus initio censuit, et sine multitudine reducatur, quem ad modum homines religiosi Sibyllae placere dixerunt. Sed haec sententia sic et illi et nobis probabatur, ut 8
ex eventu homines de tuo consilio existimaturos videremus: si cecidisset, ut volumus et optamus, omnes te et sapienter et fortiter, si aliquid esset offensum, eosdem illos et cupide et temere fecisse dicturos. Qua re quid adsequi possis, non tam facile est nobis quam tibi, cuius prope in conspectu Aegyptus est, iudicare. Nos quidem hoc sentimus, si exploratum tibi sit posse te illius regni potiri, non esse cunctandum; si dubium sit, non esse conandum. Illud tibi adfirmo, si rem istam ex sententia gesseris, fore ut absens a multis, cum redieris ab omnibus, conlaudere. Offensionem esse periculosam propter inter-

1. Te perspicere posse. The apodosis of the sentence begins here, and its structure changes to the indirect form, whence the conjunctive mood is adopted in its dependent clauses.

Cyprum. Cyprus was annexed to Cilicia in 58 B.C. under a 'lex Clodia.' Manut. Cp. Intr. to Part I, p. 30.

2. Si res . . videatur . . possis, 'if the state of things seems likely to give you an opportunity of maintaining Alexandria and Egypt.'

3. Habitura = 'adiutura.' Forcell. Cp. De Prov. Cons. 4. 9 'adversus in Syriam primus equitatus habuit interitum.'

4. Ptolemaide. Either Acre in Palestine or a city of Cyrenaica is referred to. The *former* would be more upon Lentulus' route to Egypt; the latter nearer to Alexandria.

6. Ut, eam cum . . firmaris, 'that, when you have restored order there, and secured the place with garrisons.' On the position of 'cum,' cp. Madv. 465 b; and for the zeugma 'pace praesidiisque,' Ib. 478, Obs. 4, and Zumpt 775.

8. Initio. Apparently in a decree passed 57 B.C., providing that the next governor of Cilicia should restore Ptolemy. Cp. Ep. 21, 3, note; Dion Cassius 39. 12-16; Plut. Pomp. 49.

9. Religiosi, 'scrupulous,' 'superstitious.' The king would not appear at Alexandria till after the army had done its work, and so the oracle forbidding him to be brought back 'multitudine,' would be obeyed to the letter, as he might travel to Alexandria with a small retinue.

10. Sic . . ut . . videremus, 'while we approve this arrangement, we saw.' 'Ita' is more common in this sense. Cp. Zumpt, L. G., 726.

11. Si cecidisset . . optamus, 'if the issue were such as we wish and pray for.' On the plup. 'cecidisset,' cp. Madv. 379.

16. Exploratum, 'certain.' Forcell.

17. Si dubium sit, 'but if it be doubtful.' 'Sin' would be more common.

19. Cum redieris. On the omission of a conjunction, cp. Ep. 21, 3, note.

20. Offensionem, 'any mishap.' Cp. 'si aliquid esset offensum' a line or two above; also 'offensionibus belli' Pro Leg. Man. 10, 28.

Propter interp. auctor. religionemque, 'on account of the expression of the

positam auctoritatem religionemque video; sed ego te, ut ad
certam laudem adhortor, sic a dimicatione deterreo redeoque ad
illud, quod initio scripsi, totius facti tui iudicium non tam ex
6 consilio tuo quam ex eventu homines esse facturos. Quod si
haec ratio rei gerendae periculosa tibi esse videbitur, placebat 8
illud, ut, si rex amicis tuis, qui per provinciam atque imperium
tuum pecunias ei credidissent, fidem suam praestitisset, et auxiliis
eum tuis et copiis adiuvares; eam esse naturam et regionem
provinciae tuae, ut illius reditum vel adiuvando confirmares, vel
neglegendo impedires. In hac ratione quid res, quid causa, quid
tempus ferat, tu facillime optimeque perspicies; quid nobis placu-
7 isset, ex me potissimum putavi te scire oportere. Quod mihi
de nostro statu, de Milonis familiaritate, de levitate et imbecillitate Clodii gratularis, minime miramur te tuis ut egregium
artificem praeclaris operibus laetari: quamquam est incredibilis
hominum perversitas—graviore enim verbo uti non libet—, qui

senate's opinion, and the religious difficulty which has intervened.'

1. **Ut ad certam . . deterreo**, 'while I exhort you to seize any safe opportunity of winning fame, I dissuade you earnestly from entering on a dangerous struggle.' Cp. a few lines above. 'Si exploratum . . omittendum.' For this sense of 'deterreo,' cp. Ep. 5, 6.

3. **Initio**, i.e. in the beginning of this section.

Ex consilio, 'by the policy, or object.' Cp. Philipp. 1. 1, 1 'consilium profectionis et revertendi meae.'

5. **Placebat** makes equally good sense if understood as the epistolary or as the ordinary imperfect.

6. **Si rex . . praestitisset**, 'if the king shall have fulfilled his promises to your friends.' The plup. depends on 'placebat.' Cp. Madv. 379.

Per provinciam atque imperium tuum, 'in the province under your government.' Cp. Ad Fam. 13. 55, 2 'in tuo toto imperio atque provincia.'

7. **Auxiliis eum tuis**. For the position of 'tuis,' cp. Livy 6. 26, 2 'precibus eventum vestris senatus quem videbitur dabit;' also Madv. 467, and 472 a.

Auxiliis . . adiuvares, 'place men and supplies at his disposal.' Lentulus might connive at Ptolemy's raising men in his province, without being personally compromised.

8. **Eam esse** depends on some verb to be supplied from 'placebat,' and meaning 'we thought.'

Regionem, 'the situation.' The word hardly seems to be used elsewhere in quite this sense.

9. **Ut illius reditum . . impedires**, 'that your aid would secure his return, and your neglect hinder it.' The imperfects seem to have almost the force of 'confirmare vel impedire posses.'

10. **Quid res . . ferat**, 'what the nature of the case, the king's interest (cp. Ep. 21, 1), and the course of events suggest.' Süpfle proposes to render **res**, 'the case in itself;' **causa**, 'its relation to other people;' **tempus**, 'the crisis.'

13. **De nostro statu**. For an account of Cicero's position at this time, cp. Intr. to Part II, §§ 3-6.

De Milonis familiaritate. Milo had exerted himself much in Cicero's cause during his banishment, and Cicero was now doing his best to requite him. Cp. Intr. to Part I, § 23; Ep. 23, 1, note.

Levitate et imbecillitate, 'the unprincipled, but futile efforts.' On the meaning of 'levitas,' cp. supra, p. 53, note on l. 9.

14. **Te tuis . . laetari**: cp. Intr. to Part I, § 23, for Lentulus' services to Cicero; also Ep. 18, 2.

15. **Quamquam**, 'and yet.' Cp. Madv. 443.

16. **Hominum perversitas**: cp. Epp. 20, 8; 25, 1 for similar complaints.

nos, quos ſavendo in communi causa retinere potuerunt, invi-
dendo abalienarunt; quorum malevolentissimis obtrectationibus
nos scito de vetere illa nostra diuturnaque ſententia prope iam
esse depulsos, non nos quidem ut nostrae dignitatis simus obliti,
sed ut habeamus rationem aliquando etiam salutis. Poterat
utrumque praeclare, si esset fides, si gravitas in hominibus consularibus; sed tanta est in plerisque levitas, ut eos non tam
constantia in re publica nostra delectet, quam splendor offendat.
Quod eo liberius ad te scribo, quia non solum temporibus his, 8
quae per te sum adeptus, sed iam olim nascenti prope nostrae
laudi dignitatique ſavisti, simulque quod video, non, ut antehac
putabam, novitati esse invisum meae; in te enim, homine omnium nobilissimo, similia invidorum vitia perspexi, quem tamen
illi esse in principibus ſacile sunt passi, evolare altius certe
noluerunt. Gaudeo tuam dissimilem ſuisse ſortunam; multum
enim interest, utrum laus imminuatur an salus deseratur. Me
meae tamen ne nimis paeniteret, tua virtute perfectum est;
curasti enim, ut plus additum ad memoriam nominis nostri
quam demptum de ſortuna videretur. Te vero emoneo cum 9
beneficiis tuis, tum amore incitatus meo, ut omnem gloriam,
ad quam a pueritia inflammatus ſuisti, omni cura atque industria consequare magnitudinemque animi tui, quam ego semper
sum admiratus semperque amavi, ne umquam inflectas cuius-

3. **Sententia**, 'principle' or 'maxim,' apparently.

4. **Non nos quidem . . obliti**, 'not indeed so far as to have forgotten my dignity.' For the position of 'quidem,' cp. Madv. 489 b.

5. **Poterat**, sc. 'fieri,' 'both objects might have been secured very well.' For the ellipse, cp. Ep. 22, 4; and for the mood and tense, 4, 1, note.

9. **Temporibus his**, 'my present fortunes.' Cp. Forcell. Madvig (Advers. Crit. II. 233) thinks the passage unintelligible as it stands, and suggests 'temporibus *iis gravem per te salutem* sum adeptus.'

10. **Iam olim**. Our notices of Cicero's life do not inform us to what he here refers. Perhaps to services rendered him before his consulship.

11. **Non . . invisum meae**, 'that it was not my want of nobility which excited dislike.'

13. **Quem tamen . . noluerunt**, 'they did not so, however, object to your being among the chief men, though they did to your being *pre-eminent* among them.' For **evolare** in this sense, cp. De Orat. 2. 52, 209. Cicero means that Lentulus' enemies had been more moderate than his own.'

16. **Utrum laus . . deseratur**. Cicero had been allowed to go into exile; Lentulus was merely left unsupported in his desire to win fame by restoring Ptolemy.

17. **Meae**, sc. 'fortunae.'

18. **Curasti enim . . videretur**. The decrees passed for Cicero's recall at the suggestion of Lentulus had done more good to his reputation than his exile had done injury to his fortune.

19. **Emoneo**, 'I urgently recommend.' The word only occurs here, apparently, and Wesenb. suggests either 'et moneo et rogo' or 'admoneo.'

23. **Inflectas**, 'change' or 'renounce.' Cp. Pro Caec. 26, 73 'ius civile . . quod neque inflecti gratia . . possit.'

quam iniuria. Magna est hominum opinio de te, magna commendatio liberalitatis, magna memoria consulatus tui: haec profecto vides quanto expressiora quantoque illustriora futura sint, cum aliquantum ex provincia atque ex imperio laudis accesserit. Quamquam te ita gerere volo quae per exercitum atque imperium gerenda sunt, ut haec multo ante meditere, huc te pares, haec cogites, ad haec te exerceas sentiasque—id quod, quia semper sperasti, non dubito quin adeptus intellegas—te facillime posse obtinere summum atque altissimum gradum civitatis. Quae quidem mea cohortatio ne tibi inanis aut sine causa suscepta videatur, illa me ratio movit, ut te ex nostris eventis communibus admonendum putarem, ut considerares, in
10 omni reliqua vita quibus crederes, quos caveres. Quod scribis te velle scire, qui sit rei publicae status, summa dissensio est, sed contentio dispar; nam qui plus opibus, armis, potentia valent, profecisse tantum mihi videntur stultitia et inconstantia adversariorum, ut etiam auctoritate iam plus valerent. Itaque perpaucis adversantibus omnia, quae ne per populum quidem sine seditione se adsequi arbitrabantur, per senatum consecuti sunt; nam et stipendium Caesari decretum est et decem legati, et ne lege Sempronia succederetur facile perfectum est. Quod

Cuiusquam iniuria, 'owing to any one's wrong-doing.' Ablat. caus., cp. Madv. 255.

1. Magna . . commendatio liberalitatis, 'your liberality does much to recommend you.' Lentulus, as aedile, had given splendid entertainments. Cp. Cic. de Off. 2. 16, 57.

5. Expressiora, 'more visible.' 'Expressus' = 'manifestus.' Forcell.

6. Ut haec multo ante meditere, 'without forgetting to reflect on the impression your success will produce here.' See the preceding sentence. Mr. Jeans, however, if I understand him rightly, seems to refer 'haec' to the advice given above, §§ 4-6.

7. Huc te pares, 'make your preparations with a view to this.' Cicero probably means, risk no failure which may endanger your prospects at Rome.

Sentiasque . . intellegas, 'and feel what, as you have always hoped for it, I doubt not you perceive after success, that you can with the greatest ease'—i.e. without any perilous military exploits—'maintain the highest position in the State.' I have been reminded of the usual force of 'obtinere' by a note in Mr. Yonge's edition.

10. Cohortatio. His exhortation that Lentulus should always keep Rome in view.

11. Illa me ratio movit, foll.: cp. for the constr., Ep. 11, 2, note. 'I will tell you that my reason was, that I thought you ought to be warned by our common experience to be wary in the rest of your life.' For the force of 'ut' in the clause explaining 'illa ratio,' cp. Madv. 372 b, Obs. 6, and 374; also Ad Att. 1. 19. 4 'unam rationem non reiciebam, ut ager . . . emeretur.'

15. Contentio dispar, 'the dispute is between parties unequally matched.'

Qui plus . . valent, i.e. the triumvirs.

19. Adsequi seems to have the force of 'adsequi posse' or 'adsecuturos.' Cp. 'expediri' Ep. 16, 6.

20. Stipendium, 'money for the payment of his troops.'

Decem legati, the power of naming ten legates, an unusually large number. Perhaps this was connected with an increase of Caesar's army to ten legions. Cicero supported these votes in favour of Caesar. Cp. Intr. to Part II, § 6.

21. Lege Sempronia. C. Gracchus had got a law enacted, providing that the senate should in each year assign provinces to the consuls who should be elected for the

eo ad te brevius scribo, quia me status hic rei publicae non delectat: scribo tamen, ut te admoneam, quod ipse, litteris omnibus a pueritia deditus, experiendo tamen magis quam discendo cognovi, tu *ut* tuis rebus integris discas neque salutis nostrae rationem habendam nobis esse sine dignitate neque
dignitatis sine salute. Quod mihi de filia et de Crassipede 11
gratularis, agnosco humanitatem tuam speroque et opto nobis hanc coniunctionem voluptati fore. Lentulum nostrum eximia spe summae virtutis adulescentem cum ceteris artibus, quibus studuisti semper ipse, tum in primis imitatione tui fac erudias; nulla enim erit hac praestantior disciplina: quem nos, et quia tuus et quia te dignus est filius et quia nos diligit semperque dilexit, in primis amamus carumque habemus.

27. To C. IULIUS CAESAR, Proconsul of Gaul (AD FAM. VII. 5).

Rome, February or March, 54 B.C. (700 A.U.C.)

1. I am going to give you a proof of my confidence, by recommending Trebatius to you, whom I should certainly have taken with me had any foreign service been assigned me. 2. I recommend him the more readily, as while I was talking over the matter with Balbus, a letter from you arrived, inviting me to recommend any friend to you. 3. I can assure you honestly, that you will find him a man of blameless character and eminent legal attainments. I do not presume to suggest what you should do for him; only admit him to your friendship.

CICERO CAESARI IMP. S. D.

Vide, quam mihi persuaserim te me esse alterum non modo 1
in iis rebus, quae ad me ipsum, sed etiam in iis, quae ad meos

next year, before their election. Cp. Pro Balbo 27. 61. Hence, in this case, it might provide that the two Gaulish provinces should be given to the consuls for 55 B.C., on the conclusion of their year of office at Rome. This would of course imply Caesar's recall at the end of 55 B.C. No one could suppose from Cicero's language here, that he had actively supported Caesar's claims. Cp. Intr. ubi supra.

Quod . . brevius . . . salute, 'I write on this topic briefly, because of my discontent; but I do write, that you may learn from my warning to neglect neither dignity nor safety: a lesson I, with all my reading, have learned more from experience than from books.'

4. Tuis rebus integris, 'before you have suffered any disaster.'

6. De Crassipede: cp. Ep. 25. 3, note; and the note on the date of this letter, p. 181.

8. Lentulum, son of Cicero's present correspondent. Cp. Ep. 23. 1, note.

9. Artibus, 'accomplishments.' Cp. Ad Fam. I. 8, 3 'nostra . . studia . . litterarum.'

IMP. Caesar had probably been greeted as 'Imperator' by his soldiers in Gaul, and the senate may have confirmed the title. Cp. De Prov. Cons. 13. 32; note E. p. 123.

14. Te me esse alterum, 'that you are a second self to me.' Cp. De Amic. 21, 80 'tanquam alter idem,' and Aristot. Eth. Nic. 9. 9. 10 ἕτερον αὐτόν.

pertinent: C. Trebatium cogitaram, quocumque exirem, mecum ducere, ut eum meis omnibus studiis, beneficiis quam ornatissimum domum reducerem. Sed postea quam et Pompeii commoratio diuturnior erat, quam putaram, et mea quaedam tibi non ignota dubitatio aut impedire profectionem meam videbatur aut certe tardare, vide, quid mihi sumpserim: coepi velle ea Trebatium exspectare a te, quae sperasset a me, neque mehercule minus ei prolixe de tua voluntate promisi, quam eram solitus

2 de mea polliceri. Casus vero mirificus quidam intervenit quasi vel testis opinionis meae vel sponsor humanitatis tuae: nam cum de hoc ipso Trebatio cum Balbo nostro loquerer accuratius domi meae, litterae mihi dantur a te, quibus in extremis scriptum erat: 'M. † itfiuium, quem mihi commendas, vel regem Galliae faciam, vel hunc † Leptae delega, si vis: tu ad me alium mitte, quem ornem.' Sustulimus manus et ego et Balbus: tanta fuit opportunitas, ut illud nescio quid non fortuitum, sed

1. **C. Trebatium.** This man is mentioned again (Ep. 62, 4; Ad Att. 9. 15. 6; 9. 17. 1), and there are several letters to him in this seventh book Ad Familiares. During the civil war between Caesar and Pompey, he seems to have tried to induce Cicero to be neutral.

Quocumque exirem. Cicero was legate to Pompey, and may have expected to have had some foreign service assigned him. Pompey still held his commission to supply Rome with corn (cp. Ep. 20, 7), and had been invested with the government of the two Spanish provinces, by a Lex Trebonia of this year (cp. Intr. to Part II, §§ 1; 8).

2. **Studiis, beneficiis.** On the asyndeton, cp. Madv. 434.

3. **Commoratio,** 'delay in leaving Rome.'

4. **Quaedam . . dubitatio,** 'a certain hesitation, of which you know the grounds.' Cicero was unwilling to renounce his close observation of Clodius.

5. **Videbatur,** apparently, 'seemed likely.'

7. **Exspectare.** For the infin. after 'velle' and similar verbs, cp. Madv. 396.

8. **Minus . . prolixe,** 'in less ample terms.' Verbs of promising are not uncommonly used intransitively with an adverb, or with an ablative after 'de,' instead of transitively, with an accusative. Nägelsbach (116, 319; 145, 415) gives several instances. Cp. also Süpfle's note.

10. **Opinionis,** 'my opinion of your feelings.'

Humanitatis, '*friendliness*.'

11. **Balbo.** L. Cornelius Balbus the elder is probably meant. He was a native of Gades, and acquired Roman citizenship by an act of Pompey, the validity of which Cicero maintained in a speech still extant. Balbus acquired great wealth in Caesar's service, and was now his financial agent at Rome. He was afterwards, in 40 B.C., the first consul of provincial extraction.

Accuratius, 'with much interest and care.' Forcell.

13. **M. itfiuium.** Wesenb. suggests 'Titinium.' A letter of Cicero to M. Titinius is quoted by Suetonius De Clar. Rhet. 2. Various names have been suggested—Furium, Rufum, Fulvium, Orfium, but it is difficult to identify any of them.

14. **Leptae delega,** 'refer him to Lepta for care and protection.' Wesenb. suggests 'delegabo,' and connects 'si vis' with what follows. Forcell. Q. Lepta is mentioned as 'praefectus fabrum' to Cicero in Cilicia (Ad Fam. 3. 20, 4: cp. Ad Att. 5. 17, 2), and may possibly have accompanied Q. Cicero from Caesar's camp to his brother's. Letters from Cicero to Lepta are found, Ad Fam. 6. 18 and 19.

15. **Sustulimus manus,** *i.e.* in wonder.

16. **Tanta . . opportunitas . . videretur,** 'so happy was the coincidence, that it seemed, shall I say? the proverbial intervention of Providence, not of fortune.' Cp. Philipp. 3. 10, 24 for the thought, though the expression is there used ironically. For this use of illud, cp. Madv. 485 b. c.

divinum videretur. Mitto igitur ad te Trebatium atque ita mitto, ut initio mea sponte, post autem invitatu tuo mittendum duxerim. Hunc, mi Caesar, sic velim omni tua comitate complectare, ut omnia, quae per me possis adduci ut in meos conferre velis, in unum hunc conferas; de quo tibi homine haec spondeo, non illo vetere verbo meo, quod, cum ad te de Milone scripsissem, iure lusisti, sed more Romano, quo modo homines non inepti loquuntur, probiorem hominem, meliorem virum, pudentiorem esse neminem; accedit etiam, quod familiam ducit in iure civili singulari memoria, summa scientia. Huic ego neque tribunatum neque praefecturam neque ullius beneficii certum nomen peto; benevolentiam tuam et liberalitatem peto, neque impedio, quo minus, si tibi ita placuerit, etiam hisce eum ornes gloriolae insignibus; totum denique hominem tibi ita trado, de manu, ut aiunt, in manum tuam istam et victoria et fide praestantem. Simus enim putidiusculi, quam per te vix licet; verum, ut video, licebit. Cura, ut valeas, et me, ut amas, ama.

2. **Invitatu.** A word apparently found here only.

4. **Possis.** For the mood, cp. on Ep. 21, 3.

6. **Non illo . . sed more Romano,** 'not with that old form which you rightly made sport of in Milo's case, but with Roman sincerity.' Cicero appears to have tried to reconcile Caesar to Milo, perhaps with a view to Milo's pretensions to the consulate. In writing to Caesar on the subject, he seems to have given Milo credit for qualities he did not possess, and to have been laughed at by Caesar for doing so. For the expression 'more Romano,' cp. Ad Fam. 7. 16, 3; 7. 18, 3.

9. **Quod familiam ducit,** 'that he is the head of his profession,' or 'of a school.' Cp. Philipp. 5. 11, 30. With a different punctuation the words might mean, 'which is most important.' Cp. de Fin. 4. 16, 45 'illam vestram sententiam quae familiam ducit,' and Manutius on this passage.

11. **Tribunatum,** 'the post of military tribune.'

Praefecturam, sociorum, castrorum, fabrorum.

Ullius beneficii certum nomen = 'ullum beneficium certum,' 'any definite distinction.' For the gen. defin. 'beneficii,' cp. Madv. 286.

14. **Gloriolae,** 'of a little glory.' Cp. Ad Fam. 5. 12, 9.

15. **De manu . . in manum,** 'from my hand direct to yours.' 'Quod in iis fit quae cara sunt et studiose servamus.' Forcell. Cp. Plaut. Trin. 4. 2. 57.

16. **Simus enim . . licebit,** 'let me be somewhat exacting, which your kindness ought to prevent, but will, I see, tolerate.'

Putidiusculi seems only to be found here. 'Putidum' means, 'in bad taste.' Cp. Ep. 7, 1.

28. To ATTICUS (AD ATT. IV. 15).

ROME, JULY, 54 B.C. (700 A.U.C.)

1. I am glad you have rewarded Eutychides with his freedom. 2. I approve of your journey to Asia, but be sure to return by the promised day. 3. I have written to you often and fully, but you seem not to have received all my letters, and I write so freely that this makes me rather uneasy. 4. The corruption of our courts has been lately shewn on the trials of Sufenas, Cato, and Procilius. I did not defend Procilius, out of consideration for Tullia, who feared a fresh breach with Clodius, his accuser. 5. A dispute between the citizens of Reate and Interamna took me lately to the former place; 6. on my return to Rome I was very well received in the theatre. 7. The great demand for money to be spent in bribery has actually doubled the rate of interest, and the result of the consular elections is very doubtful. 8. I will inform you of it if I hear in time. 9. I have plenty to do in pleading for clients of distinction. 10. Quintus, I suppose, is in Britain, and I feel rather anxious on his account, but his presence in Caesar's camp assures me the latter's friendship. Bid Dionysius come to me as soon as he can.

CICERO ATTICO SAL.

1 De Eutychide gratum, qui vetere praenomine, novo nomine
T. erit Caecilius, ut est ex me et ex te iunctus Dionysius M.
Pomponius. Valde mehercule mihi gratum est Eutychidem tua
erga me benevolentia cognosse suam illam in meo dolore συμπά-
2 θειαν neque tum mihi obscuram neque post ingratam fuisse. Iter
Asiaticum tuum puto tibi suscipiendum fuisse; numquam enim
tu sine iustissima causa tam longe a tot tuis et hominibus et
rebus carissimis et suavissimis abesse voluisses. Sed humanitatem tuam amoremque in tuos reditus celeritas declarabit; sed vereor ne lepore suo *te* detineat diutius rhetor Clodius et homo pereruditus, ut aiunt, et nunc quidem deditus Graecis litteris Pituanius. Sed, si vis homo esse, recipe te ad nos, ad quod

1. **De Eutychide.** Eutychides was a slave emancipated by Atticus, who took his master's old praenomen Titus with the nomen Caecilius which Atticus received on adoption by his uncle.

Gratum, sc. 'est quod fecisti.'

2. **Dionysius,** another freedman of Atticus (see § 10, note), received the name Marcus Pomponius on emancipation, out of compliment to Cicero.

3. **Tua . . benevolentia,** 'by your granting him his freedom as a favour to me.'

4. **συμπάθειαν.** I do not know to what Cicero here refers; perhaps to some services of Eutychides at the time of his exile.

5. **Iter Asiaticum.** Probably a journey to look after some money owing to Atticus in Asia.

10. **Rhetor Clodius:** so Orell. The best MS., which Baiter follows, has 'praetor,' but that seems unintelligible. A Sicilian rhetorician named Sex. Clodius is mentioned (Philipp. 2. 17, 43; cp. 2. 39, 101), but why he should accompany Atticus on this journey it is hard to see.

11. **Graecis litteris.** Boot thinks that Cicero refers to accounts, which would naturally be drawn up in Greek often in the East; or it may mean 'Greek papers,' as referring to business with Greeks.

12. **Pituanius.** Nothing seems to be known of this man.

tempus confirmasti; cum illis tamen, cum salvi venerint, Romae
vivere licebit. Avere te scribis accipere aliquid a me litterarum : 3
dedi, ac multis quidem de rebus, ἡμερολεγδὸν perscripta omnia;
sed, [ut coniicio,] quoniam mihi non videris in Epiro diu fuisse,
redditas tibi non arbitror. Genus autem mearum ad te quidem
litterarum eius modi fere est, ut non libeat cuiquam dare, nisi
de quo exploratum sit tibi eum redditurum. Nunc Romanas res 4
accipe: a. d. III. Nonas Quinctiles Sufenas et Cato absoluti,
Procilius condemnatus; ex quo intellectum est τρισαρειοπαγίτας
ambitum, comitia, interregnum, maiestatem, totam denique rem
publicam flocci non facere. Debemus patrem familias domi suae
occidere nolle, neque tamen id ipsum abunde; nam absolverunt
XXII., condemnarunt XXVIII. Publius sane diserto epilogo crimi-
nans mentes iudicum commoverat. Hortalus in ea causa fuit,
cuius modi solet. Nos verbum nullum. Verita est enim pusilla,
quae nunc laborat, ne animum Publii offenderem. His rebus 5

Homo, 'a man of your word.' 'Homo' is here used as a term of praise. Cp. 'quoniam est homo et nos diligit' Ad Att. 10. 11, 5; also Ep. 104. 2.

1. Cum illis, 'with Clodius and Pitusnius.'

Tamen, 'even if you leave them behind you in Asia.'

Cum salvi venerint, 'after their safe return to Rome.' 'Cum' almost = 'si.' Cp. Ep. 58, 1, note.

3. ἡμερολεγδόν, 'day by day.' Cp. Aesch. Pers. 63.

8. Sufenas. A cognomen of the 'gens Nonia.' The man here mentioned was perhaps the same as one whose name occurs Ad Att. 8. 15, 3 as that of a man who then held 'imperium.' A M. Nonius is mentioned Att. 6. 1, 13 as holding some office in the provinces in 50 B.C. For an account of C. Cato, cp. Ep. 15, 15, note.

9. Procilius was colleague of the two former as tribune in 57–56 B.C., but nothing further seems to be known of him. All three seem to have been brought to trial for the violence of their official conduct, by which they had caused a postponement of the election of consuls, and rendered an interregnum necessary. Cp. Dion Cassius 39. 27; App. Bell. Civ. 2. 17; Abeken, p. 169. Cato, in particular, was charged with a violation of the Lex Iunia Licinia, which provided for due publicity in legislation, and of the Lex Fufia, which required due regard to be paid to the auspices. Cp. Ad Att. 4. 16, 5; 4. 17, 2. He was defended by C. Licinius Calvus and M. Aemilius Scaurus. Procilius was accused by P. Clodius, whose eloquence seems to have secured his conviction. I cannot find any explanation of the allusion in patrem familias . . nolle.

τρισαρειοπαγῖται, 'our right rigorous judges.' τρισ- seems more commonly used with adjectives than with substantives in this sense, in classical Greek. But τρισάνθρωπον is found, Diog. Laert. 6. 47. 'Ariopagitae' is used ironically, Ep. 8, 5.

11. Debemus . . . nolle. Wesenb. omits 'debemus' on some MS. authority apparently, and suggests 'occidi' for 'occidere.' This would improve the sense, by making τρισαρειοπαγῖται the subject of 'nolle' as well as of 'facere,' thus stating the inference as to the disposition of the judges which might be drawn both from the acquittal of others and from the condemnation of Procilius. 'Our judges deal leniently with bribery, but do not wish to leave murder unpunished.'

12. Abunde, 'decidedly.'

13. Publius, Clodius. Often so called in Cicero's letters. Cp. Ep. 12, 4.

Epilogo = 'peroratione.' The word is used in various passages by Cicero. Cp. Forcell.

14. Hortalus. The celebrated orator Q. Hortensius Hortalus. Cp. Ep. 14, 1.

15. Pusilla. Used, apparently, as a term of endearment for Cicero's daughter Tullia.

actis Reatini me ad sua Τέμπη duxerunt, ut agerem causam contra Interamnates apud consulem et decem legatos, quod lacus Velinus, a M'. Curio emissus, interciso monte, in Nar defluit; ex quo est illa siccata et humida tamen modice Rosia. Vixi cum Axio, qui etiam me ad Septem aquas duxit. Redii Romam Fonteii causa a. d. VII. Idus Quinct. Veni in spectaculum, primum magno et aequabili plausu—sed hoc ne curaris; ego ineptus, qui scripserim—; deinde Antiphonti operam: is erat ante manumissus quam productus. Ne diutius pendeas, palmam tulit; sed nihil tam pusillum, nihil tam sine voce, nihil tam . . . verum haec tu tecum habeto. In Andromacha tamen maior fuit quam Astyanax, in ceteris parem habuit neminem. Quaeris nunc de Arbuscula:

1. Τέμπη, i.e. the valley of the Velinus between Reate and Interamna; so called, apparently, as rivalling the Thessalian Tempe in beauty. The dispute was probably about the regulation of some of the channels through which the water was carried off. Cp. Pro Scauro 12, 27.

2. Decem legatos. Ten commissioners or assessors appointed to assist the consul in his judgment, but how appointed we cannot say. We here get a notice of some of the ordinary business of the consuls.

3. A. M'. Curio. These words have generally been supposed to refer to the conqueror of Pyrrhus, on whose great work, forming the cascade of Terni, cp. Mommsen 1. 463; Nieb. Rom. Hist. 3. 415. But, as Cicero seems to be referring to a recent grievance, Zumpt supposed that a namesake of M'. Curius, living nearer to Cicero's time, was the author of the work here referred to. Cp. Smith's Dict. of Biogr. 1. 902, sub nom. 'Dentatus.' This seems needless, for perhaps the words quod . . defluit are merely inserted to remind Atticus of the relative position of the two places, and to shew the probability of quarrels arising.

Ex quo est . . Rosia, 'since when the famous Rosia has been drained, though it still retains some moisture.' The plain called Rosia or Rosea was one of notorious fertility, and consisted, probably, in part of land reclaimed from the lake Velinus. Cp. Tac. Ann. 1. 79. On the occasion referred to in that passage, the people of Reate protested against an obstruction of the course of the Velinus, and may now have desired Cicero's aid to avert a similar measure. Mr. Jeans says that 'at Rieti is still shewn a mutilated statue, said to be erected by the people in honour of Cicero's services in this very trial.'

4. Cum Axio. Axius was a wealthy Roman senator. Cp. Ad Att. 10. 11, 2; Varro de R. R. 3, 3.

5. Septem aquas. Some springs, distant about five miles from the lake. Axius may have had another villa there. The Septem aquae are mentioned by Dionys. Hal. Rom. Ant. 1. 14.

Fonteii. M. or M'. Fonteius, propraetor of Gallia Narbonensis from 77 to 75 B.C., was defended by Cicero in 69 B.C., on a charge of maladministration. Pomptini has been suggested, as C. Pomptinus triumphed over the Allobroges. Cp. Ad Att. 4. 16, 12; Ad Q. F. 3. 4, 6.

7. Aequabili, 'uniform,' 'general.' Manutius suggests 'unmixed with hisses.'

8. Antiphonti. Possibly a freedman of Milo. It was not, apparently, usual to give slave actors their freedom till after proof of their talent: Antiphon, therefore, was greatly favoured.

Operam, sc. 'dedi.'

10. Pusillum, 'mean,' 'insignificant.'

11. In Andromacha, 'in the character of Andromache,' which he filled in a play of Ennius so named. This shews that men took female parts in tragedy at Rome.

Maior, either 'taller,' or 'more important.'

Quam Astyanax. The best MS. has 'quam Astya,' which Schütz supposes to be the name of another actor.

12. Parem. The context seems to require some word meaning 'equally bad.' Cicero may be writing ironically.

Arbuscula, a well-known female dancer. Cp. Hor. Sat. 1. 10, 77, and Orelli's note.

valde placuit. Ludi magnifici et grati. Venatio in aliud tempus 7
dilata. Sequere nunc me in campum: ardet ambitus; *σῆμα δέ τοι ἐρέω*. Faenus ex triente Idibus Quinctilibus factum erat bessibus. Dices 'istuc quidem non moleste fero.' O virum! O civem! Memmium Caesaris omnes opes confirmant; cum eo Domitium consules iunxerunt, qua pactione, epistolae committere non audeo. Pompeius fremit, queritur, Scauro studet; sed utrum fronte an mente, dubitatur. Ἐξοχὴ in nullo est; pecunia omnium dignitatem exaequat. Messalla languet, non quo aut animus desit aut amici, sed coitio consulum *et* Pompeius obsunt. Ea comitia puto fore ut ducantur. Tribunicii candidati iurarunt se arbitrio Catonis

1. Ludi, 'Apollinares in Circo.' Billerb.

Venatio. The fights with wild animals; spectacles for which Cicero had no taste. Cp. Ad Fam. 7. 1. 3; also Ep. 9. 1.

2. In campum, sc. 'Martium,' 'to the scene of the elections.'

Σῆμα δέ τοι ἐρέω μάλ' ἀριφραδές, οὐδέ σε λήσει.—Hom. Il. 23. 326.

3. Faenus . . bessibus. The rate of interest called 'centesimae usurae,' was one per cent. per month; one 'as' for every hundred 'asses' per month. Lower rates of interest were expressed by taking fractions of the 'as,' as though for one per cent. per month the expression 'asses usurae,' instead of 'centesimae usurae,' had been used. Thus, if 'asses usurae' = 1 per cent. per month = 12 per cent. per year.

trientes = ⅓ per cent. per month = 4 per year
besses = ⅔ ,, ,, = 8 ,,

Cicero (Ad Att. 1. 12, 1) complains that he cannot borrow from a particular money-lender at a lower rate than 'centesimae,' and in another passage (Ad Fam. 5. 6, 2) says, 'omnino semissibus magna copia est.'—I think, therefore, that there is no difficulty in taking the words 'triente' and 'bessibus' here in their ordinary sense, though the rates seem rather lower than might be expected to have prevailed when the demand for money was great. Nor can I see how Dean Merivale (1. 441) gets the meaning '8 per cent. per month' out of the words.—I have been led to reconsider my opinion on this passage by Mr. J. R. King's remarks in the Academy for Feb. 15. 1871.

5. Memmium: cp. Ep. 15, 16, note.

Domitium: cp. Ep. 23. 6.

6. Consules. The consuls, Appius Claudius Pulcher and L. Domitius Ahenobarbus, agreed to support C. Memmius and Cn. Domitius. For an account of the pactio here referred to, cp. Ad Att. 4. 18, 2 'consules flagrant infamia, quod C. Memmius candidatus pactionem in senatu recitavit, quam ipse et suus competitor Domitius cum consulibus fecissent, uti ambo H.S. quadragenа consulibus darent, si essent ipsi consules facti, nisi tres augures dedissent, qui se adfuisse dicerent, cum lex curiata ferretur, quae lata non esset, et duo consulares, qui se dicerent in ornandis provinciis consularibus scribendo adfuisse, cum omnino ne senatus quidem fuisset.' Cp. Merivale 1. 439, 440.

7. Utrum fronte an mente. For the expression, cp. Ep. 29. 17, and on Pompey's dissimulation in general, Ad Att. 4. 9. 1, 'ut loquebatur;' Ad Fam. 8. 1. 3, 'solet enim aliud sentire et loqui.' That men's doubts were justified in this instance we learn from Ad Q. F. 3. 8, 3 'Scaurum . . iampridem Pompeius abiecit.' The Scaurus here referred to was a M. Aemilius Scaurus, of whom little is known, except that Cicero defended him on a charge of 'repetundae,' in a speech of which large fragments remain. Cp. § 9, note.

8. Ἐξοχή, 'distinction,' 'eminence.'

9. Messalla: cp. Intr. to Part II, §§ 11; 13; Ep. 33. 1, note.

Non quo aut animus . . obsunt. For the combination of the indicative expressing a real reason, with the conjunctive giving an imaginary reason, cp. Madv. 357 b, Obs.

11. Ducantur, 'be delayed.' Cp. Ep. 88, 2 'bellum ducere.' Cicero's expectations were fulfilled, as the year 53 B.C. opened with a succession of interregna. Cp. Intr. to Part II, § 13.

Tribunicii candidati . . tribueretur. This bond is also mentioned, Ad Q. F. 2. 15 b (Baiter 14), 4.

Se . . petituros, 'that they will submit their conduct as candidates to the judgment of Cato.' I cannot agree with Mr. Jeans

petituros: apud eum HS. quingena deposuerunt ut, qui a Catone
6 damnatus esset, id perderet et competitoribus tribueretur. Haec
ego pridie scribebam, quam comitia fore putabantur; sed ad te,
quinto Kal. Sextil. si facta erunt et tabellarius non erit profectus,
tota comitia perscribam, quae si, ut putantur, gratuita fuerint, plus
9 unus Cato potuerit quam *omnes leges* omnesque iudices. Messius defendebatur a nobis de legatione revocatus; nam eum Caesari legarat Appius. Servilius edixit ut adesset. Tribus habet Pomptinam, Velinam, Maeciam. Pugnatur acriter; agitur tamen satis. Deinde me expedio ad Drusum, inde ad Scaurum: parantur orationibus indices gloriosi. Fortasse accedent etiam consules designati,
10 in quibus si Scaurus non fuerit, in hoc iudicio valde laborabit. Ex

that the words mean 'only to go to the poll if approved by Cato.'

3. Scribebam, epistolary tense. The election of tribunes seems to have taken place in July. Cp. Ep. 31, 2. Wesenb. suggests the addition of 'ea' after 'comitia'—'ea' = tribunicia.

5. Ut putantur, sc. 'futura.' For the personal use of the passive of 'puto,' cp. De Amic. 2, 6 'quia prudens . . putabatur.' The change of tense from 'putabantur' above is accounted for by the impression here mentioned not being entertained on one day only. Cp. Madv. 345.

Gratuita, 'pure from bribery.' Cp. Pro Planc. 22. 54 'gratuita suffragia.'

6. Messius: cp. Ep. 20, 7, note.

7. Revocatus, 'summoned back for trial.' Schütz following Manutius, who adds 'a propinquis ut opinor, aut ab amicis,' seems to think that the 'legatio' would protect him against such a summons, but Billerb. and Merivale (1. 437) do not agree with him.

8. Legarat = 'legatum assignarat' (Forcell.), 'had got him a post as legate.'

Appius. Probably cos. 54 B.C. Servilius, one of the praetors for this year. For an account of him, cp. Ep. 9. 10, note.

Tribus habet, 'the tribes from which his judges are to be taken are.' Cp. Intr. to Part II, § 8; Pro Planc. 15 and 16.

9. Agitur . . satis. Forcell. explains these words as = 'satagitur,' 'I have enough to do;' Manut. as = 'aliquid proficitur.'

10. Drusum. Perhaps father of the empress Livia. He was accused of 'praevaricatio,' or collusion with an opponent on a trial. Cp. Ad Att. 4. 16, 5 and 8; Ad Q. F. 2. 16, 3.

Scaurum: cp. Ad Att. 4. 16, 8; Ad. Q. F. 3. 1, 11 and 16. He was acquitted on a charge of 'repetundae.' Cp. the conclusion of Asconius' commentary on the oration Pro Scauro, p. 139; Ad Att. 4. 16, 7.

11. Indices: 'titles,' 'tables of contents.' The different 'volumina' of his speeches would naturally be distinguished by the names of the men for or against whom they were delivered. For the meaning of 'index,' cp. Ad Att. 4. 4 b. 1, where Cicero gives the Greek σιλλύβους as an equivalent for 'indices;' also, perhaps, Philipp. 1. 8, 20 'legis index.'

Gloriosi. This word is used in a good sense in various passages, e.g. Phil. 2. 12, 27. 'I am getting fine names to put on the volumes of my works;' or, perhaps, 'titles for my works which will do me honour.'

Accedent etiam consules designati, 'the consuls elect will perhaps be added to my clients.' Bribery has been so general, that the successful candidates, whoever they were, would probably be prosecuted. Calvinus and Messalla were actually successful. The year 54 B.C. closed without any election of consuls, and several interregna followed. Hence Messalla and Calvinus entered on their office at once, and there was no interval after their election in which the prosecutions with which they were threatened could be instituted. Cp. Ad Q. F. 3. 8, 3; Ad Att. 4. 16, 8; Intr. to Part II, § 13. Messalla was afterwards condemned in 51 B.C. See Ep. 33, 1.

12. In hoc . . laborabit, 'he will come off badly;' 'it will go very hard with him in his trial,' i.e. the one for which Cicero had promised his advocacy. Judges might be less willing to convict a consul elect, though he was not legally exempt from prosecution.

Ex Q. fratris litteris. Cicero's brother

Q. fratris litteris suspicor iam eum esse in Britannia: suspenso animo exspecto, quid agat. Illud quidem sumus adepti, quod multis et magnis iudiciis possumus iudicare nos Caesari et carissimos et iucundissimos esse. Dionysium velim salvere iubeas et eum roges et hortere, ut quam primum veniat, ut possit Ciceronem meum atque etiam me ipsum erudire.

29. To P. LENTULUS SPINTHER (AD FAM. I. 9).

Rome, Autumn, 54 B.C. (700 A.U.C.)

1. I was glad to learn from your letter that you were satisfied with my gratitude. I should be guilty indeed if I failed to do you any service in my power; and I wish you had been present to see how I understand my duty. 2. For your own sake I am glad that you now hold a post of high command, but your presence would have enabled us to act in concert, and to punish our enemies. One of them, however, has saved us the trouble; his mad attempts have made him harmless for the future. 3. You have learned, at less expense than I did, how to appreciate the good faith of certain people: and this brings me to your enquiries. 4. You do not complain of my reconciliation with Caesar and Appius; but wish to know why I pleaded for Vatinius. I must reply by a general exposition of my policy.

After my restoration from exile I thought myself peculiarly indebted, not only to you but to my country, and often expressed my sense of obligation both in public and in private, 5. though even then I perceived that some who ought to have been active in securing me compensation for my losses were lukewarm or jealous; 6. and though, as you often said, I was under great obligations to Pompey, I adhered to my old party. 7. In defending Sestius, I spoke with the greatest freedom in Pompey's presence, 8. and shewed equal firmness in the senate. On April 5, in the year before last, I gave notice of a motion which was a direct attack on the policy of Pompey and Caesar. This caused great agitation; and 9. Pompey, who at first shewed no displeasure, after a meeting with Caesar at Luca, remonstrated energetically with my brother in Sardinia, and reminded him of his promises on my behalf. 10. This news from my brother, and a demand from Pompey that I should keep myself unpledged as to the motion above referred to, made me reflect whether I ought not to think of private as well as of public

Quintus now held a high command in Caesar's army. Cp. Intr. to Part II, §§ 11; 13.

1. In Britannia. Caesar was in Britain from the spring till the early autumn of 54 B.C., after a shorter visit in the previous year. Cp. Ad Att. 4. 16, 13; Caes. Bell. Gall. 5. 8–23; Merivale 1. 471–476; Mommsen 4. 1, 257–260. Q. Cicero went with him. Cp. Ad Att. 4. 17, 3.

4. Dionysium. Three contemporaries of this name, at least, are mentioned in Cicero's letters: (1) a freedman of Atticus, see § 1; (2) the one here referred to; and (3) another literary slave of Cicero. In the earlier letters to Atticus, the first is often referred to; the second is often noticed in the later letters to Atticus, and was the teacher of the young Ciceros; the third is mentioned Ad Att. 9. 3, 1; Ad Fam. 5. 9, 2; 5. 10, 1, &c. Cp. Orelli's Onomasticon, sub nom.

Autumn. From the language of § 25 of this letter it seems that Appius was already looking forward to his provincial administration, and perhaps we may infer that the year of his consulship was drawing to its close.

duty. And I was farther influenced by the malicious pleasure which some of the optimates took in my estrangement from Pompey, and by the court which they paid to Clodius. 11. Still, if the leaders of the opposite party had been worthless men, nothing should have induced me to support them in any degree. But one of them was Pompey, whose public services had been most eminent; and I did not think I should be charged with inconsistency if I slightly changed my policy in favour of one to whose support I had devoted much of my life. 12. Thus I had to regard Caesar also with favour, as his cause was bound up with Pompey's: his old friendship with me and my brother and his recent liberality made me all the more disposed for such a course; and I thought that, after his great exploits, a struggle with him would have been mischievous to the State. I considered myself also pledged to some extent by what had passed between Caesar, Pompey, and my brother. I remembered a saying of Plato, and thought how it had been verified in our history, first by the senate's behaviour in the years between my consulship and Caesar's, 13. and afterwards in another way, by the real or affected alarm of some of my apparent friends. 14. I am aware that the latter afterwards did good service to me in procuring my restoration; 15. but afterwards they courted Clodius, and seemed to wish, by treating my just claims in a niggardly spirit, to prevent my asserting my independence. 16. In this they were misled by a mistaken inference from the case of Metellus Numidicus. 17. However, there has been no undue assumption about my behaviour; I only strive to serve such men as may be in need of my help.

The support I have given to Caesar is represented as a defection from my old party. But, my dear Lentulus, you will find the whole aspect of politics changed; 18. and wise citizens ought to change their views accordingly. Plato preferred to abstain from public life altogether; my position is different from his, and Caesar's public services and private liberality both give him a claim on my support. 19. I can now answer your questions about Vatinius and Crassus.—I was urged by Caesar to defend Vatinius, and my testimony on his behalf was not stronger than that which you have borne in favour of various people. I had a further reason for my conduct; my support of Vatinius was a fair retaliation for that which certain nobles gave to Clodius. 20. Crassus, after we had been reconciled, aroused my indignation by unexpectedly undertaking the defence of Gabinius and attacking me. But I heard that some people were exulting at the prospect of a permanent breach between us, and so I listened to the earnest entreaties of Pompey and Caesar that I would be reconciled to him. 21. I should probably have acted as I have done even if no personal reasons had intervened; but I will own that Caesar's remarkable gratitude and generosity have influenced me, and I need powerful protection against the plots of my enemies. 22. Had you been present you would, I think, have approved my conduct.

23. As you wish to see anything I may have written since your departure, I will send you a few speeches, a work called 'De Oratore,' in three books, and a poem in three books on my misfortunes. 24. I attend carefully to your interests here. Quintus will be very grateful if you can do anything to secure his property in your province. I shall be glad to hear any particulars about your private life and your son's studies. 25. Appius declares himself resolved to go at once as your successor to Cilicia, and I think you had better not delay your return, though others think differently.

26. P.S. I have just had your letter about your dispute with the 'publicani;' I wish you could have avoided it, but I approve and will defend your measures.

M. CICERO S. D. P. LENTULO IMP.

Periucundae mihi fuerunt litterae tuae, quibus intellexi te per- 1
spicere meam in te pietatem: quid enim dicam benevolentiam,
cum illud ipsum gravissimum et sanctissimum nomen pietatis
levius mihi meritis erga me tuis esse videatur? Quod autem tibi
grata mea erga te studia scribis esse, facis tu quidem abundantia
quadam amoris, ut etiam grata sint ea, quae praetermitti sine
nefario scelere non possunt; tibi autem multo notior atque
illustrior meus in te animus esset, si hoc tempore omni, quo
diiuncti fuimus, et una et Romae fuissemus. Nam in eo ipso, 2
quod te ostendis esse facturum quodque et in primis potes et ego
a te vehementer exspecto, in sententiis senatoriis et in omni
actione atque administratione rei publicae floruissemus: de qua
ostendam equidem paulo post, qui sit meus sensus et status, et
rescribam tibi ad ea, quae quaeris; sed certe et ego te auctore
amicissimo ac sapientissimo et tu me consiliario fortasse non
imperitissimo, fideli quidem et benevolo certe, usus esses:—quamquam tua quidem causa te esse imperatorem provinciamque bene
gestis rebus cum exercitu victore obtinere, ut debeo, laetor:—
sed certe qui tibi ex me fructus debentur, eos uberiores et praesentiores praesens capere potuisses. In eis vero ulciscendis, quos

IMP. See § 1, note.

4. Levius . . meritis, 'too weak to describe your claims upon me.'

5. Facis . . ut . . non possunt, 'you in your overflowing affection treat the barest discharges of duty as acts deserving of gratitude.'

8. Illustrior, 'more evident.'

Hoc tempore omni. Nearly three years, for Lentulus seems to have left Rome before the close of 57 B.C. Cp. Ep. 21, which seems to imply that he had not been present at any of the debates in the senate during January 56 B.C.

9. In eo ipso, 'in that course of action which you declare you will follow,' that is, in debate and legislation.

10. Quod . . in primis potes, sc. 'facere.'

11. Sententiis senatoriis, 'our expressions of opinion as senators.'

12. Actione . . rei publicae, 'in political action and administration.' For this sense of the gen. 'rei publicae,' cp. Nägelsb. 2, 21.

De qua, sc. 're publica.'

13. Meus sensus et status, 'my opinion and position.' Both were unfavourable, and hence the qualifying sed certe with which Cicero introduces his statement of the possible results of Lentulus' presence at Rome.

14. Ad ea quae quaeris. Lentulus had questioned Cicero as to some of his recent acts in support of the triumvirs. Cp. § 4.

Sed certe . . capere potuisses. The sense of this passage seems to be, 'Bad as the times were, we could have helped each other, and though I rejoice at the distinction you have won in your province, yet you would have enjoyed clearer and more abundant fruits of my gratitude had you been here.'

17. Te esse imperatorem, 'that you enjoy the title "imperator,"' which Lentulus had probably received for successes over some robber tribes who infested his province, as Cicero did afterwards. Cp. Ad Att. 5. 20, 3; Note E, p. 123.

19. Praesentiores. 'Praesens' is vari-

tibi partim inimicos esse intellegis propter tuam propugnationem
salutis meae, partim invidere propter illius actionis amplitudinem
et gloriam, mirificum me tibi comitem praebuissem: quamquam
ille perennis inimicus amicorum suorum, qui tuis maximis beneficiis ornatus in te potissimum fractam illam et debilitatam vim
suam contulit, nostram vicem ultus est ipse sese; ea est enim
conatus, quibus patefactis nullam sibi in posterum non modo
3 dignitatis sed ne libertatis quidem partem reliquit. Te autem
etsi mallem in meis rebus expertum quam etiam in tuis, tamen in
molestia gaudeo eam fidem cognosse hominum non ita magna
mercede, quam ego maximo dolore cognoram; de qua ratione tota
iam videtur mihi exponendi tempus dari, ut tibi rescribam ad ea,
4 quae quaeris. Certiorem te per litteras scribis esse factum me
cum Caesare et cum Appio esse in gratia, teque id non reprehendere adscribis; Vatinium autem scire te velle ostendis quibus
rebus adductus defenderim et laudarim. Quod tibi ut planius
exponam, altius paulo rationem consiliorum meorum repetam
necesse est. Ego me, Lentule, initio rerum atque actionum

ously explained as meaning 'evident' and 'effective.' Cp. Forcell. and Halm's note on In Cat. 3. 9. 21. Either sense would suit this passage very well.

1. Partim .. partim. The enemies of Lentulus either hated him for his support of Cicero's restoration, or, without any particular dislike to Cicero, envied Lentulus the distinction he had won by befriending him.

4. Ille perennis inimicus. These words are by some referred to C. Cato, by others to Ap. Claudius Pulcher.

6. Nostram vicem .. ipse sese, lit. 'has punished himself on our account;' 'has avenged our wrongs on himself and saved us trouble.' Cp. Mr. J. E. Yonge's note on this passage, and Livy 34. 32 'ne nostram vicem irascaris.'

Ea est enim .. reliquit. If C. Cato is meant, Cicero refers probably to his outrageous conduct as tribune for 56–55 B.C., for which he was afterwards tried but acquitted. Cp. § 4 of the preceding letter. If Ap. Claudius, to the bargain which he as consul made with two of the consular candidates for the next year. Cp. § 7 of the preceding letter, and note. It is hardly probable, however, that in either case the liberty of the offender would be endangered by a conviction, and if the allusion has been rightly explained, Cicero must have written with rhetorical exaggeration. This letter is one of the most elaborate in the whole collection.

8. Te autem .. cognoram, 'though I could wish you had learned from my experience only, I yet rejoice that your troubles have taught you what value to set on men's honour, without such heavy sufferings as those which taught me this lesson.'

10. Eam .. quam, = 'talem,' 'qualem,' Ep. 45. 3, note.

Non ita magna mercede, 'at a cost not so very high.' On the ablat., cp. Madv. 258. 'Ita' has no corresponding particle, cp. Philipp. 2. 42, 108 'non ita multis,' 'not so many'—though there is a general contrast with maximo dolore. On the thought, cp. Ep. 26, 8.

11. De qua ratione, 'about my whole position in this affair,' i.e. in his breach with the optimates, owing to a discovery of what he thought bad faith on their part.

12. Exponendi .. quae quaeris, 'of giving an explanation which should serve as an answer to your enquiries.'

15. Vatinium: cp. Intr. to Parts I, § 18; IV, §§ 4; 5; and Ad Q. F. 2. 16, 3. Cicero defended him in August, 54 B.C.

16. Laudarim, 'bore testimony to his character.'

17. Altius paulo, 'from a point somewhat remote.' Cp. De Legg. 1. 6, 18 'alte .. et .. a capite repetere.'

Rationem, 'the ground.'

18. Initio, abl. of time: see Madv. 276; and cp. Ep. 23. 2, note.

tuarum non solum meis sed etiam rei publicae restitutum putabam et, quoniam tibi incredibilem quendam amorem et omnia in te ipsum summa ac singularia studia deberem, rei publicae, quae te in me restituendo multum adiuvisset, cum certe me animum merito ipsius debere arbitrabar, quem antea tantum modo communi officio civium, non alicui erga me singulari beneficio debitum praestitissem. Hac me mente fuisse et senatus ex me te consule audivit et tu in nostris sermonibus collocutionibusque ipse vidisti. Etsi iam primis temporibus illis multis rebus meus 5
offendebatur animus, cum te agente de reliqua nostra dignitate aut occulta non nullorum odia aut obscura in me studia cernebam; nam neque de monumentis meis ab iis adiutus es, a quibus debuisti, neque de vi nefaria, qua cum fratre eram domo expulsus; neque hercule in iis ipsis rebus, quae quamquam erant mihi propter rei familiaris naufragia necessariae, tamen a me minimi putabantur, in meis damnis ex auctoritate senatus sarciendis eam voluntatem, quam exspectaram, praestiterunt. Quae cum viderem — neque erant obscura —, non tamen tam acerba mihi haec accidebant, quam erant illa grata, quae fecerant. Itaque quam- 6
quam et Pompeio plurimum, te quidem ipso praedicatore ac teste,

Actionum tuarum, 'of your exertions in my cause.'

3. **Deberem .. praestitissem.** The conjunctive is used because Cicero is describing a previous state of his own mind. Cp. Madv. 357 a, Obs. 1.

5. **Ipsius**, sc. 'reipublicae.'

Quem .. praestitissem, 'which I had displayed before in discharge of the common duty of citizens, not as a return for any special favour conferred upon me.'

7. **Senatus .. audivit**: cp. the orat. Post Red. in Sen.,—if it be genuine.

8. **Sermonibus collocutionibusque.** Forcell. seems to treat these words as equivalent to each other.

9. **Primis temporibus**, 'in the time immediately following my restoration.'

10. **De reliqua nostra dignitate.** He probably refers to the grants for rebuilding his villas. Cp. Ad Att. 4. 2, 5 'consules .. aestimarunt .. cetera valde illiberaliter.'

11. **Occulta non nullorum odia**: cp. Ep. 20. 8, note.

Obscura in me studia, 'doubtful zeal in my cause.'

12. **De monumentis meis.** Cicero may here refer (1) to his own house or a portion of it, (2) to the neighbouring colonnade of Catulus destroyed by Clodius but rebuilt by the senate's order, (3) perhaps to some building which Cicero as consul was commissioned by the senate to erect in commemoration of the suppression of Catiline's conspiracy. Manutius, (followed by Müller, Mr. Yonge, and Mr. Parry, in notes on this passage or on § 15 below,) speaks of an 'atrium libertatis' which Cicero was commissioned to build near the bottom of the Palatine hill. Müller refers to Ad Q. F. 1. 1, 9. 26. Other passages relating to this matter are—Ad Att. 4. 2; 4. 3. 2; Ad Q. F. 2. 9. 2 (2. 7. 2 Baiter); De Harusp. Resp. 27. 58.

13. **De vi nefaria.** The rebuilding of Cicero's house was interrupted with violence by Clodius on Nov. 3rd, 57 B.C. Cp. Ad Att. 4. 3. 2.

16. **In meis .. sarciendis**, that is, 'the making good my losses under a vote of the senate.' Cp. Ad Att. 4. 2, 5.

18. **Non tamen .. quae fecerant**, 'though I saw what they were doing—and indeed it was no secret—I was not so much annoyed by their present conduct as grateful for their past services.'

20. **Te quidem .. ac teste**, 'as you yourself declared and testified.'

debebam et eum non solum beneficio, sed amore etiam et perpetuo quodam iudicio meo diligebam, tamen non reputans, quid ille vellet, in omnibus meis sententiis de re publica pristinis
7 permanebam. Ego sedente Cn. Pompeio cum ut laudaret P. Sestium introisset in urbem, dixissetque testis Vatinius me fortuna et felicitate C. Caesaris commotum illi amicum esse coepisse, dixi me eam Bibuli fortunam, quam ille adflictam putaret, omnium triumphis victoriisque anteferre; dixique eodem teste alio loco, eosdem esse, qui Bibulum exire domo prohibuissent et qui me coëgissent: tota vero interrogatio mea nihil habuit nisi reprehensionem illius tribunatus; in qua omnia dicta sunt libertate animoque maximo de vi, de auspiciis, de donatione regnorum.
8 Neque vero hac in causa modo, sed constanter saepe in senatu: quin etiam Marcellino et Philippo consulibus Nonis Aprilibus mihi est senatus adsensus, ut de agro Campano frequenti senatu Idibus Maiis referretur. Num potui magis in arcem illius causae invadere aut magis oblivisci temporum meorum, meminisse actionum? Hac a me sententia dicta magnus animorum motus est factus cum eorum, quorum oportuit, tum illorum etiam, quorum

Praedicator is a rare word, but occurs Pro Balbo 2, 4.

1. Beneficio, 'on account of his service to me.' Cp. Ep. 26, 9, note on 'iniuria.'

4. Sedente, 'sitting on the bench assigned to "laudatores."' Billerb.

Ut laudaret: cp. 'laudarim,' § 4, note.

5. P. Sestium: cp. Intr. to Part II, § 2, for an account of his trial.

Introisset. Pompey held a commission to supply Rome with corn, and this would require him to be away from Rome a good deal. By entering the 'urbs' Pompey would forfeit his 'imperium,' unless a special exemption had been granted him. Cp. Note F, also Ep. 23, 3, note; and on the different meaning of 'urbs' and 'Roma,' which I had overlooked in the note on this passage in my first edition, Ep. 5, 4, note.

6. Illi, sc. Caesari. Billerb. thinks Vatinius is meant, but would not this require 'ipsi'?

7. Dixi me .. anteferre. No remark quite to this effect exists in the speeches Pro Sestio and In Vatinium as we have them. Bibulus, however, is mentioned In Vat. 9; 10.

Ille. Vatinius.

8. Eodem teste, 'in presence of the same man.' Pompey? or Vatinius?

9. Alio loco, 'in another part of my speech.'

Eosdem esse .. prohibuissent: cp. Intr. to Part I, §§ 17; 18, and references there given, for an account of the stormy scenes of 59 B.C. when Vatinius was tribune.

10. Qui me coëgissent, 'who had compelled me to leave my home' and go into exile.

Interrogatio. Cicero's speech against Vatinius was made under the pretext of cross-examining him.

12. Maximo. For its gender, which follows that of the nearest substantive, cp. Madv. 214 a.

De vi .. regnorum: cp. Intr. l. c.; and In Vat. 12, 29.

13. In senatu, sc. 'dixi.'

14. Nonis Aprilibus. For an account of Cicero's behaviour in this matter, cp. Intr. to Part II, §§ 3; 4, and Ep. 25, 1.

16. Arcem illius causae, 'the stronghold of the triumvirs' party.'

17. Temporum, 'my sufferings.' Wiel. Billerb. Forcell.

Actionum, 'my previous public career.' His sufferings might have taught him caution; but he preferred to act according to the promise of his earlier life.

19. Cum eorum .. numquam putaram, supp. 'motum fieri,' and 'motum factum iri.'

numquam putaram. Nam hoc senatus consulto in meam senten- 9
tiam facto Pompeius, cum mihi nihil ostendisset se esse offensum,
in Sardiniam et in Africam profectus est eoque itinere Lucam ad
Caesarem venit. Ibi multa de mea sententia questus est Caesar,
quippe qui etiam Ravennae Crassum ante vidisset ab eoque in me
esset incensus. Sane moleste Pompeium id ferre constabat; quod
ego, cum audissem ex aliis, maxime ex meo fratre cognovi. Quem
cum in Sardinia Pompeius paucis post diebus, quam Luca disces-
serat, convenisset, 'te' inquit 'ipsum cupio; nihil opportunius
potuit accidere: nisi cum Marco fratre diligenter egeris, dependendum tibi est, quod mihi pro illo spopondisti.' Quid multa?
questus est graviter; sua merita commemoravit; quid egisset
saepissime de actis Caesaris cum ipso meo fratre quidque sibi is
de me recepisset, in memoriam redegit seque, quae de mea salute
egisset, voluntate Caesaris egisse ipsum meum fratrem testatus
est; cuius causam dignitatemque mihi ut commendaret, rogavit
ut eam ne oppugnarem, si nollem aut non possem tueri. Haec 10
cum ad me frater pertulisset et cum tamen Pompeius ad me cum
mandatis Vibullium misisset, ut integrum mihi de causa Campana

On the ellipses, cp. Madv. 280, Obs. 2, and 478, Obs. 3. On the genitives eorum and illorum, governed by motus animorum, cp. Zumpt L. G. 423, note. 'Illorum' is supposed by Wiel. and Billerb. to refer to the leaders of the optimates, 'eorum' to the triumvirs. But from what follows in § 9 is it not more natural to refer 'eorum' to Caesar and Crassus, and 'illorum' to Pompey and his immediate friends?

2. Cum . . nihil . . offensum, 'without having shewn any sign that he was offended.'

3. In Sardiniam . . profectus est, 'set out on a journey to Sardinia and Africa,' two of the most important corn provinces. He would probably sail from the port of Pisae or from Labro or Liburnum (Leghorn?). Cp. Ad Q. F. 2. 5. 3. On the meeting at Luca, now Lucca, cp. Intr. to Part II, §§ 3: 4.

5. Etiam Ravennae, 'even at Ravenna,' before the three met at Luca. Cp. Mommsen 4. 1, p. 307.

9. Te ipsum cupio, sc. 'videre,' 'It is just you I wish to see.' Cp. Madv. 479 d.

10. Diligenter egeris, 'entreat earnestly,' 'make urgent representations to.' See note on Ep. 5, 8, p. 38.

Dependendum . . spopondisti, 'you must pay what you promised in his name,' i.e. 'you must suffer for his failure to fulfil your promise made on his behalf, that he would acquiesce in our government.'

12. Quid egisset . . fratre, 'the negotiations he had carried on with my brother about the acts of Caesar,' i.e. about the pledges to be given by M. Cicero, that he would not attack those acts as informal.

13. Is, Quintus.

14. De mea salute, 'in promoting my recall from exile.'

16. Cuius causam, sc. Caesaris.

18. Tamen, 'nevertheless,'—although he had commissioned my brother to speak to me.

19. Vibullium. L. Vibullius Rufus was an officer who served under Pompey against Caesar. He is mentioned Ad Q. F. 3. 1, 5. 18, and Caes. Bell. Civ. 1. 15 and 23. Cp. Ep. 49, note.

Ut integrum . . reservarem, 'that I should keep my hands free with regard to the lands in Campania till his own return.' For the substantive use of neuter singulars, cp. Nägelsb. 21, 63.

De causa, = 'de re.' 'Causa accipitur . . pro quocunque negotio.' Forcell.

ad suum reditum reservarem, collegi ipse me et cum ipsa quasi re publica collocutus sum, ut mihi tam multa pro se perpesso atque perfuncto concederet, ut officium meum memoremque in bene meritos animum fidemque fratris mei praestarem, eumque, quem bonum civem semper habuisset, bonum virum esse pateretur. In illis autem meis actionibus sententiisque omnibus, quae Pompeium videbantur offendere, certorum hominum, quos iam debes suspicari, sermones referebantur ad me; qui cum illa sentirent in re publica, quae ego agebam, semperque sensissent, me tamen non satis facere Pompeio Caesaremque inimicissimum mihi futurum gaudere se aiebant. Erat hoc mihi dolendum, sed multo illud magis, quod inimicum meum—meum autem? immo vero legum, iudiciorum, otii, patriae, bonorum omnium—sic amplexabantur, sic in manibus habebant, sic fovebant, sic me praesente osculabantur, non illi quidem ut mihi stomachum facerent, quem ego funditus perdidi, sed certe ut facere se arbitrarentur. Hic ego, quantum humano consilio efficere potui, circumspectis rebus meis omnibus rationibusque subductis summam feci cogitationum mea-
11 rum omnium, quam tibi, si potero, breviter exponam. Ego, si ab improbis et perditis civibus rem publicam teneri viderem, sicut et meis temporibus scimus et non nullis aliis accidisse, non modo praemiis, quae apud me minimum valent, sed ne periculis quidem

1. **Collegi me**, 'I collected myself,' 'came to my senses.'

Quasi, 'so to say.'

2. **Tam multa .. perfuncto**, 'having suffered and done so much in her cause.'

3. **Ut officium .. praestarem**, 'to do my duty by shewing myself grateful to men who had deserved well of me, and by fulfilling my brother's promise.'

Bene meritos, sc. Pompey and his friends.

5. **Bonum virum**, 'a man of honour' in fulfilling engagements made on his behalf.

6. **In illis .. offendere**, 'with regard to all those proceedings of mine which I mentioned before, and to all my expressions of opinion which seemed to offend Pompey.'

7. **Certorum hominum**: cp. Ep. 20, 8, note.

8. **Cum illa .. sensissent**, 'though their political views were, and always had been, in accordance with the measures I proposed.' Cp. Ep. 25 for the facts referred to.

12. **Inimicum meum**. Cicero refers to Clodius.

13. **Amplexabantur**. This verb is common in the metaphorical sense.

14. **In manibus habebant**, = 'fovebant.' Forcell. It seems to be a rare phrase.

Osculabantur. For a similar use of 'osculor,' cp. Pro Muren. 10, 23.

15. **Non illi quidem .. arbitrarentur**, 'that they did not indeed excite my wrath—for I have none left—but certainly thought they did so.' For the position of 'quidem' with personal pronouns, cp. Ep. 26, 7, note.

18. **Rationibus subductis**, 'having cast up the account.' Cp. Ep. 36, 11.

Summam feci .. omnium, 'arrived at a result of all my reflections.'

21. **Meis temporibus**. Cicero had witnessed the cruelties of Cinna and Sulla.

Non nullis aliis may refer to the times of Saturninus, who was tribune when Cicero was six years old, and to those of the Gracchi.

compulsus ullis, quibus tamen moventur etiam fortissimi viri, ad eorum causam me adiungerem, ne si summa quidem eorum in me merita constarent. Cum autem in re publica Cn. Pompeius princeps esset, vir is, qui hanc potentiam et gloriam maximis in rem publicam meritis praestantissimisque rebus gestis esset consecutus cuiusque ego dignitatis ab adulescentia fautor, in praetura autem et in consulatu adiutor etiam exstitissem, cumque idem auctoritate et sententia per se, consiliis et studiis tecum, me adiuvisset meumque inimicum unum in civitate haberet inimicum, non putavi famam inconstantiae mihi pertimescendam, si quibusdam in sententiis paulum me immutassem meamque voluntatem ad summi viri de meque optime meriti dignitatem adgregassem.
In hac sententia complectendus erat mihi Caesar, ut vides, in 12
coniuncta et causa et dignitate. Hic multum valuit cum vetus amicitia, quam tu non ignoras mihi et Quinto fratri cum Caesare fuisse, tum humanitas eius ac liberalitas brevi tempore et litteris et officiis perspecta nobis et cognita. Vehementer etiam res ipsa publica me movit, quae mihi videbatur contentionem, praesertim maximis rebus a Caesare gestis, cum illis viris nolle fieri et, ne fieret, vehementer recusare. Gravissime autem me in hanc mentem impulit et Pompeii fides, quam de me Caesari dederat, et fratris mei, quam Pompeio. Erant praeterea haec animadver-

1. **Ad eorum . . adiungerem**, 'would support their party.' Cp. Ad Fam. 1. 8, 2 'me ad eius rationes adiungo.'

4. **Esset, vir is, qui.** Wesenb. punctuates, 'esset vir, is qui.'

6. **In praetura . . in consulatu.** In his praetorship Cicero had supported the Manilian law; in his consulship he proposed a 'supplicatio' for ten or twelve days in honour of Pompey's successes over Mithridates. Cp. De Prov. Cons. 11, 27, and Intr. to Part I, § 8.

7. **Cumque idem . . adiuvisset**, 'and since, also, he had served me by his own influence and expressions of opinion, and by wise counsels and zealous exertions which you shared.'

9. **Inimicum**: cp. § 10, note.

10. **Si quibusdam . . adgregassem**, 'if I changed my language a little sometimes in expressing my opinions, and shewed a disposition to promote the dignity of a man who had deserved well of me.' On the tenses, cp. Madv. 379. 'Adgregare,' = 'coniungere,' 'adiacere.' Forcell.

13. **In hac sententia . . dignitate**, 'having come to this decision I had necessarily to become intimate with Caesar, whose interest and honour were identified with those of Pompey.'

14. **Hic**, 'in this matter.' Forcell.

16. **Tum humanitas . . cognita**, 'his kindness and generosity with which I have become familiar within a short time.' On the abl. 'brevi tempore,' cp. Madv. 276 b, and on the combination of ablatives in different senses, Ib. 278 a. Caesar had appointed Q. Cicero one of his legates in Gaul, and had lent M. Cicero large sums of money. Cp. §§ 18 and 21, and Ad Att. 7. 8, 5: also Mommsen 4. 2, pp. 313, 314.

19. **Cum illis viris**, 'with Caesar and Pompey.'

21. **Pompeii fides.** Apparently a promise made by Pompey to Caesar, that Cicero would relinquish his opposition to their measures. It was very likely a repetition to Caesar of that which Q. Cicero had made on his brother's behalf to Pompey. Cp. § 9.

tenda in civitate, quae sunt apud Platonem nostrum scripta divinitus, quales in re publica principes essent, tales reliquos solere esse civis. Tenebam memoria nobis consulibus ea fundamenta iacta iam ex Kalendis Ianuariis confirmandi senatus, ut neminem mirari oporteret Nonis Decembr. tantum vel animi fuisse in illo ordine vel auctoritatis; idemque memineram nobis privatis usque ad Caesarem et Bibulum consules, cum sententiae nostrae magnum in senatu pondus haberent, unum fere sensum
13 fuisse bonorum omnium. Postea, cum tu Hispaniam citeriorem cum imperio obtineres neque res publica consules haberet, sed mercatores provinciarum et seditionum servos ac ministros, iecit quidam casus caput meum quasi certaminis causa in mediam contentionem dissensionemque civilem; quo in discrimine cum mirifica senatus, incredibilis Italiae totius, singularis omnium bonorum consensio in me tuendo exstitisset, non dicam, quid acciderit—multorum est enim et varia culpa—, tantum dicam brevi, non mihi exercitum sed duces defuisse. In quo, ut iam sit in iis culpa, qui me non defenderunt, non minor est in iis, qui reliquerunt, et, si accusandi sunt, si qui pertimuerunt, magis etiam reprehendendi, si qui se timere simularunt: illud quidem certe nostrum consilium iure laudandum est, qui meos cives et a me conservatos et me servare cupientes, spoliatos ducibus servis

1. In civitate, 'with regard to the state.' Wiel.

Apud Platonem. In the Laws, Bk. 4. p. 711. B, C. The sense is freely given by Cicero.

3. Tenebam memoria . . auctoritatis, 'I remembered that in my consulship such a basis was laid on the first of January for a firm position to be maintained by the senate, that no one ought to wonder at the spirit which that body shewed, and at the authority which it enjoyed on the 5th of December,' the day on which the senate sanctioned the execution of Catiline's accomplices. Cp. Intr. to Part I, § 11.

9. Postea. In 58 B.C. Lentulus seems to have been praetor in 60 B.C., and to have obtained the government of Hispania Citerior next year through Caesar's influence. Cp. Caes. Bell. Civ. 1. 22.

11. Mercatores . . ministros, 'men who bought provinces by giving their aid to seditious practices.' Piso and Gabinius obtained Macedonia and Syria through the influence of Clodius in great measure. Cp. Intr. to Part I, § 19.

12. Quasi certaminis causa, 'as an apple of discord.' Wiel. Billerb.

15. Non dicam . . culpa, 'I will not say what result followed, as that would involve the censure of many in various degrees.'

17. Duces. He complained especially of Q. Arrius and Q. Hortensius. Cp. Ad Q. F. 1. 3. 8; Ad Att. 3. 9. 2; Intr. to Part I, § 22.

18. Qui me non defenderunt . . simularunt. It is difficult to explain these allusions; I think 'qui me non defenderunt,' and perhaps 'qui pertimuerunt,' refer to the consuls and Pompey; 'qui reliquerunt' and 'si qui simularunt' to the leaders of the optimates.

20. Illud . . consilium, 'my well-known resolution.' For this sense of 'illud,' cp. Madv. 485 b. Cicero means his resolution to retire from Rome, rather than involve his countrymen in a civil war. Cp. Intr. to Part I, § 20.

21. Qui . . maluerim. 'Qui,' = 'cum ego.' Cp. Madv. 366.

22. Servis armatis. A contemptuous

armatis obiici noluerim declararique maluerim, quanta vis esse
potuisset in consensu bonorum, si iis pro me stante pugnare licuisset, cum adflictum excitare potuissent; quorum quidem animum
tu non perspexisti solum, cum de me ageres, sed etiam confirmasti
atque tenuisti. Qua in causa—non modo non negabo, sed etiam 14
semper et meminero et praedicabo libenter—usus es quibusdam
nobilissimis hominibus fortioribus in me restituendo, quam fuerant
idem in tenendo; qua in sententia si constare voluissent, suam
auctoritatem simul cum salute mea recuperassent. Recreatis
enim bonis viris consulatu tuo et constantissimis atque optimis
actionibus tuis excitatis, Cn. Pompeio praesertim ad causam adiuncto, cum etiam Caesar rebus maximis gestis singularibus
ornatus et novis honoribus ac iudiciis senatus ad auctoritatem eius
ordinis adiungeretur, nulli improbo civi locus ad rem publicam
violandam esse potuisset. Sed attende, quaeso, quae sint conse- 15
cuta: primum illa furia muliebrium religionum, qui non pluris
fecerat Bonam deam quam tres sorores, impunitatem est illorum
sententiis adsecutus, qui, cum tribunus pl. poenas a seditioso civi
per bonos viros iudicio persequi vellet, exemplum praeclarissimum

description of the rabble who followed Clodius.

2. Si .. licuisset, 'if their natural leaders had allowed them to act on my behalf.'

3. Cum .. potuissent, 'by their having been able to raise me when fallen.'

Excitare is common in this sense in Cicero's writings. The meaning of the passage is, 'The success of my friends in restoring me from exile shewed how easily they might have saved me from having to go into exile.'

4. Cum de me ageres, 'when you were pleading my cause in the senate.'

5. Tenuisti, 'maintained.'

6. Quibusdam: cp. Ep. 20, 8, note.

8. In tenendo, 'in keeping me at Rome.' Cp. Ep. 54. 3 'ille (Pompeius) restituendi mei, quam retinendi studiosior.' But Cicero does not, probably, refer to Pompey in this passage.

Qua in sententia .. voluissent, 'and if they had been willing to persevere in that attitude,' i.e. of friendship to me.

11. Actionibus, 'your proposals and official conduct.' Billerb.

Ad causam adiuncto, 'having enlisted himself in support of the same cause.' 'Adiungor ad,'='amplector,' 'sequor.' Forcell. Cp. § 11.

12. Singularibus honoribus: cp. Ep. 26, 10.

14. Locus, 'an opportunity.'

16. Furia, 'the mad assailant.' Clodius is meant of course. Cp. Ad Q. F. 3. 1, 11 'uti ullum ad illam furiam verbum rescriberet.' On the gender of 'qui,' cp. Madv. 315 b.

17. Tres sorores. Two sisters married to L. Lucullus and Q. Metellus Celer; one cousin, Terentia, married to Q. Marcius Rex. Billerb.

Illorum, the nobles of whom he complains so often. For their relations with Clodius at this time, cp. Ep. 23. 4, and Mommsen 4. 2, 297.

18. Sententiis, 'by their votes in the senate,' i.e. by their failure to support Lentulus Marcellinus in his proposal that Clodius should be tried by a special commission before the next comitia. Cp. Ad Q. F. 2. 1, 2.

Tribunus plebis: probably L. Racilius, or perhaps Milo. Cp. Ad Q. F. l. c. The occurrence referred to took place in 56 B.C.

19. Per bonos viros, 'by an appeal to the judges,' or perhaps 'to the well-disposed senators.'

Exemplum .. sustulerunt, 'prevented a signal punishment of sedition, which would

in posterum vindicandae seditionis de re publica sustulerunt; idemque postea non meum monumentum—non enim illae manubiae meae, sed operis locatio mea fuerat—, monumentum vero senatus hostili nomine et cruentis inustum litteris esse passi sunt. Qui me homines quod salvum esse voluerunt, est mihi gratissimum; sed vellem non solum salutis meae, quem ad modum medici, sed, ut aliptae, etiam virium et coloris rationem habere voluissent: nunc, ut Apelles Veneris caput et summa pectoris politissima arte perfecit, reliquam partem corporis inchoatam reliquit, sic quidam homines in capite meo solum elaborarunt,
10 reliquum corpus imperfectum ac rude reliquerunt. In quo ego spem fefelli non modo invidorum, sed etiam inimicorum meorum, qui de uno acerrimo et fortissimo viro meoque iudicio omnium magnitudine animi et constantia praestantissimo Q. Metello L. f. quondam falsam opinionem acceperunt, quem post reditum dictitant fracto animo et demisso fuisse; [est vero probandum,] qui et summa voluntate cesserit et egregia animi alacritate afuerit neque sane redire curarit, eum ob id ipsum fractum fuisse, in quo cum omnes homines tum M. illum Scaurum singularem virum con-

have been most famous for our country in after times.'

1. **Monumentum**: cp. § 5, note.

3. **Manubiae**, 'trophies.' Originally 'money raised by the sale of booty.' Forcell.

Operis locatio mea. Lange (Röm. Alt. 3. 328) thinks that the words refer to some building erected in 63 B.C. by Cicero, under the direction of the senate.

4. **Hostili nomine**, 'the name of Clodius.' This inscription seems to have been put up after the disorders mentioned Ad Att. l. c.

Passi sunt, i.e. by failing to support Racilius and Milo effectively.

5. **Qui**, = 'et ii.' Cp. Madv. 448.

7. **Aliptae**, 'slaves employed to attend bathers.' Forcell. who, however, remarks that Cicero uses it here for a trainer, the usual Greek word for which is παιδοτρίβης.

Virium et coloris, 'my strength and complexion.'

9. **Inchoatam**, '*only* begun.'

10. **In capite . . reliquerunt**, 'have exerted themselves only to save my rights of citizenship, and disregarded my fortune and dignity.' 'Caput' is here of course used in two senses. For the different meanings of the term 'poena capitalis,' cp. Ep. 4. 1, note.

13. **Qui . . acceperunt**, 'who heard at some past time a false account about Q. Metellus.' For an account of this Metellus, surnamed Numidicus, cp. Sall. Iug. 43 foll.; Plut. Marius 29. It is hard to see why Cicero's enemies should have based their expectations on this precedent. It would seem more natural that they should draw inferences from their knowledge of Cicero's own character. Probably Cicero only introduces the parallel for his own indirect exaltation. Cp. Pro Sestio 16, 37; Post Red. ad Quir. 3. 6. The general sense is, 'my enemies were mistaken in supposing I should act as they fancied Metellus had acted.'

14. **Acceperunt.** Wesenb. 'acceperant.'

16. **Qui et summa . . superasset**, 'to think that one who retired with the utmost readiness, and lived abroad with the greatest cheerfulness, and shewed no anxiety to return, was broken in spirit on account of that act by which he shewed more constancy than M. Scaurus.' For the use of the inf. in exclamations, cp. Ep. 18. 1, note.

19. **M. Scaurus**, censor, princeps senatus, and twice consul. He is always mentioned

stantia et gravitate superasset! sed, quod de illo acceperant aut etiam suspicabantur, de me idem cogitabant, abiectiore animo me futurum, cum res publica maiorem etiam mihi animum, quam umquam habuissem, daret, cum declarasset se non potuisse me uno civi carere; cumque Metellum unius tribuni pl. rogatio, me universa res publica, duce senatu, comitante Italia, promulgantibus octo tribunis, referente consule, comitiis centuriatis, cunctis ordinibus, hominibus incumbentibus, omnibus denique suis viribus reciperavisset. Neque vero ego mihi postea quicquam adsumpsi 17
neque hodie adsumo, quod quemquam malevolentissimum iure possit offendere: tantum enitor, ut neque amicis neque etiam alienioribus opera, consilio, labore desim. Hic meae vitae cursus offendit eos fortasse, qui splendorem et speciem huius vitae intuentur, sollicitudinem autem et laborem perspicere non possunt. Illud vero non obscure queruntur, in meis sententiis, quibus ornem Caesarem, quasi desciscere me *a* pristina causa. Ego autem cum illa sequor, quae paulo ante proposui, tum hoc non in postremis, de quo coeperam exponere. Non offendes eundem bonorum sensum, Lentule, quem reliquisti, qui confirmatus consulatu nostro, *non* numquam postea interruptus, adflictus ante te con-

with praise by Cicero, but in very different terms by Sallust, Iug. 15. He seems to have been a man of lax principles, but moderate and judicious in his political conduct; that he advocated the reforms of Drusus in 91 B.C. This passage seems to imply that he took an oath prescribed by the Lex Appuleia in 100 B.C., which Metellus refused. Cp. Plut. Marius 29; App. Bell. Civ. 1. 31 Μέτελλος δὲ οὐκ ὤμοσε μόνος.

1. Sed, resumptive, 'I say.' Cp. Ep. 23, 2, note.

5. Unius tribuni pl. Q. Calidius is referred to. Cp. Pro Planc. 28, 69.

7. Octo tribunis. The tribunes could only legally propose bills to the tribes, and hence their 'promulgatio' as well as the consul's motion in the senate, is to be distinguished from the law passed by the centuries to which Cicero actually owed his recall. Cp. Intr. to Part I, § 23.

8. Incumbentibus, 'exerting themselves.' This absolute use of the word is rare, but cp. Ep. 31, 3.

9. Reciperavisset, = 'recuperavisset,' 'recovered,' 'recalled.'

Adsumpsi, = 'adrogavi,' 'took upon myself.'

11. Neque etiam alienioribus. For a similar sentiment, cp. Pro Muren. 3, 8.

12. Hic meae .. cursus, 'this devotion to professional duties.' See the preceding sentence.

15. Illud vero .. causa, 'the complaints they do not conceal are, that my expressions of opinion in honour of Caesar shew a kind of defection from my old party.' Cp. De Prov. Cons. 8, 18; 11, 28 for Cicero's proposals in honour of Caesar.

17. Cum illa sequor .. exponere, 'I am influenced partly by the reasons I stated a little while ago (in §§ 9-12), and not least by a further important consideration, which I had begun to explain to you' before the digression about Metellus.

Hoc refers to the jealousy of some leaders of the optimates (cp. §§ 10; 13; 15), on which he now enlarges more at length.

18. Non offendes, 'you will not find on your return.' 'Offendere' = 'invenire, reperire, quasi in rem incidendo.' Forcell., who also quotes this passage.

Bonorum: 'boni' is often used as equivalent to 'optimates,' the friends of the old aristocratic constitution.

19. Sensum, 'disposition.' Cp. Ad Fam. 1. 8, 2 'sensum in re publica.'

20. Non numquam postea interrup-

sulem, recreatus abs te, totus est nunc ab iis, a quibus tuendus fuerat, derelictus; idque non solum fronte atque voltu, quibus simulatio facillime sustinetur, declarant ii, qui tum nostro illo statu optimates nominabantur, sed etiam sententia saepe iam tabellaque docuerunt. Itaque tota iam sapientium civium, qualem me et esse et numerari volo, et sententia et voluntas mutata esse debet; id enim iubet idem ille Plato, quem ego vehementer auctorem sequor, tantum contendere in re publica, quantum probare tuis civibus possis; vim neque parenti nec patriae adferre oportere. Atque hanc quidem ille causam sibi ait non attingendae rei publicae fuisse, quod, cum offendisset populum Atheniensem prope iam desipientem senectute, [cumque eum nec persuadendo nec cogendo regi posse vidisset,] cum persuaderi posse diffideret, cogi fas esse non arbitraretur. Mea ratio fuit alia, quod neque desipiente populo nec integra re mihi ad consulendum capesseremne rem publicam implicatus tenebar; sed laetatus tamen sum, quod mihi liceret in eadem causa et mihi utilia et cuivis bono recta defendere. Huc accessit commemoranda quaedam et divina Caesaris in me fratremque meum liberalitas: qui mihi, quascumque res gereret, tuendus esset; nunc in

tus. These words refer to various occurrences in the years 62, 61, 60 B.C.: perhaps especially to the affair of Clodius, and to the disputes of the senate and equites. Cp. Intr. to Part I, §§ 14; 15.

Adflictus, 'utterly depressed.'

Ante te consulem, i.e. in the years 59, 58 B.C.

2. Idque non solum .. sustinetur, 'and this they shew not merely on their brows and in their aspect, where a false pretence can be most easily made.' I think Cicero means that the leading optimates not only pretended to have changed their opinions in order to win favour from their old opponents, but took actual steps in violation of their old convictions. 'Sustinetur,' = 'geritur.' Forcell.

3. Nostro .. statu. Wesenb. suggests the insertion of 'in' before 'nostro.'

4. Sententia .. tabellaque, 'their votes in the senate and on the bench.' Cp. § 15.

6. Sententia et voluntas, 'view of things and desire.'

7. Plato: cp. Crito 50 E, 51 B and C; Sall. Iug. 3.

8. Tantum .. possis, 'to exert yourself in politics only, so far as you can gain the approval of your fellow-citizens for your measures.'

11. Offendisset, 'had met with,' 'fallen on,' or simply 'found:' as above, § 17. Cp. Plat. Ep. 5. 322 A and B Πλάτων ὀψὲ ἐν τῇ πατρίδι γέγονε, καὶ τὸν δῆμον κατέλαβεν ἤδη πρεσβύτερον καὶ εἰθισμένον ὑπὸ τῶν ἔμπροσθεν πολλὰ καὶ ἀνόμοια τῇ ἐκείνου ξυμβουλῇ πράττειν.

12. Desipientem senectute: cp. Aristoph. Eq. 42

Δῆμος πυκνίτης δύσκολον γερόντιον.

13. Persuaderi, impers., sc. 'populo.' The apodosis begins with 'cogi fas esse.'

14. Ratio, 'position.'

15. Neque desipiente populo, 'as the people with which I had to deal had not yet come to its dotage,' abl. abs.

Nec integra re .. tenebar, 'I was already committed, and had no power of freely considering the question whether I should take part in politics.'

17. In eadem causa, 'on the same question,' viz. whether Caesar's command should be continued; the expediency of which continuation Cicero maintained at length in his speech 'De Provinciis Consularibus.'

18. Huc, 'to the grounds already stated,' of self-defence and public interest.

20. Qui mihi .. videretur, 'where

tanta felicitate tantisque victoriis, etiamsi in nos non is esset, qui est, tamen ornandus videretur. Sic enim te existimare velim, cum a vobis meae salutis auctoribus discesserim, neminem esse, cuius officiis me tam esse devinctum non solum confitear, sed etiam gaudeam. Quod quoniam tibi exposui, facilia sunt ea, quae 10
a me de Vatinio et de Crasso requiris; nam de Appio quod scribis sicuti de Caesare te non reprehendere, gaudeo tibi consilium probari meum. De Vatinio autem, primum reditus intercesserat in gratiam per Pompeium, statim ut ille praetor est factus, cum quidem ego eius petitionem gravissimis in senatu sententiis oppugnassem, neque tam illius laedendi causa quam defendendi atque ornandi Catonis. Post autem Caesaris, ut illum defenderem, mira contentio est consecuta. Cur autem laudarim, peto a te, ut id a me neve in hoc reo neve in aliis requiras, ne tibi ego idem reponam, cum veneris: tametsi possum vel absenti; recordare enim, quibus laudationem ex ultimis terris miseris. Nec hoc pertimueris; nam a me ipso laudantur et laudabuntur iidem. Sed tamen defendendi Vatinii fuit etiam ille stimulus, de quo in iudicio, cum illum defenderem, dixi me facere quiddam, quod in Eunucho parasitus suaderet militi:

public services and private liberality would each severally justify the honour I have shewn him.' On the aid which Cicero received from Caesar, cp. infra, § 21.

3. Cum a vobis . . discesserim, = 'vobis exceptis' (Forcell.) 'that after you, the authors of my safety, I am more indebted to Caesar than to any one else.' 'Vobis' probably refers to Pompey and Lentulus.

5. Facilia sunt . . meum: cp. § 4, note.

8. Primum . . Pompeium, 'the first step to our friendly relations was a reconciliation brought about by Pompey just after Vatinius was elected praetor,' i.e. in 55 B.C. Cp. Intr. to Part II, § 8.

Reditus . . in gratiam. On the order of the words, cp. Zumpt L. G. 788. The verb comes early in the sentence in familiar style.

9. Statim ut. Mr. J. E. Yonge remarks that 'ut' is not strictly dependent on 'statim.'

12. Catonis. M. Cato stood for the praetorship against Vatinius. Cp. Ad Q. F. 2. 9. 3.

13. Mira contentio, 'most urgent representations.'

14. Neve . . neve: for the simple 'ne . . neque,' cp. Madv. 459. A rare usage.

15. Idem reponam, 'put the same question to you in return.' 'Reponere,' = 'par pari referre.' Forcell.

Vel absenti, sc. 'reponere.' Cp. Ep. 23. 2, note, for the ellipse.

Recordare . . miseris, 'for just remember in whose favour you have sent letters of eulogy from the most distant regions.' Cicero needed not to wait for Lentulus' return to see how he behaved. Lentulus, apparently had often written letters from Spain or Cilicia, testifying in favour of worthless men.

18. Ille stimulus. The pronoun refers to what follows; cp. Ep. 5. 3, note.

19. Me facere . . militi, 'that I was doing what the parasite recommends to the soldier in the Eunuchus.' Cp. Terent. Eunuch. 3. 1. 50. On the tense of 'suaderet,' which follows that of 'dixi,' cp. Madv. 383. The parasitus is Gnatho; the miles Thraso. The import of the advice quoted is, 'If your mistress arouses your jealousy by speaking of Phaedria, repay her by mentioning Pamphila.'

> ubi nominabit Phaedriam, tu Pamphilam
> continuo. Si quando illa dicet 'Phaedriam
> intro mittamus comissatum,' Pamphilam
> cantatum provocemus. Si laudabit haec
> illius formam, tu huius contra; denique
> par pro pari referto, quod eam mordeat.

sic petivi a iudicibus ut, quoniam quidam nobiles homines et de me optime meriti nimis amarent inimicum meum meque inspectante saepe eum in senatu modo severe seducerent, modo familiariter atque hilare amplexarentur, quoniamque illi haberent suum Publium, darent mihi ipsi alium Publium, in quo possem illorum animos mediocriter lacessitus leviter repungere; neque solum dixi, sed etiam saepe facio deis hominibusque adprobantibus.'
20 Habes de Vatinio, cognosce de Crasso. Ego, cum mihi cum illo magna iam gratia esset, quod eius omnes gravissimas iniurias communis concordiae causa voluntaria quadam oblivione contriveram, repentinam eius defensionem Gabinii, quem proximis [superioribus] diebus acerrime oppugnasset, tamen, si sine ulla mea contumelia suscepisset, tulissem; sed, cum me disputantem, non lacessentem laesisset, exarsi non solum praesenti, credo, iracundia—nam ea tam vehemens fortasse non fuisset —, sed, cum inclusum illud odium multarum eius in me iniuriarum, quod ego effudisse me omne arbitrabar, residuum tamen insciente me fuisset, omne repente apparuit. Quo quidem tempore ipso quidam homines, et iidem illi, quos saepe *nutu* significationeque appello, cum se maximum fructum cepisse dicerent ex libertate mea meque

7. Quidam . . inimicum meum: cp. § 15, note.

9. Severe seducerent, 'led aside with a serious air,' as if for conference. Cp. Pro Muren. 24, 49 'seductiones testium.'

11. Alium Publium. The praenomen of Vatinius was Publius.

12. Leviter repungere, 'prick them gently in return.' 'Repungere' seems only to be found here.

13. Dixi, sc. 'me facturum.'

14. Habes de Vatinio. Forcell. says 'habere,' = 'audire,' 'intelligere' in such passages as this. 'Enough of Vatinius.' Cp. Ep. 8, 6, note on p. 57.

Cognosce: cp. Ep. 36, 9 'nunc cognosce de Bruto.'

17. Contriveram, 'had trodden under foot,' 'effaced.' Forcell.

Defensionem Gabinii. Crassus had defended Gabinius when he and Piso were accused of misgovernment in 56 B.C.

18. Sine ulla mea contumelia, 'without any abuse of me.' For this use of the possessive pronoun, cp. Madv. 297 b, Obs. 1.

19. Disputantem, merely 'debating,' 'arguing.' Forcell.

22. Inclusum illud odium . . iniuriarum, 'the secret hatred inspired by many wrongs of his to me.' On the genit. 'iniuriarum,' cp. Ep. 4, 2, note.

24. Omne . . apparuit, 'came suddenly to light in its full extent,' sc. 'illud odium.'

25. Nutu significationeque appello, 'describe by signs and hints.' On the expression, cp. Nägelsbach 137, 397. Cicero never names the men to whose jealousy he ascribed in part his change of policy. Cp. §§ 13–15.

26. Cum se . . dicerent, 'though they

tum denique sibi esse visum rei publicae, qualis fuissem, restitutum, cumque ea contentio mihi magnum etiam foris fructum tulisset, gaudere se dicebant mihi et illum inimicum et eos, qui in eadem causa essent, numquam amicos futuros: quorum iniqui sermones cum ad me per homines honestissimos perferrentur cumque Pompeius ita contendisset, ut nihil umquam magis, ut cum Crasso redirem in gratiam, Caesarque per litteras maxima se molestia ex illa contentione adfectum ostenderet, habui non temporum solum rationem meorum, sed etiam naturae, Crassusque, ut quasi testata populo Romano esset nostra gratia, paene a meis Laribus in provinciam est profectus; nam, cum mihi condixisset, cenavit apud me in mei generi Crassipedis hortis. Quam ob rem eius causam, quod te scribis audisse, magna illius commendatione susceptam defendi in senatu, sicut mea fides postulabat. Acce- 21
pisti, quibus rebus adductus quamque rem causamque defenderim, quique meus in re publica sit pro mea parte capessenda status; de quo sic velim statuas, me haec eadem sensurum fuisse, si mihi integra omnia ac libera fuissent: nam neque pugnandum arbitrarer contra tantas opes neque delendum, etiam si id fieri posset, summorum civium principatum nec permanendum in una sententia conversis rebus ac bonorum voluntatibus mutatis, sed temporibus adsentiendum. Numquam enim *in* praestantibus in re publica gubernanda viris laudata est in una sententia perpetua

affirmed that they had derived great advantage from my independence.' Cp. Madv. 358, Obs. 3, for this use of 'cum.'

1. Qualis fuissem, 'like my old self.'

2. Ea contentio, 'my dispute with Crassus.'

Foris, 'among the people.'

3. Dicebant, 'yet said.' An adversative conjunction would make the sense clearer, but is often omitted. Cp. Ep. 21, 3, note, on p. 166.

Illum, sc. Crassum.

Eos, sc. Pompeium et Caesarem.

6. Ita contendisset .. umquam magis. On the ellipse, cp. Madv. 478; Zumpt L. G. 774, and note.

8. Habui .. naturae, 'I paid regard to the suggestions not only of circumstances but of my nature.' Man. thinks that 'temporum' here means 'of my calamities.'

10. Ut quasi testata .. gratia, 'that our good understanding might be, so to say, solemnly attested.' Cp. Ep. 8, 2 on 'testata.'

11. Condixisset, 'had offered to visit me.' Forcell. explains 'condicere' by 'denunciare alicui se apud eum cenaturum ipso volente.'

12. Apud me. Cicero probably furnished an entertainment, for which Furius Crassipes lent his gardens.

Generi: cp. Ep. 24, 2, note.

13. Eius causam. Cicero defended the conduct of Crassus in the senate, but did not really approve of it. Cp. Ad Fam. 5. 8, 2 and 4; Ad Att. 4. 13, 2. Crassus set out for his province late in 55 B.C. Cp. Intr. to Part II, § 8.

Magna illius commendatione, 'under strong recommendation from Caesar,' or perhaps 'from Pompey.'

15. Quamque rem causamque, 'each measure and cause' which I have been blamed for defending.

16. Quique meus .. status, 'and what is my political position as an individual.'

20. Summorum civium. Caesar and Pompey.

permansio, sed, ut in navigando tempestati obsequi artis est, etiam si portum tenere non queas, cum vero id possis mutata velificatione adsequi, stultum est eum tenere cum periculo cursum, quem ceperis, potius quam eo commutato quo velis tamen pervenire, sic, cum omnibus nobis in administranda re publica propositum esse debeat id, quod a me saepissime dictum est, cum dignitate otium, non idem semper dicere, sed idem semper spectare debemus. Quam ob rem, ut paulo ante posui, si essent omnia mihi solutissima, tamen in re publica non alius essem atque nunc sum: cum vero in hunc sensum et adliciar beneficiis hominum et compellar iniuriis, facile patior ea me de re publica sentire ac dicere, quae maxime cum mihi tum etiam rei publicae rationibus putem conducere. Apertius autem haec ago ac saepius, quod et Quintus, frater meus, legatus est Caesaris et nullum meum minimum dictum, non modo factum, pro Caesare intercessit, quod ille non ita illustri gratia exceperit, ut ego eum mihi devinctum putarem. Itaque eius omni et gratia, quae summa est, et opibus, quas intellegis esse maximas, sic fruor ut meis; nec mihi aliter potuisse videor hominum perditorum de me consilia frangere, nisi cum praesidiis iis, quae semper habui, nunc etiam potentium
22 benevolentiam coniunxissem. His ego consiliis, si te praesentem habuissem, ut opinio mea fert, essem usus eisdem; novi enim

1. Permansio, 'perseverance.' Cp. De Invent. Rhet. 2. 54. 164.

Artis est, 'shews skill.' Cp. Madv. 282.

2. Id. sc. 'portum tenere.'

4. Tamen, 'nevertheless,' 'even at the expense of changing your course.' The word corresponding to 'tamen' is often omitted. Cp. Forcell.

7. Non idem . . debemus, 'we ought, not indeed always to hold the same language, but always to have the same end in view.'

8. Posui, 'stated,' common in this sense in Cicero.

9. Solutissima, 'quite free from embarrassments.' The superlative is rare.

Non alius . . atque . . sum, 'no other man than I am.' Cp. Madv. 444. b.

10. Cum vero, 'but now that.'

In hunc sensum, 'to my present disposition.'

Beneficiis hominum, 'the services' of Pompey in promoting his recall, and of Caesar in lending him money.

11. Iniuriis, 'the intrigues' of certain nobles with Clodius.

Facile patior . . conducere, 'I am content to hold and express such opinions on politics as I think most likely to serve both my own interests and those of the State.' On the expression 'facile patior,' cp. Ep. 3. 2 and 3, notes.

15. Intercessit, merely = 'accidit.' Forcell.

16. Exceperit, for the tense, as referring to a definite historical fact, cp. Madv. 382, Obs. 1.

19. Hominum perditorum, in primis Clodii. Billerb.

20. Cum praesidiis . . habui. Cicero refers probably to the attachment of the more judicious nobles, and of the majority of the middle classes both at Rome and in the country towns.

Potentium, of Caesar, Pompey, and Crassus.

22. Eisdem. This word seems here to mean 'equally,' 'all the same.' I cannot remember an exact parallel, but cp. Madv. 488; Zumpt L. G. 681; and instances in Forcell.

temperantiam et moderationem naturae tuae, novi animum cum mihi amicissimum, tum nulla in ceteros malevolentia suffusum, contraque cum magnum et excelsum, tum etiam apertum et simplicem. Vidi ego quosdam in te tales, quales tu eosdem in me videre potuisti: quae me moverunt, movissent eadem te profecto. Sed, quocumque tempore mihi potestas praesentis tui fuerit, tu eris omnium moderator consiliorum meorum; tibi erit eidem, cui salus mea fuit, etiam dignitas curae. Me quidem certe tuarum actionum, sententiarum, voluntatum, rerum denique omnium socium comitemque habebis, neque mihi in omni vita res tam erit ulla proposita, quam ut quotidie vehementius te de me optime meritum esse laetere. Quod rogas, ut mea tibi scripta mittam, quae post 23
discessum tuum scripserim, sunt orationes quaedam, quas Menocrito dabo, neque ita multae; ne pertimescas. Scripsi etiam—nam me iam ab orationibus diiungo fere referoque ad mansuetiores Musas, quae me maxime sicut iam a prima adulescentia delectarunt—scripsi igitur Aristotelio more, quem ad modum quidem

2. **Nulla . . suffusum**, 'concealing no ill-will towards the rest of our countrymen.' 'Suffusus' is rarely used in this sense, but cp. Ovid. Trist. 2, 565 'a salibus suffusis felle refugi.'

3. **Simplicem**: contrasted with the duplicity of the 'quidam' presently mentioned.

4. **Quosdam in te tales**, sc. 'se gerere.' Cp. Madv. 300 a; 324 a; and for the fact, Ep. 21, 2 and 3. Bibulus seems to be especially referred to.

5. **Quae . . eadem.** On the position of these pronouns, cp. Madv. 321.

Moverunt, 'influenced.'

6. **Mihi potestas . . fuerit**, 'I shall have an opportunity of meeting you.' Cp. the expression 'potestatem sui facere,' Ep. 18, 13.

7. **Eidem**: cp Ep. 20, 1, note. 'You, moreover, who formerly cared for my safety will now provide for my dignity also.'

8. **Dignitas** is a difficult word to translate—'position,' 'general respect,' perhaps come near its meaning.

Tuarum actionum . . omnium, 'in all your proposals, expressions of opinion and wishes, in short in everything.'

13. **Discessum tuum**, 'your departure' to assume the government of Cilicia, which happened in 57 or 56 B.C. Cp. Ep. 21, 1; Ep. 22, 2, note.

Orationes. Those still extant are—Pro P. Sestio, In Vatinium, De Haruspicum Responsis, Pro M. Caelio, De Provinciis Consularibus, Pro L. Balbo, In Pisonem, Pro M. Scauro (fragmentary), Pro Cn. Plancio.

Menocrito. This man seems to have been a freedman of Lentulus, not elsewhere mentioned.

14. **Ne pertimescas.** Cp., for a similar affectation of modesty, Ad Fam. 7. 1, 3 'dummodo is tibi quidvis potius quam orationes meas legerit.' As Mr. J. E. Yonge remarks this construction is really a dependent one. Cp. Hor. Carm. 4. 9. 1.

15. **Me . . diiungo**, 'I sever myself from the company of my speeches,' which Cicero personifies to form a contrast to the 'Musae' below.

Mansuetiores Musas, 'gentler studies.' Neither oratory nor philosophy came within the province of the Muses, unless in the larger sense in which the Greeks spoke of *μουσική*. Cicero is here speaking of his poetical, philosophical, and rhetorical works.

16. **Me maxime.** Wesenb. proposes to insert 'nunc' after 'me.'

17. **Igitur**, resumptive: cp. Madv. 480.

Aristotelio more. The form of the dialogue 'De Oratore' does not correspond with that of any of the treatises of Aristotle which we possess, but Plutarch (Adv. Colot. 1115, B) speaks of *ἐξωτερικοὶ διάλογοι* of Aristotle (see also his life of Dion 22). Diogenes Laertius also (xii.), in his list of the works of that philosopher, mentions several which, judging by their titles, seem

volui, tres libros [in disputatione ac dialogo] 'de oratore,' quos arbitror Lentulo tuo fore non inutiles; abhorrent enim a communibus praeceptis et omnem antiquorum et Aristoteliam et Isocratiam rationem oratoriam complectuntur. Scripsi etiam versibus tres libros de temporibus meis, quos iam pridem ad te misissem, si esse edendos putassem; sunt enim testes et erunt sempiterni meritorum erga me tuorum meaeque pietatis; sed [quia] verebar non eos, qui se laesos arbitrarentur—etenim id feci parce et molliter—, sed eos, quos erat infinitum bene de me meritos omnes nominare; quos tamen ipsos libros, si quem cui recte committam invenero, curabo ad te perferendos. Atque istam

to have been dialogues. Cicero, too (Ad Att. 13. 19, 4) says that his 'Academica' 'Ἀριστοτέλειον morem habent, in quo sermo ita inducitur ceterorum, ut penes ipsum sit principatus.' This description does not, it is true, apply to the books 'De Oratore;' but Bernays (p. 137) thinks that Cicero in the passage now under consideration (Ad Fam. 1. 9, 23) refers to the less dramatic character of the Aristotelian dialogues as compared with the Platonic. Madvig (on Cic. de Fin. Excursus vii. p. 840) doubts if Cicero knew much of any works of Aristotle except the dialogues and rhetorical works, and Mr. Grote thinks that it was from reading the dialogues that Cicero formed the opinion of Aristotle's style expressed in the Prior Academics (2. 38, 119) 'flumen orationis aureum fundens Aristoteles'—cp. 'Aristotelia pigmenta,' Ep. 9, 1. On the whole subject, see Grote's Aristotle, 1. 43 foll.; a review of that work in the Edinburgh Review for October, 1872; the article on Aristotle in Smith's Dict. of Biogr. (1. 322) (by A. Stahr); and Jacob Bernays, Die Dialoge des Aristoteles, Berlin, 1863.

Quem ad modum quidem volui, 'according to my wish at least.' Cicero means that he would allow others to judge how far he had succeeded.

1. In disputatione . . dialogo. Wesenb. thinks that these words are genuine, except the preposition 'in.'

2. Lentulo tuo, 'your son Lentulus.' Cp. Ep. 26, 11, note.

A communibus praeceptis. The rules generally given were perhaps more directly and exclusively practical than those inculcated by Cicero. In his treatise 'De Oratore' he makes L. Crassus argue against M. Antonius (the orator) in favour of the necessity of general knowledge and cultivation for an orator.

3. Aristoteliam . . complectuntur, 'embody the theories of rhetoric set forth by Aristotle and by Isocrates.' Aristotle's treatise on rhetoric is well known; that of Isocrates is said to have perished with the exception of a few fragments; cp. Smith, Dict. of Biogr. 2. 633, and Cic. de Inv. Rhet. 2. 2, 7; the last reference I owe to Mr. Yonge's note.

5. De temporibus meis, 'about my exile and restoration.' Cp. § 8 of this letter for the meaning of 'tempora.' The poem on his consulship was written much earlier, for he quotes it Ad Att. 2. 3, 3, while the services of Lentulus (cp. l. 7) were rendered in 57 B.C., and could not have been referred to in the earlier poem, unless indeed Cicero added to it at a later time, which is possible. Baiter, xi. 130, thinks that the poem on his consulship is here referred to.

7. Meritorum . . pietatis: cp. Intr. to Part I, § 23, and Ep. 21, 1.

Sed quia . . nominare. Wesenb. retains 'quia,' thinking that some such words as 'vetui divulgari' have dropped out after 'nominare.'

Verebar, 'I was apprehensive of,' 'feared how they might be affected.'

8. Qui se laesos arbitrarentur: cp. note on § 13. He refers perhaps especially to Pompey (cp. Ep. 54, 3), and to Hortensius (Ad Att. 3. 9, 2).

Id feci, sc. 'culpavi,' the verb to be supplied from 'laesos.'

9. Erat infinitum, 'it was an endless task,' and therefore impossible.

10. Si quem . . invenero, 'if I find any messenger to whom I can prudently entrust them.'

11. Istam . . partem . . nostrae . . 'the results of my activity in this department of my ordinary life,' i.e., in his literary pursuits.

quidem partem vitae consuetudinisque nostrae totam ad te defero: quantum litteris, quantum studiis, veteribus nostris delectationibus, consequi poterimus, id omne ad arbitrium tuum, qui haec semper amasti, libentissime conferemus. Quae ad me de tuis 24 rebus domesticis scribis, quaeque mihi commendas, ea tantae mihi curae sunt, ut me nolim admoneri, rogari vero sine magno dolore vix possim. Quod de Quinti fratris negotio scribis te priore aestate, quod morbo impeditus in Ciliciam non transieris, conficere non potuisse, nunc autem omnia facturum, ut conficias, id scito esse eius modi, ut frater meus vere existimet adiuncto isto fundo patrimonium fore suum per te constitutum. Tu me de tuis rebus omnibus et de Lentuli tui nostrique studiis et exercitationibus velim quam familiarissime certiorem et quam saepissime facias existumesque neminem cuiquam neque cariorem neque iucundiorem umquam fuisse quam te mihi, idque me non modo ut tu sentias, sed ut omnes gentes, etiam ut posteritas omnis intellegat, esse facturum. Appius in sermonibus antea dictitabat, 25 postea dixit etiam in senatu palam, sese, si licitum esset legem curiatam ferre, sortiturum esse cum collega provincias; si curiata lex non esset, se paraturum cum collega tibique successurum;

1. **Nostrae . . nostris . . conferemus.** The last word must mean '*I* will lay before you,' hence 'nostrae' probably is equivalent to 'meae.' Otherwise the words 'qui haec semper amasti' might suggest that Cicero speaks of himself and Lentulus as 'nos.' On the use of 'noster' for 'meus,' cp. Madv. 4⅔.

2. **Studiis.** I do not see what force this word has here. Mr. Jeans renders it 'philosophic work;' Metzger translates 'litteris . . studiis,' 'wissenschaftliche Beschäftigung.'

4. **De tuis rebus domesticis.** I cannot explain this allusion, Lentulus' letter not having been preserved.

6. **Admoneri,** 'to be reminded of them;' **rogari,** 'to be asked to attend to them.'

7. **De Quinti fratris negotio.** Probably Cicero refers to a wish of Quintus to buy land from some Roman resident in Cilicia. Müller.

Priore aestate, in 55 B.C.

8. **In Ciliciam,** 'into Cilicia proper.' The province of Lentulus included various other districts. Cp. Intr. to Part II, § 17.

9. **Conficere,** 'to effect a settlement.' The verb is used thus absolutely, Ep. 24, 2 'de nostra Tullia spero cum Crassipede nos confecisse.'

10. **Esse eius modi,** 'is such a valuable service.'

Adiuncto isto fundo. The land which Quintus wished to buy was apparently adjacent to his patrimonial estate—perhaps near Arpinum.

12. **Nostrique:** cp. note on the previous section.

Exercitationibus, 'practice' of oratory, composition, etc. Forcell.

15. **Idque me . . facturum.** The more natural order of the words according to our notions would be 'meque esse facturum non modo ut tu id sentias sed ut.' Cicero probably meant that he would either record the services of *Lentulus* in a special work (Müller), or mention them in his speeches upon all occasions.

17. **In sermonibus,** 'in private conversation.'

18. **Si licitum esset,** i.e. if no tribune interposed his veto.

19. **Sortiturum,** 'would cast lots with his colleague' for the two consular provinces. This was the regular course; and this passage seems to imply that it could only be taken after the enactment of a 'Lex Curiata.'

20. **Paraturum,** 'would make an arrange-

legem curiatam consuli ferri opus esse, necesse non esse; se, quoniam ex senatus consulto provinciam haberet, lege Cornelia imperium habiturum, quoad in urbem introisset. Ego, quid ad te tuorum quisque necessariorum scribat, nescio; varias esse opiniones intellego: sunt qui putant posse te non decedere, quod sine lege curiata tibi succedatur; sunt etiam, qui, si decedas, a te

ment.' Cp., for this use of the verb, Sall. Iug. 43, according to one reading; also Forcell. sub voc. Manutius says that it is equivalent to 'pacisci:'—Wesenb. suggests 'comparaturum.'

Tibique successurum, 'and would go as your successor to Cilicia.'

1. **Legem curiatam.** Cicero (De Rep. 2. 13, 25) considered this law to represent the ancient popular confirmation of the election of kings, continued under the commonwealth for 'magistratus cum imperio' (De Leg. Agrar. 2. 11, 26). This approval by the 'curiae' had long become a mere form, and its only importance was that the tribunes could interfere with public business by opposing its enactment. Cp. Smith, Dict. of Antiq., 'Imperium,' p. 629. Mommsen (Rom. Hist. 1. 69; 81; 82; Römische Forschungen, p. 271) thinks it was even originally more of a mere form than would be gathered from Cicero's language.

Opus esse, necesse non esse, 'was desirable (or proper) but not necessary.' Forcell. explains 'opus esse' as = 'quod fieri debet.' On the omission of an adversative conj., cp. Madv. 437 d, Obs. Cicero (De Leg. Agrar. 2. 12, 30) insists on the necessity of the law to confer 'imperium.' Appius seems to have relied on a clause (1) of the Lex Cornelia L. Sullae, mentioned on the next page, and he may have interpreted this law as dispensing with the necessity of a 'Lex Curiata.' Lange, Röm. Alterth. 1. 630, calls this interpretation sophistical, but Fischer, Röm. Zeittafeln, on 81 B.C., refers to this passage as shewing that the Lex Cornelia *did* grant such dispensation. The passage quoted (from Ad Att. 4. 18, 2) in a note on Ep. 28, 7, however, goes rather against this view. It would appear a fair inference from this passage that the 'Lex Curiata' need not be proposed for a magistrate until he was on the point of departing for his province after, or towards the close of, his year of office at Rome. But Mommsen (Staatsrecht, I, pp. 51, note 4; 54, 55, notes) remarks that the enactment of such a law was necessary to enable the praetors to preside in the civil courts, and the consuls to convene the 'comitia centuriata;' and it is noteworthy that during the year now under consideration the 'comitia centuriata' do not seem to have been convened, at least for elections. Cp. Intr. to Part II, §§ 11; 13: Dion Cassius, 40, 45. Becker (Röm. Alterth. 2. 2, 62; 63) thinks that 'imperium' was usually conferred on the consuls for their year of office, either by anticipation or soon after their election, and that a fresh 'Lex Curiata' was passed before they departed for their provinces as proconsuls.

2. **Ex senatus consulto.** The decree by which the senate, under the Lex Sempronia C. Gracchi, fixed the provinces of the future consuls. Cp. Ep. 26, 10; De Prov. Cons. 2, 3.

Lege Cornelia, sc. L. Sullae de provinciis ordinandis. This law has been already referred to. It provided apparently (1) That all provincial governors should retain their 'imperium' till they returned to Rome; (2) That they must leave their provinces within thirty days of the arrival of their successors; (3) That a limit should be fixed to the money allowed by the provincials as travelling expenses to deputations sent to Rome for the purpose of eulogising their late governors; and possibly (4) That a 'Lex Curiata' should not be essential for a provincial governor who had had a province assigned him by the senate. But on the last point see note on 'opus esse' above. On the whole subject compare with the present passage Ad Fam. 3. 6, 3 and 6; 3. 10, 6.

4. **Varias esse opiniones**, i.e. as to what Lentulus ought to do; see the following words.

5. **Sunt qui putant**: 'putent' would be more usual, the indicative being rarely used in such passages except where a definitive pronoun or adjective of number is added, e.g. 'multi;' cp. Madv. 365, Obs. 1. But Mr. Yonge, following Kleyn, thinks that the indicative may be used in an express classification.

Non decedere, 'not leave your province,' even though Appius should present himself as your successor.

6. **A te relinqui posse . . praesit**, 'that you can leave an officer in charge of

relinqui posse qui provinciae praesit. Mihi non tam de iure certum est—quamquam ne id quidem valde dubium est—quam illud, ad tuam summam amplitudinem, dignitatem, libertatem, qua te scio libentissime frui solere, pertinere te sine ulla mora provinciam successori concedere, praesertim cum sine suspitione tuae cupiditatis non possis illius cupiditatem refutare. Ego utrumque meum puto esse, et quid sentiam ostendere et quod feceris defendere.

Scripta iam epistola superiore accepi tuas litteras de publicanis, 20
in quibus aequitatem tuam non potui non probare: facilitate quidem vellem consequi potuisses, ne eius ordinis, quem semper ornasti, rem aut voluntatem offenderes. Equidem non desinam tua decreta defendere; sed nosti consuetudinem hominum; scis quam graviter inimici ipsi illi Q. Scaevolae fuerint; tibi tamen sum auctor, ut, si quibus rebus possis, eum tibi ordinem aut reconcilies aut mitiges: id etsi difficile est, tamen mihi videtur esse prudentiae tuae.

the province.' Cicero was much embarrassed in choosing a temporary successor for himself in Cilicia. Cp. Ad Att. 6. 5, 1 and 2; 6. 6, 3, foll.

2. Quamquam ne id . . dubium est. Cicero evidently hints that Lentulus would act illegally in remaining in his province after the arrival of Appius.

3. Amplitudinem, dignitatem, libertatem. Cicero thought the position of a leading senator at home more dignified and independent than that of a provincial governor; and when he himself went to govern Cilicia was anxious to stay there as short a time as possible. Cp. Ad Att. 5. 15, 1; 5. 21, 3; Ad Fam. 2. 10, 4.

6. Cupiditatis, 'eagerness for office,' which Appius shewed by his readiness to assume the government of Cilicia without the sanction of a 'Lex Curiata,' and which Lentulus would have shewn by declining to leave his province on the arrival of a successor.

Refutare, 'to resist.' Cp. De Prov. Cons. 13, 32 'illas nationes . . refutandas . . bello.'

Ego utrumque . . defendere, 'I think it my duty both to declare what I think you ought to do, and to defend what you actually do.'

9. Epistola superiore, 'the foregoing letter,' to which Cicero now adds a postscript after receipt of one from Lentulus.

10. Facilitate, 'by readiness to oblige.'

11. Quidem, 'however.' Cp. Nägelsbach 125, 543.

Eius ordinis, of the publicans.

12. Ornasti: cp. Ad Att. 1. 17, 9 'eree aliae deliciae equitum vix ferendae] quas ego non solum tuli, sed etiam ornavi,' foll.

Rem aut voluntatem offenderes, 'come into collision with the [real or fancied, J. E. Y.] interests or wishes.'

13. Decreta. Probably decrees by which the publicans thought their interests were endangered. Cicero probably refers to them a few lines above, where he praises the 'aequitas' of Lentulus.

Consuetudinem hominum, sc. 'publicanorum.' Cicero perhaps refers to their abuse of judicial power.

14. Q. Scaevolae. Q. Mucius Scaevola governed Asia 99 B.C., and exerted himself to protect the provincials from extortion. This offended the equites, from whom alone the judges were then taken at Rome; and P. Rutilius Rufus, the upright legate of Scaevola, was brought to trial and condemned on a false charge of 'repetundae.' Cp. Ad Att. 5. 17, 5; Livy, Epit. 70; Velleius 2. 13; Cic. In Pison. 39, 95. Cicero incorporated many provisions of the provincial edict of Scaevola in his own. Cp. Ad Att. 6. 1, 15.

17. Prudentiae tuae, 'not too hard for your sagacity.' Metzg.

30. To C. SCRIBONIUS CURIO (AD FAM. II. 6).
ROME, 53 B.C. (701 A.U.C.)

1. Any seeming haste in my despatch of this letter must be excused by the importance of its subject; 2. and the greatness of your past services to me warrants my asking of you a favour, for which I should be very grateful. 3. I am most anxious for Milo's success in his canvass for the consulship, and I think your aid is just what is wanted to secure it: our other resources are ample, 4. and we only want a leader. In Milo you will find a friend of the greatest spirit and constancy. 5. I need not explain to you how deeply I am interested in this matter, and if you grant my request you will place me under a lasting obligation.

M. CICERO S. D. C. CURIONI.

1 Nondum erat auditum te ad Italiam adventare, cum Sex. Villium, Milonis mei familiarem, cum his ad te litteris misi; sed tamen cum adpropinquare tuus adventus putaretur, et te iam ex Asia Romam versus profectum esse constaret, magnitudo rei fecit, ut non vereremur ne nimis cito mitteremus, cum has quam primum ad te perferri litteras magno opere vellemus. Ego, si mea in te essent officia solum, Curio, tanta, quanta magis a te ipso praedicari quam a me ponderari solent, verecundius a te, si quae magna res mihi petenda esset, contenderem; grave est enim homini pudenti petere aliquid magnum ab eo, de quo se bene meritum putet, ne id, quod petat, exigere magis quam rogare et in mercedis potius quam beneficii loco

2 numerare videatur. Sed quia tua in me vel nota omnibus vel ipsa novitate meorum temporum clarissima et maxima beneficia exstiterunt, estque animi ingenui, cui multum debeas, eidem plurimum velle debere, non dubitavi id a te per litteras petere,

C. Scribonius Curio, to whom Cicero wrote this letter, was son of the Curio mentioned Ep. 7, 5, p. 50. His talents and his extravagance and debauchery were equally remarkable. In politics he was inconsistent, but appears to have been now on good terms with Cicero. For more particulars about him, cp. Ep. 11, 1, note; Intr. to Parts II. §§ 26, 27; III. § 9.

1. Te . . adventare. Curio was now in Asia as quaestor. Billerb.

Sex. Villium. This Villius is only here mentioned, apparently, unless Horace refers to him Sat. 1. 2, 64.

2. Misi. On the perfect used for the present in letters, cp. Zumpt L. G. 503.

4. Magnitudo rei, 'the greatness of my object.'

5. Cum has . . vellemus, 'as I wish this letter to reach you as soon as possible.'

7. Solum = 'sola,' 'my services to you only, and not also yours to me.' Cp. Philipp. 2. 32, 81 'nos . . nuntiationem solum habemus.' 'Primum' is used in the same way. Cp. Livy 6. 11, acc. to Weissenborn's text, 'Manlius primum omnium ex patribus popularis factus.'

9. Contenderem, 'should solicit it.' 'Id' omitted. Cp. Zumpt L. G. 765-766.

13. Sed quia . . exstiterunt, 'since your services to me have been some of them known to all, and others most famous and important from the very strangeness of my disasters.' Sed quia opposed to si solum in the preceding sentence.

quod mihi omnium esset maximum maximeque necessarium; neque enim sum veritus ne sustinere tua in me vel innumerabilia non possem, cum praesertim confiderem nullam esse gratiam tantam, quam non vel capere animus meus in accipiendo vel in remunerando cumulare atque illustrare posset. 3 Ego omnia mea studia, omnem operam, curam, industriam, cogitationem, mentem denique omnem in Milonis consulatu fixi et locavi, statuique in eo me non officii solum fructum sed etiam pietatis laudem debere quaerere; neque vero cuiquam salutem ac fortunas suas tantae curae fuisse umquam puto, quantae mihi est honos eius, in quo omnia mea posita esse decrevi. Huic te unum tanto adiumento esse, si volueris, posse intellego, ut nihil sit praeterea nobis requirendum. Habemus haec omnia: bonorum studium conciliatum ex tribunatu propter nostram, ut spero te intellegere, causam; volgi ac multitudinis propter magnificentiam munerum liberalitatemque naturae; iuventutis et gratiosorum in suffragiis studia propter ipsius excellentem in eo genere vel gratiam vel diligentiam; nostram suffragationem,

1. **Esset.** On the tense, following that of 'dubitavi,' cp. Madv. 383.

2. **Sustinere,** 'to bear the weight of.'

Tua, sc. 'beneficia,' which Wesenb. proposes to insert after 'innumerabilia.'

4. **Quam non . . posset,** 'that my heart cannot receive it with appreciation, and repay it with interest that shall be famous. **Capere** = 'find room for' (Man.); = χωρεῖν. J. E. Y.

7. **Fixi et locavi,** 'have attached and devoted.'

8. **Officii fructum,** 'the advantage which I may derive from this service' (Metzg., Hofm.). Mr. Jeans renders 'the solid fruits of such service as I can render.' He thinks that 'the fruits' looked for are simply success. 'A recompense for his service' (Wiel.). 'The satisfaction of doing my duty' (J. E. Yonge). May not such a verb as 'praestare' be supplied from **quaerere**? The meaning then would be, 'not only to bestow the service on which he has a claim, but to seek praise for my gratitude,' or 'affection' (so in subst. Manut.), which would not be content with the mere discharge of a debt.

11. **In quo . . decrevi,** 'on whom I am persuaded that my all depends.'

Unum, 'beyond all others.' J. E. Y.

13. **Habemus haec omnia,** 'all the following points are secured.'

14. **Ex tribunatu:** cp. Intr. to Part I, §§ 21; 23.

15. **Volgi ac multitudinis,** sc. 'studium conciliatum.'

16. **Munerum.** Milo gave splendid shows in 54 B.C., hoping to win the favour of the populace, and so to improve his prospects as an aspirant to the consulship. Cp. Ad Q. F. 3. 8, 6; 3. 9, 2, and Pro Milon. 35. 95.

Iuventutis, the young nobles, of whom Cicero generally speaks with fear and dislike. Cp. Ad Att. 1. 19, 8; 2. 7, 3; Merivale 1. 97, 98. On their influence at elections cp. Pro Muren. 35, 73, where the expression **gratiosus in equitum centuriis** occurs. It seems to mean 'influential at elections.'

17. **Ipsius,** sc. Milonis.

In eo genere: Billerb. renders 'among that class.' Is it not rather = 'in ea re,' 'in canvassing,' or, as Manut. 'in suffragiis.' Examples of this sense of 'genus' are given by Forcell. Milo had been an active supporter of his friends, who would repay him in kind.

18. **Nostram suffragationem,** 'my own support or recommendation.' Cp. Livy 10. 13, where, of the recommendation of P. Decius by Q. Fabius to the people, it is said, 'iusta suffragatio visa.'

si minus potentem, at probatam tamen et iustam et debitam et
4 propterea fortasse etiam gratiosam. Dux nobis et auctor opus
est et eorum ventorum, quos proposui, moderator quidam et
quasi gubernator; qui si ex omnibus unus optandus esset, quem
tecum conferre possemus, non haberemus. Quam ob rem, si
me memorem, si gratum, si bonum virum vel ex hoc ipso, quod
tam vehementer de Milone laborem, existimare potes, si dignum
denique tuis beneficiis iudicas, hoc a te peto, ut subvenias huic
meae sollicitudini et huic meae laudi vel, ut verius dicam,
prope saluti tuum studium dices. De ipso T. Annio tantum
tibi polliceor, te maioris animi, gravitatis, constantiae bene-
volentiaeque erga te, si complecti hominem volueris, habiturum
esse neminem; mihi vero tantum decoris, tantum dignitatis
adiunxeris, ut eundem te facile agnoscam fuisse in laude mea,
5 qui fueris in salute. Ego, ni te videre scirem, cum ad te haec
scriberem, quantum officii sustinerem, quanto opere mihi esset
in hac petitione Milonis omni non modo contentione, sed etiam
dimicatione elaborandum, plura scriberem: nunc tibi omnem
rem atque causam meque totum commendo atque trado. Unum
hoc sic habeto: si a te hanc rem impetraro, me paene plus
tibi quam ipsi Miloni debiturum; non enim mihi tam mea
salus cara fuit, in qua praecipue sum ab illo adiutus, quam

1. Probatam . . debitam, 'approved by the public, and due to Milo's claims upon me.'

2. Dux . . opus est. On this constr. cp. Madv. 266.

3. Ventorum, 'the winds that will fill our sails,' i.e. the resources I mentioned. Cp. Ep. 9, 6 'Caesarem cuius . . venti . . sunt secundi.'

Proposui, 'I set before you.' According to Forcell., Caesar uses the word more often than Cicero in this sense.

4. Optandus esset, 'had to be chosen.'

6. Bonum virum, 'a man of honour.' Cp. Ep. 29, 10.

9. Huic meae laudi . . saluti, 'this cause, in which my honour, or rather my safety, is at stake.' Cicero had still reason to fear Clodius, against whom Milo would be his most efficient protector. For this use of 'laus,' see below in this section in laude mea, 'where my honour is concerned.'

10. De ipso T. Annio. Milo was son of C. Papius Celsus, but was adopted by his mother's father, T. Annius. The Annii came originally from Setia (cp. Livy 8. 5): the Papii from Lanuvium (cp. Ascon. in Milonian. 141 and 158).

12. Complecti, 'to embrace the cause of,' 'receive warmly.' The word is more often used with an ablative of the manner, as in Ep. 15, 4: but cp. Ad Fam. 2. 8, 2, 'da te homini; complectetur.'

14. Laude, 'the praise I shall win by shewing myself grateful to Milo.' Manut.

15. In salute, 'when my safety was at stake,' in 58–57 B.C.

16. Quanto opere . . elaborandum, 'how I must exert myself, at the cost of the greatest toil and of the most perilous conflicts.'

18. Omnem rem atque causam, 'the whole affair in dispute.' 'Res,' the whole affair; 'causa,' the disputed point therein. Hofm.

19. Unum . . habeto, 'be assured of this one point.' Habere = 'scire, sibi persuadere.' Forcell. Cp. Ep. 26, 4, note.

22. Quam pietas . . iucunda, 'as the

pietas erit in referenda gratia iucunda; eam autem unius tui studio me adsequi posse confido.

31. TO ATTICUS (AD ATT. V. 11).
ATHENS, JULY 6, 51 B.C. (703 A.U.C.)

1. In future I will write, even at the risk of your not getting my letters. I hope you will do all you can to prevent my term of office being prolonged. 2. I cannot approve Marcellus' treatment of the citizen of Comum, which I fancy offended Pompey as much as Caesar. 3. I hope Pompey will not go to Spain, and have asked Theophanes to dissuade him from doing so. 4. I leave Athens to-day; all my principal officers are here except Tullius, and I have some light vessels for the voyage. The Parthians seem to be quiet. 5. My behaviour on my progress through Greece has been much admired, and I have nothing to complain of in my attendants. I do not know what may happen, however, if I am detained in my province more than a year. 6. I have attended to your requests, and have as much regard for Xeno as you have. I think, however, that a letter to Memmius will serve him better than anything else. 7. Console Pilia; I saw a letter of hers, written with much feeling.

CICERO ATTICO SAL.

Hui, totiensne me litteras dedisse Romam, cum ad te nullas 1
darem? At vero posthac frustra potius dabo, quam, si recte dari potuerint, committam ut non dem. Ne provincia nobis prorogetur, per fortunas! dum ades, quicquid provideri *potest*, provide: non dici potest, quam flagrem desiderio urbis, quam vix harum rerum insulsitatem feram. Marcellus foede in Co- 2

affection I shall shew in requiting him will give me pleasure.'

1. Eam, sc. 'pietatem,' 'the means of shewing that affection.'

Tui, 'Tuo' seems to have been the first reading of the MS., and Madvig. on Cic. de Fin. 2. 23. 76, prefers it. So too Wesenb.

3. Hui .. nullas darem? 'can I have written so often to Rome without writing to you?' quoting a reproach of Atticus probably. On the constr., see Ep. 12, 1, note. 'Hui,' an exclamation of astonishment. Cp. Epp. 42, 3.

4. Frustra .. non dem, 'I will rather write in vain than be guilty of not writing when it can be done with prudence.'

Recte, probably = 'to trustworthy messengers.' Cp. Ep. 6, 1 and 4, on Cicero's anxiety in such cases.

6. Dum ades, 'while you are at Rome.'

8. Harum rerum insulsitatem, 'the distastefulness in my present way of life.' Cp. Ad Att. 13. 29, 2 'in villa cuius insulsitatem "bene" noram.' Forcell. gives as equivalents, 'ineptia,' 'stultitia.'

Marcellus foede, sc. 'fecit.' Cp. Ep. 23, 2, note. In the following clause, the combination of 'gesserit' with 'erat' is curious. The words must mean, 'supposing him not to have been a magistrate, he was yet a Transpadane.' Merivale (2. 72, 73) thinks 'gesserit,' the reading of the best MS., inadmissible, and follows the reading 'gesserat' which Orellius and Wesenb. have adopted. This of course would commit Cicero to a statement that the man had not held office. The language of the other authorities hardly decides the question of fact. Cp. App. Bell. Civ. 2. 26, with Plut. Caes. 29. The incident referred to happened as follows. The consul, M. Claudius Marcellus, having met with a citizen of Novum Comum at Rome, ordered him to be scourged, as an insult to Caesar, who had established a colony at that town. Plut. Caes. 29. The Transpadane Gauls

mensi: etsi ille magistratum non gesserit, erat tamen Trans-
padanus. Ita mihi videtur non minus stomachi nostro *quam*
3 Caesari fecisse; sed hoc ipse viderit. Pompeius mihi quoque
videbatur, quod scribis Varronem dicere, in Hispaniam certe
iturus: id ego minime probabam, qui quidem Theophani facile
persuasi nihil esse melius quam illum nusquam discedere. Ergo
Graecus incumbet; valet autem auctoritas eius apud illum pluri-
4 mum. Ego has pr. Nonas Quinctiles proficiscens Athenis dedi,
cum ibi decem ipsos fuissem dies. Venerat Pomptinus; una
Cn. Volusius, aderat quaestor; tuus unus Tullius aberat. Aphracta

either universally (Mommsen 3. 248), or to a large extent (A. W. Zumpt, Studia Romana, 37-42), had received the Latin franchise from Cn. Pompeius Strabo, father of Pompey the Great, in 89 B.C., and Caesar's establishment of a colony at Novum Comum would enable that place to rank as a Latin community apparently. The 'Lex Vatinia' of B.C. 59, had empowered Caesar to establish a colony at Comum, which should enjoy the Latin, perhaps the Roman, franchise. Cp. Suet. Iul. 28; Ad Fam. 13. 35. 1. Now the citizen of a Latin city who had held a magistracy in it, acquired a right to the Roman franchise, with its exemption from corporal punishment. But Cicero's disapproval of the act of Marcellus seems to shew that the immunity of the Latins was extended further by custom than by law. A Lex Livia, carried by M. Drusus, the rival of C. Gracchus, proposed to exempt the Latins altogether from such punishment (cp. Plut. C. Gracchus 9). According to Mommsen (4. 2, 360), Caesar had conferred the *full* Roman franchise on the Transpadanes, but the Roman government might fairly treat such an act as invalid, and Drumann, 3. 383, thinks that the senate by resolution declared it so. But the passages which Drumann quotes from Plutarch (Caes. 29) and Suetonius (Iul. 28) do not seem to me to establish this point. Neither Caesar, however, nor Pompey, whose father had patronised the Transpadanes (cp. Drumann, 3. 383), was likely to regard the act of Marcellus with indifference. On the whole affair cp. App. Bell. Civ. 2. 26; Strabo 5. 1, 6; Mommsen 4. 2, 351. Caesar's interest in the Transpadani probably dated from an early period in his political career. Suetonius (Iul. 8) speaks of him as intriguing with the inhabitants of certain Latin colonies on his return to Italy after acting as quaestor in Spain; and those Latin colonies were probably cities of the Transpadani.

For notices of M. Marcellus, consul for this year, cp. Intr. to Parts II, § 17; IV, § 6.

2. Stomachi .. fecisse; cp. Ep. 29, 10 'non illi quidem ut mihi stomachum facerent.'

Nostro, Pompeio.

3. Ipse, M. Marcellus.

4. Videbatur .. probabam. These may be taken either as epistolary or ordinary imperfects. I prefer the latter construction.

Varronem. Varro would be likely to be well informed as to Pompey's intentions, for Pompey had appointed him one of his legates for Spain. Neither, however, had yet left Italy. Manut.

In Hispaniam: cp. Intr. to Part II, §§ 14; 15. Pompey had left the administration of Spain to his legates since his second consulship.

5. Qui quidem .. persuasi, 'and I certainly persuaded.'

6. Illum nusquam discedere, 'that Pompey should remain constantly at Rome.' Cp. Philipp. 1. 1, 1 'nec vero usquam discedebam.'

7. Incumbet, 'will exert himself.' More usual with specification of the object. Cp. Ep. 29, 16, note.

Apud illum, sc. 'Pompeium.'

8. Has, sc. 'litteras.'

Dedi and the following tenses seem to be epistolary.

9. Decem ipsos, 'precisely ten.' Cp. Madv. 487, Obs. 1.

Pomptinus. C. Pomptinus was praetor 63 B.C., and supported Cicero zealously against Catiline; he afterwards governed Gallia Narbonensis, and was now one of Cicero's legates.

10. Cn. Volusius. Q. Volusius is mentioned Ep. 36, 6. It is doubtful if Cicero had two Volusii among his officers, or if the praenomen is wrongly given in one passage.

Rhodiorum et dicrota Mytilenaeorum habebam et aliquid ἐπακτρίων. De Parthis erat silentium. Quod superest, di iuvent!
Nos adhuc iter per Graeciam summa cum admiratione fecimus, 5
nec mehercule habeo quod adhuc quem accusem meorum: videntur mihi nosse [nos,] nostram causam et condicionem profectionis suae; plane serviunt existimationi meae. Quod superest,
si verum illud est οἵαπερ ἡ δέσποινα, certe permanebunt; nihil
enim a me fieri ita videbunt, ut sibi sit delinquendi locus: sin
id parum profuerit, fiet aliquid a nobis severius; nam adhuc
lenitate dulces sumus et, ut spero, proficimus aliquantum. Sed
ego hanc, ut Siculi dicunt, ἀνεξίαν in unum annum meditatus
sum: proinde pugna, ne, si quid prorogatum sit, turpis inveniar.
Nunc redeo ad quae mihi mandas: † in praefectis excusatio iis, 6
quos voles, deferto: non ero tam μετέωρος, quam in Appuleio
fui. Xenomen tam diligo quam tu, quod ipsum sentire certo
scio. Apud Patronem et reliquos barones te in maxima gratia

Quaestor. Probably L. Mescinius Rufus, to whom Ad Fam. 5. 20 is addressed.

Tullius. L. Tullius, legate of Cicero, and apparently a friend of Atticus. Cp. Ad Att. 5. 4. 2, and Ep. 36, 5, from which we may infer that L. Tullius had been recommended to Cicero by Q. Titinius, a common friend of Atticus and Cicero. Cp. Manut.

Aphracta, 'undecked vessels.' Not a classical Greek word in this sense.

1. Dicrota, 'biremes. The Greek word occurs Xen. Hell. 2. 1, 28, but is not used there of a distinct class of vessels.

ἐπακτρίων, 'of ordinary boats,' not classical.

2. De Parthis. A Parthian invasion had been feared in the eastern provinces of Rome ever since the disaster of Crassus in 53 B.C.

Quod superest, 'for the future,' = 'in eo quod superest.'

3. Summa cum admiratione, 'amid the greatest admiration.'

5. Nostram causam, 'my pretensions' or 'interest.'

Condicionem .. suae, 'the terms on which they are to attend me.'

7. Illud, 'the proverb.'

οἵαπερ ἡ δέσποινα, τοία καὶ ἡ κύων: cp. Plat. Rep. Bk. 8, p. 563 C.

Permanebunt, 'will persevere in good conduct.' Cp. the use of 'permansio,' Ep. 29, 21.

9. Id, 'my example.'

11. Ut Siculi dicunt. Perhaps ἀνεξία was a Sicilian word. It appears not to be found in classical Greek authors. It may mean either 'forbearance,' or 'endurance of temptation.'

12. Proinde pugna .. inveniar, 'exert yourself, then, for my recall at the proper time, lest a prolonged trial prove fatal to my moderation.'

13. In praefectis .. deferto. For the corrupt words excusatio iis, Orell. suggests 'exceptis negotiatoribus;' Metzg. 'excusatio ni sit,' 'unless I have a good plea for rejecting them;' Gronov. (approved by Boot) 'negotiator ni sit.' The sense seems clear, that Atticus might recommend any one for the post of prefect against whom there was no general objection, e.g. of his being a money-dealer. Cp. Ep. 36, 10, notes.

14. Tam μετέωρος, 'so anxious or scrupulous.' It is quite classical in the first sense.

Appuleio. An Appuleius is mentioned Ad Att. 12. 13, 2, but little seems to be known of him.

15. Xeno and Patron were Epicurean philosophers now living at Athens. Cp. Ad Att. 5. 10, 5; Ad Fam. 13. 1, 2.

16. Barones, 'blockheads:' Forcell. says that the word 'significat stultum, bardum, fatuum, hebetem.' The word is common in Cicero's philosophical works.

posui, et hercule merito tuo feci; nam mihi is ter dixit te scripsisse ad se, mihi ex illius litteris rem illam curae fuisse, quod ei pergratum erat. Sed cum Patron mecum egisset, ut peterem a vestro Ariopago, *ὑπομνηματισμὸν* tollerent, quem Polycharmo praetore fecerant, commodius visum est et Xenoni et post ipsi Patroni, me ad Memmium scribere, qui pridie, quam ego Athenas veni, Mytilenas profectus erat, ut is ad suos scriberet posse id sua voluntate fieri; non enim dubitabat Xeno quin ab Ariopagitis invito Memmio impetrari non posset. Memmius autem aedificandi consilium abiecerat, sed erat Patroni iratus; itaque scripsi ad eum accurate, cuius epistolae misi ad te exemplum.

7 Tu velim Piliam meis verbis consolere; indicabo enim tibi; tu illi nihil dixeris: accepi fasciculum, in quo erat epistola Piliae: abstuli, aperui, legi; valde scripta est *συμπαθῶς*. Brundisio quae tibi epistolae redditae sunt sine mea, tum videlicet datae sunt, cum ego me non belle haberem; nam illam † *νομαν-*

1. **Merito tuo feci**, 'you deserved I should do it.' Abl. caus., cp. Ep. 26, 9. note, on p. 187.

Is, Patron.

2. **Mihi ex illius . . curae fuisse**, 'that I, in consequence of letters received from him, had attended to the matter in which he was interested.' The allusion is explained by the next sentence. Cp. Ad Fam. 13. 1. Patron wished to obtain the remains of the house of Epicurus, which had been granted to C. Memmius by a decree of the Areopagus, made in the archonship of Polycharmus (see below), and Cicero wrote to Memmius, then living in exile at Mytilene, to ask him to yield to the wishes of Patron.

4. **Vestro Ariopago.** Cicero often refers to Atticus' love of Athens. Cp. Appendix 3. § 1.

ὑπομνηματισμόν, used by Polyb. 2. 40. 4. for 'a memorandum.'

Tollerent. On the omission of 'ut,' cp. Madv. 372 b. Obs. 4; Ep. 8. 14, note.

6. **Ad Memmium.** Memmius had been convicted of bribery in 51 B.C. For other notices of him, cp. Ad Att. 4. 15. 7; 4. 16. 8; 6. 1. 23; Ad Q. F. 3. 2. 3; Ad Fam. 13. 1. Lucretius dedicated to him his poem 'De Rerum Natura.' Cp. Lucr. 1. 27; 43.

7. **Ad suos**, 'to his friends and agents at Athens.'

10. **Aedificandi**, 'of building on the site of the house of Epicurus.' Cp. Ad Fam. 13. 1. 3.

11. **Accurate**: cp. Ep. 30, 6, note, on p. 162.

12. **Piliam.** Pilia was the wife of Atticus, and seems to have written to Q. Cicero to ask him to behave more kindly to his wife Pomponia. Cicero opened the letter, as he confesses to Atticus, but wishes him not to tell Pilia ('indicabo enim tibi,' foll.)

Meis verbis, 'in such words as I generally use,' not 'in my name.' For Cicero did not wish Pilia to know that he was aware of her troubles. Boot.

13. **Fasciculum**, 'a packet of letters.'

14. **Abstuli**, 'took it from the bundle.'

συμπαθῶς . . **valde**, 'in a tone of lively sympathy.' Cp. Ad Att. 11. 44. 1. The adverb does not seem to be common in classical Greek.

15. **Quae tibi epistolae . . datae sunt.** Probably letters from Cicero's family to that of Atticus. Cicero passed through Brundisium on his way to the East. Cp. Ad Att. 5. 8. 1. Mr. Tyrrell (Intr. p. lxxx) restores the reading of the Medicean MS. 'datas,' which he says is in accordance with the usage of Comic poets, the accusative being governed by 'scilicet.'

16. **Haberem.** On the mood, cp. Madv. 358.

***νομανδρία* me.** Some word meaning 'hackneyed' seems to be wanted. Schütz prefers *νομαρχίας* = 'praefecturae,' 'employed in my letters about the prefectures,' i.e. 'when, in answer to applications for such offices, I said I had no leisure to attend to

ὀρία me excusationem ne acceperis. Cura ut omnia sciam, sed maxime ut valeas.

32. To ATTICUS (AD ATT. V. 16).

SYNNAS OR SYNNADA, AUGUST, 51 B.C. (703 A.U.C.)

1. I write hastily, while actually on the road. 2. I arrived in this miserable province on the last day of last month, and hear nothing but complaints of exaction, and find many traces of my predecessor's oppression. 3. The unhappy communities are, however, relieved by the moderation and self-control which I practise myself and enforce upon my officers, and my popularity exceeds all belief. 4. Appius has retired to the most remote part of the province. No authentic news about the Parthians. Bibulus still delays to enter his province. I am hastening to my camp.

CICERO ATTICO SAL.

Etsi in ipso itinere et via discedebant publicanorum tabellarii 1
et eramus in cursu, tamen surripiendum aliquid putavi spatii, ne me immemorem mandati tui putares; itaque subsedi in ipsa via, dum haec, quae longiorem desiderant orationem, summatim tibi perscriberem. Maxima exspectatione in perditam et plane 2
eversam in perpetuum provinciam nos venisse scito pridie Kal. Sextiles, moratos triduum Laodiceae. triduum Apameae, totidem dies Synnade. Audivimus nihil aliud nisi imperata ἐπικεφάλια

them.' Billerb. suggests *νομίμην*, 'usual.' Boot suggests *νομικὴν τριβήν*, 'that ordinary excuse for delay,' i.e. that I was too busy to write. Manutius reads *νομασίαν*, which he explains as = vilo dignam, referring to the plea of his being very busy.

1. Ne acceperis, 'do not be content with.' Cp. Madv. 386. Or perhaps 'metuo' is to be supplied: 'I fear you may have received' (from one of my family) 'the hackneyed excuse of my being too busy to write.'

3. In ipso itinere et via, 'while I am on the march, and, indeed, on the road,' i.e. not at a halting-place. Hofm.

Discedebant . . eramus. Epistolary tenses.

Tabellarii, the messengers sent home by the publicani. They are frequently mentioned by Cicero. Provincial governors used them in order to spare their own official messengers, 'statores.' Süpfle. Cp. Ad Fam. 2. 19. 1; Note C, p. 121.

5. Mandati, 'your charge to write whenever I could.'

6. Dum . . perscriberem, conj., as intimating design. Cp. Madv. 360.

7. Maxima exspectatione, 'amid the most eager expectation.' Cp. Madv. 257.

9. Laodiceae. This Laodicea stood on the Lycus in Phrygia, near the borders of Caria, but was annexed politically to Cilicia.

Apameae. Apamea was also in Phrygia, at the junction of the Marsyas and Maeander, north-east of Laodicea.

10. Synnade. Synnas, or Synnada, was in central Phrygia. Cicero gives different accounts of his halts elsewhere. Cp. Ad Att. 5. 20, 1; Ad Fam. 15. 4, 2.

ἐπικεφάλια, 'poll taxes.' The word *ἐπικεφάλαιον* occurs, Arist. Oecon. 2. 15, 3. Cicero describes it, Ad Fam. 3. 8, 5 'acerbissimam exactionem capitum atque ostiorum.' Appian, Mithrid. 83, says of L. Lucullus in Asia *τέλη δ' ἐπὶ τοῖς θεράπουσιν καὶ ταῖς οἰκίαις ὥριζε*, and Hofm. understands the first words as describing a poll tax. But I think that they might mean a tax on the rich, proportioned to the extent of their establishments.

[solvere non posse], ὠνὰς omnium venditas, civitatum gemitus, ploratus, monstra quaedam non hominis, sed ferae nescio cuius
3 immania. Quid quaeris? taedet omnino vitae. Levantur tamen miserae civitates, quod nullus fit sumptus in nos neque in legatos neque in quaestorem neque in quemquam; scito non modo nos foenum aut quod de lege Iulia dari solet non accipere, sed ne ligna quidem, nec praeter quattuor lectos et tectum quemquam accipere quicquam, multis locis ne tectum quidem, et in tabernaculo manere plerumque: itaque incredibilem in modum concursus fiunt ex agris, ex vicis, ex domibus omnibus; mehercule etiam adventu nostro reviviscunt, iustitia, abstinentia, clementia
4 tui Ciceronis: ita opiniones omnium superavit. Appius, ut audivit nos venire, in ultimam provinciam se coniecit Tarsum usque; ibi forum agit. De Partho silentium est, sed tamen concisos equites nostros a barbaris nuntiabant ii, qui veniebant. Bibulus ne cogitabat quidem etiam nunc in provinciam suam accedere; id autem facere ob eam causam dicebant, quod tardius

1. ὠνάς, 'properties,' to be sold in order to enable the owner to pay the taxes claimed. Hofm. But Andocides (de Myst. 10; 12) seems to use the word as meaning 'contracts' for farming taxes, etc., and perhaps this passage may mean that those who had made such contracts had to get rid of them at a sacrifice,—as Mr. Jeans has kindly suggested to me.

2. Monstra quaedam . . immanis, 'certain accounts of outrageous deeds, not of a man, but of some wild beast.' 'Quasi leo Marathonius aut aper Calydonius in eas grassatus esset.' J. F. Gronovius, ap. Boot. Cp. In Verr. 2. Act. 3. 73. 171, for a similar expression.

3. Taedet omnino vitae. These words may either refer to the sufferings of the natives of the province (Manut.) or to the distress they caused to Cicero.

4. Nullus fit sumptus .. in quemquam, 'they have not to incur any expense for me or for my legates, quaestors, or any one of my train.' On the repetition of the negatives, cp. Madv. 460, Obs. 2.

6. Lege Iulia. One of the laws of Caesar's first consulship forbade provincial governors when travelling to claim anything without compensation, but wood, salt, and hay. As Cicero specifies two items, his meaning seems to be that, far from claiming hay or the other supplies allowed by the Julian law, he did not even claim wood. For the force of 'non modo . . sed ne quidem,' cp. Madv. 461 b. Cicero refers also to the Julian law, In Pison. 37. 90.

7. Quemquam, 'any of my officers.'

8. Et in tabernaculo. 'Et' = 'but.' Cp. Madv. 433. Obs. 2; 458 c.

9. Manere depends upon 'scito.'

11. Etiam adventu . . tui Ciceronis, 'on my very arrival they seem to derive fresh life from the justice, forbearance, and clemency of your friend Cicero.' 'Adventu' is the ablat. of time. Cp. Ep. 8. 11, note. Wesenb. suggests 'iam' for 'etiam;' and, following Kayser, 'reviviscunt: iustitia, abstinentia, clementia tui Ciceronis opiniones omnium superavit.'

12. Opiniones, 'expectations.'

Appius Claudius Pulcher, Cicero's predecessor as governor of Cilicia.

14. Forum agit, 'presides in a court of justice.'

15. Qui veniebant, 'who came from Syria,' where C. Cassius, in command of the remains of the army of Crassus, obtained successes against the Parthians. Cp. Mommsen 4. 2, 338, 339. The rumour of disaster to which Cicero refers seems to have been unfounded. Bibulus was sent as proconsul to Syria 51 B.C., and took the command from Cassius. Cp. Intr. to Part II, §§ 20; 23. The imperfects, from nuntiabant to the end of the letter, seem to be epistolary.

17. Facere ob eam causam . . decedere. The omission of 'eum' before 'facere' seems an irregularity. Cp. Madv.

vellet decedere. Nos in castra properabamus, quae aberant bidui.

33. M. CAELIUS RUFUS TO CICERO (AD FAM. VIII. 4).

ROME, AUGUST 1, 51 B.C. (703 A.U.C.)

1. You have much news to hear. For instance, C. Marcellus has been elected consul, and P. Dolabella quindecimvir. The last event has been a great disappointment to L. Lentulus Crus. 2. C. Curio is canvassing for the tribuneship, in the room of Servaeus, and many people are anxious at the prospect of his success, but I think they are mistaken; a slight from Caesar has had great effect upon him. 3. I have put off writing, that I might report the result of all the elections, but there have been delays in many cases. My own prospects are good. 4. People were rather surprised lately by the commencement of a discussion in the senate about Caesar's provinces. The question will be resumed on Pompey's return. He used expressions shewing great respect for the senate. 5. Please to attend to my requests about the bill of Sittius and the panthers which I want. We hear that the king of Alexandria is dead; what do you think should be done about his kingdom?

CAELIUS CICERONI SAL.

Invideo tibi: tam multa quotidie, quae mirere, istoc perferuntur: primum illud, absolutum Messallam; deinde eundem condemnatum; C. Marcellum consulem factum; M. Calidium 1

401. Obs. 2. Bibulus delayed entering his province, because he wished not to have to leave it so soon as would be necessary if he entered it at the proper time. According to a decree of the senate, mentioned Ad Fam. 3. 3, 2, ex-magistrates were to hold their provinces for a year, dating from the day of their entry. Cp. Ad Att. 5. 15, 1.

M. Caelius Rufus, the writer of this letter, was defended by Cicero in 56 B.C. on charges of sedition and of poisoning. Cp. Intr. to Part II, § 5. He was a man of little constancy; when tribune in 52 B.C. he supported Milo; in 51 and 50 B.C. we find him in friendly correspondence with Cicero; afterwards he joined Caesar, and urged Cicero to be neutral in the civil war between him and Pompey. But he soon became discontented, intrigued with Milo to raise an insurrection in Italy, and was put to death near Thurii by some foreign cavalry in 48 B.C. Cp. Intr. to Part III, § 12.

3. Invideo tibi, 'I envy you having so much news to hear.'

4. Messallam. M. Valerius Messalla was elected consul for 53 B.C. after an interregnum, to hold office at once. He was accused of bribery, but the 'supplicatio' for Caesar's victories interposed to prevent his being brought to trial, and he held office for the latter part of 53 B.C. with Cn. Domitius Calvinus. Cp. Intr. to Part II, § 13; Ad Q. F. 3. 8, 3. In 51 B.C., after being once acquitted, he seems to have been convicted, probably under the Lex Licinia Pompeia de Sodaliciis. Cp. Rein, Criminalrecht, pp. 731, 732. He was probably afterwards a legate of Caesar in the African war.

5. C. Marcellum, son of a C. Marcellus, and cousin of the two Marcelli, who were consuls 51 and 49 B.C. There are letters to him, Ad Fam. 15. 10 and 11.

M. Calidium. Calidius is mentioned as an eminent orator, Brut. 79, 274. He appeared as advocate for Gabinius (Ad Q. F. 3. 2, 1); supported Milo in 52 B.C. (Ascon. in Milonian. 143); and took part in the discussion of the senate on Caesar's recall, when he pleaded for moderation (cp. Caes. Bell. Civ. 1. 2).

ab repulsa postulatum a Galliis duobus; P. Dolabellam XV. virum factum. Hoc tibi non invideo, caruisse te pulcherrimo spectaculo et Lentuli Cruris repulsi voltum non vidisse. At qua spe, quam certa opinione descenderat! quam ipso diffidente Dolabella! et hercules, nisi nostri equites acutius vidissent, paene
2 concedente adversario superasset. Illud te non arbitror miratum, Servaeum, designatum tribunum pl., condemnatum, *in* cuius locum C. Curio petit. Sane quam incutit multis, qui eum facilitatemque eius non norunt, magnum metum; sed, ut spero et volo et ut se fert ipse, bonos et senatum malet; totus, ut nunc est, hoc scaturit. Huius autem voluntatis initium et causa est, quod eum non mediocriter Caesar, qui solet infimorum hominum amicitiam

1. Ab repulsa, 'after his defeat,' probably as a candidate for the consulship. He had been praetor in 57 B.C. Manut. Cp. Post Red. in Sen. 9, 22, and for this sense of 'ab,' cp. Forcell., and Livy 44. 34 'ab his praeceptis.'

A Galliis duobus. M. and Q. Gallius apparently, sons of a Q. Gallius, whom Cicero defended in 64 B.C. against a charge of bribery brought by Callidius. Cp. Brut. 80; Ascon. Orat. in Tog. Cand. p. 113. A fragment of Cicero's speech is extant. A Gallius is also mentioned among the friends of Antony. Philipp. 13. 12, 26.

P. Dolabellam. Perhaps the same who afterwards married Tullia. Cp. Intr. to Part II, § 26.

XV virum, sc. sacris faciundis. These officers kept the Sibylline books, and presided at the ludi saeculares. Cp. Tac. Ann. 11, 11; Hor. Carm. Saec. 70. Originally the office was discharged by two men, necessarily patricians; but these were increased to ten, five patricians and five plebeians, in 369 B.C. (cp. Livy 6. 37 and 42), and afterwards, probably by Sulla, to fifteen (cp. Smith, Dict. of Antiq. p. 387).

3. Lentuli Cruris. L. Lentulus Crus was consul 49 B.C., and a strong opponent of Caesar. After the battle of Pharsalus he fell into the hands of the government of Alexandria, and was put to death. Cp. Epp. 13, 16; 87, 2.

4. Descenderat, sc. 'to the place of election.'

5. Nostri equites. The equites, from their wealth and strong class feeling, had great influence at elections. 'Nostri,' perhaps, refers to their attachment to Cicero, of which he often boasts. Cp. Ep. 9, 8. Manutius remarks that Caelius' father, like Cicero's, had not risen above the position of an 'eques.' Cp. pro Cael. 2. 3.

Acutius vidissent, either 'had been too clear-sighted for that,' or 'more clear-sighted than Dolabella.' Cp. Philipp. 2. 15. 39 'plus vidisse.' I cannot discover why the equites were so bitter against Lentulus.

Paene . . superasset, 'he would have succeeded almost without opposition from Dolabella.'

7. Servaeum. A man named Servaeus is mentioned (Pro Font. 5. 19) as an officer of Fonteius. The condemnation of the one here mentioned would prevent his entering upon office apparently.

8. C. Curio: cp. Ep. 30, first note.

Sane quam, 'certainly' = 'valde quidem.' Forcell.

Facilitatem, 'his docility' or 'good nature.'

9. Ut spero . . ipse, 'to judge from my hopes and wishes, and from his present demeanour.'

10. Malet, 'he will prefer to support.' A rare use of the word.

Hoc scaturit, 'he overflows with this feeling,' or, perhaps, as Manut. 'with eagerness to be tribune.' The word occurs here only, apparently, in a metaphorical sense.

11. Huius voluntatis, 'of this disposition of his.'

12. Non mediocriter . . valde contempsit, 'has shewn great contempt for him in no ordinary way.' So Metzg. renders 'mediocriter.' Or 'valde' may be resumptive after the intervening words. Benedict, ap. Schngar ad loc. Manutius says that Cicero adds the word 'valde,' 'fortasse ut magis augeat.' For this sense of 'contemnere,' cp. Pro Muren. 7, 15 'contempsisti L. Murenae genus, extulisti tuum.'

sibi qualibet impensa adiungere, valde contempsit; qua in re
mihi videtur illud perquam venuste cecidisse, quod a reliquis
quoque [usque eo] est animadversum, ut Curio, qui nihil consilio
facit, ratione et insidiis usus videretur in evitandis iis consiliis,
* * qui se intenderant adversarios in eius tribunatum: Laelios
et Antonios et id genus valentes dico. Has ego tibi litteras 8
eo maiore misi intervallo, quod comitiorum dilationes occupatiorem me habebant et exspectare in dies exitum cogebant, ut
confectis omnibus te facerem certiorem. Ad Kalendas Sext.
usque exspectavi. Praetoriis morae quaedam inciderunt. Mea
porro comitia quem eventum sint habitura, nescio; opinionem
quidem, quod ad Hirrum attinet, incredibilem aedilium pl. comitiis nacta sunt. Nam M. Coelium Vinicianum mentio illa fatua,

1. Adiungere amicitiam, 'to win the friendship of.' Cp. Pro Muren. 20, 41 'adiungit benevolentiam.'

2. Illud refers to ut Curio . . videretur. On the mood and tense of 'videretur,' cp. Madv. 373 and 382.

Perquam venuste, 'very neatly.' 'Perquam maxime augel.' Forcell. Cp. De Orat. 2. 49. 201 'perquam breviter perstrinxi.' 'Venuste' seems rarely to occur in the earlier Latin writers.

3. Usque eo. If these words be retained they probably mean, 'up to this time.' Wesenb. omits them.

4. Iis = 'eorum' probably. Cp. Madv. 314. Wesenb. suggests 'eorum,' or 'consiliariis.'

5. Qui se intenderant . . tribunatum, 'who had prepared themselves to oppose his election to the tribuneship.' For the double accus. se . . adversarios, cp. Madv. 227, and for the gender of 'qui,' ib. 315 b.

Laelios. A D. Laelius accused L. Flaccus in 59 B.C., and afterwards commanded some of Pompey's ships in the civil war, cp. Caes. Bell. Civ. 3. 5. and 100. He is also mentioned Ad Att. 11. 7. 2.

6. Antonios. Three brothers of this family are mentioned—Marcus, the triumvir, Caius, and Lucius. I cannot find that either of the two last sought the office of tribune at this time, unless the three brothers are referred to Ad Fam. 2. 18, 2 'tres fratres summo loco natos . . quos video deinceps tribunos plebis per triennium fore.' Perhaps the plural is used of one person, as in Tac. Ann. 1. 10 'interfectos Romae Varrones, Egnatios, Iulos.' Cp., also, Iuv. Sat. 1, 109; 10, 108.

Id genus valentes, 'influential' or 'energetic people of that sort.' Manutius explains 'valentes' as = 'animo et vigilantia praestantes.' Cp. Ad Att. 7. 3, 5 'tribunos valentes.' On the construction of 'id genus,' = 'eius generis,' cp. Madv. 238.

7. Occupatiorem me habebant, 'kept me employed more than usual.' For the two accusatives, cp. preceding section, note.

8. Exitum, the result of the comitia. Caelius was only able to report that of the consular comitia. He was himself a candidate for the curule aedileship.

11. Opinionem . . . incredibilem, 'wonderful hopes of success.' Cp. Ad Fam. 1. 6, 2 'non falsam opinionem tuam.' The word does not seem, however, to be often used without a qualifying epithet to denote *good* expectations.

12. Quod ad Hirrum attinet, 'so far as the opposition of Hirrus is concerned.' C. Lucceius, or Lucilius, Hirrus recommended in 53 B.C. that Pompey should be made dictator. Cp. Ad Q. F. 3. 8, 4. He did not support Cicero's claims for a 'supplicatio.' Cp. Ad Fam. 8. 11, 2. He raised troops for Pompey in Italy during the civil war, Ep. 49.

Aedilium plebis comitiis, 'at the time of election of the aediles of the plebs.' On the ablat., cp. Ep. 8, 11, note.

13. M. Coelium Vinicianum. This man seems only to be mentioned here and Bell. Alex. 77.

Mentio illa fatua, 'his stupid suggestion,' that Pompey should be made dictator. The proposals of Hirrus and Vinicianus seem to have been made in the same year, and were not popular. Cp. Merivale, 1. 535; Drumann 4. 528.

quam deriseramus olim, et promulgatio de dictatore subito deiecit
et deiectum magno clamore insecuta est; inde Hirrum cuncti iam
non faciendum flagitare. Spero te celeriter et de nobis, quod
4 sperasti, et de illo, quod vix sperare ausus es, auditurum. De
re publica iam novi quicquam exspectare desieramus; sed cum senatus habitus esset ad Apollinis a. d. XI. Kal. Sext. et referretur de stipendio Cn. Pompeii, mentio facta est de legione ea, quam expensam tulit C. Caesari Pompeius, quo numero esset, quoad peteretur. † Cum Pompeius 'esse in Gallia,' coactus est dicere Pompeius se legionem abducturum, sed non statim sub mentionem et convitium obtrectatorum; inde interrogatus *est* de successione C. Caesaris, de qua [hoc est de provinciis] placitum est, ut quam primum ad urbem reverteretur Cn. Pompeius, ut coram eo de successione provinciarum ageretur; nam Ariminum ad exercitum Pompeius erat iturus, et statim iit. Puto Idibus Sext. de ea re actum iri. Profecto aut transigetur aliquid,

1. Deiecit, 'defeated.' Forcell., who quotes Livy.

2. Insecuta est. This is very harsh as applying to 'promulgatio.' If the words are to be translated as they stand they must mean 'led to his being greeted with outcries after his defeat.' Ernesti suggests the insertion of 'plebs.'

3. Non faciendum, 'should not be elected.'

4. De illo, sc. Hirro.

Quod, i.e. 'that he has been defeated.'

De re publica . . desieramus, 'we had ceased to expect any novelty in public affairs.'

6. Ad Apollinis. Cp. Ep 23. 3, note.

7. De stipendio, 'about a vote of money for the troops.' For a notice of a similar vote in Caesar's favour, cp. Ep. 26, 10.

8. Expensam tulit, 'lent.' Cp. Livy 6. 20, and for the fact, Caes. Bell. Gall. 6. 1; Mommsen 4. 1, 341 and 353; Merivale 1. 489. The legion was lent to replace men lost in a contest with the Eburones in 53 B.C. Intr. to Part II, §§ 12; 13.

Quo numero esset, 'what place it held,' i.e. 'whether it was reckoned to belong to Pompey's or Caesar's army.' Wiel. Billerb. Cp. Philipp. 2. 29, 71 'quo numero fuisti;' Ib. 3. 6, 16 'homo nullo numero.'

9. Quoad peteretur, 'for how long its services were demanded.'

Esse in Gallia, sc. 'dixisset.' Cp. Madv. 479 b. The repetition of the name Pompeius after 'dicere' seems strange. Wesenb. suggests 'quae cum esset in Gallia,' omitting the first Pompeius.

10. Sub mentionem . . obtrectatorum, 'just after hints and abusive attacks made by Caesar's traducers.'

12. De successione C. Caesaris, 'as to the appointment of a successor to C. Caesar.' Cp. Appendix 6, § 5.

Placitum est. Cp. Ep. 107, § 2; Cic. de Rep. 1. 12, 18.

14. Coram eo. Either Pompey might be released from the restriction of the laws, or the senate might be held without the 'pomoerium,' so that he might attend it without forfeiting his 'imperium.' Manut.

Nam explains 'reverteretur.' 'I say should have returned, for.' Cp. Ep. 26, 2, note.

Ariminum, the first important town south of the Rubicon. Pompey seems to have assembled a force there; whether for service in Spain or in Italy seems doubtful. Cp. Drumann 4. 532.

15. Erat iturus, 'was about to depart,' on the day of the debate.

16. De ea re, 'about the appointment of a successor to Caesar.'

Aut transigetur . . intercedetur, 'either some arrangement will be made,' or 'there will be scandalous opposition by a tribune,' which Pompey, by his threat mentioned in the next sentence, seemed to anticipate.

aut turpiter intercedetur. Nam in disputando coniecit illam vocem Cn. Pompeius, omnes oportere senatui dicto audientes esse. Ego tamen sic nihil exspecto, quo modo Paulum, consulem designatum, primum sententiam dicentem. Saepius te admoneo 6 de syngrapha Sittiana; cupio enim te intellegere eam rem ad me valde pertinere; item de pantheris, ut Cibyratas arcessas curesque, ut mihi vehantur; praeterea nuntiatum nobis *est* et pro certo iam habetur, regem Alexandrinum mortuum; quid mihi suadeas, quo modo regnum illud se habeat, quis procuret, diligenter mihi perscribas. K. Sext.

34. M. CAELIUS RUFUS TO CICERO (AD FAM. VIII 8).

ROME, EARLY IN OCTOBER, 51 B.C. (703 A.U.C.)

1. Your acquaintance, C. Sempronius Rufus, has been declared guilty of bringing a malicious charge: I assisted in his discomfiture. 2. M. Servilius has been charged with extortion and corruption before the praetor M. Laterensis, but 3. owing to the ignorance of that magistrate no decision has been come to upon his case, and he is left rather discredited to stand another trial. 4. The senate has adopted various important resolutions about Caesar's provinces, after ascertaining Pompey's wishes in the matter. I send you copies of a decree and of three resolutions. 5. Decree. That the consuls for next year shall bring forward the question

1. Coniecit. Rare without mention of the person against whom the expression is directed. Here it seems simply to mean 'uttered.'

2. Dicto audientes esse = 'obtemperare.' Cp. In Verr. 2. Act. 5. 32, 85: Livy 5. 3: Zumpt, L. G. 412.

3. Ego tamen . . dicentem, 'there is nothing to which I look forward with so much interest as to hearing Paulus giving his opinion first (in the senate) as consul elect.' L. Aemilius Paulus, consul in 50 B.C., seems to have been a man of small capacity. Caesar purchased his support for a considerable sum. Cp. Intr. to Part II, § 27; Suet. Iul. 29; Mommsen 4. 2, 354.

5. De syngrapha Sittiana. P. Sittius seems to have given a bill to Caelius, and may now have been in Cicero's province, or have had funds there. Sittius afterwards did Caesar good service in Africa, at the head of a Mauretanian force. Cp. Bell. Afric. 36; 95: Mommsen 4. 2, 442.

Ad me valde pertinere, 'interests me very much.'

6. De pantheris. Caelius wanted to conciliate the people, with a view to his election as aedile, by providing wild beasts for a combat in the arena.

Cibyratas. Cibyra was a town on the borders of Phrygia and Cilicia. The word 'Cibyratae' is here probably used of hunters from Cibyra, who would be wanted to catch the panthers. Cp. Ad Att. 6. 1, 21 'alienum esse existimatione mea Cibyratas imperio meo publice venari;' also Ad Fam. 8. 9, 3.

8. Regem Alexandrinum. Caelius refers to Ptolemy XII Auletes, restored by Gabinius in 55 B.C. Cp. Intr. to Part II, § 9.

Quid mihi suadeas, 'what steps you recommend me to take.' Perhaps the king had owed Caelius money.

9. Quis procuret, 'who administers his property.' Pothinus, an eunuch, did so. Cp. Plut. Pomp. 77: App. Bell. Civ. 2, 84; Caes. Bell. Civ. 3. 108.

of the Gallic provinces on March 1, and press its discussion in every way. 6-8. Resolutions. (1) That no one interpose any obstacle to the discussion of this question in the senate: (2) That the claims of Caesar's soldiers to a discharge be brought before the senate: (3) That provision be made for the government of Cilicia and of the other eight praetorian provinces by men of praetorian rank. 9. Pompey says he will not hesitate after March 1 to aid in providing Caesar with a successor; and other expressions of his shew a determination to resist the interference of tribunes. He is clearly on bad terms with Caesar; the latter is anxious for a compromise, and 10. Curio is preparing to resist him. I have to thank Curio for some African panthers; let me have some from Asia, too. I hope you will attend to my claim upon Sittius.

CAELIUS CICERONI SAL.

1 Etsi de re publica quae tibi scribam habeo, tamen nihil quod magis gavisurum te putem habeo quam hoc: scito C. Sempronium Rufum, [Rufum,] mel ac delicias tuas, calumniam maximo plausu tulisse. Quaeris 'qua in causa?' M. Tuccium, accusatorem suum, post ludos Romanos reum lege Plotia de vi fecit hoc consilio, quod videbat, si extraordinarius reus nemo accessisset, sibi hoc anno causam esse dicendam: dubium porro illi non erat, quid futurum esset. Nemini hoc deferre munusculum maluit quam suo accusatori. Itaque sine ullo subscriptore descendit et Tuccium

1. **Quod .. gavisurum.** This accusative with 'gaudeo' seems rare, except in Caelius' letters. It is found, however, with other verbs of similar meaning. Cp. Madv. 229.

2. **C. Sempronium Rufum.** For an account of this man, and of Vestorius, cp. below, and Ep. 38, 10. If the second 'Rufum' be genuine, it may express surprise or pleasure. 'Rufus, I say.'

3. **Mel ac delicias tuas,** 'your favourite and darling.' This is apparently the only passage where 'mel' is used in a metaphorical sense by a classical prose author.

Calumniam .. tulisse, 'has been convicted of bringing a calumnious accusation,' Hofm. Wiel. Billerb. Forcellini's explanation hardly suits the sense of this passage.

Maximo plausu, 'amid the greatest applause.' Cp. on the ablat., Madv. 257.

4. **M. Tuccium.** This man seems not to be elsewhere mentioned.

Accusatorem. This word seems to be used of a plaintiff on a civil charge sometimes. Partit. Orat. 32, 110.

5. **Post ludos Romanos.** The Roman games seem to have lasted from the 4th to the 12th of September. Cp. Smith's Dict. of Antiq. p. 715.

Lege Plotia. This law was probably passed 89 B.C., and provided that trials for 'vis' need not be suspended on festivals. Cp. Pro Caelio 1, 1. It was supplemented by a Lex Lutatia in 78 B.C. (?) Ib. 29, 70; Rein, C. R. 736, foll.

6. **Extraordinarius,** 'a defendant whose trial would claim precedence of other suits.' Trials 'de vi' seem to have claimed this precedence. Forcell. explains 'extraordinarius' as said of those 'de quibus nihil est lege constitutum.' But this passage clearly implies that a man accused 'de vi' would be 'reus extraordinarius;' and there were definite statutes about 'vis.'

Hoc anno. Perhaps Sempronius would prefer a new praetor; perhaps he was merely anxious to gain time without any definite hopes.

7. **Quid futurum esset,** i.e. that he would be convicted.

8. **Hoc .. munusculum,** 'this little favour,' of a prosecution.

9. **Sine ullo subscriptore,** 'without any one to support his charge.' The 'subscriptores' were the subordinate advocates for the prosecution (cp. Ep. 13, 3, note; Div. in Caec. 15), and to appear without such support, though in accordance with old precedent (cp. Pro Cluent. 70, 199), may in

reum fecit. At ego, simul atque audivi, invocatus ad subsellia rei occurro; surgo, neque verbum de re facio: totum Sempronium usque eo perago, ut Vestorium quoque interponam et illam fabulam narrem, quem ad modum tibi pro beneficio dederit, † si quod iniuriis suis esset, ut Vestorius teneret. Haec quoque magna 2
nunc contentio forum tenet: M. Servilius postquam, ut coeperat, omnibus in rebus turbarat nec quod non venderet quicquam reliquerat maximaque nobis traditus erat invidia, neque Laterensis praetor expostulante Pausania, nobis patronis, QVO EA PECVNIA PERVENISSET, recipere voluit, Q. Pilius, necessarius Attici nostri,

this case have been thought to shew weakness.

1. Invocatus .. occurro, 'I hasten to present myself uninvited (Forcell.) at the side of the accused.' For this sense of 'occurro,' cp. Philipp. 1. 4. 9; Livy 31. 29; 36. 24. Caelius apparently only wished to annoy Sempronius.

Ad subsellia rei. A space at the end of a basilica was set apart for judicial business; sometimes rectangular, sometimes a semicircle projecting from one or both the ends of the building. The praetor's seat would be in the middle of this space; the 'subsellia rei' would probably run round one side of it. See Ep. 24. 1, note, and Smith, Dict. of Antiq., sub voc. 'Basilica,' pp. 198, 199.

2. Totum . . . perago. 'Peragere reum' is properly 'to prosecute to a conviction.' Cp. examples in Forcell. This passage perhaps means, 'I accuse Sempronius so uncompromisingly.' Manutius gives 'exagito,' 'vexo' as equivalents for 'perago.' On the adverbial use of 'totus' and similar adjectives, cp. Ep. 2, 2, note.

3. Interponam, 'introduce.'

Illam fabulam, 'the old story.' Cp. Ad Att. 5. 2, 2: 14. 14. 2. Rufus apparently had owed Vestorius some money, and had been invited to settle the dispute by Cicero's arbitration. He then seems to have made it a favour to Cicero that he forbore to oppose the just claims of Vestorius.

4. Quem ad modum .. teneret, 'how as a favour to you he allowed Vestorius to retain whatever he had possession of, to the injury of Sempronius.' In substance from Bian. Hofm. reads 'iniuriis suum esset,' Wesenb. 'si quid iniuria ipsius (Rufi) esset,' Victorius 'si quid iuris sui esset,' in which case I suppose 'sui' would refer to Vestorius.

5. Iniuriis, similar to 'ingratiis' in construction.

Iniuriis suis. 'Si quid esset suo damno suaque iniuria quod Vestorius teneret, quasi ademptum sibi aliquid ac teneri a Vestorio diceret quod aliqua eius iniuria fieret.' Manut.

Haec, 'the following.'

6. Forum tenet, 'occupies the attention of the courts.'

M. Servilius. Orell. says he was tribune in 60 B.C. There were both patrician and plebeian Servilii.

Ut coeperat .. turbarat, 'had carried through all his career the extravagance with which he had begun.' 'Conturbo' is more common in this sense. Cp. Ad Att. 4. 7. 1.

7. Quod non venderet, 'omnino;' or perhaps, as Mr. Jeans renders, 'which was not for sale.' On the conj., cp. Madv. 364.

8. Maxima .. invidia, 'and had been given me as a client with a very bad reputation.' For the ablat., cp. Madv. 257.

Laterensis: cp. Ep. 11, 2.

9. Expostulante, 'in spite of the representations of.'

Pausanias seems not to be elsewhere mentioned. Hofm. suggests that he may have been agent for the Asiatic provincials on the trial of C. Claudius. Or perhaps he was one of the creditors of Servilius.

Nobis patronis, 'while I was counsel for the defence.'

QVO EA PECVNIA PERVENISSET recipere, 'to receive a demand for enquiry "what had become of that money";' i.e. whither the unjust gains of Claudius had gone. The words printed in capitals seem to be a regular form denoting the object of a legal inquiry. The Lex Iulia de Repetundis of 59 B.C. allowed the injured parties to require restitution from any one who was proved to have profited by a governor's unjust gains. Cp. Pro Rab. Post. 4. 8.

10. Q. Pilius. Probably connected with Atticus by marriage. He is only mentioned here and Ad Att. 4. 17, 3 [4. 18, 5. Bait.]

de repetundis eum postulavit: magna ilico fama surrexit et de damnatione ferventer loqui est coeptum. Quo vento proiicitur Appius minor, ut indicaret pecuniam ex bonis patris pervenisse ad Servilium praevaricationisque causa diceret depositum HS. LXXXI. Admiraris amentiam: immo si actionem stultissimasque

2 de se, nefarias de patre confessiones audisses? Mittit in consilium eosdem illos, qui lites aestimarant, iudices. Cum aequo numero sententiae fuissent, Laterensis leges ignorans pronuntiavit, quid singuli ordines iudicassent, et ad extremum, ut solent, NON REDIGAM. Postquam discessit et pro absoluto Servilius haberi

1. **De repetundis**, sc. 'pecuniis,' 'for extortion' or misgovernment. The suit was brought for the restitution of money said to have been illegally exacted; but charges of oppression in general were introduced by the prosecutor, if the speeches against Verres are a fair specimen of the pleadings on such occasions. A permanent court for the trial of such cases was first established in 149 B.C.

Eum, sc. Servilium. It seems likely that Pausanias wished to prosecute Servilius as having shared the unjust gains of C. Claudius, and that when the praetor refused to entertain the charge, Q. Pilius prosecuted Servilius directly for 'repetundae.' Cp. Hofm.

2. **Loqui est coeptum.** Forcell. makes 'loqui' passive, but Hofm. says that 'coeptum est' = 'coeperunt.'

Quo vento proiicitur, 'is impelled by that rumour.' Forcell.

3. **Appius minor.** Younger son of C. Claudius and nephew of P. Clodius. Manutius on this passage suggests that he and his brother may have been adopted by Ap. Claudius Pulcher, consul in 54 B.C.; but Schütz doubts this. C. Claudius governed Asia in 55-54 B.C. (cp. Pro Scauro 31-35), and seems to have been dead at the time of Milo's trial for the murder of Clodius in 52 B.C. Cp. Ascon. Argum. in Milonian. p. 143.

4. **Praevaricationis . . causa.** The most natural sense of these words would be, that Servilius was the accuser of C. Claudius, and promised to betray his clients. But perhaps it suits the general sense better to suppose that Servilius received the money to bribe the accuser, and kept it himself instead. 'Praevaricatio' was the legal term for collusion of an accuser with the defendant.

Depositum, 'had been placed in the hands of Servilius.'

H. S. LXXXI. Probably LXXX = octogies, but the sum seems very large, more than £70,000. Cp., however, In Verr. Act. 1. 13. 38.

5. **Immo si**, 'how much more would you have wondered if.' Cp. Hofm.; Madv. 454.

Actionem, 'his pleading.'

6. **Confessiones**, 'of his own and his father's misconduct in Asia' probably. About himself such confessions would be foolish; about his father, unnatural.

Mittit in consilium, sc. Appius. 'He allows the same judges who had assessed his father's fine to act in this case.' This must surely be an exaggeration; it is hardly likely that precisely the same body of judges would have acted in two different years. Manutius suggests that the trial for 'praevaricatio' would come on 'extra ordinem,' as a supplement to the trial of the elder Appius. Forcell. says the phrase 'mittere in consilium' was used of the presiding magistrate; but the passage he quotes from In Verr. 2. Act. 1. 9, 26, shews that it may also apply to the parties on the conclusion of the proceedings; cp. also Pro Cluent. 30, 83. For the phrase 'lites aestimare,' 'to fix the amount to be repaid by the defendant,' cp. Pro Muren. 20, 42; In Verr. Act. 1. 13, 38. It corresponded to the Attic τίμησις, and was most important in trials for extortion and peculation, and of course in all civil suits.

7. **Cum aequo . . fuissent**, 'when the votes of the whole court had been equally divided,' though very likely a majority in two orders had acquitted Servilius.

9. **Singuli ordines**, the senators, equites, and tribuni aerarii. Cp. Intr. to Part I, § 5; II, § 8.

Ut solent, i.e. in cases of acquittal.

10. **Non redigam**, 'I shall not require the restitution of the money.' These words were very likely the regular form for declaring an acquittal in cases of 'repetundae,'

coeptus est legisque unum et centesimum caput legit, in quo ita erat, QVOD EORVM IVDICVM MAIOR PARS IVDICARIT, ID IVS RATVMQVE ESTO, in tabulas absolutum non rettulit, ordinum iudicia perscripsit; postulante rursus Appio cum L. Lollio transegit et se relaturum dixit. Sic nunc neque absolutus neque damnatus Servilius de repetundis saucius Pilio tradetur. Nam de divinatione Appius, cum calumniam iurasset, contendere ausus non est Pilioque cessit, et ipse de pecuniis repetundis a Serviliis est postulatus et praeterea de vi reus a quodam suo emissario, Sex. Tettio, factus. Recte hoc par habet. Quod ad rem publicam pertinet, omnino 4.
multis diebus exspectatione Galliarum actum nihil est; aliquando tamen, saepe re dilata et graviter acta et plane perspecta Cn. Pompeii voluntate in eam partem, ut eum decedere post Kalendas

but I cannot find them elsewhere in this sense. Cp., however, Div. in Caec. 17. 56 'bona vendit, pecuniam redigit.'

Postquam discessit, sc. Laterensis, 'after he went home.'

1. **Legis,** 'Iuliae de repetundis' probably. It would appear that this law required an absolute majority of the whole court for acquittal or conviction, and did not provide for the case of equal division.

3. **In tabulas . . perscripsit,** 'did not record an acquittal in his register, but wrote out the verdicts of the different orders.'

4. **Postulante rursus Appio,** 'when Appius renewed his charge,' apparently on the ground that Servilius had not been acquitted.

Cum L. Lollio transegit, foll., 'after a conference with L. Lollius, Laterensis said he would record Servilius as acquitted.' But the words 'neque absolutus neque damnatus' seem to imply that he did not do so at once, or that the proceeding was considered informal. L. Lollius seems to be only mentioned here. For 'transigo' as a neuter verb, cp. In Verr. 2 Act. 2. 32, 79 'qui cum reo transigit.'

6. **De repetundis . . tradetur,** 'will pass with a damaged reputation into the hands of Pilius for prosecution on a charge of "repetundae."'

Nam, 'I say of Pilius, for.' Cp. Ep. 9, 8, note.

De divinatione, 'on the discussion who should be named accuser.' The judges who decided this seem not necessarily to have been the same body who afterwards tried the main issue. Cp. In Verr. 2 Act. 1. 6, 15.

7. **Calumniam iurasset,** 'had made oath that he had good grounds for his prosecution.' The defendant might require the prosecutor to take such an oath. Cp. Smith, Dict. of Antiq., p. 235.

Contendere, 'to dispute the point,' 'to come into court.'

8. **A Serviliis.** Probably the M. Servilius of this letter, and some relation.

9. **A quodam suo emissario,** 'by a certain spy of his own.'

10. **Recte . . habet,** 'this pair is well matched.' Cp. Pro Muren. 6, 14 'bene habet,' Ep. 77, 1 'minus belle habuit.' For this sense of 'par,' cp. De Opt. Gen. Orat. 6, 17 'gladiatorum par nobilissimum;' Hor. Sat. 2. 3. 243 'par nobile fratrum.'

11. **Exspectatione Galliarum,** 'because people are waiting to see what will be done about the Gallic provinces,' where Caesar's term of government was drawing to a close.

Aliquando . . placeret, 'at length, after frequent postponements, and serious discussion of the question, when it had been clearly ascertained to be Pompey's wish that after the first of March the senate should decree Caesar's recall.' On the conj. 'placeret,' cp. Ep. 26, 9, note, and for 'in eam partem,' sc. 'inclinante,' Ad Att. 16. 1. 6 'has scripsi in eam partem ne me motum putares.' As to the facts, the Lex Pompeia Licinia of 55 B.C. probably provided that the appointment of a successor to Caesar should not be discussed before March 1, 50 B.C. Cp. below, § 5; Ad Fam. 8. 9. 5: Caes. de Bell. Gall. 8. 53; Appendix 6, §§ 1; 4, and Intr. to Part II, §§ 21; 27.

Martias placeret, senatus consultum, quod tibi misi, factum est auctoritatesque perscriptae.

5 S. C. Auctoritates. Pr. Kal. Octobres in aede Apollinis scrib. adfuerunt L. Domitius Cn. f. Fab. Ahenobarbus, Q. Caecilius Q. f. Fab. Metellus Pius Scipio, L. Villius L. F. Pom. Annalis, C. Septimius T. f. Quirina, C. Lucilius C. f. Pup. Hirrus, C. Scribonius C. f. Pop. Curio, L. Ateius L. f. An. Capito, M. Eppius M. f. Ter. Quod M. Marcellus cos. v. f. de provinciis consularibus, d. e. r. i. c., uti L. Paulus C. Marcellus coss., cum magistratum inissent, ex Kal. Mart., quae in suo magistratu futurae essent, de consularibus provinciis ad senatum referrent, neve quid prius ex Kal. Mart. ad senatum referrent, neve quid coniunctim de ea re referretur a consulibus, utique eius rei causa per dies comitiales senatum haberent senatusque cons. facerent, et, cum de ea re senatum referretur a consulibus, qui eorum in CCC. iudicibus

1. Misi, epistolary = 'mitto.'

3. Auctoritates: cp. Ep. 22, 4, note. One decree and three resolutions follow.

4. Scribendo adfuerunt, sc. 'senatus consulto.' 'There were present at the drawing up of the decree.' Cp. Ad Att. 7. 1, 7; Ad Fam. 15. 6. 2; 12. 29. 2.

On L. Domitius and Q. Scipio cp. Ep. 1, 3, notes.

Fabia, sc. 'tribu.' For the ablat., cp. Madv. 275, Obs. 3. The other tribes mentioned are Pomptina, Quirina, Pupinia, Popilia, Aniensis, Teretina.

5. L. Villius, only mentioned here. The surname Annalis probably dates from the year 180 B.C., when the Lex Villia Annalis passed. Cp. Livy 40. 44.

6. C. Septimius, perhaps a praetor of 57 B.C., who supported Cicero's restoration from exile. Cp. Post Red. in Sen. 9, 23.

C. Lucilius . . Hirrus, perhaps the Hirrus mentioned Ep. 33, 3. It seems doubtful if his name was Lucilius or Lucceius.

7. C. Scribonius . . Curio: cp. Ep. 30, first note.

8. L. Ateius . . Capito. Only here mentioned by Cicero. Caesar pardoned an Ateius in Africa. Cp. Bell. Afric. 89.

M. Eppius served under Pompey in the civil war, and was pardoned by Caesar in Africa. Cp. Ep. 50, 1; Bell. Afric. l. c.

Quod, 'whereas.'

9. M. Marcellus: cp. Intr. to Part II, § 17; Epp. 31, 2, note; 90, 3; 93; 101.

V. f. = 'verba fecit,' said of a magistrate who laid a question before the senate for discussion.

De provinciis consularibus: cp. Appendix 6, § 5.

D. e. r. i. c. = 'de ea re ita censuerunt.' The tenses which follow shew that the principal verb must be in the past tense.

10. L. Paulus: cp. Ep. 13. 2, note.

C. Marcellus: cp. Ep. 33. 1, note.

13. Ex Kal. . . essent, i.e. from March 1, 50 B.C.

14. Coniunctim, 'in combination with it.' The question was to be brought before the senate simply, without having any other bound up with it. The force of 'coniunctim' may be seen by a reference to the account of the discussion of the Licinian Rogations. Cp. Livy 6. 39.

15. Per dies comitiales. After the enactment of the Lex Pupia, first mentioned in 56 B.C., it seems not to have been usual to hold meetings of the senate on days on which the comitia could be held. Cp. Ad Q. F. 2. 2. 3; 2. 13. 3; Ad Fam. 1. 4. 1; Caes. Bell. Civ. 1. 5. The author of the Lex Pupia was probably M. Pupius Piso Calpurnianus, consul in 61 B.C., though some assign it to a Cn. Pupius, tribune in 236-5 B.C.

17. Eorum, sc. 'senatorum.'

In ccc iudicibus. Probably cccl x

essent, eos adducere liceret. Si quid de ea re ad populum plebemve lato opus esset, uti Ser. Sulpicius M. Marcellus coss., praetores tribunique pl., quibus eorum videretur, ad populum plebemve ferrent: quod *si* ii non tulissent, uti, quicumque deinceps essent, ad populum plebemve ferrent. i. n.

Pr. Kal. Octobres in aede Apollinis scrib. adfuerunt 6
L. Domitius Cn. f. Fab. Ahenobarbus, Q. *Caecilius* Q. f. *Fab.* Metellus Pius Scipio, L. Villius L. f. Pom. Annalis, C. Septimius T. f. Quirina, *C. Lucilius C. f. Pup. Hirrus*, C. Scribonius C. f. Pop. Curio, L. Ateius L. f. An. Capito, M. Eppius M. f. Teretina. Quod M. Marcellus cos. v. f. de provinciis, d. e. r. i. c., senatum existimare neminem eorum, qui potestatem habent intercedendi, impediendi, moram adferre oportere, quo minus de r. p. p. R. Q. ad senatum referri senatique consultum fieri possit: qui impedierit, prohibuerit, eum senatum existimare contra rem publicam fecisse. Si quis huic s. c. intercesserit, senatui placere auctoritatem perscribi et de ea re ad senatum populumque referri. Huic s. c. intercessit

the right number. Cp. Ep. 59, 2, note; Vell. 2. 76; Plut. Pomp. 58. Billerb. thinks the first or senatorial 'decuria' of judges, as constituted by the Lex Pompeia of 55 B.C., is referred to. The object of the decree was to make it lawful to summon such senators as belonged to this body from the courts in which they served to attend the senate's debates.

1. Si quid . . lato opus esset, 'if any enactment were required.' Cp. Madv. 266, Obs.

Ad populum plebemve, 'by the people assembled by centuries or tribes.' The expression seems to have been retained from a time at which only plebeians voted in the 'comitia tributa.' See, among other passages, Livy 2. 56. Mommsen (Röm. Forsch. 1. 194 foll.), referring especially to a quotation from Laelius Felix in A. Gellius, N. A. 15. 27, maintains that 'plebs' in such passages as the present is equivalent to, not 'comitia tributa,' but 'concilium plebis,' an assembly of the tribes from which patricians were excluded and the only one convoked by plebeian magistrates. Cp. Ep. 20, 6, note.

2. Ser. Sulpicius, an eminent jurist, was consul with M. Marcellus. Cicero had a very high opinion of him. Cp. Ad Fam. 4. 1–6; Philipp. 9; and several passages in the oration of Pro Murena.

5. Quicumque deinceps essent, 'their successors in those several offices.'

6. I. n. = 'intercessit nemo.' The tribunician veto could not legally be exercised in discussions about the consular provinces, as a Lex Sempronia C. Gracchi forbade it. Cp. De Prov. Cons. 7. 17, and Appendix 6, § 4.

12. Teretina. This word is also written Terentina. Cp. Livy 10. 9.

15. De r. p. p. R. Q. = 'de re publica populi Romani Quiritium.'

16. Senati. On this form, cp. Madv. 46, Obs. 2.

18. Fecisse. On the tense, cp. Madv. 407.

19. Auctoritatem . . referri, 'that a resolution should be drawn up, and the senate and people consulted on the affair.' The next step would be 'agere cum tribunis' to negotiate with the protesting tribunes. Cp. Philipp. 2. 21, 52.

20. Intercessit. For the sing., cp. Madv. 213 a.

C. Caelius, L. Vinicius, P. Cornelius, C. Vibius Pansa, *tribuni pl.*

7 Item senatui placere de militibus, qui in exercitu C. Caesaris sunt: qui eorum stipendia emerita aut causas, quibus de causis missi fieri debeant, habeant, ad hunc ordinem referri, ut eorum ratio habeatur causaeque cognoscantur. Si quis huic s. c. intercessisset, senatui placere auctoritatem perscribi et de ea re ad hunc ordinem referri. Huic s. c. intercessit *C.* Caelius, C. Pansa, tribuni pl.

8 Itemque senatui placere in Ciliciam provinciam, in VIII reliquas provincias, quas praetorii pro praetore obtinerent, eos, qui praetores fuerunt neque in provinciam cum imperio fuerunt, quos eorum ex s. c. cum imperio in provincias pro praetore mitti oporteret, eos sortito in provincias mitti placere; si ex eo numero, quos *ex* s. c. in provincias ire oporteret, ad numerum non essent, qui in eas provincias proficiscerentur, tum uti

1. Of the four protesting tribunes only C. Vibius Pansa seems to be mentioned elsewhere. Cicero speaks of him as a friend Ad Q. F. 3. 5, 5, and Ad Fam. 6. 12. On his conduct after Caesar's death, cp. Intr. to Part V, §§ 12; 15–17.

4. Qui eorum, sc. 'de iis qui.' Cp. Madv. 321, and Obs.

Stipendia emerita . . habeant, 'have completed their time of service, or have other pleas for discharge.' The full number of campaigns is said to have been twenty for the infantry, and ten for the cavalry. Cp. Smith, Dict. of Antiq., sub voc. 'Exercitus,' p. 499.

Causas, quibus de causis. On the pleonasm, cp. Zumpt, L. G. 743; also § 8 below, note. 'The 'causae' would be pleas for discharge, such as sickness, and, perhaps, distinguished services. A discharge obtained on the ground of sickness was called 'missio causaria.' Forcell. The object of this resolution probably was to hold out inducements to Caesar's soldiers to desert him.

11. In octo reliquas. These would be 1. Sicily; 2. Sardinia, with Corsica; 3. Macedonia, with Achaia; 4. Asia; 5. Africa; 6. Crete; 7. Cyrene; 8. Bithynia. Cp. Mommsen, Rechtsfrage, pp. 45, 46. Cilicia was to be a praetorian province after the expiration of Cicero's term of office.

12. Praetorii, 'men who had been praetors;' an analogous term to 'consulares.'

13. Obtinerent. Wesenb. has obtin(er)ent.

Eos qui . . mitti placere, 'that from the number of those who have been praetors, and have not governed provinces, such as ought, according to the decree of the senate, to be sent to govern provinces as propraetors should be sent by lot.' The second 'eos' and the second 'placere' seem pleonastic.

In provinciam . . fuerunt. On the accusat., cp. In Verr. 2 Act. 5. 38, 98 'in potestatem futurum;' Ad Att. 15. 4. 2 'quo die in Tusculanum essem futurus,' according to the Medicean MS. Wesenb., however, suggests 'in provinciis . . iverunt.'

14. Ex s. c. = 'ex senatus consulto.' For the facts, cp. Intr. to Part II, § 17; Appendix 6, § 4; Ad Fam. 3. 2, 2.

15. Eos sortito, the pronoun 'eos' is resumptive after a parenthesis. Cp. Madv. 489 a.

16. Ex eo numero = 'ex eorum numero.' Cp. Ep. 32. 2, note.

17. Quos, plural, as referring to a noun of multitude. Cp. Madv. 215 a.

Ad numerum non essent, 'there were not enough.' Forcell. Cp. Ad Q. F. 2. 13, 2, (12, 2 Bait.) 'ad numerum iudices habere.'

18. Tum uti . . proficiscerentur, 'then the praetors of the following years should be

quodque collegium primum praetorum fuisset neque in provincias profecti essent, ita sorte in provincias proficiscerentur; si ii ad numerum non essent, tunc deinceps proximi cuiusque collegii, qui praetores fuissent neque in provincias profecti essent, in sortem coniicerentur, quoad is numerus effectus esset, quem ad numerum in provincias mitti oporteret; si quis huic s. c. intercessisset, auctoritas perscriberetur. Huic s. c intercessit C. Caelius, C. Pansa, tribuni pl.

Illa praeterea Cn. Pompeii sunt animadversa, quae maxime confidentiam attulerunt hominibus, ut diceret se ante Kal. Martias non posse sine iniuria de provinciis Caesaris statuere, post Kal. Martias se non dubitaturum. Cum interrogaretur, si qui tum intercederent, dixit hoc nihil interesse, utrum C. Caesar senatui dicto audiens futurus non esset an pararet qui senatum decernere non pateretur. 'Quid, si' inquit alius 'et consul esse et exercitum habere volet?' At ille quam clementer: 'quid, si filius meus fustem mihi impingere volet?' His vocibus, ut existimarent homines Pompeio cum Caesare esse negotium, effecit; itaque iam, ut video, alteram utram ad condicionem descendere volt 8

sent, according to the priority of election of each college.' On the plural 'essent,' cp. Madv. 215.

5. In sortem coniicerentur, 'should be admitted to the allotment.' The expression is used by Livy of the 'provinciae,' 30. 1.

6. Is numerus . . quem ad numerum. On the repetition of the subst., cp. note on § 7 above; Madv. 315, and Obs. 2.

7. Mitti oporteret, sc. 'rectores.' The import of this decree seems to be that if there were not nine 'praetorii' of five years' standing, the deficiency should be made good by taking successively 'praetorii' of four, three, and two years' standing. Its object was, by assigning as many provinces as possible to 'praetorii,' to diminish the number of provinces disposable for 'consulares,' and so to strengthen the arguments for Caesar's recall in order to provide for such 'consulares' as might wish to govern provinces. The combination of the indic. fuerunt in the early part of the decree with conjunctives in the rest of it, may perhaps be accounted for by Caelius quoting the actual words of the decree in the words qui praetores . . fuerunt, and giving the rest of it in his own words.

10. Illa, 'the following demonstrations.' Cp. Madv. 485 b.

Confidentiam, 'confidence that there was an understanding between Pompey and the optimates.' It is more often used by Cicero in a bad sense for 'effrontery.'

11. Ut diceret, 'how he said.' Cp. Hor. Carm. 1. 9. 13; Madv. 356.

12. Sine iniuria: cp. § 4, note.

13. Si qui tum intercederent, sc. 'quid faciendum esset.'

15. An pararet eum, sc. 'tribunum.' Billerb. On the omission of a demonstrative, cp. § 7, above.

16. Quid si. On the ellipse, cp. Madv. 479 d.

Et consul esse . . volet. The position of Pompey himself in 52 B.C., when he was sole consul and his legates governed the Spanish provinces, was more commanding than that here suggested for Caesar.

17. At ille, Pompeius, sc. 'respondit.' Cp. Madv. l. c.

Quam clementer] of course ironical.

Quid, si . . impingere volet, = either 'absurd,' or 'I should chastise such presumption.'

19. Negotium = 'inimicitiam.' Forcell.

20. Descendere = 'se accommodare' (Forcell.), 'is willing to agree to one of

Caesar, ut aut maneat neque hoc anno sua ratio habeatur, aut, si designari poterit, decedat. Curio se contra eum totum parat; quid adsequi possit, nescio: illud video, bene sentientem, etsi nihil effecerit, cadere non posse. Me tractat liberaliter Curio et mihi suo munere negotium imposuit; nam si mihi non dedisset feras, quae ad ludos ei advectae erant Africanae, potuit supersederi. Nunc, quoniam dare necesse est, velim tibi curae sit, quod a te semper petii, ut aliquid istinc bestiarum habeamus, Sittianamque syngrapham tibi commendo. Libertum Philonem istoc misi et Diogenem Graecum, quibus mandata et litteras ad te dedi: eos tibi et rem, de qua misi, velim curae habeas; nam, quam vehementer ad me pertineat, in iis, quas tibi illi reddent, litteris descripsi.

35. M. CAELIUS RUFUS TO CICERO. (AD FAM. VIII. 6).

ROME, FEBRUARY, 50 B.C. (704 A.U.C.)

1. Appius has been accused by Dolabella. I hope you will show the sincerity of your reconciliation with Appius by doing what you can in your province to promote

these alternatives, either to remain in his province without claiming to be allowed to sue for the consulship this year, or to leave his province if he can secure his election as consul.' On ut . . decedat, cp. Ep. 26, 9, note.

1. Hoc anno. These words cannot mean 'in this present year,' for the consular election was already over. Cp. § 5. It would seem most natural to refer them to 50 B.C., as Hofmann does; but Mommsen, Rechtsfrage, p. 53, and note, understands them to mean 'in the year in question,' i.e. 49 B.C. Cp. Appendix 6, § 2, and Ad Fam. 8. 11, 3, where Caelius, writing in June 50 B.C., says that Pompey was anxious 'ut Caesar Id. Novembr. decedat.'

Sua ratio = 'sui ratio:' cp. De Off. 1. 39, 139. The phrase 'rationem habere' was used of the presiding magistrate at elections, when he accepted votes for any one as a candidate. It occurs frequently in Livy.

2. Se contra . . parat, 'is preparing his whole strength to resist him.'

3. Bene sentientem . . non posse, 'that one of sound views cannot have a fall.'

5. Suo munere . . imposuit, 'has imposed a burden by his gift,' i.e. the burden of adding to it. Caelius remarks just below, that he need not have exhibited any wild beasts at all but for the present he had received. Cp. Ep. 33. 5.

6. Ludos. Games celebrated by Curio perhaps in honour of his deceased father. Cp. Ad Fam. 2. 2; 2. 3, 1; cp. also 'theatrum Curionis' Ad Fam. 8. 2, 1.

Potuit = ἐξῆν ἄν: cp. 'ut potero' Ep. 22, 4, note; and for the indic., Ep. 4. 1, note.

Supersederi, 'be dispensed with,' i.e. the panthers.

8. Aliquid bestiarum: cp. Madv. 285, b.

Istinc, 'from Cilicia.'

9. Sittianam syngrapham: cp. Ep. 33. 5. It probably was the 'res de qua misi' mentioned just below.

Philon, of Pessinus in Galatia, a freedman of Caelius.

10. Diogenes: cp. Ad Fam. 2. 12, 2 'Diogenes tuus, homo modestus, a me . . discessit.'

FEBRUARY. So Baiter. Soringar, in his edition of the correspondence between Cicero and Caelius, suggests March as the probable date, guided by a combination of Ad Att. 6. 2, 6 with Ad Fam. 2. 16, 5 and 8. 7, 2.

his interest. Dolabella has separated from his wife during the proceedings. 2. I remember your parting instructions, but think you had better be silent on the subject at present. 3. Pompey is said to be anxious for Appius. All trials have ended in acquittals lately, and there is great political apathy. Curio is quite inactive. 4. We hear that Bibulus has lost some men on Mount Amanus. P.S. 5. Curio has gone over to Caesar's side and is much abused. Let Appius know that I have made representations to you on his behalf. I think you had better not decide about Dolabella.

CAELIUS CICERONI SAL.

Non dubito quin perlatum ad te sit, Appium a Dolabella reum 1 factum, sane quam non ea, qua existimaveram, invidia: neque enim stulte Appius; qui, simul atque Dolabella accessit ad tribunal, introierat in urbem triumphique postulationem abiecerat, quo facto rettudit sermones paratiorque visus est, quam speraverat accusator. Is nunc in te maximam spem habet. Scio tibi eum non esse odio: quam velis eum obligare, in tua manu est; cum quo *si* simultas tibi non fuisset, liberius tibi de tota re esset. Nunc, si ad illam summam veritatem legitimum ius exegeris, cavendum tibi erit ne parum simpliciter et candide *de*posuisse inimicitias videaris. In hanc partem porro tutum tibi erit, si quid volueris, gratificari; nemo enim necessitudine et amicitia te deterritum ab officio dicet. Illud mihi occurrit, quod inter postu-

1. Reum factum: of 'ambitus' and 'maiestas:' cp. Epp. 38, 10, note; 42, 1, note.

2. Sane quam: cp. Ep. 33, 2, note.

Non ea .. invidia, 'without so much ill-feeling against the accused as I had expected.' Wiel. On the ablat., cp. Ep. 34, 2, note.

Neque enim .. Appius, sc. 'fecit:' cp. Ep. 34, 9, note on 'at ille.'

3. Accessit ad tribunal, 'preferred his charge.'

4. Introierat in urbem. By thus entering the city Appius laid down his 'imperium,' and shewed confidence in his cause. Cp. the case of Caesar on his return from Spain, Intr. to Part I, § 15; and Note E, p. 123.

5. Rettudit sermones, 'has taken the edge off gossip.'

7. Odio. The word seems to mean serious and lasting hatred. Cicero and Appius had nearly quarrelled, but Cicero was placable.

Quam velis .. est, 'it depends on yourself to place him under any obligation you wish:' i.e. 'any service you do him now will be much valued.' Cicero would have many opportunities of suppressing evidence against Appius by using his influence with the inhabitants of Cilicia. Cp. the behaviour of L. Metellus as successor to Verres, In Verr. 2 Act. 3. 53. 122.

8. Liberius, sc. 'eligere quid faceres.'

9. Si ad illam .. exegeris, 'if you make your well-known and rigorous justice the standard of your lawful privileges;' 'if you make exact justice the standard of your exercise of your legal powers.' Cp. Forcell. for this sense of 'exigere:' also Livy 34. 31. The sense is, 'if you will not stretch a point in a friend's interest.'

Veritatem. Veritas = 'justice:' cp. Pro Quinctio 2, 10.

10. Parum simpliciter et candide, 'with a want of frankness and sincerity.'

11. In hanc partem .. gratificari, 'you will be safe in doing any favour you can to Appius in this matter.' Cicero was not supposed to be on the best terms with Appius, though they had been formally reconciled. Hence he would not be suspected of partiality.

13. Illud, 'the following fact.'

2 lationem et nominis delationem uxor a Dolabella discessit. Quid mihi discedens mandaris, memini; quid ego tibi scripserim, te non arbitror oblitum. Non est iam tempus plura narrandi. Unum illud monere te possum: si res tibi non displicebit, tamen hoc tempore nihil de tua voluntate ostendas, et exspectes quem ad modum exeat ex hac causa; denique invidiosum tibi sit, si emanarit; porro, *si* significatio ulla intercesserit, clarius, quam deceat aut expediat, fiat. Neque ille tacere eam rem poterit, quae suae spei tam opportuna acciderit quaeque in negotio conficiendo tanto illustrior erit; cum praesertim is sit, qui, si perniciosum sciret esse loqui de hac re, vix tamen se contineret.

3 Pompeius dicitur valde pro Appio laborare, ut etiam putent alterum utrum de filiis ad te missurum. Hic nos omnes absolvimus; et hercules consaepta omnia foeda et inhonesta sunt. Consules autem habemus summa diligentia; adhuc senatus con-

Postulationem .. delationem. The first word means properly the application for leave to prosecute; the last, the first step in the actual prosecution: i.e. the report of the defendant's name to the magistrate who would preside at the trial.

1. Quid mihi . . mandaris, 'your parting instructions' as to finding a suitable husband for Tullia. Cp. Ad Att. 5. 4, 1; Ad Fam. 7. 32, 3.

2. Quid . . scripserim. Caelius had probably mentioned Dolabella's disagreement with his wife and suggested him as a husband for Tullia.

4. Res, 'the proposal.'

5. Et = 'sed:' cp. Ep. 32, 3, note.

Quem ad modum .. causa, 'how Dolabella comes out of this case,' i.e. how he acquits himself as an accuser of Appius.

6. Denique . . emanarit, 'in a word it would bring you into disrepute if it were divulged.' Wesenb. suggests 'vide ne quam invidiosum sit.'

7. Porro .. fiat, 'moreover if you give any hint of your intentions they will become clearer than will suit either your credit or your interest,' i.e. 'it will be divulged, for Dolabella has no reticence; and it will be unbecoming for you just after your reconciliation with Appius to ally yourself with his accuser; inexpedient to offend so powerful a man as Appius.' On the tenses of sit . . emanarit . . fiat, cp. Madv. 347 b.

8. Ille, Dolabella.

9. Suae spei .. acciderit, 'will come so opportunely to further his hope.' It does not appear whether Caelius refers to his hope of getting Appius convicted, or to his general political prospects.

In negotio conficiendo, 'by helping to effect his object.' The marriage, and the success of his prosecution, would each make the other famous.

10. Cum .. is sit .. contineret, 'and that especially as he is a man who could not restrain himself even if he knew garrulity would injure him.' Cp. Madv. 364 for 'is ea qui' with the conj.

11. Putent, sc. 'homines.' For the omission, cp. Zumpt L. G. 381.

13. Alterum utrum de filiis. Pompey had two sons, the elder named Gnaeus, the younger Sextus. Both served in the civil wars; Gnaeus was killed shortly after the battle of Munda, 45 B.C. Sextus took an important part in politics after Caesar's death, and was long master of Sicily. Horace calls him 'dux Neptunius' Epod. 9, 7. He was killed in 35 B.C. at the age of 39, and must therefore have been about 24 when Caelius wrote this letter. Cp. Intr. to Parts III, § 10; IV, §§ 4; 12; V, §§ 11; 18.

Missurum, i.e. to intercede for Appius.

Hic . . absolvimus, 'we at Rome are acquitting everybody who comes into court.'

14. Consaepta .. sunt, 'everything base and scandalous is well protected.'

15. Summa diligentia, abl. qualitatis. The words are of course used in irony.

sultum nisi de feriis Latinis nullum facere potuerunt. Curioni nostro tribunatus conglaciat. Sed dici non potest, quo modo hic 4
omnia iaceant: nisi ego cum tabernariis et aquariis pugnarem, veternus civitatem occupasset. Si Parthi vos nihil calficiunt, nos *non* nihil frigore rigescimus. Tamen, quoquo modo potuit, sine Parthis Bibulus in Amano nescio quid cohorticularum amisit. Hoc sic nuntiatum est. Quod tibi supra scripsi Curionem valde 5
frigere, iam calet; nam ferventissime concerpitur; levissime enim, quia de intercalando non obtinuerat, transfugit ad populum et pro Caesare loqui coepit, legemque viariam, non dissimilem

1. De feriis Latinis: cp. Ep. 24. 2, note. A decree to fix their date would be merely formal.

2. Conglaciat, 'is getting benumbed,' 'is very inactive and idle.' The word seems only to occur here in this sense.

Quo modo . . iaceant, 'what slackness, or listlessness, there is here.' Cp. Ad Att. 7. 23, 3 'iota Capua et omnis hic dilectus iacet.' Wieland remarks on this passage, 'It was the deep calm before the outbreak of a terrible tempest.' A modern reader may remember the early summer of 1870.

3. Cum tabernariis, 'with the small shopkeepers.' Cp. Forcell., and Pro Flacc. 8. 18. Perhaps those especially are meant whose trades required a good deal of water. They may have bribed the aquarii, or managers of the public water supply, to favour them, and have so required the intervention of Caelius as aedile. Cp. Smith, Dict. of Antiq., sub voc. 'Aedilis,' p. 18.

4. Veternus, 'lethargy.'

Calficiunt, 'warm you,' 'give you exercise.' Cp. Ad Q. F. 3. 2, 1 'Gabinium . . calefecerat Memmius;' Nägelsb. 117, 336.

5. Non nihil . . rigescimus, 'we are getting rather dull.'

Sine Parthis, 'without having Parthians to fight.'

6. In Amano. Mt. Amanus separated most of old Cilicia from Cyrrhestica and Commagene.

Cohorticularum. A diminutive only used here. 'A few poor cohorts.' On the losses of Bibulus, cp. Ad Att. 5. 20, 4.

7. Quod . . scripsi, 'whereas I wrote.' Cp. Ep. 26, 2, note. A postscript begins here.

8. Calet, 'is in hot water enough,' 'is busy enough.' Cp. Ad Att. 4. 16, 11 (4. 18, 3. Bait.) 'iudicia calent;' Ep. 28, 7 'ardet ambitus.'

Concerpitur, = 'dictis laceratur.' Forcell.

9. De intercalando. The power of inserting intercalary months seems to have rested with the pontifices under a Lex Acilia of 181 B.C. Cp. Macrob. Saturn. 1. 13; Smith's Dict. of Antiq. sub voc. 'Calendarium,' p. 230. Curio may have belonged to their body. An intercalary month should have been inserted in 50 B.C., as there had not been one in 51. See Appendix viii. Its insertion would have given Curio more time for bringing forward his proposals, as it would have been inserted after February 23, and it had been arranged that the discussion on the consular provinces should begin on March 1. Cp. Ep. 34. 4–5, notes; Lange, Röm. Alt. 3. 382–383. Curio may also have wished to secure a prolongation of his own term of office, and perhaps to defer the day when Caesar would be required to surrender his provinces. In any case the refusal of his request gave him an excuse for changing his party. Caelius either did not know, or did not choose to tell Cicero, that Caesar's bribes accounted for Curio's change of policy. Cp. Intr. to Part II, § 27. Cicero was very anxious not to have his proconsular government lengthened as it would have been by the insertion of an intercalary month.

10. Legem . . viariam, 'a law for the repair of the roads.' Such a work might easily be made a reason for the appointment of a commission with very large powers. According to Appian (Bell Civ. 2. 27.) Curio brought forward this law in the expectation that Pompey and his friends would oppose it, and so give him an excuse for changing sides. For an account of the agrarian law of Rullus, cp. Intr. to Part I, § 9. The similarity of the bill of Curio to that of Rullus may have consisted in the large powers which it would have conferred

agrariae Rulli, et alimentariam, qua iubet aediles metiri, iactavit: hoc nondum fecerat, cum priorem partem epistolae scripsi. Amabo te, si quid, quod opus fuerit, Appio facies, ponito me in gratia. De Dolabella integrum tibi reserves, suadeo; et huic rei, de qua loquor, et dignitati tuae aequitatisque opinioni hoc ita facere expedit. Turpe tibi erit pantheras Graecas me non habere.

36. TO ATTICUS (AD ATT. V. 21).

LAODICEA, FEB. 13, 50 B.C. (704 A.U.C.)

1. I am glad you have arrived safely in Epirus. 2. The successes of C. Cassius have been much exaggerated, and the movements of the Parthians are very threatening. Under these circumstances, 3. I fear that the dispute between Caesar and Pompey may indirectly lead to the prolongation of my term of office; and you seem to have some such apprehension yourself. 4. Your letters do not reach me very regularly. I will do what I can for M. Laenius. 5. I am much obliged to you for what you told M. Octavius; use the same language in all doubtful cases. My moderation and integrity are unprecedented, and all my officers, except L. Tullius, follow my example. 6. At the beginning of winter I put Quintus in charge of Cilicia and my winter camp, and sent Q. Volusius to Cyprus. 7. I left Tarsus on January 5, and crossed the Taurus; my arrival in the districts beyond that mountain had been eagerly expected. I have relinquished fees which were a heavy burden to our subjects, and I allow no expensive honours to be paid me. 8. The distress caused by famine has been greatly mitigated by my exertions; I have induced many holders of corn to bring out their stores. 9. I mean to devote three months to the judicial business of my northern and western districts, and then to spend June in Cilicia, and July in returning through my province; I ought to leave it on July 30, and hope my brother will consent to act as

on its proposer. Cp. App. Bell. Civ. 2. 27, with Cic. De Leg. Agr. 2. 8–13. From an allusion in Ad Att. 6. 1, 25, it has been inferred that Curio's proposal would, if adopted, have imposed a tax or toll on such as travelled with a numerous retinue, but perhaps the reference in that passage is to another bill.

1. Alimentariam. This word seems only to occur here: it may mean a law for the distribution of corn to the people; such a law would usually be called 'frumentaria.' Cp. Ep. 11, 3.

Metiri, 'to distribute to the people by measure.' Cp. Caes. Bell. Gall. 1. 16.

Iactavit, 'has brought forward ostentatiously.'

3. Amabo te, 'I beseech you,' an elliptical expression = 'si facias quod volo amabo te,' Lindem. ap. Forcell. Cp. also Ad Q. F. 2. 10, 4; (2. 8, 4 Bait.); Ad Att. 2. 2, 1.

Si quid . . facies, 'if you do anything for the benefit of Appius.' Cp. Madv. 241 for the dat.

Ponito . . gratia, 'let him know how I have served him.' Cp. Ep. 31, 6, and for Cicero's anxiety to have his own services appreciated in a similar case, cp. Ep. 14, 1.

4. Integrum tibi reserves: cp. Ep. 29, 10, note.

Huic rei, either 'the trial of Appius,' Billerb.; or 'the marriage of Tullia,' Metzg.

5. Dignitati . . opinioni, 'for your dignity and reputation for fairness.' Cicero would damage both by virtually expressing approval of Dolabella's conduct. Cp. note on § 2.

Hoc ita facere, 'to manage the affair thus,' i.e. 'integrum tibi reservare.'

6. Pantheras: cp. Ep. 33, 5, note.

Graecas, i.e. from the Hellenized East, opposed to Africa, whence Caelius had received panthers as a present from Curio. Cp. Ep. 34, 10.

my successor. 10. Now for the affair of Brutus. He recommended to me two men who have lent money to the people of Salamis; one of them, Scaptius, visited my camp, and I promised to do what I could for him. I refused, however, to give him a command, and ordered some horsemen, whom Appius had placed at his disposal, to leave Cyprus. 11. Afterwards a deputation from Cyprus came to me, and I asked them to pay Scaptius. They said they were quite willing to do so, but Scaptius claimed most usurious interest, which was specified in his bond: my edict had named a more moderate rate. 12. I thought Scaptius misconstrued the decrees of the senate on which he relied. He afterwards tried to represent the debt as larger than it really was, but the Salaminians shewed him his mistake, and were eager to pay what they really owed. I yielded, however, to Scaptius, so far as to leave the case unsettled. 13. I am sure any fair judge would say that Brutus ought not to complain, especially considering some decrees recently made on the subject, which, by the way, Lucceius fears may impair the public credit. 14. I agree with you as to the 'secret' you mention. You will not hear from Quintus for some time, owing to the heavy snow. I do what I can for Thermus, as you wished. Deiotarus says that P. Valerius is insolvent. Let me know how the calendar is fixed for next year.

CICERO ATTICO SAL.

Te in Epirum salvum venisse et, ut scribis, ex sententia 1
navigasse vehementer gaudeo, non esse Romae meo tempore
pernecessario submoleste fero, hoc me tamen consolor: non
spero te istic iucunde hiemare et libenter requiescere. *C.* Cas- 2
sius, frater Q. Cassii, familiaris tui, pudentiores illas litteras
miserat — de quibus tu ex me requiris, quid sibi voluerint —
quam eas, quas postea misit, quibus per se scribit confectum
esse Parthicum bellum: recesserant illi quidem ab Antiochia
ante Bibuli adventum, sed nullo nostro εὐημερήματι, hodie vero

1. **Meo tempore pernecessario.** The last word seems not to occur elsewhere in this sense, 'at a time when my interests urgently require your presence.' Cp. for the pron., Ep. 29, 20, note. The senate were to discuss, on or soon after March 1, the provision to be made for the government of the provinces. Cp. Ad Att. 5. 20, 7 'est totum, quod Kalendis Martiis futurum est,' foll.; Ep. 34, 6 and 9, notes. Cicero often expresses his anxiety to leave Cilicia as early as he legally could do so. Cp. Epp. 31, 5; 36, 3.

3. **Submoleste** occurs only here, apparently.

Hoc, 'by the following expectation.'

4. **Spero.** On the use of this verb with the infin. pres., cp. Ep. 1, 1, note, and Madv. 395, Obs. 3.

Istic, 'where you are,' in Epirus.

5. **Q. Cassii.** Q. Cassius Longinus, tribune in 50–49 B.C., vetoed the senate's commands to Caesar early in that year, and afterwards commanded in Spain for Caesar. Cp. Appendix 6, § 5; Intr. to Part III, § 13.

Pudentiores illas . . bellum, 'that first letter of C. Cassius, as to the meaning of which you consulted me, was more modest than his later one, in which he writes that he has put an end to the Parthian war.' The C. Cassius here mentioned was quaestor to M. Crassus in Syria; commanded the remains of his army till the arrival of Bibulus; and was subsequently one of Caesar's murderers. Cp. Intr. to Parts II, § 20; IV, §§ 3; 13; 15; V, §§ 2; 4; 11, alib.

8. **Illi,** Parthi, to be supplied from 'Parthicum bellum.' Cp. Madv. 317 d, Obs. 1.

9. **Nullo nostro εὐημερήματι,** 'with no great success to us.' For the Greek word, cp. Polyb. 3. 72.

hiemant in Cyrrhestica maximumque bellum impendet; nam et Orodi, regis Parthorum, filius in provincia nostra est, nec dubitat Deiotarus, cuius filio pacta est Artavasdis filia, ex quo sciri potest, quin cum omnibus copiis ipse prima aestate Euphraten transiturus sit. Quo autem die Cassii litterae victrices in senatu recitatae sunt, id est Nonis Octobribus, eodem meae tumultum nuntiantes. Axius noster ait nostras auctoritatis plenas fuisse, illis negat creditum. Bibuli nondum erant allatae, quas certo
3 scio plenas timoris fore. Ex iis rebus hoc vereor, ne, cum Pompeius propter metum rerum novarum nusquam dimittatur, Caesari nullus honos a senatu habeatur, dum hic nodus expediatur, non putet senatus nos, antequam successum sit, oportere decedere nec in tanto motu rerum tantis provinciis singulos

1. **In Cyrrhestica.** Cyrrhestica was a district on the borders of Syria and Cilicia. It lay west of the Euphrates and south of Commagene. Politically, it seems to have been attached to Syria. Cp. Metzg., Billerb., and Ad Att. 5. 18, 1.

2. **Nostra** need only mean 'Roman.' Cp. Ad Fam. 8. 10, 1, where Caelius, who was at Rome, calls Cilicia 'provinciam nostram.' For an account of the operations of Cassius, see Mommsen 4. 2, 339. Cicero depreciates his successes, but they had really been considerable. Orodes, king of Parthia, had put to death Surena, the victor of Carrhae, and had sent his own son Pacorus, and a chief named Osaces, to invade Syria (cp. Ad Att. 5. 18, 1), and Cassius had defeated them near Antioch. Osaces died not long afterwards of his wounds (cp. Ad Att. 5. 20, 3: Intr. to Part II, § 20). **Orodi** is, perhaps, a genitive, cp. Madv. 42, 2. If a dative, perhaps it falls under the rule Madv. 246. The form Orodi recurs Ad Fam. 15. 1, 2, but Orodis is found, Ad Att. 5. 18, 1.

3. **Artavasdis.** Artavasdes was king of Armenia. In 53 B.C., he offered Crassus auxiliary cavalry, and a free passage through his country, which, however, Crassus declined.

Ex quo, either 'from Artavasdes' (Wiel., Metzg.), or 'from the son of Deiotarus.' The Deiotarus here mentioned was the one whom Cicero defended before Caesar in a speech still extant. He was tetrarch of Galatia, and afterwards received the title of king, and fought on Pompey's side at Pharsalus. Cp. Caes. Bell. Civ. 3, 4.

4. **Ipse**, Orodes, whose son Pacorus married a sister of Artavasdes. Cp. Ad Fam. 15. 3. 1.

6. **Nonis Octobribus.** This date presents difficulties. When Cicero wrote the letter Ad Fam. 15. 1 from his province, towards the close of September 51, he had not heard of the success of Cassius, and the latter's despatch must have been carried with unusual speed if it reached Rome on October 7. Wesenb. suggests 'Nonis Novembribus;' Hofm. (ap. Wesenb.) 'datae N. Oct.' See also Lange, Röm. Alt. 3. 380.

Meae. Probably the despatch which we possess as Ad Fam. 15. 2.

7. **Q. Axius**: cp. Ep. 28, 5, note.

Auctoritatis plenas fuisse, 'produced a great impression.'

8. **Illis**, sc. 'Cassii litteris.'

9. **Ex iis rebus . . praeesse**, 'I fear lest Pompey being detained at Rome as a protection against revolution, and Caesar receiving no honour from the senate, until this difficulty be settled the senate may think that I ought not to leave my province till a successor has been appointed, and that the provinces ought not to be entrusted each to one legate.' The 'refusal of honour to Caesar,' refers probably to Pompey's opposition to the proposals suggested on Caesar's behalf. Ep. 34. 9. While the result of the discussion about Caesar's provinces was uncertain, and Pompey was detained at Rome (cp. Ad Att. 5. 18, 1), the most important provinces of the west would be without regular governors, and the senate might object to extend such a provisional system to the East, and so insist on Cicero's remaining in Cilicia. Spain was governed by legates in Pompey's absence (Intr. to Part II, § 14).

13. **In tanto motu rerum.** These words refer to the Parthian war and the impending revolution.

legatos praeesse. Hic, ne quid mihi prorogetur, quod ne intercessor quidem sustinere possit, horreo, atque eo magis, quod tu abes, qui consilio, gratia, studio multis rebus occurreres. [Sed] dices me ipsum mihi sollicitudinem struere: cogor, et velim ita sit. Sed omnia metuo. Etsi bellum ἀκροτελεύτιον habet illa tua epistola, quam dedisti nauseans Buthroto: 'tibi, ut video et spero, nulla ad decedendum mora.' Mallem 'ut video;' nihil opus fuit 'ut spero.' Acceperam autem satis celeriter Iconii 4
per publicanorum tabellarios a Lentuli triumpho datas. In his γλυκύπικρον illud confirmas, moram mihi nullam fore, deinde addis, si quid secus, te ad me esse venturum. Angunt me dubitationes tuae; simul et vides, quas acceperim litteras. Nam quas Hermoni, centurionis Canuleii, ipse scribis te dedisse, non accepi. Laenii pueris te dedisse saepe ad me scripseras: eas Laodiceae denique, cum eo venissem, tertio Idus Februar. Laenius mihi reddidit, datas a. d. X. Kal. Octobres. Laenio tuas commendationes et statim verbis et reliquo tempore *re* probabo. Eae litterae cetera vetera habebant, unum hoc novum, de Ciby- 5

1. Ne quid mihi . . possit, 'lest my government should be prolonged by a measure against which even the tribunes' veto would be of no avail.' The veto was illegal in questions affecting the consular provinces. Cp. Ep. 34, 8, note.

2. Sustinere, 'to resist.' Cp. Philipp. 8, 1, 1.

3. Multis rebus occurreres, 'might provide for many difficulties.'

4. Sollicitudinem struere, 'am creating anxieties.'

Cogor . . ita sit, 'I cannot help it, and hope you may be right.'

5. Etsi, 'however.' Cp. Madv. 443.

ἀκροτελεύτιον, 'a concluding clause;' usually of a verse.' Cp. Thucyd. 2, 17.

6. Nauseans, 'still suffering from the voyage.'

7. Mora, sc. 'erit,' which Wesenb. inserts.

Ut video, sc. 'scripsisses.'

8. Autem, 'moreover.'

9. A Lentuli triumpho datas, 'sent just after the triumph of Lentulus.' Cicero refers to P. Lentulus Spinther, consul 57 B.C., who preceded Appius Claudius as governor of Cilicia. The letters of the first book 'Ad Familiares' are addressed to him, with one exception.

10. γλυκύπικρον illud, 'that mixture of sweet and bitter which I found in the last words of your previous letter, i.e. in the ἀκροτελεύτιον mentioned above. The word γλυκύπικρον is found in Sappho 40. (Bergk).

Confirmas, 'you repeat.'

11. Si quid secus, 'if things turn out otherwise in any way.'

12. Quas . . litteras, 'what letters I have received,' and therefore what I have not.

13. Hermoni. Apparently Hermon was a slave or freedman of Canuleius. Wesenb. inserts 'liberto.'

14. Laenii. It does not appear to whom Cicero refers. A M. Laenius protected him at Brundisium in 58 B.C. Cp. Pro Planc. 41, 97; Pro Sestio 63, 131; Ad Fam. 13. 63.

Pueris, 'slaves.' Cp. Ad Att. 5. 20, 8 'quas Laenii pueris scribis datas.'

17. Et statim verbis, sc. 'probavi.' For the omission of the verb, cp. Madv. 478.

Probabo, 'will shew my value for.'

18. Unum hoc novum, 'the only new topic they mention.'

De Cibyratis pantheris: cp. Ep. 33, 5. M. Octavius, curule aedile elect with Caelius, probably asked Atticus if he thought Cicero would send him some panthers, and Cicero is obliged to Atticus for saying he thought not.

ratis pantheris. Multum te amo, quod respondisti M. Octavio te non putare; sed posthac omnia, quae certa non erunt, pro certo negato. Nos enim et nostra sponte bene firmi et mehercule auctoritate tua inflammati vicimus omnes—hoc tu ita reperies—cum abstinentia, tum iustitia, facilitate, clementia. Cave putes quicquam homines magis umquam esse miratos quam nullum teruncium me obtinente provinciam sumptus factum esse nec in rem publicam nec in quemquam meorum, praeterquam in L. Tullium legatum. Is, ceteroqui abstinens, [sed] Iulia lege transita, semel tamen in diem, non, ut alii solebant, omnibus vicis, [praeter eum semel nemo accepit] facit ut mihi excipiendus sit, cum teruncium nego sumptus factum; praeter eum
6 accepit nemo. Has a nostro Q. Titinio sordes accepimus. Ego aestivis confectis Quintum fratrem hibernis et Ciliciae praefeci; Q. Volusium, tui Tiberii generum, certum hominem et mirifice abstinentem, misi in Cyprum, ut ibi pauculos dies esset, ne cives Romani pauci, qui illic negotiantur, ius sibi dictum nega-
7 rent; nam evocari ex insula Cyprios non licet. Ipse in Asiam profectus sum Tarso Nonis Ianuariis, non mehercule dici potest,

2. Te non putare, sc. 'me missurum.'

Omnia . . negato, 'say no as to everything of which you are not certain,' i.e. as to my ability and wish to execute the commission in question.

4. Auctoritate tua. Cp. e.g. Ad Att. 5. 20, 6 'laboras ut etiam Ligurino μώμῳ satis faciamus.'

8. In rem publicam, 'no public objects.' Cicero must mean, 'besides the regular supplies;' he cannot mean that he kept up his public establishment at his own expense. For the double negatives nullum . . nec, cp. Ep. 32, 3, note.

9. L. Tullium: cp. Ep. 31, 4, note.

Is, ceteroqui . . . vicis, 'he, in other respects abstinent, has transgressed the Julian law (cp. Ep. 32, 3, note), but only once in each day, not in every village, like others.' This seems a rare sense of 'transita;' the best MS. has 'transitam,' which makes no sense. Wesenb. suggests 'sed qui . . transitans,' i.e. on his way through towns. He would also insert a preposition before 'omnibus vicis.'

11. Facit ut . . sit, 'must be excepted.' Cp. Madv. 481 b.

13. Has . . sordes, 'the discredit of this covetousness.'

A . . Q. Titinio. Q. Titinius, a Roman knight, and common friend of Cicero and Atticus, had apparently recommended Tullius as legate to Cicero. A son of Titinius is mentioned, Ep. 62, 1.

14. Aestivis confectis, 'after the summer campaign.' The military successes detailed in Ad Att. 5. 20, and Ad Fam. 15. 4, were obtained towards the close of 51 B.C. Hence 'aestiva' must be taken rather loosely. Cp. Forcell., and Ad Fam. 3. 9, 4.

15. Q. Volusium. This Volusius, perhaps the same with one mentioned Ep. 31, 4, defended an Illyrian pirate, on his trial before Vatinius, in 44 B.C. Cp. Ad Fam. 5. 10 a, 2. Who his 'father-in-law Tiberius' was, seems not to be known.

18. Evocari probably means, 'to be summoned to a court held elsewhere.' Cp. In Verr. 2. Act. 3. 28, 68. Cicero would go therefore to Cyprus to decide cases pending between Cyprians and Roman citizens.

In Asiam. Cicero means, 'to the districts north of Taurus,' which belonged geographically to Asia in the Roman sense, but were politically annexed to Cilicia. Cp. infra § 9; Ep. 32, 2; Intr. to Part II, § 17.

qua admiratione Ciliciae civitatum maximeque Tarsensium;
postea vero quam Taurum transgressus sum, mirifica exspectatio Asiae nostrarum dioecesium, quae sex mensibus imperii mei nullas meas acceperat litteras, numquam hospitem viderat.
Illud autem tempus quotannis ante me fuerat in hoc quaestu; civitates locupletes, ne in hiberna milites reciperent, magnas pecunias dabant, Cyprii talenta Attica CC., qua ex insula—non ὑπερβολικῶς, sed verissime loquor—nummus nullus me obtinente erogabatur. Ob haec beneficia, quibus illi obstupescunt, nullos honores mihi nisi verborum decerni sino; statuas, fana, τέθριππα prohibeo, nec sum in ulla re alia molestus civitatibus, sed fortasse tibi, qui haec praedicem de me. Perfer, si me amas; tu
enim me haec facere voluisti. Iter igitur ita per Asiam feci, 8
ut etiam fames, qua nihil miserius est, quae tum erat in hac mea Asia—messis enim nulla fuerat—, mihi optanda fuerit: quacumque iter feci, nulla vi, nullo iudicio, nulla contumelia auctoritate et cohortatione perfeci, ut et Graeci et cives Romani, qui frumentum compresserant, magnum numerum populis pollice-
rentur. Idibus Februariis, quo die has litteras dedi, forum 9
institueram agere Laodiceae Cibyraticum et Apamense, ex Idibus Martiis ibidem Synnadense, Pamphylium—tum Phemio dispiciam

1. **Qua admiratione**, 'amid what admiration.' On the abl., cp. Ep. 34. 2, note.

3. **Nostrarum dioecesium**, 'so far as my districts extended.' For the word, cp. Ep. 58, 4; Ad Fam. 13. 53, 2. It is used in classical Greek only of the administration, not of the district administered. On the genitive (defin.), cp. Madv. 286, Obs. 1.

4. **Meas . . litteras**, 'demands from me.' On this use of the poss. pron., cp. Ep. 34. 9, note.

Numquam hospitem viderat, 'had had no one quartered on them.' The 'hospites' would be soldiers or others employed on the public service, probably.

5. **Illud . . tempus . . fuerat**, 'the half year, from summer to winter, had been employed after the following fashion.'

8. **ὑπερβολικῶς**, 'with exaggeration.' Quite classical.

9. **Erogabatur**, not, I think, epistolary. 'Erogare' means 'to draw money.' Wesenb. has 'erogabitur.'

10. **τέθριππα**, 'statues in chariots drawn by four horses,' of bronze or marble. The word is quite classical.

12. **Tibi**, sc. 'molestus sum.'

13. **Voluisti**: cp. § 5 'auctoritate tua.'

14. **Ut etiam fames . . optanda fuerit**, 'that I had reason to be glad even of the famine which has prevailed in my Asiatic districts,' that is, 'my visit was a pleasure, though it took place under such painful circumstances.'

In hac mea Asia, i.e. in the districts mentioned in § 7.

15. **Fuerat**, i.e. in 51 B.C.

16. **Auctoritate**, 'but by my influence.' On the omission of an adversative conj., cp. Ep. 29, 25, note.

18. **Compresserant**, 'had secreted.' Cp. Ad Att. 5. 21, 2; 10. 4, 6; In Verr. 2 Act. 3. 77. 179.

Numerum, 'amount,' commonly used of provisions. I presume the corn was to be sold at a moderate price.

Populis, 'the different cities.'

19. **Forum . . agere . . Apamense**, 'to try at Laodicea cases from Cibyra, and Apamea.'

21. **Phemio**. Phemius seems to have been a musician; perhaps a freedman of Atticus. Mr. F. Madan has pointed out to me that the name occurs as that of a musician. Hom. Odyss. 1. 154.

Dispiciam, 'I will look about for.'

κέρας—, Lycaonium, Isauricum; ex Idibus Maiis in Ciliciam, ut ubi Iunius consumatur, velim tranquille a Parthis. Quinctilis, si erit, ut volumus, in itinere est per provinciam redeuntibus consumendus: venimus enim *in* provinciam [Laodiceam] Sulpicio et Marcello consulibus, pridie Kalendas Sextiles; inde nos oportet decedere a. d. III. Kalendas Sextiles. Primum contendam a Quinto fratre, ut se praefici patiatur, quod et illo et me invitissimo fiet; sed aliter honeste fieri non potest, praesertim cum virum optimum, Pomptinum, ne nunc quidem retinere possim: rapit hominem [enim] Postumius Romam, fortasse etiam Postumia. Habes consilia nostra. Nunc cognosce de Bruto.
10 Familiares habet Brutus tuus quosdam creditores Salaminiorum ex Cypro, M. Scaptium et P. Matinium, quos mihi maiorem in modum commendavit. Matinium non novi; Scaptius ad me in castra venit: pollicitus sum curaturum me Bruti causa, ut ei Salaminii pecuniam solverent; egit gratias. Praefecturam petivit: negavi me cuiquam negotianti dare, quod idem tibi ostenderam. Cn. Pompeio petenti probaram institutum meum, quid dicam? Torquato de M. Laenio tuo, multis aliis: si praefectus vellet esse syngraphae causa, me curaturum ut exigeret.

1. *κέρας*, 'a musical horn.' Cp. Liddell and Scott, sub voc. I presume those of Pamphylia were famous.

In Ciliciam, sc. 'ire.'

2. A Parthis, 'as regards the Parthians.' Cp. Madv. 253, Obs.

3. Si erit, ut volumus, i.e. 'if I am not obliged to outstay my year of office.' 'Esse' is here used in the same sense as in 'bene est.' Cp. Ep. 4, 1.

6. A. d. III. Kalendas Sextiles, 'July 30.' The best MS. has 'IIII. Kal. Sext.,' but Cicero entered his province on the 31st (cp. Ad Att. 5. 15, 1), and could have no pretext for leaving on the 29th (cp. also, Ad Att. 6. 2, 6; 6. 3, 1).

Contendam, 'strive to obtain.'

7. Praefici, 'to be left in charge of the province,' on the departure of Marcus.

9. Pomptinum: cp. Ep. 31, 4, note.

10. Postumius was on very intimate terms with Cicero, and a friend of Pomptinus. He took part with Caesar in the civil war. Cp. Ad Att. 7. 15, 2; Ad Fam. 6. 12, 2; Pro Sestio 52, 111.

Postumia, wife of Servius Sulpicius. Pomptinus, apparently, was her lover.

11. Nunc cognosce: cp. Ep. 29, 20, 'now let me tell you.'

13. Ex Cypro, with Salaminiorum, 'of the people of Salamis in Cyprus.' Cp. the expression 'Magnetes a Sipylo' Tac. Ann. 2. 47.

M. Scaptium. Another M. Scaptius is mentioned Ad Att. 6. 1, 4, as a praefect in Cappadocia.

P. Matinium. Of this man nothing more seems to be known.

Maiorem in modum, 'earnestly.'

17. Negavi me . . dare, 'I said that it was not my practice to give,' or 'that I would not give.' Cp. audire in § 11.

18. Cn. Pompeio . . meum, 'I had shewn the soundness of my rule to Pompey, when he asked for a similar place.' On the fact, cp. Ad Att. 6. 1, 6.

19. Torquato . . aliis, sc. 'petenti . . petentibus.' Cicero probably refers to L. Manlius Torquatus, praetor 49 B.C., and son of the consul in 65 B.C. He sided with Pompey in the civil war (see Ep. 50, 1), and was killed in Africa (cp. Bell. Afric. 96).

M. Laenio: cp. § 4, note.

20. Syngraphae causa, i.e. 'to get his debt paid.' According to the Pseudo-Asconius (on In Verr. 2 Act. 1. 36, 91), 'syngrapha' means a bill which might be given without any value received by the giver.

Gratias egit, discessit. Appius noster turmas aliquot equitum
dederat huic Scaptio, per quas Salaminios coërceret, et eundem
habuerat praefectum; vexabat Salaminios. Ego equites ex Cypro
decedere iussi: moleste tulit Scaptius. Quid multa? ut ei fidem 11
meam praestarem, cum ad me Salaminii Tarsum venissent et
in iis Scaptius, imperavi ut pecuniam solverent. Multa de
syngrapha, de Scaptii iniuriis: negavi me audire. Hortatus sum,
petivi etiam pro meis in civitatem beneficiis, ut negotium con-
ficerent; denique dixi me coacturum. Homines non modo non
recusare, sed etiam hoc dicere, se a me solvere; quod enim
praetori dare consuessent, quoniam ego non acceperam, se a
me quodam modo dare, atque etiam minus esse aliquanto in
Scaptii nomine quam in vectigali praetorio. Collaudavi homines.
'Recte,' inquit Scaptius 'sed subducamus summam.' Interim
cum ego in edicto tralaticio centesimas me observaturum haberem
cum anatocismo anniversario, ille ex syngrapha postulabat quaternas. 'Quid ais?' inquam 'possumne contra meum edictum?'

Exigeret, 'should get his debt paid' = 'exigendo obtineret.' Forcell.

1. Turmas aliquot equitum. For an account of the misdeeds of these troops, cp. Ep. 38, 8.

4. Ut ei fidem meam praestarem, 'to fulfil my promise to him' of getting his debt paid.

6. Multa de syngrapha, sc. 'dicerent.'

10. A me, 'from my own funds.' Cp. Pro Plancio 42, 103 'a vobis persolvere.' As Cicero had not received what they usually paid to governors, they would pay the money asked for by Scaptius out of what they had thus saved.

11. Praetori. Cilicia had been for some years a consular province, but perhaps the Salaminians used the old title for a provincial governor, the oldest provinces having been governed by praetors; or praetor, as Manutius thinks, may be used here as a general title = 'governor.' His note is 'Praetori] Proconsuli: antiquo more rum omnes magistratus, quibus pareret exercitus, Praetor appellabantur.'

Consuessent, conj., as a quotation. Cp. Madv. 369.

Non acceperam, 'had not been in the habit of receiving.' The verb is in the indic., as giving Cicero's statement of his own conduct.

12. Minus .. praetorio, 'their debt to Scaptius amounted to much less than the exactions of governors had usually cost them.'

14. Subducamus summam, 'let us compute the amount.' Forcell.

15. Tralaticio, 'customary.' Cp. Ep. 19, 2, note. This provision with regard to the rate of interest seems to have originated during the administration of L. Lucullus. Cp. Plut. Lucull. 20; Mommsen 4. 2, 526.

Centesimas. The words 'centesimae usurae' have been variously explained; one per cent. per month, or twelve per cent. per annum, seems most likely to be the meaning of the expression.

16. Cum anatocismo anniversario. This expression is explained by Ernesti as meaning that compound interest was to be paid on the first year only, and simple interest in following years. But Boot quotes Savigny as explaining it thus; that the interest was only to be added to the principal at the end of each year, not at the end of each month. Thus a man who borrowed 1000 sesterces at 12 per cent., if he failed to pay the interest at the proper time, would be liable for the interest of 1120 sesterces in the second year, and of 1254 in the third, and so on.

Quaternas, sc. 'centesimas' = 48 per cent. per annum.

17. Contra meum edictum? sc. 'quaternas dare.' Cp. on the ellipse Ep. 23. 2, note.

At ille profert senatus consultum Lentulo Philippoque consulibus, VT QVI CILICIAM OBTINERET IVS EX ILLA SYNGRAPHA DICERET.

12 Cohorrui primo; etenim erat interitus civitatis: reperio duo senatus consulta isdem consulibus de eadem syngrapha; Salaminii cum Romae versuram facere vellent, non poterant, quod lex Gabinia vetabat. Tum iis Bruti familiares, freti gratia Bruti, dare volebant quaternis, si sibi senatus consulto caveretur. Fit gratia Bruti senatus consultum, VT NEVE SALAMINIIS NEVE QVI EIS DEDISSET FRAVDI ESSET: pecuniam numerarunt. [Et] postea venit in mentem faeneratoribus nihil se iuvare illud senatus consultum, quod ex syngrapha ius dici lex Gabinia vetaret. Tum fit senatus consultum, VT EX EA SYNGRAPHA * * * esset quam ceterae, sed ut eodem. Cum haec disseruissem, seducit me Scaptius; ait se nihil contra dicere, sed illos putare talenta CC. se debere; ea se velle accipere, debere autem illos paulo minus: rogat, ut eos ad ducenta perducam. 'Optime' inquam. Voco illos ad me, remoto Scaptio. 'Quid vos? quantum' inquam 'debetis?' Respondent 'CVI.' Refero ad Scaptium. Homo clamare. 'Quid opus est' inquam 'quam *ut* rationes conferatis?' Adsidunt, subducunt; *ad* nummum convenit. Illi se numerare velle, urgere, ut acciperet. Scaptius me rursus seducit, rogat, ut rem sic relinquam. Dedi veniam homini impudenter

1. Lentulo Philippoque consulibus. In 56 B.C.

2. EX ILLA SYNGRAPHA. 'In accordance with the stipulations of that bill,' i.e. recognising it as valid. Cp. the next section.

3. Erat interitus civitatis, 'that provision involved the ruin of the community.'

5. Versuram facere, 'to borrow money.'

6. Lex Gabinia. This law forbade all lending of money to provincials at Rome. It was probably passed when Gabinius was tribune, 68-67 B.C. Cp. Orell. Onomast. tom. iii., sub voc. The decree of the senate here mentioned was probably passed to protect both the lenders and the borrowers from the consequences of their breach of the law, but Cicero contends that it could not interfere with the rules laid down by himself in his province. It appears that Brutus was the real lender, though he wished the contract to be made in another name. Cp. Ad Att 6. 1, 6.

9. Pecuniam numerarunt, sc. 'Bruti familiares.'

12. VT EX EA SYNGRAPHA . . eodem. Boot suggests 'ut ex ea syngrapha ius diceretur non ut alio iure ea syngrapha esset quam ceterae syngraphae sed ut eodem.' That is, the bill, though given irregularly, was not to be void; but according to Cicero the terms of the senate's decree bound the lender to be content with the rate of interest fixed in the province by the governor's edict. Cp. Ep. 38, 7, notes.

16. Ad ducenta perducam, 'induce them to pay two hundred.'

17. Quid vos? sc. 'dicitis.'

19. Quid opus . . conferatis? 'what is wanted but that you should cast up,' or perhaps as Mr. Jeans renders 'compare your accounts?' Wesenb. suggests the omission of 'quam ut' and the insertion of 'licet' after 'conferatis.'

20. Subducunt, 'they add up.'

Ad nummum convenit, sc. 'subductio,' 'the accounts agree to a penny.'

22. Ut rem sic relinquam, 'that I would leave the affair unsettled.' He hoped Cicero might have a more accommodating successor.

Dedi veniam, 'I indulged him.'

petenti; Graecis querentibus, ut in fano deponerent postulantibus, non concessi. Clamare omnes qui aderant, nihil impudentius Scaptio, qui centesimis cum anatocismo contentus non esset; alii, nihil stultius. Mihi autem impudens magis quam stultus videbatur: nam aut bono nomine centesimis contentus
erat aut non bono quaternas centesimas sperabat. Habes meam 13
causam, quae si Bruto non probatur, nescio, cur illum amemus, sed avunculo eius certe probabitur, praesertim cum senatus consultum modo factum sit, puto, postquam tu es profectus, in creditorum causa, ut centesimae perpetuo faenore ducerentur: hoc quid intersit, si tuos digitos novi, certe habes subductum. In quo quidem, ὁδοῦ πάρεργον, *L.* Lucceius M. f. queritur apud me per litteras summum esse periculum, ne culpa senatus his decretis res ad tabulas novas perveniat; commemorat, quid olim mali C. Iulius fecerit, cum dieculam duxerit; numquam rei publicae plus. Sed ad rem redeo. Meditare adversus Brutum causam meam, si haec causa est, contra quam nihil honeste dici potest, praesertim cum integram rem et causam reliquerim.
Reliqua sunt domestica. De ἐνδομύχῳ probo idem, quod tu, 14

1. Ut in fano deponerent. If this deposit in a temple were made in accordance with a judicial sentence, interest would cease to become due from the day on which it was made. Billerb., Wiel.; cp. also Ad Fam. 13. 56, 3.

3. Anatocismo, 'addition of interest to the principal.'

5. Nam aut bono .. sperabat, 'either he was satisfied with 12 per cent., hoping to have the principal repaid, or hoped to repay the principal out of interest at 48 per cent.' Bono and non bono nomine perhaps mean, 'a debt recognized and unrecognized by law,' in this passage.

6. Habes: cp. Ep. 29, 20, note.

8. Avunculo. M. Cato was half-brother of Servilia, the mother of Brutus. Cp. Ep. 38, 8, and Iuv. Sat. 14. 43 'sed nec Brutus erit Bruti nec avunculus usquam.'

9. Modo, 'lately.' Cp. Mommsen 4. 2, 326.

In creditorum causa, 'relating to the position of creditors.'

10. Ut centesimae .. ducerentur, 'that 12 per cent. simple interest should be the standard rate.' Cp. Ep. 38, 7; Forcell. sub voc. 'Fenus.'

11. Hoc quid intersit,' 'the difference between this and the lowest offer of the Salaminians,' i.e. the Salaminians offered more than strictly could be required of them.

Tuos digitos, 'the activity of your fingers in calculation.'

Habes subductum, 'you have already computed.' Cp. Madv. 427 for the difference between this and 'subduxisti.'

12. In quo, 'as to which matter.'

ὁδοῦ πάρεργον, 'by the way.' Cp. Ad Att. 7. 1, 5.

L. Lucceius. Not the historian to whom Cicero addressed the letter Ad Fam. 5. 12, for the latter is called Q. F.

14. Ad tabulas novas, cp. Ep. 71, 2, note.

15. C. Iulius. Cicero generally speaks of the subsequent dictator as C. Caesar. Perhaps this is the C. Iulius Caesar mentioned by Asconius, in Scaurianam, p. 136.

Dieculam duxerit, 'allowed the time of payment to be deferred a little.' Boot. Cp. Ter. Andr. 4. 1, 27.

16. Plus, sc. 'mali factum esse.'

Meditare .. dici potest. 'Consider how to plead my cause against Brutus, if one can speak of pleading a cause when nothing can be said on the other side.'

18. Integram, 'undecided.' Cicero had left the case of Brutus and the Salaminians to his successor's decision.

19. Reliqua, 'my remaining topics.'

Postumiae filio, quoniam Pontidia nugatur; sed vellem adesses. A Quinto fratre his mensibus nihil exspectaris; nam Taurus propter nives ante mensem Iunium transiri non potest. Thermum, ut rogas, creberrimis litteris fulcio. P. Valerium negat habere quicquam Deiotarus rex, eumque ait se sustentare. Cum scies, Romae intercalatum sit necne, velim ad me scribas certum, quo die mysteria futura sint. Litteras tuas minus paulo exspecto, quam si Romae esses, sed tamen exspecto.

87. TO M. CAELIUS RUFUS (AD FAM. II. 13).

LAODICEA, EARLY IN MAY, (?) 50 B.C. (704 A.U.C.)

1. I am much pleased with your letters, though I wish they came more often. 2. I feel much affection for Appius, and I saw, as soon as our quarrel was made up, that he had the same regard for me. I wonder how you can doubt my wish to be on good terms with him. 3. I can assure you I expected Curio's change of party. I intend, as I have finished my judicial and financial business, and earned the good opinion of all classes, to set things in order in Cilicia, and then return to Rome, where I am most anxious to be.

M. CICERO IMP. S. D. M. CAELIO AEDILI CUR.

1 Raras tuas quidem—fortasse enim non perferuntur—, sed suaves accipio litteras, vel quas proxime acceperam quam prudentes! quam multi et officii et consilii! etsi omnia sic consti-

De ἐνδομύχῳ, 'about the family secret,' i.e. his plans for the marriage of Tullia. The word occurs in another sense, Soph. Philoct. 1457.

1. Postumiae filio, sc. 'eam nubere.' Servius Sulpicius the younger, whose mother Postumia was, is here referred to.

Pontidia. She seems to have suggested another match for Tullia, perhaps with a son of her own. Cp. Ad Att. 6. 1, 10. Nothing more seems to be known of her.

Nugatur, 'is trifling with me.'

Adesses, 'were in Rome.'

2. Taurus. Q. Cicero had been left in Cilicia, and his messengers could not cross the Taurus in winter.

3. Thermum: cp. Ep. 1, 2, note. He governed Asia as propraetor 53–50 B.C. Cp. Ad Fam. 2. 17, 6; Ad Att. 5, 13, 2. It does not appear how he was in want of Cicero's support.

4. P. Valerium: cp. Ad Fam. 14. 2, 2; Ad Att. 16. 7, 1. Perhaps Atticus had asked Cicero to procure repayment through Deiotarus, with whom Valerius was, of money due from the latter to Atticus.

6. Intercalatum sit, 'if an intercalary month has been inserted.' Cp. Ep. 35, 5; Appendix 8. For Cicero's anxiety on this subject, cp. Ep. 35, 8, note.

7. Certum. The accusative is rare in this sense. 'Pro certo' is more common.

Mysteria, the festival of the Bona Dea, on which cp. Ep. 6, 3, note.

MAY. Part of § 3 of this letter (mihi erat in animo . . . Nonis Maiis) compared with Ep. 38, §§ 4–6, suggests that the two letters were written between May 1 and 7. The allusions generally are to the two letters, 34 and 35.

IMP.: cp. Intr. to Part II, § 20.

10. Vel = 'even.' Cp. Madv. 436, Obs.

11. Quam multi . . consilii, 'how full of friendly advice!' Cp. Madv. 287 for the genit. qualitatis.

Omnia . . admonebas, i.e. in my relations with Appius and with Dolabella. Cp. Ep. 35, 2 and 5.

tueram mihi agenda, ut tu admonebas, tamen confirmantur nostra consilia, cum sentimus prudentibus fideliterque suadentibus idem videri. Ego Appium—ut saepe tecum locutus sum—valde diligo 2
meque ab eo diligi statim coeptum esse, ut simultatem deposuimus, sensi; nam et honorificus in me consul fuit et suavis amicus et studiosus studiorum etiam meorum. Mea vero officia ei non defuisse tu es testis, cui iam κωμικὸν μάρτυρα, ut opinor, accedit Phania, et mehercule etiam pluris eum feci, quod te amari ab eo sensi. Iam me Pompeii totum esse scis; Brutum a me amari intellegis. Quid est causae, cur mihi non in optatis sit complecti hominem florentem aetate, opibus, honoribus, ingenio, liberis, propinquis, adfinibus, amicis collegam meum praesertim et in ipsa collegii laude et scientia studiosum mei? haec eo pluribus scripsi, quod *non* nihil significabant tuae litterae subdubitare *te*, qua essem erga illum voluntate. Credo te audisse aliquid: falsum est, mihi crede, si quid audisti. Genus insti-

4. **Ut simultatem deposuimus.** The quarrel to which Cicero here refers seems to have taken place before the consulship of Appius, in 54 B.C. Perhaps it arose out of the part taken by Appius in some disturbances in 57 B.C. Cp. Ad Att. 4. 3. 4. The reconciliation was effected by Pompey. Quintil. Inst. Orat. 9. 3. 41.

6. **Studiosus .. meorum**, 'devoted to the same pursuits with myself.' Appius wrote a book on the augur's office, of which he dedicated the first book to Cicero. Cp. Ad Fam. 3. 4. 1; 3. 9. 3. There is also a hint of Appius' literary tastes, Ad Fam. 3. 1. 1.

7. **Cui** = 'Caelio.'

κωμικὸν μάρτυρα, 'a well-schooled witness' (Metzg.), i.e. 'one who had learned his part of mediator as thoroughly as a comedian learns his on the stage.' This seems far-fetched. Manutius thinks that the words mean 'intervening suddenly to remove difficulties,' like a character in a comedy who 'patefacta veritate sedat omnes turbas.' Cicero expresses a very favourable opinion of this Phania, who was a freedman of Appius. Cp. Ad Fam. 3. 1.

8. **Accedit**, 'adds his testimony.'

9. **Pompeii.** Gnaeus, eldest son of the great Pompey, married one of the daughters of Appius; another was married to M. Brutus. Cp. Ad Fam. 3. 4. 2. These connections would be additional reasons for Cicero's wishing well to Appius.

10. **Cur mihi non in optatis sit**, 'why I should not desire.'

11. **Complecti**, sc. 'amare,' 'to regard with much affection.'

Hominem, sc. Appium.

Florentem, 'distinguished.' Cp. Nägelsb. 128, 363.

Honoribus. He was consul 54 B.C., and censor 50 B.C. Cp. Ep. 41. 4.

12. **Liberis.** Appius had three daughters, and had apparently adopted the two sons of his brother Caius. Cp. Ep. 34. 1, note.

Propinquis. I cannot be sure to whom Cicero refers. Appius' brother Caius had governed Asia as propraetor, but was now dead.

Adfinibus: see above for his daughters' marriages.

Collegam, as augur.

13. **In ipsa .. mei**, 'and who, in his learned work in praise of our body, shews a desire to please me.' On this work of Appius' see De Leg. 2. 13, 32; Ad Fam. 3. 9. 3; 3. 11, 4; and Billerbeck's note on this passage.

14. **Subdubitare**, 'were rather doubtful.' The word seems only to occur here and Ad Att. 14. 15. 2. Caelius had written of Appius, 'scio tibi eum non esse odio' (Ep. 35. 1), words not suggestive of a warm friendship between Appius and Cicero.

15. **Te audisse aliquid**, 'that you have heard something of a quarrel between us.'

16. **Institutorum et rationum mearum**, 'of my rules and plans. Cp. Ad Fam.

tutorum et rationum mearum dissimilitudinem non nullam habet cum illius administratione provinciae: ex eo quidam suspicati fortasse sunt, animorum contentione, non opinionum dissensione me ab eo discrepare; nihil autem feci umquam neque dixi, quod contra illius existimationem esse vellem. Post hoc negotium autem et temeritatem nostri Dolabellae deprecatorem me pro
3 illius periculo praebeo. Erat in eadem epistola 'veternus civitatis;' gaudebam sane et congelasse nostrum amicum laetabar otio. Extrema pagella pupugit me tuo chirographo. Quid ais? Caesarem nunc defendit Curio? quis hoc putarat praeter me? nam, ita vivam, putavi. Di immortales! quam ego risum nostrum desidero! Mihi erat in animo, quoniam iurisdictionem confeceram, civitates locupletaram, publicanis etiam superioris lustri reliqua sine sociorum ulla querela conservaram, privatis summis infimis fueram iucundus, proficisci in Ciliciam Nonis Maiis et, cum prima aestiva attigissem *rem* militaremque conlocassem, decedere ex senatus consulto. Cupio te aedilem videre miroque desiderio me urbs adficit et omnes mei tuque in primis.

3, 8, 7. Cicero speaks in more decided terms about Appius' conduct elsewhere; cp. Ep. 32, 2.

2. Cum illius . . provinciae, 'with his provincial administration.'

3. Animorum . . discrepare, 'that the divergence in our conduct arose from mutual animosity, and not from a difference in opinion.' On the ablatives contentione . . dissensione, cp. Ep. 26, 9, note on p. 187. 'Discrepare' = 'discordare,' 'diversum esse.' Forcell.

5. Hoc negotium, foll., 'this affair of the trial, in which our friend Dolabella has behaved so rashly.'

7. Erat in eadem . . civitatis, 'in the same letter (Ep. 35) you wrote of a "lethargy of the state."'

8. Congelasse, 'had grown inactive.' The word seems only to occur here in the metaphorical sense. Cp. 'conglaciat' (Ep. 35, 3).

Amicum, sc. Curionem.

9. Pupugit . . chirographo, 'annoyed me by its autograph contents.' Caelius appears to have added a few lines in his own hand (§ 5) to Ep. 35, which was written by his secretary.

11. Ita vivam, 'as truly as I hope to live.' Cp. Madv. 444 a, Obs. 3.

Risum nostrum desidero, 'I miss the laugh we might have had over it.'

12. Erat. This and the following tenses down to conlocassem, are epistolary.

13. Reliqua, 'the arrears.' On the merits of Cicero's provincial government, see Ep. 38, 4-6, notes.

16. Prima aestiva. 'Prima' = 'primum' (cp. Madv. 300 b), 'as soon as I have visited the summer quarters, and arranged my military affairs.'

Militaremque. This, as Mr. Yonge remarks, can hardly be right. In Baiter's list of various readings I find 'militemque, Orellius, militarem que rem alii.' Wesenb. suggests 'rem que militarem conlocassem,' or 'militarem que conlocassem rem.'

Conlocassem: 'conlocare = ordinare, componere.' Forcell. A Parthian inroad was still not impossible.

17. Ex senatus consulto. This decree was probably passed to carry out a 'Lex Pompeia' of 52 B.C. Cp. Intr. to Part II, § 17. A decree of somewhat similar import to the one here mentioned is given Ep. 34, 8. Cicero says in various places, that he considers himself to be holding his province for one year only. Cp. Ad Att. 5. 9. 2; 5. 15, 1; Ep. 36, 9: and such appears to have been the import of the decree of the senate above referred to. Cp. Ad Fam. 15. 9. 2; 15. 14. 5.

38. To ATTICUS (AD ATT. VI. 2).

LAODICEA, MAY, 50 B.C. (704 A.U.C.)

1. I answer your last page first. I am much annoyed by what Statius is reported to have said. It is quite false; I wish for more bonds of union with you, not fewer. 2. Quintus is liable to hasty anger, but is soon appeased again. Every member of our families must do his best to keep up a good understanding; my nephew can do most. 3. I now answer your first page. Dionysius and I were both misled by Dicaearchus about the geography of Peloponnesus. I found out that Phliuntii is wrong, please substitute Phliasii in your copy. 4. I am glad you are pleased to hear of the merits of my administration. From Feb. 13 to May 1, I have been attending to the judicial business of all my districts, except those of Cilicia Proper, and have secured great results. I respect the privileges of the different communities and have relieved them much, both by the economy of my government 5. and by procuring restitution of money embezzled by their own magistrates. I have thus enabled the towns to satisfy the farmers of the revenue, and my accessibility is generally popular. 6. I mean to spend June in Cilicia—I hope at peace—and July in returning through my province. I am glad to see from the gazettes up to March 7, that no delay is likely to be offered to my departure. 7. I return to the affair of Brutus. I did all I could for him with propriety, both in Cilicia and Cappadocia; and persuaded the Salaminians to offer the whole principal of their debt, with the interest legally due; but Scaptius, on behalf of Brutus, insisted on payment in full according to the bond, which was illegal. 8. I wonder that after your previous language you can propose that I should place soldiers at the disposal of Scaptius. 9. Appius was more complaisant, but the people of Salamis complained bitterly of his conduct. You have shewn too much consideration for Brutus; I may have shewn too little. 10. I am doing all I can to serve Appius. You know that Caelius is coming here as my quaestor. I hope my return to Italy will not be delayed. I was already aware of the foolish conduct of Sempronius. Your messenger, Philogenes, is in a hurry, so farewell.

CICERO ATTICO SAL.

Cum Philogenes, libertus tuus, Laodiceam ad me salutandi 1
causa venisset et se statim ad te navigaturum esse diceret, has ei litteras dedi, quibus ad eas rescripsi, quas acceperam a Bruti tabellario; et respondebo primum postremae tuae paginae, quae mihi magnae molestiae fuit, quod ad te scriptum est a Cincio de Statii sermone, in quo hoc molestissimum est, Statium dicere a me quoque id consilium probari. *Probari* autem? de isto hactenus. Dixerim me vel plurima vincla tecum summae con-

1. **Philogenes**: cp. Ad Att. 5. 13. 2. He was now probably engaged in looking after his patron's affairs in Asia.

5. **A Cincio**: cp. Ep. 2. 1, note.

6. **In quo . . probari**, 'in this matter what annoys me most is that Statius says I approve my brother's design,' i.e. of divorcing Pomponia. Cp. Ad Att. 6. 3, 8. Statius and Cincius had apparently met and discussed the affairs of the families to which they were attached.

7. **Probari autem**, 'do I say approved? no more of that.' Cp. Ad Att. 5. 13. 3; Livy 21. 44 'transcendes autem?'

8. **Dixerim**, 'let me say.' Cp. Ep. 26, 5, note. Kayser and Wesenb. would re-

iunctionis optare, etsi sunt amoris artissima; tantum abest, ut
2 ego ex eo, quo astricti sumus, laxari aliquid velim. Illum autem multa de istis rebus asperius solere loqui saepe sum expertus, saepe etiam lenivi iratum: id scire te arbitror; in hac autem peregrinatione militiave nostra saepe incensum ira vidi, saepe placatum. Quid ad Statium scripserit, nescio: quicquid acturus de tali re fuit, scribendum tamen ad libertum non fuit. Mihi autem erit maximae curae, ne quid fiat secus, quam volumus quamque oportet; nec satis est in eius modi re se quemque praestare, ac maximae partes istius officii sunt pueri Ciceronis sive iam adulescentis; quod quidem illum soleo hortari. Ac mihi videtur matrem valde, ut debet, amare teque mirifice. Sed est magnum illud quidem, verum tamen multiplex pueri ingenium,
3 *in* quo ego regendo habeo negotii satis. Quoniam respondi postremae tuae paginae prima mea, nunc ad primam revertar tuam. Peloponnesias civitates omnes maritimas esse, hominis non nequam, sed etiam tuo iudicio probati, Dicaearchi tabulis credidi: is multis nominibus in Trophoniana Chaeronis narratione

move the full stop at 'hactenus,' and place a comma after 'dixerim.'

Vel plurima, 'even as many as possible.'

1. **Etsi sunt . . artissima**, 'though we have the most intimate union of affection.'

Tantum abest ut . . sumus, 'far from wishing that to be relaxed at all which already connects us.' On 'tantum abest ut' with the conj., cp. Madv. 440 a, Obs. 1.

2. **Illum**, sc. Quintum.

3. **De istis rebus**, 'about the conduct of his wife.' In another passage Cicero praises his brother's forbearance under great provocation. Ad Att. 5. 1, 3 and 4.

7. **Scribendum . . non fuit.** On the indic., cp. Madv. 348, Obs. 1.

9. **Se quemque praestare**, 'that each of us should engage to do all in his own power' in appeasing Quintus. Cicero means they should urge each other to do all they could. Manutius appears to connect these words with the preceding, and explains them as = 'me tibi eum praestare qui esse debeo,' i.e. 'it is not enough that one's own conduct is free from blame, but one must use one's influence on others.'

10. **Ac**, adversative: cp. Madv. 433, Obs. 2. Que is used in a similar sense, Ep. 82, 2, and et, Ep. 32, 3; Wesenb. has [ac].

Maximae . . pueri Ciceronis, 'the largest share in this work of reconciliation belongs to the young Cicero,' i.e. to the younger Quintus, who was now 17 years old probably. Cp. Ad Att. 5. 20, 9. On the genitive 'pueri,' cp. Madv. 281, Obs.

11. **Quod**, 'to which effect.' Cp. Madv. 228 c.

12. **Est magnum . . ingenium**, 'the nature of the youth is powerful' or 'vigorous indeed, but variable.' Forcell. gives 'varium, duplex, inconstans' as synonyms for 'multiplex,' in a similar passage. On the order of the words, cp. Madv. 469 b.

16. **Maritimas**, 'on the sea coast.'

17. **Nequam**, 'worthless.'

Dicaearchi. Dicaearchus, of Messene in Sicily, was a Peripatetic philosopher, pupil of Aristotle, and contemporary of Theophrastus. He paid much attention to geography. Polybius and Strabo (cp. Strab. 2. 104; 3. 170) criticised his statements on this subject. Cicero mentions him as preferring the practical to the contemplative life. Ep. 10, 3.

Tabulis, probably 'maps,' with a play on its other meaning, 'account books.'

18. **Credidi**, 'gave credit for the statement,' 'believed it on their authority.' Cp. Ep. 8, 10; Zumpt L. G. 413.

Multis nominibus, 'on many grounds.' Cp. Ad Fam. 2. 1, 1 'nomine neglegentiae.'

In Trophoniana . . narratione, sp-

Graecos in eo reprehendit, quod mare tantum secuti sunt, nec ullum in Peloponneso locum excipit. Cum mihi auctor placeret—etenim erat *ἱστορικώτατος* et vixerat in Peloponneso—, admirabar tamen et vix adcredens communicavi cum Dionysio; atque is primo est commotus, deinde, quod de isto Dicaearcho non minus bene existumabat quam tu de C. Vestorio, ego de M. Cluvio, non dubitabat quin ei crederemus: Arcadiae censebat esse Lepreon quoddam maritimum; Tenea autem et Aliphera et Tritia *νεόκτιστα* ei videbantur, idque *τῷ τῶν νεῶν καταλόγῳ* confirmabat, ubi mentio non fit istorum. Itaque istum ego locum totidem verbis a Dicaearcho transtuli. Phliasios autem dici sciebam, et ita fac ut habeas; nos quidem sic habemus. Sed primo me *ἀναλογία* deceperat Φλιοῦς, Ὀποῦς, Σιποῦς, quod Ὀπούντιοι, Σιπούντιοι. Sed hoc continuo correximus. Laetari te nostra mode- 4

parently in a dialogue or narrative about the cave of Trophonius, in which Chaeron was the (chief) speaker. The work is mentioned by Athenaeus, 13. 594; 14. 641.

1. Quod mare tantum secuti sint, 'for keeping so much to the sea coast.' Wesenb. has 'tam.'

2. Locum. This word seems to have been omitted in Baiter's edition by an error of the press. Orelli and Wesenb. insert it.

3. *ἱστορικώτατος*, 'most learned in history.' Plutarch, Themist. 13, uses the word in the sense of 'historical;' in classical Greek it would rather mean 'most inquisitive.'

4. Adcredens = 'credens,' both neut. and act.

Cum Dionysio. Dionysius was Cicero's freedman; he is the No. 2 of Ep. 28, 9, note.

6. De C. Vestorio. Vestorius was a banker at Puteoli, often mentioned in the letters of Book 4 to Atticus, and on friendly terms both with the latter and with Cicero.

M. Cluvio. Cluvius was another money-lender at Puteoli, of which the old name was Dicaearchia. Boot. Cp. Smith's Dict. of Geogr. 2. 678. Cicero compares the credit due to Dicaearchus on geography with that due to these bankers in money matters.

7. Arcadiae .. maritimum, 'he (prob. Dionysius) thought that a place called Lepreon, on the coast, belonged to Arcadia.' The Lepreon on the borders of Elis and Messenia may have stood on the sea in early times, and had been a member of the Arcadian confederacy. Cp. Paus. 5. 5. 3.

8. Tenea was in the territory of Corinth; Aliphera in Arcadia; Tritia was one of the twelve Achaean cities.

9. *νεόκτιστα*, 'of late foundation,' a classical word.

τῷ τῶν νεῶν καταλόγῳ: sc. Hom. Il. 2.

11. Transtuli, 'transferred to my book on the Commonwealth.' Cp. De Rep. 2. 4. 8. Atticus had criticised the accuracy of the statement, apparently; Cicero notices a similar criticism on another point. Ad Att. 6. 1. 8. The statement which Cicero here reports from Dicaearchus or from Dionysius must have been curious. The argument from Lepreon implies that the statement of Dicaearchus would have been justified if the Arcadian confederacy had had a single seaport; yet the anxiety of Dionysius to disprove the antiquity of Tenea and other places, would shew that the existence of a single inland city in a confederacy was held fatal to the sweeping assertion of Dicaearchus; in which case the existence of Tegea and Mantinea, to go no farther, might seem sufficient to disprove it. The whole discussion illustrates the inadequacy of the materials at the disposal of ancient writers.

Phliasios .. habemus, 'I know that the people of Phlius are called Phliasii, and do you correct your copy accordingly (ita fac ut habeas, cp. Forcell.); mine is already corrected.'

12. Sed primo .. *Σιπούντιοι*, 'but when I first wrote I was deceived by a false analogy; as Opus and Sipus make Opuntii and Sipuntii, I thought Phlius would make Phliuntii.' The present MS. of the treatise 'De Republica' seems to have 'Phliuntii.'

ratione et continentia video: tum id magis faceres, si adesses. Atque hoc foro, quod egi ex Idibus Februariis Laodiceae ad Kal. Maias omnium dioecesium praeter Ciliciae, mirabilia quaedam effecimus: ita multae civitates omni aere alieno liberatae, multae valde levatae sunt; omnes suis legibus et iudiciis usae, αὐτονομίαν adeptae, revixerunt. His ego duobus generibus facultatem ad se aere alieno liberandas aut levandas dedi: uno, quod omnino

6 nullus in imperio meo sumptus factus est—nullum cum dico, non loquor ὑπερβολικῶς—nullus, inquam, ne teruncius quidem. Hac autem re incredibile est quantum civitates emerserint. Accessit altera. Mira erant in civitatibus ipsorum furta Graecorum, quae magistratus sui fecerant: quaesivi ipse de iis, qui annis decem proximis magistratum gesserant; aperte fatebantur. Itaque sine ulla ignominia suis humeris pecunias populis rettulerunt; populi autem nullo gemitu publicanis, quibus hoc ipso lustro nihil solverant, etiam superioris lustri *reliqua* reddiderunt; itaque publicanis in oculis sumus. 'Gratis' inquis 'viris!' Sensimus. Iam cetera iuris dictio nec imperita et clemens cum admirabili facilitate; aditus autem ad me minime provinciales; nihil per cubi-

2. Hoc foro, 'at this session,' from Feb. 13 to May 1.

3. Praeter Ciliciae, 'except of Cilicia proper.' 'Praeter' is used adverbially. Cp. Madv. 172, iii, Obs. 2.

5. Omnes . . revixerunt, 'all being allowed their own laws and courts, and so having regained a kind of independence, have recovered much strength.' Cp. Ad Att. 6. 1, 15 'illud, in quo sibi libertatem censent Graeci datam ut Graeci inter se disceptent suis legibus.' This *freedom* did not exempt from obedience to the commands of the Roman governor, but allowed the cities to use their own, not Roman, laws for their domestic affairs. Cp. A. W. Zumpt C. E. 2. 156, 157.

6. His . . duobus generibus, 'in the two points I will now mention.'

8. In imperio meo, 'during my government.' Cp. Ep. 36, 5, note.

9. Hac . . re, 'by this circumstance,' abl. instr. Cp. Madv. 254.

10. Accessit altera, sc. 'res.' The construction has changed slightly, we should expect 'altero' corresponding to 'uno.'

11. Ipsorum furta . . fecerant, 'peculations of the Greeks themselves, I mean of their magistrates.' 'Ipsorum,' opposed to the Roman officers.

12. Annis decem proximis. On the ablat., cp. Madv. 276.

14. Ignominia, 'exposure.'

Suis humeris, 'of their own accord.' Boot. He quotes pro Milon. 9. 25; pro Flacco 37. 94. But those passages rather suggest 'from their own resources,' i.e. 'without borrowing,' as Mr. Jeans understands the phrase.

16. Reliqua, 'the arrears.' Cp. Ep. 37. 5.

17. In oculis sumus, 'I am a favourite with.' Forcell. Cp. Tusc. Disp. 2. 26, 63.

Gratis . . viris. Boot thinks these words are ironical, as the equites, to whose order the publicani belonged, had not supported Cicero effectively against Clodius.

Iam, 'moreover.'

19. Provinciales, 'such as had been usual in the province' (cp. Tac. Ann. 15. 31), where a foreign prince asks for his brother, 'ne . . complexu provincias obtinentium arceretur foribusve eorum adsisteret.'

Nihil per cubicularium, 'no one need apply to a chamberlain in order to get an audience,' supp. 'agebatur.'

cularium; ante lucem inambulabam domi, ut olim candidatus.
Grata haec et magna mihique nondum laboriosa ex illa vetere
militia. Nonis Maiis in Ciliciam cogitabam; ibi cum Iunium 6
mensem consumpsissem—atque utinam in pace! magnum enim
bellum impendet a Parthis—, Quinctilem in reditu ponere;
annuae enim mihi operae a. d. III. Kal. Sextil. emerentur: magna
autem in spe sum mihi nihil temporis prorogatum iri. Habebam
acta urbana usque ad Nonas Martias, e quibus intellegebam
Curionis nostri constantia omnia potius actum iri quam de provinciis: ergo, ut spero, propediem te videbo. Venio ad Brutum 7
tuum, immo nostrum; sic enim mavis: equidem omnia feci, quae
potui aut in mea provincia perficere aut in regno experiri. Omni
igitur modo egi cum rege et ago quotidie, per litteras scilicet;
ipsum enim triduum quadriduumve mecum habui turbulentis in
rebus, quibus eum liberavi. Sed et tum praesens et postea cre-
berrumis *litteris* non destiti rogare et petere mea causa, suadere
et hortari sua: multum profeci, sed quantum, non plane, quia
longe absum, scio. Salaminios autem—hos enim poteram coër-

1. **Inambulabam domi**, 'I walk up and down in my house as of old when a candidate,' i.e. I allow every one free access.

2. **Grata haec . . militia**, 'these acts of condescension are popular and highly valued,' and my old service (as an advocate and politician) has thus far prevented my being annoyed by performing them.'

3. **Ibi cum**. On the position of 'cum.' cp. Madv. 465 b.

5. **In reditu ponere**, 'to occupy July with my journey home,' i.e. with my return to the western frontier of the province, probably. For he presently remarks that his year expired on July 30.

6. **Annuae . . operae . . emerentur**, 'my year's service expires.' Cp. Ad Att. 6. 5. 3.

8. **Acta urbana**: see Ep. 36, 6, note, on p. 108.

9. **Curionis . . constantia**. Curio apparently had already begun to insist that Pompey should be deprived of his provinces if Caesar were deprived of his. Cicero does not seem to have suspected that Caesar had bought Curio's services. Cp. Mommsen 4. 2. 354, for the facts.

Omnia potius . . provinciis, 'that the last things on which discussions would take place in the senate would be questions of provincial administration.'

10. **Ut spero . . videbo**. Cicero had feared that the senate might require him to stay more than a year in his province: and Curio's opposition to all discussion about the provinces had relieved him of this anxiety.

Ad Brutum . . nostrum, foll., 'to your, or as you prefer, our—friend Brutus and his claims.' Atticus seems to have written complaining of Cicero's strictness.

11. **Equidem . . experiri**, 'I have exerted myself in effecting everything I could in my province, and in attempting all I could in the neighbouring kingdom.'

12. **In regno**, sc. Ariobarzanis, 'in Cappadocia.' Cp. Ad Att. 5. 18, 1 and 4; 5. 20, 6.

13. **Egi cum rege . . scilicet**, 'have made representations to the king, and am still making them—I mean by letter.' '**Per litteras scilicet**' corrects '**omni modo**.' '**Cum rege**,' sc. Ariobarzane.

14. **Triduum quadriduumve**, '*only* for three or four days.'

Turbulentis in rebus, 'while there was disorder in his country.' Cp. Ad Fam. 15. 2, 4–6; Ad Att. 5. 20, 6.

16. **Mea causa**, 'out of consideration for me.'

17. **Sua**, 'for his own interest,' which would be promoted by his paying his debts.

cere—adduxi, ut totum nomen Scaptio vellent solvere, sed centesimis ductis a proxuma quidem syngrapha, nec perpetuis, sed renovatis quotannis. Numerabantur nummi: noluit Scaptius. Tu, qui ais Brutum cupere aliquid perdere? quaternas habebat in syngrapha. Fieri non poterat, nec, si posset, ego pati possem. Audio omnino Scaptium paenitere; nam quod senatus consultum esse dicebat, ut ius ex syngrapha diceretur, eo consilio factum est, quod pecuniam Salaminii contra legem Gabiniam sumpserant; vetabat autem Auli lex ius dici de ita sumpta pecunia: decrevit igitur senatus, ut ius diceretur *ex* ista syngrapha. Nunc ista
8 habet iuris idem, quod ceterae, nihil praecipui. Haec a me ordine facta puto me Bruto probaturum, tibi nescio; Catoni certe probabo. Sed iam ad te ipsum revertor: ain tandem, Attice, laudator integritatis et elegantiae nostrae,

ausus es hoc ex ore tuo — —,

inquit Ennius, ut equites Scaptio ad pecuniam cogendam darem, me rogare? an tu si mecum esses, qui scribis morderi te interdum, quod non simul sis, paterere me id facere, si vellem? 'Non amplius' inquis 'quinquaginta.' Cum Spartaco minus multi primo fuerunt: quid tandem isti mali in tam tenera insula non fecissent? non fecissent autem? immo quid ante adventum meum

1. Perpetuis; cp. Ep. 36. 13. 'without compound interest.'

3. Renovatis quotannis, probably = 'cum anatocismo anniversario.' See Ep. 36, 11, note.

Numerabantur, 'were just about to be paid.' See Madv. 337, Obs. 1.

4. Tu, sc. 'is es,' 'is it you,' or 'can you defend this.' Wesenb. has 'tu qui (= qui) ais,' and Manutius interprets the passage similarly, 'qui verum est id quod scribis,' 'how can you say.'

Aliquid perdere, 'to put up with some loss.'

5. Fieri non poterat, 'payment on such terms was impossible.'

6. Scaptium paenitere, 'that Scaptius is sorry for his covetousness.'

Nam quod . . sumpserant, 'for as to the statement that (cp. Ep. 26, 2, note) a decree of the senate legalized the bringing of an action under that bill, I answer that the decree was passed because the people of Salamis had borrowed money in violation of the Gabinian law.' That is, the object of the decree was to exempt the lender and the people of Salamis from penalties for lending and borrowing at all; not to authorise an exceptional rate of interest. Cp. Ep. 36, 12, note. It appears then that the governor's edict fixed the rate of interest which could be recovered on all contracts which became subjects of litigation during his year of office, even if the contracts had been concluded previously.

9. Auli, sc. Gabinii.

10. Nunc ista habet . . praecipui: cp. Ep. 36, 12, note.

12. Nescio, sc. 'an probaturus sim.' On 'probare' with acc. and dat., cp. Madv. 242, Obs. 1.

14. Elegantiae, 'propriety,' 'purity.' Cp. Pro Sull. 28, 79.

16. Inquit. Wesenb. has 'ut inquit.'

17. Morderi, 'are tormented.' Cp. Tusc. Disp. 3. 34, 82.

19. Cum Spartaco, supp. 'and yet he did mischief enough.' The number of the original followers of Spartacus is variously given. Florus, 3. 20, supports Cicero.

20. Tenera, 'unwarlike,' 'effeminate.'

21. Non fecissent autem, 'do I say "would not have done"?' Cp. § 1, note.

non fecerunt? Inclusum in curia senatum habuerunt Salaminium
ita multos dies, ut interierint non nulli fame; erat enim praefectus Appii Scaptius et habebat turmas ab Appio. Id me igitur
tu, cuius mehercule os mihi ante oculos solet versari, cum de
aliquo officio ac laude cogito, tu me, inquam, rogas, praefectus ut
Scaptius sit? Alias hoc statueramus, ut negotiatorem neminem,
idque Bruto probaveramus. Habeat is turmas? cur potius quam 9
cohortes? sumptu iam nepos evadit Scaptius. 'Volunt' inquit
'principes.' Scio: nam ad me Ephesum usque venerunt flen-
tesque equitum scelera et miserias suas detulerunt; itaque statim
dedi litteras, ut ex Cypro equites ante certam diem decederent,
ob eamque causam, tum ob ceteras Salaminii nos in caelum
decretis suis sustulerunt. Sed iam quid opus equitatu? solvunt
enim Salaminii: nisi forte id volumus armis efficere, ut faenus
quaternis centesimis ducant. Et ego audebo legere umquam aut
attingere eos libros, quos tu dilaudas, si tale quid fecero? Nimis,
nimis, inquam, in isto Brutum amasti, dulcissime Attice, nos
vereor ne parum. Atque haec scripsi ego ad Brutum scripsisse
te ad me. Cognosce nunc cetera. Pro Appio nos hic omnia 10
facimus, honeste tamen, sed plane libenter; nec enim ipsum
odimus et Brutum amamus, et Pompeius mirifice a me conten-

1. Inclusum . . habuerunt: cp. Ep. 36, 13, note, for the construction.

4. De aliquo officio ac laude, 'about anything right and honourable.'

5. Praefectus. In the provinces a military officer seems to be denoted by this title. Cp. Ep. 27, 3, note on 'praefectura.'

6. Alias, 'at another time,' 'previously.'

Neminem, sc. 'praefectum faceremus.'

8. Sumptu . . Scaptius, 'Scaptius is becoming quite extravagant in his expenditure,' ironical. He would probably offer to pay the troops placed at his disposal, and cavalry would be more expensive than infantry.

Volunt . . principes, '"the nobles of Salamis will have it so" he (Scaptius) says.'

9. Scio, 'no doubt,' ironical.

11. Ob eamque causam tum ob ceteras, 'and both for that reason and for others.' The combination of 'que' and 'tum' is curious.

13. Solvunt, 'are ready to pay.' Cp. Madv. 339, Obs.

15. Et, admirantis: 'and shall I then venture.' Cp. Ad Att. 7. 23. 1 'et non omnes nostra corpora opponimus.'

16. Eos libros; cp. Ad Att. 6. 1, 8. Cicero refers to his treatise 'De Re publica.'

Dilaudas = 'varie vel valde laudas.' Forcell. It seems only to occur here.

18. Ne parum, scil. 'amaverimus.'

Haec scripsi, foll.: Cp. Ep. 14, 1, as illustrating Cicero's anxiety to have his services mentioned in a similar case.

19. Cetera, 'what else have I to say.'

Pro Appio; cp. Epp. 37, 1; 35, 1 and 5, notes; Rein, Crim. R. 564; 733. Appius had been accused of 'ambitus' and of 'maiestas,' and seems to have been acquitted on both charges. Cp. Ad Fam. 3. 11, 1–3; 3. 12, 1. Cicero, as governor of Cilicia, would have opportunities for discouraging witnesses from appearing against him. Manutius.

20. Honeste . . libenter, 'with a due regard for my own honour, but with evident good-will to him.'

Tamen qualifies 'omnia.'

Nec enim . . et: cp. Ep. 6, 4, note.

21. Brutum. M. Brutus was son-in-law to Appius. Cp. Ep. 37, 2, note.

Contendit, 'exerted himself much to obtain it.' Forcell. A common use of the word in Cicero's writings.

dit, quem mehercule plus plusque in dies diligo. C. Caelium quaestorem huc venire audisti. Nescio, quid sit; sed Pammenia illa mihi non placent. Ego me spero Athenis fore mense Septembri. Tuorum itinerum tempora scire sane velim. Εὐήθειαν Sempronii Rufi cognovi ex epistola Corcyraea: quid quaeris? invideo potentiae Vestorii. Cupiebam etiam nunc plura garrire, sed lucet: urget turba, festinat Philogenes. Valebis igitur et valere Piliam et Caeciliam nostram iubebis litteris et salvebis a meo Cicerone.

39. M. CATO TO CICERO (AD FAM. XV. 5).

ROME, ABOUT JUNE, 50 B.C. (704 A.U.C.)

1. On public and on private grounds alike I recognized with pleasure in the senate the merits and success of your administration. 2. The form which my approval took was in my judgment that most honourable to you; if you prefer that which the majority of the senate adopted I am glad; but this compliment will not necessarily be followed by a triumph, nor is a triumph really the highest distinction. 3. My regard for you induces me to express my views at greater length than usual.

1. Quem . . diligo. Pompey was now preparing for his impending struggle with Caesar. Hence these words may have a political bearing.

C. Caelium. C. Caelius Caldus went out to serve as quaestor in Cilicia under Cicero, and the latter afterwards left him in charge of the province, notwithstanding his youth and some defects of character. Cp. Ep. 42, 3 and 4.

2. Quaestorem . . venire, 'is coming as quaestor.' Cp. Madv. 320. He was probably one of the quaestors for 51–50 B.C. No very definite rule seems to have obtained as to the succession of quaestors in the provinces; C. Cassius remained more than a year in Syria after Crassus' death. Cp. Intr. to Part II, § 16.

Nescio, quid sit, 'I do not know what to make of this affair,' referring to what follows. Boot. Wesenb. punctuates 'audisti: nescio quid sit; sed—.'

Sed Pammenia . . non placent, 'but I am not pleased with what has been done about the house of Pammenes.' Cp. Ad Att. 5. 20, 10. Pammenes was perhaps a ward or *protégé* of Atticus or Cicero, whose property was endangered by a law-suit. A Greek orator or writer of the name is mentioned Brut. 97. 332; Orat. 30, 105 as a contemporary of Cicero.

4. Tuorum itinerum tempora, 'the probable dates of your journeys.' Cicero wished to meet Atticus on his own way to Rome.

Εὐήθειαν, 'simplicity,' 'stupidity.' Cp. below, and Ep. 34, 1, for more particulars about Rufus.

5. Corcyraea. Atticus had visited Corcyra on his way to Epirus, apparently. Cp. Ep. 36, 1.

Invideo . . Vestorii, 'I envy Vestorius the power his wealth gives him.' When Cicero had been at Puteoli, on his way to assume the government of Cilicia, Rufus had avoided him, though under considerable obligations to him. Cicero supposed that he feared to meet Vestorius, and therefore avoided publicity, and ironically says that he envies Vestorius the power which could frighten Rufus into discourtesy.

7. Turba, 'the crowd of clients and petitioners.'

Valebis . . iubebis . . salvebis, fut. indic. for imperat., cp. Madv. 384, Obs.

8. Piliam: cp. Ep. 31, 7.

Caeciliam. Caecilia, more often called Attica, was daughter of Atticus. Cp. Ep. 117, 8, note.

M. CATO S. D. M. CICERONI IMP.

Quod et res publica me et nostra amicitia hortatur, libenter 1
facio, ut tuam virtutem, innocentiam, diligentiam cognitam in
maximis rebus domi togati, armati foris pari industria administrare gaudeam: itaque, quod pro meo iudicio facere potui,
ut innocentia consilioque tuo defensam provinciam, servatum
Ariobarzanis cum ipso rege regnum, sociorum revocatam ad studium imperii nostri voluntatem sententia mea et decreto laudarem, feci. Supplicationem decretam, si tu, qua in re nihil 2
fortuito, sed summa tua ratione et continentia rei publicae provisum est, dis immortalibus gratulari nos quam tibi referre
acceptum mavis, gaudeo: quod si triumphi praerogativam putas
supplicationem et idcirco casum potius quam te laudari mavis,
neque supplicationem sequitur semper triumphus et triumpho

1. Quod with 'hortatur.' Cp. Ep. 38, 2, note.

2. Facio, ut .. gaudeam: cp. Ep. 36, 5, note.

Cognitam .. togati, 'proved in the most critical events of your domestic administration.' Cp. 'cedant arma togae' in Cicero's poem on his consulship. The 'toga,' as the dress usually worn at Rome, was the emblem of domestic administration; the 'sagum,' or military cloak, of war.

3. Armati foris. These words refer to the government of Cilicia alone, for Cicero had never held a military command abroad before his proconsulate. Cato is comparing Cicero's government of a province with his consulship, but the order of the words is rather harsh.

Administrare. The MS. has 'administrari,' which, however, seems hardly ever to be used in the sense of 'adhiberi,' which it must bear here. Cp., however, Cicero de Domo Sua 27, 71; Nägelsbach 114, 313. For 'administrare' as a neuter verb, cp. Sall. Iug. 92; Caes. Bell. Gall. 4. 29.

4. Pro meo iudicio, 'in accordance with my conviction,' 'conscientiously.'

5. Ut .. laudarem. Cato had proposed a complimentary vote in Cicero's honour, but not a formal 'supplicatio.'

Defensam. 'Contra metum Parthici belli.' Manut. Cp. Ad Fam. 15. 4. 14.

6. Ariobarzanis: cp. Intr. to Part II, § 20. Besides the services there mentioned, Cicero induced the powerful high priest of Bellona at Comana to withdraw from Cappadocia. Cp. Ad Fam. 15. 4. 6.

Sociorum .. voluntatem, 'that the hearts of our allies have been won back to a cheerful acquiescence in our rule.'

7. Sententia mea et decreto, 'my speech and vote,' when your services were discussed in the senate. 'Decernere' is used of the individual senator as well as of the whole body. Cp. In Cat. 4. 5. 10 'is .. et supplicationem mihi decrevit.'

8. Qua in re .. provisum est, supply in the first clause 'factum' from 'provisum,' and in the second 'a word meaning "all"' from 'nihil.' Süpfle. On the zeugma, cp. Madv. 478, Obs. 4.

10. Gratulari = 'grates agere.' Forcell.

Tibi referre acceptum, sc. 'id quod provisum est.' Hofm.

11. Praerogativam, 'the necessary preliminary,' which a triumph will follow as surely as the other centuries do the vote of the first. For this metaphorical sense of 'praerogativa,' cp. In Verr. Act. 1. 9. 26. For the usual meaning, Smith's Dict. of Antiq. 339.

12. Et idcirco .. mavis, 'and therefore (because you think a triumph will follow it) you wish Fortune rather than yourself to get the credit.' Cato identifies casus with the gods to whom the 'supplicatio' was addressed.

13. Neque .. et .. iudicare, 'I remark that a thanksgiving is not always followed by a triumph, and that a declaration of the

multo clarius est senatum iudicare potius mansuetudine et innocentia imperatoris provinciam quam vi militum aut benignitate deorum retentam atque conservatam esse; quod ego mea sententia
2 censebam. Atque haec ego idcirco ad te contra consuetudinem meam pluribus scripsi, ut, quod maxime volo, existimes me laborare, ut tibi persuadeam me et voluisse de tua maiestate, quod amplissimum sim arbitratus, et, quod tu maluisti, factum esse gaudere. Vale et nos dilige et instituto itinere severitatem diligentiamque sociis et rei publicae praesta.

40. To M. CATO (AD FAM. XV. 6).

WRITTEN FROM THE EAST, AUGUST (?), 50 B.C. (704 A.U.C.)

1. I value your approbation most highly, and if there were several Catos in the Commonwealth I should seek for no further recognition of my services. 2. I am sorry you were not convinced by the grounds alleged in my previous letter to justify my demand of a triumph; but I hope that if the senate grants me one you will share my pleasure at the decision.

M. CICERO S. D. M. CATONI.

1 'Laetus sum laudari me' inquit Hector, opinor apud Naevium, 'abs te, pater, a laudato viro:' ea est enim profecto iucunda laus, quae ab iis proficiscitur, qui ipsi in laude vixerunt. Ego vero vel

senate,' foll. On neque .. et, cp. Ep. 6, 4. p. 45, note, and on the omission of words meaning 'I remark that,' cp. Pro Muren. 7. 15 'sin autem sunt amplae et honestae familiae plebeiae, et proavus L. Murenae et avus praetor fuit.'

4. Contra consuetudinem .. pluribus, 'at some length, contrary to my usual practice.'

6. Voluisse .. arbitratus, 'supported that measure, with regard to the honours to be paid you, which I thought would bring you most distinction.' This sense of 'velle' is illustrated by the form in which a law was submitted to the people 'velitis iubeatis Quirites,' etc. On the mood of sim, cp. Ep. 3, 3, note on 'quod verrerere.'

7. Et quod tu .. gaudere, 'and yet that I am glad the course you preferred was adopted.' 'Et' almost = 'sed.' Cp. Ep. 38, 8, note on 'ac.'

8. Instituto itinere, 'in the path you have begun to tread,' abl. modi. Cp. Ep. 34, 2, note.

THE EAST. I cannot ascertain the date of this letter. Ad Att. 6, 7 seems to shew that Cicero had heard of the vote of a 'supplicatio' before he sailed for Rhodes (cp. Intr. to Part II, § 24), and Cato's letter was probably written soon after the vote.

10. Laetus sum .. viro; cp. Ad Fam. 5. 12, 7. Kühner, on Tusc. Disp. 4. 31, 67, says that the words form a trochaic tetrameter catalectic.

Opinor. Süpfle says that 'opinor' and 'ut opinor' do not express uncertainty, but the unimportance of the fact in question. Cp. Ad Fam. 3. 6, 3 'diebus qui tibi .. lege, ut opinor, Cornelia constituti essent.' Man. thinks that Cicero affects ignorance, so as not to seem a habitual reader of poetry.

12. In laude, 'with credit.' Cp. In Verr. Act. 1. 17. 51 'esse in laude.'

Ego vero, emphatic. Cp. Madv. 482 and 454 for 'vero.' 'I certainly.'

Vel gratulatione .. dictae, 'both by the congratulation of your letter and the

gratulatione litterarum tuarum vel testimoniis sententiae dictae nihil est quod me non adsecutum putem; idque mihi cum amplissimum, tum gratissimum est, te libenter amicitiae dedisse, quod liquido veritati dares. Et, si non modo omnes, verum etiam multi Catones essent in civitate nostra, in qua unum exstitisse mirabile est, quem ego currum aut quam lauream cum tua laudatione conferrem? nam ad meum sensum et ad illud sincerum ac subtile iudicium nihil potest esse laudabilius quam ea tua oratio, quae est ad me perscripta a meis necessariis. Sed causam meae 8
voluntatis, non enim dicam cupiditatis, exposui tibi superioribus litteris, quae etiamsi parum iusta tibi visa est, hanc tamen habet rationem, non ut nimis concupiscendus honos, sed tamen, si deferatur a senatu, minime aspernandus esse videatur. Spero autem illum ordinem pro meis ob rem publicam susceptis laboribus me non indignum honore, usitato praesertim, existimaturum. Quod si ita erit, tantum ex te peto, quod amicissime scribis, ut, cum tuo iudicio, quod amplissimum esse arbitraris, mihi tribueris,

testimony of your opinion expressed in the senate.' On the ablatives, cp. Epp. 26, 9; 37, 8, notes; and with the genitives, Ep. 5, 2, 'aliquod testimonium tuae vocis.'

2. Nihil est . . putem, 'think I have obtained every possible honour.' The negative form gives a certain awkwardness to this sentence.

3. Te libenter . . dares, 'that friendship made you take pleasure in what you granted without hesitation to truth.' For this sense of liquido, cp. Süpfle, and In Verr. 2 Act. 4. 56, 124 'confirmare hoc liquido, iudices, possum.' The words contain a slight expression of discontent, 'you praised me no more than the facts constrained you to do.' To Atticus (7. 2, 7) Cicero is more outspoken: 'Cato . . in me turpiter fuit malevolus: dedit integritatis . . mihi testimonium quod non quaerebam; quod postulabam negavit.'

4. Dares, conj., as expressing Cicero's thoughts. Cp. Ep. 36, 11, note.

Si non modo . . Catones, 'if, I do not say all, but many of our countrymen were Catos.'

6. Currum . . lauream, the insignia of a triumph.

7. Nam ad meum . . iudicium, 'according to my own feelings, or to your remarkably uncorrupt and refined judgment.' Illud marks something exceptional. Süpfle.

8. Laudabilius, 'more honourable for me.' Wiel. and Metzg.

9. Quae est . . necessariis, 'has been sent me by my friends at some length.' The speech was probably that referred to by Cato in the preceding letter. Caelius had written Cicero an account of its substance. Ad Fam. 8. 11, 2.

11. Hanc . . rationem, 'has this reasonable ground, or justification.' Cicero had explained to Cato in a previous letter that honours conferred by the senate would restore him the dignity he had held before his exile. Cp. Ad Fam. 15. 4. 14 'huic meae voluntati in qua inest aliqua vis desiderii ad sanandum vulnus iniuriae.'

12. Non ut nimis . . videatur, 'that the honour seems one not indeed to be desired too eagerly, but yet certainly not to be rejected if offered.' On the position of 'ut,' cp. Madv. 465 b, Obs.

15. Usitato praesertim: cp. Ad Fam. 15. 4. 14 'tantum ut multi nequaquam paribus rebus honores summos a senatu consecuti sint.' Lentulus Spinther triumphed for successes probably not greater than Cicero's (cp. Ep. 36, 4); and Appius Claudius, Cicero's predecessor, once hoped for a triumph (cp. Ep. 35, 1; Abeken 273).

16. Tantum, 'only thus much.' Cp. Ep. 15, 8, p. 96, note on 'quantum.'

Quod amicissime scribis, 'what you write in the most friendly terms to say you did in the case of the "supplicatio."' Cp. § 3 of the preceding letter.

si id, quod maluero, acciderit, gaudeas: sic enim fecisse te et sensisse et scripsisse video, resque ipsa declarat tibi illum honorem nostrum supplicationis iucundum fuisse, quod scribendo adfuisti; haec enim senatus consulta non ignoro ab amicissimis eius, cuius honor agitur, scribi solere. Ego, ut spero, te propediem videbo, atque utinam re publica meliore quam timeo!

41. M. CAELIUS RUFUS TO CICERO (AD FAM. VIII. 14).

ROME, SEPTEMBER OR OCTOBER 50 B.C. (704 A.U.C.)

1. No possible achievements in your province can recompense you for missing the sights to be seen here now; for instance, the vexation of Domitius on seeing Antony elected augur. 2. I fear we are on the eve of civil war; Pompey will not allow Caesar to be elected consul unless he first gives up his command; Caesar thinks he cannot safely do this unless Pompey does the same. I am in much doubt which side to take, and so I dare say are you. 3. In civil war, one must consider the strength as well as the rights of the contending parties. 4. Appius is most rigorous as a censor, strange to say. Unless either Pompey or Caesar take the command against the Parthians, a serious quarrel is imminent.

CAELIUS CICERONI SAL.

1 Tanti non fuit Arsacen capere et Seleuceam expugnare, ut earum rerum, quae hic gestae sunt, spectaculo careres: numquam

1. **Sic enim . . video,** 'for I see that your acts and feelings and the language of your letter expressed this pleasure.'

3. **Quod scribendo adfuisti,** 'in that you were present when the decree (granting me a supplicatio) was drawn up.' This would shew interest in Cicero's distinction. 'Scribendo' is the dat. of the gerund. Cp. Ep. 34. 5.

6. **Utinam re publica . . timeo!** sc. 'ne futura sit.' On the abl. abs. cp. Ep. 1, 2, note on p. 28. The quarrel between Pompey and Caesar was approaching a crisis, and Curio had interposed to prevent such a settlement as Cicero would have preferred. Epp. 37. 3; 35. 5. notes.

SUPPLEMENT. The date of this letter is difficult to ascertain. A comparison of what is said by Caelius (Ad Fam. 8. 12, 4) about the election of Domitius as future with § 1 of this letter suggests that Ad Fam. 8. 12 was written before the letter now under consideration. But Ad Fam. 8. 12 cannot have been written before the middle of the ludi Circenses in September. Cp. § 4 of that letter. On the other hand Hirtius (Caes. De Bell. Gall. 8. 50) suggests an earlier date for Antony's election as augur, and what is said in § 4 of this letter about the Parthian war as still going on is capable, when compared with the language of Ep. 47, 3, of a similar interpretation. But the war might be merely suspended, and its renewal probable; and on the whole I am disposed to think that the letter was perhaps written late in September. Compare Buringar's edition of the correspondence between Caelius and Cicero, p. 74, and Lange, Röm. Alt. 3. 388 foll.

7. **Tanti non fuit . . careres,** 'to capture Arsaces and storm Seleucea would not have been a sufficient compensation for missing the sight of what goes on here.' On the general structure of the sentence, cp. Madv. 294, Obs 3; and for the indic. 'fuit,' Ep. 4. 1, note on p. 34.

Arsacen, a title, apparently, of the kings of the Arsacid dynasty. The name of the actual sovereign of Parthia was Orodes. Cp. Intr. to Part II, §§ 9; 20; Ep. 36, 2.

Seleucea, a city of Greek origin, only separated by the Tigris from Ctesiphon, the Parthian capital.

8. **Numquam . . doluissent . . vidis-**

tibi oculi doluissent, si in repulsa Domitii voltum vidisses.
Magna illa comitia fuerunt et plane studia ex partium sensu
apparuerunt; perpauci necessitudinem secuti officium praestiterunt. Itaque mihi est Domitius inimicissimus, ut ne familiarem
quidem suum quemquam tam oderit quam me, atque eo magis,
quod per iniuriam sibi putat *auguratum* ereptum, cuius ego auctor
fuerim. Nunc furit tam gavisos homines suum dolorem unumque
modo me studiosiorem Antonii: nam Cn. Saturninum adulescentem ipse Cn. Domitius reum fecit, sane quam superiore a vita
invidiosum; quod iudicium nunc in exspectatione est, etiam in
bona spe, post Sex. Peducaei absolutionem. De summa re publica 2
saepe tibi scripsi, me annuam pacem non videre, et quo propius
ea contentio, quam fieri necesse est, accedit, eo clarius id periculum apparet. Propositum hoc est, de quo, qui rerum potiuntur,

ses, 'your eyes would never have suffered again if you had seen how Domitius looked when defeated.' Cp. Ter. Phorm. 5. 9, 64. L. Domitius Ahenobarbus, the consul of 54 B.C., was a candidate for the place in the college of augurs vacated by the death of Q. Hortensius on which cp. Ep. 42, 2. Under the 'Lex Domitia,' repealed by Sulla, but afterwards re-enacted, vacancies in the college were filled as follows: candidates were nominated each by two augurs, and their names submitted to seventeen tribes, chosen by lot. The candidate who obtained a majority of the votes was then elected by the college of augurs. Cp. Intr. to Part I, § 9.

2. Magna, 'important.'

Et plane . . apparuerunt, 'and it was clear that people exerted themselves for party purposes.'

3. Necessitudinem . . praestiterunt, 'were induced by private friendship to discharge their personal obligations.'

4. Ut ne familiarem . . quam me, 'that he hates me as much as he ever hated even one of his friends.' Ironical.

6. Per iniuriam, because a younger and less distinguished man was preferred to him. Antony was a 'quaestorius;' Domitius a 'consularis.'

Cuius . . fuerim, 'of which he supposes I was the author.' On the conj., cp. Ep. 9, 12, note on p. 72. Caelius was on intimate terms with Curio (cp. Ep. 76, 1), to whose influence Cicero ascribed Antony's election as augur (cp. Philipp. 2. 2, 4).

7. Nunc furit . . Antonii, 'now he is in a rage at the delight people take in his vexation, and that only one has shewn more zeal for Antony than I have.' The 'unus' was probably Curio, or perhaps Saturninus (Wesenb.) Cp. Philipp. 2. 2, 4. On the infin. and accus. after 'furit,' cp. Madv. 397 1 and for the accus. after 'gavisos,' Ib. 223 c. On the abl. 'me,' cp. Ep. 66, 2, note.

8. Nam introduces an illustration of the anger of L. Domitius and his family.

Cn. Saturninum. Cn. Appuleius Saturninus was son of L. Saturninus of Atina, propraetor of Macedonia 58 B.C. He had probably supported Antony in this contest; see above on l. 7. Both father and son are mentioned in the oration Pro Plancio 8, 19.

9. Ipse Cn. Domitius, son of the L. Domitius mentioned above, and of Porcia, Cato's sister. He fought against Caesar at Pharsalus, and afterwards joined the conspiracy against his life. Cp. Philipp. 2. 11, 27. Wesenb. suggests 'adolescens ipse,' saying that Cn. Domitius has not been mentioned before; Metzg. renders 'ipse' 'in person.'

Sane quam: cp. Ep. 33, 2, note.

10. In bona spe, 'with good hopes for the defendant.'

11. Post Sex. Peducaei absolutionem. This Peducaeus was son and namesake of a propraetor of Sicily in 75–74 B.C., whom Cicero mentions with praise in his speech against Verres (2 Act. 4. 64, 142). The son seems also to have enjoyed Cicero's esteem. Cp. Epp. 48, 3; 61, 2. Caelius appears to have thought his acquittal unjust, but what the charge against him was seems not to be known. The elder Peducaeus was dead early in 49 B.C. Cp. Ep. 68, 1.

14. Propositum hoc est, 'the point in

sunt dimicaturi, quod Cn. Pompeius constituit non pati C. Caesarem consulem aliter fieri, nisi exercitum et provincias tradiderit; Caesari autem persuasum est se salvum esse non posse, *si* ab exercitu recesserit. Fert illam tamen condicionem, ut ambo exercitus tradant. Sic illi amores et invidiosa coniunctio non ad occultam recidit obtrectationem, sed ad bellum se erupit; neque, mearum rerum quid consilii capiam, reperio; quod non dubito, quin te quoque haec deliberatio sit perturbatura. Nam mihi cum hominibus his et gratia et necessitudo est: causam
2 illam, non homines odi. Illud te non arbitror fugere, quin homines in dissensione domestica debeant, quam diu civiliter sine armis certetur, honestiorem sequi partem, ubi ad bellum et castra ventum sit, firmiorem, et id melius statuere, quod tutius sit. In hac discordia video Cn. Pompeium senatum quique res iudicant secum habiturum, ad Caesarem omnes, qui cum timore aut mala spe vivant, accessuros, exercitum confe-

quatione.' 'Propositum' = πρόβλημα. Ep. 45, 2.

2. Consulem aliter fieri, foll.: see Intr. to Part II, § 27.

3. Caesari . . recesserit. Caesar would probably have been prosecuted on some charge connected with his consulship or provincial government if he had been deprived of his official position even for a short time; and, as Pompey was dominant at Rome, his conviction would probably have ensued. Cp. Mommsen 4. 2, 349; Merivale 2. 55; Suet. Iul. 30.

4. Illam refers to what follows. Cp. Ep. 34. 9, note.

5. Tradant, 'deliver up' to officers appointed by the senate.

Illi amores . . coniunctio, 'their old intimacy and unpopular union,' referring to the combination of 59 B.C., and to the marriage of Pompey with Julia. Intr. to Part I, §§ 16; 18.

Non . . recidit . . sed . . se erupit, 'have not sunk into a secret jealousy, but have broken out into war.' For 'se erupit,' cp. Caes. Bell. Civ. 2. 14; and for the sing. 'recidit . . erupit,' Madv. 213 b.

7. Mearum . . capiam, 'what decision I shall come to about my own conduct or position.' On the genit., cp. Madv. 283.

Quod non dubito, 'as to which I doubt not.' Cp. Madv. 229 a. Acc. to Manut. 'quod' = 'sed.' Wesenb.'s punctuation 'reperio—quod non . . perturbatura—; nam' rather improves the sense.

8. Nam, in explanation of his difficulty in deciding.

9. Cum hominibus his, 'with Pompey's friends' I think.

Causam illam . . odi, 'while I hate Caesar's cause, but not his supporters.' On the omission of an adversative, cp. Ep. 36, 8, note.

11. Civiliter, 'with constitutional weapons.'

14. Quique res iudicant. Manutius explains these words of the judges, who were taken from the wealthy or middle classes. Pompey had in his second consulship, 55 B.C., enacted a law by which the tribunals were reconstituted, and Cicero (Ep. 59, 2) speaks of the judges as a body which would have supported Pompey but for his mistakes. But in Q. Cicero's letter De Pet. Cons. (2, 8), the words seem rather to mean, 'who judge things fairly;' and Wiel. and Metzg. give them that sense here.' Mr. Jeans renders 'judicially minded people.' If the first explanation be correct, Pompey's influence with the judges might account for Caesar's unwillingness to stand a trial.

16. Exercitum conferendum non esse, 'that there is no comparison between their armies,' Caesar's being much the best. I cannot agree with Mr. Jeans in thinking this a strange admission for Caelius to make, and the event surely proved the superior quality of Caesar's troops.

rendum non esse. Omnino satis spatii est ad considerandas utriusque copias et eligendam partem. Prope oblitus sum, quod 4 maxime fuit scribendum: scis Appium censorem hic ostenta facere? de signis et tabulis, de agri modo, de aere alieno acerrime agere? persuasum est ei censuram lomentum aut nitrum esse: errare mihi videtur; nam *dum* sordes eluere volt, venas sibi omnes et viscera aperit. Curre, per deos atque homines! et quam primum haec risum veni, legis Scantiniae iudicium apud Drusum fieri, Appium de tabulis et signis agere; crede mihi, est properandum. Curio noster sapienter id, quod remisit de stipendio Pompeii, fecisse existimatur. Ad summam, quaeris, quid putem futurum: si alteruter eorum ad Parthicum bellum non eat, video magnas impendere discordias, quas ferrum et vis *di*iudicabit; uterque et animo et copiis est paratus. Si sine tuo peri-

1. **Ad . . . eligendam partem**, 'for choosing one's side.'

3. **Fuit scribendum**: cp. Ep. 38, 2, note.

Ostenta facere, 'is shewing a portentous activity.'

4. **De signis . . agere**, 'is making the strictest enquiry as to the number of statues and pictures men have, and the amount of their lands and debts.' The 'censoria potestas' would enable Appius to censure extravagant expenditure on works of art. As to the 'extent of landed property,' perhaps he tried to put in force again the law of Ti. Gracchus, which his grandfather had co-operated in passing. As to the 'debts,' a Lex Sulpicia of 88 B.C. provided that no senator should be in debt to the amount of more than 2000 denarii, on pain, I presume, of expulsion. This law may not have been repealed like the rest of those of Sulpicius, or may have been replaced by a similar one. Cp. Plut. Sulla, 8. In all these cases the censor would probably have the power of stigmatising or degrading the guilty.

5. **Persuasum . . nitrum esse**, 'he is persuaded that his censorship will act as soap or nitre to cleanse his character.'

Lomentum was a mixture of bean-meal and rice, used to cleanse and smooth the face. Forcell.

6. **Errare . . aperit**, 'I think he makes a mistake, for in his anxiety to wash off dirt he opens his veins and his flesh,' i.e. exposes himself to attack.

8. **Legis Scantiniae**. The name is sometimes given as Scatinia. The date of this law is uncertain. It was directed 'in eos qui nefanda Venere uterentur,' and is mentioned by Juvenal (Sat. 2. 44), and, according to one reading, by Cicero (Philipp. 3. 6, 16).

9. **Apud Drusum**. This Drusus, clearly an abandoned man, was probably the same as the one mentioned Ep. 28, 9, q. v.

Appium . . agere. Appius may have appropriated several works of art as governor or officer in the provinces. Cp. Ep. 32, 2; De Domo 43. 111.

10. **Quod remisit . . Pompeii**, 'in withdrawing his objection to a vote for the pay of Pompey's troops.' Billerb.

11. **Ad summam**, 'in a word' = 'breviter.' Forcell.

12. **Eorum**, Pompeii et Caesaris.

Non eat, pres. in fut. sense. Cp. Ep. 6, 1, note, and Madv. 347 b.

13. **Video**. It seems to have been suggested as a compromise, that either Caesar or Pompey should take the command against the Parthians, and so spare the Commonwealth the dangers threatened by their rivalry in Italy. But the control of affairs at Rome was now mainly in Pompey's hands; if he had gone to the East he would have relinquished that control; if he had allowed Caesar to go, the latter would have been secured against prosecution for some time, and would have had opportunities of acquiring distinction, wealth, and influential connections.

***Di*iudicabit**. Wesenb. thinks the addition of di- needless, and refers to Ad Att. 15. 25 'causa consilium nostri itineris iudicabit.'

culo fieri posset, magnum et iucundum tibi Fortuna spectaculum parabat.

42. To ATTICUS (AD ATT. VI. 6).

SIDA, EARLY IN AUGUST, 50 B.C. (704 A.U.C.)

1. I was rather surprised to hear that my daughter had engaged herself to Dolabella, with her mother's approval; I had thought of Ti. Nero. 2. Why did you make a present of corn to the Athenians? I am sure you share my regret at the death of Hortensius. 3. I have left Caelius in charge of my province. I anticipate your criticisms, but could do no better. To have left my brother would have provoked censure, and there seems no danger of war. 4. Pompey and Caesar have both made more extraordinary appointments. I hope you will support my claims to a triumph.

CICERO ATTICO SAL.

1 Ego, dum in provincia omnibus rebus Appium orno, subito
sum factus accusatoris eius socer. 'Id quidem' inquis 'di adprobent!' Ita velim, teque ita cupere certo scio; sed crede mihi, nihil minus putaram ego, qui de Ti. Nerone, qui mecum egerat, certos homines ad mulieres miseram, qui Romam venerunt factis sponsalibus. Sed hoc spero melius; mulieres quidem valde intellego delectari obsequio et comitate adulescentis: cetera noli
2 ἐξακανθίζειν. Sed heus tu, πυροὺς εἰς δῆμον Athenis? placet hoc
tibi? etsi non impediebant mei certe libri; non enim ista largitio

2. Parabat, epistolary tense. On the mood, cp. Madv. 348 b.

SIDA. Cp. Intr. to Part II, § 24; Ad Fam. 3. 12, 4.

3. Omnibus rebus . . orno, 'do all I can to support his credit.' Cp. Epp. 35, 2; 38, 10, notes.

4. Accusatoris. P. Dolabella accused Appius. Cp. Ep. 35, l. c. He married Tullia, with her mother's approval, while Cicero was negotiating with Ti. Nero, father of the emperor Tiberius.

5. Ita velim, sc. 'esse.'

6. Qui . . miseram. Madvig (Adv. Crit. II. 236) says 'si sic sententias Cicero vinxisset, scripsisset sine dubio: "qui (etiam) de Ti. Nerone miseram."' Puto fuisse, 'ego; quin de Ti. Nerone miseram.'

De Ti Nerone, v. sup. Cicero had a good opinion of Ti. Nero (cp. Ad Fam. 13. 64, 1), who after Caesar's death opposed Augustus in the war of Perusia; escaped to Sextus Pompeius in Sicily, and afterwards to Antony in Greece; returned to Rome, and, at Augustus' request, divorced the future empress Livia. Cp. Suet. Tib. 4; Tac. Ann. 1, 10; 6, 51.

7. Mulieres. Terentia and Tullia are meant.

8. Sponsalibus, 'the betrothal.' It was a contract, often but not always made before marriage, and its fulfilment could be enforced at law. Cp. Smith's Dict. of Antiq. p. 741, sub voc. 'Matrimonium.'

9. Adulescentis, sc. Dolabellae.

Cetera . . ἐξακανθίζειν, 'to pull out all the thorns (i.e. faults), which deface his character in other respects.' Boot. The Greek word is found in Theophrastus.

10. πυροὺς . . Athenis, sc. διαδίδως. Cicero at first censures his friend's behaviour, as an instance of 'largitio frumentaria,' but corrects himself, remembering that Atticus was not a citizen of Athens, but only on hospitable terms with its people. Cp. for the facts Appendix 3, § 1, and Corn. Nepos, Atticus 2, 6.

11. Etsi non . . libri, 'though it was no violation of the precepts of my work on the Commonwealth.' Cp. Ep. 34, 9 'eos libros quos tu dilaudas.'

Largitio . . liberalitas. These words are contrasted, De Orat. 2. 25, 105.

fuit in cives, sed in hospites liberalitas. Me tamen de Academiae προπύλῳ iubes cogitare, cum iam Appius de Eleusine non
cogitet? De Hortensio te certo scio dolere, equidem excrucior;
decreram enim cum eo valde familiariter vivere. Nos provinciae 3
praefecimus Caelium: 'puerum' inquies 'et fortasse fatuum et
non gravem et non continentem.' Adsentior: fieri non potuit
aliter. Nam quas multo ante tuas acceperam litteras, in quibus
ἐπέχειν te scripseras, quid esset mihi faciendum de relinquendo,
eae me pungebant; videbam enim, quae tibi essent ἐποχῆς causae,
et erant eaedem mihi: puero tradere? fratri autem? illud non
utile nobis; nam praeter fratrem nemo erat, quem sine contumelia quaestori, nobili praesertim, anteferrem. Tamen, dum
impendere Parthi videbantur, statueram fratrem relinquere aut
etiam rei publicae causa contra senatus consultum ipse remanere,
qui posteaquam incredibili felicitate discesserunt, sublata dubitatio est. Videbam sermones: 'hui, fratrem reliquit! num est
hoc non plus annum obtinere provinciam? quid, quod senatus
eos voluit praeesse provinciis, qui non praefuissent? at hic
triennium.' Ergo haec ad populum. Quid, quae tecum? Num- 4

2. προπύλῳ. The word is neut., and quite classical. Cicero thought of building a porch in the Academy at Athens, and Appius of doing the same at Eleusis.

Cum, 'although.' Cicero means that one reason for such an expenditure—a wish to rival Appius—had been removed.

3. De Hortensio. M. Caelius had written (Ad Fam. 8. 13, 2) that that great orator was at the point of death. Cicero heard of his death at Rhodes (Brut. 1, 1).

5. Caelium: cp. Ep. 38, 10.

Fortasse, 'minuendi vim habet.' Boot. Cp. Ep. 70, 2 and 6. 'It may be.'

7. Nam quas . . eae. On the order of the words, cp. Madv. 319.

8. ἐπέχειν te, 'that you were in doubt.'

De relinquendo, 'as to the successor I should leave.'

9. Ἐποχῆς. Ἐποχή was a technical term used by some of the Sceptical philosophers, followers of Pyrrhon, for the 'suspension of judgment,' which they considered the proper frame of mind in matters of speculation. Cp. Diog. Laert. 9, 107; and Ritter and Preller's note on that passage in their History of Philosophy, p. 402.

10. Tradere, sc. 'provinciam.' For the infin., cp. Ep. 12, 1.

Fratri autem, 'should I prefer my brother?' Boot remarks that 'autem' is said 'cum aliqua indignatione, ut Gr. δή.'

Illud, 'the latter.'

11. Nam introduces a suggestion which is to be dismissed. 'No other course was open, for.' Cp. Ep. 26, 2, note.

Sine contumelia. Pomptinus had left Cicero, and it does not appear that any of his other legates had held any magistracy, so that it would be a slight to his quaestor to prefer any one of them to him.

14. Senatus consultum: cp. Ep. 37, 3, note; also below in this section.

15. Incredibili felicitate, 'by a remarkable piece of good fortune.' On the abl., cp. Ep. 26, 9, note. Cicero was unwilling to admit the diplomatic success of Bibulus, who fomented a quarrel between Pacorus and his father, Orodes. Cp. Dion Cassius 40, 30; and, for Cicero's jealousy of Bibulus, Ad Att. 6. 8, 5; 7. 2, 7.

16. Videbam sermones, 'I saw what people would say.' 'Video' = 'praevideo.' Metzg.

18. Eos . . praefuissent, 'those men qualified by office who had not yet governed provinces.' Cp. Ep. 34, 8, note.

At hic triennium, sc. 'Asiae praefuit.' Quintus Cicero governed Asia for three years. Cp. Ad Q. F. 1. 1, 2 and 46.

19. Haec ad populum, 'these reasons I can give to the public.'

quam essem sine cura, si quid iracundius aut contumeliosius aut neglegentius, quae fert vita hominum. Quid, si quid filius puer et puer bene sibi fidens? qui esset dolor? quem pater non dimittebat teque id censere moleste ferebat. At nunc Caelius, non dico equidem quid egerit, sed tamen multo minus laboro. Adde illud: Pompeius, eo robore vir, iis radicibus, Q. Cassium sine sorte delegit, Caesar Antonium; ego sorte datum offenderem, ut etiam inquireret in eum, quem reliquissem? Hoc melius, et huius rei plura exempla, senectuti quidem nostrae profecto aptius. At te apud eum, di boni! quanta in gratia posui, eique legi litteras non tuas, sed librarii tui. Amicorum litterae me ad triumphum vocant, rem a nobis, ut ego arbitror, propter hanc *παλιγγενεσίαν* nostram non neglegendam: qua re tu quoque, mi Attice, incipe id cupere, quo nos minus inepti videamur.

Quae tecum, sc. 'proferam.'

1. **Si quid . . neglegentius**, 'in case he should display passion, affront people, or neglect his duty.' Cp. Ep. 15, 6.

2. **Quae fert vita hominum**, 'faults men are liable to.'

Si quid filius, sc. 'faceret.' On the ellipse, cp. Madv. 479 c. 'Filius,' the younger Quintus.

3. **Non dimittebat**, 'did (or does?) not intend to send away.' Cp. Madv. 337, Obs. 1.

4. **Id**, i.e. 'that he ought to send him away.'

5. **Non dico . . quid egerit**, 'I do not discuss his antecedents.' Boot.

Multo minus laboro. 'I am much less anxious.' For the misconduct of Caelius, a stranger, would not annoy him like that of his nephew.

6. **Eo robore . . radicibus**, 'a man of such power, and of such deeply-rooted influence.' On the ablat., cp. Ep. 35, 3.

7. **Sine sorte**, 'not regularly assigned to him.' Q. Cassius was placed in charge of a province by Pompey 51-50 B.C. For his subsequent history, cp. Ep. 36, 1, note. For Caesar's relations with M. Antonius, here referred to, cp. Caes. Bell. Gall. 8, 2; Cic. Philipp. 2. 20, 50. Cicero means that he could not do wrong in following an example set by such eminent men as Pompey and Caesar.

Ego . . offenderem, 'was I to give offence to one who had been regularly assigned to me?'

8. **Ut etiam . . reliquissem**, 'to make him act as a spy and informer upon my representative.' Cp. Pro Muren. 23, 47, for this use of 'ut,' expressing result, and Ib. 21, 45, for the meaning of 'inquirere.'

Hoc, 'the step I have taken.'

9. **Senectuti . . aptius**, 'and is assuredly better suited to my time of life,' which naturally longs for peace.

11. **Librarii tui**. The secretary of Atticus seems to have been with Cicero, who dictated to him a letter in praise of Caelius, and then read it to Caelius as having been written by Atticus, who, as appears from this letter, had in reality expressed himself very differently.

12. **Propter hanc παλιγγενεσίαν**, 'on account of the restoration to my political position, in which I have made some progress (hanc).' The Greek word occurs, Joseph. Antiq. 11. 3, 9. Cicero refers mainly to the increased dignity which his provincial government, and the recognition of his services by the senate, would secure for him; but partly also to his general position since his restoration from exile. Cp. Ep. 20, 8 'alterius vitae quoddam initium ordimur.'

14. **Id cupere . . videamur**, 'to entertain a wish which may make me seem less foolish.' Cicero's ambition might seem less absurd if his friends shared it on his behalf.

43. To his Wife, Terentia (Ad Fam. XIV. 5).

Athens, October 18, 50 B.C. (704 A.U.C.)

1. I arrived here on October 14, after a tedious voyage, and received your letter at once. Your previous letters had all reached me. I wish to get to Italy as soon as I can, though the aspect of affairs is so gloomy. I hope you will come as far to meet me as you can without danger to your health. 2. I am sorry for the death of Precius; as for his legacy, ask Atticus or Camillus to attend to my interests. I hope to be in Italy about November 14.

TULLIUS S. D. TERENTIAE SUAE.

Si tu et Tullia, lux nostra, valetis, ego et suavissimus Cicero 1
valemus. Pr. Idus Oct. Athenas venimus, cum sane adversis ventis usi essemus tardeque et incommode navigassemus. De nave exeuntibus nobis Acastus cum litteris praesto fuit uno et vicensimo die, sane strenue. Accepi tuas litteras, quibus intellexi te vereri ne superiores mihi redditae non essent: omnes sunt redditae diligentissimeque a te perscripta sunt omnia; idque mihi gratissimum fuit. Neque sum admiratus hanc epistolam, quam Acastus attulit, brevem fuisse; iam enim me ipsum exspectas sive nos ipsos, qui quidem quam primum ad vos venire cupimus, etsi, in quam rem publicam veniamus, intellego: cognovi enim ex multorum amicorum litteris, quas attulit Acastus, ad arma rem spectare, ut mihi, cum venero, dissimulare non liceat, quid sentiam. Sed, quoniam subeunda fortuna est, eo citius dabimus operam ut veniamus, quo facilius de tota re

1. **Lux nostra**; cp. Ep. 17. 2, where the same term is applied to Terentia.

Suavissimus Cicero. It would be more usual to couple another substantive—e. g. 'puer'—with Cicero. But cp. Ep. 77. 3 'mi iucundissime Cicero.' In this passage Cicero is speaking of his son Marcus. Cp. Ad Fam. 14. 4. 3; 16. 16, 1.

4. **Acastus.** A slave of Cicero, often mentioned in his letters to Tiro and to Terentia. Also Ad Att. 6. 9. 1.

Uno et vicensimo die, 'in twenty-one days from Rome.'

5. **Sane strenue,** 'with good speed.' Cp. Ad Att. 14. 18, 1 'sane celeriter;' and 16. 6, 1 'strenue.' Manut. On another occasion a letter took forty-six days to reach Athens from Rome (cp. Ad Fam. 16. 21, 1), but that seems to have been an unusually long time.

10. **Sive nos ipsos,** 'or rather, us in person;' that is, my son and me.

13. **Ad arma rem spectare,** 'that things look towards war.' Cp. Ad Fam. 4. 2. 3 'consilia ad concordiam spectaverunt.'

Ut . . non liceat. On the tense, cp. Ep. 6, 1. note, p. 42.

14. **Quoniam . . fortuna est,** 'since we must submit to what fortune has in store for us,' i.e. 'must run some risk,' as it was impossible to avoid offending either Pompey or Caesar. Manut. Cp. De Prov. Cons. 17. 41 'excipere fortunam.'

Eo citius . . deliberemus, 'I shall exert myself to arrive more speedily, that I may deliberate about the whole case with more ease.' I have followed Wesenb. in removing a comma after 'operam.' On the position of 'citius,' apart from its verb 'veniamus,' cp. Madv. 468.

deliberemus. Tu velim, quod commodo valetudinis tuae fiat,
2 quam longissime poteris obviam nobis prodeas. De hereditate Preciana, quae quidem mihi magno dolori est—valde enim illum amavi—, sed hoc velim cures: si auctio ante meum adventum fiet, ut Pomponius aut, si is minus poterit, Camillus nostrum negotium curet. Nos cum salvi venerimus, reliqua per nos agemus; sin tu iam Roma profecta eris, tamen curabis, ut hoc ita fiat. Nos, si di adiuvabunt, circiter Idus Novembres in Italia speramus fore. Vos, mea suavissima et optatissima Terentia, si nos amatis, curate ut valeatis. [Vale.] Athenis a. d. XV. Kal. Novemb.

44. To ATTICUS (AD ATT. VII. 7).

Written from Campania, December, 50 B.C. (704 A.U.C.)

1. Dionysius does not seem very grateful for my recommendation, but I will not retract it. 2. Philogenes' letter to you was quite correct. 3. I hope Pomptinus had no unpleasant reason for entering Rome. I expect to be at the gates on Jan. 4; do not move at any risk to your health. 4. I think there will be no opposition to my triumph, unless Caesar instructs his friends among the tribunes to oppose it. I care little about it; especially as I hear there is some notion of sending me to Sicily as still holding the 'imperium.' I shall however, evade that commission. 5. You say

1. Quod . . fiat, 'so far as it can be done without injury to your health.'

Commodo is the ablat. modi. Cp. Ep. 34, 2; and for 'quod fiat,' cp. Madv. 364, Obs. 2.

2. De hereditate Preciana. A lawyer named Precianus is named as a friend of Cicero, Ad Fam. 7. 8, 2, and perhaps this legacy came from him. For Cicero's sentiments about legacies, cp. Ad Att. 6. 9, 2: also Philipp. 2. 16, 40 'Hereditates mihi negasti venire. Utinam hoc tuum crimen verum esset! plures amici mei et necessarii viverent.'

4. Sed, 'however.' Resumptive, as often, after a digression. Cp. Ep. 23, 2, p. 172.

Auctio. The property was probably to be sold for division among the creditors and legatees.

5. Pomponius, Atticus. Cicero was anxious that his wife's freedman Philotimus should have nothing to do with the business. Cp. Ad Att. 6. 9, 2.

Camillus. C. Furius Camillus, a friend of Cicero, is mentioned as being thoroughly well acquainted with the law of suretyship. Cp. Ad Fam. 5. 20, 3.

7. Sin tu iam Roma .. fiat, 'but if you have already left Rome (when you receive this letter), take care that this is done as I wish (by writing to proper people). On curabis, cp. Ep. 38, 10, note.

8. Si di adiuvabunt. Not a common expression with Cicero.

9. Vos, Terentia and Tullia. The plural may be used where one person is directly addressed, if it be intended to include others. Cp. De Orat. 1. 9, 38; Virg. Aen. 1. 140.

Campania, December. Our evidence for fixing the date and place of this letter seems to be that Cicero had received (§ 1) a letter from Atticus written not earlier than Dec. 16; that he does not mention his interview with Pompey on Dec. 25 (on which cp. Ad Att. 7. 8, 4); that he was near Trebula on Dec. 9 (see Ad Att. 7. 3, 12), and at Formiae on December 25. The letter was probably written about December 20. See Intr. to Part II, § 25.

that all good citizens have made up their minds what I shall do. But I hardly know where to look for good citizens. 6. 'Do you think that Caesar's demands ought to be granted?' No; but past supineness has made it very difficult to resist now. 7. 'War is preferable to slavery.' But the issue of a war must in any case be disastrous. 'What then shall you do?' I shall follow instinctively that party which seems to defend the constitution. The issue of war is uncertain; massacres and exactions will certainly follow the triumph of Caesar. I have written much to you about politics, but it may be summed up thus; I shall do as Pompey, that is, as you, think right. Greet Alexis for me.

CICERO ATTICO SAL.

'Dionysius, vir optimus, ut mihi quoque est perspectus, et 1
doctissimus tuique amantissimus, Romam venit XV. Kalend. Ian.
et litteras a te mihi reddidit:' tot enim verba sunt de Dionysio
in epistola tua. Illud † putato non adscribis 'et tibi gratias egit:'
atqui certe ille agere debuit, et, si esset factum, quae tua est
humanitas, adscripsisses. Mihi autem nulla de eo παλινῳδία datur
propter superioris epistolae testimonium. Sit igitur sane bonus
vir; hoc enim ipsum bene fecit, quod mihi sui cognoscendi
penitus etiam istam facultatem dedit. Philogenes recte ad te 2
scripsit; curavit enim quod debuit. Eum ego uti ea pecunia
volui, quoad liceret; itaque usus est menses XIIII. Pomptinum 3
cupio valere, et, quod scribis in urbem introisse, vereor quid sit;

1. Dionysius: cp. Epp. 38, 3; 65, 2.

Vir optimus, probably referring to Cicero's recommendation of him to Atticus. Cp. 'mihi quoque.' Cicero did not use the word 'optimus,' however. Cp. Ad Att. 7. 4, 1.

Ut . . perspectus, 'for which I also have known him,' Atticus wrote.' On the dative mihi, cp. Madv. 250 a; Ep. 132, 4, note.

4. Illud † putato. So the best MS. Boot suggests 'illud optatum,' 'what I so much wished to hear.'

5. Debuit. Cicero was apparently indignant that Dionysius shewed no gratitude for his recommendation.

6. Nulla . . datur, foll., 'I cannot retract what I have said of him, because of the testimony borne by my previous letter.' Cp. Ad Att. 7. 4, 1 'Dionysium . . misi ad te . . quem quidem cognovi cum doctum tum sane plenum officii . . plane virum bonum.'

Datur = 'conceditur.' Cicero was reconciled to Dionysius subsequently (cp. Ad Att. 7. 8, 1): but had again occasion to reproach him with ingratitude (Ib. 8. 10).

9. Etiam istam, 'even that contained in your letter,' i.e. in Atticus' silence as to any expression of gratitude by Dionysius.

Recte, 'truly.' The meaning of the following words is not very clear, but Cicero seems to have placed in the hands of Philogenes some money belonging to himself or to Atticus, with liberty to use it for some time. Cp. Ad Att. 5. 13, 2. It appears that Atticus had given Philogenes bills on some merchants in Asia.

11. Pomptinum cupio valere, 'I wish Pomptinus may be restored to health.' On the acc. and infin. after 'cupio,' cp. Ep. 27, 1, note, p. 189. Cicero seems to have heard that his legate, Pomptinus (cp. Ep. 31, 4, note), was ill.

12. Vereor quid sit, 'I am anxious about his reason for doing so.' Pomptinus would naturally have waited to attend the triumphal entry of his general Cicero, if there was any prospect of a triumph: his entering Rome beforehand shewed that he hardly thought a triumph possible.

nam id nisi gravi de causa non fecisset. Ego, quoniam IIII. Non. Ian. compitalicius dies est, nolo eo die in Albanum [venire], *ne* molestus familiae veniam: tertio Non. [Ian.] igitur; inde ad urbem pridie Nonas. Tua λῆψις quem in diem incurrat, nescio,
4 sed prorsus te commoveri incommodo valetudinis tuae nolo. De honore nostro, nisi quid occulte Caesar per suos tribunos molitus erit, cetera videntur esse tranquilla; tranquillissimus autem animus meus, qui totum istuc aequi boni facit, et eo magis, quod iam a multis audio constitutum esse Pompeio et eius consilio in Siciliam me mittere, quod imperium habeam. Id est Ἀβδηριτικόν. Nec enim senatus decrevit nec populus iussit me imperium in Sicilia habere; sin hoc res publica ad Pompeium defert, qui me magis quam privatum aliquem mittat? itaque, si hoc imperium
5 mihi molestum erit, utar ea porta, quam primam videro. Nam, quod scribis mirificam exspectationem esse mei neque tamen

1. Compitalicius dies. The Compitalia were a moveable feast in honour of the Lares, celebrated especially by the slaves and dependants of different families. Cp. Smith's Dict. of Antiq. sub voc., 'Compitalia,' p. 341.

Albanum. The estate of Pompey near Alba. From a comparison of this passage with Ad Att. 7. 5. 3. it appears that Cicero had intended to go there 'III. Non. Ian.'

3. Molestus familiae. Ut ne hilaritatem die festo meus adventus interpellaret. Manut. Wesenb. has 'ne molestus sim familiae veniam III. Non. [Ian.] igitur.'

4. λῆψις. 'Attack' of quartan fever, a classical word.

5. Te commoveri, 'that you should travel,' not usual, apparently, without mention of a starting-place.

Incommodo: cp. Ep. 43. 1, note.

De honore, sc. 'triumpho.'

6. Nisi quid .. molitus erit, 'unless Caesar shall secretly interpose some difficulty by the help of the tribunes devoted to him.' Antony and Q. Cassius are meant. Cp. Appendix 6, § 5.

7. Cetera .. tranquilla, 'there seems to be acquiescence everywhere else.' Forcell.

8. Qui .. aequi boni facit, 'which takes in good part whatever is done in the matter.' On the genit., cp. Madv. 294. Obs. 2. 'Quae' is usually added to 'aequi boni.' The words = 'aequo animo patitur.' Forcell. Cicero says elsewhere that he only desired a triumph because Bibulus was eager for one, whose services had not been greater than his own. Cp. Ad Att. 6. 8, 5; 7. 2, 6 and 7.

9. Eius consilio, 'his advisers.' The word is more commonly used of judges acting under a magistrate; but cp. Ep. 8, 4 and 5, notes. On the datives Pompeio .. consilio, cp. p. 278, note on l. 1.

10. Ἀβδηριτικόν, 'foolish.' Cp. Ad Att. 4. 16, 6; also Juvenal, Sat. 10, 50—who, however, refers to Democritus of Abdera in refutation of the popular prejudice. Cicero states the following dilemma as to the commission proposed for him. 'If the senate or people is to provide for the government of Sicily, neither has named me. If Pompey is commissioned to provide for its government, why need he send a man invested with the "imperium"?' If Pompey were invested with a general control of the provinces, or of any of them, he might send legates to govern them who need not necessarily be possessed of 'imperium' at the time of their appointment. Caesar had offered to make Cicero his legate when the latter was a private citizen (cp. Ep. 11, 3), and Pompey had entrusted the government of the Spanish provinces to legates for some time. Cp. Intr. to Part II, § 14.

14. Utar ea porta .. videro, 'I shall get rid of my "imperium" by entering Rome by the nearest gate.' Cp. Ep. 35, 1, note; note F, p. 123.

15. Exspectationem mei, 'anxiety to see what line I shall adopt.'

quemquam bonorum aut satis bonorum dubitare, quid facturus sim, ego, quos tu bonos esse dicas, non intellego—ipse nullos novi—, sed ita, si ordines bonorum quaerimus. Nam singulares sunt boni viri, verum in dissensionibus ordines bonorum et genera quaerenda sunt. Senatum bonum putas, per quem sine imperio provinciae sunt?—numquam enim Curio sustinuisset, si cum eo agi coeptum esset, quam sententiam senatus sequi noluit, ex quo factum est ut Caesari non succederetur—an publicanos? qui numquam firmi, sed nunc Caesari sunt amicissimi,—an faeneratores? an agricolas? quibus optatissimum est otium, nisi eos timere putas, ne sub regno sint, qui id numquam, dum modo otiosi essent, recusarunt. Quid ergo? exercitum retinentis, cum legis 6
dies transierit, rationem haberi placet? Mihi vero ne absentis quidem. Sed, cum id datum est, illud una datum est. 'Annorum enim decem imperium et ita latum *placet?*' Placet igitur etiam

3. Sed ita . . quaerimus, 'but only if we are looking out for well-disposed classes,' i.e. my remark only holds good in that case.

Singulares . . quaerenda sunt, 'there are well-disposed individuals, but in times of civil dissension we ought to look out for well-disposed orders and classes.' Wesenb. suggests the insertion of 'multi' after 'viri.' Ordines I think, has a more direct reference to political privileges than genera. Forcell. gives 'unus,' 'solus' among the synonyms for 'singularis.'

5. Per quem, 'through the fault of which,' i.e. through its want of decision.

Per quem . . provinciae sunt, 'provinces are without governors invested with proper powers.' Cilicia, *for* instance, was governed by a quaestor (cp. Ep. 42, 3); the two Spains by legates (sup. § 4, note); and no provision had been made for the future government of Caesar's provinces.

6. Numquam . . sustinuisset, 'Curio would never have persevered in his opposition if he had been formally asked to give way.' On this sense of 'agere cum,' cp. Ep. 34, 6, note on p. 238; Ad Fam. 8, 13, 2; Philipp. 2. 21, 52. Curio's opposition to the proposed recall of Caesar had apparently interfered with the arrangements to be made about other provinces. Cp. Ep. 38, 6, p. 262. In 51 B.C. tribunes attached to Caesar had vetoed proposals affecting the government of provinces generally. Cp. Ep. 34, 8, p. 240. Cicero probably mistook Curio's character in supposing he would have yielded to remonstrance.

7. Quam sententiam, the proposal of M. Marcellus that negotiations should be opened with the tribunes, to induce them to withdraw their veto in the summer of 50 B.C. Which proposal the senate rejected: 'frequens senatus in alia omnia iit,' Ad Fam. 8, 13, 2.

9. Firmi, 'trustworthy.' They had been alienated by rigour which some of the leading optimates shewed in enforcing a contract unfavourable to the equites. Cp. Ep. 9, 8, note.

12. Cum legis dies transierit? 'after the time fixed by law shall have expired?' Cp. for the facts, Appendix 6, § 2. The genitive is possessive or conjunctive. Cp. Madv. 280.

13. Ne absentis quidem, sc. 'rationem haberi,' on which phrase cp. Ep. 34, 9, note.

14. Id, sc. absentis rationem haberi; illud, exercitum retinentis rat. hab. These words are very important in their bearing on the occasion of the civil war. Cp. Appendix 6, § 3.

15. Enim, 'why?' Atticus interposes.

Ita latum, 'carried by such unconstitutional means.' Cp. Intr. to Parts I, § 17; II, §§ 7; 8: with the references there given, and Dion Cass. 39. 19–31; Suet. Iul. 20; 22; Vell. 2. 44 and 46, for the circumstances under which the 'Lex Vatinia' and 'Lex Pompeia Licinia' were carried.

Placet? Wesenb. has 'placet.'

Placet igitur, 'then I also approve' or 'must approve.' Cicero means that the responsibility for the various acts done by or for the triumvirs could not be divided.

me expulsum et agrum Campanum perisse et adoptatum patricium a plebeio, Gaditanum a Mytilenaeo, et Labieni divitiae et Mamurrae placent et Balbi horti et Tusculanum. Sed horum omnium fons unus est: imbecillo resistendum fuit, et id erat facile; nunc legiones XI., equitatus tantus, quantum volet, Transpadani, plebes urbana, tot tribuni pl., tam perdita iuventus, tanta auctoritate dux, tanta audacia. Cum hoc aut depugnandum est aut habenda

7 e lege ratio. 'Depugna' inquis 'potius quam servias.' Ut quid? si victus eris, proscribare? si viceris, tamen servias? 'Quid ergo' inquis 'acturus es?' Idem quod pecudes, quae dispulsae sui generis sequuntur greges: ut bos armenta, sic ego bonos viros aut eos, quicumque dicentur boni, sequar, etiam si ruent. Quid sit optimum male contractis rebus plane video: nemini est enim exploratum, cum ad arma ventum est, quid futurum sit, at illud

1. Agrum Campanum: cp. Ep. 10, 1, note.

Patricium (P. Clodium) a plebeio (P. Fonteio). P. Scipio a patrician was adopted by Q. Metellus a plebeian (cp. Epp. 1, 3, note; 34, 5), but the author of the speech 'De Domo' complains of other irregularities in the case of Clodius. De Dom. 13; 14.

2. Gaditanum, sc. L. Cornelium Balbum (the elder Balbus: cp. Ep. 27, 2, note) a Mytilenaeo, sc. Theophane (cp. Ep. 31, 3). If, as must have been the case, both Balbus and Theophanes were Roman plebeians, I cannot see why the difference of birthplace should have made the adoption irregular. Perhaps Cicero wishes to notice the degradation of the Roman franchise.

Labieni. T. Atius Labienus was one of the ablest of Caesar's officers. Cp. Caes. Bell. Gall. 1. 21, alib. He was tribune in 64-63 B.C., and accused C. Rabirius of 'perduellio.' Cp. Intr. to Part I, § 9. At the beginning of the civil war Labienus deserted Caesar, which changed Cicero's opinion of him. Cp. Ep. 47, 1. Labienus fell in the campaign of Munda. See Intr. to Part IV, § 13.

Divitiae. Labienus seems to have rebuilt the town of Cingulum, in Picenum, at his own expense. Cp. Smith's Dict. of Geogr. 1. 615; Caes. Bell. Civ. 1, 15.

Mamurrae. A Mamurra had acted as 'praefectus fabrum' or chief engineer, to Caesar in Gaul. He had a splendid house on the Caelian, and his prosperity seems to have excited much hostility. Cp. Pliny H. N. 36. 6, 7; Hor. Sat. 1. 5. 37; Suet. Iul. 73; Catull. Epigr. 29, for further notices of him.

3. Horti et Tusculanum, 'garden in the suburbs of Rome and villa at Tusculum.' Cp. Ad Att. 9. 13, 8; Pro Balbo 25, 56. The land for his garden was a gift from Pompey. Cp. Ad Att. l. c.

4. Fons unus, sc. the submission of the Romans to the joint sovereignty of Caesar and Pompey from 59-52 B.C.

5. Transpadani: cp. Ep. 31, 2, note.

6. E lege. The law Cicero refers to was one proposed by the whole body of tribunes in 52 B.C. Cp. Intr. to Part II, § 14; Appendix 6, § 3.

Ut quid, sc. 'efficias.'

9. Servias. Cicero often expresses a want of confidence in Pompey; uterque regnare vult he says of him and Caesar. Ep. 56, 2.

10. Dispulsae, 'scattered.'

12. Etiam si ruent, 'even if they rush into danger,' 'rush blindly on.' Nageisb. 127, 355.

13. Male contractis rebus, 'now that affairs are in a mischievous complication.'

Plane video, foll., 'I see clearly that to do all we can for peace is our best course. For the issue of war is uncertain; the disastrous consequences of defeat are certain.'

14. Exploratum, 'ascertained.' Cp. Ep. 70, 6. On the dat. nemini, cp. ib. and sup. § 1, note.

Cum ad arma ventum est, 'when we have come to blows' indicat. as a general remark. Cp. Madv. 335, b, Obs. 1. Wesenb., however, suggests 'sit' (1) because the sentence is in orat. obl., (2) because the fut. exact. is needed before 'fore.'

omnibus, si boni victi sint, nec in caede principum clementiorem hunc fore, quam Cinna fuerit, nec moderatiorem quam Sulla in pecuniis locupletium. Συμπολιτεύομαί σοι iam dudum, et facerem diutius, nisi me lucerna desereret. Ad summam, 'DIC M. TVLLI.' 'Adsentior Cn. Pompeio,' id est T. Pomponio. Alexim, humanissimum puerum, nisi forte, dum ego absum, adulescens factus est—id enim agere videbatur—, salvere iubeas velim.

45. To ATTICUS (AD ATT. VII. 9).

FORMIAE, END OF DECEMBER, 50 B.C. (704 A.U.C.)

1. You are amused at my writing so often, but I shall go on till we meet. 2. Tell me what you think on the following important question: either some concession must be made to Caesar, or public business must be interrupted, or a civil war must begin: which of these evils do you think the least? You will probably say, a moderate concession to Caesar, and 3. I quite agree with you; but even that would be a great misfortune. 4. People say the concession to which I refer will not satisfy Caesar; the demands attributed to him are most shameless. If we fight, chance will determine the time of our beginning hostilities, and the time of beginning will suggest our policy.

CICERO ATTICO SAL.

'Quotidiene' inquis 'a te accipiendae litterae sunt?' Si habebo, 1
cui dem, quotidie. 'At iam ipse ades.' Tum igitur, cum venero, desinam. Unas video mihi a te non esse redditas, quas L. Quinc-

1. Hunc, Caesarem. This prediction was utterly falsified by the event. Cp. Epp. 57; 91, 8-10.

3. Συμπολιτεύομαι, 'discuss politics with you,' not classical in this sense.

4. Lucerna, 'the oil in my lamp.'

Ad summam .. T. Pomponio, 'In a word, if my opinion is asked, I shall say, "I agree with Cn. Pompeius, that is, with M. Pomponius."'

Dic M. Tvlli would be the words used by a presiding officer in asking Cicero's opinion in the senate, and his supposed answer adsentior, foll., implies that he thought Atticus and Pompey agreed in their views. He still calls his friend Pomponius, notwithstanding his adoption by Q. Caecilius. Cp. Ad Att. 3. 20; Ad Fam. 14. 5. 2.

5. Alexim. This Alexis was probably son and namesake of a freedman and secretary of Atticus. Cp. Ad Att. 7. 2, 3; 12. 10.

7. Id .. agere, 'to be thinking of that,' probably of assuming the 'toga virilis,' when he would become 'adulescens.' This was generally done at the age of 14. Cp. Smith's Dict. of Antiq., sub voc., 'Impubes,' p. 631.

9. Cui dem, 'a messenger.'

At iam ipse ades. Atticus is supposed to remark, 'why write when we shall meet so soon.' Cp. § 3 of the preceding letter for an account of Cicero's movements.

10. Unas. The plural of 'unus' is used with plural substantives denoting a compound object, which can be repeated and counted. Cp. Madv. 76 c, Obs.

Quas .. cum ferret, 'in bearing which.' Cp. Madv. 358.

L. Quinctius, apparently tribune in 74–73 B.C. He defended Oppianicus on a charge of poisoning, and is not generally mentioned with praise by Cicero. Cp. Pro Cluent. 27. 74; 28. 77.

tius, familiaris meus, cum ferret, ad bustum Basili volneratus et spoliatus est. Videbis igitur, num quid fuerit in iis, quod me scire opus sit, et simul hoc διευκρινήσεις πρόβλημα sane πολιτικόν: cum sit necesse aut haberi Caesaris rationem, illo exercitum vel per senatum vel per tribunos pl. obtinente, aut persuaderi Caesari, ut tradat provinciam atque exercitum et ita consul fiat, aut, si id ei non persuadeatur, haberi comitia sine illius ratione, illo patiente atque obtinente provinciam, aut, si per tribunos pl. non patiatur, tamen quiescat, rem adduci ad interregnum, aut, si ob eam causam, quod ratio eius non habeatur, exercitum adducat, armis cum eo contendere, illum autem initium facere armorum aut statim nobis minus paratis aut tum, cum comitiis, amicis eius postulantibus, ut e lege ratio habeatur, impetratum non sit, ire autem ad arma aut hanc unam ob causam, quod ratio non habeatur, aut addita causa, si forte tribunus pl. senatum impediens aut populum incitans notatus aut senatus consulto circumscriptus aut sublatus aut expulsus sit dicensve se expulsum ad illum

1. **Ad bustum Basili.** A tomb on the Appian way near Rome, often the scene of assaults. Cp. Ascon. in Milonian. 49. p. 155.

3. **Hoc . . πρόβλημα sane πολιτικόν**, 'the following question, which may be truly called a problem of statesmanship.' The word πρόβλημα was generally used of philosophical enquiries.

Διευκρινήσεις, 'judge rightly,' not apparently a classical word.

In the following passage Cicero attempts to state all the possible courses which events could take. Either, he says

A. Caesar might keep the peace, and then

1. Retain his army till elected consul for 48 B.C.
2. Resign it, and then be elected consul.
3. Retain it, and waive his claim to the consulship for 48 B.C.
4. Retain it, and employ his friends among the tribunes to impede an election of consuls for 48 B.C. till an interregnum ensued.

Or B. He might appeal to arms,

1. Because he was not allowed to sue for the consulship when absent.
2. For that reason, combined with some affront offered to his friends among the tribunes,

He might begin war at once, or after the comitia had been held for the election of consuls for 48 B.C.; and his opponents might either maintain the capital, or try to reduce it and Caesar by famine. Cicero does not seem to have anticipated the extreme haste and violence by which Pompey and his friends gave Caesar a plausible pretext for beginning hostilities. Cp. Appendix 6, § 5.

4. The infinitives **haberi, persuaderi . . ire**, all seem to depend on **sit necesse**.

8. **Si non patiatur, tamen quiescat**, 'si' = 'etiamsi:' cp. Ep. 89, 2, note; 'if he employ tribunes to oppose this, but yet abstain from violence.' Wesenb. suggests 'et' after 'patiatur.'

11. **Armis . . contendere.** Wesenb. inserts 'nos' after 'armis,' arguing that the verb 'contendere' would otherwise be in the passive voice, like the preceding infinitives.

16. **Notatus**, 'censured,' 'stigmatised.' Cp. Caes. Bell. Civ. 1. 5; 1. 7. In 49 B.C. an appeal was made to the magistrates and citizens to support the constitution, which implied that the conduct of some of the tribunes endangered it. Cp. Appendix 6, § 5.

Circumscriptus, 'limited' in the exercise of his functions. Cp. Philipp. 2. 22, 53: Pro Milon. 33. 88. This was Caesar's actual plea for beginning hostilities.

17. **Sublatus**, 'suspended,' as had been the case with Q. Metellus Nepos in 62 B.C. Cp. Intr. to Part I, § 12.

Sit. The conj. is used because Cicero

confugerit, suscepto autem bello aut tenenda sit urbs aut ea re-
licta ille commeatu et reliquis copiis intercludendus,—quod horum
malorum, quorum aliquod certe subeundum est, minimum putes:
dices profecto persuaderi illi, ut tradat exercitum et ita consul fiat.
Est omnino id eius modi, ut, si ille eo descendat, contra dici nihil 3
possit, idque eum, si non obtineat, ut ratio habeatur retinentis
exercitum, non facere mirer; nobis autem, ut quidam putant,
nihil est timendum magis quam ille consul. 'At sic malo' inquies
'quam cum exercitu.' Certe. Sed istud ipsum, dico, magnum
malum putat aliquis, neque ei remedium est ullum. 'Cedendum
est, si id volet.' Vide consulem illum iterum, quem vidisti consulatu priore. 'At tum imbecillus plus' inquit 'valuit quam tota
res publica.' Quid nunc putas? et eo consule Pompeio certum est

speaks from another's point of view. Cp. Ep. 36, 11, note, p. 252.

Dicensve se expulsum. Cicero says that Antony and Q. Cassius were 'nulla vi expulsi' Ad Fam. 16. 11, 2. Mr. Jeans remarks: 'notice the weak alternative marked by "ve," after a succession of strong alternatives marked by "aut."'

1. **Aut tenenda sit.** These words depend on 'cum' after *voluntate*. It would be more regular had Cicero written 'urbem teneri,' but the sentence had become so long that he preferred to introduce another finite verb.

2. **Ille**, Caesar.

Commeatu .. intercludendus, 'should be cut off from supplies of provisions and from other resources.' Cp. Epp. 61, 4; 62, 2.

Quod horum .. putes. Here the apodosis begins. It corresponds to 'cum sit necesse.' The mood of sit and putes is accounted for by the words occurring in an indirect question. Cp. Ep. 34, 9, note, p. 241.

3. **Putes: dices.** I prefer Wesenberg's punctuation 'putes. Dices.'

4. **Persuaderi.** For the infinit., cp. Madv. 388 a.

Ut tradat .. fiat, 'that he should resign his command before the next consular election, and then stand for the consulship.' Cicero seems to contemplate an understanding between Caesar and his leading opponents, such as should prevent any serious opposition to Caesar's election. Hence he uses the word 'fiat,' implying that if Caesar stood he would be elected.

5. **Est omnino id .. possit**, 'that certainly ('in alle Wege' Metzg.) is a settlement to which no objection can be made if he will concede so much.'

6. **Si non obtineat .. mirer.** This is Kayser's suggestion. The MS. reading 'obtinet .. miror' surely would imply either confusion of thought or forgetfulness in the writer, and can hardly be construed. 'Si non obtinet' would naturally be followed by 'facturum puto;' 'non facere miror' would naturally be preceded by 'cum non obtinuerit.'

8. **Sic**, sc. 'consulem.'

9. **Istud ipsum**, 'that very thing,' his being consul.

10. **Aliquis**, Pompey, probably, whom Cicero had met at Formiae on Dec. 25. Cp. Ad Att. 7. 8, 4.

Cedendum est, 'we must give way to Caesar,' Atticus is supposed to say. Wesenb. has 'ullum: cedendum,' and gives the words down to 'priore' to Cicero.

11. **Vide consulem .. priore**, 'see him such a consul again as you saw him in his first consulship.'

Quem = 'qualem.' On the proceedings of Caesar in his first consulship, 59 B.C., cp. Intr. to Part I, § 17.

12. **Imbecillus**, 'in his day of weakness.'

13. **Quid nunc putas**, sc. 'eum valiturum.'

Et eo consule .. Hispania, 'during his consulship, too, Pompey is resolved to be in Spain.' For 'certum est' with the dat., cp. De Orat. 2. 33, 144 'cum diceret sibi certum esse discedere.' Cicero here, as in Ep. 31, 3, writes as though he thought it would be mischievous for Pompey to go to Spain. But after Caesar's triumph he wrote that he had been in favour of Pompey's

esse in Hispania. O rem miseram! si quidem id ipsum deterrimum est, quod recusari non potest, et quod ille si faciat, iamiam

4 a bonis omnibus summam ineat gratiam. Tollamus igitur hoc, quo illum posse adduci negant: de reliquis quid est deterrimum? concedere illi, quod, ut idem dicit, impudentissime postulat. Nam quid impudentius? Tenuisti provinciam per decem annos, non tibi a senatu, sed a te ipso per vim et per factionem datos; praeteriit tempus non legis, sed libidinis tuae, fac tamen, legis; ut succedatur, decernitur: impedis et ais 'habe meam rationem.' Habe nostrum. Exercitum tu habeas diutius, quam populus iussit, invito senatu? 'Depugnes oportet, nisi concedis.' Cum bona quidem spe, ut ait idem, vel vincendi vel in libertate moriendi. Iam si pugnandum est, quo tempore, in casu, quo consilio, in temporibus situm est; itaque te in ea quaestione non exerceo. Ad ea, quae dixi, adfer, si quid habes; equidem dies noctesque torqueor.

going to Spain as a means of averting civil war. Cp. Ep. 91. 5. Perhaps, however, he may there refer to advice given after the war had begun. He met Pompey on January 17, 49 B.C. Cp. Ep. 63, 2, and Intr. to Part III, § 3.

1. Id ipsum . . gratiam, 'that concession which cannot be refused to him, and his acceptance of which would win the greatest gratitude from all well-disposed citizens.' For the tense of ineat, cp. Ep. 35. 2.

3. Tollamus . . hoc, 'let us dismiss this settlement from consideration.'

5. Quod . . postulat, i.e. to retain his army till after he had been elected consul, or perhaps till his consulship began.

Idem, Pompeius. 'Idem' is used with reference perhaps to 'aliquis' p. 284, l. 10, perhaps to 'Pompeio certum est esse in Hispania,' p. 284, l. 13, as Manutius thinks.

6. Tenuisti . . habe nostrum. Cicero here addresses Caesar on the extravagance of his demands. On the facts referred to, cp. Ep. 44. 6, note; Intr. to Part I, § 17; Part II, § 8; Appendix 6, § 2. The past tenses do not necessarily shew that Caesar's government had expired when Cicero wrote, as Cicero may write as he would have spoken when the question should be discussed.

8. Tempus non legis, foll., cp. 'legis dies,' p. 280.

9. Decernitur, 'the senate votes for the appointment of a successor.' For this hypothetical use of the indicative cp. Pro Muren. 30, 62 'Petent aliquid publicani? cave quidquam habeat momenti gratia.'

10. Habe nostrum sc. 'rationem,' 'do you shew some regard for us.' The words are not used technically as in the preceding clause. Wesenb. reads 'Habe tu nostram.'

Habeas. The mood expresses disapprobation. Cp. Madv. 353.

11. Invito senatu. The senate by declining to send a successor might prolong the government of a proconsul or propraetor beyond the time fixed by law.

Depugnes oportet. Caesar is supposed to say to Pompey.

12. Idem, Pompeius.

13. Quo consilio . . situm est. This remark was verified by the event. The senate by sending Caesar a defiance at Pompey's suggestion before the Italian levies had assembled, made it impossible to defend Rome. Cp. Intr. to Part III, § 1.

15. Adfer, si quid habes, 'let me hear any advice you have to give.' Cp. Madv. 493 a.

NOTE F. *On the Commission granted to Pompey in September 57 B.C.*

Cp. supra, pp. 135; 162; 163; 166; 173.

The following words in Ep. 21, 3 'Crassus tres legatos decernit nec excludit Pompeium; censet enim etiam ex iis qui cum imperio sint,' seem to imply that Pompey was possessed of 'Imperium' in the beginning of the year 56 B.C. Now I am not aware of any public commission which he received in the interval between his return from the East in 61 B.C. and his second consulship in 55 B.C., except the two following: (1) That of superintending, as one of a Commission of Twenty, the allotment of the Campanian domains (cp. pp. 17; 83): and (2) the supervision of the supply of corn with which he was entrusted in Sept. 57 B.C. It is doubtful if the 'Imperium' was conferred upon him in connection with the first of these commissions. With regard to the second, Dion Cassius (39, 9) speaks of his receiving proconsular power; Appian (Bell. Civ. 2. 18) misdates the commission, but speaks of Pompey as αὐτοκράτορα τῆς ἀγορᾶς: and Plutarch (Pomp. 49) uses language suggesting that he was invested with 'Imperium.'

On the other hand, it is clear that Pompey entered the 'urbs' on various occasions during the spring of 56 B.C. (cp. Epp. 23, 2; 5; 24, 1; 29, 7); and unless special privileges had been granted him he must have forfeited his 'Imperium' thereby. Cp. Note E, p. 123. It is not surprising, therefore, that Becker (Handbuch der Röm. Alt. 2. 2, 66–69) should infer that Pompey had been invested with 'Potestas' only, and not with 'Imperium.' But Becker does not notice the words quoted above from Ep. 21, 3. Mr. Yonge, on Ad Fam. 1. 9, 7, hints that a special permission allowed Pompey to enter the city without forfeiting his 'Imperium;' this is possible, but I do not see any evidence of it beyond the passages which cause the difficulty: Lange, Röm. Alt. 3. 308, thinks that Pompey received the ordinary proconsular 'Imperium' for five years. On the whole, our materials perhaps do not justify a decided opinion on either side.

APPENDIX VI.

ON THE LEGAL QUESTION AT ISSUE BETWEEN CAESAR AND THE SENATE.

THIS turned partly upon distinct statutes, partly upon general constitutional principles.

§ 1. The 'Lex Vatinia' of 59 B.C. gave Caesar the government of Cisalpine Gaul with Illyricum, and an army of three legions, for a term of five years, to expire on March 1[1], 54 B.C. Then, perhaps on the death[2] of Q. Metellus Celer, proconsul of Gallia Narbonensis, the senate added that province, with another legion, to Caesar's government. This grant was renewed annually; and an attempt to get one of his two provinces assigned by anticipation to another governor in March 54 failed[3]. In 55 a tribune, C. Trebonius, got a law enacted securing the government of Syria to Crassus for five years, and that of the two Spains to Pompey for a like period. Perhaps they had already obtained these provinces for one year by regular allotment[4]. Then the two consuls, Pompey and Crassus, proposed a law extending Caesar's government of the two Gauls for five years[5].

§ 2. From what day did this second term of five years date? Three have been suggested.

1. Jan. 1, 54 B.C.
2. March 1, 54 B.C.
3. The day of the enactment of the consular law in 55 B.C., supposed to have been Nov. 13.

For 1, little can be said, except that it was the day on which magistrates began their year of office.

For 2, that it is the most in accordance with passages in Cicero[6], Velleius[7], Appian[8], and Plutarch[9], which speak of a real addition of five years to Caesar's government.

For 3, that

(*a*) Dion Cassius[10], writing of 51 B.C., says that Caesar's government

[1] De Prov. Cons. 15. [2] A. W. Zumpt, Studia Romana, 75. [3] Intr. to Part II, § 6. [4] A. W. Zumpt, S. R. pp. 79–80: who, however, thinks that Pompey only obtained Farther Spain by regular allotment. [5] Caes. Bell. Gall. 8. 53; Dion Cassius 39. 33–36; App. Bell. Civ. 2. 18. [6] Ad Att. 7. 7. 6; Philipp. 2. 10, 24. [7] 2. 46. [8] Bell. Civ. 2. 18. [9] Pomp. 52. [10] 40. 59.

would expire next year; and in another place[1], that the law of 55 added *in reality* three years to his term. The latter statement would in any case be incorrect; but of course less so if the term granted by the law expired in 50, than if it expired in 49, B.C.

(*b*) M. Caelius uses language[2] of which the most natural construction is that Pompey was prepared to demand Caesar's recall on Nov. 13, 50 B.C.

(*c*) Cicero, writing in the end of 50 B.C., speaks[3] of Caesar as having already held his province for the time allowed by law.

§ 3. In any case the term granted to Caesar by the 'Lex Pompeia Licinia' would expire before the usual time arrived for holding the consular comitia in 49 B.C., the earliest at which he could legally[4] sue for a second consulship. It is true that, according to the usage which had prevailed for some years before 52 B.C., a successor to him would only be sent out at the end of 49[5]; but if he were required to sue for the consulship in person in the summer of that year, he would have to relinquish the advantage which constitutional usage thus gave him; and if he left the protection of his army before he was elected consul, he would run great risk of prosecution on various charges. Foreseeing this, he requested the tribunes in 52 to propose a law, permitting him to sue for the consulship without a personal canvass. Pompey supported this proposal, and it was carried[6]. Cicero, both directly[7] and indirectly[8], furnishes evidence in support of A. W. Zumpt's[9] conjecture, that the tribunes' law provided that Caesar might retain his command till after the consular comitia in 49 had been held; Caesar's own language[10] has the same tendency; Appian[11] takes a different view. The enactment of the 'Lex Pompeia de iure magistratuum'[12] altered Caesar's position for the worse in two ways. (1) It revoked by a general provision the permission granted him to sue for the consulship while absent from Rome. (2) By providing that an interval of five years should elapse between a magistrate's year of office at Rome and his government of a province, it relieved the senate from the difficulty which that

[1] 39. 33: cp. A. W. Zumpt, S. R. 65–89; 156–196. [2] Ad Fam. 8. 11, 3: but cp. 8. 8, 4 and 9. [3] Ad Att. 7. 9, 4. But cp. sup. p. 285, note on l. 6. [4] The Lex Genucia of 343 B.C. had provided that no man should be elected a second time to any office, unless after an interval of ten years since his last election, and Sulla had revived this law from desuetude. App. Bell. Civ. 1. 100; Livy 7. 42. [5] Mommsen, Rechtsfrage, 33 f. 42; 43; Lange, Rom. Alt. 3. 367; 368. Cp. Cic. De Prov. Cons. 15. [6] Cic. Philipp. 2. 10, 24; App. Bell. Civ. 2. 25; Dion Cassius 40. 51. [7] Ad Att. 7. 7. 6. [8] Ib. 8. 3, 3; cp. 9. 11 A, 2; Philipp. l. c. [9] S. R. 172–174. [10] Bell. Civ. 1. 9. [11] Ib. 2. 25. [12] Intr. to Part II, § 14. Lange thinks that these two provisions were contained in distinct laws, the second in a 'Lex Pompeia de provinciis.' Rom. Alt. 3. 367; and his view receives some support from the language of Dion Cassius (40. 56).

body might have felt in sending Caesar a successor on March 1, 49 B.C., a difficulty which would have arisen from the previous usage that the government of provinces should be assumed by proconsuls or propraetors immediately after the conclusion of their year of office at Rome, and therefore on the first of January[1]. Under the new system a governor might enter on his government at any time. Cicero's government of Cilicia began on July 31[2].

The clause inserted by Pompey, on his own authority, in the law after its enactment, to release Caesar from its restrictions, could hardly be considered valid[3].

§ 4. Thus Caesar had no legal claim to retain his provinces for longer than the time granted him by the 'Lex Pompeia Licinia' of 55 B.C. He had, however, an equitable claim as against Pompey, whose negligence or treachery had withdrawn a privilege granted with his own sanction; and he had various constitutional modes of securing attention to his demands.

It does not appear that the 'Lex Pompeia de iure magistratuum' was retrospective; hence, as it passed in 52 B.C., no 'consulares' or 'praetorii' would be qualified under it till 46. Perhaps the senate was to provide[4] for the government of the provinces during the interval. Now

(*a*) The 'Lex Sempronia de provinciis' of C. Gracchus provided that the provinces of the future consuls should be fixed before their election; and though recent legislation, and the frequent assignation of provinces by special votes may have diminished its authority, it seems to have been thought desirable to deliberate on the appointment of a successor to any province some time before a vacancy occurred. But Pompey thought[5] himself pledged to Caesar not to allow any motion to be put to the senate with reference to the Gallic provinces before March 1, 50 B.C., which would much shorten the time available for discussion.

(*b*) It would be difficult, perhaps, to find men of consular rank to succeed Caesar in both his provinces, and if this were not done, any tribune might interpose[6] to prevent the nomination of a 'praetorius' to succeed him in either.

(*c*) A majority of the senate was indisposed for decided measures[7].

§ 5. Under these circumstances, the preliminary discussion about Caesar's recall opened on[8] Sept. 29, 51 B.C. The senate passed a

[1] above, § 3 and note 5. [2] Ep. 32, 2. [3] Intr. to Part II, § 14; Suet. Iul. 28; Mommsen, Rechtsfrage, 48. Mr. Long, however, Decline of Roman Republic, 4. 366, 367, does not notice the apparent invalidity of this amendment. [4] Ad Fam. 8, 8, 8. [5] Ad Fam. 8. 8, 9. [6] De Prov. Cons. 7. 17. The tribunes' veto could not legally be interposed in discussions on provinces to be held by consuls. [7] Ad Att. 7. 7, 5. [8] Ad Fam. 8. 8, 5.

decree 'that the assignment of the consular[1] provinces should occupy the undivided attention of the senate from March 1, 50 B.C. till some decree had been passed providing for their government.' Other motions, proposing

(1) That strong measures should be taken against any tribunes who might interfere with the senate's proceedings. (2) That Caesar's soldiers should be invited to apply for discharges. (3) That nine provinces, excluding the two Gauls, should be entrusted to the government of 'praetorii'—were vetoed[2] by tribunes.

In 50 B.C. a struggle, of which the particulars have been already[3] noticed, took place between Pompey's friends and Curio. It must be remembered, that Pompey held his provinces[4] by virtue of a law passed in 52, and might fairly decline to surrender them in obedience to a mere expression of opinion on the part of the senate.

On the first day of 49 B.C., Curio[5] appeared in Rome with very moderate proposals from Caesar; his friends among the tribunes compelled the consuls to read the proposals in the senate, but the consuls declined to put them to the vote.

The senate was intimidated by the two consuls, and by Scipio acting as Pompey's spokesman: and many of Pompey's soldiers filled the capital[6].

Caesar was required to hand over his provinces to two successors by a certain day. Two tribunes, M. Antonius and Q. Cassius, vetoed this demand, and their veto was probably regular, as one of the two successors selected was only of praetorian rank[7]. The veto was answered, however, by a vote[8] investing the consuls and other magistrates with extraordinary powers; on which Antony and Cassius fled from Rome. Much irregularity[9] seems to have marked the provisions subsequently made by the senate for the government of the provinces.

[1] Ad Fam. 8. 8, 5. Consular provinces in this passage must mean those which, under the 'Lex Pompeia de iure magistratuum,' would be governed by consulares. For its usual meaning—those to be assigned to the next consuls—is excluded by the enactment of that law which interposed an interval of five years between the consulship and the government of a consular province. Intr. to Part II, § 14. [2] Ad Fam. 8. 8, 6–8. [3] Intr. to Part II, § 27. [4] Ib. § 24. [5] Caes. Bell. Civ. 1. 1 and 2; App. Bell. Civ. 2. 32. [6] Ib. 2 and 3. [7] Ad Fam. 16. 12, 3, note. [8] Caes. Bell. Civ. 1. 5; Cic. Philipp. 2. 21, 52–53. [9] Caes. Bell. Civ. 1. 6. Mr. Long, Decline of the Roman Republic 4. 178; 442, says or implies that the two terms of provincial government granted to Caesar by the 'Lex Vatinia' and 'Lex Pompeia Licinia' respectively expired at the end of 54 and at the end of 49 B.C. But this opinion seems to me inconsistent with the language of Cicero Ad Att. 7. 9. 4. M. Paul Guiraud, in a learned and ingenious essay noticed in the preface to this edition, holds that the first term dated from Caesar's arrival in his province towards the end of March, 58 B.C., but that the second was only to last three years, as stated by Dion Cassius, 39. 33. See pp. 46 and 99 foll., of M. Guiraud's Essay. But I find it hard to reconcile this view with the following passages: Ad Att. 7. 7, 6; 9. 11 A, 2; Caesar, Bell. Civ. 1. 9.

APPENDIX VII.

Distribution of the Roman forces at the beginning of the civil war between Caesar and Pompey in 49 B.C.

Caesar had nine veteran legions—eight in Transalpine Gaul, one in Cisalpine[1]. He had also some German and Gaulish cavalry[2] and auxiliary infantry. Pompey had in Italy two veteran[3] legions of doubtful fidelity, and was authorized to levy as many fresh troops as he chose. It was hoped[4] that 130,000 men could be raised, but not more than half that number seem actually to have been brought together. For Pompey sailed from Brundisium with 20 cohorts[5], and had sent on the consuls with 30[6]; this would give a total of 25,000 men; Cicero speaks[7] of 30,000 as a number reported for Pompey's whole force. Now Caesar[8] says that Pompey had lost in Spain and Italy 130 cohorts of Roman citizens; and deducting 70 cohorts for 7 legions[9] in Spain, this statement would make his losses in Italy amount to 60 cohorts, or 30,000 men. And 30,000 + 25,000 or 30,000 carried to Epirus, would give a total of at most 60,000 mustered in Italy.

In Spain, besides the seven legions just mentioned, a large auxiliary force[10] had been raised for Pompey by his officers, Afranius and Petreius.

The other provinces were under Pompey's control, but the forces stationed there were not very important. Sicily furnished[11] some troops to Pompey in Epirus, but neither that island nor Sardinia offered much resistance to Caesar's officers[12]. In Africa, P. Atius Varus levied two legions for Pompey, and excluded the lawful governor Q. Aelius Tubero[13]. Varus could count on effective support from Juba of Numidia[14].

In the East, all the dependent princes were inclined to support Pompey, who had conquered Mithridates and re-organized the Roman empire in Asia[15]. The Roman forces in that quarter were small and scattered. After the defeat of Crassus the army of Syria can hardly have counted more than 10,000 regular[16] infantry, and it does not seem to have been reinforced before the civil war began. In Cilicia, Cicero as

[1] Caes. Bell. Gall. 8. 54. [2] Caes. Bell. Civ. 1. 18; 39. [3] Ad Att. 7. 20, 1; 8. 12 A, 2. [4] App. Bell. Civ. 2. 34. [5] Caes. Bell. Civ. 1. 25. [6] Plut. Pomp. 62. [7] Ad Att. 9. 6, 3. [8] Bell. Civ. 3. 10. [9] Ib. 1. 38. [10] Caes. Bell. Civ. 1. 39. [11] Ib. 3. 4. [12] Ib. 1. 30. [13] Ib. 1. 31. [14] Ib. 2. 25. [15] Mommsen 4. 2, 368 and 401. [16] Plut. Crass. 31; Mommsen 4. 2, 337.

proconsul in 51 B.C., complained[1] that he had only 'nomen duarum legionum exilium,' and probably no fresh troops had been sent there since his departure. Nor does it appear that any large bodies of regular troops were stationed in Macedonia, Achaia, or the province of Asia, when hostilities began[2].

Pompey may have had an understanding with the Parthians[3], enabling him to strip the eastern provinces of their garrisons, and the subject princes furnished him with considerable forces, especially of cavalry[4].

[1] Ad Att. 5. 15, 1. [2] Caes. Bell. Civ. 3. 4 and 78. [3] Ib. 3. 31 and 82; Dion Cassius 41. 55; Mommsen 4. 2, 370. [4] Caes. Bell. Civ. 3. 4; Ad Fam. 9. 9, 2.

PART III.

From the beginning of the civil war between Caesar and Pompey to Cicero's return to Italy after the battle of Pharsalus. Jan. 1, 49 B.C. to Oct., 48 B.C.

INTRODUCTION.

§ 1. The events of the first few days of 49 B.C., have been already[1] noticed. Cicero took no part in the senate's discussions, but perhaps[2] privately recommended conciliation to Pompey. He arrived before Rome on Jan. 4[3], and remained some days without the walls, perhaps[4] still cherishing hopes of a triumph.

Caesar, when he heard how the senate had received his offers, assembled[5] his soldiers at Ravenna, and addressed them. They answered with enthusiasm; and, after sending messages to his other legions to follow with all speed from Transalpine Gaul, he marched to Ariminum, where he found the two[6] tribunes who had interposed in his favour and Curio, also the praetor L. Roscius[7] and L. Caesar, son of one of his legates, who were charged with friendly messages from Pompey. Caesar asked them to carry proposals from him to Pompey. He offered to disarm if his rival would dismiss his Italian levies and retire to Spain, but was told

[1] Appendix 6, § 5. [2] Ad Att. 7. 3. 5; Plut. Caes. 31. [3] Ad Fam. 16. 11, 2. [4] Ib. l. c.; Ad Att. 7. 10. [5] The thirteenth legion. Cp. Caes. Bell. Civ. 1. 7; App. Bell. Civ. 2. 32 and 33. It numbered 5000 foot and 300 horse. [6] Cp. Appendix 6, § 5. This was about Jan. 10 or 11. For the decree giving the consuls power to protect the safety of the state passed Jan. 6. Caesar could hardly have heard of it under three days, and it was the ground of his beginning hostilities. On the other hand, Pompey knew of the invasion on or about Jan. 19: cp. Caes. Bell. Civ. 1. 5 and 14; Ad Att. 7. 13, 7; 9. 10, 4. [7] Caes. Bell. Civ. 1. 8.

that he must first himself recross the Rubicon [1]. He had just suffered a severe blow in the defection of Labienus [2], but the example was not followed, and the rapidity of his successes must have surprised men who had been told [3] that his troops only wanted a pretext for desertion. His forces occupied successively Ancona, Arretium, Iguvium, and Auximum: it was near the place last mentioned that the first bloodshed [4] took place. The news of these events caused the consuls and other magistrates to retire [5] from Rome without even securing the public treasury. Pompey [6] had already started to take the command of his two legions, which had been moved from Capua to Luceria, but he spent a day or two at Teanum [7].

§ 2. Caesar was presently joined by the 12th legion, and marched on amid the general sympathy of the population till he reached Corfinium, where his destined successor in Transalpine Gaul, L. Domitius Ahenobarbus, awaited his approach at the head of a considerable force [8]. Antony occupied Sulmo [9], and its garrison of 3500 men was incorporated with Caesar's army, which was further increased by the arrival of the 8th legion, of 11,000 Gaulish levies, and of 300 horse. Domitius, finding that Pompey did not mean to come to his relief, prepared to escape; but his men mutinied, and delivered him and the town to Caesar on Feb. 21, after a siege of seven days [10]. Caesar dismissed the officers unhurt, but retained the men in his own service [11]. They subsequently formed the army with which Curio occupied Sicily [12] and invaded Africa.

Pompey, with the two legions which he had found in Apulia, and the levies of southern Italy, marched to Brundisium, whither Caesar followed [13] on March 9. Caesar's forces were increased by desertions from the enemy, but he renewed his attempts [14] to negotiate, which proved fruitless. His army now amounted to six legions, three of which consisted of veterans. The consuls had already sailed for Dyrrhachium on March 4, with a large [15] force, and Pompey followed them on the 17th with the remainder of his army, which he embarked very skilfully [16].

§ 3. When Cicero saw how Pompey and his friends were taken by surprise, he retired to Campania, and received [17] charge of the sea coast

[1] This answer was agreed on at a council held at Teanum Sidicinum late in January: cp. Caes. Bell. Civ. 1. 8–11; Ad Fam. 16. 12, 3; Ad Att. 7. 13. 7: 7. 14, 1. [2] Ad Att. 7. 11, 1. [3] Caes. Bell. Civ. 1. 6. [4] Ib. 1. 11–13. [5] Ib. 1. 14. [6] Ib. l. c. [7] Ad Att. 7. 13. 7: 7. 14, 1. [8] Caes. Bell. Civ. 1. 15–17. [9] Ib. 1. 18. [10] Ad Att. 8. 14, 1. [11] Caes. Bell. Civ. 1. 19–23. [12] Ib. 1. 25. [13] Ad Att. 9. 13 A, 1. [14] Caes. Bell. Civ. 1. 24–26. [15] Ad Att. 9. 6, 3. [16] Ib. 9. 13 A, 1; 9. 6, 3; 9. 15, 6, or A; Caes. Bell. Civ. 1. 25–27. The two detachments together numbered about 25,000 or 30,000 men in all. [17] Ad Att. 8. 3, 4; Ad Fam. 16. 12, 5.

and of the levies of troops made there. Capua was his head quarters apparently. His fasces were still wreathed with laurel for his successes in Cilicia, and the notoriety[1] this gave his movements increased the anxiety which all his letters of this time express[2], and which was aggravated by his doubts, how he could secure the safety of his wife and daughter without, by sending them to[3] Rome, declaring his distrust of Pompey's prospects. While moving about he had interviews[4] with Pompey, and with the consuls: the dates of his movements seem to have been as follows:—

He left Rome between January 12[5] and 21; was at Minturnae[6] on the 23rd, and went to Capua[7] on the 25th, where he probably received, through Trebatius[8], an invitation from Caesar to return to Rome. He stayed at Capua till the 28th, when he left for Formiae[9], and was rejoined by his wife[10] and daughter on February 2; revisited Capua on the 5th at the invitation of the consuls, and stayed there[11] two days, returning to Formiae on the 7th, where he received a letter[12] from Pompey inviting him to go to Luceria. He left Formiae as though to comply with this request, but presently returned[13], and remained in Formiae till early in March[14] apparently. He probably received there a letter[15] from Caelius, in praise of Caesar's clemency.

§ 4. His letters follow one another very quickly during these months. He expresses anxiety[16] as to the fate of his wife and daughter, finally deciding[17] to keep them with him for the present. He disapproves of the terms offered by Caesar, yet thinks it most expedient[18] to grant them; desponds at the sight of the general confusion at Capua and Formiae, the weakness and irresolution of Pompey and the failure[19] of his levies; renews his old complaints of the past blindness of Pompey in allowing Caesar's rise[20], and of the impracticability of Cato[21]; testifies to the indifference or despondency of large classes[22] and districts, and to Caesar's popularity in the country towns and villages[23]. He admires the speed and vigour of Caesar[24], fears the cruelties[25] which might follow the triumph of Pompey, and reminds[26] the latter significantly how he had suffered before

[1] Ad Att. 7. 11, 5, alib. [2] esp. Ad Att. 7. 10; 8. 1, 3. [3] Ib. 7. 23, 2; 8. 2, 3. Cp. Ad Fam. 14. 18, 1, where he leaves it to Terentia to decide what she will do. [4] Cp. Ep. 63, 2, note, for an account of one of them. [5] Ad Att. 7. 12, 1; Ad Fam. 16. 11, 3. [6] Ad Att. 7. 13, 6. [7] Ib. 7. 15, 1. [8] Ib. 7. 17, 3. [9] Ib. 7. 16, 2. [10] Ib. 7. 18, 1. [11] Ib. 7. 21, 1. [12] Perhaps Ib. 8. 11 A.; cp. Ib. 8. 1, 1. [13] Ib. 8. 3, 7. [14] Ib. 8. 15, 1; 8. 16, 2. [15] Ad Fam. 8. 15. [16] Ib. 14. 14 and 18: cp. Ad Att. 7. 13, 3. [17] Ib. 7. 23, 2; 8. 2, 3. [18] Ib. 7. 17, 2: cp. Ad Fam. 6. 6, 5; 16. 12, 4. [19] Ad Att. 7. 12, 2; 7. 13, 1; 7. 20, 1; 7. 21, 1 and 2. [20] Cp. Ad Att. 7. 3, 4 and 7. 7, 6, with 8. 1, 4 and 8. 3, 3. [21] Ib. 7. 13, 2. [22] Ib. 7. 7, 5; 7. 21, 1. [23] Ib. 8. 13, 2; 8. 16, 1 and 2. [24] Ib. 8. 9, 4. [25] Ib. 8. 11, 2-4. [26] Ib. 8. 11 D, 7.

for his patriotism, owing to Pompey's desertion. He therefore felt reluctant to leave[1] Italy, or even to follow Pompey to Luceria, and seems to have done nothing[2] in support of his party at Capua, an attitude which he represented rather differently to Pompey[3] and to Caesar[4]. He criticised, probably without much judgment, the military conduct[5] of Pompey, especially his desertion of the capital and failure[6] to relieve Domitius, and was easily deterred by rumours of danger from attempting to comply[7] with invitations to Luceria and to Brundisium.

§ 5. On the other hand, Cicero was disgusted[8] with many of Caesar's followers, and regarded his conduct as sheer rebellion[9]. Hence he felt little inclination to appear in the senate at Rome[10], and at times was more confident than usual of the success of Pompey, especially after some demonstrations in his favour at Capua[11], and the arrival of Labienus[12] at Teanum, who appears to have confirmed a general impression of the disaffection[13] of Caesar's army to its general. On January 27, Cicero, in a letter to Tiro[14], enlarged on the preponderance of the loyal forces. He was also encouraged[15] at times by exaggerated statements of the numbers and efficiency of the army of Domitius at Corfinium, and of successes obtained in the Pyrenees by Afranius over Caesar's lieutenants. Dread of the opinion of the optimates, and an old feeling of dependence, seem, however, to have mainly weighed[16] with him in favour of going to the camp of Pompey; and he thought he was hardly treated with sufficient respect[17] by Caesar's dependents, especially by the two Balbi.

Accordingly he ordered ships to be prepared both at Brundisium and at Caieta, but still delayed[18] to embark.

§ 6. Amid all this excitement Cicero did not forget his freedman Tiro, whom he had left ill at Patrae, and often urged[19] him to be careful of his health. With another dependent[20], Dionysius, he was on less friendly terms: complained[21] of his ingratitude and insolence, and was gratified by his departure, while acknowledging his merits as a teacher[22].

§ 7. Cicero probably spent April and May on the coast of Campania or in the neighbourhood of Arpinum. Caesar visited him[23] near Formiae,

[1] Ad Att. 7. 20, 2; 7. 23, 2; 8. 1, 3; 8. 2, 4; 8. 3, 3 5; 8. 14, 2; 8. 15, 2. [2] Ib. 7. 21, 2; 7. 23, 3; 8. 3, 5. [3] Ib. 8. 11 D. [4] Ib. 9. 11 A, 2. [5] Ib. 7. 13, 1; 8. 3, 3. [6] Ib. 8. 3, 7; 8. 8, 2; 8. 9, 3. [7] Ib. 8. 11 A. D. 1 cp. 8. 1, 1; 8. 6, 2. [8] Ib. 7. 3, 5; 9. 18, 2. [9] Ib. 7. 11, 1. [10] Ib. 7. 17, 3 and 4. [11] Ib. 7. 11, 4. [12] Ib. 7. 13, 7. [13] Ib. 7. 16, 2. [14] Ad Fam. 16. 12, 4; cp. Appendix 7. [15] Ad Att. 7. 26, 1; 8. 3, 7. [16] Ib. 7. 12, 3; 7. 20, 2; 8. 1, 3 and 4; 8. 3, 2; 8. 12, 6; 8. 16, 1 and 2. [17] Ib. 8. 9, 4. [18] Ib. 8. 3, 6; 8. 4, 3. [19] Ad Fam. 16. 11, 1; 16. 12, 6. [20] Not a slave, for Dionysius had slaves of his own; cp. Ad Att. 8. 10. [21] Ib. 7. 7, 1; 8. 4, 1 and 2; 8. 10. [22] Ib. 8. 10. [23] Ib. 9. 18.

and entreated him to attend in the senate at Rome. Cicero, however, did not consent. This interview must have taken place towards the close of March [1]. Cicero wavered long as to the course of conduct he should pursue. He seems never [2] to have really forgiven himself for not making greater exertions to join Pompey, and to have been persuaded that the only chance, though a slender one, for the constitution lay in his triumph [3]. He was also much disappointed [4] by the unremitting energy of Caesar's operations, which allowed no time for negotiations. And, as has been before remarked [5], the notion of living on friendly terms with Gabinius and others of his old enemies, seemed intolerable. His disgust [6] at the violence of some of Pompey's adherents was as great as ever, and he disapproved the project of starving Rome into submission; but the licentious [7] and arrogant conduct of Caesar's officers was a more present annoyance. He was anxious [8], too, not to seem merely to depend on the result of the Spanish campaign, and the representations of Caesar [9], Antony [10], Caelius [11], and Tullia [12], did not persuade him to be neutral. At times he even seems to have thought of raising an insurrection against Caesar in Italy, but declined the overtures made him by three cohorts at Pompeii, as he suspected a snare [13]. To the last [14] he seems to have hesitated between joining Pompey and retiring to some neutral place. He finally embarked at Caieta [15] on June 7, and sailed for Greece. On his arrival in Pompey's camp, the state of affairs he found, and Cato's reproach [16] for his folly in going there, must have disconcerted him still more. He was shocked by the ferocity [17] of the language he heard, and distrusted both the efficiency of the army and the skill of its leaders. Accordingly [18] he took no prominent part in operations; or, as Plutarch [19] expresses it, Pompey would not entrust him with any important commission, being annoyed at his querulousness. Cicero revenged himself by sarcasms [20] on Pompey's tactics and officers.

§ 8. Caesar, after the interview with Cicero mentioned above, went to Rome and attempted to procure the senate's sanction to negotiations with Pompey. The senate approved the plan, but no one offered to act as envoy [21]; according to Caesar [22], the threats which Pompey

[1] Ad Att. 9. 15, 6 or A, where an account is given of Caesar's proposed resting-places. [2] Ib. 9. 6, 4; 9. 10, 2 and 3. [3] Ib. 10. 4, 3. [4] Ib. 9. 14, 1 and 2; 9. 18, 1. [5] supra, § 5; Ad Att. 9. 7, 5: 10. 8, 3. [6] Ib. 9. 7, 4; 9. 9, 2. [7] Ib. 10. 10, 5: 10. 13, 1. [8] Ib. 10. 8, 2; Ad Fam. 2. 16, 6. [9] Ad Att. 10. 8 B. [10] Ib. 10. 8 A. [11] Ad Fam. 8. 16. [12] Ad Att. 10. 8, 1. [13] Ib. 10. 16, 4. [14] Ib. 10. 18, 2; Ad Fam. 2. 16, 2. [15] Ad Fam. 14. 7, 3; cp. Ad Att. 8. 3, 6. [16] Plut. Cic. 38. [17] Ad Fam. 7. 3, 2. [18] Ad Att. 11. 4, 1. [19] Plut. Cic. 38. [20] Ib. l. c. [21] Caes. Bell. Civ. 1. 32 and 33. [22] Bell. Civ. 1. 33.

had uttered on his departure from Rome caused this reluctance. Caesar also, in spite of the opposition of L. Metellus, a tribune, forced the doors of the 'more sacred treasury[1],' of which the contents were reserved for the emergency of a Gaulish invasion. He then started for Spain, according to Caelius[2] much incensed against the senate. The hostile attitude of Massilia[3], into which L. Domitius Ahenobarbus threw himself, detained him for thirty days, while he made preparations for a siege and began the construction of a fleet. He committed further operations to D. Brutus and C. Trebonius. Meanwhile his legate, C. Fabius, had forced[4] the Pyrenees at the head of three legions. Caesar presently joined him, and began operations at once against L. Afranius and M. Petreius, who commanded a large[5] force near Ilerda. This may have been early in June[6], according to the calendar. The campaign which followed was marked by great alternations of success, but terminated after forty[7] days with the capitulation[8] of the Pompeian forces. Caesar then marched against M. Varro in Baetica, where the people were so well disposed towards the invader, that Varro could make no effective resistance, and all Spain submitted to Caesar. He placed it under Q. Cassius, one of the tribunes of this year, with an army of four[9] legions, and set out for Rome.

On his way he received the submission of Massilia, which had been besieged[10] with great energy by D. Brutus and Trebonius. He there heard[11] that he had been named dictator by M. Lepidus, one of the praetors, and continued his journey to Rome. On his way he had to suppress a serious mutiny[12] at Placentia. After his arrival at Rome he presided at consular comitia[13], and was himself elected with P. Servilius Isauricus; introduced an equitable measure for the settlement of debts; altered[14] in various cases his appointments of provincial governors; restored some of the exiles who had been condemned under the Leges Pompeiae in 52 B.C. (except Milo); and at the close of the year set off for Brundisium.

§ 9. In other quarters the events of the year had been unfavourable to

[1] Caes. Bell. Civ. 1. 33; Ad Att. 10. 8. 6; App. Bell. Civ. 2. 41. [2] Ad Fam. 8. 16. 1. [3] Caes. Bell. Civ. 1. 34-36. [4] Ib. 1. 37. [5] See Appendix 7; also Caes. Bell. Civ. 1. 38, 39. [6] Caesar (Bell. Civ. 1. 48) says that the winter supply of corn was exhausted, and the harvest not ripe. Cp. note 8. [7] Caes. Bell. Civ. 2. 32. [8] Ib. 1. 41-87. The capitulation was nominally on August 2, but the calendar was nearly two months in advance of the seasons. Appendix 8; Fischer, Römische Zeittafeln, sub anno. [9] Caes. Bell. Civ. 2. 17-21. But Hither Spain seems shortly afterwards to have been entrusted to M. Lepidus, now praetor. Bell. Alex. 59; App. Bell. Civ. 2. 48; Dion Cassius 43. 1. [10] Caes. Bell. Civ. 1. 56-58; 2. 1-16. [11] Ib. 2. 21. [12] App. Bell. Civ. 2. 47; Dion Cassius 41. 26-35. [13] Caes. Bell. Civ. 3. 1; App. Bell. Civ. 2. 48; Dion Cassius 41. 36-38. [14] App. l. c.

Caesar. Curio, after occupying Sicily[1], crossed over into Africa, and obtained at first great successes, but was afterwards defeated and his army destroyed[2] by Juba, king of Numidia, co-operating with Pompeian officers. About the same time Dolabella and C. Antonius, a younger brother of Marcus, were defeated in Illyricum by M. Octavius and L. Scribonius Libo. Antonius was made prisoner[3].

Pompey, in the meantime[4], was collecting and organizing a large force in Epirus and Macedonia. A considerable fleet gave him the command of the Adriatic. He wintered at Thessalonica[5].

48 B.C.

§ 10. Cicero spent the first months of this year in the camp of Pompey. While there he received letters from Caelius[6] and Dolabella[7]. The first expressed regret for having taken Caesar's side; the last begged Cicero to return to Italy now that he had seen how small were Pompey's chances of success. During the battle of Pharsalus Cicero was at Dyrrhachium[8], in bad health. Labienus brought the news of the defeat there[9], and the partisans of Pompey crossed over to Corcyra, where, probably[10], Cato asked Cicero, as the senior consular present, to take the command. Cicero declined, and was threatened with death by Cn. Pompeius the younger. Cato, however, protected him, and Cicero sailed to Brundisium, where he remained for some time[11].

He seems to have written few letters from Epirus, and was perhaps afraid[12] to write freely. Such as we have shew[13] much anxiety[14] for his wife, who appears to have been embarrassed by want of money, which Cicero could not understand; regret[15] for his mistake in leaving Italy; and despondency[16] at his party's prospects. He advanced considerable[17] sums to Pompey. Subsequent letters[18] illustrate still more strongly the discontent and melancholy which then possessed him. From the taunts of Antony it seems that Cicero's petulance and gloom gave general offence[19]. He does not comment in detail on the events of the war, but

[1] Cato evacuated it without a struggle, nor did M. Cotta succeed in holding Sardinia, which Q. Valerius occupied for Caesar. Cp. Ad Att. 10. 16, 3; Caes. Bell. Civ. 1. 30. [2] Caes. Bell. Civ. 2. 23-44. Curio himself fell. [3] App. Bell. Civ. 2. 47; Dion Cassius 41. 40. [4] Appendix 7; Caes. Bell. Civ. 3. 3-5. [5] Dion Cassius 41. 44. [6] Ad Fam. 8. 17. [7] Ib. 9. 9. [8] Plut. Cic. 39. [9] De Divin. 1. 32, 68. [10] Plut. Cic. 39, and Cat. 55. [11] Plut. Cic. 39. Perhaps he went previously to Patrae, cp. Ad Fam. 13. 17, 1; Ep. 79 (Ad Att. 11. 5), 4, note. [12] Ad Att. 11. 4. 2. [13] Ib. 11. 1-4. [14] Ib. 11. 2, 2; 11. 4. 1. [15] Ib. 11. 3, 1; 11. 4. 1. [16] Ib. 11. 4. 1. [17] Ib. 11. 3. 3. [18] Ad Fam. 4. 7, 2; 6. 1, 5; 7. 3. 2; Ad Att. 11. 6, 2 6. [19] Philipp. 2. 16. 39: Mommsen 4. 2, 397.

refers in one place[1] to the foolish confidence inspired by Caesar's defeat near Dyrrhachium.

§ 11. In the winter Caesar had succeeded in conveying seven legions to Epirus, and was afterwards joined by Antony with four more, all, however, much thinned by battles, long marches, and unhealthy quarters. He attempted to blockade Pompey's lines at Petra, near Dyrrhachium, but a serious reverse forced him to give up this plan, and he marched into the interior, where he was joined by Cn. Domitius Calvinus, whom he had detached into Macedonia. Pompey also formed a junction with his father-in-law, Scipio, whom he had recalled from Syria. A decisive battle was fought near Pharsalus on August 9[2]; and, in spite of Caesar's great inferiority of numbers, especially in cavalry, it resulted in a complete victory for him. L. Domitius Ahenobarbus fell in the rout; Pompey, giving up his cause for lost, fled to Egypt; his friends dispersed[3].

§ 12. In Italy some trouble was caused by the turbulent proceedings of M. Caelius Rufus, one of the praetors. He had previously[4] expressed to Cicero his discontent with Caesar, and now proposed[5] various laws, granting to debtors terms more favourable than Caesar had offered them. Caelius was opposed by C. Trebonius, one of his colleagues, and by the consul Servilius, and was suspended by the senate. In revenge he sent messages to Milo, who came to Italy, and the two together attempted to stir up a servile war. Both, however, were killed without effecting anything[6]. In a letter to Cicero, mentioned above, Caelius had affirmed that discontent with Caesar was general, except among the great money-lenders. Dion Cassius[7] describes opinion as really divided, but apparently favourable to Caesar. He allows, however, that Pompey's probable cruelty after success was feared. Appian[8] says that the people was anxious for a peaceable settlement, and knew that in case of a decisive battle the victor must become its master. These two statements are consistent with each other, and probable, but we do not know on what contemporary authority they rest.

§ 13. In Africa, after the death of Curio, the Pompeians and Juba had apparently not been disturbed.

In Spain, the governor left by Caesar, Q. Cassius Longinus[9], was

[1] Ad Fam. 7. 3. 2. [2] Calendarium Amiternum. ap. Mommsen Corpus Inscr. Lat. 1. 324. [3] Ad Fam. 4. 7. 2 and 3; Caes. Bell. Civ. 3. 1–103, exc. 20–32; App. Bell. Civ. 2. 87. [4] Ad Fam. 8. 17. [5] This must have taken place early in 48 B.C. Cp. Caes. Bell. Civ. 3. 1 and 3. 20 and 21; App. 2. 48; Dion 42. 22–25. Caesar had only provided that arbitrators should be appointed, and creditors compelled to receive land in payment at the value it bore before the war. [6] Caes. Bell. Civ. 3. 22. [7] 42. 17 and 18. [8] Bell. Civ. 2. 48. [9] Dion Cassius 42. 15 and 16.

very oppressive, and a plot was formed against his life. The conspirators attacked him when he was reviewing his army at Corduba. Cassius, however, escaped, though severely wounded, and renewed his severities. Part of his army then mutinied, and placed M. Marcellus Aeserninus, the quaestor, at its head. He did not disown his allegiance to Caesar, and was supported by M. Lepidus, proconsul[1] of Hither Spain. These disorders were put a stop to next year by the arrival of Trebonius to assume the government of Spain as proconsul[2], whereon Cassius departed, and was drowned near the mouth of the Iberus. Precious time had been lost for Caesar, for he had wished that Cassius should invade Africa from Spain[3].

[1] Bell. Alex. 59 and 63. [2] Bell. Alex. 64; Dion Cassius 43. 29. He was praetor in 48 B.C. (cp. Caes. Bell. Civ. 3. 20), but like Lepidus, who had been praetor in 49 B.C., is called proconsul as a provincial governor. [3] Bell. Alex. 51; 56.

SELECT LETTERS

OF

M. TULLIUS CICERO.

PART III.

46. To ATTICUS (AD ATT. VII. 10).

NEIGHBOURHOOD OF ROME, JAN. 17 (?), 49 B.C. (705 A.U.C.)

I have decided to go away at once. Hitherto our leaders seem to have behaved unwisely enough. If Pompey stays in Italy we shall all stay with him; if not, we must consider what to do. Write to me often.

CICERO ATTICO SAL.

SUBITO consilium cepi, ut ante quam luceret exirem, ne qui conspectus fieret aut sermo, lictoribus praesertim laureatis. De reliquo neque hercule quid agam nec quid acturus sim scio; ita sum perturbatus temeritate nostri amentissimi consilii. Tibi vero quid suadeam, cuius ipse consilium exspecto? Gnaeus

This letter must apparently have been written between Jan. 12 (cp. Ad Fam. 16. 11, 3) and Jan. 19 (cp. Ad Att. 7. 12, 1). Probably Jan. 17 (cp. Ep. 63, 4).

1. Ut . . exirem. Cicero must mean, 'to leave *the neighbourhood* of Rome.' For he had not forfeited his 'imperium,' as he would have done by entering Rome. Cp. Ep. 54. 5 and 6; p. 37, note on l. 15.

2. Conspectus, 'attention.'

Lictoribus . . laureatis, 'especially as my fasces are still laurelled' for successes in Cilicia. This would attract more notice to his movements.

4. Nostri amentissimi consilii, 'the frantic decision of our party.' Referring either to their hasty defiance of Caesar, or to their leaving Rome unguarded.

Tibi . . suadeam. Perhaps Atticus had asked Cicero's advice.

noster quid consilii ceperit capiatve nescio, adhuc in oppidis coartatus et stupens. Omnes, si in Italia consistat, erimus una; sin cedet, consilii res est. Adhuc certe, nisi ego insanio, stulte omnia et incaute. Tu, quaeso, crebro ad me scribe vel quod in buccam venerit.

47. To ATTICUS (AD ATT. VII. 11).

CAMPANIA, JAN. 19, (?) 49 B.C. (705 A.U.C.)

1. I am astonished by the news of Caesar's proceedings. 2. Even to wish for sovereignty in a free state is an atrocious crime. 3. What do you think of Pompey's decision to give up the capital? I should disapprove of it, 4. but that his flight has excited much sympathy with him and indignation against Caesar. I have the chief command in Campania and the adjacent coast districts for Pompey, not a troublesome office.

CICERO ATTICO SAL.

Quaeso, quid hoc est? aut quid agitur? mihi enim tenebrae 1
sunt: 'Cingulum' inquit 'nos tenemus, Anconem amisimus; Labienus discessit a Caesare.' Utrum de imperatore populi Romani an de Hannibale loquimur? o hominem amentem et miserum, qui ne umbram quidem umquam τοῦ καλοῦ viderit! Atque haec ait omnia facere se dignitatis causa. Ubi est autem dignitas nisi ubi honestas? honestum igitur habere exercitum

1. In oppidis, 'among the towns' of Campania probably. Cp. Intr. to Part III, §§ 1; 2, for an account of Pompey's movements.

2. Coartatus et stupens, 'embarrassed and confounded' by the number of his partisans who thronged there. The word 'coartatus' seems to be rare in Cicero's writings.

Consistat. Wesenb. 'consistet.'

3. Consilii res est, 'it is a matter for consideration.'

Stulte omnia et incaute, sc. 'facta sunt.'

4. Vel quod in buccam venerit, 'even the first thing that comes into your head.' Forcell. Cp. Ep. 84, 2, note.

6. Quid hoc est? 'what is the meaning of this?' referring to what follows. On the indic. in questions, cp. Madv. 356, Obs. 3. Cicero prefers to state the question directly, rather than to make it depend on quaeso.

Mihi enim tenebrae sunt. Tenebrae is, I think, the predicate. On the plural 'sunt,' cp. Madv. 216. 'It is quite obscure to me.' Forcell.

7. Cingulum. In Picenum, about 20 m. S.W. of Ancona, now Cingoli. It had been rebuilt by Labienus. Cp. p. 281, note on l. 2.

Inquit: cp. Ep. 45. 3. Perhaps Cicero forwarded to Atticus a letter containing the news on which he comments.

Anconem: cp. Iuv. Sat. 4. 40.

'Ante domum Veneris quam Dorica sustinet Ancon.'

'Ancona' is the more usual form. Cp. Ep. 52, 2.

8. Labienus: cp. Ep. 44. 6, note.

10. τοῦ καλοῦ = 'honesti,' 'of moral beauty.'

11. Dignitatis, 'his proper position.' Cicero rather plays upon the word in what follows. 'How can there be honour without honourable conduct?'

nullo publico consilio? occupare urbes civium, quo facilior sit aditus ad patriam? χρεῶν ἀποκοπάς, φυγάδων καθόδους, sescenta alia scelera moliri,

τὴν θεῶν μεγίστην ὥστ' ἔχειν τυραννίδα— ?

Sibi habeat suam fortunam? unam mehercule tecum apricationem in illo lucrativo tuo sole malim quam omnia istius modi regna, vel potius mori millies quam semel istius modi quicquam cogi-
2 tare. 'Quid si tu velis?' inquis. Age quis est, cui velle non liceat? Sed ego hoc ipsum velle miserius esse duco quam in crucem tolli; una res est ea miserior, adipisci quod ita volueris. Sed haec hactenus; libenter enim in his molestiis ἐνσχολάζω
3 † *cocon*. Redeamus ad nostrum: per fortunas! quale tibi consilium Pompeii videtur? hoc quaero, quod urbem reliquerit. Ego enim ἀπορῶ. Tum nihil absurdius. Urbem tu relinquas? ergo idem, si Galli venirent. 'Non est' inquit 'in parietibus res publica.' At in aris et focis. 'Fecit Themistocles; fluctum

1. **Nullo publico consilio**, 'without any public authority.' On the ablat., cp. Ep. 34, 2, note.

2. **Patriam**, 'his own city.' Cp. De Leg. 2. 2, 5. where Cicero speaks of himself as having two 'patriae'—Arpinum by birth, Rome by citizenship.

χρεῶν ἀποκοπάς, 'an abolition of debts.' Cp. Demosth. adv. Timocr. 746.

φυγάδων καθόδους, 'restorations of exiles.' As these would often be political offenders, a comprehensive restoration would be a revolutionary measure. A. Gabinius, T. Munatius Plancus, and Q. Pompeius Rufus, were now political exiles. Cp. Philipp. 1. 1. 3. where Cicero, in praise of Antony, represents him as answering to the question 'num qui exsules restituti? unum . . praeterea neminem.' Cp. also Mommsen 4. 2, 316.

Sescenta, 'countless.' Very common. Cp. p. 80.

4. **τὴν θεῶν, κ.τ.λ.**: Eur. Phoen. 506.

5. **Unam . . apricationem**, 'one day's basking with you.'

6. **Lucrativo**. I can hardly explain this word. Boot says, 'sol lucrativus dici potuit et is quem Atticus negotiis surripuisset, et is quo ut frueretur aliquo loci impedimento amoto effecisset.' Quintil. Inst. Orat. 10. 7. 27) uses 'opera lucrativa' in a sense apparently = 'opera subseciva.' 'Lucrativus' is a legal term properly, applied to things acquired by bequest or gift. Forcell. It seems not to occur elsewhere in Cicero's writings.

8. **Quid si tu velis**, sc. 'regnare.'

Age quis est . . liceat, 'who is there who may not desire it!' Cp. Iuv. Sat. 10, 95

> 'Quidni
> Haec cupias? et qui nolunt occidere quemquam
> Posse volunt.'

9. **Hoc ipsum velle**, 'the mere wish for such power.' Cp. Ep. 83, 2 'ut ipsum vinci contemnerent.'

11. **Enim . . ἐνσχολάζω † cocon.** Baiter suggests σῶς ὤν, 'talk thus idly while I am safe,' referring to his rather declamatory attack on Caesar in this letter.' Wesenb. suggests σοι. 'Enim,' 'enough of this declamation, it can be justified as a relief to my spirits.' 'I have indulged myself with it, for.' The word ἐνσχολάζω is found in Arist. Pol. 7. 12, 7, in the sense of spending time in a place.

12. **Nostrum**, sc. 'Pompeium.'

13. **Hoc . . reliquerit**, 'I mean his leaving the capital.' On the mood, cp. Epp. 3. 3; 9. 11, notes, on pp. 33, 73.

14. **Tum**, sc. 'videtur,' 'at one time I think.'

Relinquas: on the mood, cp. Ep. 45. 4, note.

15. **Idem**, sc. 'faceres.' An imaginary dialogue between Pompey and Cicero follows.

16. **At in aris et focis**, Cicero replies.

enim totius barbariae ferre urbs una non poterat.' At idem Pericles non fecit, annum fere post quinquagesimum, cum praeter moenia nihil teneret, *et* nostri olim urbe reliqua capta arcem tamen retinuerunt:

οὕτω που τῶν πρόσθεν ἐπευθόμεθα κλέα ἀνδρῶν.

Rursus autem ex dolore municipali sermonibusque eorum, quos 4
convenio, videtur hoc consilium exitum habiturum: mira hominum querela est—nescio istic, sed facies ut sciam—, sine magistratibus urbem esse, sine senatu; fugiens denique Pompeius mirabiliter homines movet: quid quaeris? alia causa facta est; nihil iam concedendum putant Caesari. Haec tu mihi explica
qualia sint. Ego negotio praesum non turbulento; volt enim 5
me Pompeius esse, quem tota haec Campania et maritima ora habeat ἐπίσκοπον, ad quem dilectus et summa negotii referatur; itaque vagus esse cogitabam. Te puto iam videre, quae sit ὁρμὴ Caesaris, qui populus, qui totius negotii status; ea velim scribas ad me, et quidem, quoniam mutabilia sunt, quam saepissime; acquiesco enim et scribens ad te et legens tua.

Fluctum . . totius barbariae, 'the flood of all the forces of the East,' i.e. of Xerxes' army. The word is not necessarily used of Asiatics, and perhaps there is here an allusion to the hordes who were supposed to be following Caesar. See Ep. 48, 3. Wesenb. has 'Themistocles.' Fluctum, &c., making Cicero's comment begin with 'Fluctum,' which perhaps improves the sense.

2. Quinquagesimum. The invasion of Xerxes took place 480 B.C.; that of Archidamus 431 B.C.

3. Olim. After the battle of the Allia, 390 B.C.

5. οὕτω που κ.τ.λ.: Hom. Il. 9. 524. But οὕτω καὶ seems the usual reading.

6. Rursus . . habiturum. Here the statement of another view about the plan pursued begins. 'On the other hand, to judge from the indignation of the municipal towns, and from the language of people whom I meet, I think the plan will succeed.'

7. Exitum. This word is not often used of a good result without some epithet to qualify it. Cp. 'meliores . . exitus' Ep. 70, 6.

8. Nescio istic, sc. 'an ita sit,' 'I know not if the case be the same at Rome.' Ernesti proposes 'an istic.'

9. Fugiens . . Pompeius . . movet, 'people are strangely affected by the sight of Pompey as a fugitive.' On the use of the participle as an adjective, cp. Madv. 424.

10. Alia causa facta est, 'the whole aspect of the case is changed.' Forcell. Cp. Ep. 92, 4.

11. Haec . . qualia sint, 'what will come of all this.'

12. Turbulento, 'troublesome.'

14. ἐπίσκοπον, 'superintendent.' Quite classical.

Ad quem dilectus . . referatur, 'to have the chief authority in the recruiting, and the general direction of affairs.' Cp. the use of 'referre' with 'ad senatum' and 'ad populum,' meaning 'to consult.' Wesenb., however, doubts if 'referatur' can have the sense here needed, and suggests 'deferatur.' On the facts, cp. Ep. 52, 5.

15. Vagus esse, 'to move about from place to place.'

Cogitabam. Epistolary tense.

Videre. Quia Romae es. Manut.

Quae sit ὁρμὴ Caesaris, 'at what point Caesar is aiming.' Wiel., Billerb.

16. Qui populus, sc. 'sit,' 'how the people is disposed.'

18. Acquiesco, 'I become tranquil.'

48. To ATTICUS (AD ATT. VII. 13).

CALES, JAN. 23 (?), 49 B.C. (705 A.U.C.)

1. I am delighted with the behaviour of Labienus. Piso, too, deserves credit. One can hardly call this struggle against the ambition of one man a civil war; but he is formidable, and our mistakes have been serious. 2. I cannot learn from Pompey what he means to do, and he seems quite at a loss himself. Our forces are not effective enough for war, yet the time for negotiation has passed. 3. I am in doubt how to provide honourably for the safety of my family, and should like to hear your advice. You and Peducaeus must consider what propriety requires from you. 4. Let me know what does take place, and what you think will take place.

CICERO ATTICO SAL.

1 De Vennonianis rebus tibi assentior. Labienum ἥρωα iudico; facinus iam diu nullum civile praeclarius, qui, ut aliud nihil, hoc tamen profecit: dedit illi dolorem; sed etiam ad summam profectum aliquid puto. Amo etiam Pisonem, cuius iudicium de genero suspicor visum iri grave. Quamquam genus belli quod sit vides: ita civile est, ut non ex civium dissensione, sed ex unius perditi civis audacia natum sit. Is autem valet exercitu, tenet multos spe et promissis, omnia omnium concupivit. Huic tradita urbs est, nuda praesidio, referta copiis: quid est, quod ab eo non metuas, qui illa templa et tecta non patriam, sed praedam putet? quid autem sit acturus aut quo modo, nescio, sine senatu, sine magistratibus: ne simulare qui-

1. Vennonianis, 'of C. Vennonius.' He was a friend of Cicero and Atticus, and died in or before the year 46 B.C. He is mentioned Ad Att. 6. 1, 25; Ad Fam. 13. 72, 2.

ἥρωα iudico, 'I esteem a hero.' On the double acc., cp. Madv. 227 c.

2. Facinus . . praeclarius, sc. 'factum est,' 'no more noble act in discharge of a citizen's duty.'

Ut aliud nihil, sc. 'profecerit.' Cp. Madv. 440 a, Obs. 4, for 'ut' in the sense of 'granting that;' 479 d, Obs. 5, on the ellipse; and 229 b, on the acc. hoc, denoting extent, with neuter verbs.

3. Ad summam, 'for the main interest of our party.'

4. Pisonem. L. Calpurnius Piso, consul in 58 B.C. He and Cicero had been bitter enemies, but were now on good terms, and seem to have remained so to the end. Intr. to Part. I, §§ 18–20; Part II, § 8; Philipp. 1. 4, 10; 8. 10, 28.

5. Genero, Caesare. Caesar had married Piso's daughter Calpurnia.

Quamquam, 'and yet this is of the less importance.'

6. Ita civile . . natum, 'though a civil war, it is not one of parties, but has been caused by the ambition of one man,' and therefore the judgment of eminent citizens like Piso will have the less weight with the followers of that man. On ita . . ut, cp. Ep. 30, 1, note.

12. Ne simulare . . πολιτικῶν, 'he will not be able, even in his hypocrisy, to

dem poterit quicquam πολιτικῶς. Nos autem ubi exsurgere poterimus aut quando? quorum dux quam ἀστρατήγητος, tu quoque animadvertis, cui ne Picena quidem nota fuerint, quam autem sine consilio, res testis: ut enim alia omittam decem annorum peccata, quae condicio non huic fugae praestitit? Nec vero 2
nunc quid cogitet scio, ac non desino per litteras sciscitari. Nihil esse timidius constat, nihil perturbatius; itaque nec praesidium, cuius parandi causa ad urbem retentus est, nec locum ac sedem praesidii ullam video: spes omnis in duabus insidiose retentis, paene alienis legionibus. Nam dilectus adhuc quidem invitorum est et a pugnando abhorrentium; condicionum autem amissum tempus est. Quid futurum sit, non video; commissum quidem a nobis certe est sive a nostro duce, ut e portu sine gubernaculis egressi tempestati nos traderemus. Itaque de Cice- 3
ronibus nostris dubito quid agam; nam mihi interdum amandandi videntur in Graeciam; de Tullia autem et Terentia, cum mihi barbarorum adventus ad urbem proponitur, omnia timeo, cum autem Dolabellae venit in mentem, paulum respiro. Sed velim consideres, quid faciendum putes: primum πρὸς τὸ ἀσφαλές —aliter enim mihi de illis ac de me ipso consulendum est—, deinde ad opiniones, ne reprehendamur, quod eas Romae velimus

observe constitutional forms,' e.g. Caesar could not legally get himself named dictator, as both the consuls had followed Pompey. Cp. Ad Att. 9. 15, 2; and, for another difficulty of Caesar, Ep. 62. 3.

1. Exsurgere, 'to raise our heads.' Frequent in this metaphorical sense.

2. Quam ἀστρατήγητος, 'how little of a general.' Apparently not used in this sense by any other writer.

3. Picena, 'the state of affairs in Picenum,' a district devoted to Pompey, and with the state of which he ought to have been thoroughly familiar.

Quam .. sine consilio, 'how destitute of a policy.'

5. Condicio, 'terms' or 'agreement.' Forcell.

Nec vero .. scio, 'nor, indeed, do I even yet know his plans.'

7. Praesidium, 'armed force.'

8. Retentus, 'detained in Italy,' whereas he might have been governing Spain. Cp. Intr. to Part II, §§ 14: 18.

Locum ac sedem praesidii, 'any place for the rendezvous of our forces.'

9. Duabus .. legionibus. They had been withdrawn from Caesar, nominally for service against the Parthians. Cp. Intr. to Part II, § 17; Ep. 33. 4; Mommsen 4. 2, 353.

Insidiose, 'under a false pretence' of being employed against the Parthians. The best MS. has 'invidiose,' which might mean, 'in a way which caused ill-feeling.'

11. Invitorum, gen. object.: cp. Madv. 283. The passage is important, as illustrating the state of feeling in Italy.

Condicionum, 'for negotiations.' Nägelsb. 64, 173.

12. Commissum .. ut, 'we have brought it to pass that.' The word suggests blame. Forcell.

14. De Ciceronibus, 'about my son and nephew.' Cp. Ad Att. 7. 12, 3 'frangor saepe misericordia puerorum.'

17. Barbarorum. Of Caesar's Gauls. Cp. Lucan Phars. 1. 475, 6, and Merivale 2. 111 and 112.

18. Dolabellae, now Tullia's husband. On the gen. after 'venit in mentem,' cp. Madv. 291, Obs. 3.

20. De illis, 'about my family.'

21. Ad opiniones: ad = πρός, 'with a view to what people will think.' Forcell.

esse in communi bonorum fuga. Quin etiam tibi et Peducaeo—scripsit enim ad me—quid faciatis videndum est; is enim splendor est vestrum, ut eadem postulentur a vobis, quae ab amplissimis civibus. Sed de hoc tu videbis, quippe cum de me ipso
4 ac de meis te considerare velim. Reliquum est ut et quid agatur, quoad poteris, explores scribasque ad me, et quid ipse coniectura assequare, quod etiam a te magis exspecto: nam acta omnibus nuntiantibus a te exspecto futura. Μάντις δ' ἄριστος—. Loquacitati ignosces, quae et me levat ad te quidem scribentem et elicit tuas litteras.

49. POMPEY TO CICERO (AD ATT. VIII. 11 A).

LUCERIA, FEB. 10, (?) 49 B.C. (705 A.U.C.)

I hear that L. Domitius is on his way to join me with thirty cohorts. You had better come to us at Luceria.

CN. POMPEIUS PROCOS. S. D. M. CICERONI IMP.

Q. Fabius ad me venit a. d. IIII. Idus Febr. Is nuntiat L. Domitium cum suis cohortibus XI. et cohortibus XIIII., quas Vibullius adduxit, ad me iter habere; habuisse in animo proficisci Corfinio

1. **Peducaeo.** Probably Cicero means the Sex. Peducaeus mentioned Ep. 41, 1. Cp. note there. Atticus had held no public office, but his wealth, and intimacy with eminent men, placed him, Cicero says, on a level with the noblest, and his behaviour would therefore be strictly criticised.

4. **Tu videbis** = 'vide.' Cp. Ep. 38, 10, note; 'tu' is emphatic, 'you for yourself.'

Quippe . . velim, 'as you may well do, for I want your advice on my affairs also,' and therefore you surely are competent to manage your own.

5. **Reliquum est . . ut . . explores;** cp. on the conj., Madv. 373.

6. **Quoad poteris.** These words are not in a dependent clause like **quid agatur.** 'Reliquum est ut explores' = 'explora.'

Quid . . assequare. On the mood, cp. Madv. 356.

7. **Etiam . . magis,** 'even more than a report of news.'

Acta . . futura, 'all can tell me what has happened; I expect you to tell me what *will* happen.'

8. **Μάντις δ' ἄριστος ὅστις εἰκάζει καλῶς.** A fragment of Euripides. Cp. Plut. de Defect. Orac. 432 C, ed. Wyttenbach. Cicero translates the line (De Divin. 2. 5, 12) 'bene qui coniciet vatem hunc perhibebo optumum.'

11. **Q. Fabius** Vergilianus had been a legate of Appius Claudius in Cilicia, and was now a partisan of Pompey. Cp. Ad Fam. 3. 3. 1; 3. 4. 1.

12. **Cohortibus XI.** Pompey (Ad Att. 8. 12 A, 1) speaks of Domitius as having twelve cohorts; hence Wesenb. proposes to read XII here.

Vibullius. L. Vibullius Rufus has been mentioned Ep. 29, 10. His present commission was to raise forces in Picenum for Pompey. Cp. Caes. Bell. Civ. 1. 15. He was devoted to Pompey, but had not authority enough to overrule the obstinate L. Domitius, for an account of whose proceedings, cp. Intr. to Part III, § 2; Mommsen 4. 2. 375. Vibullius afterwards served under Afranius and Petreius in Spain. Cp. Caes. Bell. Civ. 1. 34.

a. d. v. Idus Febr., C. Hirrum cum v. cohortibus subsequi. Censeo, ad nos Luceriam venias; nam te hic tutissime puto fore.

50. To POMPEY (AD ATT. VIII. 11 B).

FORMIAE, FEB. 15 OR 16, 49 B.C. (705 A.U.C.)

1. I am glad to hear better news from Picenum than I expected. If you think my district can be held, I will stay here, though the towns are unprotected. 2. I went to Capua as you wished; Libo and T. Ampius were acting with great energy there. I remained at Capua till the consuls left; returned there shortly afterwards, and left again for Formiae, where I now am. 3. If you wish to concentrate all our forces, I will join you.

M. CICERO IMP. S. D. CN. MAGNO PROCOS.

A. d. xv. Kalend. Martias Formiis accepi tuas litteras, ex 1
quibus ea, quae in agro Piceno gesta erant, cognovi commodiora
esse multo, quam ut erat nobis nuntiatum, Vibulliique virtutem
industriamque libenter agnovi. Nos adhuc in ea ora, cui praepositi sumus, ita fuimus, ut navem paratam haberemus; ea enim audiebamus et ea verebamur, ut, quodcumque tu consilium cepisses, id nobis persequendum putaremus. Nunc quoniam auctoritate et consilio tuo in spe firmiore sumus, si teneri posse putas Tarracinam *et* oram maritimam, in ea manebo, etsi praesidia in oppidis nulla sunt; nemo enim nostri ordinis in his locis est praeter M. Eppium, quem ego Minturnis esse volui, vigilantem hominem et industrium: nam L. Torquatum, virum fortem et cum auctoritate, Formiis non habemus, ad te profectum arbitramur. Ego omnino, ut proxime tibi placuerat, Capuam 2
veni eo ipso die, quo tu Teano Sidicino es profectus; volueras

1. C. Hirrum: cp. Epp. 33. 3: 34. 5, notes.

Subsequi, 'is following closely.'

Censeo . . venias: cp. Ep. 66. 3, note.

2. Tutissime. For adverbs as predicates, cp. Ep. 4. 1, note.

6. Cui praepositi sumus. The best MS. has 'ubi p. s.' The verb 'praeponere' is found without a dative following in Caesar (Bell. Civ. 3. 89) and Livy (37. 41). Dominationi sententiae inservit. Forcell.

9. Auctoritate, 'assurance.' Forcell.

13. M. Eppium: cp. Ep. 34. 5.

14. Torquatum: cp. Ep. 36, 10. He was now praetor, hence 'cum auctoritate' below. Manutius supposes an elder Torquatus to be referred to, for he says 'ut consolarem,' and no Torquatus had been consul since 65 B.C.

16. Omnino, 'assuredly,' 'I assure you.' Cp. Ep. 44. 3, note on p. 284. Metzg. has 'wirklich.'

17. Eo ipse die, Jan. 23rd. Cp. Ad Att. 7. 13, 7.

7. Ita fuimus . . ut . . haberemus. 'Ita, ut' = 'quidem, sed,' cp. p. 26, note.

enim me cum M. Considio pro praetore illa negotia tueri. Cum eo venissem, vidi T. Ampium dilectum habere diligentissime, ab eo accipere Libonem, summa item diligentia et in illa colonia auctoritate. Fui Capuae, quoad consules. Iterum, ut erat edictum a consulibus, veni Capuam ad Nonas Februar. Cum fuissem
3 triduum, recepi me Formias. Nunc, quod tuum consilium aut quae ratio belli sit, ignoro: si tenendam hanc oram putas, quae et opportunitatem et dignitatem habet et egregios cives, et, ut arbitror, teneri potest, opus est esse qui praesit; sin omnia unum in locum contrahenda sunt, non dubito quin ad te statim veniam, quo mihi nihil optatius est, idque tecum, quo die ab urbe discessimus, locutus sum. Ego, si cui adhuc videor segnior fuisse, dum ne tibi videar, non laboro, et tamen, si, ut video, bellum gerendum est, confido me omnibus facile satis facturum.
4 M. Tullium, meum necessarium, ad te misi, cui tu, si tibi videretur, ad me litteras dares.

Teano Sidicino. There was another Teanum in Apulia. The place here mentioned stood on the Latin way, about fourteen miles N.W. of Casilinum, and five miles N.W. of Cales.

Volueras . . me . . tueri. On the constr., cp. Ep. 44. 3, note.

1. Cum M. Considio. M. Considius had been named in the beginning of this year by the senate to succeed Caesar in Cisalpine Gaul. Cp. Ep. 52. 3.

Illa negotia tueri: cp. Ad Fam. 10. 11. 1 'locum munus tuere.' 'Illa negotia' means the superintendence of the levy. Cp. Ep. 47. 5.

2. T. Ampium. T. Ampius Balbus was a zealous adherent of Pompey; apparently he was tribune 64-63 B.C., and praetor in 59 B.C. He had governed Cilicia before Lentulus (Ad Fam. 1. 3. 2), served under Pompey at Pharsalus, and was afterwards pardoned by Caesar (cp. Ad Fam. 6. 12; Orell. Onomast., sub nom.).

3. Accipere, sc. 'milites delectos.' Billerb.

Libonem. L. Scribonius Libo. Cp. Ep. 21. 3, note.

Colonia. Capua, perhaps, became a colony by virtue of the 'Lex Iulia Agraria' of 59 B.C. Cp. Philipp. 2. 40. 101; Intr. to Part I, § 17; and Ep. 10. 1, note.

5. Ad Nonas, 'on the 5th.'

Fuissem = 'commoratus essem.' Forcel'. supp. 'ibi.'

7. Ratio, 'the plan.'

8. Opportunitatem, 'a good geographical position.' Cicero probably means, for keeping up communication with Spain, and for threatening Caesar's hold of the capital.

Dignitatem, 'importance.' Capua had been the second city of Italy.

10. Non dubito . . veniam, 'I am resolved to come to you at once.' Cicero did not do so, however. On the tense of 'veniam,' cp. Madv. 378 a. Obs. 2. On Cicero's conduct, cp. Intr. to Part III, §§ 3 and 4.

13. Dum ne tibi videar, sc. 'segnior.' For this sense of 'dum,' 'provided that,' cp. Madv. 351 b, Obs. 2.

Et tamen . . satis facturum, 'and yet (though I do not value the opinion of others much), if we are to have war, as I see we are, I am confident of satisfying every one.' Cicero means, that when he had given up all hope of peace, he would be most energetic in war.

15. M. Tullium. Perhaps a freedman. Cp. Ad Att. 5. 4. 1; 13. 22. 4 'Tullium scribam nihil fuit quod appellares.'

51. POMPEY TO L. DOMITIUS AHENOBARBUS (AD ATT. VIII. 12 D).

LUCERIA, FEB. 17, 49 B.C. (705 A.U.C.)

1. I learn from your letter that what I feared has happened. Caesar intends not to offer you battle at once, but to cut you off from me. I do not trust my forces enough to attempt to relieve you. 2. Exert yourself to the utmost to join me even now; my new levies cannot assemble rapidly, and if they could, would be worth little opposed to veterans.

CN. MAGNUS PROCOS. S. D. L. DOMITIO PROCOS.

Litterae mihi a te redditae sunt a. d. XIII. Kal. Martias, in 1
quibus scribis Caesarem apud Corfinium castra posuisse. Quod
putavi et praemonui fit, ut nec in praesentia committere tecum
proelium velit et omnibus copiis conductis te implicet, ne ad
me iter tibi expeditum sit atque istas copias coniungere optimorum civium possis cum iis legionibus, de quarum voluntate
dubitamus: quo etiam magis tuis litteris sum commotus; neque
enim eorum militum, quos mecum habeo, voluntate satis confido, ut de omnibus fortunis rei publicae dimicem, neque etiam,
qui ex dilectibus conscripti sunt *a* consulibus, convenerunt. Qua 2
re da operam, si ulla ratione etiam nunc efficere potes, ut te
explices, huc quam primum venias, ante quam omnes copiae
ad adversarium conveniant; neque enim celeriter ex dilectibus
huc homines convenire possunt, et, si convenirent, quantum iis

3. **Fit, ut . . velit.** On the constr., cp. Ep. 48, 4, note.

4. **Et omnibus . . dubitamus.** 'et' adversative (cp. Ep. 38, 2 note), 'what I anticipated and forewarned you of is happening; Caesar is unwilling to offer you battle at once; he has combined all his forces to blockade you, so that you may not be able to come to me without impediment, and join your forces with mine.'

5. **Atque,** 'and so.' It gives prominence to the second clause. Cp. Madv. 433.

Istas copias . . optimorum civium, 'your forces, which are composed of the most loyal citizens.' The army of Domitius consisted of recruits from central Italy and Picenum, on whom Pompey relied to overawe his two veteran legions which had served some time under Caesar. Cp. Appendix 7, and Ep. 48, 2, note. On the gen. 'civium,' cp. Ep. 36, 7, note.

6. **Iis.** Wesenb. 'his.'

8. **Voluntate.** On the abl., cp. Madv. 244 a, note p. 264.

9. **Ut de omnibus . . dimicem,** 'to risk a battle involving the whole fortunes of the state.'

12. **Huc.** The omission of a conjunction is curious. Orell. proposes to insert 'que;' Wesenb. 'et;' but may not haste of composition account for the omission? Cp. Ep. 72, 2, 'improbes.'

14. **Si convenirent . . sit.** On the imperf. 'convenirent,' as expressing what does not take place, cp. Madv. 347 b. The sentence is elliptical, and requires words meaning 'it would be in vain for,' to complete it. Cp. Virg. Ecl. 9. 45, and Conington's note.

committendum sit, qui inter se ne noti *quidem* sunt, contra veteranas legiones non te praeterit.

52. TO HIS FREEDMAN TIRO (AD FAM. XVI. 12).

CAPUA, JAN. 27, 49 B.C. (705 A.U.C.)

1. You may judge of our danger when I tell you that we have abandoned Rome to fire and plunder. 2. I have done all I could for peace, but others were eager for war. 3. Caesar has offered us terms, which we have accepted with a proviso; 4. if he agrees to this, peace may be maintained. In case of war chances would be in our favour, especially as Labienus, his best officer, has deserted him. 5. I have at present only the superintendence of the coast from Formiae southwards, but in case of war I shall have a military command. I am annoyed that Dolabella is with Caesar. I hope this bad news will not injure your health. 6. I have asked A. Varro to take care of you, and he has promised to do so. Do not sail in stormy weather, but come to me as soon as you can without danger to your health. My son is near Formiae, my wife and daughter are at Rome. Capua, Jan. 27.

TULLIUS S. D. TIRONI SUO.

1 Quo in discrimine versetur salus mea et bonorum omnium atque
universae rei publicae, ex eo scire potes, quod domos nostras et
patriam ipsam vel diripiendam vel inflammandam reliquimus: in
eum locum res deducta est, ut, nisi qui deus vel casus aliqui sub-
2 venerit, salvi esse nequeamus. Equidem, ut veni ad urbem, non
destiti omnia et sentire et dicere et facere, quae ad concordiam
pertinerent; sed mirus invaserat furor non solum improbis, sed
etiam iis qui boni habentur ut pugnare cuperent, me clamante
nihil esse bello civili miserius. Itaque cum Caesar amentia

1. Qui . . sunt, indic. as a simple explanation. Cp. Madv. 362 a.

TIRONI. M. Tullius Tiro was a freedman, for whom Cicero and all his family had the greatest regard; Cicero was often anxious about his health. Tiro had received a good education, and is thought to have formed in part the collection of Cicero's correspondence which we possess. Cp. p. 121; Ad Att. 16. 5. 5; Ad Fam. 16. 15; 16. 16; 16. 17; 16. 21; 16. 26.

3. Patriam ipsam: cp. Ep. 47. 1, note. Reliquimus, 'we, the friends of Pompey, have left.'

7. Ut veni ad urbem: cp. Epp. 44. 4; 46, notes. The phrase 'ad urbem esse' was used to describe the position of an officer holding 'imperium,' who was waiting close to Rome, but had some reason for not wishing to enter the 'urbs.' Cp. Epp. 5. 4; 29. 28; 35. 6, notes, and note E, p. 123.

8. Omnia . . pertinerent, 'to fashion all my sentiments, words, and acts with a view to concord.' 'Pertinerent:' on the mood, cp. Ep. 34. 2, note; and on the tense, p. 92, and Madv. 383: it follows 'destiti.'

9. Invaserat seems only here to be used with the dative by Cicero. Forcell quotes Varro and Lucretius for its use with that case.

10. Me clamante, 'in spite of my outcries.'

11. Cum . . raperetur. On the mood, cp. Ep. 45. 1, note.

quadam raperetur et oblitus nominis atque honorum suorum Ariminum, Pisaurum, Anconam, Arretium occupavisset, urbem reliquimus; quam sapienter aut quam fortiter, nihil attinet disputari;
quo quidem in casu simus, vides. Feruntur omnino condiciones 3
ab illo, ut Pompeius eat in Hispaniam; dilectus, qui sunt habiti, et praesidia nostra dimittantur; se ulteriorem Galliam Domitio, citeriorem Considio Noniano—his enim obtigerunt—traditurum; ad consulatus petitionem se venturum, neque se iam velle absente se rationem haberi suam; se praesentem trinum nundinum petiturum. Accepimus condiciones, sed ita, ut removeat praesidia ex iis locis, quae occupavit, ut sine metu de his ipsis condicionibus
Romae senatus haberi possit. Id ille si fecerit, spes est pacis, 4
non honestae—leges enim imponuntur—, sed quidvis est melius quam sic esse ut sumus. Sin autem ille suis condicionibus stare noluerit, bellum paratum est, eius modi tamen, quod sustinere ille non possit, praesertim cum a suis condicionibus ipse fugerit, tantum modo ut eum intercludamus, ne ad urbem possit accedere,

1. **Honorum**, 'the high offices he had held.'

Ariminum, now Rimini; **Pisaurum**, now Pesaro, and **Ancona**, were on or very near the Adriatic coast.

2. **Arretium**, now Arezzo, in north Etruria.

3. **Nihil attinet disputari**, 'there is no good in discussing.' Cicero's own opinion was not on the whole favourable to the policy of abandoning Rome. Cp. Ep. 54. 3 with 47. 3 and 4.

4. **Omnino**: cp. Epp. 45. 3; 80, 2, notes.

5. **Ut Pompeius eat in Hispaniam**: cp. Epp. 45. 3, note; 91, 5, note. He was now proconsul of Spain, which was administered for him by his legates. Cp. Caes. Bell. Civ. 1. 9.

Dilectus, 'the new levies.'

6. **Praesidia**, 'the forces in garrison.'

Domitio, L. Ahenobarbo, consul 54 B.C.

7. **Considio Noniano**: cp. Ep. 50, 2, note. He had been praetor but not consul.

Obtigerunt, 'were assigned' by a vote of the senate in this case. Cp. Caes. Bell. Civ. 1. 6. The arrangement was probably made just before Caesar crossed the Rubicon.

8. **Absente se**, more emphatic than 'absentis.' Cp. Phil. 11. 10, 23.

9. **Rationem .. suam**: cp. Ep. 34, 9, note, p. 243.

Trinum nundinum, acc. of duration: (cp. Madv. 235) 'during the space which the law requires, that between three market days.' According to the inclusive way of counting adopted at Rome this period need not be more than seventeen days; the first, ninth, and seventeenth, being 'nundinae.' Cp. Ep. 1, 1, note.

10. **Accepimus condiciones**, foll., 'we accepted his terms, but on condition that.' For this sense of 'ita ut,' cp. Ep. 50, 1, note. The decision here referred to seems to have been adopted at a council held at Teanum on Jan. 23 or 24. Cp. Intr. to Part III, § 1, and notes; Ad Att. 7. 14, 1; 7. 15, 2. Caesar (Bell. Civ. 1. 10 and 11) enlarges on the unfairness of the demands addressed to him.

Ex iis locis quae occupavit, i.e. from the places south of the Rubicon which Caesar had occupied: see above, § 1.

14. **Sin autem .. bellum paratum est**. The perf. indic. used of a certain future result, cp. Madv. 340, Obs. 2.

Suis condicionibus stare, 'to abide by his own terms.' On the ablative, cp. Madv. 267.

15. **Tamen** introduces a consolatory reflection.

17. **Tantum modo ut**, 'provided only that.' Süpfle. But Hofmann translates the words 'may we only,' making 'ut' = 'utinam:' cp. Ep. 63, 4. But that passage is a quotation from a longer one, and may itself be open to either construction.

quod sperabamus fieri posse; dilectus enim magnos habebamus putabamusque illum metuere, si ad urbem ire coepisset, ne Gallias amitteret, quas ambas habet inimicissimas praeter Transpadanos, ex Hispaniaque sex legiones et magna auxilia Afranio et Petreio ducibus habet a tergo: videtur, si insaniet, posse opprimi, modo ut urbe salva. Maximam autem plagam accepit, quod is, qui summam auctoritatem in illius exercitu habebat, T. Labienus, socius
5 sceleris esse noluit: reliquit illum et *est* nobiscum, multique idem facturi esse dicuntur. Ego adhuc orae maritimae praesum a Formiis. Nullum maius negotium suscipere volui, quo plus apud illum meae litterae cohortationesque ad pacem valerent; sin autem erit bellum, video me castris et certis legionibus praefuturum. Habeo etiam illam molestiam, quod Dolabella noster apud Caesarem est. Haec tibi nota esse volui, quae cave ne te
6 perturbent et impediant valetudinem tuam. Ego A. Varroni, quem cum amantissimum mei cognovi, tum etiam valde tui studiosum, diligentissime te commendavi, ut et valetudinis tuae rationem haberet et navigationis et totum te susciperet ac

1. Sperabamus and the following imperfects are epistolary tenses.

3. Quas ambas, i.e. the Cisalpine and Transalpine provinces. This statement was not true, so far as we can judge by results.

Transpadanos. Cp. Epp. 31, 2; 44, 6, notes.

4. Sex legiones. Caesar (Bell. Civ. 1. 38) mentions seven, but one of these was levied in Spain (Ib. 1. 85). M. Varro governed Baetica. Cp. Intr. to Part III, § 8; Appendix 7.

5. Si insaniet, 'if he perseveres in his mad enterprise.'

Modo ut urbe salva, sc. 'opprimatur,' 'only may his destruction not involve the ruin of the capital.' Cp. p. 314, l. 17.

7. T. Labienus: cp. Ep. 44, 6, note.

9. Orae maritimae .. a Formiis, 'I have the superintendence of the coast from Formiae southwards.' Cicero's head quarters were at Capua. Cp. Ep. 54, 4. Süpfle, however, thinks he visited Formiae so often that he might regard it as his chief station. To illustrate the ambiguity of Cicero's conduct at this time, cp. Epp. 50; 54, 5; 64; and Ad Att. 8, 11, D.

10. Nullum maius, foll. Cp. Epp. 54, 5; 91, 6; Ad Fam. 4. 7, 2, as illustrating Cicero's behaviour.

Apud illum, 'with Caesar.'

12. Video .. praefuturum, 'I see that I shall be put in charge of a camp and of certain legions.' On this sense of 'certus' = 'quidam,' cp. Forcell. As a consular, Cicero would have received a high command in Pompey's army, probably, had he not delayed too long to join him. After the battle of Pharsalus Cato urged him to take the command of the forces assembled at Corcyra. Cp. Plut. Cic. 39.

13. Dolabella noster: cp. Ep. 47, 1.

15. Perturbent .. tuam, 'disturb you so as to interfere with your recovery.'

Valetudinem, 'recovery.' Süpfle. Cp. Nägelsb. 8. 31. 'Valetudo' is a neutral word, used both of health and sickness. Tiro was now recovering from a fever. Cp. Ad Fam. 16. 11, 1.

A. Varroni. The name of this man in full would be A. Terentius Varro Murena, as he passed by adoption from the family of the Licinii Murenae into that of the Terentii Varrones. He served under Pompey in the civil wars, and was perhaps father of the Murena who was consul with Augustus in 23 B.C., and was executed for alleged conspiracy. Cp. for notices of him, Caes. Bell. Civ. 3. 19; Cic. Ad Fam. 13. 22, 1; Pro Caecina 9, 25; Drumann 4. 193; and of the son Hor. Carm. 2, 10; Dion Cassius 54, 3; Velleius 2. 91.

18. Totum te = 'te omnino;' cp. Ep. 29, 27, and Tusc. Disp. 5. 2, 5 '[philosophiae] nos .. penitus totosque tradidimus.'

tueretur: quem omnia facturum confido; recepit enim et mecum locutus est suavissime. Tu, quoniam eo tempore mecum esse non potuisti, quo ego maxime operam et fidelitatem desideravi tuam, cave festines aut committas, ut aut aeger aut hieme naviges: numquam sero te venisse putabo, si salvus veneris. Adhuc neminem videram, qui te postea vidisset quam M. Volusius, a quo tuas litteras accepi: quod non mirabar; neque enim meas puto ad te litteras tanta hieme perferri. Sed da operam, ut valeas et, si valebis, cum recte navigari poterit, tum naviges. Cicero meus in Formiano erat, Terentia et Tullia Romae. Cura, ut valeas. IIII. K. Februar. Capua.

53. To TIRO (AD FAM. XVI. 15).

DATE UNCERTAIN.

1. Aegypta has just arrived, and gives a good account of you. I am sorry, however, to hear that you are too ill to write: pray take every care of yourself. 2. P.S. Hermia has just come with a letter from you; its irregular writing does not surprise me. I send you Aegypta and a cook to wait upon you.

TULLIUS TIRONI SAL.

Aegypta ad me venit pr. Idus Apr. Is etsi mihi nuntiavit te 1
plane febri carere et belle habere, tamen, quod negavit te potuisse ad me scribere, curam mihi attulit, et eo magis, quod Hermia, quem eodem die venire oportuerat, non venerat. Incredibili sum sollicitudine de tua valetudine, qua si me liberaris, ego te omni

1. Recepit, 'he promised:' rather stronger than 'pollicitus est.' Forcell.

2. Eo tempore, foll. Probably = 'in the critical days at the beginning of this year.'

6. M. Volusius, only here mentioned apparently.

7 Quod non mirabar, foll. Cicero was not surprised that he heard so little from or about Tiro, for he thought that his own letters were much delayed on their way to Tiro.

8. Tanta hieme, 'now that it is the depth of winter.' 'Bei so tiefem Winter,' Metzg. Cp. 'multa nocte' Ad Q. F. 2. 9, 2, and Nagelsb. 70, 188. Wiel. translates 'during this stormy weather.' On the ablat. (modi), cp. Madv. 257.

9. In Formiano, 'in my villa near Formiae.' It is mentioned also Ad Att. 4. 2, 5.

TULLIUS TIRONI. As the date of this letter is uncertain and unimportant, I have inserted it here as an illustration of Cicero's care for Tiro, to whom the preceding letter was addressed.

12. Aegypta, a freedman of Cicero, mentioned Ad Att. 8. 15, 1; 12. 37. 1.

13. Belle habere. Cp. Ep. 77. 1 'minus belle habuit.'

14. Hermia: cp. Ep. 15, 12, note.

16. Sollicitudine. On the ablat., cp. Ep. 38, 3. note.

Omni cura liberabo = 'manumittam te.' Manut. There are allusions to some promise of the kind in Ad Fam. 16, 10, 2; 16. 14, 2.

cura liberabo. Plura scriberem, si iam putarem lubenter te legere posse. Ingenium tuum, quod ego maximi facio, confer ad te mihi tibique conservandum. Cura te etiam atque etiam diligenter. Vale.

2 Scripta iam epistola Hermia venit. Accepi tuam epistolam vacillantibus litterulis, nec mirum, tam gravi morbo. Ego ad te Aegyptam misi, quod nec inhumanus est et te visus est mihi diligere, ut is tecum esset, et cum eo coquum, quo uterere. Vale.

54. To ATTICUS (AD ATT. VIII. 3).
NEAR CALES, ABOUT FEB. 19, 49 B.C. (705 A.U.C.)

1. I am anxious for your advice as to what I ought to do if Pompey leaves Italy. I will set both sides of the question before you as fairly as I can. 2. Pompey's services to me, and our intimacy, seem to make it a duty to stand by him, and if I remain at Rome I must fall into the power of Caesar. His language is friendly, but how can I live without influence and with a prospect of disgrace in case of Pompey's success? 3. On the other hand, Pompey's mistakes have been many and serious, and he has never taken my advice: to omit his earlier errors, what can be worse than his present flight from Rome? 4. 'But he will recover it.' When? His measures have hitherto been ill-conceived and disastrous. I reluctantly took charge of Capua, and could mark the general apathy. 5. How can I join Pompey at this season? 6. If I stay at Rome I shall do no worse than Q. Mucius did under the tyranny of Cinna. But the 'imperium' which I retain would even then embarrass me. I hope you will not infer from all this that my choice is made, but will advise me impartially. I have a vessel ready at Caieta, and another at Brundisium. 7. I have just received news that Caesar is opposed at Corfinium by Domitius with an effective army. I do not think Pompey will desert Domitius, though his measures look suspicious. We hear reports, which I do not believe, of successes won by Afranius over Caesar's officers. I write from Formiae.

CICERO ATTICO SAL.

1 Maximis et miserrimis rebus perturbatus, cum coram tecum mihi potestas deliberandi non esset, uti tamen tuo consilio volui;

1. Si iam putarem . . posse, 'if I thought you were already well enough to read with pleasure.'

2. Confer = 'adhibe' (Forcell.), 'employ.'

6. Vacillantibus litterulis, 'with its letters written by a trembling hand,' = 'tremente manu exaratis,' Forcell. On the abl., see the preceding section.

Tam gravi morbo. On this ablat., cp. Ep. 1, 2, note, on p. 88.

7. Nec . . et. On this combination, cp. Ep. 6, 4, note on p. 45.

8. Coquum. Probably one of Cicero's slaves, who would be able to prepare proper food for an invalid.

10. Esset, epistolary tense.

deliberatio autem omnis haec est, si Pompeius Italia cedat, quod eum facturum esse suspicor, quid mihi agendum putes, et, quo facilius consilium dare possis, quid in utramque partem mihi in mentem veniat, explicabo brevi. Cum merita Pompeii summa 2
erga salutem meam familiaritasque, quae mihi cum eo est, tum ipsa rei publicae causa me adducit, ut mihi vel consilium meum cum illius consilio, vel fortuna *mea cum illius fortuna* coniungenda esse videatur. Accedit illud: si maneo et illum comitatum optimorum et clarissimorum civium desero, cadendum est in unius potestatem, qui, etsi multis rebus significat se nobis esse amicum, et ut esset, a me est—tute scis—propter suspitionem huius impendentis tempestatis multo ante provisum, tamen utrumque considerandum est, et quanta fides ei sit habenda et, si maxime exploratum sit eum nobis amicum fore, sitne viri fortis et boni civis esse in ea urbe in qua, cum summis honoribus imperiisque usus sit, res maximas gesserit, sacerdotio sit amplissimo praeditus, nomen futurus, subeundumque periculum sit, cum aliquo fore dedecore, si quando Pompeius rem publicam recuperarit. In hac 3
parte haec sunt; vide nunc, quae sint in altera: nihil actum est a Pompeio nostro sapienter, nihil fortiter; addo etiam, nihil nisi contra consilium auctoritatemque meam. Omitto illa vetera, quod istum in rem publicam ille aluit, auxit, armavit, ille legibus

1. Omnis haec est . . putes, 'is all about the question what you think I ought to do in case Pompey leaves Italy.' On the use of 'haec,' cp. Madv. 314. The arguments for accompanying Pompey begin with 'cum merita Pompeii,' and end with 'recuperarit.'

6. Consilium, 'decision.' Cp. Ep. 46 'subito consilium cepi.'

8. Illud: cp. Ep. 34, 9, note.

Illum comitatum . . civium, 'that company of good citizens' which will follow Pompey. On this use of the pronoun, cp. Madv. 485 b and c.

9. Unius, sc. Caesaris.

10. Multis rebus, 'in many relations.' Süpfle.

11. A me est . . provisum: cp. Intr. to Part II, §§ 4–6; Epp. 25, notes; 29, 12, note.

12. Utrumque refers to the clauses which follow, beginning with et . . et.

15. Esse in ea urbe . . recuperarit, 'to remain in a city in which after filling the highest posts he will be a mere shadow, and will incur the risk of being disgraced in case of Pompey's restoring the old constitution.' So Wiel. and Forcell. For this sense of 'nomen,' cp. Ad Att. 5. 15, 1 'me nomen habere duarum legionum,' and Livy 7. 29 'nomen magis quam vires.'

16. Sacerdotio = 'auguratu.' Cicero was elected augur on the death of P. Crassus, son of the triumvir, in 53 B.C. Cp. Plut. Cic. 36.

17. Cum aliquo fore dedecore, 'of being disgraced to some extent.' Would not 'ne cum al. ded. sit' be more usual? Cp. Madv. 376. The sense, however, seems plain.

18. In hac parte haec sunt, 'on this side of the question there is this to be said,' 'such are the weights in this scale.' Cp. Ep. 129, 2 'nullius partis esse.'

22. Istum, Caesarem.

Ille, Pompeius.

Ille legibus . . auctor, sc. 'fuit.' On the dat., cp. Madv. 241, Obs., and 415. The laws referred to are those of Caesar's consulship. Cp. Intr. to Part I, § 17; Ep. 10, 2, note.

per vim et contra auspicia ferendis auctor, ille Galliae ulterioris adiunctor, ille gener, ille in adoptando P. Clodio augur, ille restituendi mei quam retinendi studiosior, ille provinciae propagator, ille absentis in omnibus adiutor, idem etiam tertio consulatu, postquam esse defensor rei publicae coepit, contendit, ut decem tribuni pl. ferrent, ut absentis ratio haberetur, quod idem ipse sanxit lege quadam sua, Marcoque Marcello consuli finienti provincias Gallias Kalendarum Martiarum die restitit: sed, ut haec omittam, quid foedius, quid perturbatius hoc ab urbe discessu sive potius turpissima fuga? quae condicio non accipienda fuit potius quam relinquenda patria? malae condiciones erant; fateor,
4 sed num quid hoc peius? 'At recuperabit rem publicam.' Quando? aut quid ad eam spem est parati? Non ager Picenus amissus? Non patefactum iter ad urbem? non pecunia omnis et publica et privata adversario tradita? Denique nulla causa, nullae

1. Contra auspicia: cp. Ep. 10, 1. c. Bibulus had declared 'se servaturum de caelo,' for a great part of the year, which would render legislation irregular during that time.

Galliae . . adiunctor, 'added the Farther to the Nearer Gaul' as a part of Caesar's government. The senate made this addition (cp. Intr. to Part I, § 17), but Cicero hints that Pompey had suggested it.

2. Ille gener, sc. Caesaris.

In adoptando . . augur, 'declared as augur that he saw no obstacle to the adoption of Clodius' by Fonteius. On which, cp. Intr. to Part I, § 18.

3. Restituendi . . studiosior, 'was more earnest in promoting my recall from exile than in trying to prevent my going into exile.' Cp. for the words, Ep. 29, 14, and for the facts, Intr. to Part I, §§ 20 and 21.

Propagator, 'prolonged his tenure of' by the Lex Pompeia Licinia in 55 B.C. In this sense the word seems only to occur here.

5. Contendit . . ferrent, 'exerted himself to induce the ten tribunes to propose.' 'Contendere' = 'laborare.' Forcell.

6. Quod idem sua, 'and that very provision he sanctioned by a certain law of his own,' perhaps referring to the clause appended by Pompey to his law 'de iure magistratuum' in 52 B.C. Cp. Intr. to Part II, § 14.

7. Finienti . . die, 'when he proposed to limit Caesar's government by the first of March,' 'to fix March 1 as the last day of Caesar's government.' Cp. Ep. 34, 5 and 9. It is doubtful whether March 1, 50 or 49 B.C. is referred to. In my first edition I said 'probably the earlier date;' but I now agree with Lange (3. 374) in preferring the latter.

11. Condiciones. According to Suetonius (Iul. 29); Appian (Bell. Civ. 2. 32); and Plutarch (Caes. 31): Caesar's final offers before the beginning of hostilities in January 49 B.C. were—to surrender Transalpine Gaul and the greater part of his army at once; Cisalpine Gaul and the remainder of his army on his election to the consulship, or to give up his command if Pompey would do the same.

12. Num quid hoc peius, sc. 'esse potuit,' 'could anything be worse than this hasty surrender of the capital.'

13. Ad eam spem, 'to realize that hope.' On 'ad' with such words as 'paratum,' cp. Madv. 247 b. Obs. 6, and on the gen. parati, Ib. 285 b.

14. Pecunia omnis. The consuls in their panic had forgotten to carry away the contents of the treasury. Cp. Intr. to Part III, § 1, and Ad Att. 7. 21, 2; Ep. 71, 6, note.

15. Nulla causa: cp. Ad Att. 9. 6, 4 'causa temere instituta.' 'No definite object.' Wiel. The objects, for instance, of Pompey, Cato, and the consul Lentulus, would differ very much.

vires, nulla sedes, quo concurrant qui rem publicam defensam velint: Apulia delecta est, inanissima pars Italiae et ab impetu huius belli remotissima; fuga et maritima opportunitas visa quaeri desperatione. † In te cepi Capuam, non quo munus illud defugerem, sed in ea causa, in qua nullus esset ordinum, nullus apertus privatorum dolor, bonorum autem esset aliquis, sed hebes, ut solet, et, ut ipse sensissem, multitudo et infimus quisque propensus in alteram partem, multi mutationis rerum cupidi, dixi ipsi me nihil 5
suscepturum sine praesidio et sine pecunia; itaque habui nihil omnino negotii, quod ab initio vidi nihil quaeri praeter fugam: eam si nunc sequor, quonam? Cum illo non; ad quem cum essem profectus, cognovi, in iis locis esse Caesarem, ut tuto Luceriam venire non possem. Infero mari nobis, incerto cursu, hieme maxima navigandum est. Age iam, cum fratre an sine eo cum filio? an quo modo? in utraque enim re summa difficultas erit, summus animi dolor. Qui autem impetus illius erit in nos absentes fortunasque nostras? Acrior quam in ceterorum, quod

1. **Nulla sedes**, 'no rendezvous' or 'rallying point.'

Defensam velint. On the constr., cp. Madv. 396, Obs. 1.

2. **Delecta est**, 'has been chosen' for the assembly of our forces.

Inanissima, 'the least populous.'

Impetu, 'the onward movement.' Forcell.

3. **Fuga . . desperatione**, 'it seemed that our leaders in their desperation were seeking for an easy access to the sea, and for means of flight.' Cp. Livy 45. 30 'maritimas opportunitates.' On the personal construction of 'videor' with the infin., cp. Madv. 400 a, and Obs.

4. **In te**: 'invite' would make good sense, and has some MS. authority. Wesenb. adopts it.

Cepi, 'assumed the command at.'

Non quo . . esse solet, 'not that I wished to evade that commission, but because the cause in which I had to act was regarded with such indifference.'

8. **Cupidi**, sc. 'essent.'

On the historical allusions in the two preceding sections, cp. Intr. to Part III, §§ 1–3.

Ipsi, sc. Pompeio. If the preceding passage from **non quo** to **cupidi** be genuine, there surely should be a full stop after **cupidi**, unless, indeed, the words 'sed in ea . . pecunia' correspond to 'non quo,' foll. Wesenb. punctuates 'cupidi:'

9. **Sine praesidio**, 'without an armed force.'

10. **Quod ab initio . . fugam.** Manutius connects these words with **dixi . . pecunia**, in which case **itaque . . negotii** must be a parenthetical or subordinate clause.

11. **Eam si nunc . . quonam?** 'If I now follow that flying company, whither shall I go?' Cp. Philipp. 2. 22, 54 'exsequi cladem illam fugamque.'

Cum illo, 'sc. 'Pompeio non possum fugere.'

12. **Essem profectus**, 'had set out.' Cp. Ep. 30, 1, p. 219, l. 4.

13. **Infero mari**, 'by the western, or Tuscan sea.' On the ablat. (of the direction), cp. Madv. 274.

Incerto cursu, 'to an unknown destination.'

Hieme maxima, 'in the depth of winter.' Cp. Ep. 52, 6.

15. **In utraque re . . dolor**, 'either alternative will involve great difficulties and much suffering.' Cicero would neither wish to part from his relatives, nor to expose them to the risks of camp life.

16. **Qui autem . . nostras**, 'with what violence will Caesar behave to me and my fortunes during my absence.'

putabit fortasse in nobis violandis aliquid se habere populare. Age iam, has compedes, fasces, inquam, hos laureatos efferre ex Italia quam molestum est! Qui autem locus erit nobis tutus, ut iam placatis utamur fluctibus, ante quam ad illum venerimus?
6 qua autem aut quo, nihil scimus. At si restitero et fuerit nobis in hac parte locus, idem fecero, quod in Cinnae dominatione Philippus, quod L. Flaccus, quod Q. Mucius, quoquo modo ea res huic quidem cecidit, qui tamen ita dicere solebat, se id fore videre, quod factum est, sed malle quam armatum ad patriae moenia accedere. Aliter Thrasybulus, et fortasse melius; sed est certa quaedam illa Mucii ratio atque sententia, est illa etiam [Philippi], et, cum sit necesse, servire tempori et non amittere tempus, cum sit datum. Sed in hoc ipso habent tamen iidem fasces molestiam: sit enim nobis amicus, quod incertum est, sed sit: deferet triumphum. Non accipere, † ne periculosum sit, in-

1. In nobis . . populare, 'that he recommends himself to the populace by outrages offered to me.' This is significant as shewing that a large part of the Roman populace cherished resentment against Cicero for his treatment probably of Lentulus and perhaps of Clodius.

2. Fasces . . laureatos: cp. Ep. 46, note.

4. Ut iam placatis . . fluctibus, 'supposing that I have a calm passage.' On the conjunct., cp. Ep. 48, 1, note.

Ad illum, sc. Pompeium.

5. Qua . . aut quo, 'by what route or whither.'

Fuerit . . locus, 'if I shall be allowed a place of rest here in Italy.'

6. Quod . . Philippus, sc. 'fecit.' L. Marcius Philippus, consul in 91 B.C., repealed, in the interest of the equites, the measures of M. Livius Drusus. On Sulla's return to Italy, Philippus repaired to his camp, and was well received there. Cp. Mommsen 3. 138; 224; 331; 348.

7. L. Flaccus was the interrex who proposed a law for conferring dictatorial powers upon Sulla. Cp. De Leg. Agrar. 3. 2, 5 and 6. Mommsen (3. pp. 327; 348) identifies him with the L. Valerius Flaccus who was consul in 100 B.C.

Q. Mucius Scaevola governed the province of Asia with remarkable integrity in 98 B.C., was consul in 95 B.C., and afterwards pontifex maximus. In 82 B.C. the praetor L. Damasippus murdered him by the order of C. Marius the younger. For another notice of him, cp. Ep. 29, 26, note.

Quoquo modo . . cecidit, 'however that choice turned out for him,' indic. of an actual fact = though it turned out badly.

8. Id fore, i.e. that he would be murdered.

10. Aliter Thrasybulus, sc. 'fecit.' He left Athens on the installation of the thirty tyrants, but returned to deliver it from their sway. Cp. Xen. Hellen. 2. 3. 42; 2. 4.

Est certa quaedam . . sententia, 'the policy and resolution of Mucius is quite adequately grounded.' Hofm.

11. Est illa etiam, 'there is another also' (my own); 'illa' referring to what follows.

12. [Philippi.] Baiter is surely right in putting this word in brackets. For Cicero only six lines above has spoken of Mucius and Philippus as behaving alike, whereas he is here distinguishing between two different lines of conduct.

Et cum sit necesse . . datum, 'of yielding to circumstances as long as it is necessary, and yet not losing a chance when it is offered.' I think Cicero means that he would be more supple than Mucius in adversity, and less passive when an opportunity for action offered.

13. In hoc ipso, 'even if I behave thus.'

14. Sit enim . . amicus, 'for suppose Caesar should prove my friend.'

15. Non accipere . . ad bonos. Forcell. says that 'non' may have the force of 'nonne;' (cp. p. 319, l. 13 'non ager Pice-

vidiosum ad bonos. O rem, inquis, difficilem et inexplicabilem! atqui explicanda est. Quid enim fieri potest? Ac ne me existimaris ad manendum esse propensiorem, quod plura in eam partem verba fecerim, potest fieri, quod fit in multis quaestionibus, ut res verbosior haec fuerit, illa verior. Quam ob rem ut maxima de re aequo animo deliberanti, ita mihi des consilium velim. Navis et in Caieta est parata nobis et Brundisii. Sed ecce nuntii scribente 7
me haec ipsa noctu in Caleno, ecce litterae, Caesarem ad Corfinium, Domitium Corfinii cum firmo exercitu et pugnare cupiente. Non puto etiam hoc Gnaeum nostrum commissurum, ut Domitium relinquat, etsi Brundisium Scipionem cum cohortibus duabus praemiserat, legionem *a* Fausto conscriptam in Siciliam sibi placere a consule duci scripserat ad consules; sed turpe Domitium deseri implorantem eius auxilium. Est quaedam spes, mihi quidem non magna, sed in his locis firma, Afranium in Pyrenaeo cum Trebonio pugnasse, pulsum Trebonium, etiam Fabium tuum trans-

non amicum,' and Ep. 89, 1), and Hofm. makes ne = 'ut non,' referring to Tusc. Disp. 2. 5, 14. See also Livy 31. 7. Cp. Madv. 352. The sense will then be, 'will not my acceptance, even supposing it involve no danger, bring me into disrepute with good citizens?' Orell. proposes 'non accipere me periculosum est; accipere invidiosum;' Wesenb. 'non accipere vereor ne periculosum sit, accipere invidiosum ad bonos.' Mr. Jeans thinks it needless to insert 'vereor,' but would insert 'accipere,' before 'invidiosum.'

1. O rem . . inexplicabilem. On the acc., cp. Madv. 236. 'Hard and insoluble problem.'

2. Quid enim fieri potest? 'for what else can be done?' no third course is open. Schütz. proposes to insert 'aliter.'

3. In eam partem, 'to that end,' 'on that side.'

4. In multis quaestionibus, 'in many discussions.'

Res verbosior . . verior, 'the course last dwelt upon (that of remaining in Italy) may have more copious arguments in its favour, but the other sounder.'

7. In Caieta, 'off my estate at Caieta.' Hofm. Cp. Ad Att. 1. 4. 3 'Caietanum' . . ornabo.' 'Misenum' is similarly used for an estate, Philipp. 2. 19. 73. But as the words are followed by 'Brundisii,' may not 'in Caieta' mean merely 'in the port of Caieta?'

8. In Caleno. This estate of Cicero seems to be only mentioned here. Cp. Appendix 5, § 1.

Ad Corfinium, sc. 'esse,' is before Corfinium.' That town, situated in the territory of the Peligni, had been the capital of the Italians in the Marsic or Social war. It was now held for Pompey by L. Domitius Ahenobarbus. Cp. Ep. 51, 1; Intr. to Part III, § 2.

10. Commissurum ut, 'will be guilty of.' Cp. Ep. 48, 2, note.

11. Scipionem: cp. Ep. 1, 3, note.

12. Fausto. L. Sulla, surnamed Faustus, was a son of the dictator. He was put to death towards the close of the African campaign by Caesar's partisans. Intr. to Part IV, § 10; Bell. Afric. 95.

13. A consule, 'by one of the consuls.' Cp. Ad Att. 8. 12, A, 3.

Turpe . . deseri. On the acc. with infin. as a subject, cp. Madv. 388 a; 398 a.

15. Afranium: cp. Ep. 1, 1, note.

Cum Trebonio. C. Trebonius now held a high command in Gaul for Caesar, and afterwards directed the siege of Massilia with D. Brutus. Subsequently he joined the conspiracy of Brutus and Cassius; governed Asia for some months after Caesar's death; and was treacherously murdered by Dolabella. Cp. Intr. to Parts III, § 8; V, §§ 4; 14.

16 Fabium. C. Fabius was another of Caesar's principal officers. Orell. proposes Fadium, which Baiter adopts. But M. Fadius Gallus was then in Italy. Cp. Ad Att. 8. 12, 1.

Transisse, 'has deserted to us.' Cp. In

isse cum cohortibus, summa autem, Afranium cum magnis copiis adventare: id si est, in Italia fortasse manebitur. Ego autem, cum esset incertum iter Caesaris, quod vel ad Capuam vel ad Luceriam iturus putabatur, Leptam ad Pompeium misi *et* litteras, ipse, ne quo inciderem, reverti Formias. Haec te scire volui scripsique sedatiore animo, quam proxime scripseram, nullum meum iudicium interponens, sed exquirens tuum.

55. To ATTICUS (AD ATT. VIII. 9).

FORMIAE, FEB. 25, 49 B.C. (705 A.U.C.)

1. I am not annoyed by the publication of my letter to Caesar, and I think its language justified by the end I had in view. 2. Pompey has used expressions quite as complimentary, and your conduct, and that of many others, has been quite as equivocal as mine. 3. I wish to be at Arpinum on the 28th, and then to spend some days in my various villas. I am very glad you approve of the line of conduct I propose to follow. The clemency of Caesar, compared with Pompey's desertion of his friends, is doing our cause much harm. 4. The two Balbi both assure me that Caesar's views are moderate and pacific. I suppose Pompey may have reached Brundisium by now, but the 'monster' shews remarkable energy.

CICERO ATTICO SAL.

1 Epistolam meam quod pervolgatam scribis esse, non fero moleste: quin etiam ipse multis dedi describendam; ea enim et acciderunt iam et impendent, ut testatum esse velim, de pace quid senserim. Cum autem ad eam hortarer eum praesertim hominem, non videbar ullo modo facilius moturus, quam si id, quod cum hortarer, convenire eius sapientiae dicerem. Eam si 'admirabilem' dixi, quoniam eum ad salutem patriae hortabar, non sum veritus ne viderer adsentari, cui tali in re lubenter

Verr. 2 Act. I. 16, 40 'ad adversarios transeas;' also Ep. 71, 2. The reports to which Cicero refers were false. Cp. Intr. to Part III, § 8; Caes. Bell. Civ. 1. 37 and 40.

1. Summa autem, either 'spes est,' or 'the general import of the rumours is.'

3. Esset .. putabatur, epistolary tenses. Ad Capuam. The preposition is inserted because the neighbourhood of Capua is meant. That place and Luceria were held for Pompey, and Caesar could not count on being admitted within the walls of either. Cp. Madv. 232.

4. Leptam: cp. Ep. 27, 2, note. Et litteras = 'cum litteris.'

5. Ne quo inciderem, sc. 'in Caesarem.'

6. Proxime, 'last.' Forcell.

7. Interponens, 'expressing.' Forcell.

8. Epistolam meam. Cicero means a letter he wrote to Caesar. The passages quoted from it in this letter are found in Ep. 64; but if that be really the letter here referred to, there is some confusion about the dates.

9. Quin etiam, 'nay, even.'

10. Testatum: cp. Ep. 29, 20, note.

13. Quod cum hortarer, 'which I advised him to do.' Cp. Ep. 38, 2, note.

me ad pedes abiecissem. Qua autem est 'aliquid impertias temporis,' non est de pace, sed de me ipso et de meo officio ut aliquid cogitet; nam quod testificor me expertem belli fuisse, etsi id re perspectum est, tamen eo scripsi, quo in suadendo plus auctoritatis haberem, eodemque pertinet, quod causam eius probo. Sed quid haec nunc? utinam aliquid profectum esset! 2
ne ego istas litteras in contione recitari velim, si quidem ille ipse ad eundem scribens in publico proposuit epistolam illam, in qua est 'pro tuis rebus gestis amplissimis.' Amplioribusne quam suis, quam Africani? Ita tempus ferebat; si quidem etiam vos duo tales ad quintum miliarium,—quid nunc ipsum unde se recipienti, quid agenti, quid acturo? quanto autem ferocius ille causae suae confidet, cum vos, cum vestri similes non modo frequentes, sed laeto voltu gratulantes viderit? 'Num igitur pec-

1. **Qua autem est . . cogitet**, 'but where the words "bestow some time" occur, I meant "on thoughts—not of peace but—of myself and of my obligations to Pompey."' To entreat any citizen 'to bestow some time' on thoughts of peace would be humiliating to Cicero. The words **de pace** may be taken differently; 'that does not refer to peace.' Wesenb. has 'quod autem est,' 'whereas I say.' With the use of 'est' in l. 1, cp. Ep. 37, 3, p. 257.

3. **Nam quod . . haberem**, 'for as to my protest that I have taken no part in the war, though that rests on good evidence (and therefore I might mention it simply for my own sake), my object in making it was to give more weight to my recommendation (of peace).' On this sense of 'nam,' cp. Ep. 9, 8, note.

5. **Eodemque pertinet .. probo**, 'and the same is the object of my saying that I approve his plea.' Cp. Ep. 64, 2. For this sense of 'pertinet,' cp. In Verr. 2 Act. 5. 10, 25 'summa illuc pertinet ut sciatis.' The expressions of Cicero's letter to Caesar had apparently been criticised as too adulatory in tone. A more serious charge might be based on the difference of its language from that of the two letters to Pompey, Ad Att. 8. 11 B and D.

6. **Quid haec nunc**, sc. 'commemoro.'

7. **Velim.** The pres. conj. is used of things still possible, where in English we should use the imperf. Cp. Ep. 38, 2, note.

Si quidem, 'seeing that.'

Ille ipse, Pompeius.

8. **In publico proposuit** = 'promulgavit' (Forcell.), 'published.'

9. **In qua est**, 'in which the words occur.' This letter was an answer of Pompey's to Caesar's demands (cp. Ep. 52, 3): it is mentioned, apparently, Ad Att. 7. 17, 2, and was drawn up by Sestius.

10. **Suis**, sc. Pompeii. Cicero cavils at the use of the superlative **amplissimis**, apparently. Cp. Ad Att. 7. 26, 2 'at quibus verbis! "pro tuis rebus gestis amplissimis."'

Ita tempus ferebat, 'such language was required by circumstances.' 'Ferre = requirere postulare.' Forcell.

Si .. vos duo tales .. miliarium, 'if two such men as you and Sex. Peducaeus think of going as far as the fifth milestone to meet Caesar.' For the coupling together of Atticus and Peducaeus, cp. Ad Att. 7. 13, 3; 7. 14, 3; 7. 17, 1.

11. **Quid nunc ipsum**, 'why just now?' Cp. Madv. 487, Obs. 1.

Unde se recipienti, sc. Caesari, 'considering whence he is returning.' The best MS. has apparently 'quod ad nunc ipsum unde se recipienti.' Boot's suggestion, adopted by Baiter, is 'quid nunc ipsum de se recipienti,' 'what pledges is Caesar willing to take' as to his future conduct? 'Unde' seems, however, to make good sense. Caesar was returning from a victory won over his countrymen. Wesenb. suggests 'qum,' sc. 'Romam' for 'quod' or 'quid' before 'nunc ipsum.' If 'quid' and 'unde' be retained there should I think be a comma after 'ipsum.'

12. **Ille**, Caesar.

14. **Frequentes**, 'thronging to meet him.'

Num igitur peccamus? Atticus is supposed to ask.

camus?' Minime vos quidem; sed tamen signa conturbantur, quibus voluntas a simulatione distingui posset. Quae vero senatus
2 consulta video? sed apertius, quam proposueram. Ego Arpini volo esse pridie Kal., deinde circum villulas nostras errare, quas visurum me postea desperavi. Εὐγενῆ tua consilia et tamen pro temporibus non incauta mihi valde probantur. Lepido quidem—nam fere συνδιημερεύομεν, quod gratissimum illi est—numquam placuit ex Italia exire, Tullo multo minus; crebro enim illius litterae ab aliis ad nos commeant. Sed me illorum sententiae minus movebant; minus multa dederant illi rei publicae pignora; tua me hercule auctoritas vehementer movet; adfert enim et reliqui temporis recuperandi rationem et praesentis tuendi. Sed, obsecro te, quid hoc miserius quam alterum plausus in foedissima causa quaerere, alterum offensiones in optima? alterum existimari conservatorem inimicorum, alterum desertorem amicorum? et mehercule quamvis amemus Gnaeum nostrum, ut et facimus et debemus, tamen hoc, quod talibus viris

1. Minime vos quidem. Cicero means that he had no right to reproach them, though in another place he had said that as much would be expected from them as from the noblest. Cp. Ep. 48, 3. In another passage (Ad Att. 7. 17, 1) he remarks ironically, that they might fairly be angry with Pompey, as the war had caused a great depreciation of property.

Conturbantur, 'are confused.'

2. Quibus .. distingui posset, 'which might enable us to distinguish men's real from their pretended sentiments.'

Quae vero senatus consulta. I cannot find an account of any decrees passed between Pompey's departure from Rome and Caesar's arrival there. But probably they were ambiguous and timid.

3. Apertius, sc. 'scribo.'

4. Pridie Kal., sc. Mart.

Quas .. desperavi, 'which I despaired of ever visiting again.' Probably when Caesar crossed the Rubicon Cicero feared confiscation.

5. Εὐγενῆ, 'generous.' Γενναῖον is more common in this sense; but cp. Soph. Ant. 38; Philoct. 874.

6. Lepido. M'. Aemilius Lepidus Livianus was consul in 66 B.C., when Cicero was praetor.

7. συνδιημερεύομεν, 'pass our days together.' The word occurs Arist. Rhet. 2. 4.

8. Tullo. A L. Volcatius Tullus was consul in 66 B.C., and another was praetor in 46 B.C., and consul in 33 B.C. Cicero probably refers to the former.

Crebro enim .. commeant, 'I often have letters of Tullus forwarded to me by people to whom he writes.'

10. Movebant, epistolary tense.

11. Pignora, 'pledges of attachment.' Cicero's past services were pledges for his future conduct. Cp. In Cat. 4. 5. 9 'habemus .. a C. Caesare .. sententiam tamquam obsidem .. voluntatis.'

Tua .. auctoritas. Atticus advised Cicero not to be in a hurry to leave Italy. Cp. Ep. 63, 6.

12. Reliqui temporis .. tuendi, 'of keeping what I have now, and of recovering in future what I have lost.' Metzg. For 'tempus' used in this sense, cp. Ep. 99, 3.

13. Alterum plausus .. in optima. On the acc. and inf. as a subject, cp. Ep. 54, 7, note, p. 321. Caesar's vigour and moderation had won general applause (see Ep. 59, 2; Caes. Bell. Civ. 1. 23), while Pompey was blamed for not marching to the aid of Domitius at Corfinium. Cp. Ad Att. 8. 7, 1.

14. Offensiones quaerere, 'to incur unpopularity.' Cp. Livy 25. 6 'ignominia quaereretur.'

15. Conservatorem, especially at Corfinium. Cp. Intr. to Part III, § 2.

17. Talibus viris. Domitius and his comrades at Corfinium, among whom was

non subvenit, laudare non possum; nam sive timuit, quid ignavius? sive, ut quidam putant, meliorem suam causam illorum caede fore putavit, quid iniustius? sed haec omittamus; augemus enim dolorem retractando. VI. Kal. vesperi Balbus minor ad 4
me venit, occulta via currens ad Lentulum consulem, missu Caesaris, cum litteris, cum mandatis, cum promissione provinciae, Romam ut redeat, cui persuaderi posse non arbitror, nisi erit conventus. Idem aiebat nihil malle Caesarem, quam ut Pompeium adsequeretur—id credo—et rediret in gratiam: id non credo et metuo ne omnis haec clementia ad † unam illam crudelitatem colligatur. Balbus quidem maior ad me scribit nihil malle Caesarem quam principe Pompeio sine metu vivere: tu puto haec credis. Sed, cum haec scribebam v. Kalend., Pompeius iam Brundisium venisse poterat: expeditus enim antecesserat legiones XI. *Kal.* Luceria. Sed hoc τέρας horribili vigilantia, celeritate, diligentia est. Plane quid futurum sit nescio.

Cicero's friend P. Lentulus Spinther. Of Domitius himself Cicero had no good opinion. Cp. Ad Att. 8. 1, 3 'quorum nemo nec stultior est quam L. Domitius.' This charge against Pompey seems groundless; he had only two legions of doubtful fidelity, and some raw levies to oppose to Caesar's veterans. Cp. Ep. 51, 2.

2. Meliorem .. fore putavit. Pompey might expect to gain in two ways: by the horror which cruelty on Caesar's part would excite, and by the removal of an impracticable partisan in Domitius. But the insinuation that he contemplated such a result seems simply malignant.

4. Retractando, 'by handling it anew,' 'by recurring to his cause.' Cp. the use of 'manus adferre,' Ep. 16, 2, note.

vi. Kal., sc. Mart., = 'Feb. 24.'

Balbus minor. Nephew and namesake of the better-known Balbus, mentioned Ep. 27, 2. The nephew shewed great pride and cruelty as quaestor in Baetica after Caesar's death. Cp. Ad Fam. 10. 32, 1–3.

6. Cum promissione provinciae. Caesar might promise to use his influence to secure for Lentulus the administration of a lucrative province, and, as Lentulus was much embarrassed (see Ep. 80, 6; Caes. Bell. Civ. 1. 4), such an offer would be very grateful to him.

7. Ut redeat, 'on condition of his return.' Cp. Ep. 54, 5, note.

Nisi erit conventus, sc. Lentulus. Cp. Ad Att. 10. 4, 11 'opus fuit Hirtio convento.'

8. Ut .. adsequeretur. Caesar might wish to overtake Pompey in order to bring him to an engagement, Cicero suggests. Balbus probably meant that he wished for a *friendly interview*.

10. Ne omnis haec .. colligatur, 'lest Caesar be acquiring all this reputation for clemency with a view to the one act of cruelty he contemplates,' i.e. the execution of Pompey, which suspicion seems to have been groundless. 'Sullanam' and 'Cinnanam' have been suggested as emendations for 'unam.' For 'colligere clementiam,' cp. De Amic. 17. 61 'benevolentiam colligere;' De Legg. 1. 19. 50 'rumorem bonum colligere.' 'Clementia' seems to mean 'a *reputation* for clemency.'

12. Principe Pompeio. These words are not used I think in a technical sense, and merely mean 'while Pompey is the chief man in the state,' 'under the pre-eminence of Pompey.'

13. Puto (ironical), 'I suppose.' Forcell.

15. Legiones. The two legions which he had recalled from Caesar (see Ep. 48, 2, note), and others of recruits. He crossed the Adriatic with five (cp. Intr. to Part III, § 2, note 16).

τέρας, 'monster.' Not apparently used quite in this sense in classical Greek.

56. To ATTICUS (AD ATT. VIII. 11).

FORMIAE, FEB. 27, (BAITER) 49 B.C. (705 A.U.C.)

1. I am not so much agitated as you suppose, and spend all my time in studying the portrait of a statesman drawn in my work on the Commonwealth. 2. Pompey is not such a man: he only cares for sovereignty, and intends to assail Italy with the forces of the East, and to rule like Sulla. If he and Caesar had desired it, a peaceful settlement was quite possible. 3. I give you, as you requested, my views of the future. We neutrals have to dread the vengeance of both parties. 4. Italy will next summer be the scene of a ruinous struggle, and I see no topic of consolation. 5. Caesar is well satisfied with me, and is anxious to persuade the consul Lentulus to stay in Italy. 6. I send you two hasty letters from Pompey, with my replies. 7. I am anxious to know the result of Caesar's march to Brundisium. Let me hear what good citizens say at Rome, and send me the book of Demetrius of Magnesia, upon concord.

CICERO ATTICO SAL.

1 Quod me magno animi motu perturbatum putas, sum equidem, sed non tam magno quam tibi fortasse videor; levatur enim omnis cura, cum aut constitit consilium aut cogitando nihil explicatur; lamentari autem licet. Illud tamen totos dies; sed vereor ne, nihil cum proficiam, etiam dedecori sim studiis ac litteris nostris. Consumo igitur omne tempus considerans, quanta vis sit illius viri, quem nostris libris satis diligenter, ut tibi quidem videmur, expressimus. Tenesne igitur, moderatorem illum rei publicae quo referre velimus omnia? nam sic quinto, ut opinor, in libro loquitur Scipio: 'ut enim guber-

1. Quod me . . putas, 'as for your thinking.' Cp. Ep. 26, 2, p. 182.

3. Cum aut constitit . . explicatur, 'when one has either come to a fixed decision, or can do no good by deliberating.' Cp. Billerb., Wiel. On the tenses, cp. Madv. 335 b. Obs. 1; and on the mood, Ep. 44, 7, note.

4. Illud tamen, either 'facio,' sc. 'lamentor,' or, referring to the following words, supp. 'itero,' 'I keep repeating for whole days the following words,' sc. sed vereor . . nostris, which Orell. marks as a quotation. Boot removes the full stop at 'licet' and substitutes 'quidem' for 'tamen.' Madvig (Advers. Crit. 2. 236) also suggests 'quidem.'

5. Ne, nihil cum proficiam etiam . . . sim, 'lest since I do no good, I may even be a disgrace,' i.e. not merely useless, but a scandal.

7. Quanta vis sit . . expressimus, 'how great is the nature, or character, of the statesman whom I have described carefully enough, as you think, in my book on the Commonwealth.'

8. Ut tibi . . videmur: cp. Ep. 54, 4, note, p. 320.

Tenesne igitur . . omnia? 'Do you remember what I would have the statesman already referred to make the standard of his whole conduct?' For this sense of 'teneo,' cp. Virg. Ecl. 9. 45 'numeros memini si verba tenerem;' and of referre, Cic. De Leg. 1. 1. 5 'cum in illa ad veritatem . . . referantur . . pleraque.' The passage Cicero quotes from the 'Commonwealth' is only preserved here.

9. Nam = γάρ, 'you may remember, for.'

natori cursus secundus, medico salus, imperatori victoria, sic huic moderatori rei publicae beata civium vita proposita est, ut opibus firma, copiis locuples, gloria ampla, virtute honesta sit; huius enim operis maximi inter homines atque optimi illum esse perfectorem volo.' Hoc Gnaeus noster cum antea num- 2
quam, tum in hac causa minime cogitavit: dominatio quaesita ab utroque est, non id actum, beata et honesta civitas ut esset. Nec vero ille urbem reliquit, quod eam tueri non posset, nec Italiam, quod ea pelleretur, sed hoc a primo cogitavit, omnes terras, omnia maria movere, reges barbaros incitare, gentes feras armatas in Italiam adducere, exercitus conficere maximos. Genus illud Sullani regni iam pridem appetitur, multis, qui una sunt, cupientibus. An censes nihil inter eos convenire, nullam pactionem fieri potuisse? hodie potest; sed neutri σκοπὸς est ille, ut nos beati simus: uterque regnare volt. Haec a te invitatus 3
breviter exposui; voluisti enim me, quid de his malis sentirem, ostendere. Προθεσπίζω igitur, noster Attice, non hariolans, ut illa, cui nemo credidit, sed coniectura prospiciens:

iamque mari magno . . . .

Non multo, inquam, secus possum vaticinari; tanta malorum impendet Ἰλιάς. Atque hoc nostra gravior est causa, qui domi

2. **Proposita est, ut . . honesta sit,** 'is set before him as his object, viz. that their life (or the commonwealth) be secured in respect of power' or (Jeans) 'in their possessions.' 'Rich in material resources, distinguished by fame, and ennobled by the practice of virtue.' On the ablatives, cp. Madv. 253.

5. **Perfectorem,** 'author.' Cp. De Orat. 1. 60, 257 'perfectorem dicendi esse ac magistrum.'

6. **In hac causa,** 'on this question,' i.e. his dispute with Caesar.

8. **Ille urbem reliquit,** sc. Pompeius.

Quod . . non posset: cp. for the mood, Ep. 28, 7, note.

10. **Movere,** 'to agitate,' 'ransack' for men and ships, or perhaps 'terras' and 'maria' mean 'land and sea forces.' Cicero had probably received information from Luceria of the language held there in Pompey's councils. Cp. infra, § 4; and Ep. 59, 2 'nescio quas eius Lucerias horreant;' C. Cassius wrote to Cicero from Luceria to advise him to be neutral. Cp. Ep. 83, 4.

12. **Genus illud Sullani regni . . . appetitur,** 'he has long been desiring a sovereignty like that of Sulla.' Cp. Ep. 61, 4.

13. **Eos,** Caesar and Pompey.

Convenire, sc. 'potuisse,' 'do you think that no agreement could have been made before this? one might be made even now.'

14. **σκοπός:** cp. Ep. 11, 1.

17. **Προθεσπίζω,** cp. Aesch. Prom. Vinct. 219.

Hariolans, 'under divine inspiration.'

18. **Illa,** Cassandra. Cicero means that he does not claim inspiration, but only political sagacity.

19. **Iamque mari magno classis cita**
Texitur: exitium examen rapit:
Adveniet, fera velivolantibus
Navibus complebit manus litora.

The passage is given De Divin. 1. 31, 67, and appears to be from a tragedy on the fall of Troy, entitled Alexander, by Ennius. Boot.

20. **Non . . secus,** 'not very differently from Cassandra.'

Malorum . . Ἰλιάς, 'as many woes as she foretold for her country.' Cp. Demosth. De Fals. Leg. 387 κακῶν Ἰλιάς.

sumus, quam illorum, qui una transierunt, quod illi alterum
4 metuunt, nos utrumque. Cur igitur, inquis, remansimus? vel
tibi paruimus vel non occurrimus vel hoc fuit rectius. Conculcari, inquam, miseram Italiam videbis proxima aestate † aut
utriusque in mancipiis ex omni genere collectis, nec tam *pro-
scri*ptio pertimescenda, quae Luceriae multis sermonibus denun-
tiata esse dicitur, quam † universam interitus: tantas in confli-
gendo utriusque vires video futuras. Habes coniecturam meam;
tu autem consolationis fortasse aliquid exspectasti: nihil invenio,
5 nihil fieri potest miserius, nihil perditius, nihil foedius. Quod
quaeris, quid Caesar ad me scripserit, quod saepe, gratissimum
sibi esse quod quierim, oratque in eo ut perseverem. Balbus
minor haec eadem mandat. Iter autem eius erat ad Lentulum
consulem cum litteris Caesaris praemiorumque promissis, si
Romam revertisset; verum, cum habeo rationem dierum, ante
6 puto tramissurum, quam potuerit conveniri. Epistolarum Pompeii duarum, quas ad me misit, neglegentiam meamque in rescri-
bendo diligentiam volui tibi notam esse: earum exempla ad te
7 misi. Caesaris hic per Apuliam ad Brundisium cursus quid
efficiat, exspecto: utinam aliquid simile Parthicis rebus! Simul

1. Qui una transierunt, 'who crossed the sea with Pompey.'

Alterum, 'only one of the combatants.'

2. Vel tibi paruimus . . rectius, 'I answer, either because I took your advice, or because I failed to meet Pompey, or because this was really the best course.'

3. Conculcari . . mancipiis. 'Ab utriusque mancipiis' perhaps makes sense with the slightest departure from the best MS., and is the reading of one early edition. Orell. suggests 'utrimque mancipiis,' which would give the same sense. 'You will see unhappy Italy trodden under foot next summer, and by slaves on both sides,' i.e. by men fighting for rival pretenders. Tacitus (Ann. 1. 2) says that after the battle of Philippi, 'nulla iam publica arma,' i.e. there were only struggles of individuals for empire. Wesenb. suggests 'et quasi utriusque vi mancipiis.'

5. Ex omni genere collectis. Caesar had enlisted Gauls. Pompey hoped to draw large forces from the East. Intr. to Part III, § 9; Appendix 7.

6. Multis sermonibus, 'in many speeches of Pompey and his friends.'

7. Universam, 'universae' (Klotz), sc. 'Italiae;' or 'in universum' (Kayser) would make good sense.

10. Perditius. This comparative seems to be uncommon; but cp. Ep. 105, 1.

11. Quod saepe, 'the same as often before.'

13. Haec eadem mandat. The best MS. has 'mandata,' sc. 'fert.' 'Gives me the same advice.'

Ad Lentulum: see Ep. 55, 4.

14. Si . . revertisset. On the tense, depending on 'erat,' cp. Madv. 379.

15. Cum habeo rationem . . conveniri, 'when I count the days, I think Lentulus will cross the sea with Pompey before Balbus can possibly have met him.'

16. Epistolarum . . duarum. A and C appended to this letter in the complete editions.

17. Neglegentiam, 'carelessness.' Probably Cicero refers to the haste and brevity with which the two notes referred to were written.

19. Cursus, 'hasty march.'

Quid efficiat. For the tense, cp. Madv. 378; Ep. 50, 3, note.

20. Parthicis rebus. Cicero may refer to the recklessness and disaster of Crassus,

aliquid audiero, scribam ad te: tu ad me velim bonorum sermones; Romae frequentes esse dicuntur. Scio equidem te in publicum non prodire, sed tamen audire te multa necesse est. Memini librum tibi adferri a Demetrio Magnete ad te missum [scio] *περὶ ὁμονοίας*. Eum mihi velim mittas. Vides, quam causam mediter.

67. To ATTICUS (AD ATT. VIII. 13).

FORMIAE, MARCH 1, 49 B.C. (705 A.U.C.)

1. The weakness of my eyes compels me to employ a secretary, and I write briefly, having nothing to say. If Caesar overtakes Pompey in Italy, there is some chance of peace. The moderation and watchfulness of Caesar have made a profound impression, 2. and the country people whom I meet care for nothing but their private interests. The mistakes of our friends have been most pernicious to the common cause.

CICERO ATTICO SAL.

Lippitudinis meae signum tibi sit librarii manus et eadem 1
causa brevitatis, etsi nunc quidem quod scriberem nihil erat: omnis exspectatio nostra erat in nuntiis Brundisinis. Si nactus hic esset Gnaeum nostrum, spes dubia pacis, sin ille ante tramisisset, exitiosi belli metus. Sed videsne, in quem hominem

or perhaps to the sudden disappearance of the Parthians from Syria, owing to the intrigues of Bibulus. Cp. Ep. 42, 3. Manutius thinks that the allusion is to the slight results produced by Parthian invasions in general, the invaders often disappearing after making great demonstrations.

1. Sermones, sc. 'scribas.'

2. Frequentes esse, sc. 'bonos.'

In publicum, 'into the streets' = 'in locum publicum.' Forcell.

4. Tibi adferri, 'I remember the sending of it to you' as a present circumstance. Cp. Madv. 408 b, Obs. 2.

A Demetrio. Demetrius of Magnesia, a rhetorician, who was a contemporary and friend of Cicero and Atticus. Cp. Ad Att. 4. 11, 2; 8. 12, 6; 9. 9, 2. He also wrote *περὶ ὁμωνύμων*. Cp. Diog. Laert. 1. 11, 38. The work here referred to was probably an *ἐπίδειξις* on concord, and may be referred to Ad Att. 4. 11, 2.

5. Quam causam mediter, sc. 'tueri.' 'what part I intended to play.' Cicero might find materials in the work of Demetrius for an argument in favour of peace between Pompey and Caesar.

MARCH 1. Cicero, Ad Att. 8. 14, 1, speaks of himself as writing 'epistolas quotidianas.' Now Ad Att. 8. 16 was written on March 4.

7. Lippitudinis, an inflammation of the eyes, generally with rheum.

Manus, 'handwriting.' If Cicero's eyes had not been weak he would have written an autograph letter.

Eadem causa, sc. 'lippitudo.'

9. Omnis exspectatio . . Brundisinis, 'I await with undivided interest the news we may expect from Brundisium.' On the use of an adjective in such a sense, cp. Madv. 300 c, Obs. 3.

Si nactus hic . . metus, 'If Caesar has overtaken Pompey, there is some hope of peace; if not, a ruinous war is to be feared.' The plup. 'nactus esset' follows 'erat,' to be supplied with 'spes' as an epistolary tense. 'Nactus' is not very common in this sense.

11. In quem hominem inciderit res publica, 'what a formidable man the State has fallen in with' or 'into the hands of.' The word is more common in such phrases as 'incidere in insidias,' 'incidere in manus

incident res publica? quam acutum, quam vigilantem, quam paratum? si mehercule neminem occiderit nec cuiquam quicquam ademerit, ab iis, qui eum maxime timuerant, maxime

2 diligetur. Multum mecum municipales homines loquuntur, multum rusticani: nihil prorsus aliud curant nisi agros, nisi villulas, nisi nummulos suos. Et vide, quam conversa res sit: illum, quo antea confidebant, metuunt, hunc amant, quem timebant. Id quantis nostris peccatis vitiisque evenerit, non possum sine molestia cogitare. Quae autem impendere putarem, scripseram ad te, et iam tuas litteras exspectabam.

58. The elder BALBUS to CICERO (AD ATT. VIII. 15 A.)

Probably written about March 1, 49 B.C. (705 A.U.C.)

1. I entreat you, Cicero, to do your best to bring about an understanding between Pompey and Caesar. 2. I am much indebted to you for dissuading the consul Lentulus from leaving Italy. I wish he had been more accessible to me before: but even now, if he will be guided by you and return to Rome, all may go well. 3. I am sure you will approve of Caesar's behaviour at Corfinium, and glad that you were pleased by my nephew's visit. I am confident that Caesar will fulfil all promises made by himself, or by my nephew on his behalf.

BALBUS CICERONI IMP. SAL.

1 Obsecro te, Cicero, suscipe curam et cogitationem dignissimam tuae virtutis, ut Caesarem et Pompeium perfidia hominum distrac-

ridiculus.' But cp. Ep. 68, 6 'in vituperatores meos incidimus.'

1. Si mehercule . . ademerit, 'if he puts no one to death and extorts nothing from any one,' as we may anticipate from his conduct hitherto.

3. Qui eum . . timuerant. The country people. Cp. Ep. 47, 4.

5. Rusticani, 'country proprietors,' elsewhere, apparently, identified with the municipales, or citizens of the municipal towns. Cp. In Verr. 2 Act. 1. 48, 127.

Villulas, 'their paltry farms.' Cp. Ad Att. 8. 12 B, 2, where Pompey suggests that Domitius may be hampered by men, 'qui te impediant ut villas suas servent.'

6. Quam conversa res sit, 'how the state of affairs is changed.' The best MS. has 'est,' which might perhaps be defended by a passage in the oration Pro Sex. Rosc. Amer. 43, 125 'hoc videamus; eius hominis bona qua ratione venierunt.'

8. Nostris, 'on our side.' Cicero probably refers to the hasty rupture with Caesar; the abandonment of Rome; and the violent language of the friends of Pompey. Intr. to Part III, §§ 1-4.

9. Autem, 'however,' though my reflections are so painful.

Putarem. On the mood, cp. p. 300, note on l. 3.

Scripseram, 'I wrote.' Ep. 56 is the letter referred to.

Balbus. Cp. Ep. 27, 2, note.

12. Tuae virtutis. The ablative is much more common with 'dignus.' See, however, Pro Balbo 1. 5, where some MSS. have 'dignum rei videtur.'

Distractos, 'torn asunder.' Antony charged Cicero with fostering this estrangement. Cp. Philipp. 2. 9. 23; 2. 10, 24.

tos rursus in pristinam concordiam reducas. Crede mihi Caesarem non solum fore in tua potestate, sed etiam maximum
beneficium te sibi dedisse iudicaturum, si huc te reiicis. Velim
idem Pompeius faciat, qui ut adduci tali tempore ad ullam condicionem possit, magis opto quam spero; sed, cum constiterit
et timere desierit, tum incipiam non desperare tuam auctoritatem plurimum apud eum valituram. Quod Lentulum [consulem] 2
meum voluisti hic remanere, Caesari gratum, mihi vero gratissimum medius fidius fecisti; nam illum tanti facio, ut non Caesarem magis diligam; qui si passus esset nos secum, ut consue-
veramus, loqui et non se totum etiam et etiam ab sermone
nostro avertisset, minus miser, quam sum, essem. Nam cave
putes hoc tempore plus me quemquam cruciari, quod eum, quem
ante me diligo, video in consulatu quidvis potius esse quam
consulem. Quod si voluerit tibi obtemperare et nobis de Caesare
credere et consulatum reliquum Romae peragere, incipiam sperare
etiam consilio senatus, auctore te, illo relatore, Pompeium et
Caesarem coniungi posse. Quod si factum erit me satis vixisse
putabo. Factum Caesaris de Corfinio totum te probaturum scio: 3
quo modo in eius modi re, commodius cadere non potuit quam

2. **Fore in tua potestate**, 'will place himself at your disposal,' will comply with your wishes in all things.' Cp. Ad Fam. 5. 4. 2, where Cicero promises Metellus Nepos 'omnibus in rebus me fore in tua potestate.'

3. **Si huc te reiicis** = 'si intendis animum in hanc rem' (Forcell.), 'if you devote your thoughts to this end.'

5. **Magis opto quam spero . . ut**: cp. Madv. 372 a, and Caes. Bell. Civ. 3. 85 'hoc sperans ut . . uteretur.'

Cum constiterit. 'Cum' almost = 'si,' 'if he halts anywhere.' This sense of 'cum' may be explained by supposing an ellipse, 'when he halts,'—which is not very likely, —'then,' and not till then.

7. **Lentulum**. The consul L. Lentulus. V. infra.

8. **Meum**. In another passage, Ad Att. 9. 7 B, 2, Balbus speaks of having received great favours from Lentulus.

Hic, sc. 'in Italy.'

10. **Qui**, Lentulus.

13. **Plus me quemquam . . quam consulem**, 'that any one suffers more than I do at seeing a man whom I love almost more than myself, behave during his consulship as anything rather than a consul.'

15. **Tibi obtemperare**: cp. supr. l. 7 'quod Lentulum . . voluisti hic remanere.'

16. **Peragere**, 'to pass,' 'complete.' Cp. De Senect. 19, 70 'peragenda fabula est;' Virg. Aen. 4. 653 'cursumque peregi.'

17. **Etiam consilio . . posse**, 'that even with the sanction of the senate, at your suggestion, and with Lentulus to put the question, Pompey and Caesar may be reconciled.'

18. **Posse** is often used where we might expect a future. Cp. Madv. 410, Obs. 1. This is different from the usage noticed p. 26, note on l. 3.

19. **Totum**. Manutius refers this to the whole of Caesar's operations at Corfinium, not merely to his treatment of the prisoners made there. He argues that Cicero might be pleased to hear that Caesar's promptitude had prevented the pitched battle and consequent bloodshed which must probably have taken place if Domitius had joined Pompey with his forces.

20. **Quo modo in eius modi re** = 'ut in tali re,' 'considering the circumstances.'

Cadere, 'turn out.' I cannot find a precisely similar use of this verb, without a subject. Cp. Epp. 33. 2; 54. 6; Madv. 218 b and d, Obs. 2.

ut res sine sanguine confieret. Balbi mei tuique adventu delectatum te valde gaudeo: is quaecumque tibi de Caesare dixit quaeque Caesar scripsit, scio, re tibi probabit, quaecumque fortuna eius fuerit, verissime scripsisse.

59. TO ATTICUS (AD ATT. VIII. 16).

MARCH 4, 49 B.C. (705 A.U.C.)

1. I have made arrangements for everything except a secret and safe journey to the upper sea; I must get away soon to avoid detention. Not that I am attracted by Pompey, whose generalship is no better than his statesmanship, but I fear public opinion, though foolishly. 2. Caesar is the idol of the country towns, and Pompey's threats have caused general alarm. If Caesar, after expelling Pompey from Italy, returns to Rome by the Appian way, I shall go to Arpinum.

CICERO ATTICO.

1 Omnia mihi provisa sunt praeter occultum et tutum iter ad mare superum; hoc enim mari uti non possumus hoc tempore anni: illuc autem, quo spectat animus et quo res vocat, qua veniam? cedendum enim est celeriter, ne forte qua re impediar atque alliger. Nec vero ille me ducit, qui videtur, quem ego hominem ἀπολιτικώτατον omnium iam ante cognoram, nunc vero

Quam ut . . confieret, 'than that the affair should be settled without bloodshed.' For confieret, cp. Caes. Bell. Gall. 7. 58; Virg. Aen. 4. 116; and Ep. 98, 1, note. On the conjunct. after 'cadere,' see Ep. 33, 2. On the facts, cp. Intr. to Part III, § 2.

1. Balbi mei tuique. The younger Balbus. Cp. Ep. 55. 4, note.

2. Quaecumque tibi . . dixit. On the indic., describing an idea which is left indefinite, cp. Madv. 362 a.

3. Scio, re tibi probabit . . scripsisse, 'I know, he will prove to you by his acts, he has written most truly.' The words 're tibi probabit' may be explained either as a parenthesis, or by the omission of a copulative conjunction, for which cp. Madv. 434. It would be more usual to insert 'se' before 'scripsisse;' but cp. De Nat. Deor. 1. 34, 96 'ducebit . . ut . . vinceremur . . sic animi praestantia vinci;' also Madv. 401. Cicero seems to have been annoyed by the tone of this letter, and to have distressed Balbus. Cp. Ad Att. 8. 15. 3 'Balbi Cornelii litterarum exemplum . . misi ad te, ut meam vicem dolerem, cum me derideri videres.'

6. Superum, as often, the Adriatic.

Enim, 'I say the upper, for.'

Hoc tempore. The lower sea, apparently, was unsafe in spring. Cp. Ad Att. 10. 17. 3 'nunc quidem aequinoctium nos moratur.'

7. Illuc, to Brundisium. Cp. § 2.

Quo spectat . . vocat, 'whither my feeling inclines, and I am invited by the state of the case.'

Qua, 'by what route.'

9. Alliger, 'be hampered.' Cp. Pro Cluent. 55, 151 'populum Romanum . . alligare novo quaestionis genere.'

Nec . . ducit . . ἀστρατηγικώτατον, 'I am not, however, attracted by Pompey, whom I knew long ago to be nothing of a statesman, and now have discovered to be nothing of a general.' 'Ducere' is not often used in the active in this sense. But cp. Hor. Sat. 2. 2, 35 'ducit te species.' The two Greek superlatives seem to be found only here. With Cicero's complaints of Pompey's generalship, cp. Epp. 48, 1; 54. 4; 55. 3, notes.

etiam *ἀστρατηγικώτατον*. Non me igitur is ducit, sed sermo
hominum, qui ad me *a* Philotimo scribitur; is enim me ab optimatibus ait conscindi. Quibus optimatibus, di boni! qui nunc
quo modo occurrunt! quo modo autem se venditant Caesari!
Municipia vero deum, nec simulant, ut cum de illo aegroto vota
faciebant. Sed plane, quicquid mali hic Pisistratus non fecerit, 2
tam gratum est, quam si alium facere prohibuerit; *hunc* propitium
sperant, illum iratum putant. Quas fieri censes *ἀπαντήσεις* ex
oppidis! quos honores! 'Metuunt' inquies. Credo sed mehercule
illum magis: huius insidiosa clementia delectantur, illius iracundiam formidant. Iudices de CCCLX., qui praecipue Gnaeo
nostro delectabantur, ex quibus quotidie aliquem video, nescio
quas eius Lucerias horrent: itaque quaero, qui sint isti optimates,
qui me exturbent, cum ipsi domi maneant. Sed tamen, quicumque sunt, *αἰδέομαι Τρῶας*. Etsi, qua spe proficiscar video,
coniungoque me cum homine magis ad vastandam Italiam quam

2. *A* Philotimo. Philotimus was a freedman of Terentia, whose behaviour in some money matters had displeased Cicero, but who was subsequently received back into favour by him. Cp. Intr. to Part II, § 18; also Ad Att. 5. 8. 3; 7. 22, 2; 7. 23, 1; 7. 24. Cicero derides his over-confidence in the cause of the optimates. Ep. 61, 6; Ad Att. 10. 9. 2.

3. Conscindi, sc. 'conviciis.' It is more usual to insert such an ablative. Cp. Ep. 12, 3, note.

Qui nunc . . Caesari (quo modo servit admirationi, Forcell.), 'how eagerly do they hasten to meet and court Caesar.' On this use of 'qui,' connecting two sentences, cp. Madv. 448. On the indic. 'occurrunt,' cp. § 3 of the previous letter, note.

5. Deum, sc. 'Caesarem ducunt.' Cp. Ep. 48, 1, note, for the double acc.

De illo aegroto, 'for Pompey when sick' at Neapolis, probably about January, 50 B.C. Cp. Vell. 2. 48; Cic. Tusc. Disp. 1. 35. 86; Iuv. Sat. 10. 283-286

'Provida Pompeio dederat Campania febres
Optandas,' foll.

6. Hic Pisistratus, Caesar. A reference to the mild government which distinguished Pisistratus from the majority of Greek tyrants. Cp. Thucyd. 6. 54; Herod. 1. 59-63; Aristot. Pol. 5. 12. Cicero had expressed a doubt whether Caesar would imitate Phalaris or Pisistratus. Cp. Ad Att. 7. 20, 2.

Non fecerit, 'has, in their opinion, abstained from doing.' Cp. Ep. 9. 12, note.

7. Prohibuerit, the tense of this verb follows gratum est. Cp. Madv. 349. 'People thank him as much for abstaining from harm himself as if he had prevented another from doing it.'

Propitium, sc. 'fore.' On the ellipse, cp. Madv. 479.

8. Illum, Pompey. He would be angry at having been so languidly supported by the Italians.

ἀπαντήσεις, 'meetings.' See Polyb. 5. 26 for the word. 'What throngs do you suppose come to meet him.'

11. Iudices de CCCLX. The reference is to judges enrolled by Pompey in his second or third consulship. Cp. Vell. 2. 76, 1; Plut. Pomp. 55; Mommsen 4. 2, 324 and 328; Ep. 34. 5, note.

12. Nescio quas eius Lucerias, 'certain threats of his from Luceria.' Baiter suggests, 'Lucerinas minas.' On the fact, see Ep. 56. 4.

14. Qui me exturbent . . maneant, 'that they should try to drive me from Italy, though they remain at home themselves.' On the conj., see Ep. 34. 2, note; also Ad Att. 7. 17, 3 'quis enim tu es qui dicas.'

15. αἰδέομαι Τρῶας. Hom. Il. 6. 442; 22. 105.

ad vincendum parato. † domum quem exspecto. Et quidem cum haec scribebam, IIII. Nonas, iam exspectabam aliquid a Brundisio. Quid autem aliquid? quam inde turpiter fugisset et victor hic qua se referret et quo; quod ubi audissem, si ille Appia veniret, ego Arpinum cogitabam.

60. CAESAR TO CICERO (AD ATT. IX. 6 A).

EARLY IN MARCH, 49 B.C. (705 A.U.C.)

I was in a great hurry when Furnius brought me your letter, but could not deny myself the pleasure of writing to thank you for your conduct, and to express a hope that I may find you at Rome on my arrival there, and have the benefit of your support and counsel.

CAESAR IMP. S. D. CICERONI IMP.

Cum Furnium nostrum tantum vidissem, neque loqui neque audire meo commodo potuissem, properarem atque essem in itinere, praemissis iam legionibus, praeterire tamen non potui, quin et scriberem ad te et illum mitterem gratiasque agerem, etsi hoc et feci saepe et saepius mihi facturus videor: ita de me mereris. Imprimis a te peto, quoniam confido me celeriter ad urbem venturum, ut te ibi videam, ut tuo consilio, gratia, dignitate, ope omnium rerum uti possim. Ad propositum revertar: festinationi meae brevitatique litterarum ignosces; reliqua ex Furnio cognosces.

1. Domum. Kayser suggests 'eo denique;' Manutius 'demum.' Both would give the same meaning: 'in a word, such as I expect to find him,' i.e. 'from whom I know what to expect.' Cp. Billerb., Wiel.

2. Scribebam and the following tenses are epistolary.

3. Quid autem aliquid? On the ellipse of 'dicam,' cp. Madv. 479 d, Obs. 1, 'but why do I say "something?"' 'I expect to hear of his base flight, and by what route and whither the victor is returning.'

4. Appia, sc. via.

5. Arpinum, sc. 'ire.' Cp. Ad Fam. 7. 4 'in Pompeianum statim cogito;' also Epp. 36, 9; 106, 4.

6. Furnium. C. Furnius was tribune in 51–50 B.C. Cp. Ad Fam. 8. 10, 3, where, as Ad Att. 5. 18, 3, he is mentioned as a friend of Cicero. He served in the army of L. Plancus in 43 B.C., and is often mentioned in the correspondence of Plancus and Cicero. Ad Fam. 10. 1–24.

7. Meo commodo, 'without inconvenience to myself.' Abl. modi, see Madv. 257.

Properarem. On the omission of a conjunction, cp. Madv. 434, and Obs. 1.

8. Praeterire .. quin et scriberem, foll.: cp. Madv. 375 c, Obs. 1.

10. Ita de me mereris, 'for you deserve such a return from me.' Cp. Ad Fam. 2. 5, 2 'ne cum veneris non habeas iam quod cures ita sunt omnia debilitata.'

11. Quoniam, foll. On the order of the words, cp. Madv. 476 a, and Obs. 3 and on the indic. after 'quoniam,' Ib. 357 a.

12. Consilio .. omnium rerum, 'your advice, influence, and aid in all my measures.' On the gen. 'rerum,' cp. p. 101, l. 8, note. Cicero comments upon Caesar's language. See Epp. 62, 3; 64.

13. Ad propositum revertar, 'I shall return to this subject.' Boot. The words 'ad propositum' seem to have a somewhat different sense in Ep. 105, 2; see note there. The meaning 'to return to the point' would, I think, be more naturally expressed by 'revertor' or 'ut revertar:' cp. Ep. 92, 3.

14. Ignosces: cp. Ep. 11, 3, note on p. 80.

61. TO ATTICUS (AD ATT. IX. 7).

FORMIAE, MARCH 13, 49 B.C. (705 A.U.C.)

1. I was cheered to some extent by your letter, but have long ceased to hope for a happy issue from our troubles. 2. I am glad to learn that Peducaeus approves my conduct. I will follow your advice and stay at Formiae till Caesar has gone to Rome. 3. I had already asked Caesar to allow me to be neutral, as you suggest; but if he refuses my request, I fear that Pompey will hardly be pleased at my proposing negotiation. 4. For he intends to reduce Italy to obedience by famine, devastation, and exactions. I fear Caesar's adherents will imitate him, and my obligations to Pompey will prevent my remaining in Italy. 5. I give up my hopes of a triumph quite willingly, and stay quietly in this neighbourhood till I can sail to join Pompey. I regard his probable tactics with abhorrence, but anything is better than witnessing what Caesar's friends will probably do in Italy. 6. I am glad that good citizens approve my conduct, and will enquire about Lentulus. 7. Write what you can, even if you have little to say.

CICERO ATTICO SAL.

Scripseram ad te epistolam, quam darem IIII. Idus; sed eo die 1
is, cui dare volueram, non est profectus. Venit autem eo ipso
die ille 'celeripes,' quem Salvius dixerat: attulit uberrimas tuas
litteras, quae mihi quiddam quasi 'animulae stillarunt;' recreatum
enim me non queo dicere. Sed plane τὸ συνέχον effecisti; ego
enim non iam id ago, mihi crede, ut prosperos exitus consequar:
sic enim video, nec duobus his vivis nec hoc uno nos umquam
rem publicam habituros. Ita neque de otio nostro spero iam nec
ullam acerbitatem recuso. Unum illud extimescebam, ne quid
turpiter facerem, vel dicam, iam fecissem. Sic ergo habeto, salu- 2

1. IIII. Idus, 'on March 12.'

3. Celeripes . . dixerat, 'your swift-footed messenger, of whom Salvius spoke.' The word 'celeripes' appears not to occur elsewhere, and perhaps Cicero quotes it from Salvius. The latter was secretary and reader to Atticus. Cp. Ad Att. 13. 44. 3: 16. 2, 6.

4. Quae mihi . . stillarunt, 'which gave me a little life, drop by drop as it were.' Apparently a quotation from a poet. Animula recurs Ep. 98, 4. Forcell. says the diminutive 'usurpatur vel contemptus vel blanditiae causa.'

Recreatum, 'restored to health.'

5. τὸ συνέχον, 'the next best thing.' Manut. Polybius (2. 12) says of one of the provisions of a treaty τὸ συνέχον ὃ μάλιστα πρὸς τοὺς Ἕλληνας διέτεινεν, where the words seem to mean 'most important.'

6. Non iam id ago . . consequar, 'I am no longer seeking to secure a prosperous result.' On 'id agere,' cp. Ep. 44. 7, note.

7. Duobus his, i.e. Caesar and Pompey.

Hoc uno, sc. 'vivo.' He refers probably to Caesar.

8. Rem publicam, 'a constitutional government.'

Nec ullam . . recuso, 'nor do I refuse to submit to any cruelty.'

9. Extimescebam. The imperfect, I think, describes Cicero's state of mind before he received Atticus' letter.

10. Vel dicam, 'or, let me speak out.' Metzg.

tares te mihi litteras misisse, neque solum has longiores, quibus nihil potest esse explicatius, nihil perfectius, sed etiam illas breviores, in quibus hoc mihi iucundissimum fuit, consilium factumque nostrum a Sexto probari, pergratumque mihi tu fecisti, a quo diligi me et, quid rectum sit, intellegi scio. Longior vero tua epistola non me solum, sed meos omnes aegritudine levavit; itaque utar tuo consilio et ero in Formiano, ne aut ad urbem ἀπάντησις mea animadvertatur aut, si nec hic nec illic eum videro,
3 devitatum se a me putet. Quod autem suades, ut ab eo petam ut mihi concedat ut idem tribuam Pompeio, quod ipsi tribuerim, id me iam pridem agere intelleges ex litteris Balbi et Oppii, quarum exempla tibi misi; misi etiam Caesaris ad eos sana mente scriptas, quo modo in tanta insania. Sin mihi Caesar hoc non concedat, video tibi placere illud, me πολίτευμα de pace suscipere, in quo non extimesco periculum: cum enim tot impendeant, cur non honestissimo depecisci velim? Sed vereor ne Pompeio quid oneris imponam,

1. Has longiores, the letter mentioned in § 3 as 'uberrimae.'

2. Explicatius, 'more detailed.' Cicero seems to have received two letters from Atticus within a short space of each other.

4. A Sexto, sc. Peducaeo: see Epp. 41, 1; 48, 3; 65, 10.

5. A quo . . scio. 'I see your affection for me does not blind you to what is right.' That is, Atticus' friendship was free from weakness, and jealous of his friend's honour.

7. Ero, 'shall remain till Caesar's return.'

Ad urbem, 'near to Rome.' Metzg. and Billerb. both translate 'on his way to Rome.' But Cicero *did* meet Caesar on his way to Rome, and seems only to have wished to avoid needless publicity.

8. ἀπάντησις, 'my going to greet Caesar.' Cp. Ep. 59, 2 for the Greek word.

Hic, at Formiae.

Illic, at or near to Rome.

10. Idem tribuam . . tribuerim, 'shew as much regard for Pompey as I have shewn for himself,' by abstaining from acts of hostility against either.

Id me . . intelleges, 'you will see that I have long been pleading for that.'

11. Ex litteris: cp. Ad Att. 9. 7 A, 1 'de eo quod ad nos scripsisti tibi consilium dabimus . . nos si id quod nostro iudicio Caesarem facere oportere existimamus, ut simul Romam venerit agat de reconciliatione gratiae suae et Pompeii, id eum facturum ex ipso cognoscemus, te hortaremur ut velles iis rebus interesse, quo facilius et maiore cum dignitate per te, qui utrique es coniunctus, res tota conficeretur.'

Oppii: cp. Ep. 70, 7.

13. Quo modo in tanta insania, 'considering how mad a course he is pursuing.' 'Quomodo' = 'ut:' cp. Ep. 58, 3. Caesar's letter is found Ad Att. 9. 7 C.

14. Illud, 'the other course referred to in our correspondence.'

πολίτευμα, 'a negotiation.' Cp. Demosth. de Cor. p. 263 κατέστησεν οὐδὲν ἐστι πολίτευμα ἐμόν, where it means 'a political measure.'

15. In quo, 'in the discharge of which duty.'

Tot, sc. 'pericula.'

16. Honestissimo depecisci. An elliptical expression: 'to bargain for escape from the other dangers which beset me by incurring that which is most honourable:' cp. Ter. Phorm. 1. 3. 14 'iam depecisci morte cupio.'

Ne Pompeio . . imponam, 'lest I give Pompey some trouble.' I presume Cicero means that Pompey was so committed to a war policy that any proffer of mediation would only embarrass him.

μή μοι γοργείην κεφαλὴν δεινοῖο πελώρου

intorqueat; mirandum enim in modum Gnaeus noster Sullani regni similitudinem concupivit. Εἰδὼς σοι λέγω. Nihil ille umquam minus obscure tulit. 'Cum hoccine igitur' inquies 'esse vis?' Beneficium sequor, mihi crede, non causam [ut in Milone, ut in . . . sed *haec* hactenus]. 'Causa igitur non bona est?' 4
Immo optima, sed agetur, memento, foedissime: primum consilium est suffocare urbem et Italiam fame, deinde agros vastare, urere, pecuniis locupletium *non* abstinere; sed cum eadem metuam ab hac parte, si illim beneficium non sit, rectius putem quidvis domi perpeti. Sed ita meruisse illum de me puto, ut ἀχαριστίας crimen subire non audeam: quamquam a te eius quoque rei iusta defensio est explicata. De triumpho tibi adsentior, 5
quem quidem totum facile et libenter abiecero: egregie probo fore ut, dum vagamur, ὁ πλόος ὡραῖος obrepat. 'Si modo' inquis 'satis ille erit firmus.' Est firmior etiam quam putabamus; de isto licet bene speres: promitto tibi, si valebit, tegulam illum in

1. μή μοι κ.τ.λ. Odyss. 11. 634. The words refer to Ulysses' unwillingness to stay by the Ocean and talk with more of the shades.

2. Intorqueat, 'should hurl in my face.' Forcell.

Sullani regni similitudinem, 'a despotism resembling Sulla's.'

3. Εἰδώς, 'from certain knowledge.' Cicero had probably heard violent language from Pompey at Teanum, or had had such language reported to him from Luceria. Cp. Epp. 59, 2; 62, 2; 85, 4; Intr. to Part III, § 4.

4. Tulit = 'ostendit, palam fecit.' Forcell. Cp. Pro Planc. 14, 34 'dolorem hic tulit paulo apertius.' It seems to mean much the same as 'prae se tulit.'

5. Beneficium . . . non causam, 'I am influenced by the remembrance of past services, not by the goodness of his cause.' 'Sequi' = 'spectare in agendo.' Forcell.

[Ut in Milone . . hactenus]. If these words are genuine, they imply that Cicero had not really thought Milo's behaviour [in killing Clodius?] laudable.

6. Ut in . . Manutius suggests the insertion of 'Gabinio.' Cicero had been induced to defend Gabinius. Cp. Intr. to Part II, § 20.

Causa igitur, foll. Atticus is supposed to ask.

8. Suffocare . . fame, i.e. by intercepting supplies from the corn provinces. Cp. Ep. 62, 2. 'Suffocare' seems not to be used in a metaphorical sense elsewhere.

10. Ab hac parte, 'from Caesar's friends,' and cannot therefore join them.

Illim, 'on Pompey's side.' On the tense of 'sit,' cp. Ep. 8, 3, note, p. 36. Wesenb. suggests 'erit.'

11. Quidvis domi perpeti, 'to await at home whatever may come.'

12. ἀχαριστίας, 'ingratitude,' a classical word.

Eius quoque rei . . explicata, 'you have set forth an adequate defence even of such behaviour,' i.e. of apparent ingratitude. Cp. De Orat. 1. 56, 237 'cuiusque rei facilis est et prompta defensio.'

13. De triumpho. The triumph which Cicero had desired for his successes in Cilicia, and which he now intended either to renounce or to make a plea for not entering Rome.

15. Fore ut . . obrepat. On the construction, cp Madv. 410. 'Your remark, that while we are moving from place to place the favourable time for sailing will come.'

ὁ πλόος ὡραῖος, lit. 'it is fair weather for sailing.' The words are introduced apparently without regard to strict grammar.

16. Est firmior . . putabamus, 'his language shews greater strength than we expected.'

De isto, 'on that point.' Boot.

Italia nullam relicturum. 'Tene igitur socio?' Contra mehercule
meum iudicium et contra omnium antiquorum auctoritatem, nec
tam ut illa adiuvem quam ut haec ne videam cupio discedere;
noli enim putare tolerabiles horum insanias nec unius modi fore:
etsi quid te horum fugit, legibus, iudiciis, senatu sublato, libidines,
audacias, sumptus, egestates tot egentissimorum hominum nec
privatas posse res nec rem publicam sustinere? Abeamus igitur
inde qualibet navigatione, etsi id quidem, ut tibi videbitur, sed
certe abeamus; sciemus enim, id quod exspectas, quid Brundisii
6 actum sit. Bonis viris quod ais probari quae adhuc fecerimus,
scirique ab iis *nos* non profectos, valde gaudeo, si est nunc ullus
gaudendi locus. De Lentulo investigabo diligentius: id mandavi
7 Philotimo, homini forti ac nimium optimati. Extremum est, ut
tibi argumentum ad scribendum fortasse iam desit—nec enim alia
de re nunc ulla scribi potest; et de hac quid iam amplius inveniri
potest?—sed quoniam et ingenium suppeditat—dico mehercule ut
sentio—et amor, quo et meum ingenium incitatur, perge, ut facis,
et scribe quantum potes. In Epirum quod me non invitas, comitem non molestum, subirascor, sed vale: nam ut tibi ambu-

Si valebit, 'if he prevails.' Valere = pollere. Forcell.

Tegulam .. relictorum, 'he will leave no house still roofed.'

1. 'Tene igitur socio?' 'with you for an ally?' Atticus asks.

Contra .. auctoritatem, 'If I accompany him, it will be against my own judgment and the example set by all the men of old,' e.g. Q. Mucius Scaevola, L. Philippus, and others. Ep. 54, 6.

3. Nec tam .. ne videam, 'and not so much to aid the cause of Pompey as to avoid the sight of Caesar's friends (horum.)'

6. Nec privatas .. sustinere, 'that neither the resources of individuals nor of the state can satisfy the cravings of so many needy men.'

8. Qualibet navigatione. Billerb. explains 'by whatever passage,' i.e. whether by the upper or lower sea. See Ep. 62, 1.

Id quidem .. videbitur, sc. 'fiet,' 'you shall decide on the time and mode.'

9. Sciemus enim .. actum sit, 'we shall know what has taken place at Brundisium,' and so shall have no further reason for delay.

10. Bonis viris, in a political sense: cp. Ep. 6, 3. He may refer especially to Pedncaeus and Sulpicius.

12. De Lentulo, 'about the intentions, or conduct, of Lentulus.' Cp. Ep. 64, 3.

13. Nimium optimati, 'ultra aristocratic' (ironical), or 'too much of a party man to be trusted.' Cp. Ad Att. 10. 9. 1 'adventus Philotimi .. quam saepe pro Pompeio mentientis.'

Extremum est .. quantum potes, 'lastly, if topics for writing fail you, as I can well suppose, yet, as you lack neither ability nor interest in me, write as often as you can.'

Ut .. desit. 'Ut' = 'although:' cp. Ep. 10, 1, note, p. 73.

14. Nec enim .. et. For this combination of negative and affirmative particles, cp. p. 45, note on l. 6.

16. Suppeditat = 'abundat.' Forcell. sc. 'tibi' Manut.

17. Quo et .. incitatur, 'by which even my invention is quickened.'

18. In Epirum. Atticus was apparently about to visit his property in Epirus, as to which, cp. Ep. 16, 1, notes, App. 3, 6, alib. He can hardly have expected that that country would so soon be the seat of war.

19. Subirascor, cp. Ep. 127, 1.

Nam ut tibi, foll. Atticus may have

landum, ungendum, sic mihi dormiendum; etenim litterae tuae mihi somnum attulerunt.

62. To ATTICUS (AD ATT. IX. 9.)

FORMIAE, MARCH 17 (705 A.U.C.)

1. I have received three letters from you, and will answer them according to their dates. I agree with your suggestions about my movements. There is nothing I like so much as your letters of advice. 2. I come now to your second letter. Our reports from Brundisium were false in two points. I am sorry the consuls have left Italy; their departure makes war inevitable, and its beginning will be attended by famine; Pompey's friends intend to blockade Italy. I should certainly not join such a party but for my personal obligations to its leader. You rightly warn me to shew a becoming independence when I meet Caesar. I shall not go to Arpinum till Caesar has passed by this place. 3. Philotimus has been slow in returning to you. Domitius, I think, is near Cosa as you say; no one seems to know his plans. What a worthless man is he who says that a praetor can preside at the election of consuls! but he acts in character. Perhaps Caesar is anxious for my presence in the senate as a sanction to such a step. May I die first! 4. You are quite right in your gloomy anticipations about the war. Tell Trebatius that I shall be very glad if he will visit me before Caesar comes to this neighbourhood. I am glad that you think of buying Phamea's estate at Lanuvium; but fear that landed property is very insecure just now.

CICERO ATTICO SAL.

Tres epistolas tuas accepi postridie Idus; erant autem IIII., III., 1
pridie Idus datae: igitur antiquissimae cuique primum respondebo. Adsentior tibi, ut in Formiano potissimum commorer, etiam de supero mari, *tem*ptaboque, ut antea ad te scripsi, ecquonam modo possim voluntate eius nullam rei publicae partem attingere. Quod laudas, quia oblivisci me scripsi ante facta et delicta nostri amici,

been under medical treatment, and may have made obedience to his doctor's advice an excuse for brevity.

2. **Somnum attulerunt**, 'have brought me sleep' by mitigating my anxiety. Cp. § 1; Ad Att. 8. 1. 4 'ego si somnum capere possem tam longis te epistulis non obtunderem;' also 8. 14. 1; 9. 9. 4.

3. **Postridie Idus**, March 16.

4. **Antiquissimae cuique**, 'to each according to priority of date.' Cp. Madv. 495.

5. **Adsentior tibi ut . . commorer**, 'I approve your suggestion that I should remain here.' On the construction, cp. Madv. 372 a and 374.

Etiam de supero mari, 'also that I should choose the Adriatic for embarkation.' This may perhaps determine the meaning of 'qualibet navigatione' Ep. 61, 5 as = 'by any route.'

6. **Ut antea ad te scripsi**, Ep. 61, 3; or perhaps Ad Att. 9. 6. 6.

7. **Voluntate eius**, 'without displeasing Caesar.' On the abl. cp. Madv. 257.

Nullam rei publicae . . attingere, 'to take no part in public affairs.'

8. **Quia . . me scripsi**: cp. Madv. 357. Cicero might have expressed this, of course, in the oratio obliqua.

Ante facta . . amici, 'the old acts and offences of our friend' (Pompey). On the use of adverbs with neut. participles, cp. Madv. 425, c; and on the facts referred to here, see Ep. 54, 3.

ego vero ita facio: quin ea ipsa quae a te commemorantur secus ab eo in me ipsum facta esse non memini; tanto plus apud me valere beneficii gratiam quam iniuriae dolorem volo. Faciamus igitur, ut censes, colligamusque nos: σοφιστεύω enim, simul ut rus decurro, atque in decursu θέσεις meas commentari non desino; sed sunt quaedam earum perdifficiles ad iudicandum. De optimatibus sit sane ita, ut vis, sed nosti illud Διονύσιος ἐν Κορίνθῳ. Titinii filius apud Caesarem est. Quod autem quasi vereri videris ne mihi tua consilia displiceant, me vero nihil delectat aliud nisi consilium et litterae tuae; qua re fac, ut ostendis: ne destiteris ad me quicquid tibi in mentem venerit scribere: mihi nihil potest
2 esse gratius. Venio ad alteram nunc epistolam. Recte non credis de numero militum: ipso dimidio plus scripsit Clodia. Falsum etiam de corruptis navibus. Quod consules laudas, ego quoque animum laudo, sed consilium reprehendo; discessu enim illorum

1. **Ego vero**: cp. Ep. 40, 1, note.

Ea ipsa. The old personal injuries which Cicero had suffered from Pompey. The previous clause perhaps refers also to Pompey's political blunders.

4. **Colligamusque nos**, 'and collect myself,' 'hold myself ready to carry out any decision.'

σοφιστεύω, 'discuss philosophical or political controverted questions.' The word is quoted from Plutarch by Liddell and Scott in the sense 'to give lectures.'

Ut rus decurro, 'in walking about my estate.' Metzg.

5. **θέσεις**, 'theses,' 'subjects for discussion,' such as are found Ad Att. 9, 4. Cp. Orat. 14. 46.

Commentari, 'to think over.'

6. **De optimatibus . . vis**, 'as to the approval of my neutrality by the optimates I am willing to believe you.' Cp. Ep. 61, 6.

7. **Διονύσιος ἐν Κορίνθῳ.** A proverbial saying, by which the Lacedaemonians are said to have reminded Philip of Macedon of the inconstancy of fortune. Cp. Plut. περὶ ἀδολεσχίας, p. 511. Dionysius II retired to Corinth after his expulsion from Syracuse by Timoleon. Cp. Ep. 87, 1; Tusc. Disp. 3. 12, 27; Plut. Timol. 13-15. Here perhaps the saying means, 'But if Caesar were to fail, what would the optimates say?' Mr. Jeans thinks that one of the passages referred to above, Tusc. Disp. 3. 12, 27 shews that the saying illustrates Dionysius' clinging to power, and hence that the meaning here is 'you know that they will always care most for their own power.' This seems to me far fetched.

8. **Titinii.** Q. Titinius was half brother of C. Fannius, one of the judges of Verres (cp. In Verr. 2 Act. 1. 49. 128), and is mentioned by Cicero as a friend (Ep. 36, 5). The son is called Pontius Titinianus (Ad Att. 9. 19. 2).

9. **Me vero, sqq.**, 'on the contrary, nothing pleases me.' Cp. 'ego vero' above, and Madv. 437 d.

10. **Fac . . ne destiteris**: cp. Ep. 31, 7, note. Madvig (Opusc. Acad. II. 104) remarks 'aut scribendum videtur *non destiteris* aut sic interpungendum post *ostendis*, ut per se addatur *ne destiteris*.'

12. **Alteram**, that written on the 13th. Cp. § 1.

13. **De numero militum**, 'about the number of soldiers' said to have embarked with Pompey. Cp. Ad Att. 9. 6. 3.

Ipso dimidio plus, 'too much by just one half,' i.e. as 3 to 2. Clodia had mentioned 30,000, and Caesar, Bell. Civ. 3. 4, says that Pompey had taken five legions with him from Italy, which would number 15,000 or 20,000 men probably. Cp. Intr. to Part III, § 2, note. Clodia was mother-in-law to L. Metellus, one of the tribunes for 50-49 B.C., and seems to be only mentioned by Cicero here and Ad Att. 9. 6, 3.

14. **De corruptis navibus**, 'about the ships having been disabled' by Pompey. Ad Att. l. c.

15. **Discessu.** On the abl., cp. Madv. 255. Atticus seems to have praised the consuls for their decision to leave Italy with Pompey. Cp. Caes. Bell. Civ. 1. 25.

actio de pace sublata est, quam quidem ego meditabar. Itaque postea Demetrii librum de concordia tibi remisi et Philotimo dedi; nec vero dubito quin exitiosum bellum impendeat, cuius initium ducetur a fame. Et me tamen doleo non interesse huic bello! in quo tanta vis sceleris futura est, ut, cum parentes non alere nefarium sit, nostri principes antiquissimam et sanctissimam parentem, patriam, fame necandam putent. Atque hoc non opinione timeo, sed interfui sermonibus: omnis haec classis Alexandria, Colchis, Tyro, Sidone, Arado, Cypro, Pamphylia, Lycia, Rhodo, Chio, Byzantio, Lesbo, Smyrna, Mileto, Coo ad intercludendos commeatus Italiae et ad occupandas frumentarias provincias comparatur. At quam veniet iratus! et iis quidem maxime, qui eum maxime salvum volebant, quasi relictus ab iis, quos reliquit. Itaque mihi dubitanti, quid me facere par sit, permagnum pondus adfert benevolentia erga illum, qua dempta perire melius esset in patria quam patriam servando evertere. De septemtrione plane ita est; metuo ne vexetur Epirus. Sed quem tu locum Graeciae non direptum iri putas? Praedicat enim palam et militibus ostendit se largitione ipsa superiorem quam hunc fore. Illud me praeclare admones, cum illum videro, ne nimis indul-

1. Actio de pace, 'the chance of any negotiation for peace.' For Pompey said that he could not entertain any proposals while the consuls were absent. Caes. Bell. Civ. 1. 26.

2. Demetrii librum . . dedi, 'I sent back the work of Demetrius to you by the hands of Philotimus.' The book has been mentioned already Ep. 56, 7. Cicero probably wanted it as a source of common places on the blessings of peace.

3. Cuius initium, foll., 'which will begin with a famine.'

5. Cum, 'although.'

8. Opinione. Ablat. causae, 'from conjecture.'

Interfui sermonibus: cp. Ep. 61, 3.

Omnis haec classis, 'all our fleet.'

9. Alexandria. On this and the following local descriptive ablatives, cp. Ep. 23, 5, note.

Colchis. The name of the people is put for that of the country.

Arado. Aradus was in Northern Phoenicia, between Tripolis and Marathus.

10. Coo, ablat. of Cos.

11. Frumentarias provincias. Africa, Sicily, and Sardinia, were the provinces from which the largest supplies of corn came. Egypt was still nominally independent.

12. Quam veniet iratus! sc. Pompeius.

13. Qui eum . . volebant, 'who were most anxious for his safety,' i.e. either for peace, or for resistance to be made in Italy.

14. Quos reliquit, 'whom he abandoned' by his flight.

15. Qua dempta, 'for were this removed.'

16. Servando, 'by attempts to preserve it.'

De septemtrione. Boot supposes this word to mean 'Macedon and Epirus,' which might suffer from the presence of Pompey's army, and where Atticus had land. Cp. Epp. 6, 1; 8, 15. Others suppose it to mean 'the north wind.' Cp. Ad Att. 9. 6, 3 [Pompeius] 'conscendisse dicitur a. d. IV. Non. Mart. Ex ea die fuere septemtriones venti.' Cp. for this sense of the word, Livy 26, 45 'acer . . septemtrio ortus.' The passage would then mean 'you are right in supposing that this north wind will blow little good to Epirus.'

17. Ita est. On the adverb as predic., cp. Ep. 4, 1, note.

19. Quam hunc, 'than Caesar, who is called 'hic' as locally nearer to the writer than his enemy was.

20. Illud refers to what follows: cp. Ep. 5, 9, note.

genter et ut cum gravitate potius loquar: plane sic faciendum. Arpinum, cum eum convenero, cogito, ne forte aut absim, cum veniet, aut cursem huc illuc via deterrima. Bibulum, ut scribis, audio venisse et redisse pridie Idus. Philotimum, ut ais epistola tertia, exspectabas; at ille Idibus a me profectus est: eo serius ad tuam illam epistolam, cui ego statim rescripseram, redditae sunt meae litterae. De Domitio, ut scribis, ita opinor esse, ut et in Cosano sit et consilium eius ignoretur. Iste omnium turpissimus et sordidissimus, qui consularia comitia a praetore ait haberi posse, est idem, qui semper in re publica fuit. Itaque nimirum hoc illud est, quod Caesar scribit in ea epistola, cuius exemplum ad te misi, se velle uti 'consilio' meo; age, esto: hoc commune est; 'gratia;' ineptum id quidem, sed, puto, hoc simulat ad quasdam senatorum sententias; 'dignitate;' fortasse sententia consulari. Illud extremum est, 'ope omnium rerum;' id ego suspicari coepi tum ex tuis litteris aut hoc ipsum esse aut non multo secus: nam permagni eius interest rem ad interregnum non

Illum, Caesar, as more remote in idea and belonging to the other party. Cp. 'haec clausis' above, and Madv. 485 a, Obs.

Ne nimis indulgenter, sc. 'loquar.'

2. Arpinum . . cogito, sc. 'ire;' cp. Ep. 36, 9, note.

Cum eum convenero, '*after* I have met Caesar,' whom Cicero wished to see at Formiae.

Cum veniet, 'when he arrives' at Formiae on his way from Brundisium.

3. Aut cursem . . deterrima, 'or be hurrying from place to place while the road is very bad.'

4. Venisse et redisse, 'has arrived (? at Rome) from Syria and set off again,' probably to take command of the fleet, or to join Pompey, as Boot.

Epistola tertia, written on March 14. Cp. § 1.

5. Ad tuam . . rescripseram, 'in answer to that letter of yours to which I had written a reply at once.' Cicero perhaps refers to Ep. 61.

7. De Domitio. Cicero refers to L. Domitius Ahenobarbus, the defender of Corfinium. On whom, cp. Ep. 1. 3 and 4, note on p. 29.

Esse ut sit: cp. Ep. 33. 2, note.

In Cosano, 'on his estate near Cosa' in Etruria.

8. Iste. Perhaps M. Lepidus, one of the praetors for this year, and afterwards a member of the second triumvirate. For an account of him, cp. Ep. 105. 1, note.

11. Hoc illud est, 'this explains that passage in Caesar's letter,' 'this is the affair about which Caesar wrote.' Cp. Ep. 60.

12. Age, esto, foll., 'well, let that pass—it is a general compliment.'

13. Hoc simulat . . sententias, 'he makes this pretence with a view to the votes of certain senators' who had previously looked to Cicero as their leader. Boot. For this sense of 'ad,' cp. Ep. 48, 3, note.

14. Dignitate, 'position,' 'distinction.'

Fortasse sententia consulari, 'perhaps that which the expression of a consular's opinion would lend to his cause.' Klotz ap. Baiter suggests 'sententiae consularis;' the best MS. is reported to have 'sententia consularis.'

15. Illud extremum est, 'the last passage is,' 'illud' referring to something coming after it, as often.

16. Aut hoc ipsum esse, 'either refers to this very question,' the holding of the consular comitia by a praetor.

Aut non multo secus, 'or to something not very different.' Cp. Pro Milon. 10, 29 'hora fere undecima aut non multo secus.'

17. Nam permagni . . . venire. This would be of importance to Caesar on two grounds; first, because an interregnum could

venire; id adsequitur, si per praetorem consules creantur. Nos autem in libris habemus non modo consules a praetore, sed ne praetores quidem creari ius esse, idque factum esse numquam; consules eo non esse ius, quod maius imperium a minore rogari non sit ius, praetores autem, cum ita rogentur, ut collegae consulibus sint, quorum est maius imperium. Aberit non longe quin hoc a me decerni velit neque sit contentus Galba, Scaevola, Cassio, Antonio:

τότε μοι χάνοι εὐρεῖα χθών!

sed quanta tempestas impendeat, vides. Qui transierint sena- 4
tores, scribam ad te, cum certum habebo. De re frumentaria recte intellegis, quae nullo modo administrari sine vectigalibus

only begin when the actual consuls went out of office; secondly, because the interrex might be hostile and influence the election against him.

2. In libris, sc. 'auguralibus;' books containing an account of the rules of the augural system. Cp. De Dom. 15, 39.

A praetore .. creari, 'should be elected under the presidency of a praetor.' The same thing is afterwards expressed by 'rogari.'

4. Eo non esse ius, sc. 'a praetore creari.'

Eo = 'ideo.' Cp. Madv. 256, Obs. 3.

5. Non sit ius. The conjunctive is used because the passage is a quotation. Cp. Madv. 368: 369.

Ita rogentur .. sint, 'are elected to be colleagues of the consuls.' This perhaps was derived from the original institution of the praetorship, when the praetor may have held a position of greater equality with the consuls than he afterwards enjoyed. Cp. Livy 6. 42; 7. 1. According to Mommsen (Staatsrecht 2. 71, cp. 176) the consuls were called 'praetores maiores,' or even less correctly 'praetores maximi' after the institution of the praetorship. The term 'praetor maximus' applied more correctly to the dictator. Cp. Livy 7. 13.

7. Hoc, 'that a praetor may preside at consular elections,' referring to the beginning of this section 'qui consularia comitia a praetore ait haberi posse.' On the point at issue, cp. A. Gell. N. A. 13. 15, a quotation from Messala.

A me decerni. Caesar seems to have desired the sanction of Cicero's judgment as augur.

Galba. Orell. (Onom. sub nom.) thinks that P. Sulpicius Galba is meant, and that he was now augur. He was one of the judges of Verres. Cp. Ep. 1, 1, note. Or the reference may be to Ser. Sulpicius Galba, one of Caesar's officers in Gaul, but afterwards one of his assassins. Cp. Caes. Bell. Gall. 8. 50; Ep. 135.

Scaevola, Q. Mucius Scaevola, son of the augur under whom Cicero had studied law (cp. Intr. to Part I. § 1), and second cousin of the pontifex maximus murdered by order of the younger Marius. He was tribune in 55–54 B.C. (cp. Ad Att. 4. 16, 7), and now augur. He had been one of Q. Cicero's 'cohors' in Asia, and afterwards apparently legate of Ap. Claudius in Cilicia. Cp. Ad Fam. 3. 5. 5.

8. Cassio. Q. Cassius Longinus, now tribune (cp. Appendix 6, § 5), and apparently augur. He was brother to the more celebrated C. Cassius who conspired against Caesar, and whom Orell. supposes to be meant here as having been augur at the time referred to. But C. Cassius was with Pompey probably. Cp. Ep. 83, 4 note.

Antonio. M. Antonius, afterwards triumvir.

9. τότε μοι χάνοι εὐρεῖα χθών! Hom. Il. 4. 182.

10. Quanta tempestas impendeat, 'what a storm of danger threatens us!'

Transierint, 'have crossed the sea with Pompey.'

11. Certum habebo, 'shall have sure intelligence on the point.' Cp. Ep. 128, 1 'hiemem credo adhuc prohibuisse quo minus de te certum haberemus.'

De re frumentaria, 'about the commissariat of Pompey's army.' Billerb., Metzg.

12. Sine vectigalibus, 'without regular revenues.' Metzg. has 'ohne besondere Auflagen,' 'without special imposts.'

potest, nec sine causa et eos, qui circum illum sunt, omnia postulantes et bellum nefarium times. Trebatium nostrum, etsi, ut scribis, nihil bene sperat, tamen videre sane velim; quem fac horteris ut properet; opportune enim ad me ante adventum Caesaris venerit. De Lanuvino statim, ut audivi Phameam mortuum, optavi, si modo esset futura res publica, ut id aliquis meorum, neque tamen de te, qui maxime meus *es*, cogitavi; sciebam enim te quoto anno et quantum in solo solere quaerere, neque solum Romae, sed etiam Deli tuum digamma videram: verum tamen ego illud, quamquam est bellum, minoris aestimo, quam aestimabatur Marcellino consule, cum ego istos hortulos propter domum Antii quam tum habebam, iucundiores mihi fore putabam et minore impensa, quam si Tusculanum refecissem. Volui † .NSQ. Egi per praedem, ille daret, Antii cum haberet venale: noluit. Sed nunc omnia ista iacere puto propter nummorum caritatem. Mihi quidem erit aptissimum vel nobis potius,

1. Eos qui circum . . . postulantes, 'the friends of Pompey and their immoderate demands' for taxation, forced loans, etc.

2. Trebatium: cp. Ep. 27.

4. Opportune . . venerit, 'it will be convenient if he visits me before Caesar's arrival' at Formiae. Cicero would be glad to have Trebatius' advice. Manut.

5. De Lanuvino, 'about the estate of Phamea near Lanuvium.' This Phamea was a freedman, and grandfather, apparently, of the famous singer, M. Tigellius. Cp. Ad Att. 13. 49, 1; Ad Fam. 7. 24; Hor. Satt. 1. 2, 3; 1. 3. 4. Orell. Onom. sub nom. Tigellius.

6. Si modo . . res publica, 'if only constitutional government were likely to continue.'

Ut id aliquis meorum, sc. 'emeret,' which Wesenb. inserts.

8. Quoto anno, 'in how many years you would be repaid.'

Quantum in solo, 'how much the produce of the soil is.' Metzg. 'Res soli' = 'quae terra nituntur ut aedes, agri, plantae et ceterae res immobiles quae solo continguntur.' Forcell. Mr. Jeans renders 'the whole stock.' Boot, following Manutius, thinks the words mean 'how soon it would repay you the money you had spent on it,' supplying 'possimus.' But the ellipse would be harsh and the 'et' superfluous.

9. Deli. Cicero visited Delos on his voyage to Cilicia in 51 B.C. Cp. Ad Att. 5. 12, 1.

Digamma, perhaps = F. for 'fenus,' which may have been written on the account-books of Atticus. Boot, however, doubts if Atticus would have any account-books at Delos, and offers no explanation of the passage.

10. Illud, sc. 'praedium.'

Minoris aestimo, 'set a smaller value on,' probably on account of the troubled state of public affairs.

11. Marcellino consule, i.e. in 56 B.C.

Istos, 'those gardens.' Cicero's memory seems to have failed him here. For he had meant to buy, not the estate here mentioned, but one called Troianum. Cp. Ad Att. 9. 13, 6.

13. Minore impensa, sc. 'fore,' 'would cost less.' Cp. Ep. 6, 2, on the ablat.

Refecissem, 'had restored' after its devastation by Clodius. On which, cp. Intr. to Part I, § 20.

14. Volui, sc. 'emere.'

.NSQ. So the best MS., Wesenb., Boot, and Orell., read H.S.Q., which Boot explains as = 'quingentis sestertiis' = about £4300. Klotz. reads H.S.D., which would give the same amount.

Egi per praedem, foll., 'I applied to a surety to pay the money, as the proprietor offered the estate for sale at Antium.' Boot thinks the passage inexplicable, but suggests no emendation. Wesenb. suggests 'egi per * praedium ut ille venderet:' * representing a name which has dropped out.

15. Omnia ista . . caritatem, 'that all

si tu emeris. Sed eius dementias cave contemnas: valde est venustum. Quamquam mihi ista omnia iam addicta vastitati videntur. Respondi epistolis tribus, sed exspecto alias; nam me adhuc tuae litterae sustentarunt. D. Liberalibus.

63. To ATTICUS (AD ATT. IX. 10).

FORMIAE, MARCH 18, (705 A.U.C.)

1. I have nothing really to say, but to converse with you by letter is my only relief. 2. I regret that I did not follow Pompey as a soldier follows his general. I saw him full of alarm just after the middle of January, and his subsequent errors have estranged me from him. Now my old affection revives, and I am eager to fly to him. Yet what cruel threats he used! how he appealed to the example of Sulla! 3. History has branded men who have sought restoration to their country by foreign aid: and even Marius, Sulla, and Cinna, who appealed to their own countrymen, did much harm after their triumph. But now that Pompey has left Italy all seems changed, and I am only anxious to hasten to his side. You approve of my delay; 4–6. I have just turned over a roll of your letters, which I preserve carefully. Your constant advice was, 'If Pompey leaves Italy do not follow him;' and, when I thought you hinted that I had better depart, you wrote to deprecate such a course. 7. Then you suggested that I should remain if M'. Lepidus and L. Volcatius did so; and they have remained. In your other letters 8, 9. you gave no hint that my conduct had been at all discreditable. 10. You told me that Pedacaeus approved my plans. I hope you will defend my conduct before others, as you approved it yourself. We hear nothing of Caesar's return. Reading over your letters has calmed me a good deal.

CICERO ATTICO SAL.

Nihil habebam, quod scriberem; neque enim novi quicquam 1
audieram et ad tuas omnes rescripseram pridie; sed, cum me
aegritudo non solum somno privaret, verum ne vigilare quidem
sine summo dolore pateretur, tecum ut quasi loquerer, in quo
uno acquiesco, hoc nescio quid nullo argumento proposito scribere institui. Amens mihi fuisse videor a principio et me una 2
haec res torquet, quod non omnibus in rebus labentem vel potius

landed property is depreciated on account of the scarcity of money.'

1. Sed eius dementias, foll., 'but do not disregard his foolish extravagance,' 'do not take his so-called improvements at his own valuation.' In substance, Metzg.

Eius, sc. Phameae.

3. Addicta vastitati, 'sentenced to devastation' in the impending civil war. Cp. Ep. 56, 4.

4. Litterae seems to be used here of more than one letter. Cp. Ep. 79, 3, note.

Sustentarunt, 'have been my support.'

D. = dedi.

Liberalibus, 'the festival of Liber, March 17. Cp. Ovid, Fasti 3. 713.

5. Habebam, epistolary tense. Cp. Ep. 1, 1, note.

9. Nullo argumento proposito, 'without setting before myself any special subject.'

11. Omnibus . . labentem, 'though all his measures shewed a want of firmness, or rather a hasty despair.'

ruentem Pompeium tamquam unus manipularis secutus sim. Vidi hominem XIIII. *Kal.* Febr. plenum formidinis: illo ipso die sensi, quid ageret; numquam mihi postea placuit, nec umquam aliud ex alio peccare destitit. Nihil interim ad me scribere, nihil nisi fugam cogitare. Quid quaeris? sicut ἐν τοῖς ἐρωτικοῖς alienant immundae, insulsae, indecorae, sic me illius fugae neglegentiaeque deformitas avertit ab amore; nihil enim dignum faciebat, qua re eius fugae comitem me adiungerem. Nunc emergit amor, nunc desiderium ferre non possum, nunc mihi nihil libri, nihil litterae, nihil doctrina prodest: ita dies et noctes tamquam avis illa, mare prospecto, evolare cupio; do, do poenas temeritatis meae. Etsi quae fuit illa temeritas? quid feci non consideratissime? Si enim nihil praeter fugam quaereretur, fugissem libentissime, sed genus belli crudelissimi et maximi, quod nondum vident homines quale futurum sit, perhorrui. Quae minae municipiis! quae nominatim viris bonis! quae denique omnibus, qui remansissent! quam crebro illud
2 'Sulla potuit, ego non potero?' Mihi autem haeserunt illa: male Tarquinius, qui Porsenam, qui Octavium Mamilium contra

1. Unus manipularis, 'like one of his private soldiers,' i.e. without criticising his measures. This use of 'unus' illustrates the derivation of an indefinite article from it in modern languages. Cp. De Orat. 1. 29, 132 'sicut unus paterfamilias.'

2. XIIII. Kal. Febr., 'on Jan. 17.' This meeting probably took place somewhere between Rome and Formiae; Cicero was at Formiae on the 21st. Cp. Ad Att. 7. 12, 2.

3. Quid ageret, 'his intention' of leaving Italy to return with a foreign army.

4. Scribere . . cogitare, infin. hist. Cp. Madv. 392.

5. Quid quaeris? 'in a word.' Cp. Ep. 7, 6.

6. Insulsae. Lexicons translate 'est ineptus, insuavis.' Forcell.

Illius, Pompeii.

7. Deformitas, 'unseemliness.'

Nihil . . dignum faciebat, foll., 'his conduct gave me no sufficient reason for joining him in flight.' On the mood of 'adiungerem,' cp. Madv. 363; and for this use of qua re, Ib. 440 b, Obs. 1, and 372 b, Obs. 6.

10. Doctrina, 'philosophy.' On the sing. prodest, cp. Ep. 34, 6, note, p. 238.

11. Tamquam avis illa, 'like the bird in Plato.' Cp. Plat. Ep. 7. 348 A, where the philosopher wishes that he could fly away like a bird from the gardens in which he was detained by Dionysius.

12. Temeritatis, 'of my rash confidence' in the possibility of peace.

Etsi, 'and yet.'

13. Quaereretur, sc. 'a Pompeio.' On the tense, cp. Madv. 347 b. Obs. 2.

14. Genus belli, foll., 'the nature of a war which must be most cruel and extensive.' Cp. § 3.

16. Quae minae . . remansissent! 'what threats were uttered against the country towns! against good patriots individually! in a word, against all who should remain!' On the plup. 'remansissent,' cp. Ep. 56, 5, note.

Nominatim: cp. Ad Att. 11. 7, 3 'ut me caperet et Laelium nominatim.' With the general sense of the passage, cp. Epp. 56, 2; 62, 2.

18. Sulla potuit, sc. 'armis recuperare rem publicam.' Manh. Pompey probably hoped to imitate Sulla's victorious return from the East.

Mihi . . haeserunt illa, 'I could not get rid of the following thoughts.' 'Haerere' = 'inhaerere,' 'infixum esse.' Forcell. On the dat., cp. Madv. 241, and § 4 below. 'In mente' is often added to the dative.

19. Male, sc. 'fecit.' Cp. p. 70, note on l. 7.

patriam, impie Coriolanus, *qui* auxilium petiit a Volscis, recte Themistocles, qui mori maluit, nefarius Hippias, Pisistrati filius, qui in Marathonia pugna cecidit arma contra patriam ferens. At Sulla, at Marius, at Cinna recte. Immo iure fortasse; sed quid eorum victoria crudelius? quid funestius? Huius belli genus fugi, et eo magis, quod crudeliora etiam cogitari et parari videbam. Me, quem non nulli conservatorem istius urbis, quem parentem esse dixerunt, Getarum et Armeniorum et Colchorum copias ad eam adducere? me meis civibus famem, vastitatem inferre Italiae? Hunc primum mortalem esse, deinde etiam multis modis posse exstingui cogitabam, urbem autem et populum nostrum servandum ad immortalitatem, quantum in nobis esset, putabam, et tamen spes quaedam me oblectabat fore, ut aliquid conveniret potius, quam aut hic tantum sceleris aut ille tantum flagitii admitteret. Alia res nunc tota est, alia mens mea: sol, ut est in tua quadam epistola, excidisse mihi e mundo videtur. Ut aegroto, dum anima est, spes esse dicitur, sic ego, quoad Pompeius in Italia fuit, sperare non destiti: haec me fefellerunt,

Mamilium contra patriam, sc. 'concitavit.' Wesenb. puts * after 'patriam,' and thinks that 'arcessivit,' or some similar verb, has dropped out.

3. Cecidit. Justin. (2. 9) says that Hippias fell at Marathon; Herodotus and Thucydides say nothing on the subject.

4. At Sulla, 'yes, but Sulla.' Cp. Madv. 437 c. I have adopted Boot's punctuation.

Cinna. L. Cornelius Cinna, consul 87–84 B.C. For his history, cp. Livy, Epitt. 79–83; Vell. 2. 20–24; and for that of Sulla, Livy, Epitt. 77–90, and Plutarch's life.

Recte, sc. 'arma contra patriam tulit.' 'Recte,' sometimes = 'utiliter,' 'as their interests demanded.' Forcell.

Immo iure fortasse, 'nay, perhaps they had right on their side.' Cp. Madv. 454. Boot, however, following Manutius, thinks that 'recte' conveys more approbation than 'iure,' and that Cicero means, 'they did not do rightly, though perhaps there was some justification for them.' On the meaning of 'patria,' cp. Ep. 7. 3, note. Mr. Jeans renders 'iure' 'right in principle,' i.e. in not appealing to foreign invaders. He thinks that 'recte' conveys stronger approbation than 'iure.'

5. Huius belli genus, 'a war of this kind.' Cp. § 2.

6. Crudeliora, 'worse atrocities' than had marked earlier struggles.

7. Me . . adducere? 'was I to lead?' Cp. Ep. 11. 1, note, on the construction.

Non nulli: Cato, Plut. Cic. 23; Pompey, Cic. Philipp. 2. 5. 12; Catulus, Pro Sest. 57. 121.

8. Getarum, foll. The rudest tribes of the East are mentioned on purpose, and the campaigns of Pompey in the East may have given him great influence with them.

10. Hunc, i.e. Pompey. Matth., who thinks Cicero is excusing himself for preferring his country to a friend. Manutius, in one note seems to think that Pompey, in another that Caesar is referred to.

12. Quantum in nobis esset, 'so far as in me lay.' Cp. Madv. 364, Obs. 2, on the mood.

13. Et tamen, 'moreover.' Metzg.

14. Hic, sc. Caesar.

Tantum sceleris, 'so great a crime' as attempting to usurp sovereignty.

Ille, Pompey.

Tantum . . flagitii, 'such a scandalous enormity' as employing barbarians to ravage Italy. Forcell. defines 'flagitium' as 'quodvis facinus cum dedecore infamiaque coniunctum.' Boot and Matthiae give the sense of the passage as I have given it.

15. Alia: cp. Ep. 47. 4.

16. Ut est: cp. Ep. 55. 1, note.

18. Haec me fefellerunt, 'these anticipations deceived me.'

et, ut verum loquar, aetas iam a diuturnis laboribus devexa ad
otium domesticarum me rerum delectatione mollivit. Nunc, si
vel periculose experiundum erit, experiar certe, ut hinc avolem.
Ante oportuit fortasse; sed ea, quae scripsi, me tardarunt et
4 auctoritas maxime tua. Nam cum ad hunc locum venissem,
evolvi volumen epistolarum tuarum, quod ego *sub* signo habeo
servoque diligentissime. Erat igitur in ea, quam X. K. Febr.
dederas, hoc modo: 'sed videamus, et Gnaeus quid agat et
illius rationes quorsum fluant: quod si iste Italiam relinquet,
faciet omnino male et, ut ego existimo, ἀλογίστως: sed tum
demum consilia nostra commutanda erunt.' Hoc scribis post
diem quartum, quam ab urbe discessimus. Deinde VIII. K.
Febr.: 'tantum modo Gnaeus noster ne, ut urbem ἀλογίστως
reliquit, sic Italiam relinquat.' Eodem die das alteras litteras,
quibus mihi consulenti planissime respondes; est enim sic: 'sed
venio ad consultationem tuam. Si Gnaeus Italia cedit, in urbem
redeundum puto; quae enim finis peregrinationis?' Hoc mihi
plane haesit, et nunc ita video, infinitum bellum iunctum miser-
5 rima fuga, quam tu peregrinationem ὑποκορίζῃ. Sequitur χρησμὸς

1. Devexa ad otium, 'declining towards a peaceful evening.' There is a combination of two thoughts—'declining to its evening,' and 'disposed for rest'—which makes the passage difficult.

2. Domesticarum . . delectatione, 'the pleasure arising from my domestic life.' On the gen., cp. Ep. 4, 2, note.

3. Experiar ut avolem: cp. Madv. 372 a.

4. Oportuit: cp. Ep. 4, 1, note, on the mood.

Ea, quae scripsi, 'the reasons I have written.'

5. Cum . . venissem, 'when I had written thus far.' Metzg.

6. Volumen, 'the roll,' 'collection' of your letters = 'quia unum quasi corpus conficiunt.' Forcell.

7. Erat: cp. 'ut est,' above.

8. K. Febr., 'Jan. 21.'

9. Illius . . fluant, 'at what Caesar's plans aim.' 'Fluere' = 'spectare.' Forcell.

Iste, Pompeius.

10. ἀλογίστως, 'unreasonably.' The adverb seems rare.

Tum demum . . erunt, 'it will be only then that we shall have to change our plans.'

11. Post diem quartum. Cicero seems, then, to have left the neighbourhood of Rome on Jan. 17.

13. Tantum modo . . relinquat, 'provided only that Pompey do not leave Italy as he has left Rome.' 'Tantum modo' = 'dum modo.' Forcell.

15. Est enim sic (cp. § 1), 'it runs as follows.'

16. Consultationem tuam, 'the point on which you consult me.' Metzg. 'Consultatio' = 'actus petendi consilii.' Forcell. Cp. Ad Att. 7. 12. 4, for Cicero's question.

Italia. On this ablat. cp. Madv. 262; Zumpt, 468.

17. Quae enim, sc. 'esset si eum sequeremur.'

18. Haesit, 'made a deep impression on me.' Cp. § 3.

Ita video, sc. 'fore,' 'I foresee the following result.'

Infinitum bellum, sc. 'fore.' For a similar ellipse cp. Epp. 15. 10, note; 59, 2, note.

Iunctum miserrima fuga: cp. De Orat. 2. 58, 237 'insignis improbitas et scelere iuncta.'

19. Peregrinationem, 'as a tour,' 'residence abroad.'

ὑποκορίζῃ, 'call euphemistically,' 'gloss over.' Liddell and Scott.

χρησμὸς, 'prophecy.'

VI. *K.* Februarias: 'ego, si Pompeius manet in Italia nec res ad pactionem venit, longius bellum puto fore; sin Italiam relinquit, ad posterum bellum ἄσπονδον strui existimo.' Huius igitur belli ego particeps et socius et adiutor esse cogor, quod et ἄσπονδον est *et* cum civibus. Deinde VII. Idus Febr., cum iam plura audires de Pompeii consilio, concludis epistolam quandam hoc modo: 'ego quidem tibi non sim auctor, si Pompeius Italiam relinquit, te quoque profugere; summo enim periculo facies nec rei publicae proderis, cui quidem posterius poteris prodesse, si manseris.' Quem φιλόπατριν ac πολιτικὸν hominis prudentis et amici tali admonitu non moveret auctoritas? Deinceps III. Idus Febr. iterum mihi respondes consulenti sic: 'quod quaeris a me fugamne † fidam an moram desidem utiliorem putem, ego vero in praesentia subitum discessum et praecipitem profectionem cum tibi, tum ipsi Gnaeo inutilem et periculosam puto, et satius esse existimo vos dispertitos et in speculis esse; sed medius fidius turpe nobis puto esse de fuga cogitare.' Hoc turpe Gnaeus noster biennio ante cogitavit; ita sullaturit animus eius et proscripturit iam diu. Inde, ut opinor, cum tu ad me quaedam γενικώτερον scripsisses et ego mihi a te [quaedam] significari putassem, ut Italia cederem, detestaris hoc diligenter XI. K. Mart.: 'ego vero nulla epistola significavi, si Gnaeus Italia cederet, ut tu una cederes, aut, *si* significavi, non dico fui inconstans, sed

1. Nec res .. venit = 'et res non venit.' Cp. Ep. 9. 4, note.

2. Longius .. fore, 'I think the war will be prolonged' in Italy.

3. Ad posterum .. existimo, 'I think the materials for a desperate war at a later time are being collected.'

ἄσπονδον, quite classical.

5. VII. Idus Febr., 'Feb. 7.'

7. Non sim auctor, 'I should not advise you.' Cp., on the tense, Ep. 5, 3, note.

8. Te .. profugere. On the mood, cp. Madv. 396. The conjunctive would be more common. Ib. 372 a.

Summo .. periculo, sc. 'tuo,' 'at the greatest risk to yourself.'

10. φιλόπατριν, 'patriot.' Polyb. 1. 14. πολιτικὸν, 'statesman.'

13. Fugamne † fidam, 'a flight, which would shew your loyalty to Pompey.'

Desidem is Kayser's suggestion for the MS. 'defendam.' He also suggests 'citam' for 'fidam,' but the latter is apparently the MS. reading, and gives a tolerable sense.

16. Vos, 'you and Pompey.'

Dispertitos, foll., 'in different places, and on the watch.'

18. Biennio ante. Pompey can hardly have foreseen the exact course things would take, but he may have spoken of a war between East and West as possible.

Sullaturit .. et proscripturit, 'is eager to imitate Sulla, and to repeat his proscriptions.'

19. Inde, 'for this reason,' because of the intentions of Pompey.

20. γενικώτερον, 'in more general terms.' Orell. See Ep. 7, 2, note on p. 48, l. 1.

A te .. significari, 'that you indicated to me.' Forcell. Cp. Ep 19, 1.

21. Detestaris .. diligenter, 'you are careful to protest against this.'

23. Non dico = 'non modo.' Cp. Zumpt, L. G. 724.

Inconstans, 'inconsistent.'

demens.' In eadem epistola alio loco: 'nihil relinquitur nisi
fuga, cui te socium neutiquam puto esse oportere nec umquam
7 putavi.' Totam autem hanc deliberationem evolvis accuratius
in litteris VIII. Kal. Mart. datis: 'si M'. Lepidus et L. Volcatius remanent, manendum puto, ita ut, si salvus sit Pompeius
et constiterit alicubi, hanc *νεκυίαν* relinquas et te in certamine
vinci cum illo facilius patiaris quam cum hoc in ea, quae per-
spicitur futura, colluvie regnare.' Multa disputas huic sententiae
convenientia; inde ad extremum 'quid si' inquis 'Lepidus et
Volcatius discedunt? plane *ἀπορῶ*. Quod evenerit igitur et quod
egeris, id *στερκτέον* putabo.' Si tum dubitaras, nunc certe non
8 dubitas, istis manentibus. Deinde in ipsa fuga v. Kal. Martias:
'interea non dubito quin in Formiano mansurus sis; commodissime enim *τὸ μέλλον* ibi *καραδοκήσεις*.' Ad K. Martias, cum
ille quintum iam diem Brundisii esset: 'tum poterimus delibe-
rare, non scilicet integra re, sed certe minus infracta, quam si
una proieceris te.' Deinde IIII. Non. Martias *ὑπὸ τὴν λῆψιν*

1. Alio loco, sc. 'scribis.' Cp., on the ellipse, Ep. 15. 10, note.

Nihil relinquitur, sc. Pompeio.

3. Totam . . evolvis, 'you enter on, or enlarge on, this whole discussion more carefully.' Nägelsbach (105. 291) gives 'instituere' as an equivalent for 'evolvere;' Forcell. gives 'explicare, narrare.'

4. VIII. Kal. Mart., 'on Feb. 22.'

M'. Lepidus and L. Volcatius had been consuls together in 66 B.C. The first is mentioned Ad Att. 7. 23. 1; and both, Ib. 8. 15. 2.

5. Ita ut, foll., 'with the proviso, that if Pompey escapes Caesar's pursuit and makes a stand anywhere.' On this force of 'ita ut,' cp. Ep. 1. 1, note; Zumpt, L. G. 726.

6. Hanc νεκυίαν, 'this troop of shadows.' Caesar's followers were represented as ruined men, whom hopes of plunder attracted just as the blood poured out by Ulysses drew together the ghosts—νεκύων ἀμενηνὰ κάρηνα—in Odyss. 11. 23–50. The word νεκυία properly means a necromantic rite (Liddell and Scott), and was given as a name to the book of the Odyssey in which such a rite is described.

7. Cum illo, sc. Pompeio.

In ea . . regnare, 'to reign amid all the mass of wickedness which we see will come together.'

9. Ad extremum, 'at the end of the letter.'

10. Plane ἀπορῶ, 'I am quite at a loss' what advice to give.

Quod evenerit . . putabo. 'I shall think it right to be satisfied with whatever happens and whatever you do.'

11. στερκτέον is quoted by Liddell and Scott from Dinarchus, but seems rare.

12. In ipsa fuga, 'when Pompey was actually flying.'

14. τὸ μέλλον . . καραδοκήσεις, 'watch there eagerly to see how things go.' The word is quite classical, Liddell and Scott.

Ad K. Martias, 'on the first of March.' Cp. Ep. 66, 1 'mihi vero ad Nonas bene maturum videtur fore.' Wesenb., however, says that 'ad' cannot be used in this sense of the past, and suggests 'atque K.' Mart.

15. Ille, Pompeius.

16. Non scilicet integra . . proieceris te, 'not without committing yourself to some extent to be sure, but with less embarrassment than if you hurry off with Pompey.' Even a short delay would offend Pompey. 'Scilicet habet vim affirmandi.' Forcell.

Infracta keeps up the metaphor of 'integra.'

17. IIII. Non. Martias, 'March 4.'

ὑπὸ τὴν λῆψιν, 'just before your attack of fever.' Cp. Ep. 44. 3. ὑπὸ = 'about the time of.' Liddell and Scott.

cum breviter scriberes, tamen ponis hoc: 'cras scribam plura et
ad omnia; hoc tamen dicam, non paenitere me consilii de tua
mansione, et, quamquam magna sollicitudine, tamen, quia minus
mali puto esse quam in illa profectione, maneo in sententia et
gaudeo te mansisse.' Cum vero iam angerer et timerem, ne 9
quid a me dedecoris esset admissum, III. Nonas Mart.: 'tamen
te non esse una cum Pompeio non fero moleste; postea si opus
fuerit, non erit difficile, et illi, quoquo tempore fiet, erit ἀσμένιστον. Sed hoc ita dico, si hic, qua ratione initium fecit, eadem
cetera aget, sincere, temperate, prudenter, valde videro et con-
sideratius utilitati nostrae consuluero.' VII. Idus Martias scribis 10
Peducaeo quoque nostro probari, quod quierim, cuius auctoritas
multum apud me valet. His ego tuis scriptis me consolor, ut
nihil a me adhuc delictum putem. Tu modo auctoritatem tuam
defendito: adversus me nihil opus est, sed consciis egeo aliis.
Ego, si nihil peccavi, reliqua tuebor: ad ea tu te hortare et me
omnino tua cogitatione adiuva. Hic nihildum de reditu Caesaris
audiebatur. Ego his litteris hoc tamen profeci: perlegi omnes
tuas et in eo acquievi.

3. **Quamquam magna sollicitudine**, sc. 'mansisti,' 'though your remaining causes you great anxiety.' Billerb.

6. **III. Nonas Mart.**, sc. 'scribis.'

8. **Non erit difficile**, sc. 'esse una.'

ἀσμένιστον, 'acceptable,' a rare word. Cp. Liddell and Scott.

9. **Ita**, 'with this proviso.'

Hic Caesar.

10. **Sincere**, 'straightforwardly.'

Valde videro, 'shall look very carefully into the matter.' 'Videre' = 'cogitare.' Forcell.

11. **Utilitati nostrae**, 'our interest.' Cp. Ad Q. F. 1. 1. 24 'eorum quibus praesit commodis utilitatique servire.'

VII. Idus Martias, 'March 9.'

12. **Peducaeo**: cp. *Ep.* 61, 2.

14. **Auctoritatem . . defendito**, 'defend your advice' when it is criticised by others.

15. **Consciis egeo aliis**, 'I want others to be aware that I am acting under your advice.' Bosius ap. Boot.

16. **Reliqua tuebor**, 'I will take care of myself for the future.'

Tu te hortare, 'address yourself to the task of making others see the propriety of your advice to me.' Matth. Cp. 'auctoritatem defendito,' above.

17. **De reditu Caesaris**, sc. 'a Brundisio.' Cp. Introd. to Part III, §§ 7 and 8.

18. **Tamen**, 'respondet particulis etsi, licet, etc., vel tacitis.' Forcell. Here 'si nihil aliud' may be supplied.

19. **In eo acquievi**, 'have obtained rest thereby.' Cp. Epp. 47, 5: 94, 2. On a similar passage, Ad Att. 13. 13, 3 'crebro regusto tuas litteras; in his acquiesco,' Forcell. remarks that the words = 'his me consolor.'

64. To CAESAR (AD ATT. IX. 11 A).

FORMIAE, MARCH 19 APPARENTLY, (705 A.U.C.)

1. I hope that the meaning of your letter was that you were anxious to secure my services as a mediator for peace. 2. You could find no one better qualified for that office, as on the one hand I always protested against the attempts of your enemies to withdraw what the people had granted you, and have taken no part in this war; while on the other I am most anxious to maintain the honour of Pompey. For many years I have placed you and him first among my friends. 3. I hope, therefore, that amidst your pressing cares you will have some regard to my honour, and will allow me to preserve my neutrality. I lately heard from Lentulus, and repeat my thanks for your generosity to him. You see how grateful I am to him; let me be equally so to Pompey.

CICERO IMP. S. D. CAESARI IMP.

1 Ut legi tuas litteras, quas a Furnio nostro acceperam, quibus mecum agebas, ut ad urbem essem, te velle uti consilio et dignitate mea, minus sum admiratus: de gratia et de ope quid significares, mecum ipse quaerebam, spe tamen deducebar ad eam cogitationem, ut te pro tua admirabili ac singulari sapientia de otio, de pace, de concordia civium agi velle arbitrarer, et ad eam rationem existimabam satis aptam esse et naturam et
2 personam meam. Quod si ita est et si qua de Pompeio nostro tuendo et tibi ac rei publicae reconciliando cura te attingit, magis idoneum, quam ego sum, ad eam causam profecto reperies neminem, qui et illi semper et senatui, cum primum potui, pacis auctor fui, nec sumptis armis belli ullam partem attigi, iudicavique eo bello te violari, contra cuius honorem populi Romani

This answer to Caesar's note is not mentioned in Ep. 63, and therefore was probably not written before March 18. Its expressions seem to identify it with one quoted Ad Att. 8. 9, 1 (Ep. 55). Perhaps Ad Att. 8. 9 may be a combination of two letters written at different times, for it is hardly likely that Cicero wrote two very similar letters to Caesar within a month, and the date of Ad Att. 8. 9 is given as Feb. 25. Hofm., Billerb.

4. Spe tamen . . arbitrarer, 'my hopes, however, led me to entertain the thought that you wished me to argue in favour of peace.' On the conjunct., cp. Madv. 374.

7. Ad eam rationem, 'for such a task.' Metzg.

8. Personam, 'my position.'

9. Tuendo, 'maintaining in his proper place.'

11. Cum primum potui, i.e. after my return from Cilicia.

12. Sumptis armis, 'after hostilities had begun.'

Belli . . attigi, 'took any part in the war.' This statement seems to have been true, but can hardly be reconciled with the language of Ep. 50.

13. Contra cuius honorem . . nitebantur, 'as envious and hostile men were trying to deprive you of an honour.'

Populi . . beneficio, i.e. 'lege decem tribunorum.' See Ep. 44. 6, note.

beneficio concessum inimici atque invidi niterentur. Sed ut eo tempore non modo ipse fautor dignitatis tuae fui, verum etiam ceteris auctor ad te adiuvandum, sic me nunc Pompeii dignitas vehementer movet; aliquot enim sunt anni, cum vos duo delegi, quos praecipue colerem et quibus essem, sicut sum, amicissimus. Quam ob rem a te peto vel potius omnibus te precibus oro 2
et obtestor, ut in tuis maximis curis aliquid impertias temporis huic quoque cogitationi, ut tuo beneficio bonus vir, gratus, pius denique esse in maximi beneficii memoria possim; quae si tantum ad me ipsum pertinerent, sperarem me a te tamen impetraturum, sed, ut arbitror, et ad tuam fidem et ad rem publicam pertinet, me ex paucis et *ad* utriusque vestrum et ad civium concordiam per te quam accommodatissimum conservari. Ego, cum antea tibi de Lentulo gratias egissem, quod ei saluti, qui mihi fuerat, fuisses, tamen lectis eius litteris, quas ad me gratissimo animo de tua liberalitate beneficioque misit, eandem me salutem a te accepisse *putavi* quam ille; in quem si me intellegis esse gratum, cura, obsecro, ut etiam in Pompeium esse possim.

3. Auctor. Cicero had used his influence with Caelius in favour of the law just referred to. Cp. Ad Att. 7. 1, 4.

Pompeii dignitas, 'the just claims of Pompey's position.'

4. Aliquot . . anni . . amicissimus. Cicero probably refers to his reconciliation with the triumvirs in 56 B.C. Cp. Intr. to Part II, § 4. On 'cum' with the indic. as used here, cp. Madv. 358, Obs. 1.

7. Ut . . aliquid impertias temporis, 'that you will devote some time to considering how I may, by your indulgence, shew myself honest, grateful, and affectionate in remembering a very great service.' On the conj. 'impertias,' cp. Madv. 372 a; and p. 349, l. 3, note; and on 'possim,' not one § 1 of this letter.

8. Bonus vir, 'a man of honour.' The phrase is contrasted with 'bonus civis,' Ep. 29. 10.

9 Maximi beneficii. Cicero refers to Pompey's services in promoting his restoration from exile.

Quae si . . pertinerent, 'if this request only concerned myself.'

11. Ad tuam fidem . . pertinet, 'it affects the confidence felt in your assurances, and the public interest.' Süpfle, Metzg.

12. Me ex paucis . . conservari, 'that I, as one of the few impartial men, should be preserved in as good a position as possible for promoting a friendly understanding.' Cicero means that if Caesar respected his neutrality, people would feel confidence in Caesar's peaceful assurances.

13. Cum antea . . egissem, 'though I had thanked you before for your treatment of Lentulus,' whom Caesar had released after the capitulation of Corfinium. Cp. Caes. Bell. Civ. 1. 23.

14. Qui mihi fuerat, sc. 'saluti.' Lentulus had done all he could as consul in 57 B.C. to promote Cicero's restoration from exile. Cp. Intr. to Part I, § 23.

16. Eandem . . quam ille, sc. 'accepit.' The finite verb is usually expressed. 'Quam illum' would be admissible in an elliptic sentence. Cp. Madv. 303 b; 402 b; Ep. 3. 3, note.

17. In quem si . . possim, 'if this shews you my gratitude to him, make it possible for me to be grateful to Pompey too,' to whom I am equally indebted. A delicate plea on behalf of Cicero's neutrality.

65. TO ATTICUS (AD ATT. IX. 12).

FORMIAE, APPARENTLY, MARCH 21 (705 A.U.C.)

1. Lepta tells me that Pompey is blockaded in Brundisium, and the mouth of the harbour closed. I am much distressed by this news. Your advice is admirable, and your invitation to Epirus very kind. 2. I wonder at the conduct of Dionysius, and wish I could punish him. 3. Now what do you advise? Shall I fly to Pompey, or appeal to the country towns in his interest? 4. I feel quite in despair, and would rather have shared his misfortunes than his prosperity.

CICERO ATTICO SAL.

1 Legeram tuas litteras XIII. K., cum mihi epistola adfertur a Lepta, circumvallatum esse Pompeium, ratibus etiam exitus portus teneri: non medius fidius prae lacrimis possum reliqua nec cogitare nec scribere. Misi ad te exemplum. Miseros nos! cur non omnes fatum illius una exsecuti sumus? ecce autem a Matio et Trebatio eadem, quibus Minturnis obvii Caesaris tabellarii. Torqueor infelix, ut iam illum Mucianum exitum exoptem. At quam honesta, at quam expedita tua consilia, quam evigilata tuis cogitationibus qua itineris, qua navigationis, qua congressus sermonisque cum Caesare! omnia cum honesta, tum cauta. In

On the date, cp. § 1 with Ad Att. 9. 13. 2.

1. XIII. K., 'March 20.'

Adfertur, praes. hist. Cp. Madv. 336.

A Lepta; cp. Ep. 54. 7.

2. Circumvallatum, 'is invested' (by land) at Brundisium.

Ratibus . . teneri, 'are closed by rafts.'

Exitus. Properly speaking, there was only one entrance to the harbour of Brundisium from the sea, and this Caesar tried to close by building moles from each side, and beginning a floating bridge to connect them. Cp. Caes. Bell. Civ. 1. 25. But this single entrance presently divided into two branches, between which the town lay; and this circumstance may have suggested the use of the plural to Lepta or to Cicero. Cp. Smith's Dict. of Geogr. vol. 1, s. v. 'Brundusium,' pp. 444 446.

3. Non . . nec . . nec: cp. Ep. 8, 8, note.

Reliqua, 'anything further.'

4. Exemplum, 'a copy of Lepta's letter.'

Cur non . . sumus? 'why have we not all gone to share his fate to the end?' Boot. Cp. Philipp. 2. 22, 54 'exsequi cladem illam fugamque.'

5. A Matio. C. Matius was one of Caesar's most estimable and moderate adherents. Cp. Epp. 113; 114. On Trebatius, cp. Ep. 27.

6. Eadem, sc. 'adferuntur.'

Quibus . . tabellarii, 'whom Caesar's messengers met at Minturnae,' and who therefore have good information.

7. Torqueor: cp. Ep. 45. 4.

Illum Mucianum exitum, 'the well-known death of Mucius.' Cp. Ep. 54. 6.

At, 'but on the other hand.' Cp. Madv. 437 c.

8. Expedita, 'clear.' Metzg.

Quam evigilata . . cum Caesare, 'how elaborated by watching and thought about my journey and voyage, and the meeting and conversation (cp. Ep. 67. 1) I expect with Caesar.' 'Evigilare' is explained by Forcell. as = 'vigilando conficere.'

9. Itineris may mean, 'about my journey to the camp of Pompey generally.'

Navigationis, 'about the time and port of departure.' Cp. Epp. 54. 5; 61. 5. On the genitives, Ep. 16, 3, note on p. 105; and on qua . . qua, Ep. 12, 3, note.

10. In Epirum vero foll., 'then your invitation to your estate in Epirus was cer-

Epirum vero invitatio quam suavis, quam liberalis, quam fraterna! De Dionysio sum admiratus, qui apud me honoratior 2
fuit quam apud Scipionem Panaetius, a quo impurissime haec nostra fortuna despecta est. Odi hominem et odero; utinam ulcisci possem! sed illum ulciscentur mores sui.

Tu, quaeso, nunc vel maxime, quid agendum nobis sit, cogita. 3
Populi Romani exercitus Cn. Pompeium circumsedet, fossa et vallo saeptum tenet, fuga prohibet: nos vivimus et stat urbs ista; praetores ius dicunt; aediles ludos parant; viri boni usuras perscribunt; ego ipse sedeo. Coner illuc ire, ut insanus? implorare fidem municipiorum? boni non sequentur; leves irridebunt; rerum novarum cupidi, victores praesertim et armati, vim et manus adferent. Quid censes igitur? ecquidnam est tui 4
consilii ad finem huius miserrimae vitae? Nunc doleo, nunc torquear, cum cuidam aut sapiens videor, quod una non ierim, aut felix fuisse. Mihi contra; numquam enim illius victoriae socius esse volui; calamitatis mallem fuissem. Quid ego nunc tuas litteras, quid tuam prudentiam aut benevolentiam implorem? actum est: nulla re iam possum iuvari, qui ne quod optem quidem iam habeo nisi ut aliqua inimici misericordia liberemur.

tainly friendly, generous and brotherly in the highest degree.' On 'vero,' cp. Madv. 437 d.

2. De Dionysio, 'about Dionysius.' Perhaps, 'that you still have a word to say for him.' Cp. Ad Att. 9. 15, 5.

3. Panaetius, a Stoic philosopher of Rhodes, and friend of the younger Scipio. Cp. Ep. 112, 4; Pro Muren. 31. 66.

A quo . . despecta est, 'who has shewn a most indecent contempt for me in my present position.' Dionysius had left Cicero, and refused for some time to return to him. Cp. Epp. 44. 1; 74. 1. Cicero was reconciled to him afterwards.

5. Mores sui: cp. Ad Att. 9. 15. 5 'illum male sanum semper putavi, nunc etiam impurum et sceleratum puto.'

9. Viri boni: cp. Ep. 6, 3. Perhaps the farmers of the revenue and great money lenders are especially referred to. Cicero had generally been on good terms with them, but had often complained of their want of political firmness and disinterestedness. Cp. Ep. 9. 8; 44, 5.

Usuras = 'pecuniam datam sub usuris.' Forcell.

10. Perscribent = 'enter in their books.' 'Perscribi dicuntur quaecumque in tabulas accepti et expensi referuntur.' Forcell.

Sedeo, 'sit quiet here.'

Illuc, 'to Brundisium.'

Implorare fidem municipiorum? 'to appeal to the municipal towns for aid?' (Metzg.) i.e. to try and levy a force with which he might break through Caesar's lines.

11. Leves, 'the unprincipled.' Cp. the use of 'levitas,' Ep. 15, 4.

13. Ecquidnam . . consilii, foll., 'what advice have you to give for putting an end to this most unhappy way of life?' On the gen. (generis) cp. Madv. 285 b.

14. Ad finem. So Orell. and Boot. in his text. But Boot suggests 'ecquidnam est vi consilii finis huius miserrimae vitae?' The best MS., which Baiter follows, seems to have 'ad finis.'

16. Mihi contra, sc. 'videtur esse.' 'Contra' used adverbially as a predicate. Cp. Madv. 172. Obs. 1; Ep. 4, 1.

Illius, Pompeii.

19. Actum est, 'I am ruined.'

20. Inimici, Caesaris.

Liberemur, 'be released from embarrassment,' by Caesar's allowing him either to leave Italy or to remain neutral. Metzg. By Caesar's putting him to death. Schütz.

66. TO ATTICUS (AD ATT. IX. 16).

FORMIAE, MARCH 26 (705 A.U.C.)

1. I hear that Caesar stays to-morrow at Sinuessa; I send you a letter which he has written to me in answer to one praising his clemency at Corfinium. You see that its expressions vary a little from those of his last.

2. Caesar to Cicero. You are quite right in supposing that I have no thought of cruelty. Nor do I care for the rumours about the ingratitude of those whom I have spared. It pleases me that both they and I should act in character. 3. I shall be glad if you will meet me at Rome, that I may have the benefit of your advice and resources as usual. Your son-in-law, Dolabella, is a most agreeable companion.

CICERO ATTICO SAL.

1 Cum quod scriberem ad te nihil haberem, tamen, ne quem diem intermitterem, has dedi litteras. A. d. VI. K. Caesarem Sinuessae mansurum nuntiabant; ab eo mihi litterae redditae sunt a. d. VII. K., quibus iam 'opes' meas, non, ut superioribus [litteris], 'opem' exspectat. Cum eius clementiam Corfiniensem illam per litteras collaudavissem, rescripsit hoc exemplo:

'CAESAR IMP. CICERONI IMP. SAL. DIC.

2 Recte auguraris de me—bene enim tibi cognitus sum—nihil a me abesse longius crudelitate; atque ego cum ex ipsa re magnam capio voluptatem, tum meum factum probari abs te triumpho gaudio. Neque illud me movet, quod ii, qui a me

1. **Cum**, 'although.'

Quod scriberem . . nihil haberem. 'Nihil habeo quod' = 'mihi deest quod;' 'nihil habeo quid' = 'nescio quid.' Hofm., cp. Ernest. ap. Forcell. sub voc. 'habeo,' and p. 109, note on l. 8.

3. **Sinuessae.** Sinuessa was on the coast between the Liris and the Volturnus. It is now called Mondragone.

Nuntiabant = 'nuntiant.' See Ep. 1, 1, note.

4. **Opes.** Caesar probably referred to Cicero's influence and connections, but Cicero insinuates that Caesar wanted funds.

Ut superioribus: see Ep. 60.

5. **Exspectat**, 'says he hopes to avail himself of.'

Clementiam, foll., 'his celebrated display of clemency at Corfinium.' Cp. Intr. to Part III, § 2.

6. **Per litteras**, cp. Ep. 64, 3, p. 354.

Hoc exemplo, 'of the following purport.' Cp. Ep. 6, 2, note, for the ablat. (qualitatis).

7. **Auguraris**, 'divine.' The word is often used in a metaphorical sense (cp. 'quantum ego opinione auguror' Pro Muren. 31. 65); but Caesar may have chosen it because Cicero was one of the augurs (cp. Ep. 71, 6).

8. **Longius crudelitate.** 'Quam' with the accus. would be more in accordance with usage. Cp. Madv. 304. Obs. 1.

Cum . . tum: cp. Ep. 26, 3, note.

Ex ipsa re, 'from the exercise of clemency in itself.'

9. **Meum factum probari, foll.** On the construction, cp. Ep. 7, 3, note, on p. 48, l. 13.

10. **Triumpho gaudio**: cp. Pro Muren. 21, 51.

Illud: cp. Ep. 5, 9, note.

dimissi sunt, discessisse dicuntur, ut mihi rursus bellum inferrent; nihil enim malo quam et me mei similem esse et illos sui. Tu 2
velim mihi ad urbem praesto sis, ut tuis consiliis atque opibus, ut consuevi, in omnibus rebus utar. Dolabella tuo nihil scito mihi esse iucundius. Hanc adeo habebo gratiam illi; neque enim aliter facere poterit: tanta eius humanitas, is sensus, ea in me est benevolentia.'

67. TO ATTICUS (AD ATT. IX. 18).

ARPINUM, MARCH 28 OR 29 (705 A.U.C.)

1. I followed your advice both in the firmness of my language to Caesar, and in declining to go to Rome. He was very pressing, and finally asked me 'to think over the matter.' 2. I was disgusted with his companions. His forces and his vigilance are alike formidable. 3. He said that if I did not support him he must try others, and would shrink from no expedient. He then left for Pedum, I for this place, where I expect a letter from you. 4. You have nothing to wait for now that Caesar and I have met, and I hope you will speak out.

CICERO ATTICO SAL.

Utrumque ex tuo consilio: nam et oratio fuit ea nostra, ut 1
bene potius ille de nobis existimaret, quam gratias ageret, et in eo mansimus, ne ad urbem. Illa fefellerunt, facilem quod putaramus: nihil vidi minus. Damnari se nostro iudicio, tardiores

II, sup. L. Domitius Ahenobarbus, cp. Intr. to Part III, §§ 8, 11.

2. Quam et me . . sui, 'than that I should preserve my character, and they theirs.' On the accus. and inf., cp. Ep. 15, 11, note.

Tu velim . . praesto sis. On the omission of 'ut' after 'velim,' cp. Madv. 372 b, Obs. 2.

4. Dolabella tuo. Dolabella was now Cicero's son-in-law. Cp. Epp. 42, 1; 72, 1.

Nihil . . esse iucundius. 'Nihil de personis dictum non insolens est.' Forcell.

5. Hanc adeo, foll. 'Hanc gratiam' = 'huius rei gratiam' (Boot), 'I shall be indebted to him even for this service,' i.e. for your coming to Rome to advise me. Hofm., Metzg.

Neque enim, foll., 'for he will certainly employ his influence to this end.'

6. Tanta eius, foll., 'so great is his kindliness, such his disposition and his good will towards me.'

Is sensus . . est = 'ita de me sentit.' Boot. Cp. Ep. 29, 2 and 17 for this meaning of 'sensus.' On the mood of 'est,' cp. Ep. 60 'ita de me mereris.'

Caesar was to stay at Sinuessa March 27 (cp. preceding letter, § 1), and he was to be at Rome before April 1. Cicero went to Arpinum at once after the meeting mentioned in this letter, and seems to have written there. Cp. § 3; Ad Att. 9. 15, 6; 9. 17, 1.

8. Utrumque ex tuo consilio, sc. 'fecimus:' cp. Ep. 56, 1, note.

Ut bene, foll., 'that Caesar would entertain more respect than gratitude.'

9. In eo mansimus, 'I persevered in my resolution.'

10. Ne ad urbem, sc. 'iremus.'

Illa fefellerunt, foll., 'I was deceived in the expectations I had formed of his indulgence.'

11. Damnari se, foll., 'he said it was a hostile decision on my part, and that the other senators would be less willing to attend if I did not.' 'Damnari,' pres. after the hist. pres. 'dicere,' cp. Madv. 408 b.

fore reliquos, si nos non venerimus, dicere; ego, dissimilem
illorum esse causam. Cum multa: 'veni igitur et age de pace.'
Meone, inquam, arbitratu? 'An tibi' inquit 'ego praescribam?'
Sic, inquam, agam, senatui non placere in Hispanias iri nec
exercitus in Graeciam transportari, multaque, inquam, de Gnaeo
deplorabo. Tum ille: 'ego vero ista dici nolo.' Ita putabam,
inquam, sed ego eo nolo adesse, quod aut sic mihi dicendum est
multaque, quae nullo modo possem silere, si adessem, aut non
veniendum. Summa fuit, ut ille, quasi exitum quaerens, 'ut de-
liberarem.' Non fuit negandum. Ita discessimus. Credo igitur
hunc me non amare; at ego me amavi, quod mihi iam pridem
2 usu non venit. Reliqua, o di! qui comitatus! quae, ut tu soles
dicere, *νέκυια*! in qua erat † ero sceleri! o rem perditam! o copias
desperatas! Quid, *quod* Servii filius, *quod* Titinii in iis castris
fuerunt, quibus Pompeius circumsederetur! Sex legiones; multum

1. Si nos non venerimus. Cicero uses the tense which Caesar himself must have used. Caesar would say 'si tu non veneris.' Wesenb. has 'venireenus.'

Ego, sc. 'respondere.'

Dissimilem, foll., 'that their position was different,' as not having been such prominent politicians. Cp. Ep. 55, 3.

2. Cum multa, sc. 'locuti essemus,' or, 'locutus essem.'

Veni igitur, foll., 'come then and make proposals for peace,' Caesar is supposed to say.

3. Meone . . arbitratu? 'after my own fashion?' 'as I choose?' ablat. modi. Cp. Ep. 24, 1 'arbitratu nostro.'

An occurs in answers which are expressed as questions. Cp. Madv. 453.

4. In Hispanias . . . transportari, 'that you should march to Spain, nor that an army should be transported to Greece' to act against Pompey. Cp. for the accus. and infin., Ep. 15, 11, note. 'Hispanias,' plural as referring to the Spanish provinces now governed by Pompey's legates. In earlier editions I said 'the *three* Spanish provinces.' But it is doubtful if there were three distinct Roman provinces in Spain before the time of Augustus, though Pompey administered the government by the hands of three legates. Cp. Mommsen, Staatsrecht, 1. 101. Mommsen, Hist. 4. 1, 1/6 speaks of Caesar after his praetorship as governor of Farther Spain simply.

5. Multaque . . deplorabo, 'I shall express my sympathy with Pompey at some length.'

6. Ista dici nolo, 'I do not want anything of that sort to be said.' Cp. Ep. 15, l. c.

7. Eo . . quod: cp. Ep. 62, 3, note.

8. Multaque, sc. 'dicenda.' Cp. Madv. 478.

9. Summa fuit, 'the end of it all was.' Metzg.

Ut ille, sc. 'peteret.'

Quasi exitum quaerens, 'as though seeking to end the discussion with courtesy.' Metzg.

10. Non fuit negandum, 'I could not refuse this.'

11. At ego . . non venit, 'but I was satisfied with myself—a pleasure which I have not enjoyed for a long time.'

12. Usu venit: cp. Pro Quinctio 15, 49. Forcell. writes 'ovvenire' = 'contingere.'

Reliqua, 'for the rest,' 'übrigens,' Metzg. Adverbial accusative. Cp. Madv. 237 c, Obs. 3.

13. *νέκυια*: cp. Ep. 63, 7.

Ero sceleri. Orell. suggests *ἐρεσχελίᾳ*, a late word for 'raillery.' Cp. Liddell and Scott. Hofm. 'erat area sceleris,' 'in what an arena of crime did he move.' Kayser '*κέρας* scelerum,' *κέρας* = 'cornu copiae.' Wesenb. has 'Eros Celeris:' sc. libertus?

14. Quid, quod, foll.: cp. Madv. 479 d, Obs. 1. 'What do you say to the fact that the sons of Servius and of Titinius are with him?'

Servii. Of Ser. Sulpicius Rufus, to whom or from whom are the letters 90; 98; 99; 101. On Titinius, cp. Ep. 62, 1.

15. Sex legiones, sc. 'habet Caesar.'

vigilat, audet: nullum video finem mali. Nunc certe promenda tibi sunt consilia: hoc fuerat extremum. Illa tamen κατακλεὶς 3
illius est odiosa, quam paene praeterii, si sibi consiliis nostris uti non liceret, usurum, quorum posset, ad omniaque esse descensurum. 'Vidisti igitur virum, ut scripseras? ingemuisti?' Certe. 'Cedo reliqua.' Quid? continuo ipse in Pedanum, ego Arpinum; inde exspecto equidem λαλαγεῦσαν illam tuam. 'Tu, malum,' inquies 'actum ne agas.' Etiam illum ipsum, quem sequimur, multa fefellerunt. Sed ego tuas litteras exspecto; nihil est enim 4
iam, ut antea, 'videamus, hoc quorsum evadat:' extremum fuit de congressu nostro, quo quidem non dubito quin istum offenderim; eo maturius agendum est. Amabo te, epistolam et πολιτικήν! valde tuas litteras nunc exspecto.

1. Nunc certe, 'now certainly you must disclose your opinion.'

2. Hoc fuerat extremum, 'this [i.e. the result of my conference with Caesar] was the last thing you were to wait for before giving it.' Metzg. Boot, referring to Gronovius, explains 'extremum' as meaning 'this,' i.e. how I should behave when I met Caesar 'was the last piece of advice you had given me.'

κατακλεὶς illius, 'Caesar's final words.' Metzg. Orell. gives 'clausula' as an equivalent for κατακλείς.

5. Vidisti igitur virum, foll., 'you have seen the man, as you said you would.' Hofm. These words, of course, are put into the mouth of Atticus. Boot thinks they mean 'you have seen the "hero" as you wrote.' Atticus, criticising Cicero's language—or perhaps 'you have found Caesar, as you expected, insolent?'

Certe, 'certainly,' says Cicero.

6. Cedo reliqua, 'tell me what followed,' says Atticus.

Ipse, Caesar.

In Pedanum, sc. 'profectus est;' cp. Ep. 36, 9. 'He went to his estate at Pedum,' a town between Tibur and Praeneste.

7. Inde, for 'ibi,' 'at Arpinum.' Hofm. quotes Livy 8. 6 'ut ab utra parte cedere Romanus exercitus coepisset inde se consul devoveret.'

λαλαγεῦσαν illam tuam, sc. 'epistolam,' 'your letter that is to warn me to start in spring' [with the swallows], λαλαγεῖν, 'to chirrup like a swallow,' Liddell and Scott, who quote Theocritus. Hofm. reads πλαταγεῦσαν, 'oracular,' from πλαταγώνιον, or πατάγουσαν, 'noisy,' hence 'imperious, 'decisive.' The best MS. seems to have ΛΑΛΤΕΛCΑΝ or ΛΑΛΤΕΛCΑΝ. Boot suggests ἀποτελοῦσαν in the sense of 'conclusive.' Mr. Jeans thinks that λαλαγεῦσαν may mean 'bright, cheerful, chatty,' and renders 'babillage.'

Malum: cp. Madv. 236.

8. Actum ne agas, 'do not do that for which the time has passed.' Cp. De Amic. 22, 85 'praeposteris enim utimur consiliis, et acta agimus quod vetamur vetere proverbio.' Atticus might say that it was too late to join Pompey with credit.

Etiam illum, foll., 'Pompey shewed no more foresight than I have shewn, and ought to make allowances,' Cicero answers.

9. Nihil est enim, sc. 'quod dicas.' On which constr., cp. Madv. 372 b, Obs. 6. 'You cannot say now as you did before, "Let us see how such and such an affair will turn out!"' Cp. Ep. 63. 4, for a similar expression of Atticus.

10. Extremum fuit, foll., 'the last point,' on which we corresponded. Metzg. 'for which I was to wait before deciding.' Billerb.

12. Amabo te = 'precor.' Cp. Ep. 35, 5; Ad Att. 2. 2, 1; Ad Q. F. 2. 10, 4.

Epistolam, sc. 'mitte.'

πολιτικήν! 'discussing political subjects.'

13. Valde, 'with great anxiety.'

68. TO ATTICUS (AD ATT. X. 1).

NEAR ARPINUM, APRIL 3 (705 A.U.C.)

1. I have been much comforted by your approval and by that of Peducaeus. 2. I am still anxious for your advice, though my duty seems clearer to me than it did, and I have almost decided on remaining neutral; 3. for I doubt if any honest negotiation for peace is possible. If, however, Caesar sends for me I shall consult you again. 4. You and Peducaeus have set me a good example. I am not satisfied with my conduct and position. Another will probably be preferred to me as an envoy to Pompey.

CICERO ATTICO SAL.

1 III. Nonas cum in Laterium fratris venissem, accepi litteras et paulum respiravi, quod post has ruinas mihi non acciderat: per enim magni aestimo tibi firmitudinem animi nostri et factum nostrum probari; Sexto enim nostro quod scribis probari, ita laetor, ut me quasi patris eius, cui semper uni plurimum tribui, iudicio comprobari putem, qui mihi, quod saepe soleo recordari, dixit olim, Nonis illis Decembribus, cum ego 'Sexte, quidnam ergo?'

> 'μὴ μάν, inquit ille, ἀσπουδί γε καὶ ἀκλειῶς [ἀπολοίμην],
> ἀλλὰ μέγα ῥέξας τι καὶ ἐσσομένοισι πυθέσθαι.'

eius igitur mihi vivit auctoritas, et simillimus eius filius eodem est apud me pondere, quo fuit ille; quem salvere velim iubeas
2 plurimum. Tu tuum consilium etsi non in longinquum tempus differs—iam enim illum emptum pacificatorem perorasse puto, iam

1. **Laterium**, an estate of Q. Cicero near Arpinum. Cp. Appendix 5, § 1.

Litteras, sc. 'tuas,' which Wesenb. adds.

2. **Post has ruinas**, 'after the fall of the constitution.' Cp. Ad Fam. 5. 17. 1 'in ruinis rei publicae nostrisque.'

Per enim magni, tmesis: cp. Madv. 203, Obs.

3. **Firmitudinem . . probari**, 'that you approve the firmness of my demeanour,' on which, cp. Ep. 67. 1.

4. **Sexto enim.** The 'enim' seems superfluous. Cicero may have written hastily, and have forgotten that he had already accounted in the previous sentence for the relief Atticus' letter had afforded him. Sextus Peducaeus is often called by his praenomen only. Cp. Ep. 61. 1.

7. **Nonis illis Decembribus.** The day of the execution of Catiline's accomplices, 63 B.C. Cp. Intr. to Part I, § 11.

Quidnam ergo? sc. 'faciendum est.' Billerb., following Manut., suggests that after the senate had pronounced for the execution, Cicero asked Peducaeus if he should carry out the sentence at once. The Greek quotation is from Hom. Il. 22. 304–5.

9. **Inquit ille.** These words are inserted pleonastically to resume the sense after cum . . ergo. Cp. Madv. 480.

11. **Eius . . vivit auctoritas**, 'the expression of his judgment lives in my memory.' Cp. Philipp. 2. 5, 12 'cuius semper in hac re publica vivet auctoritas.'

13. **Non in longinquum**, foll. Atticus seems to have recommended Cicero to wait and see what would take place in the senate after Caesar's return to Rome.

14. **Illum emptum pacificatorem:** cp. 'iste nummarius' in § 3. Cicero insinuates that Caesar had bribed some senator to propose negotiations with Pompey. Curio

actum aliquid esse in consessu senatorum—*senatum* enim non puto—, tamen suspensum me inde tenes, sed eo minus, quod non dubito, quid nobis agendum putes. Qui enim Flavio legionem et Siciliam dari scribas et id iam fieri, quae tu scelera partim parari iam et cogitari, partim ex tempore futura censes? Ego vero Solonis, popularis tui, ut puto etiam mei, legem neglegam, qui capite sanxit, si qui in seditione non alterius utrius partis fuisset, *et*, nisi si tu aliter censes, et hinc abero et illim; sed alterum mihi est certius, nec praecipiam tamen: exspectabo tuum consilium et eas litteras, nisi alias iam dedisti, quas scripsi ut Cephalioni dares. Quod scribis, non quo aliunde audieris, sed 8
te ipsum putare me attractum iri, si de pace agatur, mihi omnino

is generally supposed to be the man referred to. But may not M. Lepidus be meant? Cp. Ep. 62, 3.

Perorasse, 'has concluded his speech' in the senate.

1. In consessu senatorum: cp. Ad Fam. 4. 1, 1 'conventus senatorum.' Cicero probably uses these disparaging terms because the consuls and most of the more eminent senators were absent. Cp. Mommsen 4. 2, 379.

2. Inde, 'on your decision.' Wesenb. suggests 'suspensum animum de eo tenes.'

3. Non dubito, foll. Cicero apparently thought that Atticus, by dwelling so much on the violence of Caesar's friends, was anxious to dissuade him from coming to Rome.

Qui enim, foll., 'for since you write that Sicily with one legion is being offered to Flavius, what crimes must you suppose are being plotted?' The natural order of the words seems to be inverted. A similar construction occurs Ad Q. F. 1. 1, 17 'qui in eiusmodi rebus . . castus esse velim . . quo me animo in servis esse censes.' Dari appears to be emphatic 'a Caesare quasi a rege:' Manut. For an account of L. Flavius here mentioned, cp. Intr. to Part I, § 15: Ad Att. 1. 18, 6; Ad Q. F. 1. 2, 10. M. Cato held Sicily for Pompey, and there was a rumour that Flavius would be sent to dislodge him; a commission afterwards given to Curio.

5. Ex tempore, 'as circumstances allow,' or suggest.' Cp. Ad Fam. 12. 19, 3 'haec melius ex re et ex tempore constitues.' Or perhaps more probably 'at once.' Cp. Pro Arch. 8. 18 'magnum numerum optimorum versuum . . dicere ex tempore.'

6. Popularis. Atticus had passed many years at Athens (cp. App. 3. § 1), and had received an offer of citizenship there in return for a present of corn. Cp. Corn. Nep. Att. 3, 1.

Etiam mei. Cicero had spent some time at Athens in early manhood, and his familiarity with Greek literature attached him to the place. Cp. Intr. to Part I, § 2.

7. Qui capite sanxit: cp. A. Gell. N. A. 2. 12; Grote's Hist. of Greece, 2nd edit., 3. 191, foll. Cicero seems to overstate the rigour of the law. 'Capite' = 'capitali poena' apparently.

8. Nisi si: cp Ep. 17, 1, note on p. 109.

Et hinc . . illim, 'I shall be absent from both camps.' 'Hinc,' from Caesar's; 'illim,' from Pompey's.

9. Alterum, sc. 'hinc abesse.'

Nec praecipiam tamen, sc. 'hoc,' 'I shall not, however, decide on it prematurely.'

10. Quas scripsi . . dares, 'which I asked you in my last to give to Cephalio.' Cp. Ad Att. 9. 19, 4. Cicero had asked for an account of what was going on, and for Atticus' advice. Cephalio seems to have been a slave employed by Atticus as a messenger.

11. Non quo aliunde, foll., 'not as though you had heard it from another source.' Cicero might have continued 'sed quod ipse putas,' but prefers to change the construction, putare depending on scribis. Mainly from Boot.

12. Me attractum iri, 'that I should be drawn to Rome.' Cp. Forcell., and Ovid Metam. 5. 93 (according to one reading), 'quandoquidem in partes, ait, attrahor.'

Si de pace agatur. On the pres. conj. in dependent propositions with future sense, cp. Madv. 378 a.

non venit in mentem, quae possit actio esse de pace, cum illi certissimum sit, si possit, exspoliare exercitu et provincia Pompeium, nisi forte iste nummarius ei potest persuadere, ut, dum oratores eant et redeant, quiescat. Nihil video, quod sperem aut quod iam putem fieri posse. Sed tamen hominis hoc ipsum probi est. Magnum est et τῶν πολιτικωτάτων σκεμμάτων, veniendumne sit in consilium tyranni, si is aliqua de re bona deliberaturus sit; qua re, si quid eius modi evenerit, ut arcessamur—quod equidem non curo; quid enim essem de pace dicturus, dixi; ipse valde repudiavit—, sed tamen, si quid acciderit, quid censeas mihi faciendum, utique scribito; nihil enim mihi adhuc accidit, quod maioris consilii esset. Trebatii, boni viri et civis, verbis te gaudeo delectatum, tuaque ista crebra ἐκφώνησις 'ὑπέρευ' me sola adhuc delectavit. Litteras tuas vehementer exspecto, quas quidem
4 credo iam datas esse. Tu cum Sexto servasti gravitatem eandem, quam mihi praecipis. Celer tuus disertus magis est quam sapiens. De iuvenibus quae ex Tullia audisti vera sunt. † Maconi istud,

2. Provincia, Spain, which Pompey had governed for some years as proconsul, and where his legates now commanded an army of seven legions. Cp. Intr. to Part II, §§ 8; 14; Part III, § 8; Appendix 7.

3. Iste nummarius: cp. § 2, note, and for the word, p. 98, l. 4.

4. Oratores, 'the negotiators' between Caesar and Pompey, = 'legati.' Forcell.

5. Sed tamen . . est, 'but this very conduct is worthy of an honest man.'

Hoc ipsum, I presume, means 'to argue for peace even under unpromising circumstances.' The words are introduced as from one persuading Cicero to act as mediator. I have adopted Orelli's punctuation.

6 Magnum . . σκεμμάτων, 'it is a great question, and one truly to be classed among political problems.' Cp. Ad Att. 9. 4. 2 for examples of similar disputed questions. Σκέμματα occ. Plat. Rep. 435 C. I have adopted Orelli's reading as making sense with the slightest departure from that of the MS., which appears to have 'magnum sit τῶν πολ. σκ.'

8. Qua re, 'since there is this difficulty.'

Ut arcessamur, 'so that I should be sent for to Rome.'

Quod . . non curo, 'for which I am not anxious, = 'curae habeo.' Cp. Sall. Iug. 14, 'curare iniurias sociorum.'

9. Dixi, 'I told Caesar.' Cp. Ep. 67, 3.

Valde repudiavit, 'was by no means satisfied therewith.' 'Repudiare' = 'respuere,' 'reiicere.' Forcell.

10. Sed tamen, resumptive: cp. Ep. 15. 16, p. 102. The words might either of them stand alone in this sense.

11. Quod maioris consilii esset, 'such as to require more consideration.' On the mood, cp. Ep. 1, 1, note; and on the genit. Epp. 46; 77, 3.

12. Trebatii: cp. Ep. 27.

Verbis, 'expressions.'

13. Tuaque . . ὑπέρευ, 'your frequent exclamation "most admirable."' Atticus had probably often used this expression in his letters to Cicero about the latter's conduct. ἐκφώνησις is not, apparently, a classical word. ὑπέρευ occ. Plat. Theaet. 185 D.

14. Litteras tuas: cp. the end of § 2.

15. Gravitatem. This refers probably to Atticus' behaviour in an interview with Caesar.

16. Celer tuus. Probably a freedman of Atticus. See Ep. 78, 1. Billerbeck suspects that he gave bad advice to Cicero's son and nephew.

17. De iuvenibus, about the young Marcus and Quintus. The former was now 14 years old, and had laid aside the 'toga praetexta.' He could not, however, be properly called 'iuvenis' yet. Cp. Ad Att. 1. 2, 1; 9. 19, 1. Forcell. sub voce. 'iuvenis,' 'adolescens.' The young Quintus was a year or two older. Cp. Ad Att. 5. 20, 9.

Quae . . vera sunt. This allusion is

quod scribis, non mihi videtur tam re esse triste quam verbo: haec est ἄλη, in qua nunc sumus, mortis instar: aut enim mihi libere inter malos πολιτευτέον fuit aut vel periculose cum bonis; aut nos temeritatem bonorum sequamur aut audaciam improborum insectemur. Utrumque periculosum est, at hoc, quod agimus, turpe, nec tamen tutum. Istum, qui filium Brundisium de pace misit—de pace idem sentio, quod tu, simulationem esse apertam, parari autem bellum acerrime—, me legatum iri non arbitror, cuius adhuc, ut optavi, mentio facta nulla sit: eo minus habeo necesse scribere aut etiam cogitare, quid sim facturus, si acciderit, ut leger.

69. M. CAELIUS RUFUS TO CICERO (AD FAM. VIII. 16).

EARLY IN APRIL (704 A.U.C.)

1. Your letter announcing your probable decision has filled me with terror. I write at once to dissuade you from any hasty step. You will bear me witness that I warned you how Caesar had been irritated by opposition. 2. Think of your family; do not place us who are your friends, though partisans of Caesar, in an embarrassing position; do not incur the suspicions of both parties; do not join men after defeat whom you would not join when their prospects were doubtful. 3. Wait, at least, till you hear what happens in Spain, which I believe will very soon be in Caesar's power. 4. Caesar has begged me to urge you to remain; if I were not obliged to attend him, I should have done all I could by personal entreaty to detain you. 5. If you cannot bear the taunts of the optimates and the insolence of some of Caesar's friends, await the issue of the struggle in some town remote from the seat of war.

obscure. It may refer to efforts made by them to reconcile the elder Quintus and Pomponia. Cp. Ep. 38 1–2, notes. Manut. thinks that the import of the remark is that Cicero was unwilling to have them taught by Dionysius. Cp. Ad Att. 10. 2, 2.

Maconi. Orell. suggests ἐνδόμυχον, 'the family secret;' Boot φάρμακον, 'the remedy,' some violent decision which Atticus wished Cicero to take.

2. ἄλη, 'anxiety.' The general sense of what follows seems to be, that he ought either to have followed Pompey to Greece, or to have taken a more independent line in Italy, and to have inveighed against Caesar. But Boot thinks the passage corrupt.

3. πολιτευτέον. I cannot find that this word occurs in classical Greek. Its construction with fuit seems to resemble that of the neuter gerundive. On which, cp. Ep. 38, 2.

6. Istum. According to one view, Servius Sulpicius Rufus (cp. Ad Att. 9. 18, 2; 9. 19. 2), in which case the first de pace must be ironical. Boot encloses it in brackets. Manutius suggests that L. Cornelius Balbus is referred to, but no son of his is mentioned elsewhere: the younger Balbus was his nephew. Cp. Ep. 55. 4, note, and Pliny, H. N. 5. 5, 36.

8. Legatum iri, 'will be sent as envoy' to Pompey. We should expect these words to follow 'istum,' or the position of 'non' to be changed. But cp. Ad Fam. 15. 4. 12 'quae ego in beneficii loco non pono sed in veri testimonii.' Wesenb. has 'legatum iri, non me arbitror.'

9. Cuius . . nulla sit, 'as no mention has yet been made of me.'

Habeo necesse scribere: cp. Madv. 423, Obs. 2.

CAELIUS CICERONI SAL.

1 Exanimatus tuis litteris, quibus te nihil nisi triste cogitare
ostendisti neque id quid esset perscripsisti neque non tamen,
quale esset quod cogitares, aperuisti, has ad te ilico litteras
scripsi. Per fortunas tuas, Cicero, per liberos te oro et obsecro,
ne quid gravius de salute et incolumitate tua consulas. Nam
deos hominesque amicitiamque nostram testificor me tibi praedixisse neque temere monuisse, sed postquam Caesarem convenerim sententiamque eius, qualis futura esset parta victoria,
cognoverim, te certiorem fecisse. Si existimas eandem rationem
fore Caesaris in dimittendis adversariis et condicionibus ferendis,
erras: nihil nisi atrox et saevum cogitat atque etiam loquitur:
iratus senatui exiit; his intercessionibus plane incitatus est; non
2 mehercules erit deprecationi locus. Qua re si tibi tu, si filius
unicus, si domus, si spes tuae reliquae tibi carae sunt, si aliquid
apud te nos, si vir optimus, gener tuus, valemus, quorum fortunam
non debes velle conturbare, ut eam causam, in cuius victoria salus

For an account of Caelius, cp. Ep. 33, note.

1. Exanimatus = 'exterritus.' Forcell. Cp. Hor. Carm. 2. 17, 1.

Tuis litteris. This letter of Cicero has not been preserved.

2. Quid esset .. quale esset. Cicero had hinted at the nature of his plans without precisely disclosing them.

Neque non tamen = 'et tamen:' cp. Ad Fam. 3. 12, 2 'neque non me tamen mordet aliquid.'

6. Me .. praedixisse, 'that I gave you notice.' This verb is found often without an accusat. Cp. De Har. Resp. 25. 53.

7. Temere, 'without grounds.'

Postquam C. convenerim, 'after meeting Caesar' at Ariminum. Cp. Ep. 76, 1. In the oratio directa, Caelius would have said 'conveni,' and this may account for the use of the perfect conj. (cp. Ramshorn 186, II. 1 b), but the transition to futura esset is strange.

8. Sententiam .. victoria, 'what his views would be after success.' With the construction cp. the words of Caelius (Ad Fam. 8. 10, 3) 'nosti Marcellum quam tardus .. sit;' Cicero on the contrary (Ib. 4. 1, 2), writes 'rem vides quo modo se habeat.'

9. Eandem, 'the same as he has pursued hitherto.'

Rationem, 'policy,' 'conduct.' See Ep. 9. 6, note.

10. In dimittendis adversariis, 'in letting his enemies go,' as Caesar had done with L. Domitius, P. Lentulus, and others. Cp. Caes. de Bell. Civ. 1. 23.

In .. condicionibus ferendis, 'in offering terms of peace.' Cp. Pro Rosc. Amer. 11, 30 'hanc condicionem misero ferunt.' On the facts, cp. Caes de Bell. Civ. 1. 9 and 26; Intr. to Part III, §§ 1 and 2.

11. Loquitur, with accus.: cp. Ep. 15. 5, note.

12. Senatui, dat. after 'iratus:' cp. Madv. 244 a.

Exiit, 'has left Rome.' See Ep. 17. 1. On Caesar's movements, cp. Intr. to Part III, § 8. He must have left about April 3 or 4.

Intercessionibus, especially by that of L. Metellus, a tribune. Cp. Caes. Bell. Civ. 1. 33, and Ep. 71, 6, note.

Incitatus, 'enraged,' rarely used by Cicero in exactly this sense; it occurs Caes. Bell. Gall. 1. 4 'civitas ob eam rem incitata.'

14. Domus = 'domestici.' Manut.

15. Valemus. The plural is rare in such a combination as this. But cp. Ad Att. 2. 17, 1 'quid ager Campanus, quid effusio pecuniae significant,' and Madv. 213 b, Obs. 2. The sentence breaks off after 'valemus;' the apodosis is perhaps to be supplied from 'denique .. stultitiae est.' Cp. Wesenb., who reads 'habeamus—; denique.'

Fortunam .. conturbare, 'to throw our prospects into confusion.'

16. Ut .. cogamur: cp. Madv. 355 note, for this use of the conjunctive.

nostra est, odisse aut relinquere cogamur aut impiam cupiditatem
contra salutem tuam habeamus. Denique illud cogita: quod
offensae fuerit in ista cunctatione, te subisse; nunc te contra
victorem Caesarem facere, quem dubiis rebus laedere noluisti, et
ad eos fugatos accedere, quos resistentes sequi nolueris, summae
stultitiae est. Vide ne, dum pudet te parum optimatem esse,
parum diligenter, quid optimum sit, eligas. Quod si totum tibi 3
persuadere non possum, saltem, dum, quid de Hispaniis agamus,
scitur, exspecta; quas tibi nuntio adventu Caesaris fore nostras.
Quam isti spem habeant amissis Hispaniis, nescio; quod porro
tuum consilium sit ad desperatos accedere, non medius fidius
reperio. Hoc, quod tu non dicendo mihi significasti, Caesar 4
audierat ac, simulatque 'have' mihi dixit, statim, quid de te
audisset, exposuit: negavi me scire; sed tamen ab eo petii ut
ad te litteras mitteret, quibus maxime ad remanendum commoveri
posses. Me secum in Hispaniam ducit; nam, nisi ita faceret,
ego prius, quam ad urbem accederem, ubicumque esses, ad te
percurrissem et hoc a te praesens contendissem atque omni vi

1. Aut impiam . . habeamus, 'or cherish an unnatural desire hostile to your safety,' i.e. for the triumph of our own party.

2. Quod offensae . . subisse, 'that you have already incurred whatever odium your delay may have involved,' i.e. Cicero had already hesitated too long to be trusted by Pompey and his friends. On the mood of fuerit, completing the idea expressed in the infinitive clause, cp. Madv. 369, and on the genitive with 'quod,' Ep. 26, 1.

3. Te contra victorem . . facere, 'to oppose a victor.' On this sense of 'facere,' cp. Forcell. and Pro Quinct. 1, 1 'quae res in civitate duae plurimum possunt, eae contra nos ambae faciunt in hoc tempore;' and on the use of the accus. and infin. as a subject, Ep. 54, 7, note.

4. Noluisti, 'stating a fact; nolueris, a characteristic: quos = 'men whom.' Cp. Ep. 1, 1, note.

5. Summae stultitiae est. The construction changes slightly: 'esse' depending on 'cogita' would have preserved its uniformity.

6. Parum optimatem, 'not enough of a friend to the "best cause."' There is, of course, a play on the words 'optimates' and 'optimum.' The substantive is rarely found in the singular, Oudend. ap. Sorinegr. Forcell. only refers to this passage, but cp. Ep. 61, 6.

7. Totum, 'altogether.' Cp. Madv. 300 c.

8. Dum . . scitur, 'while it is being ascertained.' Cp. Pro Sest. 38, 82 'quoad scitum est Sestium vivere;' and for the tense, Epp. 61, 5; 74, 8; Virg. Ecl. 9, 23. Madvig gives the present a future signification in such passages, and explains 'dum' by 'until,' 339, Obs. 2 b.

9. Quas . . fore nostras, 'which I announce to you will be ours on Caesar's arrival.'

Adventu may be either the abl. of the cause (Ep. 12, 3) or of the date (Ib. notes).

10. Isti, 'the Pompeians.'

11. Accedere. The gerund would perhaps be more regular, but cp. Madv. 417, Obs. 2.

12. Hoc, 'your intention to join Pompey.' Hofm.

Non dicendo, 'by your silence' or, 'not by words,' but by look or gesture. Boot gives 'subobscure' as an equivalent; so, too, Hofm. and Metzg. 'without speaking out.'

15. Quibus . . posses, 'such as should be best suited to induce you to stay.' Cp. Ep. 1, 1; Madv. 364. Caesar did write to Cicero about this time. Cp. Ep. 73.

18. Hoc . . contendissem, 'I should have striven to persuade you to adopt this course.' 'Contendere aliquid' = 'enitī ut ab aliquo obtineas.' Forcell.

3 te retinuissem. Etiam atque etiam, Cicero, cogita, ne te tuosque omnes funditus evertas, ne te sciens prudensque eo demittas, unde exitum vides nullum esse. Quod si te aut voces optimatium commovent aut non nullorum hominum insolentiam et iactationem ferre non potes, eligas censeo aliquod oppidum vacuum a bello, dum haec decernuntur, quae iam erunt confecta. Id si feceris, et ego te sapienter fecisse iudicabo et Caesarem non offendes.

70. To CAELIUS (AD FAM. II. 16).

Apparently written near Cumae, April, 49 B.C.

(705 A.U.C.)

1. I should have been much distressed by your letter, if I were not hardened by reflection and experience. I do not understand your inference from my letter; I complained of the times, but do you suppose I wish to take part in a civil war? 2. I am anxious, indeed, for retirement; for the sight of unworthy men prospering annoys me, and my fasces attract attention. You know I have estates near the sea; my staying on them makes me suspected of wishing to sail. I would gladly do so to a neutral district. 3. When you visited me at Cumae, I said I would do anything rather than take part in a civil war; why should I change my mind? I am eager that my anxiety for peace should be generally known. 4. I do not, however, fear the dangers with which you threaten me, for I would gladly suffer anything to avert evil from the Commonwealth. 5. My son will be no worse off than other citizens, probably: I am anxious about Tullia and her husband. 6. I am not dissembling; I wish for a place in a free Commonwealth if possible; if not, for peace in retirement. Perhaps my anticipations are too gloomy. 7. Both Oppius and Curtius are ambitious of high office. Pray attend to my request about Dolabella, and do all you can for me and mine.

M. CICERO IMP. S. D. M. CAELIO.

1 Magno dolore me adfecissent tuae litterae, nisi iam et ratio ipsa depulisset omnes molestias et diuturna desperatione rerum obduruisset animus ad dolorem novum; sed tamen, qua re acci-

1. Cogita, 'reflect.'

2. Evertas, 'ruin,' common in this sense.

Te . . eo demittas, 'get yourself into a position.' = 'descendas.' Forcell.

3. Voces optimatium; the criticisms of the optimates on his neutrality. Cp. Intr. to Part III, § 5.

4. Non nullorum hominum, especially of Gabinius. Cp. Ep. 71, 3.

6. Dum haec decernuntur, 'while this quarrel is being decided.' Cp. § 3, note; Forcell. Caelius refers to the war in Spain.

Iam, 'presently.' Cp. Brut. 46, 171 'id tu Brute iam intelleges cum in Galliam veneris.'

8. Ratio ipsa, 'my own reflection.' Hofm., Metzg.

10. Obduruisset . . . novum, 'had grown callous to a new pang.' Cicero uses this verb with 'ad,' 'contra,' and a dative.

derit ut ex meis superioribus litteris id suspicarere, quod scribis,
nescio: quod enim in illis fuit praeter querelam temporum?
quae non meum animum magis sollicitum habent quam tuum.
Nam non eam cognovi aciem ingenii tui, quod ipse videam, te
id ut non putem videre: illud miror, adduci potuisse te, qui me
penitus nosse deberes, ut existimares aut me tam improvidum,
qui ab excitata fortuna ad inclinatam et prope iacentem desciscerem,
aut tam inconstantem, ut collectam gratiam florentissimi
hominis effunderem a meque ipse deficerem et, quod initio semperque
fugi, civili bello interessem. Quod est igitur meum 'triste 2
consilium'? ut discederem fortasse in aliquas solitudines? nosti
enim non modo stomachi mei, cuius tu similem quondam habebas,
sed etiam oculorum in hominum insolentium indignitate fastidium;
accedit etiam molesta haec pompa lictorum meorum
nomenque imperii, quo appellor: eo si onere carerem, quamvis
parvis Italiae latebris contentus essem. Sed incurrit haec nostra
laurus non solum in oculos, sed iam etiam in voculas malevolorum.
Quod cum ita esset, nil tamen umquam de profectione

1. Ex meis .. litteris: cp. Ep. 69, 1.

2. Temporum, object. gen.; cp. Ep. 16, 3, note.

3. Sollicitum habent = sollicitant. Forcell. On the constr., cp. Madv. 237, a.

4. Eam, 'so weak.'

Aciem, 'penetration' = 'acumen.' Forcell.

Quod ipse .. videre. This order of the word is usual when a demonstrative pronoun stands alone. Cp. Madv. 321.

7. Ab excitata fortuna, sc. Caesaris, 'from the exalted fortune of Caesar,' a rare use of the word, opposed to 'inclinata.'

Ad inclinatam . . . iacentem, sc. Pompeii, 'which has received a shock and is almost prostrate.' Cp. Vell. 2. 52, 3 'inclinatam . . aciem.'

8. Collectam .. hominis, 'the favour of a most prosperous man (Caesar) which I have won.'

Ut .. effunderem = 'to forfeit *at once*.' Nägelsb. 130, 375.

9. A meque .. deficerem, 'to be untrue to myself,' rare. Cp., however, De Amicit. 11. 37 'si a virtute defeceris.'

Initio, abl. of the date. Cp. Ep. 12, 3, note.

10. Meum 'triste consilium.' Cicero does not quote the actual words of Caelius, but refers to the import of the opening sentences of Ep. 69.

11. Ut discederem, foll. On the general construction, cp. Ep. 13, 3, note. The imperfect is used because the resolution is supposed to have been taken at a past time. Süpfle, Hofm.

12. Stomachi, 'my natural indignation.'

Quondam. Caelius had once belonged to the optimates (cp. Brut. 79, 273), and would then probably have disliked some of Caesar's associates as much as Cicero did.

13. In hominum .. indignitate, 'at the sight of the revolting behaviour of insolent men.' Süpfle. Cp. Nägelsb. 46, 127.

14. Pompa lictorum: cp. Intr. to Part III, § 3; also Ep. 46, and many other passages.

16. Incurrit .. in, 'meets with.' 'Incurrere' frequently = 'incidere.' Cp. Forcell.

17. Voculas, 'gibes.' Nägelsb. 8, 32.

18. Quod cum ita esset, 'nevertheless.' The imperf. is used because of the tense of 'cogitavi.' Cp. Ep. 15, 8, note.

De profectione . . adprobantibus, 'of a departure without your approval.' The ablative abs. is used rather strangely as an attribute of 'profectio.' Cp. Sal. Iug. 10 'parvum ego te, . . amisso patre, . . accepi.'

nisi vobis adprobantibus cogitavi. Sed mea praediola tibi nota sunt; in his mihi necesse est esse, ne amicis molestus sim. Quod autem in maritimis facillime sum, moveo non nullis suspitionem velle me navigare; quod tamen fortasse non nollem, si possem ad otium: nam ad bellum quidem qui convenit? prae-
3 sertim contra eum, cui spero me satis fecisse, ab eo, cui iam satis fieri nullo modo potest. Deinde sententiam meam tu facillime perspicere potuisti iam ab illo tempore, cum in Cumanum mihi obviam venisti: non enim te celavi sermonem T. Ampii; vidisti, quam abhorrerem ab urbe relinquenda, cum audissem. Nonne tibi adfirmavi quidvis me potius perpessurum quam ex Italia ad bellum civile exiturum? Quid ergo accidit, cur consilium mutarem? nonne omnia potius, ut in sententia permanerem? Credas hoc mihi velim, quod puto te existimare, me ex his miseriis nihil aliud quaerere nisi ut homines aliquando intellegant me nihil maluisse quam pacem, ea desperata nihil tam fugisse quam arma civilia: huius me constantiae puto fore ut numquam paeniteat. Etenim memini in hoc genere gloriari solitum esse familiarem nostrum Q. Hortensium, quod numquam bello civili interfuisset: hoc nostra laus erit illustrior, quod illi tribuebatur ignaviae; de
4 nobis id existimari posse non arbitror. Nec me ista terrent, quae

1. **Vobis** = 'Caesar's and my common friends.'

Praediola, 'little estates.' The word occurs in various passages of Cicero's works. Cp. Ad Att. 16. 3. 4.

2. **Ne amicis . . sim**, 'that I may not give my friends the trouble of entertaining me.'

3. **Facillime** = 'liberrime.' Süpfle, Hofm.

Sum = 'commoror.' Forcell.

4. **Tamen**, 'indeed.'

5. **Nam**, I think here = 'but.'

Ad bellum, sc. 'navigare.'

Convenit = 'utile est.' Forcell.

6. **Contra eum**, sc. Caesarem.

Ab eo, 'on the side of Pompey,' whom Cicero had mortally offended by his hesitation.

8. **Cum . . obviam venisti**. Möller and Hofm. both refer these words to the time when Cicero returned from his province at the close of 50 B.C. His movements at that time are described, Intr. to Part II, §§ 24, 25.

9. **Sermonem T. Ampii**, sc. Balbi. He was a decided partisan of Pompey, and no doubt his words were violent. The Caesarians called him 'the trumpet of civil war.' Cp. Ad Fam. 6. 12, 3; see also Ep. 50, 2, note.

10. **Cum audissem**, 'when I had heard' that Rome had been abandoned by Pompey (Süpfle), or was to be so abandoned (Matth.).

11. **Quam . . exiturum**. 'Ut exirem' would be more according to usage, but cp. Ep. 54, 3 'quae conditio non accipienda fuit potius quam relinquenda patria.'

13. **Nonne omnia potius**, sc. 'acciderunt.' On the dat. and accus. with 'credo,' cp. Ep. 38, 3, note.

14. **Me . . quaerere**, 'that I seek no other gain from these miseries.'

18. **In hoc genere**, 'on this ground,' 'genus aliquando pro re ponitur.' Forcell.

19. **Bello civili**. That of Sulla and the party of Marius.

20. **Quod . . ignaviae**, 'because neutrality in his case was attributed to cowardice.' On the double dat., cp. Madv. 249.

mihi a te ad timorem fidissime atque amantissime proponuntur;
nulla est enim acerbitas, quae non omnibus hac orbis terrarum
perturbatione impendere videatur, quam quidem ego a re publica
meis privatis et domesticis incommodis libentissime vel istis
ipsis, quae tu me mones ut caveam, redemissem. Filio meo, 5
quem tibi carum esse gaudeo, si erit ulla res publica, satis amplum
patrimonium relinquam memoriam nominis mei; si autem nulla
erit, nihil accidet ei separatim a reliquis civibus. Nam quod
rogas ut respiciam generum meum, adulescentem optimum mihique carissimum, an dubitas, qui scias, quanti cum illum tum vero
Tulliam meam faciam, quin ea me cura vehementissime sollicitet?
et eo magis, quod in communibus miseriis hac tamen oblectabar
specula, Dolabellam meum vel potius nostrum fore ab iis molestiis,
quas liberalitate sua contraxerat, liberum. Velim quaeras, quos
ille dies sustinuerit, in urbe dum fuit, quam acerbos sibi, quam
mihi ipsi socero non honestos. Itaque neque ego hunc Hispa- 6
niensem casum exspecto, de quo mihi exploratum est ita esse, ut
tu scribis, neque quicquam astute cogito: si quando erit civitas,
erit profecto nobis locus; sin autem non erit, in easdem solitu-

1. **Ad timorem proponuntur**, 'are set before me to alarm me,' = 'timoris causa.' Cp. Ad Q. F. 1. 1, 11 'potestate quam tu ad dignitatem permisisses.' Cicero is here referring to what Caelius had said. Ep. 69, 1.

3. **Quam .. redemissem.** 'Redimere' takes an accusative sometimes of the thing averted, sometimes of the person delivered. Cp. In Verr. 2 Act. 5. 44, 117 'metum virgarum .. pretio redemit.'

4. **Vel istis ipsis**: cp. Ep. 69, 5, where Caelius had hinted that Cicero would risk his life and the safety of his family by joining Pompey.

6. **Si erit ulla res publica**, 'if any constitutional government shall exist.'

Satis amplum patrimonium. On the accus. in apposition, cp. Ep. 33, 1, note.

8. **Nam**: cp. Ep. 9, 8, note.

10. **An dubitas** = 'dubitare non debes:' cp. Ep. 67, 1, note.

Tum vero: cp. Ep. 26, 3, note.

11. **Ea .. cura**, 'anxiety on his account.' Cp. 'iis consiliis' Ep. 33, 2, note. Madv. 314.

12. **Hac .. specula**, 'this little hope.' Not that the hope itself was weak, but that its fulfilment would be a poor compensation for public disasters. Hofm. The word occurs Pro Cluent. 26, 72. **Tamen** corresponds to a particle implied in the words 'in communibus miseriis.' Cp. Ep. 29, 11, note.

13. **Molestiis**, i.e. 'his pecuniary troubles.' Cicero probably hoped that Caesar's help would enable Dolabella to satisfy his creditors. Cp. Mr. Yonge's note. For an account of Dolabella's attacks on public credit at a later time, see Intr. to Part IV, § 5.

14. **Liberalitate.** A friendly expression for Dolabella's extravagance.

Quos .. dies, foll., 'what days he suffered' from the importunity of his creditors—'dies pro actis diei.' Cp. Forcell.

16. **Mihi .. honestos.** Cicero's reputation would suffer for his son-in-law's extravagance.

Neque .. exspecto, 'I am neither waiting for the issue of the contest in Spain.'

17. **Casus** = 'eventus.' Forcell. Cp. Tac. Ann. 6. 44 'quibus proelium et fortunati casus placebant.'

De quo .. scribis, 'as to which I am sure the case is as you write.' Cp. Ep. 69, 3, for Caelius' opinion.

18. **Neque .. cogito**, 'nor do I entertain any artful plan,' e.g. of ruling his conduct according to fortune.

Civitas = 'res publica.' For the thought, cp. § 5.

dines tu ipse, ut arbitror, venies, in quibus nos consedisse audies.
Sed ego fortasse vaticinor et haec omnia meliores habebunt exitus:
recordor enim desperationes eorum, qui senes erant adulescente
7 me; eos ego fortasse nunc imitor et utor aetatis vitio. Velim
ita sit. Sed tamen! . . . togam praetextam texi Oppio puto te 8
audisse; nam Curtius noster dibaphum cogitat, sed eum infector
moratur. Hoc adspersi, ut scires me tamen in stomacho solere
ridere. *De* Dolabella, quod scripsi, suadeo videas, tamquam si
tua res agatur. Extremum illud erit: nos nihil turbulenter, nihil
temere faciemus; te tamen oramus, quibuscumque erimus in
terris, ut nos liberosque nostros ita tueare, ut amicitia nostra et
tua fides postulabit.

71. TO ATTICUS (AD ATT. X. 8).

NEAR CUMAE, MAY 2, 49 B.C. (705 A.U.C.)

1. I am aware that we ought no longer to correspond on dangerous topics, but I wish to tell you what I think about Tullia's advice, which she says you approve. 2. If I were going to determine my conduct by the issue of the war in Spain, that advice would be wise; but if Caesar triumphs 3. it will be intolerable for me to see some of his partisans acting as senators, and perhaps I shall not be allowed to be neutral. 4. Then the whole dispute will not be settled in Spain; Pompey is collecting a large fleet, and will attack Italy by sea; must I take part in resisting him? 5. Danger there must be in either course; it is best to incur that which is most honourable. 'I did not cross the sea with Pompey,' true; but it was difficult; and I feared that he and Caesar might renew their old alliance at my expense. 6. Caesar's power cannot last long; he has already given great offence, and his followers inspire no confidence. 7. If I am mistaken I shall only have to suffer for my mistake as

2. Vaticinor, 'rave,' 'utter idle prophecies.' Cp. Pro Sest. 10, 23, where 'vaticinari' and 'insanire' are coupled.

3. Desperationes. Apparently only here used in the plural.

4. Utor aetatis vitio, 'indulge the weakness of my age.'

5. Sed tamen—'but yet I cannot suppress my anxiety.' Wesenb. has 'sit; sed tamen.'

Togam praetextam, 'the embroidered robe of office.'

Oppio: cp. Ep. 61, 5. C. Oppius and M. Curtius Postumus were two friends of Caesar, who, it is insinuated, hoped to rise to dignities through his influence. Oppius is often mentioned in Cicero's letters, and a letter from him and Balbus to Cicero has been preserved (Ad Att. 9, 7 A). It does not appear that he ever held high office, though he was a most intimate friend of Caesar. A Postumus Curtius is mentioned Ad Att. 9. 2 a, 3.

6. Nam, 'I do not say the same of Curtius, for.' Cp. § 5.

Dibaphum, 'the doubly-dyed robe' of the augur. Cp. Ad Att. 2. 9. 2 'sacerdotii διβάφῳ.' It was purple and saffron. See Smith, Dict. of Antiq. sub voc. 'toga,' p. 1137.

Infector, 'the dyer,' i.e. Caesar. The word does not seem to occur elsewhere in Cicero's writings.

7. Adspersi, 'added this sprinkling of jest.' The word occurs frequently in Cicero's writings. Cp. Ad Q. F. 2, 10, 2 'epistola hoc adspersit molestiae.'

8. Quod scripsi, 'as I wrote above.' Cp. § 5.

Videas = 'cures.' Cp. Ad Att. 5. 1, 3 'ut prandium nobis videret.'

9. Turbulenter, 'violently,' a rare form apparently.

many wise men have suffered; 8. but I am persuaded Caesar must fall, sooner or later: may it be during my life! I surely, then, ought not to submit to unworthy masters. 9. I recommend all my domestic interests to your care, and shall embark with the first fair wind. Tullia's affection never blinds her to the claims of honour upon me. 10. Let me hear any news you receive from Spain. I must ask Antony to let me retire to Melita, but a letter I forward you from him is not promising.

CICERO ATTICO SAL.

Et res ipsa monebat et tu ostenderas et ego videbam, de iis 1
rebus, quas intercipi periculosum esset, finem inter nos scribendi
fieri tempus esse; sed, cum ad me saepe mea Tullia scribat orans,
ut quid in Hispania geratur exspectem, et semper adscribat idem
videri tibi idque ipse etiam ex tuis litteris intellexerim, non puto
esse alienum me ad te, quid de ea re sentiam, scribere. Consi- 2
lium istud tunc esset prudens, ut mihi videtur, si nostras rationes
ad Hispaniensem casum accommodaturi essemus; quod fieri nequit; necesse est enim aut, id quod maxime velim, pelli istum
ab Hispania, aut trahi id bellum, aut istum, ut confidere videtur,
apprehendere Hispanias. Si pelletur, quam gratus aut quam
honestus tum erit ad Pompeium noster adventus, cum ipsum
Curionem ad eum transiturum putem? Si trahitur bellum, quid
exspectem aut quam diu? Relinquitur, ut, si vincimur in Hispania,
quiescamus: id ego contra puto; istum enim victorem magis
relinquendum puto quam victum et dubitantem magis quam
fidentem suis rebus. Nam caedem video, si vicerit, et impetum

2. Quas, an abbreviation for 'de quibus litteras.' Billerb.

Esset. On the tense, cp. Ep. 1. 1, note.

3. Fieri: cp. Madv. 389.

4. Et semper . . tibi, 'and always adds that your opinion is the same.'

6. Alienum, 'out of place.' It is much more common with a case following it. Forcell. e.g. 'ab hoc loco.'

Consilium . . prudens, 'your advice would be wise, I think, if I intended to fashion my plans according to the issue of the war in Spain.'

7. Tunc = 'ita,' but 'tum' is generally used in this sense. Hofm. Wesenb. has 'tum.'

8. Quod fieri nequit. Because, whatever the course of the Spanish war, it could not change his decision. Wesenb. doubts if 'nequit' is Ciceronian in this sense, and suggests 'non potest,' 'non debet' or 'non oportet.'

9. Istum, Caesarem.

11. Apprehendere, 'should make himself master of.' Rare. Forcell.

Quam gratus, foll., of course ironical.

12. Cum . . putem, 'when I should suppose that even Curio would go over to him.'

13. Si trahitur: cp. Madv. 348 e, Obs. 4: and 353.

14. Relinquitur = the only possibility remaining in which the result of the war in Spain might affect my decision is.

15. Id ego contra puto, 'I hold the contrary opinion about that.' 'Contra' is used adverbially, and 'esse' omitted. Cp. De Off. 2. 2, 7 'alia probabilia, contra alia dicimus.'

16. Dubitantem . . rebus, 'in a doubtful position, rather than in one of confidence in his fortunes.' To be taken in close connection with victum: but the expression seems odd, and Boot suggests 'nec' for 'et.'

17. Caedem video, sc. 'fore.' Cp. Ep. 63, 4, note.

in privatorum pecunias et exsulum reditum et tabulas novas et
turpissimorum honores et regnum non modo Romano homini,
3 sed ne Persae quidem cuiquam tolerabile. Tacita esse poterit,
indignitas nostra? pati poterunt oculi me cum Gabinio sententiam dicere? et quidem illum rogari prius? praesto esse clientem
tuum Clodium? C. Ateii Plaguleium? ceteros? Sed cur inimicos
colligo, qui meos necessarios a me defensos nec videre in curia
sine dolore nec versari inter eos sine dedecore potero? Quid, si
ne id quidem est exploratum, fore, ut mihi liceat—scribunt
enim ad me amici eius me illi nullo modo satis fecisse, quod
in senatum non venerim—, tamenne dubitemus an ei nos etiam
cum periculo venditemus, quicum coniuncti ne cum praemio qui-
4 dem voluimus esse? Deinde hoc vide, non esse iudicium de
tota contentione in Hispaniis, nisi forte iis amissis arma Pompeium abiecturum putas, cuius omne consilium Themistocleum

1. **Reditum**, 'restoration.' The exiles would often be political offenders. Cp. Ep. 47. 1, note.

Tabulas novas, 'a total or partial abolition of debts.' Cp. In Cat. 2. 8, 18.

2. **Turpissimorum**: i.e. of such men as Gabinius; see the next section.

3. **Tacita . . nostra**, 'will my indignation allow me to keep silence?' Boot, however, remarks that this sense of 'indignitas,' though common in Livy, seems not to be found elsewhere in Cicero. He therefore suggests 'tanta' for 'tacita,' 'can I fall so low?'

4. **Sententiam dicere**, i.e. as a senator.

5. **Illum rogari prius**. Gabinius, as an old supporter of Caesar, might be asked his opinion before Cicero, both being consulars. A good deal depended on the will of the presiding officer. Cp. Ep. 6, 2, note. In the year 43 B.C. the consul Pansa asked Q. Fufius Calenus his opinion first. Cp. Philipp. 5. 1, 1.

6. **Clodium**. This is generally referred to Sextus Clodius, a dependent of the Clodian family, who had been banished for taking part in the disturbances of 52 B.C. Cp. Epp. 109; 110. The nature of his connection with Atticus is obscure; P. Clodius is called 'sodalis' of Atticus. Cp. Ad Att. 2. 9. 1; 2. 15, 2.

C. Ateii. A C. Ateius is mentioned Ad Fam. 13. 29. 2; De Divin. 1. 16, 29; and Plaguleius, on whom cp. De Dom. 33, 89, may have been a worthless *protégé* of his. The best MS. has Catell.

7. **Colligo**, 'count up.' Metag.

Meos necessarios, 'my own friends,' i.e. men like Vatinius, whom he had defended at Caesar's request. Cp. Intr. to Part II, § 10.

9. **Liceat**, sc. 'in senatum venire.' The independence which Cicero had shewn in not appearing in the senate at Caesar's request (see next note) might make Caesar exclude him when he wished to attend.

10. **Quod . . non venerim**. The tense of 'venerim' is accounted for by 'satis fecisse' after 'scribunt' being a present perfect. Cp. Ep. 10, 2; Zumpt, L. G. 514, 515. On the facts cp. Ep. 67, 1.

11. **Tamenne . . esse?** 'shall I still think of recommending myself, even at some risk, to a man whom I was unwilling to join for my own profit?' that is, at an earlier time, when Caesar would have been very grateful for Cicero's support. On this use of 'ne,' cp. Madv. 453; Zumpt 354. 'Tamenne interrogantis est, et urgentis.' Forcell.

13. **Non esse iudicium**, foll., 'that the decision of the whole contest does not depend on the fate of the Spanish provinces.' For this sense of 'esse in,' cp. Ep. 8, 2, note. Or, 'will not take place in.' 'Iudicium esse' = 'decerni.' Boot. The phrase seems only to occur here.

15. **Themistocleum**, 'like that of Themistocles,' in the interpretation he put on the oracle as to the 'wooden walls.' Cp. Herod. 7. 143 and 144.

est; existimat enim, qui mare teneat, cum necesse *esse* rerum
potiri. Itaque numquam id egit, ut Hispaniae per se tenerentur;
navalis apparatus ei semper antiquissima cura fuit. Navigabit
igitur, cum erit tempus, maximis classibus et ad Italiam accedet,
in qua nos sedentes quid erimus? nam medios esse iam non
licebit. [Classibus] adversabimur igitur? quod maius scelus vel
tantum denique? quid turpius? An qui † valde hic in absentes
solus tuli scelus, eiusdem cum Pompeio et cum reliquis principibus non feram? Quod si iam misso officio periculi ratio 5
habenda est, ab illis est periculum, si peccaro, ab hoc, si recte
fecero, nec ullum in his malis consilium periculo vacuum inveniri
potest, ut non sit dubium quin [turpiter facere] cum periculo
fugiamus, quod fugeremus etiam cum salute. Non simul cum
Pompeio mare transiimus. Omnino *non* potuimus: exstat ratio
dierum. Sed tamen—fateamur enim quod est—ne contendimus
quidem, ut possemus. Fefellit ea me res, quae fortasse non
debuit, sed fefellit: pacem putavi fore, quae si esset, iratum
mihi Caesarem esse, cum idem amicus esset Pompeio, nolui;

2. Per se, 'by himself in person.' Those provinces had been governed by legates of Pompey since 55 B.C. Boot. Cp. Intr. to Part II, §§ 8; 14.

3. Antiquissima, 'most important' = 'potissima.' Forcell.

5. Sedentes. 'Sedere' = 'otiosum esse.' Forcell.

Medios . . licebit, 'I shall not be allowed to be neutral any longer.' For this sense of 'medios,' cp. Forcell.; and on the accus. and infin. after 'licet,' Madv. 393 c, Obs. 2.

7. Denique = 'omnino' (Forcell), 'at all.'

An qui, foll. These words are clearly corrupt. Kayser suggests 'an qui valde huic obstans eius solus tuli scelus, eiusdem;' Hofmann 'an invadentis in absentes solus tuli scelus.'

8. Tuli = 'resisted.' Cp. Caes. Bell. Gall. 3. 19 'factum est . . ut ne unum quidem nostrorum impetum ferrent.' Cicero refers probably to his behaviour in an interview with Caesar. Cp. Ep. 67.

Cum Pompeio, foll., 'with Pompey and the other nobles by my side.'

9. Misso officio, 'dismissing the notion of duty.' Cp. Ep. 12, 1; also Pro Muren. 15. 33. 'misso praelia;' also Ep. 12, 1.

10. Ab illis, 'from the friends of Pompey.'

Ab hoc, 'from Caesar.'

12. Ut non sit dubium, 'so that I have no scruple.' In this sense the words are usually followed by an infinitive. Madv. 375 c, Obs. 2; who mentions, however, Pro Leg. Man. 23. 68 'nolite dubitare quin huic uni credatis omnia.'

Cum periculo fugiamus, sc. 'id,' 'a course now that it is dangerous.' On the omission of 'id,' cp. Madv. 321.

14. Transiimus. An objection by a critic of Cicero's conduct. 'I shall be told "I did not cross the sea with Pompey." It was quite impossible.' On this use of the perf. indic., cp. Ep. 48, 4. The best MS. has 'transierimus,' which can hardly be construed.

Exstat ratio dierum, 'a calculation of the days is open to any one,' 'is public.' 'Exstare' = 'apparere.' Forcell. Cicero complained (Ad Att. 9. 8 a. 2) that Pompey only informed him of his plans when Caesar had already cut off the communication between them.

16. Fefellit me, foll, 'I was mistaken about a point where perhaps I ought to have avoided mistakes, but did not. I thought there would be peace.'

17. Quae si esset. On the tense, cp. Madv. 382.

18. Cum idem . . Pompeio, 'at the same time that he was a friend of Pompey.' Cp., on this use of 'idem,' Ep. 20, 1, note.

senseram enim, quam iidem essent. Hoc verens in hanc tarditatem incidi. Sed assequor omnia, si propero; si cunctor, amitto.
6 Et tamen, mi Attice, auguria quoque me incitant quadam spe non dubia, non haec collegii nostri ab Atto, sed illa Platonis de tyrannis: nullo enim modo posse video stare istum diutius, quin ipse per se etiam languentibus nobis concidat, quippe qui florentissimus ac novus VI. VII. diebus ipsi illi egenti ac perditae multitudini in odium acerbissimum venerit, qui duarum rerum simulationem tam cito amiserit, mansuetudinis in Metello, divitiarum in aerario. Iam, quibus utatur vel sociis vel ministris, si ii provincias, si ii rem publicam regent, quorum nemo duo menses potuit patrimonium suum gubernare? Non sunt omnia colligenda, quae tu acutissime perspicis, sed tamen ea pone ante oculos: iam intelleges id regnum vix semestre esse posse. Quod si me fefellerit, feram, sicut multi clarissimi homines in re publica excellentes tulerunt, nisi forte me Sardanapali vicem [in suo

1. **Iidem**, 'like each other,' Boot. 'Of one mind,' Hofm., Metzg. 'Like what they were in 59 B.C.' Billerb. The latter meaning is supported by Ep. 25, 1. But Mr. Jeans remarks that the words 'qui fuerant' follow in that passage. Cicero feared that he might be sacrificed by Caesar and Pompey, as in 59–58 B.C. Cp. Ad Att. 8. 11 D, 7.

In hanc . . incidi. 'Incidere in' = 'to make a mistake, or get into a difficulty, through negligence or mischance.' Cp. In Verr. 2 Act. 1. 11, 31 'qua stultitia fuissem si . . in eam diem ego cum potuissem vitare incidissem.' Cp. below, § 7.

2. **Assequor omnia**, 'I make good everything' = 'abunde resarciam quidquid omissum est.' Gronov. ap. Boot. On the tense, cp. Madv. 339, Obs. 2 a.

3. **Et tamen**, 'moreover.' Billerb.

4. **Non haec . . ab Atto**, 'not the familiar auguries of our college derived from Attus Navius.' 'Ab' is used here nearly in the same sense as in quotations. Cp. Ad Fam. 9. 21, 1 'nihil tibi opus est illud a Trabea.' On the historical allusion, cp. Livy 1. 36.

Platonis: cp. Rep. 8. 562, foll.; Cic. De Rep. 1. 43.

6. **Quin . . concidat**, 'without falling.' Cp. Ep. 60.

Languentibus nobis, 'if we sit still.' Cp. In Pison. 33, 82 'languet iuventus nec . . . in laudis et gloriae cupiditate versatur.'

7. **Novus**, 'a new comer,' after his long absence in Gaul.

Sex septem, a proverbial expression. Cp. Hor. Epp. 1. 1, 58 'sed quadringentis sex septem millia desunt.' The reference is to the short interval between Caesar's return to Rome from Brundisium and his departure for Spain. Cp. Intr. to Part III, § 8. He gave offence to the needy by the moderation of the plan he proposed for relief of debtors, and to the citizens in general by his harsh treatment of Metellus and by his seizure of the contents of the treasury. Cp. Mommsen 4. 2, 378–382; Intr. l. c.

8. **Multitudini.** On the dat., cp. Madv. 241, Obs. 3.

10. **Iam** = 'praeterea.' Forcell., and Ep. 8. 4.

Quibus utatur, sub. 'cogita,' or perhaps 'necesse est,' 'what allies he has,' or 'must use.' Metzg. would supply the first. Wesenb. suggests 'vietur.'

12. **Gubernare**, 'keep the management of,' i.e. avoid bankruptcy. This is a sneer at men like Curio, Dolabella, and Antony.

13. **Colligenda**, 'to be strung together' in this letter. Metzg., Billerb.

Ea, The things which Cicero thinks it needless or unsafe to mention.

14. **Quod si me fefellerit**, 'If I am mistaken in this.' Cp. Ep. 67, 1, note. Supp. 'haec opinio,' Manut.

16. **Nisi forte . . Themistocleo**, 'unless you suppose I had rather die like Sardanapalus than like Themistocles.' As the words 'nisi forte' introduce something in opposition to feram, they would naturally be followed by 'malcero,' for Cicero's

lectulo] mori malle censueris quam exsilio Themistocleo, qui cum fuisset, ut ait Thucydides, τῶν μὲν παρόντων δι' ἐλαχίστης βουλῆς κράτιστος γνώμων, τῶν δὲ μελλόντων ἐς πλεῖστον τοῦ γενησομένου ἄριστος εἰκαστής, tamen incidit in eos casus, quos vitasset, si eum nihil fefellisset. Etsi is erat, ut ait idem, qui τὸ ἄμεινον καὶ τὸ χεῖρον ἐν τῷ ἀφανεῖ ἔτι ἑώρα μάλιστα, tamen non vidit, nec quo modo Lacedaemoniorum nec quo modo suorum civium invidiam effugeret nec quid Artaxerxi polliceretur. Non fuisset illa nox tam acerba Africano, sapientissimo viro, non tam dirus ille dies Sullanus callidissimo viro C. Mario, si nihil utrumque eorum fefellisset. Nos tamen hoc confirmamus illo augurio, quo diximus, 8
nec nos fallit nec aliter accidet: corruat iste necesse est aut per adversarios aut ipse per se, qui quidem sibi est adversarius

patience would only be discredited by his really despairing, not by Atticus' expectation that he would despair. A similar passage occurs, however, De Senect. 6, 17 'non viribus .. res magnae geruntur sed consilio auctoritate sententia; quibus non modo non orbari sed etiam augeri senectus solet: nisi forte ego vobis . . . cessare nunc videor.' Hofm. The general drift of the passage is, 'I will bear the consequences of any miscalculation I may make, even if they involve a death in exile; and I shall not make a greater mistake, nor fare worse, than many wise men have done before me.

Sardanapali vicem, 'like Sardanapalus.' A rare sense of the word. Forcell. Cp. Zumpt, L. G. 458. On the accus., cp. Madv. 237 c, Obs. 3. The death of Sardanapalus is described by Diod. Sic. 2. 27, and by Ctesias ap. Athen. 12. 7. In the latter passage κλῖναι are mentioned as having been placed on his funeral pile; and this may perhaps justify the retention of the words in suo lectulo. But they convey an idea so contrary to the usual associations with the death of Sardanapalus, and their combination with 'Sardanapali vicem' is so harsh, 'like Sardanapalus in his bed,' that I have followed Boot in putting them in brackets. Their insertion may have been suggested by Ad Att. 10. 14. 3, or Ad Fam. 9. 18, 2. Athenaeus (l. c.) quotes from Clitarchus a story that Sardanapalus died in old age, but the import of Cicero's remark surely is, 'unless I prefer suicide to exile.' Mr. Jeans thinks that the bracketed words present no difficulty, if we (1) supply some such word as 'excidisti,' and (2) suppose that the contrast intended is one between death at home and death in exile. The expression 'in lectulo mori' is found Ep. 87, 2; Ad Att. 10. 14, 3. Wesenb. has 'in meo lectulo.'

1. Exsilio Themistocleo, abl. modi; cp. Madv. 257.

Qui, of course, Themistocles. Wesenb. suggests the insertion of 'in' before 'exsilio.'

2. Ut ait Thucydides: cp. Thuc. 1. 138. Cicero quotes from memory, for Thucydides has τῶν τε παραχρῆμα .. and τῶν μελλόντων ἐπί. In the next passage Thucydides has τό τε ἄμεινον ἢ χεῖρον, and προεώρα.

8. Quid . . . polliceretur, 'what he would have to promise' (Wiel., Metzg.), i.e. to reduce Greece to subjection under the king of Persia. Cp. Corn. Nep. Themist. 10; Plut. Themist. 31. On the tense of 'polliceretur,' cp. note on 'quae si essent,' supra, § 5 and Madv. 378 a, 2.

Illa nox. The younger Scipio was found dead in his bed the day after he had addressed the people in perfect health. His wife Sempronia and C. Carbo were both suspected of his murder. Cp. Vell. 2. 4; Cic. Somn. Scip. 2, 12 (De Rep. 6, 12); Livy, Epit. 59.

9. Ille dies Sullanus, 'the day of Sulla's triumph,' which was followed by his own exile and the death of P. Sulpicius. Cp. App. Bell. Civ. 1. 55-60; Vell. 2. 17-19.

11. Hoc, i.e. 'my own inference from Caesar's conduct.'

Illo augurio, sc. Platonis.

Quo diximus, attraction for 'quod.' Cp. Hor. Sat. 1. 6, 15; Livy 1. 29 'quibus quisque poterat elatis.'

12. Nec nos fallit, sc. 'and I am not mistaken, and the issue will be as I expect.' For 'fallit' without a subject, cp. Ep. 108, 2.

13 Per se, 'by his own errors.' For

unus acerrimus; id spero vivis nobis fore. Quamquam tempus est nos de illa perpetua iam, non de hac exigua vita cogitare. Sin quid acciderit maturius, haud sane mea multum interfuerit, utrum factum videam, an futurum esse multo ante viderim. Quae cum ita sint, non est committendum, ut iis paream, quos contra me
9 senatus, ne quid res publica detrimenti acciperet, armavit. Tibi sunt omnia commendata, quae commendationis meae pro tuo in nos amore non indigent. Nec hercule ego quidem reperio, quid scribam; sedeo enim *πλουδοκῶν*: etsi nihil umquam tam fuit scribendum quam nihil mihi umquam ex plurimis tuis iucunditatibus gratius accidisse quam quod meam Tulliam suavissime diligentissimeque coluisti—valde eo ipsa delectata est, ego autem non minus—, cuius quidem virtus mirifica. Quo modo illa fert publicam cladem! quo modo domesticas tricas! quantus autem animus in discessu nostro! est *στοργή*, est summa *σύντηξις*: tamen nos
10 recte facere et bene audire volt. Sed hac super re nimis, ne meam ipse *συμπάθειαν* iam evocem. Tu, si quid de Hispaniis

the thought, cp. Philipp. 2. 45, 116 'tali te, mihi crede, diutius non ferent.'

Qui quidem .. est. On the mood, cp. Ep. 3. 3, note.

1. Unus strengthens the superlative. Cp. Ad Fam. 15. 16, 3; Philipp. 2. 3, 7; Ad Att. 3. 23, 5.

2. Illa perpetua .. hac exigua. The pronouns seem to compare what is future with what is present. Cp. Madv. 485 a.

Iam, 'at my age,' even if my life is not shortened by violence.

Sin quid .. maturius, 'if anything befall me previously,' i.e. 'if I die.' Cp. Philipp. 1. 4, 10 'si quid mihi humanitus accidisset.' The words refer to Cicero's desire to witness Caesar's fall, expressed just above. 'Maturius' = 'id quod festinatius fit: cui opponitur sero, tarde, lente.' Forcell.

5. Iis, i.e. Caesar and his friends.

Quos contra. On the position of 'contra,' cp. Pro Muren. 4. 9, 'illum ipsum quem contra veneris.'

Me senatus .. armavit. Cicero, as a proconsul, having 'imperium,' was included in the commission mentioned Ad Fam. 16. 11, 2; Caes. Bell. Civ. 1. 5; Appendix 6, § 5.

6. Tibi .. commendata, 'I have entrusted all I have to you.'

7. Commendationis. On the genit., cp. Madv. 295, Obs. 3.

Pro tuo .. amore, 'considering your affection for me.' Cp. Madv. 446.

9. Sedeo .. *πλουδοκῶν*, 'for I remain merely waiting for fine weather,' which would account for his not moving about to collect news. The Greek word seems not to occur elsewhere.

Etsi. Hofm. has collected various passages where this word seems to mean 'however,' or 'but:' e.g. Ad Att. 9. 7, 6: 9. 19, 1.

10. Iucunditatibus, 'courtesies' = 'iucundis officiis.' Forcell.

13. Cuius, Tulliae. Hofm. remarks that a relative does not always refer to the nearest substantive.

Publicam cladem, 'the State's calamity,' 'the civil war.'

14. Tricas = 'nugas' (Forcell.), 'troubles,' 'difficulties,' perhaps 'extravagances.'

Quantus .. nostro, 'how high a spirit she shews in view of my approaching departure' to the camp of Pompey. On this sense of 'in,' cp. Ep. 36, 13, note.

15. *σύντηξις*, lit. 'transfusion,' 'commotion.' Not classical apparently.

16. Hac super re nimis, foll., 'I dwell too much on this, and must take care not to rouse my own feelings.' Metzg. Or, 'too much of this; I must cease, lest,' etc. 'Super' with the abl. = 'de,' is not common in Cicero, and only occurs in his letters. Hofm.

17. *συμπάθειαν*. Not classical, apparently.

Evocem. The metaphorical sense of

certius et si quid aliud, dum adsumus, scribes et ego fortasse discedens dabo ad te aliquid, eo etiam magis, quod Tullia te non putabat hoc tempore ex Italia. Cum Antonio item est agendum, ut cum Curione, Melitae me velle esse, huic bello nolle interesse: eo velim tam facili uti possim et tam bono in me quam Curione. Is ad Misenum VI. Nonas venturus dicebatur, id est hodie, sed praemisit mihi odiosas litteras hoc exemplo.

72. ANTONY TO CICERO (AD ATT. X. 8 A).

MAY 1 (?) (705 A.U.C.)

1. My remarkable affection for you makes me pay attention to rumours which I should otherwise disregard, and I write, the more earnestly on account of our past disagreement, to dissuade you from leaving Italy. Both Caesar and I have the highest regard for you. 2. Do not join Pompey, who only served you after injuring you; do not fly from Caesar, who is most interested in your well being.

'ANTONIUS TRIB. PL. PRO. PR. CICERONI IMP. SAL.

Nisi te valde amarem, et multo quidem plus, quam tu putas, 1
non extimuissem rumorem, qui de te prolatus est, cum praesertim falsum esse existimarem; sed quia te nimio plus diligo, non possum dissimulare mihi famam quoque, quamvis sit falsa, magni

Fin. 2. 31. 99 'probitatem .. non .. praemiorum mercedibus evocatam.'

Si quid, sc. 'audieris.'

1. Dum adsumus, 'while I am still in Italy.' Cp. Ep. 69. 5, note, on the tense.

2. Te non putabat, sc. 'abiturum,' epistolary imperfect. Cp. Ep. 1, 1, note.

3. Cum Antonio .. est agendum, 'I must make representations to Antony.' The accus. and infin. which follows is curious, and to be accounted for, probably, by 'agendum est' being considered equivalent to 'dicendum est.' Cp. Suet. Tib. 54 'egit cum senatu non debere talia praemia tribui.' On the meaning of 'agere cum aliquo,' cp. Ep. 5. 8, note.

4. Ut cum Curione. Cicero had asked Curio at an interview on April 14 to allow him to pass through Sicily on his way to Greece. Cp. Ad Att. 10. 4. 10.

6. Is, i.e. Antony.

Ad Misenum, 'to his estate at Misenum,' near Baiae (cp. Philipp. 2. 19. 48); or, 'to the neighbourhood of Misenum' (cp. Madv. 232, and Ep. 54. 7, note).

7. Odiosas = 'molestas, graves.' Forcell. Cp. Philipp. 1. 11. 27 'video .. quam sit odiosum habere iratum eundem et armatum.'

Hoc exemplo, 'of which I add a copy.' Metzg.

TRIB. PL. PRO. PR. A tribune of the people was bound not to leave Rome for a whole day during his year of office (cp. Macrob. Sat. 1. 3); but this restriction has been disregarded by C. Gracchus (Plut. C. Gracchus 10; 11), and Antony had received from Caesar a commission to govern Italy during his leader's absence, with the title of propraetor. He travelled about for some time in the discharge of his official duties (cp. Ep. 74. 5).

9. Rumorem. Of Cicero's intention to join Pompey. Manut.

Prolatus, 'published,' 'put in circulation.' Cp. Ad Att. 15. 13. 1 'orationem .. eius .. proferendae arbitrium tuum.'

10. Nimio plus 'too much by far.' Cp. Hor. Carm. 1. 33. 1

'Albi ne doleas plus nimio.'

esse. *Te iturum esse* trans mare credere non possum, cum tanti facias Dolabellam *et* Tulliam tuam, feminam lectissimam, tantique ab omnibus nobis fias, quibus mehercule dignitas amplitudoque tua paene carior est quam tibi ipsi; sed tamen non sum arbitratus esse amici non commoveri etiam improborum sermone, atque eo feci studiosius, quod iudicabam duriores partes mihi impositas esse ab offensione nostra, quae magis a zelotypia mea quam ab iniuria tua nata est. Sic enim volo te tibi persuadere, mihi neminem esse cariorem te excepto Caesare meo,
2 Caesarem maxime in suis M. Ciceronem reponere. Qua re, mi Cicero, te rogo, ut tibi omnia integra serves, eius fidem improbes, qui tibi, ut beneficium daret, prius iniuriam fecit, contra ne profugias, qui te, etsi non amabit—quod accidere non potest—, tamen salvum amplissimumque esse cupiet. Dedita opera ad te Calpurnium, familiarissimum meum, misi, ut mihi magnae curae tuam vitam ac dignitatem esse scires.'

Eodem die a Caesare Philotimus litteras attulit hoc exemplo.

5. **Etiam improborum sermone**, 'by the talk even of unscrupulous people.'

6. **Feci studiosius**, 'I have acted the more earnestly,' 'fulfilled this duty with the more zeal.'

Quod iudicabam . . nostra, 'because I think our quarrel requires more of me,' i.e. he was the more bound to be watchful of Cicero's interest, as any neglect might be attributed to personal motives.

Duriores partes mihi impositas esse = 'plus a me exigi.' Boot. On the insertion of ab before 'offensione,' cp. Ep. 5, 10, note.

7. **Zelotypia**, 'jealousy.' It occurs Tusc. Disp. 4. 8, 18, but in Greek letters. Cicero gives 'obtrectatio' as a Latin equivalent. Antony's jealousy arose from Cicero having been elected augur before him. Cp. Intr. to Part II, § 13; Philipp. 2. 2, 4.

8. **Iniuria tua**, 'any wrong done by you.' Cp. Madv. 297 a.

10. **Caesarem.** Baiter inserts before this word from Cratander's edition the words 'neque illud me iudicare.' But neither Boot nor Hofmann sees any difficulty in the reading of the best MS., which I have followed. With the asyndeton, cp. p. 44, lines 5 and 6.

10. **Reponere.** This seems equivalent here to the simple verb 'ponere.' Cp. De Nat. Deor. 2. 21, 54 'non possumus ea ipsa (sidera) non in deorum numero reponere.'

11. **Eius**, Pompeii.

Fidem improbes, 'set no value on his honour.' Metzg. 'Pompeio ne te credas.' Manut. Pompey had promoted or sanctioned Cicero's banishment. Cp. Intr. to Part I, § 20.

12. **Qui tibi . . fecit**, 'who wronged you first that he might serve you afterwards.' Cp. Ep. 54, 3 'ille restituendi mei quam retinendi studiosior.'

Ne profugias, sub. 'eum,' sc. Caesarem. Cicero seems not to use this verb with an accusative after it. On the omission of 'eum,' cp. Ep. 54, 7, note.

13. **Etsi** = 'etiamsi.' Hofm.

Quod accidere non potest, sc. 'ut te non amet.'

14. **Dedita opera**, = *ἐκ προνοίας* (Forcell.), 'on purpose.'

Calpurnium. Perhaps the L. Piso mentioned Philipp. 10. 6, 13.

73. CAESAR TO CICERO (AD ATT. X. 8 B).

APRIL 16, 49 B.C. (705 A.U.C.)

1. I do not think you are likely to act imprudently, but what I hear induces me to write and beg you not to join my enemies. Your doing so, now especially, would be a most serious blow to me. 2. What attitude can befit an honest man and good citizen better than neutrality during a civil war?

'CAESAR IMP. SAL. D. CICERONI IMP.

Etsi te nihil temere, nihil imprudenter facturum iudicaram, 1
tamen permotus hominum fama scribendum ad te existimavi et pro nostra benevolentia petendum, ne quo progredereris proclinata iam re, quo integra etiam progrediendum tibi non existimasses; namque et amicitiae graviorem iniuriam feceris et tibi minus commode consulueris, si non fortunae obsecutus videbere —omnia enim secundissima nobis, adversissima illis accidisse videntur—, nec causam secutus—eadem enim tum fuit, cum ab eorum consiliis abesse iudicasti—, sed meum aliquod factum condemnavisse, quo mihi gravius abs te nil accidere potest; quod ne facias, pro iure nostrae amicitiae a te peto. Postremo, quid 2
viro bono et quieto et bono civi magis convenit quam abesse a civilibus controversiis? quod non nulli cum probarent, periculi causa sequi non potuerunt: tu explorato et vitae meae

2. Fama. Cp. 'rumorem.' Ep. 72, 1.

3. Ne quo progredereris, metaph. 'that you will not take any step.' Metzg., Forcell. The tense is epistolary, depending upon 'existimavi.' Cp. Ep. 1, 1, note.

Proclinata iam re, 'now that affairs have taken a decisive turn.' Cp. Caes. Bell. Gall. 7. 42 'adiuvat rem proclinatam Convictolitavis.'

6. Si non . . videntur, 'if you shall not seem to have yielded to circumstances (as you will not), for everything goes on as I could wish.' For this use of enim, cp. Forcell.

Fortunae obsecutus. 'Obsequi' = 'morem gerere, inservire.' Forcell.

8. Nec causam secutus, 'nor to have been influenced by the superior merits of his cause.' If Cicero now joined Pompey, he could not be influenced by prudence, nor by original preference for his cause, but must have been displeased by Caesar's conduct during the war. On 'secutus,' cp. Ep. 61, 3.

9. Abesse iudicasti, 'you decided to be absent.' A similar construction is found Ad Fam. 7. 33, 2 'mihi enim iudicatum est . . otio perfrui.'

Meum aliquod factum. On this use of the poss. pron., cp. Ep. 77, 1, note.

11. Pro iure, 'foll.,' 'in accordance with the right which our friendship gives me.' On this sense of the prep., cp. Zumpt, L. G. 318.

13. Quod non nulli . . potuerunt, 'a course which some men, though they approved of it, could not adopt, owing to the dangers which beset them.' e.g. the threats of Pompey against neutrals. Cp. Intr. to Part III, § 7; Ep. 80, 2.

14. Explorato . . iudicio, 'as the evidence which my life furnishes of my intentions, and the judgment which a friend should pronounce, are both clear.' Metzg. Hofm.

testimonio et amicitiae iudicio neque tutius neque honestius reperies quicquam quam ab omni contentione abesse. XV. Kal. Maias ex itinere.'

74. To ATTICUS (AD ATT. X. 16).

Near Cumae, May 14, (?) 49 B.C. (705 A.U.C.)

1. Dionysius visited me early in the morning; I was quite prepared to forgive him if his futile excuses had not shewn that he looks down on me in my present position. 2. I am now merely waiting for a fair wind. Let me hear all rumours and all your anticipations. 3. Cato has abandoned Sicily needlessly; I hope Cotta may put him to shame by holding Sardinia. 4. I have received offers from the commanders of a small force to put Pompeii into my hands, but I suspect a snare. 5. Hortensius visited Terentia while I was away, and spoke of me with respect. Antony's progresses are made in disreputable company. 6. Now that you have got rid of the ague and its consequences, come to me in Greece, and meanwhile write occasionally.

CICERO ATTICO SAL.

1 Commodum ad te dederam litteras de pluribus rebus, cum ad me bene mane Dionysius [fuit], cui quidem ego non modo placabilem me praebuissem, sed totum remisissem, si advenisset, qua mente tu ad me scripseras; erat enim sic in tuis litteris, quas Arpini acceperam, cum venturum facturumque quod ego vellem; ego volebam autem vel cupiebam potius esse cum nobiscum; quod quia plane, cum in Formianum venisset, praeciderat, asperius ad te de eo scribere solebam. At ille perpauca locutus hanc summam habuit orationis, ut sibi ignoscerem, se rebus suis impeditum nobiscum ire non posse. Pauca respondi, mag-

3. Ex itinere, 'on the march,' i.e. to Spain. Cp. Intr. to Part III, § 8.

On the date, May 14, cp. Ad Att. 10. 17, 1.

4. Commodum, 'opportunely.' Cp. Ad Att. 13. 9, 1 'commodum discesseras heri.'

Ad me. If 'fuit' is genuine, 'ad' must be equivalent to 'apud,' a sense not uncommon. Cp. Forcell.

5. Bene mane, 'very early.' 'Bene' = 'valde.' Cp. In Verr. 2 Act. 1. 70, 169 'bene penitus.'

6. Totum remisissem, 'should have forgiven him all.' 'Totum' is used thus absolutely Ad Q. F. 3. 1. 1 'totum in eo est . . tectorium ut concinnum sit.'

Qua mente = 'ea mente qua.' Madv. 321 and 319.

7. Erat enim sic, 'for it is written as follows.' On this sense of 'est,' cp. Ep. 37, 3; and on the tense, Ep. 1, 1, note.

10. Cum . . venisset. This was late in February. Cp. Ad Att. 8. 5, 1.

Praeciderat, 'had refused.' Cp. Ad Att. 8. 4, 2 'numquam reo cuiquam . . tam praecise negavi quam hic mihi plane . . praecidit.'

12. Hanc summam . . orationis, 'made a speech of this substance.'

Ut sibi ignoscerem: cp. on the mood, Madv. 372 a with 374.

13. Nobiscum ire, 'to accompany me to Greece.'

num accepi dolorem, intellexi fortunam ab eo nostram des-
pectam esse. Quid quaeris? fortasse miraberis: in maximis
horum temporum doloribus hunc mihi scito esse. Velim ut
tibi amicus sit: hoc cum tibi opto, opto ut beatus sis; erit
enim tam diu. Consilium nostrum spero vacuum periculo fore; 2
nam et dissimulavimus et, ut opinor, acerrime adservabimus.
Navigatio modo sit, qualem opto, cetera, quae quidem consilio
provideri poterunt, cavebuntur. Tu, dum adsumus, non modo
quae scieris audierisve, sed etiam quae futura providebis scribas
velim. Cato, qui Siciliam tenere nullo negotio potuit, et, si 3
tenuisset, omnes boni ad eum se contulissent, Syracusis profectus est ante diem VIII. K. Mai., ut ad me Curio scripsit.
Utinam, quod aiunt, Cotta Sardiniam teneat! est enim rumor.
O, si id fuerit, turpem Catonem! Ego, ut minuerem suspi- 4
tionem profectionis aut cogitationis meae, profectus sum in
Pompeianum a. d. IIII. Idus, ut ibi essem, dum quae ad navigandum opus essent pararentur. Cum ad villam venissem, ventum est ad me: centuriones trium cohortium, quae Pompeiis
sunt, me velle postridie [convenire]—haec mecum Ninnius
noster—; velle eos mihi se et oppidum tradere. At ego tibi

1. Fortunam . . esse, 'that he slighted me on account of my position.'

2. Fortasse miraberis, sc. 'id quod dicturus sum.'

3. Hunc, sc. 'dolorem.'

4. Ut beatus sis, 'that you may be prosperous.'

5. Tam diu, 'so long, and no longer.'

Consilium nostrum, 'my intention' of leaving Italy.

6. Dissimulavimus, 'I have concealed my intention.' This appears to be the reading of the best MS.; Baiter and Wesenb. have 'dissimulabimus.'

Adservabimus, 'shall keep them secret.' 'Adservare' = 'summa diligentia custodire et occultare.' Boot. On ut opinor, cp. Ep. 40, 1, note.

7. Navigatio: cp. Ep. 61, 5, note.

Quae quidem . . poterunt, 'so far at least as it will be possible for forethought to provide for them.' Cp. Ep. 10, 2, note, on the position of 'quidem.' The conjunctive would be more common after 'quae quidem' in this sense. Cp. Madv. 364, Obs. 2.

8. Dum adsumus, 'while I am still in Italy.' Cp. 'dum scitur' Ep. 69, 3.

10. Cato: cp. Intr. to Part III, § 9, notes.

Nullo negotio = 'sine ullo negotio.' Cp. 'nulla reda, nullis impedimentis' Pro Milon. 10, 28: Madv. 257.

Potuit: cp. Ep. 4, 1, note.

11. Ad eum, for 'ad quem.' Cp. Madv. 323 b.

13. Cotta. M. Aurelius Cotta seems only to be mentioned by Cicero here and Ad Att. 12. 22, 2, where he is spoken of as a learned man.

Est enim rumor, sc. 'eum ita facturum.' On the occurrences here referred to, cp. Intr. to Part III, p. 291, note 11. Cicero had not yet forgiven Cato for opposing the vote of a 'supplicatio' in his honour. Cp. Ad Fam. 15. 5, with Ad Att. 7. 2, 7.

16. Pompeianum: cp. Ep. 9, 11, note.

17. Ventum est ad me, 'I received a deputation, which said.' On the accus. and infin. which follow, cp. below, § 5 'misit . . puerum se ad me venire;' and Madv. 395.

19. Me velle postridie. Perhaps 'convenire' is superfluous. Cp. Ep. 29, 9 'te . . ipsum cupio.' Boot.

Haec mecum, sc. 'locutus est.' On the ellipse, cp. Ep. 33, 4, note. L. Ninnius Quadratus was a great friend of Cicero. Cp. Ep. 19, 4, and Intr. to Part I, § 20.

20. Tibi, 'I promise you.' Cp. Ep. 7, 5.

postridie a villa ante lucem, ut me omnino illi ne viderent. Quid enim erat in tribus cohortibus? quid, si plures? quo apparatu? cogitavi eadem illa Caeliana, quae legi in epistola tua, quam accepi, simul et in Cumanum veni, eodem die, et [simul] fieri poterat, ut temptaremur; omnem igitur suspitionem
5 sustuli. Sed dum redeo, Hortensius venerat, et ad Terentiam salutatum deverterat; sermone erat usus honorifico erga me. Tamen eum, ut puto, videbo; misit enim puerum se ad me venire. Hoc quidem melius quam collega noster Antonius,
6 cuius inter lictores lectica mima portatur. Tu, quoniam quartana cares, et nedum novum morbum removisti, sed etiam gravedinem, te vegetum nobis in Graecia siste, et litterarum aliquid interea.

1. A villa. It does not appear where; perhaps at Cumae.

2. Quid enim . . cohortibus, 'what was the value of three cohorts?' Cp. Ep. 9, 12, note.

Quid, si plures? sc. 'essent, temptandum erat?'

Quo apparatu? sc. 'temptaturi eramus aliquid?' Abl. instr.: cp. Madv. 254.

3. Eadem illa Caeliana, 'the same exploits of Caelius of which I wrote before.' Cp. Ad Att. 10. 12, 6, alib. The allusion is obscure. It is often referred to a Caelius who raised a force to oppose Sulla in Italy, and who is apparently noticed, according to one reading, in Plut. Pomp. 7. It is just possible that Cicero may have already heard that M. Caelius Rufus was discontented with Caesar. Cp. Intr. to Part III, § 12.

5. Fieri . . temptaremur, 'it was possible that people were trying to entrap me.' On the mood, cp. Madv. 373.

Omnem . . suspitionem sustuli, 'I removed all ground for suspicion,' which Caesar's friends would have felt if he had even listened to the proposals made.

6. Dum redeo; sc. 'in Cumanum,' Manut. Cp. for the tense Ep. 69, 3, note.

Hortensius, son of the great orator. He was a man of dissipated character (cp. Ad Att. 6. 3, 9; 10. 4, 6), who now served Caesar, but after his death supported and obeyed Brutus as governor of Macedonia, and was put to death after Philippi by Antony's order, in revenge for the death of C. Antonius, whose execution Hortensius had ordered. Philipp. 10, 5 and 6; Plut. Brut. 28.

Ad Terentiam . . deverterat, 'had visited Terentia to greet her.' Cp. Madv. 411, on the use of the supine.

8. Tamen, 'though he had called without finding me at home.' Cp. Ep. 29, 21, note. Wesenb. has 'iam.'

Misit . . venire: cp. § 4, note.

9. Hoc quidem melius, sc. 'fecit.' Cp. p. 327, l. 4, note, on the ellipse.

Collega, as augur. Antony's election is referred to Ep. 41, 1.

10. Mima: cp. Ad Att. 10. 10, 5 'hic tamen Cytherida secum lectica aperta portat, alteram uxorem;' also Philipp. 2. 24, 58.

Quartana: cp. Ad Att. 10. 15, 4 'te a quartana liberatum gaudeo.' It was a fever returning every fourth day. Forcell.

11. Nedum. Forcell. thinks that this is used in a sense resembling that of 'non dicam' and a similar sense is found in a letter of Balbus and Oppius, Ad Att. 9, 7 A, 1. But it seems not to be Ciceronian, and Wesenb. thinks that something has dropped out, e.g. 'non modo.' He reads 'et . . novum.'

Novum morbum. Perhaps the disorder was *δυσουρία*, mentioned Ad Att. 10. 10, 3.

12. Gravedinem, 'cold in the head,' 'catarrh.' Perhaps an usual consequence of the sickness from which Atticus had been suffering. Boot reads 'novum morbum removisti,' omitting 'nedum,' and putting 'sed etiam gravedinem' in brackets. The best MS. has 'novum vel nedum.'

Te vegetum . . siste, 'present yourself to me,' 'let me find you in good health in Greece.' 'Vegetus' = 'incolumis, vividus.' Forcell.

Et litterarum aliquid, sc. 'mitte,' 'and meanwhile write to me.' Cp. on the ellipse Epp. 9, 8; 15, 10, notes.

75. To TERENTIA (AD FAM. XIV. 7).

ON SHIPBOARD IN THE PORT OF CAIETA, (?) JUNE 7, 49 B.C. (705 A.U.C.)

1. I can relieve you and Tullia from all anxiety as to my health, thanks to the aid of some god, to whom I hope you will make a fitting acknowledgment. 2. I think I have a good vessel, and write on board; I will recommend you and Tullia to several friends by letter. I know your firmness, and will spare exhortations. I hope you will be free from annoyance in Italy, and that I shall be able to serve the state with others like myself. 3. Take care of your health, and, if possible, stay in villas remote from any military post. Marcus sends his good wishes.

TULLIUS TERENTIAE SUAE SAL. PLURIMAM.

Omnes molestias et sollicitudines, quibus et te miserrimam 1
habui, id quod mihi molestissimum est, *et* Tulliolam, quae nobis nostra vita dulcior est, deposui et eieci; quid causae autem fuerit, postridie intellexi, quam a vobis discessi: χολὴν ἄκρατον noctu eieci; statim ita sum levatus, ut mihi deus aliquis medicinam fecisse videatur, cui quidem tu deo, quem ad modum soles, pie et caste satis facies [id est Apollini et Aesculapio]. Navem 2
spero nos valde bonam habere; in eam simulatque conscendi, haec scripsi. Deinde conscribam ad nostros familiares multas epistolas, quibus te et Tulliolam nostram diligentissime commendabo. Cohortarer vos, quo animo fortiore essetis, nisi vos fortiores cognossem quam quemquam virum. Et tamen eius modi spero negotia esse, ut et vos istic commodissime sperem

CAIETA. In Ep. 54, 6, Cicero had written that he had ships ready at Caieta and at Brundisium in case he decided to sail for Pompey's camp.

1. Quibus . . habui, 'owing to which I kept you in a very uneasy state.' Cp. Nägelsb. 110, 300; Pro Flacco 29, 71 'cur unus te Apollonidenses . . miseriores habes quam aut Mithridates aut . . pater tuus habuit umquam.' On the abl. 'quibus,' cp. Ep. 74, 4, note.

3. Quid . . fuerit, 'what has been the reason' for my ill-health. On the tense cp. Ep. 71, 3, note; and on the gen. 'causae,' Madv. 285 b.

4. Postridie . . discessi. He had apparently parted from them at his villa near Cumae. Cp. Ep. 74, 4-8.

χολὴν ἄκρατον. He uses Greek words perhaps for delicacy's sake, or, as Mr. Jeans says, as Latin is used now: cp. Ep. 104, 1.

5. Eieci = 'evomui.' Forcell.

Medicinam fecisse, 'to have administered a remedy.' 'Facere' = 'adferre.' Forcell. Cp. De Orat. 2. 44, 186 'adhibere medicinam.'

7. Satis facies = 'gratias ages.' Frey. 'coles.' Forcell. On the mood and tense, see Ep. 11, 3.

11. Quo = 'ut eo,' 'that by so much.' Cp. Madv. 440 b, Obs. 1.

12. Et tamen: cp. Ep. 71, 6.

13. Spero esse, foll. Cicero here twice uses the present infinitive with 'spero.' Cp. Ep. 1, 1, note.

Istic, 'in Italy.'

Commodissime . . esse: cp. Ad Fam. 14. 18, 1 'tuto esse;' also Epp. 4, 1; 49, notes.

esse et me aliquando cum similibus nostri rem publicam defensuros. Tu primum valetudinem tuam velim cures; deinde, si tibi videbitur, villis iis utere, quae longissime aberunt a militibus. Fundo Arpinati bene poteris uti cum familia urbana, si annona carior fuerit. Cicero bellissimus tibi salutem plurimam dicit. Etiam atque etiam vale. D. VII. Idus Iun.

76. M. CAELIUS RUFUS TO CICERO (AD FAM. VIII. 17).

ITALY, EARLY IN 48 B.C. (706 A.U.C.)

1. Would that I had been at Formiae when you sailed! I have acted too much from private feeling, and you should have warned me before. I do not distrust our prospects of success, but detest my associates. 2. If people did not fear your cruelty, we should long ago have been driven from Rome. Nearly everybody is for Pompey, and I have done much to bring about this change of feeling. You are letting a great chance escape you. If you wait for a pitched battle, you will do just what Caesar with his hardy troops would wish.

CAELIUS CICERONI SAL.

1 Ergo me potius in Hispania fuisse tum quam Formlis, cum tu profectus es ad Pompeium! Quod utinam aut Appius Claudius *in hac parte fuisset aut* in ista parte C. Curio, cuius amicitia me paulatim in hanc perditam causam imposuit; nam mihi sentio bonam mentem iracundia et amore ablatam. Tu porro, cum ad te proficiscens Arimino noctu venissem, dum mihi pacis mandata

1. Defensuros, 'will defend with success.' Hofm. Cp. Livy 26. 27 'aedes Vestae vix defensa est.' On the plural 'defensuros,' cp. Madv. 215 c. Wesenb. points out that this construction is not Ciceronian, and prefixes † to 'defensuros.'

3. Utere, apparently future, v. sup. on 'satis facies.' Wesenb. however, as 'cures' has gone before, reads 'utare.'

A militibus, sc. Caesarianis.

4. Cum familia urbana, 'with the slaves of our town establishment.' They could be maintained more cheaply at Arpinum than at Rome, probably. The estate at Arpinum has been mentioned Ad Att. 5. 1. 3. Cp. De Legg. 2. 1; Appendix 5, § 1.

5. Cicero bellissimus, young Marcus. On this use of the superlative with a proper name, cp. Ep. 43, 1, note.

The date of Ep. 76 seems to be fixed by the allusion in § 2 to Caesar's army as apparently already in presence of Pompey's, and on the other hand, by the death of Caelius having apparently taken place early in 48 B.C. Cp. Intr. to Part III, § 12, p. 300, notes 5 and 6.

7. Ergo. 'Servit eleganter conquestioni et indignationi.' Forcell.

Me potius . . fuisse, 'to think that I should rather have been.' Cp. Ep. 12, 1, note.

8. Quod utinam, foll. 'Quod' = 'sed.' Cp. Madv. 449.

9. In hac parte, 'on Caesar's side.'

Me . . imposuit, 'led me by degrees to embark in this desperate cause.' 'Imposuit' = 'inlecit.' Forcell.

11. Iracundia et amore, 'by anger against Appius and affection for Curio.'

12. Proficiscens Arimino perhaps only means 'from Ariminum.' Caelius had been sent to Liguria by Caesar early in the civil war (cp. Ad Fam. 8. 15, 2), and probably rejoined his commander at Ariminum. Where Cicero received his visit does not appear. On the tense of das and agis, cp. Ep. 69, 3, note.

das ad Caesarem et mirificum civem agis, amici officium neglexisti
neque mihi consuluisti. Neque haec dico, quod diffidam huic
causae, sed crede mihi, perire satius est quam hos videre. Quod 2
si timor vestrae crudelitatis non esset, eiecti iam pridem hinc
essemus; nam hic nunc praeter faeneratores paucos nec homo
nec ordo quisquam est nisi Pompeianus. Equidem iam effeci,
ut maxime plebs et, qui antea noster fuit, populus vester esset.
'Cur hoc?' inquis. Immo reliqua exspectate; vos invitos vincere
coegero. *Geram* alterum me Catonem: vos dormitis, neque
adhuc mihi videmini intellegere, quam nos pateamus et quam
simus imbecilli. Atque hoc nullius praemii spe faciam, sed, quod
apud me plurimum solet valere, doloris atque indignitatis causa.
Quid istic facitis? proelium exspectatis, quod firmissimum habet?
Vestras copias non novi; nostri valde depugnare et facile algere
et esurire consuerunt.

1. **Et mirificum civem agis**, 'and in playing the part of an excellent citizen,' by trying to effect a pacification.

2. **Diffidam**: cp. Ep. 28, 7, note, for the mood.

3. **Hos**, Caesar's friends. Caelius was offended because Trebonius received the 'praetura urbana' while he only had the 'peregrina.' Cp. Dion Cass. 42, 22; Vell. 2. 68; Livy Epit. 111.

4. **Vestrae crudelitatis**, 'of the cruelty of Pompey and his friends.'

Hinc, 'from Rome,' or 'from Italy.'

5. **Faeneratores.** The great capitalists, who were pleased by Caesar's measures for the maintenance of public credit. Intr. to Part III, §§ 8; 12; Caes. Bell. Civ. 3. 1; Mommsen 4. 2, 379 380.

7. **Plebs**, 'the rabble.' Cp. Ep. 8, 11 'misera ac ieiuna plebecula.'

Populus, 'the sounder part of the population.' The words can hardly be explained here as on p. 238, l. 4, note.

Esset. On the tense, cp. Madv. 383.

8. **Reliqua**, 'the sequel' of my conduct.

Vos invitos vincere coegero, 'I shall compel you to conquer against your will,' a sneer at the mismanagement of the Pompeians.

10. **Quam nos pateamus**, 'how exposed we are.' Cp. De Off. 1. 21, 73 'minus multa patent in eorum vita quae fortuna feriat.' Caelius perhaps meant that Pompey should land in Italy instead of continuing the struggle in Greece.

11. **Quod apud me**, foll. The neuter seems rather irregular, but cp. Ep. 6, 3 'id;' also Madv. 315 b.

12. **Indignitatis**, 'indignation.' Cp., however, Ep. 71, 3, note.

13. **Istic**, i.e. 'in Epirus.'

Quod firmissimum habet, sc. Caesar. 'On the result of which Caesar may rely with the greatest confidence.' This use of 'firmus' seems peculiar, but cp. Ep. 12, 4, note on 'firmissimum habere.' Wesenb. doubts whether these words can bear such a meaning, and prints the MS. reading 'quod firmissimum † haec.'

14. **Valde depugnare**, 'to fight stoutly.'

Facile = 'libenter.' Forcell. Cp. Caes. Bell. Civ. 3. 47-49, for instances of the endurance of Caesar's soldiers.

77. DOLABELLA TO CICERO (AD FAM. IX. 9).

FROM CAESAR'S CAMP IN EPIRUS, MAY, (?) 48 B.C. (706 A.U.C.)

1. I can give you good accounts of your family. I hope you will believe that in exhorting you to be neutral in this war, I am and have been only influenced by friendship. 2. You see that Pompey has done nothing worthy of his fame and resources; I hope you will set some limit to your devotion to him. 3. You had better retire to some neutral city, where I should join you. Caesar will, I am sure, receive any requests from you with favour, and I will plead your cause with him. I hope you will secure the safe return of my messenger.

DOLABELLA S. D. CICERONI.

1 S. v. g. v. et Tullia nostra recte v. Terentia minus belle habuit, sed certum scio iam convaluisse eam. Praeterea rectissime sunt apud te omnia. Etsi nullo tempore in suspitionem tibi debui venire partium causa potius quam tua tibi suadere, ut te aut cum Caesare nobiscumque coniungeres aut certe in otium referres, praecipue nunc iam inclinata victoria, ne possum quidem in ullam aliam incidere opinionem nisi in eam, in qua scilicet tibi suadere videar, quod pie tacere non possim: tu autem, mi Cicero, sic haec accipies, ut, sive probabuntur tibi sive non probabuntur, ab optimo certe animo ac deditissimo tibi et cogitata et scripta esse

For notices of Dolabella, cp. Intr. to Parts II. § 26; IV. § 6; V. § 3; Epp. 38. 1 and 2; 42, 1. He supported Caesar actively in the civil war. The date of this letter is taken from Baiter.

1. S. v. g. v. = 'si vales gaudeo; valeo.'

Minus belle habuit, 'has been unwell.' Cp. Ep. 53. 1: and 'recte hoc par habet' Ep. 34. 3. 'Se habere' is also used in similar passages. Cp. Ad Att. 12. 37. 1 'Atticam .. belle se habere.'

2. Certum, adverbial: cp. Pro Scauro 15. 34 'sive patricios sive plebeios esset —nondum enim certum constituerat.'

3. Apud te, 'in your home.' Dolabella would have later news of Cicero's family than Cicero himself as Italy was held by Caesar's friends.

6. Inclinata, 'half won.' Cp. Ep. 21, 3.

In .. aliam incidere opinionem. Hofm. hesitates between 'come to any other opinion' and 'meet with any other reputation.' Süpfle adopts the last, which is supported by Ad Fam. 8. 10, 2 'in eam opinionem Cassius veniebat .. finxisse bellum.' Wesenb. agrees with Süpfle, and makes the words = 'in ullam aliam suspitionem tibi venire.' Mr. Jeans agrees in substance with Süpfle, and remarks that the apodosis begins with 'praecipue nunc.'

7. In qua scilicet, foll. These words are very curious; 'scilicet ut videar' would be more regular 'than of being thought to recommend what I cannot with propriety omit to mention.' Wesenb. omits 'in' before 'qua.' On the conj. 'videar,' cp. Ep. 5, 8. 'Scilicet' = 'to be sure,' 'I mean,' 'that is.' See Epp. 11. 4; 58, 7.

9. Ab optimo .. animo. The preposition seems superfluous; but cp. Madv. 255, Obs. 1.

iudices. Animadvertis Cn. Pompeium nec nominis sui nec rerum 2
gestarum gloria neque etiam regum ac nationum clientelis, quas
ostentare crebro solebat, esse tutum, et hoc etiam, quod infimo
cuique contigit, illi non posse contingere, ut honeste effugere
possit, pulso Italia, amissis Hispaniis, capto exercitu veterano,
circumvallato nunc denique; quod nescio an nulli umquam nostro
acciderit imperatori. Quam ob rem, quid aut ille sperare possit
aut tu, animum adverte pro tua prudentia; sic enim facillime
quod tibi utilissimum erit consilii capies. Illud autem *a* te peto,
ut, si iam ille evitaverit hoc periculum et se abdiderit in classem,
tu tuis rebus consulas et aliquando tibi potius quam cuivis sis
amicus: satis factum est iam a te vel officio vel familiaritati, satis
factum etiam partibus et ei rei publicae, quam tu probabas.
Reliquum est *ut*, ubi nunc est res publica, ibi simus potius quam, 3
dum illam veterem sequamur, simus in nulla. Qua re velim,
mi iucundissime Cicero, si forte Pompeius pulsus his quoque locis
rursus alias regiones petere cogatur, ut tu te vel Athenas vel in
quamvis quietam recipias civitatem; quod si eris facturus, velim
mihi scribas, ut ego, si ullo modo potero, ad te advolem. Quaecumque de tua dignitate ab imperatore erunt impetranda, qua est

1. Animadvertis, 'you must be aware.' Metzg.

2. Neque etiam, 'nor yet.' For its force after nec, cp. Caes. Bell. Civ. 1. 5 'nec . . sui periculi deprecandi . . neque etiam extremi iuris . . retinendi.'

Regum et nationum clientelis, cp. Appendix 7, and Caes. Bell. Civ. 3. 3-4.

3. Ostentare, 'to boast of.' Forcell.

Neque . . esse tutum, 'cannot look for safety to.' Cp. De Dom. 42, 109 'religionibus tuis.'

5. Italia. For the omission of a preposition, cp. § 3 'his quoque locis;' also Ep. 63. 4; Madv. 262.

Capto exercitu veterano, i.e. the army of Afranius and Petreius in Spain. Cp. Intr. to Part III, § 8.

6. Circumvallato, dat. agreeing with 'illi.' For the facts, Cp. Intr. to Part III, § 11.

Quod nescio an nulli, foll., 'which perhaps has happened to no general of ours.' Cp. Madv. 453. And on nostro imperatori = 'e nostris imperatoribus,' Cp. Caes. Bell. Civ. 3. 96 'paucos suos ex fuga nactus,' and Madv. 284. Obs. 7.

8. Animum adverte, 'consider.' With the whole clause, cp. De Nat. Deor. 3. 37, 89 'non tu animadvertis . . quam multi votis vim tempestatis effugerint.'

9. Quod . . consilii capies. On the gen., cp. Ep. 75. 1, note; on the omission of 'id,' Ep. 34. 7, note.

10. Se abdiderit, 'shall have retired.'

12. Satis factum est, foll., 'you have satisfied the claims of duty and intimacy,' freq. in this sense. Forcell.

13. Ei rei publicae, 'that constitution' (Süpfle,) (Hofm.).

14. Reliquum est ut. 'Ut' is perhaps needless. Cp. Ad Fam. 15. 21, 5 'reliquum est tuam profectionem amore prosequar.' Baiter has inserted it from Lambinus in both places.

Res publica, 'the seat of political life,' 'the government.'

15. Dum . . sequamur. 'Dum' = 'while,' 'so long as,' 'in our devotion to the commonwealth of the past.' Cp. on the mood of 'sequamur,' Madv. 360, Obs. 2. The indicative would, I think, be more regular. Cp. Ep. 61, 3.

16. His quoque locis: cp. § 1 'Italia.' This shews that Dolabella was now with Caesar.

20. De tua dignitate, 'about maintaining you in a proper position.' On

humanitate Caesar, facillimum erit ab eo tibi ipsi impetrare; et meas tamen preces apud eum non minimum auctoritatis habituras puto. Erit tuae quoque fidei et humanitatis curare, ut is tabellarius, quem ad te misi, reverti possit ad me et a te mihi litteras referat.

78. To ATTICUS (AD ATT. XI. 4).

CAMP NEAR DYRRHACHIUM, JUNE OR JULY, 48 B.C. (706 A.U.C.)

1. I have received three letters from you. I hope you will aid my family in their difficulties. I have had nothing to write about, as I do not approve of our measures, and take no part in directing them. Would that I had conferred with you in person before leaving Italy!

2. Isidorus will tell you the news; the rest of our task seems equally easy. I hope you will attend to what especially interests me. I am far from well; if I get better I shall join Pompey, who is very sanguine. Brutus is doing what he can for us. Consider well what should be done about the 'second payment.'

CICERO ATTICO SAL.

1 Accepi ab Isidoro litteras et postea datas binas: ex proximis cognovi praedia non venisse; videbis ergo, ut sustentetur per te.

the meaning of 'dignitas,' cp. Epp. 29. 51; 47. 1; 64. 2, notes.

Qua est humanitate, descriptive abl., 'considering Caesar's courtesy.' Cp. Madv. 446.

1. Ipsi, 'by yourself.'

Impetrare, sc. 'ea:' for the omission of which, cp. note on 'quod' in the preceding section.

Et meas tamen, foll., 'however, I think that my entreaties will have much weight with him.' On 'tamen' in such passages, cp. Ep. 29. 21, note.

2. Non minimum = 'maximum.' Forcell.

3. Erit tuae quoque fidei, foll., 'moreover your honour and good feeling will bid you take care that my messenger is allowed to return to me,' instead of being detained by Pompey's partisans. On the gen. 'fidei,' cp. Madv. 282, Obs. 2. 'Quoque' = 'on your part,' as a return for my services. Süpfle.

JUNE or JULY. The first portion of this letter seems to have been written before, the second after Caesar's defeat before Petra, on which cp. Intr. to Part III, § 11. Now Caesar (Bell. Civ. 3. 49) says that the corn was beginning to ripen before that disaster, and (ib. 81) that the harvest in Thessaly was nearly ripe when he reached Metropolis. Cicero seems to have remained at Dyrrhachium after Caesar's departure from the neighbourhood of that place. Cp. Intr. to Part III, § 10.

6. Isidoro. Isidorus seems to have been a slave or freedman of Atticus. He is only mentioned in this letter.

Binas. Distributive numerals are generally used with plural substantives denoting compound objects, which can be repeated and counted. Cp. Madv. 76 c. But of one letter 'unas litteras,' not 'singulas,' is said. Cp. Ep. 45. 1, note; also Ep. 79. 3, note.

7. Praedia. Some estates which Cicero had wished to sell for the benefit of Tullia and Terentia. Cp. Ad Fam. 14. 6.

Videbis = 'curabis.' Forcell. Cp. Ep. 70. 7, note.

Ut sustentetur, sc. Tullia (Boot), 'be supported.'

De Frusinati, si modo futuri sumus, erit mihi res opportuna. Meas litteras quod requiris, impedior inopia rerum, quas nullas habeo litteris dignas, quippe cui nec quae accidunt nec quae aguntur ullo modo probentur. Utinam coram tecum olim potius quam per epistolas! Hic tua, ut possum, tueor apud hos. Cetera Celer. Ipse fugi adhuc omne munus, eo magis, quod ita nihil poterat agi, ut mihi et meis rebus aptum esset.

Quid sit gestum novi, quaeris: ex Isidoro scire poteris; reliqua 2
non videntur esse difficiliora. Tu id velim, quod scis me maxime velle, cures, ut scribis, ut facis. Me conficit sollicitudo, ex qua etiam summa infirmitas corporis; qua levata ero una cum eo, qui

1. De Frusinati, 'about the property near Frusino,' which was a town situated on a feeder of the Trerus, about 15 miles S.E. of Anagnia. Cicero had sold this land, reserving power to repurchase it apparently, which he now seems to have been anxious to do. Cp. Ad Att. 11. 13. 4. Manut.

Si modo futuri sumus, 'if I am still to exist.' 'Futuri' = 'victuri.' Forcell. Cp. Ad Fam. 6. 3. 4 'si non ero sensu omnino carebo.' Wesenb. suggests 'salvi futuri,' but does not adopt it in his text.

2. Meas litteras quod requiris, 'as to your wanting letters from me.' 'You are surprised at my writing so seldom, but.' Metzg. 'Requirere' = 'to miss.' Cp. Ep. 15. 8. On 'quod requiris' cp. Ep. 8, 14, note; and on 'meas' in this sense, Epp. 72, 1; 77, 2, notes.

Quas nullas: cp. Ep. 77. 1, note on 'nostro.'

3. Quippe cui .. probentur, 'as I am not at all satisfied either with what is going on or with the measures taken.' The indicatives are used after the indefinite pronoun 'quae;' the conj. 'probentur' as giving a reason. Cp. Madv. 366, Obs. 2, and 362 a.

Accidunt casu; aguntur, 'ex consilio et voluntate Pompeii.' Manut.

4. Utinam coram tecum, sc. 'deliberavissem.' Cp. Ad Att. 12. 3. 1 'si tecum olim coram potius quam per litteras .. deliberavissem.' Cicero probably thought that Atticus would have dissuaded him strongly from leaving Italy.

5. Tua, 'your estates.' Atticus' property in Epirus has often been mentioned in Cicero's letters; e.g. 6. 1; 16, 6.

Apud hos, sc. Pompeianos.

Cetera Celer, sc. 'dicet.' He was a freedman of Atticus. Cp. Ep. 68, 4.

6. Omne munus, 'any office.' Wieland.

Ita nihil .. aptum esset, 'because no duties were open to me, suited to myself and to my interests.' Either he was not offered a high enough command, which would degrade himself, or he feared by accepting one to irritate Caesar, and so injure his prospects.

§ 2. With this section either the letter is resumed after a long interval, or a new one begins.

8. Quid sit gestum novi .. scire poteris. Cicero here refers probably to a defeat of Caesar near Dyrrhachium, described Caes. Bell. Civ. 3. 66–72. After that affair Caesar marched into the interior, and Pompey followed him, while sickness detained Cicero near Dyrrhachium (cp. Plut. Cic. 39). This accounts for Cicero's language below, ero una cum eo, foll. Cp. Intr. to Part III, § 10.

Reliqua, 'the rest of our task.' Cicero does not say if he shares the general confidence expressed by videntur. On 'reliqua,' cp. Ep. 76, 2, note.

9. Id .. quod scis me maxime velle. Probably that he would take care of Terentia and Tullia.

10. Ut scribis, ut facis, 'as you write that you do, and really do.' Cp. Tac. Dial. de Orat. 23 'ut potestis et facitis.'

Ex qua etiam, foll., 'and great bodily weakness arising from it.' Wesenb. suggests the insertion of 'est' after 'corporis.'

Sollicitudo. Anxiety either (1) as to the results of Pompey's excessive confidence—cp. Ep. 88, 2—or (2) as to the probable behaviour of Pompey and his supporters after decisive success: the last is Manutius' suggestion.

11. Qua levata, 'but when this has been alleviated.' 'Levatus' might also be used. Forcell.

Cum eo, Pompeio.

negotium gerit estque in spe magna. Brutus amicus; in causa versatur acriter. Hactenus fuit quod caute a me scribi posset. Vale. De pensione altera, oro te, omni cura considera, quid faciendum sit, ut scripsi iis litteris, quas Pollex tulit.

1. **Negotium gerit**, 'is actively engaged.'

Brutus. M. Iunius Brutus, now with Pompey. Cp. Plut. Brut. 4.

Amicus, sc. 'mihi est.'

In causa, foll. 'is serving our party with energy.' Billerb.

2. **Versatur** = 'agit.' Forcell.

Hactenus fuit . . . posset, 'only thus much can I write without imprudence.' On the tense of 'posset,' cp. Ep. 1, 1, note; and on the mood, Ep. 21, 3, note. Cicero was probably a good deal threatened by violent partisans of Pompey. Cp. Intr. to Part III, § 10; Ep. 80, 2.

3. **De pensione altera**, 'about the payment of the second instalment' of Tullia's portion to Dolabella. Boot, on Ad Att. 11. 3, 1; cp. 11. 2, 2.

4. **Iis litteris**, perhaps Ad Att. 11. 3. Man.

Pollex, a slave whom Cicero employed as a messenger. Cp. Ad Fam. 14, 6; Ad Att. 8. 5, 1.

PART IV.

CICERO UNDER THE GOVERNMENT OF CAESAR.

OCTOBER, (?) 48 TO MARCH 15, 44 B.C.

INTRODUCTION.

48–47 B.C.

§ 1. AFTER his landing in Italy, Cicero remained for some months at Brundisium, where he heard[1] of the fate of several of the leaders of his party. He was disquieted by many troubles; it was with some difficulty that he obtained[2] leave to remain in Italy from Antony, Caesar's representative; his brother and nephew, who had gone to make their peace with Caesar in Asia, seem to have calumniated[3] him; his daughter's marriage was unhappy[4], and he had some difficulty in paying her dowry; while he was by no means satisfied with the conduct of Terentia[5], to whose extravagance he attributed, in great measure, his existing embarrassments. Above all, however, he was seriously alarmed by the aspect of public affairs. He had returned to Italy under the impression that the war was virtually at an end[6]; but Caesar's delay at Alexandria[7], and the reports which were circulated of the growing strength of the optimates in Africa[8] dispelled this hope, and he accused himself of precipitation—especially as a proclamation of Antony, which gave him leave by name to remain in Italy, would mark him out for the suspicion of the optimates in case of their ultimate success[9].

Harassed by these anxieties, he remained at Brundisium till the September of 47 B.C., when Caesar[10] landed at Tarentum after his victories

[1] Ad Att. 11. 6. 5 and 6. [2] Ib. 11. 9, 1. [3] Ib. 11. 9, 2; 11. 10, 1. [4] Ib. 11. 23, 3; 11. 24, 1: cp. 11. 2, 2. [5] Ad Att. 11. 16, 5; 11. 24, 3; cp. Ad Fam. 4. 14, 3. [6] Ad Fam. 15. 15, 2. [7] Below, § 3: Ad Fam. 15. 15, 2; Ad Att. 11. 16, 1. [8] Ad Att. 11. 10, 2; 11. 12, 3. [9] Ib. 11. 7, 2. [10] Ad Fam. 14. 21; Plut. Cic. 39.

over Ptolemy and Pharnaces. Cicero hastened to meet him, was kindly received, and seems to have got leave to fix his residence wherever he chose. He probably spent the rest of the year [1] in Rome, or at some of his villas in the neighbourhood.

§ 2. His letters from Brundisium are perhaps more depressed in tone than any others; and as Abeken [2] remarks, this is probably to be accounted for by his feeling more self-reproach than he had felt at the time of his exile in 58 B.C. Then he found some relief in attacking others for their perfidy; now he could only blame himself. His two principal correspondents were Atticus and Terentia. Perhaps he hardly ventured to write to any less intimate friends. He expressed [3], however, to C. Cassius his discontent at the prolongation of the war.

His brother Quintus had made [4], though in rather ambiguous terms, an apology for his hostility. Afterwards, however, when Caesar seemed inclined to pardon Marcus, Quintus warmly congratulated [5] his brother; and a good understanding seems to have been re-established between the brothers—at least outwardly, though Marcus had reason to find fault again subsequently [6].

§ 3. Caesar, after the battle of Pharsalus, pardoned many of his opponents, including M. Brutus [7]. He then with a small force followed Pompey [8], and received in Asia the submission of C. Cassius, who had commanded a squadron in the Ionian sea at the time of the decisive battle, and had made partially successful attacks on the naval forces which were being organized for Caesar at Messana and Vibo [9]. Caesar did not overtake Pompey, and the latter having reached the roadstead of Alexandria with a few ships, was treacherously murdered there on Sept. 28 [10] by order of the young king Ptolemy's advisers. Caesar received the news of the crime with horror, and hastened to Alexandria, where he arrived early in October [11]. He secured two rival claimants for the throne of Egypt, Ptolemy and his sister Cleopatra; but had to wage a long and doubtful struggle with Arsinoe [12], younger sister of Ptolemy, who was supported by the royal army and by the populace of Alexandria. So embarrassing was Caesar's position, that he released Ptolemy in the hope that he might act as mediator; but the young king took the lead among Caesar's enemies. Mithridates of Pergamus, however, advanced to Caesar's support from Asia with a considerable force [13];

[1] Ad Att. 11. 7; Ad Fam. 14. 20. [2] p. 318. [3] Ad Fam. 15. 15. [4] Ad Att. 11. 13, 2. [5] Ib. 11. 23, 2. [6] Ib. 12. 5, 1. [7] Caes. Bell. Civ. 3. 98; cp. Ad Fam. 6. 6, 10; Plut. Caes. 46. [8] Caes. Bell. Civ. 3. 102–106. [9] Ib. 3. 101, cp. App. Bell. Civ. 2. 88. [10] Ib. 104; Plut. Pomp. 79; Vell. 2. 53; Pliny H. N. 37, 2; Ad Att. 11. 6, 5. [11] Plut. Pomp. 80; Caes. Bell. Civ. 3. 106; Livy Epit. 112. [12] Livy Epit. 112; Bell. Alex. 1-25. [13] Bell. Alex. 26–32.

Ptolemy's army was routed on March 27, and the young king himself drowned in trying to escape[1]. Resistance now ceased. Caesar made Cleopatra queen of Egypt, detained Arsinoe as a prisoner, and departed in July[2] for Asia, where the successes of Pharnaces demanded his presence. That prince, son of the famous Mithridates, had defeated[3] Cn. Domitius Calvinus, whom Caesar had left in charge of Asia Minor. But Caesar obtained a decisive success on August 2 at Zela in Pontus, and after making provision for the government of Asia, landed in September at Tarentum[4].

§ 4. In Illyricum the fortune of war had been variable. After the battle of Pharsalus, Caesar had left Q. Cornificius there with two legions, and that army was subsequently re-inforced by Cicero's old enemy, A. Gabinius. The latter suffered some reverses at the hands of the Dalmatians, and afterwards died of fatigue and vexation. M. Octavius, who commanded a naval force in the Adriatic for the optimates, attempted subsequently, in conjunction with the natives, to occupy the province, but was baffled by the energy of P. Vatinius[5], who fitted out a naval force hastily at Brundisium and defeated Octavius. Thus the province remained in the hands of Cornificius, and Octavius sailed to Africa, whither many of the leaders of the optimates had already betaken themselves.

Among them were Cn. Pompeius the younger, Metellus Scipio, Afranius, Petreius, Faustus Sulla, and Labienus. Cato, too, carried a body of troops by sea from Corcyra to Cyrene, and thence led them by a toilsome march to the province of Africa[6]. At his suggestion, Cn. Pompeius retired to Mauretania, and thence to the Balearic islands and to Spain, to take advantage of the disaffection which had been caused there by the misgovernment and dissensions of Caesar's officers[7].

§ 5. Italy had been disturbed during these months. When the news of Pompey's death reached Rome, the senate voted that Caesar, empowered to deal according to his own pleasure with members of the conquered party, and to make peace and war on his own authority, should be named dictator for a year, and should have power to name the curule magistrates for several years in advance[8]. M. Antonius, who had landed with some troops for the defence of Italy, was named his master of the horse rather irregularly, for it was usual for the dictator to

[1] Bell. Alex. 31-32; cp. 65; Fasti Maff. ap. Mommsen, C. I. L. 1. 304. [2] Bell. Alex. 33-41. [3] Ib. 65; Plut. Caes. 50; Livy Epit. 112. [4] Bell. Alex. 74-78: cp. Ad Fam. 14. 20 and 22; Plut. Cic. 39; App. Bell. Civ. 2. 91. Caesar used the celebrated words 'veni vidi vici' with regard to this victory. Cp. Plut. Caes. 50: with Livy Epit. 113, and Suet. Iul. 37. [5] Bell. Alex. 42-47. [6] App. Bell. Civ. 2. 87; Bell. Afric. 13; Plut. Cat. 56; Lucan Phars. 9. 587, foll. [7] Bell. Afric. 22-23; Bell. Hisp. 1; Bell. Alex. 48-64. [8] Dion Cassius 42. 20.

name his own master of the horse, and there was no time to send to Caesar at Alexandria[1]. Antony was thus again entrusted with the government of Italy[2], as in 49 B.C. He seems to have abstained from acts of cruelty, and treated Cicero in particular with much consideration[3]; but the measures of defence which he had to adopt were probably burdensome to several towns, and, if we may believe Cicero, his licentiousness and arrogance caused general disgust[4].

No ordinary curule magistrates were elected for the year 47 B.C. till towards its close. P. Dolabella, now tribune[5], raised an agitation[6] in favour of an abolition of debts, which threatened to become serious, but was checked by Antony, who introduced a body of troops into the capital and slaughtered 800 of the rioters. The agitation was not, however, completely appeased till the return of Caesar from the East[7].

A mutinous spirit, also, prevailed among the veterans quartered in Campania[8], and the efforts of Caesar's officers to quell it were met by outrage. Caesar met the mutineers probably in October, and when they clamoured for a discharge granted it at once. They were confounded, and asked permission to remain in his service, which he granted with some difficulty.

For the last months of the year, Q. Fufius Calenus, and P. Vatinius, were elected consuls[9]. Caesar shewed himself anxious to win over as many of the optimates as possible; he named C. Cassius one of his legates; entrusted Cisalpine Gaul to the government of M. Brutus, and Greece to that of Ser. Sulpicius Rufus[10].

46–45 B.C.

§ 6. During this year and the next there was comparatively little connection between the personal history of Cicero and the course of public events, and he employed himself principally in the composition[11] of philosophical and rhetorical treatises.

He used his influence, however, eagerly on behalf of his friends[12] in the vanquished party, and for their sake and his own kept up as good an understanding as he could with various friends of Caesar[13], especially with Hirtius, Dolabella, and Cornificius. Partly perhaps to quiet his

[1] Philipp. 2. 25, 62; A. W. Zumpt, S. R. 212. Plutarch, however, (Ant. 8) says that Caesar named Antony his master of the horse and sent him to Italy. Lange, 3. 421 follows Plutarch. [2] Philipp. l. c.; Plut. Ant. 9. [3] Ad Att. 11. 7, 2: cp. Philipp. 1. 4, 11; 2. 24. 59. [4] Philipp. 2. 25, 62; Plut. Ant. 9. [5] He had gone over to the plebs, to enable him to hold that office; cp. Dion Cassius 42. 29. [6] Bell. Alex. 65: cp. Ad Att. 11. 12, 4; 11. 23, 3; Livy Epit. 113; Plut. Caes. 51; Ant. 9. [7] App. Bell. Civ. 2. 92; Dion Cassius 42. 33. [8] App. Bell. Civ. 2. 92–94; Plut. Caes. 51; Suet. Jul. 70. [9] Dion Cassius 42. 55. [10] Ad Fam. 6. 6, 10; 4. 4, 2; 15. 15, 3. [11] Ib. 4. 3, 3; 9. 1, 2; 9. 18, 3. [12] Ib. 6. 6, 13; 6. 8, 1; 6. 14, 1; 6. 12, 1. [13] Ib. 6. 12, 2; 9. 16, 2; 9. 18, 1 and 3.

own uneasy feelings he vindicated in various letters[1] the policy he had pursued before the civil war, which he represented as having been one of conciliation—and his determination to retire from the struggle after a decisive battle.

Many of his letters were written to console friends living in exile, and to hold out hopes to them of a speedy return to their country. Such were those to Caecina, Torquatus, and Plancius[2]. He expressed his gratitude in the senate for the pardon of M. Marcellus[3], and subsequently pleaded with much independence for that of Q. Ligarius[4], who was accused before Caesar of having shewn peculiar hostility to him in Africa. Next year he defended Deiotarus of Galatia, accused of having plotted against the life of Caesar[5].

His expressions of opinion on public affairs in the letters of this time are very guarded, and he seems to have been moved by conflicting feelings; on the one hand[6], by regret for the fall of the old constitution, and for the loss of his old influential position; on the other[7], by an involuntary admiration of Caesar's magnanimity. His dislike[8] of some of Caesar's most prominent adherents remained unchanged, and may have contributed to dissuade him from mixing in public affairs. He had little desire[9], however, for the triumph either of the optimates in Africa, or of the sons of Pompey in Spain; his hasty abandonment of his party in the autumn of 48 B.C. would not have been forgiven in either case. Caesar's victory at Thapsus relieved him from this apprehension for a time; and he seems to have spent the last half of 46 in comparative cheerfulness[10].

§ 7. His family troubles, however, continued. Towards the close of this year, or at the beginning of the next, he thought it advisable to divorce Terentia[11]. What grounds for displeasure she had given him besides her alleged extravagance it is hard to say. His letters to her during the previous year had been short and rather cold[12].

Cicero was still much in want of money; and to relieve himself from his difficulties, married his young and wealthy ward, Publilia[13]. She seems to have been jealous of Tullia, and to have received little affection from her husband.

The severest blow which he suffered was the death[14] of his daughter

[1] Ad Fam. 6. 6, 5; 7. 3, 3; 15. 15, 1; Ad Att. 11. 6, 2. [2] Ad Fam. 6. 1–8; 4. 14 and 15. [3] Ib. 4. 4, 4; Pro Marcello. [4] Ad Fam. 6. 14; Ad Att. 13. 19, 2; Pro Ligario. [5] Ad Fam. 9. 12, 2; Pro Deiot. [6] Ad Fam. 4. 14, 1; 4. 6, 2. [7] Ib. 4. 4, 4; 6. 6, 10. [8] Ib. 4. 4, 5; 12. 18, 2. [9] Ad Att. 11. 7, 3; 11. 12, 3. [10] Ib. 12. 4, 1; 12. 6, 2; Ad Fam. 9. 17 and 18. [11] Plut. Cic. 41; Dion Cassius 46. 18. [12] Ad Fam. 14. 20–24. [13] Ib. 4. 14; Plut. Cic. 41. [14] Plut. Cic. l. c.; Ad Fam. 6. 18, 5; 4. 5, 1.

early in 45 B.C. Her unhappy marriage with Dolabella had been ended by a divorce[1], and shortly afterwards she gave birth to a child, but did not long survive. Her father was long inconsolable; her society[2] had been his principal comfort, and neither philosophy[3] nor the consolatory letters[4] of friends could give him much relief. He cherished for some time a wish to build a shrine[5] in her honour, but does not appear to have carried it out. The society of his young wife was now more than ever distasteful to him; he refused[6] to see her with much harshness, and presently divorced her.

His son Marcus seems to have been restless, and to have wished either to take service under Caesar in Spain[7], or to live separately from his father at Rome. Finally, however, he acceded to his father's suggestion, that he should go to study at Athens[8], for which place he set out in March, 45 B.C. The youth seems to have complained of his father's parsimony[9]; probably without good grounds. Cicero's brother had already paid court to Caesar by allowing his son to become a Lupercus[10], and to attend Caesar on his Spanish campaign.

§ 8. About this time Cicero seems to have thought of sending to Caesar a letter[11]—probably on the state of the commonwealth, but was dissuaded from doing so by Caesar's friends, who doubted the acceptability of his recommendations. He also wrote some complimentary but independent remarks on Caesar's 'Anticato,' which were sent to Caesar with the approval of Oppius and Balbus.

At the very end of the year 45 B.C. Cicero received a visit from Caesar at his villa near Puteoli, of which he has given a lively account[12]. He seems to have enjoyed the interview, but not to have been anxious for its repetition.

§ 9. During Caesar's stay in Italy after the defeat of Pharnaces he quelled, as has been already mentioned, the mutinous spirit of his veterans, and re-established tranquillity in the capital. He also filled up the ranks of the senate[13], which had been greatly thinned by the civil war; increased the number of the praetors from eight to ten[14]; and added one member to each of the great priestly colleges[15].

[1] Ad Att. 11. 23, 3. [2] Ib. 12. 15; Ad Fam. 4. 6, 2. [3] Ad Att. 12. 14. 3. [4] Ib. 12. 13. 1; 12. 14. 3 and 4; 13. 20. 1. Caesar, Sulpicius, Lucceius (Ad Fam. 5. 13), and M. Brutus were among those who wrote to him. [5] 'Fanum.' He would thus escape the penalties for excessive expenditure on sepulchral monuments: cp. Ad Att. 12. 36, 1; 12. 12, 1. [6] Ib. 12. 32, 1; Plut. Cic. 41. [7] Ad Att. 12. 7, 1. [8] Ib. 12. 24, 1. [9] Ib. 12. 7. 1; 12. 32. 2. [10] Ib. 12. 5. 1; 12. 7. 1. [11] Ib. 13. 27. 1; 13. 31, 3; 13. 50, 1. [12] Ib. 13. 52. [13] Suet. Iul. 41: Dion Cassius 43. 51. [14] Dion Cassius l. c. [15] Ib.

He then went to Lilybaeum[1], and after spending some days there, sailed for Africa on Dec. 25. After three days he landed at Adrumetum[2], and pitched his camp at Ruspina on the first day of the new year[3].

§ 10. Caesar was consul for the third time at the beginning of this year, with M. Aemilius Lepidus as his colleague. As both were patricians, this was a violation of the 'Leges Liciniae Sextiae[4].' Towards the close of the year Caesar was perhaps dictator for the third time, with Lepidus for his master of the horse. Cp. Appendix 10, 4.

Caesar's force was for some time small, composed in great measure of raw recruits, and in cavalry especially inferior to the enemy[5]. The optimates could bring into the field 70,000 regular infantry, composed, indeed, in great measure of hasty levies and emancipated slaves, with an immense number of cavalry and light troops, and several elephants furnished by their ally Juba. Nor were capable officers wanting in their ranks; Afranius, Petreius, and Labienus had all served with distinction; and the resolute endurance of Cato had been recently attested[7]. But the chief command fell, according to constitutional rules, to Scipio, who was incapable and obstinate[8]; Juba, proud of his victory over Curio, set up pretensions which it was embarrassing either to admit or to resist[9]; the provincials were harassed by oppression[10]; and the Gaetulians and Mauretanians[11] retained a kindly remembrance of Marius, which disposed them to regard with favour the representative of his party.

Still, for some time Caesar's position was difficult. In an engagement fought soon after his landing, the advantage remained with his enemies[12], and he was obliged to remain nearly inactive for more than two months. Gradually, however, his position improved as reinforcements came in from Sicily[13]; and a diversion made in his favour by P. Sittius, a Roman adventurer, and by Bocchus of Mauretania[14], compelled Juba to withdraw for a time to protect his own dominions. The provincials, too, as far as they dared, shewed their good will to Caesar[15].

At last, early in April, he felt strong enough to risk a general battle.

[1] Bell. Afric. 1-2; Cic. de Divin. 2. 24, 52; Plut. Caes. 52. [2] Bell. Afric. 3. [3] Ib. 6. [4] Livy 6. 35 and 42. [5] Bell. Afric. 1; 3; 5; 10. [6] Intr. to Part III, § 8; Caes. Bell. Civ. 2. 26, alib. [7] Supra, § 4. [8] Bell. Afric. 4; Plut. Cat. Min. 57. [9] Plut. Cat. l. c.; Bell. Afric. 57; Ad Att. 11. 7, 3. [10] Bell. Afric. 26. [11] Ib. 35. [12] Ib. 13-17. [13] Ib. 34. [14] Ib. 25. [15] Ib. 26; 33.

The armies met near Thapsus[1], and Caesar obtained a decisive victory. His orders to give quarter were disobeyed, and the slaughter was very great.

Soon after the battle Cato killed himself[2] at Utica, and the leaders of the defeated party perished almost without exception by their own hands or by those of the enemy. Scipio, Petreius, Juba, Afranius, and Faustus Sulla, none of them long survived Cato[3]. Labienus fled to Spain, and there co-operated with the sons of Pompey[4].

§ 11. Caesar, having speedily made such arrangements in Africa as seemed most necessary[5], and having reduced Numidia to the form of a province[6], sailed for Sardinia on June 13[7], and thence to Italy. He entered Rome on July 26.

In August he celebrated four splendid triumphs[8] for his victories in Gaul, Egypt, Pontus, and Africa. Representations of the deaths of Scipio and Cato were carried in the procession, which gave much offence. The triumphs were accompanied or followed by liberal grants[9] of money and food to the soldiers and people, and by street improvements on a great scale; among which were the laying out of the Forum Iulium, and the erection of a temple to Venus Genitrix[10]. Caesar also allotted lands to his veterans as he had promised, but these were not contiguous, and thus there was less interference with existing rights of possession[11] than had been usual in such cases.

For an account of the honours now voted to Caesar, of his legislation, and of his amendment of the Calendar, see Appendices 8–10. Owing to the amendment of the Calendar, the nominal and real dates correspond from the beginning of 45 B.C.

§ 12. Towards the close of 46 B.C. Caesar started for Spain[12], where the sons of Pompey, aided by Labienus, had gained great strength. The war was obstinately maintained for nearly three months, and was decided by a desperate battle fought at Munda (in Baetica) on March 17, 45 B.C.[13] Cn. Pompeius and Labienus died in the battle, or soon afterwards; but Sextus Pompeius escaped, and maintained himself in Spain till Caesar's

[1] On April 6. Bell. Afric. 79–85; Mommsen, 4. 2. 445. [2] Bell. Afric. 88; Plut. Cat. Min. 70. [3] Bell. Afric. 91–96; Livy Epit. 114; Ad Fam. 9. 18, 2. [4] Bell. Hisp. 31. [5] Bell. Afric. 90, foll.; Dion Cassius 43. 14. [6] Bell. Afric. 97. [7] Ib. 98; Ad Fam. 9. 7, 2. [8] Vell. 2. 56; Suet. Iul. 37; Livy Epit. 115; Plut. Caes. 56; App. Bell. Civ. 2. 101; Dion Cassius 43. 19. [9] Suet. Iul. 38; App. Bell. Civ. 2. 102. [10] App. Bell. Civ. 2. 102; Dion Cassius 43. 22; Suet. Iul. 44. [11] Suet. Iul. 38; App. Bell. Civ. 2. 94; Dion Cassius 42. 54. [12] Bell. Hisp. 2; App. Bell. Civ. 2. 103; Dion Cassius 43. 32. [13] Bell. Hisp. 29–31; Livy Epit. 115; Dion Cassius 43. 37 and 38.

death[1]. C. Asinius Pollio remained as Caesar's legate in the Farther Spain[2]. C. Octavius, afterwards emperor, attended his great uncle Caesar in this campaign[3].

Caesar was detained in Spain till late in the summer[4]; returned to Italy in September, and entered Rome in triumph in October[5]. Two of his legates, Q. Fabius and Q. Pedius, triumphed[6] shortly afterwards for successes in Spain. Fabius was elected consul for the last months of this year with C. Trebonius[7]; but Fabius died while in office, and was succeeded for one day only by C. Caninius Rebilus, a piece of scrupulous formality which occasioned much amusement[8].

The distribution of lands to the veterans continued during this year[9]. Caesar's triumphal festivities were marked by one incident which seems to have made a painful impression; a knight named D. Laberius, known as a writer of farces, was obliged to represent a character in one of his own[10] pieces on the stage.

The election of consuls for 44 B.C. was marked, according to Cicero, by perfidy to Dolabella[11], who had been led by Caesar to hope for the consulship, but for whom Caesar substituted himself. Dolabella's election would have been a violation of the 'Leges Annales[12],' but Cicero does not notice this.

44 B.C.

§ 13. The earliest months of this year were employed by Caesar, now consul for the fifth time and dictator for the fourth, in preparations for an expedition against the Parthians[13]. He had formed a considerable camp in Macedonia[14], and had sent the young Octavius to Apollonia, probably that he might become acquainted with the soldiers, while pursuing his studies.

Meanwhile the conspiracy was being formed which proved fatal to Caesar. Both the old parties in the State were represented among the conspirators. C. Cassius and M. Brutus had both served under Pompey[15]; D. Brutus and C. Trebonius had been active on behalf of Caesar[16]. Seneca remarks[17], 'Divum Iulium plures amici confecerunt

[1] Bell. Hisp. 32; 39; Livy Epit. 115; Plut. Caes. 56; App. Bell. Civ. 2. 105.
[2] Dion Cassius 45. 10.
[3] Ib. 43. 41; Suet. Oct. 8; Vell. 2. 59.
[4] Ad Att. 13. 45. 1.
[5] Livy Epit. 116; Vell. 2. 56.
[6] Acta Triumph. Capit. ap. Mommsen, Corpus Inscr. Lat. 1. 461; Dion Cassius 43. 42.
[7] Suet. Iul. 80; Dion Cassius 43. 46.
[8] Dion Cassius l. c.; Ad Fam. 7. 30. 1; Suet. Iul. 76.
[9] Ad Fam. 13. 4.
[10] Suet. Iul. 39; Macrob. Sat. 2. 7; Ad Fam. 12. 18, 2.
[11] Philipp. 2. 32. 79.
[12] App. Bell. Civ. 3. 88.
[13] Ib. 2. 110; 3. 24; Plut. Caes. 58; Suet. Iul. 44; Dion Cassius 43. 51.
[14] App. Bell. Civ. 2. 110; 3. 9; Plut. Brut. 22; Livy Epit. 117; Vell. 2. 59.
[15] Supra, § 3.
[16] Intr. to Part III, § 8.
[17] De Ira 3. 30, 4 and 5.

quam inimici.' Two feelings probably animated the Caesarian members of the conspiracy: jealousy of such of their comrades as enjoyed a larger measure of their leader's favour, and apprehension that Caesar might assume the title of king. The increasing haughtiness of his demeanour strengthened suspicion; and the royal title was to the Romans of this period associated with oriental despotism[1]. M. Brutus probably believed that he was acting in the public interest. C. Cassius is said to have been jealous of the favour shewn to M. Brutus by Caesar. Both the two last-mentioned conspirators held office under Caesar as praetors when they conspired against him[2].

§ 14. Early in the year Caesar's statue[3] on the Rostra was decorated by some officious friend with a laurel crown bound with a ribbon. The tribunes Flavus and Marullus removed the crown, and though Caesar took no measures against them he was annoyed. Somewhat later[4], as he was returning on Jan. 26 from celebrating the 'Feriae Latinae,' he was greeted as king by some of the crowd who met him. He made the adroit reply, 'non Rex sum sed Caesar;' but when the two tribunes mentioned above arrested the man who had first greeted him as king, Caesar was very indignant, and caused them to be deposed and excluded from the senate. On the day of the 'Lupercalia[5],' Feb. 15, Antony offered Caesar a diadem half concealed under a laurel crown, and though Caesar refused it, his sincerity was doubted. On Antony's proposal, the name of the month Quintilis was now changed to Iulius[6]. All these occurrences probably estranged the people's affections, and confirmed the conspirators in their resolution.

On some day before the 'Lupercalia[7],' comitia were held for the election of a consul to hold office after Caesar should have departed for Parthia. Dolabella was the candidate favoured by Caesar, but Antony, who presided, adjourned the proceedings after several centuries had voted, declaring as augur that the day was unfavourable. This proceeding, according to Cicero, was irregular[8].

It is doubtful if Caesar executed in this year his intention of sending numerous colonists to Corinth and to Carthage. Appian[9] assigns the measure to Augustus, but other authorities[10] to Julius, and the majority of them to this year.

[1] Ad Att. 14. 1, 2; 14. 2, 3; Suet. Iul. 79; Livy Epit. 116; App. Bell. Civ. 2. 108-111; Plut. Caes. 60; 61. [2] Plut. Caes. 62; Brut. 7; Ad Fam. 11. 3, 1; Philipp. 1. 15, 36; App. Bell. Civ. 2. 112. [3] Plut. Caes. 61; App. Bell. Civ. 2. 108; Dion Cassius 44. 9. [4] App. l. c.; Plut. l. c.; Suet. Iul. 79; Dion Cassius 44. 10. [5] Plut. Caes. 61; Ant. 12; Cic. Philipp. 2. 34. [6] Cens. de Die Nat. 22; App. Bell. Civ. 2. 106; Dion Cassius 44. 5. [7] Philipp. 2. 32 and 33. [8] Ib. [9] Punica 8. 136. [10] Suet. Iul. 42; Plut. Caes. 57; Dion Cassius 43. 50.

Caesar proposed, apparently, to leave Rome soon [1]. His presence was required in the East, not only to chastise the Parthians, but to restore order in Syria. For Sextus Caesar, whom he had entrusted with the command of a legion in that province, had been killed in the year 46 B.C. by his soldiers, at the instigation of Q. Caecilius Bassus [2], who presently got together a numerous army, composed partly of the mutinous troops of his predecessor, partly of new levies. The generals sent against him by Caesar had not been able to suppress the rebellion [3].

§ 15. The senate was convened for March 15 [4], probably to hear and approve Caesar's preparations for his expedition, and his provisions for the government of Italy and the provinces till his return. It was reported that a proposal would be made on that day to declare Caesar [5] king, and alleged prophecies were [6] circulated, not perhaps for the first time, that the Parthians could only be conquered by the Romans if the latter were commanded by a king.

The meeting of the senate took place in a building near the theatre [7] of Pompey, and consequently outside the walls. Caesar, in spite of omens [8] and warnings, was present, attended by Antony, who, however, was drawn aside by Trebonius [9], probably from fear of his courage and devotion to Caesar, or from a wish to spare needless bloodshed. L. Tillius Cimber presented [10] a petition to Caesar on behalf of his brother, then in exile; and Caesar's refusal to grant it was the signal for a general attack upon him by the conspirators. He fell, pierced with twenty-three wounds. Antony fled to his home, and the senate broke up in confusion [11].

[1] App. Bell. Civ. 2. 110; 111; Plut. Caes. 58; Dion Cassius 43. 51; 44. 15. [2] Livy Epit. 114; App. Bell. Civ. 3. 77; Dion Cassius 47. 26. [3] Philipp. 11. 13. 32; App. l. c.; Dion Cassius 47. 27. [4] Philipp. 2. 35, 88; Suet. Iul. 80. [5] Plut. Caes. 64; App. Bell. Civ. 2. 113: cp. 111; Dion Cassius 44. 15. [6] Dion Cassius l. c.; App. Bell. Civ. 2. 110; Suet. Iul. 79; Cic. de Divin. 2. 54; Merivale 2. 470, foll. [7] Plut. Caes. 66; App. Bell. Civ. 2. 115; Dion Cassius 44. 16. [8] Suet. Iul. 81; Plut. Caes. 63; Vell. 2. 57; App. Bell. Civ. 2. 115; Dion Cassius 44. 17. [9] Philipp. 2. 14. 34; Plut. Caes. 66; Ant. 13; Vell. 2. 58; App. Bell. Civ. 2. 117; Dion Cassius 44. 19. [10] Plut.; Dion Cassius; App. ll. cc.; Vell. 2. 56. [11] Philipp. 2. 35, 88; Plut. Caes. 67; Ant. 14; App. Bell. Civ. 2. 118; Dion Cassius 44. 20.

SELECT LETTERS

OF

M. TULLIUS CICERO.

PART. IV.

79. To ATTICUS (AD ATT. XI. 5).

BRUNDISIUM, EARLY IN NOVEMBER, 48 B.C. (706 A.U.C.)

1. The reasons which have suggested this hasty return to me have been painful but weighty. You are evidently rather confounded by my haste. 2. I do not think I should do much good by travelling to Rome in the way you propose. 3. Great discomfort, both of mind and body, prevents my writing many letters; I shall be glad if you will write for me. 4. Vatinius and others I have no doubt would serve me if they could. My brother was lately at Patrae, very ill-disposed towards me. I think his son has joined him there, and that both have gone away, with others.

CICERO ATTICO SAL.

1 QUAE me causae moverint, quam acerbae, quam graves, quam novae, coëgerintque impetu magis quodam animi uti quam cogitatione, non possum ad te sine maximo dolore scribere; fuerunt quidem tantae, ut id, quod vides, effecerint.

On landing at Brundisium, Cicero seems to have written to his family and to Atticus, and to have received answers from them. He replied to Atticus and to Terentia, and his answer to the latter was dated November 4. Cp. Ad Fam. 14. 12. It is probable, therefore, that this letter was written about the same time.

1. Quae me causae moverint, 'what causes induced me' to return to Italy.

2. Novae, 'strange.' Cicero refers, perhaps, partly to his quarrel with Quintus, (cp. Intr. to Part IV, § 1), partly to the threats (and violence) of the Pompeians at Corcyra and elsewhere. Cp. Ep. 78, notes.

Impetu . . uti, 'to be guided by impulse rather than by reflection.'

4. Id, quod vides, i.e. 'my sudden return to Italy.'

Itaque nec quid ad te scribam de meis rebus nec quid a te petam, reperio. Rem et summam negotii vides. Equidem ex tuis litteris intellexi et iis, quas communiter cum aliis scripsisti, et iis, quas tuo nomine, quod etiam mea sponte videbam, te subita re quasi debilitatum novas rationes tuendi mei quaerere. Quod scribis placere, ut propius accedam iterque per 2
oppida noctu faciam, non sane video, quem ad modum id fieri possit; neque enim ita apta habeo deversoria, ut tota tempora diurna in iis possim consumere, neque ad id, quod quaeris, multum interest, utrum me homines in oppido videant an in via. Sed tamen hoc ipsum, sicut alia, considerabo quem ad modum commodissime fieri posse videatur. Ego propter incre- 3
dibilem et animi et corporis molestiam conficere plures litteras non potui; iis tantum rescripsi, a quibus acceperam. Tu velim et Basilo et quibus praeterea videbitur, etiam Servilio conscribas,

1. **Itaque . . reperio,** 'accordingly, since what I have done was sudden and undesigned, I have no plans to explain to you, nor do I know in what to ask your assistance.'

2. **Rem et summam negotii,** 'the whole state of the case.'

3. **Litteris.** For the use of this word signifying more letters than one, cp. Ep. 62, 4, note.

Quas communiter . . . scripsisti, 'which you wrote, and addressed as from several other friends besides.' It is to be presumed that Atticus submitted his letter to these friends for their approval, and then prefixed their names with their leave. Specimens of such letters are to be found Ad Fam. 16. 3, foll.

4. **Quod . . videbam,** 'what I needed no assistance to be convinced of,' referring to what immediately follows.

5. **Subita re,** i.e. 'by my sudden return.'

Novas rationes. Ever since the battle of Pharsalus, Atticus seems to have been employing his influence for Cicero's protection, and now the latter's return to Italy would require a change of Atticus' mode of action. Cp., on Atticus' exertions, Ad Att. 11. 7. 5; 11. 9. 1.

6. **Quod scribis placere:** cp. Ep. 8. 14, note.

Accedam, i.e. to Rome.

Iterque . . faciam, i.e. to travel along the Appian way from Brundisium to Rome, taking care to pass through the towns by night. Cicero remarks that he knew of no lodgings where he might pass the whole of each day, and so travel by night only; and that, with a view to the avoidance of publicity (ad id quod quaeris), it would make little difference where he was seen, if he had to travel by day at all. Manutius appears to consider 'per oppida' = 'from town to town:' i.e. Cicero was to spend the days in doors, and only travel by night.

8. **Deversoria.** Cicero owned houses in various places which he called by this name, but he can hardly have had such lodgings all along the road from Rome to Brundisium. He probably here refers to inns, or to friends' houses.

11. **Hoc ipsum, sicut alia,** 'this plan, like others you have suggested.'

13. **Corporis molestiam.** The air of Brundisium seems to have affected Cicero's health. Cp Ad Att. 11. 22, 2.

Plures litteras, 'many letters.' The Latin word sometimes corresponds to the English plural, even without a distributive numeral. Madv. 52; cp. sup. § 1, note, and Ep. 62, 4, note.

15. **Basilo.** L. Minucius Basilus, who had served under Caesar in Gaul (Caes. Bell. Gall. 6. 29), and seems to have remained faithful to him during the civil war, ultimately joined the conspiracy against him, and was afterwards murdered by his own slaves for his cruelty (Ad Fam. 6. 15; cp. App. Bell. Civ. 2. 113; 3. 98).

Quibus praeterea videbitur, sc. 'scribendum esse.'

Etiam Servilio. These words would come more naturally before 'et quibus,' but Cicero may have forgotten Servilius, and

ut tibi videbitur, meo nomine. Quod tanto intervallo nihil omnino ad vos scripsi, his litteris profecto intelleges rem mihi
4 deesse, de qua scribam, non voluntatem. Quod de Vatinio quaeris, neque illius neque cuiusquam mihi praeterea officium deesset, si reperire possent, qua in re me iuvarent. Quintus 5
aversissimo a me animo Patris fuit; eodem Corcyra filius venit. Inde profectos eos una cum ceteris arbitror.

80. TO ATTICUS (AD ATT. XI. 6).

BRUNDISIUM, NOV. 27, 48 B.C. (706 A.U.C.)

1. The anxiety which I see you feel on my behalf increases my trouble, but I am glad to learn that you and others approve my conduct. 2. I do not regret having left the seat of war, but wish I had retired to some place out of Italy. 3. I hear that Caesar is disposed to treat me with great consideration; pray tell Pansa and other friends of Caesar that I have acted by their advice. 4. Tullia's health causes me great anxiety. 5. I never doubted what Pompey's end would be, but must lament such a death for such a man. 6. For others who have fallen I have less pity. 7. I hear that my brother has gone to Asia to sue for pardon. Write to me whenever you have anything to say.

not cared to correct his omission. P. Servilius Isauricus is mentioned with respect in the Philippics. Cp. 11. 8, 19; 11. 10, 25; 13. 2, 5. Cp., also, Ep. 9. 10, note. He was now Caesar's colleague as consul.

1. **Ut tibi videbitur**, 'as you shall think proper.'

Meo nomine, 'as from me.' Cp. 'tuo nomine' in § 1.

2. **His litteris.** We might have expected 'ex his litteris.' But the simple ablative is sometimes used after 'verba intelligendi.' Cp. Ad Fam. 1. 5 b, 1 'ex te et litteris multorum . . cognosse arbitror.' Boot.

Rem mihi deesse: cp. § 1, and note on 'itaque.'

3. **De Vatinio.** Atticus had apparently asked how Vatinius, governor of Brundisium for Caesar (cp. Caes. Bell. Civ. 3. 100), behaved to Cicero. On the previous relations of Cicero and Vatinius, cp. Intr. to Part II, §§ 2; 10.

4. **Cuiusquam.** Probably 'of any friend of Caesar.'

5. **Si reperire . . iuvarent.** Perhaps Caesar's absence made his officers unwilling to act without special instructions. Or Cicero may be speaking ironically. 'They would serve me if they only knew how.'

Quintus . . . fuit. Perhaps Quintus, who was hot-tempered, was annoyed by his brother's vacillation, and would have preferred that his brother should either never have gone to Pompey's camp, or should not have despaired so soon.

6. **Aversissimo . . . animo . . . fuit**, 'expressed his discontent with me loudly' (Wiel.) when I last heard of him.

Patris. The unfriendly language used by Quintus there, is mentioned again Ad Att. 11. 16, 4. Patrae was a city in the west of Achaia. Mr. Jeans' translation implies an opinion that Marcus Cicero accompanied his brother there from Corcyra, and Drumann. 6, 238, note 41, refers to Ad Fam. 13. 17, 1 in support of this opinion.

Filius. The younger Quintus, apparently.

Venit = 'ivit.' Cp. Ad Fam. 1. 10 'illo si veneris.'

7. **Profectos eos.** 'That they have gone to Asia' to sue for pardon from Caesar. Cp. Ep. 80, 7.

Cum ceteris, i.e. 'with the other repentant Pompeians.'

CICERO ATTICO SAL. DICIT.

Sollicitum esse te cum de tuis communibusque fortunis, tum 1
maxime de me ac de dolore meo sentio; qui quidem meus dolor
non modo non minuitur, cum socium sibi adiungit dolorem
tuum, sed etiam augetur. Omnino pro tua prudentia sentis,
qua consolatione levari maxime possim; probas enim meum
consilium negasque mihi quicquam tali tempore potius faciendum fuisse. Addis etiam—quod etsi mihi levius est quam
tuum iudicium, tamen non est leve—ceteris quoque, id est,
qui pondus habeant, factum nostrum probari. Id si ita putarem, levius dolerem. 'Crede' inquis 'mihi.' Credo equidem, 2
sed scio, quam cupias minui dolorem meum. Me discessisse
ab armis numquam paenituit: tanta erat in illis crudelitas,
tanta cum barbaris gentibus coniunctio ut non nominatim, sed
generatim proscriptio esset informata, ut iam omnium iudicio
constitutum esset omnium vestrum bona praedam esse illius
victoriae. 'Vestrum' plane dico; numquam enim de te ipso
nisi crudelissime cogitatum est. Qua re voluntatis me meae
numquam paenitebit; consilii paenitet. In oppido aliquo mallem resedisse, quoad arcesserer: minus sermonis subissem, minus
accepissem doloris; ipsum hoc me non angeret. Brundisii
iacere in omnes partes est molestum. Propius accedere, ut
suades, quo modo sine lictoribus, quos populus dedit, possum?

3. **Cum socium . . . tuum.** On the accus. of adjectives as predicates, cp. Ep. 33, 2, note; Madv. 227 a.

9. **Id si ita putarem,** sc. 'esse.' Cp. Ep. 71, 2. Or is 'ita' pleonastic? Cp. Zumpt, L. G. 748.

11. **In illis,** 'among the Pompeians.' In illustration of the following passage, cp. Intr. to Part III, §§ 7; 10; also Epp. 61, 4; 62, 1; 63, 3, and Ad Att. 11. 7. 3, where he says of the war in Africa, 'iudicio hoc sum usus, non esse barbaris auxiliis fallacissimae gentis rem publicam defendendam.'

13. **Ut non nominatim . . informata,** 'that a proscription had been planned, not against individuals, but against whole classes.'

14. **Generatim** = 'universim, generaliter' (Forcell.); 'informata' = 'mente concepta' (Boot). Cp. Ep. 1, 2.

Omnium iudicio, 'in the opinion of all' the Pompeians.

15. **Illius victoriae,** 'of the victory of Pompey.'

16. **Vestrum,** 'of you who remained in Italy.'

Plane, 'expressly.' Nägelsb. 86, 235.

17. **Voluntatis,** 'of my wish to retire from the struggle.'

18. **Consilii,** 'of the way in which I have carried out my wish.'

In oppido aliquo, 'in some town out of Italy,' apparently, from the context.

19. **Quoad arcesserer,** 'until I was sent for by Caesar,' 'until I had leave to return.'

Minus sermonis subissem, 'I should in that case have been subjected to less criticism.' On the omission of a clause with 'si,' cp. Madv. 347 c.

20. **Ipsum hoc,** 'my present trouble,' i.e. self-reproach for having acted unwisely. Boot.

21. **In omnes partes** = 'omnino.' Forcell.

22. **Sine lictoribus.** Cicero had not entered Rome (i.e. the 'urbs') since leaving

qui mihi incolumi adimi non possunt; quos ego nunc paulisper
cum bacillis in turbam conieci ad oppidum accedens, ne quis
3 impetus militum fieret. † Recipio tempore me domo. Te nunc
ad oppidum et quoniam his placeret modo propius accedere, ut
hac de re considerarent: credo fore auctores. Sic enim reci-
piunt, Caesari non modo de conservanda, sed etiam de augenda
mea dignitate curae fore, meque hortantur, ut magno animo
sim, ut omnia summa sperem: ea spondent, confirmant, quae
quidem mihi exploratiora essent, si remansissem. Sed ingero
praeterita. Vide, quaeso, igitur ea, quae restant, et explora
cum istis, et si putabis opus esse et si istis placebit, quo magis
factum nostrum Caesar probet quasi de suorum sententia factum,
adhibeantur Trebonius, Pansa, si qui alii, scribantque ad Caesarem me, quicquid fecerim, de sua sententia fecisse.
4 Tulliae meae morbus et imbecillitas corporis me exanimat,
quam tibi intellego magnae curae esse, quod est mihi gratissi-

Cilicia, and consequently, not having forfeited his 'Imperium,' he was still attended by the lictors whose presence had so much embarrassed him. Cp. Ep. 46.

Quos populus dedit. Cicero had probably been invested with 'Imperium' by a Lex Curiata, and may here refer to that fact. He had received his commission to govern Cilicia from the senate. Intr. to Part II, § 17.

1. Incolumi, 'while I retain my political rights.' Cp. Ep. 16, 2. In this case Cicero means his 'Imperium.' Hofm.

2. Cum bacillis, 'with their staves.' Opposed to 'fasces,' as single staves to a bundle. Forcell. Cp. De Leg. Agr. 2. 34, 93.

In turbam conieci, 'caused to mingle with the crowd.' A rare sense of the word; 'se conicere' is common. Forcell. says 'conicere' sometimes = 'agere.'

Oppidum, Brundisium.

3. Militum, of the garrison, which might be offended at the sight of a Pompeian surrounded by the ensigns of office.

The words from recipio to considerarent are evidently corrupt. The sense seems to be, that Cicero would resume the attendance of his lictors at a proper time, and wished to know what Oppius and some one else thought of the propriety of his drawing nearer to Rome. Billerb., Boot, Wesenb. suggests in a note 'Recipio tempore me ad Romam. Te nunc ad Balbum et ad Oppium, quoniam iis placet me propius accedere . . . considerent;' or, '[Recipio me domo.] Te nunc ad Oppium et * * * quoniam iis placeret me . . . considerarent' ut exciderit aliquid unde penderet 'quoniam . . . consid.'

6. De augenda . . dignitate. Probably by granting him a triumph. Cp. Hofm. on 'praeterita' below.

9. Si remansissem, 'if I had remained in Italy,' instead of joining Pompey in Epirus.

Ingero praeterita, 'I force past events on you,' 'trouble you with matters for which the time is past.' The verb is very rare in Cicero. Forcell. gives as equivalents, 'immittere, inicere praesertim hostilem impetum et crebram . . alicuius rei commemorationem.'

10. Vide . . ea quae restant, 'consider what I can still effect.' Boot, Hofm.

11. Cum istis. Apparently with the persons referred to in the obscure passage at the opening of this section.

13. Trebonius: cp. Ep. 84, 7, note.

Pansa: cp. Ep. 34, 7, note; also Intr. to Part V, and several letters in that part.

14. Fecerim. On the tense, cp. Ep. 71, 3, note.

15. Tulliae . . morbus: cp. Ad Fam. 14. 9. She was now ill at Rome, but seems to have recovered before the spring of the next year.

Exanimat, 'terrifies.' Cp. Ad Att. 10. 9, 1 'adventus Philotimi . . . exanimavit omnes qui mecum erant.' Also Ep. 69, 1, and Hor. Carm. 2. 17, 1.

mum. De Pompeii exitu mihi dubium numquam fuit; tanta 5
enim desperatio rerum eius omnium regum et populorum animos
occuparat, ut, quocumque venisset, hoc putarem futurum. Non
possum eius casum non dolere; hominem enim integrum et
castum et gravem cognovi. De Fannio consoler te? perniciosa 6
loquebatur de mansione tua; L. vero Lentulus Hortensii domum
sibi et Caesaris hortos et Baias desponderat. Omnino haec
eodem modo ex hac parte fiunt, nisi quod illud erat infinitum;
omnes enim, qui in Italia manserant, hostium numero habebantur. Sed velim haec aliquando solutiore animo. Quintum 7
fratrem audio profectum in Asiam, ut deprecaretur; de filio
nihil audivi. Sed quaere ex Diochare, Caesaris liberto, quem
ego non vidi, qui istas Alexandreas litteras attulit. Is dicitur
vidisse [an] euntem, an iam in Asia. Tuas litteras, prout res

1. **De Pompeii exitu.** Pompey was murdered off Alexandria, Sept. 28, 48 B.C., the day before his 58th birthday. Cp. Vell. 2. 53, 4.

3. **Hoc,** 'what has happened.' Cicero often uses the pronoun in this sense.

Non possum, foll. Cicero's regret is rather coldly expressed; partly, perhaps, owing to his view of Pompey's conduct before and during the civil war, partly to complaints of longer standing. Cp. Ep. 54. 3 and 7.

5. **De Fannio.** This Fannius is perhaps identical with one mentioned Ad Att. 7. 15, 2, and 8. 15, 3, as commissioned to occupy Sicily for the Pompeians. He seems to have died in or soon after the battle of Pharsalus.

Perniciosa . . . tua, 'he held very threatening language about your stay in Italy.'

6. **L. Lentulus.** The consul of 49 B.C. He was put to death at Alexandria by the Egyptian government shortly after the murder of Pompey. Cp. Caes. Bell. Civ. 3. 104.

Hortensii. The younger Hortensius is referred to, about whom cp. Ep. 74. 5.

7. **Hortos,** some gardens near Rome, probably.

Baias, 'an estate at Baiae.' Such properties were sometimes called simply by the name of the place near which they were situated. Cp. Philipp. 2. 19, 48, Misenum; also Ep. 71. 10.

Desponderat, 'had bargained for,' 'had made his own by anticipation,' as his share of the spoil.

Haec, 'such confiscations.' Cp. Philipp. 2. 25 and 26, on the exactions of the Caesarians.

8. **Ex hac parte,** 'on the victorious side.'

Illud, 'what the Pompeians threatened.'

Erat. On the mood and tense, cp. Ep. 9. 7, note.

9. **Habebantur,** 'were esteemed,' and would have been treated. On the facts, cp. Ep. 61, 4. alib.

10. **Solutiore animo,** sc. 'disseramus.'

11. **In Asiam:** cp. § 4 of the preceding letter. Quintus, apparently, did not know how Caesar had hastened to Alexandria.

Ut deprecaretur, sc. 'iram Caesaris.' We should expect 'deprecetur.' But the ambiguity of the Latin past tense profectum, which might mean either 'went,' or 'has gone,' leads to this irregularity, even where, as here, it means 'has gone.' Cp. Zumpt, L. G. 514, note 1.

Filio. The younger Quintus. Cp. Ad Att. 11. 7, 7 'Quintum filium vidi qui Sami viderat, patrem Sicyone—quorum deprecatio est facilis.'

12. **Ex Diochare.** 'Diocharinae epistolae' are mentioned Ad Att. 15. 45. 1.

13. **Istas Alexandreas litteras,** 'that letter from Alexandria.' On this use of the adjective, cp. Ad Att. 8. 13, 1 'nuntiis Brundisinis.' Cicero elsewhere uses the form 'Alexandrinus,' and hence Boot and Baiter substitute 'Alexandrinas' for the reading in the text, which is, apparently, that of the best MS. Caesar seems to have sent a letter from Alexandria by the hand of Diochares, which Atticus had seen or mentioned to Cicero, 'istas.'

14. **Vidisse,** sc. 'Q. filium.'

Euntem, 'on his way to Asia.'

postulat, exspecto; quas velim cures quam primum ad me perferendas. IIII. K. Decembr.

81. To ATTICUS (AD ATT. XI. 9).

BRUNDISIUM, JAN. 3, 47 B.C. (707 A.U.C.)

1. You are quite right in saying that I have been hasty, and the leave granted me to remain in Italy prevents my retiring elsewhere. I can only blame myself for my devotion to a hopeless cause. 2. I did as my nearest friends wished: how has my brother repaid me! I learned that he had been writing letters full of abuse of me, and opened some which quite bore out what I had heard. I send them to you: forward them or not as you choose. Pomponia has his seal. 3. I hope you will attend to Tullia's wants; she has no other protector. I write on my birthday, an unhappy anniversary!

CICERO ATTICO SAL.

1 Ego vero et incaute, ut scribis, et celerius, quam oportuit, feci nec in ulla sum spe, quippe qui exceptionibus edictorum retinear; quae si non essent sedulitate effectae et benevolentia tua, liceret mihi abire in solitudines aliquas: nunc ne id quidem licet. Quid autem me iuvat, quod ante initum tribunatum veni, si ipsum, quod veni, nihil iuvat? iam quid sperem ab

An, 'or perhaps.' Nearly = 'aut.' Boot, Hofm.

Tuas litteras, 'a letter from you.' On this use of a possessive pronoun, see Ep. 72, 1, note.

3. Ego vero, 'yes, I.' 'Vero,' though at the beginning of a letter, has its usual force of a corroborative reply, as 'ut scribis' shews. Cp. Ep. 99, 1.

4. Feci, 'acted,' in returning to Italy.

Exceptionibus edictorum, 'the exceptions made in my favour in various edicts,' i.e. the permission to remain in Italy granted by them. Cp. Ad Att. 11. 7, 2 'ille (Antonius) edixit ita ut me exciperet et Laelium nominatim.' This annoyed Cicero; he would have preferred to have had the permission granted in general terms, and not to have been mentioned by name.

5. Retinear, 'am detained here.' To leave Italy again would have seemed to slight Caesar's clemency. Cp. 'ne id quidem licet,' below, and Ad Att. 11. 7, 2.

7. Ante initum tribunatum, 'before the present tribunes came into office,' which they did on Dec. 10. Atticus may have congratulated Cicero on having returned to Italy before that date, because the new tribunes had carried, apparently, a law against absentees. Cp. lege, below. Cicero affects to believe that this law might be enforced against him retrospectively. In substance, from Wieland.

8. Ipsum, quod veni, 'my having returned at all,' without reference to the date. There is something tautologous in this, or rather, perhaps, a false antithesis. We should expect words meaning, 'If I am no better off than those who have remained abroad.'

Iam, 'moreover.' Cp. Ep. 5, 2.

Ab eo, 'from Antony,' most probably; some say 'from Dolabella.'

eo, qui mihi amicus numquam fuit, cum iam lege etiam sim confectus et oppressus? *quoti*die iam Balbi ad me litterae languidiores, multaeque multorum ad illum, fortasse contra me. Meo vitio pereo; nihil mihi mali casus attulit; omnia culpa contracta sunt. Ego enim, cum genus belli viderem, imparata et infirma omnia contra paratissimos, statueram, quid facerem, ceperamque consilium non tam forte quam mihi praeter ceteros concedendum. Cessi meis vel potius parui, ex quibus unus 2
qua mente fuerit, is, quem tu mihi commendas, cognosces ex ipsius litteris, quas ad te et ad alios misit, quas ego numquam aperuissem, nisi res acta sic esset: delatus est ad me fasciculus; solvi, si quid ad me esset litterarum: nihil erat; epistola Vatinio et Ligurio altera; iussi ad eos deferri; illi ad me statim ardentes dolore venerunt, scelus hominis clamantes; epistolas mihi legerunt plenas omnium in me probrorum. Hic Ligurius furere: se enim

1. Lege etiam, 'by a law, as well as by Antony's proclamation.' It may have been proposed by the new tribunes, of whom Dolabella was one. Manut. Without knowing its terms it is impossible to explain this passage. It may have forbidden any who had served in Pompey's army to return to Rome; in which case Cicero, by the words ipsum quod veni nihil iuvat, would mean that his position was as bad at Brundisium as it would have been if he had stayed in Greece. Or the law may merely have excluded such persons from Italy, in which case Cicero must be affecting to fear that it might be retrospective, in contradiction to what he implies in 'retinear' above. He writes in depression and vexation, and his words should not be too closely criticised. He had little reason to fear Dolabella, if it was true, as he had written to Antony, that Caesar had signified to Dolabella his wish that Cicero should return to Italy. Cp. Ad Att. 11. 7, 2.

2. Balbi: cp. Epp. 77. 81 44. 6, notes.

Languidiores, 'more lukewarm.'

3. Ad illum, 'to Caesar.' Boot. How Cicero learned that so many letters were written to Caesar, we cannot tell. Cp. Ad Att. 11. 7, 5; 11. 8, 1: Manut. suggests that the bearers would embark at Brundisium where Cicero was.

Meo vitio, 'by my own fault.' Cp. the next sentence.

5. Genus belli, 'the nature of the contest.' Cp. Pro Leg. Man. 2-7.

Imparata . . paratissimos, 'that our forces were weak and unready in all respects, and those of our enemy admirably prepared.'

6. Statueram, quid facerem: cp. Madv. 356, Obs. 2, 'I had settled what to do.'

7. Mihi . . concedendum. Because he had opposed violent measures, and was under no special obligations to Pompey.

8. Unus, his brother Quintus. See below.

9. Commendas. In one of his letters, apparently. Atticus might fear more for Quintus than for his brother. See below in this section.

11. Sic, 'as I am going to tell you.'

Fasciculus, 'a packet of letters.' Cp. Ep. 31, 7.

12. Solvi, si quid, 'I broke it open, (to see) whether.' For a similar ellipse, see Ep. 98, 4. The conj. of 'possum' with an infinitive is most common in this construction. Cp. Madv. 451 d.

Epistola, sc. 'missa erat,' 'there was a letter for Vatinius.'

13. Ligurio. 'A. Ligurius, Caesaris familiaris, mortuus est, bonus homo et nobis amicus' Ad Fam. 16. 18, 3: cp. Ad Q. F. 3. 7, 2.

14. Scelus hominis clamantes, 'exclaiming, "what shameful conduct."' On the accus., cp. Ep. 67, 3, note. 'Homo' is here used depreciatingly. Cp. De Offic. 3. 6, 31.

15. Hic, 'hereupon.' Common in Cicero in this sense.

Furere, hist. inf. Madv. 392.

scire summo illum in odio fuisse Caesari; hunc tamen non modo favisse, sed etiam tantam illi pecuniam dedisse honoris mei causa. Hoc ego dolore accepto volui scire, quid scripsisset ad ceteros; ipsi enim illi putavi perniciosum fore, si eius hoc tantum scelus percrebruisset. Cognovi eiusdem generis, ad te misi; quas si putabis illi ipsi utile esse reddi, reddes; nil me laedet. Nam, quod resignatae sunt, habet, opinor, eius signum Pomponia. Hac ille acerbitate initio navigationis cum usus esset, tanto me dolore adfecit, ut postea iacuerim, neque nunc tam pro se quam contra
8 me laborare dicitur. Ita omnibus rebus urgeor, quas sustinere vix possum vel plane nullo modo possum; quibus in miseriis una est pro omnibus, quod istam miseram patrimonio, fortuna omni spoliatam relinquam: qua re te, *ut* polliceris, videre plane velim; alium enim, cui illam commendem, habeo neminem, quoniam matri quoque eadem intellexi esse parata, quae mihi. Sed, si

1. Scire, orat. obliq. Madv. 403, and Obs. 2.
Illum, i.e. Quintus.
Hunc, i.e. Caesar.
2. Favisse, 'had shewn regard for him,' by appointing him his legate in Gaul. Cp. Intr. to Part II, § 21.
Tantam .. pecuniam dedisse: cp. Ep. 29, 18, note.
Honoris mei causa, 'as a compliment to me.'
3. Quid scripsisset, sc. Quintus.
4. Ipsi . . illi, Quinto.
5. Percrebruisset, 'should have become generally known.' On the plup., depending on putavi fore, cp. Ep. 56, 5, note.
Cognovi . . generis, sc. 'epistolas esse.'
6. Illi . . utile, 'to Quintus' own advantage.'
Reddi, 'should be delivered to those to whom they are addressed.'
Reddes: cp. p. 80, note on l. 2.
Nam: cp. Ep. 9, 3, note. 'Never mind their having been opened, for.'
7. Quod resignatae sunt, 'as to their having had their seals broken,' which would of course surprise the recipients. On 'quod,' cp. Ep. 8, 14, note.
Habet .. Pomponia. *Pomponia*, wife of Quintus, had apparently been entrusted with his seal, and seems to have been at Rome, so that Atticus might borrow the seal and reveal the letters. See the remarks of Merivale on this curious incident, in a note to his translation of Abeken, p. 321.

Hac . . acerbitate, 'the same bitterness of feeling.'
8. Initio navigationis, 'at the beginning of our voyage' from Corcyra. Ablat. of the date, cp. Ep. 8, 11, note. The two brothers apparently sailed in company for some time, perhaps to Patrae, and then parted, Quintus for Asia, Marcus for Italy. Cp. Ep. 79, 4.
9. Ut postea iacuerim, 'that I have been quite out of spirits ever since.' On the force of the tense, cp. Madv. 382, Obs. 1; and on this meaning of 'iacere,' Ad Fam. 9. 20, 3 'cura .. ut valeas ne ego te iacente bona tua comedim.'
11. Vel = 'vel potius.' Nägelsb. 84, 233.
Una est pro omnibus, 'grieves me as much as all the rest put together.' Cp. Ad Att. 2. 5, 1 'Cato . . qui mihi unus est pro centum millibus.'
12. Istam miseram, i.e. Tullia. On her troubles, cp. Epp. 71, 9; 78, 1; 80, 4.
Patrimonio. Cicero feared, or pretended to fear, that Caesar might confiscate his property and Terentia's, thus depriving Tullia of her 'patrimonium,' while Dolabella was embarrassed and unable to do much for her.
13. Relinquam, i.e. 'at my death.'
Videre = 'convenire' (Forcell.), 'to have an interview with you here.'
14. Illam, i.e. Tullia.
15. Matri. Severity to women had been little practised in the Roman revolutions, though an instance may be found in the

me non offendes, satis tamen habeto commendatam patruumque in ea, quantum poteris, mitigato. Haec ad te die natali meo scripsi, quo utinam susceptus non essem aut ne quid ex eadem matre postea natum esset! Plura scribere fletu prohibeor.

82. TO ATTICUS (AD ATT. XI. 12).

BRUNDISIUM, MARCH 8, 47 B.C. (707 A.U.C.)

1. I have always told Caesar that I left Italy because I found men's criticisms intolerable, 2. and wrote lately to assure him that Quintus had had no influence on my movements. 3. I shall hold similar language if I meet Caesar. I am very anxious about the state of affairs in Africa and Spain, and so I think are you, though you are unwilling to alarm me. 4. Write to Antony on my behalf, if you think it desirable. I am ashamed of Dolabella. Write to me even if you have nothing to say. I have accepted Galeo's bequest.

CICERO ATTICO SAL.

Cephalio mihi a te litteras reddidit a. d. VIII. Idus Mart. ves- 1
pere. Eo autem die mane tabellarios miseram, quibus ad te dederam litteras: tuis tamen lectis litteris putavi aliquid rescribendum esse, maxime, quod ostendis te pendere animi, quamnam rationem sim Caesari allaturus profectionis meae tum, cum ex

treatment of Licinia, wife of C. Gracchus. Cp. Plut. C. Gracchus, 17. Cicero's fears were hardly justified, even leaving Caesar's clemency out of consideration.

Si me non offendes. Graevius (ap. Boot) supposes that Cicero hints at suicide; but Boot, that he merely alludes to an intention of leaving Brundisium.

1. Habeto . . mitigato. According to Madv. 109 and 384, these are futures.

Patruumque, i.e. the elder Quintus.

2. In ea, 'towards her.' Cp. Madv. 230, *In*, b, Obs. 1.

Mitigato, 'appease.' Forcell.

Die natali meo, the third of January. It was his fifty-ninth birthday. Cp. Intr. to Part I, § 1.

3. Scripsi, 'I have written.'

Utinam . . non. 'Ne' is much more common, but perhaps 'non' is considered as forming one verb with 'susceptus essem.' Cp. Madv. 351 b, Obs. 1.

Susceptus, 'taken from the ground' by his father, in token of recognition. 'Sublatus' is also used in this sense.

Aut ne quid . . natum esset, 'or that no other offspring had been born afterwards of the same mother.' An outburst of vexation against his brother.

5. Cephalio, a letter carrier in the service of Atticus. Cp. Ep. 68, 2.

Mihi . . litteras reddidit . . dederam litteras. 'Dare' is used of letters either with the nom. of the writer and dat. of the bearer, or with the nom. of the bearer and dat. of the receiver. The letter of his own to which Cicero refers is Ad Att. 11. 11.

8. Te pendere animi, 'that you are very anxious.' On this genitive, cp. Madv. 296 b, Obs. 3.

9. Rationem . . allaturus. 'Adferre rationem' is a common phrase. Cp. De Fin. 5. 10, 27.

Profectionis meae . . discesserim, 'of my departure, I mean when I left Italy.' The adverb 'tum' is apparently joined with a substantive, but the expression is a concise one for 'quae tum facta est.' Cp. Madv. 301 c, Obs. 2.

Italia discesserim. Nihil opus est mihi nova ratione; saepe enim ad eum scripsi multisque mandavi me non potuisse, cum cupissem, sermones hominum sustinere, multaque in eam sententiam. Nihil enim erat, quod minus eum vellem existimare, quam me tanta de re non meo consilio usum esse. Posteaque, cum mihi litterae a Balbo Cornelio minore missae essent illum existimare Quintum fratrem lituum meae profectionis fuisse—ita enim scripsit—, qui nondum cognossem, quae de me Quintus scripsisset ad multos, etsi multa praesens in praesentem acerbe dixerat et fecerat, tamen nihilo minus his verbis ad Caesarem scripsi:

2 'De Quinto fratre meo non minus laboro quam de me ipso, sed eum tibi commendare hoc meo tempore non audeo; illud dumtaxat tamen audebo petere abs te, quod te oro, ne quid existimes ab illo factum esse, quo minus mea in te officia constarent minusve te diligerem, potiusque semper illum auctorem nostrae coniunctionis fuisse meique itineris comitem, non ducem: qua re ceteris in rebus tantum ei tribues, quantum humanitas tua amicitiaque

1. **Nova ratione**, 'of any new plan' or 'mode of defence.'

2. **Scripsi multisque mandavi**, 'I wrote and charged many friends to write.'

Cum cupissem, 'though I had been anxious to do so.'

3. **Sermones hominum**, 'what people said of my conduct.' See Ep. 59, 1.

Multaque in eam sententiam, 'and much more to the same effect.'

4. **Nihil enim .. usum esse**, 'the last thing I could wish Caesar to think would be that I did not act independently.' Cicero has just said that he assured Caesar that he was influenced by the opinion of his party, but apparently he feared that his brother might be charged with having induced him to leave Italy.

6. **Balbo**, cp. Ep. 58, 4, note.

Illum, sc. Caesarem. For the omission of words meaning 'to the effect that' after **missae essent**, see Ep. 74, 4, note.

7. **Lituum .. fuisse**, 'had given the signal for my departure.' The words are probably a quotation from Balbus or from Caesar. Cp. Ad Fam. 6. 12, 3, where T. Ampius Balbus is said to have been called 'tuba civilis belli.'

8. **Qui nondum cognossem .. scripsi**, 'I wrote as follows to Caesar, not knowing how Quintus had written of me.' From etsi to nihilo minus inclusive seems to be parenthetical, and tamen pleonastic. The general drift seems to be, that Cicero was not induced to desert his brother's interest by the latter's violent language, but might have been more affected by a knowledge of his letter.

13. **Hoc meo tempore**, 'in my present unhappy position.' Cp. Epp. 1, 4; 29, 8, note.

14. **Quod te oro**. 'Quod' is here a relative, illud being its antecedent. The sentence is rather pleonastic. Cp. id te .. rogo below. On the accus. 'quod,' cp. Madv. 228 b, Obs. 1.

15. **Quo minus .. constarent**, 'to prevent my services to you continuing without interruption.' Forcell. gives 'permanere' as a synonym for 'constare.' On the construction, cp. Madv. 375, b.

16. **Potiusque**, 'but rather.' Cp. Madv. 433, Obs. 2.

Nostrae coniunctionis, 'of an union between you and me.'

17. **Meique .. non ducem**, 'and that when I left Italy he was my companion and not my leader.'

Ceteris in rebus, 'in all other respects' (Wiel.), i.e. without considering his supposed influence upon me.

18. **Tribues**: cp. Ep. 11, 3, note.

vestra postulat; ego ei ne quid apud te obsim, id te vehementer etiam atque etiam rogo.'

Qua re, si quis congressus fuerit mihi cum Caesare, etsi non 3
dubito, quin is lenis in illum futurus sit idque iam declaraverit,
ego tamen is ero, qui semper fui. Sed, ut video, multo magis est
nobis laborandum de Africa, quam quidem tu scribis confirmari
quotidie magis ad condicionis spem quam victoriae. Quod utinam
ita esset! sed longe aliter esse intellego, teque ipsum ita existimare arbitror, aliter autem scribere, non fallendi, sed confirmandi
mei causa, praesertim cum adiungatur ad Africam etiam Hispania.
Quod me admones, ut scribam ad Antonium et ad ceteros, si quid 4
videbitur tibi opus esse, velim facias id, quod saepe fecisti; nihil
enim mihi venit in mentem, quod scribendum putem. Quod me
audis erectiorem esse animo, quid putas, cum videas accessisse ad
superiores aegritudines praeclaras generi actiones? Tu tamen
velim ne intermittas, quod eius facere poteris, scribere ad me,
etiam si rem, de qua scribas, non habebis; semper enim adferunt
aliquid mihi tuae litterae. Galeonis hereditatem crevi; puto enim

1. Ego ei . . obsim, 'that he may not suffer for my behaviour.'

2. Etiam atque etiam, 'repeatedly,' hence 'pressingly,' 'earnestly.' Forcell.

3. Congressus, 'interview.'

Etsi non dubito . . fui, 'though I do not doubt that Caesar is kindly disposed to my brother I shall continue to intercede for him, and not try to lay the blame of my mistake on him.'

5. Sed ut video . . de Africa, 'I see that we ought to be far more anxious about Africa' than about Caesar's reception of us. The republicans were collecting large forces in Africa, and if they prevailed against Caesar, Cicero's hasty return to Italy would disgrace him in the eyes of the victors, and perhaps expose him to danger. Cp. Intr. to Part IV, § 4, on the facts.

6. Quam confirmari, foll., 'which you say is gaining strength, but after such a fashion as to give more hopes of a treaty (Nagelsb. 64, 173) than of a victory.' Cp. Ep. 100, 2 'si armis aut condicione positis,' foll.

8. Longe aliter esse, sc. 'id.' On the adverb as pred., cp. Ep. 4, 1. Cicero feared the triumph of such men as Labienus and the sons of Pompey, and thought that Atticus was cherishing vain hopes of a settlement by negotiation. Cp. Intr. to Part IV, § 6.

9. Confirmandi, 'of encouraging.' 'Confirmare' = 'solari.' Forcell. On the sense, cp. Ep. 80, 2.

10. Praesertim cum refers to the main drift of the sentence 'te ita existimare,' foll.

Hispania. Disaffection had been caused in Spain by the misconduct of Caesar's lieutenant, Q. Cassius Longinus. Cp. Intr. to Parts III, § 13; IV, § 4.

12. Id quod saepe fecisti, i.e. written letters in my name. Cp. Ep. 79, 3.

14. Quid putas, 'what do you think of the probability of such a rumour?'

15. Praeclaras generi actiones. Cicero refers to Dolabella's attacks upon the public credit. Cp. Intr. to Part IV, § 5; Dion Cassius 42, 29–32.

16. Quod eius, foll. On the construction, cp. Madv. 284.

18. Galeonis. Galeo seems to be only mentioned here.

Crevi, 'have decided to accept.' After a will had been read a certain time was allowed in most cases for the heir named in it to decide if he would accept the inheritance. If it was much encumbered he might be unwilling to do so. Smith, Dict. of Antiq. sub voc. 'Heres,' p. 599.

cretionem simplicem fuisse, quoniam ad me nulla missa est. VIII. Idus Martias.

83. To C. CASSIUS (AD FAM. XV. 15).

BRUNDISIUM, 47 B.C. (707 A.U.C.)

1. We both agreed that the issue of a single pitched battle should decide our conduct. 2 but our calculations have been baffled by the delay in Caesar's movements, which has resulted from the hostility of the Alexandrians and of Pharnaces, and from the obstinacy of his Roman enemies. 3. Our decision was the same; our position has been different; you have been with Caesar, I have been a witness of the misery of Italy and of its capital. 4. Write me word of all that you see and anticipate. Would that I had obeyed your advice two years ago!

M. CICERO S. D. C. CASSIO.

1 Etsi uterque nostrum spe pacis et odio civilis sanguinis abesse a belli pertinacia voluit, tamen, quoniam eius consilii princeps ego fuisse videor, plus fortasse tibi praestare ipse debeo quam a te exspectare: etsi, ut saepe soleo mecum recordari, sermo familiaris meus tecum et item mecum tuus adduxit utrumque nostrum ad id consilium, ut uno proelio putaremus, si non totam causam, at certe nostrum iudicium definiri convenire. Neque quisquam hanc nostram sententiam vere umquam reprehendit praeter eos, qui arbitrantur melius esse deleri omnino rem publicam quam

1. Cretionem simplicem, 'an acceptance and nothing more.' Cicero means that he got nothing by the bequest. Boot, Stöpfle, Röm. Privatrecht, 829, note.

Nulla, sc. 'hereditas.' Forcell. and Wiel., however, with whom Mr. Parry and Mr. Jeans agree, follow Manutius in thinking that the words mean 'I think I am sole heir, for I have received no notice from other claimants.' In that case 'cretio' meaning 'a formal declaration to accept' (on the part of another 'heres') must be supplied with 'missa est.'

3. Uterque nostrum. On the different use of 'nostrum' and 'nostri,' cp. Madv. 297 c, Obs.

Abesse . . pertinacia, 'to keep away from a war to be waged with obstinacy,' 'from an obstinate perseverance in war.' After Pharsalus both sides would fight obstinately, and there would be little mercy shewn. Hofm. On the movements of Cassius and Cicero after the battle, cp. Intr. to Part IV, § 3. Cicero had been the first of the two to decide on neutrality.

5. Plus . . praestare, 'to furnish more' in the way of advice—which, however, in § 4, Cicero asks of Cassius.

6. Etsi, 'however.' Cp. Epp. 36, 3; 723, 9, notes.

Sermo . . mecum tuus, 'my remarks to you and yours to me in friendly intercourse.'

8. Ad id consilium ut . . putaremus, 'to this conclusion, that we thought.' For similar pleonasms, cp. Madv. 481 b.

Si non totam . . iudicium, 'if not the whole quarrel, at least our own judgment' what to do.

10. Vere, 'really.'

Eos qui . . manere. The violent Pompeians.

imminutam et debilitatam manere: ego autem ex interitu eius nullam spem scilicet mihi proponebam, ex reliquiis magnam.
Sed ea sunt consecuta, ut magis mirum sit accidere illa potuisse, 2
quam nos non vidisse ea futura nec, homines cum essemus, divinare potuisse. Equidem fateor meam coniecturam hanc fuisse, ut illo quasi quodam fatali proelio facto et victores communi saluti consuli vellent et victi suae, utrumque autem positum esse arbitrarer in celeritate victoris: quae si fuisset, eandem clementiam experta esset Africa, quam cognovit Asia, quam etiam Achaia te, ut opinor, ipso legato ac deprecatore; amissis autem temporibus, quae plurimum valent, praesertim in bellis civilibus, interpositus annus alios induxit, ut victoriam sperarent, alios, ut ipsum vinci contemnerent. Atque horum malorum omnium culpam fortuna sustinet: quis enim aut Alexandrini belli tantam moram huic bello adiunctum iri aut nescio quem istum Pharnacem Asiae terrorem illaturum putaret? Nos tamen in consilio pari 3

2. Scilicet, 'naturally,' 'of course.' Cp. Ep. 11, 4.

3. Sed ea . . potuisse, 'our conduct then was reasonable; but subsequent events have prevented our enjoying the full benefit of our prudence; and no one could have foreseen the turn things have taken.' Cicero refers to the prolongation of the war in Egypt and Pontus. Cp. Intr. to Part IV, § 3.

4. Homines cum essemus, 'as we were but men.' 'Homo' here implies 'imbecillitatem et peccandi facilitatem,' as in passages quoted by Forcell.

5. Meam coniecturam . . ut . . vellent. On this use of 'ut' in explaining substantives, cp. Ep. 13, 3, note. 'My conjecture was that the conquerors were willing.' A condensed expression for 'ut putarem velle.' Hofm. The usual construction follows in 'ut arbitrarer,' on which cp. note on § 1.

6. Et victores . . suae, 'that the conquerors would shew their care for the general interest by offering easy terms, and the conquered for their own by laying down their arms.'

7. Utrumque . . positum . . victoris, 'but thought that the fulfilment of both these hopes depended on Caesar's following up his advantages with speed.'

8. Quae si fuisset, sc. 'celeritas,' 'and if he had done so.'

9. Africa . . Asia . . Achaia. These words refer to the Pompeian refugees in the three countries mentioned, some of whom had been forgiven by Caesar. Cp. Ad Att. 11. 14, 1 'Achaici deprecatores . . quibus non erat ignotum, *etiam quibus erat*;' Ib. 11. 20, 2 'omnino dicitur (Caesar) nemini negare.'

Etiam, i.e. because Achaia had been the scene of actual war. Hofm.

10. Te . . legato, foll., 'with you for their representative and spokesman,' abl. abs.

11. Temporibus = *τῶν καιρῶν*, 'the proper times for action.' Cp. Pro Muren. 21, 43 'amisso iam tempore.'

12. Interpositus annus, 'the year which has intervened' since the battle of Pharsalus, which was fought Aug. 9, 48 B.C. Cp. Intr. to Part III, § 21.

Induxit, 'beguiled,' a common sense of the word.

13. Ipsum vinci, 'defeat itself.' Cp. Ep. 47, 2; Nägelsb. 31, 104.

14. Fortuna: cp. the beginning of this section.

Alexandrini . . moram: cp. Intr. to Part IV, § 3. On the genit. 'belli,' cp. Ep. 27, 3, note.

15. Pharnacem: cp. Intr. to Part IV, § 3, and Caes. Bell. Alex. 35-41.

16. Putaret, almost = 'putavisset:' cp. Ep. 63, 2 'quaereretur,' and Zumpt, L. G. 528, note 2.

In consilio pari, 'though our plans were the same.' Cicero rather misrepresents what had happened, perhaps. For except from this passage we should not suppose that Cassius decided to lay down

casu dissimili usi sumus: tu enim eam partem petisti, ut et consiliis interesses et, quod maxime curam levat, futura animo prospicere posses; ego, qui festinavi, ut Caesarem in Italia viderem—sic enim arbitrabamur—eumque multis honestissimis viris conservatis redeuntem ad pacem currentem, ut aiunt, incitarem, ab illo longissime et absum et afui. Versor autem in gemitu Italiae et in urbis miserrimis querelis, quibus aliquid opis fortasse ego pro mea, tu pro tua, pro sua quisque parte ferre
4 potuisset, si auctor adfuisset. Qua re velim pro tua perpetua erga me benevolentia scribas ad me, quid videas, quid sentias, quid exspectandum, quid agendum nobis existimes. Magni erunt mihi tuae litterae; atque utinam primis illis, quas Luceria miseras, paruissem! sine ulla enim molestia dignitatem meam retinuissem.

his arms on hearing the news of Pharsalus. His submission at the Hellespont (cp. p. 394) may have been the result of a momentary impulse.

1. Casu dissimili, foll., 'have met with a different fate.'

Eam partem petisti, 'you joined a party [in which].' Cp. Ep. 129, 2 'cum vero non liceret mihi nullius partis esse.'

Ut et consiliis interesses, 'where you could take part in deliberations.'

Ut . . prospicere posses. Cassius perhaps attended Caesar during the war of Alexandria, and certainly acted as his legate at some time between 48 and 46 B.C. Cp. Ad Att. 11. 15. 2; Ep. 91. 10.

4. Sic enim arbitrabamur, sc. 'fore,' 'for we thought he would soon be there,' as not foreseeing the Alexandrine war, and that with Pharnaces.

Multis . . conservatis: cp. § 2. Cicero refers to Caesar's clemency after the battle of Pharsalus. Cp. Intr. to Part IV, § 3; Caes. Bell. Civ. 3. 98. M. Brutus and C. Cassius were among those whom he spared.

5. Currentem . . incitarem, 'spur him though already willing.' A proverbial expression. Cp. Ad Q. F. 1. 1, 45; Philipp. 3. 8, 19; De Orat. 2. 44, 186. Cicero tries to make out that his conduct had been more patriotic than that of Cassius.

6. Versor autem, 'while I am surrounded by.'

7. Gemitu . . querelis. These complaints were probably caused, partly by the licentious conduct of Antony, partly by the quarrels of Trebellius and Dolabella. Cp. Intr. to Part IV, § 5.

9. Si auctor adfuisset, 'had one been present to give us the protection of his name,' i.e. Caesar. Hofm.

10. Quid videas, quid sentias, 'what your views and feelings are on our prospects.'

11. Nobis, dat. of the agent. Cp. Madv. 250 b.

12. Luceria. Pompey's head-quarters were at Luceria for some time before he left Italy in 49 B.C. Cp. Epp. 49; 54, 4–5. Cassius seems to have been there with him, and to have warned Cicero in the letter here referred to, 'primis illis,' not to leave Italy.

13. Dignitatem . . retinuissem. He could probably have maintained an honourable neutrality, or if he had wished to appear in the senate might have held a good position there, and have obtained a triumph. Cp. Epp. 54, 6; 67, 1; 73, 8. On the meaning of 'dignitas,' cp. Ep. 47, 1, note.

84. TO ATTICUS (AD ATT. XII. 1).

NEAR ARPINUM, MAY (?) 25, 46 B.C. (708 A.U.C.)

1. I hope to be at the appointed place on the 28th. I would gladly see Tullia and Attica at once; remember me to the latter, and to Pilia. 2. I have just received your letter, and am sorry to hear of Attica's feverish attack. I shall, however, visit you on the day on which you expect me.

CICERO ATTICO SAL.

Undecimo die postquam a te discesseram, hoc litterularum 1
exaravi egrediens e villa ante lucem, atque eo die cogitabam in Anagnino, postero autem in Tusculano; ibi unum diem. V. Kalend. igitur ad constitutum; atque utinam continuo ad complexum meae Tulliae, ad osculum Atticae possim currere! quod quidem ipsum scribe, quaeso, ad me, ut, dum consisto in Tusculano, sciam, quid garriat, sin rusticatur, quid scribat ad te, eique interea aut scribes salutem aut nuntiabis, itemque Piliae. Et

MAY. I had followed Baiter (with whom Schütz and Billerb. agree) in giving this date. But as no month is mentioned in the letter, and as Ep. 85 seems not to have been written later than April (see the introductory note on it), I now think that the present letter may belong to an earlier month, perhaps March.

1. Undecimo die postquam. For this and similar modes of expressing dates, cp. Madv. 276, Obs. 6.

Hoc litterularum. The subst. seems to be only here used in this sense by Cicero. On the gen., cp. Ep. 75, 1, note.

2. Exaravi, epistolary; cp. Ep. 1. 1, note. The word occurs again Ad Att. 13. 38, 1. It means, 'scratched on the waxed tablets.' Mr. Tyrrell, however, Intr. p. lv, thinks that the word might be applied to a letter written with pen and ink.

Egrediens, 'on leaving,' 'just before leaving.'

E villa, probably at Arpinum, which would suit the following dates.

In Anagnino, sc. 'manere.' Such ellipses are common in letters. Cp. Ep. 106, 4. One of Cicero's numerous villas apparently was at Anagnia, the old chief town of the Hernici.

3. V. Kalend. Boot remarks 'cuius mensis Kalendae fuerint non liquet.'

4. Ad constitutum, sc. 'eram venturus.' 'Constitutum' often stands alone, and its sense must be determined by the context. Sometimes (cp. Ad Att. 11. 16, 2) 'constitutum' is a substantive, when 'ad const.' would mean 'by appointment.' According to Boot on the passage last quoted, it means 'anything settled,' whether time, place, or business. Here he says 'ad constitutum' = 'in locum ubi tecum constitui'—which makes very good sense. Forcell. explains it 'ad constitutam diem.'

Atque utinam . . currere. Perhaps the place where Cicero and Atticus were to meet was unhealthy or otherwise inconvenient for the family of Atticus.

5. Quod quidem ipsum, 'as to this very thing.' Grammatically these words refer to 'osculum Atticae,' but in substance to Attica herself. She was now 4 or 5 years old. Cp. Ad Att. 6. 5, 4, and Appendix 3. § 7.

7. Quid garriat, 'what she prattles about.'

Sin rusticatur, 'or if she is in the country,' Atticus apparently being at Rome. 'Rusticari,' = 'ruri degere.' Forcell.

Quid scribat. Attica must have been carefully educated, or she might dictate her letters, as her elders did generally.

8. Interea, 'on the strength of this letter, before I hear from you again.'

Scribes, 'write' if she is away; nuntiabis, 'tell her' if she is with you. On the 2nd pers. fut. ind. in this sense, cp. Ep. 11, 3, note.

Piliae: cp. Ep. 31, 7, alib.

tamen, etsi continuo congressuri sumus, scribes ad me, si quid habebis.

2 Cum complicarem hanc epistolam, noctuabundus ad me venit cum epistola tua tabellarius, qua lecta de Atticae febricula scilicet valde dolui. Reliqua, quae exspectabam, ex tuis litteris cognovi omnia; sed quod scribis 'igniculum matutinum γεροντικόν,' γεροντικώτερον est memoriola vacillare: ego enim IIII. Kal. Axio dederam, tibi III., Quinto, quo die venissem, id est prid. Kal. Hoc igitur habebis, novi nihil. Quid ergo opus erat epistola? Quid? cum coram sumus et garrimus quicquid in buccam? Est profecto quiddam λέσχη, quae habet, etiam si nihil subest, collocutione ipsa suavitatem.

1. Tamen, etsi, 'yet even, although,' often written 'tametsi,' but defended by Boot in this place.

3. This section is a postscript.

Complicarem, 'was fastening up' for despatch. Cp. note C on Part I.

Noctuabundus. This word only occurs here, and presents a difficulty: for such words are generally derived from verbs, and we know of no verb 'noctuare.' Boot accordingly suspects the word. But perhaps Cicero was deceived by a false analogy. Cp. Ep. 38, 3. He did not often form such words from verbs of the first conjugation, though we find 'volutabundus' in a fragment of de Rep. II, 41, 68. The meaning of such words is equivalent to that of a present active. Cp. Madv. 115 g. here 'travelling all night.' 'Noctu vagans.' Forcell.; qui de multa nocte ambulasset, Manut.

4. De Atticae febricula, 'about Attica's slight attack of fever.' The word is rare. Atticus seems to have mentioned the illness in the letter just referred to. It was tedious. Cp. Ad Att. 12. 6, 4.

Scilicet: cp. Ep. 12, 4. note.

5. Reliqua . . omnia, 'all the other news I was waiting for.' What Cicero refers to we cannot tell.

6. Igniculum . . γεροντικόν, 'that to want a little fire in the morning is a sign of old age.' Cicero had probably asked Atticus to have a little fire made for him in the morning when he should stay with him. 'This,' Atticus said, 'is a sign of old age.' Cicero rose early (cp. § 1), and the Calendar was really about two months in advance of the true season. Cp. Appendix 8. The word γεροντικόν occurs Plat. Legg. 761 C.

γεροντικώτερον . . vacillare, 'it is a surer sign of old age that one's poor memory should falter.'

7. Memoriola only occurs here; it is used to express pity and depreciation. Cicero refers to Atticus having forgotten his engagement. See the next words.

Vacillare = 'dubitare,' 'labare.' Forcell.

Ego enim . . prid. Kal. 'as yours does, for I had originally intended to spend the 29th with Axius, the 30th with you, and the 31st with Quintus.' But when I found you had mistaken the day, and were expecting me on the 28th, I wrote above (cp. p. 420, l. 3) to say I would be with you on the 28th. Cicero was probably to visit Atticus in a suburban villa, as he was to be with Quintus on the day he reached Rome—quo die venissem. These dates are calculated on the supposition that the month was March or May.

Axio: cp. Ep. 28, 5.

Dederam, 'had assigned to.' The object is IV. Kal.

8. Hoc . . habebis . . nihil, 'take this retort and expect no news.' Hoc refers to Cicero's sally about his friend's bad memory. 'Habebis' is used in the gladiatorial sense. Boot. Cp. Ad Att. 1. 10, 1 'cape hoc tibi pro illo tuo.'

9. Quid ergo . . epistola? 'If there is no news, why write?' Atticus is supposed to say.

Quid cum. foll., sc. 'opus est.' Cicero replies, 'And pray what is the use of our chattering when we are together and say whatever comes uppermost?'

10. Quicquid in buccam, sc. 'venerit.' Cp. Ep. 46; Ad Att. 1. 12, 4.

Est profecto quiddam λέσχη, 'talk has doubtless a certain value.' Cp. Ad Att. 13. 44, 2 'est quiddam . . animum levari.' The Greek word is quite classical.

11. Etiam si nihil subest, 'even if there is nothing in it.'

85. TO ATTICUS (AD ATT. XII. 2).

ROME, APRIL (?), 46 B.C. (708 A.U.C.)

1. We hear various rumours about the war in Africa, but on no good authority. 2. Hirtius and other friends of Caesar are enjoying themselves at Praeneste, and Balbus goes on with his building. I hope you will visit me directly after your arrival.

CICERO ATTICO SAL.

Hic rumor est Statium Murcum perisse naufragio, Asinium 1
delatum vivum in manus militum, L. naves delatas Uticam reflatu
hoc, Pompeium non comparere nec in Baliaribus omnino fuisse,
ut Paciaecus adfirmat; sed auctor nullus rei quisquam. Habes
quae, dum tu abes, locuti sunt. Ludi interea Praeneste: ibi 2
Hirtius et isti omnes; et quidem ludi dies VIII. Quae cenae!

Collocatione ipsa, 'by the very act of our talking together,' abl. caus.

Arrn. The war in Africa was decided by a battle at Thapsus on April 6, of which Cicero does not seem to have heard. Hence this letter can hardly have been written later than April. Intr. to Part IV, § 10.

1. Statium Murcum. L. Statius Murcus was one of Caesar's officers, and is mentioned Caes. Bell. Civ. 3. 15. The report here referred to was false, for Murcus afterwards commanded a force in Asia. Cp. Ad Fam. 12. 11, 1; Philipp. 11. 12, 30.

Asinium. C. Asinius Pollio, one of Caesar's officers, was celebrated both as a poet and as a historian. Cp. Hor. Carm. 2. 1. He did good service in Sicily and Africa; governed Baetica for Caesar, and maintained a doubtful attitude there after Caesar's death. Cp. Intr. to Part V, §§ 15; 18 and 19; Ad Fam. 10. 31-33; 11. 9; App. Bell. Civ. 3. 40 and 46. He is called 'praetorius' by Velleius (2. 73), writing of 44 B.C.

2. Militum, 'of the forces holding Africa against Caesar.'

L. naves . . hoc, 'that 50 ships have been carried (in)to Utica by this contrary wind,' i.e. that which caused the shipwreck. Reflatus is a rare word. Utica was held by Caesar's enemies. Cp. Bell. Afric. 22; 87. Boot suspects that the real reading is 'L. navem.' 'L.' being an abbreviation of the genitive of a praenomen. The best MS. appears to have 'L. navis delata in.' As the report seems to have been false, there is no necessity for giving it a probable form.

3. Pompeium, i.e. Cn. Pompeius, the eldest son of the great Pompey. On his proceedings, cp. Intr. to Parts III, § 10; IV, §§ 4 and 12; Auct. Bell. Hisp. 1.

4. Paciaecus. L. Iunius Paciaecus, a Spaniard of Baetica, but apparently a Roman citizen, opposed the sons of Pompey in Spain. Cp. Bell. Hisp. 3: also Ad Fam. 6. 18, 2.

Auctor, 'warrantor,' 'one to attest.' Forcell.

5. Ludi. Perhaps these games were in honour of Fortune, to whom there was a famous temple at Praeneste. The ablative of names of towns in 'e' ends in 'e.' Cp. Madv. 42. 3 b.

Praeneste is neuter generally, but sometimes feminine by synesis, 'urbs' being understood. Cp. Madv. 41. 1; Verg. Aen. 7. 682; 8. 561; and on the local ablative, Madv. 273 a.

6. Isti omnes, 'all Caesar's friends,' i.e. who were in Italy.

Et quidem ludi, 'and games too.' Cp. Philipp. 2. 31, 81 'id decrevit senatus et quidem incolumis.'

Dies octo, accus. of duration of time. Cp. Ep. 52, 3, note.

Quae cenae! quae deliciae! 'Deliciae,' 'luxury.' On the tastes of Hirtius and others of Caesar's friends, cp. Ep. 87, 3.

quae deliciae! Res interea fortasse transacta est. O miros homines! At Balbus aedificat; τί γὰρ αὐτῷ μέλει; verum si quaeris, homini non recta, sed voluptaria quaerenti nonne βεβίωται; tu interea dormis. Iam explicandum est πρόβλημα, si quid acturus es. Si quaeris quid putem, ego † fructum puto. Sed quid multa? iam te videbo, et quidem, ut spero, de via recte ad me; simul enim et diem Tyrannioni constituemus et si quid aliud.

86. To M. VARRO (AD FAM. IX. 5).

ROME, JUNE, 46 B.C. (708 A.U.C.)

1. I think the 7th will be quite early enough. 2. I do not regret my past conduct, and have no patience with those who remain neutral themselves and censure me for want of vigour. 3. I shall see you near Tusculum before the 7th if possible; if not, I shall follow you to Cumae.

1. Res . . transacta est, 'meanwhile, it may be, the issue of the war has been decided.'

O miros homines! 'strange people!' Cicero was shocked by their apparent indifference at such a crisis. But probably they had better information as to Caesar's prospects, or at any rate felt more confidence than the Roman public.

2. Aedificat, 'is building,' probably a splendid villa. Cp. Ep. 44, 6, where 'Balbi horti et Tusculanum' are mentioned with evident jealousy.

τί γὰρ αὐτῷ μέλει; 'for what does he care for the state?'

Verum si quaeris . . βεβίωται; 'but if you ask my opinion, if a man makes pleasure and not duty his object has he not lived his life?' referring to Balbus. βεβίωται seems to mean 'have had enough of life.' Cp. Ep. 112, 3. In the case of a life of pleasure, Cicero hints, a little would be enough.

3. Voluptaria = τερπνά. Forcell.

Tu interea dormis, 'you meanwhile are doing nothing,' an allusion to the Epicureanism of Atticus. 'Dormire' = 'cessare, inertem esse.' Forcell.

4. Iam explicandum . . acturus es, 'you must answer the question before you at once if you are to do any good.' These words are very obscure. They may mean either 'you must make up your mind which party is likely to prevail in Africa if you intend to secure your interests with either' (Schütz), or, 'you must speedily choose between ease and patriotism.' For πρόβλημα in a similar sense, cp. Ep. 43, 2.

5. Ego fructum puto. Instead of 'fructum,' some word meaning 'settled' is wanted, referring to the struggle in Africa. Cp. Ad Fam. 9. 7, 4 'ego confectum existimo.' Wesenb. suggests 'ego transactum negotium puto' or 'ego fractum illum puto.' Manutius explains the existing text as = 'I think enjoyment preferable.'

6. De via recte ad me, sc. 'venientem,' 'coming to me at once on your arrival in Rome,' or 'after your journey.' 'Recte,' and more commonly 'recta,' are used in the sense of 'at once;' 'via' being understood in the latter case. Cp. Ep. 25, 3.

Simul enim, foll., 'for so we shall be able to settle our important affairs the sooner.'

7. Diem Tyrannioni, foll., 'shall fix a day for Tyrannio,' i.e. apparently for his treatise to be read. Cp. Ad Att. 12. 6, 2: from a comparison of which passage with Servius de Accentibus 20, Boot infers that Tyrannio's book was on accents. For an account of Tyrannio, cp. p. 177, note on l. 17.

Et si quid aliud, sc. 'agendum erit, agemus,' the verb being supplied from 'constituemus.'

VARRO (M. Terentius), after the close of the Spanish campaign in 49 B.C., went to Greece, and was at Dyrrhachium during the battle of Pharsalus (De Divin. 1. 32, 68). He was pardoned by Caesar, and entrusted with the formation of a public library at Rome (Suet. Iul. 44): was proscribed by

CICERO VARRONI.

Mihi vero ad Nonas bene maturum videtur fore, neque solum 1
propter rei publicae, sed etiam propter anni tempus: qua re istum
diem probo; itaque eundem ipse sequar. Consilii nostri, ne si 2
eos quidem, qui id secuti non sunt, non paeniteret, nobis paenitendum putarem; secuti enim sumus non spem, sed officium; reliquimus autem non officium, sed desperationem: ita verecundiores fuimus quam qui se domo non commoverunt, saniores quam qui amissis opibus domum non reverterunt. Sed nihil minus fero quam severitatem otiosorum et, quoquo modo se res habet, magis illos vereor, qui in bello occiderunt, quam hos curo,

the second triumvirate (App. Bell. Civ. 4. 47), but managed to escape, and died 28 B.C., aged 88 or 89. Cp. Hieron. in Euseb. Chron. Olymp. 188; Clinton, Fasti Hell. 28 B.C. (III. 231).—Pliny, H. N. 29. 4, says that he wrote in his 83rd, or according to some MSS. in his 88th year.

1. Mihi vero .. fore, 'yes, I think the Nones (of July) will be quite early enough' for our meeting with Caesar. On 'vero,' cp. Ep. 81, 1, note. On 'ad Nonas,' 'on the Nones,' cp. Zumpt, L. G. 296; Ad Att. 13. 45, 2. It resembles the expression 'ad diem.' Some such phrase as 'Caesari nos obviam ire' should be supplied. On the structure of the proposition, cp. Madv. 218 d. The month referred to was probably July. Cp. Intr. to Part IV, § 11, on Caesar's movements. It seems to have been uncertain by what route and when he would return from Africa (cp. Ad Fam. 9. 7, 2), and Varro had suggested that he and Cicero should go to Baiae to await Caesar's arrival (cp. Ad Fam. 9. 2, 5). Caesar spent, however, twenty-eight days on his journey to Rome.

Neque solum .. tempus. The last word is used ambiguously; 'on account not only of the state of public affairs, but of the season of the year.' In Ad Fam. 9. 2, 5, Cicero had told Varro that they had better delay visiting Baiae till they would be thought to have gone there for retirement, and not for amusement—'ploratum, potius quam natatum.' The state of public affairs forbade them to join the crowd of idlers during the fashionable time; and apparently Rome had not yet become unhealthy. The Calendar was much in advance of the real season, so that the Nones of July may well have fallen in spring. Cp. Ep. 84, 2, note.

3. Eundem ipse sequar, 'I shall abide by the same day myself.' A rare sense of the verb.

Consilii nostri, 'our decision not to persevere in the struggle till its end.'

Ne si eos .. paeniteret, 'not even if those who did not follow it did not regret theirs (as they do).' On words inserted between 'ne' and 'quidem,' cp. Madv. 457.

5. Secuti enim .. desperationem, 'we were guided, not by hope, but by gratitude (in joining Pompey); we turned our backs, not on duty, but on despair (in returning to Italy),' i.e. we obeyed the call of gratitude while there was any, even if a poor, hope of success; we abandoned a cause that had become altogether desperate. For 'sequi,' in the sense in which it is here used, cp. Ep. 61, 5.

6. Verecundiores, 'were more sensitive' to the call of honour.

7. Qui se .. non commoverunt. Those who never left Italy, such as Ser. Sulpicius, P. Servilius, L. Volcatius, and others are meant. Ad Att. 9. 10, 7: 9. 19, 2.

Saniores, 'less infatuated' = σωφρονέστεροι. Forcell.

8. Quam .. reverterunt, 'than those who after the ruin of their party did not return home,' but either stayed in Greece or Asia, or renewed the war in Africa.

9. Severitatem otiosorum, 'the harsh judgment of those who have remained neutral.' Cp. Ad Fam. 9. 6, 3 'crudeliter enim otiosissimi minabantur.'

Quoquo modo se res habet, 'whatever happens' (Wiel.), i.e. even if my anticipations are falsified by the event; 'however things stand.'

10. Illos vereor, 'feel respect for those,' 'feel shame at the thought of those.'

Quam hos curo, 'than regard those, now with us,' the 'otiosi' just mentioned. 'Curo' = 'curae habeo.' Forcell.

5 quibus non satis facimus, quia vivimus. Mihi si spatium fuerit in Tusculanum ante Nonas veniendi, istic te videbo; si minus, persequar in Cumanum et ante te certiorem faciam, ut lavatio parata sit.

87. TO L. PAETUS (AD FAM. IX. 18).

ROME OR TUSCULUM, JULY, 46 B.C. (708 A.U.C.)

1. I am glad to hear that you approve my imitation of Dionysius in opening something like a school. 2. I secure myself protectors by acting thus, and have no reason to envy any of our leaders, unless perhaps Cato, whose death I can imitate if the worst happens. 3. My employment improves my health too; nor are the entertainments of my pupils to be despised. Come and see me. 4. If you are embarrassed for want of money, I will gladly accept your services as second teacher.

CICERO S. D. PAETO.

1 Cum essem otiosus in Tusculano, propterea quod discipulos obviam miseram, ut eadem me quam maxime conciliarent familiari suo, accepi tuas litteras plenissimas suavitatis, ex quibus intellexi probari tibi meum consilium, quod, ut Dionysius tyran-

1. **Quibus non satis facimus**, foll., 'who are discontented with us for surviving,' i.e. who say that we have secured our lives by flight. Cp. Ad Fam. 9. 2, 2, where Cicero says that he and Varro ought to avoid publicity for 'qui victoria se efferunt quasi victos nos intuentur; qui autem victos nostros moleste ferunt, nos dolent vivere.'

Spatium, 'time,' 'leisure.'

2. **In Tusculanum**. Varro, then, would be at Tusculum till the Nones, when he would leave for Cumae. Cicero says that he would visit him at Tusculum if he had time; if not, that he would follow him to Cumae, where, apparently, Varro had a villa. Cicero did not, however, go to Cumae, and Caesar does not seem to have landed in that neighbourhood. Cp. Ad Fam. 9. 6, 1.

3 **Ut lavatio parata sit**, 'so that a bath may be ready for me.' 'Lavatio' = 'instrumentum balneare' (Forcell.) would include all that a bather would want. It is a rare word in Cicero. He seems to have been fond of warm baths. Cp. Ad Fam. 9. 16, 9 'ego tibi unum sumptum adferam quod balneum calfacias oportebit.'

L. Papirius Paetus was a learned and witty Epicurean, who seems to have taken no part in politics, and to have been wealthy. Cp. Ad Att. 1. 20, 7; Ad Fam. 9. 16, 7; 9. 20, 1. A comparison of the first paragraph of this letter with the last leaves some doubt if it was written at Rome or Tusculum; but the latter is most probable. Caesar returned to Rome on July 26 (Bell. Afric. 98), and as Cicero's 'pupils' had already left him to greet their leader when this letter was written, its date must probably be placed late in July.

5. **Otiosus**, 'with nothing to do.'

Discipulos, i.e. Hirtius and Dolabella, whom he calls 'dicendi discipulos' Ad Fam. 9. 16, 7.

6. **Obviam**, sc. Caesari ex Africa redeunti. Manut.

Eadem, sc. 'via,' to be supplied from 'obviam.' Süpfle.

Conciliarent familiari suo, 'might recommend me to their friend,' i.e. might make as favourable a report to Caesar of my disposition as they could. 'Conciliare' = 'commendare.' Forcell. 'Familiaris' is sometimes used as a substantive = 'necessarius.' Forcell. Cp. Ad Fam. 3. 1, 3 'est ex meis domesticis atque intimis familiaribus.'

8. **Meum consilium, quod . . coe-**

nus, cum Syracusis pulsus esset, Corinthi dicitur ludum aperuisse, sic ego [sublatis iudiciis] amisso regno forensi ludum quasi habere coeperim. Quid quaeris? me quoque delectat consilium; multa 2
enim consequor: primum, id quod maxime nunc opus est, munio me ad haec tempora. Id cuius modi sit, nescio; tantum video, nullius adhuc consilium me huic anteponere, nisi forte mori melius fuit: in lectulo, fateor, sed non accidit; in acie non fui. Ceteri quidem, Pompeius, Lentulus tuus, Scipio, Afranius foede perierunt. 'At Cato praeclare.' Iam istuc quidem, cum volemus, licebit; demus modo operam ne tam necesse nobis sit quam illi fuit;

perim. On the conj., cp. Madv. 357 a, latter part. The force of 'quod' is perhaps slightly different in Ep. 47. 3. Cicero is probably quoting what Paetus had said.

Dionysius tyrannus. The younger Dionysius, after his expulsion from Syracuse. Cicero appears to be the earliest authority for this story. It is told in different forms by Plutarch, (Timoleon 14), and Justin, (21. 5). Grote (xi. 217) expresses no opinion as to its truth.

1. Aperuisse. 'Aperire' seems an unusual word to use with 'ludus.'

2. [Sublatis iudiciis]. If these words are genuine, they may refer to a suspension of the regular action of the tribunals during the civil war. Pompey in 52 B.C., and Caesar introduced considerable changes into the constitution and procedure of the courts, but the date of Caesar's changes is uncertain. Mommsen 4. 2, 325 and 483–485.

Amisso regno forensi: cp. Ep. 1. 1, note, and Quintil. Inst. Orat. 10. 1. 112 'quare non immerito ab hominibus aetatis suae regnare in iudiciis dictus est (Cicero).'

Ludum .. habere, 'to keep as it were a school.' His instruction of Hirtius and Dolabella in rhetoric could only metaphorically be called keeping a school.

3. Quid quaeris: cp. Ep. 7. 6, note.

Me quoque, 'me as well as you.' Cp. 'tibi probari,' above.

4. Primum. This first reason occupies the remainder of the section.

Munio me ad haec tempora, 'I secure myself with regard to the dangers of the times.' 'Ad' is used 'de consilio seu fine.' Forcell. He denies that it can have the force of 'adversum.' Cicero means that the influence of his pupils would be his protection.

5. Id cuius modi sit, 'the value of this protection.'

Tantum video, 'thus much I know.' 'Video' = 'intelligo.' Forcell.

6. Nullius, 'no one's,' among the Pompeians. Explained by 'ceteri quidem,' below.

Adhuc, common with pres. Forcell.

Melius fuit: cp. Madv. 348 c, Obs. 1.

7. In lectulo. This may refer to his illness at Dyrrhachium. Cp. Intr. to Part III, § 10, and also Ep. 71. 7, note, for the phrase 'in lectulo mori.' 'I wish a peaceful death had spared me the sight of what we see.'

Non accidit, 'it was not my fortune.'

In acie, sc. Pharsalica. He means that he had not shewn cowardice in the field.

Ceteri .. perierunt, 'our other leaders perished miserably, and I cannot envy them.' None of those presently mentioned died by the hand of an enemy in fair battle.

8. Lentulus tuus, according to Manut. L. Lentulus Crus, consul of 49 B.C. On his death, cp. Caes. Bell. Civ. 3. 104; or, as Orell. P. Lentulus Spinther, Cos. 57 B.C., who appears to have perished in the civil war: Philipp. 13. 14. 29.

Scipio: cp. Intr. to Part IV, § 10: Bell. Afric. 96; Livy Epit. 114.

Afranius: Intr. l. c.; Bell. Afric. 95.

Foede, 'miserably.' For there was nothing dishonourable about the death of any of them.

9. At Cato praeclare, sc. 'mortuus est.' Cp. Ep. 63. 3, note on 'at Sulla,' foll.

Iam istuc .. licebit, 'I shall still be able to do as he did whenever I please.' 'Iam,' from its position seems to be transitional; 'well' would suit the sense. The form 'istic' for 'iste' is found in a report of a conversation with Matius, Ep. 105. 1. On the personal construction of 'licere' with neuter pronouns, cp. Madv. 218 a, Obs. 2.

10. Demus modo .. agimus, 'only let me take care, as I do, not to be compelled to do it, as he was.' Cato's uncompromising

3 id quod agimus. Ergo hoc primum. Sequitur illud: Ipse melior
fio; primum valetudine, quam intermissis exercitationibus amiseram; deinde ipsa illa, si qua fuit in me, facultas orationis,
nisi me ad has exercitationes rettulissem, exaruisset. Extremum
illud est, quod tu nescio an primum putes: plures iam pavones
confeci quam tu pullos columbinos. Tu istic te Hateriano iure
delectas; ego me hic Hirtiano. Veni igitur, si vir es, et disce
a me προλεγομένας, quas quaeris: etsi sus Minervam. Sed quo
4 modo, videro. Si aestimationes tuas vendere non potes neque
ollam denariorum implere, Romam tibi remigrandum est: satius

opposition to Caesar had left him no choice after defeat; Cicero was conciliating some members of the victorious party.

1. **Ergo hoc primum**, sc. 'consequor.' Cp. the beginning of this section.

Sequitur illud, 'next comes the following advantage.' On 'illud,' cp. Ep. 5. 3, note.

Ipse melior fio = 'convalesco,' 'I myself am getting better.' Forcell.

2. **Primum valetudine . . . deinde ipsa illa.** A slight, but easily intelligible, anacoluthon. 'Valetudo' is a neutral word (cp. Ep. 52, 5); here its meaning is fixed by amiseram.

Intermissis exercitationibus, a curious illustration of Roman habits. The declamations seem to have supplied the place of out-of-door exercise. Cp. Philipp. 2. 17, 42, where Cicero accuses Antony of practising declamation in order to get rid of the effects of intemperance.

3. **Deinde . . . exaruisset**, 'secondly, whatever flow of oratory I could command would have been dried up.' The metaphorical sense of 'exaresco' is common in Cicero. Cp. Brut. 4, 16.

4. **Extremum . . . est**, 'thirdly and lastly.' Cicero varies his introductory phrases for the three heads: 'primum,' 'sequitur illud,' 'extremum . . est.'

5. **Nescio an**: cp. Ep. 77, 2, note.

Plures . . . columbinos, 'I have got through more peacocks than you have young pigeons.' Peacocks were a notorious luxury at Rome. Cp. Hor. Sat. 2. 2, 23, alib.

6. **Confeci.** 'Conficere' = 'consumere.' Forcell.

Istic, i.e. at or near Neapolis. Cp. Ad Fam. 9. 15, 3 and 4; 9. 23.

Hateriano iure, 'the law of Haterius,' who may have been a jurisconsult staying at Neapolis.

Iure . . . Hirtiano, 'the gravy which Hirtius provides.' 'Ius,' meaning both 'law' and 'gravy,' suggests a similar pun, In Verr. 2 Act. 1. 46, 121 'ius Verrinum.' On the luxurious tastes of Hirtius, cp. Ad Fam. 9. 16, 7, where Cicero calls him one of his teachers in the art of dining.

7. **Si vir es**, 'if you are a man of spirit' with a proper enthusiasm for good living.

8. **προλεγομένας** sc. **θέσεις**, 'introductions' to the higher culinary art: again a word equally applicable to jurisprudence. Orell., Onom.

Quas quaeris. Paetus may have asked for some hints on cookery.

Sus Minervam, sc. 'doceret si a me disceres.' The proverb is found, De Orat. 2. 57, 233; Acad. Post. 1. 4, 18.

Quo modo, sc. 'sis futurum sit ut discas.' Baiter.

9. **Aestimationes tuas**, 'the property assigned you on a valuation.' 'Aestimatio pro re aestimata.' Forcell. Cp. a similar use of 'emptio,' Ad Att. 1. 5. 7 'Epiroticam emptionem gaudeo tibi placere.' Caesar's measures for the relief of debtors and for the restoration of public credit had forced a large amount of land into the market at once, and there was naturally a difficulty in getting a good price for it. Cp. Appendix 9. 1. 11; Ad Fam. 9. 16, 7 'non eo sis consilio ut cum me hospitio recipias aestimationem te aliquam putes accipere; etiam haec levior est plaga ab amico quam a debitore;' also Ep. 96, 4.

10. **Ollam denariorum**, 'your money-pot.' Süpfle and Billerb. The latter sees an allusion to the money-pot of Euclio in the Aulularia of Plautus.

Romam tibi remigrandum est, 'you must make your way back to Rome,' where plenty of friends will be glad to give you a dinner. 'Remigrare' is a common word. Forcell.

est hic cruditate quam istic fame. Video te bona perdidisse; spero idem istuc familiares tuos. Actum igitur de te est, nisi provides. Potes mulo isto, quem tibi reliquum dicis esse, quoniam cantherium comedisti, Romam pervehi. Sella tibi erit in ludo tamquam hypodidascalo proxima; eam pulvinus sequetur.

88. TO M. MARIUS (AD FAM. VII. 3).

ROME, JULY OR AUGUST, (?) 46 B.C. (708 A.U.C.)

1. I often think of our meeting three years ago; we then both of us hesitated what I ought to do with a view both to safety and to honour. I thought most of the last, 2. and regret my choice, not so much for the danger it involved, as because of the incapacity and ferocity of those whom I joined. I advised Pompey first to negotiate for peace, which he declined; then to avoid a pitched battle, which he might have done but for the confidence inspired by a partial success. His subsequent flight 3. relieved me from any obligation to persevere in the struggle; and I thought submission to the conqueror the least bad of the courses open to me. 4. I console myself with my intellectual resources, and with reflection on my past distinctions. 5. My regard for you leads me to explain myself to you thus at length, 6. that you may be able to vindicate my conduct when you hear it severely criticised.

M. CICERO S. D. M. MARIO.

Persaepe mihi cogitanti de communibus miseriis, in quibus tot 1
annos versamur et, ut video, versabimur, solet in mentem venire illius temporis, quo proxime fuimus una; quin etiam ipsum diem memoria teneo: nam a. d. III. Idus Maias, Lentulo et Marcello

1. Hic, 'in this neighbourhood.' It is not perhaps necessary to suppose that the letter was written at Rome on comparing 'Romam . . hic.' A writer at Tusculum might speak of Rome as 'in this neighbourhood,' as compared with Campania.

Cruditate, sc. 'mori,' 'to die of indigestion,' caused by good living.

Istic, i.e. 'on the Bay of Naples.'

Bona perdidisse, 'have lost your property,' by having to take land at a price above its real value.

Spero idem istuc, sc. 'passos esse,' 'I suppose your friends at Neapolis are in the same plight,' so that their hospitality cannot keep you there. On 'spero' with past tenses = 'opinor,' cp. Forcell., and Ep. 1, 4. 'Istuc,' on this form, cp. note on § 2.

2. Nisi provides, 'unless you provide for yourself,' e.g. by serving me as my under teacher.

3. Quoniam cantherium comedisti, 'since the expenses of your establishment have eaten up your back.' 'Cantherium,' 'a gelding.' Forcell. Comedisti, 'comedere'—'absumere.' Ib.

4. In ludo, 'in my school of rhetoric.' Cp. § 1, note.

5. Hypodidascalo. This word is only here used by Cicero, but is found in Plato, Ion 536 A.

Proxima, 'next my own.'

Eam pulvinus sequetur, 'you shall presently receive a cushion too,' as a mark of honour.

M. MARIO. Of this M. Marius little is known. He was a native of Arpinum, rich, and rather infirm in health. He seems to have lived little in Rome. Cp. Ad Q. F. 2. 10, 3; Ad Fam. 7. 1. 1 and 5; 7. 4.

6. Tot annos. From Caesar's first consulship? (Manut.) or from the beginning of the civil war?

7. Solet . . una, 'I am reminded of the last time we met.' On the genit. after 'in mentem venire,' cp. Madv. 291, Obs. 3.

9. A. d. III. Idus Maias, 'May 13, 49 B.C.' According to Ep. 74, 4, Cicero arrived at his villa at Pompeii on May 12th.

consulibus, cum in Pompeianum vesperi venissem, tu mihi sollicito animo praesto fuisti; sollicitum autem te habebat cogitatio cum officii, tum etiam periculi mei: si manerem in Italia, verebare ne officio deessem; si proficiscerer ad bellum, periculum te meum commovebat. Quo tempore vidisti profecto me quoque ita conturbatum, ut non explicarem, quid esset optimum factu; pudori tamen malui famaeque cedere quam salutis meae rationem ducere.

2 Cuius me mei facti paenituit non tam propter periculum meum quam propter vitia multa, quae ibi offendi, quo veneram: primum neque magnas copias neque bellicosas; deinde, extra ducem paucosque praeterea—de principibus loquor—, reliquos primum in ipso bello rapaces, deinde in oratione ita crudeles, ut ipsam victoriam horrerem; maximum autem aes alienum amplissimorum virorum. Quid quaeris? nihil boni praeter causam. Quae cum vidissem, desperans victoriam primum coepi suadere pacem, cuius fueram semper auctor; deinde, cum ab ea sententia Pompeius valde abhorreret, suadere institui, ut bellum duceret: hoc interdum probabat et in ea sententia videbatur fore et fuisset fortasse, nisi

1. **In Pompeianum**, 'to my villa at Pompeii.' Cp. Ep. 74. 4; Appendix 5, § 1. M. Marius also seems to have had a villa at Pompeii. Cp. Ad Fam. 7. 4.

Tu mihi .. praesto fuisti, 'you were there to meet me.' Cp. Ep. 16, 7; Pro Muren. 20, 42 'Romae . . amicis praesto fuisti.'

2. **Sollicitum .. te habebat.** On the double accus., cp. Ep. 78. 1, note 'and your anxiety arose from considering.'

Autem, used in the continuation of a discourse. Cp. Ep. 7. 1. note, p. 47.

3. **Officii**, 'my duty to Pompey and to his party.'

4. **Si proficiscerer .. commovebat**: cp. Madv. 348 b. Or perhaps, with Hofm., we may take the conditional clause as qualifying or explaining the word 'periculum.' Hofm. quotes De Divin. 2. 1, 1 'nulla maior occurrebat [res] quam si optimarum artium vias traderem meis civibus.'

5. **Ita .. factu**, 'so agitated, that I could not decide which course was the best.' On the use of the supine in 'u,' cp. Madv. 412.

6. **Explicarem.** 'Explicare' = 'expedire rem intellectu difficilem.' Forcell.

Pudori .. famaeque cedere, 'to yield to the claims of honour and of public opinion.'

7. **Rationem ducere**: cp. Ad Att. 8. 11 D, 7 'duxi meam rationem.' 'Habere rationem' is more common.

9. **Vitia multa .. offendi**, 'the numerous defects which I found there,' i.e. in Pompey's camp.

10. **Neque magnas copias neque bellicosas.** With the last epithet, cp. the concluding words of this section. Pompey's army must have been considerably increased after Cicero's arrival in his camp, for at Pharsalus it more than doubled Caesar's. Cp. Intr. to Part III, § 11; Caes. Bell. Civ. 3. 88 89. The accus. 'copias' is governed by 'offendi,' and so is aes alienum. The MS. has reliqui for 'reliquos,' which involves a slight break in the construction. On the language and hopes of Pompey's partisans, cp. Epp. 80, 2; 91, 6. Several of them, e.g. L. Lentulus Crus (Caes. Bell. Civ. 1. 4), Faustus Sulla, Libo, and Scipio (Ad Att. 9. 11, 4), hoped to get rid of their debts in the confusion caused by the war.

11. **In ipso bello rapaces**, e.g. Scipio, who levied very heavy contributions in Asia. Caes. Bell. Civ. 3. 32.

12. **In oratione**, 'in their language.' Hofm.

14. **Nihil boni**, sc. 'inveni,' to be supplied from 'offendi.'

15. **Suadere pacem**, 'to recommend peace.'

17. **Ut bellum duceret**, 'to protract the war.' Cp. Ep. 28, 7, for this sense of 'duco.'

18. **In ea sententia .. fore**, 'to abide by that judgment.'

quadam ex pugna coepisset suis militibus confidere. Ex eo tempore vir ille summus nullus imperator fuit: signa tirone et collecticio exercitu cum legionibus robustissimis contulit; victus turpissime amissis etiam castris solus fugit. Hunc ego mihi belli finem 3
feci, nec putavi, cum integri pares non fuissemus, fractos superiores fore; discessi ab eo bello, in quo aut in acie cadendum fuit aut in aliquas insidias incidendum aut deveniendum in victoris manus aut ad Iubam confugiendum aut capiendus tamquam exsilio locus aut consciscenda mors voluntaria: certe nihil fuit praeterea, si te victori nolles aut non auderes committere. Ex omnibus autem iis, quae dixi, incommodis nihil tolerabilius exsilio, praesertim innocenti, ubi nulla adiuncta est turpitudo; addo etiam, cum ea urbe careas, in qua nihil sit, quod videre possis sine dolore: ego cum meis, si quicquam nunc cuiusquam est, etiam in meis esse malui. Quae acciderunt, omnia dixi futura; veni 4

1. Quadam ex pugna, 'in consequence of a certain engagement,' i.e. that near Dyrrhachium, alluded to in Ep. 78, 2.

2. Nullus imperator, 'nothing of a general.' Cp. Ep. 48, 1, where Pompey is called ἀστρατήγητος; Ep. 59, 1, ἀστρατηγικώτατον. This use of 'nullus' is not quite the same as in Ad Att. 11. 24, 4 'Philotimus nullus venit,' where it = 'non,' but is found Tusc. Disp. 2. 5, 13 'nullum . . argumentum.'

Tirone et collecticio exercitu, 'having an untrained and motley army.' Abl. abs., cp. Madv. 277, Obs. 2. 'Tiro' is used as an adjective, Philipp. 11. 15, 39 'non tam veteranos metuendos arbitror quam quid tirones milites.' On the composition of Pompey's forces, cp. Caes. Bell. Civ. 3. 4.

3. Robustissimis, 'most efficient.' For Caesar's army was weak in numbers. Cp. Intr. to Part III. § 11.

4. Hunc . . finem feci, 'I made this the limit of my service.' Cp. Ep. 83, 1.

7. In aliquas insidias incidendum, as had been the fortune of Pompey, L. Lentulus and others.

Deveniendum in victoris manus, i.e. by a compulsory surrender, as did M. Brutus. Opposed to victori se committere below, which means, 'to throw one's self voluntarily on the victor's mercy,' as did C. Cassius, cp. p. 394.

8. Aut capiendus tamquam exsilio locus, 'or must choose some place, as if for a residence in banishment.' 'Tamquam,' because such self-expatriation would not be legal 'exsilium.' The case of Marcellus is probably referred to. Cp. § 5, note.

9. Nihil fuit praeterea, 'there was no course except one of these.'

10. Nolles . . auderes, conj. potentialis. Hofm. Boot.

11. Ubi . . est turpitudo. On the mood, cp. Madv. 362 a.

13. Cum ea urbe careas. 'Urbe carere,' in the sense of exile, is common. Cp. Philipp. 1. 2. 6. 'Cum' = 'in case,' 'in so far as.' Wiel.

14. Ego cum meis, foll., 'I wished to live with my own family, if one can now call anybody one's own, and also on my own property.' Müller. This seems to be the import of the words as they stand, but involves an untrue charge against Caesar, who had shewn no wish to molest the relations of his adversaries. If 'et' were prefixed to 'si,' the sense would be improved, for Cicero, as one who had been in Pompey's camp, might naturally fear fine or confiscation. Hofm. does not alter the text, but makes the words 'si quicquam' foll. refer to 'etiam in meis.' Manutius attaches quite a different sense to these words. He makes 'cum' mean, 'in possession of,' expressing security; 'in,' 'upon,' as a mere occupant; etiam, 'or if it must be so,' expressing indignation. The first 'meis' he explains as = 'propinquis et amicis.'

15. Veni domum . . . esset, 'I came home, not that I hoped to find life there very satisfactory.' On the meaning of non quo . . esset, cp. Ep. 28, 7, note.

domum, non quo optima vivendi condicio esset, sed tamen, si esset aliqua forma rei publicae, tamquam in patria ut essem, si nulla tamquam in exsilio. Mortem mihi cur consciscerent, causa non visa est; cur optarem, multae causae; vetus est enim, ubi non sis qui fueris, non esse cur velis vivere. Sed tamen vacare culpa magnum est solacium, praesertim cum habeam duas res, quibus me sustentem, optimarum artium scientiam et maximarum rerum gloriam; quarum altera mihi vivo numquam eripietur,
8 altera ne mortuo quidem. Haec ad te scripsi verbosius et tibi molestus fui, quod te cum mei, tum rei publicae cognovi amantissimum. Notum tibi omne meum consilium esse volui, ut primum scires me numquam voluisse plus quemquam posse quam universam rem publicam; postea autem quam alicuius culpa tantum valeret unus, ut obsisti non posset, me voluisse pacem; amisso exercitu et eo duce, in quo spes fuerat uno, me voluisse etiam reliquis omnibus; postquam non potuerim, mihi ipsi finem fecisse belli; nunc autem, si haec civitas est, civem esse me; si non, exsulem esse non incommodiore loco, quam si Rhodum *me*
9 aut Mytilenas contulissem. Haec tecum coram malueram; sed quia longius fiebat, volui per litteras eadem, ut haberes, quid

1. **Sed tamen**, foll., 'but that, if anything like a free Commonwealth was to remain, I might live as in my country.' Cp. § 5 'civem esse me.'

4. **Vetus est enim**, sc. 'dictum.' Cp. Pro Quinct. 17, 55; Nägelsb. 31, 64. The quotation which follows is thought to be from an old tragedian, with slight variation.

5. **Non esse cur** = 'non esse causam cur.' Cp. Forcell. on 'est quod;' Madv. 372 b., Obs. 6.

7. **Maximarum rerum gloriam**, 'distinction won by the greatest exploits.' Gen. poss., cp. Ep 4, 2, note on p. 35.

8. **Altera**, sc. 'scientia.'

9. **Altera**, sc 'gloria.'

Verbosius, 'at considerable length.' Cp. Ep. 54, 6.

Tibi molestus fui, 'have thus troubled you.'

11. **Omne meum consilium**, 'the grounds of my whole conduct.'

12. **Primum**, not followed by 'deinde' or any such word but by a change in the form of the sentence. Hofm.

Plus quemquam posse, foll., 'that a single man should be more powerful than the State.' On the constr., cp. Ep. 15, 11, note.

13. **Alicuius**, sc. Pompeii. Cp. on the substance of this charge, Ep. 54, 3.

14. **Unus**, sc. Caesar.

Obsisti, impers.

15. **Amisso exercitu**, i.e. at Pharsalus.

Voluisse etiam reliquis, sc. 'pacem.' Süpfle. But does not the contrast between 'reliquis omnibus' and 'mihi ipsi' suggest that we should supply 'finem facere belli' from below, with Müller?

16. **Postquam non potuerim**, 'now that I have failed in that.' The sequence of the tense here changes, from the historic to the primary.

18. **Rhodum**. Rhodes was an agreeable island with a refined population. Its people, however, refused an asylum to some of the fugitives from Pharsalus. Caes. Bell. Civ. 3, 102.

19. **Mytilenas**. Both the singular and plural forms of this word are found in Roman authors. Cp. Hor. Carm. 1, 7, 1; Epp. 1, 11, 17. M. Marcellus had gone to Mytilene. Cp. Ad Fam. 4, 7, 4; Brut. 71, 250. Both Rhodes and (Vell. 2, 18) Mytilenae were (nominally) independent states (Manut.), so that a Roman could go into exile at either.

Coram, sc. 'loqui.'

Malueram. On the mood, cp. Ep. 12, 3, note.

20. **Quia longius fiebat**, 'as it was

diceres, si quando in vituperatores meos incidisses; sunt enim qui, cum meus interitus nihil fuerit rei publicae profuturus, criminis loco putent esse, quod vivam, quibus ego certo scio non videri satis multos perisse: qui, si me audissent, quamvis iniqua pace, honeste tamen viverent; armis enim inferiores, non causa fuissent. Habes epistolam verbosiorem fortasse, quam velles; quod tibi ita videri putabo, nisi mihi longiorem remiseris. Ego, si, quae volo, expediero, brevi tempore te, ut spero, videbo.

80. To L. PAETUS (AD FAM. IX. 17).

ROME, AUGUST, (?) BAIT. 46 B.C. (708 A.U.C.)

1. How absurd your question was about the towns and lands in your neighbourhood. I ought rather to ask you what will become of us all, but I see that we ought to be grateful for every day that we escape ruin. 2. My own property seems to be endangered, but I have chosen to accept life as a gift, and must be grateful to the giver. He wishes, perhaps, to rule with moderation, but is embarrassed by his connections, 3. and must fashion his policy according to the demands of the times. In conclusion, I have heard no rumours of the danger you fear.

CICERO PAETO.

Non tu homo ridiculus es, qui, cum Balbus noster apud te fuerit, 1

getting too long,' i.e. 'the interval before we met;' or, 'as time was going on,' I could not wait for a meeting. Here the construction is impersonal, but another is admissible. Cp. De Legg. 1. 7. 22 'non faciam longius.' On the mood, cp. Madv. 357 a, and on the tense, ib. 337.

Eadem, sc. 'tibi exponere.'

Ut haberes quid diceres, 'that you might know what to say.' On 'habeo quid,' cp. Ep 66, 1, note.

1. In vituperatores meos; cp. Ep. 86, 2, note.

2. Cum meus interitus, foll., 'though my death would have been of no service to the State.' On the tenses, cp. Ep. 10, 2, note.

3. Quibus . . perisse, 'who, I know for certain, do not think that victims enough have fallen.'

4. Qui si me audissent. 'Pacem suadentem,' cp. § 2. Manut. This must refer to those who had fallen, though the construction is harsh. Cp. with the general sense of the passage, Ep. 94, 1.

Quamvis iniqua pace, abl. abs. (cp. § 2, note), 'however hard the terms of peace.'

Armis enim . . fuissent, 'for they would have yielded to their enemy's superiority in arms, not in the justice of his pretensions,' and so there would have been no discredit in their submission to brute force. The argument seems rather ingenious than convincing.

6. Habes epistolam, 'there is a letter for you.' Cp. De Orat. 2. 88, 361 'habetis sermonem bene longum.'

7. Quod tibi . . putabo, 'and I shall think you agree with me as to its tediousness.' 'Quod'='et id.' Cp. Ep. 26, 1, note. Either 'quod' or 'ita' seems superfluous. Cp. Zumpt, L. G. 748.

8. Si quae volo expediero: cp. Ad Att. 12. 5. 4. The words seem to refer to his anxiety about Tullia's divorce; perhaps also to his own money difficulties. Cp. Intr. to Part IV, §§ 1 and 7; Appendix 5, § 3.

9. Non='nonne.' Cp. Pro Rosc. Com. 2, 5 'suarum perscriptionum . . adversaria proferre non amentia est?' Wesenb. has 'ne.'

Cum Balbus noster apud te fuerit, 'though you have had a visit from our friend Balbus.' Cp. Ad Fam. 9. 19, where the visit is described.

ex me quaeras, quid de istis municipiis et agris futurum putem? quasi aut ego quicquam sciam, quod iste nesciat, aut, si quid aliquando scio, non ex isto soleam scire. Immo vero, si me amas, tu fac ut sciam, quid de nobis futurum sit; habuisti enim in tua potestate, ex quo vel ex sobrio vel certe ex ebrio scire posses. Sed ego ista, mi Paete, non quaero: primum quia de lucro prope iam quadriennium vivimus, si aut hoc lucrum est aut haec vita, superstitem rei publicae vivere; deinde, quod scire *ego* quoque mihi videor, quid futurum sit: fiet enim quodcumque volent qui valebunt; valebunt autem semper arma. Satis igitur nobis esse debet quicquid conceditur: hoc si qui pati non potuit, mori debuit.

2 Veientem quidem agrum et Capenatem metiuntur; hoc non longe abest a Tusculano. Nihil tamen timeo: fruor, dum licet; opto, ut semper liceat. Si id minus contigerit, tamen, quoniam ego vir fortis idemque philosophus vivere pulcherrimum duxi, non possum eum non diligere, cuius beneficio id consecutus sum; qui si cupiat

1. De istis municipiis et agris, 'about the municipal towns and lands in your neighbourhood,' i.e. in Campania. Paetus seems to have feared that Caesar might make a new assignation of lands among his veterans at the expense of previous proprietors; which, however, Caesar avoided. Cp. App. Bell. Civ. 2. 94; Ep. 102, notes.

Istis, 'which you are concerned about.'

2. Quasi . . sciam. On the mood and tense, cp. Madv. 349 Obs.

4. Quid de nobis . . sit, 'what is to become of ourselves.' Cicero had still some doubts, apparently, as to Caesar's intentions, though he had written with much confidence to Paetus. Ad Fam. 9. 16, 2 and 3.

Habuisti enim, sc. 'hominem,' 'for you have had a man at your disposal.'

5. Ex ebrio. I cannot find that Balbus is elsewhere charged with intemperance. But he is said (Ad Fam. 6. 19, 2) to have suffered 'pedum doloribus,' which may have been caused by excess. On the repetition of 'ex,' cp. Madv. 470; Zumpt. L. G. 745. The present case, however, seems not to come under the rules there given.

6. Ego ista . . non quaero, 'I do not trouble myself about these matters,' i.e. the assignations of land. Wiel.

De lucro . . vivimus, 'our life has for nearly four years been clear gain,' i.e. what we had no right to reckon on. It had been due to the mercy of a conqueror. Cicero dates apparently, with some exaggeration, from the beginning of 49 B.C. With the expression 'de lucro,' cp. Hor. Carm. 1. 9, 14 'quem fors dierum cumque dabit lucro Appone.'

9. Qui valebunt, 'those who shall prevail.' Cp. Ep. 61, 5.

10. Autem: cp. Ep. 7, 1, note.

11. Quicquid conceditur, 'whatever the conqueror allows us.'

Hoc si quis . . debuit, 'all who could not be content with this ought to have died.' 'Hoc' = 'this state of things.' 'Si quis' is more common than 'si qui' without a substantive. Cp. Madv. 90. 1.

12. Veientem, of Veii.

Capenatem, 'of Capena,' a town of Etruria, about eight miles from Soracte, between it and the Tiber. The site of Veii would be about twenty-three miles N.W. of Tusculum.

Metiuntur, sc. 'agrimensores Caesariani,' 'are measuring for assignation.'

Hoc . . Tusculano, 'this comes very near the territory of Tusculum,' and threatens my villa there. 'Hoc' refers to the substance of the previous sentence. Cp. note on the previous section.

13. Fruor, 'I enjoy my property.'

Opto, ut: cp. Ep. 58, 1, note.

14. Vir . . philosophus, 'a brave man, and a philosopher to.' Ironical.

15. Vivere . . duxi, 'have thought life more precious than anything else.' For the infin. as an object, cp. Ep. 47, 2.

16. Eum, Caesarem.

Si cupiat . . non habet: cp. Madv.

esse rem publicam, qualem fortasse et ille volt et omnes optare debemus, quid faciat tamen non habet; ita se cum multis colligavit.
Sed longius progredior; scribo enim ad te. Hoc tamen scito, non 2
modo me, qui consiliis non intersum, sed ne ipsum quidem principem scire, quid futurum sit; nos enim illi servimus, ipse temporibus: ita nec ille, quid tempora postulatura sint, nec nos, quid ille cogitet, scire possumus. Haec tibi antea non rescripsi, non quo cessator esse solerem, praesertim in litteris, sed, cum explorati nihil haberem, nec tibi sollicitudinem ex dubitatione mea nec spem ex adfirmatione adferre volui. Illud tamen adscribam, quod est verissimum, me his temporibus adhuc de isto periculo nihil audisse: tu tamen pro tua sapientia debebis optare optima, cogitare difficillima, ferre quaecumque erunt.

90. To SERVIUS SULPICIUS (AD FAM. IV. 4).

ROME, SEPTEMBER (?) 46 B.C. (708 A.U.C.)

1. I accept of your excuses for writing many copies of one letter, but cannot admit that of want of talent. 2. Your letter strengthens my approval of your decision to accept the government of Achaia. Each of us thinks that sight most grievous which is before his own eyes; but you have greater freedom in writing than I have. 3. I am glad, however, to have been present when Caesar granted Marcellus his pardon

352; also Ad Att. 5. 4, 1 'si iam res placeat agendi tamen viam non video.' 'Si' = 'etiamsi.' Forcell.

1. Esse rem publicam, 'that a free government should exist.'

2. Ita se cum multis colligavit, 'to such an extent has he entangled himself with many people.' 'Colligare' = 'irretire.' Forcell. The order of the words is virtually transposed; 'ita se cum multis colligavit ut quid faciat non habeat' is what we might expect. Cp. Livy 2. 27 'tergiversari res cogebat: adeo in alteram caussam .. collega .. praeceps erat.' 'Ita' = 'adeo.' Forcell. Cp. Ep. 60 'ita de me mereris.' Caesar was obliged to reward his partisans, which could hardly be done without injury to the constitution.

3. Longius progredior, 'I am running on too long.' With this use of 'progredior,' cp. De Orat. 3. 30, 119 'nunc ad reliqua progrediar.'

Scribo enim ad te, 'for I am writing to you, who know more than I do.'

Non modo me. On 'non modo,' cp. Epp. 10, 2; 16, 4; notes.

4. Consiliis, Caesarianorum.

Ipsum .. principem, i.e. Caesar, of whom Cicero here speaks with remarkable candour.

5. Ipse temporibus, sc. 'servit.' Cp. De Prov. Cons. 1. 2 'non iracundiae serviam.'

7. Non rescripsi, i.e. in answer to your enquiry. Cp. § 1.

8. Cessator = 'iners, piger.' Forcell.

10. Ex adfirmatione = 'enuntiatione,' 'by a declaration.' Forcell. A rare word.

11. His temporibus, 'at present.'

De isto periculo, 'about the danger to which you refer,' i.e. of assignations of lands in Campania.

12. Tu tamen .. erunt, 'it will be right for you, however, in your wisdom to hope for the best, to look on the hardest fate as possible, to bear whatever comes.'

SEPTEMBER (?). This letter was written after Caesar's return to Rome from the African campaign. He reached Rome on July 26. Cp. Intr. to Part IV, § 11.

at the request of the senate. 4. I declared my thankfulness at some length, and so I fear I may have more difficulty in abstaining from public life in future; but I mean to keep a good deal of my time for literature. 5. Your official business prevents your indulging a similar taste, but the long nights will give you more leisure. Your son shews me much attention, and often converses with me about your plans. I think we ought to consult Caesar's wishes in every way, for his generosity is the one redeeming feature of the times.

M. CICERO S. D. SER. SULPICIO.

1 Accipio excusationem tuam, qua usus es, cur saepius ad me litteras uno exemplo dedisses, sed accipio ex ea parte, quatenus aut neglegentia aut improbitate eorum, qui epistolas accipiant, fieri scribis ne ad nos perferantur: illam partem excusationis, qua te scribis orationis paupertate—sic enim appellas—isdem verbis epistolas saepius mittere, nec nosco nec probo; et ego ipse, quem tu per iocum—sic enim accipio—divitias orationis habere dicis, me non esse verborum admodum inopem agnosco: εἰρωνεύεσθαι enim non necesse est: sed tamen idem—nec hoc εἰρωνευόμενος—
2 facile cedo tuorum scriptorum subtilitati et elegantiae. Consi-

SER. SULPICIO. On Servius Sulpicius, cp. Intr. to Parts II, § 17; V, § 12, several passages in the oration Pro Murena, and nearly the whole of the 9th Philippic.

1. Qua usus es. Cobet. om.

Cur dedisses. According to Hofm. the fault excused is more often expressed by the genitive than by a clause beginning with 'cur.'

2. Uno exemplo, 'with the same contents.' Süpfle. Cp. 'iisdem verbis' below, and 'eodem exemplo' Ad Fam. 9. 16, 1. Sulpicius had apparently excused himself for sending several letters with the same contents, on two grounds; first, that he could not rely upon his messengers; secondly, that his pen was not fluent. Cicero accepts the first reason, but not the second.

Ex ea parte quatenus, 'only in so far as you say.'

3. Neglegentia .. perferantur, 'that the carelessness or dishonesty of those entrusted with your letters prevents their reaching us regularly.' This would be especially likely to happen when the distance was so considerable, Sulpicius being in Achaia. Cicero often expresses want of confidence in those who carried his letters. Cp. Epp. 6, 1; 12, 5, alib.

4. Illam partem .. qua, 'but that part of your plea wherein,' opposed to 'ex ea parte, quatenus' above.

5. Orationis .. paupertate, 'owing to an insufficient command of language.' Not Ciceronian, apparently, as the words 'sic enim appellas,' 'for such are the words you use'—seem to imply.

Isdem verbis, abl. qualitatis: cp. Ep. 6, 2, note.

6. Nec nosco nec probo, 'I neither admit nor allow.' Süpfle, Matth. '[Noscere] est interdum probare, et admittere, agnoscere.' Forcell.

7. Per iocum .. accipio, 'jestingly, for so I understand it.'

8. εἰρωνεύσασθαι, 'to shew any mock modesty.' The verb occurs Arist. Pol. 3, 2, 2; the character is described Arist. Eth. Nic. 4. 7, 3.

9. Nec hoc εἰρωνευόμενος, sc. 'dico.' Cicero refers to what follows 'cedo,' foll.

10. Subtilitati. Forcell. gives 'puritas,' 'venustas,' 'naturalis quasi color,' as synonyms for 'subtilitas,' 'purity, naturalness, absence of affectation.' See also Quint. Inst. Orat. 12. 10, 58. (Hofm.)

Elegantiae, 'propriety.' In Orat 23. 79 'elegantia' is coupled with 'munditia' and opposed to 'fucati medicamenta candoris.' It was a lawyer's word, and Sulpicius was a great lawyer. Cicero praises his style, Brut. 41, 152; 42, 153.

Consilium recusavisse, 'the grounds on which you decided to accept your present

lium tuum, quo te usum scribis hoc Achaicum negotium non recusavisse, cum semper probavissem, tum multo magis probavi lectis tuis proximis litteris; omnes enim causae, quas commemoras, iustissimae sunt tuaque et auctoritate et prudentia dignissimae. Quod aliter cecidisse rem existimas atque opinatus sis, id tibi nullo modo adsentior; sed quia tanta perturbatio et confusio est rerum, ita perculsa et prostrata foedissimo bello iacent omnia, ut is cuique locus, ubi ipse sit, et sibi quisque miserrimus esse videatur, propterea et tui consilii paenitet te et nos, qui domi sumus, tibi beati videmur, at contra nobis non tu quidem vacuus molestiis, sed prae nobis beatus. Atque hoc ipso melior est tua quam nostra condicio, quod tu, quid doleat, scribere audes, nos ne id quidem tuto possumus, nec id victoris vitio, quo nihil moderatius, sed ipsius victoriae, quae civilibus bellis semper est insolens. Uno te vicimus, quod de Marcelli, collegae tui, salute 8

government of Achaia.' Sulpicius, who had taken no part in the civil war, seems to have retired to Asia after the battle of Pharsalus, and there to have received from Caesar a commission to govern Achaia. Cp. Ep. 98, 4. So Süpfle. The details of his appointment are wanting. Hofm. infers from Philipp. XIII. 14, 29 that Sulpicius joined Pompey in Greece, but Mr. King (see his note on that passage) does not think this a necessary inference.

1. Achaicum. A. W. Zumpt, Comment. Epigr. 2. 227-231 has argued with great ingenuity that Achaia or southern Greece was still attached to the province of Macedonia; but Cicero's language is hard to reconcile with this, and would rather imply that Achaia was now a separate province, perhaps constituted in 48 or 47 B.C.

5. Quod aliter . . adsentior, 'as to your opinion that the affair has turned out differently from your expectations, I cannot agree with you at all.' Sulpicius very likely found his position embarrassing. Many Pompeian refugees were in his province, including probably several old friends of his own; and his relations with them and with the triumphant Caesarians must have been awkward. Cicero, however, replies that if Sulpicius is disappointed he is unreasonable, for that he would be no better off in Italy. Wesenb. has 'opinatus esses,' arguing that Sulpicius would have said 'opinatus eram.'

6. Id . . adsentior. This cogn. accus. is not uncommon with such verbs as 'adsentior.' Cp. Madv. 229 a.

Sed quia, foll. The apodosis begins with 'propterea.'

8. Ut . . videatur explains the sentence from 'tanta' to 'omnia,' 'that each one thinks the place he is in most miserable, and himself the most wretched of men.'

10. Non tu quidem: cp. Ep. 26, 7, note.

11. Prae nobis, 'compared with us' at Rome.

Hoc ipso 'this very point' that you *can* complain shews that *your* complaint is unreasonable.

12. Quod. T. has 'quo.'

Nos ne id . . possumus. Cicero very likely thought that the letters of Sulpicius as a public officer, would be less liable to be tampered with than his own—yet he writes freely enough; and Sulpicius was not without apprehensions on this point. Cp. § 1.

14. Ipsius victoriae: cp. Ad Fam. 4. 9. 3 'miserius nihil quam ipsa victoria, quae etiamsi ad meliores venit tamen eos ipsos ferociores impotentioresque reddit.' Cp. also Ep. 89, 2 note.

15. Uno te vicimus, 'in one point we (at Rome) have had an advantage over you.'

Marcelli. Sc. M. Marcelli, cos. 51 B.C. Cp. Epp. 31, 2; 34. 5; 95. He and Sulpicius had been consuls together.

Salute, 'restoration from exile.' Cp. Ep. 29, 10 for the word; and the following sections of this letter for the fact.

paulo ante quam tu cognovimus, etiam mehercule quod, quem ad modum ea res ageretur, vidimus. Nam sic fac existimes: post has miserias, id est post quam armis disceptari coeptum est de iure publico, nihil esse actum aliud cum dignitate; nam et ipse Caesar accusata acerbitate Marcelli—sic enim appellabat—laudataque honorificentissime et aequitate tua et prudentia repente praeter spem dixit, se senatui roganti de Marcello ne hominis quidem causa negaturum. Fecerat autem hoc senatus, ut, cum a L. Pisone mentio esset facta de Marcello et C. Marcellus se ad Caesaris pedes abiecisset, cunctus consurgeret et ad Caesarem supplex accederet. Noli quaerere: ita mihi pulcher hic dies visus

1. **Etiam . . vidimus**, 'yes, and what is more, in witnessing how that affair was brought about.'

2. **Fac existimes**: cp. Madv. 372 b, Obs. 4.

3. **Disceptari.** A legal term, here transferred to war.

4. **Nihil . . aliud cum dignitate**, 'that this is the only dignified proceeding which has taken place.' In contrast, probably, with the general servility of the senate.

Et ipse Caesar, 'even Caesar with his own lips.' Hofm. remarks that there is no corresponding clause, and consequently a slight anacoluthon. We should expect 'et senatus.'

5. **Acerbitate**, 'bitterness'='nimia severitate.' Forcell. For illustrations of Marcellus' hostility to Caesar, compare the passages quoted in a note on p. 436, l. 15.

Sic enim appellabat, 'for that was the word he used.' The phrase expresses surprise. Cp. § 1, note.

6. **Aequitate . . prudentia**, 'your fairness and prudence.' Sulpicius had during his consulship urged strongly the misery of civil war, and pleaded against measures calculated to drive Caesar to despair. Cp. Intr. to Part II, § 17; Ad Fam. 4. 3, 1.

7. **Ne hominis . . negaturum**, 'that he would not make even his personal quarrel with Marcellus a ground for opposing the senate's request.' Matth., Süpfle. Forcell. says that this use of 'homo' for a pronoun (here 'ipse') is 'elegans et frequens usus.' He quotes no other examples from Cicero, but see Ep. 7. 7, note, pp. 81–82, where, however, the word is used without emphasis. Hofm. reads 'ominis.' The original reading of M. seems to be 'neominis.' 'Ominis' would mean 'though this intercession for Marcellus was no good omen for their co-operation.'

8. **Fecerat . . ut . . consurgeret.** On the pleonasm, cp. Ep. 16. 2, note.

A L. Pisone. Piso was consul 58 B.C. Cp. Ep. 48. 1, note. He behaved with much independence in the troubled times between 50 and 43 B.C. Cp. Epp. 48, 1; 117, 5–7; Philipp. 1. 4. 10; 12. 6. 14.

9. **C. Marcellus**: cp. Ep. 95, where M. Marcellus speaks of him as his 'frater.' The consul of 50 B.C. was first cousin; of 49 B.C. brother, to M. Marcellus. Hence we should naturally suppose the latter to be referred to here, with Orell., Onom. But Billerb and Drumann (2. 399, cp. 401) suppose that he died about the time of the battle of Pharsalus. He is certainly reckoned among the dead by Cicero in 43 B.C. (cp. Philipp. 13. 14, 29); and M. Marcellus may have spoken of his cousin as 'frater.' Cp. the use of the word in Post Red. in Sen. 10, 25, and Orelli's comment thereon in his Onomasticon, sub nom. Metellus Celer. The proceedings in the senate seem to have been as follows. L. Piso, probably when some other business was before the senate, had mentioned M. Marcellus; on which the whole senate had entreated Caesar to pardon him, and Caesar had declared that he would not oppose the senate's wishes. Thereon the question seems to have been formally put, whether M. Marcellus should be allowed to return. He had been probably excluded from Italy by a proclamation of Caesar, forbidding all who had served Pompey in Epirus to appear there. Cp. Ad Att. 11. 7. 2.

11. **Noli quaerere**='quid quaeris?' Forcell. On which, cp. Ep. 7. 6, note.

Ita mihi pulcher . . est. Merivale (note on Abeken, p. 336) thinks that Cicero's extravagant expressions of delight are to be accounted for by his now being finally relieved from the fear of proscription.

est, ut speciem aliquam viderer videre quasi reviviscentis rei
publicae. Itaque cum omnes ante me rogati gratias Caesari 4
egissent praeter Volcatium—is enim, si eo loco esset, negavit se
facturum fuisse—, ego rogatus mutavi meum consilium: nam
statueram non mehercule inertia, sed desiderio pristinae dignitatis, in perpetuum tacere. Fregit hoc meum consilium et
Caesaris magnitudo animi et senatus officium; itaque pluribus
verbis egi Caesari gratias, meque metuo ne etiam in ceteris
rebus honesto otio privarim, quod erat unum solacium in malis.
Sed tamen, quoniam effugi eius offensionem, qui fortasse arbitraretur me hanc rem publicam non putare, si perpetuo tacerem,
modice hoc faciam aut etiam intra modum, ut et illius voluntati
et meis studiis serviam. Nam etsi a prima aetate me omnis
ars et doctrina liberalis et maxime philosophia delectavit, tamen
hoc studium quotidie ingravescit, credo et aetatis maturitate ad

2. **Omnes ante me rogati.** On the order of precedence in the senate, cp. Epp. 6, 2; 71, 3, notes. On the present occasion Caesar would be the only consul elect, as he held office alone for the first five months of 45 B.C.; and as he was also consul he would put the question. If his colleague Lepidus was present, the latter may have been asked his opinion early in the debate.

3. **Volcatium.** L. Volcatius Tullus had been consul 66 B.C. During the civil war he remained in Italy and offered no opposition to Caesar. Cp. Epp. 55, 3; 63, 7. He seems to have been on bad terms with Marcellus.

Si eo loco esset, 'if he were in Caesar's place,' Hofm. with whom Mr. Jeans agrees. Süpfle, Müller, Schütz; 'in Marcellus' place' Matth., Orell., ap. Billerb., i.e. 'that if he had done as much as Marcellus to offend Caesar he would not accept pardon.'

4. **Mutavi meum consilium,** 'broke my resolution.' He explains below what it had been.

5. **Non mehercule .. dignitatis,** 'not from inactivity, but from pain at the loss of my former position,' as a leading senator. The ablatives are causal. Cp. Madv. 255.

6. **Fregit hoc meum consilium,** 'was too much for my resolution,' a rare phrase.

7. **Caesaris magnitudo animi.** On the double gen., cp. Ep. 29, 8, note.

Senatus officium, 'the senate's dutifulness' (Süpfle) or 'loyalty' to one of its members.

Pluribus verbis. Perhaps in the Oratio pro Marcello, of which the genuineness has been questioned.

8. **In ceteris rebus,** 'on other occasions.' Wiel.

9. **Honesto otio privarim,** 'have deprived myself of honourable leisure.' For now that he had spoken once, Caesar would expect him to speak often.

10. **Eius offensionem,** 'the displeasure of Caesar,' gen. possess. Cp. In Verr. 1. Act. 12, 35 'in odium offensionemque populi Romani irruere.'

11. **Me hanc rem publicam non putare,** 'that I did not recognise the present system as constitutional.' On the gender of 'hanc,' cp. Madv. 313.

12. **Hoc faciam** = 'shall take part in public affairs.' I cannot think that Süpfle is right in referring these words to tacere: the general drift of the passage seems to me to be 'since I have now escaped Caesar's displeasure I shall not often have to repeat the proceeding by means of which I did so.' A few speeches in the senate would satisfy Caesar.

Intra modum = 'minus quam modice.' Cp. Ad Fam. 9. 26, 4 'epulamur una non modo non contra legem . . sed . . intra legem.' See too A. Gell. N. A. 12. 13, 23-24, quoted by Hofm. on the present passage.

Ut .. serviam, 'so as to consult both his wishes and my own tastes.'

13. **A prima aetate,** 'from the beginning of my youth,' i.e. the 16th or 17th year. Süpfle.

15. **Hoc studium .. ingravescit,** 'this

prudentiam et his temporum vitiis, ut nulla res alia levare
5 animum molestiis possit; a quo studio te abduci negotiis intellego ex tuis litteris, sed tamen aliquid iam noctes te adiuvabunt. Servius tuus vel potius noster summa me observantia colit; cuius ego cum omni probitate summaque virtute, tum studiis doctrinaque delector. Is mecum saepe de tua mansione aut decessione communicat: adhuc in hac sum sententia, nihil ut faciamus nisi quod maxime Caesar velle videatur. Res sunt eius modi, ut, si Romae sis, nihil praeter tuos delectare possit. De reliquis, nihil melius ipso est, ceteri et cetera eius modi, ut, si alterum utrum necesse sit, audire ea malis quam videre. Hoc nostrum consilium nobis minime iucundum est, qui te videre cupimus, sed consulimus tibi. Vale.

taste of mine [(for literature and philosophy)] grows stronger every day.' The verb, which is stronger than 'augetur' or 'crescit' (Süpfle), seems to be more often used in a bad than in a good sense. See instances in Forcell. The metaphor might be preserved by rendering it 'has daily more weight.'

Credo . . vitiis is parenthetical, 'owing I suppose to my age growing ripe for [or 'in respect to'] wisdom, and to these evils of the times,' abl. caus. For prepositions depending on a subst. cp. Madv. 298 a; Ep. 34, 4. Wesenb. has 'iis' for 'his,' referring to what follows.

Maturitate. 'Maturitas' seems rarely to be used, as here, in a metaphorical sense.

Ad = 'quod attinet ad.' Forcell., 'in Bezug auf' Hofm. Cp. Madv. 253, and Obs. where, however, the use of ad with *adjectives* is spoken of.

1. **Ut . . possit** gives the result of 'ingravescit.'

2. **Negotiis**, 'by the duties of your office.'

3. **Aliquid . . adiuvabunt**, 'but the longer nights will soon help you a little.' This letter seems to have been written in what was autumn by the Calendar, summer according to the real season; but it would take some time to reach Sulpicius, and when the latter received it the days may have begun to shorten considerably. I presume that official business ceased at sunset.

4. **Servius tuus.** The son and namesake of Cicero's correspondent. He had supported his father in the prosecution of Murena, and served in Caesar's army during the civil war, but is generally mentioned by Cicero with much regard. Cp. Pro Muren. 26, 54; Ad Att. 9. 19, 2; Philipp. 9. 3, 5.

5. **Omni probitate**, 'thoroughly honourable feeling,' in substance, Hofm.

Studiis: cp. Ep. 56, 1 'studiis ac litteris nostris.'

6. **De tua mansione . . communicat**, 'converses with me about your continued residence in Achaia or departure from it.' 'Decedo' is a technical word for leaving a province. Cp. Ep. 15, 1, note. 'Communicat' is rarely used as here. But cp. Ep. 26, 3.

7. **In hac sum sententia . . ut**: cp. Madv. 374.

Faciamus; it is uncertain whether this refers to Cicero and Sulpicius, or to Cicero alone.

8. **Si Romae sis.** Perhaps this is a general remark, not applying only to Sulpicius, 'if one is at Rome.' Cp. Madv. 370.

9. **Delectare.** Baiter proposes to insert 'te,' but the verb is used absolutely by Seneca, Ep. 39, 6 'ubi turpia non solum delectant, sed etiam placent.' Cp. also Ad Q. F. 2. 15, 1, where the MS. has 'litterae . . incredibiliter delectarunt.'

De reliquis, 'as for the rest.' Cp. nihil praeter tuos above. The 'reliqui' include Caesar, as opposed to the 'ceteri et cetera' just below.

10. **Ceteri et.** T. has 'est Caesare, cetera.'

Si alterum utrum necesse sit, 'if one or the other alternative must be chosen.' 'Necesse' an indecl. adj. Forcell.

11. **Nostrum consilium** seems to mean 'my advice,' that you stay in Greece.

91. To A. CAECINA (AD FAM. VI. 6).

Rome, September or October, (?) 46 B.C. (708 A.U.C.)

1. I have delayed writing to you in the hope that I might congratulate you, and not have to console you. 2. Meanwhile I write to cheer you, by the confident expression of this hope, as you did to me in exile. 3. As your Etruscan augury has not deceived you, my political predictions 4. will be as true henceforth as they have been hitherto. I warned Pompey against his first connection, and also against his final breach, with Caesar, 5. advised him to retire to Spain as a means of averting civil war, 6. and after hostilities had begun, remained neutral as long as I could. 7. Believe, then, my predictions as to the future; 8. I base them partly on Caesar's own character, partly on the usual course of events in civil war. Caesar is very placable; and his admiration for your talents and respect for the wishes of an important district of Italy, will incline him to clemency. 10. I will now speak of the general state of affairs. No one dares to insult men of our party; some of us have been advanced to posts of honour, others pardoned; and 11. the same favour will be shewn to all. 12. If you took up arms in complete confidence of success you do not deserve much credit; if otherwise, you should bear defeat with fortitude. 13. I might console you for your absence by telling you what disorder prevails here. Meanwhile I promise you all the services I can render. I have much influence with Caesar and his friends, and will use it all on your behalf.

M. CICERO S. D. A. CAECINAE.

Vereor ne desideres officium meum, quod tibi pro nostra et 1 meritorum multorum et studiorum parium coniunctione deesse non debet, sed tamen vereor ne litterarum a me officium requiras, quas tibi et iam pridem et saepe misissem, nisi quotidie melius exspectans gratulationem quam confirmationem animi tui com-

A. CAECINAE. Caecina was a knight of Volaterrae, of literary tastes, and easy fortune. He supported Pompey in the civil war, and wrote a bitter attack on Caesar, which so exasperated the latter, that though he granted Caecina his life in the African campaign, he refused him permission to return to Italy; and though Caecina sought to appease him by writing a book in which he extolled his clemency, it is doubtful if Caecina returned to Italy before Caesar's death. Cicero's speech 'Pro A. Caecina' most probably was delivered for his father, but Hofm. thinks that it was for himself. Cp. Ad Fam. 6. 9, 1; Bell. Afric. 89; Orell. Onom. sub nom.

1. Desideres officium meum, 'complain of my failing in the discharge of my duties towards you.'

2. Studiorum parium. Perhaps these words refer to their common interest in 'divinatio.' Cp. § 3. Süpfle, Müller.

3. Sed tamen . . requiras, 'but though this ought to reassure you in general, you may complain of my failing in a correspondent's duties.' 'Requirere' here = 'desiderare.'

4. Quotidie melius exspectans, 'looking daily for better things.' Nagelsb. 12. 71 gives 'melius' a substantive force in this passage, allowing that it is a rare usage.

5. Gratulationem . . maluissem, 'I had preferred to make my letter one of congratulation on your return rather than of encouragement in exile,' i.e. to wait till I could congratulate you.

Confirmationem. 'Confirmatio' = 'actus consolandi.' Forcell.

plecti litteris maluissem. Nunc, ut spero, brevi gratulabimur;
2 itaque in aliud tempus id argumentum epistolae differo. His autem litteris animum tuum, quem minime imbecillum esse et audio et spero, etsi non sapientissimi, at amicissimi hominis auctoritate confirmandum etiam atque etiam puto; nec iis quidem verbis quibus te consoler ut adflictum et iam omni spe salutis orbatum, sed ut eum, de cuius incolumitate non plus dubitem quam te memini dubitare de mea. Nam cum me ex re publica expulissent ii, qui illam cadere posse stante me non putarant, memini me ex multis hospitibus, qui ad me ex Asia, in qua tu eras, venerant, audire te de glorioso et celeri reditu meo con-
3 firmare. Si te ratio quaedam mira Tuscae disciplinae, quam a patre, nobilissimo atque optimo viro, acceperas, non fefellit, ne nos quidem nostra divinatio fallet, quam cum sapientissimorum virorum monumentis atque praeceptis plurimoque, ut tu scis, doctrinae studio, tum magno etiam usu tractandae rei publicae
4 magnaque nostrorum temporum varietate consecuti sumus; cui quidem divinationi hoc plus confidimus, quod ea nos nihil in his

1. Nunc . . etiam puto. 'As things stand'—i.e. 'as I think further silence might be misconstrued'—though I have not given up the hope of your speedy return, I do not like to wait any longer.

2. Argumentum, 'subject.' Cp. Ad Att. 10. 13, 2 'argumentum epistolae.'

4. Hominis, i.e. Cicero's own.

5. Nec iis quidem verbis . . sed ut eum, 'not in words of consolation as to one in a desperate position, but as to one,' foll. The negative would perhaps be more naturally attached to adflictum, unless another verb is to be supplied from consoler, e.g. 'horter.' The general sense is plain enough.

7. Incolumitate. This word seems to have been specially applied to the retention or recovery of political privileges. Cp. Ep. 80, 2 'mihi incolumi.'

8. Dubitare. The present infinitive is not uncommon after 'memini,' even when past time is referred to. Madv. 408 b, Obs. 2, says that it is generally used of things coming within our personal experience. In English we might say with equal propriety, 'I remember your doubting' ('te dubitare'), and 'I remember that you doubted' ('te dubitavisse').

9. Ii. The triumvirs and Clodius. Cp. Intr. to Part I, § 20.

10. Hospitibus. Probably residents in Asia who were connected with Cicero by ties of hospitality, and visited him at Thessalonica or Dyrrhachium on their way to Rome.

In qua tu eras. Caecina was probably looking after his money affairs there. Cp. Ad Fam. 6. 8, 2.

11. Audire: cp. 'dubitare' above.

Confirmare, 'to speak positively about.' Cp. Ad Fam. 3. 10, 1 'de me tibi sic . . promitto atque confirmo.'

12. Ratio, 'theory' or 'system.' Süpfle.

Tuscae disciplinae. Etruria was the district from which 'haruspices' were summoned to interpret the meaning of any strange portents which occurred at Rome. Cp. de Divin. 1. 2, 3; In Cat. 3. 8, 19.

14. Quam . . consecuti sumus. Cicero means that his power of prediction depended partly on his study of the works of philosophers, partly on his political experience.

15. Monumentis atque praeceptis, 'writings and [oral, Hofm.] teaching.' So the MS. The words are again coupled together, De Off. 3. 33, 121. Baiter has 'monitis.'

16. Doctrinae, 'philosophy.' Cp. Nägelsb. 2. 19.

17. Nostrorum temporum, 'of my fortunes.' 'Negotia,' 'eventus' are among the synonyms given by Forcell. Cp. Ad Fam. 13. 29, 2 'varietates meorum temporum.'

18. Quod ea nos . . fefellit: cp. Corn.

tam obscuris rebus tamque perturbatis umquam omnino fefellit.
Dicerem, quae ante futura dixissem, ni vererer ne ex eventis
fingere viderer; sed tamen plurimi sunt testes me et initio, ne
coniungeret se cum Caesare, monuisse Pompeium, et postea,
ne se *di*iungeret: coniunctione frangi senatus opes, diiunctione
civile bellum excitari videbam. Atque utebar familiarissime
Caesare, Pompeium faciebam plurimi; sed erat meum consilium
cum fidele Pompeio, tum salutare utrique. Quae praeterea pro- 5
viderim, praetereo; nolo enim hunc de me optime meritum
existimare ea me suasisse Pompeio, quibus ille si paruisset, esset
hic quidem clarus in toga et princeps, sed tantas opes, quantas
nunc habet, non haberet: eundum in Hispaniam censui; quod si
fecisset, civile bellum nullum omnino fuisset. Rationem haberi
absentis non tam pugnavi ut liceret, quam ut, quoniam ipso consule pugnante populus iusserat, haberetur. Causa orta belli est:
quid ego praetermisi aut monitorum aut querelarum! cum vel
iniquissimam pacem iustissimo bello anteferrem. Victa est 6
auctoritas mea, non tam a Pompeio—nam is movebatur—quam

Nep. Att. 16 'non enim Cicero ea solum quae vivo se acciderunt futura praedixit sed etiam quae nunc usu veniunt cecinit ut vates.'

2. Dicerem .. viderer, 'I would say what I had predicted, were I not afraid of seeming to invent from the result.'

3. Initio, i.e. in 59 B.C. Cicero makes a similar boast Philipp. 2. 10, 23. But he does not refer to any such warning in his letters of that date in Ad Att. 2. On the ablat. 'initio,' cp. Epp. 8, 11; 12, 3, pp. 61; 82, notes. It marks a date.

4. Et postea. Perhaps at the end of 50 B.C. Cp. Philipp. 2. 10, 24 'atque illa vox est nota multis "utinam Cn. Pompei cum C. Caesare societatem aut numquam coisses aut numquam diremisses!"'

6. Utebar .. plurimi. Cicero distinguishes his personal liking for Caesar from the respect he felt or affected for Pompey on more public grounds. He does not therefore think it needful to defend himself from a charge of *disloyalty* to Caesar in the following passage sed erat .. utrique, but merely says that his advice, if followed, would have done him no injury.

8. Quae praeterea providerim, 'the other instances of foresight which I displayed.' 'Provideo' = 'ante video.' Forcell. Cicero refers to his anxiety at the beginning of the war that concessions should be made to Caesar.

9. Hunc .. meritum, i.e. 'Caesar, to whom I owe so much.'

10. Esset hic quidem .. non haberet. Cicero thought that if Caesar had been elected consul for 48 B.C., and had resigned his provinces, the commonwealth might have been saved. Cp. Ep. 45. 2-3.

12. Eundum in Hispaniam censui, sc. 'a Pompeio.' Cp. Intr. to Part III. §§ 1; 4; Ep. 52, 3. But in Epp. 45, 3; 31, 3; also Ad Fam. 3. 8, 10, Cicero seems not to have looked forward to such a proceeding on Pompey's part with pleasure. Hofm. remarks that Cicero was not present at the debates of the senate immediately before the civil war began, and that therefore if the word 'censui' implies a formal vote it must refer to deliberations about peace after the war had begun.

13. Rationem haberi absentis: cp. Ep. 34, 9, note; also Appendix 6, § 3.

14. Ipso consule, sc. Pompeio tertium consule. Cp. Intr. to Part II, § 14.

16. Cum vel iniquissimam .. anteferrem: cp. Ad Fam. 5. 21, 2 'quavis tota condicione pacem accipere malui quam viribus cum valentiore pugnare.' 'Iniquissimam,' 'on the most unfair terms.'

ab iis, qui duce Pompeio freti peropportunam et rebus domesticis
et cupiditatibus suis illius belli victoriam fore putabant. Susceptum bellum est quiescente me, depulsum ex Italia manente
me, quoad potui; sed valuit apud me plus pudor meus quam
timor; veritus sum deesse Pompeii saluti, cum ille aliquando non
defuisset meae. Itaque vel officio vel fama bonorum vel pudore
victus, ut in fabulis Amphiaraus, sic ego prudens et sciens
'ad pestem ante oculos positam' sum profectus; quo in bello
7 nihil adversi accidit non praedicente me. Qua re quoniam, ut
augures et astrologi solent, ego quoque augur publicus ex meis
superioribus praedictis constitui apud te auctoritatem augurii et
divinationis meae, debebit habere fidem nostra praedictio. Non
igitur ex alitis involatu nec e cantu sinistro oscinis, ut in nostra
disciplina est, nec ex tripudiis solistimis aut soniviis tibi auguror,
sed habeo alia signa, quae observem; quae etsi non sunt certiora
8 illis, minus tamen habent vel obscuritatis vel erroris. Notantur

1. **Peropportunam . . . putabant.** Cicero has made this complaint before. Cp. Ad Att. 9. 11. 4 'quid Faustum quid Libonem praetermittunturum sceleris putes? quorum creditores convenire dicuntur;' also Epp. 88. 2; and Caes. Bell. Civ. 1. 4.

3. **Quiescente me.** This is true, but inconsistent with what Cicero wrote to Pompey at the time. Cp. Intr. to Part III, § 4; also Ad Att. 8. 11 B and D.

Depulsum ex Italia. By the embarkation of Pompey for Epirus.

4. **Quoad potui.** 'Quoad sermones bonorum me reprehendentium sustinere potui.' Manut. Cicero was under no compulsion. The next sentence reveals the real state of the case.

Pudor: cp. Ep. 88, 1.

5. **Aliquando**, 'on a former occasion,' i.e. in 57 B.C.

6. **Officio**, 'by gratitude.'

Fama bonorum, 'by the talk of the well-affected,' i.e. of the optimates. Cp. Ep. 39, 1.

In fabulis, 'in the plays.' The hard fate of Amphiaraus in being involved in the ruin of his wicked allies, which his prophetic gift enabled him to foresee, is dwelt on by Aesch. Sept. c. Theb. 594 foll. The words **ad pestem . . positam** seem to be a quotation from a tragedy. Süpfle suggests from the Eriphyle of Accius. But Ribbeck, Trag. Lat. Rel. p. 236 places it among the Incert. Fabul. 145.

9. **Non praedicente me**, 'which I did not predict.'

10. **Solent, sc.** 'ex superioribus praedictis constituere auctoritatem,' to obtain credence for their present predictions by appeals to the fulfilment of others.'

Augur publicus, 'a political prophet,' or perhaps 'a prophet invested with public authority.' Süpfle. The latter rendering suits the general meaning of 'publicus' best; but Cicero says just below that he is *not* basing his predictions on the rules of the augural system.

13. **Alitis . . oscinis.** The first term was applied to birds which gave omens by their flight, the last to those whose notes were thought significant. Forcell.

Involatu, an augural term, apparently only found here.

In nostra disciplina, 'in the system of us Roman augurs.'

14. **Tripudiis solistimis.** 'Tripudium solistimum' was the term used when the sacred fowls ate so eagerly that the food fell from their mouths. Cp. Pliny, H. N. 10. 21; Livy 10. 40; Cic. de Divin. 2. 34. 72. If the food made a noise as it fell on the ground, the term **sonivium** was used with 'tripudium.' Pliny, H. N. 15. 22.

16. **Illis**, 'than those of the augural system,' which Cicero as an augur would not openly disparage. Perhaps, too, his correspondent was superstitious.

Notantur autem . . via, 'I have two

autem mihi ad divinandum signa duplici quadam via, quarum alteram duco e Caesare ipso, alteram e temporum civilium natura atque ratione. In Caesare haec sunt: mitis clemensque natura, qualis exprimitur praeclaro illo libro Querelarum tuarum; accedit quod mirifice ingeniis excellentibus, quale est tuum, delectatur; praeterea cedit multorum iustis et officio incensis, non inanibus aut ambitiosis, voluntatibus, in quo vehementer eum consentiens
Etruria movebit. 'Cur haec igitur adhuc parum profecerunt?' 9
Quia non putat se sustinere causas posse multorum, si tibi, cui iustius videtur irasci posse, concesserit. 'Quae est igitur' inquies 'spes ab irato?' Eodem *e* fonte se hausturum intellegit laudes suas, e quo sit leviter aspersus. Postremo homo valde est acutus et multum providens; intellegit te, hominem in parte Italiae minime contemnenda facile omnium nobilissimum et in communi re publica cuivis summorum tuae aetatis vel ingenio vel gratia vel fama populi Romani parem, non posse prohiberi re publica

ways for ascertaining tokens which may guide me in prediction.' Cicero goes on to say that he was guided by a consideration, first of Caesar's character, secondly of the position of public affairs.

2. **Temporum . . ratione**, 'the nature and character of our political relations at this time.' Wiel.

3. **In Caesare haec sunt.** Cicero had good hopes of success from considering (1) Caesar's natural clemency, (2) his admiration of talents like Caecina's, (3) his accessibility to reasonable requests, such as Etruria would prefer on behalf of Caecina.

4. **Exprimitur**: cp. Ep. 56, 1.

Querelarum: see the introductory remarks on this letter. Billerb. thinks it was an elegiac poem like Ovid's Tristia.

5. **Ingeniis excellentibus**, 'minds of high order.' 'Dicitur interdum [ingenium] de ipsis hominibus ingeniosis.' Forcell. Cp. Ad Fam. 4. 8, 2 'is qui omnia tenet favet ingeniis;' and, for the fact, the account of Caesar's visit to Cicero in Ep. 104, 2.

6. **Cedit multorum . . voluntatibus**, 'he yields to the combined wishes of many if they be well founded and inspired by regard, not groundless or interested.'

7. **Ambitiosis** probably means 'influenced by a desire to make friends,' or 'by party spirit.' Cp. Ad Fam. 6. 12, 2 'valent apud Caesarem non tam ambitiosae . . rogationes quam necessariae.'

Consentiens Etruria, 'the unanimous intercession of Etruria.' Caecina, as has been already mentioned, was of Etruscan birth.

8. **Cur haec igitur . . profecerunt?** Caecina is supposed to ask.

9. **Non putat . . concesserit**, 'he thinks that there are many others whose pleas he cannot resist if he makes a concession to you.' On this sense of 'sustinere,' cp. Philipp. 8. 1, 2 'parum mihi visus es eos quibus cedere non soles sustinere.'

10. **Iustius**, i.e. because of Caecina's bitter attack upon him.

11. **Eodem e fonte**, 'from the same pen.' Süpfle. Perhaps the preposition is not required. Cp. Madv. 254.

12. **Leviter aspersus** 'slightly splashed.' These words keep up the metaphor of 'eodem fonte,' but 'aspergere' is more generally followed in the passive by an ablative—e.g. 'infamia,'—in the active by an ablat. 'rei,' and acc. pers., or by an acc. 'rei,' and dat. 'personae.' Cp. Madv. 259 b.

13. **In parte Italiae**, sc. Etruria.

14. **In communi re publica**, 'in the commonwealth to which all belong,' opposed to 'in parte Italiae.' In Etruria, Cicero says, Caecina had no equal; in the state in general, no superior among his contemporaries. This seems the language of exaggeration as far as our knowledge goes.

16. **Prohiberi re publica**, 'to be excluded from political life;' elsewhere (Philipp. 13. 15, 31) 'a re publica removere' means 'to suspend from office.'

diutius; nolet hoc temporis potius esse aliquando beneficium quam
10 iam suum. Dixi de Caesare; nunc dicam de temporum rerumque
natura: nemo est tam inimicus ei causae, quam Pompeius animatus melius quam paratus susceperat, qui nos malos cives dicere
aut homines improbos audeat. In quo admirari soleo gravitatem
et iustitiam et sapientiam Caesaris; numquam nisi honorificentissime Pompeium appellat. 'At in eius persona multa fecit
asperius.' Armorum ista et victoriae sunt facta, non Caesaris.
At nos quem ad modum est complexus! Cassium sibi legavit;
Brutum Galliae praefecit, Sulpicium Graeciae; Marcellum, cui
11 maxime succensebat, cum summa illius dignitate restituit. Quo
igitur haec spectant? Rerum hoc natura et civilium temporum non
patietur, nec manens nec mutata ratio feret primum, ut non in

1. **Nolet hoc .. iam suum**, 'he will be unwilling by delay ('aliquando') to make your restoration seem a gift of time, but will make it his own by prompt concession,' i.e. Caesar would not wish to seem to have pardoned Caecina through weariness or forgetfulness.

2. **Dixi de Caesare**, 'so much for Caesar.' Cp. the beginning of § 8.

Nunc dicam, foll., 'I will now speak of the nature of the times and circumstances.' Cp. the preceding page, lines 2, 3 'alteram .. ratione.'

3. **Animatus melius quam paratus**, 'with a spirit above his resources.'

4. **Nos**, 'us Pompeians.' Cp. the end of this section.

7. **At in eius persona**, foll. On 'at' in this sense, cp. Ep. 87, 2; 63, 3, note. For 'in' with the abl. of persons, cp. De Amic. 12, 41 'amici et propinqui quid in P. Scipione effecerint.' It is used in almost the same sense Ep. 81, 3. Cp. also Madv. 230 b, Obs. 1.

Persona. This word usually means a part, or character. Cp. Pro Cluent. 29, 78 'Staieni persona .. ab nulla turpi suspicione abhorrebat;' and Prof. Ramsay's note. 'Ipse homo quatenus hanc vel illam personam gerit.' Forcell. We may perhaps translate 'against Pompey as a public man' with Süpfle.

8. **Armorum .. Caesaris**: cp. Ep. 90, 2, ad fin.

9. **Cassium sibi legavit**, 'he has made [C.] Cassius his legate.' Cp. Ep. 83, 3, notes.

10. **Brutum Galliae**. M. Brutus seems to have been entrusted with the government of Cisalpine Gaul by Caesar about the end of 47 B.C., and to have held it till 45 B.C. Compare with this letter Ad Fam. 13. 10, 11 Ad Att. 12. 27, 3; App. Bell. Civ. 2. 111.

Sulpicium, cp. Ep. 90, 2, notes.

Marcellum: cp. Ep. 90, 3 and 4.

11. **Cum summa illius dignitate**, 'under circumstances most honourable for Marcellus.' Caesar had shewn great delicacy in arranging that the recall of Marcellus should be the act of the whole senate.

Quo igitur haec spectant? Caecina is supposed to ask 'what is the import of all this?' Cicero replies, 'The nature of things in general, and of politics especially, forbids our believing—first, that members of the same party will not be treated alike—next, that honest men will be forbidden to return to a state to which so many criminals have been restored.' The reference in the last words is to a law passed in 49 or 48 B.C., on the proposal of the praetors and tribunes, restoring to their country several exiles who had been convicted under the Lex Pompeia de Ambitu in 52 B.C. Cp. Caes. Bell. Civ. 3. 1; Dion Cassius 41. 36. Several had also been recalled in 49 B.C. by Antony. Cp. Philipp. 2. 23, 56.

12. **Hoc**, explained by **primum ut .. reverterunt**. On this use of the conjunct. mood (ut .. sit) explaining a pronoun, cp. Madv. 374.

Temporum, as often, 'circumstances.'

13. **Nec manens . . . ratio**, 'nor will things, whether they remain as they are, or whether they change, allow.'

Ut non: cp. Madv. 372 b; 456 Obs. 3.

causa pari eadem sit et condicio et fortuna omnium; deinde, ut
in eam civitatem boni viri et boni cives nulla ignominia notati
non revertantur, in quam tot nefariorum scelerum condemnati
reverterunt. Habes augurium meum, quo, si quid addubitarem, 12
non potius uterer quam illa consolatione, qua facile fortem virum
sustentarem; te, si explorata victoria arma sumpsisses pro re
publica—ita enim tum putabas—, non nimis esse laudandum;
sin propter incertos exitus eventusque bellorum posse accidere,
ut vinceremur, putasses, non debere te ad secundam fortunam
bene paratum fuisse, adversam ferre nullo modo posse. Disputarem etiam, quanto solacio tibi conscientia tui facti, quantae
delectationi in rebus adversis litterae esse deberent; commemo-
rarem non solum veterum, sed horum etiam recentium vel ducum
vel comitum tuorum gravissimos casus; etiam externos multos
claros viros nominarem; levat enim dolorem communis quasi
legis et humanae condicionis recordatio. Exponerem etiam, 13
quem ad modum hic et quanta in turba quantaque in confu-
sione rerum omnium viveremus; necesse est enim minore desiderio perdita re publica carere quam bona. Sed hoc genere nihil

4. **Addubitarem**, not quite so strong as the simple verb (Forcell.), 'were inclined to doubt.'

5. **Illa consolatione**, 'the following consoling topics.'

6. **Explorata victoria**, 'with full assurance of victory.'

Sumpsisses . . . putasses . . . laudandum. We should have expected either 'sumpseris,' 'putaris' or 'fuisse.' Cp., however, Madv. 382, Obs. 2.

7. **Ita enim tum putabas**, 'for such was then your opinion.' I think these words merely refer to 'pro re publica,' 'you thought you were fighting for the constitution,'—perhaps Cicero did not wish to commit himself to a statement that Caesar was fighting against it, and so made the sentiment one entertained by Caecina in part time. Billerb. and Wiel. suppose the words to refer to 'explorata victoria.' But Cicero says that to have armed with full assurance of victory would have had nothing very creditable in it, and he would hardly be so discourteous as to say for certain that Caecina had done so, but offers him an alternative, 'If you were quite sure of victory you did nothing peculiarly creditable; if you thought defeat possible why do you repine at it?'

10. **Adversam ferre**, foll. 'Autem' or some such word might be supplied with 'adversam.' Cp Ep 6, 2, note.

12. **Litterae**, '*your learning*.'

13. **Veterum**, e.g. in early Roman history Coriolanus, Camillus, Q. Metellus Numidicus, C. Marius.

Vel ducum vel comitum tuorum, '*your own generals and comrades*.' Cp. Ep. 87, 2.

14. **Externos**, 'in foreign states,' opposed to the Romans just referred to.

15. **Claros viros.** To be taken as one notion—otherwise a conjunction would be needed to couple **multos** and 'claros.' Süpfle. Cp. Madv. 300 c, Obs. 5. Aristides, Themistocles, Cimon, and Alcibiades would be among the foreign worthies referred to.

Communis . . recordatio, 'the recollection of the law to which all are subject, and of the lot of mankind.'

18. **Viveremus.** On the tense, cp. Ep. 15, 8, note.

19. **Perdita**, explained by what has gone before, 'disorganised,' 'disordered.'

Hoc genere, 'this topic,' 'this kind of consolation.' Cicero hoped soon to welcome Caecina to Rome, and therefore thought it needless to say how little there was to regret in absence from the capital.

opus est: incolumem te cito, ut spero, vel potius, ut perspicio, videbimus. Interea tibi absenti et huic, qui adest, imagini animi et corporis tui, constantissimo atque optimo filio tuo, studium, officium, operam, laborem meum iam pridem et pollicitus sum et detuli; nunc hoc amplius, quod me amicissime quotidie magis Caesar amplectitur, familiares quidem eius, sicuti neminem. Apud quem quicquid valebo vel auctoritate vel gratia, valebo tibi: tu cura ut cum firmitudine te animi, tum etiam spe optima sustentes.

92. A. CAECINA TO CICERO (AD FAM. VI. 7).

SICILY, END OF 46 B.C. (BAIT.) (708 A.U.C.)

1. I am sorry you have not yet received my book, but my son was afraid that its publication might do harm, as I am already suffering for a literary offence. 2. Why should I be selected for Caesar's especial hostility? 3. The difficulties of composition under my present circumstances must account for the faults of my work. 4. I am especially alarmed when I consider how Caesar may regard each expression. You, in your 'Orator,' divide your responsibility with Brutus. Caution is still more needful for me. I hope you will correct my book thoroughly. 5. I have given up my journey to Asia, as you recommended. I hope you will act for me on your own judgment; my son has hardly experience enough to be taken into council with you. 6. To conclude, I hope you will do all you can for me. Do not let my book get into circulation unless so amended as not to injure me.

CAECINA CICERONI PLUR. SAL.

1 Quod tibi non tam celeriter liber est redditus, ignosce timori nostro et miserere temporis. Filius, ut audio, pertimuit, neque

1. **Vel potius ut perspicio**, 'or rather as I see for certain.' Cp. Ep. 36. 3, where a similar contrast appears.

3. **Filio.** This son is perhaps mentioned Ep. 121, 2, as on intimate terms with Octavian.

4. **Pollicitus sum et detuli**, 'I have promised and placed at his disposal.'

5. **Nunc hoc amplius**, foll., 'I now place also at your service my remarkable influence with Caesar.' 'Hoc amplius' = 'praeterea.' Forcell.

6. **Familiares**, sc. 'amplectuntur.' Cp. Ad Fam. 9. 16, 2 'sic enim colo, sic observor ab omnibus iis, qui a Caesare diliguntur, ut ab iis me amari putem.' Cicero refers especially to Hirtius and Dolabella.

Sicuti neminem, 'more than any one else.'

7. **Apud quem . . valebo tibi**, 'and all my influence with him shall be employed on your behalf.' On the dat., cp. Ep. 34, 5, note; Madv. 241. T. has 'conciliabo tibi.'

10. **Liber.** A continuation, perhaps, of the 'Querelae' referred to in the previous letter, § 8.

Redditus, merely 'sent,' 'delivered,' the 're-' implying that it was due. Cp. Ad Fam. 2. 17. 1 'litteras a te mihi stator tuus reddidit Tarsi.'

Timori. Explained by what follows. Though the book was written to pacify Caesar, Caecina did not feel sure how it might be received.

11. **Temporis**, 'my unfortunate position' (cp. Ep. 26, 2, note), which deserved pity and not blame.

iniuria, si liber exisset, quoniam non tam interest, quo animo
scribatur, quam quo accipiatur, ne ea res inepte mihi noceret,
cum praesertim adhuc stili poenas dem. Qua quidem in re
singulari sum fato; nam cum mendum scripturae litura tollatur,
stultitia fama multetur, meus error exsilio corrigitur, cuius summa
criminis est, quod armatus adversario male dixi. Nemo nostrum 2
est, ut opinor, quin vota Victoriae suae fecerit; nemo, quin etiam
cum de alia re immolaret, tamen eo quidem ipso tempore, ut
quam primum Caesar superaretur, optarit: hoc si non cogitat,
omnibus rebus felix est; si scit et persuasus est, quid irascitur
ei, qui aliquid scripsit contra suam voluntatem, cum ignorit
omnibus, qui multa deos venerati sunt contra eius salutem? Sed 3
ut eodem revertar, causa haec fuit timoris: scripsi de te parce
medius fidius et timide, non revocans me ipse, sed paene refugiens. Genus autem hoc scripturae non modo liberum, sed

1. Exisset, 'should be published.' Cp. Pro Rosc. Am. 1, 3 'nequaquam . . oratio mea exire atque in vulgus emanare poterit.'

Quoniam . . accipiatur, a parenthesis containing a general remark in which, therefore, the sequence of tenses is suspended.

2. Ne. On the order of the words, cp. Madv. 465 b, Obs. The passage of Sallust there quoted, however, stands differently in the most recent editions.

Ea res = 'id,' 'its publication.' Cp. Ep. 21, 3, note.

Inepte, 'through my own folly.' Wesenb. suggests 'inpensae' or [inepte].

3. Cum praesertim, 'all the more as.' Billerb.

Adhuc . . poenas dem, 'I am still suffering for my writings.'

4. Cum mendum . . multetur, 'while a clerical error is removed by a stroke of the pen, and a writer's folly punished by loss of reputation.' Wiel. 'Mendum' = 'error qui scribendo fit.' Forcell. Fama is difficult. Wiel. renders 'fama durch den bösen Ruf,' 'by the discredit,' in which case it would be ablat. instr. But may it not mean, 'in respect of reputation?' Cp. Madv. 253.

5. Cuius summa criminis. On the double gen., cp. Ep. 29, 8, note.

6. Quod armatus . . male dixi, 'that I abused an adversary against whom I was actually in arms.' Caecina thinks it hard that he should be punished so severely for *writing* against Caesar, who had pardoned others, and was ready to pardon him, for *fighting* against him.

Nostrum, 'of us Pompeians.'

7. Victoriae suae = 'deae et sibi propitiae futurae,' 'to Victory with prayers that she would aid him.' Schütz.

8. Immolaret. 'Immolare' means literally, 'to sprinkle with meal before sacrifice;' hence, 'to sacrifice.' It is usually followed by an accusative.

9. Hoc si non cogitat . . felix est, 'if he is unconscious of this, he is indeed happy in his ignorance.'

10. Persuasus est, almost a solecism, at least in prose. Cp. Madv. 244 b, Obs. 4. But Caecina is the writer, not Cicero.

Quid irascitur . . salutem? 'why is he angry with one who has written what may displease him, when he has pardoned all who offered prayers for his ruin?' The use of suam and eius in parallel clauses is strange. Cp. Madv. 490, c, Obs. 3.

12. Sed ut eodem revertar, 'this then, to return, was the cause of my fears,' mentioned in the second line of the letter.

13. Scripsi de te, i.e. in his book of Querelae. See Billerb.

14. Non revocans . . refugiens, 'not merely with reserve, but almost afraid of my own thoughts.' Wiel. 'Revocare se' = 'sibi temperare.' Forcell. 'Non revocavi me sponte sed refugi metu.' Manut.

15. Genus . . hoc scripturae, i.e. 'panegyric.' 'Scriptura' = 'composition.' Smith's Lat. Dict.

incitatum atque elatum esse debere quis ignorat? solutum existimatur esse alteri male dicere—tamen cavendum est, ne in petulantiam incidas—; impeditum, se ipsum laudare, ne vitium adrogantiae subsequatur; solum vero liberum, alterum laudare, de quo quicquid detrahas, necesse est aut infirmitati aut invidiae adsignetur. Ac nescio an tibi gratius opportuniusque acciderit; nam quod praeclare facere non poteram, primum erat, non attingere; secundum [beneficium], quam parcissime facere. Sed tamen ego quidem me sustinui; multa minui, multa sustuli, complura ne posui quidem. Quem ad modum igitur, scalarum gradus si alios tollas, alios incidas, non nullos male haerentes relinquas, ruinae periculum struas, non ascensum pares, sic tot malis tum vinctum tum fractum studium scribendi quid dignum
4 auribus aut probabile potest adferre? Cum vero ad ipsius Caesaris nomen veni, toto corpore contremesco, non poenae metu, sed illius iudicii: totum enim Caesarem non novi. Quem putas animum esse, ubi secum loquitur? 'Hoc probabit: hoc verbum suspitiosum est.' 'Quid, si hoc muto? at vereor, ne peius sit.'

1. **Incitatum atque elatum**, 'spirited and lofty.'

Solutum existimatur . . incidas, 'satire, too, is held to have licence allowed it, yet care must be taken lest it degenerate into scurrility,' and so it is less free than panegyric. Caecina seems to distinguish 'solutum' from **liberum**.

3. **Impeditum**, 'difficult.'

5. **Infirmitati aut invidiae**, 'to want of talent (Wiel.) or to jealousy.' 'Infirmitas animi' occ. Pro Rosc. Am. 4. 10, but not quite in this sense.

6. **Nescio an . . acciderit**, 'perhaps you will be the better pleased that I have said so little about you.'

7. **Primum erat**, foll., 'my best course was not to mention you at all.' On the mood of **erat**, cp. Madv. 348 e, Obs. 1; on the fact, cp. 'scripsi de te,' above.

8. **Secundum**, 'the next best thing I could do for you.'

Facere, used for 'attingere,' to avoid tautology, 'to do so.'

9. **Ego . . me sustinui**, 'I put a restraint upon myself,' 'resisted my natural impulse to speak freely in your honour.' 'Sustinere' = 'cohibere.' Forcell.

Multa, 'much of what I might have said in your honour.'

Minui . . sustuli, i.e. in revising the work, 'lowered the tone of, and removed.'

10. **Ne posui quidem**, 'I never set down at all.'

11. **Tollas . . pares**. On the tenses, cp. Ep. 8, 3, note.

12. **Ruinae**, 'of a fall' of the staircase? or of one who would mount it (Wiel.)?

Tot malis . . scribendi, 'a literary taste, or power, fettered and impaired by so many disasters.'

14. **Probabile**, 'deserving approbation.' Forcell.

Cum vero . . contremesco, 'when' in the course of my writing 'I have come to Caesar's name, I tremble.' On 'veni,' cp. Madv. 358.

16. **Illius iudicii**, 'of Caesar's judgment' on my work. Billerb.

Totum enim . . novi, 'for I am not thoroughly acquainted with Caesar.' Caecina here refers to Caesar's literary gifts and tastes. On 'totum' = 'omnino,' cp. pp. 174, note on l. 15; 315, note on l. 18; Madv. 300 c.

Quem putas . . loquitur? 'how do you suppose one's heart feels when it argues as follows with itself?'

17. **Hoc probabit**, sc. 'Caesar.' A thought supposed to occur to Caecina as he reads his work over to himself.

18. **At vereor, ne peius sit**, 'but I fear the change may make matters worse.'

'Age vero, laudo aliquem: num offendo? cum porro offendam, quid, si non volt?' 'Armati stilum persequitur: victi et nondum restituti quid faciet?' Auges etiam tu mihi timorem, qui in Oratore tuo caves tibi per Brutum et ad excusationem socium quaeris: ubi hoc omnium patronus facit, quid me, veterem tuum, nunc omnium clientem sentire oportet? In hac igitur calumnia timoris et caecae suspitionis tormento, cum plurima ad alieni sensus coniecturam, non ad suum iudicium scribantur, quam difficile et evadere, si minus expertus es, quod te ad omnia summum atque excellens ingenium armavit, nos sentimus. Sed tamen ego filio dixeram, librum tibi legeret et auferret, aut ea condicione daret, si reciperes te correcturum, hoc est, si totum

1. **Age vero, laudo aliquem**, 'or again, suppose that I praise some one.' Wiel.

Aliquem, e.g. Cato.

Num offendo, sc. Caesarem. Wesenb. has 'non,' thinking that even Caecina would hardly use 'num' here.

Cum porro . . non volt? 'I hope not, but if I do offend him what will happen? What if he does not wish the man to be praised whom I praise?' Orell. ap. Billerb. On **quid si**, cp. Madv. 479 d, Obs. 1. Wiel. renders 'cum . . offendam,' 'suppose I attack anybody.' But surely 'offendam' has the same sense in both clauses. Wesenb. has † offendam, and suspects that 'reprendam' was the original reading.

2. **Armati stilum persequitur**: cp. the end of § 1.

Victi . . quid faciet, sc. 'stilo.' Cp. Madv. 241, Obs. 5; 267, Obs.

3. **In Oratore tuo . . Brutum**, 'who, in your work called Orator, provide for your own safety by throwing responsibility on Brutus.' Cp. Orat. 10, 35 'hoc sum adgressus statim Catone absoluto, quem ipsum numquam attigissem tempora timens inimica virtuti nisi tibi hortanti et illius memoriam mihi caram excitanti non parere nefas esse duxissem.' This also explains 'ad excusationem socium quaeris.' The favour which Brutus enjoyed with Caesar would make the latter look with indulgence on any step taken at Brutus' suggestion.

5. **Ubi hoc omnium . . oportet**, 'when you, everybody's advocate, deem such precautions necessary, what ought I to feel who was once your client, and now need everybody's advocacy?' These words are thought by some to identify the writer of this letter with the Caecina for whom Cicero delivered a long speech still extant; but perhaps they have no such precise meaning, and merely refer to general services rendered by Cicero to Caecina. The passage explains the words 'auges etiam tu mihi timorem' just above.

6. **Calumnia timoris** = 'vanus metus.' Forcell.

7. **Ad alieni sensus**, foll., 'according to what one can guess of another's feelings,' i.e. Caesar's. Cp. Ep. 40, 1 'ad meum sensum.'

8. **Suum iudicium**, 'one's own judgment.' 'Suus' used sometimes even by the writer of himself. Cp. Madv. 490 c, Obs. 5; Nägelsb. 91, 250.

9. **Evadere**, 'to get out of the difficulty.'

Expertus es. We might expect 'tu' to be inserted. Cp. Madv. 482.

Ad omnia. On the force of the preposition, cp. Ep. 87, 2, note.

10. **Sed tamen**, — 'but notwithstanding the necessary imperfections of my book.'

11. **Dixeram**, 'I told my son.' Epistolary tense. Cp. Ep. 1, 1, note.

Auferret, 'to take it away again.' On the omission of 'ut,' cp. Ep. 31, 6, note.

Ea condicione . . reciperes, 'give it you only on condition of your undertaking,' etc. On this limiting force of the pronoun, cp. Pro Arch. 10, 25 'ea condicione ne quid postea scriberet;' Nägelsb. 84, 230. 'Ea condicione ut' = 'ita ut,' on which, cp. Ep. 9, 6, note, pp. 68, 69.

12. **Reciperes**, 'undertake.' Cp. Ep. 52, 6, note.

Si totum alium faceres. On the double accus., cp. Madv. 227 a; on 'totum,' a note above on this section; on 'alium' in this sense, cp. Ep. 47, 4, note.

5 alium facceres. De Asiatico itinere, quamquam summa *me* necessitas premebat, ut imperasti, feci. Te pro me quid horter? vides tempus venisse, quo necesse sit de nobis constitui. Nihil est, mi Cicero, quod filium meum exspectes: adulescens est; omnia excogitare vel studio vel aetate vel metu non potest. Totum negotium tu sustineas oportet; in te mihi omnis spes est. Tu pro tua prudentia, quibus rebus gaudeat, quibus capiatur Caesar, tenes; a te omnia proficiscantur et per te ad exitum perducantur necesse
6 est; apud ipsum multum, apud eius omnes plurimum potes. Unum tibi si persuaseris, non hoc esse tui muneris, si quid rogatus fueris, ut facias—quamquam id magnum et amplum est—, sed totum tuum esse onus, perficies: nisi forte aut in miseria nimis stulte aut in amicitia nimis impudenter tibi onus impono. Sed utrique rei excusationem tuae vitae consuetudo dat: nam quod ita consuesti pro amicis laborare, non iam sic sperant abs te, sed etiam sic imperant tibi familiares. Quod ad librum attinet, quem tibi filius dabit, peto a te, exeat, aut ita corrigas, ne mihi noceat.

93. TO M. BRUTUS (AD FAM. XIII. 11).

ROME, 46 B.C. (708 A.U.C.)

1. You know how eager I am to serve my townsmen of Arpinum. Now we depend in great measure on money paid us by the inhabitants of Gaul. We have commissioned three Roman knights to inspect the town property there, and to get payment of money owing. 2. I hope you will serve them to the best of your power; you will

1. De Asiatico itinere. Caecina was anxious to go to Asia to get in some old debts there, but Cicero recommended him to stay in Sicily, where Caesar's friends had given assurances that Caecina might stay in safety. Cp. Ad Fam. 6. 8, 2.

2. Premebat is, I think, epistolary.

3. Quo necesse .. constitui, 'when my fate must needs be settled' by Caesar.

Nihil est, quod .. exspectes, 'there is no reason why you should wait for my son,' to concert measures with him. On 'nihil est quod,' cp. Madv. 372 b, Obs. 6.

4. Omnia .. studio .. aetate .. metu, 'zealous haste, inexperience, or fear will prevent his thinking out every possible plan.' The ablatives are causal.

Omnia, 'all attempts to serve me.'

9. Apud ipsum multum .. potes. Caecina echoes Cicero's own remark in Ep. 91, 13. The MS. has 'ad,' not 'apud,' before eius, which may perhaps be defended by Ep. 74, 1; Pro Lig. 10, 30 'ad parentem sic agi solet;' Livy 7. 7, 'ad hostes bellum apparatur.'

10. Non hoc esse .. onus, 'that to discharge your duty you must not only do what you are asked, but undertake the burden of the whole affair.' On 'hoc,' cp. note on 'ea condicione' in § 4.

12. Perficies, 'you will effect what has to be done.'

Aut in miseria .. impono, 'unless misery makes me hope for impossibilities, or friendship presume on your kindness too shamelessly.'

14. Nam quod ita .. familiares, 'for you have been accustomed to work so hard for your friends, that they not only hope for, but demand, such services of you.'

find the people of Arpinum grateful, and 3. will do me a great favour, especially in this year, as my son and nephew, and my friend M. Caesius, have been made aediles there by my wish.

CICERO BRUTO SAL.

Quia semper animadverti studiose te operam dare, ut ne quid 1
meorum tibi esset ignotum, propterea non dubito quin scias, non
solum cuius municipii sim, sed etiam, quam diligenter soleam
meos municipes [Arpinates] tueri: quorum quidem omnia commoda omnesque facultates, quibus et sacra conficere et sarta tecta
aedium sacrarum locorumque communium tueri possint, consistunt
in iis vectigalibus, quae habent in provincia Gallia. Ad ea visen-
da pecuniasque, quae a colonis debentur, exigendas totamque rem
et cognoscendam et administrandam legatos equites Romanos mi-
simus, Q. Fufidium Q. f., M. Faucium M. f., Q. Mamercum Q. f.
Peto a te in maiorem modum pro nostra necessitudine, ut tibi 2
ea res curae sit operamque des, ut per te quam commodissime
negotium municipii administretur quam primumque conficiatur,
ipsosque, quorum nomina scripsi, ut quam honorificentissime pro
tua natura et quam liberalissime tractes. Bonos viros ad tuam 3
necessitudinem adiunxeris municipiumque gratissimum beneficio
tuo devinxeris, mihi vero etiam gratius feceris, quod cum semper
tueri municipes meos consuevi, tum hic annus praecipue ad meam
curam officiumque pertinet: nam constituendi municipii causa hoc

BRUTO. On Brutus, cp. Epp. 36, 10–12; 91, 10; Intr. to Parts IV, § 3; V, passim.

1. Ut ne: cp. Ep. 22, 4, note.

Quid meorum, 'anything concerning me.'

4. Arpinates, Cobet om.

Quorum quidem . . possint, 'all whose profits and entire revenues available for the maintenance of public worship and the repairs of their temples and other public buildings.' 'Quidem'='certainly.' Cp. Madv. 489 b.

5. Sarta tecta is a technical expression. Cp. In Verr. 2 Act. 1. 49, foll. 'Sarta (et) tecta aedes' is also found. Cp. In Verr. 2 Act. 1. 50, 131. 'Et' is omitted between 'sarta' and 'tecta.'

7. Vectigalibus. The municipal authorities of Arpinum seem to have invested their common funds in the purchase of lands in Cisalpine Gaul. The people of Atella had done the same, cp. Ad Fam. 13. 7, 1.

8. A colonis, 'from the tenants.' Cp. Forcell., sub voc.

Totamque rem . . administrandam, 'to make themselves acquainted with, and to manage, the whole affair.'

9. Legatos. Of these deputies, Q. Fufidius is mentioned Ad Fam. 13. 12, 1, as stepson of M. Caesius (cp. § 3), and as having been a military tribune under Cicero in Cilicia. The other two seem only to be mentioned here.

14. Ipsosque, quorum nomina scripsi, the three envoys named above.

Ut quam honorificentissime: cp. Madv. 465 b, Obs., on the position of 'ut.'

Pro tua natura: cp. Ep. 71, 9, note.

15. Ad tuam necessitudinem adiunxeris, 'will place under a great obligation.' Billerb. Sc. 'si ita feceris.'

17. Devinxeris: cp. Ep. 15, 4, note.

Mihi . . etiam gratius, 'what will give me more pleasure;' 'place me under an obligation all the greater.' Wiel.

18. Praecipue . . pertinet, 'has especial claims on my interest and services.'

19. Constituendi municipii causa, 'to organize the town satisfactorily.' Billerb.

anno aedilem filium meum fieri volui et fratris filium et M. Caesium, hominem mihi maxime necessarium; is enim magistratus in nostro municipio nec alius ullus creari solet; quos cohonestaris in primisque me, si res publica municipii tuo studio, diligentia bene administrata erit. Quod ut facias, te vehementer etiam atque etiam rogo.

94. To CN. PLANCIUS (AD FAM. IV. 14).

Rome, Autumn, 46 B.C. (708 A.U.C.)

1. I have received two letters from you, dated Corcyra. One congratulates me on maintaining my old position. Now I have the approval of good men, but have lost political power and independence. 2. I recall with some satisfaction my foresight as to our present misfortunes. 3. Your other letter wishes that my marriage may be happy. I should not have contracted it but for the perfidy of my old connections. 4. As to your own prospects, do not believe that you are in any special danger. I will do my utmost for you. Let me know your plans.

M. CICERO S. D. CN. PLANCIO.

1 Binas a te accepi litteras, Corcyrae datas; quarum alteris mihi gratulabare, quod audisses me meam pristinam dignitatem obtinere, alteris dicebas te velle, quae egissem, bene et feliciter evenire. Ego autem, si dignitas est bene de re publica sentire et bonis viris probare quod sentias, obtineo dignitatem meam;

The interest which Cicero took in the affairs of his native town would strengthen the hands of the local authorities. 'Constituere' = 'ordinare.' Forcell.

2. Is . . magistratus, sc. 'aedilis.' Other names for municipal magistrates were dictator, duumvir, quattuorvir. Cp. pro Milon. 10, 27; Caes. Bell. Civ. 1. 23; Appendix 12.

3. Cohonestaris = 'honore affeceris.' Forcell.

4. In primisque me, 'and on me as much as on any of them.' Cicero is not included among the 'quos,' but the careless expression 'in primis me,' is natural and intelligible.

Res publica municipii, 'this matter of public interest to that town.' Billerb.

CN. PLANCIO. Cn. Plancius, when quaestor in Macedonia, had been of great service to Cicero, who repaid him by pleading for him when accused of bribery by M. Iuventius in 54 B.C. Plancius had supported Pompey in the civil war, and was living in exile when Cicero wrote this letter. Cp. Intr. to Parts I, § 21; II, § 10.

7. Binas: cp. Ep. 78, 1, note.

Corcyrae. On the gen., cp. Madv. 296 a; acc. to Hofm. the ablative is more commonly used in dating letters. See Ep. 17, 4, note on p. 111, and Madv. 275, Obs. 2.

9. Quae egissem. These words, apparently, refer to Cicero's marriage with his young and wealthy ward Publilia. Cp. Intr. to Part IV, § 7.

10. Ego autem replies to something implied in what has gone before, e.g. 'as for your congratulation.' Süpfle.

Si dignitas est. Cicero here distinguishes a position morally dignified from one politically so. The Latin word is ambiguous.

11. Probare quod sentias, 'convince of the rectitude of your sentiments.' On the construction, cp. Ep. 38, 8, note.

sin autem in eo dignitas est, si, quod sentias, aut re efficere possis aut denique libera oratione defendere, ne vestigium quidem ullum est reliquum nobis dignitatis, agiturque praeclare, si nosmet ipsos regere possumus, ut ea, quae partim iam adsunt, partim impendent, moderate feramus, quod est difficile in eius modi bello, cuius exitus ex altera parte caedem ostentat, ex altera servitutem. Quo 2
in periculo non nihil me consolatur, cum recordor haec me tum vidisse, cum secundas etiam res nostras, non modo adversas, pertimescebam, videbamque quanto periculo de iure publico disceptaretur armis; quibus si ii vicissent, ad quos ego pacis spe, non belli cupiditate adductus accesseram, tamen intellegebam, et iratorum hominum et cupidorum et insolentium quam crudelis esset futura victoria, sin autem victi essent, quantus interitus esset futurus civium partim amplissimorum, partim etiam optimorum, qui me haec praedicentem atque optime consulentem saluti suae malebant nimium timidum quam satis prudentem existimari.

1. In eo . . est, sc. cp. Ad Att. 2. 22, 5 'totum est in eo si ante (te videro) quam ille ineat magistratum.'

2. Denique, 'even only.' Süpfle.

3. Agiturque praeclare, 'and we do very well.' Cp. Ep. 98, 3; also Forcell.

Nosmet ipsos regere, 'to school ourselves.' 'Regere' may be suggested by 'efficere' above. 'We cannot influence events, and must be content with ruling ourselves.'

4. Ut ea . . feramus, 'to bear with composure the evils, some of which are already present and others at hand.'

5. In eius modi bello, 'in a war like this,' which Caesar is waging against Pompey's sons in Spain. Hofm. however, who places the date of this letter earlier, thinks that the war in Africa is here referred to. The indicative is often found in relative clauses after 'eius modi,' where, as here, the relative is not to be resolved into 'ut' with the demonstrative. Cp. examples in Forcell.

Cuius exitus . . servitutem, 'of which the issue threatens us with a massacre at the hands of one party (Cn. and Sex. Pompeii), and with slavery at the hands of the other' (Caesar). Cp. Ad Fam. 15. 19, 4, where C. Cassius says, 'malo veterem et clementem dominum habere quam novum et crudelem experiri' (sc. Cn. Pompeium). Cp. also Intr. to Part IV, §§ 6 and 12.

6. Ostentat, 'threatens.' Not a common use of the word. But cp. Pro Cluent. 8. 25 'qui sibi . . capitis periculum ostentarat.'

7. Non nihil me consolatur. 'Non nihil' may either be the nominative, 'there is something to console me,' or the adverbial accusative. In the latter case it would come under the rule stated by Madvig, 229 b, and cum recordor would be equivalent to 'quod recordor.' Cp. Madv. 358, Obs. 2, and Forcell.

Tum, i.e. 'at the beginning of 49 B.C.' Cp. Intr. to Part III, § 4.

8. Secundas . . pertimescebam: cp. Epp. 56, 4; 59, 2; 61, 3–5.

10. Si, perhaps = 'etiamsi;' cp. Ep. 69, 2, note.

Ii, 'the Pompeians.'

Pacis spe, 'by the hope of bringing about a peace.'

11. Tamen. Hofm. remarks that this belongs in sense not to 'intellegebam,' but to the following clause; 'yet their victory would have been followed by cruelties.'

12. Cupidorum: cp. Epp. 80, 2 and 6; 88, 2; 91, 6. Hofm. renders here 'blinded by selfishness.'

14. Civium . . optimorum, 'of citizens, some of whom were most eminent, and the others most excellent also.'

Partim = 'aliorum.' It subdivides a larger class into smaller ones. Forcell.

15. Haec praedicentem, 'predicting what we now see around us.'

3 Quod autem mihi de eo, quod egerim, gratularis, te ita velle certo scio, sed ego tam misero tempore nihil novi consilii cepissem, nisi in reditu meo nihilo meliores res domesticas quam rem publicam offendissem: quibus enim pro meis immortalibus beneficiis carissima mea salus et meae fortunae esse debebant, cum propter eorum scelus nihil mihi intra meos parietes tutum, nihil insidiis vacuum viderem, novarum me necessitudinum fidelitate contra veterum perfidiam muniendum putavi. Sed de nostris
4 rebus satis vel etiam nimium multa. De tuis velim ut eo sis animo, quo debes esse, id est, ut ne quid tibi praecipue timendum putes: si enim status erit aliquis civitatis, quicumque erit, te omnium periculorum video expertem fore; nam alteros tibi iam placatos esse intellego, alteros numquam iratos fuisse. De mea autem in te voluntate sic velim iudices, me, quibuscumque rebus opus esse intellegam, quamquam videam, qui sim hoc tempore et quid possim, opera tamen et consilio, studio quidem certe rei famae saluti tuae praesto futurum. Tu velim, et quid agas et quid acturum te putes, facias me quam diligentissime certiorem.

1. **De eo, quod egerim**, 'on my second marriage.'

Te ita velle, 'that you wish it may be happy.' Cp. § 1.

2. **Nihil novi**, foll., 'I should have made no change in my plans,' i.e. by divorcing Terentia and marrying again. On the genit., cp. Madv. 285 b.

3. **Res domesticas**: cp. Intr. to Part IV, §§ 1 and 7. Cicero seems to have been involved in money difficulties, partly through the mismanagement of Terentia, partly through the demands of Pompey. And perhaps he had never got quite clear of the embarrassments attending his exile. At the end of 50 B.C. he was in debt to Caesar. Cp. Ad Att. 7. 8, 5, and Ep. 29, 18; Appendix 5, § 3.

4. **Quibus .. propter eorum.** On the order of words, cp. Ep. 13, 1, note. Both the pronouns refer, perhaps, only to Terentia, of whose extravagance Cicero seems to have complained. Cp. Ad Att. 11. 16, 5 'auditum ex Philotimo est eam scelerate quaedam facere:' also Ad Att. 11. 24, 3; 11. 25, 3; Plut. Cic. 41. Perhaps he refers also to his brother and nephew, of whose conduct he wrote with dissatisfaction in this year. Cp. Ad Att. 12. 5, 1, and see Epp. 81, 82.

8. **Veterum**, sc. 'necessitudinum.'

9. **Nimium multa**, sc. 'dixi.'

De tuis, 'about your own affairs.'

10. **Ut ne quid**: cp. Ep. 22, 4, note.

Praecipue = 'prae ceteris Pompeianis.' Müller.

11. **Si enim .. civitatis**, 'if the State is still to exist, on whatever basis,' i.e. whether under Caesar or under the sons of Pompey. This sense of 'status' seems rare. Cp. Ep. Ad Brut. 1. 15, 12 'ad collocandum aliquem civitatis statum.'

12. **Alteros** (Caesarianos) **tibi iam placatos.** Plancius had done nothing to offend the party of Pompey.

15. **Videam.** This verb is in the conj. as depending on 'iudices,' Wesenb., who, however, thinks that 'videam' may be a copyist's error.

Qui sim .. possim, 'what my position is, and how little I can do.' Cp. § 1.

16. **Studio quidem certe**, 'at least with zeal.' The words 'quidem certe' bring a new point into prominence. Cp. De Offic. 1. 39, 138 'quoniam omnia persequimur, volumus quidem certe;' also De Senect. 2, 6.

95. M. MARCELLUS TO CICERO (AD FAM. IV. 11).

MYTILENE, END OF 64 B.C. (708 A.U.C.)

1. Even my dear cousin's exhortation could not persuade me to return to Rome till you supported it. I thank you for your congratulations; 2. the society of men like you forms the only attraction Rome has for me, and I will shew you my gratitude by my conduct.

MARCELLUS CICERONI S.

Plurimum valuisse apud me tuam semper auctoritatem cum in 1
omni re tum in hoc maxime negotio potes existimare. Cum mihi C. Marcellus, frater amantissimus mei, non solum consilium daret, sed precibus quoque me obsecraret, non prius mihi persuadere potuit, quam tuis est effectum litteris ut uterer vestro potissimum consilio. Res quem ad modum sit acta, vestrae litterae mihi declarant. Gratulatio tua etsi est mihi probatissima, quod ab optimo fit animo, tamen hoc mihi multo iucundius est et gratius, quod in summa paucitate amicorum, propinquorum ac necessariorum, qui vere meae saluti faverent, te cupidissimum mei singularemque mihi benevolentiam praestitisse cognovi.
Reliqua sunt eius modi, quibus ego, quoniam haec erant tem- 2

MARCELLUS. On Marcellus, cp. Ep. 90, 3, note.

2. In hoc maxime negotio, 'in this affair especially,' i.e. his acceptance of Caesar's pardon. Marcellus seems to have been persuaded to do so by C. Marcellus and Cicero. On the circumstances of his recall, cp. Ep. 90, 3 and 4.

Potes existimare, 'you may judge' from my conduct. Explained by the next words. Cicero had urged Marcellus to return. Ad Fam. 4. 9.

3. C. Marcellus: cp. Ep. 90, 3.

5. Tuis . . litteris. Probably one that has been lost, for Ad Fam. 4. 7; 8; 9, contain no account of the proceedings in the senate.

Ut uterer vestro . . consilio, 'to follow your advice and his in preference to that of any one else,' i.e. to return to Rome.

6. Res quem ad modum sit acta, 'how my recall was effected.'

8. Ab optimo fit animo: cp. Madv. 284, Obs. 1; Epp. 77, 1, note.

Hoc, ablat. On the gender of 'iucundius,' referring to 'gratulatio,' cp. Madv. 211 b, Obs. 1.

9. In summa paucitate amicorum. Lukewarmness on the part of some of the friends or relatives of Marcellus is hinted at by Cicero, Ad Fam. 4. 8, 2 'tui suum esse, fore cum tuis si modo essent tui;' also ib. 4. 7. 6 (C.) 'Marcello non deeramus. A tuis reliquis non adhibemur.'

10. Faverent: cp. Ep. 1, 1, note, on the mood.

Cupidissimum mei, sc. 'fuisse,' unless it is to be explained as an accusative of the predicate (cp. Madv. 227 c, and Ep. 48, 1, note), in which case 'cognovi' is used in a double sense. Wesenb. suggests the insertion of 'esse' or 'fuisse.'

12. Reliqua sunt . . carebam, 'everything else is such as, seeing the times were what they were, I readily and contentedly resigned.' On the mood of 'carebam,' cp. Ep. 94, 1, note.

pora, facile et aequo animo carebam; hoc vero eius modi esse statuo, ut sine talium virorum et amicorum benevolentia neque in adversa neque in secunda fortuna quisquam vivere possit: itaque in hoc ego mihi gratulor; tu vero ut intellegas homini amicissimo te tribuisse officium, re tibi praestabo. Vale.

96. TO ATTICUS (AD ATT. XII. 21).

WRITTEN PROBABLY FROM ASTURA, IN SPRING, 45 B.C. (709 A.U.C.)

1. The letter of Brutus shews great ignorance of the case of Lentulus and his associates, and does scant justice to my services. But it is his own affair. 2. I shall be glad if you can buy me a garden; you know for what object. 3. I quite agree with you about Terentia. 4. Please attend to the business of Ovia. 5. You suggest that I should come to Rome to shew my fortitude; but I prefer the consolations of literature to those of society.

CICERO ATTICO SAL.

1 Legi Bruti epistolam eamque tibi remisi, sane non prudenter rescriptam ad ea, quae requisieras. Sed ipse viderit; quamquam illud turpiter ignorat: Catonem primum sententiam putat de animadversione dixisse, quam omnes ante dixerant praeter Cae-

1. Hoc vero .. statuo, 'I attach such importance to this assurance of your friendship.' Cp. the conclusion of the previous section.

SPRING. Mr. Jeans has pointed out that this is the first letter in this collection written after the reform of the Calendar. See Appendix VIII. The dates given henceforth correspond with the real seasons. This letter seems to have been written after the death of Tullia (cp. § 2, note), the news of which had reached Caesar in the south of Spain by April 30 (cp. Ad Att. 13. 20, 1), and before the news of the battle of Munda reached Rome on April 20 (cp. Dion Cassius, 43. 42).

6. Bruti epistolam. M. Brutus had written a treatise in honour of Cato, in which he claimed for Cato more than his due with regard to the proceedings in the senate on Dec. 5, 63 B.C. Atticus had sent Brutus some criticisms on his work, modestly expressed in the form of questions (quae requisieras), and Brutus seems to have shown obstinacy and ignorance in another letter to Atticus. Billerb. On the work of Brutus, cp. Ad Att. 13. 46, 2, where a sarcastic remark of Balbus is quoted, 'Bruti Catone lecto se sibi visum disertum.' Hofmann's note on this passage seems to take 'quae requisieras' as meaning 'what you pointed out as defective.'

Non prudenter, 'without a proper knowledge of the facts.' Cp. Philipp. 2. 3. 5 'quam cuiquam minus prudenti non satis gratus videri.'

7. Ipse viderit, 'let him correct this himself.' It seems to be implied that Brutus did not bear criticism well. 'Videris, it, int dicimus cum aliis rei cuiuspiam curam relinquimus.' Forcell.

8. Illud turpiter ignorat, 'he shews discreditable ignorance on the following points.' On this use of ille, cp. Ep. 5, 9, note.

De animadversione, 'in favour of the execution of the prisoners.' 'Animadversio' = 'punitio.' Forcell.

9. Omnes. But after Caesar's speech many of those who had spoken for capital punishment advocated delay or tried to explain away their speeches. Cp. Sall. Cat. 50 and 52; Suet. Iul. 14.

sarem, et, cum ipsius Caesaris tam severa fuerit, qui tum praetorio loco dixerit, consularium putat leniores fuisse, Catuli, Servilii, Lucullorum, Curionis, Torquati, Lepidi, Gellii, Volcatii, Figuli, Cottae, L. Caesaris, C. Pisonis, etiam M'. Glabrionis, Silani, Murenae, designatorum consulum. Cur ergo in sententiam Catonis? Quia verbis luculentioribus et pluribus rem eandem comprehenderat. Me autem hic laudat, quod rettulerim, non quod patefecerim, cohortatus sim, quod denique ante, quam consulerem, ipse iudicaverim: quae omnia, quia Cato laudibus extulerat in caelum perscribendaque censuerat, idcirco in eius sententiam est facta discessio. Hic autem se etiam tribuere multum mihi putat, quod scripserit 'optimum consulem.' Quis enim ieiunius dixit

1. **Tam severa.** Caesar had proposed that the conspirators should be punished with perpetual imprisonment and confiscation of their property. Cp. Cic. in Cat. 4. 4 and 5; Sall. Cat. 51.

Fuerit . . dixerit. The conj. may be explained by treating the passage as a quotation from Brutus' letter, or by translating cum 'though,' qui 'though he.'

Praetorio loco. Caesar was praetor designatus at the end of 63 B.C. Cp. Intr. to Part I, § 18. On the order in which senators expressed their opinions, cp. Ep. 6, 2, note; Philipp. 5. 13. 35; A. Gell. N. A. 4. 10.

2. **Consularium.** This list agrees with one given Philipp. 2. 5-6 of those who approved Cicero's measures generally, except that M. Crassus and Q. Hortensius are there mentioned, and Gellius and Torquatus omitted.

Q. Catulus was consul 78 B.C.; P. Servilius 79; L. Lucullus 74; M. Lucullus 73; C. Curio 76; L. Torquatus and L. Cotta 65; M'. Lepidus and L. Volcatius 66; L. Gellius 72; C. Piso and M'. Glabrio 67; L. Caesar and C. Figulus 64. Silanus and Murena were the consuls elect for 62 B.C.

4. **Etiam** should probably stand before 'Silani.' Boot.

5. **Cur ergo in sententiam Catonis?** sc. 'facta est discessio,' or 'itum est.' Brutus is supposed to ask this question. It might seem strange that the proposal of Cato, a tribune elect, should be adopted if so many consulars had advocated substantially the same course.

6. **Luculentioribus,** 'more distinct.' 'Luculentus' = 'perspicuus' 'dilucidus.' Forcell. Silanus, one of the consuls elect, had tried to explain away his own proposal. Cp. Cic. in Cat. 4, and Sall. ll. cc. About the meaning of Cato's there could be no mistake; he had proposed that the conspirators should be punished 'more maiorum.' Cp. Sall. Cat. 52.

7. **Hic,** Brutus.

Quod rettulerim, 'for having submitted the question to the senate.' Cp. Ep. 16, 6.

Quod . . cohortatus sim, 'for having exhorted the senate to act with vigour.'

8. **Quod . . ipse iudicaverim,** 'for having made up my own mind.' The word can hardly refer to Cicero's expression of his opinion. For he spoke in the debate after a good many senators had risen, and so the words ante quam consulerem would be out of place. Cp. In Cat. 4. 11, 24. Perhaps Cicero means that by submitting the question to the senate at all he shewed his opinion that the conspirators were outlaws, otherwise the senate could not sentence them to death. Cp. Appendix 4. 'Consulere' is 'to ask the senate's opinion.'

10. **Perscribenda,** 'should be recorded' in the report of the debate. Cp. Ep. 22, 4, note. Sallust does not make Cato so lavish of his praises, Cat. 52. See, however, Vell. 2. 35.

11. **Hic,** M. Brutus.

12. **Quod scripserit 'optimum consulem,'** 'in having called me "a very good consul" in his book.'

Enim, 'why.' 'Inservit ironiae.' Forcell. Cp. Philipp. 7. 8, 21 'occulta enim fuit eorum voluntas.'

Ieiunius = 'magis invide,' 'more grudgingly.' Forcell.

inimicus? Ad cetera vero tibi quem ad modum rescripsit! tantum
rogat, de senatus consulto ut corrigas. Hoc quidem fecisset
2 etiam si † rario admonitus esset. Sed haec iterum ipse viderit.
De hortis, quoniam probas, effice aliquid: rationes meas nosti.
Si vero etiam a Faberio † aliquid recedit, nihil negotii est; sed
etiam sine eo posse videor contendere. Venales certe sunt Drusi,
3 fortasse etiam Lamiani et Cassiani: sed coram. De Terentia
non possum commodius scribere, quam tu scribis: officium sit
nobis antiquissimum; si quid nos fefellerit, illius malo me quam
4 mei paenitere. Oviae C. Lollii curanda sunt HS. C. Negat
Eros posse sine me, credo, quod accipienda aliqua sit et danda

1. Ad cetera .. rescripsit! 'what replies he made to your other criticisms!'

2. De senatus consulto, foll., 'to correct his mistake about the decree of the senate,' of which Brutus may have given an incorrect version. He seems to have been unwilling to acknowledge any other mistake.

3. Etiam si rario, clearly corrupt. 'A Ranio' (Graevius, ap. Baiter), supposing Ranius to be a clerk or freedman of Brutus, or 'a librario' (H. A. Koch, ap. Baiter; Wesenb.) would make good sense. 'He would have corrected this even at the suggestion of a clerk.'

Haec iterum ipse viderit, 'he must take the consequences of these faults also.' See note above.

4. De hortis. Cicero was anxious to buy a piece of ground where he might build a shrine ('fanum') in honour of Tullia. Cp. Ad Att. 12. 19, 1.

5. A. Faberio. Faberius was a debtor of Cicero's. Cp. Ad Att. 12. 25, 1; 12. 51, 3.

Aliquid recedit, 'something is repaid.' But the usual word, Boot and Wesenb. say, is 'redit,' which Boot suggests. Aliquid is inserted from Cratander (ap. Baiter). Hofm. has 'si Eros etiam a Faberio recepit.'

6. Contendere. Forcell. gives 'curare' as one of its synonyms. Cp. De Off. 3. 2, 6 'quantum labore contendere potes,' = 'effect my purpose.' Boot gives 'operam dare ut hortos comparem' as the meaning.

Drusi. Perhaps the same Drusus who is mentioned Ep. 28, 9; 41, 4. He may have been the father of the empress Livia.

7. Lamiani, those of L. Aelius Lamia. He was a Roman knight of distinction, and had supported Cicero in the troubles of 58 B.C. Cp. Pro Sest. 12, 29. He is also mentioned Ad Fam. 11. 16, 2. Horace addressed the Odes 1. 26 and 3. 17 to his son. Cp. Orell. on Hor. Carm. 1. 26.

Cassiani. Billerb. supposes these gardens to have belonged to C. Cassius.

Sed coram, sc. 'haec agemus.'

8. Commodius, 'with more propriety.'

Officium, 'duty.' Cicero was anxious that Terentia should have her due. He was settling business arising out of her divorce, and seems to have discussed the provisions of his will and hers. Cp. Ad Att. 12. 18, a, 2; 12. 19, 4. He was anxious for his son's interest; she for her grandson by Tullia, Lentulus.

9. Antiquissimum: cp. Ep. 71, 4 note.

Si quid nos fefellerit, 'if I am a loser.' Wiel.

Illius .. paenitere, 'I had rather have to complain of her conduct than to regret my own,' i.e. 'if one of us must lose, let it be I.' 'Paenitere de iis quae non satis faciunt dicitur.' Forcell. 'If I fail to conciliate her I should prefer that the fault were hers.' Manut.

10. Oviae C. Lollii. On the gen., cp. Madv. 280, Obs. 4. 'Ovia' is mentioned two or three times in the letters of the 12th and 13th books to Atticus. Of her husband, C. Lollius, nothing more seems to be known: a Lollius is mentioned Ad Att. 2. 2, 3, but nothing important is said of him.

Curanda sunt HS. c., 'we must provide for the payment of 100,000 sesterces to her.' Billerb. suggests that this was a debt of Terentia's. On the way of expressing sums of money, cp. Madv. Suppl. II. The general sense of the passage is often the only guide to the meaning of 'HS.'

11. Eros, a steward of Cicero. Cp. Ad Att. 13. 30, 2; 15. 15, 3; 15. 17, 1.

Sine me, sc. 'curare.'

aestimatio. Vellem tibi dixisset: si enim res est, ut mihi
scribit, parata nec in eo ipso mentitur, per te confici potuit; id
cognoscas et conficias velim. Quod me in forum vocas, eo vocas, 2
unde etiam bonis meis rebus fugiebam; quid enim mihi cum foro,
sine iudiciis, sine curia, in oculos incurrentibus iis, quos aequo
animo videre non possum? Quod autem homines a me postulare
scribis, *ut Romae sim, neque mihi, ut absim, concedere*, aut † quatenus eos mihi concedere, iam pridem scito esse, cum unum te
pluris quam omnes illos putem. Ne me quidem contemno, meoque
iudicio multo stare malo quam omnium reliquorum; neque tamen
progredior longius, quam mihi doctissimi homines concedunt,
quorum scripta omnia, quaecumque sunt in eam sententiam, non
legi solum, quod ipsum erat fortis aegroti, accipere medicinam,

Quod accipienda .. aestimatio, 'because I must accept a valuation of some property and hand it over to her.' Under Caesar's measure for the relief of debtors they were allowed to offer land at the value it had borne before the civil war began. This value was to be fixed by public arbitrators. Cp. Caes. Bell. Civ 3. 1. Now Cicero, in order to pay Ovia, had to get in apparently a debt of his own, for which he was offered land; and Eros seems to have thought that he ought to be present at the valuation, which Cicero thought needless. Perhaps 'aestimatio' means 'the land valued,' as in Ep. 87, 4. Forcell. gives 'res aestimata' as a synonym.

1. Tibi dixisset, sc. 'num aliqua sit accipienda et danda aestimatio.' Manut.

Si . . res . . parata, 'if the affair is ready for settlement.'

2. Potuit: cp. Epp. 16, 8, note; 4. 1, note on 'debebat.'

Id cognoscas . . velim, 'I should like you to enquire into and settle this.' 'Cognoscere' in this sense is generally more definitely a legal term.

3. In forum, 'to the courts.'

4. Bonis meis rebus. I am not aware that Cicero expressed this distaste for advocacy before the civil war broke out; and enim in the next clause assigns a reason which could only exist after its beginning. Hence I think that 'bonis meis rebus' refers to his comparative happiness before the death of Tullia.

Quid . . mihi cum foro. With this phrase cp. Ep. 8, 10; Zumpt, L. G. 770; Madv. 479 d, Obs. 1.

5. In oculos incurrentibus iis, 'when men come in my way.' Wiel. Cicero refers especially to the less reputable of Caesar's friends. Cp. Ep. 71, 3, and note.

6. Homines. Caesar's friends? or people in general?

Postulare, i.e. as a proof of his resignation and fortitude.

7. Quatenus. Perhaps the reading of Lambinus (ap. Baiter) 'quadam tenus' may be adopted.

8. Iam pridem scito esse cum, 'know that I have long valued your opinion more than that of them all.' On the use of 'iam pridem,' an adverb, as a predicate, cp. Ep. 4, 1, note. 'Cum' = 'ex quo.' Forcell. Hofm. thinks that this combination occurs nowhere else in Cicero's writings. In Ad Fam. 15. 14, 1 he writes 'multi enim anni sunt cum ille in aere meo est;' Ad Att. 9. 11 A, 2 'aliquot enim sunt anni cum.' Cp. Plaut. Amph. 1. 1, 146; Adn. 2 1, 3.

10. Neque tamen progredior longius, 'however, I do not go further,' in the way of retirement from public business. 'Tamen,' though I am satisfied with your approval and my own, I can appeal to the authority of great philosophers for preferring to seek consolation from literature rather than from business.' On this use of 'tamen,' cp. Ep. 29, 21, note.

12. In eam sententiam, sc. 'scripta' 'of that purport.' Cp. Ep. 34, 4, note.

13. Quod ipsum .. medicinam, 'though this reception of a remedy itself shewed fortitude in sickness.'

Quod = 'quamquam hoc.' Madv. 448; Zumpt, L. G. 803. On the infin. as the subject of a proposition, cp. Ep. 45, 2; Madv. 378 a.

sed in mea etiam scripta transtuli, quod certe adflicti et fracti animi non fuit. Ab his me remediis noli in istam turbam vocare, ne recidam.

97. To JULIUS CAESAR (AD FAM. XIII. 16).

ASTURA, (?) APRIL, (?) 45 B.C. (709 A.U.C.)

1. My regard for P. Crassus led me to make the acquaintance of his freedman, Apollonius, 2. and after the death of Crassus my opinion of Apollonius' merits increased. I found him very useful in Cilicia. 3. He has now decided to join you in Spain, and I wish to let you know what I think of him. 4. His learning makes me think him well qualified for the task which he wishes to undertake—that of composing a Greek history of your achievements.

CICERO CAESARI SAL.

1 P. Crassum ex omni nobilitate adulescentem dilexi plurimum, et ex eo cum ab ineunte eius aetate bene speravissem, tum perbene existimare coepi iis iudiciis, quae de eo feceras, cognitis. Eius libertum Apollonium iam tum equidem, cum ille viveret, et magni faciebam et probabam: erat enim et studiosus Crassi et ad eius optima studia vehementer aptus; itaque ab eo admodum
2 diligebatur. Post mortem autem Crassi eo mihi etiam dignior visus est, quem in fidem atque amicitiam meam reciperem, quod

Aegroti. 'Aegrotus substantivi more usurpatur.' Forcell. Cp. Nägelsb. 25. 83. On the genitives 'aegroti' and **animi**, cp. Ep. 77. 3, note.

2. **Istam turbam,** 'the throng of litigants,' or merely of people at Rome, where Atticus was.

3. **Ne recidam,** 'lest I have a relapse.' Cp. Livy 24. 29 'quo mox in graviorem morbum recideret.' Cicero uses metaphorical language. 'I have adopted a regimen of literary retirement; if I change it for one of political action I may have a relapse.'

4. **P. Crassum:** cp. Intr. to Part II, §§ 7; 13. He was the younger son of M. Crassus the triumvir, and perished in his father's Parthian campaign. He had served with distinction under Caesar in Gaul, and was much attached to Cicero. Cp. Caes. Bell. Gall. 1. 52; 2. 34; 3. 20–27; Cic. Ad Fam. 5. 8, 4. Cicero succeeded to his place as augur. Cp. Plut. Cic. 36.

Ex omni nobilitate, 'out of the whole nobility.' The 'nobiles' were the descendants of men who had held some curule office. Forcell. Cp. Livy 22. 34.

5. **Ex eo,** with **speravissem.** 'De eo' is more common, and Wesenb. has it here, but cp. Bell. Afric. 45 'quid ex tuis copiis sperare debeas.'

Ab ineunte aetate: cp. Ep. 90. 4, note.

Perbene, rare.

6. **Iis iudiciis . . cognitis,** 'when I became acquainted with your expressions of opinion about him.' Caesar had entrusted P. Crassus with very important commissions. Cp. reff. above.

7. **Apollonium.** This freedman of Crassus seems to be only mentioned in the present passage.

8. **Studiosus:** cp. Ep. 6. 2, note.

9. **Ad eius optima studia,** 'to aid in his most honourable pursuits.'

10. **Post mortem . . Crassi,** i.e. of P. Crassus.

eos a se observandos et colendos putabat, quos ille dilexisset
et quibus carus fuisset. Itaque et ad me in Ciliciam venit
multisque in rebus mihi magno usui fuit et fides eius et prudentia, et, ut opinor, tibi in Alexandrino bello, quantum studio
et fidelitate consequi potuit, non defuit: quod cum speraret te 2
quoque ita existimare, in Hispaniam ad te, maxime ille quidem
suo consilio, sed etiam me auctore, est profectus. Cui ego commendationem non sum pollicitus, non quin eam valituram apud
te arbitrarer, sed neque egere mihi commendatione videbatur, qui
et in bello tecum fuisset et propter memoriam Crassi de tuis
unus esset, et, si uti commendationibus vellet, etiam per alios
eum videbam id consequi posse: testimonium mei de eo iudicii,
quod et ipse magni aestimabat et ego apud te valere eram expertus, ei lubenter dedi. Doctum igitur hominem cognovi et 4
studiis optimis deditum, idque a puero: nam domi meae cum
Diodoto Stoico, homine meo iudicio eruditissimo, multum a puero
fuit; nunc autem, incensus studio rerum tuarum, eas litteris
Graecis mandare cupiebat. Posse arbitror: valet ingenio; habet

1. **A se observandos.** The dative is much more common with gerundives. Cp. Madv. 421 a, Obs. 1; Zumpt, L. G. 651; but the present construction is found Ad Fam. 15. 4. 11 'admonendum potius te a me quam rogandum puto.' Süpfle remarks (on Ad Fam. 15. 4. 11) that the ablative and preposition are used either (1) to make more prominent the person with whom an action originates, (2) to preserve uniformity of construction—if e.g. a past participle passive has been used in a parallel clause. Cp. Pro Planc. 3. 8 'nec si a populo praeteritus est quem non oportuit idcirco a iudicibus condemnandus est qui praeteritus non est:' (3) to avoid ambiguity—where e.g. the dative might be mistaken for a dativus commodi.

Ille, P. Crassus.

2. **In Ciliciam**, during Cicero's government of Cilicia, 51–50 B.C.

4. **Ut opinor**: cp. on the force of this expression, Ep. 40, 1, note.

5. **Quod cum speraret**: cp. Madv. 449. It is a pleonastic usage, 'quod' pointing to the accus. and infin. following. Süpfle renders 'on that point.'

6. **In Hispaniam.** Caesar was now engaged in a war with the sons of Pompey in Spain. Cp. Intr. to Part IV, § 12.

7. **Cui ego .. pollicitus**, 'to whom I did not promise a recommendation.' 'Commendationem' is the emphatic word.

8. **Non quin** = 'non quo non.' On which, cp. Ep. 28, 7, note.

9. **Neque .. et**: cp. Ep. 6, 4, note.

10. **De tuis unus esset**, 'is one of your dependents.' On the abl. with 'de,' cp. Madv. 284, Obs. 1. The use of 'unus' in this indefinite sense is colloquial, and found mainly in the comic poets, unless, as here, used with a partitive preposition. Cp. Pro Milon. 24. 65 'se gladio percussum esse ab uno de illis.'

12. **Mei .. iudicii**, gen. possess.: cp. Ep. 4, 2, note.

14. **Igitur .. cognovi**, 'I may say then that I know him.'

Hominem = 'eum:' cp. Ep. 90, 3, note.

16. **Diodoto.** Diodotus was Cicero's teacher, and for many years an inmate of his house, where he continued his studies even after he had become blind. Cp. De Nat. Deor. 1. 3. 6; Tusc. Disp. 5. 39, 113. He died 59 B.C., and bequeathed Cicero 10,000,000 sesterces. Cp. Ad Att. 2. 20 6.

Meo iudicio, a form of the ablat. caus. Cp. Madv. 255, Obs. 3.

17. **Studio rerum tuarum**, 'with enthusiasm for your exploits.'

Litteris Graecis mandare, 'to write an account of in Greek.' On the phrase 'mandare litteris,' cp. De Orat. 2. 12, 51.

18. **Cupiebat**, probably the epistolary imperfect. Cp. Ep. 1, 1, note.

usum; iam pridem in eo genere studii litterarumque versatur; satis facere immortalitati laudum tuarum mirabiliter cupit. Habes opinionis meae testimonium, sed tu hoc facilius multo pro tua singulari prudentia iudicabis. Et tamen, quod negaveram, commendo tibi eum: quicquid ei commodaveris, erit id maiorem *mihi* in modum gratum.

98. SERVIUS SULPICIUS TO CICERO (AD FAM. IV. 5).

ATHENS, (?) APRIL (?) 45 B.C. (A.U.C.)

1. I grieved much for the death of Tullia, and it is hard to console you for a loss which I share: yet 2. surely, after all we have suffered as citizens, you ought to bear this private loss with firmness. Moreover 3. she had little to live for, considering the present aspect of things. 4. The sight of many famous cities lying in ruins lately made me form a juster estimate of individual life. Think, too, how many eminent men have died prematurely in our civil wars. 5. Tullia enjoyed life and honour as long as life was worth having. Let your philosophy, which has consoled others, 6. anticipate for yourself the healing work of time. She whom you lament, if she still is conscious of anything, would not have you indulge excessive grief. As a matter of prudence, do not let those in power suspect that you are really bewailing the fall of the commonwealth. Shew yourself, lastly, as firm in adversity as you have been moderate in prosperity.

SERVIUS CICERONI S.

1 Postea quam mihi renuntiatum est de obitu Tulliae, filiae tuae,

1. In eo genere studii, foll., 'in historical composition?' (Manut.) Passages like this shew how the word 'studium' tended even in Cicero's time to assume its later meaning of 'literary pursuits.' Cp. Epp. 90, 4; 92, 3.

2. Satis facere .. tuarum, 'to do justice to your immortal exploits by a work that shall last as long as their remembrance;' = 'ita scribere de rebus tuis ut scriptis suis aequet immortalitatem laudum tuarum.'

Laudum. 'Laus metonymice dicitur de recte factis.' Forcell.

3. Habes: cp. Ep. 88, 6, note.

Tu hoc .. iudicabis. On the accus., cp. Ep. 41, 3, note. On the mood and tense, cp. Ep. 11, 3, note.

4. Tamen, 'after saying I would not do so.' Cp. § 3 'commendationem non sum pollicitus.'

5. Quicquid ei commodaveris, 'whatever you do to oblige him.' 'Commodare' = 'benigne facere concedendo alicui aliquid.' Forcell. Cp. Ad Fam. 13. 48 'quibus tu quaecumque commodaris erunt mihi gratissima.'

6. Maiorem .. in modum. A rare expression, = 'in a high degree.' Wiel. The words are used in a slightly different sense Ep. 36, 10.

SERVIUS. On Servius, cp. Ep. 90.

7. Renuntiatum est, 'news was brought,' which I had a right to expect. This is the force of 're.' Cp. Ep. 92, 1, note.

De obitu Tulliae. Tullia seems to have died early in 45 B.C.—perhaps in February—, see Ep. 96, note on date, after the birth of a son. Dolabella had divorced

sane quam pro eo ac debui graviter molesteque tuli communemque
eam calamitatem existimavi, qui, si istic adfuissem, neque tibi
defuissem coramque meum dolorem tibi declarassem. Etsi genus
hoc consolationis miserum atque acerbum est, propterea quia, per
quos ea confieri debet [propinquos ac familiares], ii ipsi pari
molestia adficiuntur neque sine lacrimis multis id conari possunt,
uti magis ipsi videantur aliorum consolatione indigere quam aliis
posse suum officium praestare, tamen quae in praesentia in mentem mihi venerunt, decrevi brevi ad te perscribere, non quo ea te
fugere existimem, sed quod forsitan dolore impeditus minus ea
perspicias. Quid est quod tanto opere te commoveat tuus dolor 2
intestinus? cogita, quem ad modum adhuc fortuna nobiscum
egerit: ea nobis erepta esse, quae hominibus non minus quam
liberi cara esse debent, patriam, honestatem, dignitatem, honores
omnes. Hoc uno incommodo addito quid ad dolorem adiungi
potuit? aut qui non in illis rebus exercitatus animus callere iam
debet atque omnia minoris existimare? An illius vicem, credo, 3

her probably a short time before. The first allusion to her death is found Ad Att. 12. 12, 1; cp. also Ad Fam. 9. 11, 1. Hofm. refers to Ad Fam. 14. 5. 1 as shewing that news might reach Athens in twenty days from Rome.

1. Sane quam, 'assuredly.' Cp. Ep. 33. 2.

Pro eo ac debui, lit. 'in proportion as I was bound to do so.' Cp. Madv. 444 b. An instance of the common use of 'ac' in comparisons.

2. Istic, 'in Italy,' where Cicero was.

Neque . . coramque: cp. In Cat. 2. 13. 28 'ut neque bonus quisquam intereat paucorumque poena vos salvi esse possitis.' 'Neque . . et' is, however, much more common. Cp. Madv. 458 c.

3. Genus hoc consolationis, i.e. 'the condolence of those who themselves suffer.'

4. Miserum atque acerbum, 'painful and distressing.'

Quia. Cicero would probably have written 'quod.' Manut.

5. Confieri. 'Confici' is more common, Madv. 143. but cp. Ep. 58, 3.

[Propinquos, foll.] If these words are genuine, the accus. must be explained as used by attraction to 'quos.' Cp. Madv. 207, Obs.; Zumpt, L. G. 814.

9. Brevi. Cp. Epp. 29. 13; 91, 1 for the suppression of a substantive with 'brevi.' Hofm.

10. Sed quod . . perspicias. As these words express the real motive of Sulpicius' conduct, we should expect the indicative (see Ep. 28, 7, note); but 'perspicias' is accounted for by the insertion of 'forsitan.' Cp. Madv. 350 b, Obs 3.

11. Quid est quod: cp. 'nihil est quod' Ep. 92, 5, note.

12. Intestinus, 'private,' 'personal.' Müller. A rare sense of the word, apparently. Cp. Ep. 99, 2 for a similar opposition of public and private affairs.

14. Honestatem, dignitatem, 'reputation and position.' 'Honestas' = 'bona fama.' Matthiae. Cp. Pro Rosc. Am. 39, 114 'damnatus . . honestatem omnem amiserit.'

16. Qui, probably an adverb.

In illis rebus exercitatus, 'that has been trained in that school of public calamity in which we have been trained.' 'Ille' of something well known. Cp. Madv. 485 b.

Callere, rare in this sense. Forcell. only quotes this passage.

17. Minoris existimare. Cicero does not use 'existimare' in this way, but cp. Corn. Nep. Cato 1, 2 'magni eius opera existimata est.'

An. Hofm. reads 'at;' Mr. H. A. J. Munro, Journal of Philology, 4. 249, believes that 'credo' is a mistake for 'Cicero.' See Mr. Jeans' note. Mr. J. E. Yonge, ib. 5. 52, prefers 'at.'

Illius vicem, 'her fate,' or 'on her account.' Cp. Ep. 29, 2, note.

doles? Quotiens in eam cogitationem necesse est et tu veneris et nos saepe incidimus, hisce temporibus non pessime cum iis esse actum, quibus sine dolore licitum est mortem cum vita commutare? Quid autem fuit quod illam hoc tempore ad vivendum magno opere invitare posset? quae res? quae spes? quod animi solacium? Ut cum aliquo adulescente primario coniuncta aetatem gereret? Licitum est tibi, credo, pro tua dignitate ex hac iuventute generum deligere, cuius fidei liberos tuos te tuto committere putares! An ut ea liberos ex sese pareret, quos cum florentes videret laetaretur? qui rem a parente traditam per se tenere possent? honores ordinatim petituri essent? in re publica, in amicorum negotiis libertate sua usuri? Quid horum fuit quod non prius quam datum est ademptum sit? 'At vero malum est liberos

Credo, ironical, 'perhaps,' 'forsooth.' Cp. Pro Arch. 10, 25.

1. Et tu veneris, foll. A slight anacoluthon (Orell. ap. Müller): incidimus should be co-ordinate with 'veneris,' not with 'necesse est.' Hofm. remarks that 'et—et' may be interpolations, and 'nos saepe incidimus' originally a parenthesis. On the difference between 'venire' and 'incidere,' Oudend. ap. Müller remarks 'venimus in cogitationem ratione et prudentia: incidimus casu.' Cp. Ad Fam. 2. 7, 2 (Cicero to Curio) 'quod in rei publicae tempus non incideris sed veneris—iudicio enim tuo, non casu in ipsum discrimen rerum contulisti tribunatum tuum.' Perhaps Sulpicius means 'you most frequently [as a philosopher] have arrived at the opinion which has often occurred to me [a man of the world].'

2. Cum iis esse actum: cp. Ep. 94, 1.

3. Sine dolore, 'naturally,' opposed to a death by violence. Süpfle.

Mortem . . commutare, 'to receive death in exchange for life.' The verb more often means 'to give in exchange.' Cp. Madv. 258, Obs. 2.

5. Quae res, 'what present enjoyment.' Wiel. Cp. 'neque solum spe sed certa re' Ad Fam. 12. 25, 2.

6. Ut . . gereret. This clause, and the co-ordinate ut . . pareret explain quid in 'quid autem fuit,' foll., which is developed into quae res? quae spes?

Cum . . . adulescente. Tullia had probably been about 30 years old at the time of her death. Cp. Ad Att. 1. 3, 3. 'Adulescens' was a word used very loosely by the Romans. Cicero speaks of Brutus and Cassius as 'adulescentes' (Philipp. 2. 44, 113) at a time when both were praetors, and when Cassius had held an important command in Syria nine years before. Also of himself when consul and aged 43. Philipp. 2. 46, 118.

Aetatem gereret, 'pass her life.' 'Ageret' would be more common. Forcell., Süpfle.

7. Licitum est tibi, credo, foll., 'it was in your power no doubt to choose a son-in-law, such as your position demanded from our present set of young men—one under whose protection you would think your child safe!' ironical, of course.

Iuventute. 'Iuventus' = 'multitudo iuvenum.' Forcell.

8. Liberos, sometimes used of one child: cp. In Cat. 1. 2, 4 'necatus est cum liberis M. Fulvius consularis,' i.e. with his son. But is it not merely indefinite? we might say 'entrust your children.'

9. An ut ea . . laetaretur, 'or that she might have children in the sight of whose prosperity she might rejoice?'

Quos = 'et hos.' Cp. Ep. 96, 5, note.

10. Per se, 'in independence,' without the protection of a patron such as Caesar. Müller.

11. Possent has a future sense, 'would be able.' Cp. Madv. 378 a, 2.

Ordinatim = 'ordine, composite' (Forcell.), 'in the order prescribed by law,' from which Caesar had departed in favour of his friends. Sulpicius means, holding each office in proper order and at the proper age.

13. Prius quam datum, 'before the prospect of it has been given' by their birth.

Ademptum, i.e. by the usurpation of Caesar.

amittere.' Malum: nisi hoc peius est, haec sufferre et perpeti. Quae res mihi non mediocrem consolationem attulerit, volo tibi 4 commemorare, si forte eadem res tibi dolorem minuere possit. Ex Asia rediens, cum ab Aegina Megaram versus navigarem, coepi regiones circumcirca prospicere: post me erat Aegina, ante me Megara, dextra Piraeus, sinistra Corinthus; quae oppida quodam tempore florentissima fuerunt, nunc prostrata et diruta ante oculos iacent. Coepi egomet mecum sic cogitare: 'hem! nos homunculi indignamur, si quis nostrum interiit aut occisus est, quorum vita brevior esse debet, cum uno loco tot oppidum cadavera proiecta iacent? visne tu te, Servi, cohibere et memi-

At vero, nearly = 'at enim,' 'but certainly.' Wiel. Cp. Philipp. 2. 15, 38 'at vero Cn. Pompeii voluntatem a me abalienabat oratio mea.'

1. Malum, nisi hoc peius, sc., 'a misfortune no doubt—were it not a greater [or 'only it is a greater.' Hofm. Mr. Jeans renders 'nisi' 'but'] that they should have to suffer what we do now.' This version makes the best sense, though the construction is in favour of referring 'haec sufferre et perpeti' to the parents. But it would be no consolation to say 'were we not suffering a greater misfortune'—while it would be one to say 'if death did not deliver them from greater evils.' Cp., however, § 2, where Sulpicius certainly does dwell on the loss of liberty as making private misfortunes more endurable.

Nisi . . est: cp. Madv. 442 c; Zumpt, L. G. 526.

2. Quae res, a periphrasis for 'quod.' Cp. Ep. 21, 3, note.

3. Commemorare. This verb is often used without an accusative following it. Cp. Ad Q. F. 1. 1, 37 'ita de tua virtute . . . commemorant.' Here the sentence 'quae res . . . attulerit' forms the object.

Si forte, 'in the hope that perhaps.'

4. Ex Asia rediens. Sulpicius seems to have retired to Asia after the battle of Pharsalus, and perhaps Caesar met him after his victory over Pharnaces. Cp. Ep. 90, 2, note.

Megaram. Cicero uses this form De Divin. 1. 27, 57; but the plural Ib. 2. 65, 135.

Versus, 'towards.'

5. Regiones circumcirca = 'regiones quae circumcirca sunt.' Supfle. Cp. Ep. 82. 1, note, for this use of an adverb. The word is not Ciceronian apparently.

7. Nunc prostrata et diruta. An adversat. conjunction is omitted with 'nunc.' Cp. Ep. 6. 2, note. Of the places here mentioned Aegina perhaps had fallen gradually into decay after its surrender to Athens 456 B.C. Cp. Thucyd. 1. 108; Smith, Dict. of Geog. 1. 33. Of Megara's condition we know little but from this passage. Hofm. says that it was destroyed by Demetrius Poliorcetes, 307 B.C. Piraeus had been ruined in the Mithridatic war. Cp. Mommsen 3. 302; App. Mithr. 41; Smith's Dict. of Geog. 1. 308. Corinth had never recovered its destruction by Mummius in 146 B.C. Livy Epit. 52; Vell. 1. 13. Cp. Cic. De Leg. Agrar. 1. 32, 87. Sulpicius must have made this voyage before its restoration by Julius Caesar. On which cp. Plut. Caes. 57; Dion Cassius 43. 50; Smith's Geog. 1. 678; Intr. to Part IV, § 14.

8. Hem! indignantis. Forcell.

9. Homunculi, 'poor mortals,' rare. Cp. Tusc. Disp. 1. 9, 18 'homunculus unus e multis.'

10. Brevior esse debet, 'must be somewhat short.' On the force of the comparative, see Madv. 308.

Oppidum. This form of the gen. plur. seems not to occur elsewhere in prose. It is somewhat irregular. Cp. Madv. 37. Obs. 4. We must remember that Sulpicius, not Cicero, is the writer.

11. Cadavera. A somewhat similar metaphor occurs in Cat. 4. 6, 11 'sepulta in patria.'

Visne tu. '"Vis tu" dicit qui aliquem hortatur aut rogat aut modeste iubet' Hand. Tursell. 4. 82. Cp. Iuv. 5. 74

'Vis tu consuetis audax conviva canistris
Impleri,'

and Mr. Mayor's note. On the force of ne, cp. De Senect. 10, 31 'videtisne ut apud Homerum saepissime Nestor praedicet.' According to P. and B. it = 'nonne.'

nisse hominem te esse natum?' Crede mihi, cogitatione ea non mediocriter sum confirmatus. Hoc idem, si tibi videtur, fac ante oculos tibi proponas: modo uno tempore tot viri clarissimi interierunt; de imperio populi Romani tanta deminutio facta est; omnes provinciae conquassatae sunt: in unius mulierculae animula si iactura facta est, tanto opere commoveris? quae si hoc tempore non diem suum obisset, paucis post annis tamen ei
5 moriendum fuit, quoniam homo nata fuerat. Etiam tu ab hisce rebus animum ac cogitationem tuam avoca atque ea potius reminiscere, quae digna tua persona sunt: illam, quam diu ei opus fuerit, vixisse; una cum re publica fuisse; te, patrem suum, praetorem, consulem, augurem vidisse; adulescentibus primariis nuptam fuisse; omnibus bonis prope perfunctam esse: cum res publica occideret, vita excessisse. Quid est quod tu aut illa cum fortuna hoc nomine queri possitis? Denique noli te oblivisci

2. Hoc idem . . . proponas. With Baiter's punctuation I think 'idem' is the nom. sing. 'I should like you also to set before yourself the following thought.' Wieland's translation connects these words with what has gone before, in which case 'hoc idem' would be 'this same thought.' Hofm. puts a full stop after 'proponas.'

3. Modo, 'just lately,' 'but a short time ago.' Melmoth compares with this passage Addison's reflections in Westminster Abbey. Spectator, No. 26.

Tot viri clarissimi: cp. Ep. 87, 2.

4. De imperio . . facta est, 'the sovereignty of the Roman people has been impaired as seriously as you know.' Sulpicius means that the people's control over the empire, or perhaps the reputation of the empire, had been diminished—not the extent of the empire lessened.

5. Conquassatae, 'convulsed,' not Ciceronian, apparently, in this metaphorical sense.

In unius . . animula. The diminutives express somewhat of depreciation. Elsewhere such words seem to express compassion. Cp. Tac. Ann. 1. 59, where Arminius calls his wife 'muliercula.' 'Animula' is rare, but occurs in a quotation Ep. 61, 1; also in the well-known short poem of Hadrian 'animula vagula blandula.' Spartian. 25. For this sense of 'in' with the ablat., cp. Ep. 127, 3 'magnum damnum factum est in Servio.'

6. Quae si . . ei. The demonstrative is inserted on account of the change from the personal to the impersonal construction.

7. Diem suum obisset. Sulpicius uses this expression again (Ep. 101, 2), but 'diem obire' simply is more common.

8. Moriendum fuit. On the indic., cp. Ep. 38, 2, note.

Homo, 'a mortal.' Cp. Tusc. Disp. 3. 17, 36 'qui mortalis natus condicionem postules immortalium.'

Etiam tu, 'do you as well as I.' Cp. above, 'cogitatione ea non mediocriter sum confirmatus.'

10. Tua persona: cp Ep. 91, 10, note, 'your position and character.' Cp. also Ep. 64, 1, note.

Opus fuerit, 'was advantageous,' 'desirable.' Cp. Ep. 29, 25, note.

11. Una cum re publica fuisse, 'that her life lasted no longer than the commonwealth.' Cp. De Orat. 3. 3, 10 'ut ille qui haec non vidit et vixisse cum re publica pariter et cum illa simul exstinctus esse videatur.'

12. Adulescentibus primariis. Sc. C. Pisoni, cp. Intr. to Part I, §§ 8; 22; Furio Crassipedi, cp. Epp. 24, 2; 25, 3, notes; P. Dolabellae, cp. Ep. 42, 1.

13. Omnibus bonis prope perfunctam esse, 'that she enjoyed to the full nearly every blessing life can offer.' 'Perfungi' is used both of calamities and enjoyments. Forcell. Cp. Ad Fam. 1. 8, 3 'cum et honoribus amplissimis et laboribus maximis perfuncti essemus.'

15. Hoc nomine: cp. Ep. 38, 3, note.

Ciceronem esse et eum, qui aliis consueris praecipere et dare
consilium, neque imitari malos medicos, qui in alienis morbis
profitentur tenere se medicinae scientiam, ipsi se curare non
possunt; sed potius, quae aliis tute praecipere soles, ea tute tibi
subiice atque apud animum propone. Nullus dolor est, quem non 6
longinquitas temporis minuat ac molliat: hoc te exspectare tempus tibi turpe est ac non ei rei sapientia tua te occurrere. Quod si qui etiam inferis sensus est, qui illius in te amor fuit pietasque in omnes suos, hoc certe illa te facere non volt. Da hoc illi mortuae; da ceteris amicis ac familiaribus, qui tuo dolore maerent; da patriae, ut, si qua in re opus sit, opera et consilio tuo uti possit. Denique, quoniam in eam fortunam devenimus, ut etiam huic rei nobis serviendum sit, noli committere ut quisquam te putet non tam filiam quam rei publicae tempora et aliorum victoriam lugere. Plura me ad te de hac re scribere pudet, ne videar

1. **Ciceronem.** On the use of proper names to express character or distinction, cp. Ad Fam. 2. 4. 1 'quid est quod possit graviter a Cicerone scribi ad Curionem nisi de re publica;' Ep. 15. 15 'civis Romanus et Cato.'

2. **Neque imitari:** supply 'be willing' from 'noli.' Süpfle. The MS. has 'neque imitare,' and, as the letter is not Cicero's, perhaps there is no sufficient reason for changing it, though 'neve' would be more regular.

3. **Tenere,** 'to possess.' Not very common in the precise sense, apparently.

6. **Hoc te exspectare . . occurrere:** cp. Cicero's own advice to Tiro, Ad Fam. 5. 16, 5 'quod allatura est ipsa diuturnitas quae maximos luctus vetustate tollit id nos praecipere consilio prudentiaque debemus.'

7. **Ei rei . . te occurrere.** 'that you should anticipate the effect of time,' lit. 'go forward to meet the result.' 'Occurrere' = 'remedium adferre, praesertim cum de malo agatur quod nondum accidit' Forcell. Cp. In Verr. 2 Act. 4. 47, 105 'ratio . . occurrendum esse satietati aurium.'

Quod si qui . . sensus est, 'and if even the departed have any consciousness.' On this sense of '**inferi**' cp. In Vat. 6, 14 'inferorum animas elicere.' Sulpicius speaks very doubtfully as to a life after death.

8. **Qui illius in te amor fuit.** On this constr. = 'pro' with the ablat., cp. Madv. 446 'such was her affection for you that.'

9. **Hoc certe . . te facere,** i.e. 'that you should mourn immoderately.'

Da hoc, 'concede this,' viz. a lessening of your sorrow.

Illi mortuae, a fair instance of the use of the demonstrative as equivalent to the Greek article. Cp. Nägelsb. I. § 3. 2 b, who quotes Cic. de Orat. 2. 46, 193; De Nat. Deor. 2. 3, 7; Tusc. Disp. 5. 27, 78.

11. **Si qua in re opus sit,** 'if your aid can be of service to it in anything.'

12. **Denique.** Sulpicius has already used this word in § 5. It is probable that he intended to finish his letter with the words 'uti possit,' when a fresh topic occurred to him. The letter does not seem to have been carefully revised. Süpfle; Müller.

Quoniam . . serviendum sit, 'since we have come into such a position that we must take account of such considerations as the following.'

Devenimus. 'Devenire' = 'in locum perniciosum venire.' Forcell.

14. **Aliorum** = 'alterorum,' sc. 'Caesarianorum.' Cp. Livy 24. 27 'aliae partis hominibus,' of one of two parties—a doubtful passage, however: also Caes. Bell. Gall. 1. 1 'unam . . aliam . . tertiam.'

15. **De hac re,** 'on this subject,' i.e. the general subject of the letter. For the next sentence suggests a new topic, and does not dwell on that last mentioned.

prudentiae tuae diffidere; qua re, si hoc unum proposuero, finem faciam scribendi: vidimus aliquotiens secundam pulcherrime te ferre fortunam magnamque ex ea re te laudem apisci; fac aliquando intellegamus adversam quoque te aeque ferre posse neque id maius, quam debeat, tibi onus videri, ne ex omnibus virtutibus haec una tibi videatur deesse. Quod ad me attinet, cum te tranquilliore animo esse cognoro, de iis rebus, quae hic geruntur, quemadmodumque se provincia habeat, certiorem faciam. Vale.

99. To SERVIUS SULPICIUS (AD FAM. IV. 6).

ASTURA, APRIL (?), 45 B.C. (709 A.U.C.)

1. I wish, my dear Servius, you *had* been present at the time of my bereavement; your letter has been consolatory; your presence would have been still more so; your son, however tries to fill your place. I feel the force of what you say. But I have not the consolations which other sufferers had in better times. 2. The loss of her who was my only comfort makes even old wounds smart; and I now feel the misfortunes of the State more bitterly than ever. 3. Your sympathy and advice will be most precious, and I hope to see you as soon as possible.

M. CICERO S. D. SER. SULPICIO.

1 Ego vero, Servi, vellem, ut scribis, in meo gravissimo casu adfuisses: quantum enim praesens me adiuvare potueris et consolando et prope aeque dolendo, facile ex eo intellego, quod litteris lectis aliquantum acquievi; nam et ea scripsisti, quae

1. Prudentiae tuae diffidere, 'to distrust your wisdom,' i.e. your power of thinking for yourself and controlling yourself.

Si . . proposuero, 'when I have set before you' 'Si' = 'ubi' or 'postquam.' Forcell. Cp. also Madv. 340.

2. Pulcherrime, 'most creditably,' i.e. with moderation.

3. Apisci. The simple form is rare. As a rule the Latin authors of the best period preferred compound to simple forms of verbs.

4. Aeque, 'with equal credit.' Süpfle. So, too, Forcell. = 'ut illam.'

5. Id, sc. 'adversam ferre fortunam.'

6. Haec una, 'firmness in adversity.'

7. Tranquilliore. The reading of the MS. seems to be 'tranquilliorem,' and Wesenb. retains it.

8. Geruntur . . habeat. The last word is in the conj. because 'quemadmodum' implies a question. Cp. Madv. 356.

Provincia, cp. Ep. 90, 2, note.

10. Ego vero . . vellem. When 'vero' occurs, as here, at the beginning of a letter, it must be taken in close connection with a previous letter. Here the words are an answer to Ep. 98, 1, as 'ut scribis' shews, 'yes, I could wish, Servius.' Cp. Madv. 437 d: 454.

11. Potueris. In a direct sentence potuisti adiuvare would have been written, which in an indirect one becomes 'potueris.' Cp. Madv. 348 e, Obs. 1, with 381 and Obs.

13. Aliquantum acquievi, 'I was much calmed.' 'Acquievi' = 'me consolatus sum' cp. Forcell.

levare luctum possent, et in me consolando non mediocrem ipse animi dolorem adhibuisti. Servius tamen tuus omnibus officiis, quae illi tempori tribui potuerunt, declaravit et quanti ipse me faceret et quam suum talem erga me animum tibi gratum putaret fore; cuius officia iucundiora scilicet saepe mihi fuerunt, numquam tamen gratiora. Me autem non oratio tua solum et societas paene aegritudinis, sed etiam auctoritas consolatur; turpe enim esse existimo me non ita ferre casum meum, ut tu, tali sapientia praeditus, ferendum putas. Sed opprimor interdum et vix resisto dolori, quod ea me solacia deficiunt, quae ceteris, quorum mihi exempla propono, simili in fortuna non defuerunt. Nam et Q. Maximus, qui filium consularem, clarum virum et magnis rebus gestis, amisit, et L. Paulus, qui duo septem diebus, et vester Gallus et M. Cato, qui summo ingenio, summa virtute filium perdidit, iis temporibus fuerunt, ut eorum luctum ipsorum dignitas consolaretur ea, quam ex re publica consequebantur. Mihi autem amissis orna- 2
mentis iis, quae ipse commemoras quaeque eram maximis laboribus adeptus, unum manebat illud solacium, quod ereptum

2. **Adhibuisti**, '*you shewed*.' Cp. Tusc. Disp. 1. 29. 71 'Socrates . . adhibuit liberam ferociam.'

3. **Illi tempori**, 'to this calamity.' Cp. Ep. 1, 4, note.

Declaravit, 'shewed.'

5. **Iucundiora . . gratiora**, 'have often given greater pleasure, but have never deserved more gratitude.' Cp. Ad Att. 1. 17. 6 'fuit mihi saepe et laudis nostrae gratulatio tua iucunda et timoris consolatio grata.'

Scilicet: cp. Ep. 12, 4, note, alib.

7. **Auctoritas**, 'the weight *of your* advice.' Cp., especially, §§ 5 and 6 of the previous letter.

12. **Q. Maximus**. Q. Fabius Maximus Cunctator, the celebrated general in the second Punic war. Cp. Tusc. Disp. 3. 28, 70. His son was consul 213 B.C., and recovered Arpi for the Romans in that year. Cp. Livy 24. 43–47.

14. **L. Paulus**. Son of the Paulus who fell at Cannae. He defeated Perseus at Pydna 168 B.C., and conquered Macedonia. His two sons here referred to died about the time of his triumph. Cp De Senect. 19, 68; Vell. 1. 10. They were his two youngest sons; their elder brothers had been adopted by P. Scipio Africanus, son of the conqueror of Zama, and by Q. Fabius Maximus.

Vester Gallus. C. Sulpicius Gallus did good service against *Perseus*, under the command of L. Paulus (cp. Livy 44. 37), and was consul 166 B.C. He was a learned man, especially in astronomy. Cp. De Off. 1. 6, 19; Brut. 20, 78. The death of his son is referred to, De Amic. 2, 9. Cicero inserts his name here, probably, as a compliment to his correspondent; it does not occur in a similar list given Tusc. Disp. 3. 28, 70.

Vester, as one of the '*gens Sulpicia*.'

M. Cato, the censor. His son was 'praetor designatus' when he died in 152 B.C. (cp. Tusc. Disp. l. c.), and is mentioned De Senect. 6. 15; 19, 68; Livy Epit. 48.

15. **Qui . . perdidit** refers of course only to Cato.

17. **Ex re publica**, *from political life*.' Cp. Ep. 91, 9.

Ornamentis . . quae . . commemoras, 'the distinctions which you mention.' Cp. Ep. 98, 5 'te, patrem suum, praetorem, consulem, augurem vidisse.' Cicero must mean that he had lost the position to which such distinctions entitled him.

19. **Illud solacium**, i.e. 'the pleasure of Tullia's society.'

est. Non amicorum negotiis, non rei publicae procuratione impediebantur cogitationes meae; nihil in foro agere libebat; aspicere curiam non poteram; existimabam, id quod erat, omnes me et industriae meae fructus et fortunae perdidisse. Sed, cum cogitarem haec mihi tecum et cum quibusdam esse communia, et cum frangerem iam ipse me *et* cogerem illa ferre toleranter, habebam quo confugerem, ubi conquiescerem, cuius in sermone et suavitate omnes curas doloresque deponerem.: nunc autem hoc tam gravi volnere etiam illa, quae consanuisse videbantur, recrudescunt; non enim, ut tum me a re publica maestum domus excipiebat, quae levaret, sic nunc domo maerens ad rem publicam confugere possum, ut in eius bonis acquiescam. Itaque et domo absum et foro, quod nec eum dolorem, quem e re publica capio, domus iam consolari potest nec domesticum res
5 publica. Quo magis te exspecto teque videre quam primum cupio: maior mihi levatio adferri nulla potest quam coniunctio

1. **Non . . impediebantur cogitationes**, 'the course of my thoughts was not checked.'

Amicorum negotiis, 'by attention to my friends' affairs in the senate and in the courts of justice.

Procuratione, 'administration,' Forcell.

2. **In foro**, 'as an advocate;' perhaps also as a popular orator.

3. **Aspicere curiam non poteram.** The sight of it would remind him how different a position he had once held there.

4. **Industriae . . et fortunae**, 'the rewards of my industry and gifts of fortune,' to which Cicero allowed considerable influence in awarding public honours. Cp. Pro Muren. 17. He refers here to his public distinctions, and to the credit and influence which they should have secured him. Cp. on 'ornamenta' above.

5. **Haec**, 'this loss of position.'

Tecum et cum quibusdam, 'with you and certain others I might name.' He means such friends of the old constitution as had survived Caesar's victory.

6. **Frangerem . . ipse me**, 'was breaking down my resolution,' 'was giving way,' 'forcing myself into acquiescence.' Cp. Ep. 90, 4, 'fregit . . meum consilium.' 'Frangere' = 'vincere.' Forcell. Cp. Tusc. Disp. 1. 21, 49; Pro Sull. 6. 18.

Illa, 'the losses I have referred to.'

7. **Quo confugerem**, foll., 'a refuge and resting-place,' i.e. Tullia's society. Cp. Ep. 71, 9.

9. **Hoc tam gravi volnere**, 'owing to this heavy blow.' Ablat. caus.

Illa, 'the old wounds.' Cp. the beginning of this section.

Consanuisse, apparently used here only in a metaphorical sense. Forcell. Hofm. says that it is peculiar to the letters of Cicero.

10. **Recrudescunt**, 'smart afresh.'

Tum, 'while Tullia lived.'

A re publica maestum, 'retiring in sadness from public life.' 'Maestum a' seems to unite this meaning with 'saddened by,' but the combination is one hardly possible to be expressed in English. Cp. Verg. Aen. 6. 450

'Recens a volnere Dido.'

11. **Domo . . confugere**: cp. Madv. 275, obs. 2.

12. **Ut . . acquiescam**, 'to derive content from its prosperity.'

13. **Domo absum**, 'I stay away from home,' i.e. from his residence at Rome. It appears that Tullia had lived under his roof for some time. From the sad associations he had with his Tusculan estate, it has been argued that she died there (cp. Ad Att. 12. 46), but Ascon. in Pisonian., p. 122, and Plut. Cic. 41, indicate that she died in the house of Dolabella.

15. **Videre**: cp. Ep. 81, 3, note.

16. **Levatio**, 'relief' = 'consolatio.' Forcell. Wesenb. has 'maior enim levatio mihi,' T. has 'maius solacium afferre ratio;' M. Thurot suggests 'maius solacium levatio afferre nulla.'

consuetudinis sermonumque nostrorum; quamquam sperabam tuum adventum—sic enim audiebam—adpropinquare. Ego autem cum multis de causis te exopto quam primum videre, tum etiam, ut ante commentemur inter nos, qua ratione nobis traducendum sit hoc tempus, quod est totum ad unius voluntatem accommodandum et prudentis et liberalis et, ut perspexisse videor, nec a me alieni et tibi amicissimi. Quod cum ita sit, magnae tamen est deliberationis, quae ratio sit ineunda nobis, non agendi aliquid, sed illius concessu et beneficio quiescendi. Vale.

100. To A. TORQUATUS (AD FAM. VI. 2).

ASTURA, APRIL (?), 45 B.C. (709 A.U.C.)

1. Not forgetfulness, but either ill-health or absence from Rome has been the reason of my writing to you less frequently than I used to write. 2. The delay which has taken place with regard to your restoration is no real subject for regret; whatever may be the end of the present troubles, you have nothing more to fear than others, and may hope for better fortune. 3. Let me know how you do, and where you are likely to be.

M. CICERO S. D. A. TORQUATO.

Peto a te ne me putes oblivione tui rarius ad te scribere, 1
quam solebam, sed aut gravitate valetudinis, qua tamen iam

Coniunctio . . nostrorum, 'meetings for friendly intercourse and conversation.'

1. Consuetudinis. 'Consuetudo' = 'convictus.' Forcell.

Quamquam sperabam, 'I hope, however.' Cp. Ep. 1, 1, note.

2. Tuum adventum, 'your arrival' from your province, where Sulpicius' term of office was expiring. Süpfle.

3. Cum . . tum etiam: cp. Epp. 26, 3, note; 9, 12, note.

4. Ante, i.e. 'before Caesar's return from Spain,' which took place in the autumn of 45 B.C. Cp. Intr. to Part IV, § 12.

Commentemur = 'meditemur' (Forcell.), 'consider.'

Qua ratione, foll., 'in what way we are to pass this time in which we must altogether consult the wishes of one man.'

Traducendum = 'agendum.' Forcell.

5. Tempus, used, like 'dies,' for what passes in it.

Quod est . . . accommodandum, 'during which our behaviour must be so ordered as to suit the will of one,' etc.

7. Tibi amicissimi. Sulpicius had various claims on Caesar's good will. During his consulship he had not supported the violent proposals of his colleague, M. Marcellus; it is doubtful if he had gone to the camp of Pompey during the civil war; his son had served in Caesar's army; and he himself had accepted the government of Greece from Caesar. Cp. Ep. 90, 2 and 3, notes; Intr. to Part III, § 17: Ep. 67, 2.

Magnae . . deliberationis, 'it is a case for much discussion.' 'Deliberatio' = συμβουλεύειν. Forcell.

9. Illius . . beneficio, ablat. caus.

Quiescendi, 'of retiring from active life.' 'Quiescere' = 'in otio esse.' Forcell.

A. TORQUATO. A. Manlius Torquatus is mentioned more than once with regard by Cicero. He took part with Pompey in the civil war, and after the battle of Pharsalus lived in retirement at Athens. Cp. Ad Fam. 6. 1, 6 'in urbe ea es ubi nata et alta est ratio et moderatio vitae.' He was subsequently allowed to return to Italy, but not, apparently, to Rome. Cp. note on p. 473, l. 5, and Ad Att. 13. 9. 1.

11. Gravitate valetudinis. Perhaps

paulum videor levari, aut quod absim ab urbe, ut, qui ad te proficiscantur, scire non possim; qua re velim ita statutum habeas, me tui memoriam cum summa benevolentia tenere tuasque omnes res non minori mihi curae quam meas esse.

2 Quod maiore in varietate versata est adhuc tua causa, quam homines aut volebant aut opinabantur, mihi crede, non est pro malis temporum quod moleste feras; necesse est enim aut armis urgeri rem publicam sempiternis aut his positis recreari aliquando aut funditus interire. Si arma valebunt, nec eos, a quibus recipieris, vereri debes nec eos, quos adiuvisti; si armis aut condicione positis aut defatigatione abiectis aut victoria detractis civitas respiraverit, et dignitate tua frui tibi et fortunis licebit; sin omnino interierint omnia fueritque is exitus, quem vir prudentissimus, M. Antonius, iam tum timebat, cum

this illness was caused in part by his regret for Tullia.

Quo . . levari, 'from which, however, I think I am to some extent recovering.' On the abl., cp. Madv. 261.

1. Quod absim. Not 'absum,' because Cicero refers to the opinion he would have Torquatus hold, not to the fact.

Qui ad te proficiscantur, 'what friends or messengers are going to you,' so that I might entrust letters to them.

2. Statutum habeas, 'assure yourself.' On 'habeo,' with the past part. pass., usually only of verbs denoting insight or resolution, cp. Madv. 427.

5. Quod . . non est quod, 'there is no reason, considering the painful circumstances of these times, for you to regret that your complete restoration has been delayed.' On the force of est quod, cp. Ep. 90. 5, note.

Maiore in varietate . . . est, 'has been subject to "a more varied combination" of lenity and rigour.' Wiel. Marth., in substance. Caesar would only grant the pardon of Torquatus by degrees. Cicero speaks of him as in Italy (Ad Att. 13. 9. 1), yet as having something still to request from Caesar (Ib. 13. 20, 1; 13. 21, 2). Manut. takes rather a different view of the passage, and explains it as = 'quod varietas fuerit inter causam Torquati et voluntatemque opinionemque hominum.'

7. Aut armis . . interire. Either, says Cicero, the civil war must last for ever, or on its conclusion the Commonwealth must to some extent recover, or be utterly destroyed. In the first two cases you have nothing to fear; in the last, nothing worse than others. For the infinitives after 'necesse est,' cp. Madv. 373, Obs. 1.

9. Si arma valebunt = 'si perpetuum bellum erit' (Müller), 'if, of the three possibilities I have mentioned, continued war be that which comes to pass.'

Eos, a quibus recipieris, sc. 'in fidem,' 'those who shall accept your submission,' and thereby promise you your life. The Caesarians are meant. On this sense of 'recipere,' cp. In Cat. 4. 10, 22 'hostes . . aut oppressi serviunt, aut recepti beneficio se obligatos putant.'

10. Eos, quos adiuvisti, i.e. the Pompeians. It is doubtful, however, how this party would have treated those of their friends who did not persevere in the struggle to the end. Cp. Intr. to Part III, §§ 7; 10; Ep. 82, 3, note.

Armis . . detractis, 'after arms have been laid down upon terms, or thrown away in weariness, or wrested from one side by the other's victory.' Cicero must have written this before the news of the battle of Munda reached Rome. It was fought on March 17. Cp. Intr. to Part IV, § 12.

11. Condicione = 'pactione.' Forcell.

12. Respiraverit, 'shall have obtained relief from its sufferings.' The verb is often used metaphorically, as here.

13. Is exitus = 'utter ruin.'

14. Iam tum, 'even before the civil war of Marius and Sulla.' Manut. M. Antonius the orator was murdered by order of C. Marius and Cinna 87 B.C. Cp. Philipp. 1. 14, 34; Brut. 89; Livy Epit. 80. On his prophecy, cp. De Orat. 1. 7, 26.

tantum instare malorum suspicabatur, misera est illa quidem consolatio, tali praesertim civi et viro, sed tamen necessaria, nihil esse praecipue cuiquam dolendum in eo, quod accidat universis. Quae vis insit in his paucis verbis—plura enim committenda epistolae non erant—, si attendes, quod facis, profecto etiam sine meis litteris intelleges te aliquid habere, quod speres, nihil, quod aut hoc aut aliquo rei publicae statu timeas; omnia si interierint, cum superstitem te esse rei publicae ne si liceat quidem velis, ferendam esse fortunam, praesertim quae absit a culpa. Sed haec hactenus. Tu velim scribas ad me, quid agas et ubi futurus sis, ut aut quo scribam aut quo veniam scire possim.

101. SERVIUS SULPICIUS TO CICERO (AD FAM. IV. 12).

ATHENS, MAY 31, 45 B.C. (709 A.U.C.)

1. On landing at Piraeus on May 23rd, I found M. Marcellus there, and spent the day with him. 2. Two days afterwards I heard that he had been badly wounded

4. Quae vis . . verbis, 'the drift of these few hints.'

Plura enim . . non erant, 'which are all that I wish to entrust to a letter.' Epistolary terms.

Enim explains why Cicero did not write at greater length.

5. Si attendes, 'if you consider.' In English these words would precede 'quae vis . . insit,' 'if you consider the force of these few words.' 'Attendes,' sc. 'animum;' but the verb is often used absolutely, as here. Forcell.

6. Sine meis litteris, 'without any letter from me.' On this use of the poss. pron., cp. Ep. 72, 1, note.

Aliquid habere quod speres, 'that you have something to hope for,' i.e. complete restoration to his previous position. Cp. note on the address of the letter.

7. Aut hoc . . statu. On the ablat. abs., cp. Ep. 1, 2, note, 'if the present or any other form of legal government be maintained.' Cicero had told Torquatus Ad (Fam. 6. 1, 6) 'non debes . . dubitare quin aut aliqua re publica sis is futurus qui esse debes, aut perdita non adflictiore condicione quam ceteri.'

Aliquo seems here to mean 'any other.' Cp. In Cat. 1. 8, 20 'Catilina dubitas . . abire in aliquas terras;' Tac. Ann. 1. 4 'Tiberium . . ne iis quidem annis . . aliquid quam iram . . meditatum.' Aliquis is used in negative clauses where the negative particle is attached to the verb, or where the negation applies to a special affirmative idea. Otherwise 'ullus' or 'quisquam' is used. Cp. Madv. 494 a, Obs. 1.

8. Omnia si interierint, adversat. conj. omitted. 'Sin autem' would be more regular. Cp. on the omission, Ep. 6, 2, note.

Cum superstitem . . velis, 'since you would wish to survive the Commonwealth, not even if it should be in your power to do so.' So these words may be literally translated. In English the order of the two clauses would be changed, 'you would not wish to survive the Commonwealth, even if you could.' On the tenses of velis and liceat, cp. Ep. 5, 3, note.

9. Quae absit a culpa, 'as you have incurred it by no fault of yours.' Cp. Ep. 16, 2, note.

11. Ubi futurus sit . . quo veniam. This seems to shew that Torquatus had a good prospect of returning to Italy, for Cicero would hardly have proposed to cross the sea to him. Manut. thinks that Torquatus was already in Italy.

by P. Magius Cilo, and that the assassin had killed himself. As I drew near Piraeus at dawn, taking surgeons with me, I heard that Marcellus was dead. 3. I took back the body to Athens in my litter, and had it burned in the Academy, the most honourable place where such a ceremony could legally be performed. I also caused the Athenians to provide for the erection of a monument to Marcellus there.

SERVIUS CICERONI SAL. PLUR.

1 Etsi scio non iucundissimum me nuntium vobis adlaturum,
tamen quoniam casus et natura in nobis dominatur, visum est
[faciendum], quoquo modo res se haberet, vos certiores facere.
A. d. x. Kal. Iun. cum ab Epidauro Piraeum navi advectus essem,
ibi *M.* Marcellum, collegam nostrum, conveni eumque diem ibi
consumpsi, ut cum eo essem. Postero die cum ab eo digressus
essem eo consilio, ut ab Athenis in Boeotiam irem reliquamque
iurisdictionem absolverem, ille, ut aiebat, supra Maleas in Italiam
2 versus navigaturus erat. Post diem tertium eius diei, cum ab
Athenis proficisci in animo haberem, circiter hora decima noctis

1. **Vobis**, 'to you and to our common friends at Rome.'

2. **Quoniam . . . dominatur**, 'since you will be the less surprised from knowing that nature and chance control our lives.' The distinction between natura and casus is rather popular than philosophical. Death by disease, however sudden, would be called natural; death by the hand of an assassin, casual; though 'casus,' in the strictest sense, is confined to events which exclude human agency altogether. Cp. Forcell. Manut., however, thinks that only a death from old age could be strictly called 'natural.' On the sing. 'dominatur,' cp. Ep. 34, 6, note. But Andr. thinks that 'dominantur' should be read.

Visum est = 'placuit.' Forcell.

3. **Quoquo modo res se haberet**, 'the circumstances, however painful,' whatever may be the nature of the case.' 'Wie auch immer die Sache sich verhalten möchte.' Andr.

Vos certiores facere. The infinitive is to be accounted for as following one of the 'verba voluntatis.' Madv. 396. Wesenb. has 'faciendum . . ut facerem,' which Cobet also suggests.

4. **A. d. x. Kal. Iun.**, 'May 23.'

Piraeum. Cicero thought this form more correct in Latin than Piraea. Cp. Ad Att. 7. 3, 10.

Navi. This ablat. has an adverbial force. Süpfle. Cp. Ad Att. 14. 20, 1. On the form, cp. Madv. 42, 1 and 3.

5. **Collegam nostrum**, 'my colleague as consul?' or 'our colleague as augur?' Müller and Andr. think the former; Billerb. on § 3, and Wesenb. the latter. Ep. 90, 3, rather supports Müller.

7. **Reliquamque iurisdictionem**, 'the rest of my judicial business,' which he had to discharge before leaving his province. It was usual for the governor to make a circuit of his principal towns for this purpose. See Cicero's account of his proceedings in Cilicia, Ep. 36, 9. The province of Achaia would include nearly all Greece proper, even if Macedonia was not also under the government of Sulpicius. Cp. Ep. 90, 2, note; Smith's Dict. of Geog. 1. 17.

8. **Supra Maleas**, 'round Malea.' The singular form of this word is more common than the plural, which, however, occurs Herod. 1. 82. Malea was the S.E. promontory of Laconia.

In Italiam versus. 'Versus' is probably a preposition, correcting 'in.' 'To Italy, I mean in that direction.' Cp. Forcell.

9. **Post diem tertium eius diei.** Probably on May 26. This expression is not apparently Ciceronian, cp. Madv. 276, Obs. 6, but resembles 'postridie eius diei,' which is common in Caesar.

10. **Hora decima noctis.** This would be about two hours before day-break, or rather before 3 o'clock in the morning. Cp. Smith's Dict. of Antiq. 'hora,' p. 614.

P. Postumius, familiaris eius, ad me venit et mihi nuntiavit M. Marcellum, collegam nostrum, post cenae tempus a P. Magio Cilone, familiare eius, pugione percussum esse et duo volnera accepisse, unum in stomacho, alterum in capite secundum aurem; sperari tamen eum vivere posse; Magium se ipsum interfecisse postea; se a Marcello ad me missum esse, qui haec nuntiaret et rogaret, ut medicos *cogerem*. Coëgi et e vestigio eo sum profectus prima luce. Cum non longe a Piraeo abessem, puer Acidini obviam mihi venit cum codicillis, in quibus erat scriptum, paulo ante lucem Marcellum diem suum obisse. Ita vir clarissimus ab homine deterrimo acerbissima morte est adfectus, et, cui inimici propter dignitatem pepercerant, inventus est amicus, qui ei mortem offerret. Ego tamen et tabernaculum eius perrexi: 3
inveni duos libertos et pauculos servos; reliquos aiebant profugisse metu perterritos, quod dominus eorum ante tabernaculum interfectus esset. Coactus sum in eadem illa lectica, qua ipse delatus eram, meisque lecticariis in urbem eum referre, ibique pro ea copia, quae Athenis erat, funus ei satis amplum faciendum curavi. Ab Atheniensibus, locum sepulturae intra urbem

1. P. Postumius is apparently only here mentioned. Orell., Boot.

2. A P. Magio Cilone. Some suspected Caesar of instigating Magius, but both Brutus and Cicero disbelieved the charge, and Cicero thought that Magius killed Marcellus in a fit of rage at Marcellus having refused him help in some money difficulties. Cp. Ad Att. 13. 10. 3.

7. Medicos cogerem. T. has 'medicos ei mitterem itaque medicos coegi.'

E vestigio, 'at once.' Forcell.

8. Acidini. C. Manlius Acidinus was a youth of good family studying at Athens apparently. Cp. Ad Att. 12. 32, 2.

9. Codicillis, 'tablets,' on which letters were written. Forcell.

10. Diem suum obisse: cp. Ep. 98. 4, note.

11. Acerbissima. Perhaps 'most untimely.' Cp. Verg. Aen. 6. 428-9.

'Ab ubere raptos
Abstulit atra dies et funere mersit acerbo,'

with Conington's note. If Marcellus was elected consul as early as he was qualified for election, he would be forty-nine years old in 45 B.C.

13. Ad tabernaculum. Piraeus lay in ruins (cp. Ep. 98. 4, note), so that those who wished to spend a night there had either to pitch a tent or to stay on board ship in the harbour.

Tamen, 'though it was too late to be of service to Marcellus.' Andr.

14. Profugisse . . perterritos. Lest they should be punished for complicity with the assassin, or for failing to defend their master. A provision for the punishment of slaves in such a case was probably contained in the Leges Corneliae (L. Sullae); and a decree of the senate embodying a similar provision was adopted under Augustus—the Senatus Consultum Silanianum. Cp. Digest. 29. 5. 25. Later legislation was very severe on this subject. Cp. the case of Pedanius Secundus (Tac. Ann. 14. 42-45), on which the historian remarks that it was 'vetus mos' for the whole of a man's domestic slaves to be executed if he had been murdered in his house. Cp. Tac. Ann. 13. 32.

17. Meisque lecticariis, 'and by the hands of my bearers.' Ablat. instr.; 'per meos lect.' would be more common. Cp. Madv. 254. Obs. 3. The word 'lecticarius' occurs Pro Rosc. Am. 46, 134.

Referre. Marcellus then had probably passed through Athens on his way to Piraeus. See Andr.

18. Pro ea copia . . erat, 'so far as the means available at Athens allowed.'

ut darent, impetrare non potui, quod religione se impediri dicerent; neque tamen id antea cuiquam concesserant: quod proximum fuit, uti in quo vellemus gymnasio eum sepeliremus, nobis permiserunt. Nos in nobilissimo orbi terrarum gymnasio Academiae locum delegimus ibique eum combussimus, posteaque curavimus, ut eidem Athenienses in eodem loco monumentum ei marmoreum faciendum locarent. Ita, quae nostra officia fuerunt, pro collegio et pro propinquitate et vivo et mortuo omnia ei praestitimus. Vale. D. pr. Kal. Iun. Athenis.

102. TO Q. VALERIUS ORCA (AD FAM. XIII. 4).

ROME, OCTOBER (BAIT.), 45 B.C. (709 A.U.C.)

1. I am on very good terms with the people of Volaterrae, and shall be much indebted to you if you can save their lands from distribution to military colonists. During my consulship 2. I interposed for their protection, and Caesar exempted their territory from distribution four years afterwards. I think you should either follow his example or wait till you can refer the whole matter to him. 3. I now turn from argument to entreaty, and recommend the city to your protection in the strongest terms. 4. I should certainly appeal to the people on their behalf if the times admitted of it, and hope I may have as much influence with you as I might have with the people.

1. Quod .. dicerent: cp. Epp. 1, 3; 30, 6, notes.

2. Neque tamen, foll. These words admit some justice in the Athenians' plea; 'quod .. dicerent' would rather imply that it was a mere pretext. 'However, I may say in their defence that they had never granted the privilege to any one before.' The words are rather obscure; every step in the argument is not drawn out, but this is natural enough in a letter. The Greeks generally buried their dead without the walls of their cities. See Thucyd. 2, 34; but cp. Plut. Timol. 39. Mr. Jeans remarks, that this passage 'shows, as Mr. Long justly points out, the toleration of the Romans for the national and religious customs of the different people in their empire.'

Quod proximum fuit, 'the next best thing,' or, as Andr. 'my next request.'

3. Gymnasio. The gymnasia were places held in much esteem. Cp. Corn. Nep. Timol. 5, 4. The term was now extended so as to include schools and places of discussion, perhaps because originally the public places of exercise were chosen by philosophers for their lectures and conversations. Cp. p. 31.

4. Orbi terrarum, 'in the whole world.' Cp. In Verr. 2 Act. 4. 38, 82 'cuius amplissimum orbi terrarum clarissimumque monumentum est.' Andr. reads 'orbis.'

Academiae. The celebrated gardens where Plato taught, on the north side of Athens.

6. Curavimus, i.e. by command or request. There would be little difference between the two when made by a Roman governor.

7. Quae nostra .. fuerunt, 'the attentions which could be expected from me.' Wesenb. omits the comma after 'fuerunt' and places one after 'propinquitate.'

8. Collegio, 'our relation as colleagues.' Cp. Livy 10. 22 'nihil concordi collegio firmius ad rem publicam tuendam esse;' Ib. 10. 24 'invidiose Decium concordibus collegiis tribus.'

Propinquitate, 'intimacy.' Forcell. does not give this sense as Ciceronian, but Sulpicius may have been less precise, and I cannot find that he was connected with Marcellus by blood or marriage. Andr., however, assumes a relationship between Sulpicius and Marcellus.

M. CICERO S. D. Q. VALERIO Q. F. ORCAE LEGATO PROPR.

Cum municipibus Volaterranis mihi summa necessitudo est; 1
magno enim meo beneficio adfecti cumulatissime mihi gratiam rettulerunt; nam nec in honoribus meis *nec in* laboribus umquam defuerunt. Cum quibus si mihi nulla causa intercederet, tamen, quod te vehementissime diligo quodque me a te plurimi fieri sentio, et monerem te et hortarer, ut eorum fortunis consuleres, praesertim cum prope praecipuam causam haberent ad ius obtinendum: primum quod Sullani temporis acerbitatem deorum immortalium benignitate subterfugerunt, deinde, quod summo studio populi Romani a me in consulatu meo defensi sunt. Cum 2
enim tribuni plebi legem iniquissimam de eorum agris promulgavissent, facile senatui populoque Romano persuasi, ut eos cives,

Q. VALERIO. This Valerius had been praetor 57 B.C., and had supported Cicero's recall from exile. Post Red. in Sen. 9. 23. Next year he governed Africa as propraetor or proconsul (Ad Fam. 13. 6 a, 2), and when this letter was written he was one of the commissioners appointed by Caesar to superintend an assignation of lands in Italy, on which cp. Ep. 89. Similar letters to this are found, as 5. 7. and 8 of this 13th book Ad Familiares.

1. Municipibus. The people of Volaterrae had probably received the Roman franchise by the 'Lex Iulia' 90 B.C. Their city was an ancient and famous one in the north of Etruria, still called Volterra.

2. Magno .. beneficio adfecti: cp. notes on § 2 for the facts. On the expression 'adficere beneficio,' cp. Pro Muren. 1, 4. 'honore adfecto.'

3. Honoribus .. laboribus. These two words seem to refer to Cicero's days of good and evil fortune respectively. Cp. Ad Fam. 13. 7. for a similar contrast.

4. Defuerunt, sc. 'suffragiis,' 'failed to support me' by their votes.

Cum quibus si .. intercederet, 'and if no such tie existed between us.'

Causa = 'coniunctio.' Forcell. Cp. Pro Quinct. 15, 48 'quicum tibi .. omnes .. causae et necessitudines veteres intercedebant.' '"Intercedere" de iis dicitur per quae alteri iungimur vel alienamur.' Forcell.

5. Quod te .. diligo. Cicero's regard for Valerius induced him to warn him how Caesar had interposed for the protection of Volaterrae. Cp. next section.

6. Ut eorum fortunis consuleres, 'that you would protect them in the enjoyment of their property.'

7. Prope praecipuam causam, 'well-nigh the strongest claim.'

8. Sullani temporis acerbitatem. Volaterrae had afforded an asylum to some of the proscribed partisans of Marius, and had stood a siege of two years, surrendering at last to Sulla upon terms. Sulla had then declared its lands confiscated, but had not assigned them to new occupants; and had carried a law at Rome depriving the people of Volaterrae of their rights as Roman citizens. The courts, however, refused to recognize the validity of the latter law, and the confiscation was never actually carried out. Hence Cicero represents that the gods had interposed to protect the people of Volaterrae. Their sufferings in the cause of Marius would give them a claim upon Caesar. Cp. Pro Caec. 7, 18 and 35. 102; De Dom. 30, 79; Livy Epit. 89.

9. Summo studio populi Romani, 'with the most hearty approval of the Roman people.'

10. In consulatu meo. If this was the first service which Cicero rendered to the people of Volaterrae, it seems probable that the first obligation must have been conferred by them, for 'in honoribus' can hardly refer to a time subsequent to Cicero's consulship.

11. Tribuni plebi. Rullus took the lead among them. Cp. Intr. to Part I, § 9. Cicero pleaded again for the exemption of the lands of Volaterrae from the operation of the law of Flavius in 60 B.C. Cp. Ad Att. 1. 19. 4. Plebi, a rare gen. from 'plebes.' Forcell.

quibus fortuna pepercisset, salvos esse vellent. Hanc actionem meam C. Caesar primo suo consulatu lege agraria comprobavit agrumque Volaterranum et oppidum omni periculo in perpetuum liberavit, ut mihi dubium non sit quin is, qui novas necessitudines adiungat, vetera sua beneficia conservari velit. Quam ob rem est tuae prudentiae aut sequi eius auctoritatem, cuius sectam atque imperium summa cum tua dignitate secutus es, aut certe illi integram omnem causam reservare; illud vero dubitare non debes, quin tam grave, tam firmum, tam honestum municipium tibi tuo summo beneficio in perpetuum obligari velis.

3 Sed haec, quae supra scripta sunt, eo spectant, ut te horter et suadeam: reliqua sunt, quae pertinent ad rogandum, ut non solum tua causa tibi consilium me dare putes, sed etiam, quod mihi opus sit, me a te petere et rogare. Gratissimum igitur mihi feceris, si Volaterranos omnibus rebus integros incolumesque esse volueris: eorum ego domicilia, sedes, rem, fortunas, *quae* et a dis immortalibus et a praestantissimis in nostra re publica civibus summo senatus populique Romani studio conser-

4 vatae sunt, tuae fidei iustitiae bonitatique commendo. Si pro

1. **Fortuna**: cp. 'deorum immortalium benignitate,' in § 1.

2. **Lege agraria.** In 59 B.C. Cp. Intr. to Part I, § 17.

3. **Omni periculo . . liberavit,** 'secured against all danger' of seeing its lands assigned under an agrarian law. This might perhaps be effected by clauses inserted in the law of 59 B.C.

4. **Qui . . adiungat,** 'seeing that he is forming new connections,' i.e. by favours conferred on different cities.

6. **Auctoritatem,** 'the authority of his example.'

7. **Sectam,** 'party,' whether philosophical or political. For the latter sense, cp. Livy 8. 19 'Vitruvio sectamque eius secutis.'

Summa . . dignitate, 'without any sacrifice of independence on your part.'

8. **Illi integram . . reservare,** 'to keep the whole case for Caesar's free decision,' i.e. not to take any step that would commit Caesar.

Illud vero . . quin . . velis. On the accus. 'illud,' cp. Madv. 229 a. The words 'dubitare . . quin . . velis' mean 'hesitate to desire.' Cp. Ep. 71. 5, note, on the construction.

9. 'Grave, moribus; firmum, opibus: honestum, splendore municipum.' Manut.

11. **Eo spectant . . suadeam,** 'are by way of exhortation and advice.'

12. **Reliqua . . rogandum,** 'the purpose of what follows is to entreat you,' 'I have hitherto advised you with a view to your own interest; I now entreat you to do me a favour.' On 'pertinere ad,' cp. Ep. 55. 1, note.

13. **Quod mihi opus sit,** 'what I ought to ask.' On the difference of 'opus esse' and 'necesse esse,' cp. Ep. 29. 25, note.

15. **Feceris, si . . volueris.** The double future perfect implies that the completion of both actions will be simultaneous. Cp. Madv. 340, Obs. 2.

Omnibus rebus, foll., 'with all their property untouched and unimpaired.'

16. **Rem** = 'rem publicam.' Wiel., Forcell. Cp. Livy 1. 28 'inter Fidenatem Romanamque rem.'

17. **Praestantissimis . . civibus.** Cicero probably refers to himself and Caesar. See the preceding section. Müller.

19. **Bonitatique.** 'bonitas specialiter sumitur pro benignitate, liberalitate, clementia.' Forcell. It is noticeable that the meaning of 'bonitas' and 'malitia' was narrowed down from general goodness and badness to benevolence and unkindness.

Si pro meis . . duret, 'If circum-

meis pristinis opibus facultatem mihi res hoc tempore daret, ut ita defendere possem Volaterranos, quem ad modum consuevi tueri meos, nullum officium, nullum denique certamen, in quo illis prodesse possem, praetermitterem; sed quoniam apud te nihilo minus hoc tempore valere me confido, quam valuerim semper apud *bonos* omnes, pro nostra summa necessitudine parique inter nos et mutua benevolentia abs te peto, ut ita de Volaterranis mereare, ut existiment eum quasi divino consilio isti negotio praepositum esse, apud quem unum nos eorum perpetui defensores plurimum valere possemus.

103. To Q. CORNIFICIUS (AD FAM. XII. 18).

ROME, LATE IN 45 B.C. (709 A.U.C.)

1. I have taken advantage of every opportunity of writing to you. I am glad to learn that you will wait to see how the enterprise of Bassus turns out. Pray write to me frequently. The aspect of affairs has suddenly changed, both 2. in Syria, where it is now warlike, and here, where it is peaceable. But the peace we enjoy has several unpleasant accompaniments—which are distasteful, I believe, to Caesar himself. But I have learned to acquiesce in them; and only need some congenial companion like yourself to share my amusement at some of the things that are taking place.

CICERO S. D. CORNIFICIO COLLEGAE.

Quod extremum fuit in ea epistola, quam a te proxime accepi, 1

stances gave me at this time power to protect the people of Volaterrae as effectively as my previous influence did.'

1. Res = '*factum*.' Forcell. Cicero refers probably to the years between 63–60 B.C., when he had been one of the most influential men in the State.

3. Meos, 'my friends' or clients. Not opposed to 'Volaterranos,' but including them in a larger class.

Certamen, 'contest' with those who attempted to wrong them.

5. Hoc tempore, 'even now.'

6. Bonos. The insertion of this word seems necessary, for it would be no compliment to Valerius to say, 'I have as much influence with you now as I have always had with all,' unless, indeed, 'semper' mean 'always in better times.'

8. Mereare. The form in '-re' of the 2nd pers. sing. of passive verbs is most commonly used by Cicero, except in the present indic. Cp. Madv. 114 b.

9. Isti negotio, 'the business in which you are engaged,' i.e. the assignation of lands. Cp. the introductory note on this letter.

CORNIFICIO. This Cornificius was probably the son of one mentioned Ep. 1, 1. He took Caesar's side in the civil war, and after the battle of Pharsalus was entrusted with the government of Illyricum. Cp. Bell Alex. 42. In 44–43 B.C. we find him governing Africa, where he supported the authority of the senate, and afterwards of Octavian, against Antony. He was, however, defeated and killed by T. Sextius, acting in Antony's interest as governor of Numidia. Cp. Dion Cassius 48. 21. He is mentioned, Ep 124, 1, as joint colleague of Cicero and Antony, probably as augur. On his position at the date of this letter, cp. § 1, note.

11. Quod extremum fuit. A complaint, apparently, that Cicero did not write often enough. Cp. below 'epistolas requiris meas.'

ad id primum respondebo; animum advorti enim hoc vos magnos oratores facere nonnumquam: epistolas requiris meas; ego autem numquam, cum mihi denuntiatum esset a tuis ire aliquem, non dedi. Quod mihi videor ex tuis litteris intellegere te nihil commissurum esse temere nec ante, quam scisses, quo iste nescio qui Caecilius Bassus erumperet, quicquam certi constiturum, id ego et speraram prudentia tua fretus et, ut confiderem, fecerunt tuae gratissimae mihi litterae; idque ut facias quam saepissime, ut et quid tu agas et quid agatur scire possim et etiam quid acturus sis, valde te rogo. Etsi periniquo patiebar animo te a me digredi, tamen eo tempore me consolabar, quod et in summum otium te ire arbitrabar et ab impendentibus magnis negotiis discedere:

1. **Hoc . . facere**, i.e. answer the last remark of another first. Cp. Ep. 8. 1, where Cicero speaks of the practice as Homeric.

Vos magnos oratores. Cornificius seems to have had some pretensions to eloquence and learning. Cp. Ad Fam. 12. 17, 2. It has been thought that Quintilian assigns the Rhet. ad Herenn. to him. Cp. Inst. Orat. 3. 1, 21; 9. 3. 98.

2. **Requiris**: cp. Ep. 91, 1.

Meas, as often, = 'a me.'

3. **Cum mihi . . a tuis**, 'whenever I had received information from your friends here.'

Denuntiatum differs from 'renuntiatum,' on which, cp. Ep. 98, 1, note.

Esset. This tense is used because numquam non dedi means 'I never failed to give,' **a tuis**, 'from your agents and representatives here.' Wesenb. suggests 'est,' saying that the sense of 'quotienscumque' suits 'cum' here better than that of 'postquam.'

Ire, sc. 'ad te,' 'that some one was going to you' as a messenger. On the tense, cp. Ep. 1, 1, note.

4. **Quod mihi . . intellegere**, 'as for what I think I may infer.' Cp. Ep. 97. 3, note. 'Quod' = 'whereas.' Smith, Lat. Dict. 'Inservit continuandae orationi.' Forcell.

Nihil temere, foll. In accepting the dangerous commission offered him by Caesar.

5. **Nec ante . . constiturum.** It is doubtful where Cornificius was at this time. From Ad Fam. 12. 17, 1 'ex Syria nobis tumultuosiora quaedam nuntiata sunt: quae quia tibi sunt propiora quam nobis . .' we may infer that he held some commission in the East, and was in doubt how to act with regard to Q. Caecilius Bassus. He was subsequently entrusted with the conduct of the war in the East, and with the province of Syria, by Caesar (cp. Ad Fam. 12. 19, 1), but seems speedily to have resigned it, for in 44 B.C. he was governing Africa. Cp. introductory note on this letter.

Scisses. Videor intellegere implies a past tense, 'I seem to have gathered,' and the construction soon drops into the past tense altogether.

Quo . . erumperet, 'what that Bassus was aiming at.' Wiel.

6. **Bassus** rose in insurrection against Caesar's authority in Syria, organised a plot which led to the death of Sex. Caesar, lieutenant of the dictator, and procured Parthian support for his enterprise. Cp. Ad Att. 14. 9, 3; Pro Reg. Deiot. 9. 25; Dion Cassius 47, 26 and 27. The prospects of Bassus might influence the decision of Cornificius about accepting the government of Syria.

7. **Speraram**, 'I had hoped' before I heard from you; **et . . litterae**, 'and your letter gave me confidence.'

8. **Idque ut facias.** The context requires, apparently, a reference to 'litterae,' 'that you will continue to write.' Wiel.

9. **Quid tu agas**, 'your own proceedings;' '**quid agatur**,' the news. Cp. Ep. 18, 6, note, p. 114.

10. **Periniquo**, a rare word. It occurs Pro Leg. Man. 22, 63.

11. **Eo tempore.** Cobet om. 'tempore.'

In summum otium, 'to a most peaceful district.' This would hardly be true of Africa, where Orell. (cp. his Onomasticon) thinks that Cornificius now was.

12. **Ab impendentibus . . negotiis.**

utrumque contra accidit; istic enim bellum est exortum, hic pax consecuta, sed tamen eius modi pax, in qua, si adesses, multa te non delectarent, ea tamen, qua ne ipsum Caesarem quidem delectant; bellorum enim civilium ii semper exitus sunt, ut non ea solum fiant, quae velit victor, sed etiam, ut iis mos gerendus sit, quibus adiutoribus sit parta victoria. Equidem sic iam obdurui, ut ludis Caesaris nostri animo aequissimo viderem T. Plancum, audirem Laberii et Publilii poëmata. Nihil mihi tam deesse scito quam quicum haec familiariter docteque rideam: is

'From great troubles impending here.' Perhaps this refers to the war in Spain. But as we do not know the date of Cornificius' departure it is difficult to say for certain. The contrast of 'otium . . negotium' may be noticed. Cp. Ad Fam. 12. 17, 1 'Romae summum otium est sed ita ut malis salubre aliquod et honestum negotium.'

1. Utrumque contra accidit, 'in both points my expectations have been falsified.'

Istic, 'where you are,' in Syria.

3. Ea tamen, foll., 'which, however, I allow.' A very candid admission. Cp. Ep. 90, 2, note.

4. Ut non ea solum, foll. The following clause sed etiam ut, foll., does not precisely correspond to this: we should expect 'sed etiam ea quae velint adiutores.' On the position of ut after 'sed etiam' instead of between those two words, cp. Madv. 465 b. Obs.

5. Mos gerendus sit. 'Morem gerere' = 'obsequi.' Forcell. 'Those also must be humoured [by Caesar? or by people in general?] who have aided in winning the victory.'

6. Quibus adiutoribus, abl. abs.: cp. Ep. 88, 2, note.

Obdurui: cp. Ep. 70, 1. Cicero often uses the word in a metaphorical sense.

7. Ludis. The games which Caesar celebrated in honour of his victory in Spain. They took place, probably, in October, 45 B.C., and help to fix the date of this letter. Cp. Intr. to Part IV, § 12; Fischer, Röm. Zeitt. pp. 302, 304, sub ann. 45 B.C.

Caesaris nostri: Cicero is writing to a Caesarian.

Animo aequissimo, 'with the greatest indifference.'

Viderem T. Plancum, audirem . . poëmata. There is much pungency in this comparison of the personal worthlessness of Plancus and the badness of the poems of Laberius and Publilius. Mr. Jeans remarks that Mommsen 4. 2, 581 speaks of the 'mimes' of Laberius with high praise. So does Mr. W. B. Donne (Dict. of Biography, 2. 693); and there is much to be said for Mr. Jeans' view that what disgusted Cicero was the sight of a Roman knight acting in his own piece. But this would not apply to Publilius Syrus. And Cicero does not seem to have been on good terms with Laberius: cp. Macrob. Sat. 2. 3. 10.

T. Plancum. T. Munatius Plancus Bursa was tribune 53–52 B.C. He was banished under the 'Lex Pompeia de vi,' but restored by Caesar. He was a bitter enemy of Cicero, and, after Caesar's death, an active supporter of Antony. Cp. Ad Fam. 7. 2, 2; Ad Att. 6. 1, 10; Philipp. 6. 4, 10; 13. 12, 27. It is uncertain in what character he was prominent at Caesar's games. Süpfle suggests that it was as a gladiator.

8. Audirem, an asyndeton. Cp. Ep. 20, 6, note.

Laberii et Publilii. This form of the genitive of nouns in '-ius' and '-ium' was the later one; the old genitive was in 'i,' e.g. in Plautus and Sallust, the latter affecting archaic forms. It is also retained by Horace and Virgil.

Decimus Laberius, a writer of farces ('mimi') appeared at Caesar's request or command as an actor in one of his own pieces, but lamented his dishonour in a prologue quoted by Macrobius, Sat. 2. 7. Cp. Suet. Iul. 39. He received a present of 500,000 sesterces from Caesar, but not the prize, which was awarded to Publilius Syrus, the other farce writer here mentioned by Cicero, who had been a slave. Cp. Macrob. l. c.

9. Familiariter = 'amice et libere.' Forcell.

Docte = 'scite' (Forcell.), 'with the taste of philosophers,' who would scorn such entertainments as those to which Cicero here refers. 'Docti' = 'philosophi.' Cp. 'doctrinae,' Ep. 91, 3. Cicero had re-

tu eris, si quam primum veneris; quod ut facias, non mea solum, sed etiam tua interesse arbitror.

104. To ATTICUS (AD ATT. XIII. 52).

NEAR PUTEOLI (?), DECEMBER 19, 45 B.C. (709 A.U.C.)

1. I do not regret having entertained my formidable visitor. His numerous escort had given trouble at the villa of Philippus, but mine was protected from intrusion by sentries. Caesar heard about Mamurra. My entertainment was handsome, 2. and Caesar seemed to enjoy himself. The conversation was mainly literary. I shall shortly go to Tusculum.

CICERO ATTICO SAL.

1 O hospitem mihi tam gravem ἀμεταμέλητον! fuit enim periucunde. Sed cum secundis Saturnalibus ad Philippum vesperi venisset, villa ita completa militibus est, ut vix triclinium, ubi

marked the increasing popularity of the 'mimes,' which Süpfle thinks Caesar encouraged for political reasons.

PUTEOLI. Boot thinks that this letter was written from Formiae, as we learn from Ad Att. 15. 13. 5 that Dolabella had a villa there. But cp. infr. § 2.

3. O hospitem . . ἀμεταμέλητον. The accus. expresses astonishment. Cp. Madv. 236. 'My formidable guest's visit gave me no cause to regret it!' Cp. § 2 'habes . . ἐπισταθμείαν,' foll. The Greek word is quite classical. Liddell and Scott.

Gravem, perhaps referring to the number of Caesar's escort.

Fuit enim periucunde, 'for he was in a very good humour.' The word 'periucunde' occurs Pro Cael. 11, 25. On the adverb as a predicate, cp. Ep. 4, 1, note; Nägelsb. 144, 412.

4. Sed, 'but to come to the point.' Süpfle. It is resumptive, after the exclamation with which the passage opens.

Secundis Saturnalibus, 'on the second day of the Saturnalia,' i.e. on Dec. 18. Livy (2. 21, 1) says 'Saturnalia institutus festus dies,' from which it appears that the festival originally only lasted one day. It was held xiv Kal. Ian., i.e., before Caesar's reform of the Calendar, on December 17th according to Macrobius, Sat. 1. 10, 2, if I understand him rightly. The same writer says that the festival was prolonged for three days owing to the diversity of practice caused by Caesar's reform. But this seems hardly likely, for not only does Cicero here use the words 'secundis Saturnalibus' without any hint that they imply a recent change, but the words 'tertiis Saturnalibus' occur (Ad Att. 5. 20, 5) in a letter written before the reform of the Calendar took place. Perhaps Prof. W. Ramsay is right in suggesting [see art. 'Saturnalia,' in Smith's Dictionary of Antiquities] that the popular practice had been for some time to keep three days, but that Augustus first formally sanctioned the prolongation. Cp. Macrob. Sat. 1. 10, 4.

Andresen's note has called my attention to the insufficiency of my own note in previous editions, but I can hardly agree with him in thinking that the festival was celebrated from December 19 to December 21, before Caesar's reform of the Calendar, and from December 17 to December 19 after it.

Ad Philippum. L. Marcius Philippus was one of the consuls for 56 B.C., and stepfather of Octavian. He seems to have had a villa near Puteoli.

5. Completa militibus. The best MS. seems to have 'a militibus,' which slightly changes the meaning from 'filled with soldiers' to 'thronged by soldiers,'—the latter bringing out their action more prominently.

Ut vix triclinium, foll., 'that a room where Caesar was to dine could hardly be kept free.'

Triclinium = 'cenatio.' Forcell. It originally meant a couch for three people.

cenaturus ipse Caesar esset, vacaret; quippe hominum CIↃ CIↃ. Sane sum commotus, quid futurum esset postridie, ac mihi Barba Cassius subvenit: custodes dedit. Castra in agro; villa defensa est. Ille tertiis Saturnalibus apud Philippum ad h. VII., nec quemquam admisit: rationes opinor cum Balbo; inde ambulavit in litore. Post h. VIII. in balneum; tum audivit de Mamurra; non mutavit. Unctus est, accubuit. Ἐμετικὴν agebat; itaque et

1. **Esset.** Ubi seems to have the force of 'in qua,' and thus the mood may be explained by Madv. 364, and Obs. 1.

Quippe hominum CIↃ CIↃ, sc. 'fuerunt.' 'For there were two thousand of them:' genitivus generis. Cp. Madv. 285 a. If, as Wieland seems not to doubt, all these men were entertained in the establishment of Philippus, the passage gives a great idea of its size and resources. Cp. Merivale 7. 332 foll., for another account of a Roman villa.

2. **Sane sum commotus . . postridie,** 'I was disturbed to think what was going to happen on the next day,' sup. 'reputans' from 'commotus sum,' or, 'I was disturbed and anxiously asked myself.' Andr. Caesar had probably given Cicero notice of his intention to visit him, and Cicero did not like the prospect of entertaining so large a body of men.

Ac, 'when' = 'et statim.' Boot.

Barba Cassius is mentioned as one of the 'naufragia Caesaris amicorum' who were with Antony before Mutina. Philipp. 13. 2, 3.

3. **Custodes dedit,** 'set a guard over my villa,' explained by what follows. The soldiers were obliged to encamp in the open fields instead of crowding Cicero's villa.

4. **Ille,** Caesar.

Apud Philippum, sc. 'mansit.'

Ad horam VII., 'till a little after noon.' Cp. Ep. 101. 2, note.

5. **Admisit,** 'admitted to an interview.'

Rationes opinor, sc. 'conferebat,' or 'conficiebat,' 'he was settling accounts with Balbus' his treasurer, on whom cp. Epp. 27, 2, note; 44. 6; 58. For alleged instances of his influence with Caesar, cp. Suet. Iul. 78; Plut. Caes. 60.

6. **In litore,** 'on the shore of the bay of Baiae.' Boot suggests, very probably, that words have dropped out after post h. VIII, describing Caesar's arrival at Cicero's villa.

In balneum, sc. 'ivit.' This was probably at Cicero's villa.

Audivit de Mamurra. This obscure allusion has been explained as meaning, (1) Heard of Mamurra's death. Boot. (2) Heard of Mamurra's offences against the sumptuary laws. Manut. (3) Heard of the bitter attacks of Catullus (Epigr. 29 and 57) upon Mamurra. Lambin. and Süpfle. There is no evidence that Catullus lived later than 47 B.C.; it is doubtful therefore if one of his epigrams could be referred to as a piece of news in 45 B.C. On the whole I incline to (2), but the subject is very obscure. On Mamurra, cp. Ep. 44. 6, note. Wesenb. has 'dum audivit de Mamurra, vultum non mutavit.' Andr. thinks that the allusion is to Mamurra's death and reads 'vultum non mutavit.'

7. **Non mutavit.** 'Non mutare dicuntur qui aliquid ab alio dictum factumve laudant probantque' Forcell. But in one of the passages which he quotes the reading is doubtful. This would make good sense if we suppose that Mamurra had been convicted of transgressing the sumptuary law, and that Caesar approved his conviction. The sumptuary law is noticed Ad Fam. 7. 26, 2; Ad Att. 13. 7, 1.

Unctus est, as was usual before dinner. Cp. Hor. Carm. 2. 11, 16

'Assyriaque nardo
Potamus uncti.'

Accubuit, 'he took his place at table.'

ἐμετικὴν agebat, 'he intended to take an emetic' after dinner. Imperf. of the attempt. Cp. Ep. 42, 4; Madv. 337, Obs. 1. So Billerb., Süpfle, Matth., Andr. But the fem. ἐμετική seems not to be classical as a substantive, and the passage is otherwise very harsh. Perhaps Peerlkamp's (ap. Boot) suggestion ἐμετικόν is to be adopted, = 'agebat partes eius qui vomere vellet.' Cp. Pro Reg. Deiot. 7. 21 'cum . . vomere te post cenam velle dixisses.' ἐμετικόν is approved by Mr. H. A. J. Munro, Journal of Philology, 2. 3, p. 21, 1869. For the use of a Greek medical term, cp. Ep. 75. 1, note.

edit et bibit ἀδεῶς, et iucunde, opipare sane et apparate, nec id solum, sed

bene cocto,
condito, sermone bono et, si quaeri', libenter.

2 Praeterea tribus tricliniis accepti οἱ περὶ αὐτὸν valde copiose; libertis minus lautis servisque nihil defuit: nam lautiores eleganter accepti. Quid multa? homines visi sumus. Hospes tamen non is, cui diceres: 'amabo te, eodem ad me, cum revertere.' Semel satis est. Σπουδαῖον οὐδὲν in sermone, φιλόλογα multa. Quid quaeris? delectatus est et libenter fuit. Puteolis se aiebat unum diem fore, alterum ad Baias. Habes hospitium sive ἐπι-

1. ἀδεῶς, 'freely,' as he intended to provide against indigestion.

Opipare .. et apparate, sc. 'acceptus est,' to be supplied from 'edit et bibit,' 'he was entertained with plenty and in good style.' Forcell. gives 'copiose' as an equivalent for 'opipare;' 'magnifice' for 'apparate.'

3. Bene cocto, foll. This is a fragment from Lucilius which Cicero quotes, also de Fin. 2. 8, 25. The construction is not very clear. Forcell. sub voc. 'conditus' takes all the epithets as applying to 'sermone,' in which case the ablatives will be of the manner, in apposition to 'opipare.' Mr. Munro also appears to connect all the epithets with 'sermone.' P. and B. render 'bene cocto condito,' something well cooked and seasoned,' and say that the ablatives probably depend on some verb preceding them in the original. Mr. Jeans renders freely

'Though the cook was good,
'Twas Attic salt that flavoured most the food.'

4. Libenter, 'to his taste.'

5. Tribus tricliniis, 'in three dining rooms.' Cp. sup.

οἱ περὶ αὐτόν, 'his immediate attendants.'

Copiose = 'large, cum copia.' Forcell.

6. Nihil defuit, 'wanted for nothing.'

Nam: cp. Epp. 9, 8; 26, 2, notes.

Lautiores, sc. 'liberti.' 'lautus' = 'qui laute vivit.' Forcell.

Eleganter, 'appropriately,' 'in good taste.' = 'apte, concinne, laute.' Forcell. It is contrasted with the abundant supply of necessaries mentioned above—'nihil defuit.' The best MS. seems to have 'accepi,' and Wesenb. retains it.

7. Quid multa? 'in a word.'

Homines, 'a man who understood hospitality,' or, as Ands. 'a man of taste.' 'Homo' is also used in a good sense Ep. 28, 2 'si vis homo esse.' P. and B. say that the words mean 'we seemed on friendly terms as men should be with one another.'

Hospes tamen, 'yet though so agreeable he was not a guest,' etc.

8. Amabo te, 'if you would oblige me.' Cp. Ad Fam. 2. 7, 2 'amabo te cura et cogita;' also Ep. 35. 5.

Eodem ad me, 'come and see me the next time you pass this way.' Boot, after Peerlkamp, says that these words form an iambic line from a comic poet. In that case the 'dem' in 'eodem' must not be elided.

9. σπουδαῖον .. multa, sc. 'fuerunt.' 'Nihil de re publica multa de libris et doctrinae studiis' Boot.

φιλόλογα = 'erudita.' Orell. Cp. Ad Att. 15. 15, 2.

10. Quid quaeris: cp. p. 51, note on l. 13; p. 85, note on l. 6.

Libenter fuit: cp. § 1, note.

11. Ad Baias: cp. Ep. 71, 10, note, 'in the neighbourhood of Baiae.'

Habes, 'you now know all about.' 'Habere' in this sense of 'being informed about' is usually found in the second person. Cp. Epp. 29, 20; 88, 6.

ἐπισταθμείαν. Liddell and Scott explain this word as meaning a 'liability to have soldiers quartered upon one,' and Orell. gives substantially the same explanation. It seems to me to be equivalent to the Latin 'deductio,' 'a billeting,' and Cicero refers partly to the numerous escort which accompanied Caesar, partly to the fact that a proposal from Caesar to visit him was equivalent to a command. The Greek word is found in Diodorus and Plutarch in the military sense. Ands. thinks that Cicero uses it to express the shortness of Caesar's visit, which he could hardly call 'hospitium.'

σταθμείαν odiosam mihi, dixi, non molestam. Ego paulisper hic, deinde in Tusculanum. Dolabellae villam cum praeteriret, omnis armatorum copia dextra sinistra ad equum nec usquam alibi. Hoc ex Nicia.

1. Odiosam .. molestam, 'which as I said was distasteful to me, though not annoying.' Forcell. makes these two words synonymous.

Dixi. In the first words of this letter. Cicero means, I think, that he did not like being virtually compelled to entertain Caesar though he found him an agreeable guest enough when he did come. Orell. puts a semicolon after 'odiosam,' which does not much alter the sense 'I have described to you a visit of an unpleasant kind, though to me, as I said, it was not annoying.' For a free translation of this letter, cp. Merivale 2. 457.

Ego paulisper hic manebo deinde in Tusculanum ibo. Such ellipses are very common in letters.

2. Dolabellae villam. Probably at Baiae. Cp. Ad Fam. 9. 12, 1 (a letter written about this time) 'gratulor Baiis nostris si quidem, ut scribis, salubres repente factae sunt.'

Cum praeteriret, Caesar.

Omnis armatorum .. ad equum, 'his whole escort paraded on either side of him,' i.e. in regular military array.

3. Dextra sinistra. On the asyndeton, cp. Madv. 434.

Ad equum, sc. Caesaris, Andr.

Nec usquam alibi, 'and this happened nowhere else.' It was a special honour paid to Dolabella. Boot.

4. Hoc ex Nicia, sc. 'audivi.' Süpfle. Curtius Nicias was a grammarian of Cos, intimate both with Cicero and with Dolabella. He was with Cicero in Cilicia (cp. Ad Att. 7. 3. 10), but Cicero does not seem to have had a high opinion of him (Ib. 12. 26, 2), and Nicias subsequently attached himself to Dolabella (Ib. 13. 28, 3).

APPENDIX VIII.

On the Calendar.

Before the reformation of the Roman Calendar by Julius Caesar seven months had 29 days each; four—March, May, July, and October—had 31; and February 28, thus making up a year of 355 days. In alternate years a month was intercalated after the 23rd of February, which in the intercalated years had only 23 days. This intercalated month had alternately 27 and 28 days. Thus the quadriennial cycle would consist of 1465 days. For $355 \times 4 = 1420 + 55$ (two intercalary months) $- 10$ (five days twice deducted from February) $= 1465$. This gave four days too many, and Macrobius (Saturn. I. 13) says that in every third period of eight years only 66 days were inserted, which would correct the mistake.

Great irregularity, however, prevailed with regard to intercalation; the pontifices appear occasionally to have applied it to suit the interests of magistrates and governors who were anxious to shorten or to prolong their term of office, and in the year of Cicero's consulship the first of January of the old calendar would have corresponded to the fourteenth of March of the Julian. No intercalation seems to have taken place between that year and 52 B.C., and thus the discrepancy of the official and solar year constantly increased. In 52 B.C. the first of January of the unreformed calendar fell really on Nov. 21, 53 B.C., but an intercalary month of 27 days being inserted after the 23rd of February as usual, the nominal Jan. 1 of 51 was postponed to Dec. 3, 52.

After this year no intercalation is found till 47 B.C., which had 377 days; its last day fell on Oct. 12th of the corrected calendar. Then followed the year of transition, 708 U.C. or 46 B.C. Its Jan. 1 fell on Oct. 13, 707 U.C. of the corrected calendar, and Caesar inserted in it, besides the ordinary intercalary month, two extraordinary intercalary months numbering 29 and 28 days respectively, which were inserted between November and December, 46 B.C., and ten days. The transitional year would thus number 445 days, i.e. $355 - 5$ deducted from February $+ (29 + 28 + 28 + 10)$ intercalated, and its last day would correspond to the Julian 31st of December.

Mommsen (Römische Chronologie, pp. 276, 277) explains the change rather differently. He thinks that the official year began on March 1 till 45 B.C., and that all that Caesar did in 46 was (1) to insert between November and December two intercalary months instead of January and February: for as 46 would naturally end with February, and he intended 45 to begin with January, the repetition of two months so soon after each other would cause confusion; (2) to add ten days to the year, which seem to have been appended to the 'mensis intercalaris posterior.'

The ordinary year from 45 B.C. was one of 365 days, but to complete the quadrennial cycle the insertion of one day every four years was requisite, and this took place in February after the VI. Cal. Mart. The extra day was called 'bis VI. Cal. Mart.,' whence the term bissextile for leap year. 45 B.C. was a leap year. Cp. Mommsen, Römische Chron. 279–281. The Julian year of 365 days 6 hours exceeded the solar year by about eleven minutes. A table is appended of the days on which the first of January of the unreformed calendar fell according to one reckoned back on the Julian system to 63 B.C. inclusive.

In	63 B.C.,	March	14.		
	62 ,,	March	4.		
	61 ,,	Feb.	22.		
	60 ,,	,,	11.		
	59 ,,	,,	1.		
	58 ,,	Jan.	22.		
	57 ,,	,,	12.		
	56 ,,	,,	1.		
	55 ,,	Dec.	22.	698 U.C.	
	54 ,,	,,	12.	699 ,,	
	53 ,,	,,	2.	700 ,,	
	52 ,,	Nov.	21.	701 ,,	
	51 ,,	Dec.	3.	702 ,,	
	50 ,,	Nov.	23.	703 ,,	
	49 ,,	,,	13.	704 ,,	
	48 ,,	,,	2.	705 ,,	
	47 ,,	Oct.	23.	706 ,,	
	46 ,,	,,	13.	707 ,,	

In drawing up this table a day has been inserted according to the Julian system in 61, 57, 53, and 49—reckoning back from 45 B.C. The authorities consulted have been Korb's tables, in Orelli's Onomasticon; Suringar's Annales Ciceroniani; Smith's Dictionary of Antiquities, art. 'Calendarium;' and Th. Mommsen's Römische Chronologie.

APPENDIX IX.

CAESAR'S LAWS ENACTED FROM 49–44 B.C.

I. Laws proposed by Caesar as dictator in 49 B.C.

1. Lex Iulia (?) de exsulibus,—restored, according to some accounts, all exiles who had been sentenced under the 'Leges Pompeiae' of 52 B.C., except Milo. Caesar's own statement, however, says that it only applied to a few persons. The plea for this enactment was that the proceedings for bribery ('ambitus') under those laws had been irregular[1]. The restoration included all exiles whatever except Milo, according to Appian and Dion Cassius. The act of restoration seems actually to have been proposed by the praetors and tribunes, and Cicero charges Antony, one of the latter, with having been its author[2].

2. Lex Iulia de pecuniis mutuis[3]. Caesar proposed this law as dictator towards the close of 49 B.C. It was intended to provide a remedy for the scarcity of money caused by the civil war, and enacted that public valuers should be appointed to ascertain what the worth of land and other property had been before the civil war. Creditors were then obliged to take land at the value so ascertained in payment of their claims; whereby about a quarter of what they could otherwise have claimed was lost. Dion Cassius[4] mentions also a law limiting to 15,000 drachmae the amount of gold or silver coin which any one might possess, but he does not describe it as a new law. Tacitus[5] seems to include it under 2, but his language is not very precise, 'legem dictatoris Caesaris qua de modo credendi possidendique intra Italiam cavetur.'

3. Lex Iulia de Transpadanis[6],—granting the Roman franchise to the Gauls living beyond the Po and south of the Alps. Tacitus, however, affirms[7] that that grant was made during a time of peace.

4. Lex Rubria, passed probably at Caesar's instance to regulate the jurisdiction of the magistrates of municipal towns in Cisalpine Gaul[8].

Perhaps 5. a Lex Hirtia de Pompeianis may belong to this year. A. Hirtius was tribune in 49–48 and praetor in 47 B.C. The import of the law is doubtful; perhaps it excluded those who had served in Pompey's army from public offices[9].

[1] Caes. Bell. Civ. 3. 1; App. Bell. Civ. 2. 48; Dion Cassius 41. 36. [2] Caes. l. c.; Cic. Philipp. 2. 23, 56. [3] Caes. l. c. [4] 41. 38. [5] Ann. 6. 16. [6] Dion Cassius 41. 36. [7] Ann. 11. 24. [8] Corp. Insc. Lat. 1. pp. 115–119. [9] Philipp. 13. 16, 32.

6. Lex Antonia? de proscriptorum filiis,—admitting the children of those whom Sulla had proscribed to curule offices. Pansa was one of them[1].

This measure apparently was passed early in the year.

7, 8. Other laws, giving citizenship to the people of Gades and depriving the people of Massilia of some of their privileges, may belong to this time[2].

II. Laws of Caesar as 'dictator iterum' 47 B.C.[3]

1. Increase of the number of praetors to ten.

2. Increase of the three greatest priestly colleges by one member each.

3. Remission of a proportion of rents due for houses in Rome and Italy.

III. Laws of Caesar as 'consul III, dictator III' 46 B.C.

1. Lex Iulia iudiciaria,—providing that the judges should be taken exclusively from among the senate and the equestrian order, excluding the 'tribuni aerarii[4].'

2. Leges Iuliae de vi et de maiestate,—fixed as the penalty of those crimes 'interdictio aquae et ignis,' and forfeiture of half the offender's property[5]. As the trials would be before one of the permanent courts an appeal to the people would be ipso facto excluded.

3. Lex Iulia de collegiis: abolished all guilds and political clubs recently instituted. This law was probably designed to rescind the Lex Clodia of 58 B.C.[6] An exception from its penalties was granted to the Jews[7].

4. Lex Iulia de sacerdotiis,—apparently provided that candidates for priestly offices need not canvass in person[8]. It was perhaps connected with a law of 47, or with a law of 45 B.C. vid. sub ann.

5. Lex Iulia sumptuaria[9],—forbade the use of litters, of purple dresses, and of pearls, except to persons of a certain age or position. It restricted also the liberty of buying certain dainties. A strict watch was kept on the markets, and sometimes dishes which had been already set on table were forcibly removed by Caesar's orders.

6. Lex Iulia de provinciis,—providing that the praetorian provinces should not be held for more than one year by the same governors, nor

[1] Dion Cassius 41. 18; 45. 17; Plut. Cic. 37; Intr. to Part I, § 9; Ad Att. 2. 1, 3. note. [2] Dion Cassius 41. 24; 25. Livy Epit. 110. [3] Dion Cassius 42. 50 51; Suet. Iul. 38; 41. [4] Philipp. 1. 8, 19; Suet. Iul. 41; Dion Cassius 43. 25. [5] Philipp. 1. 9, 23; Suet. Iul. 42. [6] Intr. to Part I, § 19; Suet. Iul. 42. [7] Josephus Antiqq. 14. 10, 8. [8] Cic. ad Brut. 1. 5, 3. [9] Suet. Iul. 43; Dion Cassius 43. 25; Ad Att. 13. 7, 1; Ad Fam. 7. 26, 2; 9. 15, 5.

the consular for more than two[1]. The assignation of praetorian provinces had been already conceded to Caesar, while that of the consular provinces remained nominally with the senate[2].

7. Lex Iulia de liberis legationibus,—probably extended the time for which their privileges were enjoyed. Cicero had limited this to a year by a law proposed in his consulship[3]. Caesar also reduced the number of recipients of corn furnished at the public expense from 320,000 to 150,000[4].

IV. Leges agrariae.

Those of 59 B.C. have been already mentioned. Cp. Intr. to Part I, § 17. A. W. Zumpt thinks[5] that they remained legally valid, and might be put into operation whenever there was money in the treasury to buy land; and that as dictator Caesar actually did revive the laws of his consulship with only two alterations, viz.

1. That their operation was extended to lands out of Italy[6].

2. That 'vigintiviri' were no longer appointed to superintend their execution, which was now entrusted to Caesar's legates[7].

In any case lands were assigned to veterans in various parts of Italy[8] in 46 B.C. Such lands had probably either been previously unoccupied, or recently confiscated, or were purchased. The towns where such soldiers were settled were not necessarily called 'coloniae,' and the lands assigned were for the most part not contiguous. None but soldiers received lands in Italy[9].

V. Laws of Caesar as 'consul IV, dictator IV' (? see p. 494) 45 B.C.

1. Increase of the senate to 900[10].
2. Creation of new patrician families[11].
3. Increase of the 'triumviri monetales' to 4. Connected perhaps with a permission granted to Caesar to stamp coin with his name[12].
4. Addition of a third class, called Iuliani, to the Luperci[13].
5. Continuation of distribution of lands begun 46 B.C.[14]

[1] Philipp. 1. 8. 19; 5. 3. 7; Dion Cassius 43. 25. [2] Dion Cassius 42. 20. [3] Cp. Intr. to Part I, § 9, with Ad Att. 15. 11. 4. [4] Livy Epit. 115; Dion Cassius 43. 21; Suet. Iul. 41; App. Bell. Civ. 2. 102; Plut. Caes. 55. [5] Comment. Epigr. 1. 300 foll. [6] Intr. to Part IV, § 14; A. W. Zumpt, Comment. Epigr. 1. 301, foll. [7] Ad Fam. 13. 4. [8] Intr. to Part IV, § 11; Ad Fam. 9. 17; Dion Cassius 42. 54; Suet. Iul. 38. [9] Suet. Iul. l. c.; A. W. Zumpt, Comment. Epigr. 1. 302. [10] Ad Fam. 13. 5, 2; Suet. Iul. 41; 76; 80; Dion Cassius 43. 47. [11] Dion Cassius l. c.; Tac. Ann. 11. 25. [12] Suet. Iul. 76; Dion Cassius 44. 4; Smith, Dict. of Antiq., sub voc. 'Moneta,' p. 766. [13] Philipp. 13. 15. 31; Suet. Iul. 76; Dion Cassius 44. 6. [14] Ad Fam. 13. 4; 13. 5; 13. 7; 13. 8; Dion Cassius 43. 47.

6. Increase of the number of quaestors to 40; of praetors, first to 14 and then to 16; of aediles to 6 [1].
7. Lex Iulia municipalis. This appears to have comprised firstly, regulations as to the distribution of corn at the public expense at Rome; secondly, police regulations especially relating to the traffic in the streets of Rome; thirdly, regulations as to the qualifications and duties of magistrates and senators in municipal towns [2].

Other laws of uncertain date, but which must have been enacted within the period here referred to, are mentioned by Suetonius [3].

1. A law restraining the liberty of Roman citizens, especially of the higher classes, to travel or reside out of Italy.
2. A law providing that a third part of the herdsmen employed on estates consisting of pasture lands should be freemen.
3. A law granting citizenship to physicians and teachers of liberal arts who should settle at Rome.
4. A law increasing the severity of penalties for the higher crimes.

APPENDIX X.

ON THE HONOURS VOTED TO CAESAR.

§ 1. 1. 49 B.C.

Perhaps when Caesar met the senate on April 1 he received proconsular power throughout the whole empire, by virtue of which he disposed of different provinces [4].

Chronological writers [5] assigned to Caesar a reign of four years and seven months, evidently dated from his first dictatorship. This would fix its grant to the middle of August, 49 B.C.; a date supported by the probability that his nomination followed the announcement of his victory over Afranius and Petreius, who surrendered on August 2 [6].

His nomination took place under a law proposed by Lepidus, and he held the office, probably, 'comitiorum habendorum causa [7],' for he had no 'magister equitum.' He held the dictatorship for eleven days, and resigned it on leaving Rome for Brundisium [8]; in December, according to the Calendar, in October, according to the real season.

[1] Dion Cassius 43. 47 and 51. [2] Cp. Mommsen Corp. Inscr. Lat. I. 119-125. [3] Iul. 42. [4] A. W. Zumpt, Studia Romana, 201-204; Ad Att. 9. 17, 1; Cp. Dion Cassius 41, 15-17. [5] Cp. A. W. Zumpt, S. R. 204. [6] Intr. to Part III, § 8. [7] Ad Att. 9. 9, 3; Dion Cassius 41. 36; Caes. Bell. Civ. 2. 21. [8] Plut. Caes. 37; App. Bell. Civ. 2. 48; Dion Cassius 41. 36-39.

2. 48 B.C.

Second consulship. He was absent from Rome throughout its duration, as he entered upon it at Brundisium [1].

After Pompey's death was known at Rome, the senate and people voted to Caesar

1. The consulship for five years;
2. A dictatorship for one year [2].

The consular power would last from 48 to 44, or from 47 to 43 B.C., according as the year 48 was included or not.

He entered upon his second dictatorship 'at once,' says Dion Cassius [3]. That is, probably, as soon as he heard of his nomination. Now Pompey was killed on Sept. 28 [4], and his death might be known in Rome by the middle of October, from which time Caesar's dictatorship probably dated. M. Antonius was named his master of the horse, probably by the consul P. Servilius [5]. Caesar seems to have retained this dictatorship till the end of 47 B.C., if we may trust the statements of Dion Cassius [6] and Plutarch [7]; and Mommsen (Corpus Inscr. Lat. 1. pp. 451–453) believes that this dictatorship was conferred for an undefined period 'rei publicae constituendae causa.' Coins, with the inscription 'Cos. tert. Dict. iter.' support this view. Ib. p. 449, and Lange 3. 420.

3. 47 B.C. Second dictatorship, till the close of the year.

Third consulship (?). So Suetonius [8]. But Caesar only held a titular consulship in 47 B.C., and both the Fasti Capitolini [9] and Dion Cassius [10] place in

4. 46 B.C. Caesar's third consulship, to which he seems to have been regularly elected with Lepidus [11].

Third dictatorship, decreed to him when the news of the battle of Thapsus reached Rome. It was for ten years, and probably 'rei publicae constituendae causa.' Caesar was named by his colleague Lepidus, who named himself master of the horse, contrary to precedent [12].

The Fasti Capitolini place this dictatorship in 45 B.C.; either, as W. Henzen (Corpus Inscr. Lat. 1. pp. 448–449) thinks, because the

[1] App. Bell. Civ. 2. 48; Dion Cassius 41. 39. [2] Dion Cassius 42. 20. [3] Ib. 42. 21. [4] Intr. to Part IV. § 3. [5] Philipp. 2. 25. 62; Dion Cassius 42. 21; A. W. Zumpt, S. R. 212; Intr. to Part IV, § 5; but Lange, R. A. 3. 421–422, says he was named by Caesar as usual. [6] 42. 55. [7] Caes. 51. [8] Iul. 76; cp. A. W. Zumpt, S. R. 215; e contr. Fasti Cap. sub anno. [9] Ib. Zumpt, S. R. 200. [10] 43. 1. [11] Fasti Capitolini, sub anno. Mommsen, C. I. L. 1. 451. Suetonius, (Iul. 76) and Dion Cassius, (43. 33) take a different view. [12] Dion Cassius l. c.; cp. 43. 14.

greater part of its duration was comprised in that year,—a remark which applies equally to his second dictatorship with reference to the years 48 and 47 B.C.,—as the fourth dictatorship only began late in 45 B.C. at the earliest; or, as Mommsen (Corpus Inscr. Lat. 1. 452) thinks, because the ten years' dictatorship voted to Caesar in 46 was to begin Jan., 45 B.C.

5. 45 B.C. Fourth consulship, without a colleague.

The consulship for ten years was decreed to him when the news of the battle of Munda reached Rome[1]. He accepted the grant at first, but resigned the consulship on entering the capital early in October, when Q. Fabius and C. Trebonius were elected as 'consules suffecti[2].'

According to Dion Cassius[3], Caesar did not discharge the functions of the consulship to which he was regularly elected for long: but Appian[4] seems to affirm that he declined the ten years' consulship offered to him, and was content with that which he held by regular election from Jan. 1, 45 B.C.

He was made Praefectus Morum for three years after his African victories[5].

And received the title 'Imperator' for himself and his posterity in 45 B.C.[6]

6. 44 B.C. Fourth dictatorship. Perhaps Caesar entered upon this before the close of 45 B.C.[7] It was perpetual; perhaps an extension for life of that granted him in 46 B.C.[8] for ten years. But it was regarded apparently as a series of yearly dictatorships, as the masters of the horse changed from year to year. Cp. Fast. Capit. sub anno 44 B.C., Mommsen, C. I. L. 1. 452.

Fifth consulship[9].

§ 2. The title 'Imperator[10].'

It was used as a prefix to the names of the emperors[11]; but it is doubtful if Caesar used it thus. A. W. Zumpt thinks[12] that he only used it *after* his name, as had been the practice of the republican period, and without numbers, e.g. II, III, appended to it. Mommsen considers[13] the new 'imperium' to have been a continuation of the old consular or proconsular 'imperium' without the 'pomoerium.'

[1] Dion Cassius 43. 45. The news arrived the day before the Parilia, i.e. on April 20, Ib. 43. 42. [2] Vell. 2. 56; Suet. Iul. 76; Dion Cassius 43. 46. [3] 43. 46. [4] Bell. Civ. 2. 103; 107. [5] Dion Cassius 43. 14. [6] Ib. 43. 44. [7] The remarks on the way of dating the third dictatorship apply equally to the fourth. Cp sup. 4. [8] Dion Cassius 43. 14: Appian. De Bell. Civ. 2, 106; A. W. Zumpt, S. R. 229 foll. [9] Intr. to Part IV, § 12. [10] Note E, p. 123: Zumpt, S. R. 233 foll. [11] Suet. Iul. 76; Dion Cassius 43. 44. [12] L. c. [13] 4. 2, 470.

§ 3.

For the year 48 B.C. the usual magistrates were elected[1].

In 47 B.C. no curule magistrates were elected except for the last three months[2].

For 46 B.C. the usual magistrates were elected[3]. But on leaving for Spain Caesar appointed praefects, not praetors[4], to govern Rome in his absence.

At the end of the year 45 B.C. the usual magistrates were elected for its last few months[5].

§ 4. Tribunicia potestas.

Granted to Caesar for life in 48 B.C.[6] The most important privileges which it included were

(1) Ius auxilii ferendi.
(2) Ius intercedendi.
(3) Ius senatum consulendi[7].
(4) Ius agendi cum plebe.
(5) Personal inviolability[8].

In 45 B.C. he received the power of deciding who should be tribunes[9].

[1] A. W. Zumpt, S. R. 241. [2] Ib. 243; Dion Cassius 42. 27. [3] Dion Cassius 42. 51. [4] Ib. 43. 28. [5] Ib. 43 46; Zumpt, S. R. 245: Intr. to Part IV, § 12. [6] Dion Cassius 42. 20: cp. Zumpt, S. R. 252. [7] A. Gell. N. A. 14. 7; Smith, Dict. of Antiq. 1151. The tribunes, if no one of their own body interfered, could probably bring questions before the senate even if a consul opposed them; the Caesars probably had this power personally, without being subject to intercession. Zumpt, S. R. 262. Cp. Ad Fam. 10. 16, 1; Ep. 22, 2, note. [8] Dion Cassius (44. 5), App. (Bell. Civ. 2. 106), and Livy (Epit. 116), say that Caesar was declared inviolable 44 B.C. A. W. Zumpt suggests that this inviolability was not limited locally, while that of the tribunes could only be vindicated in the capital—and that it protected the emperor at all times—not only in his official acts. S. R. 252, foll. [9] Dion Cassius 43. 45.

PART V.

From the Death of Caesar to that of Cicero.

March 15, 44 B.C. to December 7, 43 B.C.

INTRODUCTION.

§ 1. It has been mentioned that after Caesar's murder Antony fled to his home[1], and the senate broke up in confusion[2]. Lepidus heard of the event in the forum[3]. He was master of the horse[4] and governor of Narbonensis and Hither Spain, and had a legion in the island of the Tiber. Many also of Caesar's veterans filled the city[5]. On the other hand, D. Brutus had at his disposal a body of gladiators[6]; and under their protection, after a fruitless appeal to the people[7], the conspirators occupied the Capitol, where they were presently joined by Cicero and other nobles[8], including Dolabella, who Caesar had intended should succeed him as consul for the last part of 44 B.C.

The conspirators employed the 16th apparently in making a second appeal to the people[9], and in attempting to sound the disposition of Antony and Lepidus. Meanwhile Calpurnia[10], Caesar's widow, placed at the disposal of Antony her husband's papers and a considerable sum of money.

§ 2. On the 17th an important meeting of the senate was held in the temple of Tellus[11]. Cicero took a leading part in the debate. Appeals had been made to him by the conspirators immediately after the murder[12], and Antony afterwards accused him of complicity with them. It is not likely however, that he was in the secret; nor did he, like some others, pretend to have been so[13]. He now advocated a general amnesty[14], and

[1] Intr. to Part IV, § 15. [2] Ib. [3] App. Bell. Civ. 2. 118; Dion Cassius 44. 22. [4] App. l. c.; Dion Cassius 43. 49-51. [5] App. Bell. Civ. 2. 119. [6] Ib. 2. 122; Vell. 2. 58. [7] App. Bell. Civ. 2. 119; Dion Cassius 44. 20. [8] App. Bell. Civ. l. c.; Dion Cassius 44. 22; Vell. 2. 58; Philipp. 2. 35, 89; Ad Att. 14. 10, 1. [9] App. Bell. Civ. 2. 122-124. [10] Ib. 125; Plut. Ant. 15. [11] Ad Att. 14. 14. 2; Philipp. 1. 1, 1; 2. 35, 89; App. Bell. Civ. 2. 126. [12] Philipp. 2. 12; Dion Cassius 44. 20. [13] Philipp. 2. 11, 25; App. Bell. Civ. 2. 119; Dion Cassius 44. 21. [14] Philipp. 1. 1; App. Bell. Civ. 2. 135; Dion Cassius 44. 34.

the senate adopted his proposal, combining with it, however, a ratification of Caesar's acts. An apparent reconciliation followed between Antony[1] and the conspirators. But Caesar's friends, headed by his father-in-law, L. Piso[2], procured the consent of the senate to the publication of his will and to a public funeral for his body. Brutus subsequently addressed[3] the people in defence of Caesar's murder, trying especially to quiet the apprehensions of the veterans; and his speech, which produced a good effect, was followed next day by one from Cicero[4] in defence of the amnesty.

About the same time Caesar's will was read[5], in which Octavius was adopted, and named his heir, and a sum of money, variously stated, was bequeathed to every Roman citizen. A painful feeling was excited when the name of D. Brutus was read among the 'second heirs;' and was intensified by the public funeral[6] which followed, and by Antony's address on that occasion. The people and the veterans committed many acts of violence, and the conspirators had to hide themselves or to withdraw from Rome.

But Antony presently reassured the nobles by consulting some of the more eminent of their number as to his measures[7], and by proposing the abolition of the dictatorship, which the senate gladly sanctioned. Nor did Antony oppose the adoption by the senate of a decree[8] forbidding the registration of any resolution found in Caesar's papers to confer immunities or similar special privileges on individuals or communities. The favourable impression thus created was deepened by the suppression of disorders caused by an impostor named Herophilus or Amatius, who pretended to the name of C. Marius, and was executed by Antony's order[9].

§ 3. These hopes, however, were presently dispelled by the use which Antony made of Caesar's papers[10], and of the aid of Faberius, a scribe who had been in Caesar's service, and who now forged many documents purporting to be Caesar's. Exiles were restored; privileges[11] and exemptions granted to individuals and communities; and the aid of Dolabella purchased with a large sum[12]. The populace was offended by Antony's vigorous maintenance of order, and he made its hostility a plea for sur-

[1] Philipp. 1. 1, 2; 2. 36, 90; Vell. 2. 58. [2] Ad Att. 14. 10, 1; App. Bell. Civ. 2. 136; 143; Vell. 2. 59; Dion Cassius 44. 35. [3] App. Bell. Civ. 2. 137-142. [4] Ib. 2. 142. [5] Ib. 2. 143; Dion Cassius 44. 35. [6] Philipp. 2. 36; App. Bell. Civ. 2. 143-148; Dion Cassius 44. 36-50. [7] Philipp. 1. 1; 2. 36. [8] Philipp. 1. 1, 3; 2. 36, 91. [9] Ib. 1. 2, 5; Livy Epit. 116; App. Bell. Civ. 3. 2 and 3; Dion Cassius 44. 51. The execution probably took place in April. Ad Att. 14. 8, 1. [10] Philipp. 1. 8-10; 2. 36-39; Vell. 2. 60; App. Bell. Civ. 3. 5. [11] Philipp. 1. 10, 24; 2. 36-38; Plut. Ant. 15; Dion Cassius 44. 53. [12] Ad Att. 14. 18, 1.

rounding himself with a guard[1]. The senate sanctioned this step, and the number of the guard was gradually increased to several thousands. But Antony was anxious to revive his failing popularity, and with that object procured, with the aid of his brother Lucius, now tribune, the enactment of an agrarian[2] law. He left Rome in April to superintend its execution.

Meanwhile Dolabella, who had acted as consul since Caesar's death, overthrew an altar erected in memory of Caesar by Amatius, and punished with great severity those who had assembled to worship there; a service which Cicero praised in extravagant terms[3].

§ 4. Octavius landed in Italy apparently in April[4]. He came to claim his inheritance, and to assume the name of his adoptive father. As he approached Rome he received promises of support[5] from the veterans settled in Campania, but declined them. Antony had returned to the capital when Octavius arrived there and claimed Caesar's bequest[6]. Antony had already spent the money, but Octavius borrowed from his friends enough, added to his own resources, to pay a portion at least of Caesar's legacies to the people, and to celebrate some days afterwards the games of Venus Victrix in honour of Caesar's victory at Pharsalus[7]. Owing to the opposition of Antony's friends the enactment of a 'Lex Curiata' for his adoption was delayed[8].

Trebonius had already, apparently, left for Asia, and D. Brutus for Cisalpine Gaul[9]—where, if we judge by results, he was not warmly welcomed, and undertook various petty operations[10] to gratify his soldiers with plunder. M. Brutus and C. Cassius still lingered in the neighbourhood of Rome[11].

An important meeting of the senate took place on June 1[12], when Macedonia was assigned to Antony, and Syria was assigned about the same time by a vote of the people[13] to Dolabella, who then finally broke with the republican leaders. On the 5th, apparently, M. Brutus was released from his obligation to reside in Rome as praetor[14], and, with C. Cassius, commissioned to supply corn. Both remained, however[15], in Italy to

[1] App. Bell. Civ. 3. 4 and 5; cp. Philipp. 1. 11, 27. [2] Ad Att. 14. 21, 2; Philipp. 2. 39; 5. 3, 7; 5. 7, 20. [3] Ad Att. 14. 15, 2; Ad Fam. 9. 14; Philipp. 1. 2, 5. [4] Ad Att. 14. 10, 3; 14. 12, 2; Vell. 2. 59; App. Bell. Civ. 3. 9-11. [5] App. Bell. Civ. 3. 11 and 12. [6] Ib. 3. 17 and 20. [7] Ib. 3. 23; Ad Att. 15. 2, 3: Dion Cassius 45. 6. [8] Dion Cassius 45. 5. [9] Ad Att. 14. 10, 1; 14. 13, 2; App. Bell. Civ. 3. 2. [10] Ad Fam. 11. 4. [11] App. l. c.; Ad Att. 14. 10, 1. [12] Philipp. 1. 2, 6; App. Bell. Civ. 3. 7 and 8. [13] 7 in April, Halm, Intr. to Philipp. §§ 46. 47. [14] Ad Att. 15. 9, 1; 15. 11, 1; 15. 12, 1; Philipp. 2. 13, 31; App. Bell. Civ. 3. 6 and 8. [15] Ad Att. 15. 26, 1; 15. 28; 16. 1, 1; App. Bell. Civ. 3. 24.

see what effect might be produced by the Ludi Apollinares[1] celebrated in the name of M. Brutus on the 7th of Quinctilis, now first called Iulius[2]. The people applauded, but their cheers were not followed by any important results[3].

§ 5. Since March 17[4] Cicero had been living mostly in retirement. He was soon undeceived as to the probable results of Caesar's death. His first letter[5] after that event was written in great exultation, a feeling soon exchanged for regret[6] that the deed had been done with so little regard for consequences, and that Caesar's power had passed with little diminution into the hands of Antony. Cicero left Rome[7] early in April, and exchanged friendly letters[8] with Antony as to the restoration of one Sex. Clodius from exile. His gratification at the vigorous measures of Dolabella has been already[9] mentioned.

The landing of Octavius[10] at first gave him no pleasure, and he was alarmed by the prospect of civil war[11] with D. Brutus and Sex. Pompeius, and by rumours that Antony would attempt to seize the Gallic provinces[12]. He had not as yet[13] much confidence in the consuls elect Hirtius and Pansa, but was pleased with an edict[14] of Brutus and Cassius, in which they seem to have held moderate language, dismissing the friends who came from the country towns to protect them. The regrets, however, openly expressed[15] for Caesar by Matius and others disquieted him, nor was he much reassured by a correspondence[16] with Matius.

§ 6. Cicero spent the greater part of the spring and early summer in different villas: we find him dating letters from Tusculum[17], Lanuvium[18], Puteoli[19], Sinuessa[20], Pompeii[21], Arpinum[22], Antium[23], and other places. At Antium he had an interview with Brutus and Cassius, and found both of them discontented with the commissions proposed for them, and Cassius very violent[24]. Cicero was alarmed by Antony's intrigues[25] with the veterans settled in Campania, and annoyed by the name Iulius[26] given to the seventh month. These anxieties did not, however, make him careless of his private interest; his affairs seem to have been in a

[1] Philipp. 1. 15, 36; App. l. c. [2] Ad Att. 16. 1, 1; 16. 4, 1; Cens. de Die Nat. 22. [3] Ad Att. 16. 2, 3; Philipp. 1. 15, 36. According to Appian (Bell. Civ. 3. 24) the demonstration in favour of Brutus proceeded from hired partisans of his own, and the people broke into the theatre and silenced them. [4] Supra, § 2. [5] Ad Fam. 6. 15. [6] Ad Att. 14. 4, 2; 14. 9, 2; 14. 12, 1; Ad Fam. 12. 1. [7] Ad Att. 14. 1. [8] Ib. 14. 13 A and B. [9] Supra, § 3. [10] Ad Att. 14. 12, 2. [11] Ib. 14. 13, 2; 15. 20, 3. [12] Philipp. 1. 3, 8; Ad Att. 14. 14, 4. [13] Ad Att. 14. 12, 2; 14. 19, 2; 14. 21, 4; 15. 12, 2; 16. 1, 4. [14] Ib. 14. 20, 4; Ad Fam. 11. 2. [15] Ad Att. 14. 1, 1; 14. 2, 3; 14. 22, 1. [16] Ad Fam. 11. 27 and 28. [17] Ad Att. 14. 3. [18] Ib. 4. [19] Ib. 9. [20] Ib. 8. [21] Ib. 17. [22] Ib. 15. 26. [23] Ib. 11. [24] Ib. 15. 11, 1. [25] Ib. 14. 21, 2; Philipp. 2. 39, 100. [26] Ad Att. 16. 1, 1; 16. 4, 1.

very disorderly state, and this increased his eagerness to get money owing him, from Dolabella and others, repaid [1]. Seeing little hope of doing any good by remaining at Rome, he decided on retiring to Athens [2] till the beginning of the next year. Dolabella had named him his legate with peculiar privileges on June 2 [3], and this gave him a pretext for leaving Italy. He was also anxious to see his son, then studying at Athens, of whose behaviour unfavourable rumours had reached him [4].

Early in July [5] he saw M. Brutus at Nesis, where he also heard news [6] of Sextus Pompeius, who was still in arms. He was much pleased by the behaviour of his brother Quintus [7] at this time, and the good understanding between them seems not to have been again disturbed.

§ 7. Cicero seems to have embarked about the middle of July. He touched at Vibo on the 23rd [8], and at Syracuse [9] on August 1. He set sail next day for Greece, but was presently driven back by contrary winds which he encountered off Leucopetra in the territory of Rhegium. On landing, he heard [10] that there was a fair prospect that Antony would be reconciled to Brutus and Cassius, and would renounce the Gallic provinces. He also read a satisfactory speech of Antony, and a proclamation of Brutus and Cassius, in which they expressed their willingness to retire from Rome in the interest of public tranquillity. He was not aware that an angry correspondence [11] was probably going on at that very time between Antony and Brutus and Cassius, and was eager to return to Rome in time for a meeting of the senate announced for September 1. A letter from Atticus, reproaching him [12] for deserting his country, strengthened him in this resolution.

He travelled back, accordingly, towards Rome; a meeting with Brutus at Velia [13], from whom he learned that L. Piso had spoken against Antony in the senate on the first of August, undeceived him as to political prospects, but he persevered and arrived at Rome on August 31 [14].

§ 8. Important events had happened during his absence. Antony had procured early in the summer [15] a vote of the people sanctioning an exchange of provinces between him and D. Brutus, and empowering him to transport the army of Macedonia to Cisalpine Gaul. He owed his success in this manœuvre to the co-operation of Octavius, with whom

[1] Ad Att. 14. 18, 1; 14. 19, 1; 14. 21, 4; 15. 20, 4; 16. 1, 5. [2] Ib. 16. 3; Philipp. 1. 2, 6. [3] Ad Att. 15. 11, 4; Philipp. l. c. [4] Ad Att. 14. 16, 3. [5] Ib. 16. 4, 1. [6] Ib. 16. 4, 2. [7] Ib. 16. 5, 2. [8] Ib. 16. 6, 1. [9] Philipp. 1. 3, 7. [10] Ad Att. 16. 7, 1; Philipp. 1. 3, 8; Ad Fam. 11. 3, 3. [11] Ad Fam. 11. 3. [12] Ad Att. 16. 7, 2 and 4. [13] Ib. 16. 7, 5; Philipp. 1. 4. [14] Plut. Cic. 43; cp. Philipp. 5. 7, 19. [15] App. Bell. Civ. 3. 27–30; Dion Cassius 45. 9; Appendix 11. 11.

he had effected a temporary reconciliation. An enactment[1] presently followed, extending the duration of proconsular governments from two years to six. This was in direct violation of a law of Caesar. Notice was also given[2] of measures introducing a more popular element into the courts of law, and granting the privilege of appeal to the people to criminals convicted of riot or treason ('vis' or 'maiestas').

§ 9. On September 1[3] the senate was convoked to consider the propriety of adding a day to the public thanksgivings, in honour of Caesar. Cicero sent an excuse to Antony for his absence, but Antony spoke of him with much violence. On the next day Cicero addressed the senate, Antony being absent. His speech, the first Philippic, was a criticism of Antony's policy, free, however, from personal hostility. He complained[4] especially of the promulgation of measures directly violating laws of Caesar, and of the use[5] made of Caesar's papers; artfully mixed praise and censure[6] of the presiding consul Dolabella; spoke of Hirtius[7] with much regard; and warned[8] Antony what his fate would probably be if he persisted in his actual course. Antony replied[9] on September 19 with a violent attack on Cicero's whole career, and left Rome[10] on October 9 for Brundisium, where three or four legions of the army of Macedonia had landed. They had been tampered with, probably, by agents of Octavius, and received Antony badly. The good understanding between Antony and Octavius had not lasted long; and Antony had charged[11] Octavius with plotting his assassination. Having punished[12] some of the mutinous soldiers, Antony set out for Rome attended by the fifth legion[13] ('Alaudae'). The legions of Macedonia were to proceed along the coast road to Cisalpine Gaul.

Antony returned to Rome[14] about the middle of November. He left the greater part of his troops at Tibur, but brought an escort into the capital. Having heard of the open mutiny of the Martian legion he summoned the senate for a meeting on the 28th[15], when he probably intended to ask its sanction for decisive measures against Octavius. But he heard during the sitting that the fourth legion had followed the example of the Martian[16], and contented himself with procuring a vote in honour

[1] Philipp. 1. 8, 19; 5. 3, 7; 8. 9. 28. [2] Ib. 1. 8 and 9. [3] Ib. 1. 4–6; 5. 7, 19. [4] Ib. 1. 8 and 9. [5] Ib. 1. 10. [6] Ib. 1. 12. [7] Ib. 1. 15, 37. [8] Ib. 1. 14, 34. [9] Ad Fam. 12. 2, 1; Philipp. 5. 7. [10] Ad Fam. 12. 23, 2; Ad Att. 16. 8, 2; App. Bell. Civ. 3. 40 and 43; Dion Cassius 45. 12. [11] Ad Fam. 12. 23, 2; App. Bell. Civ. 3. 39. [12] App. Bell. Civ. 3. 43; Philipp. 3. 2, 4; 3. 4, 10. [13] Ad Att. 16. 8, 2; App. Bell. Civ. 3. 44 and 45; Dion Cassius 45. 13; Appendix 11, 11. [14] Ad Att. 16. 10, 1; App. Bell. Civ. 3. 48. [15] App. l. c.; Philipp. 3. 8. [16] Philipp. 3. 3, 6; 3. 9; 5. 8–9; 13. 9, 19. Appian (Bell. Civ. 3. 45) says that he only heard of the revolt of the Martian legion as he was entering the senate house.

of Lepidus[1], and with making provision, with the apparent approval of the senate, for the government of the provinces during the year[2] 43 B.C. The most important nomination was that of his brother Gaius to supersede M. Brutus in Macedonia. Antony then retired to Tibur[3], where an attempt at mediation was made by several senators who attended him to his quarters, but failed, owing to the opposition of his brother Lucius[4]. He then set out for Cisalpine Gaul at the head of a large force[5]. D. Brutus prepared to resist[6] him, but was obliged to evacuate one town after another, and finally was besieged in Mutina.

§ 10. Octavius meanwhile had raised a considerable force of veterans in Campania; during Antony's absence he approached Rome, and on the invitation of the tribune Cannutius he entered the city and addressed the people, professing his readiness to oppose Antony. The Martian legion had occupied Alba for him; and he named Arretium as the gathering-place for his followers[7].

Cicero seems not to have appeared in Rome between the middle of October and the 9th of December[8]; he employed himself in composing a reply[9] to Antony's attack of September 19. This reply, the second Philippic, after being submitted to Atticus for criticism, was probably published after Antony had left Rome. Cicero was not satisfied with the demeanour of Octavius[10], and wrote to various provincial governors[11] to confirm them in their allegiance to the senate. His leisure was occupied in the composition of philosophical[12] works, as it had been earlier in the year. On December 20, however[13], an opportunity presented itself to him for resuming his duties as a senator. The new tribunes of the people had then come into office, and convoked the senate on that day to take steps for securing the freedom of its deliberations on January 1. Cicero, however, did not confine himself to the question, but suggested votes in honour of D. Brutus, Octavius, and others, and commented severely on the proceedings of Antony and his brother Lucius. He also proposed[14] that the provisions made by Antony for the government of the provinces during the year 43 B.C. should be treated as null and void, a suggestion which the senate seems to have approved. On the same day he addressed[15] the people, to stimulate their zeal on behalf of the senate.

§ 11. M. Brutus and C. Cassius had probably by this time entered the

[1] Philipp. 3. 9. [2] Ib. 3. 10; Appendix 11. [3] App. Bell. Civ. 3. 45 and 46; Dion Cassius 45. 13. [4] Philipp. 6. 4. 10; App. Bell. Civ. 3. 46. [5] App. l. c.; Dion Cassius l. c.; Philipp. 3. 11, 31. [6] App. Bell. Civ. 3. 49: Dion Cassius 45. 14; Philipp. 3. 4. 8. [7] Ad Att. 16. 8, 1; 16. 9; 16. 15, 3: Philipp. 3. 2, 5: App. Bell. Civ. 3. 40-42. [8] Ad Fam. 11. 5, 1: cp. 11. 25, 8, and Ad Att. 15. 13. 1. [9] Ad Att. 15. 13. 1; 16. 11, 1 and 2. [10] Ib. 16. 8: 16. 9; 16. 11, 6; 16. 15. 3. [11] Ad Fam. 10. 1: 11. 5. [12] Ad Att. 16. 11 3-4. [13] Ad Fam. 11. 6. 2; Philipp. 3 passim. [14] Philipp. 3. 15. 38; cp. Philipp. 3. 10; Ad Fam. 12. 22, 3. [15] Philipp. 4. 1, 1.

provinces[1] assigned them under Caesar's arrangements, Macedonia and Syria. Dolabella[2], to whom Syria had been granted (by a vote of the people) about the same time that Macedonia had been assigned to Antony, had also left Rome.

Sex Pompeius[3] had been induced by M. Lepidus to disband his army under a promise of the restoration of his father's property, and of his being allowed to return himself to Rome. He waited, however, for some time at Massilia to watch events[4].

§ 12. On the first of January[5] an important meeting of the senate took place. That body was convened by the two consuls Hirtius and Pansa, for discussion of the policy to be adopted towards Antony. Cicero proposed[6] to invest the consuls with full powers, and to offer an amnesty to such of Antony's followers as might leave him before the first of February. He also[7] proposed votes in honour of D. Brutus, Lepidus, Octavius, and others. The senate, however, after a long debate, decided on Jan. 4 to send envoys to Antony, who should require[8] him to evacuate the province of D. Brutus and to obey the senate and people. Ser. Sulpicius Rufus[9], L. Piso, and L. Philippus were chosen as envoys, and Cicero's proposals as to honorary votes were adopted; but he was much dissatisfied with the result of the proceedings, and expressed his discontent in a speech[10] delivered to the people after the division in the senate had taken place, and also in a letter written shortly afterwards to Cassius, in which[11], as in one to Trebonius, he complains of the weakness of the consulars, but praises the behaviour of the consuls and of the majority of the senate.

Appian[12] charges Cicero with having tampered with the instructions given by the senate to the envoys, so as to make them less conciliatory than the senate had intended them to be. This charge is not, however, preferred by any other writer, and Cicero[13] says that the instructions were drawn up in accordance with the advice of Sulpicius.

The envoys set out for Antony's camp; but as they approached it Ser. Sulpicius died[14]; his colleagues went on, but did not, according to Cicero, execute their commission with sufficient firmness. During their absence Hirtius[15] set out to take the command of the forces destined to relieve Mutina, and Cicero again addressed[16] the senate, to prove that peace was dangerous, disgraceful, and impossible.

[1] Ad Fam. 11. 2, 3; 12. 3, 2; Philipp. 10. 1, 1; 10. 4, 9; Livy Epit. 118; Vell. 2. 62; App. Bell. Civ. 3. 24 and 26; Plut. Brut. 24; Appendix 11. [2] App. Bell. Civ. 3. 7 and 8; 24 and 26; Philipp. 11. 2, 4; Appendix 11; supra, § 4. [3] Philipp. 5. 14; Vell. 2. 73; App. Bell. Civ. 4. 84; Dion Cassius 45. 10. [4] Philipp. 13. 6, 13; App. Bell. Civ. l. c. [5] Philipp. 5. 1. [6] Ib. 5. 12, 34. [7] Ib. 5. 13–19. [8] Ib. 6. 1, 3; 6. 2, 4. [9] Ib. 9. 1, 1. [10] Philipp. 6. [11] Ad Fam. 12. 4, 1; cp. 10. 28, 3. [12] Bell. Civ. 3. 61. [13] Philipp. 9. 3, 7; see Cobet's notes on the Philippics in Mnemosyne 7. 173–174. (1879). [14] Philipp. 9. 3, 7; Ad Fam. 10. 28, 3; 12. 4, 1; 12. 5, 3. [15] Philipp. 8. 2, 5. [16] Philipp. 7.

§ 13. After the return of Piso and Philippus, who had not been allowed to confer with D. Brutus[1], and brought counter proposals from Antony, the senate met to consider those proposals. Cicero was anxious[2] for an immediate declaration of war against Antony, but the senate substituted for war the less decided term 'tumult[3],' greatly to Cicero's annoyance. He tried to promote his object indirectly, by proposing[4] that the memory of Ser. Sulpicius should receive honours which had previously been only granted in the case of envoys who had been killed in the service of their country, and the senate seems to have adopted his proposal[5].

Shortly afterwards a despatch[6] arrived from M. Brutus describing his successful operations in Macedonia. During the last months of 44 and the beginning of 43 B.C., he had been actively employed, and had made[7] himself master both of Macedonia and of Illyricum. He gained over some troops which should have followed Dolabella into Asia, and levied others in Greece; a large sum of money and considerable stores of arms also fell into his hands. In these operations he was effectively supported by Cicero's son Marcus, and the poet Horace held a command in his army. Q. Hortensius, governor of Macedonia for 44 B.C., recognized Brutus as his lawful successor, and P. Vatinius in Illyricum was unable or unwilling to oppose him; but C. Antonius, brother of Marcus, landed late in 44 to assume the government of Macedonia by virtue of an appointment already referred to[8]. Brutus, however, defeated him, and wrote, as before mentioned, to announce his successes to the senate.

In the debate which followed, Q. Calenus[9] recommended that Brutus should be required to surrender his army and provinces to Vatinius and C. Antonius; but Cicero opposed[10] this strongly, and proposed that the proceedings of Brutus should be approved and his authority confirmed. The senate seems to have adopted this suggestion.

§ 14. Important events were presently reported from the East[11]. Dolabella had left Rome in the autumn of the previous year to take the command in Syria, as he had been authorized to do by a vote of the people. Some of his soldiers had been gained[12] over by Brutus on their march through Macedonia, but at the head of such as remained faithful, he marched through the province of Asia[13], captured its governor, Trebonius, by a treacherous surprise, and had him put to death. When the

[1] Philipp. 8. 7-10. [2] Ib. 8. 1, 1. [3] Ib. [4] Ib. 9. 1. 3. [5] Pomponius de Origine Iuris ap. Digest. lib. 1. tit. 2, 43, recogn. T. Mommsen. [6] Philipp. 10. 1, 1. [7] Ib. 10. 5 and 6; Plut. Brut. 24-26; App. Bell. Civ. 3. 79; Dion Cassius 47. 21 and 22. [8] Supra, § 9. [9] Philipp. 10. 3, 6. [10] Ib. 10. 11. [11] Ib. 11. 1. 1. [12] Ib. 10. 6, 13. [13] Ib. 11. 2; Ad Fam. 12. 12. 1; App. Bell. Civ. 3. 26; Dion Cassius 47. 29.

news of this event, which may have happened in February, 43 B.C., reached Rome, the senate was convoked to consider what steps should be taken in consequence. There was a general agreement as to the atrocity of Dolabella's conduct; Calenus[1] proposed that he should be declared a public enemy, and his property confiscated. The senate seems to have adopted this proposal; but Cicero was unable, owing to the opposition[2] of Pansa, to secure that the conduct of hostilities against Dolabella should be entrusted to C. Cassius, of whose successful operations in Syria Cicero had heard[3].

The conduct of the war with Dolabella was actually entrusted to the consuls[4], who were, after relieving D. Brutus, to cast lots for Syria and Asia. Many, no doubt, supported this proposal in the hope that the consuls' attention might be diverted from Mutina. Events, however, deprived the vote of any practical importance. Cicero attempted, apparently, to get it reversed at once[5] by the people, but failed, owing to the opposition of Pansa and the fears of the nearest relatives of Cassius.

On March 17 a despatch[6] arrived from Q. Cornificius, describing his resistance to the officers of Calvisius, Antony's nominee for the government of Africa. The senate approved his proceedings, but declined to adopt any severe measures against his opponents.

§ 15. After the return of Piso and Philippus from the seat of war, it was proposed[7] in the senate that a fresh embassy should be sent to Antony. Cicero had always opposed such a step; but Antony's friends now held very despondent language[8] as to his prospects, represented that he would make great concessions, and by these artifices inveigled Cicero into a promise to serve as an envoy. No sooner, however, had he made that promise than he was eager to retract it, for the language of Antony's supporters[9] presently changed. P. Servilius, another of the envoys proposed, shewed equal unwillingness to serve, and the scheme fell to the ground.

The senate paid Cicero a compliment[10] on the 19th of March, by voting for the restoration of a statue of Minerva which Cicero had dedicated in the Capitol on the eve of his exile in 58 B.C., and which had been thrown down by a storm.

On the 20th[11], apparently, Pansa left Rome at the head of his new

[1] Philipp. 11. 6, 15. [2] Ad Fam. 12. 7. 1. [3] Ib. 12. 5. 1: Philipp. 11. 13. [4] The language of Ad Fam. 12. 7. 1, supports Dion Cassius 47. 29, rather than Appian Bell. Civ. 3. 63. Cp. Philipp. 11. 9. [5] Ad Fam. 12. 7, 1. [6] Ad Fam. 12. 25. 1. [7] Philipp. 8. 7, 20. [8] Ib. 12. 1 and 2. [9] Ib. 12. 2, 4. [10] Ad Fam. 12, 25, 1: cp Plut. Cic. 31; Dion Cassius 38, 17. [11] Cp. Ad Fam. 10. 6. 3. with Philipp. 13. 7. 16, sub. Pansa was not, apparently, present during the delivery of the thirteenth Philippic: see note 2 on the next page.

levies. M. Cornutus, the praetor urbanus[1], was left in charge of the capital; and seems, on the very day[2] of Pansa's departure, to have convoked the senate for the consideration of despatches[3] from Lepidus and Plancus which recommended the adoption of a conciliatory policy towards Antony. P. Servilius[4] spoke against their recommendations, and was followed by Cicero in a long speech[5]. Cicero warned Lepidus against disloyalty, and read aloud, with a running commentary, a letter[6] lately addressed by Antony to Hirtius and Octavius. Antony complained bitterly of the hostility to the Caesarian cause which the senate's measures implied, and invited Hirtius and Octavius to combine with him against their common enemies. The result of the discussion seems to have been that the senate renounced all idea of negotiations; and Cicero wrote an account[7] of the proceedings at once to Plancus, and perhaps to Lepidus also. To Plancus he used a tone of friendly reproof; to Lepidus he coldly expressed dissatisfaction with the ingratitude which he shewed to the senate. Cicero heard about the same time, probably, from Pollio[8] that he was anxious for peace, and would oppose its disturbers; but that he regretted the absence of instructions from the home government, which, however, he was prepared to support.

Towards the close of the month another letter[9] arrived from Plancus of more satisfactory import. Plancus excused himself for the hesitation of his previous language, alleging that it was necessary to secure the affection of his soldiers and of the provincials before he committed himself by a declaration of opinion. Cicero wrote[10] to thank him, and to exhort him to persevere in his good disposition. He also wrote to C. Cassius[11], to say that D. Brutus was reduced to the last extremity by famine, and that the main hope of the Commonwealth was in the armies of Syria and Macedonia.

§ 16. Meanwhile Pansa, with four legions[12] of recruits, drew near to the seat of war. Some partial engagements[13] had already taken place; Antony's outposts had been driven from Claterna, and he afterwards evacuated Bononia without a battle to concentrate his forces nearer to Mutina. He commissioned his brother Lucius[14] to watch D. Brutus, while he himself prepared to resist the advance of Hirtius and Octavius.

[1] Ad Fam. 10. 12, 3. [2] Cicero writing to Plancus on March 20 (cp. Ad Fam. 10. 6) speaks of the despatches of Plancus and Lepidus as having been already read in the senate, while in a letter to Cornificius (Ad Fam. 12. 25, 1) he mentions Pansa as having been present in the senate on March 19, and in the thirteenth Philippic (7, 16) speaks of him as having already left Rome when the despatches of Lepidus and Plancus were considered in the senate. [3] Ad Fam. 10. 6, 1; 10. 27. [4] Philipp. 13. 21, 50. [5] Philipp. 13. [6] Ib. cap. 10, foll. [7] Ad Fam. 10. 6; 10. 27. [8] Ib. 10. 31. [9] Ib. 10. 8. [10] Ib. 10. 10. [11] Ib. 12. 6. [12] Ib. 10. 30, 1; App. Bell. Civ. 3. 66. [13] Philipp. 8. 2, 6; App. Bell. Civ. 3. 65; Dion Cassius 46. 36 and 37. [14] Dion Cassius 46. 37.

Antony had a decided superiority[1] in cavalry, but the country was not well suited for its action. On receiving news of Pansa's approach he marched out with his cavalry[2], two veteran legions, two praetorian cohorts, and other veterans to intercept him. Hirtius, however, had already sent out the Martian[3] legend and two praetorian cohorts under D. Carfulenus to escort Pansa to his camp; Ser. Galba[4], one of Caesar's murderers, went on to announce their approach, and when joined by these troops, Pansa advanced along the Aemilian way till he encountered Antony, a little to the east of Forum Gallorum, on April 15th. An obstinate engagement followed, in which Pansa was severely wounded, and his forces defeated with great slaughter; but Hirtius fell upon Antony as he returned to his lines, and inflicted great loss upon him[5]. Octavius, meanwhile, repulsed an attack made upon his camp.

Galba reported[6] this action to Cicero, and despatches from the consuls and from Octavius arrived at Rome about the same time with his letter. Reports had[7] been previously flying about of a victory of Antony; others of usurpation contemplated by Cicero. They met with little credence, however; the truth was known on April 20, and Cicero went up to the Capitol to thank the gods for the victory they had granted[8].

Next day the senate[9] met, and Cornutus read the despatch of the consuls, which begged that a thanksgiving might be ordered in honour of their victory. P. Servilius[10] argued that their request should be granted, but did not apply the term 'hostis' to Antony, nor the term 'imperatores' to the consuls. On this Cicero remarked[11] that thanksgivings could only be ordered with propriety in cases when those two words would be appropriate. He[12] proposed that thanksgivings for fifty days should be offered; that a monument should be erected in honour of the soldiers who had fallen, and that the promises made to them should be fulfilled to their surviving relatives. The senate adopted these suggestions, and declared Antony a public enemy.

Cicero had been much embarrassed at this time by the personal jealousies which prevailed at Rome. Plancus[13] was evidently discontented by the senate's inadequate recognition, as he thought it, of his services, and Cicero had some difficulty in soothing him. P. Servilius

[1] App. Bell. Civ. 3. 65 and 66. [2] Ad Fam. 10. 30, 1; App. Bell. Civ. 3. 66. [3] Ad Fam. l. c.; App. Bell. Civ 3. 66. [4] Ad Fam. l. c.; Philipp. 13. 16, 33. [5] Ad Fam. 10. 30; Philipp. 14. 9 and 10; App. Bell. Civ. 3. 69–70; Dion Cassius 46. 37. [6] Ad Fam. 10, 30. [7] Philipp. 14. 5 and 6. [8] Ib. l. c. [9] Philipp. 14. 5. [10] Ib. 14. 3, 7. [11] Ib. 8 and 9. [12] Ib. 14; App. Bell. Civ. 3. 74; Dion Cassius 46. 39. The two latter, however, in their condensed accounts, place the votes after the raising of the siege of Mutina. Cp. Livy Epit. 119; Corn. Nep. Att. 9. [13] Ad Fam. 10. 12; cp. 10. 11, 3.

Isauricus, M. Cornutus, and P. Titius, one of the tribunes, were all unfriendly to Plancus.

§ 17. After the battles near Forum Gallorum, Hirtius and Octavius had brought together the forces which they could employ against Antony[1]. After some days of inactivity, the consul's manœuvres[2] drew Antony from his entrenchments towards the close of April, and a general action followed, in which Antony was completely beaten, and compelled to raise the siege of Mutina. Hirtius, however, fell[3], and Pansa died not long afterwards of his wounds. D. Brutus was unable[4], for want of transport, and Octavius probably unwilling, to press Antony hard on his retreat; and the latter was thus able to form a junction[5] at Vada in Liguria with P. Ventidius Bassus, who had raised three[6] legions in Picenum and elsewhere, and after threatening, perhaps entering, Rome, had led his forces to North Italy. After his union with Ventidius, Antony saw himself again at the head of a formidable force, and marched rapidly[7] towards Gallia Narbonensis. The senate seems now to have summoned Lepidus and Plancus to Italy[8], but Antony[9] arrived at Forum Iulii on May 15, and encamped[10] near Lepidus, whose army was posted near Forum Voconii, and on the Argenteus[11]. Intrigues soon began for an union of the two armies, and Lepidus either was[12], or pretended to be, compelled by his soldiers' outcries to consent to it. The united armies must have numbered nearly 80,000 men, mainly veterans; and Plancus, who had crossed the Isara[13] to support Lepidus against Antony, now recrossed[14] that river, on June 4, to await in security the arrival of D. Brutus. Lepidus wrote[15] to the senate to plead compulsion as an excuse for his treachery, but was declared[16] a public enemy by its unanimous vote on June 30. He had written eight[17] days before his revolt to assure Cicero of his loyalty.

§ 18. During the past month the senate, under Cicero's guidance, had been trying, without much discretion, to impair the influence of Octavius by teaching his army to look to them for rewards, and by placing Pansa's recruits under the command of D. Brutus, who was commissioned to prosecute the war against Antony[18]. Nor was a place found for

[1] App. Bell. Civ. 3. 71; Dion Cassius 46. 38. [2] App. l. c. [3] Ib.; Vell. 2. 61; Dion Cassius 46. 39. [4] Ad Fam. 11. 10, 4; 11. 13, 2, 1. [5] Ib. 11. 10, 3. [6] App. Bell. Civ. 3. 66. [7] Ib. 3. 72; Dion Cassius 46. 50; Ad Fam. 11. 11, 1; Vell. 2. 63. [8] App. Bell. Civ. 3. 74; Ad Fam. 10. 33. 1. [9] Ib. 10. 17, 1. [10] App. Bell. Civ. 3. 83 and 84; Dion Cassius 46. 51; Plut. Ant. 18. [11] Ad Fam. 10. 34, 1 and 2. [12] Ib. 10. 23, 2; 10. 35, 1; App. and Dion. ll. cc. [13] Ad Fam. 10. 18, 4. [14] Ib. 10. 23. 3. [15] Ib. 10. 35. [16] Ib. 11. 10, 1; Dion Cassius 46. 51. [17] Ad Fam. 10. 34. [18] Vell. 2. 62; App. Bell. Civ. 3. 74; Dion Cassius 46. 40 and 41.

Octavius on a commission[1] of ten, which seems to have been appointed to distribute the rewards intended for the conquerors of Mutina. Cicero had already proposed[2] a decree in honour of Sex. Pompeius, who was now invested with the chief command at sea[3]. As the eastern provinces were almost entirely controlled by Cassius and M. Brutus, the senate's measures would naturally alarm even moderate Caesarians; and their apprehensions would be increased by the appointment of a fresh commission of ten, nominally to review the administration of Antony, but really, Appian suggests[4], to reverse Caesar's acts.

Cicero continued to urge[5] D. Brutus and Plancus to energetic co-operation, and was encouraged by news of their union, which took place early in June[6]. Their combined forces must have outnumbered[7] those of Antony and Lepidus, but comprised only four legions of veterans. They did not, therefore, venture to take the offensive[8], while their adversaries hoped to prevail without a battle. Pollio remained inactive[9] in Spain, thinking himself slighted that the senate did not seek his aid. Meanwhile the contest of intrigue was waged unremittingly in Italy. Octavius was ordered to support D. Brutus, but had been offended by the ambiguous language of Cicero, by the preference shewn for Caesar's murderers in the distribution of honours and power, and by the persistent efforts made to estrange his soldiers from him[10]. Having allowed the effects of these insults to ripen in the minds of his men, and having made overtures[11] for reconciliation to Antony and Lepidus, Octavius caused his soldiers to demand[12] the consulship for him. His youth was a legal disqualification for that office, but had been disregarded in the vote[13] of the first of January.

The dominant party in the senate made desperate appeals for aid to the officers commanding[14] in the East and in Africa. Cicero's last letter[15] preserved to us, is a request to C. Cassius to come to Italy. From Africa two legions[16] did actually land, but, as will be seen, subsequently went over to Octavius. The last letter addressed to Cicero, which is still extant, is one[17] from Plancus, dated July 28, in which Plancus speaks of his reluctance to risk a battle, and complains of the ambition of Octavius. Letters subsequently written or received by

[1] Ad Fam. 11. 14, 1; 11. 20, 1; 11. 21. [2] Philipp. 13. 21, 50. [3] Dion Cassius 46. 40. [4] Bell. Civ. 3. 82. [5] Ad Fam. 10. 13, alib.; 11. 12, alib. [6] Ib. 10. 23, 3. A few days before D. Brutus had made a most earnest appeal for reinforcements; Ib. 11. 26. [7] Ib. 10. 24, 3. [8] Ib. [9] Ib. 10. 33, 1. [10] Ib. 11. 20, 1; Vell. 2. 62; App. Bell. Civ. 3. 74; 85; 86. [11] Dion Cassius 46. 41. 43. [12] Ad Fam. 10. 24, 6; App. Bell. Civ. 3. 88; Dion Cassius 46. 42, 43. [13] Supra, § 12; Philipp. 5. 17. [14] App. Bell. Civ. 3. 85: cp. 91 and 92. [15] Ad Fam. 12. 10. [16] App. Bell. Civ. 3. 91; Dion Cassius 46. 44. [17] Ad Fam. 10. 24.

Cicero have probably been destroyed by men whose reputation would have suffered by their preservation.

§ 19. When a deputation from the army of Octavius arrived in Rome[1] to demand the consulship for him, the senate refused him leave to stand, on account of his age. His soldiers, when the deputation returned, demanded to be led to Rome, and he complied[2] with their wish. He had eight legions, with cavalry and light troops, and the news of his advance caused a great panic. It was allayed, however, for a time by the arrival of the African legions[3]; they were encamped, together with one left behind by Pansa, for the defence of the city, and new levies were ordered. But the African legions consisted in great measure of old soldiers of Caesar; Octavius probably did not spare promises, and on his approach the troops which should have opposed him submitted to him[4]. The senate was now defenceless; the praetor M. Cornutus slew himself, and Cicero went to greet Octavius, who replied to his salutation in ambiguous terms. In the night a rumour was spread[5] abroad that two legions had revolted against Octavius, and Cicero and the senate regained courage for a moment, but were speedily undeceived.

Nothing now remained but submission; the necessary forms were hurried through, and Octavius was elected consul[6] in his 20th year, with Q. Pedius for his colleague. The news of this event produced great effects in the provinces; Pollio seems at once to have declared for Antony and Lepidus. Plancus remained faithful to the senate for some time longer, till Pollio effected by his mediation a reconciliation between him and Antony[7]. D. Brutus was now quite unable to hold his ground, and desertion rapidly thinned his ranks. He resolved, therefore, to try to force his way to M. Brutus, and by a difficult route reached Aquileia, where he fell into the hands of a Gaulish chief to whom he had formerly done service, but who now killed him at Antony's bidding, probably in October[8].

§ 20. M. Brutus, meanwhile, had captured[9] C. Antonius, but treated him very well at first. He secured his position in Greece, and after

[1] App. Bell. Civ. 3. 88; Dion Cassius 46. 43. [2] App. Dion. ll. cc. [3] App. Bell. Civ. 3. 91; Dion Cassius 46. 44. [4] App. Bell. Civ. 3. 92; Dion Cassius 46. 45. [5] App. Bell. Civ. 3. 93. [6] Ib. 3. 94; Dion Cassius 46. 46. According to Suetonius (Octavius 31) in August; Dion Cassius 56. 30 says on the 19th; according to Velleius (2. 65) on September 22. Perhaps the first date is that of the senate's decree authorising him to stand; the second that of the election. Cp. Dion Cassius 55. 6; 56. 30. Lange, Röm. Alt. 3. 535–536, agrees with Suetonius and Dion Cassius. See also Corp. Inscr. Lat. 1. pp. 310; 400. [7] Vell. 2. 63; App. Bell. Civ. 3. 97; Dion Cassius 46. 53. [8] App. Bell. Civ. 3. 97 and 98; Vell. 2. 64; Dion Cassius l. c. [9] App. Bell. Civ. 3. 79; Dion Cassius 47. 21.

visiting Asia, returned to Europe, and obtained successes against some Thracian tribes, which, however, were a poor compensation for his absence from Italy at a critical moment[1]. The operations of Cassius had been more important; after the battle of Mutina the senate commissioned[2] him to act against Dolabella, whom he besieged in Laodicea. A strict naval blockade of the same place was maintained by Patiscus, Turullius, and C. Cassius, a quaestor. Some of the gates were subsequently betrayed to Cassius, and Dolabella killed himself. Cassius, after occupying the place, marched towards Egypt, but was recalled by a letter from Brutus, and went to meet him in the province of Asia[3].

§ 21. The remainder of Cicero's life may be described in a few words.

When Octavius had received the consulship, he ascended to the Capitol to make the usual vows and sacrifices; paid Caesar's bequests to the people; thanked the senate for releasing him from the restriction of the 'Leges Annales,' and procured the enactment of a 'Lex Curiata[4]' to sanction his adoption. Other laws of importance followed; one removing the outlawry of Dolabella, and another[5] directing that an enquiry should be made about the murder of Caesar, and fixing a punishment for the principals and accomplices in it. Under this law, the conspirators and others who had merely sympathised with them were condemned in their absence to exile and confiscation, which of course implied the loss of commands and provinces[6].

§ 22. Octavius now left Rome, professedly to act against Antony. But on his way a message reached him from the senate, saying that his colleague had proposed the reversal of the outlawry of Antony and Lepidus. He signified his approval, and the reversal was carried[7]. Meanwhile Antony and Lepidus, leaving L. Varius Cotyla in charge of Gaul, marched into Italy[8] at the head of a large army, and met Octavius near Bononia, where, in an island[9] formed either by the Lavinius or the Rhenus, the three generals met to provide for the government of the western part of the empire, for the prosecution of the war with Brutus and Cassius, for the removal of their own most formidable enemies, and for the reward of their soldiers

[1] Livy Epit. 122; Plut. Brut. 27; 28; Dion Cassius 47. 24 and 25. [2] Dion Cassius 46. 40. [3] Vell. 2. 69; App. Bell. Civ. 4. 60-62; Dion Cassius 47. 30; Plut. Brut. 28. [4] App. Bell. Civ. 3. 94; Dion Cassius 46. 47. [5] Lex Pedia; cp. Vell. 2. 69. [6] App. Bell. Civ. 3. 95; Dion Cassius 46. 48; Plut. Brut. 27; Vell. 2. 69. [7] Vell. 2. 65; App. Bell. Civ. 3. 96; Dion Cassius 46. 52. [8] Plut. Ant. 18; Dion Cassius 46. 54. [9] Plut. Ant. 19; App. Bell. Civ. 4. 2; Dion Cassius 46. 55 and 56.

by confiscation[1]. Their measures were agreed upon by about the end of October[2], and a despatch[3] was at once sent off to Rome bidding the consul Pedius to put to death at once seventeen of the proscribed, including Cicero. According to some accounts[4], Octavius had struggled long before sacrificing him to Antony. A terrible agitation followed the arrival of the despatch at Rome, and Pedius died[5] from excitement caused by his efforts to restore confidence.

Shortly afterwards, at the close of November, the triumvirs appeared[6], and received a commission to regulate the affairs of the Commonwealth for five years. Octavius then laid down the consulship, and P. Ventidius Bassus and C. Albius (?) Carrinas were elected consuls for the remainder[7] of 43 B.C.

§ 23. Cicero was at this time at Tusculum, and ill-provided with money; he was anxious to fly to Macedonia, and his brother and nephew entered Rome to procure supplies for the journey, but were taken and put to death[8]. Cicero himself travelled to Astura; coasted along to Circeii; returned to Astura, and thence sailed to Caieta, landed, and passed a night in his Formian villa. He was weary of suspense, and disliked the thought of a voyage in winter; but his slaves persuaded him to let them carry him to his ship. He was driven back more than once by bad weather, and returned to his villa, saying, 'Let me die in the country I have often saved.' He passed another night there; next day a party sent in search of him approached, and his slaves made a last effort to carry him to the ship, but were overtaken in a wood by soldiers, under the command of Popilius Laenas, a tribune, and Herennius, a centurion. The slaves prepared to defend their master, but Cicero forbade them, and stretched out his neck to the sword of Herennius or Popilius. The latter had once been Cicero's client in an action[9].

Cicero was killed on December 7; he had nearly completed his 64th year. His head and hand were cut off, and displayed on the Rostra at Rome, after his head had received insults from Fulvia. Antony paid to his murderers ten times the reward promised them[10].

[1] Vell. 2. 66; App. Bell. Civ. 4. 2 and 3; Plut.; Dion Cassius; ll. cc. [2] Fischer, Römische Zeittafeln, sub anno. [3] App. Bell. Civ. 4. 6. [4] Suet. Oct. 27; Vell. 2. 66; Plut. Ant. 19. [5] App. l. c. [6] Dion Cassius 47. 2: cp. 46. 55; App. Bell. Civ. 4. 7. [7] App. Bell. Civ. 4. 2; Vell. 2. 65; Fasti Consulares (apud Orell. Onomast.), sub anno. [8] Plut. Cic. 47; App. Bell. Civ. 4. 20; Dion Cassius 47. 10. [9] Dion Cassius 47. 11; M. Seneca, Controv. 3. 17. [10] Livy, Fragm. 50, e lib. 120; Plut. Cic. 47–49; Vell. 2. 64 and 66; App. Bell. Civ. 4. 19 and 20; Dion Cassius 47. 8 and 11.

SELECT LETTERS

OF

M. TULLIUS CICERO.

PART V.

105. To ATTICUS (AD ATT. XIV. 1).

MATIUS' SUBURBAN VILLA, ABOUT APRIL 7, 44 B.C. (710 A.U.C.)

1. I have come to visit Matius, who says, with some satisfaction, that Caesar's death will cause great confusion. 2. Tell me any news you hear, especially about Brutus. I remember a striking remark of Caesar's about him; and that reminds me of another, referring to my humiliation under the late system.

CICERO ATTICO SAL.

1 DEVERTI ad illum, de quo tecum mane. Nihil perditius: 'explicari rem non posse; etenim si ille tali ingenio exitum non reperiebat, quis nunc reperiet?' Quid quaeris? perisse omnia aiebat, quod haud scio an ita sit; verum ille gaudens, adfirmatque minus diebus XX. tumultum Gallicum, in sermonen se

ABOUT APRIL 7. A comparison of Ad Att. 14. 2, 4 with 14. 5, 3 makes this date seem probable.

1. Deverti, 'I have come on a visit.'

Ad illum. Probably to C. Matius. Cp. Ad Att. 14. 3, 1; and, for an account of Matius, Ep. 113, note.

De quo tecum mane, sc. 'locutus sum.' Cp., on the ellipse, p. 70, note on l. 7; p. 97, l. 13.

Nihil perditius. Probably Cicero's words, 'nothing could be more desperate' than his tone. Boot says of the words 'si Ciceronis sunt indicant *illum* = C. Matium non esse bonarum partium.'

2. Ille, sc. Caesar.

3. Non reperiebat. There is rather a harsh transition from the 'oratio obliqua' to the 'directa' in this clause.

4. Quod haud scio . . sit, 'which perhaps is the case.' Cp. Madv. 453.

Ille gaudens, sc. 'aiebat.' See above; adfirmatque. Wesenb. has 'adfirmabat quo.'

5. Tumultum Gallicum, sc. 'fore.' The word 'tumultus' was only applied by the Romans to a war in Gaul or Italy. Cp. Philipp. 8. 1. 3. The fears of Matius were not justified by the event.

post Idus Martias praeterquam Lepido venisse nemini; ad summam, non posse istaec sic abire. O pudentem Oppium! qui nihilo minus illum desiderat, sed loquitur nihil, quod quemquam bonum offendat. Sed haec hactenus. Tu, quaeso, quicquid 2
novi—multa autem exspecto—scribere ne pigrere: in his, de Sexto satisne certum, maxime autem de Bruto nostro, de quo quidem ille, ad quem deverti, Caesarem solitum dicere, 'magni refert, hic quid velit, sed quicquid volt, valde volt;' idque eum animadvertisse, cum pro Deiotaro Nicaeae diceret; valde vehementer eum visum et libere dicere; atque etiam—ut enim quidque succurrit, libet scribere—proxime, cum Sestii rogatu apud eum fuissem exspectaremque sedens, quoad vocarer, dixisse eum, 'ego dubitem quin summo in odio sim, cum M. Cicero sedeat nec suo commodo me convenire possit? atqui, si quisquam est facilis, hic est; tamen non dubito quin me male oderit.' Haec et eius modi multa. Sed ad propositum: quicquid erit, non modo magnum, sed etiam parvum, scribes; equidem nihil intermittam.

1. **Lepido**: cp. Ep. 62, 3, note; and, on his position at this time, Intr. to Part V, § 1; Appendix 11, 2.

Ad summam, 'the general import of what he said was.'

2. **Non posse . . abire**, 'that these transactions could not pass unpunished.' Cp. De Fin. 5. 3, 7 'etsi hoc . . fortasse non poterit sic abire cum hic adsit.'

Oppium: cp. Ep. 70, 7, note.

3. **Illum**, sc. Caesarem.

4. **Quicquid novi**, sc. 'audieris,' or 'acciderit.'

5. **Pigrere**. Apparently a ἅπαξ λεγόμενον.

De Sexto, Pompeio. This son of the great Pompey had maintained himself in Farther Spain after the battle of Munda, and probably Cicero wished to be informed of his movements. Later in the year he was induced by M. Lepidus to lay down his arms on favourable terms. Cp. Intr. to Part V, § 11.

6. **Satisne certum**, sc. 'sit quod auditum est.' Cp. Ad Att. 14. 4. 1; 14. 13. 2.

De Bruto nostro, 'what you hear about our friend Brutus.' On the force of 'noster,' cp. Ep. 38, 7, note. It is doubtful if M. Brutus had left Rome before this letter was written. If he had, he was probably at Antium. Cp. Intr. to Part V, §§ 2; 4; 6; Plut. Brut. 21.

7. **Ille**, sc. 'Matius.'

Magni refert, 'it is of much importance.' Plutarch (Brut. 6) gives the saying in a different and more intelligible form, *οὐκ οἶδα μὲν ὃ βούλεται*. As it is quoted by Matius, the sed seems unmeaning; we should expect 'enim.'

8. **Idque eum** (Caesarem) . . **cum** . . **diceret** (Brutus). Cicero mentions this speech, Brut. 5, 21. There is some doubt whether it was delivered at the Bithynian Nicaea in 47 B.C., or at the Ligurian in 45 B.C. Meier (Orat. Rom. Fragm. pp. 448, 449,) pronounces for the former.—In earlier editions I retained Baiter's spelling 'Nicaee.'

11. **Sestii rogatu**. From two rather obscure allusions it would appear that Sestius was tried 45 B.C. Cp. Ad Fam. 7. 24, 2; Ad Att. 13. 49, 1.

12. **Apud eum**, sc. Caesarem.

Sedens. Cicero probably sat in an ante-chamber till he was admitted to an audience by Caesar (quoad vocarer).

14. **Suo commodo**, abl. modi. For an account by Cicero himself of his feelings on such occasions, cp. Ad Fam. 6. 14, 2.

16. **Haec . . multa**, sc. 'Matius dicebat.'

Ad propositum, sc. 'revertor,' 'to resume.' Cp. the beginning of this section. 'Propositum' seems to have another meaning in Ep. 60.

106. To ATTICUS (AD ATT. XIV. 2).

NEAR ROME, APRIL 8, 44 B.C. (710 A.U.C.)

1. I was glad to hear of the demonstrations at the theatre. 2. [Matius was not so well disposed for peace as you suppose.] 3. I will explain Caesar's remark about me referred to in my last. 4. I am going to Astura, by Tusculum and Lanuvium; remember me to your wife and daughter.

CICERO ATTICO SAL. D.

1 Duas a te accepi epistolas heri: ex priore theatrum Publiliumque cognovi, bona signa consentientis multitudinis; plausus vero L. Cassio datus etiam facetus mihi quidem visus est.
2 Altera epistola de Madaro scripta, apud quem nullum φαλάκρωμα, ut putas; processi enim, sed minus diu; eius sermone enim
3 sum retentus. Quod autem ad te scripseram, obscure fortasse, id eius modi est: aiebat Caesarem secum, quo tempore Sestii rogatu veni ad eum, cum exspectarem sedens, dixisse: 'ego nunc tam sim stultus, ut hunc ipsum facilem hominem putem

APRIL 8. Cp. § 4 of this letter with Ad Att. 14. 5. 3.

1. **Theatrum Publiliumque**, 'the demonstration at the theatre when a piece of Publilius (Syrus) was being played.' Brutus and Cassius seem to have been well received at the theatre. Cp. 14. 3. 2 'populi ἐπισημασίαν et mimorum dicta perscribito.' A similar display took place at the 'ludi Apollinares' in June. Cp. Philipp. 1. 15. 36. On Publilius Syrus, cp. Ep. 103, 2, note.

2. **Plausus**: cp. Ep. 118, 2 'infinito . . fratris tui plausu.'

3. **L. Cassio**. This Cassius was tribune for 45-44 B.C., and brother of the conspirator, but not himself an accomplice in the murder of Caesar. Hence the applause given to him amused Cicero. L. Cassius had been a Caesarian (cp. Caes. Bell. Civ. 3. 34), but his conduct at this time dissatisfied Antony (cp. Philipp. 3. 9. 23).

4. **Altera epistola**, 'your second letter.'

Madaro scripta, sc. 'est.' 'Madarus,' from the Greek μαδαρός, 'bald.' Cp. Ad Att. 14. 5. 1, where Matius is called Calvena. The Greek word is used by Aristotle, Hist. An. 4. 6, ad fin. (but in a different sense apparently), and occurs in the Anthol. Pal. 11. 434.

φαλάκρωμα, foll. I cannot explain this passage as it stands. The Greek word might possibly mean, 'a mild or peaceable disposition, such as suits old age,' but is very difficult to connect with what follows, so as to make good sense. Moreover, in § 3 φαλάκρωμα seems to be a mere pun on Matius' surname Calvena. The MS., apparently, has φαλάκωμα, the first letter being reported to be a correction, and 'processit enim sed minus diutius.' J. F. Gronovius (ap. Orelli) reads σαλακώνισμα, apparently in the sense of 'luxury;' and Orelli adopts this, reading subsequently, 'processi enim sed minus. Diutius sermone,' foll., 'I had no luxurious entertainment as you suppose; I went on my way (before supper time), but not far. I was detained by a conversation with Matius.' If this reading be adopted we must suppose that Atticus had hinted that Cicero would prolong his stay with Matius for the sake of a good dinner. Boot suggests μαλακὸν κῶμα, 'quiet sleep;' and the retention of the MS. 'processit' for 'processi,' 'I did not sleep sound as you expected. It lasted for some time, but not long enough; the remarks of Matius disturbed me.' Manut. has σαλάκωμα = 'inanis iactantia,' I indulged in no foolish boasts.

6. **Quod . . ad te scripseram**: cp. § 2 of the previous letter.

7. **Id eius modi est**, 'is of the following purport.'

Aiebat, sc. Matius.

mihi esse amicum, cum tam diu sedens meum commodum exspectet?' Habes igitur φαλάκρωμα inimicissimum otii, id est Bruti. In Tusculanum hodie, Lanuvii cras, inde Asturae cogitabam. Piliae paratum est hospitium, sed vellem Atticam; verum tibi ignosco; quarum utrique salutem.

107. D. BRUTUS TO M. BRUTUS AND C. CASSIUS (AD FAM. XI. 1).

ROME (?), APRIL, 44 B.C. (710 A.U.C.)

1. I heard yesterday from Hirtius, that Antony is disposed to play us false. 2. I have applied accordingly for a 'free commission.' 3, 4. In any case I shall retire from Rome. 5. Let me know what you think. 6. My last talk with Hirtius makes me think it will be best for us to ask leave to live at Rome with a guard.

D. BRUTUS BRUTO SUO ET CASSIO SAL.

Quo in statu simus, cognoscite: heri vesperi apud me Hirtius 1
fuit; qua mente esset Antonius, demonstravit, pessima scilicet et infidelissima. Nam se neque mihi provinciam dare posse

2. Igitur is obscure, for the words of Matius just quoted do not justify such an inference. Boot suggests that they recalled to Cicero the general import of the previous letter. Or 'igitur' may mean 'I say,' resuming after a remark on another subject. Cp. Madv. 480.

Otii, id est Bruti. Rather a harsh combination. It is explained, perhaps, by the words 'non posse istaec sic abire,' in § 1 of the previous letter. If Matius wished Caesar's death to be avenged, he must wish for war with his murderers. For a similar use of 'id est,' cp. Ad Att. 4. 16, 9 'accusatorum incredibilis infantia id est L. Lentuli.'

3. In Tusculanum hodie ire, Lanuvii cras manere, inde Asturae esse. See, on the ellipses, Madv. 479. Cicero spent some time at Astura after Tullia's death (cp. Ad Att. 12. 7-45), and embarked thence shortly before his own (cp. Intr. to Part V, § 23). On his 'Lanuvinum,' cp. Ep. 62, 4, note.

4. Sed vellem Atticam, sc. 'secum duceret.' Boot.

5. Tibi ignosco, 'I forgive you for wishing to have your daughter with you.'

D. Brutus had served Caesar with ability in the Gallic and civil wars (cp. Intr. to Part III, § 8; Caes. Bell. Gall. 3. 11-14), and had been named by Caesar to hold the consulship in 42 B.C., with L. Plancus for his colleague (cp. Ad Fam. 10. 10, 2; 11. 15, 1; Suet. Iul. 76). It was he who persuaded Caesar to go to the senate house on the Ides of March (App. Bell. Civ. 2. 115; Plut. Caes. 64). This letter seems to imply that he stayed longer at or near Rome than M. Brutus and C. Cassius.

6. Hirtius. A. Hirtius was consul designate for 43 B.C., and a devoted friend of Caesar. After the Ides of March he seems to have lived in retirement, but subsequently combined with Octavian to oppose Antony. Cp. Intr. to Part V, §§ 12; 15-17. He was a man of much cultivation, and author of an eighth book appended to Caesar's work on the war in Gaul; perhaps also of the treatises 'De Bello Alexandrino' and 'De Bello Africano.'

8. Provinciam. The province of Cisalpine Gaul had been destined for D. Brutus by Caesar, and Caesar's arrangements had been confirmed by the senate on March 17; cp. Intr. to Pt. V, § 2, p. 498. Philipp. 3. 1, 1; Vell. 2. 60; Suet. Oct. 10.

aiebat neque arbitrari tuto in urbe esse quemquam nostrum; adeo esse militum concitatos animos et plebis: quod utrumque esse falsum puto vos animadvertere atque illud esse verum, quod Hirtius demonstrabat, timere eum ne, si mediocre auxilium dignitatis nostrae habuissemus, nullae partes his in re publica relin-
2 querentur. Cum in his angustiis versarer, placitum est mihi ut postularem legationem liberam mihi reliquisque nostris, ut aliqua causa proficiscendi honesta quaereretur. Hanc se impetraturum pollicitus est, nec tamen impetraturum confido: tanta est hominum insolentia et nostri insectatio; ac si dederint quod petimus, tamen paulo post futurum puto ut hostes iudicemur aut aqua et
3 igni nobis interdicatur. Quid ergo est, inquis, tui consilii? Dandus est locus fortunae; cedendum ex Italia, migrandum Rhodum aut aliquo terrarum arbitror: si melior casus fuerit, revertemur Romam; si mediocris, in exsilio vivemus; si pessi-
4 mus, ad novissima auxilia descendemus. Succurret fortasse hoc loco alicui vestrum, cur novissimum tempus exspectemus potius, quam nunc aliquid moliamur? Quia ubi consistamus non habemus praeter Sex. Pompeium et Bassum Caecilium, qui mihi

1. Aiebat, sc. 'Antonius.' The context seems to require this, but the change of subject from 'demonstravit' is strange.

2. Militum, i.e. of Caesar's veterans. Many of them seem to have come to Rome, and Lepidus had a legion in or near the city.

4. Si mediocre . . habuissemus, 'if our pretensions were even moderately supported,' i.e. by the senate and people granting them provinces.

5. Nullae partes . . relinquerentur, 'they (Antony and his party) would have no political part left to play.' Süpfle. Wesenb. does not think that 'his' can have the meaning here given to it, and suggests 'illis,' 'ipsis,' 'suis,' or 'sibi.' Andr. prefers 'illis,' and refers to § 6 of this letter for an instance of the application of that pronoun to opponents. He remarks that 'sibi' or 'suis' would be more natural, but that 'illis' is used from the writer's point of view.

6. Versarer . . postularem. These tenses are not epistolary, but refer to the time of the conversation with Hirtius. Cp. 'hanc se impetraturum pollicitus est,' below.

Placitum est: cp. Ep. 53, 4, note.

7. Legationem liberam: cp. Ep. 11, 3, note.

9. Pollicitus est, sc. Hirtius.

Hominum, sc. Caesarianorum.

10. Insectatio. Not apparently Ciceronian, 'underhand persecution.' Forcell.

11. Aqua et igni . . interdicatur. This was equivalent to banishment. Cp. p. 19, and Smith, Dict. of Antiq., sub voc. 'Exsilium,' p. 516.

12. Tui consilii. On the gen., cp. Ep. 26, 1, note.

13. Dandus est locus fortunae, 'we must yield to fortune.' Forcell. Cp. also Cic. Pro Quinct. 16, 53 'aliquid loci rationi et consilio dedisses.'

14. Rhodum: cp. Ep. 88, 5, note.

Aliquo, 'somewhere or other.' Andr. Cp. Ep. 100, 3, note.

Melior. Rather curiously used for one of three possibilities, as opposed to 'pessimus.'

16. Ad novissima auxilia, 'to the most desperate expedients,' i.e. civil war, and co-operation with Bassus and Sex. Pompeius: on whose enterprises, cp. Intr. to Part IV, §§ 12; 14; Appendix 11, 4 and 10.

Succurret, 'will occur.' Andr. Cp. Ep. 105, 2.

18. Quam . . moliamur, 'than now try some decisive measure.'

Ubi consistamus, 'a place where we may take up a safe position;' 'a rallying point.' Jeans.

videntur hoc nuntio de Caesare adlato firmiores futuri; satis tempore ad eos accedemus, ubi quid valeant scierimus. Pro Cassio et te, si quid me velitis recipere, recipiam; postulat enim hoc Hirtius ut faciam. Rogo vos quam primum mihi 5
rescribatis—nam non dubito quin de his rebus ante horam quartam Hirtius certiorem me sit facturus—; quem in locum convenire possimus, quo me velitis venire, rescribite. Post novissi- 6
mum Hirtii sermonem placitum est mihi postulare ut liceret nobis Romae esse publico praesidio: quod illos nobis concessuros non puto; magnam enim invidiam iis faciemus. Nihil tamen non postulandum putavi, quod aequum esse statuerem.

108. To ATTICUS (AD ATT. XIV. 12).

PUTEOLI, APRIL 22, 44 B.C. (710 A.U.C.)

1. The 15th of March has profited little, except to satisfy our revenge. Antony's measures go further than Caesar's ever did, and he makes money out of all grants, such as those to Deiotarus and to the Sicilians. 2. Octavius treats me with much consideration, but I fear his advisers will prevent his ever being a good citizen, and am anxious to retire to some remote spot. I am more independent now, however, than I was during Caesar's life. 3. Write me any news you hear, especially of Brutus.

CICERO ATTICO SAL.

O mi Attice, vereor ne nobis Idus Martiae nihil dederint 1
praeter laetitiam et odii poenam ac doloris. Quae mihi istim

1. Hoc nuntio, i.e. 'by the news of Caesar's death.'

Firmiores futuri, 'will grow stronger.'

Satis tempore, 'early enough.' The ablative is used adverbially. Forcell.

3. Si quid . . recipere, 'if you wish me to make any engagements with Hirtius.' Andr.

5. De his rebus, 'on the topics I have discussed,' on our prospects. Andr. thinks that the writer refers to the thought of applying for a 'libera legatio.' Cp. § 2.

7. Post novissimum . . sermonem. The following passage seems to be a postscript written after the interview mentioned just above had taken place.

9. Publico praesidio, 'with a guard granted by the State.' Billerb. Abl. modi.

Illos, 'the friends of Antony.'

10. Magnam enim . . faciemus, 'we shall make them very unpopular,' if it appears that the liberators cannot be at Rome in safety without a guard. Facere invidiam is a rare phrase, according to Forcell., but is used by Asconius ad Orat. in Tog. Cand. p. 111, invidiam facere competitori—a passage to which Professor Nettleship has called my attention. It is also used by Juvenal. Cp. Sat. 15, 123—

'Anne aliam terra Memphitide sicca
Invidiam facerent nolenti surgere Nilo?'

13. Odii poenam ac doloris, 'the satisfaction of our hate and indignation.' Gen. possess. Cp. Ep. 4. 2, note. The expression 'poena doloris' occurs in a slightly different sense in Ep. 8, 7.

Istim, 'from Rome.'

adferuntur? quae hic video? ὢ πράξεως καλῆς μέν, ἀτελοῦς δέ! Scis, quam diligam Siculos et quam illam clientelam honestam iudicem: multa illis Caesar, neque me invito, etsi Latinitas erat non ferenda, verum tamen—. Ecce autem Antonius accepta grandi pecunia fixit legem a dictatore comitiis latam, qua Siculi cives Romani; cuius rei vivo illo mentio nulla. Quid? Deiotari nostri causa non similis? Dignus ille quidem omni regno, sed non per Fulviam. Sescenta similia. Verum illuc refero: tam claram tamque testatam rem tamque iustam, Buthrotiam, non

1. ὢ πράξεως κ.τ.λ. Perhaps a quotation from some Greek play. It expresses Cicero's regret that Antony had not been killed with Caesar. Cp. Epp. 126, 1; 127, 1.

2. Quam diligam Siculos: cp. Div. in Caec. 1, 2 'cum .. ita .. ex ea provincia decessissem ut Siculis omnibus iucundam diuturnamque memoriam quaesturae nominisque mei relinquerem, factum est uti cum summum in veteribus patronis multis tum non nullum etiam in me praesidium .. arbitrarentur.' Also Intr. to Part I, § 3.

Illam clientelam, 'to have them for clients.' Cp. In Cat. 4. 11, 23 'clientelis provincialibus.'

3. Multa illis Caesar, sc. 'dedit.' Cp. Ep. 15. 10, note.

Latinitas. The grant of the 'ius Latii' to the inhabitants of Sicily by Caesar seems to be only referred to here. Cp. Merivale 2. 412. On the privileges conveyed by it, cp. Ep. 31, 2, note.

4. Non ferenda. 'An intolerable measure.' I prefer Wieland's interpretation 'etwas nicht zu duldendes' to that of Mr. Jeans 'not a proper measure to pass.'

Verum tamen. An aposiopesis. Cp. Madv. 479 d, Obs. 6. Supply, 'it was useless to oppose it.'

5. Fixit legem .. latam, 'had a law posted up as having been carried by Caesar as Dictator in the comitia.' This was inconsistent with Antony's support of a motion made in the senate by Ser. Sulpicius, to the effect 'that no decree or grant of Caesar should be registered after the Ides of March.' Cp. Philipp. 1. 1, 3.

6. Cives Romani, sc. 'facti sunt.' This law does not seem to have been carried out.

Vivo illo, sc. Caesare.

7. Deiotari .. non similis? 'was not the case of my friend Deiotarus similar?' On Deiotarus, cp. Intr. to Part IV, § 6; Philipp. 2. 37.

Omni regno, 'of any amount of sovereignty,' or 'of his whole kingdom.' Cp. Pro Sest. 27, 59 'cum .. videant .. se fortunis spoliari et regno omni posse nudari.' Antony restored to Deiotarus part of Armenia which Caesar had taken away. Cp. Philipp. 2, l. c.

8. Per Fulviam. Antony's wife, Fulvia, was charged with procuring for money decrees of Antony in favour of Deiotarus. Cp. Philipp. l. c. 'syngrapha .. per legatos .. facta in gynaeceo; quo in loco plurimae res venierunt et veneunt.'

Illuc, 'to the affair I mentioned before.' Cp. Ad Att. 14. 11, 2 'de Buthrotiis et tu recte cogitas et ego non dimitto istam curam.'

Refero. This is the MS. reading, but 'I return' seems an unusual sense of the word. Orell. has 'referor.' Wesenb. has 'me' before 'refero.' But Manut., with whom Mr. Lock agrees in defending 'refero,' explains it as meaning 'haec ideo dico ut ostendam; cum haec de Siculis et Deiotaro fiant .. rem fore non ferendam si non tam testatam rem .. Buthrotiam non tenuerimus.' Mr. Jeans remarks that 'refero' is rarely transitive, whether we regard the object as being understood or 'illuc' as being the neuter of the old form 'illic.'

Tam claram tamque testatam, 'so clear and well attested.' On the latter word, cp. Ep. 8, 2 note.

9. Buthrotiam. Caesar had imposed a heavy contribution on the town of Buthrotum in Epirus, and, when the inhabitants did not pay it, offered their lands to his soldiers. But Atticus advanced money to the Buthrotians, on receipt of which Caesar issued a decree in their favour, attested by many eminent Romans. It had, however, not been executed, and Cicero hoped that Antony might be induced to carry it out. Süpfle. Cicero afterwards wrote on behalf of the Buthrotians to Cn. Plancus, brother

tenebimus aliqua ex parte? et eo quidem magis, quo iste plura?
Nobiscum hic perhonorifice et amice Octavius, quem quidem sui 2
Caesarem salutabant, Philippus non *item*, itaque ne nos quidem;
quem nego posse *esse* bonum civem: ita multi circumstant, qui
quidem nostris mortem minitantur. Negat haec ferri posse.
Quid censes, cum Romam puer venerit, ubi nostri liberatores
tuti esse non possunt? *qui* quidem semper erunt clari, conscientia vero facti sui etiam beati; sed nos, nisi me fallit,
iacebimus. Itaque exire aveo, 'ubi nec Pelopidarum,' inquit.
Haud amo vel hos designatos, qui etiam declamare me coëge-
runt, ut ne apud aquas quidem acquiescere liceret. Sed hoc
meae nimiae facilitatis: nam id erat quondam quasi necesse;
nunc, quoquo modo se res habet, non est item. Quam*quam* 3
dudum nihil habeo, quod ad te scribam, scribo tamen, non ut
te delectem meis litteris, sed ut eliciam tuas. Tu, si quid erit
de ceteris, de Bruto utique, quicquid. Haec conscripsi X. Kal.

of the consul designate for 42 B.C., who had been commissioned by Caesar to superintend the distribution of the lands. Cp. Ad Att. 16. 16 A, B, E.

1. **Tenebimus**, 'shall maintain' what Caesar had granted. See preceding note.

Quo iste plura? 'the more grants Antony has made.'

2. **Nobiscum**, sc. 'agit.' Cp. Ep. 15. 10, note.

Octavius. The future emperor. Caesar had adopted him by his will, but the adoption had not been ratified by the curiae. Cp. Intr. to Part V, § 4. On the conduct of Octavius at this time, cp. Intr. l. c.

Sui, 'his adherents.' From the next clause they seem to have been numerous. According to Appian (Bell. Civ. 3. 11 and 12) they were freedmen or old soldiers of Caesar.

3. **Philippus** had married Atia, the mother of Octavius. Cp. Suet. Oct. 8; Vell. 2. 59 and 60. Matthiae, following Manutius, suggests that he objected to Octavius taking the name Caesar, because the curiae had not sanctioned his adoption.

4. **Quem**, sc. Octavium.

5. **Nostris**, i.e. 'to the assassins of Caesar.'

Negat haec ferri posse, 'Octavius says that the present state of things is intolerable.' Cp. Ep. 105. 1 '(adfirmat Matius) non posse istaec sic abire.' Wesenb. suggests 'minitantur, cum negant.'

6. **Quid censes**, sc. 'eventurum' or 'factorum,' cp. Madv. 479 d.

8. **Nos**, 'our party.'

Nisi me fallit, 'if I am not mistaken.' Cp. Ep. 71, 8, note.

9. **Iacebimus**, 'shall get the worst.' Cp. Ep. 3. 1.

Ubi nec Pelopidarum, 'nomen nec facta audiam.' Apparently a quotation from some old play; perhaps, as Manut. and Boot suggest, from the Atreus of Attius. Cp. Ad Fam. 7. 30, 1.

Inquit seems needless. One would expect 'ut inquit,' sc. 'poeta.' The absence of a subject to 'inquit' need present no difficulty. Cp. pp. 284, l. 12; 304, l. 7, note.

10. **Hos designatos**, i.e. Hirtius and Pansa. Cp. Ad Att. 14. 11, 2. If this passage is serious, it may refer to the lukewarmness of Hirtius and Pansa, but it is more probably ironical.

Declamare, 'to give them lessons in rhetoric.' Cp. Ep. 87, 1, note.

11. **Ut ne**: cp. Ep. 7, 5, note.

12. **Meae nimiae facilitatis.** On the gen., cp. Ep. 77, 3, note.

Quondam, i.e. 'during Caesar's life.'

13. **Non est item**, 'it is not equally so.' Not compulsion, but his own excessive good nature now induced Cicero to give lessons.

15. **Si quid erit . . quicquid**, sc. erit velim scribas.

16. **De ceteris**, 'about the other conspirators.'

accubans apud Vestorium, hominem remotum a dialecticis, in arithmeticis satis exercitatum.

109. ANTONY TO CICERO (AD ATT. XIV. 13 A).

ABOUT APRIL 20 (?), 44 B.C. (710 A.U.C.)

1. I should have preferred to ask you in person 2. to approve the restoration of Sex. Clodius, which Caesar sanctioned. Your consent will place my step-son, P. Clodius, and myself under a great obligation. 3. Let my step-son think that your quarrel with his father was only political. You will prefer, I dare say, an old age of tranquillity to one of disquiet; and I have done you services enough to have a claim for some return. I shall not, however, permit the restoration of Sex. Clodius if you object to it.

M. ANTONIUS COS. S. D. M. CICERONI.

1 Occupationibus est factum meis et subita tua profectione, ne
tecum coram de hac re agerem; quam ob causam vereor ne
absentia mea levior sit apud te: quod si bonitas tua responderit
2 iudicio meo, quod semper habui de te, gaudebo. A Caesare
petii ut Sex. Clodium restitueret: impetravi. Erat mihi in
animo etiam tum sic uti beneficio eius, si tu concessisses; quo
magis laboro, ut tua voluntate id per me facere nunc *liceat:*
quod si duriorem te eius miserae et adflictae fortunae praebes,
non contendam ego adversus te; quamquam videor debere tueri
commentarium Caesaris. Sed mehercule, si humaniter et sapienter et amabiliter in me cogitare vis, facilem profecto te praebebis et voles P. Clodium, in optima spe puerum repositum,

1. **Accubans**, 'lying at table.'

Vestorium. On C. Vestorius, cp. Ep. 34, 1, note. Cicero says that he was more familiar with accounts than with logic. He lived at Puteoli, apparently. Cp. Ad Att. 5. 2, 2.

2. **Arithmeticis.** This word seems to be rarely used in Latin for 'arithmetic.'

3. **Profectione**, 'departure from Rome.'

5. **Absentia**, 'a rare word. Here it seems to mean, 'my entreaties during my absence.' Mr. Jeans renders 'I fear that in my absence it,' the subject about which I am now writing, 'may seem to you only of lighter weight:' I presume that he refers 'levior' to 'res,' and considers 'absentia' an ablative.

Levior sit, 'have less weight.'

Responderit, 'shall correspond.' Forcell.

7. **Sex. Clodium.** Sex. Clodius, a dependant of Publius, was banished for riot 52 B.C. Cp. Ep. 71, 3; Ascon. in Milonian., p. 159.

8. **Etiam tum**, 'even after Caesar had consented.'

9. **Tua voluntate**: cp. Madv. 257, and Obs. 5.

Per me, 'by my own authority,' as Caesar had died without carrying out his purpose.

11. **Tueri commentarium Caesaris**, 'to carry out an intention of which Caesar had made a note.' On Caesar's 'commentarii,' cp. Intr. to Part V, § 3. They are often referred to in the two first Philippics.

12. **Sapienter..cogitare.** This verb seems not often to be used with adverbs.

14. **Voles..existimare**: cp. Ep. 18, 3, note.

P. Clodium. Son and namesake of

existimare non te insectatum esse, cum potueris, amicos paternos. Patere, obsecro, te pro re publica videri gessisse simultatem cum patre eius: non contempseris hanc familiam; honestius enim et libentius deponimus inimicitias rei publicae nomine susceptas quam contumaciae. Me deinde sine ad hanc opinionem iam nunc dirigere puerum et tenero animo eius persuadere non esse tradendas posteris inimicitias. Quamquam tuam fortunam, Cicero, ab omni periculo abesse certum habeo, tamen arbitror malle te quietam senectutem et honorificam potius agere quam sollicitam. Postremo meo iure te hoc beneficium rogo; nihil enim non tua causa feci. Quod si non impetro, per me Clodio daturus non sum, ut intellegas, quanti apud me auctoritas tua sit, atque eo te placabiliorem praebeas.

110. To ANTONY (AD ATT. XIV. 13 B).

Written apparently about April 25, from Puteoli, 44 B.C. (710 A.U.C.)

1. Your past services to the State, 2. and the friendly tone of your letter, 3. make me grant your request most willingly. I have never, moreover, been of a harsh disposition. 4. Train the youthful Clodius in sound views; I never felt any remarkable hostility to his father, and were he living should feel none now. 5. I grant your request, then, not from alarm for myself, but from regard for you.

Cicero's old enemy Clodius. He afterwards died of the effects of gluttony. Cp. Val. Max. 3. 5.

In optima spe . . repositum, 'of the highest promise.' A curious construction.

1. Cum potueris, 'though it has been in your power to do so.'

3. Eius: non . . familiam. Wesenb. has 'eius, non quo,' i.e. 'not out of contempt for his family.'

Hanc familiam. That of Clodius, with which Antony was now nearly connected. See below. Müller supposes it to refer to the Claudian house generally.

5. Contumaciae. The sense seems to require a word meaning 'personal dislike,' but I cannot find that 'contumacia' ever has that meaning. C. F. Hermann (ap. Baiter) suggests 'contumeliae.' Wesenb. thinks that 'contumaciae' = 'superbae contemptionis.'

6. Dirigere puerum. Antony had married Fulvia, the widow of P. Clodius, and his step-son was probably brought up in his house.

10. Sollicitam, 'troubled by anxiety,' which it might be, even if free from any serious risk. There may be a hint here of Antony's employing Cicero's old enemies against him.

Meo iure . . rogo, 'I have a good right to ask this favour of you.' 'Suo iure' = 'potestate a legibus seu iure concessa.' Forcell.

Nihil enim . . feci. Antony refers, probably, to his support of Cicero against Clodius, 53 B.C., and to his protection of Cicero after the battle of Pharsalus. Cp. Philipp. 1. 4, 11; 2. 3, 5; 2. 9, 21; 2. 20, 49.

11. Per me: see above.

CICERO ANTONIO COS. S. D.

1 Quod mecum per litteras agis, unam ob causam mallem coram
egisses: non enim solum ex oratione, sed etiam ex voltu et oculis
et fronte, ut aiunt, meum erga te amorem perspicere potuisses;
nam, cum te semper amavi, primum tuo studio, post etiam beneficio provocatus, tum his temporibus res publica te mihi ita com-
2 mendavit, ut cariorem habeam neminem. Litterae vero tuae
cum amantissime, tum honorificentissime scriptae sic me adfece-
runt, ut non dare tibi beneficium viderer, sed accipere a te ita
petente, ut inimicum meum, necessarium tuum, me invito servare
3 nolles, cum id nullo negotio facere posses. Ego vero tibi istuc,
mi Antoni, remitto, atque ita, ut me a te, cum iis verbis scrip-
seris, liberalissime atque honorificentissime tractatum existimem,
idque cum totum, quoquo modo se res haberet, tibi dandum putarem, tum do etiam humanitati et naturae meae; nihil enim umquam non modo acerbum in me fuit, sed ne paulo quidem tristius
aut severius, quam necessitas rei publicae postulavit. Accedit ut
ne in ipsum quidem Clodium meum insigne odium fuerit umquam,
semperque ita statui, non esse insectandos inimicorum amicos,
praesertim humiliores, nec his praesidiis nosmet ipsos esse spo-
4 liandos. Nam de puero Clodio tuas partes esse arbitror, ut eius

1. **Quod**, 'as to the fact that.' Cp. Ep. 8, 14, note.

2. **Voltu et oculis**, foll., 'my expression, and eyes and brow.' The words ut aiunt seem to shew that Cicero is quoting some familiar saying.

4. **Tuo studio**, 'your devotion to me.' Cp. § 3 of the previous letter, and note thereon.

Beneficio, i.e. after Pharsalus. Cp. Philipp 1. 4. 11; 2. 3. 5.

5. **Provocatus**, 'invited.'

Res publica, 'your public conduct,' or perhaps 'the public interest.' Cicero refers especially to Antony's behaviour on March 17. Cp. Intr. to Part V, § 2.

8. **Ita petente . . nolles**, 'as in making your request you express unwillingness to restore your friend against my will.'

10. **Ego vero**, 'I certainly.' Cp. Ep. 40, 2, note; also Pro Muren. 4. 9 'ego vero libenter desino.'

Istuc . . remitto, 'I give up that quarrel to please you,' 'make that sacrifice for your sake.'

13. **Totum**, 'altogether.' Cp. Ep. 2, 2, note.

Quoquo modo . . haberet, foll., 'under any circumstances I should be willing to do this for *you*, even if my disposition were sterner than it is.'

14. **Nihil enim . . postulavit**, 'there was never anything in me—I do not say cruel, but—harsher or more rigorous than the State's need required.'

Enim explains naturae meae.

16. **Accedit ut**. On this construction, cp. Madv. 373. Obs. 3.

17. **Ne . . insigne . . umquam**. Yet Cicero cherished for a long time his exultation over the death of Clodius. After more than two years had elapsed he still counted the days from that event. Cp. Ad Att. 6. 1, 26.

19. **His praesidiis**, i.e. 'the services of our dependents,' whose exile would diminish the number of their opportunities for serving their patron's interest.

20. **Nam**: 'I say nothing of the young Clodius, for,' cp. Ep. 26. 2, note.

Tuas partes esse. Because Antony was step-father to young Clodius.

animum tenerum, quem ad modum scribis, iis opinionibus imbuas, ut ne quas inimicitias residere in familiis nostris arbitretur. Contendi cum P. Clodio, cum ego publicam causam, ille suam defenderet: nostras concertationes res publica diiudicavit; si viveret, mihi cum illo nulla contentio iam maneret. Qua re, quoniam hoc a me sic petis, ut, quae tua potestas est, ea neges te me invito usurum, puero quoque hoc a me dabis, si tibi videbitur, non quo aut aetas nostra ab illius aetate quicquam debeat periculi suspicari aut dignitas mea ullam contentionem extimescat, sed ut nosmet ipsi inter nos coniunctiores simus, quam adhuc fuimus; interpellantibus enim his inimicitiis animus tuus magis patuit quam domus. Sed haec hactenus. Illud extremum: ego, quae te velle quaeque ad te pertinere arbitrabor, semper sine ulla dubitatione summo studio faciam; hoc velim tibi penitus persuadeas.

111. To DOLABELLA (AD FAM. IX. 14).

NEAR POMPEII, MAY 4, 44 B.C. (710 A.U.C.)

1. I must write to thank you for the credit your conduct has reflected upon me, for there is a general impression that I am your adviser. 2. And though I cannot fairly claim this honour, I am unwilling altogether to disclaim it. 3. L. Caesar regrets that he has not as much influence with Antony as I am thought to have with you. 4. I do not seriously pretend to any share in your glory, which I would gladly increase. 5. My love for you has been strengthened by your recent service, as my love for Brutus was by his deed on the 15th of March. 6. You need no exhortation: 7. but I must congratulate you on having been both vigorous and popular as a magistrate, and on the admirable skill of your address to the people. 8. You have delivered your country from alarm, and I hope you will employ your influence thus won in the interest of our liberators.

4. Concertationes. A milder term than 'contentiones,' according to Boot.

Diiudicavit, 'has decided' by recalling Cicero, in spite of Clodius' opposition.

6. Quae .. ea. On the order of the words, cp. Ep. 42, 3, note.

7. Puero .. dabis, 'you will make this a present from me to the young Clodius.' 'E te pecuniaria ductum, in qua "ab aliquo solvere" dicimus.' Matthiae. Cp. Ep. 36, 11, note.

Non quo .. extimescat. An answer to the hints of Antony in § 3 of the previous letter. On 'non quo,' with the conj., cp. Ep. 14, 1, note.

9. Ullam contentionem, 'a dispute with anybody.' Opposed to ab illius aetate. Wieland.

Nosmet ipsi, Cicero and Antony.

10. Interpellantibus .. his inimicitiis, 'owing to the interposition of the quarrel which you are aware of;' that is, of Fulvia's animosity to Cicero, inherited from her former husband Clodius. This excluded Cicero from Antony's house.

13. Quaeque ad te .. arbitrabor, 'and what I shall think for your true interest.' Billerb.

Antony, after his final breach with Cicero, read this letter aloud in the senate, to shew his enemy's inconsistency. Cp. Philipp. 2. 4. 7.

MAY 4. Cp. Ad Att. 14. 17, 1 and 4.

CICERO DOLABELLAE CONSULI SUO S.

1 Etsi contentus eram, mi Dolabella, tua gloria satisque ex ea magnam laetitiam voluptatemque capiebam, tamen non possum non confiteri cumulari me maximo gaudio, quod volgo hominum opinio socium me adscribat tuis laudibus. Neminem conveni—convenio autem quotidie plurimos; sunt enim permulti optimi viri, qui valetudinis causa in haec loca veniant, praeterea ex municipiis frequentes necessarii mei—, quin omnes, cum te summis laudibus ad caelum extulerunt, mihi continuo maximas gratias agant; negant enim se dubitare quin tu meis praeceptis et consiliis obtemperans praestantissimum te civem et singularem con-
2 sulem praebeas. Quibus ego quamquam verissime possum respondere te, quae facias, tuo iudicio et tua sponte facere nec cuiusquam egere consilio, tamen neque plane adsentior, ne imminuam tuam laudem, si omnis a meis consiliis profecta videatur, neque valde nego—sum enim avidior etiam quam satis est gloriae—; et tamen non alienum est dignitate tua, quod ipsi Agamemnoni, regum regi, fuit honestum, habere aliquem in consiliis capiendis Nestorem; mihi vero gloriosum te iuvenem consulem florere laudibus quasi
3 alumnum disciplinae meae. L. quidem Caesar, cum ad eum aegrotum Neapolim venissem, quamquam erat oppressus totius corporis doloribus, tamen ante, quam me plane salutavit, 'O mi Cicero,' inquit 'gratulor tibi, cum tantum vales apud Dolabellam,

DOLABELLAE. For an account of Dolabella, cp. Ep. 77, note and reff.

1. Tua gloria: cp. Intr. to Part V, § 3; also Ad Att. 14. 15. 1, where Cicero, describing the vigorous measures of Dolabella, says 'magnam ἀναθεώρησιν res habet; de saxo, in crucem, columnam tollere, locum illum sternendum locare.'

3. Cumulari . . gaudio. Andr. compares the expression, 'tunc meum cor cumulatur ira,' Pro Cael. 16, 37, a quotation from a dramatist.

4. Socium me adscribat, 'associates me.' 'Adscribere' = 'adiungere,' 'adnumerare.' Forcell.

Neminem conveni . . quin omnes. The sentence would naturally run 'quin agat,' but after the inserted clause Cicero alters its structure.

6. In haec loca, i.e. 'to the neighbourhood of the bay of Naples.'

14. Si omnis, sc. 'tua laus.' The adjective is used adverbially. Cp. p. 32, note on l. 3.

15. Gloriae; et tamen. Wesenb. omits the ; and explains 'tamen' as = 'praeterea' 'moreover my love of fame does not injure you.' Cp. Madvig on De Finibus, 2. 26, 84, where he says that the words are equivalent to 'et etiamsi illa, quae dixi, defecerint, tamen.' Itaque refertur particula ad tacitum intellectum et concessionem contrarii eius quod antea positum est. 'If you do not admit this justification, still you must see that.'

16. Ipsi Agamemnoni: cp. Hom. Il. 2. 370, foll.

17. In consiliis capiendis, 'when he took advice,' 'as a counsellor.'

18. Iuvenem: cp. App. Bell. Civ. 3. 121; Dion Cassius 44. 53.

19. L. Caesar: cp. Ep. 1, 2, note.

22. Cum tantum vales, 'on having so much influence.' The indic. is used as giving a real reason. Cp. Madv. 358, Obs. 2; also Pro Milon. 36. 99 'te quidem cum isto animo es satis laudare non possum.'

quantum si ego apud sororis filium valerem, iam salvi esse possemus. Dolabellae vero tuo et gratulor et gratias ago; quem quidem post te consulem solum possumus vere consulem dicere.' Deinde multa de facto ac de re gesta; tum nihil magnificentius, nihil praeclarius actum umquam, nihil rei publicae salutarius. Atque
haec una vox omnium est. A te autem peto, ut me hanc quasi 4
falsam hereditatem alienae gloriae sinas cernere meque aliqua ex parte in societatem tuarum laudum venire patiare. Quamquam, mi Dolabella—haec enim iocatus sum—, libentius omnes meas, si modo sunt aliquae meae, laudes ad te transfuderim quam aliquam partem exhauserim ex tuis: nam cum te semper tantum dilexerim, quantum tu intellegere potuisti, tum his tuis factis sic incensus sum, ut nihil umquam in amore fuerit ardentius; nihil est enim, mihi crede, virtute formosius, nihil pulchrius, nihil amabilius.
Semper amavi, ut scis, M. Brutum propter eius summum ingenium, 5
suavissimos mores, singularem probitatem atque constantiam: tamen Idibus Martiis tantum accessit ad amorem, ut mirarer locum fuisse augendi in eo, quod mihi iam pridem cumulatum etiam videbatur. Quis erat qui putaret ad eum amorem, quem erga te habebam, posse aliquid accedere? Tantum accessit, ut mihi nunc denique amare videar, antea dilexisse.
Qua re quid est quod ego te 6
horter, ut dignitati et gloriae servias? Proponam tibi claros viros, quod facere solent, qui hortantur? neminem habeo clariorem quam te ipsum; te imitere oportet, tecum ipse certes: ne licet quidem tibi iam tantis rebus gestis non tui similem esse.
Quod cum ita 7
sit, hortatio non est necessaria, gratulatione magis utendum est: contigit enim tibi quod haud scio an nemini, ut summa severitas

3. Deinde multa, sc. 'dixit,' which is again to be supplied after tum. Cp. p. 70, note on l. 7.

4. De facto ac de re gesta, 'about the fact and the mode of execution.' Wieland. Wesenb. has 're gesta tua,' and omits 'tum.'

6. Hanc . . cernere, 'to accept this inheritance, as it were, of another's glory to which I have no claim.' On the phrase cernere hereditatem, cp. Ep. 82. 4, note.

11. Cum . . tum: cp. Ep. 26. 3, note.

14. Formosius . . pulchrius. These two adjectives seem to be used as synonymous by Cicero, cp. De Nat. Deor. 1. 10, 24.

16. Suavissimos mores. Cicero used different language when proconsul of Cilicia. Cp. Ep. 36. 13.

18. Augendi, 'of an increase.' Cp. Nägelsb. 31, 101. 'Augere' is sometimes a neuter verb. Süpfle, Forcell.

Cumulatum, 'to have reached its greatest amount.' = 'plenum.' Forcell. The example of Brutus is apparently introduced to show that it is possible for great affection to be suddenly much increased.

21. Dilexisse, 'only to have esteemed you.' Cp. Ad Fam. 13. 47 'ut scires eum a me non diligi solum verum etiam amari.' Forcell. (s. v. 'amo') remarks, 'amare est ex appetitu; diligere ex ratione.'

27. Quod haud scio, foll., 'which perhaps has been the lot of no one else.' Cp. Ep. 77. 2, note.

Summa severitas: cp. § 1, note.

animadversionis non modo non invidiosa, sed etiam popularis esset et cum bonis omnibus tum infimo cuique gratissima. Hoc si tibi fortuna quadam contigisset, gratularer felicitati tuae; sed contigit magnitudine cum animi tum etiam ingenii atque consilii; legi enim contionem tuam: nihil illa sapientius; ita pedetemptim et gradatim tum accessus a te ad causam facti, tum recessus, ut res ipsa maturitatem tibi animadvertendi omnium concessu daret.

2 Liberasti igitur et urbem periculo et civitatem metu, neque solum ad tempus maximam utilitatem attulisti, sed etiam ad exemplum. Quo facto intellegere debes in te positam esse rem publicam tibique non modo tuendos, sed etiam ornandos esse illos viros, a quibus initium libertatis profectum est. Sed his de rebus coram plura propediem, ut spero: tu quoniam rem publicam nosque conservas, fac ut diligentissime te ipsum, mi Dolabella, custodias.

112. TO ATTICUS (AD ATT. XIV. 21).

PUTEOLI, MAY 11, 44 B.C. (710 A.U.C.)

1. I am sorry not to have heard from you, but have had a good letter from Dolabella. 2. Balbus has visited me; he gave an unsatisfactory account of Antony's proceedings, and his own disposition is questionable. 3. We clearly have war in prospect; there was more courage than wisdom shewn in the great exploit. But this is of more importance for younger men than for me. 4. I write in Vestorius' house. I shall try to gain over Hirtius and others for the good cause, but am not sanguine, and think of leaving Italy. Remember me to Attica. I am anxious to see if Dolabella will pay his debt to me.

3. **Fortuna . . magnitudine**: ablatives of the cause.

5. **Contionem.** Cicero seems to refer to a speech of Dolabella made in defence of his strong measures; but such a speech does not appear to be mentioned elsewhere.

Ita pedetemptim . . daret, 'so cautiously did you first approach and then retire from the subject that all had to allow that the case was ripe for strong measures.' 'Facti' is a participle, as the Master of University College has pointed out to me. The metaphors in these words are military. Süpfle, Andr., however, thinks that the comparison is with the ebb and flow of the tide. The general sense seems to be that Dolabella prepared his hearers skilfully to listen to his excuses, without harping too much on the subject. Cp. Merivale's account (5. 188–9) of the 'verbosa et grandis epistola' of Tiberius. Manutius thinks the meaning is that Dolabella spoke deliberately and without hurry or passion, so as to leave the impression that he had acted deliberately. 'All allowed that the case itself shewed that you had not been premature in taking such strong measures,' i.e. 'as the facts of the case and not your eloquence formed your defence.'

9. **Ad tempus,** 'for the present.'

Utilitatem attulisti, 'you have done good service.' Cp. Ep. 19, 1, note, for this sense of 'adferre.'

Ad exemplum, 'as an example for the future.'

11. **Illos viros,** i.e. 'the conspirators.'

13. **Propediem,** sc. 'disseremus.'

14. **Custodias**: i.e. against plots devised by Antony.

CICERO ATTICO.

Cum paulo ante dedissem ad te Cassii tabellario litteras, v. Idus 1
venit noster tabellarius, et quidem, portenti simile, sine tuis litteris; sed cito conieci Lanuvii te fuisse. Eros autem festinavit,
ut ad me litterae Dolabellae preferrentur, non de re mea—nondum
enim meas acceperat—, sed rescripsit ad eas, quarum exemplum
tibi miseram, sane luculente. Ad me autem, cum Cassii tabel- 2
larium dimisissem, statim Balbus. O dei boni, quam facile per-
spiceres timere otium! et nosti virum, quam tectus; sed tamen
Antonii consilia narrabat: illum circumire veteranos, ut acta
Caesaris sancirent idque se facturos esse iurarent, ut rata omnes
haberent eaque duumviri omnibus mensibus inspicerent. Questus
est etiam de sua invidia, eaque omnis eius oratio fuit, ut amare
videretur Antonium. Quid quaeris? nihil sinceri. Mihi autem 3
non est dubium quin res spectet ad castra: acta enim illa res est
animo virili, consilio puerili: quis enim hoc non vidit, regni
heredem relictum? quid autem absurdius?

hoc metuere, alterum in metu non ponere?

Quin etiam hoc ipso tempore multa ὑποσόλοικα. Pontii Neapoli-

2\. **Sine tuis litteris**: cp. Ep. 100, 3, note.

3\. **Lanuvii.** M. Brutus and Cassius were there probably, and Atticus may have gone to visit one of them. Cp. Ad Att. 14. 10, 1; App. Bell. Civ. 3. 7; Merivale 3. 77.

Eros: cp. Ep. 96, 4, note.

4\. **De re mea**, 'about my own affair,' i.e. his debt to me. Cp. Ad Att. 14. 18, 1 'Kal. Ian. debuit [Dolabella]; adhuc non solvit.'

5\. **Rescripsit**, Dolabella.

Eas, i.e. Ep. 111.

6\. **Luculente**, 'in excellent terms,' = 'clare.' 'Aptis et copiosis verbis.' Forcell.

7\. **Statim Balbus**, sc. 'venit.'

8\. **Timere otium**, 'is afraid of peace,' 'looks forward to it with alarm.'

Tectus, 'reserved,' 'cautious.' Forcell. gives 'occultus' and 'cautus' as synonyms.

9\. **Circumire veteranos**, 'is canvassing the veterans,' especially those settled in Campania. Cp. Philipp. 2. 39 and 40. 'Circumire' = 'ambire,' 'to court,' 'canvass,' Forcell., but is a rather stronger term.

10\. **Idque se . . haberent**, 'and would secure that their validity should be respected by every one.' Wesenb. has 'arma' for 'rata,' supposing the duumviri to be the magistrates of the different colonies in which the veterans had been established.

11\. **Duumviri.** These were probably to be special commissioners appointed by Antony.

12\. **De sua invidia**, 'about his unpopularity' as a friend of Caesar. Manut.

13\. **Nihil sinceri**, 'there is nothing honest in him.' i.e. Balbus.

14\. **Quin res spectet ad castra**, 'but that things hold out a prospect of war.' Cp. Ep. 43, 1, note.

Illa res, i.e. 'the murder of Caesar.'

15\. **Regni heredem**, i.e. Antony.

17\. **Hoc metuere .. ponere**, 'to fear the monarchy and not be afraid of its heir.' An iambic line, probably from a play. It is quoted also Topic 13. On the purport of the passage, cp. Ep. 113, 1.

18\. **Multa ὑποσόλοικα**, 'there are many instances of something like bad taste.' The word ὑποσολοικότερον occurs in Plutarch, Symp. 1. 2, 615 D.

Pontii. L. Pontius Aquila incurred Caesar's displeasure by his independent de-

tanum a matre tyrannoctoni possideri? Legendus mihi saepius est 'Cato maior' ad te missus; amariorem enim me senectus facit. Stomachor omnia. Sed mihi quidem βεβίωται. Viderint iuvenes.
4 Tu mea curabis, ut curas. Haec scripsi seu dictavi apposita secunda mensa apud Vestorium. Postridie apud Hirtium cogitabam, et quidem πεντέλοιπον. Sic hominem traducere ad optimates paro. Λῆρος πολύς. Nemo est istorum, qui otium non timeat. Qua re talaria videamus; quidvis enim potius quam castra. Atticae salutem plurimam velim dicas. Exspecto Octavii contionem et si quid aliud, maxime autem, ecquid Dolabella tinniat an in meo nomine tabulas novas fecerit.

menacer as tribune, Suet. Iul. 78; was one of the conspirators against him, App. Bell. Civ. 2. 113; Dion Cassius 46, 38, and did good service in the war of Mutina. Philipp. 11. 6, 14. Servilia, the mother of the 'tyrannicide' M. Brutus, was a favourite of Caesar, and it has been generally supposed that the property of Pontius near Neapolis (Neapolitanum) had been confiscated by Caesar, and granted to Servilia. But Drumann (3. 709: 710) remarks that no record of such confiscation has been preserved, and that Pontius is afterwards mentioned as lending money to D. Brutus. Cp. Dion Cassius 46. 40. Drumann suggests therefore that Pontius may have had to sell some property during the civil war, and that Servilia bought it cheap.

1. Possideri. On the infin., cp. Ep. 12, 1, note.

2. Cato maior. Cicero's work on old age. He thinks he ought to study it in order to learn how to behave.

3. Stomachor omnia, 'I am vexed at everything.' The verb does not often govern an accusative.

Mihi quidem βεβίωται: cp. Ep. 85, 2, note.

Viderint iuvenes, 'let the young see to this,' with a reference probably to the conspirators. Cp. Ad Att. 14. 22, 2, where they are called 'illi iuvenes,' and Philipp. 2. 17, 26 'in tot hominibus . . partim adulescentibus.'

4. Mea curabis, 'attend to my affairs.' Cp. Ep. 11, 3, note, for this sense of the fut.

Seu dictavi. Boot suspects these words. Cicero he thinks, would have written 'seu potius dictavi.'

Apposita secunda mensa, 'after the last course had been put on table.' Forcell.

5. Apud Vestorium: cp. Ep. 108, 3, note.

Cogitabam, sc. 'cenare.' The imperfect is probably the epistolary sense.

6. πεντέλοιπον, 'the last of five,' whom I have met here. Boot who, however, suggests 'est quidem πεντέλοιπον hic' = Hirtius solus Puteolis relictus est e quinque illis quos olim in his oris offendi. Probably Pansa, Octavius, Balbus, and Dolabella or Philippus were the other four. Cp. Ad Att. 14. 11, 2.

7. Λῆρος πολύς, 'great folly' to expect success.

Istorum, 'of Caesar's friends.'

8. Talaria, 'our winged shoes,' such as Mercury was represented as wearing. Cicero means that he had rather fly than again experience camp life as in 49-48 B.C.

Videamus, 'let us prepare' (Forcell.) or 'provide.'

Quam castra, sc. 'experiamur.'

9. Octavii contionem. Apparently a speech in which he declared that he would accept Caesar's inheritance. It seems to have been delivered early in May. Cp. Ad Att. 14. 20, 5, and 15. 2, 3, with Dion Cassius 45, 6.

10. Ecquid . . tinniat, 'jingles any money.' On Cicero's anxiety about the debts owing to him, cp. Merivale, 3. 63.

11. An . . fecerit, 'or has declared an abolition of debts with regard to my private account,' as before with regard to debts in general. Cp. Intr. to Part IV, § 5; Ad Att. 11. 23, 3.

113. TO MATIUS (AD FAM. XI. 27).

TUSCULUM, MAY 28, 44 B.C. (710 A.U.C.)

1. I was sorry to hear from Trebatius that you were discontented with me. 2. I reckon you one of my oldest friends, and though we were separated for many years, I was much indebted to your good offices with Caesar before the civil war, 3. and to your advice and 4. sympathy during its earlier events. 5. After my return to Rome you did all you could to keep up a good understanding between Caesar and me. 6. All these well-known services and the pleasure I have derived from your society, make me wonder that you should have suspected me of any breach of friendship. 7. I always defend your conduct. 8. But you must be aware that your respect for Caesar's memory is open to two constructions. I always represent it in the most favourable light, and I hope this letter will remove your suspicions of me.

[M.] CICERO MATIO SAL.

Nondum satis constitui molestiaene plus an voluptatis attulerit 1
mihi Trebatius noster, homo cum plenus officii, tum utriusque
nostrum amantissimus; nam cum in Tusculanum vesperi venissem, postridie ille ad me, nondum satis firmo corpore cum esset,
mane venit; quem cum obiurgarem, quod parum valetudini parceret, tum ille, nihil sibi longius fuisse, quam ut me videret.
'Num quidnam' inquam 'novi?' Detulit ad me querelam tuam,
de qua prius quam respondeo pauca proponam. Quantum memoria 2
repetere praeterita possum, nemo est mihi te amicus antiquior;
sed vetustas habet aliquid commune cum multis, amor non habet:
dilexi te, quo die cognovi, meque a te diligi iudicavi. Tuus
deinde discessus, isque diuturnus, ambitio nostra et vitae dissi-

MAY 28. We learn from Ad Att. 15. 4, 2 that Cicero expected to reach his villa at Tusculum on May 27, and this letter (cp. § 1) seems to have been written on the next day.

MATIO. C. Matius was a Roman knight of high education and amiable disposition. He was born about 84 B.C., and seems to have spent much of his early manhood in Greece. On his return to Rome he became very intimate with Caesar, but was not a keen partisan, and after Caesar's triumph employed his influence on behalf of members of the vanquished party. Our principal knowledge of him is derived from this letter, and from Matius' answer (Ep. 144). Cicero praises his talents and disposition very highly Ad Fam. 7. 15, 2. 'C. Matii suavissimi doctissimique hominis.' Cp. Orell. Onom.

1. Attulerit, 'adferre' is used most properly of a letter or message, but also of the feelings called out by it in the receiver. Andr.

2. Trebatius: cp. Ep. 27. 1, note.

6. Nihil . . longius fuisse. Forcell. says that 'nihil mihi est longius' = 'nihil magis cupio.' A similar phrase occurs in Verr. 2 Act. 4. 18, 39, and Pro Rab. Post. 13, 35.

7. Querelam tuam. Cicero had apparently spoken with displeasure of the regard which Matius continued to shew for Caesar's memory (cp. Ep. 105, 1; 122, 1); and Matius had been hurt by his remarks.

10. Vetustas, 'length of acquaintance.'

12. Discessus. Probably Matius' retirement to Greece. See note on MATIO above.

Ambitio nostra, 'my ambition.' Cicero chose a public life.

Dissimilitudo. Matius had not taken part in public affairs like Cicero. Manut.

militudo non est passa voluntates nostras consuetudine conglu-
tinari; tuum tamen erga me animum agnovi multis annis ante
bellum civile, cum Caesar esset in Gallia: quod enim vehementer
mihi utile esse putabas nec inutile ipsi Caesari, perfecisti, ut ille
me diligeret, coleret, haberet in suis. Multa praetereo, quae
temporibus illis inter nos familiarissime dicta, scripta, commu-
3 nicata sunt; graviora enim consecuta sunt. *Etenim* initio belli
civilis cum Brundisium versus ires ad Caesarem, venisti ad me in
Formianum. Primum hoc ipsum quanti, praesertim temporibus
illis! Deinde oblitum me putas consilii, sermonis, humanitatis
tuae? quibus rebus interesse memini Trebatium. Nec vero sum
oblitus litterarum tuarum, quas ad me misisti, cum Caesari ob-
4 viam venisses in agro, ut arbitror, Trebulano. Secutum illud
tempus est, cum me ad Pompeium proficisci sive pudor meus
coëgit sive officium sive *fortuna*: quod officium tuum, quod studium vel in absentem me vel in praesentes meos defuit? quem
porro omnes mei et mihi et sibi te amiciorem iudicaverunt?
Veni Brundisium: oblitumne me putas, qua celeritate, ut primum
audieris, ad me Tarento advolaris? quae tua fuerit adsessio,
oratio, confirmatio animi mei fracti communium miseriarum
5 metu? Tandem aliquando Romae esse coepimus: quid defuit
nostrae familiaritati? In maximis rebus quonam modo gererem

2. Multis annis. On the ablat., cp. Ep. 18, 15, note.

7. Etenim. Wesenb. thinks that this word is out of place here, and retains 'et' = 'both,' supposing that there is an anacoluthon, the corresponding clause being 'secutum illud tempus est.'

8. Cum Brundisium . . . Caesarem, 'when you were travelling towards Brundisium to meet Caesar' in the spring of 49 B.C. Cp. Ad Att. 9. 15, 6; 9. 17, 1.

In Formianum, 'to my estate at Formiae.' On which, cp. Appendix 5, § 1; and on the visit of Matius, Ad Att. 9. 11, 2. Matius left on Cicero's mind the impression that he was anxious for peace, and disgusted with many of Caesar's adherents.

9. Hoc ipsum, 'your visiting me at all.'

12. Litterarum tuarum. I now think that a letter from Matius and Trebatius to Cicero transcribed in one to Atticus may be the one referred to. It seems to have been written before they met Caesar. Andr. remarks that this meeting of Matius and Caesar occurred when Caesar was moving from Brundisium to Rome, 49 B.C. Cp. Ad Att. 9. 15, 6.

13. In . . Trebulano. There were three places in central Italy called Trebula; two in the Sabine country and one, probably that here referred to, on the borders of Samnium and Campania, about ten miles N.E. of Casilinum. The last mentioned is now called Treglia.

14. Pudor meus, 'my regard for public opinion.' Cp. Intr. to Part III, § 5.

15. Sive officium, 'or gratitude to Pompey.'

16. In praesentes meos, 'to my family who remained at Rome.'

18. Veni Brundisium: i.e. after the battle of Pharsalus. Cp. Intr. to Part III, § 10; IV, § 1.

19. Quae tua . . adsessio, 'how you gave me the comfort of your presence.' The word 'adsessio' seems only to be found here.

21. Tandem aliquando: i.e. after eleven months. Cp. Intr. to Part IV, § 1.

me adversus Caesarem usus tuo consilio sum, in reliquis officio:
cui tu tribuisti excepto Caesare praeter me, ut domum ventitares
horasque multas saepe suavissimo sermone consumeres? tum,
cum etiam, si meministi, ut haec φιλοσοφούμενα scriberem, tu me
impulisti. Post Caesaris reditum, quid tibi maiori curae fuit,
quam ut essem ego illi quam familiarissimus? quod effeceras.
Quorsum igitur haec oratio longior, quam putaram? Quia sum 6
admiratus te, qui haec nosse deberes, quicquam a me commissum,
quod esset alienum nostra amicitia, credidisse: nam praeter haec,
quae commemoravi, quae testata sunt et illustria, habeo multa
occultiora, quae vix verbis exsequi possum. Omnia me tua
delectant, sed maxime [maxima] cum fides in amicitia, consilium
gravitas, constantia, tum lepos, humanitas, litterae. Quapropter
redeo nunc ad querelam. Ego te suffragium tulisse in illa lege 7
primum non credidi; deinde, si credidissem, numquam, id sine
aliqua iusta causa existimarem te fecisse. Dignitas tua facit, ut
animadvertatur, quicquid facias; malevolentia autem hominum,
ut non nulla durius, quam a te facta sint, proferantur: ea tu si
non audis, quid dicam nescio; equidem, si quando audio, tam
defendo, quam me scio a te contra iniquos meos solere defendi.
Defensio autem est duplex: alia sunt, quae liquido negare soleam,

1. **In reliquis**, sc. 'rebus.' Cicero means that he shewed independence on points which Caesar did not consider of vital importance. Cp. Abeken 339, and note; also Ad Fam. 9. 16, 3 'ut enim olim arbitrabar esse meam libere loqui, cuius opera esset in civitate libertas, sic ea nunc amissa nihil loqui quod offendat aut illius aut eorum qui ab illo diliguntur voluntatem. Effugere autem si velim non nullorum acute aut facete dictorum famam, fama ingenii mihi sit abiicienda.' Cicero also, perhaps, refers to his intercession for Marcellus and Ligarius. Cp. Ad Fam. 4. 4, 3; 4. 7-11; 6. 13 and 14.

4. **φιλοσοφούμενα**. Among them were probably the treatises called Academica, De Finibus, and Tusculanae Disputationes. See the list of his works at the beginning of this edition.

5. **Post Caesaris reditum**, 'after Caesar's return from Spain' in 45 B.C. Cp. Intr. to Part IV, § 12.

6. **Effeceras** = 'effecisti.' But Andr. thinks that the pluperfect has its ordinary force here, and means 'you had already reconciled Caesar to me, and continued to promote good feeling between us.'

10. **Testata**: cp. Ep. 8, 2, note.

11. **Occultiora**, 'more secret grounds' or 'ties of friendship.'

Omnia .. tua, 'all your qualities.'

13. **Lepos**, 'wit,' 'grace.' Billerb.

14. **Querelam**: cp. § 1, note. Wesenb. has Quapropter—redeo nunc ad querelam—which perhaps makes better sense. Andr. adopts the same punctuation.

In illa lege: i.e. about Caesar's law for the settlement of debts. Cp. Intr. to Part III, § 8; Appendix 9, 1. Cicero had probably heard Matius accused of supporting it from selfish motives, though in reality his property had been impaired by it. Cp. Ep. 114, 2.

19. **Quid dicam nescio**, 'I do not know what to say,' 'how to explain the news failing to reach you.'

20. **Iniquos**, used as a substantive = 'ill wishers.' Cp. Pro Plancio 16, 40 'iniquos .. meos.'

21. **Defensio .. est duplex**, 'my advocacy takes two forms.'

Liquido, 'confidently,' 'outright.' Forcell. The word occurs also Ep. 40, 1.

ut de isto ipso suffragio; alia, quae defendam a te pie fieri et humane, ut de curatione ludorum. Sed te, hominem doctissimum, non fugit, si Caesar rex fuerit—quod mihi quidem videtur—, in utramque partem de tuo officio disputari posse, vel in eam, qua ego soleo uti, laudandam esse fidem et humanitatem tuam, qui amicum etiam mortuum diligas, vel in eam, qua non nulli utuntur, libertatem patriae vitae amici anteponendam. Ex his sermonibus utinam essent delatae ad te disputationes meae! Illa vero duo, quae maxima sunt laudum tuarum, quis aut libentius quam ego commemorat aut saepius? te et non suscipiendi belli civilis gravissimum auctorem fuisse et moderandae victoriae, in quo, qui mihi non adsentiretur, inveni neminem. Qua re habeo gratiam Trebatio, familiari nostro, qui mihi dedit causam harum litterarum, quibus nisi credideris, me omnis officii et humanitatis expertem iudicaris; quo nec mihi gravius quicquam potest esse nec te alienius.

114. MATIUS TO CICERO (AD FAM. XI. 28).

ROME, END OF MAY, 44 B.C. (710 A.U.C.)

1. I am glad to learn that as I supposed you do not believe the charges made against me, and I thank you for contradicting them. 2. I am aware that men call me a bad citizen for shewing regret for my friend; but in Caesar I loved the man, not the politician; I gained nothing by his triumph, and exerted myself on behalf of the conquered. 3. I may therefore fairly grieve for his death, though our so-called liberators are anxious to suppress freedom of speech on the subject. 4. I will never be false to the claims of gratitude, but am anxious for peace and order 5. as my whole past life may testify. 6. I helped the young Caesar to celebrate his games out of regard both

1. De .. suffragio, 'about your alleged support of Caesar's law already referred to.' Cp. note on l. 14 of the preceding page.

Defendam, 'I maintain.' Nägelsb. 102, 279.

Pie .. et humane, 'from devotion to Caesar, and from good feeling.'

2. De curatione ludorum. Cicero had expressed a different opinion to Atticus. Cp. Ad Att. 15. 2, 3 'ludorum .. apparatus et Matius et Postumus mihi procuratores non placent.' On the games in question, cp. Intr. to Part V, § 4.

3. In utramque partem .. posse, 'that opposite views may be taken of the propriety of your conduct.' But Andr. explains 'officium' as = curatio ludorum.

8. Illa vero duo. On 'illa' referring to something following, cp. Ep. 5, 3, note.

9. Maxima .. laudum. On the neut. plural of adjectives referring to substantives of another gender, cp. Madv. 211 b, Obs. 1.

10. Te et non .. victoriae: cp. Ad Att. 9. 11, 2 'Matius .. homo mehercule ut mihi visus est temperatus et prudens; existimatus quidem est semper auctor otii.'

13. Causam harum litterarum, 'a reason for writing this letter,' gen. object. On which, cp. Ep. 16, 3, note.

16. Te alienius. The omission of 'a' before 'te' is strange, but Forcell. gives parallel instances. Wesenb. inserts 'a.'

for himself and for his uncle. 7. My visits to Antony were only paid out of courtesy, and I cannot allow any one to dictate to me in my choice of friends: Caesar never did so. 8. I shall probably pass the rest of my life at Rhodes. I am grateful to Trebatius for making me acquainted with your disposition, and placing our friendship on a firmer footing.

MATIUS CICERONI SAL.

Magnam voluptatem ex tuis litteris cepi, quod, quam speraram 1
atque optaram, habere te de me opinionem cognovi; de qua etsi
non dubitabam, tamen, quia maximi aestimabam, ut incorrupta
maneret, laborabam. Conscius autem mihi eram nihil a me commissum esse, quod boni cuiusquam offenderet animum: eo minus
credebam plurimis atque optimis artibus ornato tibi temere quicquam persuaderi potuisse, praesertim in quem mea propensa et
perpetua fuisset atque esset benevolentia; quod quoniam, ut volui,
scio esse, respondebo criminibus, quibus tu pro me, ut par erat tua
singulari bonitate et amicitia nostra, saepe restitisti. Nota enim 2
mihi sunt, quae in me post Caesaris mortem contulerint: vitio
mihi dant, quod mortem hominis necessarii graviter fero atque
eum, quem dilexi, perisse indignor; aiunt enim patriam amicitiae
praeponendam esse, proinde ac si iam vicerint obitum eius rei
publicae fuisse utilem. Sed non agam astute: fateor me ad istum
gradum sapientiae non pervenisse; neque enim Caesarem in dissensione civili sum secutus, sed amicum, quamquam re offendebar,

7. Propensa 'inclined,' common. Forcell.

9. Ut par erat, 'as was becoming.' Muller thinks the ablative 'bonitate' is causal, but the punctuation adopted by Baiter is against this. In a fragment of Sallust (Hist. 4. 55) we find 'scalas pares moenium altitudine,' but Dietsch considers 'altitudine' to be there a form of the dative. Lambinus (ap. Baiter) suggests 'pro tua,' and Süpfle renders 'considering your kindliness,' without adding 'pro.' Andr. quotes de Divin. 2. 55. 114 'ita ut constantibus hominibus par erat' as a parallel passage, but allows that the combination is rare.

10. Nota .. sunt, 'I am well aware.' A kind of attraction for 'notum est.' Süpfle.

Enim refers to § 7 of the previous letter, 'ea tu si non audis.' It may be translated 'yes, certainly.'

11. Contulerint, sc. 'homines.' The conj. is used as though 'notum est' had gone before. Andr.

14. Proinde ac si, 'just as if.' 'Perinde' is more common. Cp. Zumpt. L. G. 282.

Vicerint, 'they had proved.' For this sense of 'vincere' Andr. quotes, among other passages, Pro Cluent. 44. 124 'vince deinde virum bonum fuisse Oppianicum.' On the tense, cp. Madv. 349; also Ad Fam. 16, 5, 1 'tam te diligit quam si vixerit tecum.'

15. Astute, 'artfully,' 'evasively.' Cp. p. 370, l. 18. Matius was unwilling to defend his conduct on any other ground than the real one of his friendship for Caesar.

Istum gradum sapientiae, 'such a height of philosophy,' as to prefer the claims of the State to those of friendship.

16. In dissensione civili, 'as the head of one side in a civil war.'

17. Quamquam re offendebar, 'though I was not pleased with the affair.' Billerb. Perhaps he thought Caesar might have given way.

tamen non deserui, neque bellum umquam civile aut etiam causam dissensionis probavi, quam etiam nascentem exstingui summe studui. Itaque in victoria hominis necessarii neque honoris neque pecuniae dulcedine sum captus, quibus praemiis reliqui, minus apud eum quam ego cum possent, immoderate sunt abusi. Atque etiam res familiaris mea lege Caesaris deminuta est, cuius beneficio plerique, qui Caesaris morte laetantur, remanserunt in civitate. Civibus victis ut parceretur, aeque ac pro mea salute

3 laboravi. Possum igitur, qui omnes voluerim incolumes, eum, a quo id impetratum est, perisse non indignari? cum praesertim idem homines illi et invidiae et exitio fuerint. 'Plecteris ergo,' inquiunt 'quoniam factum nostrum improbare audes.' O superbiam inauditam, alios in facinore gloriari, aliis ne dolere quidem impunite licere! at haec etiam servis semper libera fuerunt, *ut* timerent, gauderent, dolerent suo potius quam alterius arbitrio; quae nunc, ut quidem isti dictitant libertatis auctores, metu nobis

4 extorquere conantur. Sed nihil agunt. Nullius umquam periculi terroribus ab officio aut ab humanitate desciscam; numquam enim honestam mortem fugiendam, saepe etiam oppetendam putavi. Sed quid mihi succensent, si id opto, ut paeniteat eos sui facti? cupio enim Caesaris mortem omnibus esse acerbam. 'At debeo pro civili parte rem publicam velle salvam.' Id quidem me cupere, nisi et ante acta vita et reliqua mea spes

1. Causam dissensionis. Probably he means Caesar's claim to retain the government of Gaul.

2. Quam, sc. 'dissensionem.' Cp., on what follows, note on § 3 of the previous letter.

4. Reliqui, i.e. Caesar's other adherents.

6. Lege Caesaris: cp. § 7 of the previous letter.

Cuius legis beneficio . . . civitate. Many embarrassed men were probably relieved by Caesar's legislation from the necessity of going into exile.

11. Idem homines. Some of those whom Caesar spared apparently. Perhaps Cassius may be especially referred to. Caesar's old partisans may have been offended by the consideration he shewed for their opponents; on which cp. Ep. 91, 10.

12. Inquiunt, 'the murderers say.'

13. Alios . . gloriari. Infin. expressing indignation. Cp. Ep. 12, 1, note.

In facinore, 'about their crime.' Cp. Ep. 36, 13, note.

14. Impunite, appears to occur here only.

Haec, 'the following privileges.' Cp. Madv. 485 b.

Ut timerent: cp. Madv. 374, on the construction.

16. Ut quidem . . auctores, 'the authors, as they profess themselves, of liberty.' In substance, Andr.

Metu, 'by intimidation.' 'Metus accipitur tam active tam passive.' Forcell.

17. Nihil agunt, 'they fail,' = 'frustra operam dant.' Forcell.

21. Cupio . . acerbam. For this use of the accus. and infin. cp. p. 98, l. 18, note.

22. Pro civili parte, 'as much as a citizen can.' Ernest. ap. Matth.; 'pro civis officio.' Manut.

Rem publicam velle salvam. On the omission of 'esse,' cp. Madv. 396, Obs. 2; Zumpt. L. G. 611.

23. Reliqua . . spes, 'my hope for the future,' Süpfle; 'the hope I have left after Caesar's death,' Andr.

tacente me probat, dicendo vincere non postulo. Qua re maiorem 6
in modum te rogo, ut rem potiorem oratione ducas mihique, si
sentis expedire recte fieri, credas nullam communionem cum
improbis esse posse. An, quod adulescens praestiti, cum etiam
errare cum excusatione possem, id nunc, aetate praecipitata, com-
mutem ac me ipse retexam? Non faciam, neque quod displiceat
committam, praeterquam quod hominis, mihi coniunctissimi ac
viri amplissimi doleo gravem casum. Quod si aliter essem animatus, numquam quod facerem negarem, ne et in peccando
improbus et in dissimulando timidus ac vanus existimarer.
'At ludos, quos Caesaris victoriae Caesar adulescens fecit, cu- 6
ravi.' At id ad privatum officium, non ad statum rei publicae
pertinet; quod tamen munus et hominis amicissimi memoriae
atque honoribus praestare etiam mortui debui, et optimae spei
adulescenti ac dignissimo Caesare petenti negare non potui.
Veni etiam consulis Antonii domum saepe salutandi causa; ad 7
quem qui me parum patriae amantem esse existimant rogandi
quidem aliquid aut auferendi causa frequentes ventitare reperies.
Sed quae haec est adrogantia, quod Caesar numquam interpellavit,
quin, quibus vellem atque etiam quos ipse non diligebat, tamen

1. Dicendo vincere: cp. 'vicerint' in § 2.

2. Rem potiorem, foll., 'that you will give more weight to things than to words.' Matius appeals to his life as contradicting the remarks of his enemies. But Andr., referring to 'dicendo vincere non postulo' above, thinks that the words mean 'give more weight to facts than to *my* words.'

3. Recte fieri, 'that things should go on well,' 'that law and justice should prevail.'

5. Aetate praecipitata, 'now that my life has passed its middle point,' 'is drawing near its close.' Forcell.

6. Me ipse retexam. A harsh expression. Cp. In Verr. 2 Act. 2. 26, 63 'istius praeturam retexere.' Matius means 'undo the work of my life.'

Non faciam, sc. 'ita' or 'hoc.' 'Facio' is often used without an accusative following it.

Quod displiceat, sc. 'alicui,' 'anything likely to give offence.' Süpfle.

7. Praeterquam quod . . casum, 'except in lamenting the death of an intimate friend and a most eminent man.' This, Matius means, would be the only part of his conduct that could offend anybody. 'Praeterquam quod' = 'excepto eo quod.' Cp. Forcell.; also Ad Q. F. 2. 14, 1.

8. Si aliter essem animatus, 'if I were otherwise disposed,' i.e. 'if I wished to promote disorder.' 'Animatus' = *διακείμενος*. Forcell.

10. Vanus, 'false.'

11. Ludos. These games were properly in honour of Venus Genitrix, to whom Caesar vowed a temple on the day of Pharsalus, but their real object was to commemorate the victory. Octavius undertook to celebrate them, but Matius and others supplied the necessary funds. Cp. Suet. Oct. 10; Drumann 1. 125.

Victoriae, 'in honour of the victory.' Madv. 241.

Caesar adulescens, sc. Octavius.

19. Quae haec est adrogantia . . eos . . conari. These words are to be taken together. On the use of the accus. and inf. in such a passage, cp. p. 84, l. 1, note. The words from quod Caesar to uterer are parenthetic, and 'quod' may be rendered 'whereas,' or perhaps 'though.' Forcell. Cp. De Amic. 24, 90 '[ut] obiurgari moleste ferunt: quod contra oportebat delicto dolere.'

Interpellavit, 'interfered with.' Cp.

iis uterer, eos, qui mihi amicum eripuerunt, carpendo me efficere
6 conari, ne, quos velim, diligam? Sed non vereor ne aut meae vitae modestia parum valitura sit in posterum contra falsos rumores, aut ne etiam ii, qui me non amant propter meam in Caesarem constantiam, non malint mei quam sui similes amicos habere. Mihi quidem si optata contingent, quod reliquum est vitae, in otio Rhodi degam; sin casus aliquis interpellarit, ita ero Romae, ut recte fieri semper cupiam. Trebatio nostro magnas ago gratias, quod tuum erga me animum simplicem atque amicum aperuit et quod eum, quem semper libenter dilexi, quo magis iure colere atque observare deberem, fecit. Bene vale et me dilige.

115. To C. CASSIUS (AD FAM. XII. 1).

END OF MAY, 44 B.C. (710 A.U.C.)

1. I think constantly of you and of Brutus. You two and D. Brutus are the main hopes of the State. I have been cheered lately by Dolabella's vigour, but on the whole your deed seems to have relieved us of a monarch, but not of monarchy. 2. Do not think, then, that you have done enough, and do not plead against me the decree which present need extorted from us on March 17.

CICERO CASSIO SAL.

1 Finem nullam facio, mihi crede, Cassi, de te et Bruto nostro, id est de tota re publica, cogitandi, cuius omnis spes in vobis est et in D. Bruto; quam quidem iam habeo ipse meliorem, re

the next section 'sin casus aliquis interpellarit.'

2. Ne . . valitura sit. The fut. conj. is rarely found after 'non vereor ne,' but 'vereor' may mean 'to expect with anxiety,' and the first subordinate clause is referred to the future by the words 'in posterum.' Andr.

4. Aut ne, for 'aut' as though 'aut ne' went before instead of 'ne aut.' Andr.

Etiam ii, i.e. 'even Caesar's murderers.'

5. Mei quam sui similes. Matius contrasts his own fidelity with the treachery of several of Caesar's murderers, who had received great benefits from him.

10. Aperuit. By causing Cicero to write to Matius. Andr.

Libenter dilexi. Cp. Ad Fam. 13, 16, 1 'ut libenter quoque diligamus.' Andr.

Quo magis. 'Quo' is found at times with comparatives for 'ut' with verbs like 'facio.'

11. Bene vale. Cicero himself never uses this expression, but it is found in a letter of Curius, Ad Fam. 7. 29, 2.

This letter was written after the suppression of disorder by Dolabella, and apparently before the meeting of the senate on June 1, to which Cicero does not refer. Cp. Intr. to Part V, §§ 3 and 4. On C. Cassius, cp. Intr. to Parts II, §§ 16 and 20; IV, § 3; V, passim.

15. Quam quidem, sc. 'spem.'

Re publica . . gesta, 'now that the measures of my dear Dolabella have done excellent service to the State.' On the measures referred to, cp. Ep. 111, notes.

publica a Dolabella meo praeclarissime gesta: manabat enim illud malum urbanum et ita conroborabatur quotidie, ut ego quidem et urbi et otio diffiderem urbano; sed ita compressa *res* est, ut mihi videamur omne iam ad tempus ab illo dumtaxat sordidissimo periculo tuti futuri. Reliqua magna sunt ac multa, sed posita omnia in vobis: quamquam primum quidque explicemus. Nam, ut adhuc quidem actum est, non regno, sed rege liberati videmur; interfecto enim rege regios omnes nutus tuemur. Neque vero id solum, sed etiam, quae ipse ille, si viveret, non faceret, ea nos quasi cogitata ab illo probamus. Nec eius quidem rei finem video: tabulae figuntur; immunitates dantur; pecuniae maximae discribuntur; exsules reducuntur; senatus consulta falsa referuntur: ut tantum modo odium illud hominis impuri et servitutis dolor depulsus esse videatur, res publica iaceat in iis perturbationibus, in quas eam ille coniecit. Haec omnia vobis sunt 2
expedienda, nec hoc cogitandum, satis iam habere rem publicam a vobis: habet illa quidem tantum, quantum numquam mihi in

1. Manabat, 'was spreading.' Cp. Philipp. 1. 2, 5 'cum serperet in urbe infinitum malum idque manaret in dies latius.'

2. Illud malum urbanum, 'the well-known disorder in the capital.'

4. Ab illo . . . periculo, 'from the most degrading danger referred to above,' i.e. that of mob rule at Rome.

Dumtaxat, 'at least.' Forcell. Cp. p. 78, l. 14, note.

5. Reliqua, 'what remains for us to do,' i.e. to establish liberty on a secure basis.

6. Primum quidque, 'each question in proper order.' Cp. Nägelsbach 91, 153. Cicero hints, perhaps, that some provision for the establishment of liberty should have been made before the murder of Caesar was resolved on. Cp. Ep. 112, 3 'acta enim illa res est animo virili, consilio puerili.' Manut. thinks that Cicero means that to put down Antony was the most pressing business.

11. Tabulae figuntur, 'tablets are fixed up,' purporting to record grants of Caesar. The senate, with Antony's approval, had decreed that no such tablets should be fixed up after March 15. Cp. Philipp. 1. 1, 3.

Immunitates, 'exemptions from taxation.' Cp. Intr. to Part V, § 3; Philipp. 1. 10, 24 'immunitatibus infinitis sublata vectigalia a mortuo.'

12. Discribuntur, 'are being distributed.' Forcell. prefers the form 'describuntur.'

Exsules reducuntur: cp. Philipp. 1. l. c. 'de exsilio reducti a mortuo.' Cicero had commended Antony for his abstinence from measures such as these during the period immediately following Caesar's death. Cp. Philipp. 1. 1, 3.

13. Referuntur, sc. 'ad aerarium,' the formal way of registering decrees of the senate. The practice as to the custody of the decrees of the senate seems to have varied; after the fall of the decemvirs, it was provided that they should be kept in the temple of Ceres, under the custody of the aediles of the plebs (Livy 3. 55). But afterwards it is said that they were deposited in the treasury (Tac. Ann. 3. 51), and perhaps Cicero (De Legg. 3. 4) describes a similar custom as existing in his time. Cp. also Plut. Cat. Min. 17. Dr. Smith (Dict. of Antiq. sub voc. 'aerarium') thinks that copies were taken for the 'aerarium' of originals deposited in the temple of Ceres. That the measures taken for reporting and preserving decrees were inadequate, may be inferred from the plot referred to in Ep. 28, 7, and note.

Odium . . et . . dolor depulsus . . videatur. On the gender and number of 'depulsus,' cp. Madv. 213 a, 2; 214 a; Ep. 29, 7, note. There is a zeugma in sense, 'we seem to have gratified our hatred, and have been relieved of our indignation.'

mentem venit optare, sed contenta non est et pro magnitudine et animi et beneficii vestri a vobis magna desiderat adhuc. Ulta suas iniurias est per vos interitu tyranni; nihil amplius: ornamenta vero sua quae reciperavit? an quod ei mortuo paret, quem vivum ferre non poterat? cuius aera refigere debebamus, eius etiam chirographa defendimus? 'At enim ita decrevimus.' Fecimus id quidem temporibus cedentes, quae valent in re publica plurimum; sed immoderate quidam et ingrate nostra facilitate abutuntur. Verum haec propediem et multa alia coram: interim velim sic tibi persuadeas, mihi cum rei publicae, quam semper habui carissimam, tum amoris nostri causa maximae curae esse tuam dignitatem. Da operam, ut valeas. [Vale.]

116. BRUTUS AND CASSIUS TO ANTONY (AD FAM. XI. 3).

NEAPOLIS (?), AUGUST 4TH, 44 B.C. (710 A.U.C.)

1. Your letter, like your proclamation, is unworthy of you. We only asked 2, 3. leave to renounce some of our privileges and you replied by threats. They will have no effect upon us, and perhaps you uttered them in confidence that we should do nothing hastily. 4. We wish you to hold an honourable position in a free Commonwealth, but value our own freedom more than your friendship. Remember how short Caesar's reign was, and reflect on your own position.

BRUTUS ET CASSIUS PR. S. D. ANTONIO COS.

1 S. v. b. Litteras tuas legimus simillimas edicti tui, contumeliosas, minaces, minime dignas quae a te nobis mitterentur. Nos,

2. Adhuc. With the following words, cp. Philipp. 2. 44. 113 'res publica quae se adhuc tantummodo ulta est, nondum reciperavit.' Wesenb. has 'desiderat. Adhuc ulta.'

3. Ornamenta, 'privileges.' Cp. Ep. 99. 2.

5. Aera, 'the tablets recording his laws.' Refigere, 'to take down;' hence 'aera refigere' = 'to repeal the laws of.'

6. Chirographa, 'notes in his handwriting.' Cp. Intr. to Part V, § 3; Philipp. 1. 38, 97 'quid ego de commentariis infinitis quid de innumerabilibus chirographis loquar.'

At enim ita decrevimus, 'but you will say that we voted that they should be observed,' i.e. in the temple of Tellus on March 17. Cp. Intr. to Part V, § 2; Philipp. 1. 7, 16 'primum igitur acta Caesaris servanda censeo.' On the force of 'at enim,' cp. Ep. 15. 6, note.

8. Abutuntur, sc. 'M. Antonius et amici eius.'

9. Haec propediem, sc. 'disseremus.' Cicero saw Cassius at Antium early in June. Cp. Ad Att. 15. 11, 1.

PR. = praetores.

13. S. v. b. = 'si vales, bene,' sc. 'est;' on which formula, cp. note C, p. 121.

Litteras tuas. Apparently a letter written to intimidate Brutus and Cassius, and hasten if possible their departure from Italy. Cp. Drumann 1. 141. It seems to have been preceded by a proclamation containing much abuse of Brutus and Cassius.

Antoni, te nulla lacessiimus iniura neque miraturum credidimus,
si praetores et ea dignitate homines aliquid edicto postulassemus a
consule: quod si indignaris ausos esse id facere, concede nobis ut
doleamus ne hoc quidem abs te Bruto et Cassio tribui. Nam de 2
dilectibus habitis et pecuniis imperatis, exercitibus sollicitatis et
nuntiis trans mare missis quod te questum esse negas, nos quidem
tibi credimus optimo animo te fecisse, sed tamen neque agnoscimus quicquam eorum et te miramur, cum haec reticueris, non
potuisse continere iracundiam tuam, quin nobis de morte Caesaris
obiiceres. Illud vero quem ad modum ferundum sit, tute cogita. 3
non licere praetoribus concordiae ac libertatis causa per edictum
de suo iure decedere, quin consul arma minetur. Quorum fiducia
nihil est quod nos terreas; neque enim decet aut convenit nobis
periculo ulli submittere animum nostrum neque est Antonio postulandum, ut iis imperet, quorum opera liber est. Nos si alia hor-

1. **Miraturum**, sc. 'te.' Cp. Madv. 401, Obs. 2. The construction is somewhat irregular.

2. **Ea dignitate**, 'of such position as ours,' or as 'praetors.' Mr. W. Lock; so, too, Wiel. 'Hac' would be more in accordance with usage. On the ablat., cp. Ep. 6, 2, note.

Edicto: cp. Intr. to Part V, § 7. Brutus had probably already received permission to be absent from Italy for more than ten days during his year of office as praetor, and hence the request here mentioned probably refers to something different. Perhaps, as Andr. thinks, they wished to be relieved of the commission to buy corn, but our materials hardly warrant a decided opinion. Cp. Ad Att. 15. 9, 1 with Philipp. 2. 13, 31; and, on the public demand of Brutus and Cassius, Merivale 3. 98. Dean Merivale thinks that they wished for a formal permission to be absent from Rome.

4. **Ne hoc quidem**, 'not even such a poor boon as this.' The reference is to the request alluded to in the previous sentence. Manut. paraphrases 'hoc saltem nobis non tamquam consul praetoribus sed tamquam Bruto et Cassio tribuere deberes.' Andr. says that the proper names are emphatically used instead of pronouns. Cp. Antonio in l. 14.

Nam: cp. Ep. 9, 8, note.

De dilectibus habitis. Antony apparently pretended to have heard rumours that Brutus and Cassius were tampering with various armies—e.g. those of Syria and Macedonia—and raising troops and money, charges which, if not true at this time, were true soon afterwards.

7. **Te fecisse**, sc. 'non questum esse.'

Agnoscimus, 'admit the truth of.' Forcell. 'Nostrum esse fatemur.' Andr. Cp. Philipp. 14. 3, 8 'facinus quod nulla barbaria posset agnoscere.'

8. **Quicquam eorum**, 'any of the charges about our alleged intrigues.'

9. **De morte Caesaris obiiceres.** 'Mortem Caesaris' would perhaps be more common; but cp. Pro Planc. 31, 75 'de Cispio mihi ne tu obiicias.'

10. **Illud** refers to what follows. Cp. Ep. 6, 3, note.

11. **Per edictum .. decedere**, 'to issue a proclamation declaring that they renounce some of their rights,' i.e. by leaving Rome for more than ten days. Manut. But cp. § 1, note. Perhaps they expressed their willingness to remain absent from Italy in the interest of concord. Cp. Vell. 2. 62, 3. 'Edictum,' a public proclamation, opposed to 'epistola.' Wiel.

12. **Quin** = 'ut non.' Cp. Madv. 375 c, Obs. 4.

Quorum fiducia, 'by your confidence in those arms.' Ablat. causae.

13. **Nihil est .. terreas.** The usual sense of these words would be 'there is no reason for your trying to frighten.' Cp. Ep. 92, 5. Here it seems rather, 'there is no use in your trying to frighten.'

14. **Neque .. postulandum**, 'nor ought Antony to demand.' On the dat. after gerundives, cp. Ep. 83, 4, note.

tarentur, ut bellum civile suscitare vellemus, litterae tuae nihil proficerent; nulla enim minantis auctoritas apud liberos est: sed pulchre intellegis non posse nos quoquam impelli, et fortassis ea
4 re minaciter agis, ut iudicium nostrum metus videatur. Nos in hac sententia sumus, ut te cupiamus in libera re publica magnum atque honestum esse, vocemus te ad nullas inimicitias, sed tamen pluris nostram libertatem quam tuam amicitiam aestimemus. Tu etiam atque etiam vide, quid suscipias, quid sustinere possis, neque quam diu vixerit Caesar, sed quam non diu regnarit, fac cogites. Deos quaesumus, consilia tua rei publicae salutaria sint ac tibi; si minus, ut salva atque honesta re publica tibi quam minimum noceant, optamus. Pridie Nonas Sext.

117. To ATTICUS (AD ATT. XVI. 7).

ON SHIPBOARD, NEAR POMPEII, AUGUST 19, 44 B.C. (710 A.U.C.)

1. On August 6 I sailed from Leucopetra, but was driven back by contrary winds, and upon landing heard favourable news of Antony's intentions, which induced me to give up my intended voyage. 2. Your letter, however, surprised me; I thought you had approved my plan, 3. and your pressing appeals to me to return shewed a decided change in your views. 4. I have not deserted the Stoics for the Epicureans in this matter. 5. Your hint as to Brutus' silence was interpreted by his delight at my return. I met him at Velia; he praised Piso, regretted that I had not been present to second him, but congratulated me on escaping further censure by my return. 6. There is another reason for my coming back—the need of paying my debts. 7. I have read the proclamation of Antony, and the reply of Brutus and Cassius. The latter pleased me, but will do little good. I return to my country to die, not in the hope of guiding its counsels. 8. I was sorry to hear of Pilia's attack; remember me to her and to Attica.

1. Nihil proficerent, 'would have no effect in preventing us.'

3. Pulchre = 'bene.' Forcell. Cp. Ep. 146, 1.

Quoquam impelli, 'to be driven to any course by passion,' or perhaps 'by threats.'

Fortassis, a rare form of 'fortasse.'

Ea re, 'therefore,' referring to what follows. It seems a rare expression, but the construction is the same as that of 'eo,' on which, cp. Madv. 256, Obs. 3.

4. Iudicium . . videatur, 'that our well-considered [free. Andr.] decision (to leave Italy?) may seem the result of panic.'

In hac sententia, foll. On the construction, cp. Ep. 90, 5, note.

6. Honestum' = 'honoratum.' Andr. See too Forcell.

Vocemus. On the omission of a conjunction before this word, cp. Ep. 20, 6, note.

9. Quam non diu, 'how short a time,' i.e. not half a year after his last return from Spain. Cp. Intr. to Part IV, §§ 12-15.

10. Deos quaesumus. The accus. of a person after 'quaeso,' seems not to be Ciceronian, but occurs in Livy (40. 46) 'quaesumus vos universi;' and is common in Terence.

Sint. On the omission of 'ut,' cp. Epp. 8, 14; 11, 4; 31, 6, notes.

11. Salva . . re publica, 'if the safety and honour of the commonwealth do not suffer.'

CICERO ATTICO SAL.

VIII. Idus Sextil. cum a Leucopetra profectus—inde enim tra- 1
mittebam—stadia circiter CCC. processissem, reiectus sum austro
vehementi ad eandem Leucopetram. Ibi cum ventum exspectarem—erat enim villa Valerii nostri, ut familiariter essem et
libenter—Regini quidam, illustres homines, eo venerunt, Roma
sane recentes, in iis Bruti nostri hospes, qui Brutum Neapoli
reliquisset. Haec adferebant: edictum Bruti et Cassii, et fore
frequentem senatum Kalendis, a Bruto et Cassio litteras missas
ad consulares et praetorios, ut adessent, rogare. Summam spem
nuntiabant fore ut Antonius cederet, res conveniret, nostri Romam
redirent; addebant etiam me desiderari, subaccusari. Quae cum
audissem, sine ulla dubitatione abieci consilium profectionis, quo
mehercule ne antea quidem delectabar; lectis vero tuis litteris ad- 2
miratus equidem sum te tam vehementer sententiam commutasse,
sed non sine causa arbitrabar: etsi, quamvis non fueris suasor et
impulsor profectionis meae, adprobator certe fuisti, dum modo Kal.

1. Leucopetra. A promontory in the territory of Rhegium, looking south. Cp. Philipp. 1. 3. 7. In another passage Cicero mentions a Leucopetra Tarentinorum, more usually called Leuca. Cp. Ad Att. 16. 6. 1.

Tramittebam, 'I was trying to cross to Greece.' The verb is often used in a neuter sense. Forcell. On the force of the imperfect, cp. Ep. 19, 4, note.

4. Erat, sc. 'ibi.'

Valerii nostri. The P. Valerius mentioned Philipp. 1. 3. 8, and perhaps Ep. 36, 14. He attended Cicero on his journey.

Familiariter, 'on friendly terms.' On the use of 'esse' with adverbs, cp. Ep. 4. 1, note.

Essem, sc. 'ibi' = 'commorarer.' Cp. Ep. 70, 2.

6. Recentes, 'freshly come.' Cp. In Verr. 1 Act. 2, 5 'e provincia recens.'

Qui . . reliquisset, 'who, as he said, had left Brutus at Neapolis.' On the mood, cp. Ep. 9, 12, note; Madv. 368.

7. Haec, 'what follows.' The sentence would be differently cast in English: 'they brought a copy of the edict of Brutus and Cassius, and *the news* that there would be a full meeting of the senate on the first of September. Drumann 1. 143 thinks that the first of August is meant, and so does Merivale, 3. 98, 100. Cp. Philipp. 1. 3. 8. In that case the result of the debate cannot have been known at Leucopetra on Aug. 6.

9. Ut adessent, rogare, 'that they (Brutus and Cassius) entreated them (the consulares and praetorii) to be present in the senate.' 'Rogantes' would make the sentence simpler.

10. Ut Antonius cederet, 'that Antony would renounce his pretensions,' especially to the government of Cisalpine Gaul. Cp. Philipp. 1. 3, 8 'Antonium repudiatis malis suasoribus, remissis Galliis provinciis ad auctoritatem senatus esse rediturum.'

Res conveniret, 'an arrangement would be made.' Cp. Philipp. l. c.

Nostri, the conspirators. On their movements, cp. Intr. to Part V, §§ 1 and 4.

11. Subaccusari, 'was somewhat complained of.' Rare. Forcell.

12. Abieci, 'renounced.' Cp. Ad Att. 7. 3, 2 'rem tantam (triumphum) abiicere.'

14. Sententiam commutasse. Apparently from approval to disapproval of Cicero's journey. Cp. Ad Att. 15. 29, 2 'legationem probari meam gaudeo,' and 16. 1, 3 'meam profectionem laudari gaudeo.'

15. Non sine causa, sc. 'te fecisse.'

Etsi, 'and yet.' Cp. Madv. 443.

16. Kal. Ian. Of 43 B.C. Cp. Philipp. 1. 2, 6 'ut adessem Kal. Ian., quod initium senatus cogendi fore videbatur.'

Ian. Romae essem; ita fiebat ut, dum minus periculi videretur, abessem, in flammam ipsam venirem. Sed haec, etiamsi non prudenter, tamen ἀνεμέσητα sunt, primum quod de mea sententia acta sunt, deinde etiam si te auctore, quid debet qui consilium dat
3 praestare praeter fidem? Illud admirari satis non potui, quod scripsisti his verbis: 'bene igitur tu, qui εὐθανασίαν, bene relinque patriam.' An ego relinquebam aut tibi tum relinquere videbar? Tu id non modo non prohibebas, verum etiam adprobabas. Graviora, quae restant: 'velim σχόλιον aliquod elimes ad me, oportuisse te istuc facere.' Itane, mi Attice? defensione eget meum factum, praesertim apud te, qui id mirabiliter adprobasti? Ego vero istum ἀπολογισμὸν συντάξομαι, sed ad eorum aliquem, quibus invitis et dissuadentibus profectus sum: etsi quid iam opus est σχολίῳ? si perseverassem, opus fuisset. 'At hoc ipsum non constanter.' Nemo doctus umquam—multa autem de hoc genere scripta sunt—
4 mutationem consilii inconstantiam dixit esse. Deinceps igitur haec: 'nam si a Phaedro nostro esset, expedita excusatio esset:

1. Ita fiebat ut, foll., 'by this arrangement I was to be absent while there was less danger, and to arrive when it was at its height.'

2. Haec, 'these proceedings.'

Etiamsi non prudenter, sc. 'acta,' 'if not wise on my part.'

3. ἀνεμέσητα, 'involve no blame to you.' Quite classical.

4. Etiam si te auctore, sc. 'acta sunt.'

Quid debet .. fidem, 'what more than his honesty ought an adviser to guarantee.'

5. Illud. On the use of this pronoun with 'quod' and the indicative, cp. Madv. 398 b.

6. Bene igitur, foll. If this reading—that of the MS.—can be maintained, 'bene' is of course ironical. Orell. reads, 'veni igitur tu qui εὐθανασίαν. Veni. Relinques patriam?'

Qui εὐθανασίαν, sc. 'laudas,' or 'optas,' 'who commend (or desire) an honourable death.' The Greek word is not classical, according to Liddell and Scott. Perhaps Atticus referred to Ad Att. 15. 20, 2, 'ex hac mess exire constitui non ad fugam sed ad spem mortis melioris.' Manut. Merivale (3. 100) thinks the reference is perhaps to Tusc. Disp. 1. 45, 109.

9. Quae restant, 'what follows in your letter.'

σχόλιον, 'interpretation,' 'comment,' 'explanation.' Liddell and Scott.

Elimes = 'absolvas.' Forcell.

Oportuisse te, 'to the effect that it was your duty.'

10. Istuc facere, 'to do as you are doing,' i.e. to go to Greece.

11. Ego vero: cp. Ep. 40, 1, note.

12. Istum ἀπολογισμόν, 'the statement of reasons which you require.' The word is used by Aeschines (adv. Ctes. p. 89, Steph.).

14. Si perseverassem, 'if I had carried out my purpose,' of going to Greece.

Non constanter, sc. facis,' 'but your return itself shews inconsistency,' Atticus is supposed to say.

15. Nemo doctus umquam, 'nay, but no philosopher ever.' The adversative conjunction which we should expect is omitted here, as in Philipp. 10. 5. 12 'At ne Bruto quidem. Id enim fortasse quispiam improbus dixerit. Omnes legiones .. rei publicae sunt.'

De hoc genere, 'on this subject.'

16. Mutationem consilii, 'a change of plan.'

Deinceps igitur haec, 'then this follows in your letter.'

17. Si a Phaedro .. esset, sc. 'factum.' But the expression is rather strange. Wesenb. thinks that either 'esset' should be omitted or 'factum' inserted. Boot suggests 'esses,' 'if you were a disciple of Phaedrus,' an Epicurean philosopher, mentioned Ad Fam. 13. 1, 2; De Deor. Nat. 1. 33. 93. He was dead before this letter was written.

nunc quid respondemus?' Ergo id erat meum factum, quod Catoni probare non possem? flagitii scilicet plenum et dedecoris. Utinam a primo ita tibi esset visum! tu mihi, sicut esse soles, fuisses Cato. Extremum illud vel molestissimum: 'nam Brutus noster silet,' hoc est, non audet hominem id aetatis monere. Aliud nihil habeo, quod iis a te verbis significari putem, et hercule ita est. Nam XVI. Kal. Sept. cum venissem Veliam, Brutus audivit; erat enim cum suis navibus apud Haletem fluvium, citra Veliam milia passuum III; pedibus ad me statim: dei immortales, quam valde ille reditu vel potius reversione mea laetatus effudit illa omnia, quae tacuerat! ut recordarer illud tuum 'nam Brutus noster silet.' Maxime autem dolebat me Kal. Sext. in senatu non fuisse. Pisonem ferebat in caelum, se autem laetari, quod effugissem duas maximas vituperationes: unam, quam itinere faciendo me intellegebam suscipere, desperationis ac relictionis rei publicae, flentes mecum vulgo querebantur, quibus de meo celeri reditu non probabam; alteram, de qua Brutus et qui una erant—multi autem erant—laetabantur, quod eam vituperationem effugissem, me existimari ad Olympia. Hoc vero nihil turpius quovis rei publicae tempore,

1. Nunc, 'as it is.' Cp. Ep. 1, 4, note. Ergo (ironical), 'I suppose, then.' Catoni = 'to the model Stoic.'

3. Sicut . . soles. Is this a sarcasm on the advice which Atticus constantly gave Cicero to act with spirit?

4. Extremum illud, 'this concluding passage.'

5. Silet, 'says nothing about your behaviour.'

Id aetatis, 'of my years.' cp. Madv. 238.

6. Et . . ita est, 'and I declare that you are right.'

7. Nam, foll. The delight of Brutus on hearing that Cicero had given up his journey might interpret his previous silence.

XVI. Kal. Sept., 'August 17.'

Veliam. Velia was a town on the west coast of Lucania; the Phocaeans, who founded it, had called it Elea. The river Hales (or Heles, as Wesenb.) was a petty stream entering the sea a little to the N.W. of the town. On the movements of Cicero and Brutus, cp. Intr. to Part V, § 7.

9. Pedibus ad me, sc. 'ivit.' Cp. Ep. 15, 10, note.

10. Reversione. 'Reversio' means, as distinguished from 'reditus,' a turning back from a journey before its end has been reached. Forcell.

12. Pisonem. L. Piso, Caesar's father-in-law, and consul in 58 B.C. Cp., for an account of his behaviour at different times, Intr. to Part I, §§ 19-20; Ep. 48, 1; Intr. to Part V, § 7.

13. Se autem laetari . . effugissem, orat. obl. Cp. Madv. 369.

14. Unam . . alteram are governed by 'effugissem.' Billerb.

Me . . suscipere, 'that I incurred.' Forcell.

16. Querebantur . . probabam, 'while people bewailed it whom I could not convince that I should soon return' from Greece, whence Cicero intended to return in time to be at Rome on Jan. 1, 43 B.C. See § 2 of this letter. 'Queri' sometimes takes an accusative (Boot), but the construction of 'quam' with both 'intellegebam suscipere' and 'querebantur' is harsh.

17. Qui una erant, 'the fellow-travellers of Brutus.'

19. Ad Olympia, 'sc. 'ire,' 'that I was going to see the Olympic games.'

Hoc vero, 'than such conduct certainly.'

sed hoc ἀναπολόγητον. Ego vero austro gratias miras, qui me a
6 tanta infamia averterit. Reversionis has [speciosas] causas habes
iustas illas quidem et magnas, sed nulla iustior, quam quod tu
idem aliis litteris: 'provide, si cui quid debetur, ut sit unde par
pari respondeatur; mirifica enim δυσχρηστία est propter metum
armorum.' In freto medio hanc epistolam legi, ut, quid possem
providere, in mentem mihi non veniret, nisi quod praesens me
7 ipse defenderem. Sed haec hactenus; reliqua coram. Antonii
edictum legi a Bruto, et horum contra: scriptum praeclare. Sed
quid ista edicta valeant aut quo spectent, plane non video, nec
ego nunc, ut Brutus censebat, istuc ad rem publicam capessendam
venio; quid enim fieri potest? num quis Pisoni est adsensus?
num rediit ipse postridie? Sed abesse hanc aetatem longe a sepul-
8 cro negant oportere. Sed obsecro te, quid est quod audivi de
Bruto? Piliam πειράζεσθαι παραλύσει te scripsisse aiebat: valde
sum commotus; etsi idem te scribere sperare melius. Ita plane

1. **Sed hoc**, sc. 'tempore.'
ἀναπολόγητον, 'would be inexcusable.' Occ. Polyb. 29. 4.
Austro. The south wind had driven him back to Leucopetra. Cp. § 1.
Gratias miras, sc. 'ago.'
3. **Illas quidem**: cp. Ep. 13, 4, note.
Tu idem, 'you also.'
4. **Aliis litteris**, sc. 'scripsisti.'
Ut sit . . respondeatur, 'that you may have the means of paying your debts in full.' The phrase has been questioned, but is defended by Boot, who quotes Ad Att. 6. 1, 22 'non ut pompeiani χρύσεα χαλκείων sed paria paribus respondimus.' The passive, in a personal construction, is rare, but occurs Pro Muren. 13, 28 'minimo periculo respondentur.'
5. **δυσχρηστία**, 'difficulty' here 'in borrowing.' The word is used by Polyb. 3. 74 alib.
6. **In freto medio**, 'in the middle of the Straits' of Messina. Cicero means that he could not while on board ship take any steps to pay his debts.
7. **Quod . . defenderem.** Boot and Orell. both follow Lambinus (cp. Baiter, Adnotatio Critica) in reading 'ut.' But Forcell. gives a passage from Varro (R. R. 1. 10, med.), where 'quod' seems to have the force of 'ut'—'facile est quod habeant conservam.'
8. **Antonii edictum**: cp. Ep. 116, 1.
9. **A Bruto**, sc. 'suppeditatum.' Cp. Tusc. Disp. 1. 30, 74 'sed haec et vetera et a Graecis.' Antony's edict was a violent attack on Brutus and Cassius.
Horum, sc. 'Bruti et Cassii.' They had issued a proclamation expressing their willingness to make sacrifices for peace. It is referred to by themselves, Ep. 116, 3; by Cicero, Philipp. 1. 3, 8; and by Velleius, 2. 62, 3.
11. **Istuc**, 'to Rome.'
Ad rem publicam capessendam, 'to take part in public affairs.'
12. **Pisoni.** Cicero refers to Piso's speech in the senate on August 1. Cp § 5 of this letter and Ep. 118, 1, note.
13. **Rediit**, sc. 'in senatum.'
Sed abesse, foll. In substance, 'they say that a man of my age ought not to fear death.' Cicero was annoyed by his friends' importunity that he should play a spirited part. Cp. § 3, note. But Manut. thinks that 'a sepulcro' means 'from one's home,' where one would wish to be buried.
14. **De Bruto**, 'from Brutus.'
15. **πειράζεσθαι παραλύσει**, 'is suffering from an attack of paralysis.' Neither word seems to be quite classical in this sense, but Polybius uses the substantive metaphorically. Boot quotes Celsus as using the phrase 'temptari resolutione nervorum.' On the use of Greek for medical terms, cp. Ep. 75, 1, note.
16. **Etsi idem**, sc. 'Brutus dixit.'
Te . . melius, sc. 'fore,' 'that you wrote you hoped she would soon be better;' or 'esse,' 'that she was better.'

velim et *ei* dicas plurimam salutem et suavissimae Atticae. Haec scripsi navigans, cum Pompeianum accederem, XIIII. Kal.

118. TO C. CASSIUS (AD FAM. XII. 2).

ROME, END OF SEPTEMBER, 44 B.C. (710 A.U.C.)

1. I am glad that you approve my speech. Antony intended to have had me murdered on the 19th, when he delivered a violent and studied harangue against me. 2. Men recognize the arbitrary nature of the present government, but Antony has won over two men nearly connected with you. 3. and three eminent consulars for various reasons do not attend the senate's meetings. All our hopes, then, are fixed on you and on your associates, and I hope you are preparing for some achievement worthy of your reputation. I will do all I can to serve your relations at Rome.

CICERO CASSIO SAL.

Vehementer laetor tibi probari sententiam et orationem meam ; 1
qua si saepius uti liceret, nihil esset negotii libertatem et rem publicam reciperare. Sed homo amens et perditus multoque nequior quam ille ipse, quem tu nequissimum occisum esse dixisti, caedis initium quaerit, nullamque aliam ob causam me auctorem fuisse Caesaris interficiendi criminatur, nisi ut in me veterani incitentur : quod ego periculum non extimesco ; modo vestri facti gloriam cum mea laude communicet. Ita nec Pisoni, qui in eum primus invectus est nullo adsentiente, nec mihi, qui idem tricensimo post die feci, nec P. Servilio, qui me est consecutus, tuto in

1. Atticae, daughter of Atticus. Cp. Appendix 3. § 7.

2. Cum . . accederem : on the mood, cp. Ep. 31, 7, note.

3. Tibi probari. The letter in which Cassius expresses his approval no longer exists.

Sententiam et orationem, 'my opinion, and the speech in which it was expressed.' Cicero refers to the first Philippic, delivered on Sept. 2. Cp. Intr. to Part V, § 9. It did not conclude with a formal 'sententia,' the only words containing a formal suggestion of some resolution to be adopted occurring cap. 7, 16. So that 'sententia' probably means only 'an expression of opinion.'

4. Qua, sc. 'oratione,' if I could speak more often with the same freedom.'

Nihil esset negotii, foll., 'there would be no difficulty in recovering.' On the accus. and infin. as a subject, cp. Ep. 54, 7, note.

5. Homo amens, sc. Antonius.

7. Initium, 'a pretext.' Billerb.

8. Criminatur. In his reply to the first Philippic. Cp. Philipp. 2, 11, 25 'illud vero recens, Caesarem meo consilio interfectum.'

Veterani : cp. Intr. to Part V, § 3. After the execution of the false Marius, Antony had been allowed to raise a bodyguard of veterans, and afterwards he had visited various towns to strengthen his influence among the old soldiers settled there. Cp. App. Bell. Civ. 3. 4 ; Cic. Philipp. 2. 39-41.

9. Modo vestri . . communicet, 'if only it gives my reputation a share in the glory of your deed.' Wiel., Billerb.

10. Ita. This, as Andr. remarks, refers to the words 'caedis . . incitentur.'

Pisoni : cp. Ep. 117, 5 and 7, notes.

11. Tricensimo post die. Piso spoke on August 1 ; Cicero on September 2.

12. P. Servilio. The consul of 48 B.C.

senatum venire licet: caedem enim gladiator quaerit eiusque initium a. d. XIII. Kal. Octobr. a me se facturum putavit, ad quem paratus venerat, cum in villa Metelli complures dies commentatus esset. Quae autem in lustris et in vino commentatio potuit esse? itaque omnibus est visus, ut ad te antea scripsi, vomere suo more,
2 non dicere. Qua re, quod scribis te confidere auctoritate et eloquentia nostra aliquid profici posse, non nihil, ut in tantis malis, est profectum: intellegit enim populus Romanus tres esse consulares, qui, quia, *quae* de re publica bene senserint, libere locuti sint, tuto in senatum venire non possint. Nec est praeterea quod quicquam exspectes; tuus enim necessarius adfinitate nova delectatur: itaque iam non est studiosus ludorum infinitoque fratris tui plausu dirumpitur. Alter item adfinis novis commentariis Caesaris delenitus est. Sed haec tolerabilia: illud non ferendum, quod est, qui vestro anno filium suum consulem futurum putet ob

Est consecutus, 'followed my example.' 'Consequi' = 'imitando sequi.' Forcell. Nothing more is known, apparently, about this speech of Servilius.

2. Ad quem, sc. 'diem.'

3. In villa Metelli, Scipionis. Cp. Ep. 122, 2, note. It was at Tibur. Cp. Philipp. 5. 7. 19.

Complures. Seventeen. Cp. Philipp. 5. 7. 19.

Commentatus esset. This verb is both act. and neut.: 'had studied.' Forcell.

5. Vomere: cp. Philipp. 2. 25. 63; 2. 30. 76; 5. 7, 20 'in me absentem orationem . . evomuit.' In 'more suo' there is probably an allusion to Antony's manner as a speaker, as well as to his personal habits.

6. Quod scribis, 'as for your writing,' 'whereas you write.' Cp. Ep. 8, 14, note.

8. Tres esse consulares. Cicero, Piso and Servilius. Cp. supra.

10. Nec est . . exspectes, 'there is no reason for you to expect any other aid.' Cp. Ep. 92, 5, note; Zumpt, L. G. 562.

11. Tuus . . necessarius. M. Lepidus. He and Cassius had both married sisters of M. Brutus. Cp. Ad Fam. 12. 8, 1; 12. 10, 1; Vell. 2. 88; Tac. Ann. 3. 76.

Adfinitate nova. Lepidus' son married a daughter of Antony. Dion Cassius 44. 53; Drumann 1. 15.

Delectatur. Cp. Ad Fam. 12. 29, 1 'ut nullo prorsus plus homine delecter.' The verb is used both with the simple ablative and with 'ab.' Madvig, on De Fin. 1. 5. 14 remarks '*delector aliquo* est universe *probo, placet mihi; delector* autem *ab aliquo* est: *delectationem mihi* aliquo temporis momento *parit*.'

12. Non est studiosus ludorum, 'he has no taste for the games' of Apollo, which ought to have been celebrated by M. Brutus. Studiosus has the force of a substantive. Cp. Ep. 6, 2, note; and, on the games Intr. to Part V, § 4.

Infinitoque . . plausu: cp. Ep. 106, 1.

13. Dirumpitur = 'invidia rumpitur,' 'is bursting with vexation.' Forcell. Cp. Ad Att. 4. 16, 10 'dirumpuntur ii qui me aliquid posse doluerunt.'

Alter item adfinis. It is not known who this was. The name of C. Marcellus has been suggested.

Novis commentariis. On the use made of Caesar's papers, cp. Intr. to Part V, § 3. Antony probably declared that he had found a decree amongst them promoting the interest of the 'alter adfinis' in some way.

15. Quod est, qui. It is quite uncertain to whom Cicero refers.

Vestro anno, 'in your year,' i.e. the year in which you and M. Brutus would be legally eligible. This would be 41 B.C., as the 'leges annales' prescribed an interval of two years between the praetorship and consulship, and Cassius and Brutus were praetors in 44 B.C. The 'Lex Villia Annalis,' carried in 180 B.C., fixed 31 as the legal age for the quaestorship, 37 for the aedileship, 40 for the praetorship, 43 for the consulship. Cp. Livy 40. 44 with Cic. de Off. 2, 17. 59, where Cicero says that he held each office,

eamque causam se huic latroni deservire prae se ferat. Nam L. 2
Cotta familiaris meus fatali quadam desperatione, ut ait, minus in senatum venit; L. Caesar, optimus et fortissimus civis, valetudine impeditur; Ser. Sulpicius et summa auctoritate et optime sentiens non adest. Reliquos exceptis designatis ignosce mihi si non numero consulares. Habes auctores consilii publici; qui numerus etiam bonis rebus exiguus esset, quid censes perditis? Qua re spes est omnis in vobis, qui si idcirco abestis, ut sitis in tuto, ne in vobis quidem; sin aliquid dignum vestra gloria cogitatis, velim salvis nobis; sin id minus, res tamen publica per vos brevi tempore ius suum reciperabit. Ego tuis neque desum neque deero: qui sive ad me referent *sive non referent*, mea tibi tamen benevolentia fidesque praestabitur. Vale.

119. To Q. CORNIFICIUS (AD FAM. XII. 23).

ROME, OCTOBER, 44 B.C. (710 A.U.C.)

1. Tratorius told me of the state of affairs in your province. 2. The most important news here is the attempt of Octavian on Antony's life. Most people disbelieve it, but wise and honest men both believe the story and approve the design. Antony has gone to Brundisium to bring the legions of Macedonia here. 3. You are to be pitied for not being old enough to have seen our commonwealth in a sound condition, and now the intemperate language of Antony deprives us even of hope. 4. I am grateful to philosophy for arming me against the attacks of fortune, and exhort you to follow my example. Tratorius serves you well.

'nostro anno.' A 'Lex Cornelia (L. Sullae) de Magistratibus,' required that every candidate for the praetorship should have been quaestor, and for the consulship, praetor. Cp. App. Bell. Civ. 1. 100. With the expression 'vestro anno,' cp. De Off. l. c.; Ep. 1, 8.

1. Nam, 'you need not ask about anyone else, for.'

L. Cotta, consul 65 B.C.

2. Fatali .. desperatione, 'owing to irresistible despair.' Wiel.

Minus, 'seldom.' A rare sense of the word, apparently. Wiel., Billerb.

3. L. Caesar: cp. Ep. 1, 2.

Valetudine impeditur, sc. 'quo minus in senatum veniat.' Cp. Philipp. 8. 7, 22 'utinam L. Caesar valeret.'

4. Ser. Sulpicius: cp. Epp. 90; 98; 101, for notices of him. He had left Rome in the spring of 44 B.C. Cp. Ad Att. 14. 18, 3.

5. Exceptis designatis, sc. 'consulibus,' i.e. Hirtius and Pansa.

Si non numero consulares, 'if I do not reckon to be men of consular dignity.'

6. Habes auctores, 'here is a list of the leaders of our national council.' Cp. Epp. 7, 5 'habes res Romanas;' 29, 10 'habes de Vatinio;' also Ep. 36, 9.

Numerus. The nominative is used by attraction for 'numerum.' Cp. Madv. 319.

7. Quid censes perditis, sc. 'fore.' Cp. Epp. 59, 2; 63, 4: notes.

8. Ne in vobis quidem, sc. 'spes est ulla.' The language of the last part of the letter is throughout elliptical.

9. Velim salvis nobis, sc. 'perficiatis quod cogitatis.'

10. Sin id minus, sc. 'fiet.' Cp. Ep. 9, 8, note.

11. Tuis, i.e. 'to your family and adherents.'

12. Ad me referent, 'consult me.' Derived from the expression 'ad senatum referre,' on which cp. pp. 107, l. 16, note; 169, l. 2; 239, l. 20, note.

CICERO CORNIFICIO SAL.

1 Omnem condicionem imperii tui statumque provinciae mihi demonstravit Tratorius. O multa intolerabilia locis omnibus! Sed quo tua maior dignitas *est*, eo, quae tibi acciderunt, minus ferenda; neque enim, quae tu propter magnitudinem et animi *et* ingenii moderate fers, ea non ulciscenda sunt, etiam si non sunt
2 dolenda. Sed haec posterius. Rerum urbanarum acta tibi mitti certo scio; quod ni ita putarem, ipse perscriberem, in primisque Caesaris Octaviani conatum; de quo multitudini fictum ab Antonio crimen videtur, ut in pecuniam adulescentis impetum faceret; prudentes autem et boni viri et credunt factum et probant. Quid quaeris? magna spes est in eo: nihil est, quod non existimetur laudis et gloriae causa facturus. Antonius autem, noster familiaris, tanto se odio esse intellegit, ut, cum interfectores suos domi conprehenderit, rem proferre non audeat. A. d. VII. Id. Oct. Brundisium erat profectus obviam legionibus Macedonicis quattuor, quas sibi conciliare pecunia cogitabat easque ad urbem adducere et in cervicibus nostris conlocare.
3 Habes formam rei publicae, si in castris potest esse res publica;

1. **Omnem condicionem.** Cornificius had probably been entrusted with the government of Africa early in this year, as a successor to C. Calvisius, and now Antony had made an arrangement by which Calvisius should return to Africa. Cp. Ad Fam. 12. 22, 3; 12. 25; 12. 30, 7; Philipp. 3. 10, 26; Intr. to Part V, § 10.

2. **Tratorius.** Apparently a friend of Cornificius. He is mentioned again Ad Fam. 12. 30, 5.

Locis omnibus. Referring probably to the irregular arrangements made by Antony for the government of various provinces. Cp. Philipp. l. c.

3. **Quae tibi acciderunt**, i.e. the appointment of a successor. See above.

5. **Non .. dolenda**, 'because the violence of our enemies can only serve us.' Andr.

6. **Haec posterius**, sc. 'disseremus.'

Rerum urbanarum acta: cp. Ep. 16, 6, note.

7. **Quod ni .. putarem**, sc. 'esse,' 'and unless I knew this was so.' 'Quod' is here a pronoun equivalent to a demonstrative with a conjunction, cp. Madv. 449.

8. **Caesaris Octaviani conatum.** An alleged attempt on the life of Antony. Cp. Suet. Oct. 10; Vell. 2. 60, 3; App. Bell. Civ. 3. 39; Merivale 3. 107.

9. **In pecuniam adulescentis.** Caesar had made Octavian his heir, and the latter demanded his inheritance from Antony. Cp. Intr. to Part V, § 4.

10. **Factum**, sc. 'conatum,' 'that the attempt was made.'

11. **Probant.** Cicero (Philipp. 3. 8, 19) hints that he himself instigated Octavian.

Quid quaeris: cp. Ep. 7, 6, note.

In eo, sc. Octaviano.

13. **Noster familiaris**, of course ironical; or with reference to their old intimacy. Cp. Ad Fam. 16. 23, 2. Manut.

Interfectores suos. See above on the charge made against Octavian.

15. **A. d. VII. Id. Oct.** On Antony's movements at this time, cp. Intr. to Part V, § 9.

Legionibus .. quattuor: cp. Appendix 11, 11, and note.

17. **In cervicibus .. conlocare**, 'to seat them on our necks,' a common metaphor. Forcell.

18. **Habes**: cp. Ep. 29, 20, note.

Formam, 'outline,' 'sketch.' Billerb.

In castris, 'in a city which resembles a camp,' owing to Antony's introduction of

in quo tuam vicem saepe doleo, quod nullam partem per aetatem
sanae et salvae rei publicae gustare potuisti. Atque antehac
quidem sperare saltem licebat; nunc etiam id ereptum est: quae 4
enim est spes, cum in contione dicere ausus sit Antonius
Cannutium apud eos locum sibi quaerere, quibus se salvo locus
in civitate esse non posset? Equidem et haec et omnia, quae
homini accidere possunt, sic fero, ut philosophiae magnam habeam
gratiam, quae me non modo ab sollicitudine abducit, sed etiam
contra omnes fortunae impetus armat, tibique idem censeo
faciendum nec, a quo culpa absit, quicquam in malis numerandum. Sed haec tu melius. Tratorium nostrum cum semper
probassem, tum maxime in tuis rebus summam eius fidem diligentiam prudentiamque cognovi. Da operam, ut valeas; hoc
mihi gratius facere nihil potes.

120. D. BRUTUS TO CICERO (AD FAM. XI. 4).

CISALPINE GAUL, AUTUMN (?) 44 B.C. (710 A.U.C.)

1. I have attacked the Inalpini, wishing to satisfy my soldiers and attach them to our cause. 2. and I think I have succeeded; for they have witnessed both my energy and my liberality. If you support the claims which I have preferred in a letter to the senate, you will do good service to the common cause.

D. BRUTUS IMP. COS. DESIG. S. D. M. CICERONI.

Si de tua in me voluntate dubitarem, multis a te verbis peterem, 1

troops. Cp. Intr. to Part V, l. c.; Appendix 11, 12. Cicero's language seems exaggerated.

1. Tuam vicem, cp. Ep. 29, 2, note, p. 199.

Quod nullam partem, foll., 'that you were not born soon enough to enjoy the benefit of a healthy state of things at all.' Cicero means, probably, that the public life of Cornificius had not begun when the civil war broke out. He was Caesar's quaestor 48 B.C., and the quaestorship was considered the first step in a public career. Cp. Bell. Alex. 42. On this sense of 'gustare,' cp. De Fin. 1. 18, 58 'gustare partem ullam liquidae voluptatis;' also Ep. 8, 8, note on 'degustes.'

5. Cannutium. Ti. Cannutius was tribune for this year, and attacked Antony with much freedom. He was afterwards put to death by order of Octavian. Cp. Philipp. 3. 9. 23; Ad Fam. 12. 3. 2; Vell. 2. 64, 3.

Apud eos, sc. Bruti et Cassii amicos.

Locum sibi quaerere, 'is seeking a position for himself.' 'Locus' = 'gradus honoris.' Forcell.

10. Nec ei a quo culpa absit, foll. A demonstrative pronoun is often omitted in sentences like this, cp. Epp. 34. 7; 114. 3. notes, and here 'ei' may be easily supplied from 'tibi,' or perhaps, as Mr. W. Lock thinks, 'a quo' refers to 'quicquam.'

11. Tu melius, 'scis.' On the ellipse, cp. Ep. 9, 8, note.

Cum semper .. tum maxime: cp. Ep. 26, 3. note.

IMP. The use of this title may be explained by the victories of D. Brutus over the Inalpini.

COS. DESIG. It is implied in various passages of the Philippics and of Cicero's letters, that Caesar had nominated D. Brutus and L. Plancus to be consuls in 42 B.C.

ut dignitatem meam tuerere, sed profecto est ita, ut mihi persuasi, me tibi esse curae. Progressus sum ad Inalpinos cum exercitu, non tam nomen imperatorium captans quam cupiens militibus satis facere firmosque eos ad tuendas nostras res efficere: quod mihi videor consecutus; nam et liberalitatem nostram et animum sunt experti. Cum omnium bellicosissimis bellum gessi; multa castella cepi, multa vastavi: non sine causa ad senatum litteras misi. Adiuva nos tua sententia; quod cum facies, ex magna parte communi commodo inservieris.

121. To ATTICUS (AD ATT. XVI. 8.)

PUTEOLI, (?) EARLY IN NOVEMBER, 44 B.C (710 A.U.C.)

1. When my plans are fixed, I will tell you on what day to expect me. I hear from Octavian that he has gained over the veterans at Calatia and Casilinum, and will visit the other colonies. I do not, however, trust him much, and a secret interview which he proposes would be impracticable. 2. He sent Caecina to me to tell me of Antony's movements and to ask whether he himself should occupy Capua, or march to Rome, or repair to the legions of Macedonia. I advised his going to Rome. Would that Brutus were here! What do you advise me to do? I expect you will wish me to go to Rome.

CICERO ATTICO SAL.

1 Cum sciam, quo die venturus sim, faciam ut scias. Impedimenta exspectanda sunt, quae Anagnia veniunt, et familia aegra est. Kal. vesperi litterae mihi ab Octaviano: magna molitur.

Cp. Merivale 3. 472. On the movements of D. Brutus, cp. Intr. to Part V, §§ 4; 9: Appendix II. 1; Ep. 107. notes.

1. Est ita . . curae, 'the case is as I have persuaded myself, namely, that you take an interest in me.' On 'ita est,' cp. Ep. 122, 1.

2. Ad Inalpinos. Perhaps the tribes of the modern Savoy and Piedmont. Wiel., Billerb.

4. Militibus satis facere, 'to satisfy the expectations of my men.' Cp. the next section.

Ad tuendas nostras res, 'to support our interests.'

5. Mihi videor consecutus: cp. Madv. 400 a; Epp. 22, 4; 26. 3, note.

Liberalitatem, 'my generosity' in distributing rewards and plunder.

6. Animum, 'my courage' in the field.

7. Castella, 'villages' not necessarily fortified. Cp. Livy 22. 11 'quibus castella . . immunita essent.'

8. Tua sententia, 'by your vote in the senate.'

10. Cum sciam, fut. indic.

11. Anagnia. The old capital of the Hernici, situated above the valley of the Trerus, about half way between Praeneste and Frusino. It is now called Anagni. On Cicero's movements at this time, cp. Intr. to Part V, § 10. Boot suspects 'Anagnia' and suggests 'a Velia.'

Familia aegra est, 'there is illness among my slaves.'

12. Kal., sc. Novemb.

Ab Octaviano, sc. 'redditae sunt.'

Veteranos, qui Casilini et Calatiae *sunt*, perduxit ad suam sententiam; nec mirum: quingenos denarios dat. Cogitat reliquas colonias obire; plane hoc spectat, ut se duce bellum geratur cum Antonio. Itaque video paucis diebus nos in armis fore. Quem autem sequamur? vide nomen, vide aetatem. Atque a me postulat, primum ut clam colloquatur mecum vel Capuae *vel non longe a Capua:* puerile hoc quidem, si id putat clam fieri posse; docui per litteras id nec opus esse nec fieri posse. 2 Misit ad me Caecinam quendam Volaterranum, familiarem suum, qui haec pertulit, Antonium cum legione Alaudarum ad urbem pergere, pecunias municipiis imperare, legionem sub signis ducere. Consultabat, utrum Romam cum CIƆ CIƆ CIƆ. veteranorum proficisceretur, an Capuam teneret et Antonium venientem excluderet, an iret ad tres legiones Macedonicas, quae iter secundum mare superum faciunt, quas sperat suas esse: eae congiarium ab Antonio accipere noluerunt, ut hic quidem narrat, et ei convi-

1. **Casilini et Calatiae.** Caesar had settled some veterans at both these places. Cp. App. Bell. Civ. 3. 40; Vell. 2. 61. 1. A. W. Zumpt, Comment. Epigraph. 1. 296, thinks that the towns had been re-constituted under the Lex Iulia in 59 B.C. Casilinum was the place now called Capua, and commanded an important passage over the Volturnus. Calatia (now Le Galazze?) stood on the Appian way about 6 miles S.E. of Capua; there was another town of the same name N.E. of Capua. Cp. Dict. of Geogr. 1. 476 77.

2. **Quingenos denarios.** The denarius has been valued by different scholars at different sums from 7·92*d*. to 8·52*d*. The sum here given may therefore be from £16 10s. to £17 10s.

5. **Nomen.** Cicero could not trust one who bore the name of Caesar even by adoption.

Aetatem. Octavian was now 19, as he was born Sept. 23, 63 B.C. Cp. Suet. Oct. 5.

6. **Primum.** No corresponding particle follows, but, as Andr. says, one is implied in p. 555, l. 2.

7. **Puerile.** It was childish to suppose that the movements of such men as Cicero and Octavian would not be watched in so populous a neighbourhood.

9. **Caecinam quendam.** Cicero would hardly speak thus of the intimate friend to whom he wrote the letter 91 (Ad Fam. 6. 6). This man is probably not elsewhere mentioned. Cp., however, Ep. 91, 13, note.

10. **Cum legione Alaudarum.** This legion, which Caesar had raised in Transalpine Gaul, and had presented with the rights of Roman citizenship, was now thoroughly devoted to Antony. It probably bore the number 5. Cp. Suet. Iul. 24; Philipp. 1. 8. 20; Ad Fam. 10. 33. 4; Appendix 11. 11, note.

Ad urbem pergere: cp. Intr. to Part V, § 9.

11. **Sub signis,** 'in warlike array,' 'with colours flying.' Forcell.

Consultabat, 'he asked my advice.'

12. **CIƆ CIƆ CIƆ.:** cp. App. Bell. Civ. 3. 42.

13. **Excluderet,** 'cut off from Rome.' Billerb. Antony would pass through Capua if he followed the Appian way.

14. **Tres legiones;** cp. Intr. to Part V, and Appendix 11, ll. cc. Andr. thinks that the 'legio Martia' had already deserted Antony.

Secundum mare superum, 'by the road along the Adriatic coast.' Cp. App. Bell. Civ. 3. 44.

15. **Suas esse,** 'are devoted to him.' On the pres. infin. after 'spero,' cp. p. 26 (Ep. 1, 1), note.

Congiarium, 'a present' originally of wine and oil. More often used of gifts to the people than of gifts to the soldiers. For the latter 'donativum' is more common.

16. **Hic,** i.e. Octavian. Cp. 'ducem se profiteatur' below. But Billerb. and Wiel. think that 'hic' is Caecina.

Convitium .. fecerunt, 'abused.' Cp. p. 50, l. 4.

tium grave fecerunt contionantemque reliquerunt. Quid quaeris? ducem se profitetur nec nos sibi putat deesse oportere. Equidem suasi, ut Romam pergeret; videtur enim mihi et plebeculam urbanam et, si fidem fecerit, etiam bonos viros secum habiturus. O Brute, ubi es? quantam εὐκαιρίαν amittis! non equidem hoc divinavi, sed aliquid tale putavi fore. Nunc tuum consilium exquiro. Romamne venio, an hic maneo, an Arpinum—ἀσφάλειαν habet is locus—fugiam? Romam, ne desideremur, si quid actum videbitur. Hoc igitur explica: numquam in maiore ἀπορίᾳ fui.

122. To ATTICUS (AD ATT. XVI. 11).

PUTEOLI, (?) EARLY IN NOVEMBER, 44 B.C. (710 A.U.C.)

1, 2. Two letters have arrived from you to-day. I am glad you like my work, and you have shewn judgment in choosing passages from it. As for your criticisms on my speech, I will gladly adopt your suggestions, and hope it may soon be possible to circulate it freely. 3. I am not sorry you like Varro's πεπλογραφία, and glad that you approve my work on Old Age. 4. I have written a work in two books on Duties containing the substance of three books of Panaetius, and shall add another book from Posidonius, on conflicts of motives. I dedicate the whole to my son Marcus. 5. Thank you for telling me about Myrtilus. 6. Octavian writes to me often, and is anxious to go to Rome and meet the senate. I do not think anything can be done there before Jan. 1, but he is very popular in Campania and Samnium, and I shall visit Rome sooner than I had intended. 7. Please settle the business you referred to before the 13th. I will give Valerius introductions in Sicily as he wished. 8. I hear Lepidus' holidays will last till the 29th. I shall like to hear from you, and I send you a letter from Quintus. Remember me to Attica.

1. **Contionantem**, 'in the middle of his speech.' On the occurrences here mentioned, cp. App. Bell. Civ. 3. 43-44. The soldiers were discontented with the smallness of Antony's offers.

3. **Plebeculam**, cp. p. 60, note on l. 15.

4. **Si fidem fecerit**, 'if he shall convince them of his honesty;' 'win their confidence.' 'Fides' = 'firma opinio et persuasio quam habemus de aliquo.' Forcell.

5. **O Brute, ubi es?** M. Brutus was probably at Athens preparing to take possession of Macedonia. Cp. Intr. to Part V, § 11; Plut. Brut. 24.

εὐκαιρίαν, 'an admirable opportunity for action,' quite classical.

Hoc, 'what has happened.'

7. **Venio . . maneo**: cp. Ad Att. 13. 40, 2 'quid mihi auctor es? advolo an maneo.' The transition to '**fugiam**' is curious; Madvig (Opusc. Acad. 2. 40) explains it as one from oratio directa to obliqua. Cp. Pro Quinct. 17. 54 'postulo ut a praetore . . ut . . decernatur.'

ἀσφάλειαν habet, 'is safe.' Forcell. Cp. 'habere videtur ista res iniquitatem.' In Cat. 4. 4, 7. Its retirement made Arpinum a safe residence. Cp. Appendix 5, § 1.

8. **Romam**, sc. 'malo,' which Boot proposes to insert. Cicero, however, did not apparently visit Rome till December. Cp. Intr. to Part V, § 10.

Si quid . . videbitur, 'if any good shall seem to have been done.' Cp. Ad Att. 16. 9 'metuo ne quae ἀριστεία me absente.'

CICERO ATTICO SAL.

Nonis accepi a te duas epistolas, quarum alteram Kal. dederas, 1
alteram pridie: igitur prius ad superiorem. Nostrum opus tibi probari laetor, ex quo ἄνθη ipsa posuisti, quae mihi florentiora sunt visa tuo iudicio; cerulas enim tuas miniatas illas extimescebam. De Sicca ita est, ut scribis; † asta ea aegre me tenui. Itaque perstringam sine ulla contumelia Siccae aut Septimiae, tantum ut sciant παῖδες παίδων, sine vallo Luciliano, eum ex Galli Fadii filia liberos habuisse. Atque utinam eum diem videam, cum ista oratio ita libere vagetur, *ut* etiam in Siccae domum introeat! sed illo tempore opus est, quod fuit illis III

2. **Igitur prius**, sc. 'rescribam.'

Nostrum opus. Usually supposed to mean the books 'de gloria,' on which, cp. Ad Att. 16. 2, 6; 16. 6, 4. But I agree with Mr. Jeans that the whole section may refer to the second Philippic.

3. **ἄνθη**, 'the fine passages' called 'eclogarii,' sc. 'loci,' Ad Att. 16. 2, 6. The Greek word does not seem to be used by classical authors quite in this sense.

Posuisti, 'you have mentioned.' Forcell.

Florentiora, 'more brilliant,' with allusion to the ἄνθη or 'flores' mentioned above.

4. **Tuo iudicio**, 'owing to *your* approval,' abl. causae.

Cerulas .. miniatas, '*your* marks with red wax,' which Atticus used to point out passages to which he objected. Cp. Ad Att. 15. 14, 4 'me ad *συντάξεις* dedi quae quidem vereor ne miniata cerula tua pluribus locis notandae sint.'

5. **Sicca.** A friend of Cicero. Cp. Ad Att. 16. 6, 1 'ix Kal. igitur ad Siccam; ibi tamquam domi meae scilicet.' Septimia was probably his wife. The passage seems to imply that Antony had intrigued with Septimia, and that Cicero did not mention this in his second Philippic out of consideration for her husband. Boot.

Ita est, ut scribis, '*your* suspicion is well founded.'

Asta ea, foll. Victorius (ap. Baiter) suggests 'ast aegre;' Boot 'ab ista,' 'I could hardly help mentioning her.'

6. **Perstringam**, sc. Antonium. On the verb, cp. p. 48, l. 16, note.

7. **παῖδες παίδων.** Hom. Il. 20. 308.

Sine vallo Luciliano, 'without the obstacles Lucilius interposed.' Lucilius is said to have declared that he did not wish to be understood by everybody. Cp. De Orat. 2. 6, 25. Corradus ap. Boot.

Eum, Antonium.

8. **Galli Fadii**: cp. Philipp. 2. 2, 3; 3. 6, 17. He was a freedman, and as it was not usual for freedmen to take their patron's cognomen, Boot suggests 'Gaii' for 'Galli.' His daughter, Fadia, was Antony's first wife. Cp. King's Philippics, p. 306; Drumann 1. 517.

9. **Ista oratio**, i.e. the second Philippic.

Vagetur. On the future sense of the pres. conjunct., cp. Ep. 6, 1, note. The word seems to mean 'be published.' Cp. 'ea fama vagatur' Verg. Aen. 2. 17.

In Siccae domum: where it could not now safely enter lest Septimia should divulge its contents.

10. **Quod fuit illis III viris**, 'which we had under the triumvirs,' i.e. from 59-53 B.C.—a reference perhaps to the greater freedom which then prevailed. Boot and Billerbeck both see an allusion to Caesar and Pompey having both been three times married. The words 'tribus viris' seem to be a quotation from a letter of Atticus. Mr. Jeans paraphrases 'I want my speech to make its way into Sicca's house.. but to penetrate there we ought to have the days of "the triumvirate" back again when Antonius and two unnamed lovers who had intrigues with Sicca's wife, Septimia, used frequently to make their way in.' Professor Nettleship has furnished me with an ingenious suggestion on this passage. He would omit the comma after 'opus est,' and explain 'we want those times back *which are over* now that the three Antonii are triumvirs.' A sugges-

viris. Moriar, nisi facete! Tu vero leges Sexto eiusque iudicium
mihi perscribes. Εἷς ἐμοὶ μύριοι. Caleni interventum et Calvenae
2 cavebis. Quod vereris ne ἀδόλεσχος mihi tu, quis minus? cui, ut
Aristophani Archilochi iambus, sic epistola *tua* longissima quaeque
optima videtur. Quod me admones, tu vero etiam si reprehen-
deres, non modo facile paterer, sed etiam laetarer, quippe cum in
reprehensione sit prudentia cum εὐμενείᾳ. Ita libenter ea corrigam,
quae a te animadversa sunt. 'Eodem iure, quo Rubriana' potius,
quam 'quo Scipionis,' et de laudibus Dolabellae deruam cumulum.
Ac tamen est isto loco bella, ut mihi videtur, εἰρωνεία, quod cum
ter contra cives in acie. Illud etiam malo '† indignius esse hunc
3 vivere' quam 'quid indignius?' πεπλογραφίαν Varronis tibi pro-

tion of J. F. Gronovius, quoted by Boot, and approved, though not adopted, by Orelli supports the same explanation of 'illis' and, indirectly, of the force of 'fuit.' Perhaps the letter of Atticus to which Cicero is here replying would have explained the allusion, but it is hard to form an opinion on the matter under existing circumstances.

1. Nisi facete, sc. 'hoc dixeris.'

Leges: cp. Ep. 11, 3, note.

Sexto, sc. Peducaeo: cp. Ep. 61, 2.

2. Εἷς ἐμοὶ μύριοι, 'his judgment goes for that of ten thousand with me.' Cp. Ad Att. 2. 5. 1 'Cato . . qui mihi unus est pro centum millibus.'

Caleni. Q. Fufius Calenus is often mentioned in the Philippics as acting on behalf of Antony. For notices of him, cp. Intr. to Part IV, § 5; to Part V, §§ 13; 14; Epp. 7, 1; 11, 1, notes.

Calvenae, a nickname for Matius. Cp. Ep. 106, 2. 'Do not let yourself be surprised by Calenus and Matius while reading my speech.'

3. Ne ἀδόλεσχος, sc. 'videaris.'

4. Aristophani. Here the grammarian of Byzantium is probably meant. He lived at Alexandria in the third century before Christ.

Archilochus of Paros lived in the 8th and 7th centuries before Christ.

Iambus, here for 'a satire' or 'iambic poem.' Cp. Smith's Lat. Dict.

5. Quod me admones . . paterer. 'as for your criticisms, I should not object even to censure from you.'

7. Prudentia cum εὐμενείᾳ, 'discernment combined with good will.'

8. Eodem iure quo Rubriana: cp. Philipp. 2. 40, 103 'quo iure? quo ore? eodem, inquies, quo in heredum L. Rubrii.' Cicero seems originally to have written 'eodem iure quo Scipionis,' and to have been warned by Atticus that Antony had not acquired the estate of Scipio as he supposed. Cp. Philipp. 5. 7, 19 'ipse interea xvii. dies de me in Tiburtino Scipionis declamitavit.'

9. Deruam cumulum, 'will remove what is exaggerated.' Cicero had praised Dolabella for his courage and consistency (Philipp. 2. 30, 75), and for his vigour displayed in support of the cause of order after Caesar's death (Ib. 42, 107: cp. Ep. 111). 'Cumulus' is explained by Forcell. 'quod supra mensuram adicitur.'

10. Isto loco: Philipp. 2. 30, 75. Cicero did not expunge this passage after all.

εἰρωνεία, 'hidden meaning.' Nearly 'irony' in our sense.

Quod cum . . in acie, sc. steterit dixi: cp. Philipp. l. c. 'ter depugnavit Caesar cum civibus . . omnibus adfuit his pugnis Dolabella.'

11. Illud etiam malo, 'I prefer, too, the words you suggest in another place to mine.' Cicero did not, however, change what he had written at first. Cp. Philipp. 2. 34, 86 'quid indignius quam vivere eum qui imposuerit diadema.'

12. πεπλογραφίαν. This has been explained as follows:—The Athenians are said (cp. Smith, Antiq. sub voc. 'Panathenaea;' Schömann, Griech. Alt. 2. 447) to have embroidered on a shawl given to Athene every four years, both mythological subjects and the names of men distinguished in war or otherwise: hence Varro seems to have given the name to a portrait album with explanatory comments. This work is by some identified with one called 'Hebdomades, sive de Imaginibus.' Orell. Onomast. sub voc.;

bari non moleste fero, a quo adhuc Ἡρακλείδειον illud non abstuli.
Quod me hortaris ad scribendum, amice tu quidem, sed me scito
agere nihil aliud. Gravedo tua mihi molesta est: quaeso, adhibe.
quam soles, diligentiam. 'O Tite' tibi prodesse laetor. Anagnini
sunt Mustela ταξίαρχης et Laco, qui plurimum bibit. Librum,
quem rogas, perpoliam et mittam. Haec ad posteriorem. Τὰ περὶ 4
τοῦ καθήκοντος, quatenus Panaetius, absolvi duobus: illius tres sunt,
sed cum initio divisisset ita, tria genera exquirendi officii esse
unum, cum deliberemus, honestum an turpe sit, alterum, utile an
inutile, tertium, cum haec inter se pugnare videantur, quo modo
iudicandum sit, qualis causa Reguli, redire honestum, manere
utile, de duobus primis praeclare disseruit, de tertio pollicetur se
deinceps, sed nihil scripsit. Eum locum Posidonius persecutus *est*;
ego autem et eius librum arcessivi et ad Athenodorum Calvum
scripsi, ut ad me τὰ κεφάλαια mitteret, quae exspecto; quem velim

Pliny, Hist. Nat. 35. 2, 11; Smith, Dict. of Biogr. 3. 1216.

1. A quo, sc. Varrone.

Ἡρακλείδειον. Apparently a great work in the style of Heraclides Ponticus, which Cicero expected from Varro. Cp. Ad Att. 16. 12 'de Ἡρακλειδείῳ Varronis negotia salsa; me quidem nihil umquam sic delectavit.' In some passages, however, Cicero seems to refer to a contemplated work of his own as Ἡρακλείδειον. Cp. Ad Att. 15. 13. 3. Heraclides was a pupil of Plato.

Non abstuli, 'I have not succeeded in getting.'

2. Amice tu quidem, sc. 'agis.'

3. Gravedo: cp. Ep. 74, 6, note.

4. O Tite. The treatise De Senectute begins with these words in a quotation from Ennius, in which T. Flamininus is addressed by a guide. Cp. Livy 32. 11. In Mr. Wordsworth's Fragments and Specimens of early Latin, ed. 1874, p. 305, I find—

'O Tite si quid ego adiuvero curamve levasso
Quae nunc te coquit et versat in pectore fixa
Ecquid erit praemi?' Enn. Ann. 8.

Anagnini, 'the men of Anagnia,' referred to in Philipp. 2. 41, 106. The passage now stands 'praeterita cum duos secum Anagninos haberet, Mustelam et Laconem, quorum alter gladiorum est princeps, alter poculorum.' The names of Mustela and Laco were probably inserted by Cicero on revision, owing to a remark from Atticus on the obscurity of the allusion.

5. ταξίαρχης = 'centurio.'

Librum, probably the Topica. Cp. Ad Fam. 7. 19 'ut primum Velia navigare coepi institui Topica Aristotelea conscribere.'

6. Haec, sc. 'respondeo.' This refers to what follows. Wesenb. suggests 'Haec (habes) ad superiorem; nunc (or nunc audi) ad posteriorem.'

Ad posteriorem, sc. 'epistolam.' Cp. § 1.

τὰ περὶ τοῦ καθήκοντος = 'de officiis.'

7. Quatenus Panaetius, sc. 'scripsit.'

Absolvi duobus, sc. 'libris,' 'I have finished my work, so far as Panaetius dealt with the question, in two books.' Panaetius was a Stoic philosopher, patronised by the younger Scipio, and often mentioned by Cicero, e.g. Pro Muren. 31. 66.

8. Exquirendi officii, 'of enquiries on points of duty.'

11. Qualis causa Reguli. The construction seems rather irregular; we should expect 'ut in causa Reguli' or the insertion of 'est' before 'redire.'

13. Posidonius: cp. Ep. 9. 2, note. With the passage in general compare De Off. 1. 3. 8-10.

Persecutus est = 'perfecit.' Forcell.

14. Athenodorus of Tarsus, a Stoic, was afterwards apparently teacher of Claudius the emperor during Augustus' lifetime. He can hardly in that case have been past middle life when Cicero knew him. Cp. Ad Att. 16. 14. 4; Ad Fam. 3. 7. 5; Suet. Claud. 4.

15. τὰ κεφάλαια, 'the heads' of the work of Posidonius. It is quite a classical word.

cohortere et roges, ut quam primum. In eo est περὶ τοῦ κατὰ περίστασιν καθήκοντος. Quod de inscriptione quaeris, non dubito quin καθῆκον 'officium' sit, nisi quid tu aliud, sed inscriptio plenior 'de officiis.' Προσφωνῶ autem Ciceroni filio; visum est non
5 δυσοίκειον. De Myrtilo dilucide. O quales tu semper istos! itane
6 in D. Brutum? di istis! Ego me, ut scripseram, in Pompeianum
non abdidi, primo tempestatibus, quibus nil taetrius; deinde ab Octaviano quotidie litterae, ut negotium susciperem, Capuam venirem, iterum rem publicam servarem, Romam utique statim.

αἴδεσθεν μὲν ἀνήνασθαι, δεῖσαν δ' ὑποδέχθαι.

Is tamen egit sane strenue et agit; Romam veniet cum manu magna, sed est plane puer: putat senatum statim. Quis veniet? si venerit, quis incertis rebus offendet Antonium? Kal. Ianuar. erit fortasse praesidio, aut quidem ante depugnabitur. Puero municipia mire favent; iter enim faciens in Samnium venit Cales, mansit Teani: mirifica ἀπάντησις et cohortatio. Hoc tu putares?

1. Ut quam primum, sc. 'mittas.'

κατὰ περίστασιν, 'under circumstances.' The subst. occurs ap. Polyb. 1. 35. 10, alib.

2. De inscriptione, 'about the title of my work.'

4. Προσφωνῶ, 'I address,' i.e. dedicate my book to him. Cp. De Off. 1. 1, 1.

5. δυσοίκειον, 'inappropriate;' cp. Polyb. 5. 96, alib.

De Myrtilo: cp. Ad Att. 15. 13, 6. It seems that Myrtilus had plotted against the life of Antony, and had been executed. Both D. Brutus and Octavius seem to have been suspected of suborning him. Cp. Ep. 119, 2 with this passage.

Dilucide, sc. 'scripsisti.' The adverb seems common.

Quales tu semper istos, sc. 'Antonii amicos esse dixisti.' 'Quam Antonii amicos recte cognoscis et vere describis!' Boot.

Itane in D. Brutum? sc. 'crimen conferunt.'

6. Di istis! sc. 'mala dent!' Cp., on the ellipse, Ep. 9, 8, note.

Ego me . . non abdidi, 'I did not retire to my estate at Pompeii, as I wrote you word I intended to do.' Cp. Ad Att. 15. 13, 6 'ego autem in Pompeianum properabam.'

7. Primo. Wesenb. has 'primum.'

Tempestatibus, 'owing to the stormy weather,' abl. causae.

8. Quotidie litterae, sc. 'veniebant.'

Capuam. Octavius was now organizing a large force at Capua. Cp. Ad Att. 16. 9 '(Octavius) rem gerit palam, centuriat Capuae.'

9. Romam utique statim, sc. 'irem.'

10. αἴδεσθεν κ.τ.λ. Hom. Il. 7. 93, where the Greeks' reluctance to accept Hector's challenge is described.

12. Est plane puer, 'he is quite a boy,' full of enthusiasm.

Putat senatum statim, sc. 'a se cogi posse.' Billerb.

Quis veniet? 'what senator will attend?'

13. Incertis rebus, 'while things look so doubtful.'

Kal. Ianuar., the date when Hirtius and Pansa would come into office as consuls.

14. Erit fortasse praesidio, sc. 'Octavius senatui.'

15. Enim, 'as we have been able to see, for.'

Cales, an old Latin colony about seven miles N.W. of Casilinum, on the Latin road. It received the Roman franchise, and became a municipium, probably, by the Lex Iulia 90 B.C.

16. Teani. There were two cities of the name Teanum; one in Apulia, the other, here mentioned, an old city of the Sidicini about five miles N.W. of Cales, on the same (Latin) road.

ἀπάντησις: cp. Ep. 59, 2.

Cohortatio, 'exhortation' of Octavius by the people, to be active.

Hoc tu putares, 'could you believe

Ob hoc ego citius Romam, quam constitueram. Simul et constituero, scribam. Etsi nondum stipulationes legeram—nec enim Eros venerat—, tamen rem pridie Idus velim conficias. Epistolas Catinam, Tauromenium, Syracusas commodius mittere potero, si Valerius interpres ad me nomina gratiosorum scripserit; alii enim sunt alias, nostrique familiares fere demortui: publice tamen scripsi, si uti vellet eis Valerius, aut mihi nomina mitteret. De Lepidianis feriis Balbus ad me, usque ad III. Kal. Exspectabo tuas litteras, meque *de* Torquati negotiolo sciturum puto. Quinti

this,' potential. Cp. Ep. 8, 10, note; Madv. 350 a.

1. Ob hoc. Wesenb. suggests 'ob haec' saying that the reference is to all the reasons stated above.

Citius Romam, sc. 'ibo.'

Simul et constituero, 'as soon as I shall have fixed my plans.' For the use of 'simul et,' cp. Ep. 74. 4 'simul et in Cumanum veni.'

2. Stipulationes, 'the covenants' which Eros (on whom cp. Ep. 96, 4, note) was expected to bring. 'Stipulatio' was properly the form in which a question was proposed by one of the parties to the other, e.g. 'tu dare spondes centum sestertios?'

3. Rem. What this business was can hardly be ascertained. Boot, following Manutius, thinks that it may refer to the contemplated sale of some estate by Cicero; Corrad. (ap. Billerb.) and Billerb., to some arrangement of Dolabella's for paying his debt to Cicero. Cp. Ad Att. 15. 15, 5; 16. 3. 5.

Epistolas. Cicero seems to have been asked to give Valerius letters of introduction to various Sicilian communities, and to the chief men in them.

4. Catinam, now Catania on the east coast of Sicily, south of Mount Etna and north of Syracuse.

Tauromenium, now Taormina, near Naxos and north of Mount Etna on the east coast.

5. Valerius apparently was an interpreter employed either by C. Antonius (Cicero's fellow consul in 63 B.C.) in Macedonia, or by the senate at Rome. Cp. Ad Att. 1. 12, 2. On the employment of professional interpreters by the Romans, cp. Ad Fam. 13. 54; Caes. Bell. Gall. 1. 19.

Gratiosorum, 'of men of influence' in the different cities. Cp. Ep. 30, 3 'gratiosorum in suffragiis.'

6. Alias, 'at different times.' Forcell., Boot.

Nostri .. demortui, 'I have been deprived by death of most of my friends there.' On 'demortuus' Forcell. remarks 'in hoc verbo semper relatio ad alios inest qui morte alicuius aliqua re privantur.' Cicero had won the good will of many Sicilians when quaestor at Lilybaeum about thirty years before the date of this letter. Cp. Intr. to Part I, § 3; Ep. 108, 1.

Publice, 'to the different governments.' Cp. Ep. 3, 1 'ex litteris tuis quas publice misisti.'

7. Vellet .. mitteret, epistolary tenses. Aut seems sometimes to have the force of 'alioqui.' Forcell. He does not give any instance of its use in that sense by Cicero. But cp. Ep. 9, 3 'aut ne poscimus.'

De Lepidianis feriis, 'about the holidays fixed by Lepidus,' or 'in honour of Lepidus.' The first is the usual rendering, and it is supposed that Lepidus as chief pontiff had assigned many days in which the augurs should take the auspices (cp. Ad Att. 16. 5, 4), which would make them holidays for the senate. The pontifices had much influence in fixing the 'feriae,' though they were not independent of the magistrates. Cp. Lange, Röm. Alt. 1. 304, 305; also Smith's Dict. of Antiq. sub voce. 'Feriae,' p. 528; 'Pontifex,' 940, 941. Lepidus was elected pontifex maximus in the place of Caesar, rather irregularly. Cp. Livy, Epit. 117; Vell. 2. 63; Ep. 141, note.

8. Balbus ad me, sc. 'scripsit feriarum.' 'Balbus wrote me word that they would last till Dec. 30.' Boot. It is not said when they would begin.

Exspectabo tuas litteras, 'I shall wait for a letter from you before going to Rome.'

9. De Torquati negotiolo. I cannot tell whether the reference is to A. Manlius Torquatus, praetor 52 B.C., to whom the letter Ad Fam. 6. 1 was written, or to his brother Lucius, praetor 49 B.C., on whom,

litteras ad te misi, ut scires, quam valde eum amaret, quem dolet a te minus amari. Atticae, quoniam, quod optimum in pueris est, hilarula est, meis verbis suavium des volo.

123. To D. BRUTUS (AD FAM. XI. 5).

ROME, MIDDLE OF DECEMBER, 44 B.C. (710 A.U.C.)

1. I only returned to Rome on the 9th, and so could not write by Lupus. I have since heard good news of you from Pansa. 2. I wish to remind you how much your countrymen expect from you, and how important a position you hold. 3. Exert yourself, then, to the utmost to complete your service to your country, and count on my energetic support.

M. CICERO S. D. D. BRUTO IMP. COS. DESIG.

1 Lupus familiaris noster cum a te venisset cumque Romae quosdam dies commoraretur, ego eram in iis locis, in quibus maxime tuto me esse arbitrabar: eo factum est ut ad te Lupus sine meis litteris rediret, cum tamen curasset tuas ad me perferendas. Romam autem veni a. d. v. Idus Dec., nec habui quicquam antiquius, quam ut Pansam statim convenirem; ex quo ea de te cognovi, quae maxime optabam. Qua re hortatione tu quidem non eges, si ne in illa quidem re, quae a te gesta est post hominum memo-

cp. Ad Att. 9. 8, 1; Caes. Bell. Civ. 1. 24. The word 'negotiolum' occurs also Ad Q. F. 3. 4. 6.

Quinti litteras. This letter is no longer extant.

1. Eum, i.e. the younger Quintus.

2. In pueris, 'in children.' Cp. Hor. Epp. 1. 2, 44 'pueriisque beata creandis Uxor.' Attica was now probably about 7 years old. Cp. p. 420, l. 5, note. Her father married Feb. 12, 56 B.C. Cp. Ep. 23, 7.

3. Hilarula, 'somewhat merry.' The word apparently occurs only here.

Meis verbis = 'meo nomine.' Forcell.

Suavium. Rare, apparently, in prose. Forcell.

IMP. D. Brutus had perhaps obtained the title 'imperator' by successes gained over the Inalpini. Cp. pp. 552-553. This letter seems to have been written before the meeting of the senate on Dec. 20, on which cp. Intr. to Part V, § 10.

4. Lupus. Apparently a legate of D. Brutus, and perhaps the same with a Rutilius Lupus, tribune in 56 B.C. (cp. Ep. 21, 3), and (?) praetor 49 B.C. (cp. Caes. Bell. Civ. 1. 24).

5. In iis locis. Cicero seems to have spent the latter part of the autumn in different villas. Cp. Intr. to Part V, § 10; Ep. 121, 1.

6. Tuto . . esse. On the constr., cp. Ep. 4, 1, note.

Sine meis litteris, 'without a letter from me.' Cp., on this use of the pronoun, Ep. 72, 1, note.

8. Nec habui . . antiquius, 'and there was nothing to which I attached greater importance.' On this sense of 'antiquus,' cp. Ep. 71, 4, note.

9. De te, probably, 'about your disposition towards the Commonwealth.' Frey.

11. Si = 'si quidem.' Cp. In Cat. 1. 3, 6 'si neque nox tenebris obscurare coetus nefarios . . potest.'

In illa . . re, i.e. in the murder of Caesar.

riam maxima, hortatorem desiderasti. Illud tamen breviter significandum videtur, populum Romanum omnia a te exspectare atque in te aliquando reciperandae libertatis omnem spem ponere. Tu, si dies noctesque memineris, quod te facere certo scio, quantam rem gesseris, non obliviscere profecto, quantae tibi etiam nunc gerendae sint: si enim iste provinciam nactus erit, cui quidem ego semper amicus fui ante, quam illum intellexi non modo aperte, sed etiam libenter cum re publica bellum gerere, spem reliquam nullam video salutis. Quam ob rem te obsecro iisdem precibus, quibus senatus populusque Romanus, ut in perpetuum rem publicam dominatu regio liberes, ut principiis consentiant exitus. Tuum est hoc munus, tuae partes; a te hoc civitas vel omnes potius gentes non exspectant solum, sed etiam postulant: quamquam, cum hortatione non egeas, ut supra scripsi, non utar ea pluribus verbis; faciam illud, quod meum est, ut tibi omnia mea officia, studia, curas, cogitationes pollicear, quae ad tuam laudem et gloriam pertinebunt. Quam ob rem velim tibi ita persuadeas, me cum rei publicae causa, quae mihi vita mea est carior, tum quod tibi ipsi faveam tuamque dignitatem amplificari velim, tuis optimis consiliis, amplitudini, gloriae nullo loco defuturum.

124. TO Q. CORNIFICIUS (AD FAM. XII. 22).

END OF DECEMBER, 44 B.C. (710 A.U.C.)

1. I am carrying on an unequal contest against Antony. 2. We are sadly in want of leaders; Pansa is very well disposed, but Hirtius is recovering slowly from an illness. I will do all I can for you. 3. On the 20th the senate adopted my proposals on several affairs of importance, especially in directing all provincial governors to retain their commands till superseded by the senate. I beg you to maintain your

1. **Maxima.** A superlative defined by a relative proposition is put in the relative clause. Madv. 320, Obs.

Illud, referring to what follows. Cp. Ep. 6, 3, note. On the accus. and infin. where an actual fact is stated, and we might expect 'quod' with the indicat., cp. Madv. 398 b, Obs. 1.

3. **Aliquando** = 'tandem.' Forcell.

6. **Iste**, Antony, who was preparing to wrest Cisalpine Gaul from D. Brutus. Cp. Intr. to Part V, § 9.

11. **Ut principiis**, foll., 'so that the issue of your enterprise (the recovery of freedom) may agree with its beginning (the death of Caesar).' On the mood of consentiant, cp. p. 101, note on l. 9.

12. **Omnes potius gentes.** Hyperbolical, and even false, for it may probably be inferred from Tac. Ann. 1. 2, that the provinces were in many cases favourable to Caesar.

14. **Utar ea**, sc. 'hortatione' = 'hortabor.'

15. **Pluribus verbis**, ablat. modi.

Faciam illud . . ut, foll.: cp. Ep. 16, 2, note.

19. **Faveam**, conj., as representing a supposed opinion of D. Brutus. Cp. Madv. 368, 369.

position accordingly. 4. I wish you could have obliged me about Sempronius, but it is of little consequence.

CICERO CORNIFICIO SAL.

1 Nos hic cum homine gladiatore omnium nequissimo, collega
nostro, Antonio, bellum gerimus, sed non pari condicione, contra
arma verbis. At etiam de te contionatur, nec impune; nam sentiet, quos lacessierit. Ego autem acta ad te omnia arbitror perscribi ab aliis; a me futura debes cognoscere, quorum quidem non
2 est difficilis coniectura: oppressa omnia sunt, nec habent ducem
boni, nostrique tyrannoctoni longe gentium absunt. Pansa et
sentit bene et loquitur fortiter; Hirtius noster tardius convalescit.
Quid futurum sit, plane nescio; spes tamen una est aliquando
populum Romanum maiorum similem fore. Ego certe rei publicae
non deero et, quicquid acciderit, a quo mea culpa absit, animo
forti feram; illud profecto, quoad potero: tuam famam et digni-
3 tatem tuebor. A. d. XIII. K. Ian. senatus haud *in*frequens mihi est
adsensus cum de ceteris rebus magnis et necessariis, tum de provinciis ab iis, qui obtinerent, retinendis neque cuiquam tradendis
nisi qui ex senatus consulto successisset. Hoc ego cum rei publicae causa censui, tum mehercule in primis retinendae dignitatis
tuae; quam ob rem te amoris nostri causa rogo, rei publicae causa

CORNIFICIO. On the position of Cornificius at this time, cp. Ep. 119.

1. Cum homine gladiatore. On the use of 'homo' in apposition, cp. De Orat. 2. 46, 193 'hominis histrionis.' 'Gladiator,' 'a bravo.' Cp. Philipp. 7. 6, 17 'quem (L. Antonium) gladiatorem non ita appellavi ut interdum etiam M. Antonius gladiator appellari solet sed ut appellant ii qui plane et Latine loquuntur.'

Collega nostro, sc. 'in augurato.' Cp. Ep. 41, 1, note, and the superscription of Ep. 103, note.

3. De te, probably about the unwillingness of Cornificius to resign his province. Cp. Ep. 119. 1, note.

Contionatur. Speeches of Antony to his soldiers, or to the citizens of towns in Cisalpine Gaul, are probably referred to. Cp., on this sense of the verb, Ep. 129. 4, note.

Sentiet quos lacessierit. I presume Cicero means that the senate would reply by its decrees to the abuse which Antony heaped on Cornificius and his friends; or that he himself would retaliate on Antony.

4. Acta, 'what has happened.'

6. Oppressa omnia sunt. This letter is much more depressed in tone than the third Philippic, delivered on Dec. 20. Cp., especially, Philipp. 3. 11–14.

Nec habent ducem boni: cp. Ep. 126, 1. Cicero complains there, as often in the Philippics, of the misconduct of several of the leading senators. Cp., especially Philipp. 8. 7, 20.

7. Tyrannoctoni. M. Brutus was in Macedonia; C. Cassius perhaps in Syria. Cp. Appendix 12, 7 and 10; Intr. to Part V, § 11.

Pansa . . fortiter. Cicero speaks differently of him elsewhere. Cp. Ad Att. 16. 1, 4 'in Pansa spes? λῆρον πολὺν in vino et in somno istorum.'

8. Tardius convalescit. Hirtius was ill during the latter part of 44 and earlier part of 43 B.C. Cp. Philipp. 1. 15, 37 with 7. 4, 12 and 8. 2, 5.

9. Spes tamen una est, 'however, our only hope is.'

Aliquando: cp. p. 562, l. 3, note.

12. Illud profecto, sc. 'faciam.' Cp. on the ellipse p. 70, l. 7, note. It refers to the following clause, 'tuam famam . . tuebor.'

14. Cum de ceteris rebus: cp. Intr. to Part V, § 10; Philipp. 3. 15.

16. Nisi qui, sc. 'nisi ei qui.'

hortor, ut ne cui quicquam iuris in tua provincia esse patiare
atque ut omnia referas ad dignitatem, qua nihil esse potest prae-
stantius. Vere tecum agam, ut necessitudo nostra postulat: in 4
Sempronio, si meis litteris obtemperasses, maximam ab omnibus
laudem adeptus esses; sed illud et praeteriit et levius est, haec
magna res est: fac ut provinciam retineas in potestate rei publicae. Plura scripsissem, nisi tui festinarent. Itaque Chaerippo
nostro me velim excuses.

125. To D. BRUTUS (AD FAM. XI. 8).

ROME, JANUARY, 43 B.C. (711 A.U.C.)

1. I have no definite news to send, but think you may be glad to learn that everybody is watching your movements with interest and admiration. 2. Men offer themselves zealously for the army. I hope we shall soon hear from you. I hope you confide in my friendship.

M. CICERO S. D. D. BRUTO IMP. COS. DESIG.

Eo tempore Polla tua misit, ut ad te, si quid vellem, darem 1
litterarum, cum, quid scriberem, non habebam; omnia enim erant
suspensa propter exspectationem legatorum, qui quid egissent,
nihildum nuntiabatur. Haec tamen scribenda existimavi; primum, senatum populumque Romanum de te laborare non solum
salutis suae causa, sed etiam dignitatis tuae; admirabilis enim est
quaedam tui nominis caritas amorque in te singularis omnium

1. Ne cui . . patiare. Cornificius was to resist the usurpation of Calvisius. Cp. Ep. 119, 1.

2. Atque, adversative. It is used thus after negative clauses. Cp. Madv. 433, Obs. 2.

Omnia referas ad dignitatem, 'act in all things with a view to your dignity.' Frey. Cp. Ep. 56, 1, note.

3. In Sempronio. Perhaps the C. Sempronius Rufus mentioned in Ep. 34, 1. What the quarrel between him and Cornificius here referred to was seems not to be known.

7. Tui, 'your servants.'

Chaerippo. Chaerippus was a Greek dependent of Q. Cicero in Asia, and was on good terms with Marcus Cicero also. He seems now to have been with Cornificius in Africa. Cp. Ad Fam. 12. 30, 3; Ad Q. F. 1, 1, 4, 14; Ad Att. 4. 7, 1.

9. Polla. Valeria Polla, or Paula, wife of D. Brutus. Cp. Ad Fam. 8. 7, 2.

Misit, 'sends,' or 'has sent to invite me.' Cp. p. 90, l. 9, note.

Si quid vellem . . litterarum, 'whatever in the shape of a letter I might feel disposed to send.' On the gen. after neuters denoting measure, cp. Ep. 26, 1, note.

10. Quid scriberem non habebam: cp. Ep. 17, 1, note.

11. Suspensa, 'uncertain.' The word is rarely used in this absolute sense. See examples in Forcell.

Legatorum: cp. Intr. to Part V, § 12.

12. Nihildum = 'nondum quidquam.' Forcell.

Haec refers to what follows. Cp. Ep. 114, 3.

Primum. No corresponding word—such as 'deinde'—is found in the next section.

civium: ita enim sperant atque confidunt, ut antea rege, sic hoc tempore regno te rem publicam liberaturum. Romae dilectus habetur totaque Italia, si hic dilectus appellandus est, cum ultro se offerunt omnes: tantus ardor animos hominum occupavit desiderio libertatis odioque diutinae servitutis. De reliquis rebus a te iam exspectare litteras debemus, quid ipse agas, quid noster Hirtius, quid Caesar meus, quos spero brevi tempore societate victoriae tecum copulatos fore. Reliquum est ut de me id scribam, quod te ex tuorum litteris et spero et malo cognoscere, me neque deesse ulla in re neque umquam defuturum dignitati tuae.

126. TO C. CASSIUS (AD FAM. XII. 4).

ROME, JANUARY OR FEBRUARY, 43 B.C. (711 A.U.C.)

1. The remnants left over from your banquet on the Ides of March are troublesome. The consuls and the mass of the senate are firm enough, but the consulars, especially Piso and Philippus, shew great weakness. The people is admirably disposed, and have become popular. 2. I hear no certain news of you; we hope that both you and Brutus have considerable forces at your disposal, and that you will resist Dolabella.

CICERO CASSIO SAL.

1 Vellem Idibus Martiis me ad cenam invitasses: reliquiarum nihil fuisset. Nunc me reliquiae vestrae exercent, et quidem praeter ceteros me: quamquam egregios consules habemus, sed turpissimos consulares; senatum fortem, sed infimo quemque honore fortissimum. Populo vero nihil fortius, nihil melius, Italiaque universa; nihil autem foedius Philippo et Pisone legatis, nihil

1. **Ut antea rege,** sc. 'liberarit.' On the ellipse, cp. p. 563, l. 12, note.

4. **Desiderio . . odio,** abl. causae.

5. **De reliquis rebus . . debemus,** 'on all other points we ought to expect news from you.'

7. **Caesar meus.** Of course Octavius.

Brevi tempore societate victoriae. On the combination of ablatives in different senses, cp. Ep. 29, 12, note.

8. **Copulatos fore,** 'will have been united.' Cp. Madv. 410, Obs. 2. It is a fut. exact. of the infinitive.

9. **Neque . . dignitati tuae.** Cicero probably means that he would exert himself to procure a proper recognition of D. Brutus' services from the senate.

11. **Ad cenam,** i.e. to the murder of Caesar.

Reliquiarum nihil fuisset, 'we should have had nothing over.' Cp. Ep. 127, 1. Cicero hints that had he been in the plot Antony would have been killed with Caesar. Cp. Philipp. 2. 14. 34.

13. **Praeter ceteros** = 'magis quam' (Forcell.), '*more than* all the rest.' Prey.

14. **Turpissimos consulares.** Cicero presently mentions Piso and Philippus. He was also much discontented with Q. Fufius Calenus, and not altogether satisfied with L. Caesar. Cp. Philipp. 8. 1, 2; 10. 1, 2.

Infimo quemque honore, 'the bolder the lower their official position,' i.e. the aedilicii bolder than the praetorii, and these than the consulares. On the use of 'quisque' with superlatives, cp. Ep. 62. 1, note.

16. **Legatis:** cp. Intr. to Part V, § 12.

flagitiosius; qui cum essent missi, ut Antonio ex senatus sententia
certas res denuntiarent, cum ille earum rerum nulli paruisset,
ultro ab illo ad nos intolerabilia postulata rettulerunt: itaque ad 2
nos concurritur, factique iam in re salutari populares sumus. Sed tu quid ageres, quid acturus, ubi denique esses, nesciebam: fama nuntiabat te isse in Syriam; auctor erat nemo. De Bruto, quo propius est, eo firmiora videntur esse quae nuntiantur. Dolabella valde vituperabatur ab hominibus non insulsis, quod tibi tam cito succederet, cum tu vixdum XXX. dies in Syria fuisses; itaque constabat eum recipi in Syriam non oportere. Summa laus et tua et Bruti est, quod exercitum praeter spem existimamini comparasse. Scriberem plura, si rem causamque nossem: nunc quae scribo, scribo ex opinione hominum atque fama. Tuas litteras avide exspecto. Vale.

127. To C. TREBONIUS (AD FAM. X. 28).

ROME, JANUARY OR FEBRUARY (?) 43 B.C. (711 A.U.C.)

1. I am sorry you saved Antony on the Ides of March; he gives me trouble enough. 2. I resumed my old political activity on Dec. 20, and inspired the senate and people with fresh hopes and energy; nor have I been idle since. 3. I have no doubt you hear

Cicero apparently had already heard of the death of their colleague Sulpicius when he wrote this letter.

2. Certas res: cp. Philipp. 6. 2, 4 'mittuntur enim qui nuntient ne oppugnet consulem designatum, ne Mutinam obsideat, ne provinciam depopuletur, ne dilectus habeat, sit in senatus populique Romani potestate;' Ib. 7. 9, 26 'ad Brutum adeundi legatis potestatem fecerit, exercitum citra flumen Rubiconem eduxerit, nec propius urbem millia passuum cc admoverit.'

3. Ad nos concurritur, 'men crowd to me,' i.e. to my house, or when I appear in public.

4. In re salutari, 'though my measures are salutary,' which popular measures generally are not. Cp. Philipp. 7. 2, 4 'me . . semper adversatum multitudinis temeritati haec fecit praeclarissima causa popularem.'

5. Quid acturus, sc. 'esses.' The tenses in this passage are all epistolary. On the movements of Brutus and Cassius, cp. Intr. to Part V, §§ 11; 14; Appendix 11. 7; 10.

6. De Bruto, sc. 'de M. Bruto.' Of D. Brutus Cicero probably had trustworthy intelligence.

8. Non insulsis, 'witty.' The point of this remark was as follows:—By a 'Lex Cornelia (L. Sullae) de provinciis,' thirty days were allowed after the arrival of a successor for a governor to leave his province. Cp. Ad Fam. 3. 6, 3. But Cassius had not been in Syria at all for thirty days when Dolabella set out to go there. Cicero only touches by implication the question which of the two claimants had the best right to govern Syria. Cassius claimed the province by virtue of Caesar's arrangements (cp. App. Bell. Civ. 3. 7; 8); Dolabella by virtue of a resolution of the people (cp. App. l. c.). But Velleius (2. 60, 5) says, 'Dolabella transmarinas (provincias) decrevit sibi.'

12. Rem causamque. Cicero often combines these two words. Cp. Ep. 30, 5, where Süpfle renders them 'the state of the case;' Hofmann, 'the whole affair and the question in dispute.' Cp. also Frey on Ad Fam. 2. 7, 3, who agrees with Hofmann.

FEBRUARY. The death of Servius Sulpi-

the news, but will touch on what is most important. The consuls and senate behave admirably, but most of the consulars are weak or disloyal. D. Brutus is doing good service, and so is the young Caesar, of whom I have great hopes. If he had not raised forces to oppose Antony, Antony would have perpetrated all conceivable cruelties.

CICERO TREBONIO SAL.

1 Quam vellem ad illas pulcherrimas epulas me Idibus Martiis invitasses! reliquiarum nihil haberemus: at nunc cum iis tantum negotii est, ut vestrum illud divinum in rem publicam beneficium non nullam habeat querelam. Quod vero a te, viro optimo, seductus est tuoque beneficio adhuc vivit haec pestis, interdum, quod mihi vix fas est, tibi subirascor; mihi enim negotii plus reliquisti uni quam praeter me omnibus. Ut enim primum post Antonii foedissimum discessum senatus haberi libere potuit, ad illum animum meum reverti pristinum, quem tu cum civi acerrimo,

2 patre tuo, in ore et amore semper habuisti. Nam cum senatum a. d. XIII. Kalendas Ianuarias tribuni pl. vocavissent deque alia re referrent, totam rem publicam sum complexus egique acerrime senatumque iam languentem et defessum ad pristinam virtutem consuetudinemque revocavi magis animi quam ingenii viribus. Hic dies meaque contentio atque actio spem primum populo Romano attulit libertatis recuperandae; nec vero ipse postea tempus ullum intermisi de re publica non cogitandi solum, sed

3 etiam agendi. Quod nisi res urbanas actaque omnia ad te perferri arbitrarer, ipse perscriberem, quamquam eram maximis occupa-

cius who was appointed one of an embassy to Antony early in January, and who died on his journey to Antony's camp, is mentioned below, § 3.

TREBONIO. On Trebonius, cp. Ep. 84, 7, note; Intr. to Part V, § 14. He probably never received this letter.

1. Epulas: cp. 'cenam,' on p. 565.

2. Cum iis, sc. 'reliquiis.' Cp. p. 565.

4. Habeat, 'suggests,' 'is open to.'

Seductus est .. haec pestis. On the gender of 'seductus,' cp. p. 230, l. 5, note. On the fact referred to, cp. Philipp. 2. 14, 34; Intr. to Part IV, § 18.

6. Subirascor, 'I am somewhat angry.' Cp. Ep. 61, 7.

7. Praeter me, 'except me.' The preposition has a different meaning in Ep. 126, 1.

8. Foedissimum discessum: cp. Intr. to Part V, § 9. Cicero misrepresents the circumstances of Antony's departure. Cp. Merivale 3. 112; App. Bell Civ. 3. 45, 46.

10. Patre tuo. The father of Trebonius is called 'splendidus eques Romanus.' Philipp. 13. 10, 23.

Nam refers to 'praeter me omnibus.'

11. Deque alia re, sc. 'de praesidio ut senatum tuto consules Kal. Ian. habere possent.' Philipp. 3. 5, 13; Intr. to Part V, § 10.

12. Totam rem publicam, foll., 'I discussed the whole position of affairs in my speech,' i.e. in the third Philippic.

14. Animi .. viribus, 'by the force of enthusiasm rather than of intellect.'

18. Quod nisi, 'and unless.' On this form of 'quod,' cp. Ep. 76, 1, note.

Res .. omnia, 'the affairs of the capital and all public proceedings.' Wiel.

Acta has not, I think, here its technical meaning of 'a gazette.' Cp. Ep. 16, 3 'Anim eiusdem diei scribens ad me acta.'

tionibus impeditus. Sed illa cognosces ex aliis; a me pauca, et ea summatim: habemus fortem senatum, consulares partim timidos, partim male sentientes. Magnum damnum factum est in Servio. L. Caesar optime sentit, sed, quod avunculus est, non acerrimas dicit sententias. Consules egregii; praeclarus D. Brutus; egregius puer Caesar, de quo spero equidem reliqua. Hoc vero certum habeto, nisi ille veteranos celeriter conscripsisset legionesque duae de exercitu Antonii ad eius se auctoritatem contulissent atque is oppositus esset terror Antonio, nihil Antonium sceleris, nihil crudelitatis praeteriturum fuisse. Haec tibi, etsi audita esse arbitrabar, volui tamen notiora esse. Plura scribam, si plus otii habuero.

128. To C. CASSIUS (AD FAM. XII. 5).

ROME, FEBRUARY, (?) 43 B.C. (711 A.U.C.)

1. Marcus Brutus has achieved great things, and, if rumour tells truth as to your proceedings, the Commonwealth has the whole East under its control. 2. The war will, however, really be decided before Mutina, and we hope all will go well there. Hirtius and young Caesar, with efficient armies, confront Antony, who only holds three towns; Pansa is raising numerous recruits, and Cisalpine Gaul is zealous in our cause. The senate is firm; not so most of the consulars. 3. Sulpicius was a great loss, and cowardice, envy, and ambition, are too common among our chief men. Rome and Italy are wonderfully unanimous. I hope your valour may cause light to rise for us in the East.

CICERO CASSIO SAL.

Hiemem credo adhuc prohibuisse, quo minus de te certum 1
haberemus, quid ageres maximeque ubi esses; loquebantur omnes

2. Summatim, 'briefly,' 'compendiously.' Cp. Ep. 32, 1.

Consulares: cp. Ep. 126, 1, note.

3. In Servio: cp. Intr. to Part V, § 12.

4. L. Caesar: cp. Philipp. 8. 1, 1. He objected to a declaration of war against Antony.

6. Egregius puer. Octavius was now nineteen. Cp. p. 554, l. 3, note.

Reliqua, 'what remains of his duty,' 'the sequel.' Wesenb. has 'reliqua, hoc.'

7. Ille, Octavius.

Veteranos: cp. Intr. to Part V, § 10.

8. Legionesque duae: ib. § 9.

9. Nihil Antonium . . fuisse: cp., especially, Philipp. 3. 2.

13. Hiemem . . prohibuisse, foll. Bad weather would interfere with the despatch of news either by land or by sea. Cassius thought that his messengers were intercepted by Dolabella. Cp. Ep. 138, 1.

Certum haberemus, 'know for certain.' Cp. Ad Fam. 5. 14, 1 'non habeo certum quae te res . . retrahat.' 'Certum habere' = 'certam et indubitatam rem scire.' Forcell.

14. Loquebantur. Andr. says that when 'loqui' is followed by an accus. and infin., it is often coupled with 'vulgo' or 'omnes.' 'Loqui' with a neuter accusative is found p. 94, l. 6.

tamen—credo, quod volebant—in Syria te esse, habere copias. Id autem eo facilius credebatur, quia simile veri videbatur. Brutus quidem noster egregiam laudem est consecutus; res enim tantas gessit tamque inopinatas, ut eae cum per se gratae essent, tum ornatiores propter celeritatem. Quod si tu ea tenes, quae putamus, magnis subsidiis fulta res publica est; a prima enim ora Graeciae usque ad Aegyptum optimorum civium imperiis muniti erimus et copiis: quamquam, nisi me fallebat, res se sic habebat, ut totius belli omne discrimen in D. Bruto positum videretur, qui si, ut sperabamus, erupisset Mutina, nihil belli reliquum fore videbatur. Parvis omnino iam copiis obsidebatur, quod magno prae-
8 sidio Bononiam tenebat Antonius. Erat autem Claternae noster Hirtius, ad Forum Cornelium Caesar, uterque cum firmo exercitu; magnasque Romae Pansa copias ex dilectu Italiae comparat. Hiems adhuc rem geri prohibuerat. Hirtius nihil nisi considerate, ut mihi crebris litteris significat, acturus videbatur. Praeter Bononiam, Regium Lepidi, Parmam, totam Galliam tenebamus studiosissimam rei publicae; tuos etiam clientes Transpadanos mirifice coniunctos cum causa habebamus. Erat firmissimus senatus ex-

1. **Quod volebant**, sc. 'ita esse.'

In Syria te esse: cp. Intr. to Part V, § 11; Appendix 11. 10.

2. **Brutus**: cp. Introd. to Part V, § 13; Appendix 11. 7; Philipp. 10. 5 and 6.

4. **Essent.** The tense is used of the time when Brutus' despatch arrived. Andr.

5. **Ornatiores**, 'more famous.'

Celeritatem. M. Brutus got possession of Macedonia, apparently, about the end of 44 B.C., and had formed a considerable army and occupied nearly all Illyricum before the beginning of March, 43 B.C. (cp. Intr. to Part V, § 13; Mr. King's Intr. to Philipp. 10), when the tenth Philippic was delivered (cp. App. Bell. Civ. 3. 79; Dion Cassius 47. 21 and 22).

6. **A prima enim ora . . Aegyptum.** These words are found, with slight alteration, Philipp. 10. 5. 10.

8. **From nisi me fallebat** to the end of this section, Cicero uses the epistolary tenses. On 'fallit' impers. cp. Ep. 71, 8, note.

11. **Parvis omnino . . copiis.** This can hardly be true, for D. Brutus made no attempt to break through the besiegers' lines.

12. **Bononia**, now Bologna; **Claterna**, now Quaderna, on the Aemilian way about 10 miles S.E. of Bononia; **Forum Cornelium**, now Imola, also on the Aemilian way, about 13 miles S.E. of Claterna.

14. **Ex dilectu Italiae**: cp. Intr. to Part V, § 15; Philipp. 10. 10, 21.

15. **Rem geri**, 'active operations.'

16. **Praeter**, 'except.'

17. **Regium Lepidi**, now Reggio.

Parma retains its old name.

Totam Galliam, 'all Cisalpine Gaul.'

Tenebamus studiosissimam: cp. Ep. 132, 1 'tenuisse suspensam.'

18. **Tuos etiam clientes Transpadanos**, 'even your dependents, the people beyond the Po.' Little or nothing seems to be known of their connection with Cassius, but the relation of clientship between subject communities and eminent Romans was common. Cp. Ep. 108, 1; In Cat. 4. 11, 23. Caesar had been very popular among the people beyond the Po, and had granted them the rights of Roman citizenship, so Cicero was surprised at their devotion to the Commonwealth. Cp. Intr. to Part II, § 28; Ep. 31, 2, note; Appendix 9. 1, 3.

19. **Cum causa**, sc. 'nostra,' 'with our party.'

ceptis consularibus, ex quibus unus L. Caesar firmus est et rectus.
Ser. Sulpicii morte magnum praesidium amisimus. Reliqui partim 3
inertes, partim improbi; non nulli invident eorum laudi, quos in
re publica probari vident; populi vero Romani totiusque Italiae
mira consensio est. Haec erant fere, quae tibi nota esse vellem;
nunc autem opto, ut ab istis Orientis partibus virtutis tuae lumen
eluceat. Vale.

129. C. ASINIUS POLLIO TO CICERO (AD FAM. X. 31).

CORDUBA, MARCH 16, 43 B.C. (711 A.U.C.)

1. Brigandage and civil war interfere seriously with correspondence, but now that the season permits navigation I will write more frequently. 2. My nature and my pursuits both incline me to peace. I always regretted the outbreak of civil war, though compelled by private circumstances to act as I did. 3. I was grateful for Caesar's kindness, and tried to moderate the evils of his government; I am now prepared to resist any one who attempts to usurp absolute power. 4. I was long without instructions from Rome and Pansa's request that I would place myself at the disposal of the senate was not wise. How could I get through the province of Lepidus against his will? 5. I promised publicly at Corduba that I would only give up my province to a successor named by the senate, and have retained the 30th legion under my command with some difficulty. Peace and liberty are my great objects. 6. I hope I may enjoy your society hereafter. At present I am inclined to march into Italy to support the government.

C. ASINIUS POLLIO CICERONI S. D.

Minime mirum tibi debet videri nihil me scripsisse de re pub- 1
lica, posteaquam itum est ad arma; nam saltus Castulonensis, qui
semper tenuit nostros tabellarios, etsi nunc frequentioribus latrociniis infestior factus est, tamen nequaquam tanta in mora est, quanta qui locis omnibus dispositi ab utraque parte scrutantur tabellarios et retinent. Itaque nisi nave perlatae litterae essent,

1. Consularibus, cp. Epp. 126, 1.
Rectus, 'well intentioned;' 'non contorti aut pravi ingenii.' Andr. Not often used of persons.

2. Ser. Sulpicii morte: cp. Ep. 127, 3, note.

3. Eorum. Cicero means himself, apparently.

6. Ab istis Orientis partibus, i.e. 'where the sun rises.'

C. ASINIUS POLLIO. For an account of Pollio, cp. Ep. 85, 1, note.

9. Saltus Castulonensis. A range of mountains on the upper Baetis or Guadalquiver, near the borders of the provinces of Tarraconensis and Baetica, now the Sierra de Cazorla. Cp. Caes. Bell. Civ. 1. 38; and, on the town Castulo, Pliny, H. N. 3. 3, 17; 3. 3, 29.

12. Ab utraque parte, 'both by me and by Lepidus.' Wiel., Süpfle. An examination even by friendly sentinels might cause some delay.

omnino nescirem, quid istic fieret. Nunc vero nactus occasionem, postea quam navigari coeptum est, cupidissime et quam creberrime
2 potero scribam ad te. Ne movear eius sermonibus, quem tametsi nemo est qui videre velit, tamen nequaquam proinde ac dignus est oderunt homines, periculum non est: adeo est enim invisus mihi, ut nihil non acerbum putem, quod commune cum illo sit; natura autem mea et studia trahunt me ad pacis et libertatis cupiditatem. Itaque illud initium civilis belli saepe deflevi; cum vero non liceret mihi nullius partis esse, quia utrubique magnos inimicos habebam, ea castra fugi, in quibus plane tutum me ab insidiis inimici sciebam non futurum; compulsus eo, quo minime volebam, ne in extremis essem, plane pericula non dubi-
3 tanter adii. Caesarem vero, quod me in tanta fortuna modo cognitum vetustissimorum familiarium loco habuit, dilexi summa cum pietate et fide. Quae mea sententia gerere mihi licuit, ita feci, ut optimus quisque maxime probarit; quod iussus sum, eo tempore atque ita feci, ut appareret invito imperatum esse. Cuius facti iniustissima invidia erudire me potuit, quam iucunda libertas et quam misera sub dominatione vita esset. Ita, si id agitur, ut rursus in potestate omnia unius sint, quicumque is est, ei me profiteor inimicum; nec periculum est ullum, quod pro libertate aut
4 refugiam aut deprecer. Sed consules neque senatus consulto neque

1. **Istic**, 'at Rome.'

2. **Postea quam . . coeptum est**, 'now that navigation has begun,' which apparently was suspended during the winter.

3. **Eius**, sc. Antonii. Süpfle. Wiel., however, suspects that Pollio's quaestor, Balbus, may be meant. On the cruelty of Balbus, cp. Ad Fam. 10. 32. 1-3. Mr. Jeans thinks that Antony cannot be referred to.

6. **Non acerbum.** Cobet proposes to omit 'non,' which would make Pollio declare himself ready to endure any suffering provided that his enemy shared it.

7. **Studia**: cp. Hor. Carm. 3. 1.

8. **Illud initium**, 'the first beginning,' i.e. in 49 B.C.

10. **Ea castra**, i.e. the camp of Pompey.

11. **Inimici.** Süpfle and Billerb. both suggest 'of [C.] Cato,' whom Pollio, when 21 years old, accused in the year 54 B.C. Cp. Ep. 28. 4, note; Tac. Dial. de Orat. 34. Or is Labienus meant? Cp. Quinct. Inst. Orat. 1. 5. 8.

Eo quo minime volebam, i.e. to Caesar's camp, whereas I wished to be neutral.

12. **In extremis**, 'among the most despicable.' Wiel., Süpfle.

Plane. Wesenb. has ['plane'].

Pericula. Pollio was with Caesar when he crossed the Rubicon and fought at Pharsalus. Cp. Plut. Caes. 32; App. Bell. Civ. 2. 82.

13. **Modo cognitum**, 'only lately known.'

15. **Gerere.** He refers to his proceedings as an officer of Caesar.

16. **Quod iussus sum** = 'in eo quod iussus sum,' 'when I had to obey orders.' Cp. Caes. Bell. Gall. 3. 6 'quod iussi sunt faciunt.' I cannot find that Cicero uses this construction.

17. **Cuius facti**, 'of this conduct.' Pollio complains that people had not made allowances for his position; but adds that the unpopularity he had incurred for even involuntary compliances had shewn him how odious monarchy was.

22. **Consules**, Hirtius and Pansa.

litteris suis praeceperant mihi, quid facerem; unas enim post Idus Martias demum a Pansa litteras accepi, in quibus hortatur me, ut senatui scribam me et exercitum in potestate eius futurum: quod, cum Lepidus contionaretur atque omnibus scriberet se consentire cum Antonio, maxime contrarium fuit; nam quibus commeatibus invito illo per illius provinciam legiones ducerem? aut, si cetera transissem, num etiam Alpes poteram transvolare, quae praesidio illius tenentur? Adde huc, quod perferri litterae nulla condicione potuerunt; sescentis enim locis excutiuntur, deinde etiam retinentur ab Lepido tabellarii. Illud me Cordubae pro contione 5
dixisse nemo vocabit in dubium, provinciam me nulli, nisi qui ab senatu missus venisset, traditurum: nam de legione tricensima tradenda quantas contentiones habuerim quid ego scribam? qua tradita quanto pro re publica infirmior futurus fuerim, quis ignorat? hac enim legione noli acrius aut pugnacius quicquam putare esse. Qua re eum me existima esse, qui primum pacis cupidissimus sim —omnes enim cives plane studeo esse salvos—, deinde qui et me et rem publicam vindicare in libertatem paratus sim. Quod fami- 6
liarem meum *in* tuorum numero habes, opinione tua mihi gratius est; invideo illi tamen, quod ambulat et iocatur tecum. Quaeres,

(Manut., however, thinks that Antony and Dolabella are meant, and that Pollio is speaking of the whole time since Caesar's murder.)

1. **Praeceperant** is, I think, the epistolary tense.

Unas: cp. Ep. 45. 1, note.

3. **Me et exercitum . . futurum.** Such an offer would imply that Pollio was ready to march to Italy; an enterprise which, as he remarks just below, would be attended by great difficulties.

4. **Contionaretur**, 'said publicly.' Cp. Ad Q. F. 2. 6, [4] 6 'C. Cato contionatus est se comitia haberi non siturum.' The active sense of this verb seems, however, not to be classical (cp. Forcell.), and perhaps 'se consentire' depends only upon 'scriberet.' This is the first intimation of the possible treason of Lepidus, except, perhaps, one in Ep. 131. The speech was probably addressed to his army. Cp. Ep. 124, 1, note.

5. **Contrarium**, 'impedimentum.' A rare sense. 'Contraria' = 'quae nocent,' Forcell.

7. **Transvolare**, not, apparently, used by Cicero.

9. **Excutiuntur**, 'are thoroughly examined,' 'searched.' 'Excutere' = 'concutere scrutandi et explorandi causa.' Forcell. I suppose that Pollio refers to this difficulty of communication as an additional reason for his not attempting to march to Italy.

10. **Cordubae.** Cordoba is now called Cordova. It was the chief town of one of the four 'conventus' of Baetica, and often the governor's residence. Cp. Pliny, H. N. 3. 1, 3; App. Hisp. 65.

12. **Nam.** I am not sure of the force of this word here. Perhaps it means 'And I will press no further proofs of my loyalty upon you.'

13. **Tradenda**, sc. Lepido. Cp. Ad Fam. 10. 32, 4 'Lepidus ursit me . . ut legionem tricensimam mitterem sibi.' Pollio did not, apparently, comply with the request of Lepidus.

17. **Omnes enim . . salvos.** This seems to have been a frequent plea with those who wished for a peaceful settlement. Cp. Ep. 144; Philipp. 8. 4, 13 'ais [Calenus] eum te esse qui semper pacem optaris, semper omnes cives salvos volueris.'

18. **Familiarem meum.** Probably C. (?) Cornelius Gallus. Cp. Ad Fam. 10. 32. 5.

19. **Opinione tua**, 'than you suppose.' Wiel.

20. **Iocatur.** Cicero could still enjoy pleasantry. Cp. Ad Fam. 9. 24.

quanti *id* aestimem? Si umquam licuerit vivere in otio, experieris; nullum enim vestigium abs te discessurus sum. Illud vehementer admiror, non scripsisse te mihi, manendo in provincia an ducendo exercitum in Italiam rei publicae magis satis facere possim: ego quidem, etsi mihi tutius ac minus laboriosum est manere, tamen, quia video tali tempore multo magis legionibus opus esse quam provinciis, quae praesertim reciperari nullo negotio possint, constitui, ut nunc est, cum exercitu proficisci. Deinde ex litteris, quas Pansae misi, cognosces omnia; nam tibi earum exemplar misi. XVII. Kal. April. Corduba.

130. To PLANCUS (AD FAM. X. 6).

ROME, MARCH 20, 43 B.C. (711 A.U.C.)

1. Your despatch did not bear out the language of Furnius as to your disposition; peace should be secured by victory, not by negotiation, and you will learn from your brother and from Furnius how your proposals and those of Lepidus were received. 2. I write, however, to entreat you to separate yourself from associates with whom circumstances and not your own judgment have united you. 3. In revolutionary times men often attain a position which brings them no real credit unless they display a patriotism worthy of it—as I hope you will do.

CICERO PLANCO.

1 Quae locutus est Furnius noster de animo tuo in rem publicam, ea gratissima fuerunt senatui populoque Romano probatissima; quae autem recitatae litterae sunt in senatu, nequaquam consentire cum Furnii oratione visae sunt: pacis enim auctor eras, cum collega tuus, vir clarissimus, a foedissimis latronibus obsideretur, qui aut positis armis pacem petere debent aut, si pugnantes eam postulant, victoria pax, non pactione parienda

7. Quae praesertim, 'as they certainly.' Süpfle.

8. Ut nunc est, 'as things now stand.' Wiel.

Deinde, 'for the rest.' Wiel.

PLANCO. L. Munatius Plancus had served Caesar in the Gallic and civil wars (cp. Caes. Bell. Gall. 5. 24; Bell. Civ. 1. 40), and had been entrusted by him with the government of Transalpine Gaul, except the old province, with a promise of the consulship for 42 B.C. He was a hereditary friend of Cicero (cp. Ad Fam. 13. 29, 1). On his subsequent behaviour, cp. Intr. to Part V, §§ 18; 19; Appendix 11. 3. Velleius speaks of him with much bitterness (2. 63) 'Plancus dubia, id est sua, fide.' Plancus begged the triumvirs to proscribe his brother Plotius Plancus (cp. Vell. 2. 67, 2). According to Dion Cassius he and Lepidus jointly founded Lugdunum (Lyons) by the senate's orders. Cp. Dion 46. 50.

11. Furnius. C. Furnius, a friend of Cicero and of Caesar, is mentioned Epp. 60; 148, 7. He was now legate of Plancus, cp. Ep. 132, 5. Cicero wrote two letters to him (Ad Fam. 10. 25 and 26).

15. Collega tuus: cp. Ep. 120, note on superscription.

est. Sed de pace litterae vel Lepidi vel tuae quam in partem
acceptae sint, ex viro optimo, fratre tuo, et ex C. Furnio poteris
cognoscere. Me autem impulit tui caritas ut, quamquam nec tibi 2
ipsi consilium deesset et fratris Furniique benevolentia fidelisque
prudentia tibi praesto esset futura, vellem tamen meae quoque
auctoritatis pro plurimis nostris necessitudinibus praeceptum ad
te aliquod pervenire. Crede igitur mihi, Plance, omnes, quos
adhuc gradus dignitatis consecutus sis—es autem adeptus amplissimos—, eos honorum vocabula habituros, non dignitatis insignia,
nisi te cum libertate populi Romani et cum senatus auctoritate
coniunxeris. Seiunge te, quaeso, aliquando ab iis, cum quibus te
non tuum iudicium, sed temporum vincla coniunxerunt. Com- 3
plures in perturbatione rei publicae consulares dicti, quorum nemo
consularis habitus *est* nisi qui animo exstitit in rem publicam
consulari. Talem igitur te esse oportet, qui primum te ab
impiorum civium tui dissimillimorum societate seiungas, deinde
te senatui bonisque omnibus auctorem, principem, ducem prae-

1. Lepidi vel tuae. Cicero rebuked Lepidus (Ep. 131) for a letter of similar import to that of Plancus, which was probably discussed in the senate about this time. For Cicero notices it (Philipp. 13. 4) after the departure of Pansa from Rome (cp. Philipp. 13. 20, 46), which did not take place before March 19. Cp. Ad Fam. 12. 25, 1. Cicero implies that the letters of Lepidus and Plancus made an unfavourable impression on the senate. Negotiations with Antony seem to have been dropped, but no vote declaring him a traitor passed before the news of the battle of Forum Gallorum reached Rome. Cp. Intr. to Part V, § 16. Perhaps a formal declaration to that effect was not made till after the raising of the siege of Mutina. Cp. Livy, Epit. 119; Cornelius Nepos, Att. 9.

Quam in partem . . sint, 'the construction put upon them.'

2. Fratre tuo, sc. Cn. Planco. He held a commission from Caesar in Epirus 44 B.C. (cp. Ad Att. 16. 16, A), and was then praetor designatus. He is mentioned again Ep. 139, 3. Cicero wrote some letters to him. Cp. Ad Att. 16. 16 A. B. E.

4. Deesset. The mood may be accounted for perhaps by the general structure of the sentence, or as expressing the view of Cicero as of a third person. Cp. Madv. 368; Zumpt, L. G. 547. It is rare in Cicero's writings after 'quamquam.'

6. Pro . . necessitudinibus. Plancus had paid much attention to Cicero from his youth. Cp. Ad Fam. 13. 29, 1.

8. Amplissimos. He had probably held the lower offices, and was now 'consul designatus.'

9. Eos; resumptive after a parenthesis. Cp. Ep. 68, 1; Madv. 489 a.

Habituros, 'will have attached to them.'

Honorum vocabula, 'mere official titles.'

Dignitatis insignia, 'badges of merit,' 'of real dignity.' Süpfle. 'The stamp of a real worthiness,' 'den innern Character der Würde.' Wiel.

10. Cum libertate . . coniunxeris: cp. Ep. 128, 2 'coniunctos cum causa.'

11. Aliquando, 'at last,' after acting with them so long. Cp. Ep. 123, 2, note.

Ab iis, i.e. 'from Antony and his friends.'

12. Temporum vincla, 'bonds created by circumstances.'

Complures . . consulari. Cicero refers probably to Q. Fufius Calenus, L. Piso, and others, who opposed the adoption of vigorous measures against Antony. Cp. Ep. 127, 3; Philipp. 8. 7, 20 'quam hesternum diem nobis, consularibus dico, turpis illuxit!' Ib. 7. 2, 5 '[Pansam] nisi talis consul esset . . consulem non putarem.'

17. Auctorem, 'auctor est non qui alios sequitur sed qui movet.' 'Princeps autem plus est quam auctor et dux quam princeps.' Manut.

beas, postremo [ut] pacem esse iudices non in armis positis, sed in abiecto armorum et servitutis metu. Haec si et ages et senties, tum eris non modo consul et consularis, sed magnus etiam consul et consularis; sin aliter, tum in istis amplissimis nominibus honorum non modo dignitas nulla erit, sed erit summa deformitas. Haec impulsus benevolentia scripsi paulo severius, quae tu in experiendo ea ratione, quae te digna est, vera esse cognosces. D. XIII. Kal. Apr.

131. To LEPIDUS (AD FAM. X. 27).

ROME, MARCH 20? 43 B.C. (711 A.U.C.)

1, 2. I am sorry that you are not more grateful to the senate for the honour it has paid you. I am glad to hear that you are so anxious for peace, but I hope that you will not recommend us to sacrifice liberty to obtain it.

CICERO LEPIDO SAL.

1 Quod mihi pro summa *mea* erga te benevolentia magnae curae
est, ut quam amplissima dignitate sis, moleste tuli te senatui
gratias non egisse, cum esses ab eo ordine ornatus summis honoribus. Pacis inter cives conciliandae te cupidum esse laetor: eam
si a servitute seiungis, consules et rei publicae et dignitati tuae;
sin ista pax perditum hominem in possessionem impotentissimi
dominatus restitutura est, hoc animo scito omnes sanos, ut mortem
2 servituti anteponant. Itaque sapientius, meo quidem iudicio,
facies, si te in istam pacificationem non interpones, quae neque

5. Non . . erit, sed erit. For similar repetitions of a verb, cp. 'satisfacio,' Ep. 21, 1; Süpfle quotes also Ad Att. 14. 14. 6; De Fin. 2. 21, 68. It gives emphasis.

6. Deformitas, 'discredit.' Forcell.

7. In experiendo . . cognosces. 'if you test my words in a way worthy of yourself you will find them true.' Süpfle. On this sense of 'experiri,' cp. Forcell. Perhaps, however, it is absolute, and means 'if you wish to make an experiment.'

LEPIDO. For an account of Lepidus' position, cp. Intr. to Part V, §§ 1; 11; Appendix 11. 2. He had written, like Plancus, but perhaps in more urgent terms, to recommend peace with Antony (see § 1 of the previous letter, note), and Cicero reproves him on that account.

11. Ornatus summis honoribus. Cicero refers to votes of a 'supplicatio' on Nov. 28th, 44 B.C., of a gilded statue, and of a triumph, both apparently on Jan. 4th, 43 B.C. Cp. Intr. to Part V, § 9; Philipp. 5. 15. 41; 13. 4. 9.

12. Pacis inter cives, foll.: cp. Philipp. 13. 4.

13. Seiungis, Wesenb. has 'seiunges.'

14. Perditum hominem, i.e. Antony.

15. Hoc animo, sc. 'esse.' For a similar ellipse, see Ep. 80, 1 'id ut ita putarem.' Wesenb. inserts 'esse.'

17. Te . . . interpones = 'immiscebis' (Forcell.), 'meddle with,' 'intrude yourself into.'

In istam pacificationem, 'with the negotiations for peace which you recommend.'

senatui neque populo nec cuiquam bono probatur. Sed haec audis ex aliis aut certior fies litteris: tu pro tua prudentia, quid optimum factu sit, videbis.

132. PLANCUS TO THE MAGISTRATES, SENATE, AND PEOPLE (AD FAM. X. 8).

FARTHER GAUL, MARCH, 43 B.C. (711 A.U.C.)

1. I wish first to excuse myself for my apparent hesitation in declaring my intentions; 2. only anxiety for the public interest prevented my declaring them long ago. 3. Much time was required for securing my position in various ways. 4. My necessities must be my apology for a dissimulation which I do not deny, 5. and for the discrepancy between my despatch and my instructions to Furnius. 6. I have now five legions under my command; the population is devotedly loyal, and furnishes large forces of cavalry and light troops; I am ready to act in whatever way shall seem best for my country. 7. I hope my aid may not be wanted, even should this cause me a loss of distinction, and I recommend my soldiers to your consideration.

PLANCUS IMP. COS. DESIG. S. D. COSS. PR. TR. PL. SENATUI POPULO PLEBIQUE ROMANAE.

Si cui forte videor diutius et hominum exspectationem et spem 1
rei publicae de mea voluntate tenuisse suspensam, huic prius excusandum me esse arbitror quam de insequenti officio quicquam ulli pollicendum; non enim praeteritam culpam videri volo redemisse, sed optimae mentis cogitata iampridem maturo tempore enuntiare.
Non me praeteribat in tanta sollicitudine hominum et tam pertur- 2

1. Aut certior fies, sc. 'de his,' zeugma.

3. Videbis: for 'vide,' cp. Ep. 11. 3, note.

MARCH. Nake (page 80) says that this letter was written 'mense Martio exeunte.' Cicero appears to have received it on April 7. Cp. Ad Fam. 10. 7: 10. 12. A letter seems to have taken at least fifteen days to reach the camp of Plancus from Rome: Cicero wrote Ad Fam 10. 12 on April 11, and Plancus does not appear to have received it when he wrote Ad Fam. 10. 9, not earlier than April 26. Cp. Nake, pp. 7, 8.

IMP. It does not appear for what exploits Plancus had assumed the title of 'Imperator.' On that of COS. DESIG., cp. p. 552, note.

The address of this letter seems peculiar. Cicero (Ad Fam. 15. 1, and 2) ends with 'senatui.'

4. Si cui forte videor, foll.: cp. Cicero's expression of discontent, Ep. 130, 1.

5. Tenuisse suspensam: cp. Ep. 128, 2 'totam Galliam tenebamus studiosissimam.'

6. De insequenti officio, 'about my services in future.' Wiel.

7. Non enim, foll., 'for I do not wish my present attitude to be considered an atonement for the past,' as it might be if he failed to justify his past conduct.

Redemisse. Redimere 'to make good,' = 'luere, pro culpa satisfacere.' Forcell.

8. Sed . . enuntiare, 'but a declaration at the proper time of sentiments long cherished.' On the part. and adverb with a genitive, cp. De Amic. 2, 6 'multa eius . . vel provisa prudenter . . ferebantur.'

Maturo. 'Maturus' = 'qui debito tempore fit.' Forcell.

bato statu civitatis fructuosissimam esse professionem bonae voluntatis, magnosque honores ex ea re complures consecutos videbam; sed, cum in eum casum me fortuna demisisset, ut aut celeriter pollicendo magna mihi ipse ad proficiendum impedimenta opponerem aut, si in eo mihi temperavissem, maiores occasiones ad opitulandum haberem, expeditius iter communis salutis quam meae laudis esse volui. Nam quis in ea fortuna, quae mea est, et ab ea vita, quam in me cognitam hominibus arbitror, et cum ea spe, quam in manibus habeo, aut sordidum quicquam pati aut perniciosum con-
8 cupiscere potest? Sed aliquantum nobis temporis et magni labores et multae impensae opus fuerunt, ut, quae rei publicae bonisque omnibus polliceremur, exitu praestaremus neque ad auxilium patriae nudi cum bona voluntate, sed cum facultatibus accederemus. Confirmandus erat exercitus nobis, magnis saepe praemiis sollicitatus, ut ab re publica potius moderata quam ab uno infinita speraret; confirmandae complures civitates, quae superiore anno largitionibus concessionibusque praemiorum erant obligatae, ut et illa vana putarent et eadem a melioribus auctoribus petenda existimarent; eliciendae etiam voluntates reliquorum, qui finitimis provinciis exercitibusque praefuerunt, ut potius cum pluribus societatem defendendae libertatis iniremus, quam cum paucioribus

2. **Complures.** Perhaps M. Lepidus among others, cp Ep. 131, 1; also Octavius and L. Egnatuleius, Philipp. 5. 17, 46; 5. 19, 52.

3. **Demisisset,** cp. p. 367.

4. **Ad proficiendum,** 'in respect of the execution of my promise.' Süpfle. Cp. Caes. Bell. Civ. 1. 62 'ad transeundum impedirentur;' also Nägelsb. 123. 340. Plancus (probably) wished to sound Lepidus, and to ascertain the disposition of his own soldiers and of the provincials. Cp. § 3.

5. **In eo,** sc. 'in pollicendo.'

Opitulandum, used with a dat. Ep. 133. 2.

6. **Expeditius iter . . volui,** lit. 'that the road to the common safety should be in better condition than that which led to my private fame.' 'I wished rather to consider my country's good than my own reputation.'

7. **In ea fortuna.** He was governor of a province, imperator, and consul designatus.

Ab ea vita, 'after such a life,' 'with such antecedents.' Cp. Ep. 33. 1, note on 'ab repulsa.'

8. **Ea spe,** i.e. the hope of the consulship for 42 B.C.

9. **Sordidum quicquam . . potest,** 'can either suffer any humiliating treatment [from Antony] or desire a position dangerous to the state.'

11. **Multae impensae.** The plural is common, but not apparently in Cicero's writings.

Opus, used as a plural. Cp. Madv. 266.

14. **Magnis . . praemiis,** 'by the offer of large rewards' on Antony's behalf.

15. **Ab uno,** sc. Antonio.

17. **Largitionibus.** Especially by grants of citizenship and of exemption from taxes. Cp. Intr. to Part V, § 3; Philipp. 2. 36, 92.

Obligatae, i.e. by Antony as consul.

18. **A melioribus auctoribus.** That is, from the senate and people.

19. **Reliquorum,** 'of the other governors,' especially of Lepidus and of Asinius Pollio.

20. **Ut . . iniremus.** On the mood, cp. Ep. 15, 13, note.

21. **Cum paucioribus . . partiremur.** The sense seems to be that Plancus wished to secure so much support for his cause as should save the commonwealth from suffering the loss which must attend even victory in an obstinate struggle. Or perhaps, as Wieland thinks, 'paucioribus' = 'Antonianis.'

funestam orbi terrarum victoriam partiremur. Muniendi vero 4
nosmet ipsi fuimus aucto exercitu auxiliisque multiplicatis, ut,
cum praeferremus sensus aperte, tum etiam invitis quibusdam
sciri, quid defensuri essemus, non esset periculosum. Ita numquam diffitebor multa me, ut ad effectum horum consiliorum per-
venirem, et simulasse invitum et dissimulasse cum dolore, quod,
praematura denuntiatio boni civis imparati quam periculosa esset,
ex casu collegae videbam. Quo nomine etiam C. Furnio legato, 5
viro forti atque strenuo, plura etiam verbo quam scriptura mandata dedimus, ut et tectius ad vos perferrentur et nos essemus
tutiores, quibusque rebus et communem salutem muniri et nos
armari conveniret praecepimus. Ex quo intellegi potest curam
rei publicae summe defendendae iam pridem apud nos excubare.
Nunc, cum deum benignitate ab omni re sumus paratiores, non 6
solum bene sperare de nobis homines, sed explorate iudicare volumus: legiones habeo quinque sub signis et sua fide virtuteque rei
publicae coniunctissimas et nostra liberalitate nobis obsequentes,
provinciam omnium civitatium consensu paratissimam et summa
contentione ad officia certantem, equitatus auxiliorumque tantas
copias, quantas hae gentes ad defendendam suam salutem liber-

3. Cum praeferremus, 'when I should declare.' The conj. expresses a past frame of mind of the writer. Cp. Ep. 19, 4, note; and for the imperf. in a future sense, Ep. 71, 5, note. 'Praeferre' = 'prae nobis ferre.' Süpfle. A rare construction in Ciceronian Latin.

Invitis quibusdam. These words may either be an ablative absolute, or a dative after sciri. Cp. Madv. 250 a. The sense will be of course slightly different; in the first case 'sciri' would mean 'should be generally known.' Wesenb. has 'tum, etiam invitis quibusdam,' of course making 'invitis' an ablative.

5. Ad effectum, 'to the execution,' = 'at performance.' Cp. Forcell.

Multa .. simulasse, i.e. regard for Antony; dissimulasse, devotion to the senate. Plancus concealed his sentiments effectually, cp. Ep. 130, 1, note. 'Simulo' = 'I pretend to be or have that which I am or have not;' 'dissimulo' = 'I pretend not to be or to have that which I am or have.'

7. Denuntiatio, 'declaration,' 'fere terrendi causa.' Forcell.

8. Ex casu collegae. D. Brutus was now besieged in Mutina.

Quo nomine: cp. Ep. 38, 3, note on 'multis nominibus.'

C. Furnio: cp. Ep. 130, 1, note.

9. Plura etiam .. dedimus. Cicero had noticed a discrepancy between the despatch of Plancus and the language of Furnius. Ep. 130, 1.

12. Praecepimus, Furnio. Plancus probably charged Furnius to inform the senate what measures he wished that it should adopt.

Curam .. excubare. A military metaphor. 'That anxiety to defend the commonwealth to the best of my power has long been keeping watch in my heart.'

13. Summe. Wesenb. 'summae.'

14. Ab omni re, 'in every respect.' For this sense of 'ab,' cp. Ep. 1, 2, note.

15. Explorate, 'confidently,' 'Certo,' 'plane.' Forcell.

16. Quinque. He seems to have used only four for active operations. Cp. Epp. 140, 3; 148, 3.

18. Civitatium, a less common form of the genitive than 'civitatum.' It appears to be the MS. reading.

19. Ad officia, 'in the discharge of its duties.' Cp. § 2 'ad proficiscendum.'

tatemque conficere possunt; ipse ita sum animo paratus, *ut* vel provinciam tueri vel ire, quo res publica vocet, vel tradere exercitum auxilia provinciamque, vel omnem impetum belli in me convertere non recusem, si modo meo casu aut confirmare patriae
7 salutem aut periculum possim morari. Haec si iam expeditis omnibus rebus tranquilloque statu civitatis polliceor, in damno meae laudis rei publicae commodo laetabor; sin ad societatem integerrimorum et maximorum periculorum accedam, consilia mea aequis iudicibus ab obtrectatione invidorum defendenda commendo. Mihi quidem ipsi fructus meritorum meorum in rei publicae incolumitate satis magnus est paratus; eos vero, qui meam auctoritatem et multo magis vestram fidem secuti nec ulla spe decipi nec ullo metu terreri potuerunt, ut commendatos vobis habeatis, petendum videtur.

133. To PLANCUS (AD FAM. X. 10).

ROME, MARCH 30, 43 B.C. (711 A.U.C.)

1. Your letter has produced a very favourable impression, and the senate would have shewn its gratitude to you but for the absence of the consuls. A battle has perhaps already decided the state's fortunes. 2. If our cause prospers you will receive abundant honours, and I hope you will exert yourself to the utmost in support of your colleague. Public and private grounds alike will secure you my warm co-operation.

CICERO PLANCO.

1 Etsi satis ex Furnio nostro cognoram, quae tua voluntas, quod consilium de re publica esset, tamen tuis litteris lectis liquidius de toto sensu tuo iudicavi. Quam ob rem, quamquam in uno proelio omnis fortuna rei publicae disceptat—quod quidem, cum haec

2. Tradere, 'to hand over' to a successor appointed by the home government.

5. Si iam expeditis, foll. In English we should say, 'If when I make this offer everything has been settled satisfactorily.' Cp. Süpfle.

6. In damno .. laetabor, 'I shall rejoice in the commonwealth's gain though attended by loss to me.' On the abl. commodo, cp. Madv. 264.

8. Integerrimorum, 'not diminished in any degree.'

Consilia: cp. § 3.

11. Eos, i.e. his soldiers and the provincials.

12. Vestram fidem secuti, 'influenced by your promises,' 'relying on your good faith.'

15. Ex Furnio: cp. Ep. 130, 1, note. Furnius probably stayed some days at Rome.

16. Tuis litteris. The letter of Plancus here referred to seems to have been lost. It can hardly be Ad Fam. 10. 7, which appears to have accompanied 10. 8 (Ep. 132), and does not seem to have reached Cicero before April 7, eight days after he wrote this letter. Cp. Nake, Jahresbericht über das Luisenstädtische Gymnasium, Berlin, 1866. I have learned from this paper that the note in my previous editions gave a wrong account of this matter.

Liquidius, 'more clearly.'

18. Disceptat, 'is at stake,' = 'periclitatur,' a rare sense. Wesenb. 'disceptatur.'

legeres, iam decretum arbitrabar fore—, tamen ipsa fama, quae de
tua voluntate percrebruit, magnam es laudem consecutus; itaque
si consulem Romae habuissemus, declaratum esset ab senatu cum
tuis magnis honoribus, quam gratus esset conatus et apparatus
tuus: cuius rei non modo non praeteriit tempus, sed ne maturum
quidem etiam nunc meo quidem iudicio fuit; is enim denique
honos mihi videri solet, qui non propter spem futuri beneficii, sed
propter magna merita claris viris defertur [et datur]. Qua re, sit 2
modo aliqua res publica, in qua honos elucere possit, omnibus,
mihi crede, amplissimis honoribus abundabis; is autem, qui vere
appellari potest honos, non invitamentum ad tempus, sed perpetuae virtutis est praemium. Quam ob rem, mi Plance, incumbe
toto pectore ad laudem, subveni patriae, opitulare collegae, omnium gentium consensum et incredibilem conspirationem adiuva.
Me tuorum consiliorum adiutorem, dignitatis fautorem, omnibus
in rebus tibi amicissimum fidelissimumque cognosces; ad eas enim
causas, quibus inter nos amore sumus, officiis, vetustate coniuncti,
patriae caritas accessit, eaque effecit ut tuam vitam anteferrem
meae. III. K. Apr.

134. To CASSIUS (AD FAM. XII. 6).

ROME, APRIL (?), 43 B.C. (711 A.U.C.)

1. C. Titius will tell you the news; he has the greatest regard for you. 2. D. Brutus can hardly hold out longer at Mutina; if he prospers our fears are at an end; if not, all our hopes will rest on you and on M. Brutus.

Quod proelium decretum: cp. Livy 28. 33 'irritare magis quam decernere pugnam,' 'decided.' The decisive battle at Mutina did not, however, take place for some days afterwards. Cp. Intr. to Part V, §§ 16; 17.

3. Si consulem, foll. Hirtius had left for the seat of war, probably, in January; Pansa about March 20. Cp. Intr. to Part V, §§ 12; 15.

5. Cuius rei, 'for which declaration of the senate.'

Ne maturum . . fuit, 'has not even now fully come.'

6. Is enim denique, foll., '*that* only seems to me to be true honour.' 'Is' masc. by attraction to 'honos.' Cp. Ep. 90, 4. In the following words Cicero hints that the state now looked for deeds from Plancus, not merely for professions.

8. Sit modo . . res publica, 'If only we have some form of free government.'

10. Qui vere . . potest, sc. 'honos,' 'which may truly bear that name.'

11. Invitamentum, 'an invitation,' rare.

Ad tempus: cp. Ep. 111, 8. Here it seems to mean 'to do your duty for a time.' Manut.

12. Incumbe . . ad laudem, 'strive after fame to the utmost of your power.'

15. Dignitatis. It does not appear that Plancus had been honoured by votes like those adopted in favour of Lepidus. Cp. Ep. 132 with Ad Fam. 10. 7, 2 'cum ahi occupare possessionem laudis viderentur;' and again, 'a te peto ut dignitati meae suffragere.'

17. Quibus, ablat. case.

Vetustate, 'the length of our connection.'

April. This letter seems to have been written before the news of the battle at

CICERO CASSIO SAL.

1 Qui status rerum fuerit tum, cum has litteras dedi, scire poteris ex C. Titio Strabone, viro bono et optime de re publica sentiente; nam quid dicam 'cupidissimo tui,' qui domo et fortunis relictis
2 ad te potissimum profectus sit? Itaque eum tibi ne commendo quidem; adventus ipsius ad te satis eum commendabit. Tu velim sic existimes tibique persuadeas, omne perfugium bonorum in te et Bruto esse positum, si, quod nolim, adversi quid evenerit. Res, cum haec scribebam, erat in extremum adducta discrimen; Brutus enim Mutinae vix iam sustinebat: qui si conservatus erit, vicimus; sin—quod di omen avertant!—, omnis omnium cursus est ad vos. Proinde fac animum tantum habeas tantumque apparatum, quanto opus est ad universam rem publicam recuperandam. Vale.

135. GALBA TO CICERO (AD FAM. X. 30).

CAMP BEFORE MUTINA, APRIL 16, 43 B.C. (711 A.U.C.)

1. On the 15th Pansa, to meet whom Hirtius had sent me, was drawing near the seat of war. Antony met us with a large force, and 2. when his cavalry appeared, we could not restrain the Martian legion, and an engagement followed. 3. At first we got the better, but Antony's superiority in numbers enabling him to outflank us, 4. we fell back on our camp, which he attacked in vain, and on his return to his own met Hirtius, who with two legions destroyed nearly his whole force at Forum Gallorum,

Forum Gallorum, which reached Rome on April 20, had arrived there. Cp. Intr. to Part V, § 16.

2. C. Titio Strabone: he is apparently only here mentioned.

3. Nam quid dicam: cp. Ad Q. F. 1. 1, 10 'nam quid ego de Gratidio dicam? quem certo scio ita laborare de existimatione sua ut . . etiam de nostra laboret.' The phrase introduces what is notorious or otherwise attested.

6. Omne perfugium . . positum, 'that all the well-disposed have only you and M. Brutus to look to for aid.' Cp. Ep. 83, 2, note.

7. Quod nolim. The conj. expresses a wish modestly. Cp. Ep. 1, 3, note.

8. Cum . . scribebam . . sustinebat, 'at the time I am writing Brutus can hardly hold out any longer at Mutina.' Cp. for the absol. use of 'sustinere,' Caes. Bell. Gall. 1. 6 'sese diutius sustinere non posse.'

10. Vicimus. The perfect indicative is used even of things future when it is desired to express certainty. Cp. Ep. 52, 4 note, p. 314; Madv. 340, Obs. 2.

Sin . . avertant, aposiopesis; cp. Madv. 479 d, Obs. 6.

Omnis . . ad vos, 'everybody will hasten to you and Brutus.'

GALBA. Servius Sulpicius Galba, great grandfather of the emperor of that name, had served Caesar in Gaul, and was put forward by him as a candidate for the consulship in the year 50 B.C. Cp. Caes. Bell. Gall. 8. 50. But subsequently he was annoyed because Caesar did not grant him a consulship, and conspired against his life. Cp. Suet. Galba 3. He now commanded the Martian legion. With the narrative here given should be compared Intr. to Part V, § 16; Philipp. 14. 9; 10; and App. Bell. Civ. 3. 67–70.

the scene of the first action. Antony then retired to his camp before Mutina. 5. Hirtius to that of Pansa. We have obtained a great success, and captured several standards, but that part of our forces which was first engaged has suffered some loss.

GALBA CICERONI SAL.

A. d. XVII. Kal. Maias, quo die Pansa in castris Hirtii erat 1
futurus, cum quo ego eram—nam ei obviam processeram milia
passuum centum, quo maturius veniret—, Antonius legiones
eduxit duas, secundam et quintam tricensimam et cohortes praetorias duas, unam suam, alteram Silani, *et* evocatorum partem:
ita obviam venit nobis, quod nos quattuor legiones tironum habere
solum arbitrabatur. Sed noctu, quo tutius venire in castra possemus, legionem Martiam, cui ego praeesse solebam, et duas
cohortes praetorias miserat Hirtius nobis. Cum equites Antonii 2
apparuissent, contineri neque legio Martia neque cohortes prae-
toriae potuerunt; quas sequi coepimus coacti, quoniam retinere
eas non potueramus. Antonius ad Forum Gallorum suas copias
continebat neque sciri volebat se legiones habere; tantum equitatum et levem armaturam ostendebat. Postea quam vidit se
invito legionem ire Pansa, sequi se duas legiones iussit tironum.
Postea quam angustias paludis et silvarum transiimus, acies est

1. A. d. XVII Kal. Maias, April 15.

Erat . . eram, *not* epistolary tenses.

2. Cum quo, sc. Pansa. A relative does not always refer to the nearest substantive. Cp. Ep. 71, 9, note on p. 377, l. 13.

Obviam processeram. Pansa had set out from Rome for the seat of war about March 20. Cp. Intr. to Part V, § 15.

4. Quintam tricensimam. Quintam *et* tricensimam would be the usual expression. Andr.

Cohortes praetorias. The establishment of a select body of troops called a praetorian cohort to act as a body-guard to the general is said to have originated with the younger Scipio at the siege of Numantia. Cp. Paul. Diac. ap. Festum, p. 223 Müller. We also find references to it Sall. Cat. 60; Caes. Bell. Gall. 1. 42. Those engaged on both sides on this occasion probably consisted of 'evocati.'

5. Silani. M. Iunius Silanus (mentioned by Caesar Bell. Gall. 6. 1), appears to have held high command under Lepidus in Gaul, and to have deserted him for Antony. He afterwards, however, rejoined Lepidus, Ep. 141; Dion Cassius 46. 38. He was half-brother of M. Brutus. See Ep. 147, 1, note.

Evocatorum. 'Evocati' were soldiers who, having served their full time, were induced to enlist again. They may have been exempted from the more irksome military duties. Cp. Smith's Dict. of Antiq. 477; Dion Cassius 45. 12; Caes. Bell. Gall. 7. 65; Ad Fam. 3. 6. 5.

7. In castra, Hirtii.

8. Legionem Martiam: cp. Intr. to Part V, §§ 9; 16; Philipp. 3. 3. 6; 14. 9 and 10.

Solebam. It was commanded on this occasion by D. Carfulenus, or Carsuleius, as Appian (Bell. Civ. 3. 67) calls him. Cp. Ad Fam. 10. 33, 4; Ad Att. 15. 4. 1.

Duas cohortes. Those of Hirtius and Octavius.

10. Contineri . . potuerunt. The soldiers of the Martian legion were probably enraged by Antony's attempt to enforce discipline among them. Cp. Intr. to Part V, § 9.

12. Forum Gallorum, about eight miles S.E. of Mutina, and on the Aemilian way: now Castel Franco.

15. Tironum, i.e. of the new levies raised in Italy by Pansa. Cp. Philipp. 12. 15. 39; 14. 2. 5.

16. Angustias . . silvarum, 'a defile

3 instructa a nobis XII. cohortium; nondum venerant legiones duae: repente Antonius in aciem suas copias de vico produxit et sine mora concurrit. Primo ita pugnatum est, ut acrius non posset ex utraque parte pugnari; etsi dexterius cornu, in quo ego eram cum Martiae legionis cohortibus octo, impetu primo fugaverat legionem XXXV. Antonii, ut amplius passus * ultra aciem [quo loco steterat] processerit. Itaque cum equites nostrum cornu circumire vellent, recipere me coepi et levem armaturam opponere Maurorum equitibus, ne aversos nostros adgrederentur. Interim video me esse inter Antonianos Antoniumque post me esse aliquanto. Repente equum immisi ad eam legionem tironum, quae veniebat ex castris, scuto reiecto. Antoniani me insequi; nostri pila coniicere velle: ita nescio quo fato sum servatus, quod sum
4 cito a nostris cognitus. In ipsa Aemilia, ubi cohors Caesaris praetoria erat, diu pugnatum est. Cornu sinisterius, quod erat infirmius, ubi Martiae legionis duae cohortes erant et cohors praetoria, pedem referre coeperunt, quod ab equitatu circumibantur, quo vel plurimum valet Antonius. Cum omnes se recepissent nostri ordines, recipere me novissimus coepi ad castra; Antonius tamquam victor castra putavit se posse capere: quo cum venit, complures ibi amisit nec egit quicquam. Audita re Hirtius cum cohortibus XX. veteranis redeunti Antonio in sua castra

formed by wooded and marshy ground,' which extended along both sides of the road. Cp. App. Bell. Civ. 3. 67.

1. XII. cohortium. Ten of the Martian legion and two praetorian.

Legiones duae, sc. 'tironum.' Cp. § 2.

4. Etsi, foll., '[the battle was obstinate] although we met with great success at first.'

Dexterius. Not uncommon, though apparently needless, = 'dextrum.'

6. Amplius passus. Some editions insert D.

Ultra aciem, 'beyond the general line of battle.'

7. Processerit, sc. 'dexterius cornu.'

Cum equites, sc. Antonii. Perhaps the previous retreat had been a feint.

9. Maurorum equitibus. These horsemen were probably levied by Caesar for his projected campaign in Parthia, where they would have been very useful.

10. Post me, 'in my rear.'

11. Quae veniebat. Probably one of the two which had followed Pansa. Cp. § 2. Two others were probably left to fortify a camp. Cp. § 5, and App. Bell. Civ. 3. 69.

12. Scuto reiecto, 'with my shield behind my shoulder,' shewing that he came as a friend, or perhaps to protect himself from the missiles of the pursuers. 'Reiicere' = 'retro iacere.' Forcell.

14. In ipsa Aemilia, 'on the raised causeway of the Aemilian road,' a continuation of the Flaminian, leading from Ariminum to Bononia and Placentia: the portion between Placentia and Ariminum was constructed in 187 B.C. by M. Aemilius Lepidus, see Livy 39. 2.

16. Cohors praetoria, sc. Hirtii.

20. Tamquam victor: 'like a conqueror' without having really conquered. Andr.

Cum venit: 'venisset' would be more in accordance with usage, but the style of this letter is not very correct. Andr.

21. Nec egit quicquam. Appian however, says that Antony slaughtered a large number of Pansa's new recruits (Bell. Civ. 3. 69).

22. Cum cohortibus XX veteranis.

occurrit copiasque eius omnes delevit fugavitque eodem loco, ubi
erat pugnatum, ad Forum Gallorum; Antonius cum equitibus
hora noctis quarta se in castra sua ad Mutinam recepit; Hirtius 5
in ea castra rediit, unde Pansa exierat, ubi duas legiones reli-
querat quae ab Antonio erant oppugnatae. Sic partem maiorem suarum copiarum Antonius amisit veteranarum; nec id tamen sine aliqua iactura cohortium praetoriarum nostrarum et legionis Martiae fieri potuit. Aquilae duae, signa LX. sunt relata Antonii. Res bene gesta est. A. d. XVI. K. Mai. ex castris.

130. D. BRUTUS TO M. CICERO (AD FAM. XI. 9).

REGIUM LEPIDI, APRIL 29, 43 B.C. (711 A.U.C.)

1. Pansa is a great loss, and I hope you will exert yourself, as I shall, to avert evil consequences. By all means write to Lepidus; 2. I have little confidence in him, but I hope Plancus will be loyal. If Antony crosses the Alps I shall secure the passes, and write to you again.

D. BRUTUS S. D. M. CICERONI.

Pansa amisso quantum detrimenti res publica acceperit, non te 1
praeterit: nunc auctoritate et prudentia tua prospicias oportet, ne inimici nostri consulibus sublatis sperent se convalescere posse. Ego, ne consistere possit in Italia Antonius, dabo operam; sequar eum confestim: utrumque me praestaturum spero, ne aut Venti-

Two legions—the fourth, one of the two which revolted from Antony (cp. Intr. to Part V, § 9), and the seventh, composed of veterans recalled to arms, Philipp. 14. 10, 27.

1. Delevit fugavitque. The first word perhaps refers to the infantry, the second to the cavalry. Que here = 'or,' see instances in Forcell. Pullio had received an account similar to that here given. Cp. Ad Fam. 10. 33. 4. Appian does not describe Antony's loss as having been so great, and says that his cavalry recovered many of the wounded from the marshes where they lay (Bell. Civ. 3. 70).

Eodem loco. Wesenb. has 'eodem die eodemque loco.'

Ubi erat pugnatum, 'where the battle previously mentioned had taken place.'

3. Hora noctis quarta. About 10 or 11 P.M. according to our reckoning. Cp. Ep. 101, 2, note.

4. In ea castra: cp. § 3, note. Pansa's quaestor, Torquatus had fortified it during the first engagement.

5. Partem maiorem. But the fifth legion and some of the 'evocati' had not been engaged. Cp. § 1 with Ad Fam. 10. 33. 4.

7. Sine aliqua iactura. Galba seems to underrate the loss on his own side. Cp. Ad Fam. l. c.; App. l. c.

8. Aquilae duae. The eagles of the second and thirty-fifth legions. C. Marius first gave the eagle to the legion collectively as a standard. Cp. Pliny, H. N. 10. 4. 5; Smith's Dict. of Antiq. p. 1044.

Signa LX. 'Signum' seems properly to mean the standard of a cohort, but may be used here for the 'vexilla' of the centuries. Cp. Smith's Dict. pp. 1044-46.

10. Pansa amisso. Pansa died at Bononia on April 28, the day after the battle of Mutina. Merivale 3. 147; Drumann 1. 310. Cp. Ep. 145. 2.

14. Ventidius. P. Ventidius Bassus was taken prisoner in the Marsic or Italian war, and followed a very humble calling for

dius elabatur aut Antonius in Italia moretur. In primis rogo te, ad hominem ventosissimum, Lepidum, mittas, ne bellum nobis redintegrare possit Antonio sibi coniuncto: nam de Pollione Asinio puto te perspicere, quid facturus sit. Multae et bonae et firmae sunt legiones Lepidi et Asinii. Neque haec idcirco tibi scribo, quo te non eadem animadvertere sciam, sed quod mihi persuasissimum est Lepidum recte facturum numquam, si forte vobis id de hoc dubium est. Plancum quoque confirmetis oro, quem spero pulso Antonio rei publicae non defuturum. Si se Alpes Antonius traiecerit, constitui praesidium in Alpibus conlocare et te de omni re facere certiorem. III. Kal. Maias, ex castris Regii.

187. D. BRUTUS TO CICERO (AD FAM. XI. 10).

DERTONA, MAY 5, 43 B.C. (711 A.U.C.)

1. I thank you much for your fair judgment of my conduct. 2. You know as well as I do what confusion the consuls' death has caused, and what hopes it has encouraged. 3. Antony has enlisted slaves and other recruits, and has joined Ventidius at Vada. He has thus a large force with him. 4. Had Caesar been willing to listen to me, we should have reduced Antony to extremity; but Caesar will not obey me, nor his army him. 5. I find it almost impossible to provide for my army, which now numbers seven legions; I have spent my private fortune, and incurred heavy debts in the service of the State.

some time. Cp. Ad Fam. 10. 18, 3. He served Caesar in the civil wars, and was now leading three legions—raised apparently in Picenum—to the support of Antony, whom he joined near Vada Sabatia (now Vado, near Savona). Cp. Ad Fam. 10. 33, 4; 11. 10, 3; App. Bell. Civ. 3. 72.

2. Ventosissimum, 'most fickle.' Forcell. gives 'inconstans' as a synonym.

Mittas, 'send him a message.'

Ne . . possit. This expresses result, not direct purpose. D. Brutus probably wished Cicero to threaten Lepidus with outlawry, for the next clause shews that Brutus had little confidence in Lepidus.

4. Quid facturus sit. This is obscure, but as Pollio is coupled with Lepidus, and distinguished from Plancus, I think Brutus hints distrust of him. Cp. Vell. 2. 63 'Pollio . . Iulianis partibus fidus.' But Manutius merely remarks on the words 'te perspicere' that Cicero was a friend of Pollio.

Multae, foll. Lepidus had seven legions, cp. App. Bell. Civ. 3. 84; Pollio three, cp. Ad Fam. 10. 32, 4. But his were entirely composed of veterans, apparently.

6. Quo . . sciam . . quod . . est. On the different force of the indic. and conj., cp. Epp. 14. 1; 28, 7, notes.

8. Id de hoc dubium est. Rather a harsh construction, as Süpfle remarks, and more in the style of D. Brutus than in that of Cicero.

9. Se Alpes . . traiecerit. This double accusative is rare. Cp., however, Ep. 148. 4 'Isaram se traiecerint.'

12. Regii. 'Regium Lepidi' was on the Aemilian road, about half way between Mutina and Parma. Perhaps it was founded by the Lepidus who made the Aemilian road, on whom cp. p. 583, note on l. 14. The town is now called Reggio.

Dertona, now Tortona, stood on the north side of the Apennines, about 51 miles from Placentia, and between that place and Genua. It was about 10 miles south of the Padus.

D. BRUTUS S. D. M. CICERONI.

Non mihi rem publicam plus debere arbitror quam me tibi. 1
Gratiorem me esse in te posse, quam isti perversi sint in me,
exploratum habes; si tamen haec temporis videantur dici causa,
malle me tuum iudicium quam ex altera parte omnium istorum:
tu enim a certo sensu et vero iudicas de nobis; quod isti ne
faciant, summa malevolentia et livore impediuntur. Interpellent
me, quo minus honoratus sim, dum ne interpellent, quo minus
res publica a me commode administrari possit; quae quanto sit
in periculo, quam potero brevissime exponam. Primum omnium, 2
quantam perturbationem rerum urbanarum adferat obitus consulum
quantamque cupiditatem hominibus iniiciat vacuitas, non te fugit:
satis me multa scripsisse, quae litteris commendari possint, arbitror;
scio enim, cui scribam. Revertor nunc ad Antonium, qui 3
ex fuga cum parvulam manum peditum haberet inermium, ergastula
solvendo omneque genus hominum adripiendo satis magnum
numerum videtur effecisse; huc accessit manus Ventidii, quae
trans Appenninum itinere facto difficillimo ad Vada pervenit
atque ibi se cum Antonio coniunxit. Est numerus veteranorum
et armatorum satis frequens cum Ventidio. Consilia Antonii 4
haec sint necesse est: aut ad Lepidum ut se conferat, si recipitur;
aut Appennino Alpibusque se teneat et decursionibus per

2. **Isti perversi.** Apparently men jealous of D. Brutus. Cicero speaks of 'obtrectatores' Ad Fam. 11. 14. 1. 'Isti' 'those referred to in your letter.' Hence sint is used, not 'sunt.' Cp. Ep. 3. 3. note.

3. **Si tamen haec,** foll. This passage is obscure, and possibly corrupt. The sense seems to require 'If they speak as time-servers, and are not therefore so hostile to me as their language would seem to imply, still I value your judgment more than that of all of them.' Wieland despairs of the text, and gives for the general sense 'whatever they may say now.'

5. **A certo sensu et vero,** 'with decided and honest feelings,' 'certus dicitur qui constans.' Forcell.

6. **Livore** = 'invidia,' 'by envy.' Forcell. **Interpellent** = 'impediant.' Forcell. Cp. Ep. 114, 7.

11. **Hominibus.** D. Brutus refers, probably to the arrogant pretensions of Octavius Cp. Intr. to Part V, § 18.

Vacuitas, 'the vacancy of both consular places,' 'interregnum.' Billerb., Forcell. The word is used here only apparently in this sense.

12. **Satis . . multa . . quae . . possint,** 'as much as can be safely entrusted to a letter.' The construction is rather condensed and confused, but the sense is clear. Cp. Madv. 363; 364 and Obs.

14. **Ex fuga,** 'after his rout.'

Ergastula solvendo, 'by breaking open the workhouses where slaves were detained,' or 'by releasing the slaves so detained.' 'Ergastulum' means both the prison and its occupants. Forcell.

17. **Vada,** sc. Sabatia, now Vado, near Savona.

19. **Et armatorum,** 'and of *other* armed men,' apparently.

20. **Si recipitur,** 'If Lepidus is willing to receive him.' Cp., on the tense, Ep. 38, 9, note.

21. **Appennino Alpibusque.** It would be more usual to insert a preposition before

equites, quos habet multos, vastet ea loca, in quae incurrerit: aut rursus se in Etruriam referat, quod ea pars Italiae sine exercitu est. Quod si me Caesar audisset atque Appenninum transisset in tantas angustias Antonium compulissem, ut inopia potius quam ferro conficeretur. Sed neque Caesari imperari potest nec Caesar exercitui suo; quod utrumque pessimum est. Cum haec talia sint, quo minus, quod ad me pertinebit, homines interpellent ut supra scripsi, non impedio; haec quem ad modum explicari
5 possint aut, a te cum explicabuntur, ne impediantur timeo. Alere iam milites non possum. Cum ad rem publicam liberandam accessi, HS. mihi fuit pecuniae · CCCC · amplius. Tantum abest, ut meae rei familiaris liberum sit quicquam, ut omnes iam meos amicos aere alieno obstrinxerim. Septem numerum nunc legionum alo; qua difficultate, tu arbitrare: non, si Varronis thesauros haberem, subsistere sumptui possem. Cum primum de Antonio exploratum habuero, faciam te certiorem. Tu me amabis ita, si hoc idem me in te facere senseris. III. Non. Mai. ex castris, Dertona.

these words. Ancient geographers seem to have placed the junction of the Alps and Apennines at various places—Strabo (4. 6, 1,) at Genoa. Cp. Ep. 145, 2; Smith's Dict. of Geogr. 1, p. 154.

Decursionibus, 'by descents,' = καταδρομαῖς. Forcell.

1. Rursus. It does not appear that Antony had marched through Etruria, but the movement described would be on the whole a retrograde one.

3. Atque . . transisset. So as to anticipate and cut off Antony when he also tried to cross the mountains.

5. Conficeretur = 'deleretur,' 'should be destroyed.' Forcell.

Nec Caesar, sc. 'imperare potest.'

7. Quod ad me pertinebit, 'what shall concern my distinction.' Cp. § 1.

8. Supra. Cp. § 1 of this letter.

Haec, 'my present difficulties.'

9. A te cum explicabuntur, 'when you try to settle them.'

11. HS. . . ·CCCC·. 400,000 sestertii—the sum at which the 'census equester' was fixed—seems a small sum for D. Brutus, an eminent member of a victorious party, to have possessed at the death of Caesar; and I therefore now think that HS. ·CCCC· must be understood as = 'quadringenties,' or 40,000,000 sestertii. Wiel. renders it '400,000 sesterces in ready money.'

12. Liberum, 'unencumbered.'

13. Aere . . obstrinxerim. 'Aer. al. obstringere' = 'facere ut aliquis pecuniam mutuam sumat eaque creditori obliget,' Forcell. According to Dion Cassius (46. 40), L. Pontius Aquila had furnished him with large sums.

Septem, a genitive.

Numerum, 'a force,' 'a number.'

14. Arbitrare, 'form an opinion,' 'just consider.'

Varronis. The wealth of Varro does not seem to have been proverbial; hence some have supposed the reference to be to the wealth described in some of Varro's works.

15. Subsistere, 'to support.' Forcell.

De Antonio, 'about Antony's movements.'

16. Tu me amabis . . senseris, 'love me *only* if you shall be persuaded of my affection *for* you.' On the force of 'amabis,' cp. Ep. 11, 3, note; and of 'ita si' = 'only if,' Ep. 44, 5, note.

138. C. CASSIUS TO CICERO (AD FAM. XII. 12).

CAMP IN SYRIA, MAY 7, 43 B.C. (711 A.U.C.)

1. If you and the senate have not received letters from me, perhaps Dolabella has intercepted my messengers. 2. I have under my orders all the forces which were in Syria, and four legions which A. Allienus has brought from Egypt. I am now ready for action, and recommend my own dignity 3. and my soldiers' interests to your consideration. I also recommend to your attention the conduct of Murcus and Crispus. Bassus, on the other hand, would have resisted me, but that his soldiers compelled him to submit. 4. This army is devoted to the senate, and especially to you, owing to what I say of your good will towards it. 5. I have just heard that Dolabella has entered Syria, and shall march to meet him there.

CASSIUS PROCOS. S. D. M. CICERONI SUO.

S. v. b. e. e. q. v. Legi tuas litteras, in quibus mirificum tuum 1
erga me amorem recognovi; videbaris enim non solum favere nobis—id quod et nostra et rei publicae causa semper fecisti—, sed etiam gravem curam suscepisse vehementerque esse de nobis sollicitus. Itaque, quod te primum existimare putabam, nos oppressa re publica quiescere non posse, deinde, cum suspicarere nos moliri, quod te sollicitum esse et de salute nostra et de rerum eventu putabam, simul ac legiones accepi, quas A. Allienus eduxerat ex Aegypto, scripsi ad te tabellariosque complures Romam misi; scripsi etiam ad senatum litteras, quas reddi vetui prius, quam tibi recitatae essent, si forte mei obtemperare mihi voluerunt. Quod si litterae perlatae non sunt, non dubito quin Dola-

C. CASSIUS. On the proceedings of Cassius in Syria, cp. Intr. to Part V, §§ 11; 14; 20; Appendix 11. 10.

1. S. v. b. e.; cp. pp. 33; 131.

E. q. v. = 'ego quidem [or 'quoque' Tyrr. p. lvii] valeo.'

5. Quod te primum, foll., 'first, because I supposed you would think.' The position of 'primum' is strange.

6. Deinde . . putabam. The sense would be clearer if the words ran 'deinde quod putabam te, cum suspicarere . . sollicitum esse.'

Nos moliri, 'that we were attempting somewhat.' For the absol. use of 'moliri,' cp. Ad Fam. 6. 10, 2 'agam per me ipse et moliar.'

8. Quas A. Allienus eduxerat. They were four in number, composed, according to one account, of men who had belonged to the armies of Pompey and Crassus; according to another, of men left by Caesar to protect Cleopatra. Cp. App. Bell. Civ. 3. 78, and 4. 59.

9. Scripsi. Cp. Ad Fam. 12, 11. Man.

10. Reddi, sc. 'ad senatum.' They would probably be sent in the first instance to the relations of Cassius at Rome.

11. Mei, 'my household.' Ern. (ap. Billerb.), Wiel. The former remarks that the connections of Cassius may have been on bad terms with Cicero. His mother, Servilia his mother-in-law, and his brother disputed the wisdom of some of Cicero's measures (cp. Ad Fam. 12. 7, 1), and Cassius and Lepidus had married sisters (cp. Ep. 147, 1, note).

bella, qui nefarie Trebonio occiso Asiam occupavit, tabellarios
2 meos deprehenderit litterasque interceperit. Exercitus omnes, qui in Syria fuerunt, teneo; habui paullulum morae, dum promissa militibus persolvo. Nunc iam sum expeditus. A te peto, ut dignitatem meam commendatam tibi habeas, si me intellegis nullum neque periculum neque laborem patriae denegasse, si contra importunissimos latrones arma cepi te hortante et auctore, si non solum exercitus ad rem publicam libertatemque defendendam comparavi, sed etiam crudelissimis tyrannis eripui, quos si occupasset Dolabella, non solum adventu, sed etiam opinione et expectatione exercitus sui Antonium confirmasset.
3 Quas ob res milites tuere, si eos mirifice de re publica meritos esse animadvertis, et effice, ne quem paeniteat rem publicam quam spem praedae et rapinarum sequi maluisse. Item Murci et Crispi imperatorum dignitatem, quantum est in te, tuere: nam Bassus misere noluit mihi legionem tradere; quod nisi milites invito eo legatos ad me misissent, clausam Apameam tenuisset, quoad vi esset expugnata. Haec a te peto non solum rei publicae, quae tibi semper fuit carissima, sed etiam amicitiae
4 nostrae nomine, quam confido apud te plurimum posse. Crede mihi hunc exercitum, quem habeo, senatus atque optimi cuiusque esse maximeque tuum, de cuius voluntate adsidue audiendo mirifice te diligit carumque habet: qui si intellexerit commoda sua curae tibi esse, debere etiam se tibi omnia putabit.

1. Trebonio occiso. The death of Trebonius seems to have taken place in February; it was known at Rome by about the middle of March. Cp. Philipp. 11. 1, foll., with App. Bell. Civ. 3. 26 and 61; also Intr. to Part V, § 14; Abeken 450; Merivale 3. 135, 136.

2. Exercitus omnes. Those of Q. Caecilius Bassus, L. Statius Murcus, Q. Marcius Crispus, and A. Allienus. Cp. § 3; Philipp. 11. 12, 30; 11. 13, 32.

5. Dignitatem, 'Cupere se ostendit Syriae administrationem.' Manut.

6. Nullum neque . . neque: cp. Ep. 8, 8, note, on this combination of negatives.

9. Crudelissimis tyrannis: i.e. from Antony and Dolabella.

10. Quos, sc. 'exercitus.'

11. Opinione, 'by the opinion people would form of it.'

14. Murci. L. Statius Murcus is mentioned Ep. 85, 1; Philipp. 11. 12, 30.

15. Crispi. Q. Marcius Crispus is mentioned by Cicero, Philipp. 11. 12, 30 as holding a command in the East. Murcus certainly, and Crispus perhaps, had served under Caesar in the civil war. Cp. Caes. Bell. Civ. 3. 15; Bell. Afric. 77.

16. Nam Bassus, 'I say nothing of Bassus, for.' Cp. Ep. 26, 2, note. On Bassus, cp. pp. 403, 481.

Misere = 'nullo consilio et suo malo,' 'foolishly.' Forcell. 'Turpiter et infeliciter.' Manut.

Quod nisi, 'and unless.' On this sense of 'quod,' cp. Ep. 76, 1 note.

17. Apameam. This Apamea stood near the Orontes, about 60 miles S.E. of Antioch, and is of course to be distinguished from one mentioned Ep. 32, 2.

20. Nomine: cp. Ep. 38, 3, note, p. 259.

Crede mihi . . esse: cp. Ep. 58, 1.

22. Audiendo, 'from hearing of it,' i.e. in my speeches. On this use of the gerund, cp. Madv. 416.

23. Qui si intellexerit . . putabit,

Litteris scriptis audivi Dolabellam in Ciliciam venisse cum 8
suis copiis: proficiscar in Ciliciam. Quid egerim, celeriter ut sciam, dabo operam; ac velim, ut meremur de re publica, sic felices simus. Fac valeas meque ames. Nonis Maiis ex castris.

130. PLANCUS TO CICERO (AD FAM. X. 11).

COUNTRY OF THE ALLOBROGES, MAY 10, (?) 43 B.C. (711 A.U.C.)

1. I can never requite your support, but pray continue it. 2. When I heard on my march towards Mutina of Antony's defeat, I halted to watch events. If Antony comes alone, I can deal with him, even if Lepidus support him; if he brings any forces with him I will still do my best, and shall have good hopes if any aid be sent me from Italy. 3. I will exert myself to the utmost in our country's cause, and will try to secure Lepidus, in negotiating with whom I employ my brother, Furnius, and Laterensis.

PLANCUS CICERONI.

Immortales ago tibi gratias agamque dum vivam; nam relatu- 1
rum me adfirmare non possum: tantis enim tuis officiis non videor mihi respondere posse, nisi forte, ut tu gravissime disertissimeque scripsisti, ita sensurus es, ut me referre gratiam putes, cum memoria tenebo. Si de filii tui dignitate esset actum, amabilius

'If a mere statement of your good will has had such an effect, a persuasion that you have its interests at heart will make it think it owes you everything.'

1. **Litteris scriptis.** Here a postscript begins.

In Ciliciam: cp. Dion Cassius 47. 30. Tarsus supported Dolabella.

Cum suis copiis. Two legions, according to App. Bell. Civ. 3. 78.

2. **Proficiscar.** Cassius met Dolabella apparently somewhere between Aradus and Laodicea, and drove him into the latter place, which was a coast town about 60 miles S.W. of Antioch, and 90 miles N.W. of Aradus. Cp. Intr. to Part V, § 20.

Quid egerim, 'what I shall have done.'

4. **Ex castris.** This camp was probably somewhere in the valley of the Orontes. His previous letter had been dated March 7, Tarichese, which was at the south end of the sea of Tiberias.

The Allobroges lived mainly between the Rhone, the Isère, and the high Alps of Savoy. A line drawn from Geneva to Valence would traverse nearly all their territory.

MAY 10. This is the date given by Baiter and by Wesenberg. But Andresen, following Nake, has given reasons for thinking that the letter was written somewhat earlier. All that can be said is, firstly, that Plancus can hardly have heard before May 3 of the relief of Mutina, which happened towards the close of April and is mentioned in § 2 of this letter; secondly, that there is no mention in this letter of the bridge thrown over the Isara by Plancus on or about May 8. Cp. Ep. 140, 1, note.

5. **Relaturum,** 'to repay,' 'requite.' 'Agere gratias' is used of expressions of gratitude; 'referre gratiam' of a practical return. Forcell.

7. **Respondere.** Cp. Ep. 3. 2, note.

8. **Scripsisti.** In a letter now lost, apparently. But Andr. thinks that the reference need not be to a letter, and suggests that Plancus had in his mind pro Planc. 28. 68, where a similar thought occurs.

Cum . . tenebo, 'by keeping in remembrance.' 'Cum' = 'quod,' cp. Ep. 83. 6, note, and Forcell.

certe nihil facere potuisses. Primae tuae sententiae infinitis cum muneribus, posteriores ad tempus arbitriumque amicorum meorum compositae, oratio adsidua et perpetua de me, iurgia cum obtrectatoribus propter me notissima mihi sunt; non mediocris adhibenda mihi est cura, ut rei publicae me civem dignum tuis laudibus praestem, in amicitia tui memorem atque gratum. Quod reliquum est, tuum munus tuere et me, si, quem esse voluisti, eum
2 exitu rebusque cognoscis, defende ac suscipe. Cum Rhodanum copias traiecissem fratremque cum tribus milibus equitum praemisissem, ipse iter ad Mutinam dirigerem, in itinere de proelio facto Brutoque et Mutina obsidione liberatis audivi: animadverti nullum alium receptum Antonium reliquiasque, quae cum eo essent, habere nisi in his partibus, duasque ei spes esse propositas, unam Lepidi ipsius, alteram exercitus. Quod quaedam pars exercitus non minus furiosa est quam qui cum Antonio fuerunt, equitatum revocavi; ipse in Allobrogibus constiti, ut proinde ad omnia paratus essem ac res me moneret. Si nudus huc se Antonius confert, facile mihi videor per me sustinere posse remque publicam ex vestra sententia administrare, quamvis ab exercitu Lepidi recipiatur; si vero copiarum aliquid secum adducet et si decima legio veterana, quae nostra opera revocata cum reliquis

1. Primae tuae sententiae, foll., 'your first expressions of opinion in the senate proposed unlimited honours for me.' Cp. Ad Fam. 10. 12, 3. The words 'primae' and 'posteriores' perhaps refer respectively to the two days of debate in the senate mentioned in Cicero's letter Ad Fam. 10. 12, 3 and 4.

2. Ad tempus . . meorum. 'according to the demands of the time and the will of my friends.' Forcell. gives 'e re nata' as one equivalent of 'ad tempus.'

3. Iurgia cum obtrectatoribus, especially with P. Servilius. Cp. Ad Fam. 10. 12, 3 and 4.

7. Tuum munus. Either 'your favourite,' Wiel., or 'quae in me tuendo atque ornando partes suscepisti.'

8. Exitu rebusque. 'In the actual event.'

Suscipe = 'tuere,' 'defende.'

Rhodanum. Plancus crossed the Rhone, probably somewhere near Vienna (Vienne), on April 26, and was preparing to march into Italy by the Cottian Alps—Mont Genèvre—when he heard of the relief of Mutina. Then he encamped near the Isara (Isère), which he bridged on May 11 or 12. Cp. Ep. 140. 3; Ad Fam. 10. 9. 3.

9. Fratremque, i.e. Cn. Munatius Plancus. Cp. Ep. 130, 1.

13. In his partibus. Wesenb. has 'in has partes.' Andr. thinks that the ablative may stand, as 'receptum' in l. 2, may mean 'a possibility of retreat.'

14. Exercitus eius, sc. Lepidi. The gen. is objective. Cp. Ep. 16. 3, note.

Quaedam pars exercitus, 'a certain part of the army of Lepidus.'

15. Fuerunt. The perfect is used as implying that Antony had lost his army. Andr.

16. Proinde . . ac, 'just as.' Cp. Ep. 114, 2, note; and 'proinde quasi' Pro Quinct. 14. 45.

17. Nudus, 'without reinforcements,' which, in fact, Antony had received from Ventidius. Cp. Appendix 11. 11.

18. Sustinere, 'to resist him,' 'to hold out.' Cp. Ep. 134. 2; Caes. Bell. Gall. 2. 6.

21. Decima legio. This legion, as Drumann (1. 391) and Süpfle remark, had taken the lead both in battle and mutiny under Caesar. Cp. Bell. Gall. 1. 40 and 41, with Suet. Iul. 70. It now seems to have

est, ad eundem furorem redierit, tamen, ne quid detrimenti fiat
dabitur opera a me, idque me praestaturum spero, dum istinc
copiae traiciantur coniunctaeque nobiscum facilius perditos oppri-
mant. Hoc tibi spondeo, mi Cicero, neque animum nec diligen- 1
tiam mihi defuturam. Cupio mehercules nullam residuam sollicitudinem esse; sed si fuerit, nec animo nec benevolentiae nec patientiae cuiusquam pro vobis cedam. Do quidem ego operam, ut etiam Lepidum ad huius rei societatem incitem, omniaque ei obsequia polliceor, si modo rem publicam respicere volet. Utor in hac re adiutoribus interpretibusque fratre meo et Laterense et Furnio nostro. Non me impedient privatae offensiones, quo minus pro rei publicae salute etiam cum inimicissimo consentiam. Quod si nihil profecero, nihilo minus maximo sum animo et maiore fortasse cum mea gloria vobis satis faciam. Fac valeas meque mutuo diligas.

140. PLANCUS TO CICERO (AD FAM. X. 15).

NEAR THE ISARA, MAY, 12 (?), 43 B.C. (711 A.U.C.)

1. I hope that I have secured Lepidus for the good cause; 2. he has given his word, by Laterensis, that he will oppose Antony, and I am on my march to join him My army, 3. and especially my cavalry, will be most welcome. I have bridged the Isara, and sent my brother with cavalry to oppose L. Antonius. I shall follow myself with the rest of my army. 4. With moderately good fortune we shall succeed.

PLANCUS CICERONI.

His litteris scriptis quae postea accidissent scire te ad rem 1

belonged to the army of Lepidus. Cp. App. Bell. Civ. 3. 83; Drumann, l. c. Plancus does not hint at any disaffection in his own army, otherwise we might suppose the Tenth belonged to him.

Revocata, 'recalled to its duty.'

2. Istinc, 'from Italy.'

5 Defuturam, Fem. as agreeing with the nearest subst. Cp. Ep. 29. 7, note; Madv. 214 a.

6. Nec animo . . cedam. 'Benevolentia' and 'cuiquam' would be more in accordance with usage. But cp. Tac. Hist. 4. 2 'Lucius Vitellius . . par vitiis fratris.' Andr.

8. Huius rei, 'of this enterprise,' the liberation of the Commonwealth.

Omniaque . . polliceor, 'I promise to consult his wishes in everything.' The plural 'obsequia' seems to be rare.

10. Laterense: cp. Ep. 11. 2, note.

11. Furnio: cp. Ep. 60, note.

12. Inimicissimo, Lepido. Manut. Cp. Epp. 140, 1; 146, 1.

13. Sum. Plancus means 'I am in good spirits even with the possibility of failure before me.' Andr.

14. Maiore fortasse . . gloria, 'perhaps with all the more distinction to myself.' Wiel. He would gain more reputation by a victory over Antony and Lepidus, than by effecting a peaceful settlement.

16. His litteris scriptis, 'after the accompanying letter had been written.' The present one seems to have been sent by the same bearer as Ep. 139.

publicam putavi pertinere: sedulitas mea, ut spero, et mihi et rei publicae tulit fructum. Namque adsiduis internuntiis cum Lepido egi, ut omissa omni contentione reconciliataque voluntate nostra communi consilio rei publicae succurreret, se, liberos urbemque pluris quam unum perditum abiectumque latronem putaret
2 obsequioque meo, si ita faceret, ad omnes res abuteretur. Profeci: itaque per Laterensem internuntium fidem mihi dedit se Antonium, si prohibere provincia sua non potuisset, bello persecuturum, me ut venirem copiasque coniungerem rogavit, eoque magis, quod et Antonius ab equitatu firmus esse dicebatur et Lepidus ne mediocrem quidem equitatum habebat; nam etiam ex paucitate eius non multis ante diebus decem, qui optimi fuerant, ad me transierunt. Quibus rebus ego cognitis cunctatus non sum; in cursu bonorum
3 consiliorum Lepidum adiuvandum putavi. Adventus meus quid profecturus esset, vidi; vel quod equitatu meo persequi *Antonium* atque opprimere equitatum eius possem, vel quod exercitus Lepidi eam partem, quae corrupta est et ab re publica alienata, et corrigere et coërcere praesentia mei exercitus posset. Itaque in Isara, flumine maximo, quod in finibus est Allobrogum, ponte uno die facto exercitum a. d. IIII. Idus Maias traduxi. Cum vero mihi

2. Namque . . abuteretur. These words explain 'sedulitas.'

Adsiduis internuntiis. On this use of the ablat. instrum., cp. Ep. 101, 3, note.

Cum Lepido egi. Cp. Ep. 139, 3.

6. Abuteretur: abuti = 'large et plene uti,' 'use to the utmost.' Forcell. Cp. Ad Fam. 9. 6, 5.

Profeci, 'I succeeded.' Forcell. gives instances of a similar sense from Caesar, e.g. Bell. Civ. 3. 23 'adeo .. profecit.' Andr. remarks that this word is inserted to recall the attention to 'tulit fructum' in l. 2. The following words to 'rogavit' shew wherein the success of Plancus consisted.

11. Ex paucitate eius, 'from his slender force of cavalry.'

12. Transierunt. Wesenb. suggests 'transierant,' corresponding to 'habebat' and 'fuerant.'

13. In cursu bonorum consiliorum, 'in this patriotic course of policy.'

17. Eam partem. Especially the tenth legion. Cp. Ep. 139, 2.

18. Isara, now the Isère.

19. Ponte .. facto. This may perhaps have been near Cularo. A comparison of Ep. 146, § 3 with § 7 of the same letter would lead us to place Cularo on the right bank of the Isara, and Mr. Jeans thinks the place stood near the modern suburb of St. Laurent, on the right bank of the Isère, opposite Grenoble. The editor of Murray's Handbook for France (1873) says that that suburb occupies the site of the original Gaulish town of Cularo. Spruner and Mr. G. Long (Dict. of Geogr. 1. 716) both place Cularo on the *left* bank of the Isara, and certainly the Cularo of the third century A.D. appears to have occupied the same site as the modern Grenoble. Perhaps 'Cularone' in Ep. 146, 7 may refer to a camp just opposite the city and on the other bank of the Isara: or the town may originally have stood on both sides of the river, especially if it was not fortified till after the date of these letters. The map of Gaul in the Atlas of Ancient Geography by Dr. Smith and Mr. Grove supports this view. An inscription of the third century found at the modern Grenoble and speaking of the place as Cularo is published by Gruter, Inscriptiones clxxii, 1; cp. Dict. of Geography 1. 715. The Emperor Gratian renamed the place after himself, Gratianopolis, from which word the modern name Grenoble is derived. No very direct road seems to have led from the Isara to Forum Iulii,

nuntiatum esset L. Antonium praemissum cum equitibus et cohortibus ad Forum Iulii venisse, fratrem cum equitum quattuor milibus, ut occurreret ei, misi a. d. v. Idus Maias; ipse maximis itineribus cum quattuor legionibus expeditis et reliquo equitatu
subsequar. Si nos mediocris modo fortuna rei publicae adiuverit, 4
et audaciae perditorum et nostrae sollicitudinis hic finem reperiemus. Quod si latro praecognito nostro adventu rursus in Italiam se recipere coeperit, Bruti erit officium occurrere ei, cui scio nec consilium nec animum defuturum. Ego tamen, si id acciderit, fratrem cum equitatu mittam, qui sequatur, Italiam a vastatione defendat. Fac valeas meque mutuo diligas.

141. M. LEPIDUS TO CICERO (AD FAM. X. 34 (1. 2).)

PONS ARGENTEUS, MAY 22 (?), 43 B.C. (711 A.U.C.)

1. When I heard that Antony was on the march for my province, I marched to oppose him, and have encamped on the Argenteus. He is strong in cavalry and his infantry is numerous, but not all armed, and he loses many men by desertion. 2. Silanus and Culleo have left him, and I have spared them, but do not employ them. I shall do my duty to the senate and to the commonwealth in this war.

1. L. Antonium. This brother of the triumvir is often spoken of with disgust in the Philippics. Cp., especially, 3. 12, 31; 5. 3. 7; 8. 7. 20. He was consul 41 B.C., and, aided by his sister-in-law Fulvia, took a leading part in organizing opposition to Octavian in Italy. The struggle which followed was known as the 'war of Perusia,' for the siege of that place was its most important incident. Cp. Livy Epitt. 125 and 126; Vell. 2. 74; Suet. Oct. 9; 14; 15; App. Bell. Civ. 5. 19-50.

2. Forum Iulii, now Fréjus, on the coast of Provence, between Antibes and Toulon, looking S.E.

3. Misi. But Plancus' brother seems to have fallen ill soon afterwards (cp. Ad Fam. 10. 21, 7) and can hardly have moved far. Andr.

A. d. v. Idus. May 11. But the bridge seems only to have been ready for the passage of the army on the 12th. Hence Wesenb. suggests III. Id., and remarks that if v. Id. were the true date, 'miseram' should be substituted for 'misi.' Andr. would prefer to read a. d. VII. or a. d. VIII. in p. 593, l. 10. He follows Nake, who (pp. 9-13) argues (1) that Plancus must have bridged the Isara before he sent his brother with cavalry to meet L. Antonius; (2) that one of the two dates 'III. Idus' in p. 593, l. 20 or 'v. Idus' in l. 3 must be wrong; (3) that as Plancus does not say that his brother left him on the same day on which he himself crossed the Isara or on the next, it is probable that two days may have passed between the two events; (4) that 'III. Idus' is more likely to have been erroneously substituted for 'VII.' or 'VIII. Idus' than 'v. Idus' for 'pridie Idus' or 'Idibus.'

4. Quattuor. In Ep. 137, 6 Plancus speaks of five legions, but of four Ep. 148, 3.

5. Mediocris modo, 'only to a moderate extent.' The adjective is used as an adverb. Cp. Epp. 2. 2; 22. 1.

10. Sequatur .. defendat. Asyndeton. Cp. Ep. 20, 6, note. Wesenb. inserts 'ut' after 'sequatur.'

M. LEPIDUS IMP. ITER. PONT. MAX. S. D. M. TULLIO CICERONI.

1 S. v. b. e. e. v. Cum audissem Antonium cum suis copiis, praemisso L. Antonio cum parte equitatus, in provinciam meam venire, cum exercitu meo ab confluente [ab Rhodano] castra movi ac contra eos venire institui. Itaque continuis itineribus ad Forum Voconii veni et ultra castra ad flumen Argenteum contra Antonianos feci. P. Ventidius suas legiones tres coniunxit cum eo et ultra me castra posuit; habebat antea legionem quintam et ex reliquis legionibus magnam multitudinem, sed inermorum. Equitatum habet magnum: nam omnis ex proelio integer discessit, ita ut sint amplius equitum milia quinque. Ad me complures milites et equites ab eo transierunt et in dies singulos eius copiae

This letter must have been written after Antony and Ventidius had joined their forces near Forum Voconii. Now Antony reached Forum Iulii, distant 24 Roman miles from Forum Voconii, on May 15, and Ventidius was two days' march behind him. (Cp. Ad Fam. 10. 17. 1.) Allowing one day for the march from Forum Iulii to the neighbourhood of Forum Voconii, and two more for Ventidius to come up, we see that this letter cannot have been written before May 18. The date XII. Kal. Iun. is found in a fragment attached to this letter in the MSS. apparently, but detached from it by some of the latest editors, following Victorius.

On M. LEPIDUS, cp. Ep. 62, 3, note; Intr. to Part V, §§ 1; 11; 17; 22.

IMP. ITER. Lepidus assumed the title of imperator once, for alleged achievements in Spain 48-47 B.C.; and again for his successful negotiations with Sex. Pompeius. Cp. Intr. to Part III, § 13; to Part V, § 11; Philipp. 13. 4. 7, with Mr. King's note; Bell. Alex. 59; 63; 64; Drumann 1. 13.

PONT. MAX. Lepidus had received this office in the previous year through Antony's influence, but the appointment seems to have been somewhat irregular. Cp. Livy Epit. 117; Vell. 2. 63; Dion Cassius 44. 53; Epp. 122, 8, note.

Pons Argenteus was apparently a little N.E. of Forum Voconii (Le Canet), on the road from Aquae Sextiae (Aix) to Forum Iulii (Fréjus). The Argenteus, or Argents, enters the sea a little W. of Forum Iulii. Cp. Spruner's map of Gaul, and Smith, Dict. of Geogr. 1. 198, sub voc. 'Argenteus.'

1. S. v. b. e. e. v.: cp. p. 181, note.

3. Ab confluente. Wiel. and Billerb. both explain this of the confluence of the Rhone and Durance, near Avignon. Wesenb. suspects that the true text may be 'ab confluente Rhodani et Druentiae.'

4. Ad Forum Voconii: cp. introductory remarks.

5. Ultra, 'beyond that place,' i.e. between it and Forum Iulii. Wesenb. suspects the word here.

6. Suas legiones tres. The seventh, eighth, and ninth. Cp. Ad Fam. 10. 33. 4.

Cum eo, sc. Antonio.

7. Ultra me, 'between me and Rome,' 'further from my starting point.'

Habebat antea, Antonius.

Legionem quintam. Probably composed of the Alaudae who were devoted to Antony. Cp. Philipp. 1. 8, 20. The statement in the next lines that Antony had many soldiers from his other legions with him seems to shew that his loss at Forum Gallorum had been exaggerated by Galba. Cp. Ep. 135. 4-6.

8. Ex reliquis legionibus. The veteran second and thirty-fifth, and three of recruits, strengthened probably by an admixture of 'evocati.' Antony, in a letter quoted Philipp. 8. 8, 25, spoke of having six legions. One of the mixed legions seems to have been organized by L. Antonius. Cp. Philipp. 3. 12, 31.

11. Milites et equites. 'Miles' was used especially of the regular infantry. Cp. Livy 22. 37, where Hiero writes to the Roman senate, 'milite atque equite scire nisi Romano Latinique nominis non uti populum Romanum.'

minuuntur; Silanus et Culleo ab eo discesserunt. Nos etsi gravi- 8
ter ab iis laesi eramus, quod contra nostram voluntatem ad Antonium ierant, tamen nostrae humanitatis et necessitudinis causa eorum salutis rationem habuimus; nec tamen eorum opera utimur neque in castris habemus neque ulli negotio praefecimus. Quod ad bellum hoc attinet, nec senatui nec rei publicae deerimus. Quae postea egerimus, faciam te certiorem.

142. To PLANCUS (AD FAM. X. 13).

ROME, MAY, 43 B.C. (711 A.U.C.)

1. The senate's decree will shew how anxious I have been to secure your services a proper recognition. 2. I hope you will go on as you have begun. Whoever overpowers Antony will be the real finisher of the war.

CICERO PLANCO.

Ut primum potestas data est augendae dignitatis tuae, nihil 1
praetermisi in te ornando, quod positum esset aut in praemio virtutis aut in honore verborum: id ex ipso senatus consulto poteris cognoscere; ita enim est perscriptum, ut a me de scripto dicta sententia est, quam senatus frequens secutus est summo studio magnoque consensu. Ego quamquam ex tuis litteris, quas mihi 2
misisti, perspexeram te magis iudicio bonorum quam insignibus gloriae delectari, tamen considerandum nobis existimavi, etiamsi tu nihil postulares, quantum tibi a re publica deberetur. Tu con-

1. Silanus: cp. Ep. 135. 1, note.
Culleo (Q. Terentius) had been posted on the Alps by Lepidus, nominally to prevent Antony from leaving Italy, but probably with secret orders to grant him a passage. He and Silanus both probably acted as go-betweens for Antony and Lepidus (cp. App. Bell. Civ. 3. 83). Culleo has been mentioned Ep. 16, 5.

4. Eorum salutis rationem habuimus, 'I spared their lives.'

8. Augendae dignitatis. It is not clear to what these words refer. Probably some decree in honour of Plancus had recently passed. M. Cornutus, praetor urbanus, and P. Servilius seem to have opposed any distinct recognition of his services (cp. Ad Fam. 10. 12, 3 and 4; 10. 16, 1), and Cicero had to exhort him to consider virtue its own reward. Plancus seems to have wished for a place on the commission of ten already referred to (Intr. to Part V, § 18: Ad Fam. 10. 22, 2).

9. In praemio . . verborum, 'in substantial rewards for merit, or in honourable expressions.'

11. De scripto. On some occasions senators wrote out beforehand the proposal they intended to make in the senate. Cp. Philipp. 1. 1, 3; 3. 8, 20; 10. 2, 5.

13. Tuis litteris. Probably Cicero refers to Ad Fam. 10. 9; cp. Nake, pp. 31-32.

16. Contexes. On the mood, cp. Ep. 11, 3, note. 'Let the end of your work be worthy of its beginning'—'efficies ut extrema eandem cum primis formam, speciem referant.' Forcell.

texes extrema cum primis: qui enim M. Antonium oppresserit, is bellum confecerit; itaque Homerus non Aiacem nec Achillem, sed Ulixem appellavit πτολιπόρθιον.

143. D. BRUTUS TO CICERO (AD FAM. XI. 23).

EPOREDIA, MAY 25, 43 B.C. (711 A.U.C.)

1. We are getting on very well. Lepidus seems to be well disposed; three such armies ought to give you confidence. 2. What I reported to you before must have been an invention intended to frighten you. I shall stay in Italy till I hear from you.

D. BRUTUS S. D. M. CICERONI.

1 Nos hic valemus recte et, quo melius valeamus, operam dabimus. Lepidus commode nobis sentire videtur. Omni timore deposito debemus libere rei publicae consulere. Quod si omnia essent aliena, tamen tribus tantis exercitibus, propriis rei publicae, valentibus, magnum animum habere debebas, quem et semper

2 habuisti et nunc fortuna adiuvante augere potes. Quae tibi superioribus litteris mea manu scripsi, terrendi tui causa homines loquuntur: si frenum momorderis, peream, si te omnes, quot sunt, conantem loqui ferre poterunt. Ego, tibi ut antea scripsi, dum mihi a te litterae veniant, in Italia morabor. VIII. K. Iunias Eporedia.

1. Itaque = 'as the last service done seems most important.'

3. πτολιπόρθιον. Homer applies the epithet πτολιπόρθιον to Achilles in various passages (e.g. Il. 8. 372; 15. 77); but Cicero is probably thinking of others, where the services of Ulysses are most highly praised (e.g. Odyss. 9. 504, 530; 22. 230). The point of this passage is, I think, that as Ulysses had the credit of the capture of Troy, not Ajax and Achilles, who both fell before it was taken, so would Plancus, if he gave the final blow to Antony, have rather than Hirtius or Pansa the fame of finishing the war.

I cannot, with Mr. Jeans, see any suggestion to use craft.

EPOREDIA. Its site is occupied by the modern Ivrea, on the Dora Baltea (Duria) in Piedmont.

4. Nos, 'I and my army.'

6. Omnia, 'all other forces.' The meaning must depend on that of tribus tantis exercitibus. Two of them, no doubt, were those of Decimus himself and of Plancus, the third may have been that of Octavius (Manut., Wiel., Billerb.) or of Lepidus.

8. Animum .. augere. A rare phrase, with a personal subject to the principal verb. 'Fortuna adiuvans augere potest' would be more common.

9. Quae tibi .. scripsi: cp. Ad Fam. 11. 20, 1 and 2. D. Brutus had reported to Cicero a conversation with Segulius Labeo, who had spoken of Octavius and the veterans as discontented.

11. Si frenum momorderis, 'If you champ the bit,' 'shew a high spirit.' 'Si te ferocem et recusantem ostenderis.' Forcell. 'Si eos contempseris.' Manut. Cp. Ad Fam. 11. 24. 1.

12. Conantem loqui, '[illegible] loquentem.' Manut.

13. Italia. See Ep. 145, 3, note.

14. Eporedia. On the ablative, cp. Ep. 17, 4 note, p. 111.

144. M. LEPIDUS TO THE SENATE AND PEOPLE (AD FAM. X. 35).

PONS ARGENTEUS, MAY 30, 43 B.C. (711 A.U.C.)

1. I protest that I should soon have convinced you of my devotion, but that my army mutinied and declared for peace. 2. I beseech you, therefore, to forget all private quarrels, and not to treat as a crime the merciful disposition of myself and of my army. Act as is best for the safety and dignity of all.

M. LEPIDUS IMP. ITER. PONTIFEX MAX. S. D. SENATUI POPULO PLEBIQUE ROMANAE.

S. v. liberique vestri v. b. e. e. q. v. Deos hominesque testor, 1
patres conscripti, qua mente et quo animo semper in rem publicam fuerim et quam nihil antiquius communi salute ac libertate iudicarim; quod vobis brevi probassem, nisi mihi fortuna proprium consilium extorsisset: nam exercitus cunctus consuetudinem suam in civibus conservandis communique pace, seditione facta, retinuit meque tantae multitudinis civium Romanorum salutis atque incolumitatis causam suscipere, ut vere dicam, coëgit. In qua re ego 2
vos, patres conscripti, oro atque obsecro, ut privatis offensionibus omissis summae rei publicae consulatis neve misericordiam nostram exercitusque nostri in civili dissensione sceleris loco ponatis. Quod si salutis omnium ac dignitatis rationem habueritis, melius et vobis et rei publicae consuletis. D. III. Kal. *Iun.* a Ponte Argenteo.

On the titles of Lepidus, and on the abbreviations in l. 1, cp. Ep. 141, note.

4. **Brevi probassem**, i.e. by resisting Antony.

Fortuna. Appian (Bell. Civ. 3. 83 and 84) represents that the army of Lepidus was debauched by emissaries from that of Antony. It is probable that Lepidus offered no great resistance to his soldiers, but neither Appian (l. c.) nor Velleius (2. 63) charges him with premeditated treachery. A son of Lepidus had been betrothed to Antony's daughter (Ep. 118, 2; Dion Cassius 44. 53), and Antony flattered Lepidus by promising to act under his orders (Vell. l. c.).

5. **Consuetudinem suam.** Perhaps there is here an allusion to Caesar's orders at Pharsalus 'ut civibus parceretur.' Cp. Suet. Iul. 75; Caes. Bell. Civ. 3. 98; cp. also Philipp. 8. 4, 13, where Cicero represents Calenus as saying, 'cum te esse qui . . semper . . omnes cives salvos volueris.'

6. **Communique pace**, sc. 'conservanda.'

9. **Privatis offensionibus.** Perhaps with especial reference to the quarrel between Cicero and Antony.

12. **Dignitatis.** Perhaps of Antony and himself as 'consulares.'

145. D. BRUTUS TO CICERO (AD FAM. XI. 13 a).

GRAIAN ALPS (?) MAY OR BEGINNING OF JUNE, 43 B.C. (711 A.U.C.)

1. I wish you to read this letter carefully. I could not follow Antony at once, for want of transport, and from uncertainty as to the position of affairs. 2. Next day I should have visited Pansa, but heard of his death. My forces were exhausted, and Antony, who had two days' start, marched much faster than I could, and first halted at Vada. 3. Ventidius joined him there, and I heard that his followers were eager to decide the contest in Italy. 4. I anticipated them, however, in occupying Pollentia, and the speed of my march has rather disconcerted them. Planeus and I are confident that we are a match for the enemy; 5. you may trust us, and hope for the best, but do what you can to send us reinforcements and supplies, that we may resist the guilty combination of public enemies.

D. BRUTUS IMP. COS. DESIG. S. D. M. CICERONI.

1 Iam non ago tibi gratias; cui enim re vix referre possum, huic verbis non patitur res satis fieri: attendere te volo, quae in manibus sunt; qua enim prudentia es, nihil te fugiet, si meas litteras diligenter legeris. Sequi confestim Antonium his de causis, Cicero, non potui: eram sine equitibus, sine iumentis; Hirtium perisse nesciebam; Caesari non credebam
2 prius, quam convenissem et collocutus essem. Hic dies hoc

GRAIAN ALPS. This letter as we have it seems to be compounded of two fragments written at different times and from different places. The first portion of it, from the beginning to 'cum equitibus' or perhaps to 'puto consistere' seems to be a reply to Ad Fam. 11. 13, and to have been written while D. Brutus was on the march from Pollentia to Eporedia: he wrote in good spirits from the latter place on May 25, cp. Ep. 143. With regard to the rest of the letter, it seems from the latter part of § 4 that D. Brutus was already acting in concert with Plancus, and from Ep. 146, 3, that Plancus, in his camp at Cularo, expected D. Brutus to join him on June 8 or 9. This portion of the letter, then, was probably written from a camp on the upper Isara, perhaps at or near Darentasia (Moutiers). The writer seems to refer to the treachery of Lepidus in § 5, and that seems to have been consummated late in May. Cp. Epp. 142, 144. Cp. the Journal of Philology, vol. viii. 16, pp. 169 foll.

2. Non patitur res, 'the nature of the case does not allow.' Billerb.

Attendere, sc. 'ea,' 'to observe.' Cp. Ep. 100, 3; Philipp. 2. 12, 30 "stuporem hominis . . attendite.'

Quae in manibus sunt. 'Quae' is relative, not interrogative; hence the indic. Cp. Zumpt, L. G. 553; Madv. 356, Obs. 1. Forcell. gives as an equivalent for these words, 'ea circa quae in praesentia laboramus.'

3. Qua enim prudentia es = 'pro tua prudentia' (Ep. 131, 2) or 'quae est tua prudentia,' both of which are more common. (Cp. Ep. 98, 6, note.)

4. Diligenter. D. Brutus writes in rather obscure terms and therefore invites Cicero to read attentively. Cp. § 5.

6. Nesciebam. H. adds 'Aquilam perisse nesciebam.'

7. Prius, quam convenissem. These words, which only describe a past state of mind in Decimus, do not imply that he actually met Octavius, but from Ep. 137, 4 it is perhaps probable that he did so, though Appian (Bell. Civ. 3. 73) says that Octavius refused to meet him.

Hic dies, i.e. 'the day of the battle.' Cp. Intr. to Part V, § 17.

modo abiit. Postero die mane a Pansa sum arcessitus Bononiam. Cum in itinere essem, nuntiatum mihi est eum mortuum esse. Recurri ad meas copiolas; sic enim vere eas appellare possum: sunt extenuatissimae et inopia omnium rerum
pessime acceptae. Biduo me Antonius antecessit, itinera multo
maiora fugiens quam ego sequens: ille enim iit passim, ego
ordinatim. Quacumque iit, ergastula solvit, homines adripuit,
constitit nusquam prius, quam ad Vada venit; quem locum
volo tibi esse notum: iacet inter Appenninum et Alpes, inpe-
ditissimus ad iter faciendum. Cum abessem ab eo milia pas- 3
suum XXX. et se *ei* iam Ventidius coniunxisset, contio eius ad
me est adlata, in qua petere coepit a militibus, ut se trans
Alpes sequerentur; sibi cum M. Lepido convenire. Succlamatum est ei frequenter, a militibus Ventidianis—nam suos
valde quam paucos habet—, sibi aut in Italia pereundum esse
aut vincendum; et orare coeperunt, ut Pollentiam iter facerent. Cum sustinere eos non posset, in posterum diem iter
suum contulit. Hac re mihi nuntiata statim quinque cohortes 4
Pollentiam praemisi meumque iter eo contuli: hora ante prae-

1. **Bononiam.** Pansa lay there disabled by a wound. Cp. App. Bell. Civ. 3. 69.

3. **Copiolas,** 'my handful of men.' The word seems to be found here only.

4. **Extenuatissimae,** 'very much reduced.' Rare in this sense. The language of this passage hardly agrees with that of § 3, or with that of other letters written about this time. Cp. Ad Fam. 11. 20, 4; 11. 23, 1.

5. **Pessime acceptae,** 'have been brought into an evil plight.' 'Acceptae' = 'tractatae.' Forcell. Cp. Ad Fam. 12. 14, 4 'Dolabella . . in oppugnando male acceptus;' also Ter. Ad. 2. 1. 12.

Itinera . . sequens, 'making much greater marches in his flight than I in my pursuit.' Cp. Smith's Lat. Dict. sub voc. 'iter'; Madv. 223 c, Obs. 4. Wesenb. suggests either the insertion of 'facit' before 'itinera,' or the substitution of 'fuga faciens' for 'fugiens.' Forcell. quotes the passage as it stands, saying 'notat aliquando (iter) modum itineris faciendi.' H. inserts 'facit' after 'itinera.'

6. **Passim,** 'spreading his troops over the country;' opposed to **ordinatim,** 'in regular array.' For the description of Antony's march, cp. Ep. 137, 3. 'Passim' seems not to be Ciceronian in this sense; 'ordinatim' not in any. The latter word, however, is used by Sulpicius (Ep. 98, 3) and by Caesar (Bell. Civ. 2. 10), who also (Bell. Civ. 2. 38) uses 'passim' in the sense in which it is used here.

13. **Sibi . . convenire,** 'that he had an understanding with Lepidus.' D. Brutus had suspected this a month before. Cp. Ep. 136, 1.

Succlamatum est ei, 'his speech was followed by cries.' Not a Ciceronian word, but used by Livy both of friendly and hostile interruptions. Cp. 3. 50, 10; 21. 18, 14.

14. **Frequenter,** either 'often,' or 'by numbers.' Forcell. recognises both senses; Wieland adopts the latter.

15. **Valde quam.** Forcell. quotes no other instance of this combination, which he says has the same force as 'nimis quam' in the next section.

16. **Pollentiam.** On the left bank of the Tanarus (Tanaro), about 35 miles S. by E. of Augusta Taurinorum (Turin). It is mentioned by Pliny, H. N. 3. 5. 7, and is now a small place called Polenza or Polenzo.

17. **In posterum . . contulit,** 'he put off his march till the next day.' 'Conferre' = 'differre.' Forcell. Cp. Ad Att. 6. 1, 24 'de rebus urbanis, de provinciis quae omnia in mensem Martium sunt conlata.'

sidium meum Pollentiam venit quam Trebellius cum equitibus. Sane quam sum gavisus; in hoc enim victoriam puto consistere. In spem venerant, quod neque Planci quattuor legiones omnibus suis copiis pares arbitrabantur neque ex Italia tam celeriter exercitum traiici posse credebant. Quos ipsi adhuc satis adroganter Allobroges equitatusque omnis, qui eo praemissus erat a nobis, sustinebant, nostroque adventu sustineri facilius posse confidimus. Tamen, si quo etiam casu Isaram se traiecerint, ne quod detrimentum rei publicae iniungant,
3 summa a nobis dabitur opera. Vos magnum animum optimamque spem de summa re publica habere volumus, cum et nos et exercitus nostros singulari concordia coniunctos ad omnia pro vobis videatis paratos. Sed tamen nihil de diligentia remittere debetis dareque operam, ut quam paratissimi et ab exercitu reliquisque rebus pro vestra salute contra sceleratissimam conspirationem hostium confligamus; qui quidem eas copias, quas diu simulatione rei publicae comparabant, subito ad patriae periculum converterunt.

1. **Trebellius.** L. Trebellius Fides was tribune in the same year with Dolabella, 48–47 B.C., and resisted his colleague's attacks upon public credit. After Caesar's death he was a decided partisan of Antony. Cp. Philipp. 6. 4: 11. 6, 14: 13. 12, 26.

2. **Sane quam**: cp. Ep. 33, 2, note.

In hoc . . consistere, 'depends on this.'

3. **In spem venerant,** 'they had begun to hope.' 'venire in spem = sperare.' Forcell. Not often used without the thing hoped for being expressed.

Quattuor legiones: cp. Ep. 140, 3, note.

4. **Ex Italia.** Italy is here spoken of in its modern sense, as including the modern Piedmont and Lombardy. Cp. p. 597. l. 13; Merivale 3. 157, note; and § 3 of this letter. A. W. Zumpt, S. R. 31 has produced some strong evidence to shew that 'Italia' even at an earlier date than that of this letter was considered to include Gallia Cisalpina.

Tam celeriter, 'so quickly as has been the case.' 'Tam dicitur cum ellipsi oppositi membri,' says Forcell. Cp. De Off. 1. 31, 73.

5. **Ipsi,** 'by themselves.'

6. **Satis adroganter,** 'boldly enough.'

Allobroges: cp. Ep. 139, note.

Equitatusque omnis: cp. Ep. 140, 3.

7. **A nobis,** 'by Plancus and me.'

Sustinebant, epistolary imperfect.

9. **Iniungant** = 'imponant.' Forcell.

10. **Vos.** Cicero and his friends at Rome.

11. **Et nos,** 'both Plancus and me.'

14. **Et ab exercitu,** foll., 'in respect of soldiers and of everything else.' For this sense of 'ab,' cp. Ep. 1. 2, note. The position of 'que' is irregular.

16. **Qui quidem.** The reference is probably to Lepidus mainly; for, though the words diu . . **comparabant,** 'which they were raising for a long while, nominally for the defence of the Commonwealth,' 'spent much time in raising, as they pretended, for the defence of the Commonwealth,' Billerb., suit Octavius better than Lepidus, the defection of Octavius can hardly have taken place early enough to be known already to D. Brutus. Cp. Intr. to Part V, § 18. But see also Ad Fam. 11. 10, 4; 11. 20, 1.

146. PLANCUS TO CICERO (AD FAM. X. 23).

CAMP AT CULARO, JUNE 6, 43 B.C. (711 A.U.C.)

1. I never really trusted Lepidus, but was unwilling to incur the charge of suspecting him unfairly. 2. I marched to within forty miles of the camp of Antony and Lepidus, and then halted, when I heard that they had moved twenty miles nearer. 3. I withdrew across the Isara on June 4, and broke down the bridge. I expect D. Brutus in three days. 4. Laterensis has shewn much loyalty, but not enough penetration. On hearing of the treason of Lepidus he attempted his own life, but I hope may survive. 5. My escape has annoyed the public enemies a good deal. 6. Do what you can to support us; let Caesar's army come to our aid, with or without himself. 7. My regard for you increases daily, and I hope that I may have opportunities hereafter of proving this to you.

PLANCUS CICERONI.

Numquam mehercules, mi Cicero, me paenitebit maxima 1
pericula pro patria subire, dum, si quid acciderit mihi, a reprehensione temeritatis absim. Confiterer imprudentia me lapsum,
si umquam Lepido ex animo credidissem; credulitas enim error
est magis quam culpa, et quidem in optimi cuiusque mentem
facillime inrepit: sed ego non hoc vitio paene sum deceptus:
Lepidum enim pulchre noram. Quid ergo est? pudor me, qui
in bello maxime est periculosus, hunc casum coëgit subire; nam,
nisi uno loco essem, verebar ne cui obtrectatorum viderer et
nimium pertinaciter Lepido offensus et mea patientia etiam
alere bellum. Itaque copias prope in conspectum Lepidi An- 2
toniique adduxi quadragintaque milium passuum spatio relicto
consedi eo consilio, ut vel celeriter accedere vel salutariter recipere me possem. Adiunxi haec in loco eligendo, flumen op-
positum ut haberem, in quo mora transitus esset, Vocontii sub

On the situation of Cularo, cp. Ep. 140, 3, note.

2. **Si quid acciderit mihi**, 'If I meet with any disaster.' Cp. Ep. 71, 8, note.

A reprehensione . . absim, 'I be free from the charge of rashness.' On this sense of 'abesse a,' cp. Ep. 16, 2, note.

6. **Non hoc . . deceptus**, 'this is not the fault by which I have been so nearly taken in.' Süpfle.

7. **Pudor**, explained by the next sentence, 'fear of public opinion.'

9. **Nisi . . essem**, 'if I did not meet Lepidus.'

10. **Patientia**, 'inactivity.' Wieland.

13. **Salutariter** = 'exercitu salvo et incolumi,' 'without loss.' Forcell.

14. **Haec**, 'the following advantages,' i.e. (1) the protection of a river; (2) a safe retreat through the country of the Vocontii.

Flumen. Perhaps the Verdon, a feeder of the Druentia or Durance, separating the modern department of the Var from that of the Basses Alpes. But Andr. thinks that it was the Druentia itself.

15. **Vocontii**. This people lived between the Druentia and the Isara. The modern Avignon and Grenoble would perhaps mark the extreme west and east of their territory.

Sub manu = 'prope.' Forcell.

manu ut essent, per quorum loca fideliter mihi pateret iter.
Lepidus desperato adventu meo, quem non mediocriter capta-
bat, se cum Antonio coniunxit a. d. IIII. Kal. Iunias, eodemque
die ad me castra moverunt; viginti milia passuum cum abessent,
3 res mihi nuntiata est. Dedi operam deum benignitate, ut et
celeriter me reciperem et hic discessus nihil fugae simile haberet, non miles ullus, non eques, non quicquam impedimentorum
amitteretur aut ab illis ferventibus latronibus interciperetur.
Itaque pridie Nonas Iunias omnes copias Isaram traieci pontesque, quos feceram, interrupi, ut spatium ad colligendum se homines haberent et ego me interea cum collega coniungerem, quem
4 triduo, cum has dabam litteras, exspectabam. Laterensis nostri
et fidem et animum singularem in rem publicam semper fatebor;
sed certe nimia eius indulgentia in Lepidum ad haec pericula
perspicienda fecit eum minus sagacem. Qui quidem cum in fraudem se deductum videret, manus, quas iustius in Lepidi perniciem
armasset, sibi adferre conatus est; in quo casu tamen interpellatus et adhuc vivit et dicitur victurus. Sed tamen de hoc parum

1. **Fideliter**, 'through a loyal district.' So, in substance, Süpfle. Perhaps 'fideliter pateret' may be translated 'would be loyally kept open.'

2. **Desperato adventu.** But Plancus wrote a short time before (Ad Fam. 10. 21, 2) that Lepidus had asked him to halt on the Isara, and felt strong enough to deal with Antony single handed.

4. **Ad me**, '*towards* me.'

Moverunt. This is only true of Antony, for Lepidus was still on the 30th at his old quarters near Pons Argenteus. Cp. Ep. 144, 2, and Andresen's note on this passage.

5. **Deum benignitate** = 'dis faventibus.' Abl. caus.

6. **Celeriter.** His retreat probably began on May 30th or 31st, for Antony joined Lepidus on the 29th, and Plancus heard of their junction when they (or rather Antony, see above) had marched 20 miles (§ 2). Now Cularo, whence this letter was written on June 6, was about 150 miles from Pons Argenteus, and as Plancus had halted 40 miles short of the latter place (§ 2), he must have retreated 110 miles, crossed the Isara, and broken his bridges, in six days at most, perhaps in five. Cp. Ep. 140, 3, note.

7. **Non miles . . non eques**: cp. Ep. 141, 1, note.

8. **Ferventibus** = '*furiosis*.' Forcell. A rare use of the word.

9. **Pontesque**: cp. Ep. 140, l. c. Only one has been mentioned before. Cp. Ep. 140, 3 and Ad Fam. 10. 21, 2. He had secured one of them with forts at each end, so that D. Brutus might follow him with safety. Cp. Ad Fam. 10. 18, 4.

10. **Ut spatium . . colligendum.** Wesenb. thinks that a double 'et' is required by the form of the sentence (et et spatium), and that 'colligendum,' for which he substitutes 'colligendi,' is here a solecism.

Homines. Perhaps he refers principally to his own soldiers, whose loyalty might be shaken by the sudden defection of Lepidus.

11. **Cum collega**, sc. D. Bruto.

12. **Triduo cum has dabam litteras**, 'in three days from the date of this letter.' Süpfle. Cp. Ep. 145 for the movements of D. Brutus.

Laterensis. He had written, just before attempting his own life, to warn Plancus against the designs of Lepidus. Cp. Ad Fam. 10. 21, 3.

13. **Fatebor** = 'testabor,' 'praedicabo.' Forcell.

17. **In quo casu** = 'discrimine,' 'in which perilous act.'

Interpellatus: cp. Ep. 114, 7.

18. **Parum mihi certum est.** Laterensis died of his wound (Vell. 2, 63), and had a statue and public funeral voted him by the senate (cp. Dion Cassius 46, 51).

mihi certum est. Ego magno cum dolore parricidarum elapsus 5
sum iis; veniebant enim eodem furore in me quo in patriam,
incitati. Iracundias autem harum rerum recentes habebant: quod
Lepidum castigare non destiteram, ut exstingueret bellum; quod
colloquia facta improbabam; quod legatos fide Lepidi missos
ad me in conspectum venire vetueram; quod C. Catium Vestinum, tribunum mil., missum ab Antonio ad eum cum litteris
exceperam: in quo hanc capio voluptatem, quod certe, quo magis
me petiverunt, tanto maiorem iis frustratio dolorem attulit. Tu, 6
mi Cicero, quod adhuc fecisti, idem praesta, ut vigilanter ner-
voseque nos, qui stamus in acie, subornes. Veniat Caesar cum
copiis, quas habet firmissimas, aut, si ipsum aliqua res impedit,
exercitus mittatur; cuius ipsius magnum periculum agitur: quicquid aliquando futurum fuit in castris perditorum contra patriam,
huc omne iam convenit. Pro urbis vero salute cur non omnibus
facultatibus, quas habemus, utamur? Quod si vos istic non de-
fueritis, profecto, quod ad me attinet, omnibus rebus abunde
rei publicae satis faciam. Te quidem, mi Cicero, in dies meher- 7
cules habeo cariorem sollicitudinesque meas quotidie magis tua
merita exacuunt, ne quid aut ex amore aut ex iudicio tuo perdam.

1. **Parricidarum**, 'traitors.' Cp. Philipp. 14. 10, 27; 3. 13, 31 'confiteor eos . . plus . . quam parricidas esse, si quidem est atrocius patriae parentem quam suum occidere;' Ib. 2. 7, 17; and Mr. King's note.

3. **Iracundias . . habebant**, 'their angry feelings had been lately aroused by the following causes.' The plural 'iracundias' seems very rare. But cp. Ad Q. F. 1. 1, 13. 39.

4. **Castigare** = 'castigando impellere.' Billerb.

5. **Colloquia**, conferences between Antony and Lepidus, or between their soldiers. Cp. Ep. 144, notes; Intr. to Part V, § 17.

Legatos, sc. Antonii. Cp. App. Bell. Civ. 3. 83.

Fide Lepidi, 'under the safe conduct of Lepidus.' Cp. Ep. 13, 2, note on 'fides publica.'

6. **C. Catium Vestinum**. This man seems to be only here mentioned. The Vestini were a people of central Italy living N.E. of the Marsians, S.E. of the Picentines.

7. **Ad eum**, sc. Lepidum. Manut.

8. **Exceperam**, 'I had intercepted.'

In quo, 'on account of which.' Cp. p. 67, l. 15, note.

10. **Nervose**, 'energetically' = 'fortiter.' Forcell.

11. **Subornes**, 'supply,' 'subinde instruas.' Forcell. Not Ciceronian apparently.

12. **Quas habet firmissimas**, 'which are very efficient' (unter die schlagfertigsten). Wiel.

13. **Cuius ipsius**, sc. Caesaris, 'whose own safety is much imperilled.' With this use of a relative not referring to the last substantive cp. Ep. 135, 1, note. Plancus then did not believe that any agreement had yet been made between Antony and Octavian.

Quicquid aliquando . . convenit, 'all the desperadoes who were likely at any time to take the field against their country have met here,' i.e. in the camp of Antony and Lepidus.

15. **Cur non . . utamur**. A protest against any reluctance to transfer the forces of Octavian to the critical spot.

17. **Omnibus rebus**, 'in every respect.' Billerb.

20. **Exacuunt**, 'stimulate.'

Ex iudicio tuo, 'of your good opinion,' 'consideration.' Billerb.

Opto ut mihi liceat iam praesenti pietate meorum officiorum tua beneficia tibi facere iucundiora. VIII. Idus Iun. Cularone, ex finibus Allobrogum.

147. To C. CASSIUS (AD FAM. XII. 10).

ROME, JULY, 43 B.C. (711 A.U.C.)

1. Lepidus has been declared a public enemy by the senate. We hear good news about Dolabella, 2. and hope that you are coming to Italy with your army. We wish to hear not only of your efforts but of their *results*, and 3. are most anxious for your presence. Our success was secure had not Lepidus given Antony a refuge. We have great hopes that the consuls elect may prosper, but 4. all really depends on you and on M. Brutus; we shall need your aid even if we conquer our enemies without you.

CICERO CASSIO SAL.

1 Lepidus, tuus adfinis, meus familiaris, pr. K. Quinctiles sententiis omnibus hostis a senatu iudicatus est ceterique, qui una
cum illo a re publica defecerunt; quibus tamen ad sanitatem rede-
undi ante K. Sept. potestas facta est. Fortis sane senatus, sed
maxime spe subsidii tui. Bellum quidem, cum haec scribebam,
sane magnum erat scelere et levitate Lepidi. Nos de Dolabella
quotidie, quae volumus, audimus, sed adhuc sine capite, sine auc-
2 tore, rumore nuntio. Quod cum ita esset, tamen litteris tuis, quas
Nonis Maiis ex castris datas acceperamus, ita persuasum erat civitati, ut illum iam oppressum omnes arbitrarentur, te autem in
Italiam venire cum exercitu, ut, si haec ex sententia confecta
essent, consilio atque auctoritate tua, sin quid forte titubatum,

1. Praesenti pietate .. iucundiora, 'to make your services more agreeable to you,' i.e. to make you a return for your services—' by affection shewn in kindnesses done at Rome.'

2. Cularone; see note at the beginning of this letter.

4. Tuus adfinis. Lepidus had married Iunia, and Cassius Iunia Tertulla—both daughters of D. Silanus, cos. 62 B.C. and of Servilia, and half-sisters of M. Brutus. Cp. Ad Att. 14. 20, 2; Dion Cassius 44. 34; Vell. 2. 88. Their brother M. Silanus has been mentioned Ep. 135. 1; he was consul 25 B.C.

6. Quibus. I agree with Wiel. in thinking that this does not include Lepidus himself.

Sanitatem, 'bonam mentem,' 'rectum consilium,' 'a sound state of mind.' Forcell.

8. Scribebam . . erat, 'epistolary tenses.'

9. De Dolabella: cp. Intr. to Part V, § 20; Appendix 11. 10. From a letter of Cassius, a quaestor, to Cicero (Ad Fam. 12. 13, 4), it would seem that Laodicea was invested about June 13.

10. Sine capite, 'without any definite source.' 'Caput' = 'origo unde aliquid manat et exit in vulgus.' Forcell. Cp. Pro Planc. 23, 57 'si quid sine capite manabit.'

11. Litteris tuis: Ep. 138.

14. Haec, 'the war with Antony and Lepidus.'

15. Titubatum, cp. de Orat. 3. 50, 192.

ut fit in bello, exercitu tuo niteremur; quem quidem ego exercitum
quibuscumque potuero rebus ornabo; cuius rei tum tempus erit,
cum, quid opis rei publicae laturus is exercitus sit aut quid iam
tulerit, notum esse coeperit: nam adhuc tantum conatus audiuntur,
optimi illi quidem et praeclarissimi, sed gesta res exspectatur,
quam quidem aut iam esse aliquam aut adpropinquare confido.
Tua virtute *et* magnitudine animi nihil est nobilius; itaque opta- 3
mus, ut quam primum te in Italia videamus: rem publicam nos
habere arbitrabimur, si vos habebimus. Praeclare viceramus, nisi
spoliatum, inermem, fugientem Lepidus recepisset Antonium;
itaque numquam tanto odio civitati Antonius fuit, quanto est
Lepidus: ille enim ex turbulenta re publica, hic ex pace et victoria
bellum excitavit. Huic oppositos consules designatos habemus, in
quibus est magna illa quidem spes, sed anceps cura propter incertos
exitus proeliorum. Persuade tibi igitur, in te et in Bruto tuo esse 4
omnia, vos exspectari, Brutum quidem iam iamque. Quod si, ut
spero, victis hostibus nostris veneritis, tamen auctoritate vestra
res publica exsurget et in aliquo statu tolerabili consistet; sunt
enim permulta, quibus erit medendum, etiam si res publica satis
esse videbitur sceleribus hostium liberata. Vale.

148. PLANCUS TO CICERO (AD FAM. X. 24).

CAMP AT CULARO (?), JULY 28, 43 B.C. (711 A.U.C.)

1. I must express, however imperfectly, my gratitude for all your services. 2. You have tried to promote my soldiers' interests, as the public welfare demanded. 3. and hitherto I have maintained my position. Caution is needful, for our forces, though

2. Ornabo: cp. the requests of Cassius, Ep. 138, 3 and 4.

5. Gesta res, 'some achievement,' 'a result,' i.e. the overthrow of Dolabella.

6. Esse aliquam, 'has been effected to some extent.'

9. Vos, Cassius and M. Brutus. Cp. § 4.

Viceramus. An elliptical mode of expression. 'We had gained a great success, which would have been decisive,' or perhaps, as Andresen says, it is rhetorical exaggeration describing what had nearly happened as having actually happened. Cp. Madv. 348, c.

13. Consules designatos. Plancus and D. Brutus. Mauritius thinks that Octavius is passed over out of regard for Cassius, who had been one of the murderers of Julius Caesar. But may not Cicero's reason for omitting his name have been that he did not trust him? Cp. note on l. 19 below.

14. Illa quidem. A pronoun is often prefixed rather pleonastically to 'quidem.' Cp. Madv. 489, b.

16. Iam iamque. Brutus' province, Macedonia, was of course much nearer than that of Cassius.

18. Exsurget..consistet. Bold metaphors: 'will arise from its depression and be settled in a satisfactory position.' 'Exsurget' = 'erigetur,' 'recreabitur.' Forcell. Cp. Ep. 48, 1, note, on exsurgere.

19. Permulta, foll. Perhaps these words refer to Cicero's suspicions of Octavian.

very numerous, are for the most part inexperienced: 4. If you can send us the army of Africa, or the young Caesar's, we may risk a battle with confidence. 5. You know how friendly I have always been to the young Caesar for various reasons, 6. but I must say that our present difficulties are entirely owing to his breach of promises and foolish ambition. 7. All who have influence with him ought to exert it in the interest of the state. 8. Our position here is difficult, as a battle would be dangerous, and retreat might involve loss to the Commonwealth.

PLANCUS IMP. COS. DESIG. S. D. CICERONI.

1 Facere non possum, quin in singulas res meritaque tua tibi gratias agam, sed mehercules facio cum pudore; neque enim tanta necessitudo, quantam tu mihi tecum esse voluisti, desiderare videtur gratiarum actionem, neque ego libenter pro maximis tuis beneficiis tam vili munere defungor orationis, et malo praesens observantia, indulgentia, adsiduitate memorem me tibi probare. Quod si mihi vita contigerit, omnes gratas amicitias atque etiam pias propinquitates † in tua observantia, indulgentia, adsiduitate vincam; amor enim tuus ac iudicium de me utrum mihi plus dignitatis in perpetuum an voluptatis quotidie sit adlaturus, non
2 facile dixerim. De militum commodis fuit tibi curae; quos ego non potentiae meae causa—nihil enim me non salutariter cogitare scio—ornari volui a senatu, sed primum, quod ita meritos iudicabam, deinde, quod ad omnes casus coniunctiores rei publicae esse volebam, novissime, ut ab omni omnium sollicitatione aversos

This letter is the last written to Cicero which we possess; Ad Fam. 12. 10 the last written by him. Abeken suspects that many were destroyed by Augustus (cp. p. 470 of his work).

1. In = 'for,' 'on account of.' Cp. Ad Q. F. 2. 6, 5 'in eam tabulam magni risus consequebantur.' In singulas res, 'point by point.' Andr.

5. Tam vili . . orationis, 'so worthless a gift as this of words,' gen. defin. Cp. Ep. 10, 2, note.

7. Amicitias . . propinquitates: for 'amicos' and 'propinquos.' The words do not seem to be used quite in this sense by Cicero, but we find 'convictiones' and 'apparitiones' used of persons (Ad Q. F. 1. 1, 12). Cp. also Pro Quinct. 30, 93 'ab afflicta amicitia transfugere atque ad florentem aliam devolare.'

8. In tua observantia, 'in courting you.' Cp. Ep. 29, 20 'sine ulla mea contumelia.' Wesenb. agrees with Baiter in regarding these words as suspicious, and puts 'in tua . . adsiduitate' in brackets.

Indulgentia, 'devotion.' Billerb., Wiel.

9. Amor . . ac iudicium, 'the affection shewn in your opinion of me.'

10. Adlaturus, masc. as agreeing with the more important word 'amor.' Cp. Ad Fam. 10. 21, 5 'mihi . . non modo honorem sed misericordiam quoque defuturam.' Cp. Madv. 214 d, Obs. 3.

11. De militum commodis. Perhaps Plancus refers especially to grants of land promised to those who should be loyal to the commonwealth. Cp. Ad Fam. 11. 20, 3; 11. 21, 2 and 5; Philipp. 5. 19, 53; 14. 14, 38. It is probable, though not stated, that such promises were made to the soldiers of Plancus.

13. Scio. Wesenb. has 'scis.'

Ornari volui: cp. Ep. 132, 7.

14. Ad omnes casus. On the force of 'ad,' cp. p. 426, note.

15. Novissime, 'lastly.' Not Ciceronian, apparently, in this sense.

Omni omnium sollicitatione, 'all the seductions which anybody,' especially Antony and Lepidus, 'can employ.' On the

eos tales vobis praestare possem, quales adhuc fuerunt. Nos adhuc 3
hic omnia integra sustinuimus. Quod consilium nostrum, etsi
quanta sit aviditas hominum non sine causa † talis victoriae scio,
tamen vobis probari spero. Non enim, si quid in his exercitibus sit offensum, magna subsidia res publica habet expedita,
quibus subito impetu ac latrocinio parricidarum resistat. Copias
vero nostras notas tibi esse arbitror: in castris meis legiones
sunt veteranae tres, tironum vel luculentissima ex omnibus una;
in castris Bruti una veterana legio, altera bima, octo tironum:
ita universus exercitus numero amplissimus est, firmitate exiguus;
quantum autem in acie tironi sit committendum, nimium saepe
expertum habemus. Ad hoc robur nostrorum exercituum sive 4
Africanus exercitus, qui est veteranus, sive Caesaris accessisset,
aequo animo summam rem publicam in discrimen deduceremus.
Aliquanto autem propius esse quod Caesarem videbamus, nihil
destiti eum litteris hortari, neque ille intermisit adfirmare se
sine mora venire; cum interim aversum illum ab hac cogitatione
ad alia consilia video se contulisse. Ego tamen ad eum Furnium
nostrum cum mandatis litterisque misi, si quid forte proficere
posset. Scis tu, mi Cicero, quod ad Caesaris amorem attinet, 5

attempts to tamper with Plancus and his army, cp. Epp. 132, 3; 146, 2 and 5.

Aversos is, I think, a participle here.

2. Omnia . . sustinuimus, 'we have kept everything as it was.' Frey. 'Have not involved the commonwealth in any risk' = 'proelium vitavimus.' Manut. 'Sustinere = 'conservare,' 'tueri.' Forcell.

3. Talis. Perhaps 'fatalis,' 'desidere,' should be read with H. A. Koch, ap. Baiter. If the MS. reading be retained, quanta may mean 'how little' (cp. 'quantum,' l. 11; Ep. 15, 8, note on p. 96): 'how little men desire the mere maintenance of our position.' Wesenb. inserts 'belli.' 'Talis' would then = 'civilis.' Professor Nettleship suggests 'alterius' (ahis) for 'talis'; Andr. suggests 'ut ais' as referring to a letter of Cicero to Plancus.

5. Subsidia . . expedita, 'reserves ready for action.'

6. Impetu, dat.: cp. Madv. 46, Obs. 3: Nägelsb. 56, 151.

8. Luculentissima, 'finest.' Wiel.

9. Bima, 'which has seen more than one year's service.' Appian (Bell. Civ. 3. 49) seems to have considered this a veteran legion.

10. Firmitate, 'steadiness,' not common without a qualifying genitive.

Exiguus, 'slight,' 'weak.'

11. Autem. Andresen remarks that 'enim' would suit the context better.

Nimium saepe, e.g. at Pharsalus, cp. Ep. 88, 2; Intr. to Part III, §§ 10; 11; Thapsus, Intr. to Part IV, § 10; and Forum Gallorum, Ep. 135, notes; Intr. to Part V, § 16. For an account of the forces of Plancus and D. Brutus, cp. Appendix 11, 1 and 3.

13. Africanus exercitus: cp. Intr. to Part V, §§ 18 and 19; Appendix 11, 5.

Accessisset . . deduceremus, epistolary tenses in place of the lit. exact. and simple fut. indic. Cp. Ep. 56, 5, note.

14. Summam rem publicam, 'the highest interests,' 'the existence' of the commonwealth.

15. Propius esse, sc. 'quam Africanum exercitum.'

Videbamus, 'we' (D. Brutus and I) 'see.'

Nihil destiti, 'I have not ceased.'

18. Ad alia consilia, i.e. to his designs upon the consulship. Cp. § 6.

Furnium: cp. Ep. 130, 1, note.

20. Quod ad Caesaris Octaviani amorem.

societatem mihi esse tecum: vel quod in familiaritate Caesaris
vivo illo iam tueri eum et diligere fuit mihi necesse; vel quod
ipse, quoad ego nosse potui, moderatissimi atque humanissimi
fuit sensus; vel quod ex tam insigni amicitia mea atque Caesaris
hunc filii loco et illius et vestro iudicio substitutum non proinde
6 habere turpe mihi videtur. Sed—quicquid tibi scribo, dolenter
mehercule magis quam inimice facio—quod vivit Antonius hodie,
quod Lepidus una est, quod exercitus habent non contemnendos,
quod sperant, quod audent, omne Caesari acceptum referre possunt.
Neque ego superiora repetam; sed ex eo tempore, quo
ipse mihi professus est se venire, si venire voluisset, aut oppressum
iam bellum esset aut in aversissimam illis Hispaniam
cum detrimento eorum maximo extrusum. Quae mens eum, aut
quorum consilia, *a* tanta gloria, sibi vero etiam necessaria ac
salutari, avocarit et ad cogitationem consulatus bimestris summo
cum terrore hominum et insulsa cum efflagitatione transtulerit,
7 exputare non possum. Multum in hac re mihi videntur necessarii
eius et rei publicae et ipsius causa proficere posse; plurimum,
ut puto, tu quoque, cuius ille tanta merita habet, quanta

1. In familiaritate Caesaris, 'as an intimate friend of Julius Caesar.'

2. Illo .. illius refer to the elder Caesar; eum .. ipse .. hunc to Octavian.

5. Vestro. Octavian's adoption was only sanctioned in the comitia curiata after his return to Rome from North Italy, apparently in August. Cp. App. Bell. Civ. 3. 94; Dion Cassius 46. 47. However, Cicero had always called him Caesar in the Philippics (cp. 3. 6, 15; 5. 17, 46), and most of the other friends of Octavian had done so even before (cp. Ep. 108, 2). Plancus therefore perhaps refers to the informal recognition.

Proinde, 'as such,' i.e. 'as his son.' Wiel.

7. Facio. This verb is used like its English equivalent instead of repeating a more definite verb. Cp. Andresen's note on this passage, and Ep. 90, 4.

10. Superiora, 'his earlier shortcomings,' in failing to press Antony hard after the battle of Mutina.

Ex eo tempore .. esset. With the order of the words, cp. Pro Tull. 4. 9; and see Madv. 476 c. But this passage seems rather confused. The words may mean—either 'The war would have been at an end since the time when he promised to come—if he had been willing to come,' or 'If he had been willing to come at the time he promised the war would have been already at an end.'

11. Oppressum, 'put an end to.'

12. Aversissimam. Wesenb. has 'adversissimam.'

Illis, 'to Antony and his party.' Spain had been attached to Pompey and his family for many years. Cp. Intr. to Part IV, § 22; Appendix 1, § 2; 7; 11, 4.

14. Sibi: 'ipsi' would be more common. Frey.

Vero, 'moreover.' 'Servit transitionibus.' Forcell.

Necessaria. Because he had much to fear from Antony.

15. Bimestris. An exaggeration. For Octavian was elected at latest on Sept. 22. Cp. Intr. to Part V, § 19, note 6.

16. Efflagitatione, a rare word. It occurs Ad Fam. 5. 19, 2. On the facts here referred to, cp. Intr. l. c.; Suet. Oct. 26; App. Bell. Civ. 3. 88; Dion Cassius 46. 43.

17. Exputare, very rare = 'coniectando adsequi.' Forcell.

Necessarii. His mother Atia, his stepfather L. Philippus and his brother-in-law C. Marcellus, the consul of 50 B.C., may be especially referred to. Cp. Ep. 108, 2; Philipp. 3. 6, 17.

19. Cuius, 'from whom,' gen. possess.

Merita = 'beneficia,' 'services,' referring

nemo praeter me; numquam enim obliviscar maxima ac plurima me tibi debere. De his rebus ut exigeret cum eo, Furnio mandavi. Quod si, quantam debeo, habuero apud eum auctoritatem, plurimum ipsum iuvero. Nos interea duriore condicione bellum sustinemus, quod neque expeditissimam dimicationem putamus neque tamen refugiendo commissuri sumus, ut maius detrimentum res publica accipere possit. Quod si aut Caesar se respexerit aut Africanae legiones celeriter venerint, securos vos ab hac parte reddemus. Tu, ut instituisti, me diligas rogo proprieque tuum esse tibi persuadeas. V. Kal. Sext. ex castris.

to Cicero's proposals in the senate in honour of Octavian—those e.g. recorded Philipp. 5. 17; 14. 14. 37.

2. Ut exigeret, 'to treat.' The word does not seem to be Ciceronian in this sense, but Forcell. quotes Seneca and Pliny for it.

3. Habuero .. iuvero: on the tenses cp. p. 479, note on l. 15. 'Iuvero:' the aid of Plancus would be valuable to Octavian because of the hostility of Antony to the latter. Cp. Epp. 146, 6; 148, 6, notes.

4. Duriore; 'eo duriore' would be more in accordance with usage.

5. Expeditissimam = 'facillimam.' Forcell. The superlative is found also Ad Fam. 11. 24. 2.

7. Se respexerit, 'shall have regard to his true interest'='ad consilia sibi et rei publicae salutaria redierit.' Forcell.

9. Ab hac parte, 'in this quarter' of the empire.

APPENDIX XI.

STATE OF THE ROMAN PROVINCES AND ARMIES FROM THE DEATH OF CAESAR TO THAT OF CICERO.

1. Cisalpine Gaul. D. Brutus had been appointed[1] by Caesar to govern this province, and went there in April, 44 B.C.[2] At the time of the siege of Mutina he seems to have had two legions of old soldiers and one of recruits at his disposal, with a numerous body of gladiators[3]. He took the command of Pansa's new levies after the death of their general, and these with recruits whom he raised himself brought his total force up to ten legions[4]—of which, however, Plancus only allows one to have been composed of veterans. Four of his legions subsequently joined Antony, and six Octavian[5].

2. Narbonensian Gaul with Hither Spain. M. Lepidus held these two provinces, but entrusted their government to his legates for some time[6]. He had a legion close to Rome at the time of Caesar's murder[7], and four[8] in Gaul later in the same year. Next year we find him near Forum Iulii at the head of seven, one being the famous[9] tenth.

3. Northern Gaul (Gallia Comata). This province, which had been added to the empire by Caesar, was divided in 44 B.C. between A. Hirtius and L. Munatius Plancus. The former, however, left his district to his officers[10], and in 44–43 B.C. we find the whole province subject to Plancus, who commanded an army of four or five legions there[11].

4. Farther Spain (Baetica and Lusitania). After the battle of Munda Sex. Pompeius retired among the Lacetani and subsequently raised forces which he combined with fugitives from the battle. He fought with some success against Pollio[12], but Lepidus[13] induced him to lay

[1] App. Bell. Civ. 2. 124.
[2] Ad Att. 14. 13. 2.
[3] App. Bell. Civ. 3. 49.
[4] Ib. 3. 76; Ad Fam. 10. 24. 3.
[5] App. Bell. Civ. 3. 97.
[6] Ib. 2. 107; Dion Cassius 43. 51.
[7] App. Bell. Civ. 2. 118.
[8] Ib. 3. 46.
[9] Ib. 3. 84; Ad Fam. 10. 11, 2.
[10] Ad Att. 14. 9. 3.
[11] Ad Fam. 10. 8, 6; 10. 15. 3.
[12] Philipp. 5. 14.
[13] Dion Cassius 45. 10. Cp. Intr. to Part IV, § 18.

down his arms, and he retired to Massilia[1] to watch events. During the campaign of Mutina, C. Asinius Pollio governed Farther Spain with three legions[2], of which the 28th and 30th were two.

5. Africa. There were two Roman provinces in Africa; Old Africa and New Africa or Numidia; the first was governed by Q. Cornificius[3], the second by T. Sextius. We are not told what force Cornificius had at his disposal; but Sextius seems to have had three legions, and to have obeyed an order[4] of the senate to send two of them to Rome, and place the third under the orders of Cornificius. The two which were sent to Italy presently went over to Octavian[5].

6. Sicily was governed by A. Pompeius Bithynicus till he was forced to yield up his province to Sex. Pompeius towards the close of 43 B.C.[6]

7. Macedonia at the time of Caesar's death was subject to Q. Hortensius, son[7] of the great orator. In the autumn of 44 B.C., M. Antonius got it assigned to his brother[8] Gaius, who landed with one legion near Dyrrhachium, but found the province already in possession of M. Brutus, who defeated and captured him[9]. Brutus had been designated by Caesar to govern Macedonia after his praetorship[10], and now assembled a considerable force there, consisting (1) of old soldiers of Pompey recalled to arms[11], (2) of men left behind by Dolabella[12], (3) of the troops of C. Antonius and P. Vatinius[13], (4) of a legion commanded by an officer[14] of M. Antonius, (5) of two legions raised in Macedonia[15]; in all eight legions. Achaia seems to have been annexed to Macedonia.

8. Asia. C. Trebonius had been appointed to govern Asia by Caesar[16], and held it during some months in 44–43 B.C. After his murder[17] no special governor seems to have been appointed for Asia.

9. Bithynia. L. Tillius Cimber governed Bithynia by Caesar's appointment[18] in 44–43 B.C., but marched with a small force to join Cassius in Syria[19].

[1] Philipp. 13. 6, 13; App. Bell. Civ. 4. 84. [2] Ad Fam. 10. 32. 4. [3] Ib. 12. 21 30. [4] App. Bell. Civ. 3. 85 and 91. [5] Ib. 3. 92. [6] Ib. 4. 84; Ad Fam. 6. 16; 17; 16. 23, 1; Livy Epit. 123. [7] Philipp. 10. 5, 11; 10. 6, 13. [8] Ib. 3. 10, 26. [9] App. Bell. Civ. 3. 79; Dion Cassius 47. 21. [10] App. Bell. Civ. 3. 2. [11] Plut. Brut. 25. [12] Or diverted from him; Philipp. 10. 6, 13. [13] Plut. Brut. 26; Dion Cassius 47. 21; App. Illyr. 13. Vatinius had three legions, but they had suffered greatly in encounters with the natives. [14] Philipp. 10. 6, 13. [15] App. Bell. Civ. 3. 79. [16] Ad Fam. 12. 16; App. Bell. Civ. 3. 2. [17] Ib. 4. 58; Ad Fam. 12. 12, 1; Philipp. 11. 1–3; Livy Epit. 119; Dion Cassius 47. 29. [18] Ad Fam. 12. 13, 3; App. Bell. Civ. 3. 2. [19] Dion Cassius 47. 31.

10. Syria. Caesar had left one legion there under Sex. Iulius Caesar, who failed, however, to command the respect of his men, and perished in a mutiny which perhaps was caused by the intrigues of Q. Caecilius Bassus, who then took the command of his forces, and probably increased them [1]. Caesar, however, sent against Bassus three legions under the command of L. Statius Murcus, who was supported by an equal force under Q. Marcus Crispus, governor of Bithynia. On the arrival of Cassius in Syria, both the opposing armies placed themselves under his orders, and A. Allienus, who at Dolabella's command raised four legions in Egypt and led them into Syria, was alarmed by the superiority of Cassius' forces, and submitted to him [2]. Cassius subsequently besieged Dolabella at Laodicea [3], and Dolabella killed himself when Cassius' soldiers entered the place.

11. M. Antonius seems to have had no regular force at his disposal till, after the execution of Amatius, the senate empowered him to raise soldiers for his protection [4]. Afterwards, early in June, apparently, he seems to have procured a decree of the senate [5] assigning to himself Macedonia, and to Dolabella Syria, with the command against the Parthians. Six legions had been assembled by Caesar in Macedonia for the war, which would naturally have been commanded by Dolabella; but rumours of threatening movements among the Getae enabled Antony to persuade the senate to detain them all in Macedonia except one [6], which probably followed Dolabella. Finally, in July, apparently, Antony obtained Cisalpine Gaul by a vote of the centuries in exchange for Macedonia, Octavian supporting his claims [7]. Subsequently Antony brought over four or five legions [8] from Macedonia into Italy, but two of them, the Martia and fourth, presently deserted to Octavian [9]. With the others, supported by one of veterans recalled to arms, and apparently by two of recruits, Antony began the siege of Mutina [10]. After his defeat before that place, he was joined by P. Ventidius with three legions, the 7th, 8th, and 9th [11], and after he had crossed the Alps, first

[1] Ad Fam. 12. 11; App. Bell. Civ. 3. 77. [2] Ib. l. c.; Philipp. 11. 12, 30; App. Bell. Civ. 3. 77 and 78; Dion Cassius 47. 28. [3] Intr. to Part V, § 20. [4] App. Bell. Civ. 3. 4 and 5. [5] Ib. 3. 7 and 8. [6] App. Bell. Civ 3. 24 and 25. [7] Ib. 3. 30. [8] Our accounts are not consistent. There were six legions at first in Macedonia (App. Bell. Civ. 3. 24), of which Dolabella kept one (Ib. 25), and another submitted to Brutus (Philipp. 10. 6, 13). This would leave four for Antony, yet Appian (Bell. Civ. 3. 43; 46) makes him transport five to Italy. Of the six with which he began the siege of Mutina, two, the 2nd and 35th, (cp. Ad Fam. 10. 30, 1) had probably belonged to the army of Macedonia. Perhaps the 5th (Alaudae) had been previously in Italy, and Appian may have been led into a mistake by supposing that this was one of the legions of Macedonia. Three of them landed at first, and were followed by a fourth. Cp. Ad Att. 16. 8, 2; App Bell. Civ. 3. 43 and 46; Drumann 1. 203 and 210. [9] Philipp. 3. 3. [10] App. Bell. Civ. 3. 46; Philipp. 8. 8, 25. [11] App. Bell. Civ. 3. 66; Ad Fam. 10. 33, 4.

Lepidus with seven[1] legions, then Pollio with three[2], and subsequently Plancus with four or five[3], joined him; four also of the legions of D. Brutus went over to him in Gaul or Italy[4]. Antony and Lepidus, when they marched to Italy, left six legions in Gaul under L. Varius Cotyla[5]; and we are told[6] that at the meeting of the triumvirs near Bononia at the close of 43 B.C., Antony had sixteen legions, Octavian seventeen, and Lepidus ten. These, however, may have included some new Italian levies.

12. Octavian, towards the close of 44 B.C., had at his disposal two veteran legions of the army of Macedonia, the 4th and Martia, two of veterans recalled to arms, which were brought up to their full complement by recruits[7], one of recruits and a praetorian cohort, composed probably of veterans. With this force he marched to the neighbourhood of Mutina, and wintered there; Hirtius joined him at the beginning of the next year[8], and Pansa brought up four legions of recruits in April[9], while he left one[10] to guard Rome. These forces suffered heavy losses in the battles of Forum Gallorum and Mutina[11]. When Octavian preferred his claim to the consulship, he had, according to Appian[12], eight legions, which were joined by three[13] encamped for the protection of Rome, and by six which abandoned D. Brutus. Thus the seventeen[14] are accounted for which he had when he met Antony and Lepidus as above mentioned.

APPENDIX XII.

On the Meaning of the Words 'Colonia,' 'Municipium,' and 'Praefectura.'

(See pages 161; 222-223; 452-453; 554.)

In attempting to determine this question it will be convenient to distinguish the periods before and after the enactment of the 'Lex Iulia de Civitate Sociorum' in 90 B.C.

[1] Ad Fam. 10. 35; App. Bell. Civ. 3. 84. [2] Ad Fam. 10. 32, 4; Vell. 2. 63. 3. [3] Vell. l. c.; Ad Fam. 10. 8, 6; 10. 15, 3. [4] App. Bell. Civ. 3. 97. [5] Plut. Ant. 18. [6] App. Bell. Civ. 4. 3. He says that the meeting was near Mutina, but cp. Intr. to Part V, § 22; Suet. Oct. 96; Dion Cassius 46. 55. [7] Ib. 3. 47; Ep. 135, notes. One of the two mixed legions was numbered 'the seventh,' a number which was also borne by one of those of Ventidius. Cp. Philipp. 14. 10, 27, with Ad Fam. 10. 33, 4. This seems to imply that there might already be more legions than one bearing the same number, as was certainly the case in the reign of Augustus. Cp. Smith's Dict. of Antiq. sub voc. 'Exercitus,' p. 492. [8] Dion Cassius 46. 36. But Appian (Bell. Civ. 3. 65) seems to make them march together. [9] Ad Fam. 10. 30, 1; App. Bell. Civ. 3. 69. [10] App. Bell. Civ. 3. 91. [11] Intr. to Part V. §§ 16 and 17; Ep. 135, 5, note. [12] Bell. Civ. 3. 88. [13] Ib. 3. 92. [14] Ib. 4. 3.

A. In the period which elapsed between the complete conquest of Italy by the Romans and the enactment of the 'Lex Iulia,' Italian cities must, with very few exceptions, have belonged to one of the following classes :—

I. Coloniae Civium Romanorum. The most ancient of these consisted of a small number of Roman citizens sent to act as garrisons, usually in towns on the sea coast. The colonists retained their full Roman citizenship and combined with it, probably, the right of managing their local business. Cp. Madv. Opusc. Acad. 1. 243–245; Marquardt, Römische Staatsverwaltung, 1. 36. The original population probably became 'cives sine suffragio.' Praefects were sent from Rome to administer justice in many of such colonies (cp. Fest. 233, Müller), perhaps originally in all [1], but whether to the Roman settlers, or to the original population, or to both, does not appear. It is probable that in all cases the colonial and original population had amalgamated, and that the latter had received the full franchise, before the enactment of the 'Lex Iulia.' Cp. Marquardt, 1. 37.

Colonies of Roman citizens were also established beyond the limits of Italy proper, the earliest at Parma and Mutina, in Cisalpine Gaul, in 183 B.C. These were established principally for military reasons, and seem to have undergone no change of status before the time of Cicero. Cp. Livy 39. 55; Madv. Opusc. Acad. 1. 302.

Others were established or proposed, nearly all in Italy, by C. Gracchus and by M. Livius Drusus the elder, as a means of relieving the distress of the poor at Rome. Cp. Plut. C. Gracch. 8; 9; Livy Epit. 60; App. Bell. Civ. 1. 23; 24; A. W. Zumpt, C. E. 1. 230–239; Madv. Opusc. Acad. 1. 303.

A. Gellius (N. A. 16. 13) says that the 'coloniae civium Romanorum' had less independence than the municipia.

[1] C. G. Zumpt (cp. the list of authorities at the end of this appendix) thinks that the larger colonies of Roman citizens were never 'praefecturae,' but that all other early communities of Roman citizens outside Rome were so. Cp. as to Minturnae, Velleius (2. 19), who speaks of 'duoviri' there; also Plutarch (Marius 39). A 'praefectus Mutinensis' is mentioned in the 'Lex Rubria' (cp. Corp. Inscr. Lat. 1. 116 (205)), which was enacted in 49 B.C.; but 'quattuorviri iuri dicundo' are also mentioned as existing there. These appear to have been locally elected magistrates, and must of course be distinguished from the functionaries of the same name appointed at Rome to act in Campania, on whom see below. Cp. Ad Att. 5. 2. 3; A. W. Zumpt, Comment. Epigr. 1. 54. At Puteoli, another colony of Roman citizens, mentioned by Festus among the 'praefecturae,' 'duoviri' are mentioned as existing in 105 B.C. (Corp. Inscr. Lat. 1. 163 foll. (577)); cp. Cic. de Leg. Agrar. 2. 31, 86; also at Cumae in 49 B.C., cp. Ad Att. 10. 13, 1. Now the existence of such functionaries seems inconsistent with that of a praefect sent from Rome to administer justice. Festus (p. 233) says that the 'praefecturae' had no magistrates. Mr. D. B. Monro agrees with the opinion expressed by Mommsen in his Münzwesen (p. 336, note 130, Berlin, 1860), and thinks that the colonies of Roman citizens were originally praefecturae, but changed their constitution during the second century B.C.

II. Municipia. The term 'municipium' is supposed by Marquardt (1. 28) to have originally denoted the status of 'cives sine suffragio,' and to have been transferred to the various communities the members of which held that status. Such communities appear to have been divided into two classes; one of them retaining more of local self-government than the other. Paulus Diaconus (Fest. 127, Müller) gives Tusculum, Lanuvium, and Formiae, as examples of the first or more favoured class; Aricia, Caere, and Anagnia, of the other. Livy, however, couples Aricia with Lanuvium (8. 14), and Cicero's language in one passage tends to support Livy (Philipp. 3. 6, 15).

To some of these municipia praefects were sent from Rome to administer justice. At first such officers were appointed by the praetor urbanus, but, according to Livy (9. 20), after the year 318 B.C. four ('quattuorviri iuri dicundo') were elected[1] to act at Capua and other places. Others were still appointed by the praetor urbanus. Thus there were two classes of 'praefecturae,' or towns to which such officers were sent (cp. Festus 233, Müller), and a considerable number of towns might for some time be called with equal propriety 'municipia' or 'praefecturae.' The four praefects appointed to act in Campania were reckoned among the viginti sex viri—on whom cp. Smith, Dict. of Antiq. p. 1196.

It is to be noticed that no names of old Latin towns nor of old colonies of Roman citizens occur in the list of praefecturae given by Festus. Perhaps the inhabitants of such places had to bring their cases before the praetor urbanus for trial. It is true that a praefect is mentioned in an inscription, of the time of the emperor Claudius probably, as existing at Lavinium (cp. A. W. Zumpt, De Lavinio, etc., pp. 2; 14, 15), but perhaps no argument can be drawn from the institutions of the first century of the empire, and Mommsen thinks that he represented the municipal, not the Roman, praetor. (Staatsrecht 2. 569-570, note 8.)

All these municipia and praefecturae probably, with the exception of Capua and a few places in its neighbourhood, had received the full Roman franchise before the enactment of the 'Lex Iulia,' and most of the praefecturae may have obtained the right of electing their own magistrates on receiving such full citizenship. Cp. Marquardt 1. 34; 42; 43.

[1] In the comitia tributa. Cp. A. Gell. 13. 15. 4; Lange, Röm. Alt. 1. 750; 756. But as the names of such 'quattuorviri' are omitted in the lists of magistrates recited in the earlier laws, Mommsen thinks that Livy was mistaken in supposing that they were elected by the Roman people before the seventh century of the city. Cp. Mommsen, Hist. of Rome, 1. 435; Corp. Inscr. Lat. 1. 45-47 (197).

The status of the praefecturae would thus be a transitional one: but cp. pp. 619–620.

The position of Capua between the first establishment of its connection with Rome and its revolt in the second Punic war (343–216 B.C.) presents some difficulty. It is said by Livy (8. 14) to have received the 'civitas sine suffragio' in 338 B.C., cp. Velleius 1. 14; but it is still spoken of as a 'civitas foederata' by Livy at later periods (9. 6; 23. 5), and it appears that a magistrate, the meddix tuticus, was still elected there up to the year 211 B.C. Cp. Livy 23. 35; Mommsen, Oskische Studien, 112. Perhaps the gradual disappearance of the old municipal relation led to a confusion of it with that of the civitates foederatae. Cp. Marquardt 1. 31.

The inhabitants of the municipal towns of the older kind served in legions of their own, but under tribunes, thus holding an intermediate position between that of the full Roman citizens and that of the allies. They are sometimes called Roman citizens (Fest. 142), sometimes not (Paul. Diac., Fest. 127). In the latter case the title is probably denied them as not being enrolled in the tribes. Cp. Marquardt 1. 32, and notes.

III. Nomen Latinum. This consisted of—

1. Old Latin towns, of which Tibur, Praeneste, and perhaps Laurentum[1], alone, so far as we know, retained their old privileges to a considerable extent after the revolt and subjugation of Latium in 338 B.C. Cp. Livy 8. 11; 14.
2. Coloniae Latinae. The population of such of these as were founded after the subjugation of Latium probably consisted partly of Latins, partly of indigent Romans who sacrificed some of their privileges as citizens to obtain a grant of land in such colonies. Cp. Madv. Opusc. Acad. 1. 263. The composition of the population of the earlier Latin colonies—at least of those founded before 384 B.C.—is more doubtful.

All the Latin communities appear to have enjoyed the rights of Roman citizens with regard to the tenure and acquisition of property (ius commercii). Cp. Cic. Pro Caec. 35, 102. Whether they, or any of them, had the right of intermarriage with Roman citizens (ius connubii) is doubtful. Cp. Livy 1. 49; 4. 3; Dionys. Hal. Rom. Ant. 6. 1; Mommsen, Rom. Hist. 1. 110; 351; 359; 433; Madv. Opusc. Acad. 1. 274–279.

[1] A. W. Zumpt (De Lavinio et Laurentibus 10; 14) believes that Lavinium was the political centre of the people called Laurentes. If he is right, of course the name of Lavinium must be substituted for that of Laurentum in the text.

Any citizen of such towns could acquire the Roman full citizenship in two ways especially.—

1. By having held office in his own city. Cp. supr. p. 223 and reff.

2. By leaving a son to represent him there[1]. Livy 41. 8.

The cities of the Latins held a place, though the most favoured place, among the 'civitates foederatae.' Cp. Cic. Pro Balb. 24, 54; Philipp. 3. 6, 15.

IV. Other allied communities. The condition of these was determined by special treaties, and in some cases it was so favourable that they were unwilling to change it for that of full Roman citizens (Cic. Pro Balb. 8. 21; Livy 23. 20).

Capua, Atella, Calatia and Tarentum, after their revolt and reduction in the second Punic war, and the Brutii after the close of that war, seem to have held an exceptionally bad position. Cp. Livy 26. 16; App. Annib. 61; A. Gell. N. A. 10. 3; Strab. 6. 3, 4 or C 281; Marquardt 1. 46.

B. I. The 'Lex Iulia de civitate sociorum,' enacted in 90 B.C., conferred the full Roman franchise on all the communities in Italy proper which had remained faithful to Rome in the Marsic war up to that time, provided that the several communities were willing to accept it. Its provisions applied to all the Latin colonies then existing in Italy and in Cisalpine Gaul, and subsequent legislation extended the privileges of Roman citizenship still more widely. It is probable that at the time of Cicero's greatest activity as an advocate and politician all communities in Italy proper had received the full Roman franchise, and had, with the exception of recent colonies of Roman citizens, become 'municipia.'

II. Thus a new class of municipia was formed, the third of those mentioned by Paulus Diaconus (Fest. 127). It comprised the old Latin and other allied towns, the Latin colonies, and probably a large majority of the old municipia and praefecturae. The rights of the new municipia were settled by 'leges municipales,' of which the Lex Rubria, passed in 49 B.C. (cp. p. 489), and the Lex Iulia municipalis, passed in 45 B.C. (cp. p. 492), were among the most important. All the new municipia had some rights of local self-government. Cp. Marquardt 1. 62–67; 475 foll. The proper definition of municipes in the later sense is 'Roman citizens not belonging by extraction to the city of Rome.' Ib. 34.

[1] Marquardt (1. 55) believes that this privilege, with some others, was withdrawn from colonies founded in and subsequently to 268 B.C.

III. A new class of 'coloniae civium Romanorum' was shortly afterwards formed, consisting of the settlements of veterans made in different parts of Italy by Sulla—an example afterwards imitated by the dictator Caesar and by Augustus. These did not, it is true, form in all cases new political communities; but Praeneste is spoken of by Cicero as a colony (In Cat. 1. 3, 8), and so is Capua (Pro Sest. 4; Philipp. 2. 40), where a considerable number of veterans and of indigent Roman citizens was settled under Caesar's agrarian law of 59 B.C. (cp. supr. pp. 16; 17; 73); Casilinum also is called a colony (Philipp. l. c. Cp. supr. p. 654).

IV. A new class of 'Latini' came into existence in the year 89 B.C., when a law of the consul, Cn. Pompeius Strabo, raised several towns of the Transpadani to that position. The same privilege was extended to other towns subsequently, e.g. to Novum Comum, where Caesar established or augmented a colony not consisting of Latins by birth or Romans. Such communities could of course only be called Latin colonies in a peculiar sense. Cp. supr. p. 223 and reff.; Madv. Opusc. Acad. 1. 276; 277; Suet. Iul. 8; Ascon. in Pisonian. 120; 121.

V. Cicero (Pro Sest. 14, 32) speaks of 'coloniae,' 'municipia,' and 'praefecturae' as forming three classes of towns in Italy in his time. In speaking of 'coloniae,' he must refer to colonies of Roman citizens, but perhaps also, less properly, to Latin colonies [1]. When it is his object to speak accurately he shews a clear appreciation of the distinction between Latin colonies and municipia—or rather of the change effected in the condition of Latin colonies by the enactment of the 'Lex Iulia' (cp. Philipp. 13. 8, 18).

VI. Of the towns which had originally been 'praefecturae,' Cicero speaks of Reate and Atina as still bearing that name (In Cat. 3. 2, 5; Pro Planc. 8, 19). Arpinum, which had been a 'praefectura,' he calls 'municipium' (supr. pp. 452–453); Puteoli and Cumae had undergone changes in their constitution, and perhaps were no longer called 'praefecturae' (cp. Cic. de Leg. Agrar. 2. 31, 86; Ad Att. 10. 13, 1).

Caesar (Bell. Civ. 1. 15) speaks of being well received by the praefecturae' of Picenum in 49 B.C.; which seems to shew that such cities held an important place in that region.

[1] I now doubt whether any of the older Latin colonies, that is, of those founded before the enactment of the 'Lex Iulia,' were still called colonies, even in popular language, after the enactment of that law. The language of Cicero as to Brundisium is hardly decisive (Ad Att. 4. 1, 4). Asconius, it is true (In Pisonian. 3. 120), wonders at Cicero's calling Placentia a municipium, which had been a Latin colony.

VII. To recapitulate.

(1) The terms 'colonia,' 'municipium,' 'praefectura' were not, perhaps, mutually exclusive.

(2) A majority—perhaps all—of the 'municipia' and 'coloniae civium Romanorum' of the earlier period (i.e. of that which ended in the year 90 B.C.) were also 'praefecturae,' and some of them retained the latter title in Cicero's time.

(3) The term 'municipium,' *and no other*, applied in Cicero's time to such old Latin and other allied communities in Italy as had received the full Roman franchise in B.C. 90, or later; and perhaps when Cicero speaks of 'coloniae,' 'municipia,' and 'praefecturae,' he uses the term 'municipium' in this narrower sense.

(4) The term 'colonia' applied in Cicero's time, when used of towns south of the Rubicon or of the Po,

(*a*) To the more recent 'coloniae civium Romanorum;'

(*b*) Perhaps to 'coloniae Latinae,' less properly, in consideration of their original constitution.

See, in addition to authorities already quoted, Festus sub voc. 'Municeps,' 142, Müller[1]; Paul. Diac. (Festus 131, Müller); Niebuhr, Rom. Hist. 2. 60 (3rd edition), On the Rights of Isopolity and Municipium; Smith's Dict. of Antiq. sub vocc. 'Colonia,' 315–319; 'Latinitas,' 669, 670; C. G. Zumpt, Ueber den Unterschied der Benennungen Municipium, Colonia, Praefectura— in the Treatises of the Berlin Academy for 1839; Marquardt, Römische Staatsverwaltung, vol. 1; Mr. Long's Decline of the Roman Republic, 2. 174–178; Cavedoni, Dichiarazione degli antichi marmi Modenesi, Modena 1828, pp. 220 foll.; Mommsen, Römisches Münzwesen (Berlin 1860), p. 336, note 130. In compiling this Appendix, I have derived great assistance from a selection of passages from ancient authors illustrating Roman antiquities, printed for private circulation by Mr. D. B. Monro, Fellow of Oriel College.

[1] Lipsiae, 1839.

INDEX I.

OF GREEK WORDS AND PHRASES.

Ἀβδηριτικόν, 279.
ἀγών, 58.
ἀδόλεσχος, 557.
αἰδέομαι Τρῶας, 334.
αἴδεσθεν μὲν ἀνήνασθαι, κ.τ.λ., 559.
αἰνιγμός (ἐν αἰνιγμοῖς), 84.
ἀκκίζεσθαι, 84.
ἄκρατος, 384.
ἀκροτελεύτιον, 248.
ἄλη, 364.
ἅλις, δρυός, 81; σπουδῆς, 70.
ἀλλ' ἀεί τινα φῶτα, κ.τ.λ., 92.
ἀλογίστως, 349.
Ἀμάλθεια, 63, cp. 42; Ἀμαλθεῖον, 63.
ἀμεταμέλητος, 483.
ἀνάθημα, 31.
ἀναλογία, 260.
ἀναπολόγητος, 547.
ἀνεμέσητος, 545.
ἀνεξία, 224.
ἄνθη (metaph.), 556.
ἀνοίκειον, 559.
ἅπαξ θανεῖν, 99.
ἀπάντησις, 334, 337, 559.
ἀποθέωσις, 62.
ἀπολιτικώτατος, 333.
ἀπολογισμός, 545.
ἀπορία, 555; ἀπορῶ, 305, 351.
ἀποσπασμάτια, 66.
ἀπρακτότατος, 51.
Ἄρειος πάγος, 49.
ἀριστοκρατικῶς, 47.
ἀσμένιστος, 352.
ἄσπονδος, 350.
ἀστρατήγητος, 308; ἀστρατηγικώτατος, 334.
ἀσφάλεια, 84, 555; ἀσφαλῶς, 92; πρὸς τὸ ἀσφαλές, 308.
ἀττικώτερα, 45.
αὐτονομία, 261.
ἀχαριστία, 318.

βεβίασται, 423, 531.
βίος πρακτικός, 76; θεωρητικός, 76.

γενναίως, 48; γενναιότερον, 350.
γεροντικόν, γεροντικώτερον, 421.
γλυκύτερον, 248.

διευκρινεῖν, 283.
Διονύσιος ἐν Κορίνθῳ, 341.
δυσχρηστία, 547.

εἰδώς σοι λέγω, 338.
εἰρωνεία, 557; εἰρωνεύεσθαι, 435.
εἷς ἐμοὶ μυρίοι, 557.
ἐκφώνησις, 163.
ἑλικτὰ καὶ οὐδέν, 90.
ἐμετική, 484.
ἐμπεριπατεῖσθαι, 49.
ἐν τοῖς ἐρωτικοῖς, 347.
ἐνδόμυχον, 254.
ἐνθυμήματα, 49.
ἐνσχολάζω, 305.
ἐξακανθίζειν, 273.
ἐξοχή, 194.
ἐπεὶ οὐχ ἱερήϊον, κ.τ.λ., 30.
ἐπέχειν, 274.
ἐποχή, 274.
ἐπικεφάλια, 226.
ἐπίπεμπτος, 224.
ἐπισημασία, 61.
ἐπίσκοπος, 306.
ἐπισταθμεία, 485.
ἐρωτικά, τά, 347.
ἔσπετε νῦν μοι, κ.τ.λ., 56.
εὐγενῆ, 325.
εὐήθεια, 265.
εὐημέρημα, 246.
εὐθανασία, 545.
εὐκαιρία, 555.
εὐκαίρως, 175.
εὐμένεια, 557.

ἡμερολεγδόν, 192.
Ἡρακλείδειον, 557.
ἥρως, 307.

θέσεις, 341.

Ἴλεως, 328.
ἱστορικώτατον, 260.

καθῆκον, τό, 559; περὶ τοῦ κατὰ περίστασιν καθήκοντος, ib.
καλόν, τό, 304.
καραδοκεῖν, 351.
καρποί, 49.
κατακλείς, 360.
κατάλογος, τῶν νεῶν, ὁ, 260.
κατασκευαί, 49.
καχέκτης, 51.
κέρας, 251.
κεφάλαια, τά, 558.
κωμικὸς μάρτυς, 256.

λαλαγεῦσα, 360.
λεπτόν, κατά, 78.
λέσχη, 421.
λήκυθος, 48.
λῆρος πολύς, 531.
λῆψις, 279; ὑπὸ τὴν λῆψιν, 351.

μάντις δ' ἄριστος, κ.τ.λ., 309.
μέλλον, τό, 351.
μετέωρος, 224.
μὴ μὰν ἀσπουδί γε, κ.τ.λ., 361.
μή μοι γοργείην, κ.τ.λ., 338.

νεκυία, 351, 359.
νεάκτιστα, 260.
νομανδρία (?), 225.

ὁδοῦ πάρεργον, 254.
οἱ περὶ αὐτόν, 485.
οἷάπερ ἡ δέσποινα, 224.
ὁμόνοια, περὶ ὁμονοίας, 330.
Ὀπούς, Ὀπούντιοι, 260.
ὀρθὰν τὰν ναῦν, 99.
ὁρμή, 306.
οὕτω που τῶν πρόσθεν, κ.τ.λ., 306.

παῖδες παίδων, 556.
παλιγγενεσία, 275.
παλινῳδία, 179, 278.
πανήγυρις, 47.
παραλύουσι πειράζεσθαι, 547.
παρρησία, 58.
πεντέλαιπος, 531.
πολυγραφία, 557.
περίοδος, 49.
περίστασις, 559.
πλόος ὡραῖος, ὁ, 338.
πλουδοκῶν, 377.
πολιτείᾳ, 70.
πολίτευμα, 337.
πολιτευτέον, 364.

πολιτικός, 283, 350, 360; ἐν τοῖς πολιτικοῖς, 45; πολιτικώτερος, 66; πολιτικώτατον, 363; πολιτικῶς, 308.
πρόβλημα, 423; πρόβλημα πολιτικόν, 283.
προθεσπίζω, 328.
προλεγόμενα, 427.
προσεπονομεῖσθαι, 175.
πρόπυλον, 274.
πρὸς τὸ πρότερον, 54.
πρόσθε λέων, κ.τ.λ., 76.
προσπάσχειν τῷ καλῷ, 81.
προσφωνῶ, 559.
πτολιπόρθιος, 597.
πυροὺς εἰς δῆμον, 273.

σεμνότερος, 65.
σῆμα δέ τοι ἐρέω, 194.
Σιπούς, Σιπούντιοι, 260.
σκέμμα, τῶν πολιτικωτάτων σκεμμάτων, 363.
σκοπός, 78, 328.
σοφίζεσθαι, 74.
σοφιστεύω, 341.
σπουδαῖον, 485.
στιφρείαν, 351.
στοργή, 377.
συμπάθεια, 191, 377.
συμπαθῶν, 225.
συμπολιτεύεσθαι, 282.
συνδημερεύειν, 325.
συντάσσεσθαι, 545.
σύντηξις, 377.
σχέδιον, 545.
σῶμα, 66.

τὰ περὶ τοῦ καθήκοντος, 558.
ταξιάρχης, 558.
τὰς τῶν κρατούντων, 90.
τέθραπτα, 250.
Τέμπη, 193.
τέρας, 126.
Τεῦκρις, 51, cp. 46.
τὴν θεῶν μεγίστην, κ.τ.λ., 305.
τί γὰρ αὐτῷ μέλει, 423.
τὸ ἄμεινον καὶ τὸ χεῖρον, κ.τ.λ., (Thucyd.) 376.
τοποθεσία, 45, 63.
τοτέ μοι χάνοι εὐρεῖα χθών, 344.
τοῦ πλοῦ, 304.
τρισαριστοπαγίται, 192.
τυφλώττω, 81.
τῶν μὲν παρόντων, κ.τ.λ., Thucyd. on Themist., 376.

ὑπερβολικῶς, 259, 261.
ὑπέρου, 363.
ὑπόθεσις, 49, 179.

ὑπασπορίζεσθαι, 349.
ὑπόμνημα, 65; ὑπομνηματισμός, 225.
ὑπεσάλευκα, 530.
ὕστερον πρότερον, Ὁμηρικῶς, 52.

φαλάκρωμα, (?) 517, 518.
φιλόλογα, 485.
φιλόπατρις, 67, 350.
φιλοσοφητέον, 62.
φιλοσοφούμενα, 534.

Φλιοῦν, 260.
φυγάδων κάθοδοι, 305.
φυσᾷ γὰρ οὐ σμικροῖσιν, κ.τ.λ., 74.

χολή, ἄκρατος, 384.
χρεῶν ἀποκοπαί, 305.
χρησμός, 349.

ὦ πρόξενος καλῆς, κ.τ.λ., 521.
ὠναί, 225.

INDEX II.

A or ab = 'after,' 229, 577; 'in respect of,' 27, cp. 251; 'dating from,' 'derived from,' 375; 'on the side of,' 369; personifying an abstract noun, 40; 'supplied by,' 547; a me, 'from my own funds,' 252.

Abbreviations, list of, xiv; used at the beginning of letters, 32, 121, 588, 595; or in official documents, 237–240.

Abesse, a scelere, 104; a sepulcro, 547.

Abire, consulatu, 56; 'sic,' 'to pass unpunished,' 516.

Ablative case—form in 'i,' 475, 477, l. 4; of neuter names of towns in 'e,' 472; of the cost, 199; absolute, emphatic for genitive, 314; after 'alienum,' without a preposition, 535; after 'confidere,' 312; after 'stare,' 314; with comparatives, where 'quam' would be more common, 357, cp. 270; of the date, 61, 68; of direction, 120; of the quality, 43, 241, 316; of duration of time, 101, 261, 422; with 'facere' (quid puero fiet), 114; with 'a' after gerundives, 462; local, 422; without a preposition after 'iunctum,' 349; of a man's tribe, 174, 237; without a preposition, after 'verba intelligendi,' 407; of names of countries and similar words after verbs of motion, 349, cp. 388; and of such words without a preposition denoting rest, 586; of the place from which a letter is written, 111; of 'voluntas,' 523; of extent, where the genitive would generally be used, 477; of the instrument, where we should expect 'per' with the accusative, 476; combination of ablatives in different senses, 82, 204.

Ablegare, 79.

Abrogare, 107, 117, 171.

Absentia, used in a peculiar sense, 523.

Abstract for concrete, 607.

Absurde, 97.

Abunde, 'decidedly,' 192.

Abuti, 593.

Ac, adversative, 259; how different from 'et,' 43; ac non, 55; ac potius, 105; = 'et statim,' 484.

Acceptae (= tractatae) pessime, 600.

Accessus (metaph.), 529.

Accidere, of misfortunes, 377.

Accommodare, tempus, 472; accommodatum ad, 99.

Accurate, 162, 225; accuratius, 189.

Accusative case, after proxime (?), 37; adverbial, 359, 376; 'certum' for 'pro certo,' 255; and dative, after 'credere,' 259; of duration of time, 422; in exclamations, 122, 369, 483; of neuter pronouns with 'adsentiri,' 436; and 'dubitare,' 479; 'gaudere,' 233; 'hortari,' 259, 266; 'orare,' 415; fugere and sequi itinera, 600; of the person, after 'quaesumus,' 543; double, after 'iudicare,' 307; after 'cognoscere,' 456; after 'facere,' 450; after 'rogare,' 416; with the infinitive, *see* Infinitive.

Acerbissima mors, 476.

Acerbitas, of a person, 'bitterness,' 437.

Acies (metaph.), 368.

Acquiescere, 352, 469.

Acta, 'occurrences,' 105; 'gazette,' 108, 262.

Actio, 'a pleading,' 235; actiones in other senses, 74, 199–201, 416; actio rei publicae, 198.

Ad, nearly = 'against,' 426 (?); = 'in answer to,' 86; = 'apud,' 322, cp. 378, 381; 'in respect of,' 108, 438,

439; and with gerundive, 577; in a final sense, 370, cp. 319; in dates = 'upon,' 424; ad equum, 486; ad numerum, 'enough,' 239; ad summam, 'in a word,' 272, 282, cp. 516; in another sense, 307; 'ad tempus,' 'for the present,' 529; 'to suit circumstances,' 585.
Adclamatio, 172.
Adcredens, 260.
Adesse = comparere in iudicio, 171.
Adferre utilitatem, 115, 529; molestiam, 532.
Adfligere se, 82.
Adgregare voluntatem, 204.
Adhibere dolorem, 470.
Adhuc, with a verb in the present, 426.
Adjectives, used as adverbs, especially in the predicate, 32, 168, cp. 214, 257, and 366; rarely used alone with proper names, 276; instead of the ablative with a preposition, 330; with a substantive of another gender, 456, 535; two with one substantive without a copulative conjunction, 446; one with two substantives, agreeing in gender with the nearest, 592; formation of, from Greek names of towns, 260.
Adiunctor, provinciae, 319.
Adiungere, amicitiam, 230, cp. 479; viros ad necessitudinem, 452; adiungi ad causam, 206, cp. 204.
Adligati (edere ad adligatos), 175; alligata voluntas, 78.
Administrare (neut.), 266.
Adroganter, 601.
Adservare, 382.
Adsessio, 533.
Adspergere (metaph.), 371, cp. 444.
Adsumere = adrogare, 208.
Adverb, as predicate, 34, 310; separated from the verb it qualifies, 276; with a neuter participle = a substantive, 340; with substantives, 414, 466.
Adversative particles omitted, 42, 166.
Adversus rem publicam, 61.
Adulescens, 465.
Advocatus, 'a supporter,' 171; advocati, 'partisans,' 55, 82.
Aedilis, a municipal magistrate, 453.
Aequabilis, 193.
Aeque, 469.
Aequi boni facere, 279.
Aerarii, in two senses, 54.
Aerati, 54.
Aes, in two senses, 72; aera, 'tablets,' 541.
Aestimationes, 427, cp. 460.
Aestiva, 249.
Aetas, 'youth or early manhood,' 438; aetatem gerere, 465.
Agere, 'to argue,' 19, cp. 173; 'to think of,' 282; cum aliquo, 'to go to law with,' 29; 'to negotiate with,' or entreat, 38; 'to attempt,' 111; cum re publica, 'to take care of the state's interest,' 43; ἐμπεσεῖν, 484; nihil, 537; followed by accusative and infinitive, 378; actum agere, 360; agi, 'to be intended,' 87; praeclare, 454, cp. 465; 'to be going on,' 172; cp. 'quid agatur' and 'quid agatis,' 114; agitur satis, 195.
Agnoscere, 'to admit the truth of,' 542.
Alaudae, 502, 554, 595.
Alienum, 'out of place,' 372.
Aliptae, 207.
Aliquando = tandem, 562.
Aliquis, in negative sentences, 474: = aliquis alius, 474, cp. 519; aliquis esse, 109, 606.
Alius = 'different,' 306, 450, 451; = alter, 468.
Alligare, 'to hamper,' 333.
Alter ego, 106, 188; alterum se, 163; altera vita, 164.
Altius, 'from a more remote point,' 199.
Amabo te = 'I beseech you,' 245.
Ambitiosus, 91, 444.
Amplexari (metaph.), 203.
Amplissimus, different from 'optimus,' 454.
An, in answers, 359; in simple supplementary questions, 373; = 'or perhaps,' 410–411.
Anacoluthon, 92, 362, cp. 40.
Anatocismus anniversarius, 252.
Ancora soluta, 41.
Animadversio, 'punishment,' 457.
Animatus, 445, 538.
Animula, 116, 467.
Animus, opposed to 'ingenium,' 567.
Annales, an official journal, 76.
Annus vester, 'your year for office,' 549.
Antecedent, attracted to the case

of the relative, 85; implied in a possessive pronoun, 160; omitted, 239, l. 4; put after the relative, 85; and with the demonstrative omitted, 381; repeated in the relative clause, 239.
Antiquare, 49, 50.
Antiquissima, 'most important,' 374.
Aperire ludum, 426.
Aperte tecte, 49.
Aphracta, 223-224.
Apisci, 469.
Aposiopesis, 521, 581.
Apparate, 485.
Appellare, 'to address,' 168; sic, 'to use such a term,' 435, 437.
Apprehendere, 'to master,' 372.
Apricatio, 305.
Apud, nearly = 'against,' 79.
Aquae (Arpinatis), 59, 60.
Aquarii, 244.
Aquilae, 584.
Arcula, 61.
Ardere (metaph.), 194.
Arithmetica, 521.
Arx (metaph.), 201.
Aspirare, 70, 87.
Assequi, 'to make good,' 375.
Astute, 93, 370, 536.
Asyndeton, of verbs, 162, 335, 482; of substantives, 189, 333; of adverbs, 486.
At, 'yes but,' 348, 426; at enim, 94; at vero, nearly = at enim, 465-466.
Atque, how different from 'et,' 312; adversative, 564; = 'than,' 213.
Attendere, 474; transit., 599.
Attingere, of an attack of sickness, 113.
Attraction, accusative substituted for nominative by, 33, cp. 464; nominative for accusative of a substantive attracted to a relative, 550; plural for singular of a participle, 536; of a demonstrative pronoun, in gender, to a following substantive, 438; of the relative 'quo' for 'quod,' 376.
Auctor, 'one to attest,' 422; 'a backer or supporter,' 419; 'an adviser or originator of measures,' 574.
Auctoritas, of official documents or resolutions, 53, 99, 170, 217; 'assurance,' 310.
Augere, as a neuter verb, 528; augere animum, 597; auctus, 31.
Augur publicus, 443.
Aut, perhaps = 'alioqui,' 560.
Autem, continuing a narrative, 47; expressing surprise, 258.
Auxilium dignitatis, 529.

Bacillum, 409.
Barbaria, 306.
Barbatuli, 49.
Barones, 224.
Beatus, 'wealthy,' 47; cp. 382, l. 4.
Bellus, 30.
Bene = 'cheaply,' 46; 'valde,' 381.
Biduo, eo, 162.
Bima, 'of two years' service,' 608.
Bona dea, 13, 43, 206.
Boni or boni viri, in a political sense, 44, 47, 56, 173, 206, cp. 356; 'bonus vir,' distinguished from 'bonus civis,' 203.
Bonitas, 479.
Brachio molli (metaph.), 68.
Buccam, venire in, 304, 421.

Cadavera, oppidum, 466.
Cadere, used impersonally, 332.
Caeciliana fabula, 63.
Caeliana, 383.
Calere (metaph.), 244.
Calficere (metaph.), 244.
Callere (metaph.), 464.
Calumnia, 'a malicious plea,' 165; timoris, 'vain fear,' 450; 'calumniam ferre,' 233; iurare, 236.
Campus, 194.
Cantherium, 438.
Caput (civis), 34; = poena capitalis, 362; legis, 107; = origin, 605; used in two senses in one sentence, 207; supra caput, 94.
Carcer, 59.
Carere urbe, said of exiles, 430.
Castella, 553.
Castigare = castigando impellere, 604.
Casus, how different from natura, 475; = discrimen, 603.
Cavere, with accusative, 'to provide securities,' 116.
Causa, 'a claim,' 478; 'object,' 'watchword,' 319; 'a party,' 569; 'a case,' 94, cp. 30; 'position,' 359; = coniunctio, 478; 'state of the case,' 306; (?) = 'res,' 202; how different from 'res,' 566.
Celare, 'to keep in the dark,' 39.
Celebritas, 'populousness,' 114.
Celeripes, 336.

Centesimae usurae, 252, cp. 194.
Cernere hereditatem, 416, 528.
Certus, of men, 'trustworthy,' 182; (of a resolution) adequately grounded, 321; sensus, 'decided,' 586; certi = 'quidam,' 203, 315; certum, as an adverb, 387; certum esse, with the dative, 86, 284; certum habere, 344, 568; certiorem facere, 113.
Cervicibus, conlocare in, 551.
Cerulae miniatae, 556.
Chirographum, 257, 541.
Circuli, 78.
Circumforaneus, 72.
Circumire, 'to canvass,' 530.
Circumrodere (metaph.), 179.
Circumscribere, a political term, 283.
Circumvectio, 76.
Circumventus, 34.
Cistophorus, 77.
Civiliter, 271.
Civitas, libera, 114; form 'civitatium,' 578.
Clamare (transit.), 412.
Claudus homo, 62.
Clientela, 521, cp. 388.
Clivus Capitolinus, 69.
Coartatus, 304.
Codicilli, 476.
Cogere (absol.), 83.
Cognoscere, 460; cognosce, 'let me tell you,' 251, cp. 29, l. 9, 211.
Cohonestare, 453.
Cohors praetoria, 582.
Cohorticulae, 244.
Collecticius (exercitus), 430.
Collegium, 'colleagueship,' 477; for the body of the tribunes or praetors, 117, 240; collegia, 'clubs,' 19, 105.
Colligare se (metaph.), 434.
Colligere, benevolentiam, 96; clementiam, 326; gratiam, 368; se, 203, 341; 'to count up,' 373, 375; ad colligendum se, 603.
Colonia, civium Romanorum, 615, 619-620; Latina, 617, 619-620.
Comedere (metaph.), 428.
Comissatores coniurationis, 61.
Comitiales dies, 237.
Commemorare, without an accusative, 466.
Commentari, 472, 549.
Commentarius, 64; Caesaris, 523, 549.
Committere ut, suggesting blame, 308, 322.
Commodare, 75, 463.
Commodum, an adverb, 381.
Commoveri, 'to travel,' 279.
Communia praecepta, 215.
Communicare, neut., 182; transit., 'to grant a share of,' 549.
Communiter scribere, 406.
Commutare cum (construction of), 465.
Comparare se, 174, cp. 241.
Comparatio, 102.
Comparative, used of one of three courses, 519; without 'eo' where we should expect that word, 610.
Comperisse omnia, 50.
Compitalicius dies, 279.
Complecti, 'to treat,' 94; 'to embrace the cause of,' 221.
Complicare epistolam, 121, cp. 421.
Comprimere, 'to secrete,' 250.
Concerpere, 244.
Concertationes, 526.
Concidere = dicendo evertere, 177.
Concidere (metaph.), 56, 58, 60.
Concord, masc. used with reference to two substantives, a masc. and neut., 607. *See* also Adjective, Attraction, Gender, Plural, Singular.
Concursatio, 'canvassing,' 166, 167.
Condicere, 212.
Condicio, 'agreement,' 308; vivendi, 431, l. 1; condicione, 'under an agreement,' 473; ea condicione si, 450.
Conferre, 'to discuss together,' 91; = adhibere, 317; in posterum diem, 'to put off,' 600.
Conficere, aestiva, 249; 'to destroy,' 587; 'to get through,' 427; = 'facere,' 452, l. 5; cum aliquo, 'to settle with' (neut.), 178, cp. 216.
Confidentia, 240.
Confidere, with accus. of pronoun understood, 481, l. 7 (?).
Confieri, 333, 464.
Confirmare, 'to encourage,' 174, 416; 'to repeal,' 248; confirmare de, 441; confirmari, 'to gain strength,' 416; confirmatio, 'encouragement,' 440.
Confluens, of a place, 595.
Congelare (metaph.), 257.
Congiarium, 554.
Conglaciare (metaph.), 244.
Conicere, 'to utter a threat,' 232; in sortem, 240; in turbam, 409.

Coniunctim, 237.
Conjunction omitted, 312, 335; cp. Asyndeton.
Conjunctive mood, (1) of verbs of affirming or denying, 162; (2) expressing disapprobation, 285; (3) expressing past thoughts of the writer, 200; or (4) the words or thoughts of another, 33, 52, 169; or (5) completing an idea expressed by an infinitive clause, 366; or (6) 'as he thought,' 'as he said,' 544; (7) apparently unnecessary, of 'dico,' 29; (8) as a potential, 60, 372, l. 13 (?); (9) after relatives meaning 'though,' 44; or stating a reason or cause, 390, 426; (10) in indirect questions, 309; (11) after 'ubi,' 484; (12) after 'quo' or 'quod' of a reason not the real one, 194; (13) with 'forsitan,' of a fact, 464; (14) after 'si'='etiamsi,' 38, 433; (15) explaining what is referred to by a pronoun, 445; (16) of 'volo' and its compounds, 29; (17) and after such verbs, 62, 80; (18) after 'nihil,' 'non,' 'quid' est quod, 451, 464, 473; (19) with 'ut' after 'accedit,' 525; or 'adsentior tibi,' 340; or 'cadere,' 332–333; or 'fieri potest,' 383; or in final propositions generally, 349, 381; (20) or after 'opto' and 'spero,' 332; (21) after 'ita—ut' limiting the verb in the principal clause, 26, 78; (22) after 'ut' meaning 'supposing that,' 73; (23) after 'quamquam,' 574.
Present tense, in future sense, 42, 311; in dependent clauses after the future infinitive, 362; where we should use the imperfect, 36, 243, 433; 2nd person singular of a person whose existence is only assumed, 439; with 'ne,' 214; with 'dum,' 388; = imperat., 38; cum audiam, 'on hearing,' 95.
Imperfect, almost = infin. with 'possum,' 185; expressing what does not take place, 312; where we use the present after verbs in the past, 92, 220, 386, 410; where we should use the pluperfect, 347; with 'cum,' meaning 'when,' 225; or 'though,' 211–212, cp. 36; = 'was to' in indirect questions, 412, l. 6; of future time, in dependent relative questions, 465.
Perfect, in modest expressions, 183; how different from imperfect in final clauses, 413; where we should use the pluperfect, 75, 334, 536; pass., for a second future, 116, l. 6.
Pluperfect, where we should use the perfect, 184; after 'cum' meaning 'when,' 172, ll. 9, 10; with 'ne' almost = an imperative, 66; for the fut. exact. when the principal verb is in the past, 329; used for the perfect after 'esse' and a gerundive, 446.
Fut. exact. 2nd person sing. = imperat., 226.
Coniungere se cum libertate, 574; coniunctos cum causa, 569.
Conlocare = 'ordinare,' 257.
Conquassatus (metaph.), 467.
Consaepta, 243.
Consalutatio, 78.
Consanescere (metaph.), 471.
Conscindere (metaph.), 82, 334.
Consequi, 'to follow the example of,' 548–549.
Consessus senatorum, 362.
Consilium, 'authority,' 305; 'object,' 185; 'plan,' 106, l. 5; 'decision,' 305, 318; meo consilio uti, 'to act on my own responsibility,' 415, l. 5; 'a body of judges,' 47, 55, 56, 76 (?); of counsellors, 76 (?).
Consistere (metaph.), 58; 'to be settled,' 606; mente, lingua, ore, 172; cum aliquo, 'to confer with,' 86; in hoc, 'to depend upon this,' 601; 'to take up a position,' 519.
Conspectus, 303.
Consputare, 172.
Constare, 'to be fixed,' 327; = permanere, 415.
Constitutum, neut. subst., 420.
Constrictio, 180.
Consuetudo, 472.
Consulere, 'to consider' (re consulta), 76.
Contemnere, 'to shew contempt for,' 229–230.
Contendere, = curare, 459; = laborare, 319; ab aliquo, 219, 251; and with accus., 366.
Conterere (metaph.), 211.
Contexere, extrema cum primis, 596.
Contio, 'a speech,' 47; contionem

dare, 162; habere, 18; in contionem producere, 47; 'the rostra,' 101.
Contionalis, 60.
Contionari, 555, 563, 572.
Contionarius, 174.
Contiuncula, 74.
Contra rem publicam, 173; contra venire, 30; contra used as an adverb, 316, 372, 482.
Contrahere vela (metaph.), 53; contractis male rebus, 281.
Contrariae, 'inconsistent,' 96; contrarium, 'inexpedient,' 572.
Contubernales, 178.
Contumacia, 524.
Convenire, after res, 544; = 'utile esse,' 369; personal construction of, in the passive, 326; cum aliquo, 'to have an understanding with,' 600.
Convitium facere, 50, 554.
Copiolae, 600.
Copiose, 485.
Corrumpere rem, 'to ruin a project,' 169, 170.
Credere, in a double sense, 60; with dat. and accus., 259; iron., 465.
Creditores, 165.
Cretio simplex, 417.
Criminari, 548.
Cruditas, 478.
Cubicularius, 261-262.
Culeum, insuere in, 94.
Cum = quod, 175, cp. 26, 527; almost = 'si,' 332, cp. 410; placed after the beginning of a sentence, 182, cp. 262; = ex quo, 469; cum praesertim, 448; cum . . . tum etiam, 472; or tum vero, 72, 183.
Cumulare, 220, l. 5; gaudio, 527.
Cumulatum, 'to have reached its height,' 528; cumulatissime, 177.
Cumulus, 'something extra,' 56; cumulum deruere (metaph.), 557.
Cupiditas, 'ambition,' 169, 218; 'passion,' 94.
Curare, 'to provide,' 178; 'to care for,' with a personal object, 424.
Currentem incitare, 419.
Cursus, 'a career,' 30; vitae, 208, l. 12; bonorum consiliorum, 593.
Custodia publica, 100.

Damnum fieri, 59, 568.
Dare litteras, construction of, 414; diem, 'to assign for a visit,' 421; dare se (ut se initia dederint), 119.
Dative case, in -u of the fourth declension, 608; ethical, 50; 'for the benefit of,' 245, 447, l. 7, note; in 'honour of,' 538; of the person, after 'cupio' and such verbs, 98, 167; after 'iratus,' 165; after 'dicto audientes esse,' 232; with gerundive, after 'auctor esse,' 318; after 'intervenire,' 92; after 'invadere' (rare), 313; after 'in odium venire,' 375; after passives, especially gerundives, 278, 318, l. 2, 419, 578; double, after 'tribuere,' 369; and ablative, after 'facere,' 450.
De, with the ablat. preceding an accus. and infin., 45.
Debere, absol., 'to be indebted to,' 167.
Decedere, 'to leave a province,' 92, 217; de suo iure decedere, 542.
Decernere, 'to vote for' (of an individual), 162; 'to decide,' 580.
Declarare, 'to shew,' 470.
Declinare, 81; declinatio, 84.
Decuriati, 175.
Deducere rem eo, or in eum locum, 78, 86; summam rem publicam in discrimen, 608, l. 14.
Deesse, 'to disappoint,' 177.
Defendere, 'to maintain,' 535.
Deficere, a se ipso, 368.
Deformitas, 'unseemliness,' 347; discredit, 575.
Degustare, 58.
Deicere, 'to defeat,' 231.
Delatio, 243.
Delectare (absol.), 'to give pleasure,' 439; pass., with the ablat., 549.
Delegare, 189.
Deliberatio, 472; deliberatius, 39, l. 8.
Deliciae, 233; = 'luxury,' 422-423.
Deminuere, 'to alienate,' 98.
Deminutio de imperio populi Romani, 467, l. 4.
Demisse, 79.
Demitigari, 44.
Demittere se aliquo, 367.
Demortui, 560.
Denique = 'omnino,' 374; = 'only' or 'even only,' 454, 580, l. 6.
Denuntiare, 481; denuntiatio, 578.
Depecisci, 337.
Dependere and spondere in a metaphorical sense, 202.

Deponere provinciam, 66.
Deprecator, 418, l. 10.
Derivata (metaph.), 73.
Derogare, 117.
Descendere, 'to come to the place of election,' 229; metaph., 240, 284.
Describere, 'to describe' without naming, 173.
Desiderare, 257; se ipsum, 104, ll. 12, 13.
Desiderium, said of a person, 110.
Desperationes, 371.
Despondere (metaph.), 410; cp. desponsam, 58.
Detestari, 350.
Detrahere de, 93, l. 6.
Devenire, in eam fortunam, 468.
Deversoria, 406, cp. 133.
Devertere ad, 383, 515.
Devexa ad otium, 349.
Devincire familiaritate, 93.
Devorare (metaph.), 60, 179.
Dexterius, 583.
Dialectica, 523.
Dialogus (Aristotelis), 214–215.
Dibaphum, 371.
Dicacitas, 43.
Dicrota, 224.
Dicta, 68.
Dicto audientes esse, 232.
Diecula, 254.
Dies, of a period, 104; of the events of a day, 370, l. 15; Sullanus, 376; diem dicere, 102; consumere, 169; prodicere, 171; diem suum obire, 467; post diem tertium eius diei, 475; legis, 'a time fixed by law,' 280.
Digamma, 345.
Digiti, 254; digito caelum attingere, 69.
Dignitas, 214, 304, 311, 343, 453, 542; dignitatem habere, 93; dignitatis insignia, 574.
Diiudicare, 272 (?), 526.
Dilaudare, 264.
Dilectus, 314.
Diligentia, 115.
Diligere, how different from 'amare,' 528.
Dilucide, 559.
Dimittere, 'to release,' 365.
Dioecesis, 250.
Direptum iri (metaph.), 92.
Dirumpi, with ablat., 549.
Discedere, 'to come off,' 102, cp. 171; sc. de sententia, 'to change one's mind,' 76; discedere ab, 'to make an exception of,' 210.
Disceptare, 'to be at stake,' 579; disceptatio, 39.
Discessio, 71; discessionem facere, 169.
Discipuli (metaph.), 425.
Discrepare, of persons, 257.
Discribere, 67, 540.
Discutere, 'to dispel fears of, 89.
Displiceo mihi, 79.
Disputare, 211.
Dissimulare and simulare, 578.
Dissolutio, 39.
Distinere, 118; distineri, 'to be busy,' 47.
Distractos (metaph.), 331.
Distributive numerals, with substantives only used in the plural, 389.
Dividere, 'to submit a motion in parts,' 168.
Divinatio, a legal term, 236.
Divinitus, 58.
Divinum, 'providential, 189, 190.
Divisores, 61.
Docte, 482.
Dodrans, 51.
Dolus malus, 29.
Domesticus dolor, 35.
Dominus, 82.
Dormire (metaph.), 423.
Dubitare an, 373; dubitare or dubium esse quin, 479; cp. 374, l. 12.
Ducere, 'to attract,' 333; 'to delay,' 194, 429.
Dumtaxat, 78, cp. 540.
Duumviri, 530, 615.

E vestigio, 476.
Ea re = 'eo,' 543.
Edicta, 84; cp. 542.
Effectus, 'execution,' 578.
Efflagitatio, 609.
Effundere (metaph.), 368.
Ego vero, 104; at the beginning of a letter, 411, 469.
Eiectio, 78.
Eiicere = 'explodere,' 86; = 'evomere,' 384.
Eius modi = 'tale,' 73.
Elaborare, 99.
Elapsum de manibus, 57.
Elatum, of style, 449.
Eleganter, 485.
Elegantia, of conduct, 263; of style, 435.

Elimare, 545.

Ellipse, of 'causa' with 'est cur,' or 'est quod,' 431, 549; of 'via,' 180, 425; of 'cogita,' 375; of tenses of 'dicere,' 231, 335; of 'hoc dico,' 44; of 'esse' with an adverb in the predicate, 408, and with the perfect infin. pass., 106; of other tenses of 'esse,' 38, 86; of 'facio,' 327; of 'fieri' after 'ut potest,' 170; of 'fore,' 334; and with an accus. after 'videre,' 349; of a gerundive in the plural to be supplied from a gerund, 359; of 'ire,' 251, 335; of a participle, 547, l. 9; of a particle corresponding to 'tam,' 601; of substantives to be repeated from another clause, 354, l. 14; of a verb, after 'ut nihil magis,' 212, cp. 113; or 'ut aliud nihil,' 307; to be supplied in one tense from another, 248; or to be easily supplied from a substantive, 31, 70, 92, 172; or in the infin. after 'possum' and other verbs, 57, 77; or in a finite mood from the infinitive, 354; in the active voice from one in the passive, 587; of 'ut scirem' before 'si quid,' 412; of words meaning 'I remark that,' 266; or answering to 'ne quaeras,' 28; or explaining 'gratum,' 191; of the subject of 'inquit,' 284, 304; in familiar discourse, 274, ll. 18, 19; in phrases with 'quid,' 240, cp. 46, l. 1, 84, l. 9, 179, 248, 359; in the phrase 'tu qui,' 263; of a clause after a pluperfect indicative, 606.

Emerere, 262; emerita, 239.

Emergere (metaph.), 261, l. 10.

Emissarius, 236.

Emittere (metaph.), 66.

Emonere, 186.

Enim, ironical, 458; referring to a reason not expressed, 83, cp. 380, l. 7; ='why,' 280.

Eo—quo or quod, 'for the reason that,' 105, 344, l. 4.

Eodem loci='ibidem,' 45; 'eodem ad me' (ellipt.), 485.

Epigrammata, 62.

Epistolary tenses, 26.

Epulae (metaph.), 567.

Equitatus, of the equestrian order, 69.

Ergastula, 586.

Ergo, expressing indignation, 385; or irony, 546.

Erogare, 100, 250.

Erumpere, 'to aim at,' 481; and with 'se,' 271.

Eruptio, 88.

Esse='commorari,' 311, 544; 'to be in circulation,' 65; 'to involve,' 253; 'to be written,' 'to stand in a letter,' 257, 324; in ea opinione =(res), 87; in optatis, 'to be an object of desire,' 256; ='vivere,' 390; repetition of a tense of, 575; 'est cur' or 'est quod,' 431, 549; ut nunc est, 573; fuit='which is over,' 556; esse omitted with accus. after 'volo,' etc., 537.

Et, adversative, 227, cp. 259; expressing wonder, 264; et litteras=cum litteris, 323; et quidem, 'and that too,' 422; et tamen, 'moreover,' 375.

Etiam, 'still,' 77; 'yes,' 45, cp. 437; etiam atque etiam, 416.

Etiamsi, with indicat., 93.

Etsi, 'and yet,' 347, 544; 'however,' 248, 377; 'etiamsi,' 179; with the perfect conjunct. in a hypothetical sentence, 222–223.

Evadere, 'to turn out,' 360; 'to get out of a difficulty,' 450.

Evigilata, 355.

Evocare, a legal term, 249; συμπάθειαν (metaph.), 377; evocati, 582.

Evolare (metaph.), 186.

Evolvere, 351.

Ex cruce detrahere, 95; ex eo esse, 97, l. 2.

Exacuere, 604.

Exagitare, res, 167.

Exanimare (metaph.), 409.

Exarare, 420.

Exarescere (metaph.), 427.

Exceptiones, 411.

Excipere, how different from 'accipere,' 48; 'to intercept,' 604.

Excitata fortuna, 168; cp. 'excitare,' 206.

Excubare (metaph.), 578.

Excutere (metaph.), 572.

Exemplo, uno, 435; ad exemplum, 529.

Exercitatio, 216, 427.

Exercitus (metaph.), 83, l. 14.

Exhaurire sermonem, 92.

Exhibere=facessere, 65.

Exigere, 160, cp. 251–252; ius

legitimum, 242; 'to negotiate,' 610.
Exire, 'to go on foreign service,' 189; 'to leave the neighbourhood of Rome,' 303; 'to be published,' 448.
Exitus, 'success,' 300; exitu rebusque, 591.
Expedire, 'to settle,' 108; expedita, 'clear,' 355; expeditius iter, 577; expeditissimus, 610.
Expensam ferre, 231.
Explicatius, 337.
Exploratum, 'certain,' 184, cp. 109, 281, 446; explorate, 'confidently,' 578.
Expressiora, 187.
Exprimere, 'to describe,' 127, 444.
Exputare, 609.
Exsecratio, 78.
Exsequi, 'to fulfil,' 105.
Exsilio privare, 59.
Exstare = apparere, 174.
Exsurgere (metaph.), 308, 606.
Extenuatissimae, 600.
Extraordinarius reus, 233.
Extremus, 'worst,' 77; in extremis, 571.
Extrudere bellum, 609.
Exulceratae, res (metaph.), 167.

Faba mimus, 62.
Fabula Caeciliana, 63.
Facere, 'to elect,' 231; 'to comply,' 62; 'to sacrifice,' 43; se, 'to call one's self,' 84; convitium, 50, 554; invidiam, 420; medicinam, 384; 'hoc ita facere,' 'to manage the affair thus,' 245; 'contra . . . facere,' 'to oppose,' 366; used instead of another verb repeated, 438, 449; or instead of a verb to be supplied from a participle, 215; facere ut, pleonastic, 103, 104, 249; fac existimes, 437, cp. 103; factus, 'schooled,' 87; facteon, 62.
Facetiae, 95.
Facile = libenter, 386.
Faeneratores, 386.
Faenus, 194, 252–254; perpetuum, 254, cp. 263.
Faex Romuli, 79, cp. 60.
Fallit, impers., 376.
Fama multare, 448.
Fames, 'want,' 57.
Familia, 'a household of slaves,' 113; urbana, 385; 'a school,' 76; familiam ducere, 190.
Familiaris, as a substantive, 425, 550, 560, 605, l. 4.
Familiaritas, 93; familiariter, 482, 544.
Fanum, deponere in fano, 254.
Fasciculus, 225, 412.
Fastidiose, 65.
Fatalis, 550.
Fateri = 'testari,' 603.
Fatum, 112.
Febricula, 421.
Feriae, Latinae, 244; Lepidianae, 560.
Ferre, 'to withstand,' 374; 'to require,' 324; = 'ostendere,' 338; graviter, 98.
Fervens = 'furiosus,' 603.
Fideliter, 603.
Fides, 'honour,' 389; fides publica, 86, cp. 604; fidem facere, 555; 'praestare,' 'to fulfil a promise,' 252.
Fieri longius, 431.
Figere (metaph.), 220.
Finire, 'to propose as a limit,' 319.
Firmitas (exercitus), 608.
Fistula (metaph.), 61.
Florens, 256; florentiora, 556.
Fluctus (metaph.), 305–306.
Fluere (metaph.), 349.
Foede, 'miserably,' 426.
Forsitan, 464.
Fortasse, 274; fortassis, 543.
Forum, 'a session,' 227, 261; forum agere, ib.; forum tenere, 'to occupy the attention of the courts,' 234.
Frangere (metaph.), 58, 67; me, 471; meum consilium, 438.
Frater, perhaps 'cousin,' 456, l. 3, cp. 437.
Fraus, 'penalty,' 117; in fraudem conjici, 108.
Fremere, 163.
Frenum mordere (metaph.), 597.
Frequenter, 600.
Frigere, 'to be ill received,' 47.
Fronte an mente,' 194; frontem ferire, 26.
Frumentariae provinciae, 342.
Fucus, 25–26.
Fumo comburere, 95.
Furia, of Clodius, 206.
Fustem impingere, 240, l. 18.

Gender, of an adject., pronoun, or participle with two substantives, 58, 201, cp. 549, 607; determined

by sense rather than grammar, 206, 230; neut., of an adjective referring to masc. or fem. substantives, 456; of a pronoun, referring to a sentence, 44.
Generatim, 408.
Genitive case, of nouns in -ius or -ium, 482; double, in different senses, 160; or where one governs the other, 201-202; 'generis,' 182, 356, 384, 455, 484; of the quality, 101, 255; of the place where a letter is written, 453; objective, 105, 308, l. 11; cp. 271, where it = ablative with 'de'; with 'existimare,' 464; partitive, 57; possessive, 15, cp. 57 (doloris); 280 (legis); of the price, 279; after 'indigere,' 377; with active participles, 99; with a passive participle and adverb, 576; after 'in mentem venire,' 428; with 'esse' of that to which a thing belongs as suitable, 213, 389; cp. consilii res est, 304; after 'dignus,' 331; of 'animus,' 414; of the name of a husband, 459; unusual forms of, 40.
Genus = res, 93, 220, 261, 369; 'a mode of appointment,' 53; genera, with 'ordines,' 280; perhaps = 'parties' (or 'professions'?), 81; genus Sullani regni, 328.
Germanus, 180.
Gerund, used as an ablat. caus., 589.
Gerundive, ablat. of, without 'in,' 162; with force of pres. part. pass., ib.
Gladiator, 'a bravo,' 563; gladiatoribus, 68, cp. 61.
Gloriola, 190.
Gloriosus, in a good sense, 195; gloriosius, 69.
Graecus = 'eastern,' 245.
Gratiae, in a peculiar sense, 30.
Gratiosi in suffragiis, 220.
Gratuita, comitia, 195.
Gratus, how different from 'iucundus,' 470; gratum, elliptical phrase with, 191.
Gravedo, 383, 556.
Gubernare patrimonium, 375.
Gustare (metaph.), 552.
Gymnasium, 31, 477.

Habere = adferre, 184; with adjectives or past participles passive, 254, 368, 384, 473; 'to have as a reading,' 260, l. 12; habere belle, 316, 387; recte, 236; summam orationis, 381; habeo necesse scribere, 364; nihil habeo 'quid' and 'quod,' 357, cp. 109; se res sic habet, 102; habes = 'audis,' 'intellegis,' 57; epistolam, 432; habebis, in a gladiatorial sense, 421; sic habeto, 90, 183; habes res Romanas, 51, cp. 550.
Hactenus, 391.
Haerere (metaph.), 147, 149.
Hariolans, 328.
Haud scio an, 515.
Hem, indignantis, 466.
Hermathena, 30.
Hic, pron. referring to what follows, 537, cp. 415; referring to the present, 'ille' to the future, 377; haec gratia = huius rei gratia, 358; haec, on the following subject, 318; = 'the present state of things,' 454; hoc = 'this only,' 451.
Hic, adv. = 'in hac re,' 106.
Hiems, hieme tanta, 316; maxima, 320.
Hilarula, 561.
Hirudo (metaph.), 60.
Homo, in a good sense, 191-192, 485; in a bad sense, 412, cp. 418; of a woman, 467; in apposition to another substantive, 563; instead of a pronoun, 51-52, 437.
Homunculus, 466.
Honestas, 'reputation,' 464.
Honestus = 'honoratus,' 543.
Honos, 'public office,' or election to it, 32; honores, 'days of honour,' 478.
Hora, 484; noctis, 475.
Hortari (hortare te), 352.
Hospes, of people lodged at the public expense, 250.
Huc, for this object, 187.
Hui, 222.
Huius modi, 'of the kind described,' 176.
Humaniter, 32.
Humeris suis, 261.
Hypodidascalus, 428.
Hypothetical clause supplied from context, 408.

Iacere (metaph.), 'to be prostrate,' 33; or 'listless,' 244; or 'out of spirits,' 413.
Iactare, legem, 245.

Iacturam facere (metaph.), 70; cp. 467, l. 6.
Iam, transitional, 37, cp. 261; 'well,' 426; iam tum, 473.
Iambus, of an iambic poem, 557.
Id, aetatis, 546; causae = ea causa, 182; id genus, 230; id ipsum, introducing an addition, 169.
Idem, 'also,' 'on the other hand,' 58, l. 2, 160; 'and yet,' 118; pleonastic (?) with 'hic,' 213, l. 22; position of, with 'qui,' 214; 'in the same position,' 60; 'of one mind,' 'similar,' or perhaps, 'consistent,' 375.
Ieiunius, 458.
Igitur, 214, 462, 518.
Igniculus, 421.
Ignorare, 59.
Ille, referring to something following, 37, 240; or before mentioned, 85; or exceptional, 268; or future, 377; or remote, 343; or well known, 464; pointing to 'quod' with the indic., 545; ille . . qui = talis . . qualis, 284, l. 11; pleonastic with 'inquit' after a long parenthesis, 361.
Illustre, 45; illustrior, 'more evident,' 198.
Immissus (metaph.), 59.
Immo si, 'much more if,' 235.
Immolare, 448.
Immunitates, 540.
Impeditum, 419.
Impelli, 'to be driven by passion or by threats,' 543.
Impensae, plur., 577.
Imperative, form of in -to, 414.
Imperator, imperium, 122.
Impetus, animi, 405; belli, 320.
Imponere, in causam, 385; volnus (metaph.), 57.
Impressio, 39.
Improbare, 179.
Impunitas, 116; impunite, 537.
In, *with accus.*, 'against,' 69, cp. 75; in buccam venire, 304, cp. 421; in iudicium venire, 70; in eam partem, 236, cp. 460; in locum mortui, 84, l. 2; in oculos incurrere, 460; in provinciam esse, 219; in tempus, 'to suit the time,' 81, l. 13; 'for,' 'on account of,' 607; *with ablat.* = 'as to,' 174, 254, cp. 26, 86; with 'persona' nearly = 'against,' 445; in bona spe esse, 270; in caelo esse (metaph.), 81; in eo esse, 'to depend on that,' 53; in hoc esse = 'hoc agere,' 68; in manibus esse, 599; in—habere = fovere, 203; in eo, 'on that account,' 67; 'thereby,' 352; in eo est si, 454; in eo, 'in this matter,' 108; cp. 'in quo,' 115; in ea, 'towards her,' 414; in meis, how different from cum meis, 430; in oculis esse, 261; in officio esse, 114; in potestate alicuius esse, 332; positum esse in, 'to depend upon,' 72; in primis, 453; iacturam facere in, 467, l. 6; in damno, 'at the cost of,' 579.
Inambulare, 262.
Inanis, 'thinly peopled,' 320.
Incidere, how different from 'venire,' 465; in hominem, 330; in opinionem, 387; in tarditatem, 375.
Incitatum, 449; incitatius, 85.
Inclinata fortuna, 368; res, 166, l. 10; victoria, 387.
Incolumis, in a political sense, 104; incolumitas, 104, 441.
Inculcatum, 116.
Incumbere, ad laudem, 580; in causam, 105; in eam rem, 119; incumbentibus, absol., 208, cp. 223.
Incurrere in, 368, cp. 460.
Index, 'an informer,' 85, l. 6, cp. 174, l. 13; indices, 'titles,' 195.
Indicative mood, after 'cum' as a general remark, 281; or giving a real reason, = 'inasmuch as,' 527; or 'at the time when,' 419; or 'since,' of time, 354; after 'nisi,' 466; after 'quasi,' in a quotation, 81; after 'quia,' 431; after 'quod,' giving a real reason, 65; after 'quoniam,' of an actual fact, 315; hypothetical, without 'si,' 285, l. 6 (?); in antecedent with a question in the consequent, 372; with 'quae quidem,' 382; with indefinite relative pronouns or adverbs, 430; with adjective or neuter gerundive, of what ought or ought not to have been done, 69, 107, 259, 426, 449; or of past tenses of 'possum,' 'debeo,' etc., 34, 69, 107, 349; with 'qui,' as a simple explanation, 33, 313; with 'quo quo modo' of an actual fact, 321; in relative clauses after 'eius modi,' 454, cp. 456–457.

Present tense, with future signification, 264, 375, 555, l. 7; historic, 355; with 'dum,' 366, 383; in antecedent of hypothetical sentences with the future in the consequent, 111; and with the conjunctive in the consequent, 372; and in the consequent with the conjunctive in the antecedent, 434, cp. 273.
Imperfect, epistolary, 26; of intentions or possibilities, 117, cp. 263,275,484.—Perfect, used for pluperfect, 54, 384, l. 4; used hypothetically of a certain result, 114, cp. 107.—Pluperfect, for conjunctive, 83, cp. 273; with 'postquam,' giving a date, 420; after 'quod,' giving a real reason, 65.—Future, second person sing. = imperative, 80, 265.—Second Future, double, import of, 479.
Indicium, 88.
Indignitas, 368; = indignatio (?), 373, 386.
Inductus, 108, cp. 179, l. 6, and 'induxit,' 418, l. 12.
Infector (metaph.), 371.
Inferi, 'the departed,' 468.
Inferum mare, 330.
Infinite mood, after verbs expressing emotion, 48; or meaning 'to inform,' 382; as a substantive, 384, 305; after passive verbs and 'debeo' used personally, 170, l. 5, 183, 320, 387, l. 3; with accus., as a subject, 322; or after verbs of advising, 350; after 'habeo necesse,' 364; after 'necesse est,' 473; after subire periculum, 318; after words expressing a duty or purpose, 'tempus esse,' 372, cp. 377; 'iudicare,' 380; historic, 347, 412; in 'oratio obliqua,' 413; expressing surprise or indignation, 81, 110; with accus. after 'nolo,' 'volo,' 'cupio,' etc., 98, 113; stating an actual fact, 562; without pronominal subject, referring to the principal verb, 333; or even when the subject of that verb is different, 542, l. 1; when the genitive of the gerund would be more usual, 366. Present tense of, after 'memini,' 411; cp. 330, l. 4; = imperfect, after a historic present, 358, l. 11; after 'spero,' 26, 112; of 'proficiscor' almost = future, 26; cp. 108 (expediri); 187 (adsequi); 332 (posse); 246 (hiemare). Perfect tense of, where the main sentence refers to future time, 238; perfect participle with 'fore' = fut. exact., 565.
Infirmitas, 'want of talent,' 449.
Infitiari, 98.
Inflectere, magnitudinem animi, 186.
Infracta, res, 351.
Ingenia, 441.
Ingerere praeterita, 409.
Ingravescere, in a good sense, 438.
Iniqui, as a substantive, 534.
Iniungere = imponere, 601.
Iniuriis suis, a legal term, 234.
Inquirere in, 275.
Inscriptio, 'a title,' 559.
Insectatio, 519.
Insignia dignitatis, 574.
Insinuare, insinuari in, 85.
Instituta, 'rules,' 256; cp. 251, l. 18.
Instituta res, 68.
Insulsus, 347, 566; insulsitas, 222.
Integrum esse, 38; sibi reservare, 302, 245; omnia integra sustinere, 608.
Intendere, 'to maintain,' 169; 'to threaten,' 80; se, 230.
Intercalare, 244.
Intercedere = accidere, 213, cp. 170; 'to give security,' 56; 'to veto,' 24; = 'intervenire' (?), 478, l. 4.
Interior, 'up the country,' 'eastern,' 96.
Intermortuus, 49.
Interpellare, 'to interfere with,' 526, 538, 586.
Interponere, 'to introduce in a discussion,' 214, cp. 323; se, 'to intrude,' 575.
Interpres, 560.
Interrogatio, 201.
Interrogative clause with affirmative sense, 362, ll. 3–5.
Intervenire = interesse, 92.
Intestinus dolor, 364.
Intime, 'cordially,' 93.
Intra modum, 438.
Invitamentum, 580.
Invitatus, a subst., 190.
Invocare (corrupt), 66; invocatus = non vocatus, 234.
Involatus, 443.
Inurere (metaph.), 57.
Ipse, 'without aid or instructions,' 97, 389; 'precisely,' 223.
Iracundiae (pl.), 604.

Ire, in alia omnia, 168; in sententiam, 169, ll. 6, 7.
Is ... qui = talis ... qualis, 199; cp. 'ille qui,' 284; is where we might expect 'qui,' 382; or hic, 542.
Iste, 'that mentioned in your letter,' 84, 278; of things interesting the person addressed, 48, 52, 84; form in '-ic,' 426.
Ita, 'so very much,' 105; with 'si,' limiting a remark, 280; with 'ut' and the conjunct. in the same sense, 26, 68–69, 78, 102, 104, 310; ita vivam, 257; pleonastic, with 'videri,' 432, l. 7; with 'id,' 408; with the indicative, answering to a clause to be supplied from the context, 335, l. 10; itaque, 'and so,' 175; ita est, 556.
Item, 'in like manner,' 82, cp. 87.
Iter, how different from 'via,' 226; with 'fugere' and 'sequi,' 600.
Iucundus, how different from 'gratus,' 470; 'iucunditates,' 377.
Iudicare, not the praetor's business, 98; = decernere, followed by a simple Infinitive, 380, l. 9; qui res iudicant, 271.
Iudices ccc, 237, cp. 334.
Iudicium esse (in) = decerni, 373.
Iurare morbum, 27.
Iure meo, 524.
Ius, in two senses, 427.
Iuvenis, 363.
Iuventus, 465.

Labores, 'sufferings,' 478, l. 3.
Languere (metaph.), 375; languidiores litterae, 412.
Lanista, 54.
Largitio, agraria, 73; opposed to liberalitas, 273.
Latiar, 178.
Latinitas, 521, cp. 223, 617–620.
Lavatio, 425.
Laudare, 'to bear witness to character,' 199, 201.
Laus, in laude vivere, 267; laudes, 'exploits,' 463, l. 2.
Laute, 79; lautiores, 485.
Lecticarii, 476.
Lectulus (mori in lectulo), 376, cp. 426.
Legare, 'to procure a post as legate' (for another), 195.
Legationes, audiences to foreign envoys, 51, 171; legatio libera, 28, 79.
Legatus, 'a military officer,' 28, 79, l. 8; 'a commissioner,' 166; in an informal sense, 418; 'a deputy,' 161; decem legati, of assessors or commissioners, 193.
Legio, decima, 591; Martia, 502, 508, 582–584; quarta, 502, 583–584; quinta (Alaudae), 502, 584; quinta et tricensima, 582. *See* also pp. 611–614.
Levare, 'to mitigate,' or 'relieve,' 390; pass., 'to recover from,' 473.
Levatio, 471.
Levis, levitas, 53, 69, 94, cp. 185, 356.
Lex Aurelia, 4; Campana (Iulia), 78; Leges Clodiae, 19, 105, 107, 116, 117; Lex Cornelia, 217; Gabinia, 5; eiusdem de pecuniis mutuis, 253; Iulia de civitate sociorum, 618; Leges Iuliae, 17, 78, 227, 489–492, 534; Lex Manilia, 6; Leges Pompeiae, 4, 142, 143, 147, 148; Lex Porcia, 131; Roscia, 66, 83; Scantinia, 272; Sempronia, 187, 289; Trebonia, 142; Vatinia, 17; agraria (Rulli), 8, 66, 244–245; alimentaria, 245; curiata, 217; frumentaria, 83; viaria, 244.
Liberalitas, used euphemistically of extravagance, 370.
Liberare periculo, 479.
Liberi, perhaps of one child, 465.
Liberum, 'unencumbered,' 587.
Librarius, 275.
Licet, used personally, 426; licitum est, 465.
Lictores laureati, 303.
Lippitudo, 330.
Liquido, 268.
Litterae, 'rescripts,' 96; in the plural sense, 406, cp. 389, l. 6; (?) of literary works, 48; litterulae, 317, 420.
Lituus (metaph.), 415.
Livor, 586.
Locus, 'an opportunity,' 206, cp. 93; 'a position,' 552; 'a passage,' 201; 'a topic,' 58; consularis locus, 68; locum dare fortunae, 519.
Lomentum, 272.
Loqui, followed by accus., 94, l. 6; by accus. and infin., 568, l. 14; loqui est coeptum, 235.
Lucere (metaph.), 'to be remarkable,' 105.
Lucrativus sol, 305.

Luculente, 530; luculentior, 458; luculentissima, of a legion, 608.
Lucus Pisonis, 176.
Ludus, 'a school,' 426; gladiatorius, 56; talarius, 54.
Lux, 'distinction,' 65; a term of endearment, 110, 276.
Lycurgei, 44.

Maculosi (metaph.), 54.
Magister (auctionis), 29.
Magistratus (apud), 61.
Magnus, 'important,' 270.
Maiorem in modum, 251, 463; maiora, 'too tragic,' 99–100.
Male consularis, 68; malum! an exclamation, 360.
Malitia, 117.
Malle, 'to prefer the side of,' 229.
Manare (metaph.), 540.
Mancipia (metaph.), 329.
Manens, as an adjective, 445.
Manipularis, 347.
Manubiae, 207.
Manus, adferre (metaph.), 104; tollere, in wonder, 189; de manu in manum, 190; in manibus esse, 599; in manibus habere, 203; sub manu, 602; 'a body of supporters,' 28, 102.
Materiam dare, 93.
Maturum, 'suitable,' 576; maturius, 'previously,' 377; maturitas (metaph.), 438, 439.
Medicina, 69; medicinam facere, 'to administer a remedy,' 384.
Medius, 'neutral,' 374.
Medius fidius, 98–99.
Megara, declension of, 466.
Mel (metaph.), 233.
Melior fio = 'convalesco,' 427; melius, as a subst., 440.
Memoriola, 421.
Mensa secunda, 531.
Mercatores, provinciarum (metaph.), 205.
Metellina oratio, 45.
Metiri, 'to distribute,' 245.
Metus, 'intimidation,' 537.
Miles, opposed to 'eques,' 595, 603.
Militia (metaph.), 262.
Minuere, 'to soften down,' 'lower the tone of,' 449.
Minus, 'seldom,' 550.
Misellus, 119.
Misere, 'foolishly,' 589; miserum misere perdere, 119.
Mittere = nuntiare, 90; 'to say nothing of,' 81, cp. 374; 'in consilium,' 235.
Modo, 'just lately,' 467.
Molestus, opposed to odiosus, 486; moleste, 71.
Moliri, used absolutely, 588.
Molli brachio (metaph.), 68.
Monstra, 'outrageous acts,' 237.
Monumentum, 200; 'a record,' 99, cp. 441.
Moods, curious change of, 166.
Moratus, 90.
Morderi (metaph.), 263.
Morem gerere, 482; more Romano, 'honestly,' 190; cp. 'more maiorum,' 25–26.
Morosus, 177.
Movere, 'to ransack' (?), 328; moveri = moleste ferre, 48.
Muliercula, 467.
Mulli barbati, 69.
Multa, how different from 'poena,' 117.
Multitudo comparata, 118–119.
Mundi habitatores, 176.
Municipes, townsmen, 452, L. 4.
Municipium, 614–620; constituere, 452, L. 19; municipales, 331.
Munire (metaph.), 426; munitior, 79, 173.
Munus, 'a public duty,' 390; munera, 'shows,' 220.
Munusculum (ironical), 233.
Musae mansuetiores, 214.
non Mutare, 484.
Mutue, 33.
Myrothecium, 64.
Mysteria, of the festival of the Bona Dea, 255.

Nam, anticipating and answering an objection or suggestion, 70, 182, 274; introducing an illustration, 270; in an elliptical passage, 58, 327.
Nancisci, 'to overtake,' 330.
Nanneiani, 56.
Narratio, 'a dialogue,' 259.
Natura, 475.
Naufragia (metaph.), 108–109.
Navi, 475.
Navigatio, 139.
Ne, for 'ut non,' 321–322; neve .. neve, for 'ne .. neque,' 210; ne .. quidem, in a subordinate proposition, 474, L. 9; separated by other words, ibid. and 424.

Necesse, as an adjective, 439.
Nedum = non modo, 383.
Negative, position of, 39; followed by an affirmative, 45, 264; double, not always = an affirmative, 58, cp. 227.
Negotiari, 251, l. 17; negotiatores, 77.
Negotiolum, 560.
Negotium, 'a commission or office,' 436, l. 1; = inimicitia, 240; dare magistratibus, 56; gerere, 391; nullo negotio, 382.
Neque—et, 45; ne-que—que, 464; = 'and yet not,' 66; neque etiam, after two negatives, 388; neque non tamen = et tamen, 365.
Nervose, 604.
Nescio an nulli, 388.
Neuter, of a substantive referring to a person, 46; see also under 'gender.'
Nihil = non, 67; nihil agere, 537; nihil est, in elliptic sentences, 360; nihil est quod, 451, 542; nihil habeo quod, and quid, 357; nihildum = nondum quidquam, 564; nihil sibi longius fuisse, 532.
Nisi forte, in arguments, 375, cp. 426, l. 6; nisi si, 109.
Nitrum, 272, l. 5.
Nobilitas, 461.
Noctuabundus, 421.
Nodus (metaph.), 247, l. 11.
Nolle alicui, 167; noli quaerere = quid quaeris, 437.
Nomen, 'a debt,' 254; 'a ground,' 259; 'a shadow,' 318; pleonastic, with a genitive, 190.
Nomenclator, 97.
Nominare (technical), 87.
Nominatim, 'individually,' 107, 347, 408.
Non = nonne, 319, l. 13, 321, 414, 432; for 'ne' with 'utinam,' 414; position of, with 'ut,' 60, l. 1; curious position of, 364, l. 8; non dico = non modo, 350; non habeo quid or quod, 109; non ita, with an adjective and with no corresponding particle, 199; non minimum, 389; non modo, 'I do not say,' 106, l. 4; with sed ne, 75, l. 9; non mutare, 484; non religam, a legal phrase, 235.
Noscere, 'to admit,' 435.
Nostra (provincia) = 'Romana,' 247.
Nostrum, nostri, as genitives of 'nos,' 417.
Notare, 'to censure,' 283.
Novissime, 'lastly,' 607.
Nudus (metaph.), 54, 591.
Nugae, 'worthless men,' 94.
Nullus = non, 93, l. 4; cp. 430.
Number, of an adjective or participle with two substantives, 540.
Numerals, distributive, with substantives only used in the plural, 389; ordinal, quintam tricensimam for quintam et tric., 582.
Numerus, 'an amount of coin,' 250; ad numerum, 239; quo numero esset, 231.
Nummarii, 58.
Nummus, ad nummum, 253.
Nunc = 'under existing circumstances,' 30; ipsum, 324.
Nundinae, 47.
Nuntium remittere, 44.
Nutu (metaph.), 211.

O Tite, 558.
Obducere, 27.
Obdurescere (metaph.), 367, 482.
Obiicere, with 'de' and the ablat., 542.
Obire diem suum, 467, 476.
Obrogare, 117.
Obscure, 'under a disguise,' 84.
Obsequi fortunae, 380.
Obsequia, pl., 592.
Observare, 29, 42; observantia, 'courting,' 607.
Obstringere se aere alieno, 587.
Obstructa (metaph.), 108.
Obtinere, 'to maintain,' 'defend,' 75.
Obviam ire, in a double sense, 68.
Occallere (metaph.), 80.
Occupatior, 230.
Occurrere, 'to anticipate,' 468; 'to provide for,' 248; 'to present one's self,' 234.
Odiosus, 378; odiosa ἱστοπάθεια, 485.
Odium, 242.
Offendere, 'to meet with,' 208, 429; animum, 'to give offence to,' 33, cp. 192, l. 16, 218; offensus, 'odious,' 81.
Offensio, 'a mishap,' 184; offensiones quaerere (unpopularity), 325.
Olla denariorum, 427.
Olympia, 'the Olympic games,' 546.
Omnino, 'certainly,' 284; omnino non = ne vix quidem, 116, l. 9.
Opera, dedita opera, 379; operae, 'hired partisans,' 11, 59, 172.

Operto, in, 59.
Opinio, 'hope of success,' 230; opinione tua, 'than you think,' 572.
Opinor, ut opinor, 267, cp. 41.
Opipare, 485.
Opitulari, with dat., 580, l. 13; absol., 577.
Oppidum, as a gen. pl., 466.
Opportunitas, 189, 311; maritima, 320.
Opprimere bellum, 609.
Optimates, 120; in the sing., 366.
Opus esse, with nom. or accus. case, 221, cp. 77, l. 3; with the plural, 577; with the accus. and infin. pass., 88, 217; with the ablat. of participles, 238; how different from 'necesse esse,' 217, cp. 77.
Oratio, directa and obliqua, combined in one sentence, 515; cp. p. 555 for a harsh transition from one to the other.
Oratiunculae, 65.
Orator, 'a negotiator,' 363; Cicero's treatise so called, 450.
Ordinatim, 465, 600.
Ordo, 'rank as a senator,' 116; ordines, among judges, 235.
Ornamenta, 470.
Ornare praetores, 171; ornari, 'to receive attentions from,' 161, cp. 167, 189, l. 15, 218; ornatiores, 569.
Oscen, 443.
Osculari (metaph.), 203.
Ostendere, se optime ostendunt, 102.
Ostenta facere, 272.
Ostentare, 'to boast of,' 388; 'to threaten,' 454.

Pactio (at the consular election in 54 B.C.), 194.
Paenitere, construction of, 459.
Pammenia, 265.
Pantherae, 232.
Par (?), with the ablat., 536; 'a pair,' 236.
Parare, 216; se contra aliquem, 241.
Parasitus, 210.
Parricidae, 604.
Pars, 'a side of a question,' 318, 322, cp. 371; in omnes partes, 'in every way,' 408; pro civili parte, 537; quam in partem, 574.
Participle, *present*, as an adjective, 306; with nearly a future sense, 420, l. 2; *past passive* in the accus. after 'velle,' 320; with 'fore,' 565; *fut. act.*, instead of 'ut,' with the conjunct., after 'quam,' 369; with past tense of the indicative, or with perf. conj., instead of the pluperfect conjunctive, 92, 432; *neut. pass.* with adverb, followed by genitive, 576.
Partim, 454.
Passim, 'in disorder,' 600.
Pastoricia fistula (metaph.), 61.
Patere (metaph.), 386.
Pati facile, 33, 213.
Patientia, 'inactivity,' 602.
Patria, 'one's own city,' 48, 305.
Patrimonium, 413.
Paucitas, 'a small number,' 593.
Paupertas orationis, 435.
Peccare in aliquem, 105, l. 11.
Pedetemptim, 529.
Pedisequi, 74.
Pellectio, 41.
Pensio, 391.
Per se, 'independently,' 465.
Peraeque, 81.
Peragere, 'to accuse unsparingly,' 234; 'to complete,' 332.
Perbene, 461.
Perblandus, 96.
Percrebrescere, 413, cp. 26, l. 4.
Percupidus, 182.
Perditum perdere, 114; perditius, 329, 515.
Peregrinatio, 349.
Perfector, 328.
Perferre, 'to bring news,' 112.
Perfidelis, 84.
Perfringere (metaph.), 119.
Perfungi, 'to enjoy,' 467.
Perhibere, 30.
Periniquus, 481.
Perire (metaph.), 76.
Permanere, 'to persevere,' 224; permansio, 213.
Pernecessarius, 246.
Perpetua oratio, 58, 68; and, in another sense, 172; perpetuum faenus, *see* Faenus.
Perplacet, 118.
Perquam, 230.
Perscribere, 115, 170; usuras, 356.
Perscriptio, 37.
Persequi = perficere, 558.
Persona, 353, 445, 467.
Perspicere, 'to look through,' 97.
Perstringere, 48-49.
Persuasus est, 448.

Pertexere, of a speaker, 48.
Pertinere, 'to have for an object,' 311, 324, l. 5; 'to affect,' or 'interest,' 71, 232; ad curam, 452; ad spem, 115.
Pervelim, 29.
Petere, 'to seek a man's friendship,' 112.
Petitio, 'a canvass,' 25.
Petiturire, 52.
Phaselus, 41.
Philorhetor, 45.
Pietas, 113; a stronger word than 'officium,' 164.
Pigmenta (metaph.), 64.
Pigrari (pigrere) used personally, 516.
Pingere (metaph.), 48, cp. 180.
Piscinae, 69, l. 14.
Pistrinum, 100.
Plaga (metaph.), 71.
Plagiarius, 95.
Plane, 'expressly,' 408.
Plebs and populus, 238, 386; plebi, from form 'plebes,' 478; plebecula, 60, 555.
Plena manu (metaph.), 90.
Pleonasm, 'fore ut' with conjunct., instead of a future, 338; 'inquit ille,' after a long parenthesis, 361; of 'ita,' 432; of a substantive with a relative, 239, 240; of a verb with 'ut' or 'ne' after 'facere,' 104, cp. 181, l. 5, foll., 249; or after 'loqui,' 47–48; of a verb after a long dependent clause, 239, l. 16; of words meaning 'to think,' 87, 417.
Plumbeus gladius, 54.
Plural, after nouns of multitude, 239; of a predicate, after subjects connected by 'cum,' 385; after various disconnected subjects, 365; of pronouns, in addressing one person, 277; of 'sum' agreeing with a predicate in the plural, 304; change from to the singular, 110.
Poena doloris, 57, 521.
Polliceri, absol. and transit., 101, 102.
Ponere, 'to inscribe,' 62; 'to quote,' or 'mention,' 556; 'to state,' 213; in gratia, 245; in reditu, 262, cp. 42; positum esse in, 'to depend upon,' 72, cp. 418, 581.
Pontes, for voting, 50.
Populares, 81.
Populus, distinguished from 'plebs,' 238, cp. 386; 'a city community,' 250.
Portorium, 74, 76.
Postquam, in dates, 420.
Postulare, 'to accuse,' 101, cp. 174, 235, l. 1, 236.
Postulatio, 242–243; postulationes, in another sense, 55.
Potestas est, with genit., 182, 214; potestatem sui facere, 101, l. 11; in potestate [alicuius] esse, 332.
Praecidere, 381.
Praecipitare, neut., 108; praecipitata aetas, 538.
Praecipue, 455.
Praedicator, 200–201.
Praediola, 369.
Praefectura, 190; in another sense, how related to 'municipium,' 616–620.
Praefectus, 224, 264.
Praeferre = prae se ferre, 578.
Praeliari (metaph.), 52.
Praerogativa (metaph.), 266.
Praesens, 'evident,' 198.
Praestare, 'to guarantee,' 110; 'se,' 'to engage to do what one can,' 259; 'to furnish,' as advice, 417.
Praesto esse, 108.
Praeter, 'contrary to,' 115, cp. 57, l. 4; as an adverb, 261; 'more than,' 565; praeterquam quod, 538.
Praetermissus, 160.
Praetor, for propraetor or proconsul, 98, 252.
Praevaricatio, 235.
Prensare, 'to canvass,' how different from 'profiteri,' 25, 26.
Preposition, put after its case, 377; repeated, 433; with an ablative, instead of a local adjective, 251; with its case, depending upon a substantive, 236, 438–439; used adverbially, 356, 372.
Primum, without a corresponding word, 564.
Princeps, the first, 44, 69, 163.
Privatus dictator, 101.
Privilegium, 106–107.
Pro civili parte, 537; pro eo ac, 464; pro iure nostrae amicitiae, 380, cp. 377, 452, l. 11; pro necessitudine, 38; pro omnibus esse, 413.
Probare, 'to test, or revise,' 65; 'to shew value for,' 248; 'to make good' ('aliquid alicui'), 30, cp. 251, l. 18, 263.

Probe, 104, 105.
Procedere, 517.
Proclinata re, 380.
Proconsul, title of, 34.
Procurare, 232; procuratio, 471; procuratores, 97.
Producere in contionem, 47; in rostra, 87.
Proferre ita, 'to use such an expression,' 92.
Proficere, nihil, 543; quiddam, 26; absol. 'to succeed,' 593; ad proficiendum, 577.
Profiteri, absol., 101.
Prognostica, 72.
Progredi (metaph.), 380; longius, 434, 460.
Proiici, 'to be impelled,' 235.
Proinde, 'as such,' 609; ac, 536, 591.
Prolixa, 28; proline, 189.
Promising, verbs of, used intransitively, 189, cp. 101.
Promulgatio, 115, l. 9.
Pronouns, *demonstrative*, agreeing with substantives, instead of genitive, 210, 239; genitive of, for 'suus,' 448, note, 449, l. 16; inserted to avoid ambiguity, 467; omitted, 239, l. 4; pleonastic, referring to what follows, 174; or with 'quidem,' 606; curious pleonastic use of 'id,' 585; resumptive after a parenthesis, 239, 574; in the second of two relative clauses, instead of a relative, 382; = the Greek article, 468; ea condicione, '*only* on condition of,' 450; *personal*, inserted for emphasis, 36; omitted where we might expect it, 450; *possessive*, agreeing with subst. instead of a genitive or ablative with a preposition, 36, 241, cp. 285, 379, 388, 474; = a personal pronoun in objective sense, 311; suus, 'one's own,' opposed to 'alienus,' 450; position of, 185; *relative*, prefixed to an antecedent, 274, 362, cp. 368, quod .. id; referring to the contents of a sentence, 15, 166; in two clauses, one causal, prefixed to the main proposition, 362, l. 3; = a conjunction with a demonstrative, 15, 182, 205, 460; relative propositions describing character, 189. *See* also Hic, Ille, Ipse, Iste, Qui, Quid, Quod.
Pronuntiare, 'to promise,' 62; 'to read out,' 168.
Propagator (provinciae), 319.
Proper name used to express character, 268, 468, cp. 101, l. 9; (?) 542, l. 4.
Propinquitas, 'intimacy,' 477.
Propius nihil est factum, 101.
Proponere, 'to threaten,' 81; in publico, 324.
Propositum, 'a question, or subject,' 270, 335.
Proscripturire, 350.
Providere, transit., 442.
Provincia, 120; provinciae quaestorum, 171; provinciam deponere or praetermittere, 36, 37, 66; number of the Roman provinces in Cicero's time, 124–128, 219, 436, 611–614.
Provinciales aditus, 261; provincialia negotia, 72.
Provocatus, 'invited,' 182.
Proximum, 'next best,' 477; proximum habere, 30; proxime, of time, 32, cp. 428, l. 8.
Prudenter, 457.
Pseudocato, 51.
Publicus, augur, 443; in publico proponere, 324; in publicum, 330; publice, 'sent to public bodies,' 32, 560.
Pudor, 34, 79.
Puer, of Octavian, 568; pueri, 'children,' of either sex, 561; 'pupils,' 41; 'slaves,' 248, cp. 26, l. 6.
Pugnare (metaph.), 224.
Pulchellus, 59.
Pulchre, 543; pulcherrime, 469.
Pullus miluinus, 95; pulli columbini, 427, l. 6.
Pungere (metaph.), 73, 257.
Purgare, 'to acquit,' 104; 'to sift,' 97.
Pusilla, a term of endearment, 192; pusillum, a term of reproach, 193.
Putare, constructed personally in the passive, 195; ironical, 326; putes .. dicere, 60.
Putidum, 46; putidiusculi, 190, l. 16.

Qua .. qua, 'both .. and,' 81.
Qua re, in final propositions, 347, l. 8.
Quaerere, 'to care for,' 431.
Quamquam, 'and yet,' 64, 185.
Quantum, 'how little,' 96.

Quartana, 383.
Quaternae (sc. centesimae usurae), 252.
Que, adversative, 415; = 'or,' 584.
Queri, with accus., 546.
Qui, connecting two sentences, 334; qui sim = 'how weak I am,' 455; almost = 'qualis,' 306, l. 16; after 'si' for 'quis,' 433; qui illius in te amor fuit, 468; = 'though they,' 96.
Quid, 'anything more,' 45; quid censes, 522; quid dicam, 581; quid ergo est, quid aliud, in abrupt sentences, 84; quid mihi cum, 460; quid quaeris, 'enough,' 51, 55, 73; quid quod, 359; quid si, 'what if,' 98, 450, l. 2; *see* also Ellipse; est quiddam, 'is of some good,' 421.
Quidem, with pronouns, 74, 186, 259, 452; meaning 'however,' 218; its position, 88; quidem certe, 455.
Quiescere, 472.
Quin, with conjunct. after 'dubium est,' 374; = ut non, 542; non quin = non quo non, 462; quin etiam, 323.
Quindecimvir, 229.
Quippe cui, 390.
Quirinalia, 173.
Quisque, with superlatives, 340.
Quisquiliae, 57.
Quo = quia, 90; = ut eo, 384; quo ea pecunia pervenisset, a legal phrase, 234.
Quo minus, after 'recusare,' 78; after 'factum esse,' 415.
Quo modo, expressing surprise, 334, l. 4; quo modo in eius modi re, 332; quo quo modo se res habet, 424.
Quod, as a relative with an antecedent of a different gender, 386; = 'and,' 385; 'as to the fact that,' 'whereas,' 62, 182, 217, 244; 'as to which,' 100, 271; pointing to an infinitive following, 172, cp. 462, 481; or to a conjunctive, 538; perhaps = 'ut,' 547; with the indicative, how different from the accusative and infinitive, 96; quod iussus sum, 571; pointed to by a demonstrative, 165, l. 14; quod fiat, 272, cp. 25; quod superest, 224; = a demonstrative with a conjunction, 551.
Radices (metaph.), 275.
Ratio, 'interest,' 26; in plur., 36–37; 'policy,' 69, 170; 'position,' 25, 199; 'reflection,' 367; 'system' or 'theory,' 215, cp. 441; 'task,' 353; rationes, 'plans,' 256–257; 'accounts,' 353; 'in ratione,' 'in the matter of,' 32; rationem adferre, 'to give an account of,' 414; ducere, 429; habere, 212; as a political term, 241; 'to count,' 329.
Recedit, in a corrupt passage, 459.
Recens, 'freshly come,' 544.
Recessus (metaph.), 529.
Recidere, 'to have a relapse,' 461; 'in,' 'to be left over for,' 28.
Reciperare = recuperare, 208.
Recipere, 'to receive a charge' (of a magistrate), 234, l. 10; 'to promise,' 316; in fidem recipere, 473.
Reclamare, 86.
Reconciliare gratiam, 34, l. 2.
Recrudescere, 471.
Recte, 'truly,' 378; 'with prudence,' 160, 222, cp. 182, l. 4; distinguished from 'iure,' 348; 'at once,' 423.
Rectus, used of persons, 570; recta, ellipt., 180.
Recuperare se ipsum, 113, l. 11.
Reddere, 'to give,' of a book or letter, 417.
Redemptor, 178.
Redigere, 'non redigam,' a legal phrase, 235.
Redimere, 'to make atonement for,' 576; rem manifestam, 60; double construction of, 170.
Referre, with 'quo,' 'to make the standard of,' 327, 564; ad populum, 238; ad senatum, 107, cp. 238, l. 20; ad aliquem, 306, note; gratiam, 'to requite;' how different from 'agere,' 590; ironical, 172; ad aerarium, 540; in tabulas, 'to record,' 236; illuc refero, 521.
Reflatus, 423.
Refractoriolus, 65.
Refrigescere (metaph.), 28, 68.
Refugere, se, 448, l. 15.
Refutare, 218.
Regere nosmet ipsos, 'to school ourselves,' 454.
Regio, 'situation,' 185.
Regnum forense, 426; iudiciale, 27.
Reiecto (iudicum), 54.

Reiicere = differre, 171; se huc, 332; scuto reiecto, 583.
Relevare (metaph.), 41.
Religio, 'sacrilege,' 47; religionem tollere, in another sense, 163, cp. 166.
Reliqua, 'arrears,' 357; 'sequel,' 386, cp. 355, 568.
Reliquiae (metaph.), 565, 567.
Remissio animi, 39.
Remittere, 'to grow less earnest,' 76; 'to make a concession,' 98, cp. 272.
Removere, 44.
Renuntiare, 463; in another sense, 70.
Repetundae, 235.
Reponere = ponere, 379; = par pari referre, 210.
Repudiare, 'to shrink from,' 84; 'to be dissatisfied with,' 363.
Repungere, 211.
Requirere, 'to miss,' 96, cp. 440; = sciscitari, 457.
Res, how different from 'causa,' 185; 'circumstances,' 480, l. 1; opposed to 'spes,' 465; rei servire, 'to take account of a thing,' 468, l. 13; = res publica, 479: quae res, periphrastic for 'quod,' 166.
Res publica. 'constitution,' 101, l. 7, 388; 'political life,' 92, l. 11, 349, 441, cp. 519, l. 5; 'seat of government,' 388; 'some public business,' or 'object,' 249, 451, cp. 539; a condensed expression, 601; 'state of public affairs,' 260, l. 6; 'constitutional government,' 336, 345, 370, 434, l. 1; res publica summa, 608; rem publicam capessere, 547; totam complecti, 567.
Rescindere (metaph.), 104.
Residere (plus officii), 33.
Respicere se, 610.
Respondere, 'to make a defence,' 56; 'to correspond,' 523; 'to make a return,' 33, 37, 590; par pari, 547.
Restitui, 'to regain a position,' 108.
Retexere se ipsum (metaph.), 538.
Retinere, 'to keep,' as a friend, 183.
Retractando (metaph.), 326.
Retundere, sermones, 342.
Reversio, different from 'reditus,' 546.
Reviviscere (metaph.), 227, 261.
Revocare, 'to win back,' 266, l. 6; 'to recall for re-examination,' 88; or for trial, 195; se ipsum, 448.
Rex, used of Caesar and other Romans, 102, 535, l. 3.
Rhetorum pueri, 41.
Rigescere (metaph.), 244.
Robur (metaph.), 275.
Rogare, 'to ask opinions in the senate,' 169; populum, 'to supplicate the people,' 107.
Ruere, 'to rush into danger,' 281.
Rusticani, 331.
Rusticari, 420.

Saepire (metaph.), 116.
Sal, different from 'facetiae,' 95.
Salus = 'restoration from exile,' 202, 436.
Salutariter, 602.
Sampsiceramus, 75.
Sancire, 'to provide by enactment,' 116.
Sane quam, 229.
Sane strenue, 276.
Sanguinem mittere (metaph.), 60.
Sanitas (metaph.), 605.
Sanus, 'of sound mind,' 424.
Sapere, 'to notice anything,' 112.
Sarcire, 'to make good,' 200.
Sarta tecta, 452.
Satis facere, 'to give his due to,' 384, cp. 188, 463.
Saturnalia secunda, 483.
Saucius (metaph.), 236, l. 6.
Scaturire, 229.
Scilicet, 'I mean,' limiting a previous statement, 262; 'of course,' 83, 98, 118, 387, 418.
Scio (ironical), 264.
Scribendo adesse, 237.
Scripto, sententiam dicere de, 596.
Scriptura, 'composition,' 448.
Scuto reiecto, 583.
Secta, 479.
Sed, resumptive, 94, 102, 172; sed etiam, perhaps = quin etiam, 107.
Sedere = otiosum esse, 374.
Seducere, 'to lead aside,' 211.
Senate, order of proceedings in, 39, 40, 42, 43.
Sensus certus et verus, 586.
Sententia, 'opinion,' 209, 548; 'principle,' 186; 'vote,' 56, cp. 39, 209, 373.
Septemtrio, 342.
Sequi, causam, 338, 380; diem, 424;

fidem vestram, 579; mare, 260; spem, 424.
Servare de caelo, 75.
Servire, officiis, 94; temporibus, ib. and 434; voluntati, 438.
Sescenta, 80.
Severitas otiosorum, 424.
Sex septem (proverb.), 375.
Si, put later in the sentence than seems natural, 609, l. 11; position of, with 'quidem,' 424; = etiamsi, 38, 433, 434; = postquam, 469; = si quidem, 180, 561; = sin, 184; si dii adiuvabunt, 277; si forte, 466; si quid (ellipt.), 412; si vero, 113.
Sic, = tale, 54; with a verb limited by 'ut' with the conjunctive, 184.
Significare, 'to declare,' 88, l. 11; 'to hint at' or 'indicate,' 115, l. 6, 350.
Significatio, 'expression of opinion,' 33; 'hint,' 115, 211, 243, l. 7.
Signa, militaria, 584; sub signis, 554.
Signifer (metaph.), 69.
Silentio, 'without interruption,' 172, l. 5.
Simpliciter, 'frankly,' 242.
Simul cum, in a corrupt passage, 62; simul et, 560.
Simultatem vereri, in a quotation from Terence, 81.
Singular, of a verb or participle following two substantives, 61, 238; even if one be in the plural, 271; of 'sum' if the subject be plural and the predicate singular, 44.
Singulares, 280.
Sittybi, 180.
Sodalitates, 175.
Solistimum tripudium, 443.
Solum (subst.), quantum in solo, 345.
Solum = sola, 219.
Solutissima, 213.
Solutus, 'exempt from the operation of a law,' 118; 'free from restraint,' of writing, 449; generally, 'independent,' 42.
Sonivius, 443.
Sordes, 'covetousness,' 249; 'contemptible position,' 54.
Sors, sine sorte, 275.
Spe devorare, 60; in spe esse, 46, cp. 270; in optima spe repositus, 523-524; in spem venire, 601.
Spectare ad arma, 276; ad castra, 530.
Specula, 370.
Sperare ex aliquo, 461; spero, with infin. pres., 26, 72; or perfect, 176, l. 3, 428.
Sponsalia, 273.
Squalor, 34, 35.
Statim quod, 'as soon as,' 99.
Status civitatis, 455.
Stillare (metaph.), 336.
Stilus (metaph.), 418, l. 3.
Stipulationes, 560.
Stomachari, with accus., 531.
Stomachum facere, 203, l. 15, 223; perdere, 203, l. 16.
Strictim, 'hastily,' 65.
Struere sollicitudinem, 248.
Studiosus, apparently used as a substantive, 43, 58.
Studium, 438; of literary pursuits, 463; contentionis, 58; scribendi, 449, l. 13.
Suadere, with accus. of a thing, 429; after a verb used personally, with the same subject, 387.
Suavium, 561.
Sub, 'just after,' 231; sub manu, 'at hand,' 602.
Subaccusare, 544.
Subdubitare, 256.
Subducere, 'to add up,' 252-254; (metaph.), 203.
Subesse, nihil subest, 421.
Subirasci, 339, 567.
Subire, 'to subject one's self to,' 109, cp. 276, l. 14.
Sublevare, 34.
Submoleste, 246.
Subornare, 604.
Subringi, 179.
Subscribere, 87-88.
Subscriptor, 233.
Subsellia alicuius, 177, 234.
Subsequi, 310.
Subsistere, transit., 'to support,' 587.
Subtilis, 'precise,' 45; 'refined,' 268.
Subtilitas, 435.
Subturpicula, 179.
Succlamatum est, 600.
Suffocare, 338.
Suffragatio, 220.
Suffusus (metaph.), 214.
Sullaturire, 350.
Summam facere, with genit., 203.
Summatim, 568.

Summo discessu, 56.
Superficies, 163.
Superior pars provinciae, 94; superiora, 'earlier,' 609.
Superlative in relative clauses, 562.
Supersederi, 241.
Superum mare, 333, 554.
Supine, in -um, 383, l. 7; in -u, 429, l. 5.
Suppeditat, 339.
Supra caput, 94.
Sus Minervam, 427.
Suscipere (liberos), 414; 'to incur,' 546.
Suspensa (metaph.), 564.
Suspitionem tollere, 383.
Sustinere = cohibere, 449; 'to contribute to the support of,' 111; 'to bear the weight of,' ib., 220; = 'gerere,' 209; 'to maintain,' 608; 'to resist,' 248, 444, 601, l. 7; absol. 'to hold out,' 280, 581.
Syngrapha, 232, 251, 252.

Tabella, 50, 209.
Tabellarii, 114, 121, 226.
Tabernarii, 244.
Tabulae, 'accounts,' 55; 'maps,' 259; 'records,' 236, 540; novae, 254, 373, 531; tabula Valeria, 110.
Talaria (metaph.), 531.
Tam, with no corresponding particle, 601; tam esse, 'to be so numerous,' 97.
Tam diu, 'only so long,' 382.
Tamen, apparently pleonastic, 415, l. 10; resumptive, 102; without a corresponding particle, 54, cp. 213, 352, 389; tamen etsi, 421.
Tantum modo = dum modo, 349.
Tantus, with the indicative, the corresponding word being suppressed, 358; 'only so much,' 183, 268; tanta hieme, 316.
Tectus (metaph.), 530.
Temere, 'to anybody,' 182.
Tempus, 'circumstances,' 324, cp. 94, l. 4; 'a time of need,' 182, cp. 39, l. 9, 215; 'a misfortune,' 201, cp. 441; 'the events of a time,' 472; cp. 'tempus Caninianum, 183; reliquum tempus, 325; tempore, as an adverb, 520; ex tempore, 362; temporis causa, 586.
Tenebrae (metaph.), 304.
Tenera, 'effeminate,' 263.
Tenere, 'to be master,' 78; 'to cling to,' 79; 'to obtain,' 165, l. 18; 'to possess,' 463, l. 10; cp. 468, l. 3; 'to remember,' 90, 327; followed by accus. of adjective, 362; neminem voluntate, 82; teneri, 'to be held in check,' 77; 'to be liable to,' 175.
Terrae filius, 45.
Testatum, 53, cp. 212, 521, 534.
Themistocleum consilium, 371.
Timere ut, 111.
Tinnire, 531.
Tiro, as an adjective, 430.
Titubatum (metaph.), 605.
Tmesis, 361.
Toculliones, 72.
Togatus, 264.
Tollere, 'to dismiss from consideration,' 285; 'to suspend,' 383.
Totum, used as a subst., 381; as an adverb, 315, 366.
Tradere exercitum, 271; se alicui, 174.
Traducere tempus, 472.
Traiicere, with double accusative, 585, 601, l. 9.
Tralaticius, 116, 252.
Tramittere, used absolutely, 544.
Tranquilla esse (metaph.), 279.
Transigere, cum aliquo, 236; rem, 'to decide a struggle,' 423.
Transire, 'to desert,' 322; 'to transgress,' 249.
Transvolare, 572.
Tres viri, 'illis III viris,' 556.
Tribum ferre, 70; tribus habere, a legal term, 195.
Tribunes, initiative powers of in the senate, 166, 495; their year of office, how dated, 8.
Tributa exigere, 95.
Tricae, 377.
Triclinium, 483.
Triduo cum, 'in three days from,' 603.
Trinum nundinum, 314.
Tripudium (solistimum), 443.
Triumphare (metaph.), 55, cp. 357.
Trudere, 'to push forward,' 61.
Tueri negotia, 311.
Tum vero, 183.
Tumultus (Gallicus), 515.
Tunc = ita, 372.
Turbare, 'to be extravagant,' 234.
Turbulenter, 371.
Tyrannoctonus, 531, cp. 563.

Umquam = ullum, 169.
Una cum . . . esse, 'to be contemporary with,' 467.
Unus, perhaps = 'especially,' 25-26; almost = an indefinite article, 347; de tuis, 462; omnium, strengthening a superlative, 119; una = 'only,' 563; uno loco esse, 'to meet,' 602, l. 9; plural of, with substantives only used in the plural, 282, cp. 389.
Urbanus, 28.
Urbs, ad urbem, 313.
Usque eo, of time, 230.
Usurae, 356, cp. 252.
Ut = 'granting that,' 307; with ablat. abs., 79; in indirect questions, 55, 118, 240; position of, 102, 172, 268, l. 12, 452, 482; perhaps = utinam, 314, l. 17; ut ne, pleonastic, 51, cp. 170, l. 6; ut non, how different from 'ne,' 104, l. 1, 445; ut opinor, 41; ut scribis, ib.; ut, repeated instead of 'et,' 390.
Uti rogas, a political phrase, 50.
Utilitatem adferre, 115, cp. 529.
Utinam non, instead of 'utinam ne,' 414.

Vacillare (memoriola), 421; vacillantes litterulae, 317.
Vacuitas, 586.
Vagari, of a speech, 'to be published,' 556.
Vagus esse, 306.
Valde, 'stoutly,' 186; valde magnum facere (ironical), 96; valde quam, 600.
Valere, 'to prevail,' 'last,' 471.
Valetudo, a neutral word, 112, 315; valetudinem impedire, 315; amittere, 437.
Vallum Lucilianum, 556.
Vaticinari, 371.
Vectigal constituere, 75.
Vectigal praetorium, 252, l. 13.
Vegetus, 383.
Vel, 'even,' 255; = 'vel potius,' 413.
Velle, with accus. and infin., 431; alicuius causa, 165; with the force of a substantive, 305; visne, 466.
Venas et viscera aperire (metaph.), 272.
Venatio (in Circo), 194.
Venditare, 53; in another sense, 63.
Venire, in iudicium, 70; in spem, 601; venire = ire, 407; ventum est ad me, 382.
Ventosus (metaph.), 585.
Ventus, 'a rumour,' 235; venti (metaph.), 221; cp. venti secundi, 69.
Venuste, 'neatly,' 230.
Verb, understood, 104; repeated, 164, ll. 7-8, 575.
Verba facere, 237; meis verbis = meo nomine, 561; = 'in such words as I use,' 225.
Verbals in -bundus, 421.
Verbosior, 322; verbosius, 431.
Vere, 'really,' 'rightly,' 417.
Verecundiores, 424.
Vereri, with a personal object, 215, 424.
Veritas, 'justice,' 242.
Vero, adversative (me vero nihil delectat), 341; at the beginning of a letter, 469; emphatic, 356; in transitions, 609; with personal pronouns, 267, 341.
Versari in causa, 391.
Versuram facere, 253.
Versus, as a preposition, 466, cp. 475.
Verus, 'fair,' 70; 'honest,' 586.
e Vestigio, 476.
Vestitum mutare, 107, cp. 171-172.
Veternus (metaph.), 244.
Veto of the tribunes, illegal in debates on the consular provinces, 238, 248; means of evading it in other cases, 238, l. 18, note.
Vetus est, 'it is an old saying,' 431.
Vetustas, 532.
Via, utor via, 82; de via, 180, 423.
Viaria lex, 244.
Viaticum, 180.
Vicem, nostram, 'instead of us,' 199, cp. 552; with the genitive, = 'like,' 375-376; ? 'fate,' 464.
Vicensima, a tax, 74.
Victoria sua, 448.
Vicus, 114.
Videre, 'to foresee,' 274, cp. 279, l. 12; 'to have an interview with,' 413; = intellegere, 436; 'to provide,' 371, 531; 'to shew penetration or foresight,' 55, 229; 'to take care,' 389, cp. 352, 371; viderit, 457.
Villulae, 331.
Vincere, 'to have an advantage over,' 436; 'to prove,' 536.

Vindex, 72.
Vir, 'a man of spirit,' 427.
Vis, 'nature,' 'character,' 327; e.g. verborum, 474, l. 4; the name of a crime, 88.
Vivere de lucro, 433.
Vocabula honorum, 574.
Voculae, 368.
Voltu et oculis, 525.
Volumen, 349; cp. volumina, 97, l. 3.
Voluntas, 'good will,' 31, 266.
Voluptaria, 423.
Vomere (metaph.), 549.

Zelotypia, 379.
Zeugma, 184, l. 6, 576; of negative and affirmative ideas, 266; of verbs, 423.

INDEX III.

OF PROPER NAMES.

Academia, 274, 477.
Acastus, slave of Cicero, 276.
Achaia, a Roman province, 125, 239, 418, 436; Achaici, 42.
Achilles, in Homer's poems, 597.
Acilius, M'. Glabrio, 6, 458.
Aedui, 16, 149.
Aegina, 466.
Aegypta, a freedman of Cicero, 316, 317.
Aegyptus, 184, 300, 394, 569, 588.
Aelii Lamiae, 176; L. Aelius Lamia, 19; Lamiani horti, 159.
Aelius, P. or Sex. Ligus, 21.
Aelius, Q. Tubero, 291.
Aemilia via, 583.
Aemilius, M. Lepidus, praetor 49 B.C., afterwards consul and triumvir, 298, 301, 343, 493, 497, 509–512, 516, 549–560, 572–576, 585, 586, 591–596, 597, 598, 600–606, 611.
Aemilius, M'. Lepidus Livianus, consul 66 B.C., 125, 351, 458.
Aemilius, L. Paulus, the conqueror of Perseus, 470.
Aemilius, L. Paulus, consul 50 B.C., 86, 154, 157, 232, 243.
Aemilius, M. Scaurus, consul 115 B.C., 207.
Aemilius, M. Scaurus, son of the above, curule aedile in 58 B.C., 21, 194, 195.
Aesopus, a tragic actor, 100, 101.
Afranius, L., consul 60 B.C. (Auli filius), 14, 27 (?), 61, 162, 166, 298, 315, 322, 400, 426.
Africa, province of, 125; hostilities there, 299, 395, 399, 416, 418; Africanus exercitus (in 43 B.C.), 608–610, cp. 612.
Agamemnon, in the Iliad, 527.
Agesilaus, in Xenophon's work, 96.
Aiax, in Homer's poems, 597.
Alaudae, 502, 554, 613.
Albanum, of Pompey, 279.
Alexandria, 342, 393–395, 410, 418, 462; see also Aegyptus, Ptolemaeus.
Alexis, 282.
Aliphera, 260.
Allienus, A., 588, 613.
Allobroges, 11, 15, 42, 99, 590, 591, 601, 605.
Alpes, 572, 585, 586, 600.
Amalthea, 43, 71; Amaltheum, 62; see also the Index of Greek Words.
Amanus (Mons), 152, 244.
Amatius, C., or Herophilus, 498.
Ambiorix, 146.
Amphiaraus (in fabulis), 443.
Ampius, T. Balbus, 311, 415, note.
Anagnia, 553.
Anagnini, 558; Anagninum, 133, 420.
Ancharius, Q. Priscus, 142.
Ancon(a), 304, 314.
Andromache, 193.
Anneius, M., 151.
Annius, T. Milo, as tribune in 57 B.C. promotes Cicero's restoration from exile, 23; quarrels with Clodius in 57–56 B.C., 135–137, 171–172; stands for the consulship in 53 B.C., 146–147, 219 222; orders the murder of Clodius, is convicted, and goes into exile 52 B.C., 147–148; tries to raise an insurrection against Caesar, but is killed in 48 B.C., 300.
Antandros, 93.
Antiochia, in Syria, 246.
Antiochus, a philosopher, 2.
Antiphon, 193.
Antium, and estate of Cicero there, 64, 133, 345.
Antonii, 230.
Antonius, C., consul in 63 B.C., 7–9, 12, 18, 26.
Antonius, C., brother of the triumvir, 299, 503, 505, 511.
Antonius, L., brother of the triumvir, 499, 501, 507, 594, 595.

Antonius, M., the famous orator, 1, 473.
Antonius, M., the triumvir, accuses Milo, 148; elected augur, 158, 269, 270; as tribune 49 B.C. vetoes a decree of the senate against Caesar, 290; represents Caesar in Italy, 378, cp. 344; his debauchery, 383; protects Cicero after his return to Italy in 47 B.C., 396; behaviour of, after Caesar's death, 497–502; besieges D. Brutus in Mutina, 503–509; is defeated and crosses the Alps, 509; reconciled to Lepidus, 509; and to Octavian, 512; orders the death of Cicero, 513. *See* also the letters of Part V, passim.
Apamea, in Phrygia, 226; in Syria, 589.
Apelles, 207.
Apollinis aedes, 173, 231, 237.
Apollonis or Apollonidae, in Mysia, 98.
Apollonius, a freedman of P. Crassus, 461.
Appenninus (Mons), 586, 600.
Appia via, 335.
Appuleius, 224.
Appuleius, Cn. Saturninus, 270.
Appuleius, L., propraetor of Macedonia, 20.
Apulia, 320.
Aquilius, C. Gallus, 26–27.
Aradus, 342.
Arbuscula, 193.
Archias, A. Licinius, 12, 63.
Archilochus, 557.
Archimedes, 2.
Argenteus, a river, 595; pons, A., 598.
Ariminum, 231, 314, 385.
Ariobarzanes, 153, 266.
Ariopagus, 225.
Ariovistus, 20.
Aristarchus, 48.
Aristophanes (a grammarian), 557.
Aristoteles, Aristotelio more, 214.
Armenii, 348.
Arpinum, and the estate of Cicero there, 61, 77, 133, 325, 335, 343, 360, 385, 555; Arpinates, 452.
Arretium, 314, 503; Arretina mulier, 2.
Arsaces, 269.
Artavasdes, 247.
Artaxerxes, contemporary with Themistocles, 376.
Asia, a Roman province, 77, 124, 250, 418, 589.
Asinius, C. Pollio, 401, 422, 507, 510, 511, 570–573, 585.
Astura, villa of Cicero near, 133, 513, 518.
Astyanax, 193.
Ateius, C., 373.
Ateius, L. Capito, 237.
Athenae, 2, 65, 123, 388, 475–477. *See* also under Pomponius and Tullius.
Athenodorus, Calvus, a philosopher, 558.
Atilius, S. (?) Serranus, 21, 22.
Atius, T. Labienus, 9, 153–154, 158, 281, 294, 296, 304, 307, 315, 395, 399, 400.
Atius, P. Varus, 291.
Attalus, of Hypaepi, 100.
Attica, Caecilia, daughter of T. Pomponius Atticus, 131, 265, 420, 421, 518, 548, 561.
Aufidius, M. Lurco, 61.
Auli filius, 27, 61.
Aurelius, C. Cotta, 2.
Aurelius, L. Cotta, 4, 7, 22, 458, 550.
Aurelius, M. Cotta, 382.
Autronius, P. Paetus, 7, 45.
Axius, Q., 105, 193, 421.

Baiae, 59, 410.
Baliares insulae, 395, cp. 422.
Basili bustum, 283.
Belgae, 146.
Bibracte, 21.
Bithynia, 124, 127.
Blaudus, 93–94.
Boeotia, 475.
Bononia, 512, 569, 600.
Britannia, 143, 145–146, 196.
Brundisium, 23, 161, 322, 330, 393, 394, 408, 533, 551.
Buthrotum, 248, 521.
Byzantium, 342.

Caecilia, *see* Attica.
Caecilius, L., 94.
Caecilius, Q., uncle of Atticus, 29.
Caecilius, Q. Bassus, 403, 481, 519, 589, 613.
Caecilius, L. Metellus, tribune in 49 B.C., 298, 375.
Caecilius, M. Metellus, 64.
Caecilius, Q. Metellus Celer, 10, 13, 14–16, 34–40, 67.
Caecilius, Q. Metellus Creticus, 6, 126.

Caecilius, Q. Metellus Nepos, 11-13, 21, 33, 34-40.
Caecilius, Q. Metellus Numidicus, references to, 55, 207.
Caecina, 554.
Caecina, A., 5.
Caecina, A., (?) son of the above, 440-451.
Caeliana, 381.
Caelius, C., tribune in 51 B.C., 239.
Caelius, C. Caldus, quaestor of Cicero, 265, 274.
Caelius, M. Rufus, 140, 228-245, 255-257, 269-273, 364-371, 383 (?), 385.
Caelius, M. Vinicianus, 230.
Caesius, L., 93.
Caesius, M., aedile at Arpinum, 453.
Caesonius, M., 26.
Caieta, 323, 384, 513.
Calatia, 554.
Cales, 559; estate of Cicero at, 133, 323.
Calidius, M., 228.
Calpurnia, wife of Caesar, 17, 497.
Calpurnius, 379.
Calpurnius, M. Bibulus, 16, 17, 75, 81, 84, 155, 237, 244, 247, 343.
Calpurnius, C. Piso, consul in 67 B.C., 28, 458.
Calpurnius, Cn. Piso, 7.
Calpurnius, L. Piso Bestia, 175.
Calpurnius, L. Piso Caesoninus, consul in 58 B.C., 17-19, 24, 141, 142, 307, 437, 498, 501, 504, 546-548, 565.
Calpurnius, C. Piso Frugi, son-in-law of Cicero, 7, 22, 88.
Calvena, *see* Marius.
Calvus, nickname for M. Crassus, 56.
Campania, 16, 17, 73, 138, 139, 201, 202. *See* also Capua.
Caninius, L. Gallus, 168, 170, 183.
Caninius, A. Satyrus, 29.
Cannutius, Ti., 552.
Canuleius, a centurion, 248.
Capena porta, 161.
Capenas ager, 433.
Capua, 83, 295, 310, 311, 316, 320, 554, 559.
Carinae, house of Q. Cicero in, 176.
Cascellius, M., 94.
Casilinum, 554.
Cassiani horti, 459.
Cassivellaunus, 136.
Cassius Barba, 484.
Cassius, C. Longinus, defeats the Parthians in 51 B.C., 152, 246; dissuades Cicero from joining Pompey in 49 B.C., 419; submits to Caesar in 48 B.C., 394; legate of Caesar, 396, 445; conspires against him, 401-403; secures Syria for the Senate in 43 B.C., 503, 504-505, 510, 569, 589; besieges Dolabella, 512; letters of Cicero to him, 417, 539, 548, 565, 568, 581, 605; of Cassius to Cicero, 588; of D. Brutus to M. Brutus and Cassius, 518; of M. Brutus and Cassius to Antony, 541.
Cassius, L., his brother, 517.
Cassius, Q., brother of the two preceding, 246, 275, 300, 301, 344.
Castulonensis saltus, 570.
Catienus, T., 95.
Catina, 560.
Catius, C. Vestinus, 604.
Cato maior, a work of Cicero, 531, cp. 558.
Celer, a freedman of Atticus, 363, 390.
Cephalio, a slave of Atticus, 362, 414.
Chaerippus, 564.
Chaeron, 259-260.
Chios, 342.
Cibyra, Cibyratae, 232; cp. 248, 250.
Cilicia, a Roman province, 124, 127, 151-155, 184, 246-255, 258-266, 462, 590.
Cincius, L., 26, 258.
Cingulum, 304.
Claterna, 569.
Claudia, wife of Q. Metellus Celer, 38, 68.
Claudius, Ap. Pulcher, consul 54 B.C., 144, 150, 153, 195, 199, 216, 227, 242, 256, 264, 385.
Claudius, Ap. Pulcher, minor, 235.
Claudius, Ti. Nero, 156, 273.
Claudius, C. Marcellus, consul 50 B.C., 153, 154, 157, 228, 243, l. 15, 437 (?).
Claudius, C. Marcellus, consul 49 B.C., 158, 290, 311, 428, l. 9, 437 (?).
Claudius, M. Marcellus, consul 51 B.C., 148, 222, 232, 319, 397, 436-438, 445, 456, 475-477.
Cleopatra, 394, 395.
Clodia, mother-in-law of L. Metellus, 341.
Clodius, P. Pulcher, an intruder in the house of Caesar, 13, 43-44;

trial of, 14, 47, 59, 52–57; quaestor in Sicily, 67; quarrels with Cicero, *ib.*; procures Cicero's exile, 19, 20; quarrels with Milo, 23, 135–137, 171–174; intrigues with the optimates in 56 B.C., 206, 211; murdered, 147.
Clodius, P., son of the preceding, 523, 525.
Clodius, Sex., 373 (?), 523–526.
Clodius, Sex., a rhetorician, 191.
Cluentius, A. Avitus, or Habitus, 6.
Cluvius, M., of Puteoli, 260.
Colchi, 342, 348.
Considius, Q. Gallus, 88–89.
Considius, M. Nonianus, 311, 314.
Corcyra, 64, 155, 299, 407, 453.
Corduba, 570, 572, 573.
Corfinium, 294, 309, 313, 322.
Corinthus, 341, 436, 466.
Cornelia, wife of Pompey, 147.
Cornelius, C., tribune in 67 B.C., 5, 7, 175.
Cornelius, M., 41.
Cornelius, P., tribune in 51 B.C., 239.
Cornelius, L. Balbus, maior, 16, 141, 189, 281, 326, 331, 412, 423, 432, 484, 539, 560.
Cornelius, L. Balbus, minor, 326, 333, 415.
Cornelius, C. Cethegus, 11.
Cornelius, L. Cinna, consul 87–84 B.C., 348.
Cornelius, P. Dolabella, accuses Ap. Claudius, 242; marries Tullia, 156, 243, 273; elected quindecimvir, 229; fights for Caesar in the civil war, 308, 315, 358, 370, 379, 557; urges Cicero to leave Pompey's camp, 388; causes troubles in Italy in 47 B.C., 396, 416; divorces Tullia, 398, 403; proceedings at his election in 44 B.C., 402; his vigour in the cause of order after Caesar's death, 499, 527–529, 539; his debt to Cicero, 501, 531; his reconciliation with Antony, 499; notices of, in the second Philippic, 557; orders the murder of Trebonius in Asia, 505, 589; attempts to occupy Syria and Cilicia, 505, 566, 590; his death, 512, 605, 613.
Cornelius, L. Lentulus Crus, consul 49 B.C., 102, 156, 158, 290, 326, 329, 333, 410, 426 (?), 428, l. 9.
Cornelius, Cn. Lentulus Marcellinus, consul 56 B.C., 165, 168, 201, 345.
Cornelius, L. Lentulus Niger, flamen, 86, 141.
Cornelius, L. Lentulus Niger, son of the preceding, 86.
Cornelius, P. Lentulus Spinther, consul 57 B.C., 21, 22, 136, 141, 153, 164–170, 181–188, 196–218, 248, 339 (?), 354, 426 (?).
Cornelius, P. Lentulus Spinther, son of the preceding, 171, 188, 216.
Cornelius, P. Lentulus Sura, praetor 63 B.C., 11, 59, 131–132.
Cornelius, Cn. Lentulus Vatia, 175.
Cornelius, P. Scipio, afterwards Q. Metellus Scipio by adoption, consul 52 B.C., 29, 147, 237, 300, 322, 395, 399, 400, 426, 557.
Cornelius, P. Scipio Africanus minor, 33, 324 (?), 327, l. 10, 376.
Cornelius, L. Sulla Felix, 3, 3, 347, 348; Sullanus dies, 376; Sullanum regnum, 328, 338; Sullanum tempus, 478.
Cornelius, L. Sulla Faustus, son of the preceding, 322, 395, 400.
Cornelius, P. Sulla, 7, 12.
Cornificius, Q., 26, 44.
Cornificius, Q., son of the preceding, 395, 480, 506, 550, 562–564, 612.
Cornutus, C., tribune in 61 B.C., 51.
Cornutus, M., praetor in 43 B.C., 509, 511.
Cos, 342.
Cosa (Cosanum), 343.
Cosconius, C., 84.
Cossinius, L., 65.
Creta, 6, 126; made a province, 127.
Cularo, 593, 602, 605, 606.
Cumae (Cumanum Ciceronis), 133, 369, 383, 425.
Curius, M'., 193.
Curius, Q., 10, 12 (?), 27.
Curtius, Nicias, 486.
Curtius, M. Postumus, 371.
Cyprus, 20, 150, 184, 249–254, 262–264, 342.
Cyrene, a Roman province, 125, 239.
Cyrrhestica, 247.
Cyrus, in Xenophon's Cyropaedia, 96.
Cytheris, 383.

Dalmatia, 124, 395.
Deiotarus, king of Galatia, 152, 247, 255, 397, 516, 521.

Delos, 345.
Demetrius, of Magnesia, 330, 342.
Demosthenes, 65.
Dertona, 585, 587.
Dicaearchus, 76, 259, 260.
Diochares, 410.
Diodotus, a freedman of Lucullus, 99.
Diodotus, a Stoic philosopher, 1, 134, 462.
Diogenes, a friend of M. Caelius Rufus, 241.
Dionysius II, of Syracuse, 341, 425–426.
Dionysius, freedman of Atticus, 191.
Dionysius, slave (?) of Cicero, 196, 260, 278, 356, 381.
Dionysopolitae, 93.
Diphilus, a tragic actor, 82.
Domitius, L. Ahenobarbus, consul in 54 B.C., 29, 61, 144, 194, 270, 294, 296, 298, 300, 312, 314, 322, 343.
Domitius, Cn. Ahenobarbus, 270.
Domitius, Cn. Calvinus, consul 53 B.C., 146, 175, 194, 395.
Doterio (?), 61.
Drusus, *see* Livius.
Dyrrhachium, 21, 23, 114, 299, 300, 389, 390.

Eburones, 146.
Eleusis, 274.
Ennius, Q., quoted, 263, 558.
Ephesus, 100, 151.
Epidaurus, 475.
Epirotici, 42.
Epirus, 41, 42, 128–130, 339, 342. *See* also Buthrotum, Dyrrhachium.
Eporedia, 597.
Eppius, M., 237, 310.
Eros, 459, 530, 560.
Etruria, 444, 587.
Euphrates, 247.
Eutychides, freedman of Atticus, 191.

Faberius, 459.
Faberius, 498.
Fabius, 68.
Fabius, C., a legate of Caesar, 322.
Fabius, C., 95.
Fabius, Q. Maximus, a legate of Caesar, 401.
Fabius, Q. Maximus Cunctator, mentioned, 470.
Fabius, Q. Maximus, son of the preceding, 470.
Fabius, Q. Vergilianus, 309.
Fadius, M. Gallus, 332, note on l. 16.
Fadius, C. or Q. Gallus (?), a freedman, father-in-law of Antony, 556.
Fadius, T. Gallus, tribune in 57 B.C., 21, 118.
Fannius, C., 87, 410.
Faucius, M., 452.
Favonius, M., 50, 70, 171.
Flavius, L., tribune in 60 B.C., 15, (?) 97–99, (?) 362.
Fonteius, M., 5, 193.
Formiae, 295, 315, 385; estate of Cicero there, 113, 116, 337, 349, 513, 533.
Forum, Cornelium, 569; Gallorum, 582; Iulii, 594; Voconii, 595.
Frusino, estate of Cicero at, 390.
Fufidius, Q., 452.
Fufius, Q. Calenus, tribune in 61 B.C., consul 47 B.C., 47, 53, 54, 78, 396, 505, 506, 557.
Fulvia, 521, 526.
Fundanius, C., 98.
Furius, C. Camillus, 277.
Furius, Crassipes, 141, 178, 180.
Furius (?), L. Philus, a name given by Cicero to Atticus, 84.
Furnius, C., 335, 353, 573, 578, 579, 592, 608.

Gabinius, A., consul 58 B.C., 5, 18–20, 24, 143–145, 211, 253, 373, 395.
Galeo, 134, 416.
Gallia, Cisalpina, 9, 10, 28, 34, 124, 452, 499, 503–509, 569, 585–587, 597, 600.
Gallia, Transalpina, 15–16, 20, 24, 72, 141, 143, 146, 149, 153, 158, 263, 509–511, 576–579, 590–596, 598–605, 607. *See* also Iulius.
Galli duo (M. and Q.), 229.
Gellius, L., consul 72 B.C., 458.
Getae, 348.
Graecia, 383; as a Roman province, 125, 436, 445. *See* also Achaia, Athenae, Corinthus.

Hales, a river, 546.
Haterianum ius, 427.
Hector (in Naevius' poem), 267.
Helvetii, 16, cp. 20.
Helvia, mother of Cicero, 1.
Hephaestus, of Apamea, 93.
Heraclides, of Pontus, allusion to, 557.
Herennius, murderer of Cicero, 513.
Hermia, 99.

Hermippus, 93.
Hermon, 248.
Hippias, son of Pisistratus, mentioned, 348.
Hirtius, A., consul 43 B.C., 396, 422, 425, 504, 509, 518, 520, 522, 531, 561, 565, 568, 569, 582–584, 586, 592; Hirtianum ius, 427.
Hispania, 3–4, 125, 142, 148, 205, 223, 285, 291, 315, 322, 366, 370, 372–373, 385, 388, 400, 416, 462, 510, 609. See also Aemilius, M. Lepidus, Asinius, Pompeius.
Hispo, 113.
Homerus, 597.
Hortensius, Q. Hortalus, consul 69 B.C., 4, 14, 43, 53–55, 90, 104, 155, 165, 274, 369.
Hortensius, Q., son of the preceding, 383, 410, 505.
Hypaepi, 100.
Hyrcanus, 24.

Iconium, 248.
Inalpini, 553.
Interamna, on the Liris, (?) 67; Interamnates, on the Nar, 193.
Isara, a river, 593.
Isauricum forum, 251.
Isidorus, a slave or freedman of Atticus, 389, 390.
Isocrates, 64.
Italia, extent of, 601.
Iuba, king of Numidia, 299, 300, 379, 400, 430.
Iudaea, 24, 127, 141, 150.
Iulia, daughter of Caesar, 17, 143, 145.
Iulius, C., 254.
Iulius, C. Caesar, consul 59 B.C., suspected of complicity with Catiline, 10, 12; opposes the execution of his accomplices, 11, cp. 457; outrage in his house, 13, 43–44; his prospects of the consulship, 69; behaviour of, as consul, 16–18, 73–89, 102; victories of, in Gaul, 20, 24, 136, 141, 143, 146, 149, 153–154; in Britain, 143, 145–146; conference of with Pompey at Luca in 56 B.C., 138, 202; prolongation of the government of, 142, 287; Cicero recommends Trebatius to him, 188; granted leave to sue for consulship without going to Rome, 148; proposals to recall him, 153, 157, 231, 236–241, 271, 289, 290; invades Italy in 49 B.C., 293, 304; surrender of Confinium to, 294, 332; of Pompey's army in Spain to, 298, 388; victory of, at Pharsalus, 300; danger of, at Alexandria, 394, cp. 418; pardons Cicero, 394; victory of, at Thapsus, 400; and at Munda, 400; visits Cicero at Puteoli, 398, 483; honours voted to, 492–495; laws of, 298, 489–492; letters of, to Cicero, 335, 337, 380; and of Cicero to him, 188, 353, 461; sayings of, about Cicero and Brutus, 516, 517; death of, 401.
Iulius, C. Octavianus, see Octavius.
Iulius, L. Caesar, consul 64 B.C., 7, 27, 31, 458, 527, 550, 568, 570.
Iunius, D. Brutus, serves under Caesar in the civil war and besieges Massilia, 298; conspires against Caesar, 401; behaviour of, after Caesar's death, 497; one of Caesar's heirs, 498; occupies Cisalpine Gaul for the senate, 499; correspondence of, with M. Brutus and C. Cassius, 518; with Cicero, 552, 561, 564, 584–587, 597, 599; charge against him, 559; besieged in Mutina by Antony, 503–509, 569, 581; relieved, 509, 584, 591; (?) confers with Octavian, 599; crosses the Alps to join Plancus, 510, 603, 606; deserted by his troops, 511; death of, 511.
Iunius, L. Brutus, consul 509 B.C., mentioned, 88.
Iunius, M. Brutus, by adoption Q. Servilius Caepio, one of the murderers of Caesar—denounced by Vettius, 86; his covetousness, 154, 251–254, 262–264; Cicero's regard for him, 256; in Pompey's camp, 391; pardoned by Caesar, 394; governor of Cisalpine Gaul, 396, 445, 452; letter of Cicero to, 452; writes of Cicero's consulship, 457; Caesar's judgment of, 516; conspires against Caesar, 401; meets Cicero at Velia, 501, 546; operations and position of, in Macedonia, 503–505, 511, 566, 569, 581; letter of D. Brutus to, 518; of him and C. Cassius to Antony, 541.
Iunius, L. Paciaecus, 422.
Iunius, D. Silanus, consul 62 B.C., 10, 27, 458.

Iunius, M. Silanus, 582, 596.
Iuventius, M. Laterensis, 79, 592, 603.

Laberius, D., 482.
Lacedaemonians, enmity of, to Themistocles, 376.
Laco, 558.
Laelii, 230.
Laelius, C. Sapiens, 33.
Laenius, (M.?), 248.
Lanuvium, 518, 530; estate there, 345.
Laodicea, in Phrygia, 226.
Laterium, an estate of Q. Cicero, 133, 361.
Lepreon, 260.
Lepta, Q., 189, 323.
Lesbos, 342.
Leucopetra, 544.
Licinius, a kidnapper, 95.
Licinius, a slave, 100.
Licinius, L. Crassus, the great orator, 1.
Licinius, M. Crassus, consul 70 and 55 B.C., joins Pompey in his legislation of 70 B.C., 4; praises Cicero in 61 B.C., 48; forms one of the so-called first triumvirate, 16; proposal of, as to the restoration of Ptolemy, 166; rivalry of with Pompey in 56 B.C., 172, 173; reconciled to him, 138, 139, cp. 202; and to Cicero, 211–212; second consulship of, 142, 143; command in Syria, defeat and death of, 145, 146.
Licinius, P. Crassus, son of the preceding, 24, 141, 146, 161.
Licinius, (?) Crassus Dives, 88.
Licinius, L. Lucullus, consul 74 B.C., 6, 19, 63, 124, 127, 458.
Licinius, M. Lucullus, brother of the preceding, by adoption M. Terentius Varro Lucullus, consul 73 B.C., 63, 124, 165, 182, 458.
Licinius, C. Macer, 6; another, 177.
Licinius, L. Murena[1], consul 62 B.C., 10, 11, 458.
Ligurius, A., 412.
Lilybaeum, 2.
Livius (?) Drusus, 195, 272, 459.
Lollius, C., 459.
Lollius, L., 216.
Lollius, M. Palicanus, 27.
Luca, 138, 202.
Lucceius, L. Q. F., 51, 141, 256.
Lucceius, L., M. F., 254.
Lucceius, or Lucilius, C. Hirrus, 230, 237, 310.
Luceria, Pompey's head-quarters for a time in 49 B.C., 294, 310, 320, 323, 329, 334, 419.
Lucilius, the satirist, allusion to, 556.
Lupus, 561. *See* also Rutilius.
Lutatius, Q. Catulus, 12, 15, 43, 57, 89, 458.
Lycaonia, 150, 251.
Lycia, 342.

Macedonia, a Roman province, 9, 18, 20, 24, 124, 141, 142, 292, 300, 436, 505, 569; Macedonicae legiones, 551. *See* also Antonius (C.), Calpurnius (L. Piso), Iunius (M. Brutus).
Madarus, *see* Matius, C.
Maecia tribus, 195.
Magius, P. Cilo, 476.
Maleae, 475.
Mallius or Manlius, C., 12.
Mamercus, Q., 452.
Mamilius, Octavius, 347.
Mamurra, 281, 484.
Manilius, C., tribune in 66 B.C., law of, 6.
Manlius, C. Acidinus, 476.
Manlius, A. Torquatus, 472–474, (?) 560.
Manlius, L. Torquatus, consul 65 B.C., 458.
Manlius, L. Torquatus, son of the preceding, 310, (?) 251.
Marathon, battle of, 348.
Marcius, C. Coriolanus, 348.
Marcius, L. Censorinus, (?) 99.
Marcius, Q. Crispus, 589, 613.
Marcius, C. Figulus, consul 64 B.C., perhaps identical with Q. Minucius Thermus, 7, 27, 31, 458.
Marcius, L. Philippus, consul in 91 B.C., 321.
Marcius, L. Philippus, son of the preceding, consul 56 B.C., 201, 484, 504, 522, 565.
Marcius, Q. Rex, 14, 60.
Marius, C., seven times consul, 348, 376.
Marius, M., 428.
Matinius, P., 251.
Matius, C., 355, 500, 515–518, 532–539, 557.
Megara, 466.
Megaristus, of Antandrus, 93.

[1] In the best editions this name is spelt Murena, not Muraena.

Melita, 378.
Memmius, C. Gemellus, 102, 194, 225.
Menocritus, 214.
Mescinius, L. Rufus, quaestor of Cicero in 51 B.C., 151.
Messius, C., 163, 195.
Miletus, 342.
Minturnae, 310.
Minucius, L. Basilus, 406.
Minucius, A. Thermus, 18.
Minucius, Q. Thermus, 27, (?) 255. *See* also Marcius, C. Figulus.
Misenum, villa of Antony near, 378.
Mithridates, Eupator, king of Pontus, 3, 6, 124, 126, 127.
Molon, 1, 2, 71.
Mucia, wife of Pompey, 14, 38.
Mucius, Q. Scaevola, augur, 1.
Mucius, Q. Scaevola, pontifex maximus, 1, 121; Mucianus exitus, 355.
Mucius, Q. Scaevola, tribune in 54 B.C., 344.
Munatius, Cn. Plancus, 574, 591, 592, 594.
Munatius, L. Plancus, brother of the preceding, commands in northern Gaul after Caesar's death, 611; for a long time professes devotion to the senate, 507–511, 576, 590–594, 602, 607–610; Cicero's exhortations to him, 571, 579, 596; joins D. Brutus, 510, 608; is reconciled to Antony, 511.
Munatius, T. Plancus Bursa, 149, 482.
Mustela, Tamisius, 558.
Mutina, 503–509, 560, 581, 584. *See* also Antonius, M.; Iunius, D. Brutus.
Myrtilus, 559.
Mytilenae, 431.

Naevius, Cn., the poet, quoted, 267.
Nar, 193.
Navius, Attus, reference to, 175.
Neapolis, 527, 544; Neapolitanum (Pontii), 530–531.
Nerius, Cn., 174.
Nervii, 24.
Nestor, in the Iliad, 527.
Nicaea, 516.
Nicias, of Smyrna, 91.
Nicias, Curtius, 486.
Nigidius, P. Figulus, praetor 58 B.C., 102.
Ninnius, L. Quadratus, tribune in 58 B.C., 19, 21, 118, 182.
Nonius, M. (?) Sufenas, 192.
Numerius, Q. Rufus, tribune 57 B.C., 21.
Numestius, Numerius, 85.
Nymphon, of Colophon, 94.

Octavius, C., father of the emperor, 72, 96.
Octavius, afterwards C. Iulius Caesar Octavianus Augustus, birth of, 12; goes to Caesar's camp in Spain, 401; studies at Apollonia in Epirus, 401; returns to Italy after Caesar's death, 499, cp. 522; speech of, 531; his games, 535, 538; accused of an attempt on Antony's life, 551; correspondence of, with Cicero, 559; intrigues with the population of Campania, 554, 559; and with Antony's legions, 502, cp. 568; takes the field against Antony, 503, 565, 569; inactivity of, after the relief of Mutina, 509, 587, 604, 609; demands the consulship, 510; and marches to Rome, 511; is reconciled to Antony, 512; and joins the second triumvirate, 512.
Octavius, L. Naso, 97.
Octavius, M., curule aedile 50 B.C., 248–249, 299.
Octavius, Mamilius, 347.
Olbia, in Sardinia, 176.
Olympia, 546.
Oppius, C., 337, 371, 516.
Orodes, king of Parthia, 247.
Ovia, 459.

Pammenes, 265.
Pamphylia, 150, 342; forum Pamphylium, 250.
Panaetius, a philosopher, 356, 558.
Papirius, C. Carbo, contemporary with C. Gracchus, 174.
Papirius, L. Paetus, 72, 425, 432.
Parma, 569.
Parthi, 126, 127, 146, 152, 155, 224, 227, 244, 246, 292, 401; Parthicae res, 329.
Patrae, 407.
Patron, an Epicurean philosopher, 100, 225.
Pausanias, 234.
Peducaeus, Sex., propraetor of Sicily in 76–75 B.C., 2, 161.
Peducaeus, Sex., son of the preceding, 279, 309, 324, 337, 352, 361, 363, 556.
Pedum, estate of Caesar near, 360.

Pelopidae, in a quotation, 522.
Peloponnesus, geography of, 259-260.
Pericles, 306.
Petreius, M., 12, 291, 298, 315, 395, 399, 400.
Phaedrus, an Epicurean philosopher, 128, 545.
Phameu, 345.
Phania, 256.
Pharnaces, son of the famous Mithridates, 127, 395, 418.
Phemius, 250.
Philip, father of Alexander the Great, 61.
Philo, an Academic philosopher, 1.
Philo, a freedman of M. Caelius, 241.
Philogenes, 258.
Philotimus, a freedman of Terentia, 134, 151, 334, 339, 342, 343, 379.
Phlius, Phliasii, 260.
Phraates, 143.
Picenum, 308.
Pilia, wife of Atticus, 139, 225, 518, 547.
Pilius, Q., 234.
Pindenissus, 152.
Piraeus, 466, 475-476.
Pisaurum, 314.
Pisistratus, of Athens, 348; Caesar compared to him, 314.
Pituanius, 191.
Plaguleius, 373.
Plancius, Cn., quaestor in 58, curule aedile in 54 B.C., 21, 113, 144, 397, 453.
Plato, the pupil of Socrates, 205, 209, 375.
Plato, of Sardis, an Epicurean philosopher, 100.
Plautius, P. Hypsaeus, 147, 166-167.
Plautus, one of the judges of Clodius, 57.
Plotius, L., 14.
Polla, wife of D. Brutus, 564.
Pollentia, 600, 601.
Pollex, a slave of Cicero, 391.
Polycharmus, 225.
Pompeia, wife of Caesar, 44.
Pompeii, 382; estate of Cicero at, 71, 133, 382, 429, 548, 559.
Pompeius, Cn. Strabo, consul in 89 B.C., 1.
Pompeius, Cn. Magnus, son of the preceding, returns from Spain, 4; measures of, as consul, in 70 B.C., 4; commissioned to act against the pirates, 5; and against Mithridates, 6, 127; campaigns of, in the East, 127-128; Cicero's respect for, 6; and discontent with, 33; returns to Rome, 14; behaviour of, there, 15, 47, 48; combines with Caesar and Crassus in 60 B.C., 16; marries Julia, Caesar's daughter, 17; behaviour of, during Caesar's consulship, 74, 75; unpopularity of, 82-84; quarrels with Clodius, 21; promotes Cicero's return from exile, 22; intrigues for a command in 57-56 B.C., 135, 138, 162, 165; conference of, with Caesar, at Luca in 56 B.C., 138, 202; second consulship of, in 55 B.C., 142; receives the government of Spain, 142; third consulship of, in 52 B.C., and estrangement from Caesar, 147, 148, 240, 271; marries Cornelia, 147; behaviour of, in Italy, in 49 B.C., 294, 303-313, 319; interviews of, with Cicero, 295, 347; his cruelty feared, 334, 338, 342, 408, 410; campaign of, in 48 B.C., 298, 300, 388, 390, 412, 429; death of, 394, 410, 426.
Pompeius, Cn., son of the preceding, 243, 299, 395, 400, 432.
Pompeius, Sex., brother of the preceding, 243, 400, 504, 510, 516, 519, 611, 612.
Pomponia, sister of Atticus, wife of Q. Cicero, 5, 72, 128, 131, 258, 259, 413.
Pomponius, T. Atticus, 128-131, and the letters to Atticus, passim.
Pomptina tribus, 195.
Pomptinus, C., praetor in 63 B.C., 223, 251, 278.
Pontidia, 255.
Pontius, Titinianus, 341.
Pontius, L. Aquila, 29, 530, 599.
Popilius Laenas, murderer of Cicero, 513.
Porcius, C. Cato, 101, 142, 171-174, 192.
Porcius, M. Cato, the censor, 470.
Porcius, M. Cato, 'of Utica,' tribune 62, praetor 54 B.C., advocates the execution of Lentulus and his associates, 457, 458; prosecutes L. Murena, 11; opposes the claims of Pompey to command against Catiline, 12; energy of, in pressing proceedings against Clodius, 44, 50; his ill-timed rigour in 60 B.C., 70; advises

Cicero to leave Italy in 58 B.C., 20; receives a commission to manage the annexation of Cyprus, 29; defeated in a contest for the praetorship in 55 B.C., 142; opposes the grant of a 'supplicatio' in honour of Cicero in 50 B.C., 156, 266-269; fails to hold Sicily for Pompey, in 49 B.C., 382; rebukes Cicero for going to Pompey's camp, 297; but requests him to take the command after Pharsalus, 299; conducts a body of troops from Cyrene to the province of Africa, 305; death of, 400, 426; name of, used proverbially, 546.
Porcius, M. Laeca, 10.
Porsena, 347.
Posidonius, a philosopher, 65, 558.
Postumia, 251; her son, 255.
Postumius, 251.
Postumius, P., 476.
Praeneste, games at, in 46 B.C., 432.
Precius (?), or Precianus, hereditas Preciana, 277.
Procilius, 193.
Ptolemaeus XII, Auletes, 17, 24, 74, 136, 143, 164-170, 183-185.
Ptolemais, 184.
Publicius (?), Q., 100.
Publilia, second wife of Cicero, 397, 398, 453.
Publilius Syrus, 482, 517.
Pupius, M. Piso, consul in 61 B.C., 13, 42-44, 50, 51, 53, 58.
Puteoli, estate of Cicero at, 133.

Quinctius, L., a friend of Cicero, 282.
Quinctius, P., defended by Cicero, 2.
Quinctius, T. Flamininus (O Tite), 558.

Rabirius, C., 9, 66, 132.
Rabirius, C. Postumus, 144.
Racilius, L., tribune in 56 B.C., 182.
Ravenna, 138, 202, 293.
Reate, people of, 193.
Regium, people of, 544.
Regium Lepidi or Lepidum, 560, 585.
Regulus, case of, 558.
Rhodanus, 591.
Rhodus, 2, 155, 342, 431, 519, 539.
Roscius, Sex., of Ameria, 2.
Roscius, Q., an actor, 5.
Roscius, L. Fabatus, 293.
Roscius, L. Otho, 5, 9, 66.
Rosea or Rosia, 193.
Rubrius, Q., estate of, 557.
Rutilius, P. Lupus, tribune in 56 B.C., 166, 169, (?) 561.

Salamis, in Cyprus, 251-254, 262-264.
Sallustius, C. Crispus, authority of, as a historian, 10.
Samnium, 559.
Sampsiceramus, a nickname for Pompey, 75.
Sardanapalus, reference to, 375, 376.
Sardinia, 125, 176, 202.
Saufeius, M., 148.
Scaptius, M., 251-254, 263-264.
Scribonius, C. Curio, consul 76 B.C., 49, 50, 53, 458.
Scribonius, C. Curio, son of the preceding, tribune 50 B.C., supports Clodius in 61 B.C., 49; opposes the triumvirs in 59 B.C., 78; denounced by Vettius, 85; Cicero, in 53 B.C., begs his support for Milo as a candidate for the consulship, 220-222; as tribune supposed hostile to Caesar, 153, 157, 241, cp. 229; but is purchased by him, 157, 244; carries a proposal in the senate that both Caesar and Pompey should resign their provinces and armies, 157; brings Caesar's last proposals to the senate in January, 49 B.C., 158, 290; has an interview with Cicero in 49 B.C., 378; writes to him, 382; a friend of M. Caelius, 385; occupies Sicily for Caesar, 297; crosses over to Africa, where he is killed in a battle with the Pompeians and Iuba, 299.
Scribonius, L. Libo, father-in-law of Sex. Pompeius, 166, 299, 311.
Seleucea, on the Tigris, 269.
Sempronius, C. Rufus, 233, 265, (?) 564.
Septem aquae, near Reate. 193.
Septimia, 556.
Septimius, C., 237.
Sequani, 16.
Sergius, L. Catilina, twice acquitted of serious charges, 59; first con-

spiracy of, 7; candidate for the consulship in 65 B.C., 27; (?) defended by Cicero, 31; attacked by Cicero in 64 B.C., 8; resumes his conspiracy, 9; leaves Rome, 10; punishment of his chief accomplices, 11, 457; defeat and death of, 12; character of, described in the speech pro Caelio, 140.
Sertorius, Q., 3, 125, 126.
Servaeus, tribune elect in 51 B.C., 229.
Servilia, mother of M. Brutus, 531.
Servilii, 236.
Servilius, M., 234-236.
Servilius, C. Ahala, reference to, 83.
Servilius, Q. Caepio, cp. Iunius, M. Brutus.
Servilius, P. Rullus, tribune 63 B.C., 8, 244-245.
Servilius, P. Vatia Isauricus, consul 79 B.C., 166, 458.
Servilius, P. Vatia Isauricus, son of the preceding, consul 48 B.C., 71, 195, 200, 406, 506-508, 548, 591.
Sestius, P., tribune 57 B.C., 12, 21, 118, 137, 174, 175, 177, 201, 516, 517.
Sicca, 20, 556.
Sicilia, Siculi, 2, 67, 68, 224, 362, 382, 521.
Sicyon, Sicyonii, 42, 71.
Sidon, 342.
Sinuessa, 357.
Sittius, P., 232, 399.
Smyrna, 342.
Solon, 362.
Spartacus, 3, 126, 263.
Spongia, one of the judges of Clodius, 57.
Statius, a freedman of Q. Cicero, 80, 92, 93, 96, 259.
Statius, L. Murcus, an officer of Caesar, 422, 589, 613.
Sufenas, *see* Nonius.
Sulla, 'nomenclator' of Q. Cicero, 97.
Sulpicius, P. Galba, 25, 26.
Sulpicius, Ser. Galba, one of Caesar's murderers, 136, 344 (?), 508, 581-584.
Sulpicius, C. Gallus, 470.
Sulpicius, Ser. Rufus, consul 51 B.C., prosecutes Murena in 63 B.C., 11; as consul argues in favour of conciliation, 150; placed in charge of Greece by Caesar, 436, 445; writes to console Cicero on the death of Tullia, 463-469; reports the murder of M. Marcellus to Cicero, 475-477; absent from Rome in 44 B.C., 550; in the following year goes on a mission to Antony, 504; his death, 504, 568, 570; letters of Cicero to him, 435, 469.
Sulpicius, Servius Rufus, son of the preceding, 359, 439, 470.
Surenas, 152.
Synnada or Synnas, in Phrygia, forum Synnadense, 226, 250.
Syracusae, 382, 426, 560.
Syria, made a Roman province, 127. *See* also M. Calpurnius Bibulus, C. Cassius, M. Licinius Crassus, Cn. Pompeius Magnus.

Tamisius Mustela, 558.
Tarentum, 393.
Tarquinius, L. Superbus, reference to, 347.
Tarracina, 310.
Tarsus, 152, 227, 249.
Tauromenium, 560.
Taurus, Mons, 250, 255.
Teanum, Sidicinum, 294, 310-311, 314, 559.
Tencteri, 143.
Tenea, in Peloponnesus, 260.
Terentia, wife of Cicero, 2; her energy on his behalf in 58 B.C., 21, 110-114; approves Tullia's marriage to Dolabella, 273; Cicero writes to her in 50 B.C., 155, 276; his anxiety on her behalf in 49 B.C., when she stayed in Italy, 295, 308, 316, cp. 387; his farewell letter to her before leaving Italy, 384; he is discontented with her on his return to her in Italy in 48 B.C., 393; divorced, 397, cp. 453, 455, 459.
Terentius, Q. Afer, the poet, quotation from, 211.
Terentius, Culleo, 106, 596.
Terentius, M. Varro, 22, 89, 105, 298, 423, 552, 587.
Terentius, M. Varro Lucullus, *see* Licinius Lucullus.
Terentius, A. Varro Murena, 315.
Tettius, Sex., 236.
Teucris, 46.

halna, one of the judges of Clodius, 57.
hemistocles, 306, 348, 373, 376.
heophanes, of Mytilenae, 223, 281.
heophrastus, of Amisus, *see* Tyrannio.
heophrastus, of Eresus, a pupil of Aristotle, 75.
heopompus, a dependent of Q. Cicero, 97.
hessalonica, 20, 108–111, 299.
hrace, 124, 512.
hrasybulus, 321.
hucydides, the great historian, 376.
hyillus, a poet, 63.
igranes, king of Armenia, 6, 124, 126, 127.
igranes, a prince of Armenia, son of the preceding, 21.
illius, L. Cimber, one of Caesar's murderers, 612.
hinius, Q., 240; his son, 341.
itius, C. Strabo, 581.
ranspadani, 124–125, 223, 281, 315, 569.
ratorius, 551, 552.
rebatius, C. Testa, 189, 295, 315, 532, 535, 539.
rebellius, L. Fides, 601.
rebonius, C., 323, 409, 567, 589.
rebula, district of, 533.
Tritia, a town of Peloponnesus, 260.
uccius, M., 233.
Tullia, daughter of Cicero, betrothed to C. Piso, 7; anxiety of Cicero for her during his exile, 109–110, 112; meets him at Brundisium in 57 B.C., 21; betrothed to Furius Crassipes, 178; married to Dolabella in 50 B.C., 156, 273; Cicero's anxiety on her behalf in 49 B.C., 295, 308, 370; her care for his safety, 372; and for his honour, 377; anxiety of Cicero in 48 B.C. as to her maintenance, 389, 413; and as to her health, 409; divorce from Dolabella, and death of, in 45 B.C., 398, 463; Cicero anxious to build a shrine to her memory, 398, 459, note on l. 4.
Tullius, L., legate of Cicero in Cilicia, 223–224, 349.
Tullius, M., a friend of Cicero, 311; defended by Cicero (?), 3.
Tullius, L. Cicero, uncle of the orator, 1.
Tullius, M. Cicero, father of the orator, 1.
Tullius, M. Cicero, the orator, birth of, 1; life of, till his election to the praetorship, 1–5; advocates the proposal of Manilius, 6; consulship of, 8–12; quarrels with Clodius, 14, 58–60, 67–68; behaviour of, during Caesar's first consulship, 18, 79, 84; leaves Rome in 58 B.C., and lives in exile for a year and a half, 20–23, 103–119; good understanding between him and Pompey after his return, 135, 162, 163; breach of, with Pompey and Caesar, 138, 201; submission of, to them, 139, 179, 203, 209; his advocacy of the claims of P. Lentulus Spinther to restore Ptolemy, 136, 164–170, 181–185; pleads for Milo in 52 B.C., 148; his government of Cilicia, 51–50 B.C., 151–155, 226–237, 246–255, 262–269; return of, to Italy, 155, 279; his hopes of a triumph, 266–269, 275; hesitation of, at the beginning of the civil war, between Caesar and Pompey, 294–297, 318–322, 346–352; sets out for Pompey's camp, June 7, 49 B.C., 297, 384; his behaviour there, 297, 299, 390; returns to Italy, 299, 405, 408; quarrel of, with his brother, *see* Quintus Cicero; pardoned by Caesar, 394; divorces Terentia, 397, cp. 453, 455, 459; death of Tullia, *see* Tullia; conduct of, after Caesar's death, 497, 498; correspondence of, with Antony, 523–526; with Dolabella, 527–529; with Matius, 532–539; sets out for Greece, 501, 544; interview of, with M. Brutus at Velia, in August, 44 B.C., 501, 546; returns to Rome and delivers the first Philippic, 502, 548; in 43 B.C. pleads in the senate for energetic measures to be taken against Antony, 504–508; corresponds with D. Brutus, C. Cassius, Q. Cornificius, Lepidus, Plancus, Pollio, Trebonius, 539–610; injudicious attempts of, to weaken Octavian, 509; after the formation of the second triumvirate attempts to escape from Italy, 513; death of, 513. *See* also, principal events in

the life of, xxxii; on his estates and other property, 133, 134; chronological list of the writings of, xxvii; names of his correspondents, xx.

Tullius, M. Cicero, son of the preceding, birth of, 7, 31; anxiety of his father for, in 58 B.C., 112, 114, 119; accompanies his father to Cilicia, 151; stays with Deiotarus, 152; visits Rhodes, 155; at Formiae in 49 B.C., 316; appointed aedile at Arpinum in 46 B.C., 453; goes to study at Athens in 45 B.C., 398; does good service to M. Brutus in Macedonia in 43 B.C., 505; the treatise 'De Officiis' addressed to him, 559.

Tullius, Q. Cicero, brother of the orator, marries Pomponia, 131; writes a long letter to his brother, 'De Petitione Consulatus,' 8; praetor in 62 B.C., 12; governs the province of Asia, 61–59 (inclusive) B.C., 14, 76, 92–103; injured in a riot in 57 B.C., 23; makes promises to Pompey on behalf of his brother, 202; goes as Pompey's legate to Sardinia, 136, 176; and as Caesar's to Gaul, 145, 213; visits Britain, 196; in great danger in Gaul in 53 B.C., 146; goes with his brother to Cilicia, 151, 152, 249; Marcus thinks of leaving him in charge of the province, 251, 274; spends the winter of 51–50 B.C. in Cilicia proper, 255; quarrels with Pomponia, 258–259; quarrels with his brother after the battle of Pharsalus, 393, 407, 412, 413; sues for pardon to Caesar, 410; Marcus intercedes for him, 415; they are reconciled, 394; pays court to Caesar in 45 B.C., 398; letter of, to his brother, in 44 B.C., 560, 561; proscribed by Antony and murdered in 43 B.C., 513.

Tullius, Q. Cicero, son of the preceding, education of, 177; accompanies his father and uncle to Cilicia, 151; character of, 259; with his father after the battle of Pharsalus, 407, 410 (?); suspected by the orator of calumniating him, 393; aedile at Arpinum in 46 B.C., 453; serves under Caesar in 45 B.C., 398; referred to in 44 B.C., 561; murdered with his father, 513.

Tullius, M. Tiro, freedman of the orator, 121, 296, 313–317.

Tusca disciplina, 441.

Tuscenius, 95.

Tusculum, estate of Cicero at, 71, 133, 345, 420, 425, 433, 518, 532; Tusculanus ager, 433.

Tyrannio, 177, 423.

Tyrus, 342.

Ulixes, in Homer's poetry, 597.

Usipetes, 143.

Utica, 400, 422.

Vada, 586, 600.

Valerius, P., 110, 255, 544.

Valerius, L. Flaccus, interrex in 82 B.C., 321.

Valerius, L. Flaccus, praetor in 63 B.C., 18, 90.

Valerius, M. Messalla Niger, consul in 61 B.C., 13, 43, 44, 51.

Valerius, M. Messalla, consul in 53 B.C., 146, 194, 228.

Valerius, Q. Orca, commissioner for dividing lands in 45 B.C., 477–480.

Valerius, an interpreter, 560.

Varius, P., 29.

Vatinius, P., tribune in 59, praetor in 55 B.C., 17, 18, 88, 142, 144, 199, 201, 210–211, 395, 407, 412; consul at the close of 47 B.C., 396; submits to M. Brutus in Illyricum, 43 B.C., 505.

Veii, territory of, 433.

Velia, 546.

Velina tribus, 195.

Velinus, a lake and river, 193.

Vennonius, C., 307.

Ventidius, P. Bassus, 509, 584, 586, 595, 600.

Vercingetorix, 149.

Vergilius, C., 20, 96.

Verres, C., 3–5.

Vestorius, C., a money-lender of Puteoli, 234, 260, 265, 523, 531.

Vettius, 179.

Vettius, L., an informer, 12, 18, 85–88.

Vibius, C. Pansa, tribune in 51 B.C., 153, 239–240; friendly to Cicero, 409; consul in 43 B.C., 504–509, 522, 531, 561, 563, 565, 569, 572, 582, 584, 600.

Vibullius, L. Rufus, 202, 309-310.
Villius, Sex., 219.
Villius, L. Annalis, 237.
Vinicius, L., tribune in 51 B.C., 239.
Visellius, C. Varro, 118.
Vocontii, 602.
Volaterrae, 477-480.
Volcatius, L. Tullus, consul in 66 B.C., 166, 325, 351, 438, 458.
Volsci, 348.
Volusius, (?) Cn., 223.
Volusius, M., 316.
Volusius, (?) Q., 249.

Xeno, an Epicurean philosopher, 224-225.
Xenocrates, contemporary with Aristotle, 55.
Xenophon, reference to the works of, 96.

Zeno, an Epicurean philosopher, 128.
Zeuxis, of Blaudus, 93, 94.

www.ingramcontent.com/pod-product-compliance
Lightning Source LLC
Chambersburg PA
CBHW021217300426
44111CB00007B/346
* 9 7 8 3 7 4 2 8 0 5 5 3 9 *